NEWSDAY

NEWSDAY

*A Candid History of the
Respectable Tabloid*

Robert F. Keeler

ARBOR HOUSE
WILLIAM MORROW

NEW YORK

Library of Congress Cataloging-in-Publication Data

Keeler, Robert F.
  Newsday: a candid history of the respectable tabloid / Robert Keeler.

    p.   cm.

  ISBN 1-55710-053-5
  1. Newsday (Hempstead, N.Y.)--History. I. Title.
PN4899.N42N525 1990
071'.47245--dc20   90-38096
                                                                                               CIP

Printed in the United States of America

First Edition

1 2 3 4 5 6 7 8 9 10

To Subscribe to Newsday
Call 1-516-454-2000

BOOK DESIGN BY WILLIAM J. DAVIS

For Judy, Rebekah and Rachel

Contents

BOOK I

CAPTAINS, COLONELS AND COPPER KINGS

BOOK II

ALICIA'S TOY

BOOK III
THE CAPTAIN AT THE HELM

BOOK IV
THE GOLDEN WEST AND THE BIG APPLE

BOOK I

Captains, Colonels And Copper Kings

CHAPTER ONE

The Honeymooners

QUIRKY HONEYMOONS HAD been so common in their complex marital histories that Harry Frank Guggenheim and Alicia Patterson saw nothing strange about launching their marriage in the middle of the desert, sipping martinis with a rocket scientist scorned by his peers as a moon-mad visionary.

It was early July, 1939, when they flew into the airport at Roswell, New Mexico, for a visit with Harry's protege, Robert Hutchings Goddard, a bald, slightly built physicist with a big dream and a small budget. By then, Goddard had accomplished the first flight of a liquid-fueled rocket: in 1926, at his Aunt Effie Ward's farm near Worcester, Massachusetts, where he taught physics at Clark University. He had also begun amassing the complex web of patents that made him the father of rocketry. But the sound that had dominated his life in the 1920s and 1930s was not applause for his past accomplishment. It was laughter at his vision for the future. Goddard had suggested in a monograph released in 1920 by the Smithsonian Institution that a rocket could someday reach the moon. That prediction appeared in headlines everywhere, creating a tidal wave of lunar goofiness, such as songs, jokes and offers to volunteer for the trip. Some reporters and scientists ridiculed Goddard as "moony" or "moon-mad." But Harry Guggenheim, a deadly serious man, wasn't laughing. To him, Goddard's work was no joke.

Throughout the 1920s, Guggenheim money had encouraged the development of commercial aviation in a variety of ways, including the sponsorship of Charles A. Lindbergh's triumphal tour of America after his solo flight to Paris. Through Lindbergh, who believed that the future of aviation had to include rocketry, Goddard genius met Guggenheim money. The first funding came from Harry's father, Daniel, allowing Goddard to come to Roswell, in search of open spaces where falling rockets would do no damage and cause no scandal.

When Daniel died, Harry kept the cash flowing to Goddard. Still, many scientists were skeptical about Goddard's work. Even Harry had reason for doubt: He had never seen one of Goddard's rockets perform successfully. In September, 1935, for example, four months after Goddard had sent a rocket 7,500 feet into the air, he decided to show off his work to his two major supporters, Harry and Lindbergh. Within three days, however, two Goddard rockets fizzled on the launch frame at Roswell. "Goddard's faith in the ultimate success of his work was contagious," Harry said later. "I promised I would come back."

Now Harry was back, this time with his new bride. On July 1, 1939, just a few days before their arrival in Roswell, Harry and Alicia had exchanged vows at the home of one of her oldest friends, in Jacksonville, Florida. That quiet ceremony joined two fabled American families. The immigrant Guggenheims had amassed breathtaking wealth through shrewd exploitation of the earth's natural resources and used that wealth to endow a diverse series of philanthropic foundations. The Pattersons had made their money in journalism, operating papers in three major cities. Alicia's great-grandfather, Joseph Medill, had made the *Chicago Tribune* into a journalistic colossus, and her cousin, Colonel Robert Rutherford McCormick, controlled it. Her father, Joseph Medill Patterson, had founded the most successful tabloid in America, the *New York Daily News*. Her aunt, Cissy Patterson, ran the *Washington Times-Herald*.

Apart from the acquisition of wealth, the histories of the two families were starkly dissimilar. So, it seemed, were Harry and Alicia. At the time of their wedding, Harry was 48 and Alicia was 32. They shared interests in horses, in flying, in hunting, but in many ways they were fundamentally different. Impeccably educated at Yale and Cambridge, Harry was a man of the world: businessman, Navy pilot, patron of aviation, former ambassador to Cuba, friend of presidents, owner of a horse-racing stable. Harry always knew exactly what he wanted, and he had an unerring sense of how to get it. Politically, he was a Herbert Hoover-Alf Landon Republican. In contrast, Alicia had been intermittently educated at a series of girls' schools, where she read voraciously but spent much of her time practicing escape and evasion. She was intelligent, pretty and fearless, but she acted like an irrepressible little girl grown into an uncertain young woman. Her accomplishments, although impressive, were scattered and directionless: a few newspaper and magazine bylines, a handful of hunting trophies and some women's flying records. Her politics were solidly New Deal.

In all, Harry and Alicia were a truly odd couple. Despite their differences, however, they had one compelling common trait: failure at marriage. They also had both experienced odd honeymoons. On Alicia's first, she got along so badly with her new husband that she sent for one of her oldest friends to join them. On her second, she and her husband took along a mechanic for their plane. On Harry's second, his architect accompanied him and his wife through Europe, looking for chunks of medieval castles for Harry's new estate on Long Island. For both Harry and Alicia, the second marriages had not worked out. In the middle of those unhappy relationships, Harry and Alicia met, fell in love, travelled to Florida for divorces, took the vows and flew to New Mexico for their honeymoon.

Even at the start of a new marriage, however, Harry could not completely divorce himself from business. Besides spending time with Alicia, Harry wanted to use the stay in Roswell for some discussions with Goddard. In 1938, Harry had brought in scientists from Guggenheim-funded aeronautical research centers, sat them down with Goddard and tried to nudge him in the direction of cooperative research. But Goddard had worked alone for so long that he resisted a team approach. Now it was time for Harry to persuade him that the quickest way to reach his dream of space flight was to harness his genius to the abilities of other scientists. That was the unspoken issue as the Guggenheims arrived at Mescalero Ranch, where Goddard and his wife, Esther, lived in a rented pueblo-style house, just 10 miles from the launch site. While they were there, the Guggenheims did manage to get in some recreation, including a trout-fishing expedition to the Rio Ruidoso, west of Roswell. But when they returned to the ranch, business intruded again. What they found waiting was a telegram from Max Annenberg, the circulation director of the *New York Daily News* and one of Joseph Medill Patterson's closest friends. Annenberg was a legendary newspaper tough guy who had built a bloody legend in the Chicago circulation wars and later joined Patterson at the *News*. There, Annenberg had become friendly with Alicia. Now, he was offering her and Harry some advice.

Since Alicia was a newspaperwoman without a newspaper of her own, they had asked Annenberg to search around for a likely property. They had turned down earlier Annenberg proposals, but this telegram brought news of one that might be suitable. It was a small paper in Nassau County, the first county east of New York City, on Long Island. The *Nassau Daily Journal* had begun publication on March 1, 1939, in the Village of Hempstead, the county's major business area. It had folded on March 10, in the face of a labor struggle. The defunct paper's equipment was still sitting in its closed offices, a converted automobile dealership. "Max's telegram was of great interest to me," Harry wrote later. "I was especially pleased with a newspaper prospect in Nassau County where my roots were and where Alicia could operate within a half hour's drive of our home. . . . I felt that she should prepare for her heritage of responsibilities and that she should use to the full her latent talents and abilities." Not to put too fine a point on it, Harry wanted to keep Alicia busy. " 'Everybody ought to have a job,' Harry said to me not long after our marriage," Alicia wrote later. " 'People who make a business out of pleasure seldom are happy.' The obvious job for me was publishing a newspaper. . . . Harry was acting from dual motives. He didn't want me running amok from sheer boredom, and he wanted to prepare me for my future role on the News, which I still expected to fill."

Her father had led her to believe that, when he died, she was likely to move into a position of power at the *Daily News*. Since emulating her father was a central theme of Alicia's life, the idea of running the *Daily News* appealed to her immensely. But that was in the future. For now, if she wanted to get any serious training for publishing a newspaper, she'd have to learn by running a paper of her own. Her new husband was willing to help her financially, ready to lend his seriousness and discipline to her love for journalism. This was as good a time as any to start, with the energy of a new marriage still flowing. But was Alicia ready for it?

"On the arrival of Max's telegram, Alicia balked," Harry wrote. "She wanted, at that moment, to give up the whole idea." Alicia had a chance to take on an adult responsibility, to go into the family business in a meaningful way. Or she could stay home and be a lady of leisure, writing book reviews for her father's newspaper and remaining totally dependent. Confronted in the middle of the desert with that choice, mulling over the prospect of running a tiny newspaper in a building that had been an auto dealership, Alicia suddenly developed cold feet. What would her great-grandfather, Joseph Medill, the fearless founder of the dynasty, think about her timidity?

CHAPTER TWO

Bourbon Joe

I

INK FIRST ENTERED the blood of Alicia Patterson's ancestors in 1819, when her great-great grandfather, James Patrick, hauled some presses by mule wagon from Pittsburgh to New Philadelphia, Ohio, and established a tiny weekly, the *Tuscarawas Chronicle*. Patrick, a recent immigrant from Belfast, became a power in Tuscarawas County: a land commissioner, Indian agent and county judge. It was his daughter who later married a young lawyer named Joseph Medill and started the dynasty.

Medill was born on a farm near St. John, New Brunswick, on April 6, 1823. His roots stretched back to families called Medille in France, Dill in England, McDill in Scotland and Medill (accented on the last syllable) in Ireland. When Medill was nine, his family moved to a farm in Stark County, Ohio. Too poor to attend college, he acquired an education on his own, by reading borrowed books. At the same time, he took his first steps into newspapering by selling *The Weekly Tribune*, the rural extension of Horace Greeley's *New York Tribune*. In 1844, Medill began studying law with two attorneys in Canton, and two years later, he was admitted to the Ohio bar. He practiced law for three years, but his enthusiasm for the profession waned, and he began to spend more time hanging around Judge Patrick's newspaper in New Philadelphia — by then renamed the *Tuscarawas Advocate* — where he discussed politics and sometimes wrote editorials. Briefly, he took a substitute teaching job. One of his students was Katharine Patrick, the judge's daughter. They got to know each other better at the newspaper, where she taught Medill typesetting. Before long, typography turned to romance, and Medill asked permission to marry Katharine, who was six years younger. But Judge Patrick made it clear that Medill would first have to establish himself financially. Then Medill took the plunge into full-time journalism, buying the *Coshocton Whig*, making himself the editor and changing its name to the *Republican*. The county was Democratic. The paper was stoutly pro-Whig and anti-slavery.

In 1852, Medill established a Whig morning paper in Cleveland called *The Daily Forest City*. Merging it with another paper run by an abolitionist, Medill named the new paper the *Cleveland Leader* and built it into a unifying voice for the anti-slavery forces in the area. Then he married Katharine Patrick, over the strong objections of her father, and moved her to Cleveland. There she gave birth to their two daughters, Kate and Elinor, who was called Nellie. At the *Leader*, his political activism gave him a seat at the creation of a new political party. A month after a meeting of anti-slavery activists at Ripon, Wisconsin, in February, 1854, Medill held a similar meeting at the *Leader*. At that meeting, some historians have concluded, Medill suggested that the new party be called "Republican." The party held its first convention that July and adopted the name.

A few months later, in the fall of 1854, Medill was offered the job of managing editor of the *Chicago Tribune*. Unimpressed by the paper's tattered facilities, he turned the job down, but the excitement of a rapidly growing Chicago gradually caught his fancy. The following spring, at the suggestion of Horace Greeley, Medill left for Chicago and met with Dr. Charles Ray, a newspaper editor from Galena, Illinois — another strong abolitionist. They decided to acquire control of the *Tribune*. Medill bought a one-third interest and Ray bought one-fourth.

Not long after Ray and Medill took command, Medill heard a fiery anti-slavery speech by a young lawyer named Abraham Lincoln and became convinced that Lincoln was the right man to lead the new Republican Party into the White House. But Medill stood in awe of no human — Lincoln or anyone else. One frequently repeated account of their relationship is that Lincoln visited Medill's office one day and made himself a bit too much at home, which moved Medill to growl: "Take your goddamned feet off my desk, Abe." Nonetheless, Medill played a major role in Lincoln's election in 1860 and afterward remained a burr in Lincoln's side, constantly goading him to free the slaves and to conduct the war against the South harshly. Having elected a president, Medill enjoyed decades of overwhelming power in Chicago, including a brief tour in politics. In 1871, a cataclysmic fire destroyed Chicago, and the *Tribune* played a leading role in the reconstruction, which brought about Medill's election as mayor, on the "Union-Fireproof" ticket. Aside from that short, unhappy term as mayor, however, the source of Medill's power was the loud voice of the *Chicago Tribune*.

For Joseph Medill, a newspaper was not a forum for balanced, rational discourse. It was a blunt instrument that he used to bludgeon those who opposed his many strong views, such as his virulent hatred of labor unions and his support for abolition before and during the Civil War. It was that issue that brought him into conflict with the inventor of the reaper, Cyrus Hall McCormick, who wasn't abolitionist enough for Medill. McCormick had left Virginia, established an industrial empire in Chicago, purchased the *Chicago Times* and used it to carry on a vigorous public debate with the *Tribune* over abolition. When McCormick ran for Congress in 1864 against Medill's candidate, the *Tribune* hammered him mercilessly — even calling into question the legitimacy of his claim to have invented the reaper. McCormick lost the election. Despite their feud, McCormick and Medill eventually became related by marriage: Medill's daughter Kate married Robert Sanderson McCormick, the nephew of Cyrus McCormick. That marriage in 1876 brought the business genius of the McCormick family together with the journalism skills of Medill. The marriage of Medill's other daughter, Nellie, united the Medills with another influential Chicago family, the Pattersons.

The Pattersons were Scottish Presbyterians who had come to America searching for religious freedom. Before Joseph Medill even arrived in Chicago, a Patterson was a strong moral force there: Robert W. Patterson, the minister at the Second Presbyterian Church. After the war, in the wake of the Chicago fire, he moved his flock north to Lake Forest, which became Chicago's most exclusive suburb, and he founded Lake Forest College. His son, Robert W. Patterson Jr., decided against the pulpit or the law and chose journalism instead. At the *Tribune*, he rose from night telegraph editor to night editor. At the same time, he started courting Nellie Medill, the daughter of the boss. Neither his father nor Joseph Medill approved of the marriage, but Nellie insisted.

Taken together, the marriage of Kate Medill to Robert Sanderson McCormick and of Nellie Medill to Robert W. Patterson Jr. forged a McCormick-Patterson-Medill empire that would control the *Chicago Tribune* until the middle of the twentieth century. But this was no smooth, wrinkle-free dynasty. The rivalry of the two redheaded Medill sisters, Kate and Nellie, made peace and quiet impossible. The two sisters were accustomed to getting their way, but each saw the other as an obstacle. Kate was smarter and cannier, and Nellie was prettier, but in many ways, they were the same. Each resented being born a woman, deprived of the normal male routes to power, and each was boundlessly ambitious for both her husband and her son and fearful that the other's men would gain an advantage. The result was a long-lasting, quarrelsome, difficult dance of succession at the *Tribune*. It all began with the sons.

Kate's son came along first, in 1877, and she named him Joseph Medill McCormick. By arming him with the name of her father, she hoped to ensure that the boy would someday inherit control of the *Tribune*. To underline her point, she always called the boy Medill, not Joseph or Joe. Nellie's son arrived less than two years later, on January 6, 1879, and she didn't miss her chance to stake a claim for him. Pointedly, almost defiantly, she named him Joseph Medill Patterson, but she called him just plain Joe. As a result of the competing ambition of their mothers, these two grandsons of Joseph Medill were born into the role of rivals for control of the *Tribune*.

Nellie's second child was a girl, Elinor, who came to be known as Cissy.

Kate's second baby was also a girl, Katrina, who died after only six months. That death jolted Kate, and when the next child came along in 1880, she was desperately anxious for a replacement. Not only did the new baby turn out to be a boy, but Kate also learned from the doctors that she couldn't have any more children. The result was a shaky start for the boy, Robert Rutherford McCormick. For years, Kate would look at her son and address him as Katrina. She decorated his flowing hair as if he were a girl and dressed him in ribbons and bows. But Bertie or Bert, as his playmates called him, was not the important son. All of Kate's hopes rested on his older brother, Medill. "My mother hated me," Bert McCormick said years later. "My mother and aunt were real bitches."

One of the primary targets of Kate's bitchiness was Nellie's husband, Robert Patterson. She knew that Nellie was disappointed in her marriage, a union of two utterly incompatible people. Nellie was large — in voice, in body, in ambition. Rob was quieter, more thoughtful, sweeter. He had strong views and unwavering journalistic principles, but he could never stand up to his wife. More and more, he coped with her disdain by drinking. Even though they would never have considered divorce, there was no love left. In fact, Patterson did better at winning Joseph Medill's approval than at winning Nellie's. In time, Medill began turning control of the paper over to him, although Patterson's brand of journalism was tamer than Medill's. Given authority over day-to-day decisions, Robert Patterson sharpened the line between editorials and news stories, a distinction that had never worried Medill very much, and worked in other ways to make the paper more professional.

For Kate McCormick, Patterson's rise was a galling omen, even at a time when her own husband's fortunes had taken a favorable turn. In 1889, Benjamin Harrison became president and sent Robert Todd Lincoln, the son of Abraham, to London as his minister. Lincoln, who had done legal work for the *Tribune* and knew how much the paper's support had meant to his father, asked Medill's son-in-law, Robert Sanderson McCormick, to become second secretary of the legation. But even while Kate's husband was learning the ways of diplomacy in London, Robert Patterson was continuing to run the *Tribune*. The McCormicks returned from London in 1893. A year later, Kate's mother, Katharine Patrick Medill, died, and Joseph Medill continued in ill health. When fire destroyed his Los Angeles winter home in 1898, Medill began spending the winter in a hotel suite in San Antonio. Later, his grandson, Bert McCormick, came down from Groton to serve as his connection with the outside world. On the morning of March 16, 1899, Bert brought the newspapers into his grandfather's bedroom, and Medill asked: "What's the news this morning?" A few moments later, Bert left the room, and Joseph Medill died.

At his death, Medill owned 1,056 of the 2,000 shares of *Tribune* stock. Rather than simply divide the shares among his survivors and risk the eventual loss of family control, Medill's will established a new entity called the Medill Trust, under three trustees: his attorney and his sons-in-law, Robert Sanderson McCormick and Robert W. Patterson. That left Kate and Nellie with plenty of income, but without real control over the *Tribune*. Patterson continued to run the paper, and Kate continued to fear that power at the *Tribune* in the next generation would elude her oldest son, Medill McCormick, and fall into the unworthy hands of Nellie's son, Joseph Medill Patterson.

II

THE STRUGGLE WITH wealth began early for Joe Patterson. As soon as he was old enough to know anything, he knew that he was rich, and that unearned flow of dollars eventually began to make him feel guilty.

Following education at private schools on Chicago's lakefront and in Paris, he went off at age 11 to a new school called Groton, a hard-edged, aristocratic academy that turned out senators and presidents. The other lords-in-training were not impressed with his family's ink-stained millions, his Little Lord Fauntleroy outfit or his Illinois accent. Victimized repeatedly by the upperclassmen, Patterson grew to despise the school, writing letters to his parents that expressed open longing for home. But his father wrote him back, suggesting sternly that it would be unmanly to quit. So he stayed. Through the sheer force of his will, Patterson overcame his lack of athletic talent and built up his body enough to play football and baseball and row on the crew. Academically, Patterson was a nonconformist. Instead of reading what was assigned, he indulged his own interests, such as the study of Civil War battles. As a result, he was stuck solidly in the middle of his class. He was graduated in 1896, soon to be followed by his cousin, Robert Rutherford McCormick, and another young aristocrat by the name of Franklin Delano Roosevelt.

Instead of starting college in the fall, Patterson spent the winter as a cowboy in Wyoming and on a cattle ranch in northern Mexico. When he finally went to Yale in 1897, he moved more comfortably in the ruling crowd than he had at Groton. Showing that he could drink, despite his grandfather Medill's legendary hatred of alcohol, he earned the nickname "Bourbon Joe." Proving that he could play politics, he won admission to Yale's exclusive underworld of secret societies. But his taste for the effete rituals of the rich filled him with self-loathing. Before his freshman year was over, he grew restless and longed to run off to the Spanish-American War, but his father refused to let him go. A few months later, in the summer of 1900, the lure of combat called to him again when he read about the Boxer Rebellion, a peasant uprising designed to chase foreigners from China, and about the international force that was trying to quell the revolt. So he lied to his parents and told them that he was going to Japan to view the plum blossoms. Later, he told his mother the truth: He was really working for one of William Randolph Hearst's papers in New York. By the time he got to the front, however, the fighting was over.

While he was in China, Patterson at least got enough of a taste of journalism to decide that he was willing to go into the family business. In the spring of

1901, he left New Haven with a Yale degree and headed home to join the battle between the *Tribune* and Hearst's newly established morning *American* and evening *Examiner*. In that war, Patterson found himself fighting on the boring side. His father's vision of journalism was far more respectable, dusty and dull than Hearst's. Typically, he told his father that Hearst was the greatest publisher in the country. But he persevered, covering cops and later writing editorials. At the same time, he had an active social life, but his bachelor days ended quickly. On November 19, 1902, he married Alice Higinbotham, the daughter of Harlow Niles Higinbotham, one of the most important businessmen in Chicago. Higinbotham, a partner in Marshall Field & Company, had run the 1893 Columbian Exposition, which put Chicago on the international map. Alice was short and delicate, with Dresden-doll good looks and a far more finely tuned sense of the social niceties than her rough-riding new husband had.

Even before that marriage into Chicago society, he began to revolt against that society, by campaigning for a seat in the state legislature as part of a municipal reform group. In January, 1903, he took a seat in the state House of Representatives and became, at the age of 24, the youngest member of the state legislature. The hottest issue in Springfield that year was municipal ownership of Chicago's streetcar system. Patterson favored it, but a solid bloc of legislators, backed by his own newspaper, opposed it. The bill passed, but it was later invalidated in the courts. Patterson did not run for a second term, apparently after finding out that his nomination had been the result of a quiet deal between the Republicans and his father, who had grown weary of Patterson's proletarian views at the *Tribune* and saw the legislative seat as a good way to get him out of town. "I was through being a statesman and went back to the *Tribune*, writing editorials a year or so, and then controlling the editorial page under my father's direction," Patterson said later. Given his father's views and his own, that was a doomed proposition from the start.

In early 1905, Patterson went to Russia, where his uncle, Robert Sanderson McCormick, was the American ambassador. Covering the start of the 1905 revolution, Patterson wrote dispatches for the *Tribune* that clearly favored the revolutionaries. That outraged his aunt, Kate McCormick, who felt more comfortable in the salons of the czar than with the proletariat. Following this radicalizing experience, he reached a watershed decision. If, as his father assured him, the *Tribune* would never change its opposition to municipal ownership of streetcars, then Joe Patterson would change. So he left the *Tribune* and cast his lot with Judge Edward Dunne, a progressive candidate for mayor who favored municipal ownership. When Dunne won, he rewarded Patterson by naming him commissioner of public works — an astounding responsibility for a 26-year-old man who had never run anything more complicated than an editorial page.

One of the first things that Patterson did was to take aim at the department store owners on State Street. Outraged by the way the stores made shopgirls work in poorly ventilated bargain basements, he measured the basements and found that some of them extended under the city's sidewalks. So he made the owners pay $500,000 to continue operating the basements under city property. His disdain for the department store tycoons grew worse after the death of Marshall Field, his own father-in-law's employer. Field left $140 million to his two grandsons, and Patterson wrote a scathing article for *Collier's* about the property rights of the rich. After about a year, he decided that pushing around department store owners and attacking municipal corruption was not enough. His ripening disgust with the system became so strong that he decided to make a dramatic break. In a pointed letter of resignation, Patterson announced that he was leaving the government and becoming a Socialist. He addressed the letter to Mayor Dunne, but Patterson was obviously aiming it equally at his family and at Chicago society. "I have hardly read a book on Socialism, but that which I have just enunciated I believe in general to be their theory," Patterson wrote. "If it is their theory, I am a Socialist."

Patterson wrote his letter from his family's opulent new mansion on Dupont Circle in Washington, where Nellie Patterson set herself up as a society hostess, while her husband continued to run the *Tribune*. A few days later, Patterson headed to New York for a convention of Socialists. His father was in New York, too, on his way back to Chicago. The next day, the *New York Times* carried an extensive story on Patterson's conversion, including interviews with father and son. It was a difficult moment for Robert Patterson, adding to the pain of his loveless marriage, alcoholism and periodic depression. But he handled it calmly. "My son is of age and has a right to an opinion of his own," he told the *Times*. "I am a firm believer in letting everybody think as he pleases, including my son."

In July, Patterson made his first speech on behalf of the Socialist Party. In August, he issued "Confessions of a Drone," a detailed statement of his view that the rich lived lazily off the wealth produced by the workers. "I have an income of between ten and twenty thousand dollars a year," Patterson wrote. "I spend all of it. I produce nothing — am doing no work." This outburst of economic conscience impressed another Chicago journalist, Carl Sandburg, who later wrote Patterson: "I still maintain that two of the nicest, cleanest, historical documents we have in this country, of our time, are your 'Confessions of a Drone' and 'The Will of Marshall Field.' " But his conversion to socialism was a shock to his family, which was grasping the fruits of capitalism with boundless energy and no discernible guilt. Patterson didn't have to look any further than his own adoring sister for confirmation of his views about wealth-consuming capitalist brats.

From Cissy Patterson's childhood, her mother had a clear destiny planned for her: to be educated correctly, to debut lavishly and to marry well. So Nellie sent her to the proper finishing schools, provided the Dupont Circle mansion as a stage for Cissy's social graces, and hoped for a rich young man to appear. That hope began to fall apart when Cissy visited her Aunt Kate at the rented palace in Vienna where Kate and Robert Sanderson McCormick lived while he represented America at the Austrian court. There, Cissy met Count Josef Gizycki, a charming, sexually magnetic, totally self-assured aristocrat from Poland. Robert

Patterson quickly found out about Gizycki's profligate lifestyle and his long list of love affairs, but romance overwhelmed facts, and Cissy married the comic-opera playboy. The marriage degenerated soon after Cissy moved into his ramshackle "castle" in Europe, where she was surrounded by his former lovers and his illegitimate children. As time went on, he wore her down with his absences, his gambling and drinking, his debts and his demands for money. Her life didn't improve even when she gave birth to a daughter, Felicia. Gizycki was certain that the child's birth would bring a flow of Patterson money, but Cissy left him, taking Felicia to London. The count hired detectives to kidnap his daughter, and the Pattersons hired detectives in a failed effort to kidnap her back. The mess ended when President William H. Taft sent a letter to Czar Nicholas, who persuaded Gizycki to return the child to Cissy.

This was the dance of capitalistic decadence that occupied Joe Patterson's family in the years surrounding his conversion to socialism. Fleeing the external symbols of wealth, he headed for a simpler lifestyle, paid for by that wealth. In the summer of 1906, he announced that he was becoming a farmer. For a year, he took courses in agriculture and German at the University of Wisconsin at Madison. Then he began to put his new agricultural knowledge into practice on his farm just outside Libertyville, north of Chicago. It was just seven miles from Lake Forest, the rich suburban village where Patterson's grandfather had established a college and where many of Alice Patterson's fashionable friends lived, but Lake Forest might as well have been on the other side of the moon. The only access to Patterson's farm was over dirt roads that became muddy brown soup in the rain. That was fine with Patterson. He could achieve all his goals right in Libertyville. His plans were to run the farm and write agricultural articles, sociological tracts and proletarian fiction. He was going to spend all his time raising children, Holsteins and hell.

CHAPTER THREE

"Keep Alicia Moving"

I

THE FIRST THING that Alicia Patterson did on this planet was to disappoint the most important man in her life.

In the middle of Joe Patterson's eventful entry into the legislature in early 1903, he and Alice had found time to conceive their first child, who was born that October and named Elinor. Patterson desperately wanted a son, but when his second child was born, on October 15, 1906, it was a girl: Alicia. In his disappointment, Patterson slammed the door, walked out and didn't return for days. His third child, born in 1913, was another girl: Josephine.

"He had wanted a boy, instead of three daughters in succession, and that meant one of the Patterson girls would have to be his substitute son," Alicia wrote later. The oldest daughter, Elinor, was an unlikely candidate — quieter, more withdrawn and well-behaved than Alicia, with a delicate beauty like her mother's. So the role of substitute son fell to Alicia, who adored her father and was willing to do anything to please him — even strenuous and dangerous activities that were usually reserved for boys. Alicia began to learn that role on the isolated farm in Libertyville, which exerted a powerful influence on her imagination. Many years later, she sat down and wrote in longhand her memories of those years.

"When I think of Libertyville I can feel the hot middle western wind hit my face and body and squeeze the moisture dry," Alicia said. "I smell black earth and cow dung and rotting apples on the ground. I feel the stiff crab grass between my fingers and the lumpy bark of an old cherry tree. Libertyville is where I spent my childhood, where I grew up. The pain and pleasure of that place is still alive in me. I cannot forget it.

"Libertyville is a small town 35 miles northwest of Chicago. When I was a girl there was a drug store, a grocery store, a variety store, a blacksmith. There must have been more than that but I forget. We lived three miles to the south on a 350-acre farm which mother christened 'Westwood.' Stubbornly we kept calling the farm Libertyville until she too finally fell into the habit. Poor mother. She forever tried to change us. I fear we were too much for her."

Alice, the mistress of "Westwood," was a delicate beauty, but she was fearless. "In fact, she took everything gallantly, from riding to hounds to going up in an old 'box car' plane, circa 1911," Alicia wrote. "Father always said she was the bravest woman in the world." Even when Patterson embraced socialism and turned his back on the society that mattered so much to his wife, she didn't flinch. A reporter asked her how she felt about the bewildering conversion, and Alice answered: "I don't know what being a Socialist is, but if that is what my husband is, I'm for it." Despite her loyalty, Alice couldn't control her husband. She could barely persuade him to leave the farm for a social event in Lake Forest. "He hated parties with grim determination and it was only by coaxing and scolding that mother ever got him to Lake Forest," Alicia wrote in her reminiscence. "She won 75% of the time, but I am sorry to relate that father, when he found himself trapped, never took his defeats with good grace. Mother often came home weeping because father had been rude to one of the guests. Home was father's castle and he was quite happy there with his family, his books and his black loam soil."

Joe and Alice also had different visions for the red brick Georgian farmhouse and the flat, treeless farm. "Mother planted elms along the half-mile drive, but they were puny specimens and took years to grow to a respectable size," Alicia wrote. "Mother's craze to make Westwood live up to its name drove her into a frenzy of tree planting that caused many a quarrel in the family. Father liked to look as far as his eye could see over the rock-growing earth. Mother wanted to close herself off from the farm land and pretend she was mistress of an English estate — a forlorn hope, as the droughts, the wind, the torrential thunderstorms and the topography refused to cooperate."

The girls also found the found the isolation difficult. There were no other children of their age nearby, except for a farmer's son, with whom they shared their toys. "I remember well the contempt he had for our governesses and it would humiliate me hideously when one of them tracked us down with orders to come and wash up," Alicia wrote. "We had a series of frauleins. It was before the first world war when German was still a fashionable language and mother was determined that we learn languages." As a result, before Alicia had turned six, her parents dispatched her and Elinor to Berlin, to stay at the *Pension Braune* and learn German. There, the girls were not alone, but their governess was not always a comfort. When Alicia developed an abscess in her ear, the governess, a Christian Scientist, was reluctant to allow an operation. The staff at the *pension* finally persuaded her, and an ear specialist operated on Alicia and relieved the infection. "As my mother used to say, can you imagine sending two small children to Germany with a Christian Scientist?" said Adrianne Baker Reilly, Elinor's daughter. "Alicia was screaming in pain."

The pain of separation and illness brought Alicia no gain: Elinor learned German and retained it, but Alicia did not. "Elinor had a couple of strikes on me aside from languages," Alicia wrote. "She was older, she was prettier, she was ladylike. Her eyes were big and violet, her light brown hair was soft and tractable, her mouth was small and heart-shaped. I lacked all of these attributes. . . . There was no one to salve my ego, and I grew more and more morose. When company came Elinor was dressed up and brought downstairs. I stayed on the nursery floor and peered through the bannisters like some little wild animal, watching and hating every minute of the gaiety below.

"Father must have sensed my misery, for one day he saw me sitting on a floor and he asked me if I wouldn't go for a walk with him. It was the most wonderful invitation I had ever had. From that day on, I would have walked around the earth if he had asked me to.

"Many was the time we marched over the dusty roads, father frowning over some deep problem which I could not hope to fathom. I hated these moments when he shut himself away. I couldn't reach him. I didn't . . . try. I trotted behind him, grateful for the occasional remark he threw my way.

"I became his slave and I would wait crouched on the top of the stairs when he would come home of an evening. Then with a hoop and a holler I would hurl myself down the steps and into his arms. Obviously my abject devotion pleased him and he began to take an interest in me."

II

THE "DEEP PROBLEMS" that Patterson pondered on his walks with Alicia flowed from a turbulent 10 years in his life.

During his first full year on the farm, Patterson was elected to the Socialist Party's national executive committee. The following year, 1908, he managed the presidential campaign of Eugene V. Debs — only nine years after the death of Joseph Medill, who had ordered the *Tribune* to use the epithet "Dictator" every time it mentioned Debs. In that campaign, Patterson fell short of everyone's expectations. Another Patterson campaign, against his former mentor, Mayor Edward Dunne, also fizzled. So it was not as a politician that he made his mark during this period, but as a writer.

Probably his best-known work was a novel called *A Little Brother of the Rich*, which later became a play by the same title. Like many first novels, it was autobiographical, with a plot that revolved around a middle-class Yale undergraduate who became wealthy after graduation, by exploiting the poor. During that time, he wrote several other plays. The most successful was *The Fourth*

Estate, a melodramatic work that featured a corrupt publisher, a crusading editor and a bank of noisy typesetting machines on stage. All his writing throbbed with concern for the downtrodden, but his fervor for socialism cooled, as he became frustrated over its inability to bring about real change. Just four years after he had converted to socialism, a chain of events began that brought Patterson back to the *Tribune*.

In his last years, Robert Patterson had fought, largely unsuccessfully, to overcome alcohol. As a result, effective control of the paper fell to James Keeley, a tough, tenacious, cigar-chewing editor who had come to the *Tribune* in 1889 and risen to general manager. Aside from Robert Patterson, the only other member of the Patterson-McCormick clans in any position of power at the *Tribune* was Medill McCormick. Earlier, he had gone off to gain experience by running the *Cleveland Leader*, Joseph Medill's old paper. His wife, Ruth, saw it as a chance to be near her politically powerful father, Mark Hanna, which would help her husband start a political career. But the *Leader* lost money, and McCormick returned to Chicago, where Kate, his mother, hoped he would take over the *Tribune*. He did increase advertising revenue and worked as the paper's literary editor, and when Robert Patterson had to check into Carl Jung's clinic in Europe, McCormick took control. But McCormick was also struggling with alcohol, and he followed Patterson to the Jung clinic. Later, McCormick left the *Tribune* and moved to Washington, which led to a career in the United States Senate.

His younger brother, Robert Rutherford McCormick, had also been out of the *Tribune* orbit, becoming a lawyer, a city alderman and president of the city's sanitary district. Despite Joe Patterson's Socialist ties and the long-standing battle between his mother and Kate McCormick, he had always gotten along well with her son Bert. The two cousins became officers on the paper when Robert Patterson returned from a European stay and named Joe Patterson secretary and Bert McCormick treasurer. Then mortality intervened. On April 1, 1910, alone in a hotel room in Philadelphia, Robert W. Patterson died. His death threw the *Tribune* into a crisis. Victor Lawson, publisher of the *Chicago Daily News* and the *Record-Herald*, was offering the stockholders $10 million for the *Tribune*. When Bert McCormick persuaded the family not to sell, Lawson threatened to cut his price from two cents to one. Lawson made good on his threat, and the temporarily dormant circulation wars heated up again.

In the earlier battles, William Randolph Hearst had hired Max Annenberg away from the *Tribune* to make sure that news dealers found room on the stands for his *Chicago American*. Annenberg used a group of street-wise armed thugs to get fair treatment for the *American*. Now that Lawson had declared war, the *Tribune* responded by hiring Annenberg back, to make *Tribune* circulation grow, despite Lawson's price cut. Annenberg used his proven techniques of marketing by mayhem. Bullets and indictments flew freely, and people died, but the *Tribune*'s circulation rose.

If the paper's circulation strategy was unorthodox, its definition of executive responsibility was bizarre: Patterson edited the paper one month and

McCormick the next. The skills of the two cousins complemented each other nicely. Bert, the president, concentrated on business affairs, such as procuring newsprint by establishing a forest-to-pressroom ownership of the production process. Joe, the chairman, focused on making the *Tribune* a paper with something in it for everyone. Among his innovations was the idea of continuing stories in comic strips, to bring readers back day after day. The cousins also pioneered the use of rotogravure printing, to publish a sepia-tone version of the modern Sunday magazine. Another innovation was the movie directory page, an idea that came from Patterson's assistant, Mary King. "I never had a good idea in my life that she wasn't at least the first half of it," Patterson once said. So he named her the Sunday editor of the *Tribune*, the first time any woman had ever held that post at a major American newspaper. By 1914, the two cousins were strong enough to do without Keeley, who left to take control of the rival *Record-Herald*. The departure of a world-class journalist should have left them feeling vulnerable, but the team of Patterson, King, McCormick and Annenberg had solidified the paper's profitability and started its circulation climbing. Soon enough, however, Patterson had bigger wars to worry about.

In 1914, during the seemingly endless series of Mexican revolutions and counter-revolutions, the *Tribune* was among the many voices demanding American intervention. When the United States Marines seized Vera Cruz, Patterson dispatched himself to Mexico as a correspondent. By the time he arrived in Vera Cruz, the fighting was over, but shortly after he returned to Chicago, another war had broken out, the War to End All Wars. This time, Patterson was not going to miss the action. Within three weeks after the outbreak of war in Europe, Patterson was in Berlin, filing blatantly pro-German dispatches. His sympathy for Germany led to his arrest by the allies on spying charges. Luckily, he had made the acquaintance of Alfred Harmsworth, Lord Northcliffe, the London publishing giant, who extricated him.

Patterson returned to the war again in 1915, this time to observe it from the allied side. The result was a series of six articles for the *Tribune*, later published as a book called *Notebook of a Neutral*. It showed that, despite his strong pro-intervention feelings on Mexico, Patterson was a stout isolationist — not because he hated the idea of war but because he believed that America was more important than any potential ally. Not many months after his return from Europe, he left again in search of action. The Mexican rebel leader Pancho Villa had crossed the border into Texas and New Mexico in 1916, leaving behind a trail of dead, and President Woodrow Wilson sent General John Pershing to chase him. Patterson had joined the Illinois National Guard as an enlisted man, and Bert McCormick had acquired a commission as a colonel from Governor Edward Dunne, the former mayor of Chicago. Soon the two cousins were in Texas, where McCormick commanded a cavalry unit and Patterson tended horses and ended up a sergeant. While they were waiting patiently near the action, the *Tribune* loudly advocated intervention in Mexico. It questioned Wilson's moves toward entering the war in Europe, but advocated a strong military buildup. Once America entered the European war in 1917, despite all their reservations about it in print, Patterson and McCormick were quick to jump into the action.

At the age of 38, Patterson could have sat out the war, but he went overseas as a lieutenant with Battery B, 149th Field Artillery, 42nd (Rainbow) Division. From early January, 1918, until the armistice in November, Patterson and his men spent 100 days in combat. Along the way, he was wounded, gassed and promoted to captain — the title that stuck with him for the rest of his life. Bert McCormick saw some combat, but his major contribution was as a staff officer to General Pershing. For the captain and the colonel, however, the most lasting trophy of the war was not a title or a battle ribbon, but a plan for the future. That decision, made in a brief moment away from the second Battle of the Marne, recast the shape of journalism in America.

Pershing had ordered McCormick back home, to help organize troops for an offensive in 1919. Before leaving for the states, McCormick wanted to meet with his cousin. On July 20, 1918, McCormick borrowed a helmet from Brigadier General Douglas MacArthur at division headquarters and headed for the meeting, at a farmhouse-command post in the village of Mareuil-en-Dole. McCormick remembered later that they left the farmhouse and conversed on a manure pile, which Patterson denied. But they both remembered clearly the subject of their talk: tabloid journalism in postwar America. Patterson had been impressed by the success of Alfred Harmsworth, Lord Northcliffe, with his new British tabloid, *The Daily Mirror*. In his conversations with Patterson, Northcliffe had said that a tabloid could succeed in New York. That idea made sense to both cousins. "I said we would get started on it right away," McCormick remembered later. The key phrase was "right away." If they didn't establish the new tabloid quickly, someone else — Hearst, perhaps, or even Northcliffe himself — would do it.

Soon after he got out of the Army, Patterson persuaded his mother and his Aunt Kate that the *Tribune* should lend the money to bring his idea to life. Then he scrambled to rent space in New York from the *Evening Mail*, put together a staff and designed the paper. Less than a year after the meeting at the farm in France, the first issue of the *Illustrated Daily News* appeared, on June 26, 1919. That first issue was far from perfect, as an editorial on the second day acknowledged: "So far, our printing has been the worst in New York," the editorial said. "Before we're through it will be the best. Watch us." Patterson worked hard to improve the paper, fussing over details as small as the insufficient supply of critical letters to the editor, which he corrected by writing some himself. Despite that hard work, the paper experienced months of uncertainty. On the first day, curious New Yorkers snapped up 150,000 copies, but as the summer wore on, circulation plummeted, to well below 30,000 copies in July and August. For a while, the *Tribune* toyed with the idea of dropping the new venture entirely. But the circulation started to turn upward in September, and by October, the *Tribune* directors had decided to keep it going.

Given Patterson's intuitive sense of what the masses wanted to read, and given the identity of his circulation director, his old friend Max Annenberg, circulation was bound to go up, even though Patterson gave the old Chicago brawler terse new ground rules for operating in New York: "No more killing, Max." By the end of 1925, the circulation of Patterson's tabloid had passed 1,000,000. And Patterson, who had been running the paper by mail and tele-gram from Chicago, moved to New York, leaving Alice Higinbotham Patterson and his family behind in Chicago.

III

IN THE MIDST of circulation battles in Chicago, world war, and the establishment of a fabulously successful newspaper in New York, Joseph Medill Patterson faced one more formidable challenge: bringing up Alicia.

From the start, "Violet Roughneck," as they called Alicia, had to show a boy's toughness, courage and athletic skill. In contrast, the beautiful Elinor escaped that boyification and became known as "Elinor Delicate." The baby, Josephine, was a tough little kid, dubbed "Rosie Roughneck," who exasperated her sisters. "I think they really thought I was a terrible brat," Josephine said. "They resented me quite a lot." Eventually, though Josephine was seven years younger than Alicia, they grew close. Josephine joined in Alicia's mis-chief, such as helping her older sister escape at night by sleeping in Ali-cia's bed to disguise her absence, and she endured many of the same rites of male passage that Alicia did.

"Father seemed to get a kick out of having me do dangerous things," Alicia said. "In fact, what with one thing and another, I kept getting so scared that finally I wasn't scared of anything anymore. And boy, when you reach that stage, you've really got release from pain!" If Alicia couldn't learn to golf the first time, she stood out in the sun for hours, practicing until she collapsed. If she didn't have the nerve to jump off the 15-foot diving board at the farm, her father watched her stand up there trembling for hours until she jumped. "He made me do the same things," Josephine said. "When God speaks, you do what he says. . . . I had a pony. So he put a jockey saddle on it without any stirrups. He said, 'That's the way you learn to grip.' He just gave this pony a whack on the rear end and off the pony went." Soon, she lost her grip, and the fall knocked the wind out of her. "I staggered back, and he said, 'Why didn't you hold on to the pony?' " Experiences like those, reinforced by their mother's own brand of fearlessness, taught Alicia and Josephine a lesson: "You're not ever supposed to admit you're afraid," Josephine said. "It was considered a sin to be afraid."

The bravery theme showed up even in the fairy tales that Patterson told about Black Mane and Silver Mane, a lion and lioness. "Black Mane was bigger and braver than any lion that ever lived, but the most awful things happened to him," Alicia wrote. "Black Mane always came out on top, but those dreadful moments when his life was hanging by a thread were agonizing. I woke up screaming at night. . . ." His emphasis on courage didn't end in her childhood.

"Long after I had grown up, father continued to exert an almost hypnotic influence on me," Alicia said later. "I would have died rather than fail him. On one trip to the Panama Canal Zone, father discovered that the best tarpon fishing was to be had at Gatun Dam, a structure 150 feet high. . . . The only way to catch one of those huge fish was to wade out atop the dam, knee-deep in rushing water, and then to cast over the edge to the rocks at the base of the spillway." Though that adventure regularly killed people, her father told her to try it. "I waded through the roaring torrent and dutifully cast until I hooked a fish," she said. "Psychiatrists may suggest that pa felt an ambivalence toward me, a mixture of love and hate, a desire to test my nervous system to the snapping point. All I know is that he helped to make me unafraid. I felt at times like the Spartan boy who kept silent though the fox was gnawing at his vitals."

As tough as he was, her father had a softer side. He'd bring home the comic strips and read them aloud, or make up stories and weave his daughters in as characters. Or he would sing to them. Or he'd sit on the stairs of their red brick house at 3 Banks Street and teach Alicia and her friend, Florence Noyes, to play chess. Whether he was driving Alicia and Josephine to conquer fear or spending gentler moments with them, "Poppy" was the center of their lives. "We worshiped him," Josephine said. Their relationship with their mother was different. "She was quite Victorian in many ways, and she wanted us to behave, but she had a hard time making us do it," Josephine said. "She didn't like noise and she didn't like mess and she thought children ought to be seen and not heard quite as much as we were." Alicia and her friend Dorothy Michelson, known as Dody, would disappear whenever Alicia's mother came around the corner. "We were scared to death of Mrs. Patterson," Dody said. "There was always nothing but a scolding." Once, when they were about 13, Dody visited with Alicia overnight, and Alicia persuaded her to join in some mischief, in Alice Patterson's absence: They would dress up in Alice's clothes and attend a risque play in downtown Chicago. "I told Mrs. Patterson about it one time, some 20 years later," Dody said, "and she did not think it was funny at all."

Growing up, the Patterson girls spent their winter months in Chicago — first in the house at 3 Banks Street, then in apartments at 232 Walton Place and 209 Lake Shore Drive, a short walk from the opulent Drake Hotel. In the summer, they moved to the farm in Libertyville. Alicia also spent large parts of her summers with the family of Florence Noyes, at their home on Campement D'Ours Island, in Ontario. No matter where she was, Alicia always managed to find trouble. In the city, she and her friends would run through the alleys, ring doorbells, throw dead cats on the doorsteps of the neighbors, hitch rides on ice wagons. In Libertyville, they would sneak into the pool on the neighboring property and flee in their bathing suits when the police arrived. On occasion, she showed that she could be as pugnacious as her father. "She called my dog a fool once, my Irish terrier," Florence Noyes said, "and we had a terrible, physical fight."

As carefully as Alicia applied herself to playfulness and boyish skills, she was less serious about studying — at least in her earliest years. In the elementary grades, she attended the University School for Girls, near the Oak Street beach, north of the Drake Hotel. From the windows, her classmates could look out the windows and notice Joe Patterson jogging, in the sloppiest clothing he could manage. That embarrassed Alicia, but more often, it was Alicia herself who raised eyebrows at the school. "She was always the ringleader," Dody Michelson said. Alicia loved practical jokes, and her friends had to be eternally vigilant. "Alicia and I once decided in seventh grade we were going to strike and get everybody else to do it too," Florence Noyes said. "This was a prank on me. And so, at a certain hour when the clock hit that moment, I stood up all by myself and said, 'I strike.' Nobody else stood up. It was all organized."

From the University School, the next stop for Alicia was Les Fougeres, a boarding school in Lausanne, Switzerland, where the daughters of the wealthy could learn to speak French and German. While Elinor and Alicia studied, their mother lived at hotels in Nice and Versailles, and Josephine attended a parochial school. Madame Chaubert, the headmistress at Les Fougeres, ran her kingdom of 50 or 60 students with a firm set of rules, especially on the subject of language. "The idea was that you were supposed to learn French and think in French," said Marian Brown, who had been with Alicia at the University School and then was her roommate for part of Marian's time at Les Fougeres. "Every evening we'd have to confess how many English words we had spoken during the day. . . . Of course, most of us transgressed constantly." But Elinor followed the rules, just as she always had. "I remember her accent being very, very nice and greatly approved of by the various teachers there," Marian Brown said. Alicia was just the opposite. "She wasn't terribly interested in learning French. She was pretty much a law unto herself."

What Alicia wanted was books in English, which were taboo at Les Fougeres. So she entered into a conspiracy with her father, encouraging him to send her books, at the same time as she was asking him to send money and chocolates. "Most likely Elinor wrote you and said that Madame didn't want you to send me anymore books," Alicia wrote. "I shouldn't think you'd listen to her because she never writes you anyway. So *please* send me some more books." Her father needed no encouragement to break rules, so he kept sending Alicia the forbidden books, and in his letters he gave her capsule descriptions of the works. "There are millions of books I want to read," she said in another letter, giving him a list that ranged from *Doctor Faustus* and *David Copperfield* to a less high-minded requisition for "lots of trashy exciting books."

Despite Alicia's disregard for discipline, her roommate detected real talent there. "She was intelligent, and she was very well read and very critical and had a very fine sort of analytical mind," Marian Brown said. "In a way, it was a wasted life, because she could have really amounted in the academic world to a great deal." But even then, her father was encouraging Alicia's deas about a non-academic career, in the family business. In one letter, he mentioned the Graduate School of Journalism at Columbia. "I don't know that this is a very good school," he wrote, "but I will find out before you ever decide where you want to go." Alicia wrote back to her father excitedly: "I am awfully interested in that journalism school and would like to go there awfully."

Well in advance of any decision about her formal schooling, her father's letters were already providing her with a correspondence course in writing. She would send him undated letters written in a sloppy, almost illegible hand, with no noticeable punctuation and erratic spelling. He would almost always send back typewritten letters, full of gentle encouragement and writing hints. "Really you oughtn't to use 'vile' and 'horrid' and 'hateful' and 'loathe' casually," he wrote. "Strong language is supposed to be saved for an emergency and then shot out all at once, not dribbled out like squeezing a sponge. It should be sort of an explosion that will do some damage in the neighborhood, tear up trees and rocks, make a hole in the ground."

The letter that prompted that comment was one of a series in which Alicia lobbied her father to get her out of Switzerland. "Mother is going to stay over here two years!!!!!!!!!!!! Isn't that awful???? I know I shall die here if I have to stay in this *vile* school more than this winter." She got her wish. In the spring of 1921, when Alicia was 14, she came home to America and went to St. Timothy's School, in Catonsville, Maryland. Right after she arrived, her father wrote his assessment of the school. "Groton was very strict and made me step around and do what I didn't want to do," he wrote. "Yale was very easy and I got away with murder. The consequence is that I look back at Groton with great affection and I am glad I went there, whereas I look back at Yale without any affection. . . . In other words, St. Timothy's is a great deal like a girls' Groton." Academically, Alicia did well, but before the year was over, she found a way to get herself booted out, as she described it, "for general obstreperousness."

Her next stop was Foxcroft, in the Virginia hunt country. Foxcroft had a Spartan regimen: The girls slept in sleeping bags on unheated porches, for example, and they wore uniforms — corduroy skirts and green corduroy coats in the winter. This time, though, Alicia didn't seem to rebel against the discipline quite as much, perhaps because Foxcroft had something that she loved dearly: horses. "Today I jumped and the teacher said I did it very well," Alicia wrote. "Just loads of people have their own horses and if you want to hunt you've got to have your own. So *please* get me one for Christmas." That fall, Alicia took some tests for matriculation at Bryn Mawr, but she didn't score well. Still, she adjusted well to Foxcroft, in and out of the classroom. She took first- and second-place honors in the Foxcroft horse show, played as a substitute on the basketball team, and served as the sports editor of the yearbook, *Tally-Ho*. At the end of two years, in the spring of 1924, she was graduated second in her class. It began to look as if Alicia might be growing up.

Just as she was turning 18, in the fall of 1924, Alicia went abroad for some additional "finishing," to Miss Risser's School for Girls in Rome. Her time there was brief. On November 4, she sent her father a cable: "Complications. Six girls expelled. . . . Cable money for passage. Distressed." The six girls included Alicia, a friend named Winifred West and Elizabeth Drake, whose father ran the Drake Hotel. Miss Risser cabled Alice Patterson and said she was dismissing Alicia from the school, and a few days later, she followed the cable with a letter that explained what had happened to prompt the mass dismissals.

"Last Sunday night six girls, including Alicia and Winifred, left the villa at midnight walking two miles through a part of the city where the streets are dark and deserted, to a garage where I am accustomed to rent my motors," Miss Risser wrote. "There they insisted upon the owner furnishing them with a car and a driver. . . . They drove all around town, and out into the country, stopping first at a very conspicuous sidewalk cafe on the Corso where they ordered cocktails. Finally, at three o'clock, he insisted on bringing them home. . . . Alicia has shown a most disappointing attitude, disdainful towards the other girls and rebellious to the very simple rules. . . . I feel that Sunday night was a sort of final challenge to the life she was expected to lead here with me, and naturally there was nothing to do but dismiss her summarily with the rest."

Alicia wrote her father an abjectly repentant letter. "I don't know what ever struck me," she wrote. "I guess I must have some wild blood in my veins alright." She and the other girls had been feeling "fearfully bored and blue and were simply pining for some excitement" when their little escape began, Alicia said. It ended ignominiously. "When we got home we found the gate locked and had to climb the wall. Unfortunately there was some cut glass stuck on the top and we all cut ourselves to pieces. I had taken off my shoes to make less noise and consequently my feet were torn to shreds and I haven't been able to walk since. . . . Forgive me if you can and I'll honestly try to reform in the future."

Her father seemed as angry at Miss Risser as he did at Alicia. In a letter to Elizabeth Drake's father, he said: "I certainly would not call this an offense for which half the children in the school should have been expelled a week or two after their arrival. I think the woman is an old fool." To his oldest daughter, the well-behaved Elinor, Patterson wrote an exasperated complaint: "What a bad girl she is! If she doesn't like a place she makes everybody unhappy, including her family. I wish she would behave better." To Alicia, who was staying in a London hotel with a chaperone while she waited for her mother and Josephine to arrive by boat, he sent a gentle letter of reproof. "Alicia, please try to be a good sensible girl from now on," he wrote. "You have hurt my feelings a good deal by getting expelled from your school in Rome. It makes me apprehensive about your future."

Her mother was less understanding. When Alice Patterson reached London, she conceived a drastic plan for taming her 18-year-old daughter. "Mother was all for sending her to a convent in the north of Scotland," Josephine remembered, "but she raised such hell that she finally persuaded mother that we were to go to Rome so we could get culture." At some point in this odyssey, Alice cabled her husband with a plea for advice, and he cabled back: "Keep Alicia moving." On their way from London to Rome, Alicia, Josephine and Alice stopped off in Biarritz, where Alicia met several men who asked her for dates. "I got two proposals in Biarritz, one from a Cuban and one from a Russian," she wrote to her father. "I liked the Cuban the best but he has such backward ideas about women. . . . Anyhow I haven't any intentions of marrying him." Her father's reaction was crude and racist. "I am glad at least that you decided not to marry the coon," he wrote. "Most Cubans are touched with the tar brush, as they say."

Having failed to finish finishing school, Alicia wandered the continent, accompanied by her mother, Josephine and a tutor, a well-educated woman whom they they called Dottaressa Gibellini. "She was a Ph.D. type who took us from museum to museum and ruin to ruin," Josephine said. "We liked it, I guess, but I remember throwing up in the Sistine Chapel once. We were just drug through the Vatican by the hour, and I was 12, and I was getting a little tired of it." As the winter receded into spring, and the last bits of her formal education ended, Alicia realized what the inevitable next step would be. Her parents would spend thousands of dollars on a gaudy debutante ball back home in Chicago, in which Alicia would join society. After years of boarding school, she was happy to be coming home, but she didn't want to "come out" into society.

"I wish to heaven you wouldn't all make me come out next winter," she wrote her father. "If you would give me that same money that you would spend on my debut, I would travel and improve my mind instead of dashing around to dumb parties that I hate anyway." But society was too important to Alice Patterson to let Alicia win that argument. So, in late 1925, at the age of 19, Alicia climbed into an orchid tulle dress, walked into the Crystal Ballroom of Chicago's Blackstone Hotel, which was filled with roses and poinsettias and 600 guests, and met Chicago society. The only thing missing was her sister Elinor, who was off in Boston, playing the role of the nun in *The Miracle*, Max Reinhardt's cast-of-thousands religious drama. When the band had stopped playing and the last guest had left, Alicia Patterson was faced with the reality that her education was over and now she had to figure out how to get on with the rest of her life.

IV

THE FIRST FEW months after Alicia's society debut were not exactly filled with momentous achievements.

"Last year she went about to various horse-shows in the middle west exhibiting jumpers. I regretted this," Joe Patterson wrote, in an article on daughters and careers. "Alicia did not go to college. I wanted her to but she wouldn't. Her education is rather sketchy. She has a good enough mind, but put it on bridge and horses." At some point, Alicia would have to turn that mind to something more serious than aimless dabbling in horses and boys.

Though Alicia and her father had once talked about the Graduate School of Journalism at Columbia, he didn't really consider that a serious option. "The thing simply never entered my head," Patterson wrote. "What an aspiring newspaper man or woman needs is as broad an education as he can get in all lines. Add to that the ability to use the typewriter, and it seems to me he has all that a school of journalism can teach him. Then it is up to his own brains, ambition and experience." So Alicia took a brief course in typing and started work at the *Daily News* office at 25 Park Place, at the age of 20. She began her journalism career, she remembered later, "in the corner clipping out filler items from other newspapers for use in the *Sunday News*." Her father put her on the Sunday paper first because the pace was more leisurely than what she would have found working on the daily paper. "She had actually never been in a subway in New York until she became a Sunday reporter," he wrote. "To her the town was taxicabs, theaters, dressmakers and parties. Now she has found out the other town of crime and statistics and pathos. Sinners, saints, Mrs. Dives and Mr. Lazarus, she meets them all. People have said to me, 'You let her see these horrors?' I do, since she wants to."

In New York, Alicia continued her pursuit of fun, staying out late in speakeasies and enjoying the company of an endless caravan of young men. But she also began developing a serious feeling for the *Daily News*, growing close to Max Annenberg and to the city editor, Harvey Deuell. In addition, of course, she had the example of Joseph Medill Patterson. "Much that I learned I learned from my father," she wrote in a speech years later. "He had the most active curiosity I have ever encountered. Nothing was too insignificant for him to notice, from the way a leaf grew on a tree to a stray alley cat prowling the roof tops. This trait helped him to understand why people do as they do, and why they laugh and cry and hate and love, and why they buy some newspapers and ignore others. He was geared with invisible antennae that alerted him to the shifting moods of the times. He changed the *News* so that it reflected and appraised these moods." Patterson did have antennae, as Alicia observed, but he didn't find out what people were thinking by sitting in his office. He got out into the streets of New York and observed. He went to the movies and listened to people talk. He stood at newsstands and watched the papers that people were buying. He went down into the subway and watched what stories people were reading. He kept the company of panhandlers on the Bowery. He travelled to Coney Island, the blue-collar amusement park by the sea in Brooklyn, where he sampled the inexpensive entertainment of the city's working people.

With her father's example in front of her, Alicia plunged into her work and began to learn something about reporting on the lives of real people. The city editor sent her on an assignment to interview a woman "whose husband had just been designated by the judge as the most pitiful case of henpecking that he had yet witnessed," Alicia remembered. "I was to find out how and why she won this distinction. I charged up the five flights of tenement stairs with fire in my eye, determination in my heart, and the will to die for the dear old *Daily News*. I pounded on the door, which was opened by my victim. The lady was enormous, forceful, uncompromising. Nothing daunted, I blurted out my question with a 'tell me or else' attitude. She growled and the door was well on the way to slamming in my face. Feeling that never again would I be able to face my city editor unless I brought home the story, I inserted my foot in the jamb. The conclusion was quick and to the point. She lifted me by the scruff of the neck and tossed me with dispatch down the five flights. I am sure that if I had been sympathetic, rather than inquisitional, I might have gotten my interview."

That learning experience was painful for the moment, but it didn't hurt as much as the lesson she learned when she covered a messy marital dispute and somehow managed to mix up the names in her story, which gave birth to a libel suit. "When she told me about it she cried, she was so sorry," Patterson wrote. But the tears didn't deter him from his plan: "After Alicia has had a little more training, I expect to discharge her and let her hunt for another job. That's a regular part of newspaper life." Soon afterward, he invited her to lunch, along with his cousin, Bert McCormick. Right there in the restaurant, they jointly fired Alicia — not only because of the libel suit, but also because they thought that a firing would be good training for her. Stunned, Alicia threw a monumental tantrum. "Bertie was horribly embarrassed," Alicia said. "I don't think he could *abide* me for years afterward. But he got pretty well over it at last." Her father looked at it casually. "Maybe one of my friends in the business . . . will hire her," he wrote, citing a long list of possible bosses for his daughter. Alicia was not as casual. Despondent, she went back to Chicago and resumed the life of a playgirl.

V

THE COMPARISON WITH her beautiful sister Elinor had always made Alicia feel plain and awkward, but that didn't stop her from being interested in boys or prevent boys from noticing her.

"She always had a lot of beaux," said Jane Warner Dick, one of her childhood friends. "She was very attractive, had a lot of sex appeal and a lot of intelligence and was very uninhibited." Growing up on the farm in Libertyville, Alicia would ride for miles toward Lake Forest, meet her friend Janet Chase halfway, and sit there chatting about the future. "Sometimes we talked about marriage, whether we would get married for love or for what," Janet said. "Alicia said she would marry for power." In keeping with that goal, Alicia particularly admired the Russian actress, Alla Nazimova, for her power over men. "There were pictures of Nazimova all over her room," her friend Dody Michelson remembered.

Despite her concern that Elinor was much more beautiful, Alicia's looks, along with her sense of fun and her drawling, somewhat husky voice, made her very attractive to men. She also had a neat trick of appearing shy, casting her eyes downward in the presence of a boy, then suddenly raising them and looking straight at him — to great effect. "I was in love with being in love," Alicia said. She was so popular, in fact, that she sometimes attracted several invitations for the same night, and she contrived an interesting approach for dealing with that. "Two of them would ask her for a date and I was brought along to entertain number one while she was talking to number two," Dody Michelson said. "Neither one sort of had the chance to say, 'Do you really love me?' "

One of the men who interested Alicia was a young lawyer from Bloomington named Adlai Stevenson. In 1926, when Alicia was wandering around loose after her coming-out party, Stevenson came to Chicago to begin the practice of law. "That's when Adlai just kind of melted into our group," Jane Warner Dick said. "We had positions on ecology and politics, and I think that's why we found Adlai very interesting, because to us he was a fountainhead of wisdom." Stevenson was six years older than Alicia, but she and her friends found him utterly charming. Some of their friends said that he even proposed marriage to Alicia, which would not have been unusual. "He was everybody's beau," Alicia's friend Florence Noyes remembered. "He proposed to everybody, including me." But Stevenson later married one of Alicia's former classmates at the University School, Ellen Borden.

Even before she left the *Daily News* and the string of boys she met in New York, Alicia had a marriage proposal of her own, from James Simpson Jr., whose father ran Marshall Field & Company, the department store empire. That proposal carried some interesting historical echoes. Marshall Field himself had made a loan to Alicia's great-grandfather, Joseph Medill, allowing him to buy a controlling share in the *Chicago Tribune*. And when Field died, Alicia's father had written a Socialist diatribe against the wealth that he left in his will. "Jim Simpson is coming to see me next Saturday to say he wants to marry Alicia," Joe Patterson wrote to his daughter Elinor. "I am not going to encourage it, but of course I won't stand in the way." Alice Patterson had more reason to favor the match. Her father had been a partner in the Field enterprises, and now her daughter had a chance to marry a handsome young man from that same wealthy milieu.

Whatever her parents felt about it, Alicia didn't act at all like a young woman convinced that this was the love of her life. One minute, everything seemed fine, with Alicia and her mother dining pleasantly at the Simpson home. The next day, within hours after the official announcement of the wedding had appeared in Chicago newspapers, a small glitch developed: A young Milwaukee archaeologist named A. Ledyard Smith, who had reportedly been "very attentive" to Alicia at a series of dances in North Milwaukee, obtained a license to marry her. The license was issued in Waukegan, Illinois, which the Associated Press described as "a place where hurry-up marriages are frequent." In the hot, gossipless dog days of August, the details of this complication spread quickly, gleefully disseminated by the competitors of the *Chicago Tribune*. Finally, poor Ledyard Smith confessed that he had gotten the license in a moment of romantic hope, and his chances of marrying Alicia had existed only in his mind. "Miss Patterson certainly did not accompany me to Waukegan, and she did not know of my plans to ask for a license," he acknowledged.

At the time of the Smith incident, Alicia was only 20, and still as wild as ever. But she decided to marry Simpson and promised to stay with him for a year. Surrounded by speckled lilies and yellow roses in the living room of the Patterson country home at Libertyville, they stood at an informal altar in front of a bay window and took the vows. The guests sipped champagne from Alicia's shoe, and everything seemed fine. But the bride was still somewhat reluctant. "The next morning, after the wedding, the doorbell rang about nine o'clock, and I went to the door, and there was Alicia," said Florence Noyes. "She just didn't want to leave us. I said, 'What are you doing here?' I was sort of embarrassed, and I guess she was, too."

Even on the *R.M.S. Laconia,* sailing toward Europe for a months-long honeymoon, Alicia didn't seem entirely comfortable being alone with her new husband. "Darling," she wrote to her father, "please come over this winter, would you? I'd give anything if you would. I miss you terribly already." Before the honeymoon, she had visited her old friends at the *Daily News,* and she wrote to tell her father she'd be coming back some day. "Gosh, I love that place," she wrote. "They all kidded me about Waukegan and mentioned that I was creating scandal instead of collecting it. . . . You know big boy I am eventually going back to that place. First I am going to get so good at the Trib that you can't out of fairness keep me off, and then I want to go back to the News. I guess it's a fever I've got like the stage."

Once the new bride and groom were in England, they began arguing vehemently over everything. One night, for example, they went to the theater in London, and Alicia insisted, to Simpson's horror, on going into a between-the-acts bar that was staunchly male-only. "Jim has given up hunting entirely, and I don't see much of him anymore — just as lucky because we are usually fighting when I do," Alicia wrote her father. "I'll say one thing — married bliss isn't all it's cracked up to be. This living happily ever after is the bunk." One source of friction was Alicia's fierce pride in her father, even though he had fired her a few months earlier. "He knows now that the only way he can get a rise out of me is by saying something about that damned yellow sheet," she wrote. "I retaliate and compliments fly thick and fast."

When the arguments got heated enough, Simpson occasionally resorted to hitting his feisty new bride, Alicia later told her friends. At one point, the strain of the relationship apparently got to her. "You didn't know did you I had been quite sick?" she wrote her father. "Sort of a nervous breakdown — I stayed in a nursing home about a week." Eventually, Alicia grew so uncomfortable with her new husband that she sent for her friend Janet Chase to join her for part of the honeymoon. A third person on any honeymoon is odd, as her father pointed out in one of his letters, but the past relationship between Janet Chase and Simpson made it even stranger. "I didn't like him very much," Janet remembered. "He proposed to me before he met Alicia. I turned him down. He didn't have any sense of humor." After Janet's arrival, the fighting continued. "One evening," Janet said, "she moved out of his bedroom and moved in with me." The hostilities evolved into something like separate honeymoons: The groom went his way, to the races, and the bride and her friend went theirs, chasing foxes in the hunt country at Melton Mowbray. "You don't know how nice it is to have her," Alicia wrote to her father. "Jim never hunts and is always tearing off to race meetings for weeks at a time, so I would be completely stranded without her."

The fox hunting charmed Alicia so much that she used part of her honeymoon time to write a piece about it for *Liberty*, the magazine that her father had started in 1924 to challenge the *Saturday Evening Post*. Patterson loved his daughter's article and agreed to pay her $275 for it — minus the cost of cabling the money to her. (That was their way. He was absurdly generous, but at the same time, he seemed to nickel-and-dime her in minor matters, to help her learn how to cope with being rich.) Though he loved the piece itself, he was not happy about the absence of her married name from her byline. "If by any chance you take my story," she had written him, "please sign it Alicia Patterson. Jim would rather and so would I."

All the signs were there, in those first weeks of the marriage, that it was, as Alicia later called it, "a self-canceling contest of wills." A year later, having stayed as long as she had promised to stay, Alicia left Jim Simpson abruptly and permanently. She filed for divorce in 1930, accusing him of desertion.

VI

IF ALICIA'S FIRST marriage did nothing else, it had at least started her off as a magazine writer. Her father had fired her from the *Daily News*, but in his role as the publisher of *Liberty*, he was happy to pay her for more pieces like "Fox Hunting in Leicestershire."

The stories she wrote were not hard-hitting investigations or even profound sociological reporting. They were basically fluffy, reasonably well written accounts of the continuing adventures of Alicia. For one series of articles, Alicia set out to see how an untrained, unemployed country girl would do in the job market. So she dubbed herself Agnes Holmberg, borrowing her identity from a real person back home in Libertyville, and went to look for work. In one piece, she sold magazine subscriptions, and she turned out not to be very good at it. In another, she got herself hired as a department store dress saleswoman and quit a week later. Escalating her adventures to a higher level of danger, Alicia decided that she wanted to learn to fly. She started taking lessons at the same time she left Jim Simpson, and continued her training at Curtiss Field and Roosevelt Field on Long Island. "My father had a Laird biplane with a J5 Wright motor," she wrote. "He was learning to fly, too, and with all due respect he was just about as dumb as I was." Together with their instructor, Fred Becker, Alicia and her father went on a 3,500-mile tour of the Caribbean in their Sikorsky amphibian. They both got their licenses in 1929, but only after a series of scrapes that Alicia detailed in *Liberty*. In later pieces, *Liberty* occasionally ran an inset photo of Alicia, right under her byline, showing her in a pilot's helmet and goggles.

Despite getting his license, Joe Patterson remained a dreadful pilot. He had overcome his fear of flying, but he never overcame his poor eye-hand coordination. Once, taking off from Roosevelt Field in the huge Sikorsky, he somehow flipped the plane on its back, destroying it. Uninjured, he switched to his other plane, the Laird, and flew off. Unlike her father, Alicia made herself into a fair pilot. But she was sloppy about navigation. Other pilots would study maps and weather charts carefully, but she would glance quickly at a map, then take off, relying on railroad tracks as her primary means of navigation. Once, she got herself lost in fog over northern New York State and ended up 180 miles off course. But she did learn the knack of flying fast in her black and gold Laird biplane. In less than two weeks at the end of 1930, she set women's speed records from Philadelphia to New York, from New York to Albany and back, and from Cleveland to New York. On the Cleveland flight, she narrowly escaped disaster, landing at Curtiss Field with a dead motor and an empty fuel tank.

Right after her record-setting flights, Alicia left for the Far East on a hunting trip, accompanied by her friend Janet Chase's sister Elizabeth. In the sheep country of Queensland, Australia, she and Libby Chase hunted kangaroos, and Alicia shot one in the neck from 50 feet. "I didn't feel nearly so jubilant as I expected," she wrote in *Liberty*. "He had such a sweet face." But she quickly overcame this feeble attack of conscience. When Libby Chase became ill and had to go home, Alicia pushed on to Southeast Asia, where she went after meaner game: a huge, buffalo-like creature called a sladang, with horns that measured four feet from tip to tip. The tribesmen who guided her were so excited by her trophy — reputedly the first sladang killed by a white woman — that they staged a ceremony with drums and dead chickens, marking a cross on her forehead in chicken blood to identify her as a god-like "hunt lady."

On her Asian trip, Alicia had to dodge yet another set of marriage rumors, this time involving Peter Grimm, the Shanghai representative of a New York firm. "It is the most absurd thing I ever heard," she told a reporter. "I met Mr. Grimm on a trip out of Saigon, and sat at the same table with him and two Englishmen. I never was alone with Mr. Grimm excepting for half an hour or so at Shanghai when we went shopping." But when she returned home, Alicia found herself moving toward a real marriage — thanks to her father and her flying.

Her new love interest was Joseph W. Brooks, a former All-America tackle at Colgate. His father had been the general manager of Western Union, and both of his grandfathers had been officers in the Confederate Army. Brooks himself, the first member of his family born north of the Mason-Dixon line, became an officer in the United States Army and served in the battle of St. Mihiel with a unit of the 42nd Division, as Joe Patterson did. Brooks was a giant of a man, but he had a gentle disposition that charmed everyone, including Joe Patterson, who became his close hunting and fishing buddy after the war. Brooks located his insurance office in the East 42nd Street building that Patterson built for the *Daily News*, and Patterson sent much of his insurance business to him. Brooks was seldom around the office, leaving the heavy lifting to his partner and reserving plenty of leisure time for himself.

"He was first of all a sportsman," said Kathleen Bishop, whose late husband, Dr. Louis F. Bishop, became a close friend of Brooks through playing racquets at the New York Racquet Club. "Everybody liked to shoot with him, everybody liked to play golf with him, because he was tops at whatever he did. . . . I never met anybody that didn't like him." The sports that appealed to him most were fishing and hunting. In 1924, Brooks and two friends from World War I had bought 600 acres along the Ausable River in the Adirondack Mountains of upstate New York, built a cabin of pine logs, called The Shanty, and added a grass airport a half mile away. They stocked the stream with trout and fished it avidly. On one weekend fishing trip to the Brooks camp, Joe Patterson asked if he could bring along Alicia. The relationship between Brooks and Alicia started slowly, but then they began flying together and growing closer.

Even though Brooks was 15 years older than she was, Alicia loved his courage, his sportsmanship, his outgoing personality. Sports came naturally to Brooks. Despite his size and his meaty hands, he had a deft touch with a trout fly. But it wasn't easy or natural for Alicia. She had to work hard to acquire any athletic skill, and her competitive fires burned into anger when she didn't do well. "When she first tried it, she'd lose her temper when she got a strike and couldn't hook the fish," Brooks said in a magazine interview. "I had a fine collection of trout rods. . . . She'd get mad and throw them into the water after the fish that got away. But she's a fine fly fisherman now." So they fished together, hunted together, flew together. In fact, it was through aviation that the world first learned that Alicia and Brooks were engaged. Alicia was in London with a friend, and Brooks was flying her Laird speedwing from Long Island to Chicago, to have some work done on the plane at the factory. En route, he crashed in South Bend, Indiana, damaging the plane. Then her father gave away the secret. "Account inquiries concerning Joe's crash thought wise announce your intention marriage coming winter," Patterson cabled Alicia. Tersely, she cabled back: "Furious at unauthorized announcement. Unable to understand why not consulted."

Like their courtship, their honeymoon had an aviation theme. It began at Roosevelt Field on Long Island, where they climbed into a Bellanca monoplane and headed off for an aerial tour of the South, including Mexico. Consistent with her first honeymoon, Alicia took someone else along: a mechanic, Charles Sutter. But it wasn't for protection from her new husband; they got along fine. While they were on the honeymoon, Alicia's father made plans for her future. Through trusts and other arrangements, Patterson was giving her an income of $25,000 a year. In addition, he had decided to provide them with a place to live, buying three acres in the fashionable Long Island community of Sands Point and outfitting a house for them, which he rented to Alicia for 99 years, at $1 a year. Beyond that, he offered Alicia a chance to get back into newspapering, preferably in the *Daily News* advertising department. "That is because you already know something about the editorial end, but the Advertising Department tells you where the money comes from and how hard it is to get," he wrote her. Writing back from a hunting lodge in Sea Island, Georgia, Alicia said: "I'll do anything you think best — only to be perfectly frank, I prefer the editorial side. The main thing is I want to learn the newspaper game backwards and forwards. Who knows? I might be a great publisher myself some day."

Two months after it began, the honeymoon ended with a bang: On the last leg of their flight, from Chicago to New York, they made a forced landing in high winds at Leroy, a small town in upstate New York. Then they hopped on a train for New York City to begin the rest of their lives together. The marriage provided some stability in Alicia's life, but it didn't entirely settle her down. With her sister Josephine and their friend Libby Chase — but without Joe Brooks — Alicia travelled to Rome, Athens, Cairo, Baghdad, Persia and India. When they reached India, Alicia wanted to hunt wild boars from horseback, an elaborate ritual known as "pig-sticking." Women were not supposed to participate in this dangerous event, but they somehow persuaded an Indian prince to let them in on the spectacle — the golden tents, the elephants, the polo ponies, the spears, the crowds of "beaters" flushing out the boars. "It's by far the hardest sport I've ever attempted," Alicia wrote her father. "It has fox hunting, shooting, fishing beaten hollow. Yes, and flying too. It combines danger, speed, accuracy, skill. The sport of kings alright."

That long trip away from her new husband did not appear to hurt her marriage to Brooks. "They got along awfully well for a while," Josephine said. Together, they made a large investment in the future, buying their own hunting lodge. On a trip to Sea Island, they had found a piece of property along the St. Mary's River that they loved. They bought 1,800 acres there for fishing and quail hunting, and on a bend in the river, they built a simple lodge of clear cypress, which became Alicia's favorite retreat from the world. Together, they travelled with a glittering crowd in New York and on Long Island that included the actress Katharine Cornell and her husband, the producer Guthrie McClintic, the journalist Heywood Broun and others. Together, Brooks and Alicia almost had a baby. But it turned out to be an ectopic pregnancy, and Alicia learned that she would never be able to have her own child. They also had their individual interests. Alicia was working again at the *News*, first in the advertising department and later as a book reviewer. Joe had his circle of friends, his camp in the Adirondacks, his racquet club. But as their marriage neared the seven-year mark, a subtle change came over them. Alicia, the playgirl, was beginning to think more and more seriously about a career. Joe was showing no signs of thinking seriously about anything except recreation. "He liked avocations, rather than vocations," Josephine said. "He didn't like to work much. . . . I know that she was very upset about the gambling, and he used to play way over his head with the big boys." Alicia began to feel that Joe was running up too many debts and counting on her to bail him out. "She told me that she had to pay his bills," said Hal Burton, who worked first with Joe Patterson and later with Alicia. "She felt she was winding up a drunken bum. . . . She was determined to get out of her marriage with Joe, much as she loved him."

Later, Alicia called these entertaining but purposeless years "a messed-up period in my life." She was having fun, but she was starting to question whether having fun was what she was really about. "As the years went on," she said, "I began to feel restive about a life based on sports. Joe and I grew apart." It was during that time that she met someone far more serious about life than Joe, someone firmly dedicated to his career. His name was Harry Frank Guggenheim.

CHAPTER FOUR

Ghetto to Gold Mine

I

THE STING OF religious hatred does not hurt any less if oppressors and oppressed are both surrounded by breathtaking scenery. Certainly, the Swiss ghetto that imprisoned the dreams of the Guggenheim family was beautiful, a gentle green valley carved out by a stream called the Surb. But their village of Lengnau was still a ghetto.

For centuries, European Jews had been forced to wander from town to town, fleeing first from massacres and then from the subtler forms of oppression by the Christian majority. The Christians even forced names on the Jews. At some point, the ancestors of the Guggenheims had passed through the German village of Guggenheimb, and that brief passage had saddled them with a name. The family lived under the yoke of anti-Semitism for generations, until one Guggenheim, a tailor named Simon, led them out of the ghetto.

Simon Guggenheim was the father of six children, one of whom had died, and he had been a widower for 11 years. Then he met a widow, Rachel Weil Meyer, who had seven children of her own. Since Jews needed government permission to marry, and Simon and Rachel didn't have enough money to arrange that approval, Simon began to think of another solution. In letters from those who had emigrated, the Lengnau Jews were hearing wonderful things about America. Jews who lived there could move about freely, choose whatever livelihood interested them, own whatever property they could afford. The place that appealed most strongly to Simon was the City of Philadelphia, which had gained a reputation for religious tolerance. So, at the end of 1847, Simon Guggenheim and Rachel Weil Meyer gathered their children and sailed to

America. Early in 1848, they reached Philadelphia. Simon and Rachel married, and the joined families moved into a small house and began to make a living.

The Guggenheims started humbly. Simon gave up tailoring and took up peddling, as his son Meyer had done in the old country. Simon sold his goods to the housewives of Philadelphia. Meyer carried his peddler's pack to the anthracite coal country. They began the process of bettering themselves by manufacturing a popular stove polish, which sharply increased their profits. They established the roots of the American Guggenheims when Meyer married his stepsister, Barbara Meyer, and they began having children — 11 of them between 1854 and 1873. One son died young, but the surviving seven became Meyer's primary agents for multiplying money — especially Daniel, his most trusted advisor in the family's new ventures, such as importing European lace. As merchants, the Guggenheims became prosperous, but it wasn't until they got into the mining business, with the purchase of a silver mine in Colorado, that they became truly rich. Then, not content to let the smelters make huge profits from their ore, the Guggenheims diversified into smelting. Along the way, they gained so much business skill that they outmaneuvered a huge Rockefeller-controlled smelting trust, American Smelting and Refining Company (ASARCO) and took control of it themselves. They moved into the gold business in Canada and copper in Alaska and Utah. At Chuquicamata, in the Chilean desert, they developed a fabulously productive copper lode, just in time to take advantage of the exploding market for copper during World War I.

In the process, the Guggenheims amassed a fortune greater than any other in America, with the possible exception of John D. Rockefeller's. Oddly, they never won total acceptance in the inner circle of New York City's richest Jewish families. But they gravitated, as the other rich families did, to a summer retreat along the New Jersey Shore, a stretch of communities that were known as "The Jewish Newport." Daniel Guggenheim and his wife, Florence, had a summer home there, in a town called Elberon. It was in the nearby town of West End, on August 23, 1890, that Florence gave birth to her second son, Harry Frank Guggenheim.

As a boy, Harry was mildly mischievous — breaking the fingers on a statue in his grandfather's home, causing minor damage to Uncle Isaac's silk hat, acquiring a speeding citation at age 15. But for most of his life, he was deadly serious about everything — in sharp contrast to his older brother, M. Robert Guggenheim, his mother's favorite, who always knew how to have fun. "Every wealthy family supports at least one gentleman in leisure," M. Robert once said. "I have elected to assume that position in mine."

Harry was graduated from Columbia Grammar School in Manhattan in 1907 and went on to Sheffield Scientific School at Yale, where he began the study of mining and metallurgy. After the first term, Harry told his father that he wanted to leave school and marry a young woman named Helen Rosenberg. Disappointed that Harry didn't want to continue in school, Daniel provided his son with an alternate education. He sent him to the ASARCO smelter at Aguascalientes, Mexico, to work for a dollar a day. During this period, they began to exchange a long series of letters that continued almost until Daniel's death in 1930. Again and again, Daniel's letters repeated the same messages: Life was a serious business. The family needed Harry's talents, and Harry had to use his time well and apply himself faithfully. Daniel was growing tired after decades of business and Harry's turn was coming. This early education from his father helped mold Harry into a relentlessly, sometimes even oppressively, serious man.

When Harry returned from Mexico, Daniel persuaded him to continue his education, at a prestigious British institution: Pembroke College, Cambridge. (The same year, Harry married Helen Rosenberg. While he was still an undergraduate, she became pregnant and gave birth to a daughter, Joan.) Everything about Cambridge appealed to Harry: the courses, the architecture, the tennis team, the lack of anti-Semitism. He worked hard at his studies and at his tennis, becoming the president of the Pembroke College Lawn Tennis Club. The Cambridge experience converted him into a lifelong Anglophile. Immediately after his graduation in 1913, Harry went into the family business. In 1916, the family reorganized the core company, M. Guggenheim's Sons, into Guggenheim Brothers, which included Meyer's five oldest sons, plus Harry and his cousin Edmond. Meyer's sons had produced almost nothing but daughters, leaving Harry and Edmond as the only logical choices in the new generation. Guggenheim Brothers also included a non-Guggenheim, William C. Potter, who was to run the operations in Chile, assisted by Harry and Edmond. So Harry went to Santiago as executive director of Chile Copper, the crown jewel of the family's copper empire.

The year after the reorganization, the war intervened. Early in 1917, Harry bought a Curtiss Flying Boat, took flying lessons and joined a small private aviation unit in training on Manhasset Bay, on Long Island. In September, he received a commission in the United States Navy Reserve and was assigned to a station at Bay Shore, on the South Shore of Long Island. During flight tests there, Harry made an error during one landing and lost his chance to qualify for his wings before he was shipped to France. In August, 1918, in Moutchic, he qualified for his wings. (Over the years, naval aviators developed an intense pride in having the earliest possible serial numbers. Without his mistake, Harry would have earned a number between 108 and 120, but he ended up with number 1129.) His service in England, Italy and France included a tour with the Navy's Northern Bombing Group, where one of his jobs was to negotiate with the Italian government to acquire some Caproni heavy bombers. At the same time, an Army officer named Fiorello LaGuardia was trying to get them for the Army. The Navy won.

When the war ended, Harry left with the rank of lieutenant commander and went back to Guggenheim Brothers, where he soon came into conflict with his father and the other "seniors" over Chile Copper. Harry had supervised the creation of the Chuquicamata operation, which had become a phenomenal success, but his family was thinking of selling it to Anaconda Copper. Demand for copper had fallen sharply after the war, and the Guggenheims wanted to go into a new industry in Chile: producing nitrates for fertilizer. On the other hand, Chuqui was capable of producing huge amounts of the cheapest copper in the world for decades. So Harry and Edmond both objected to the sale. The seniors overrode them and accepted a $70 million check from Anaconda, which gave Anaconda a narrow majority in Chile Copper. Six weeks later, Harry and Edmond resigned, enriched by the sale but angered that the seniors had declined to take their advice.

In the aftermath, Daniel tried to persuade Harry to stay on to complete his work in the tin and nitrate businesses. But Harry's hesitation about the sale turned out to be right. The Guggenheims had made a major miscalculation. They had thought they would have a monopoly on nitrates, and they did — on natural nitrates. But at the same time, a European process for producing synthetic nitrates destroyed any real hope that they had for turning the venture into a success. To make matters worse, Anaconda kept making huge profits at Chuquicamata. Harry was right. Daniel was wrong. At the same time that he was splitting with his father, Harry was completing the last act of another painful disagreement. His first marriage had ended in divorce, and just before his family sold Chile Copper, Harry had gotten married again, on February 3, 1923. His second wife was Caroline Morton Potter, known as Carol, the former wife of William C. Potter, Harry's associate in Chile Copper.

Despite his disagreement with Harry, Daniel gave his son a generous wedding present: 90 acres of land from his own estate in Sands Point. Only six years earlier, Daniel had bought the property from Howard Gould, the son of Wall Street titan Jay Gould. Over his family's objections, Howard Gould had married an actress named Viola Katherine Clemmons, who had performed with Buffalo Bill Cody's Wild West Show. To fulfill his new wife's wish, Gould set about creating a replica of Ireland's Kilkenny Castle on his property in Sands Point. His architects did finish the stables, topped with a crenellated tower. But before the entire project could be completed, Gould and his wife separated, in 1907. Gould built a $1,000,000 English manor house on his land, but he seldom used it, since he was spending most of his time in Europe. Meanwhile, Daniel Guggenheim was looking for a place in Sands Point, where two of his brothers already lived. In March, 1917, Daniel acquired the whole 250 acres of the estate for $600,000, named the main residence Hempstead House and began adapting it to his own use. To Harry, he gave 90 acres that included a bluff overlooking Long Island Sound.

On his slice of Long Island, Harry did what many wealthy Americans were doing: He built a medieval European home. On his instructions, the architect Frederick Sterner designed a house in the style of a thirteenth-century Norman manor — with Dutch brick, Norman roof tiles, semi-pointed arches, wooden beams, a protected cobblestone courtyard and some rounded exterior walls. Harry also followed another popular fashion, integrating into the structure bits and pieces of European houses, such as carved doors, columns, mantels, tiles and wrought iron work. On their extended wedding trip, Harry and Carol toured Europe, occasionally joined by Sterner, to find suitable fragments to bring home. Besides those fragments, Harry and Carol chose paintings, sculptures, tapestries, stained glass and other medieval works of art — many of them with strongly Christian themes. Fittingly, the name that Harry gave to his estate was Falaise, which is both a French word for "cliff" and the name of a town in Normandy. At Falaise, now that he had left the family business behind, Harry settled down to begin the next phase of his life.

II

ALL THAT ANYONE needs to know about Harry Guggenheim's luck is this: Once the previous generation had amassed incredible wealth, it was Harry who drew the most visible role in giving much of it away. Harry ran his father's fund for promoting commercial aviation. Harry saw Robert Goddard's work through. Harry built and launched Uncle Solomon's art museum.

After World War I, Harry was at the center of a felicitous intersection of private and public needs that helped to launch the air age in America. Daniel needed a suitable means of expressing gratitude to the country that had made him so rich, and America needed a way to make aviation outgrow barnstorming and air mail, to enter an era of regular passenger service. The agent for meeting those needs was Harry, who persuaded Daniel to spend his wealth on aviation.

As it happened, charity began at home, in New York. The catalyst was a distinguished engineer, Alexander Klemin, who had come from England to enroll in a pioneer aeronautical engineering course at Massachusetts Institute of Technology. Later, he and a professor from New York University put together a similar course at NYU. Once its first graduates found jobs, NYU Chancellor Elmer Brown wanted to make the program permanent, which would require a $500,000 endowment. So he appointed an organizing committee, including Harry Guggenheim. Some members suggested that they launch a broad public campaign to raise the money. Harry made another suggestion: Why not ask his family? The result was a letter from Brown to Daniel Guggenheim, which Harry hand-delivered. Klemin later described Daniel's response: "Don't show this letter to your uncles, Harry. I will do it myself." Daniel started by giving NYU $500,000, which endowed three chairs in aeronautics, provided salaries for lab assistants and paid for a laboratory building and a propeller lab. In October, 1925, Daniel broke ground for the new building.

The logical next step, suggested to Harry by Ivy Lee, a New York publicist who had done work for the copper industry, was the establishment of a fund for promoting aeronautics. Harry discussed the idea with Orville Wright, who liked it. Then Daniel suggested they discuss it with the government. So Harry went to see Dwight Morrow, a longtime friend and business associate of the Guggenheims, who ran President Calvin Coolidge's air board. Harry described to Morrow his plan, a fund of $2,500,000 to promote aviation through education, research and demonstrations of aeronautical safety. The result was a White House meeting in December, 1925, with Calvin Coolidge and Secretary of Commerce Herbert Hoover. Coolidge approved of the basic plan, but when Harry mentioned the need to develop faster planes, the legendarily taciturn President asked tersely: "What's the use of getting there quicker if you haven't got something better to say when you arrive?"

A month later, Guggenheim Brothers announced the creation of the Daniel Guggenheim Fund for the Promotion of Aeronautics. Harry rounded up an impressive board of trustees, including Orville Wright himself and Dwight Morrow. Harry was elected president of the fund, and in early 1926, he toured aviation facilities in Europe with the vice president, Rear Admiral Hutchinson Cone. They came back with a long list of what was needed, and the fund began to meet those needs. Over the four years of its existence, the fund established six schools of aeronautical engineering. It set up a pioneering airline between Los Angeles and San Francisco. It established a meteorological service along the route of its model airline. It sponsored a safe aircraft competition. It also recognized the importance of promoting public acceptance of the whole idea of aviation, which brought about Harry's association with Charles A. Lindbergh.

Accompanied by his wife Carol, Harry had visited Lindbergh at Long Island's Roosevelt Field as he was preparing for the flight to Paris. When he saw the cramped cockpit of Lindbergh's plane, Harry wasn't optimistic. "I remember looking in there and saying to myself, 'This fellow will never make it. He's doomed!' " Harry said. "And as I was leaving, I said to him, with far more optimism in my words than in my heart, 'Well, when you get back to the United States, come up to the fund and see me.' " After the Paris flight, Harry's colleague Dwight Morrow called and told him that the press and a long line of promoters were hounding Lindbergh. So Harry and Morrow took it on themselves to protect him. One of the deals that Lindbergh had made was for a book, but when he saw the manuscript that a ghostwriter had produced, Lindbergh found it inaccurate and unacceptable. So he decided to write it himself, and Harry and Carol gave him a quiet place to work: a northeast bedroom in their home, overlooking Long Island Sound. "I spent about three weeks at Falaise, as their guest, that summer, during which I wrote most of and completed the manuscript for my book published under the title of *We*," Lindbergh said. "Frankly, I don't think I ever would have gotten it done if they hadn't offered me that retreat." That summer, Harry suggested that the fund sponsor a cross-country tour by Lindbergh, and Dwight Morrow recommended the fund pay him $50,000. (The year before, after Commander Richard Byrd had made the first flight over the North Pole, the fund had sponsored a 7,000-mile, 45-city tour by Byrd's pilot, Floyd Bennett.) The three-month Lindbergh tour covered 23,350 miles, visiting 82 cities in 48 states. During the tour, Harry worried so much about Lindbergh's health that he even wrote letters to mayors along the route, begging them to see that Lindbergh got enough sleep.

The tour began a relationship between Harry and Lindbergh that lasted for more than four decades. Lindbergh was a frequent guest at Falaise. In fact, it was there that Lindbergh had one of his first dates with his future wife, Anne Morrow, the daughter of Harry's friend Dwight Morrow. Lindbergh agreed to take Anne on a plane ride, but feared that being seen with her in public would start a flood of rumors. "So I landed a small biplane in an estate pasture near Falaise from which we could fly without attention by the press," Lindbergh wrote. Landing and taking off at that makeshift airport wasn't easy. "It was very small," Anne Morrow Lindbergh said. "I didn't know enough about flying to be scared."

Harry's work with the fund also brought him a lifelong friendship with another daring aviator: Lieutenant James H. Doolittle, the first man to fly across America in less than a day. In early 1929, Harry announced that the fund was beginning experiments in blind flying at Mitchel Field on Long Island, and the Army assigned Doolittle to work with him. By September, the Consolidated NY-2 aircraft had all the essential instruments: an accurate altimeter, fabricated by Paul Kollsman in his garage in Brooklyn, and an artificial horizon and a directional gyrocompass developed by Elmer Sperry. On the morning of September 24, 1929, a thick fog covered Mitchel Field. The fund's maintenance chief put in a call to Doolittle and to Harry. Doolittle decided that this thick fog was the perfect opportunity to test blind flying. So he jumped in the plane, took off, navigated completely by the instruments, and 10 minutes later, landed. As the plane's wheels touched the runway, Harry arrived from Falaise. Harry was so excited that he asked Doolittle to take another flight, this time with a canvas hood over the cockpit. Harry himself closed the hood over Doolittle's head. Just 15 minutes later, Doolittle landed safely, after completing the first instruments-only flights ever. Without Harry's support, there is no way to know how long the development of that capacity might have taken. "It would come, but it would not come as quickly," Doolittle said. "He did a very great thing for aviation and for our country."

The fund provided aviation with exactly what it needed in the late 1920s. Richard Hallion, the former curator of science and technology at the National Air and Space Museum, who did a long, scholarly study of the fund's work, said that, without the fund, "I think we would have seen a very much slower development of aeronautical engineering in this country as a distinct academic enterprise." There were no other funds even remotely like Daniel and Harry's, Hallion said. "The Guggenheims were *it*."

Just before his father's fund went out of business, Harry and Lindbergh found a way for Guggenheim money to expand the frontiers of flight. On a fall day in 1929, they sat in the living room at Falaise and talked about the future. "Then one of those unpredictable incidents happened that so often bend the trends of life and history," Lindbergh wrote in his autobiography. "I was standing beside a window in the oak-beamed living room, looking out over the sound, comparing an airplane's speed with the slothlike progress of a string of gravel barges under tow." At that moment, Carol Guggenheim, who had been reading quietly while the men talked, said: "Listen to this!" She read them an article about the experiments of Robert Goddard at his aunt's farm in Massachusetts and the furor that his work had caused. When Carol had finished reading the article aloud, Harry turned to Lindbergh, smiling. "May be the answer to our problem," Harry said. "Why don't you check up on Goddard? Go have a talk with him, if you think it's worthwhile." A few days later, Lindbergh visited Goddard at Clark University. Eventually, Lindbergh persuaded the Carnegie Institution to give Goddard $5,000. For longer-term funding, Lindbergh turned back to the Guggenheims. In the spring of 1930, he went to Daniel Guggenheim to plead Goddard's case.

The Daniel Guggenheim Fund for the Promotion of Aeronautics had officially closed shop on February 1, 1930. But Daniel was willing to listen when Lindbergh visited him at Hempstead House. Lindbergh told him that Goddard needed $25,000 a year for four years. "Do you think he can accomplish enough to make it worth a hundred-thousand-dollar investment?" Daniel asked. "Well, it's taking a chance," Lindbergh answered. "But if we're ever going to get beyond the limits of airplanes and propellers, we'll probably have to go to rockets. It's taking a chance, but — yes, I think it's worth it." So Daniel set aside $50,000 for the first two years, with another $50,000 to follow if Harry and Lindbergh and an advisory committee approved. With that money, the Goddards set up shop in Roswell, New Mexico.

The death of Daniel Guggenheim in September, 1930, eventually caused a temporary grounding of the Roswell experiments. The funding shortage forced the Goddards to move back to Massachusetts and scale back his studies. Then, in 1934, another Guggenheim fund under Harry's control, the Daniel and Florence Guggenheim Foundation, agreed to pick up the funding, and the Goddards returned to New Mexico. From then until he died in 1945, Goddard had a faithful supporter in Harry.

III

HARRY GUGGENHEIM'S FIRST memory of Cuba was his jingoistic joy as an eight-year-old boy, when he heard that America was going to war over the sinking of the *Maine* in Havana harbor.

Now, in late 1929, Cuba became the center of his life. The work of the aviation fund was winding down, and he was looking for a new career. In the 1928 election, Harry had been an enthusiastic supporter of Hoover's presidential candidacy, and when Hoover won, he nominated Harry to be the next United States ambassador to Cuba. Soon after Hoover sent Harry's name to the Senate, it became clear that this was not going to be an easy job. At the same time that the Senate was considering the nomination, it was entertaining a Senate Foreign Relations Committee resolution calling for an investigation of conditions in Cuba under President Gerardo Machado y Morales, known as *El Gallo* (The Rooster). The resolution raised the possibility of American intervention, accusing Machado of crimes ranging from assassination to bribing legislators. This crisis shelved the confirmation until the Senate could decide whether the United States needed a career diplomat as ambassador to Cuba. Finally, the Senate confirmed Harry in October, 1929, and his picture appeared on the cover of *Time* magazine.

Typically, Harry tackled the new job methodically, using his own money to hire experts to help him keep track of the Cuban economy and ordering an exhaustive study of past American interventions in Cuba. When his study found that America had not acted consistently, Harry sought a clarification. Secretary of State Henry Stimson told Harry that America was not going to intervene in Cuba's internal affairs unless the island dissolved in chaos. Meanwhile, Harry was to maintain a strict and careful neutrality in the struggle between President Machado and his angry but disjointed enemies. This presented Harry with a cruel set of realities. On one side were Machado's enemies and most of the liberal American press, making it very clear that Harry's duty was to nudge Machado out. On the other side were Harry's bosses in Washington, who ordered him to stay neutral. In the middle were Harry and Machado.

Harry did what he could, intervening periodically to urge Machado to enact reforms and to spare the lives of political prisoners. But his influence was limited. Following an unsuccessful revolution in 1931, he recommended that the United States modify its policy and inform the Cuban ambassador of "our lack of sympathy with President Machado's present policies," which would relieve the United States of responsibility for Machado's actions. Stimson sent him back a firm rejection, which reduced Harry to little more than a reporter of what was going on. "After Machado realized that Guggenheim's official actions were limited to friendly advice and mere verbal pressure that lacked official Washington backing," wrote Donald Ross Brimmer in a master's thesis on Harry's performance, "Machado was free to increase his dictatorial hold on Cuba." At the same time, Harry's obedience to Stimson's neutrality directives subjected him to nasty public attacks by Machado's opponents.

Finally, after Franklin Roosevelt had been elected, Harry resigned, effective April 1, 1933. For Harry, whose life had been a long string of successes, Cuba was a painful experience, made even worse by the death of his father in the middle of it all. Harry did get some satisfaction after his tour was over. Machado was ultimately overthrown, for one thing. In addition, Harry recommended in his book, *The United States and Cuba*, that Congress make drastic changes to the Platt Amendment, a congressional enactment after the Spanish-American War that laid out the conditions under which America would intervene in Cuba. In 1934, Roosevelt persuaded Congress to do away with the Platt Amendment and followed that with a new trade treaty. Cuba was finally truly independent.

Even though he came away from Cuba with some scars, Harry's reputation survived. But his marriage did not. Harry and Carol had a daughter together, Diane, and they shared a number of interests, from campaigning for Herbert Hoover to a love for painting and sculpture. Carol had played as important a role as Harry in filling Falaise with art. She was a talented artist who had her own studio in their Manhattan apartment overlooking the East River. When Harry built his hunting lodge, Cain Hoy, in Charleston, South Carolina, Carol sculpted an impressive pair of wild turkeys that sat atop columns at the entrance, and carved wild turkeys into a mirror over the fireplace. Despite their common interests, sometime during their stay in Cuba, the marriage began to develop severe strains, and Carol's physical and mental health began to deteriorate. She returned to New York in March, 1932, while Harry stayed in Havana. A month later, one of her doctors wrote to him that she was "easily fatiguable, depressed at times, and emotionally unstable," and recommended that she not return to Havana for months.

Finally, their problems became serious enough that Carol moved out of their East 57th Street apartment in 1937. "You know perfectly well why I have taken another apartment," she wrote him, in one of a series of crisp letters that they exchanged. "The fact is you made it impossible for us to continue living together." In his replies, Harry struggled to retain his usual gentlemanly tone, but that couldn't hide the painful issues. In one letter, he accused her of "departing with several millions of dollars which had been entrusted to you for the common purposes of our joint lives. . . ." They also exchanged letters about what Carol called "the essential obligation of marriage," apparently a code phrase for sex. "You know it to be a fact that for more than two years, every suggestion from you of a 'modus vivendi' was accompanied by the express reservation that, under no circumstances, would you resume what you choose to call, 'the essential obligation of marriage,' " Harry wrote.

The years after his return from Havana were difficult times for Harry Guggenheim. His marriage was breaking up and he was without a real full-time career. But he did have his interests. In 1934, Harry spent $400 on a race horse, a yearling named Nebraska City. As time went on, he became more and more involved in buying horses, breeding them and directing the trainers who raced them. Harry eventually named his racing stable Cain Hoy, after his plantation outside Charleston. The plantation's cattle and timber operations also began to take up more of Harry's time. And he dabbled in politics, campaigning hard in 1936 for Alf Landon, the Republican presidential candidate.

The closest thing he had to a career in the late 1930s was his position as president of the Citizens Committee on the Control of Crime in New York. The request that he head this new committee came from Thomas E. Dewey, the special prosecutor who was waging a well-publicized battle against rackets in Manhattan. One of the committee's purposes was to raise money to support the families of Dewey's witnesses. Of course, in 1937, Dewey was already being discussed as a candidate for governor of New York, and any visibility that the committee gave Dewey the racket-buster was beneficial. The committee also served as a watchdog over criminal justice agencies in New York City.

Even with these interests, Harry found himself somewhat at loose ends once Carol moved out of their apartment in 1937. Suddenly, he was living something very much like a bachelor's life again. And he was beginning to spend time with an interesting younger woman, Alicia Patterson.

CHAPTER FIVE

Alicia Says Yes

THE SETTING FOR the courtship of Harry and Alicia was a 1930s version of the Gold Coast social whirl that inspired F. Scott Fitzgerald to chronicle the 1920s lifestyle of "East Egg" and "West Egg" in *The Great Gatsby*.

No one is certain how they first met, although Alicia's sister Josephine said that it was through Jean Stout, the daughter of Harry's second wife, Carol. Wherever they met, they clearly grew to know one another in the glittering summer world of Sands Point. Those who were part of this coterie spent the summers either in their own homes in Sands Point or as weekend visitors to the homes of friends. The group included, among others, the theatrical director George Abbott, the magazine illustrator Neysa McMein, and Phyllis Fraser, an actress who was dating the publisher Bennett Cerf at the time Alicia and Harry met. Alicia and her husband Joe Brooks had a place in Sands Point, just a short distance from Harry's, and they were welcome in that circle. In August, many in the group would move from Long Island to Saratoga Springs, a fashionable village north of Albany that attracted the wealthy with its mineral waters and its achingly beautiful racetrack. During the one-month racing meeting, Harry was a regular fixture at Saratoga. There, while Joe Brooks was off gambling, not being as attentive to Alicia as she wanted, Harry was paying close attention. "She said he was stunning looking and was very assiduous and he'd take her all around and he really courted her," said Dorothy Holdsworth, Alicia's secretary and close friend. "So she had found somebody who cared what she did, and she wasn't alone all the time."

Part of Harry's appeal was that he appreciated her brains. "Where he got Alicia was he told her she was intellectual, and that Joe didn't understand her great mind," said Alice-Leone Moats, who wrote book reviews for Alicia at the *Daily News* and was a friend of Alicia and Joe Brooks. "Alicia was very, very bright, but an intellectual she was not. She wasn't one who would play with ideas, which is my definition of an intellectual." Even though they were so different, there was clearly a powerful attraction, and Brooks lamented to Fred and Virginia Pasley, close friends of both Alicia and her father: "He's hypnotized her. He's hypnotized her."

At age 48, Harry still had patrician good looks, with his meticulous clothing, his militarily crisp demeanor, his icy blue eyes. "I think that he was the most interesting man that she had really met, but also sexy, and she pointed that out," Phyllis Cerf said. "He respected Alicia and gave her big jobs to do. I mean he backed her. . . . He was really behind her, and you have to love somebody like that, even though you're fighting a daughter-father relationship." That relationship, of course, was a problem. Nothing that Alicia had done in her first 32 years, with the exception of being born a woman, angered her father as much as her decision to divorce Brooks and marry Harry. To Patterson, everything was wrong with Harry: He was Jewish; he was only 11 years younger than Patterson, and he was an Old World gentleman, far more buttoned-down than Patterson. When Patterson's friend Hal Burton suggested that Harry was pleasant enough, Patterson snapped: "Goddamn old stuffed shirt." Perhaps as much as anything else, Patterson was unhappy because Alicia was planning to divorce someone that he cared about. "He was furious," Burton said, "because he thought the world of Joe Brooks." As one friend of Brooks said: "One is not unkind to dogs, horses or Joe Brooks." Some of Alicia's friends thought she was treating Brooks thoughtlessly. "She behaved very badly in that whole matter, because she didn't make a clean break with Joe," Moats said. "She kept going back to him, giving him hope. . . . We were all sore at her."

That was not the only strain in the Patterson family at the time. Joe Patterson's marriage was also a painful issue. Even before he moved from Chicago to New York, he and his trusted aide, Mary King, had become lovers, and she had become pregnant. It was an odd relationship, in which they had to preserve the formality of their employment relationship for public consumption. "Dear Miss King," he wrote her in London in early 1923, "I got your letter asking for an extension of your leave of absence. This is to state that you may have up to one year's leave of absence without interfering with your 'seniority rights.' " In essence, Patterson was giving permission to his employee/lover to take time off and give birth to his child. Less than two months later, James Patterson was born. Not quite two weeks after the birth, she wrote an almost apologetic "Dear Mr. Patterson" letter from London, announcing that she was returning to America, but not saying a word about the baby.

For the next 15 years, Alice Patterson refused to give her husband a divorce. In 1925, Joe Patterson left Alice in Chicago and moved to New York. So did Mary King, who worked for Patterson at *Liberty* and at the *Daily News*. But she didn't live with him. All this was painful for both of them. At the age of 44, Patterson had finally acquired a son, but he could neither publicly acknowledge his son's existence nor gain freedom to marry the boy's mother. Mary King had grown up a devout Catholic, but now she was an unmarried mother, and she could no longer receive Communion. The awkwardness of their situation forced Patterson and Mary King into an odd lifestyle that gave their son a painful start in the world. Mary King lived in the Riverdale section of New York City, with Jimmy and her two sisters — one of whom, Loretta, worked with her at *Liberty* and later, under the pseudonym Kate Cameron, as a movie critic at the *News*. Jimmy had nurses and governesses and the three sisters, but as far as he knew, he didn't have a mother. "I have to say I didn't know she was my mother for the early years of my life," he said. "It was never told to me that this is your mother. I know she was a big part of my life. . . . I guess I suspected it." For a while, they also neglected to inform him that Joe Patterson was his father. "I always thought of him as my father," said Patterson, who bears a strong physical resemblance to Joseph Medill Patterson. "He couldn't have denied me if he wanted to."

Eventually, when he was about seven years old, Jimmy moved into his father's new mansion in Ossining, on the Hudson River, north of New York City. (Typical of his proletarian style, Joe Patterson had told the architect Raymond Hood, who also designed the *Chicago Tribune* and *Daily News* buildings: "Make it look as if I didn't have any money." Hood created an ugly, boxy structure that looked like a battlefield bunker.) Though the son and his father were united, Mary King continued to live in Riverdale. "She never lived in Ossining until they were married," James Patterson said, "but she did come to dinner almost every night." And when dinner was over, she'd drive or take the train back to Riverdale, leaving father and son in the mansion. Adding to the confusion, it wasn't until several years after Jimmy was born that his half-sisters discovered that they had a brother. "I didn't learn of it until I was about 16 or 17," said Josephine, who was nine when he was born and later heard about him from Alicia. "Father, I don't think, ever told me." James Patterson recounted these arrangements in a quiet, matter-of-fact way that did not betray his feelings, but it could not have been easy for him. "This was very tragic," Josephine said. "I think he had a perfectly horrible early life." Somehow, he survived these strange beginnings, was graduated from the United States Military Academy and grew into a useful career as an editor at the *Daily News*.

The mere existence of Jimmy Patterson was, of course, a major complication in his father's snarled marital affairs. To disentangle himself, Patterson reached a complex pre-divorce agreement with Alice, followed by an equally detailed pre-marital agreement with Mary King. The agreement was necessary because Alice feared that her husband would treat his daughters unequally in his will — a fear that Patterson's lawyer, Weymouth Kirkland, saw when he met with Alice in late 1937. Kirkland described to her how Patterson was unhappy about the way his daughter Elinor was treating Jimmy, and he told Alice that her husband planned to change his will to give Elinor a smaller share than Alicia and Jimmy would get. The final 1938 agreement with Alice pledged that, if Patterson left any of his interest in the Tribune Company to Jimmy, he would leave equal shares to Elinor, Alicia and Josephine, and he would not treat any one of the daughters better than the other two. The agreement with Mary King outlined how he would provide for her and Jimmy. So Patterson had his divorce, but he wasn't at all pleased about the prospect of Alicia's, just a year after his own.

From some members of Harry's family, though, Alicia enjoyed solid support. Naturally enough, Diane, his daughter with Carol, didn't like Harry divorcing her mother to marry Alicia. But his two daughters by his first marriage, Joan and Nancy, appreciated Alicia. Joan was her friend even before the marriage, and felt that she was just what Harry needed. "She was good for him," Joan said, "with a lot of brains and a lot of challenge." Nancy also liked Alicia and took it on herself to calm Diane's fears. "Alicia is a very fine intelligent person," Nancy wrote. "I find her delightful to be with and very sincere and gracious. She also has a very gay and happy nature and I am sure will make Father very happy. . . . He has been very lonely and at loose ends. He is a young man and has found someone who can fill his life for him and inspire him."

Finally, Alicia and Harry decided to get their divorces in Florida. To help them meet the residency requirement, Alicia's friend Dody Michelson arranged for them to rent separate houses in Jacksonville, not far from her home. Dody had to keep reminding them to show up in their temporary homes, but once they arrived, the divorces went smoothly. Though Joe Patterson was unhappy about it, Joe Brooks didn't put any obstacles in Alicia's way. "He was willing to let her be free," said Charles Murchison, the local lawyer who represented Harry and Alicia. "He was a nice guy. He was very cooperative."

They were married at the home of Dody and her husband, John Bitter, who was then the conductor of the Florida State Symphony. It was a quiet wedding, performed by a county court judge, with no music, no frills, no crowds. Harry's public relations consultants drafted a brief announcement to keep the press at bay. And that was it — a simple, non-religious ceremony to unite two families that had left Europe to flee religious hatred. Now Guggenheim money and Patterson journalism were joined. Joe Patterson remained angry, and Alicia's sister Josephine drifted away from Alicia for a few months after the marriage. But for now, Alicia and Harry had other concerns — a honeymoon and the start of life together.

During their visit to the Goddard ranch in New Mexico, the telegram from Max Annenberg, holding out the possibility that Alicia and Harry could buy a defunct paper in Nassau County and start their own, caught Alicia at a vulnerable time. She was not exactly feeling competent. She had failed at two marriages and botched her first reporting job. But she still desperately wanted to be a real journalist — not just a book review editor for her father. Running a newspaper was almost an obligation in her family. Her father ran the *News*. Cousin Bert McCormick ran the *Chicago Tribune*. A few months earlier, even her flaky aunt had become a newspaper owner. Since 1937, Cissy Patterson had been leasing the *Washington Times* and the *Herald* from William Randolph Hearst. On January 28, 1939, she bought both papers and merged them into the *Times-Herald*. That made Alicia the only journalistically talented member of the family who didn't have her own paper.

Alicia was by no means poverty-stricken. She had a steady income from the trust that her father had established for her, and she had her salary as book review editor of the *News*. But she didn't have enough cash to buy a newspaper on her own. She couldn't even pay the $4,388 legal fee for her divorce without a little strain. "I doubt whether at the moment she will have a large enough balance in the bank to pay this account," Harry said in a letter to Murchison, the attorney. "I shall arrange a loan to her just as soon as we can get her affairs straightened out and find out where she stands." A little over a week into their marriage, this established a pattern: Harry would lend or give her money, but he kept careful track of the dollars and urged her to do the same. Now he was willing to lay out the money to buy her a paper, if she was ready. But self-doubt plagued her. "I had terrible inferiority feelings," Alicia said. "I didn't think I had anything."

As much as she wanted it, running a newspaper was a huge responsibility, and she had never shown that she had the necessary attention span or sense of duty. So, when the telegram from Max Annenberg made the prospect of running her own paper real and immediate, she balked and asked Harry to drop the whole idea. "I wonder if at that moment of decision she did not foresee the utter devotion and indeed dedication to a newspaper that would embrace all of her future life," Harry wrote two decades later. It was the first meaningful disagreement of their marriage, and he didn't back down. "I refused to be shaken by her plea to forget all about it," Harry wrote. "I told her that we had started this job and we would have to finish it."

So Alicia consented, and they headed back east to see about starting a newspaper. The honeymoon had worked out well for the Goddards, who got a new infusion of Guggenheim money a few weeks later, and for the Guggenheims, who made a decision that got Alicia started on a new life. In the years ahead of them in what would turn out to be a difficult and often painful marriage, Alicia would clash with Harry repeatedly. But she never forgot his role in that decision in the desert. "He told me once he saved her life," said Alice Albright, Alicia's niece and Josephine's daughter. That was years after their marriage, one day when Alicia, Harry and Alice were sitting at Falaise. "I remember him saying something like, 'I picked your Aunt Alicia out of the gutter,' " Alice Albright said, "and her saying something like, 'He's absolutely right.' "

BOOK II

Alicia's Toy

CHAPTER SIX

Mr. Newhouse Regrets

I.

THE LITTLE VENTURE that Harry and Alicia were contemplating at the end of 1939, opening a newspaper where another one had just failed, was like a good-news-bad-news joke.

The good news was the location. Even though it lay just east of New York City, Nassau County was still a semi-rural aggregation of potato farms and small villages, with boundless potential for growth. Eventually, residential and commercial development had to come to Long Island, a huge, fish-shaped land mass with its nose nuzzling Manhattan and its tail jutting into the Atlantic. At its western end were Brooklyn and Queens, two of the five boroughs of the City of New York. Just east of Queens was Nassau County, which contained 300 square miles — larger than Brooklyn and Queens together. Beyond Nassau lay the undeveloped expanses of Suffolk, more than 900 square miles. As the city's population growth used up the available land in Brooklyn and Queens, the tide of migration would inevitably move east into Nassau. The bad news was that S. I. Newhouse, who had already established himself as one of the craftiest newspaper profiteers of them all, had seen the same potential, established a new daily paper in the heart of this promising county, and closed it down after less than two weeks. If a shrewd operator like Newhouse couldn't make it work, who could?

Newhouse had first planted his flag on Long Island in 1932, when he bought the *Long Island Press*, which dominated Jamaica, the prime shopping area in Queens. His two major competitors in Queens were the *Long Island Star*, which circulated primarily in northwestern Queens, and the *Flushing*

Daily Journal, which covered northeastern Queens, out to the Nassau County
border. It was the publisher of the *Journal*, T. Harold Forbes, who started the
events that led to the opportunity for Harry and Alicia. Forbes was a former
vaudevillian who had appeared in George M. Cohan musicals and later built a
chain of papers in Westchester County, north of New York City. He sold those
papers in 1929 and two years later took over the *Journal*. His paper was serving
an audience in northern Queens, but Forbes looked east to Nassau, where there
was a newspaper vacuum in the communities on Long Island Sound. There
were two daily papers in Nassau, the *Daily Review* and the *Daily Star*, but they
concentrated in the central and southern parts of the county. So it was a natural
step for Forbes to move his circulation area east. Changing the paper's name to
the *North Shore Daily Journal* and moving its offices to a new building on
Northern Boulevard in Flushing, he began selling papers in the wealthy communities of Great Neck, Manhasset and Port Washington, near Harry's estate.

Forbes and his chief lieutenant in Nassau, Forrest Corson, aligned themselves with the Democrats in a county where the Republicans were so dominant
that the party had helped create the newspaper vacuum on the North Shore in
the first place. The county Republican leader, J. Russel Sprague, instructed the
publisher of the *Review*, a Republican committeeman named James E. Stiles,
not to expand northward. Sprague was feuding with the Republican leader in
that area, James Dowsey, and he didn't want to escalate the conflict by allowing
a newspaper that was virtually his mouthpiece to expand into Dowsey's turf.
Stiles docilely obeyed Sprague. The *Review* stayed away from the North Shore
and remained content to dominate the South Shore and Hempstead, the
commercial center of the county.

The goal for Forbes was to establish the *Journal* in the areas on Long
Island Sound, then expand south into Hempstead. That plan faltered at the
start, when advertisers ignored the *Journal* and stayed with the established
weeklies. On top of that problem, Forbes precipitated a strike that lasted
almost seven months. The *Journal* kept publishing, but the strikers put out
their own newspaper, picketed the *Journal* and drained away its advertising.
When the strike ended in June, 1937, the *Journal* was a cripple. It limped along
until September, 1938, when Forbes announced that the *Journal* was going out
of business and merging with the *Long Island Star*, which Newhouse had just
bought. Newhouse's ownership of the new *Long Island Star-Journal*, along
with his control of the *Long Island Press*, gave him an iron grip on Queens and
northern Nassau County.

As 1939 began, Newhouse prepared to make his move southward into
Hempstead to compete with Stiles, who by then had bought out his competitor,
the *Nassau Daily Star*, and merged it with his *Review*. First, acting as a
Newhouse emissary, Forbes found out that Stiles would not sell his paper to
Newhouse. Then Newhouse and Forbes decided to take all the old equipment
from the *Journal* building in Flushing, relocate it in Hempstead and start a new
paper of their own — the only paper that Newhouse, the newspaper-collector,
ever established. With the help of his former employee, Forrest Corson, who

had become the public relations man for the Nassau Republican Party, Forbes found a building to house the paper: a former automobile dealership at 283 Main Street, in the Village of Hempstead.

The new paper, the *Nassau Daily Journal*, made its debut on March 1, 1939. It was a six-day daily, a broadsheet that looked like the old *North Shore Daily Journal* — as it should, since many of the employees and almost all of the equipment had come from the old paper. The plan was to distribute the *Nassau Daily Journal* jointly with the *Long Island Press* in south and central Nassau and with the *Star-Journal* on the North Shore, using Teamster drivers. That idea angered the Newspaper and Mail Deliverers Union, whose members delivered the *Press* and the other dailies in New York City. "All of a sudden, we showed up one morning and there were pickets outside," said Bill Ritter, who had worked for Forbes in Flushing and came to Hempstead to operate the worn Goss press. The NMDU also threatened to strike the *Press*. That alarmed Newhouse, who had experienced labor troubles with the Newspaper Guild at both the *Press* and the *Star*. "He doesn't want anything to jeopardize the *Long Island Press*," Corson said. "So he said to Forbes, 'Cease publication.' " Forbes closed the paper on March 10.

Since the conflict focused on a handful of drivers, Ritter and other employees thought it would be a brief interruption. But they underestimated Newhouse's anti-labor feelings. "He wasn't going to tolerate unions in Nassau County," Ritter said. "He could see them in Queens, but he would not tolerate them in Nassau County at all." So the paper stayed closed, the equipment gathered dust, and the Newhouse-Forbes scheme to expand deeper into the growing market of Nassau County was abandoned — all because Newhouse detested unions.

II

FORLORNLY, T. HAROLD Forbes kept showing up at the quiet plant that he had created from an automobile showroom. It had touches of class — a marble counter, a brass plate out front and a comfortable office for Forbes — but it was empty.

One day, Forbes called Forrest Corson and asked if they could meet for lunch at the nearby Garden City Hotel. At lunch, Forbes told him that Harry Guggenheim and Alicia Patterson were looking around for a newspaper, and someone named William Mapel was doing a survey of Nassau County for them, to analyze its potential. Forbes wanted Corson to help Mapel any way he could. If Mapel reported favorably on Nassau County to the Guggenheims, Newhouse could sell them the equipment and Forbes could get on with his life. Obligingly, Corson met Mapel for lunch and started familiarizing him with the county.

At 37, Mapel was a tall, ramrod-straight man who dressed well and exuded

self-assurance. Growing up in Missouri, where his father was a Southern Meth-
odist minister, he had been graduated from the journalism school at the University of Missouri in 1925. He got his reporting and early editing experience at
small papers in Missouri, then began teaching journalism. Later, he ran the
journalism program at Washington and Lee University in Lexington, Virginia.
From there, he went to Wilmington, Delaware, as executive editor of the
Morning News and *Evening Journal*. Leaving Wilmington in a policy conflict
with the Du Pont family, he went to New York in 1937, worked for the Institute
of Public Relations, then set up his own public relations firm. No one is certain
how he came in contact with the Guggenheims, but Forbes told Corson that
George Townley, Joe Patterson's attorney, had made the arrangements.

For several days, Mapel and Corson spent many hours together. Corson
introduced him to businessmen and government officials, showed him election
district and real estate information, to give him an idea of the county's growth
potential, and took him on a tour of Nassau's wide-open spaces. "I told him I
thought that this had a wonderful potential," Corson said. "I certainly thought
that the *Review-Star* was not covering the county the way it could be covered.
And he agreed." With all its potential, large parts of Nassau were still rural.
There were more than 600 farms, mostly in the center of the county, and fewer
than 300 manufacturing plants. On the North Shore, there were dozens of large
estates. Along the South Shore, there were small villages with active shopping
districts, separated by tree-covered undeveloped areas.

Politically, the county was showing signs of sophistication. In 1936, Nassau
became the first county in the state to approve by referendum a charter form of
government, effective in 1938. Its first elected county executive was J. Russel
Sprague, whose political roots went back to the county's origins. The Republicans had ruled Nassau since it was separated from Queens in 1898 and became a
separate county, and the first Republican leader was Sprague's uncle, G. Wilbur
Doughty. When Doughty died in 1930, he passed along to Sprague his position
as supervisor of the Town of Hempstead. By 1935, Sprague had won an internal
struggle to become the county Republican chairman. Once he combined that
party position with the office of county executive, Sprague became a dominant
figure who reached out beyond the county's borders to play a major role in the
campaigns of Thomas E. Dewey for governor and president.

Commercially, the county had a growing number of retail stores, especially
in Hempstead, its most populous village. In addition, as war began in Europe, it
seemed likely that the manufacturers of aircraft and aviation equipment on
Long Island would be hiring thousands of workers and generating further hiring
by subcontractors. The county did present one problem for a daily paper,
however: Advertisers tended to view it as a collection of small markets that they
could reach through the weekly newspapers, rather than as one large market.

In studying these factors, Mapel had a wiry young assistant named Stan
Peckham, who was about eight inches shorter than his boss. Louis Stanton
Peckham was born in Clay Center, Kansas, in 1906. His first encounter with
journalism was at a private school in Minnesota called Shattuck, where he was

the editor of the *Spectator*. Following graduation from the University of Kansas at Lawrence, Peckham sold telephone service to Kansas farmers, spent some time abroad, living in Mallorca, then entered the foreign service and served in Maracaibo, in Chile and in Colombia. By the margin of one question, he failed a test for a permanent foreign service job. So when Franklin Roosevelt was elected President, Peckham was out of a job. He went to New York, worked briefly on the New York Stock Exchange and became New York City editor of *Everyweek*, a current events publication for high school students. In Manhattan, Peckham met Mapel and joined his public relations firm.

As 1939 ended and 1940 began, Mapel and Peckham worked on the survey for the Guggenheims, operating out of the former *Nassau Daily Journal* building. "Mapel did all the important interviews, all the big shots," Peckham said. "I got the small businessmen and the bartenders and the housewives." In his travels, Peckham found enthusiasm for the idea of a new paper and disdain for the *Review-Star*. Every day, he would buy a copy of the *Review-Star*, bring it to his apartment on East 68th Street in Manhattan, cut it up, and analyze it. "It was just a sloppily edited paper, badly written and a lot of wire service and canned stuff — nothing lively at all," said Peckham, who also noticed that it wasn't as fat with ads as it could have been. "They probably didn't go out after it, for one thing, and they concentrated on the South Shore. So the North Shore was left high and dry. . . . Advertisers wanted someplace to advertise besides the South Shore."

Adding up the weaknesses of the *Review-Star* and the potential of Nassau County, Mapel and Peckham concluded that a new daily paper was an excellent idea. Finally, they went to Mapel's room at the Murray Hill Hotel in Manhattan and started to write a report. "Both Bill and I wanted to work for the newspaper," Peckham said. "That was why we had such an argument. I said, 'Bill, you're watering this thing down. This looks much better than you're saying it is.' And he said, 'I've got to, because if I told him the truth, Harry Guggenheim would never believe it.' " The result was a moderately optimistic report, dated January 23, 1940, which predicted: "By the end of the second year the paper should have a paid circulation in Nassau County of 15,000 copies daily."

Once they had finished the Nassau report, they thought that Alicia might want them to look at other potential markets, since she had talked about surrounding New York City with a ring of tabloids. But that assignment didn't materialize. Alicia and Harry focused on Hempstead, studied the report and decided to go ahead. So Mapel made an appointment to meet S. I. Newhouse at one of his papers, the *Newark Star-Ledger*, and found him wandering in the halls. "When I said I wanted to make him an offer for his *Nassau Journal* property, he beckoned me into an empty office," Mapel said. "I told him I was acting for Harry Guggenheim and Alicia Patterson, who wanted to start a new paper. He said, 'Make me an offer.' " Mapel thought it would cost $100,000 to replace the equipment at the closed-down plant. "I said, '$50,000.' And he said, 'You've got yourself a plant.' " On April 5, 1940, Harry agreed to purchase the equipment of the *Nassau Daily Journal* from Newhouse and to take over the lease on the former automobile dealership.

As the word got around that Harry and Alicia were going to publish a daily paper, the conventional wisdom was that she would quickly grow weary of it. "I thought she'd see it as a toy, something to play with for a while," Newhouse said, "and that eventually I'd be able to buy it back from her." Newhouse, along with the others who subscribed to the "Alicia's toy" theory, did not understand what was driving her. "The burning ambition she had, all she gave a damn about, was to prove to her goddamn family — and she would call them her goddamn family — that she was just as good a newspaperman as any of them," Peckham said. At that stage of her life, however, people still underestimated Alicia. "They just figured she was a bored rich girl and she might drink less if she had something to do," said Edith Wyckoff, who had worked as a stringer for the *Nassau Daily Journal*. "People who knew her said, 'Wait. She's not Joe Patterson's daughter for nothing. She's not Cissy Patterson's niece for nothing.'"

CHAPTER SEVEN

What's In a Name?

I

FROM THE START, the inner workings of a newspaper were as mysterious to Harry as ledger books were to Alicia.

That became obvious to Forrest Corson and T. Harold Forbes when Alicia led Harry on a tour of the plant. Corson overheard Harry reminding her that they had to get to a cocktail party, but she insisted that he look at the composing room and the pressroom. "Harry said, 'Oh, Alicia, you're going to print the paper here?' " Corson said. "Forbes looked at me and shrugged his shoulders." Whether Harry was just being absent-minded, or whether he really didn't understand that his new property included a press, it was clear that he wasn't going to be the journalist in this operation. He had plenty of projects to keep him busy, such as trying (without success) to persuade the Pentagon to use Robert Goddard's rocket technology in the world war, and working in the presidential campaign of Wendell Willkie. So he wouldn't get in Alicia's way while she tried to create a newspaper. As Alicia described it, Harry's role was to conserve the profits for future expansion. While he worked to keep the paper from going broke, her job was to make it "readable, entertaining, comprehensive, informative, interpretive, lively, but still sufficiently serious-minded so that no Long Islander will feel compelled to read any New York City paper." In other words, it would be up to Alicia to give the paper a shape, to set the tone.

Alicia wanted her paper to be feisty and willing to shoot at kneecaps — not stuffy and tied to the establishment, like the *Review-Star*. To those who wanted to understand her vision, she recommended *Timber Line*, a 1933 book about the *Denver Post* — a gutsy, brawling paper that concentrated on vigorous local coverage and aimed its message at the masses. That was exactly the philosophy of the greatest journalist that Alicia had ever met — her father. So Joseph Medill Patterson couldn't argue with the populist tone that she wanted to set, but he did quarrel with the shape. "I favored a tabloid despite discouragement from my father, who thought a standard size paper would be more acceptable in a suburban community where the population is considered more conservative," Alicia wrote. But she liked the appearance of a tabloid and the convenience that its smaller pages offered readers. So she rejected the anti-tabloid warning from the founder of America's most successful tabloid.

Before Alicia could turn her vision into reality, she needed employees. First, she hired a general manager, William Mapel, who had convinced her and Harry to start a paper in Nassau County. Then Mapel asked his assistant, Stan Peckham, to help hire a staff and make the plant habitable. "I was permitted an enormous budget of three dollars a chair to go out and buy chairs for the city room," Peckham said. "Well, I went to a second-hand furniture store and found a big old rickety dining room set and bought all the chairs from this dining room set, which didn't last a year." Making the plant ready involved dozens of other details, such as creating additional space by removing part of the marble counter, building an office in front for Mapel and adjusting the vintage two-unit Goss press to print a tabloid. The composing room equipment also needed maintenance. "We were taking the Linotypes apart and putting them together again," said John MacCary, who came to work for the paper at age 18, more than two months before the first issue. "They overhauled them all."

To run the advertising department, they hired Charles Nicholson, who had been working as general manager of the *New Bedford News* in Massachusetts. "Nick" was a gruff, bearish man with thick, bushy eyebrows behind his glasses. Operating from a space near the front of the converted showroom, he drew up a list of about 2,500 businesses in Nassau County, identifying potential advertisers. At the start, he had nothing tangible to sell, but he could lure advertisers by telling them that the new paper would enable them to reach readers on the North Shore. "The salesmen that went over there really had it easier than around the South Shore, because they just had a few weekly newspapers as competition," said Lewis (Bus) Seaman, who joined the advertising department later in the year. Promising a daily circulation of 15,000, Nicholson and his salesmen signed up enough advertisers to guarantee that they'd at least be able to support a 16-page paper.

For circulation, Mapel picked Joe Yauch, who had grown up on Long Island and played football for Hempstead High School, then built up the home delivery system for the *Brooklyn Eagle*, a daily paper in Brooklyn that also circulated on Long Island. Yauch was a tall, sturdy, barrel-chested man, with the appearance of a football player, and the confidence to go with it. "If you haven't hired your circulator yet, don't until you interview the best — me," Yauch said in a telegram to Mapel. At the *Eagle*, Yauch had built up experience in home delivery, and Alicia planned to rely almost entirely on home delivery to get her newspaper to readers. The New York City papers were sold primarily from newsstands, but home delivery was more reliable than newsstand sales, for both the paper and its advertisers.

Selling subscriptions and developing a network of carriers to deliver the paper was probably the most important and time-consuming job that the staff of the new paper did in the summer of 1940. "We were selling a product without even having seen the product," said Vinnie Bordash, one of the first people that Yauch hired. Like the rest of the new circulation department, Bordash was young but experienced in the difficult art of selling newspaper subscriptions. He was the son of immigrants from Czechoslovakia who had settled in the City of Yonkers, just north of New York City. He had just finished high school a year earlier, in 1939, but he had been gaining newspaper experience since he became a carrier at age 12. In high school, he delivered the *Yonkers Herald-Statesman*. During the summers, he had canvassed door-to-door for subscriptions. It was while he was working for the Westchester papers that Bordash began to develop a feel for the difficult art of selling newspaper subscriptions, which requires constant, frenetic effort. Every day, hundreds of people stop subscribing for one reason or another, which makes "stop" the worst four-letter word in the language for circulation managers. Just to stay even, they have to learn the reasons for the stops and try to resell the paper to those who have dropped it, in addition to finding new subscribers. This requires a tremendous amount of paperwork, and Bordash learned well in Westchester how to handle it. "They installed a system of keeping track of subscribers and non-subscribers that was way ahead of its time," Bordash said. Despite the store of circulation wisdom that he had acquired by the age of 19, Bordash didn't see much chance, at the tail end of the Depression, that he'd get above the level of assistant district manager in Westchester. So he acted on a tip from a friend: There was a new newspaper starting in Nassau County. Bordash drove to Long Island, stopped at the corner of Fulton and Main in Hempstead and asked a policeman for directions to the new newspaper. A few minutes later, he was at 283 Main Street, standing in front of Joe Yauch. A week after that, Yauch sent him a letter, telling him to report to John J. Mullen.

In contrast to Yauch, Mullen was almost painfully thin, but he certainly knew how to sell. The common joke was that he could peddle horse manure by persuading the customer that it would make the birds sing better. Like Yauch, Mullen had worked at the *Eagle*, starting as a circulation district manager. From there, he had gone to the *New York Post* and to *PM* the innovative but short-lived Manhattan paper. Just before coming to the new paper in Hempstead, he had run a weekly in Brooklyn. Now he became the first salesman to sell a home-delivery subscription for Alicia. (Actually, the first subscriber of them all was an attorney named Thomas K. Finletter, who wrote a letter asking for a subscription on April 8, 1940, right after the first stories about the new paper appeared. Later, Finletter was a consultant to the United States delegation at the formation of the United Nations, headed President Truman's Air Policy Commission, which led to the creation of the Air Force, then served as secretary of the Air Force and as United States ambassador to NATO.) Mullen's job, while others were setting up the network of carrier boys, was to run a sales crew of adults. "You needed an adult to sell a product that didn't exist," said Bordash, who started as one of Mullen's crew members. Before the first issue, Mullen's crew had sold 5,000 subscriptions.

Meanwhile, other circulation employees were trying to hire an army of carriers, or "merchant princes," as Alicia liked to call them. Since the district managers didn't have a newspaper to show the parents and couldn't offer the boy as easy a profit as the *Review-Star* could, they offered an intangible. "We didn't sell the $2 a week that the kid was going to make," said Buddy Chernow, who had worked in circulation at the *Brooklyn Eagle* and at *PM*, and had played beer-and-pretzels baseball against Yauch, who hired him. "What I sold was the business training and 'busy boys are better boys.' " District managers also had to map out the new paper routes, trying to keep them small and manageable, to avoid discouraging the new carriers. "We wanted to keep it as near a square as possible," said Jack Rovegno, who signed on with the new paper in early July. Rovegno had grown up in Freeport and had worked for the *Review-Star* circulation department, whose policies he learned to dislike. "All I wanted to do was to beat the *Review-Star*, because I thought they were lousy," Rovegno said. "I just didn't think they were fair to the kids or the managers."

Once they signed up the young carriers, the managers counted on the boys to soften the hearts of potential readers, but they also offered the readers a bargain: The normal home delivery price would be two cents a day — a dime a week. (The newsstand price would be higher, three cents a day, to encourage people to take home delivery.) But before the paper started, any reader who signed on for 13 weeks could get the first five weeks for a nickel a week, instead of a dime. In selling the non-existent newspaper, the district managers also emphasized "doorknob delivery," which meant the promise of a dry, undamaged newspaper, rolled up neatly and stuck on a door handle or under a mat — not sitting on the driveway, soaked by rain. As for the newspaper itself, they simply told people that it would be a tabloid, filled with photographs, but not sensational. It would be vital and interesting, not as dull as the *Review-Star*. "More or less, we were selling what it *wouldn't* be," Chernow said.

In the summer of 1940, and in the paper's first few years, when it was still ragged, amateurish and inconsistent editorially, it was primarily the circulation managers that made it work. Bordash, Chernow, Rovegno and the others were all young and hungry. They had worked long enough at other papers to know how the game was played. They were just married or getting married, and they desperately *needed* this new paper to succeed, if they were to build a life for their families. They also wanted to teach the *Review-Star* about the price of complacency. By the time the first issue rolled off the press, thousands of pink order cards from the adult sales crews and yellow cards from the carrier boys had piled up in the showroom. By the first day of publication, they had generated 11,000 subscriptions. The circulation people were so aggressive and confident that they almost didn't think they needed a decent newspaper to sell. In fact, Bordash said, Buddy Chernow once cockily summed up that view for

Alicia: "Hell, all we have to do is print it on brown wrapping paper. We'd sell it."

II

THE KEY DECISION in putting together a staff of reporters and editors was Alicia's — again with the help of her father's closest friend, Max Annenberg. Looking for someone experienced and knowledgeable to run the new paper for Alicia, Annenberg went to a young *Daily News* makeup editor named Alan Hathway.

Starting on the suburban desk, Hathway had moved to the copy desk, the telegraph desk and the news desk. Hathway had a knack for the clever *News* headline, but Annenberg liked him for a different reason: Hathway made the paper run on time. Delays in the composing room had been causing the paper to be late, and the *News* had been losing circulation. So Annenberg complained, and the response of the managing editor, Harvey Deuell, was to make Hathway chief makeup editor. "When Hathway set to work, the closings improved and the presses started on time — usually," said William Casselman, who later became the executive editor of the *News*. So, Annenberg liked Hathway's work, and he consulted Hathway about Alicia's needs for a strong editor. As Hathway recalled it years later, Annenberg told him that he was sure that Hathway had a good future at the *News*, but he wasn't certain about the future of Alicia's newspaper. So Annenberg asked him who else might be suitable, and Hathway recommended Harold Davis, another *News* editor who was Hathway's neighbor in Sunnyside, Queens.

Davis was born in Lamar, Colorado, and had worked at the *Tulsa World* and later at Hearst's *New York Journal-American* before coming to the *News*. In addition to working with Hathway at the *News*, Davis also knew him through writing Doc Savage pulp novels. Hathway did a total of four Doc Savage novels and Davis did about a dozen, plus an impressive list of novels and short stories featuring other characters, said Will Murray, an expert on pulp fiction. So, both Hathway and Davis knew how to turn out copy on deadline. But they were totally different personalities. Hathway was boisterous and pugnacious. He entered a room with his head tilted forward, as if he were on his way to a fight. Davis was slight, thin and soft-spoken, with an impassive face, bleary blue eyes and a head of pale reddish hair. Most often, he wore an editor's old-fashioned green eyeshades and looked more like an accountant than a journalistic leader. But he did have good news judgment, plus blurring speed at writing and editing. On Annenberg's recommendation, Alicia hired him as the paper's first managing editor.

Alicia's *Daily News* connections had produced the location of the newspaper, the man who surveyed Nassau County for its potential and, now, the managing editor. But it didn't stop there. "There were a lot of people from the *Daily News*," said Ralph Hausrath, who wasn't one of them. His connection was

Washington and Lee University. One of his classmates told him that the former head of the school's journalism department, Bill Mapel, would be working at a newspaper in Hempstead. So Hausrath walked in and got hired in July as a copy boy. One of his fraternity mates at Washington and Lee, Seth Baker, had been a copy boy at the *News* and came to the new paper in the same role in July. Other *News* copy boys and cub reporters came as reporters. And a *News* alumnus, Herb McCory, became the chief photographer.

The showroom on Main Street quickly filled up with young, inexperienced people like Seth Baker — and some even younger. Irene McLaughlin walked into the showroom, told Harold Davis she was 19 and was immediately hired as his secretary. But she had lied. She was still 16, and she had six months to go before she'd finish high school. She hid her school books at a candy store nearby so that no one at the paper would know. She drove back and forth in a car that her father had given her, even though she only had a learner's permit. And before she turned 17, Davis had kept his promise and promoted her to a reporter's job, for which her only real qualification was the desire to be in journalism. Similarly, Virginia Sheward, a handsome, high-cheekboned young woman with a perpetual tan and the air of a horsewoman, came to the paper with nothing even resembling journalism experience. She had been graduated from college in San Francisco, became a nurse and took private cases all over the New York area. One day, she passed by the showroom in Hempstead, became intrigued by a sign promoting the new paper's search for a name and went in. She was hired to sell subscriptions by phone, but before too many months had passed, she had become a reporter. Another inexperienced reporter, Norman Lobsenz, could at least boast a journalism education. He had grown up in Brooklyn, majored in journalism at New York University, then went to the Graduate School of Journalism at Columbia University. He was hired right out of Columbia and, at age 22, immediately became a valued rewrite man.

Not everyone they hired that summer was a total novice. There was a leavening of experienced but still young journalists, such as Jackie Gilbride Gebhard, who had worked in the women's department at the *New York Herald Tribune* and the *Long Island Press*. Her husband, Ed Gebhard, had already become the new paper's first sports editor, and she had decided to see Alicia about a job for herself. "She offered me a job in the women's department, which I refused," Gebhard said. "They had hired women for the women's department but nobody on the city side." They agreed to give her a two-week tryout, covering the North Shore. "I didn't have a car then," Gebhard said. "We had only one car in the family and Geb was using it. He had already been hired. So I hired a car and a driver for two weeks while I covered my beat." The rented car cost her more in a day than she made in a week, and she had to endure some tart comments about it. But the tryout worked out, and so did Jackie Gebhard, who quickly became a star on the young staff. "She was the best reporter I had — no question about that," said Andre Fontaine, who came to the new paper that summer as an editor. Fontaine also had real experience: at the *North Shore Daily Journal*, the ancestor of the new paper, at a local weekly, at the *Press* with the Gebhards and at a short-lived new paper in Rochester. The editors who joined the staff before the first issue also included Marty Forman, the city editor, a Columbia journalism graduate who had worked at the *Review-Star*, and Forbes Fairbairn, the wire editor, who worked at various times at the *Daily News* and the *Journal-American*.

Blending together a few well-experienced editors and a corps of untrained reporters, Alicia created a staff whose collective personality tended toward puppy-like enthusiasm. "In a way," Lobsenz said, "putting that paper together in those days was sort of like Judy Garland and Mickey Rooney sitting around and saying, 'Hey, kids, let's put on a show.' "

III

FOR THE DESIGN of the new paper, Alicia sought help from the husband of one of her closest friends. Janet Chase had married an abstract expressionist named Fred Hauck, who did commercial design from his Manhattan studio, and Alicia asked him to create a distinctive appearance for her paper.

The "look" that Hauck designed was a significant departure from normal tabloid practice. The front page was like a front page in the *Daily News*: usually a large headline, in dark, blocky, sans serif-style type, and a large photograph. It was inside the paper that Hauck created innovations. Most newspapers had developed a habit of loading their headlines at the top of a page, and dangling long columns of type straight down from there, separated by column rules. The reason for broadsheet papers to do this was obvious: When the papers were folded and placed on newsstands, the only part visible to potential readers was the part above the fold. So that is where they stacked the boldest, heaviest elements of the page — to attract attention and stimulate sales. For the most part, tabloid newspapers had adopted the same vertical style. But Alicia's paper was not going to be the usual tabloid. Since it was going to be sold primarily through home delivery, the paper didn't have to struggle to attract the potential reader's eye, as papers sold at newsstands had to do. That reality gave Alicia and Hauck room to create a new design. It also shaped for many years the way the paper covered and presented news.

In the final weeks of August, Hauck put together prototypes that did away with the vertical format and replaced it with a horizontal look, which spread one- and two-line headlines around and gave equal focus to different parts of the page. In the process, Hauck also eliminated the rules between columns. "If you're going to go for horizontal makeup, you practically had to get rid of the rules," said Andre Fontaine. The effect was to allow more white to show through in the spaces between the columns, which brightened the paper and, along with the larger-than-usual typeface that they chose, made it look easier to read. For the typeface that would announce the new paper's name at the top of page one, Hauck chose Ultra Bodoni, part of a family of faces developed by the Italian typographer Giambattista Bodoni in the eighteenth century. Though the Bodoni family of type was then 150 years old, it gave the top of the new paper a surprisingly fresh, elegant and contemporary look.

At the same time, the staff was gathering biographical information and photographs on prominent people in the community, carrying around a four-page questionnaire called "Information for Your New Paper." So far, that was the only name the paper had. Rather than name the paper themselves, Alicia, Bill Mapel and Stan Peckham decided to make a contest out of it, to build reader interest. One week, posters appeared on Long Island Rail Road stations, asking: "What's In a Name?" The following week, the sign said, "What's In a Newspaper Name?" A week later, it was "What's In a Newspaper Name — Well for One Thing, $1,500," including a top prize of $1,000. They did other promotions as well, including a movie that Peckham and an office boy named Bobby Blossom made in one day, taking shots around Long Island, followed by scenes at the new newspaper. It didn't work as well as it should have, since many local theaters accepted the free film, showed the Nassau travelogue and lopped off the paper's promotion message at the end.

As the naming contest went on, thousands of entries poured in, but most of them offered names that were already being used by one or more of the local weeklies. The closer they got to the planned September 3 starting date, the more concerned they grew. At one point, Alicia's friend Neysa McMein, one of the judges for the contest, suggested that they name the paper *The County Irritant*, and Alicia at least pretended to like it. Desperate to avoid that, Mapel sat down, a little more than a week before the opening edition, and doodled on a pad. He stopped when the word "Newsday" popped out of his head. Walking into Alicia's office near the composing room, he wrote the new name down on a lined piece of paper and gave it to her. Mapel recalled later that Alicia sat silently for about 15 seconds, looking at the name he had written, before she reacted. "A light began shining in her eyes," Mapel said. Once they had a name chosen by a member of the staff, they had to figure out a way to give out the prizes in the contest. "We had to go through all these thousands of entries to look for the nearest thing," Peckham said. They found three identical entries that were close to the one Mapel had dreamed up, and a fourth that was almost the same. In a 100-word essay contest, they chose the $1,000 winner, Lawrence A. Brown, 28, a mechanical engineer from East Hempstead.

The last week before publication, they printed a complete dummy news-paper every day, from Monday, August 26, to Friday, August 30. In the same typeface that they'd eventually use for *Newsday*, they gave each day's paper a different name — Monday, Tuesday and so on through the week. They did everything except actually sell the paper. Then, just before publication, Harry and Alicia adopted a formal agreement on how she was to be paid. Though Harry had given Alicia a $4,000 "participation" in *Newsday*, it was clear that he was the owner and she was the employee. In a letter dated September 1, 1940, Harry spelled out what they had discussed. "You will devote your time to the publication of *Newsday* in the capacity of editor and publisher without salary," he wrote. "In lieu of salary, you are to receive one-half of the net profits to me from *Newsday* that may accrue in any calendar year."

It seemed a little early to be talking about profits. They hadn't shown yet that they could publish even one day's paper properly, let alone profitably. The time had come to try it.

IV

THE WEEKS OF dry runs should have produced a smooth beginning, but the first edition of *Newsday* quickly started going sour.

As the printers struggled to lock up pages on the morning of September 3, Alicia Patterson and Harold Davis stood in the composing room near Joe Curley, who was making up the inside pages. To their shock, they found that half a dozen photo engravings were missing, which prevented them from closing three pages. Alicia threw her car keys to Nick Grande, a rotund young office boy, and told him to drive as fast as he could to the engraver that *Newsday* was using, several miles away, and get back with the missing cuts. Grande hopped in her car and sped off. On Grande's way back to the office, he ran into a motorcycle cop, who pulled him over and ticketed him for speeding. Grande explained that his paper was trying to make a deadline, and the cop asked him what paper. When Grande told him it was *Newsday*, the cop became perhaps the first person, outside of the staff and the contest winners, to learn the paper's name.

The primary problem in the composing room was not the missing engravings, but the crowding. One of the rules of composing-room etiquette is that there should be no more editorial employees there than necessary. But the excitement of the paper's birth had brought a crowd of onlookers, from the publisher herself down to advertising salesmen, anxious to make last-minute adjustments to ads. "Everybody was busy as hell and nothing was happening," said Andre Fontaine, the makeup editor that first day. "We're a couple of hours from deadline, and we had no paper." So Fontaine went up to Jake Federman, a *Daily News* alumnus who was the composing room foreman, and persuaded him to invoke his power to stop all work by blowing his whistle. "Everybody was very startled," Fontaine said. "I explained to them what it meant. And Alicia said, 'Well, I want to stay.' I said, 'You can't. Do you want to make up the paper?' She said, 'I don't know how to make up the paper.' " So she left, along with the others, and Fontaine and the printers eventually got the pages closed, stereotyped and on the press. "We didn't make the deadline," Fontaine said. "At least we came fairly close to it."

Ceremoniously, as a photographer waited to record the scene, Alicia stepped up to the press and pushed the button. The first issue of *Newsday* started rolling off the presses. Stan Peckham grabbed an armful and ran out the door with Nick Grande, the office boy, to drive off quickly on two missions. Peckham's most urgent assignment was the registration of the copyright for the new paper at the county courthouse in Mineola. The weekly newsmagazine *Newsweek* had been friendly to the new paper all summer long, Peckham said. In the weeks just before the first edition, they had been anxious to know its name, so they could prepare a story to run when the paper started up. But the management of *Newsday* was fearful that *Newsweek* might try to get some kind of injunction against the name, on the basis of copyright infringement. Now that the paper was going out to the world, Peckham had to hurry. "Without even looking at it, I had to grab it and race for Mineola to register the name before *Newsweek* caught on," Peckham said. Despite his nervousness, he got the copyright registered without a hitch, leaving *Newsweek* with no chance to stop the new paper from being called *Newsday*. In the issue right after *Newsday* made its debut, *Time* carrieds a small story on the event. *Newsweek* said not a word.

From the courthouse, Peckham and Grande rushed into Manhattan, to deliver a copy of the paper to Joseph Medill Patterson. By the time the two men returned to the office in Hempstead, the staff had managed to straighten out some of the first day's mess, including a press breakdown in the middle of the run, and a series of errors. Peckham, in his rush, hadn't even noticed that the first few papers off the press, which he had delivered to Alicia's proud father, were decidedly inferior. "What we took him must have been a slap in the face," Peckham said. "We thought we were going to put out a very good paper. That's why it was so disappointing when we saw the paper the first day. Everyone was horrified. Here we thought we were so well rehearsed."

Right on page one, for example, someone had reversed the captions on two pictures. One photo showed Larry Brown, the winner of $1,000 in the contest for naming *Newsday*, grinning broadly and wrapped in a poster that asked: "What's in a Newspaper Name?" The other photo was a forlorn student, obviously distraught about having to return to school after the summer. Underneath Brown's photo was a tag, in large type, saying, "He's Happy." Next to the boy's photo was one that read, "He's Not." The arrows pointed correctly from those lines to the photographs. Embarrassingly, however, someone had stuck the wrong caption material underneath the tags. Inside the paper, the first part of a planned fiction series mistakenly began with a synopsis of what was still to come. Seth Baker, the copy boy and desk assistant who made up that page, remembered that the error was his. The night before, Baker had missed a staff party, because he was putting together the back pages. When Mapel returned from the party and asked him about the serial, Baker was angry that he was working while the others celebrated, and he wasn't in a careful mood. "So when he said, 'I don't think that's right,' I don't think I even bothered to look," Baker said. "I just figured, 'Oh, the hell with it,' and out it went."

Alicia's verdict on the first day's paper was swift: "I'm afraid it looks like hell." And as the young people on the staff drifted out that afternoon and walked a few doors away to a bar called the Anchor Inn, they indulged in gallows humor. "We were taking bets on how many days it would last before it folded,"

Virginia Sheward said. "That's how bad it was. It was a horror." Nonetheless, they had published a 32-page daily newspaper. Out of a press run of 30,000, about 11,000 copies went to home delivery subscribers, and another 5,000 or 6,000 were sold at newsstands.

Besides the errors, the first *Newsday* at least had some news. Considering that it was the day after Labor Day, in fact, the lead headline on page one was a surprisingly good news story — even if it came from the wires: "U.S. Gives British/50 Warships." The second headline on page one referred to police dropping tear gas on a jealous husband who had taken a rifle and barricaded himself for four days in the woodpile at the Sands Point estate of Harry's uncle, Solomon Guggenheim. So the first local news story was about the North Shore, the area that the *Review-Star* had always neglected. Right under the tear gas story on page two was a piece about a *Newsday* straw poll taken by 45 students, showing President Franklin Roosevelt's strength dropping in Nassau County. In addition, *Newsday* reported in almost embarrassing detail on the winners of the naming contest, including one photograph of the grand prize winner on page one, another on page three and three more of him and his family on page five. The center of the paper had a spread of photos about Long Island's aircraft industry gearing up as the war in Europe continued. And the big sports story was the opening of a new race track, Roosevelt Raceway in Westbury, just a short distance from the *Newsday* office. The 8,500 customers were witnesses to some minor history: the state's first night harness racing with parimutuel betting.

Aside from the story about the warships for England, probably the most important thing in the paper was the only editorial, outlining what the new paper stood for.

"Publishing a newspaper is a business," the editorial said. "Any business, to be successful, must have revenue. Most newspaper revenue comes from advertising. We hope, and so far the result has been gratifying, to obtain such advertising.

"However, we do wish to make this point: Our first, second and final object is to present the news. That is where Newsday is our slogan as well as our name. If we present the news honestly, we know we will have readers. If we have readers it will be profitable for advertisers to use our columns whether they agree with our policy or not." The policy was that *Newsday* would be liberal but independent. "There have been rumors that we would be a Democratic organ, meaning that we would line up behind the county Democratic organization," the editorial said. "At the present time that is not the case. We are not going to line up behind any county political organization."

Another rumor that the opening editorial wanted to set to rest was one about ownership. It didn't specifically mention the *Daily News*, but it was obviously addressing rumors that *Newsday* and the *News* were financially connected. "The ownership of Newsday is clearly stated at the top of this column," the editorial said, referring to the small print containing the names of Harry and Alicia. "No one else has any connection with it." Alicia could deny that the *News* had an ownership interest in *Newsday*, but she could hardly deny the influence. For example, the opening editorial cartoon, a naked child labelled *Newsday*, standing in front of a map of Nassau County, and toasting the readers with a glass filled with a brew called "The Truth," was drawn by the well-known *Daily News* cartoonist, C. D. Batchelor. And that same morning, Harry and Alicia had sent a grateful telegram to Joe Patterson and his wife, Mary, thanking them, Max Annenberg and a list of others, "for all the help you have given us." Even if the *News* was not the mother of *Newsday*, it certainly was the midwife at the birth.

Finally, the editorial staked out Alicia's hopes. "We are convinced this county has a bright future and we want to share in it," the editorial said. For the moment, those bright hopes were darkened by the less-than-perfect performance on the first day. The next day, just as her father had done 21 years earlier when the *Daily News* started off shakily, Alicia carried an editorial apologizing for the mess. "For our part, we have decided to be philosophical about it all," the editorial said. "Newsday, we discovered, was just like a child, and as with our favorite youngsters, it refused to be at its best in its first public appearance. So, if you will pardon a not-too-good pun, even if we err again, we will not be discouraged, for tomorrow also will be Newsday."

CHAPTER EIGHT

Newsday Goes to War

I

IF ALICIA PATTERSON was ever tempted to rule her newspaper aloofly from above, she chose the wrong building for it. The former auto showroom at 283 Main Street was just too small for management-at-a-distance.

The building was located a few doors south of the triangular intersection of Main Street and Old Franklin Street, in the Village of Hempstead. The plant sliced through that triangular block, with the front doors on Main and the rear doors on Old Franklin. At the front, there were identical doors in the middle of the building. The one on the left led to the automobile dealership operated by Dan Eldredge, at 281 Main. The door on the right was *Newsday*. The long, narrow section that *Newsday* occupied, 185 feet deep and only 56 feet wide, was narrower than the side occupied by Eldredge. The paper's offices were in the front third of the building, which was even skinnier than the section to the rear, because a driveway on the side of the building ate up 12 feet of its width. The newsroom was on the same side of the building as the driveway. The composing room was farther back, through double doors, and the pressroom was all the way to the rear, with doors on Old Franklin.

The miniature newsroom, crammed into a space about 15 feet wide, contained the office of the managing editor Harold Davis, along with the society department, the sports department, local reporters and the city desk itself. There was space enough in the narrow room for two rows of desks, about four deep, leading back to the double doors into the composing room, which was filled with rickety Linotypes. From the newsroom, an editor or reporter could walk through the doors into the composing room, turn left and be in Alicia's office. When Alicia showed up in the morning, she'd park her Cadillac in the driveway, next to a large plate glass window that gave everyone in the newsroom a perfect view of her arrival. Instead of walking around to the front door on Main Street, she'd enter the building through a side door off the driveway and walk through the composing room to her small, windowless office. There, she was smack in the middle of everything, surrounded by the clatter of typesetting. Immediately to the rear of her office was the minuscule darkroom and nearby were the steps to the men's toilet in the basement. A short distance to the rear was the rumble of the Goss press.

Early in the paper's life, Alicia decided there were more important places for her to work than in her tiny office. "I said, 'Why don't you come out and put a desk next to mine and watch what's going on? I'll funnel the copy through you,' " said Andre Fontaine, who had succeeded Marty Forman as city editor. So Alicia spent a month on the desk. "I was very impressed with that, that a woman like her, who owned the paper and who was rich . . . would come in at seven in the morning and was interested enough to learn the details of how the place worked," Fontaine said. "Even though she didn't know the technology of it, some of the details of putting out a paper, her instincts were marvelous. She'd say, 'I think we ought to look into so and so.' By God, almost every time there would be a story there." But she could also be high-handed. "There was a certain capriciousness, almost a capricious arrogance about her," Fontaine said. "Sometimes she would come up with a request or an order which was absolutely absurd. So you were sort of on pins and needles with her, until you got to know her." But before long, they developed a good, bantering relationship. "I found that she could be argued with," he said. "She had an open mind."

Just as her intuitions about stories were sound, Alicia's instincts about the location of her paper and about its tabloid form turned out to be entirely correct. But the timing of its birth, toward the end of 1940, brought *Newsday* a difficult infancy. As Alicia began marching her young staff into war with the *Review-Star*, Franklin Roosevelt was preparing to march America into war against Germany and Japan. Within weeks after *Newsday* was born, the draft started to disrupt a staff that was inexperienced enough already. After the Japanese attack on Pearl Harbor, the personnel drain became even stronger. "The turnover is terrific for me right now," she said in a newspaper interview. "When I started the paper, my personnel was young and single — unfortunately. They began to marry. Then they began to have babies. Now the husbands are going off to war. And I'm going crazy over all this changing around!" As a result, the tone of *Newsday* was improvisational and often amateurish.

From the beginning, Alicia and Davis often had to pull out of a magician's hat even the simplest elements of the paper. For example, there were not enough letters initially to fill up "The County Irritant," the letters-to-the-editor column, which got its name from her friend Neysa McMein's suggestion for the name of the paper. So Alicia's staff did what Joe Patterson's staff had done at the *Daily News* two decades earlier: Young reporters would come back from covering their beats and spend their spare time composing letters to the editor. Similarly, Alicia faced the daily tensions of finding enough subjects to fill her editorial page and enough people to write them. Since there was no full-time editorial page staff, the task of writing editorials fell to Alicia or anyone else who had the time.

Early in the paper's history, several long-term themes emerged in the editorials, such as animal rights. Paradoxically, Alicia loved to shoot quail and big game, but she became enraged when others abused animals. She also wrote a long string of editorials urging that the armed forces be allowed to draft women as well as men. "She was a hearty feminist," Stan Peckham said. "Why in hell not draft women too?" Another frequent target was the Long Island Rail Road. Everyone shared anger over the frequent accidents at points where highways crossed the tracks at ground level, and everyone felt frustration over train delays. So the LIRR was a unifying theme. It was also during the war years that Alicia began beating the drum for legalized off-track betting, even though some of Harry's horse-owning friends frowned on the idea.

Of course, Alicia couldn't ride these few hobbyhorses every day. When she was desperate for other ideas for editorials, she was not shy about asking for help from visitors to Falaise, such as the publisher Bennett Cerf and his wife, Phyllis. "So we, being houseguests, paid for our supper by writing editorials," said Phyllis Cerf, who had already had some writing experience, as an advertising agency copywriter and as a Hollywood columnist. "We would be talking, just conversationally, and she'd say, 'Oh, we could do an editorial on that. Write it.' So, we'd write it." Later, Alicia tapped Phyllis Cerf for other jobs, such as making up puzzles called "Hidden History" and writing a column. At Alicia's request, she also acted as an advisor to the staff of the women's pages. "They weren't thrilled with it, as you can imagine," she said.

This practice, asking friends to help, became a pattern. When John Bitter, the husband of her lifelong friend Dody Michelson, enlisted in the Army, for example, Alicia asked him to write periodic columns for her about Army life. She also asked her sister Josephine, who had been a reporter at the *Chicago Daily News*, to write a column, "Life with Junior," about the trials of raising children. Alicia even used the work of her friends after they were dead. For years, she made an annual ritual of running on the editorial page a short Christmas parable by her friend Heywood Broun. Perhaps her most notorious use of a friend's talents involved the artist Neysa McMein, who had made her reputation by painting covers for such magazines as *McCall's*, *Saturday Evening Post* and *Collier's*. For Alicia, she tried something altogether different: a comic strip.

At the birth of *Newsday*, the *Daily News* helped Alicia in many ways, but there was one form of assistance that her father refused to give: He was not about to let Alicia run any of his comics in *Newsday*. They were major circulation builders, and he jealously guarded his rights of territorial exclusivity. As Alicia remembered it later, he said: "I wouldn't give them to anyone else in my circulation area, so why should I give them to you?" As a result, *Newsday* had second-rate strips, and Alicia decided, if her father could invent comic strips, she could too. So Alicia and McMein created "Deathless Deer," a strip about an Egyptian princess returned to life in modern times, with drawings by McMein and story line by Alicia. It started on November 9, 1942, and on the second day, it began to reveal its amateurishness: "Deer's beauty drove men mad," the narration said. "From the four corners of the earth suitors came to ask her hand in marriage. None pleased her." So Princess Deer dismissed one of them with a stunningly anachronistic piece of dialogue: "You are too gross. Go!" By the end of the strip's first week, an avaricious enemy stabbed the princess, but her high priest administered a potion that would eventually awaken her. In the second week, the strip rushed to a time 3,000 years later, when the archaeologist Professor Hoot and his "faithful man," Frappy, discovered Deer's burial place. Frappy was a black man, drawn to look stereotypically bug-eyed as they entered the tomb. And when the mummified princess awoke, McMein drew Frappy lying on the floor, obviously fainted away in terror. He revived just in time to have Alicia put a frightened and ungrammatical piece of dialogue into his mouth: "Let's git going, Prof, afore she really gits waked up!"

In its first two weeks, the strip displayed a dazzling mixture of anachronism, tin-eared dialogue and the none-too-subtle racism that was characteristic of the era. But unaccountably, it kept running in *Newsday* until the following summer. Worse, it also ran in her father's *Daily News*, Aunt Cissy Patterson's *Washington Times-Herald* and Cousin Bert McCormick's *Chicago Tribune*. So the whole family could watch every morning, as Alicia's comic strip unfolded painfully. Alicia's staff took her seriously in most things, but Stan Peckham said that they chuckled over her comic strip. "Oh, it was awful," he said. "It was supposed to be a comic strip, but it wasn't very comic." Finally, in July, 1943, the *News* stopped carrying "Deathless Deer" because of newsprint restrictions. But Alicia had never received the letter from the managing editor, Richard Clarke, warning that it might be dropped. So she construed the termination as an unannounced slight, and she responded with a torrent of long-repressed resentment toward her father. First, she said something sarcastic about his patriotism. Then she wrote him a "Dear Father" letter, much more chilly than the loving "Dearest Poppy" letters of a few years earlier. It began with an apology for her remark about his patriotism, but it ended with a list of grievances.

"I think I lashed out the way I did because I wanted to hurt you just to even up the score," Alicia wrote. "You see you have been pushing me around for quite a spell now and the worm had to turn.

"The immediate cause for the turning was Deathless Deer. Both Neysa and I had worked so hard to make her a success that when she was booted out with never a word we felt it was hardly cricket. . . . She has been such a trial to us and we know she was lousy at first. But lately people seemed to take a fancy to her. . . . God rest her soul.

"But Deathless Deer was only the last of many kicks in the pants that you have favored me with over a number of years. And I don't mean financial kicks because you have been most extraordinarily generous to me that way. It started way back when I jumped five feet six and you never gave me the horse you promised. Then came the time when you fired me off the News and married me to Simpson. One instance I remember was after the Civil War battle field junket when you told me you never wanted to see me again. . . . After I married Harry you refused for a year to see him while you taunted me with jibes about the Jews. And then you fired me off the book review column." Alicia had continued writing book reviews for the *News* after she started *Newsday*, almost as if she was desperate to retain some connection with her father's newspaper. "When I started Newsday I thought you would be proud and happy that I was trying to follow your lead," Alicia continued. "But it took the greatest persuasion to get you even to look at the plant. And you never take any interest anymore in anything I do. So because I have loved you very much these things have hurt me perhaps more than they would hurt most daughters."

Then she got around to the wound that rankled most: Despite her years of service as a substitute son, all of her father's concern seemed focused on her half brother, Jimmy, who was nearing graduation from West Point and a possible assignment to the war zone. "Certainly you had no fear of any hurt that might befall me — which is okay," she wrote. "Now because you fear so much for Jimmy perhaps I am somewhat jealous that you never felt that way about me. I know that he is the only thing in your life that matters; that to have a son has always been your one ambition. Well I couldn't help being a girl. And I tried to overcome the handicap."

The next day, she sent a short note of conciliation. "Perhaps getting married and settling down to a different kind of a life broke the spell of our relationship," she wrote. "We used to have such a helluva time — are them days really gone forever?" Her father's response was cool and logical. First he explained the mixup about the comic strip. Then, in two terse sentences, he disposed of her complaints. "As to your other grievances, I don't see much use in discussing them," he wrote. "If they have been rankling in your heart all this time, they can't be eliminated now." Two weeks later, her father brought the whole episode to a halt with a one-sentence note: "I think I am too old to quarrel with you and hope we may make up." Even if they did, their relationship was clearly no longer the same. The days of Dearest Poppy were gone.

II

ONE BENEFIT OF the constant flux caused by the war was that the young, inexperienced people on the staff had the chance to stretch their wings and try new things.

The fluid situation, for example, allowed the young rewrite man Norman Lobsenz to expand quickly to criminal-justice features. At the request of Harold Davis, he emulated the Sunday justice series in the *Daily News*, by reading trial transcripts of interesting Long Island cases from the past and turning out 5,000-word stories on them. He also wrote editorials, handled photo captions and even chose photos. Lobsenz owed this opportunity to play photo editor largely to the detached management style of Davis, who spent his evenings a few doors away, at the Anchor Inn. "Davis would leave around 8:30 and say, 'I'll be up at the corner. In case anything happens, call me,' " said Lobsenz, who would telephone Davis at the bar and describe the photographs as they came in. "He'd sort of tell me what to use, without even seeing the stuff. Then after that went on for a while, he said, 'If there's no real problem in your mind, Norman, you decide. Don't bother calling me.' "

Often, a reporter simply had to ask for an assignment and it was his. Covering draft boards and working on a geographical beat, Seth Baker learned that he lacked the aggressiveness to be a good daily reporter, and he asked Davis to let him write features. Davis promptly gave permission — so long as Baker continued covering draft boards. Soon, Baker was also reviewing night clubs and restaurants. "You immediately had to do a lot of things," Baker said. Before he could get accustomed to the features, Baker experienced another sudden career change, when he visited his own draft board in Freeport to get the latest list of draftees. "There was my name," he said. "I was thunderstruck." He entered the service in March, 1941, just six months after joining *Newsday*.

Within a year after Pearl Harbor, half of the early news staff had gone to war, including some of the more experienced members, such as Ed Gebhard, the sports editor, Herb McCory, the chief photographer, and Ben White, a well-respected reporter who had risen to city editor. The loss of White especially hurt, because the younger reporters on the staff looked up to him. "He could do everything on a newspaper, and do it spectacularly well," said Marie Quantrell, one of the reporters of that era. White had grown up in Nassau County and had worked at a small weekly, at the *North Shore Daily Journal* and at the *New York World-Telegram & Sun*. He knew every cop and every bartender, which made him handy to have around. For example, he helped break the ice with Nassau police and public officials, who had developed a relationship with the *Review-Star* and were not always friendly to *Newsday*. Soon after White had interceded to get more cooperation from the police, he went into the service, along with Walter Kennedy, a reporter who had worked with him at the start of *Newsday* on the poll that accurately predicted that Wendell Willkie would defeat Franklin Roosevelt easily in Nassau County. White returned to *Newsday* after the war, but Kennedy died in combat.

The pit of military service also opened up beneath the feet of Stan Peckham, who handled a variety of promotional chores for Alicia, including a flower show designed to capture the loyalty of women readers, a limerick contest, and a Long Island version of the *Daily News* Golden Gloves boxing tournament — with the cooperation of the *News*. Alicia had also made Peckham a columnist. What she wanted was something local, written in the style of the literate and witty "Talk of the Town" column in *The New Yorker* — a tall order for a young man whose previous journalistic experience included little more than writing for a current-events magazine for teenagers. But Peckham's column, "Around the Corner," was a nice facsimile of that "Talk" style. A typical example was his engaging look at the history of an odd street name: Skunk's Misery Road. A year after the column started, Peckham began writing about his initial encounters with his draft board and his unsuccessful efforts to get into the Navy or the Merchant Marine. Finally, he arranged to be drafted into the Army. Peckham told Alicia that he would be sent to basic training at Camp Dix, New Jersey, but she insisted that he get the induction site changed to Camp Upton, in Suffolk County, so that he could write from there. Somehow, possibly through connections at the *Daily News*, Alicia and Harold Davis got Peckham assigned to Upton. Once Peckham was in the Army, he continued to write columns from Upton, from basic training in Virginia and from Officer Candidate School in North Carolina.

That kind of staff depletion was not as disruptive to the more established papers as it was to *Newsday*. The older papers had a core of reporters and editors who had been around for many years and were too old for the draft. At *Newsday*, that core group was far smaller. In many cases, the people that Alicia hired to replace draftees were women. In some cases, the replacements were older reporters hired away from the *Review-Star*. The loose, anything-goes atmosphere at *Newsday* proved attractive to four *Review-Star* employees, James Jenkins, Richard Wyse, Leo Hanning and Bea Jones, who came to *Newsday* early. In that wartime environment, Alicia didn't have the luxury of setting up a rigorous hiring process. "We had a staff you would not believe today," said Jacquie Villa, who came to the paper directly from Hofstra College, as a society reporter. The only question that anyone asked about her qualifications was how long she had lived on Long Island. "They wouldn't let a staff like that put out a college paper, much less a daily," Villa said. "People landed on *Newsday* from outer space." Sometimes, people even got hired by accident. Marie Quantrell, a junior at Adelphi College, showed up at the office one day in the spring of 1942 with a friend who had just been graduated. The friend was looking for a job, but Quantrell was not. Nonetheless, the switchboard operator handed them two applications, and Quantrell obediently filled one out. "The next day I received a call from Harold Davis, telling me to come down for an interview," she said. "I did, and was hired to write a column on the civil defense activities of Long Islanders." Just like that: From unemployment to columnist, overnight.

Ultimately, the influx of women even brought in a female photographer — a highly unusual commodity at that time. Edna Murray had begun to think about photography as a career, and she had puttered around in darkrooms, but that was about the extent of her knowledge. She called up *Newsday* and asked whether they had any openings in the darkroom. "I knew nothing about being a photographer," Murray said. *Newsday* sent her out on a photo assignment anyway, but she found she couldn't make her camera work. So she called Jim Martenhoff, who by the end of the war was the only other photographer on the staff. When Martenhoff arrived on the scene, he found that Murray had simply been handling the camera wrong. "I was less than pleased, because she was totally inept," Martenhoff said. "Eventually, she learned. . . . I had to treat her with kid gloves. I didn't know how to deal with women."

It was a woman, however, who delivered the first piece of solid investigative reporting for *Newsday*. Jackie Gilbride Gebhard was something of an idol to the younger reporters because she came with experience, and she was sharp in the ways of the world. "We were all in love with Jackie," Seth Baker said. Her ground-breaking investigation began one day in late 1940 in District Court, when a judge decided to move the court to a local nursing home, to hear testimony from a bedridden witness. The photographer John Dolan decided to go along, and so did Gebhard. She was appalled by the substandard conditions, and she asked a nurse about them. The nurse told her that this home was better than most, and that there were few laws governing the operation of the homes. Gebhard went back to Harold Davis and told him about the potential for a story. "This is the kind of stuff we're looking for," he told her.

To help in the investigation, Davis sent Dolan and the reporter John Gardner undercover into the homes and hired a former Secret Service agent to help check on conditions. The result was a series of first-person stories by Gebhard, Gardner and Dolan in early 1941. They found a variety of abuses, such as poor food, dirty linens and differences in the treatment given to private and welfare patients. A closing editorial advocated that the state set up a system of supervision over the homes. In April, 1941, two months after the series, Governor Herbert Lehman signed a bill giving the county health department authority to regulate the homes. The following year, one of Gebhard's original sources told her about a man named Samuel Hill, who had died at The Maples, a nursing home in Oceanside. Based on Gebhard's tip that an employee had beaten Hill, authorities exhumed the body. Police later arrested an employee, Russell Wilson, who was convicted of second-degree assault.

In the original nursing home series, no single story was particularly damaging by itself. They were all little more than anecdotal accounts of what the homes looked, smelled and sounded like on a given day. But by the sheer persistence of the effort, the series got enough attention to force a change in the law. For *Newsday*, it was a first.

III

IN THE FRUSTRATING job of guiding a patchwork staff, Alicia's chief lieutenant was a man who almost never left his little office except to go to the bar down the street.

"To me, he was very quiet," said Lucy Risedorf, one of the secretaries to Harold Davis. "He spent most of his day behind the desk." Davis was a fast and skillful writer, but he didn't enjoy managing nearly as much as he liked doing. Given the youth and inexperience of the staff, his lack of management zeal was a major defect. He also had to cope with a difficult marriage, with personal financial problems and with his stepdaughter, Joy, who helped around the office by answering phones and hindered by providing a beautiful distraction to the staff. But his real problem was his drinking. "Harold Davis used to drink iced tea all afternoon," said Matte Prince Hausrath, another of his secretaries. "When he would come back from dinner, the Anchor Inn would send a similar carton, but it wouldn't be iced tea. It would be straight Scotch."

The drinking didn't help the relationship between Davis and one of his key editors, Andre Fontaine. They clashed so much, over a variety of issues, that Alicia separated their shifts. Eventually, Davis tried to fire him. "Ed Gebhard was chairman of the Guild and he made Davis rescind the firing," Fontaine said. "There was bad blood and this feud was not a help to the paper." Eventually, Fontaine grew tired of the fighting and asked Alicia for a raise to $50 a week, which she refused. "That's when I told her I wanted to leave," Fontaine said. Alicia used her *Daily News* connections and arranged a job there for Fontaine. "Of course it was always an elegant thing to me that when she found out she had to hire somebody to replace me, she hired Alan Hathway." By then, Hathway's future at the *News* no longer looked as bright as it had when Max Annenberg had told him at the start of *Newsday* that he'd be better off staying with the *News*. Part of the time since then, Hathway had taken a leave from the *News* to write pulp fiction. His first experience at *Newsday* had been part-time work as a makeup editor, after his regular shift at the *News*. Then, when Fontaine left, Davis turned to his old friend from the *Daily News* and the Doc Savage novels and made Hathway the city editor in the middle of 1942.

The new authority figure for the young staff had spent most of his years rebelling against authority. His earliest battles were against his father, Frank Jesse Hathway, who ran a lumber camp and a hardware store without notable success. Rebelling, the younger Hathway ran away from his hometown of Sault Sainte Marie, Michigan, and got passage on a boat to China. Along the way, he managed to get himself thrown into jail in both Hong Kong and Dublin. He also ran away to join a steamer on the Great Lakes. To the younger children of his hometown, this defiance made "Happy" Hathway a hero. Hathway did go to college for two years, but he got the bulk of his education in the newspaper business, first in the rough-and-tumble world of Chicago journalism and later at the *Daily News*. At the *News*, Hathway became the first chairman of the new Newspaper Guild and represented the union in the negotiation of its first contract. He was such a fiery unionist, in fact, that he couldn't stay away from a 1937 Guild strike against the *Long Island Press*. Charging out to the picket lines, he provoked a loud confrontation with police. "So they arrested him," said Jackie Gebhard, who was in the Guild at the *Press* before coming to *Newsday*. "He spent the night in the clink."

It was his instinct for combat that would turn out to be Hathway's greatest contribution to *Newsday*. At the start, what the infant paper needed most of all was not finesse, but the kind of fighting spirit that would convince its competitors and its own staff that it had the will to survive. That made Hathway the perfect man for the job. Drunk or sober — and Hathway was often drunk — fighting was his natural state. A typical example of his belligerent attitude happened a few years after he came to *Newsday*. Hathway was on his way into a local bar with two friends when they encountered two men, who asked if he was Alan Hathway. When Hathway admitted that he was, one of the men socked him and sent him sprawling. His friends offered to grab the offender, so that Hathway could punch him back. But Hathway told them to leave the attacker alone. He picked himself up, defiantly stood in front of the man who had just decked him, and said: "I'm *still* Alan Hathway."

As pugnacious as he could be in bars, Hathway was far more aggressive with a newspaper. He had first tasted journalism in the brawling Chicago of the late 1920s, when reporters really spoke and acted the way Charles MacArthur and Ben Hecht painted them in the deathless newspaper play, *The Front Page*. So the journalism that Hathway knew best was that Chicago style: fists-first, hard-drinking, card-playing, wisecracking, get-the-story-at-all-costs newspapering.

Hathway's feel for a good story, however, didn't always include a slavish reliance on facts. One morning in 1943, for example, the foreign news was large enough for page one: 2,000 tons of British explosives raining down on Cologne, in the heart of Germany. But Hathway chose to lead the paper with something far more local: reports from police that a gorilla had escaped in Oceanside, on the South Shore. Marie Quantrell, who had been at *Newsday* a little more than a year, was in the office on rewrite that morning and began to write the story. While she typed, Hathway kept running up to her, barking out instructions and grabbing her copy, a paragraph at a time. Quickly, her copy was thrown into type and splashed across the top of page one, under a huge headline: "GORILLA LOOSE / ON S. SHORE." But as the morning wore on and Quantrell made other phone calls, she began to realize that it wasn't a gorilla after all. "Hathway just never stopped jumping, first jumping to get the story onto the streets immediately, to alert everyone to the danger of this gorilla, and then he's jumping to kill the story," Quantrell said. "He was a very fast thinker, which was probably part of his problem." By the time the final edition hit the streets, the police had killed the "gorilla," but the story still led the paper, with this headline: "BABOON TERRORIZES / S. SHORE 7 DAYS, / COP SAFARI KILLS IT." The following day's story called the beast an orangutan. Finally, they found out that it was just a rhesus monkey, and the New York City papers had a terrific time poking fun at a suburban paper's shaky grasp of the facts.

This was the kind of colossal blunder that no newspaper staff could let pass without tormenting someone. The next morning, two mischievous photographers, Jim Martenhoff and Herman Klappert, drove to a local zoo in Massapequa operated by Frank Buck. Tipping a member of the staff with a bottle of whiskey, they borrowed a stuffed gorilla that had been standing out front in a cage, stood the gorilla in the back of Martenhoff's 1937 Ford convertible and headed for *Newsday*. At the city desk, they propped up the gorilla and equipped it with a green eyeshade and a telephone. By the time Hathway returned to the office with Davis, who was cooperating in the gag, the newsroom was packed with people waiting to see Hathway's reaction — described variously by observers as good-humored or purple-faced. Martenhoff and Klappert recorded it for posterity.

Hathway's instincts didn't always lead to huge errors. More often, they spawned stories that cast *Newsday* in the role of defender of the little guy against the establishment. Of course, the paper's owners were firmly rooted in that establishment, but Alicia agreed strongly with Hathway on the need to crusade against the powerful. One of those stories involved the complex rules on gas rationing. Everyone had gas problems. Even Alicia was forced occasionally to bum a ride from Jim Martenhoff, because photographers were considered essential and could buy all the gasoline they needed. One Saturday, Hathway wandered into the office to pick up his mail. *Newsday* still did not publish a Sunday paper, and no one was in the office working. So when the phone rang, Hathway picked it up himself. The woman at the other end was complaining about a society wedding scheduled for that afternoon, in which 40 cars were scheduled to transport guests. Hathway called Augustus Weller, the head of the county's gas rationing program, and Weller told him that only the principals were allowed to drive to the ceremony. Then Hathway called the bride's mother, who told him that an elected official who was a friend of her husband had gotten them a dispensation. Finally, he called in Deborah Lane, a young reporter, on her day off. She completed the reporting by talking to the elected officials, and covered the wedding itself. The story appeared in Monday's paper, complete with the documents, the wording of the rationing rules and photos. Some of those who attended the wedding had to forfeit their ration books, which annoyed them and pleased almost everyone else who read the paper.

IV

EARLY IN THE paper's life, Hathway became the infernal engine driving it, providing it with energy and blood lust. In giving guidance to the young staff, he and his friend Harold Davis got some help from some other experienced journalists.

One of the strongest early influences was Frank Atwood, a veteran editor who had come to *Newsday* right after it started. Atwood had been a long-time night city editor at William Randolph Hearst's *New York American* and had retired to Garden City. His retirement was filled with tragedy: His daughter-in-law and infant grandson perished in a fire and his son drowned. Finally, Atwood's wife suffered a stroke and became paralyzed. The medical expenses drained his savings and forced him to return to work, at age 64. The Colonel, as everyone called him, had white hair, a stern face and, for the new reporters on the staff, an unapproachable manner. He came to the office in starched white shirts with cuff links and started work armed with a neatly aligned battalion of sharpened pencils.

To the young staff, Atwood was an intimidating figure. "When he'd call you up to the desk, you would die," Jacquie Villa said. "But I learned later that he only gave hell to the people that he thought had something in them. If somebody would turn in a story and he didn't think the reporter was going to make beans in that business, he would not say a word. He'd just turn it over to a rewrite person. But if he called you up and laid you out flat and flayed the skin off your back, he only did it to the people he thought were worth his time. . . . Once, I turned in a story on sodomy. He almost killed me. He said, 'Do you know what it means?' And I said, 'No.' And he said, 'Well, goddamn it, go back to your desk, pick up the dictionary, look at it, and we don't run those stories.' "

Besides editing the news, Atwood helped the sparse staff to generate it — compiling a weekly section of religious listings and gathering tips on police stories from a source he called "Jake." That was Emma Jackson, an elderly widow who had worked with him at the *New York American*. Jake lived in Baldwin, where she was friendly with all the police and volunteer firemen. Sometimes her tips meant something, and sometimes they were useless, but through Atwood, she became a *Newsday* fixture for years.

In the paper's early years, another older woman also provided an anchor of experience. Frances Story had worked at the defunct *New York Globe* and been an assistant magazine editor, then wrote fashion copy for Macy's department store. When *Newsday* opened, she wrote a column on "unusual business services," worked on a gardening page and rose to women's editor. During the war, she wrote "home front" features to help housewives cope with wartime shortages. And at war's end, she began writing an advice column called "Ask Frances Story," which became an important selling point for the infant newspaper. Story looked the role of a reporter, sitting at her typewriter, with a cigarette clenched in her mouth, and one side of her graying hair turning yellow from the stream of smoke. But when it came to the letters seeking advice, she was not the typical newspaper cynic. She worried over every answer.

Another newspaper veteran who helped to shape the early paper was John Frogge, a large, redheaded former Marine who had worked at the *New York Times* and opened its suburban bureau in Mineola. For the *Times*, Frogge covered Charles Lindbergh's departure for Paris from Roosevelt Field. Later, Frogge covered Nassau County for the *New York Herald Tribune*. Then, when *Newsday* opened, he wandered over to the office and insinuated himself into the young staff. Frogge remembered getting $50 a week from *Newsday*, but others said he was never permanently on the staff. Whatever his payroll status, he was constantly around the office, using the phone, writing or reporting stories for *Newsday* and for the *Tribune*. "He was our mainstay on the night desk," Quantrell said. "He was the best writer." If it was a slow news day and there was a huge hole in the paper, Frogge had the knack of making a tiny story into something interesting enough to fill it. For all his value, however, Frogge could never get along with Hathway, and when Hathway succeeded Davis as managing editor, Frogge was gone.

It would be less than gracious for Hathway to have hastened the departure of Davis, an old friend who had helped him in the pulp fiction business and had hired him at *Newsday*. "Ostensibly, Alan was Harold's best friend," said Stan Peckham, who was in the Army when Hathway replaced Davis, but had observed the two of them before he left for the service. "When I heard that he had taken Harold's job, I figured he had undercut Harold, and the hell with him. . . . I saw Harold quite a few times once I got back, and I think he blamed Alan for that." Another Hathway-watcher, Hal Burton, said: "I asked Davis if Hathway actually finagled him out of a job, and he said, 'Well, I was at the top of the slide, but I wouldn't say he pushed me. I'd just say he nudged me.' "

It is also possible that Davis simply decided to leave, without prompting, because of his drinking, marital and financial difficulties. From all appearances, his relationship with Alicia had been good. She depended heavily on him at the start, and even after he left, she showed her respect for his talents by running in *Newsday* a series of reports by Davis from Russia in 1947. The respect appeared to be mutual: Davis named a daughter Alicia. Whatever the explanation for his departure, Davis went back to the *Daily News* and Hathway became managing editor at the beginning of 1944.

The new managing editor was a man of outrageous excess. He drank too much, swore too much, flirted too much. If you were blind, you could tell Hathway had arrived for his day's work by listening to the trail of squeals from women that he pinched on his way through the building. One of his later secretaries, Janet DeMarinis, remembered that when she arrived, other women warned her. "They all said, 'Never turn your back on him, never bend over in front of him, always keep your eyes on him, especially after lunch,' " DeMarinis said. "He was a grabber and he was a pincher and he was very crude." When he was drunk, he would say virtually anything, including vulgar remarks to women. Drunk or sober, Hathway frightened the hell out of his staff. Lucy Risedorf, who was a copy girl and later the secretary to Davis and Hathway, remembers being the target of Hathway's wrath when she took too long on a sandwich run. "When I got back, he started hollering at me," Risedorf said. "I started crying like crazy. The whole office went over and hollered at him."

Beyond these undesirable personal traits, Hathway used questionable reporting and editing techniques and several times stepped over ethical boundaries, acutely embarrassing Alicia. She tried to rein in his excesses wherever she could, but she respected his journalistic skills, and Hathway did provide the kind of gutsy tone for *Newsday* that she wanted. It would not quite be accurate to call Hathway her loaded rifle, because he was not simply a passive instrument, and he could not always be precisely aimed. But he certainly was her hired gun, her contract-killer. She may not have approved of every step he took when he was going after a target, and she had to bring him up short on some occasions when he was using his intimidating power for his personal benefit. But Hathway, who became a feared figure on Long Island, could not have acquired that power without Alicia's approval. Hathway himself feared only one thing: angering Alicia. Early in this relationship, Alicia and Hathway went down

the block to the Chungking Royal, a Chinese restaurant that was one of Hathway's haunts. The owner, Arthur Lem, who later became Hathway's closest
friend, was there as Alicia and Hathway discussed his role. She told him she was
putting everything in his hands, and he outlined his ideas. "He said, 'A good
newspaper is an honest policeman on a corner,' " Lem remembered. As the
conversation went on, Hathway described how he would go after corrupt politicians, and Alicia sounded a note of caution. "The first thing he says, 'Bullshit!'
Imagine? She's his boss. He says, 'Bullshit.' " For years, Alicia and Hathway
retained that ability to yell at each other without destroying their relationship.
But the final word was hers.

One of Hathway's first decisions, even before he formally took over as
managing editor, was to find a replacement for himself as city editor. On the
surface, at least, he made an odd choice. Instead of picking someone with long
experience, he chose a short, round, Damon Runyonesque character named
Jack Altshul, who had only recently come to *Newsday*. When *Newsday* began,
Altshul was working as the editor of a small Nassau County weekly called the
Oceanside Home News. For five or six years, Altshul had been trying to crack into
the newspaper business, but without luck. That had reduced him to working for
weeklies. Then, in July, 1940, an announcement came across his desk about the
formation of a new daily newspaper. Altshul immediately applied and met with
Harold Davis, who asked him to demonstrate his skills by putting together a
comprehensive survey of sports on Long Island. Altshul did the survey and
Davis liked it, but Altshul did not get a job. Still, Davis left open a possibility for
the future. Altshul went back to weeklies, taking over as editor of a paper in the
City of Long Beach and assuming the former editor's role as stringer for the *New
York Times*, which paid 40 cents per column inch for local news, for *Newsday*,
which paid six cents per column inch, for the *Brooklyn Eagle* and others. But
1941 brought hard times. The Army rejected him for induction because of a
variety of ailments, including near-blindness in one eye. Meanwhile, the wartime newsprint shortage forced the *Times* and the *Eagle* to cut back drastically
on Long Island coverage, which severely reduced his income. Finally, in the
spring of 1942, Frank Atwood hired Altshul to do night rewrite and help run the
desk. Less than two years later, Altshul was the city editor.

Besides his loyalty to Hathway, Altshul's major strengths were his contacts
around Long Island and his ability to get along with people. He was gregarious
and fun to be around, a good conversationalist with a knack for telling Yiddish
dialect jokes. His enthusiastic gambling brought him into contact with a constellation of Runyon-style characters, which proved helpful at the end of the
war, when Alicia asked him to take over from Deborah Lane a column called
"Heads and Tales," a bits-and-pieces compilation of gossip items. While the
column did drain time away from his primary job as city editor, it had its
benefits. By sprinkling the column with mentions of restaurants and bars,
Altshul avoided having to pay for his meals. Besides, the contacts that he made
sometimes led to real news stories.

Like Hathway, Altshul learned early that excessive speed in handling a story can be disastrous. In early 1945, he got a call one morning from Don Abrew, a sports editor and part-time reporter in the short-staffed Suffolk office, which had only opened the previous summer. Abrew reported that a barber had gone berserk and used his razor to slash his wife and two children. While Bea Jones wrote the story, Altshul put together a page one headline: "Barber's Razor Slays Wife, Two Children." A few minutes later, checking with police on the arraignment of the killer, Altshul found out that no one had died. He raced outside just in time to stop the truck leaving for Suffolk with the disastrously wrong headline and story. As a result, he had to throw away 5,000 copies of the newspaper, at a time when the newsprint shortage made every scrap of paper precious. The next day, while Altshul was still recovering, Jim Jenkins, an editor with a sometimes vulgar sense of humor, made him a victim again. Jenkins noticed a headline about a bombing raid by American Super Fortresses on Japan: "50 Super Forts Bomb Tokyo." Carefully and crudely, he altered the "forts" to "farts" on the copy of the newspaper that went to Altshul's desk. Predictably, Altshul noticed it and started screaming, as he had the day before, "Stop the presses!"

Clearly, Altshul was not strong on attention to detail, and he was not a sophisticated manager. Finding himself with a wartime staff full of women, for example, he developed an unusual management tool. On the wall, he kept a calendar on which he marked down the menstrual periods of the women who worked for him. It isn't clear whether Altshul used this calendar to trap women who called in sick without mentioning that the cause of their absence was menstrual discomfort, or whether he was simply trying to predict accurately the size of his staff on a given day. Edna Murray, the photographer, who later married him, said: "You could not call in sick just because you had your period." At that time, women had little clout at *Newsday*, despite their numbers. So they had to go along with Altshul's calendar. "Today, I would have ripped it down off the wall and hung it around his neck," Jacquie Villa said. "We didn't even resent it. . . . At the time, the sexism was simply accepted. It was part of your daily life."

Despite that burden of sexism, the women on the staff did have Alicia on their side. "She was a feminist before the word was even used," said Murray, the first full-time, accredited woman photographer at *Newsday*, and among the first in the metropolitan area. "She was all for women doing whatever they wanted to do." Jacquie Villa, hired with almost no experience, also felt Alicia's encouragement. "She pushed me, and I'm sure she pushed other women on the staff," Villa said. "I wound up being women's editor when I was like 26 years old, which is fantastic. Miss P and I used to have lunch every six weeks or so, and she'd ask me if there were any problems."

Alicia's lunches with Villa were just one example of her hands-on style. In the tiny plant, she was everywhere. "She was on the composing room floor," said John MacCary, who often saw her personally supervising the layout of pages. "Page one was her pet — that and the back page. . . . She was really fussy." And she was familiar with her staff. "She knew everybody by their first name in the whole building," said Al Kunkel, one of the earliest composing room employees. The staff never knew where she might pop up. Once, Joe Curley yelled across the composing room at a printer who seemed to be hanging aimlessly around a type cabinet — only to find out that he was doing something for Alicia, who was hidden behind the cabinet. She waved and apologized to Curley for slowing down production. Occasionally, at nights, the printers would see her come back to *Newsday* in a plain dress, Paul Johansson said, to do some late work. And whenever she was curious, she'd stick her head into the darkroom, near her office, to see what kind of photos were being developed. "She was interested in what was going on," said Bill Johnke, one of the first photographers. "She didn't just stay aloof and sit in an office and push buttons."

Though her primary concern was the editorial department, she also kept in touch with the commercial side of the paper. She went to meetings of circulation supervisors after a snowstorm, to find out if there were any problems. She attended gatherings of the carrier boys. She went out and walked door-to-door with circulation supervisors, to meet with subscribers at their homes. She went out on sales calls with advertising salesmen. She occasionally even met with big advertisers. Once, Alicia went to a country club luncheon with an executive of Arnold Constable, the first major department store to advertise extensively in *Newsday*, and she called Harold Davis to get a photographer to the event. Davis reached Jim Martenhoff and Herman Klappert, who were working at Klappert's home on a victory garden that they were growing for a *Newsday* series. Both men were in old clothing, spreading chicken manure. They tried to protest that they were in no condition to go to a country club. But Davis insisted. The two photographers looked mischievously at each other and said, almost simultaneously, "I will if you will." So they went to the country club in their grubby clothes, reeking of the barnyard. As they approached the table, everyone noticed the odor. Alicia knew them, of course, but she didn't acknowledge that. "She had a very frosty look on her face, unsmiling," Martenhoff said. When the two malodorous photographers left, someone asked who they were, and she said she had never seen them before.

This hands-on style of the publisher, combined with Alan Hathway's love of journalistic hand-to-hand combat and the hunger of the young staff, created a newspaper that made a lot of mistakes, but seldom out of caution. The wartime *Newsday* was often sloppy and amateurish, but it was seldom fearful. It was a paper always anxious for a fight.

V

ALICIA PATTERSON STARTED her career as a publisher with an immature staff and an imperfect plant, but a kindly fate dealt her an absolutely perfect competitor: James E. Stiles and his *Nassau Daily Review-Star*.

The *Review-Star* was the ideal blend of complacency and complicity. It was smug and self-satisfied about its place in the world, largely because of its publisher's role in the perpetuation of one-party government in Nassau County. As a result of this close identification between the county's only other daily newspaper and its dominant political party, Alicia was able simultaneously to attack the established newspaper and to position her own paper as the people's advocate against tyrannical political rule — an utterly perfect situation for a new newspaper.

James Stiles was a graduate of Freeport High School — an achiever who played on the football team, served as the advertising manager of the school paper and got elected class president. Less than a year out of Wesleyan University, Stiles became a newspaper publisher, establishing a weekly in Freeport called the *Nassau Post*. At the start, Stiles declared: "*The Nassau Post* will be absolutely independent of parties." But the ink was barely dry on that declaration when Stiles began a pattern of almost parasitical dependence on a political party that lasted for the rest of his career. In 1915, Stiles supported a Republican candidate for village president, and when his candidate won, so did Stiles. The *Nassau Post*, only one year old, became the village's official newspaper for the publication of legal notices. The same year, Stiles was elected a Republican committeeman and threw himself and his paper behind Republican candidates in town- and county-wide elections. In 1916, the *Post* became the Republican newspaper of Nassau County, which brought Stiles the county's legal advertising. With this dependable revenue from county, town and village legal ads, Stiles started acquiring other weeklies. Eventually he merged several of them into a single weekly and on March 7, 1921, converted it into a daily, the *Nassau Daily Review*.

Stiles had already built his empire before his friend, J. Russel Sprague, even entered county politics, and Stiles played a role in Sprague's rise to power as Nassau County Republican leader. "He never hesitated in throwing his own support, and that of his newspaper, to Sprague when there were powerful forces against him, and the conflict might well have been lost," wrote Edward Uhlan, the founder of a vanity publishing house called Exposition Press, in his biography, *Dynamo Jim Stiles: Pioneer of Progress*. "Stiles' unwavering loyalty was well repaid, for there were important and decisive instances where Sprague rallied to the support of Stiles and the *Review*. Because of this unfailing teamwork, they were dubbed 'the Dauntless Duo.'" Sprague helped Stiles to beat back a state investigation of the paper's stock. Stiles helped Sprague to defeat bills in the state Legislature that would have weakened Republican control. Stiles also campaigned against a proposed county charter backed by the Democrats and worked just as hard in 1936 in support of a county charter that Sprague favored. The voters approved that charter, and Sprague was later elected the first county executive. Stiles helped in political campaigns, too. "He was generous in his contributions to campaign funds, including state and national campaigns," Uhlan wrote. "He published thousands of dollars' worth of political advertising as a contribution to the party, and to individual candidates he wanted to help."

In this relationship, when Sprague spoke, Stiles listened. Sprague told him not to expand his paper to the North Shore, and Stiles obeyed, leaving a vacuum for *Newsday* to fill. When Stiles thought about buying a chain of papers in Westchester County, Sprague told him: "Don't spread out while I am in office, Jim. We are all okay as we are." Stiles obeyed. Stiles even took Republican advice on the purchase of his competition, the *Nassau Daily Star*. During the struggle over county leadership, a Sprague ally named Fred Maidment, vice president of the Long Island Lighting Company, decided that the best way to stop the *Star* from opposing Sprague was to have the loyal Stiles buy it. His Republican friends took care of the whole negotiation, while Stiles was recuperating from a heart attack. At the close of the deal, Stiles came up short of money, and Maidment himself made him a $31,000 loan toward the $125,000 purchase. So the *Review*, which had grown from a series of weeklies into a daily newspaper with the help of revenue from legal ads, now became the *Review-Star* with the help of the Republicans.

The greatest service that the party and Sprague performed for Stiles was to make sure that he kept getting the legal ads. When *Newsday* came to town, Alicia wasted no time in pounding Stiles over the head with that point. One of Alicia's circulation supervisors, Jack Rovegno, remembered talking to her about the large amounts of money the county paid Stiles to run the legal advertising. "She said, 'I'm going to call them and give it to them for nothing,' " Rovegno said. Alicia had no plans to run legal ads for nothing, but she had every intention of offering the county a better rate than Stiles charged.

The campaign to dislodge the legal ads from Stiles began in 1941, but *Newsday* got nowhere. In early 1942, as the county prepared to advertise two years' worth of tax delinquencies at once, the stakes got higher and *Newsday* became even more shrill and "got in plenty of low blows," Uhlan wrote. Not content simply to make its case privately to the county Board of Supervisors, *Newsday* launched a series of editorials and articles designed to convince the public that the politicians were giving the store away to Stiles. The basic argument was that the *Review-Star* was running the ads in a larger-than-usual typeface, surrounded by plenty of white space, which cost the county far more than *Newsday* would charge. While unblushingly advancing its own economic interests by making a pitch for the legal ads, *Newsday* could also attack the Republicans for being careless with county money for the benefit of Stiles.

"On the opposite page is a copy of a letter that *Newsday* yesterday sent to the Nassau Board of Supervisors," one editorial began. "The letter is a bid for business, of course. Naturally we want to make money if we can. However, we do not expect to get this business, although we are offering a plan which we believe would save the county and the delinquent taxpayers nearly $75,000 in the Town of Hempstead alone." To prove the point, a few days later, *Newsday* ran a copy of the delinquent tax list as it would appear in the *Review-Star*, alongside the same list as it would appear in the condensed *Newsday* style. It also ran a copy of a letter from the state Department of Taxation and Finance, approving of the proposed *Newsday* form.

Subtlety was apparently banned for the duration of this campaign. One story, with the headline, "Loses Home, Health to Tax Greed," was an early example of what became a repeated *Newsday* technique over many years, a long story personalizing an issue by describing in numbing detail one family's ordeal. In this case, the story told how Joseph Wisnewski of Hempstead started down the slippery slope of tax delinquency by failing in 1935 to pay $16.02 in school taxes. The purpose of that story, plus a sidebar about how the delinquent tax lists worked, was to make the point that the cost of advertising tax delinquencies fell either on the delinquent taxpayer, such as the Wisnewskis, or on the person or firm that buys the property at a tax sale. So, *Newsday* argued, the high advertising rates that Stiles charged the county really hurt the average person. Despite its large size, the Wisnewski story did not say how much of the family's arrears bill was actual taxes and penalties and how much was advertising costs. But the subhead on the story called it: "A Tragic Account Of/Nassau Patronage Toll." To underline the point, an editorial cartoon two days later showed a man marked "delinquent taxpayer" carrying a heavy bag labelled "added advertising costs," and the caption above it asked, "What About This, Mr. Stiles?" Another story detailed how the *Review-Star* had made $569,216.83 since 1932 for printing the delinquent tax lists. The headline across the top of the page was: "What Is Your Answer, Mr. Stiles?" Below was a picture of Stiles sitting regally in a chair, his moon-shaped face beaming above his earth-shaped body. The photo made him look like a typical fat cat, in keeping with *Newsday*'s policy of using photographs that showed Stiles to maximum disadvantage. "We were led to understand that any unflattering photo we could get would be welcome," said Jim Martenhoff, the photographer.

Despite this campaign, the county voted again in 1942 to give the advertising for tax delinquencies in the Town of Hempstead to Stiles. The county chose the *Review-Star* again in 1943, although the form of the list moved toward the condensed form that *Newsday* recommended. Finally, in 1944, the county awarded the ads to *Newsday*. It had taken her three years to bludgeon the county Republicans into submission, but Alicia had won her first big campaign, and Stiles had lost.

The competition, of course, did not end there. The two papers continued to snipe at each other editorially. Even when Stiles ran a series of meetings in 1945 to encourage merchants in the Town of Hempstead to overcome the wartime snappishness of employees and enlist in his "Courtesy and Cooperation" campaign, *Newsday* took the occasion twice to berate him. It wasn't the "Courtesy and Cooperation" campaign that the editorials criticized, but what they described as his boosterism for Hempstead, the county's key business district, over the rest of the county. The two editorials were little more than excuses to remind readers that *Newsday* had beaten Stiles by becoming a true county-wide paper, while he was still stuck in one area. An editorial cartoon showed a fence called "Hempstead Town Line" surrounding Stiles. "With 25 years background, the Rockville Centre paper has been unable to maintain circulation leadership in the County," one editorial said. "In less than two years,

Newsday outstripped him in circulation and has steadily increased that lead to several thousand copies daily." By the end of September, 1945, the Audit Bureau of Circulations showed *Newsday* with a 12-month average net paid circulation of 45,446, compared to 37,998 for the *Review-Star*.

Newsday's circulation had stalled earlier in the war, when the home delivery price went from two cents to three cents a day. It took about two years to make up for the subscribers who had dropped the paper then. But in July, 1945, a strike by deliverers closed down the New York City newspapers, made Mayor Fiorello LaGuardia famous for his radio broadcasts of the missing comic strips, and provided *Newsday* with a golden opportunity. Partly as a result of the extra papers it sold during the strike, *Newsday*'s average circulation soared to 64,439 by September, 1946 — up from 38,039 in 1944. In contrast, the *Review-Star* stagnated.

Before *Newsday* even existed, Stiles had pushed the idea of Nassau County as one large advertising market, instead of a series of unconnected small villages. In the process, he characterized Nassau as "Metropolitan Long Island." But Stiles failed to match his greater-Nassau rhetoric with circulation reality. In obeying Sprague's command to avoid the North Shore, the *Review-Star* lost any chance to be a countywide newspaper. *Newsday* didn't miss that chance. In fact, in 1944, *Newsday* took the first step toward becoming a Long Island-wide newspaper, by establishing a tiny new edition in the southwest corner of Suffolk County. It was a shaky first step toward expansion, but at least it was expansion, while the *Review-Star* stood pat. "If the *Review-Star* had been aggressive and had not been asleep, it would not have permitted *Newsday* to start up," said David Starr, who became the editor of the *Long Island Press*. "They didn't understand that, in order to continue doing well, they had to expand."

Despite that laziness, the *Newsday* staff still looked at the *Review-Star* as the established paper, the one they had to beat. If *Newsday* was the underdog, it was an angry, growling Doberman pinscher puppy, biting at the heels of a sleepy, aging Saint Bernard. Even in the composing room, the *Newsday* staff had a hungry, competitive attitude. "This was something that everybody had a chance to build, and they were all going to make sure that this paper made it," said Al Kunkel, who had become a journeyman printer at the *Review-Star* before coming to *Newsday*.

In a sense, it was never a fair fight from the start. The only real edge that the *Review-Star* had was its longevity. *Newsday* had youth, energy, independence and money. In his biography of Stiles, Uhlan ran a list of the 54 methods that Stiles used to raise cash. If there were a biography of Alicia, her list of fundraising methods would have had only one item: "Ask Harry." Being dependent on her husband had its drawbacks, but Harry's money at least enabled her newspaper to be independent. Despite Harry's Republican beliefs, no one thought *Newsday* needed handouts from the Republican machine. "Everyone knew you weren't going to have an Alicia Patterson and a Harry Guggenheim on the pad," said Edith Wyckoff, the *Newsday* stringer.

On the top of her editorial column, Alicia liked to run a pithy little quote.

In 1947, she settled more or less permanently on a verse from the Book of Proverbs: "Where there is no vision, the people perish." But during these early years, and again briefly during the Korean War, one of her favorites was from the Revolutionary War pamphleteer, Tom Paine: "Tyranny, like Hell, is not easily conquered." It isn't clear whether she picked this because of its relevance to the Axis powers in Europe, or whether it was a sly reference to a more local axis, James Stiles and the Nassau County Republican Party. If she was referring to Stiles, she was wrong. Stiles *was* easily conquered. By the time the war in Europe was over, *Newsday* had all but won the battle. The *Review-Star* lingered for a few more years, but it was already beaten.

VI

AT THE SAME time as Alicia was warring on one front with the *Review-Star*, she was fighting a more difficult series of battles with her husband and her father.

Scarcely more than a month after the paper opened, the public got its first view of the complex marital-business relationship between Alicia and Harry Guggenheim. Blatantly imitating a device used by her father, Alicia established a feature called "The Squared Circle," which provided an opportunity for two people of starkly contrasting views to air their thoughts on a subject, side by side. One such debate matched Pietro DiDonato, a proletarian novelist speaking up for Franklin Roosevelt in his campaign for a third term, and Clarence Budington Kelland, a more conservative author and lecturer, who supported Wendell Willkie and argued that a third term was equivalent to dictatorship. Just a few weeks later, on October 22, 1940, Alicia ran an eye-catching pair of opposing views on the same question: Alicia for Roosevelt and Harry for Willkie.

"My husband and I do not see eye to eye on the coming presidential election," Alicia wrote. "Since we are joint owners of this newspaper, the only solution seemed to be to split the Squared Circle between us." Alicia had voted for Roosevelt in 1932 and 1936, but she confessed that the third-term question disposed her to be receptive to a Republican alternative, until she discovered that Willkie approved of almost all of Roosevelt's programs. "It is safe to assume, since Mr. Willkie cannot make up his own mind that the Republican Party will make it up for him," she wrote. On the left side of the page, Harry grumbled about the New Deal "using the people's money to propagandize us and keep itself in power." One of his reasons for opposing Roosevelt was the action of a group of boys who had thrown an egg at Willkie's wife. "Children do not do these things of themselves," Harry wrote, implying that their hostility was the product of the New Deal's efforts to paint its opponents as the enemies of progress. "They do these things because they are told to do them." A week later, in a second installment of the debate, Alicia argued that children didn't need the encouragement of the New Deal to throw things. "I can remember distinctly throwing overripe apples at passing cars when I was a child for no better reason than to watch the apples splatter on the nice shiny automobile," she wrote. "My parents certainly didn't spur me on to these dastardly deeds." Beyond that, the wife of one of America's richest men said that she was going to vote for Roosevelt "because he has tried to make this a country where the poor as well as the rich will share in the blessings of democracy." Harry and Alicia maintained this schizophrenic posture right up until election day.

The irony was that Alicia was busy making a name for her paper by wrestling with the Republicans, while she was married to as staunch a Republican as anyone in the county. Harry had been a friend, admirer and employee of Herbert Hoover. In 1936, when Roosevelt ran for reelection against Alfred Landon of Kansas, Harry played a major role in Landon's campaign in Nassau County. Harry ran the Minutemen, a Republican organization, spoke at a Landon campaign dinner at the Port Washington Yacht Club and held a campaign rally for Landon in a barn at Falaise.

Even though Harry and Alicia disagreed about Franklin Roosevelt, that disagreement was almost inconsequential in comparison with the breach that Roosevelt caused between Alicia and her father. Joe Patterson had stoutly supported FDR's New Deal domestic agenda at a time when conservative publishers across the country were attacking it. But when Roosevelt floated his lend-lease proposal, which gave him broad authority to provide arms to other nations in the European war, Patterson the isolationist felt personally betrayed. And when Alicia stuck with Roosevelt, that disagreement became part of the reason why her father chose not to leave her control of the *Daily News* in his will after all.

More than almost any other American journalist, Patterson understood instinctively that the fight against the despair of the Depression required not only a relentless attack by the government, but serious coverage by the press. So Patterson directed his staff to cover in depth the struggle for the nation's economic survival. And at the start of Roosevelt's first term, on March 6, 1933, a *News* editorial gave the new president a stunning blank check: "This newspaper now pledges itself to support the policies of President Franklin D. Roosevelt for a period of at least one year from today; longer, if circumstances warrant." A year later, the *News* said: "We are glad to report today that we have never regretted that pledge; that we have been in sympathy with almost everything the President has done or tried to do . . . ."

The Roosevelt-Patterson relationship during his first two terms was close and personal. Patterson ran a fund-raising drive to build a pool for the president at the White House, sailed on the presidential yacht, visited FDR at his home in Hyde Park and at the White House. Right after the 1936 campaign, Roosevelt wrote Patterson a "Dear Joe" letter crediting the *News* with helping his campaign immensely. In that same campaign, Patterson's cousin, Colonel Robert Rutherford McCormick, used the *Chicago Tribune* to go after Roosevelt with unbelievable venom. At the beginning, the Colonel had been cordial enough to his old Groton schoolmate, but well before the 1936 campaign, the *Tribune* had become nakedly hostile. In the weeks before the 1936 election, the *Tribune* carried a daily box on page one: "Only --- days to save your country — what are you going to do about it?" The switchboard operators answered the phone with a similar question. By contrast, Patterson's sister, Cissy, who became the editor of the *Washington Herald* in 1930, remained well disposed to Roosevelt through his first term and called Eleanor Roosevelt "the noblest woman I have ever known."

The need for military preparedness to avert war was a constant *Daily News* theme. All during the 1930s, in a series of Monday editorials that were headed "Two Ships for One," the *News* had urged that the American Navy be strengthened to ward off the threat of Japan. "Suppose the Japanese should some day catch up with a weak Navy, in a surprise attack," one 1935 editorial warned. "With our Navy's back broken, the rest would be easy." Roosevelt credited the *News* for the passage of the "Big Navy" bill in 1940, and sent Patterson one of the pens that he used to sign the bill. But during those same years, Patterson expressed concern over the President's moral support of Britain and France. "If it averts war, President Roosevelt will go down in history as a great statesman," the *News* said. "If it brings us into a war, his memory will most likely be cursed by future generations of Americans."

Despite those gathering clouds, the *News* urged the Democratic convention in July, 1940, to nominate Roosevelt for a third term. In August, General John Pershing floated a proposal — obviously favored by Roosevelt — that America sell Britain or Canada 50 ancient warships. At a lunch at Hyde Park, Roosevelt told Patterson in confidence that Britain would give the United States a group of bases in exchange for the old ships. When that deal became public, the *News* accepted it, apparently because the President had driven a hard bargain in getting the bases. Through the 1940 campaign, the *News* supported FDR, but a month after he was reelected, Roosevelt took the step that pushed Patterson and Cissy onto the same side of the fence as Bert McCormick. On December 19, FDR announced at a press conference that the cash-and-carry approach was not sufficient to save Britain. So he proposed a lend-lease bill that would allow him to decide that a nation's security was vital to America, then provide that nation with war supplies — on any basis he considered appropriate. "He lied to me, he lied to me," Patterson said, brought to tears by his feelings of betrayal. But the *News* did not weep. It roared. The bill, it argued, would give Roosevelt "virtual power to take us into war on the side of any country or countries he thinks we should be allied with, and to run our entire war effort without consulting Congress. . . . Therefore, the bill is a bill to make the President dictator of the United States, and hence its right name is the 'dictatorship bill' instead of the 'lease-lend' bill."

All through 1941, the isolationist-interventionist battle raged. One of the leading public figures in that America First movement was Harry Guggenheim's close friend, Charles Lindbergh. In a speech at Des Moines, Iowa, on September 11, 1941, he listed the three major groups pushing America into war: the British, the Roosevelt Administration and the Jews. His wife, Anne Morrow Lindbergh, feared that this speech would subject him to bitter criticism and worked to soften its language. "I was worried about it," she said. "He did accept the changes, but he thought I was exaggerating." In the three paragraphs on the Jews in his speech, Lindbergh tried to make clear he was not attacking them. "No person with a sense of the dignity of mankind can condone the persecution of the Jewish race in Germany," he said. "But no person of honesty and vision can look on their pro-war policy here today without seeing the dangers involved in such a policy, both for us and for them." Whatever nuances Lindbergh wove into his words, his critics accused him of making an anti-Semitic speech. Even his close friend Harry was offended. "I asked him about Lindbergh," Hal Burton said, "since I came from Lindbergh's hometown and we knew the Lindberghs very well, and he said, 'Poor Slim, they led him down the garden path.' " The friendship resumed, Burton said, but for a time, Harry stopped seeing Lindbergh. "He was mad as hell," Burton said. "And Alicia just hated Lindbergh for that."

At the end of 1941, Patterson and his wife, Mary, visited Harry and Alicia at Cain Hoy, Harry's plantation, for some hunting. While they were there, they were completely cut off from the world. "Harry had one oddity," said Burton, who was also there. "Harry absolutely refused to have a radio anywhere around the place." So they were unaware of what was happening thousands of miles away, until Patterson's wife came hurtling up to them in a jeep while they were out hunting. "She said, 'My God, you don't know what's happening?' I said, 'What?' She said, 'Pearl Harbor was bombed yesterday,' " Burton remembered. "And we'd known nothing about it."

Patterson had hated the idea of this war, but now that America was in it, he was ready to gallop off to battle again. Immediately, he made a written application to the War Department for readmission into the Army. The day after that, on December 11, Patterson went to the White House for a meeting with Roosevelt. Fred Pasley of the *News* Washington bureau had suggested to Steve Early, FDR's press aide, that the publisher should visit the President. Patterson slipped into the building quietly, avoiding reporters. "When I entered the President's room he was signing documents," Patterson wrote in a memo. "He did not speak to me for ten minutes, all the while he continued with his official signature. He then looked up. I put out my hand, which he took, and said: 'I am here, Mr. President, to tell you that I wish to support your war effort.' I then remained standing for fifteen minutes while he gave me pretty severe criticism for the way The News had conducted itself during the year 1941. He said he would give me a task, which was to read over the News editorials for 1941. This I have since done. . . . I had thought that perhaps he was testing me to see if I could accept military discipline, on account of the application of the day before. Accordingly, I stood at attention and my only answers were at intervals of 'Yes, Sir' with the following exception: When he told me to read over my editorials and realize their wrong-headedness (these are not his words, but the meaning of them) I did say: 'Mr. President, those editorials were written in peace time, not in war time.' "

This meeting with Roosevelt, which could have been the beginning of a reconciliation, humiliated and angered Patterson. "He was furious," his daughter Josephine said. "He felt it was very unfair." His struggle with the President embittered Patterson. "All I want to do now is outlive that bastard Roosevelt," he told his family. For years, Patterson had been, in many ways, a progressive. Now, as a result of his clash with FDR, he was to be branded forever a reactionary. In his home, Patterson's son James said, the publisher used to tell his wife, "I was born to love you and hate Roosevelt."

For the remainder of the war, Joe and Cissy Patterson and their cousin, Bert McCormick, were labelled "the three furies of isolationism." Their enemies even accused them of being Nazi sympathizers or of helping the Japanese. Right after the crucial Battle of Midway, all three papers ran a story describing the American Navy's knowledge of Japanese plans. The story had the effect of tipping off the Japanese that their codes had been broken. It didn't help, either, that propaganda broadcasts from Berlin and Tokyo frequently cited *Tribune* editorials.

The only member of the family who did not get painted into this anti-Roosevelt corner was Alicia. Before Pearl Harbor, in editorials that made clear that she was no isolationist, Alicia had staked out a position clearly in opposition to her father's. Perhaps the most widely cited example of Alicia's disagreement with the rest of the McCormick-Patterson axis was an editorial called "That 80 Per Cent," on September 23, 1941. The isolationists claimed that 80 per cent of the American people were against going to war, and the *Chicago Tribune* and the *Daily News* had repeated that assertion as gospel. In her editorial, Alicia took issue with that statistic: "You remember the old gag: 'Figures don't lie — but liars sometimes figure.' " She disagreed with the way the questions were asked, consulted with pollsters George Gallup and Elmo Roper and concluded that only 16.3 per cent of Americans really supported the isolationist position. A *Time* magazine article, "Daughter *v*. Father," reached the conclusion that she was all but calling her father a liar. But Alicia said: "Father and I are still very great friends." And she admitted that the *News* had been "very good" to *Newsday*. Nonetheless, she and her father disagreed on the war issue. "We just don't talk about it," Alicia said.

Even though Alicia and her father saw the war differently, she did come to his defense in the period after Pearl Harbor, when politicians and other newspapers were sniping at him. On August 3, 1942, Representative Elmer Holland, a Pennsylvania Democrat, got up on the floor of the House of Representatives and said that Joe and Cissy were "doing their best to bring about a Fascist victory — hoping that in that victory they will be rewarded." Patterson responded with the only *News* editorial that he ever signed. "Congressman Holland: you are a liar," Patterson concluded. "Make what you like of that." Alicia reprinted the original story of Holland's charges, plus her father's editorial, and she wrote a signed editorial of her own. "Joseph Medill Patterson who wrote the editorial is my father," she said. "I know him perhaps better than most daughters know their fathers. . . . Now on the floor of Congress a Democratic congressman makes the astounding statement that Joseph Patterson and his sister Eleanor Patterson are 'Hitler's followers. . . .' It is true that my father has from time to time criticized the Administration. Does that make him a traitor? If it does then anyone who questions the policies laid down in Washington is likewise treasonable. . . . Are we no longer allowed to disagree with the elected 'servants of the people?' If that is so we have lost our democracy before we have begun to fight for it."

Despite this strong editorial of support, the relationship between Alicia and her father clearly suffered as a result of Patterson's anger over her marriage to Harry and then over Franklin Roosevelt. Even though he appears to have allowed his staff at the *News* to help her, Patterson seems not to have said much to encourage her or praise her. At a lunch in Patterson's office, Hal Burton once asked him how Alicia was doing. "He said, 'Oh, she's all right. She's got a little paper out in Hempstead, but it isn't going anywhere.' " When Alicia's infant tabloid won an Ayer award for typographical excellence in 1941, beating out the *Daily News*, her father didn't even bring the subject up, she told an interviewer. Years later, she talked to one of her editors, Jack Mann, about her father's reaction to *Newsday*. "She told about the time, after *Newsday* had been started for about five years or so, that he finally came out to Hempstead to visit it," Mann said. "He walked in, and he looked around, and he walked out. He didn't say anything. She was in tears by the time that she got through saying that."

Nonetheless, Alicia continued to look up to her father and take his advice. They might disagree on the substance of editorials, but she considered him a master of the form. "I am going to follow your suggestion of getting an idea and plugging it persistently," she wrote him after he visited *Newsday*. And she continued to get help from the *Daily News* in a variety of ways. Patterson even allowed her to borrow newsprint, which was no small favor. The drafting of paper mill workers and the increased use of paper by the government, among other factors, made newsprint a scarce commodity for everyone during the war. The War Production Board rationed newsprint, based on consumption in 1941. That was particularly irksome for a new newspaper like *Newsday*, because its fast-growing circulation brought an escalating need for paper at the same time that the government was clamping a ceiling on use. The squeeze became even worse when *Newsday* started a Saturday paper on December 5, 1942. Like newspapers everywhere, *Newsday* was caught in a bind: Every day there was important news about the war, but there just was not enough paper to print it on.

The business staff did what they could, scrounging newsprint shipments from Finland to supplement the normal supply, but those Finnish shipments sometimes fell through. On one of those occasions, *Newsday* was forced to drop almost all display advertising in the week after Christmas, 1943. It offered space to advertisers who had used *Newsday* exclusively in 1943, and made room for one of its best customers, the Arnold Constable department store, but most other ads had to wait. Instead, *Newsday* printed a news story describing what the ads *would* have said. But no matter how many tricks *Newsday* tried, it often just came up short of paper and had to turn away ads. That is when Alicia had to rely on the *News*. "Alicia would borrow eight rolls off her father and return two and borrow four more," said the compositor John MacCary. The *News* occasionally helped by printing *Newsday* at its Brooklyn plant, and Patterson even approved the sale of a used press unit to *Newsday* in 1944.

Just as Alicia had to go occasionally to her father for newsprint, she had to go repeatedly to her husband whenever she needed money for the paper. And Harry was not shy about asserting financial control when he felt it was necessary. He intended to make sure that *Newsday* was fiscally sound, and from the start, he was often disappointed in Alicia's business sense. One source of Harry's unhappiness was William Mapel, the paper's first general manager. "I know Harry wanted to axe Mapel, and she interceded for Mapel quite a bit," Stan Peckham said. One day, just before Christmas, 1941, Peckham and Alicia went to lunch and Mapel invited himself along at the last minute. Mapel and Peckham had an angry argument right in front of her, and when they returned to the plant, Alicia called Peckham into her office. "She broke into tears: 'I don't know what to do. Harry thinks Mapel should be fired.' "

In the red-ink environment of wartime *Newsday*, Mapel and the other senior business officials, Joe Yauch in circulation and Charles Nicholson in advertising, worried that Harry might close down this losing proposition. One night, Nicholson received a telegram from Guggenheim, asking him and the others to appear for an emergency meeting the next morning. "I was sure this was it," Nicholson said. But at the meeting, Harry surprised them by telling a story: He had gone to a dinner at the Waldorf-Astoria in Manhattan and sat in the bar for a drink beforehand. As he sat there, he overheard a voice complaining about the plan to seat Harry at the dais. "Before I get through with him and his paper," the voice said, "they'll be sorry they ever heard of Nassau County." Harry turned around, saw the round man with the brush mustache and asked pleasantly: "Are you Mr. Stiles?" It *was* Stiles, who began to blush. "I just want you to know that I happened to overhear your remarks, and I presume they were directed at *Newsday* and myself," Harry said. "There may be room for two newspapers in the county, and we'll be happy to have two, as long as you are the second." This story didn't save Mapel's job. Harry replaced him in 1942 with Henry Page, who had been general manager of the *New York Sun*. But Harry's tale of his meeting with Stiles helped to convince the top executives at *Newsday* that he would keep the paper going.

VII

As ALICIA WATCHED her staff marching off daily to war, she showed that she had inherited a touch of her father's instinct for running to the scene of the battle.

She was a licensed transport pilot, and she had a friend named Jacqueline Cochran who could have arranged a wartime aviation job for her. Cochran was a distinguished pilot who had gathered a group of American women to join the British Air Transport Auxiliary, in which female pilots ferried new or damaged aircraft between factories and the front, to free male pilots for combat. "I considered joining Jacqueline Cochran in England," Alicia said. But Harry talked her out of it. The battle bug had bitten the old World War I aviator too, and he pulled rank on his wife. " 'I'm going back to the service,' he said to me," Alicia said. " 'You stay home and tend the store.' " And as she thought of it, Alicia realized that leaving the infant paper behind would be wrong. "What would those 130 persons I employ think of me?" she said in an interview.

So Alicia stayed and Harry left. Lieutenant Commander Guggenheim reentered the Navy on May 11, 1942, and reported first to Floyd Bennett Field in Brooklyn, where he served as an aide to the executive officer, while he awaited a command of his own. A year later, the Navy promoted Harry to commander and ordered him to establish an aircraft delivery unit at Mercer Field, near Trenton, New Jersey. "He was the first officer assigned, and I was the first enlisted man assigned," said George Schwartzkopf, his chief enlisted aide, who had met Harry at Floyd Bennett, then followed him to Trenton and, after the war, to *Newsday*. The purpose of Mercer Field was to accept delivery of newly manufactured aircraft, equip them and send them off to war. Providing combat-ready planes for the fleet was no small matter, and at war's end, Harry won a commendation for producing "a marked saving in the time necessary to process new aircraft for the Fleet. . . ."

Despite the obvious need for him at Mercer Field, Harry began to get the itch for at least a brief view of combat. Somehow, in the closing months of the war, he got himself assigned temporarily to a carrier, the U.S.S. *Nehenta Bay*, cruising off the Ryukyu Islands. The ostensible reason for his assignment was apparently to observe naval aircraft under combat conditions. But while he was on the carrier, he volunteered to serve as a turret gunner on a torpedo bomber and participate in the strafing of Japanese installations on Sakashima. A photograph taken on the flight deck shows a group of young sailors around the old aviator, who is wearing a baggy khaki flight suit, with a baseball cap and a pair of earphones on his head and a bandolier of ammunition around his shoulders — a bizarre contrast to his knife-sharp, perfectly tailored civilian clothing. This combat mission, of course, was a goofy idea for a 54-year-old officer with an important administrative job ashore. But Harry was a complex and proud man with a streak of machismo. Almost two decades earlier, Harry had written a polite but frosty note to a business associate who made joking remarks about the bravery of Jews in Harry's presence. "I do not know if from personal experience you have found Jews to lack courage," Harry wrote, "but I think if you will inform yourself you will find that throughout their history they have not been lacking in this quality." For strafing Sakashima, Harry was awarded a combat commendation ribbon.

Aside from this brief adventure in 1945, Harry's wartime experiences were routine. He'd get back to New York periodically on Navy business, and Alicia would occasionally visit him at Trenton. In between, they stayed in touch by mail. While Harry was away, Alicia ran the newspaper and handled an additional wartime responsibility: two children, refugees from the war in Europe, who had come to live with them before Harry left for the Navy. At the time, large numbers of American families were providing wartime homes for British children who might otherwise be killed in the Nazi air war against England. But even in this cause, Harry and Alicia found reason to disagree. "Alicia wanted to get some children and Harry said no," said Alicia's friend, Phyllis Cerf, who spent the summers at Falaise during the war. Harry argued that exposing poor children to the rich Guggenheim lifestyle would only make them unhappy when they returned home after the war. "So Alicia said, 'Well, if I can find a child who is accustomed to living the way we live, can I get them?' And he said yes."

The children that Alicia found were anything but poor. Their mother was Baroness Kathleen Annie Pannonica (Nica) de Koenigswarter, the great-great granddaughter of Nathan Mayer Rothschild, one of the founders of the fabulously wealthy banking family. She had married Baron Jules de Koenigswarter, a French mining engineer. Just before the Nazis invaded France, they were living at Abondant, a 60-room chateau near Dreux, 60 miles from Paris. When the Nazis arrived, the de Koenigswarter family took one of the last trains out of Paris, bound for Calais. It was difficult journey, with bombs dropping all around the train. In London, Baron de Koenigswarter became one of the first to join General Charles de Gaulle in the Free French Forces. Nica wanted to join her husband in the fight against the Nazis, but they were afraid to leave the children at Ashton, the 5,000-acre Rothschild estate in England, because of the air war. So the baroness left for New York with the children and ten British pounds — the most cash she was able to take out of the country under wartime regulations. The baroness, worried that her children would not be considered legitimate refugees because they were wealthy, had no idea how she would place them. But with the help of John Foster, an English barrister attached to the British embassy in Washington, she met the Guggenheims, a few months after they had founded *Newsday*. "They came and met the children at the Waldorf," Nica de Koenigswarter said. "They fell right in love with them. . . . They took the children, and I got myself to Africa in very short order."

At the start of the war, the two de Koenigswarter children were very young: Patrick was born in 1936 and his sister, Janka, in 1938. But they were bright and aware. Harry loved to tell the story of how they reacted when they arrived at Falaise — an estate that would awe most children, but not two young Rothschilds, who were accustomed to the splendor of Ashton. "They got out of the car and saw Falaise and said, 'Oh, what a nice little house,' " said Alicia's niece, Alice Albright. That nice little house became a safe, comfortable home for them, but Harry and Alicia didn't have to do much actual parenting, since the children had a nanny. "They were extremely well brought up and shy and intimidated by Alicia and this terrible governess, Miss Davenport," said Ursula Bitter Ulmer, Alicia's goddaughter. "We were supposed to be seen and not heard."

Even though Harry was away most of the time, Patrick has fairly vivid memories of him. "For some reason, I remember him more than I remember her," Patrick said. "He was rather intimidating." As the temporary children of the Guggenheims, Patrick and Janka were able to live a solidly upper-class lifestyle — including visits to the hunting lodges in South Carolina and Georgia, and access to Harry's horses. "I remember going with him, for example, to see the race horses training at Belmont and also at Falaise," Patrick said. At Falaise, Patrick learned to ride, and entered horse shows on Long Island. They went fishing on Long Island Sound and swimming in the pool at Falaise. They met Alicia's friends, including George Abbott, the theatrical director, Bennett Cerf and Carl Sandburg, and neighbors such as the pianist Eddie Duchin and his son Peter. They even got a chance to see the comic strips before they appeared in the paper. At Mercer Field, on a visit to Harry, they got the royal treatment. Patrick went to school in Port Washington and later at a French *lycee* in Manhattan. Janka discovered her career at Falaise, where she used to paint together with Jenny Hauck, the daughter of Alicia's friend, Janet Hauck. "I remember finding out that I wanted to be an artist, and I was drawing and painting," Janka said, "and Aunt Alicia was very encouraging."

Their temporary Aunt Alicia had gynecological problems that made it impossible for her to give birth, but she did feel some maternal urges. "At one point, she told me she wanted to adopt a child," said her friend, Dody Michelson. "I said, 'Why don't you? You could get a very nice one.' She said, 'Well, would you help me ask Harry?' I went to Harry and I said, 'She really deserves a child. You have children, but she doesn't.' I gave him all I could, but he was stony about it and would brook no interference in personal affairs." Adoption of a child who had already gone through the messy, noisy stages of infancy would have been perfect for Alicia. She didn't like infants at all. She preferred children who were old enough to behave well and to perform when called upon. "Certainly the feeling I had from Alicia as a child was, 'You be polite and do what you're told,'" Ursula Ulmer said. "A little later on, as a teenager or a young adult, it was 'Be brilliant and do something.'" Alicia's niece, Adrianne Baker Reilly, said that she, Patrick and Janka would occasionally be allowed into Alicia's presence in the mornings while she ate her breakfast in bed, but they always understood their place. "We were in awe of her, and we behaved," Reilly said. "It was very much on her terms and on her schedule. She was very controlling of people."

During the day, of course, Alicia was at work, and for most of the war, Harry was in Trenton. That left Patrick and Janka under the control of their nanny, and Walter Moulton, Harry's butler. On the surface, Walter was the quintessential proper British butler, but he had stores of humanity and humor that the children understood better than the adults. Reilly remembered that Walter would bring the tea on a circular tray, empty the tray, put it under his arm and drum it, as if he were on parade. The children would beg him for this little routine, squealing, "Walter, be a parade!" Once, Alicia came in just as he had emptied the tea tray, and when he saw her, Walter hurried to regain the reserved demeanor that he showed to adults. "I remember Alicia looking at him with just a glint of a smile," Reilly said. "And she said, 'Walter, be a parade!'"

In this setting, Patrick and Janka were almost no trouble at all — except once. Stan Peckham, by then an Army officer, was in town, awaiting shipment to Europe, and he visited Alicia at the Savoy-Plaza several times when Harry was away at Mercer Field. Once, Harry came home, and Patrick mentioned Peckham's visits. "Patrick said, 'Oh, do you know our friend, Lieutenant Peckham? He's here every night.' That set me up fine with Harry," Peckham said. At one time, Peckham conceded, his relationship with Alicia was "quite romantic." In fact, when he went into the service, she rented a post office box under the name Marjorie Muffet and urged him to write. "She thought I would write more uninhibited letters," Peckham said. "I didn't choose to write any indiscreet letters to her." But Alicia did write warm letters to Peckham. "They were affectionate, but not gushy," he said. "She knew I didn't care for gushy."

Alicia also kept in touch regularly with her former husband, Joe Brooks. Despite the divorce, they were still friends. "She was very fond of Joe," said Alicia's secretary, Dot Holdsworth. "They went fishing together at his place up in the Adirondacks, and then he would come down to Georgia for the shooting. So they saw a lot of each other. I don't know whether Harry knew it or not. I imagine he did." It was a difficult situation for Alicia, who felt some sorrow about divorcing Brooks, and it was painful for Brooks himself. "Joe Brooks never quite got over Alicia and pined for her and wanted her to leave Guggenheim," said her nephew, Joseph Patterson Albright, who used to go fishing with Brooks. When Alicia visited Brooks after the divorce, she observed the proprieties. Rita Hinds, whose father, uncle and husband, Lee, served in turn as caretakers at the Brooks property, said that on those occasions, Alicia stayed at the Whiteface Mountain House, a hotel about three miles from the Brooks camp. Still, she apparently felt some embarrassment about her continuing relationship with Brooks. Alicia's friend, Alice-Leone Moats, remembered eating lunch alone one day at the Gladstone Hotel, looking up and seeing Alicia and Brooks. "So on my way out, I stopped and said hello, and Alicia looked so uncomfortable," Moats said. "Then she called me up afterwards and said, 'Oh, please don't tell anybody that you saw us there together.' "

During Harry's absence, Alicia also spent much of her time with Jackie Gebhard, her star reporter. Gebhard's husband was away in the service, and Alicia wanted Gebhard and her son, Kevin, to live at Falaise. "I said I couldn't do that," Gebhard said. "In the first place, I couldn't afford to share the cost of servants at Sands Point, and I wouldn't do it any other way. She was furious and told me I had a false pride."

So, Alicia was left with just Patrick and Janka and occasional visits from other children. At the end of the war, Nica de Koenigswarter came back to claim her children. "The Guggenheims wanted to adopt them," the baroness said. "They didn't want to give them up." The children didn't remember it quite that vividly. "They didn't try to keep us, although I think it must have been very sad for them as well as us, because we were very fond of each other," Janka said. "I remember leaving Aunt Alicia especially." In the end, Nica de Koenigswarter, who later became known as the jazz baroness for her patronage of musicians such as Charlie Parker and Thelonious Monk, felt she had found the right place for her children: "They had a wonderful war." Alicia had her few years with Patrick and Janka, and she treated Joe and Alice Albright as surrogate children, but she never had a child of her own, except for *Newsday*. Some part of her always felt sadness about that. "You've raised a wonderful, lovable family," she told her friend Albert Wood years later. "I've only raised a money-making monstrosity."

In the war years, while Harry was away and Alicia was getting the paper off the ground, her "money-making monstrosity" didn't make much money, but it was sometimes a monstrosity. The journalism of early *Newsday*, produced by a war-depleted staff, was inconsistent. Sometimes, as with the nursing home series, it broke new ground. Sometimes, it was frivolous, as when Virginia Sheward and Millard Kaufman purposely got themselves arrested in Great Neck Plaza by wearing shorts, in violation of an anti-shorts ordinance. Sometimes, it broke taboos, such as the one against even the mention of cancer. Alicia ordered her staff to be honest in obituaries about cancer as a cause of death, and when she couldn't find models to pose for a photo spread on cancer detection, she posed in photos as the young wife, with Hathway as the husband, the general manager Henry Page as the doctor, and Page's son and niece as the children.

Despite its inconsistency, in those war years *Newsday* established an unmistakable tone: irreverent, saucy, willing to challenge the powerful. That persona contrasted nicely with the stuffy, stand-pat *Review-Star*, and *Newsday*'s quick success in exceeding its established competitor's circulation was ample proof that Alicia had set the right tone. In choosing Alan Hathway, with all his faults, as managing editor, she had picked exactly the right kind of journalist for a new paper that needed to get itself noticed. It was still an uneven newspaper, but it was strong enough and self-confident enough to start growing up.

CHAPTER NINE

The End of Infancy

I

INEXORABLY, IN THE months after World War II ended, Joseph Medill Patterson drank himself to death, and in dying, he shaped the future for his daughter Alicia, even more definitively than he had done with 40 years of parenting.

For Alicia, the postwar years brought a breathtaking procession of experiences: the beginnings of permanence and professionalism for her newspaper, increasing influence on the growth of her suburban community, nagging marital difficulties and the start of a love affair. But at the beginning of all this, it was her father's death that drew a clear demarcation line through her life, closing out the possibility of a career at the top of the *Daily News* and bonding her tightly to the little country newspaper that had started as a training ground for her anticipated role at the *News*.

The consuming goal of Joe Patterson's final years was to outlive Franklin Roosevelt. Patterson got his wish when Roosevelt died on April 12, 1945. As America mourned FDR's passing, Patterson managed somehow to fight back the tears, first in an unsentimental obituary editorial and then, a few weeks later, in a dazzlingly tasteless editorial under the headline, "Three of the Big Ones Dead in a Month." It lumped together "three departed headmen," Roosevelt, Benito Mussolini and Adolf Hitler, and added: "These occurrences, we imagine, have stimulated some long thoughts in the brains of Winston Churchill, now 70, and Josef Stalin, now 65."

The angry reaction to Patterson's treatment of FDR's death was brief, but before 1945 was over, he found himself in the middle of a long-lasting storm of anger. The cause of the furor was a savagely anti-Semitic column by his Washington columnist, John O'Donnell, on October 3, 1945. The basis of the column was a famous incident involving General George S. Patton's visit to a military hospital in Sicily in 1943. Accusing one of the patients of malingering and cowardice, Patton had slapped him and raised a furor. O'Donnell's column alleged that the soldier was Jewish and that Patton had used the word "Jew" during the incident. As a result, O'Donnell said, a Jewish cabal at the highest levels of government had later conspired to disgrace Patton and strip him of his power. O'Donnell was wrong: The soldier was not Jewish at all. The columnist eventually admitted his outrageous error of fact, and the *News* issued a tepid pseudo-apology, but the storm continued. Mayor Fiorello LaGuardia criticized the *News*, advertisers cancelled ads, subscribers cancelled subscriptions and demonstrators marched, handing out leaflets and urging people not to buy the *News*. It was a sharp blow to Patterson's journalistic pride. "He'd always insisted that you had to check the facts," said Hal Burton, who returned to the *News* after World War II. Now, despite those standards, Patterson's newspaper had been horrifyingly wrong. This storm over the O'Donnell column, Burton suggested, was partly responsible for Patterson's final decline. "That really finished Patterson as a person," Burton said. "He was just shattered by the whole thing. Really shattered."

Patterson had always been a drinker, but in his last months, he was essentially out of control. It was a difficult time for his second wife, Mary King Patterson, who had to cope not only with his drinking but with the lingering antipathy of his daughters. The derisive family term for her was "Bloody Mary," the nickname given to Queen Mary I of England, a devout Roman Catholic who persecuted Protestants vigorously. "I think they called her Bloody Mary because she was a Catholic usurper," James Patterson said of his mother. Alicia, at least, seems to have subscribed to the "usurper" view of Mary King. "She sort of lost her father to Mary," said Alicia's friend, Dody Michelson. "Before that, they had this very close relationship, and Mary sort of ended that." Alicia also resented Mary King for influencing her father to convert to Catholicism, Michelson said. Actually, Patterson had shown a strong interest in Catholicism long before he married Mary King. During World War I, he even asked his troops to tell him which of them were Catholic, so that one of them could baptize him, if necessary. A sergeant named Tom Howard, who later took the famous electric chair photograph of Ruth Snyder for the *Daily News*, raised his hand. "My father always told him to keep some water in his canteen so he could be baptized," James Patterson said.

The family's natural hostility toward Mary King Patterson did not abate in the final weeks of her husband's life, when Alicia and Josephine felt she could have done more to deal with his drinking. "They both thought my mother could have, should have prevented my father's death by putting him away or doing something like that," James Patterson said. "As my mother said to that, he was driving in to work until about a week before — well maybe two weeks, but he was in fairly good health until he kind of just collapsed." So Mary King felt that it would be impossible to commit him to an institution, but she had trouble controlling him. "You couldn't," said Dot Patterson, his daughter-in-law. "He was a very powerful man, and she tried. Lord knows, she tried." In the spring of 1946, Patterson entered Doctors Hospital in Manhattan, where he died on May 26 — just before his fiftieth anniversary Groton reunion and a little more than a year after Franklin Roosevelt's death.

Joseph Medill Patterson was a complex and contradictory man — impossible to categorize, impossible to ignore. He almost resented his wealth and the power that it brought him, but he used that power without hesitation. "It is purely because of an accident of birth that I happen to be in a position where I get my way," he once said. "*But*, I do get my way, and don't ever forget that." His management style was to suggest, "Let's do this," or "Don't you think it would be a good idea if . . . ." But the prudent employee always knew that his gentle suggestions were actually irrevocable orders. He rarely showed anger, but he was capable of making abrupt, almost arbitrary personnel changes, as he did when Paul Gallico reviewed movies too harshly to suit Patterson the movie buff, and Patterson ordered him removed from movie criticism and hidden elsewhere on the staff. He could rant fiercely about Roosevelt, yet break into tears reading a poem to his family. He was deeply anti-intellectual, but he read widely and wrote clearly and persuasively. He was courageous on the battlefield, but he suffered from a strange claustrophobia that impelled him to order an architect to install a hatchet and a phone in his private bathroom in Chicago, so he could get out in an emergency. He ran Alicia through a series of almost cruel male-making rites of passage, but he was also a thoughtful father whose letters taught her much about life and about newspapering. "I've learned everything that is worth anything from you, not only as a publisher but as my pa and a helluva swell guy," she once wrote him. "I've aped you shockingly but they say that is true appreciation."

In Patterson's last years, he and Alicia had argued over her marriage to Harry and over Roosevelt, but his death was still a terrible loss to her. "She adored her father," Dody Michelson said, "and she just wept over the fact that Mary had caused the breach between them." Some of the family's lingering ill feeling toward Mary King Patterson exploded after her husband's death. "It was kind of bitter at the funeral," James Patterson said. In an upstairs bedroom in the mansion at Ossining, before the body was to be taken out to a local Catholic church for the funeral, Josephine began to berate Mary. "I think Josephine had kept things inside for a long time," Dot Patterson said. "Alicia came forward and said, 'Jo, stop it, stop it!' " Looking back at that moment, Josephine said: "I don't think there's much she could have done. I may have been upset at the time. You always have to blame somebody."

Once the funeral was over, there was the question of the will. To begin with, there was nothing in it that gave Alicia any real power at the *News*, despite his earlier proposal to make her part of a small team of top managers after his death. "It was a wonderful plan, but it never came true, in part because father and I fell out over Franklin D. Roosevelt," Alicia wrote. Hal Burton, who was friendly with Patterson until his death and later came to work for Alicia at

Newsday, said Alicia told him that her father had called her one day toward the end of his life and said: " 'I'm not going to give you the paper. I'm going to give it to Mary and Jimmy.' She said he laughed when he said it." She felt hurt, but she also had begun to doubt whether she wanted to operate the *News*. "If she were running the *News*, she'd have to get rid of half the people on top because they were either ossified or they were so reactionary that she couldn't tolerate them on the paper," Burton said. "She said, 'Maybe it was just as well.' "

Actually, Patterson did not have the power to give her financial control of the *News*, because he didn't really own it. The *News* belonged to the Tribune Company, which in turn was dominated by something called the McCormick-Patterson Trust. When Joseph Medill died, he had established the Medill Trust, to keep the family from dissipating its control over Tribune Company stock. In 1932, a year before the Medill Trust was to expire, Joseph Medill Patterson and Robert Rutherford McCormick had established a new instrument, the McCormick-Patterson Trust, to extend that family control into the future. At his death, Patterson owned 196 7/8 of the 1,070 shares, or units, in the trust. So he did not own a controlling share in the Tribune Company. If he had wanted to, he could have arranged a position of real power for Alicia, perhaps as one of the New York trustees of the McCormick-Patterson Trust. But he didn't.

In the wake of Patterson's death, his cousin Bert McCormick persuaded Cissy Patterson to become the chairman of the News Syndicate Company. So the *Daily News* was in the firm control of other members of the family, while Alicia was little more than a spectator. Cissy tried to intercede with Bert McCormick to get Alicia a share of power, but the Colonel angrily resisted giving anything to a woman he regarded as a Roosevelt liberal. She did get a seat on the less consequential *Daily News* board, but she was distinctly in the minority. Alicia would say something, the members of the board would listen in silence, and then go on with their business as if no one had spoken. "She didn't get much of a chance to participate," said James Patterson, who served on the board with her. "We used to sit next to each other most of the time and whisper like school kids."

In the same period, Cissy Patterson suggested to Alicia that she accept control of the *Washington Times-Herald* after Cissy's death. During his life, Joe Patterson had warned Alicia against any involvement in the Washington paper, because he felt it would never be a money-maker. But Cissy thought Alicia had the right stuff. "You have done such a wonderful job with your newspaper, starting from scratch and with almost every handicap against you," Cissy had written Alicia earlier. Now, with a fog of drugs and alcohol shrouding her mind, Cissy decided that she would fulfill a wish of her dead brother if she could induce Alicia to divorce Harry, remarry Joe Brooks and take over the *Times-Herald*. So she wrote Alicia a series of letters, announcing that she wanted to leave her the paper. Stan Peckham said that Alicia asked him: " 'My God, if Aunt Cissy died and left me that newspaper, what do I do with it?' "

Cissy Patterson is believed to have gone so far as to draft a revision to her will, dropping her plan to leave control of the paper to seven of its executives, and leaving it instead to Alicia. But on July 24, 1948, before this proposed change in her will became final, Cissy died. Cissy's often-discussed plans for a new will, combined with her paranoid fears that she would be murdered, plus the apparent suicide of one of her executives, added up to lingering rumors that someone had killed her. But when all the furor died down, her daughter Felicia reached an out-of-court settlement with the executives, and they inherited the *Times-Herald*. They later sold the paper to Bert McCormick, who made it more stuffy and less profitable, then sold it to Eugene Meyer, the owner of the competing *Washington Post*.

So, in a space of two years, the last wills of her father and her aunt had foreclosed to Alicia two opportunities to leave behind her country newspaper and get into big-city journalism. But if her father's will didn't give her power in the Tribune Company, it did something for her that turned out to be far more important: It left her enough money to assume a significant role in the ownership of *Newsday*.

During his lifetime, Patterson had been generous to his daughters. The documents filed with the Surrogate Court in Westchester County show that he had given Alicia cash gifts of $72,469.91 between 1932 and 1945, plus the house and property in Sands Point, valued at $60,929. That does not include all his earlier cash gifts, or a series of trusts that he and his mother had established for Alicia. In the will itself, Patterson created five trusts to dispose of the income from his 196 7/8 shares of the McCormick-Patterson Trust, which were appraised at $6,890,625 in the probate proceeding. Alicia was entitled to the income from a 22 and 2/9ths interest in the value of his shares. The principal on her portion would have been worth more than $1.5 million before estate taxes. In addition, Patterson left her a 22 and 2/9ths share of the rest of his estate, excluding his house at Ossining. That bequest was worth another $1 million to Alicia, before taxes. Well over half of the $11.2 million net estate went to pay taxes, and there is no precise record of how much Alicia finally received. But by the end of the decade, Harry's records show Alicia receiving about $75,000 a year in income from the McCormick-Patterson Trust and her other trusts. "That means for the first time in Harry's eyes, she's really got something," said Roger Williams, an attorney at the law firm of Townley and Updike, who became an expert on Patterson's will. "Now she gets into some real money."

II

ALICIA WASTED LITTLE time in using her new financial clout. Within six months after her father's death, she wrote a formal letter to Harry, seeking a share of ownership in the paper.

"For some time, as you know from our numerous conversations, I have wanted to purchase a substantial interest in NEWSDAY, so that I might add to my responsibility for the management of the paper a feeling of proprietary interest in it as well," she wrote. "This is a natural desire on my part, since I have devoted practically all of my time and efforts to the paper for the last six years.

"The heavy losses which were sustained in the first three years of operation made it virtually impossible for me to acquire NEWSDAY on my own at that time, as I would have been unable to finance it. The inheritance which I received as a result of my father's death this year now makes it possible for me to undertake this responsibility."

Harry was willing to sell Alicia an interest, but only a minority one. "As you know," he wrote, "I desire to retain a controlling interest in the enterprise, and accordingly I am prepared to sell you a 49 percent interest in NEWSDAY, which, on the overall value of $165,000, comes to $80,850.

"As you know, when I acquired NEWSDAY in 1940, I transferred to you as a gift a $4,000 capital interest in NEWSDAY. Due largely to losses in the first few years of operation, this interest of yours has been reduced to the amount of $386.62. This sum should, therefore, be deducted from the purchase price of $80,850, leaving a net payment for you to make of $80,463.38."

It wasn't this penny-counting that annoyed Alicia, but his decision to maintain majority control. "He wanted 51 percent of everything," said Harry's nephew, Oscar Straus. The way Alicia saw it, she was actually running *Newsday*, and she deserved to have majority ownership as well. "The only thing she wanted was two percent, and she nagged him about that from day one, and he never would give it to her," said Dorothy Holdsworth, Alicia's secretary. "She knew she was going to get it after his death. She wanted it at that time, so she wouldn't have all these hassles."

The "hassles" over finances were continuous. From the moment when Harry returned from the Navy, and even before, he was dissatisfied with the way the paper was running. "You people have been running a great paper around here," he said, "but you've been running a mighty bad business." The bottom line, of course, was his major concern. In 1946, a law firm prepared a study of *Newsday* for Harry that showed losses of $161,000 in 1940, $203,000 in 1941, $145,000 in 1942 and $35,000 in 1943, totalling $705,000. In 1944, the study showed a profit of $29,000 and in 1945, a profit of $28,000. (Other documents indicate the 1944 profit may have been $38,000.) The same memo found that the Guggenheims had probably committed a technical violation of the income tax laws by failing to file partnership returns, although that didn't affect the amount of tax paid. That kind of sloppiness was part of the mess that faced Harold Ferguson, a tall, straight-as-an-arrow accountant who had audited the books as an outsider since 1942, then became the paper's controller after World War II. What he found was distressing.

The controller before Ferguson had been untidy about keeping books, said Kathryn Maynard, who had worked with Harry at Floyd Bennett Field during the war and came to *Newsday* in early 1946, without even realizing that Harry was the owner. She had found the business practices of Ferguson's predecessor appalling. "When he went out to lunch, I used to have to go through his wastepaper basket to save things," Maynard remembered. "He said, 'Well, why should I write it down? It's all in my head. . . .' There just wasn't anything kept — little slips of paper. Oh, it was awful." So it fell to Ferguson to straighten out the mess and make peace with the Internal Revenue Service. Hiring Ferguson was apparently Harry's idea, and he was Harry's man. "Alicia always felt that he sided towards Harry, which I guess is true, because he was an astute businessman," Maynard said. "Now, you tried to talk about a balance sheet to Alicia and she'd just go off on a tangent: 'Well, I don't care what it says.' You can't run a business that way."

Running the business, making the dollars-and-cents decisions that confront any firm, was a constant source of friction between Harry and Alicia. And anyone who worked for them in the position of general manager was constantly caught in the crossfire — first William Mapel, then Henry Page, then Richard Amberg, who lasted only 21 months, and Joe Yauch, who moved from the circulation department to replace Amberg in 1949. One of them is reported to have said: "I couldn't stand it. It was like being nibbled to death by ducks." And Yauch, who became weary of the fiscal struggles and left *Newsday*, advised his colleague Buddy Chernow: " 'Don't ever let yourself get caught between a woman and a man in business.' "

The financial struggles between Harry and Alicia spread beyond their business and into their home, where Harry developed a tightly structured system for keeping track of their separate incomes and expenses, with an endless flow of memos. Despite Alicia's lack of fiscal skill, she had a complicated lifestyle, including her hunting lodge at Kingsland, Georgia, a personal maid, an apartment at the Savoy-Plaza Hotel during the war years and later her own townhouse on East 74th Street. She needed help in managing all this. Harry offered that help, but not without trying to exert control over her spending. During the war years they had a constant debate-by-memo over which household expenses should be charged to him and which to her. "So in the future, therefore, I suggest that you pay your own bills and control all of your own expenses," Harry wrote in one memo. "You will pay the salary and all expenses of your personal maid, all telephone and I suggest liquor bills (formerly included in the household expenses), your car and other bills personal to you. . . . The only way that any fortune can be guarded is by placing specific responsibility on those making the expenditures. You will now have your own financial responsibilities and I shall have my own."

Once Alicia had bought her 49 percent share of the paper, her indebtedness to Harry grew, and he was not hesitant to remind her about it. "I have decided, in view of the confusion in your mind in regard to your financial status and your expressed desire to get out of debt, personally to write to you from time to time," he said in one memo, whose tone was like that of an impatient father talking to a muddle-headed teenager. "If you do not understand any of these transactions, please let me know." Not only did Harry keep careful track of what she owed, but he also watched her bank account closely, to decide how much she could afford to repay him at a given time, until she finally settled her debts, at the start of the 1950s.

As much as the conflicts with Harry grated on Alicia's nerves, his fiscal acumen did come in handy. From the beginning, for example, Harry supervised the purchase of newsprint — one of the greatest headaches *Newsday* had in the 1940s. The newsprint situation got so bad that *Newsday* began buying rolls of paper that were narrower than the size they needed. These odd-size rolls were called "dinkies," and running them on the press required constant ingenuity. "We bought anything that was on a roll, and it was up to me to run it," said Harvey Broad, the pressroom superintendent. "I got to be known as the dinky king." Broad and Allan Woods, who had risen from composing room foreman to production manager, had to figure out ways of running two or three of these dinky rolls on the same shaft. That wasn't easy. The web of paper flowing through the presses could break when adjoining small rolls wobbled and knocked into each other. "Because of their size, there wasn't much stability," said Bill Schindler, who had to work with the dinkies.

In handling such chores as the purchase of newsprint, Harry proved that he could be a working partner to Alicia, as well as a miserly adversary. When she left for Europe to cover the Berlin airlift in 1948, for example, he stayed behind and sent her chatty, friendly reports. "Well you certainly got off in a blaze of sunshine and glory," he wrote. "While you are settling the affairs of the world I will tell you about some of the trivia of New York and Long Island." The trivia included union negotiations, newsprint and a "soft soap" session that Harry had with an executive of Arnold Constable, one of the paper's most important advertisers. And at the close of one letter, Harry even found time to praise Alicia's journalism skills. "I have read the first two installments of your story," he said. "I think the copy excellent and especially like the approach. Congratulations!"

Alicia's greatest strength on her overseas trips wasn't in the writing. "She wrote in a rather direct fashion," Hal Burton said. "I wouldn't describe her as a stylist particularly." Her strength wasn't always sophistication or understanding, either. As a young reporter for *Liberty*, she had offended Central Americans by writing this about Nicaragua: "The natives are half or more Indian, which explains a lot of things. Fighting is their favorite pastime. They have no fear of death and kill each other off as casually as we would shoot crows. . . . Work to them is worse than death. They die young." Her real strength was simply her willingness to ask difficult questions and go where the story was — a product of her training to be Joe Patterson's son. "She was the most courageous woman I've ever met," said Dorothy Schiff, then the publisher of the *New York Post*, who accompanied Alicia on her 1948 European trip. "Physically and mentally, she was very daring."

On the voyage to Europe on the Queen Elizabeth, Schiff said, they encountered Milton Eisenhower, the brother of General Dwight Eisenhower, and Alicia asked him a question that Schiff would never have asked: What about Eisenhower's rumored love affair with his aide, Kay Summersby? When they reached Europe, they went together to see the graves of the soldiers who died in the invasion at Normandy. They stayed at a small hotel in a fishing village, and Schiff became nervous about some unsavory characters at the bar. "It was very scary and there was a dog that howled all night," Schiff said. "She got out a bottle of whiskey, put it on the bureau and wasn't a bit scared. I was petrified." Despite Alicia's bravado, she was compassionate toward those who were more prudent. "I was a terrible sissy physically," said Schiff, who hated to fly and travelled to Frankfurt by train, while Alicia flew in the Berlin airlift. "She was so understanding about it."

Covering the airlift, Alicia flew in a C-47 transport from Orly Airport to Wiesbaden in overcast weather. "Even the birds were walking, as the old time pilots used to say," Alicia wrote, in one part of of her 14-part series describing the airlift and her tour of Europe. Then she climbed into a C-54 at Rhein Main Airport and sat in the cockpit as the pilot flew his cargo of sugar and dehydrated potatoes to Berlin. When they approached a tower, the pilot asked Alicia to get on the radio and give the plane's position. After a moment of silence and a long whistle at the other end, an awed voice came back from the tower: "Didya hear that? A girl flying the plane!"

Alicia's reporting from Europe was impressionistic and colorful, but it made little pretense of being unbiased. She spent much of her time with the leaders of the Western powers in Berlin, and her reports reflected their views. The Americans were always "we" and the Russians were often "the Reds" and "the Commies" in these stories. This series, of course, was the ultimate expression of the ancient principle of Rank Has Its Privileges. *Newsday*, still a little country newspaper, could hardly afford a real foreign staff. So when there was a need to cover an important story overseas, it naturally fell to the editor-publisher.

While Alicia was flying through the fog and conferring with generals, Harry was home, watching the store. It was only when they were both in town that the sparks flew, as their two separate spheres collided. But luckily for Alicia's sanity, Harry continued to have other interests to distract him. In addition to his long-term interest in his plantation and his racing stable, for example, he spent a few months after the war as chairman of the New York City Airport Authority, charged with the completion and operation of LaGuardia and Idlewild airports. But he resigned only three months after his appointment, in a conflict with Robert Moses, the city's construction coordinator, who became something of a sacred cow at *Newsday*, despite this tiff with Harry. "Moses, it is now quite clear, determined to dominate the authority from the inception," Harry said in a hand-written outline of his reasons for quitting. "It will have been the first undertaking that I have started without finishing with some success."

That sort of failure irked Harry, a relentless perfectionist who wanted to get every detail right, especially when it came to business. So, even if his other interests kept him away from the plant, he was determined that

Newsday would not fail financially. Even if that determination meant continued conflict with his wife over spending, he wasn't going to back down.

III

BEYOND HER SKIRMISHES with Harry, Alicia faced a formidable array of postwar problems: the return of her staff from overseas, restless unions, a deteriorating plant that was now far too small, and the erratic growth of her new Suffolk County edition.

Before the war, the young people who signed on with *Newsday* had been happy simply to have a job. But when they returned from overseas, they were not as easily contented. They were starting families, and they needed to think about salary as well as excitement. A typical example was Ed Gebhard, who had been the sports editor before the war. When he came back, Alicia offered him the chance to run the Suffolk paper, but her salary offer was not convincing. "It was such a shockingly small amount that we decided no way," said Jackie Gilbride Gebhard. "I don't think she realized it was as tiny as it was." So, for the want of a decent salary offer, Alicia lost a valuable husband-wife team. Jackie was one of her best reporters and her husband was an experienced editor who could have done a professional job for her in Suffolk. Instead of staying with *Newsday*, the Gebhards later set up their own public relations firm.

It wasn't long before Alicia also lost the services of Ben White, the young veteran journalist who had been the city editor before he joined the service. When White returned, Jack Altshul was the city editor, and Alicia made no move to replace Altshul with White. For a while, White worked as a reporter, then left for the *Daily News*. White's wife, Theresa, said that he didn't resent not getting the city editor job back and actually preferred being a reporter. He simply got a good offer from friends at the *News*. Whatever the reason for his departure, Alicia apparently felt some remorse. So she continued to pay White a regular stipend of $25 a week after he went to the *Daily News*. In return, his wife said, he continued writing a series of editorials for *Newsday* that he had started before the war, examining life on Long Island through the eyes of a fictitious family called the Gamsons. At the *News*, White continued to be a useful resource to the young postwar *Newsday* staff, providing tips and guidance. "He was a cooperative guy — I mean a paid cooperator," said David Rosenbluth, one of the first of a long line of young reporters that *Newsday* hired right off the staff of the *Chronicle*, the student newspaper at Hofstra University, where Alicia was a member of the board of trustees. "He was very good, especially if you were a new reporter and you didn't know many cops. He could help you get in somewhere."

In some ways, it was probably just as well that White didn't regain his city editor job. "Altshul got along fine with Hathway, and Ben probably wouldn't," said Stan Peckham, who didn't want to work for Alan Hathway either. "I wrote to her from London and I said, 'I understand Alan Hathway is now managing editor and that you booted out Harold Davis. I guess that means I'd better look for another job, because I'm not going to work for Hathway.' She wrote and said, 'You don't need to worry about that, because you won't be working for him. You'll be working for me.' " So Peckham returned to *Newsday*, where he became Alicia's full-time editorial writer, but not exactly Hathway's pal. Apparently feeling threatened by Peckham's closeness to Alicia, Hathway refused even to provide him with a desk. "So Alicia blew her stack one day and said, 'I'll find you a place to sit myself,' " Peckham remembered. She scrounged a large rolltop desk from Hempstead House, the Daniel Guggenheim mansion adjoining Falaise, ordered a raised platform set up outside her office and put the desk and Peckham on it. Peckham's relationship with Hathway remained so touchy that Peckham and Alicia developed a little conspiracy to keep Hathway from finding out how closely they worked in shaping the editorials. "If she was staying out at Falaise, we'd meet in her office," Peckham said. "If she was in New York, I would ride out with her and we'd discuss them in the car on the way out. But then she would drop me off before we got to *Newsday*, and she'd drive on into *Newsday*, and I would come in five or ten minutes later, as if I just got off the train, so Hathway didn't know we'd already had our editorial conference. Meanwhile, we'd discussed everything. Sometimes, we even discussed Hathway. She sort of liked to play us against each other all the time. I kept saying, 'For God's sake, get rid of this guy.' "

At the start of *Newsday*, in the interests of labor peace, Harry and Alicia had actually invited unions to come to the plant and organize workers. But after the war, as wages and working conditions became more important, the unions became restless. The first workers to revolt were the pressmen, whose salaries were much less than what pressmen in the city were making. They had been getting $48 a week, with some supplementary payments from the union. *Newsday* increased them to $56, but they wanted $69, which was roughly what pressmen in the city earned. The words "New York City scale" were poison to Harry, who wanted nothing to do with New York City wages or work rules. Finally, the pressmen just decided not to show up one morning. It wasn't a strike. They weren't picketing or trying to prevent *Newsday* from hiring other pressmen. They were simply moving to better-paying jobs in the city. The stereotypers showed up, but later, when they saw that the pressmen were not coming in, they walked off the job too.

"So we had an edition completed down to the last plate, but no one to run the presses," Altshul wrote. "All the executives took a crack at it. Page, Hathway, Yauch and Woods got the plates on the press in the right places and Miss Patterson and even I — a mechanical moron — helped wherever we could. . . . Only once did the press sputter through the printing procedure and that for the space of six papers, so that while the public did not receive *Newsday* that day, at least we had file copies to continue an uninterrupted five-year skein." For the first time in its history, on April 15, 1946, *Newsday* failed to publish.

Alicia called around looking for someone who could help, and she came up with the name of Harvey Broad, who had worked at the *Flushing Journal* during its strike and was familiar with the *Newsday* presses, because they had come from the *Journal*. When the pressmen deserted *Newsday*, he was working as a pari-mutuel clerk, and he wanted Harry or Alicia to get him a guarantee that he could get that job back if *Newsday* didn't work out. He also wanted assurances from the international union that it had no objection to his putting together a staff of pressmen at *Newsday*. When both of those conditions had been met, Broad showed up and started hiring replacements, but there were no experienced pressmen to be had. So he looked around for recently returned veterans who were strong, reasonably intelligent and anxious for jobs. "I figured, 'What the hell. They've been in the service. I'll give them a break,' " Broad said. Broad and Allan Woods together hired a crew that was at least willing to learn. "I didn't know anything about a press," said Joseph Knoll, one of the new pressmen. But the new crew learned on the job, after *Newsday* resumed publication on April 16.

Soon after that crisis, *Newsday* had a painful struggle with the Newspaper Guild. At the expiration of the first contract, *Newsday* had demanded that the Guild organize the *Review-Star*, so that *Newsday* would not be at a competitive disadvantage. For its part, the Guild demanded wages closer to the New York City scale. In the spring of 1947, an arbiter heard the Guild's demand, but Harry and Alicia refused to accept the New York scale. "The philosophy of the Guild is that Newsday's employees perform the same kind of work as those of the Metropolitan dailies and so should receive the same wages," a management memo argued. "An extension of this view would require all newspapers throughout the nation to pay New York scale. If this philosophy were accepted and extended throughout the country all small papers would be squeezed out of existence."

The real crunch came later that year, when the Guild suddenly found itself in a weakened position. In the postwar era, the threat of Communist Party infiltration of unions and the reality of several difficult strikes helped to create the perception that significant union abuses had arisen under the Wagner Act of 1935. The Republican-controlled Congress responded to those anti-labor feelings by passing the Labor-Management Relations Act of 1947, usually called the Taft-Hartley Act, over President Harry S Truman's veto. The bill's proponents felt it simply gave management more protection against abuses by organized labor. The unions saw it as a slave labor law and opposed it bitterly. Among other provisions, it outlawed the closed shop and required union officials to swear under oath that they weren't members of the Communist Party.

Encouraged by the Taft-Hartley Act, *Newsday* decided to wave the red flag and run the Newspaper Guild out of town. The day after the contract expired, the general manager, Richard Amberg, wrote to the Guild: "We do not believe that the Guild is the true bargaining representative of our employes. Until such time as your organization may be able to establish itself as the bargaining representative in accordance with Federal law, we shall be forced to discontinue recognition of the Guild as the collective bargaining agent of our employes." In other words, the Guild no longer existed at *Newsday*, unless it could organize and win a National Labor Relations Board election. At the same time, Amberg played his red card: "The New York Guild has specifically refused to disavow Communism, and its officers have failed to file a disavowal of Communist affiliation under the Labor Management Relations Act of 1947."

On the same day that Amberg declared the death of the Guild, he announced a 10 percent wage increase. The paper followed that carrot with a series of announcements designed to persuade employees to ignore the Guild and embrace *Newsday*. First, management offered Blue Cross coverage. Then they gave a third week of vacation to those who had been with the paper five years or more, set up a loan fund and established a *Newsday* Recreation Fund. The employees met, voted not to submit to an NLRB election and affirmed their opposition to the Communist Party.

Following the death of the Guild unit, a sports reporter named Ed Comerford began trying to resurrect it. Comerford was relatively content in his work, but he believed that the staff needed a union. When he asked Alan Hathway for a leave of absence to work on an organizing campaign for the Guild, however, he found that the former Guild firebrand had undergone a complete conversion. "He was strongly anti-union," Comerford remembered. "He said, 'No way. If you go, you go, but there's no leave of absence.' " Comerford left anyway, and began working with the Guild organizer, John Weilburg, on an organizing drive. "A lot of the people, it turned out to my dismay and surprise, didn't want the Guild," Comerford said. "A lot of them viewed the New York Guild as a Communist-leaning radical outfit. I'm sure there were people who thought I was a Communist. . . . We realized as the thing went along that, if we did have an election, we were not going to win it."

Though Alicia had invited the unions to organize *Newsday* in 1940, she was not a passive observer in the efforts to cut off the Guild. She phoned Ralph Hausrath, the Suffolk editor, and asked him to come in for a meeting. At the lunch, she made it clear that she wasn't happy about the Guild drive, and she rolled out the ultimate threat to make her point. " 'If there's going to be a lot of union trouble, I'll sell the paper. We've had inquiries from the Newhouse people, and I think we could sell if we had to,' " Hausrath remembered her saying. But the drastic step of selling to S. I. Newhouse — a threat that Alicia used again several years later in her struggles with Harry — became unnecessary. In an NLRB election on June 14, 1949, the Guild lost, 34 to 24. For the next quarter century, editorial workers at *Newsday* were to be without union representation.

The other postwar labor confrontation involved the printers, who also objected to the difference between what *Newsday* paid and the scale in the city. The conflict with International Typographical Union Local 915 came to a head while Alicia was in Europe for the Berlin airlift. "On Friday the ITU left out about $1,200 of advertising by the same action that it took a few weeks ago; namely, refusing to work overtime and, of course, without any prior notice; Saturday they left out about four pages," Harry wrote to Alicia. The union's tactics left footprints in the paper — blank spots where ads might have run, filled only with notations such as "Space Reserved for Swezey and Newins." Amberg recommended that they offer a $9 weekly wage increase, but Harry favored a more radical strategy: doing away with the ITU entirely, as they had done with the Guild. "We are in a position, in which we may never be again, successfully to operate Newsday without benefit of the ITU," Harry wrote. "Should we succeed in throwing off the yoke of the ITU, over the period of the next five to ten years it will probably mean several million dollars to Newsday."

In later correspondence with the ITU, Harry indicated some willingness to move toward the $9 increase, which was the largest the printers had ever received at *Newsday*. But Carl Barra, who was brand-new in the composing room during this struggle, recalled that it was Alicia who came dashing back from Europe and granted the increase. "We all loved Alicia," Barra said. "We didn't care too much for Harry. He was tough." The union chapel chairman, Wallace Harris, said: "Of the two of them, she was more prone to deal with the ITU than he was." The crisis ended, the printers stayed, and partly as a result of this dispute, Harry came to feel that Alicia was soft on unions. "Whenever these negotiations have reached a point of extreme difficulty," he wrote her years later, "the record is quite clear that you have always weakened and have forced me to take the strong stand that has accomplished our objectives."

The ITU turned out to be a far more serious problem for the *Review-Star* than for *Newsday*. Late in 1947, months after his contract with the printers had expired, James Stiles filed a suit against the printers for a violation of the Taft-Hartley Act. The union presented the publisher with a list of working conditions and told him that, if he didn't meet them, the printers would consider themselves locked out. Stiles called it a strike, but the printers called it a lockout, and they picketed the *Review-Star* offices in Rockville Centre. *Newsday* printers joined them on the lines. Later, Stiles hired scabs, but the ITU organized them too. In the middle of all this, *Newsday*'s rapid growth created a demand for more printers in its composing room, and *Newsday* started hiring them away from the *Review-Star*.

Stiles had a more consuming interest at the time than averting a strike: his role as a director and later as chairman of the executive committee and chairman of the board of directors of the Old Country Trotting Association, which ran the Roosevelt Raceway harness track. "If Stiles had dropped his activities at the Raceway completely, and devoted all of his energies to personal negotiation with the union," wrote his biographer,

Edward Uhlan, "he perhaps might have brought about a settlement." But he didn't, and the union struck. In 1949, largely as a result of the wounds inflicted by the ITU strike, Stiles sold the *Review-Star* to S. I. Newhouse, who planned to use it as a base for the expansion of the *Long Island Press* into Nassau County. The full details of the sale to Newhouse's Newspaper Enterprises Inc. did not come out until later.

IV

NOT ALL OF Alicia's personnel problems came from unions. She also had to worry about her edition in Suffolk County, which had provided more than its share of headaches since she opened it on July 17, 1944.

Expanding eastward to Suffolk, which was more than twice the size of Nassau but far more rural and sparsely populated, had made good strategic sense. Still, it was a bad time tactically to start a new edition, since the Nassau version was still so shaky. "*Newsday* was not, in my estimation, a grand success in Nassau in 1944," said Vinnie Bordash, who had the job of boosting the Suffolk circulation from 1,800 to 5,000 in the first year. "It was still a cruddy newspaper. You had more gypsies coming in and out of *Newsday* — no stability."

Building the new paper wasn't easy. Newspaper readers in Suffolk could buy a Long Island edition of the *Brooklyn Eagle* if they wanted a daily, but most Suffolk readers got their news from a chain of weekly papers owned by the county Republican leader, W. Kingsland Macy. As time went on, Macy's papers began referring to *Newsday* as "that Nassau-minded daily," in an attempt to brand the new paper as a carpetbagger from the wicked west. At the start, neither readers nor advertisers were receptive to the Suffolk edition of *Newsday*. "I didn't like working for them," said Peter Sturcke, who sold ads for the new Suffolk edition. "They had very little circulation to start off with. It was a rough deal." Advertisers watched the results of the ads, and they weren't happy. "They didn't see any response to the small circulation they were getting," said Sturcke, who left *Newsday* after a year. Making that circulation grow was difficult, largely because the newspaper was so thin — 12 pages altogether. "I used to beg Alicia for 16 pages, particularly on the day the weeklies came out," Bordash said. "How the hell could you sell it? It wasn't serving its purpose."

The reporting staff also had its problems. Just as some government officials in Nassau, accustomed to dealing with the *Review-Star*, had been cool to *Newsday* reporters, some Suffolk officials did not cooperate with the *Newsday* staff nearly as well as they did with Macy's weekly papers. "We all had that problem," said Marie Carlson, who joined the staff a few weeks after it started. "Macy had it pretty well tied up. They didn't call him King Macy for nothing." In addition, the staff was outnumbered and untutored. Carlson, for example, came to *Newsday* with no reporting experience and was assigned to cover the Town of Babylon. What they had going for them, like the original paper in Hempstead, was enthusiasm. "We always had a feeling of adventure, because we were something new," said Marie De Carmine Quinn, who came to *Newsday* from the weekly *Bay Shore Journal* to be women's editor. Beyond the burden of inexperience, the staff also worked under less-than-ideal conditions. The first office was a storefront at 17 East Main Street in Bay Shore, one of the primary shopping villages in Suffolk. The circulation and advertising desks were in the front. Behind a partition, the reporting staff sat in a tiny space at the rear, near the toilet, which served as men's room, ladies' room and a darkroom for the photographer. At the start, they sent their copy into Hempstead on a teletype machine, and they sent longer stories and photographs in with a messenger named Gene Parker, who logged 50,000 miles a year between Bay Shore and Hempstead. Over the next few years, as the paper grew, the need for space forced them to move three times to different offices along Main Street.

They also worked under a less-than-ideal editor, a picaresque character almost as inexperienced in the ways of daily journalism as his young staff was. Bill Steele had walked into *Newsday* one day and announced to Hathway that he was looking for a job. His resume, to put it generously, was skimpy. He was a college graduate who had taken a few journalism courses and spent the next few years bouncing around America, trying to gather material for a book. In the process, he had worked on a skyscraper, fallen 16 floors into a truck filled with sand and emerged from the hospital two years later with a bad back, no book and a legitimate reason for a 4-F draft status. On the basis of this background, Hathway hired him — yet another example of Hathway Hunch Hiring. Then, after Steele had briefly covered the Village of Hempstead, Hathway got it into his head that Steele could run the Suffolk paper.

Steele had his strong points. He was intelligent, well educated and personally honest. He believed strongly in the brotherhood of man and objected if he heard someone say anything derogatory about an ethnic group. So the staff liked him. "He was very charming, very funny, very bright and sort of irrepressible," Carlson said. But he also had some weaknesses, including a drinking problem and the distraction of an affair with a younger woman who worked in the Hempstead office. But his real problems weren't personal. They involved the little matter of turning out decent stories and meeting deadlines. Steele had only Quinn, Carlson and Don Abrew to fill the paper, and sometimes he apparently used his imagination. "I think when he was drinking, it was impossible for him not to fantasize," Quinn said. Before long, Vinnie Bordash began to notice. "I read the paper from cover to cover," Bordash said. "I discovered that some of the stories were truly fictitious." So Alicia and Hathway came out and met with Bordash. Not surprisingly, Hathway defended Steele. "I said fine, but that I could give them the documentation," said Bordash. "Alicia took it from there." Steele's brief career came to a climax only three months after the new Suffolk paper started. One night, his copy was late and nobody could find him. So the Suffolk paper ended up filled with Nassau news. The next day, Steele sent a telegram from Massachusetts, announcing that he had run away with a *Newsday* copy girl and would not be back.

The replacement for Steele was a far more conservative figure, Charlie Fuller, a lanky redhead with freckles, a small mustache and a Scottish accent — as responsible as Steele was flaky. His successor was Richard Wyse, a veteran reporter from the *Review-Star*, who was married to another *Newsday* reporter, Bea Jones. Finally, after the war, Hathway settled on a longer-term solution for Suffolk. Ralph Hausrath, who had started at *Newsday* as a copy boy and gone on to become a reporter, returned from the Navy and suddenly found himself the Suffolk editor. "I really think the reason they sent me was because they knew I had been an officer in the Navy and I could crack the whip a little bit," Hausrath said. "I wanted everybody to shape up and fly right." Hausrath got tough, for example, when he came in one Sunday and found reporters for the weeklies sitting in the *Newsday* office, using *Newsday* phones — as they had apparently been doing for a while. In addition, he began firing people when it was necessary. His tight-ship techniques did not make him a popular figure, but his staff respected him. "He was all business," said Bob Pfeifle, one of his reporters. "He had his hands full, because he had all sorts of characters working for him."

One of the most colorful characters of them all was Pfeifle, who had grown up in Babylon and worked for two local weeklies. His family tried to divert him from the newspaper business into something more respectable, a career at Sears, but Pfeifle spent a bit too long at a bar one day when he should have been pursuing his future in merchandising, and that was that. When he returned from the service late in 1945, Pfeifle came to *Newsday* and worked on rewrite. Like other *Newsday* reporters and editors of that time, Pfeifle went to great lengths for a drink. Since the bars in New York City closed later than those in Nassau County, Pfeifle would have a last drink at one of the *Newsday* hangouts in Nassau, then hop in his car and head quickly west for a few more drinks at a bar in Queens and sometimes a few more in Manhattan. Then he would drive back east to his home in Suffolk County, not always perfectly sober. "It got to be a hazardous trip," Pfeifle said. Finally, Pfeifle transferred to the Suffolk office, ridding himself of the long trips but not of the drinking. Hanging out in bars was a primary reporting tool, and Pfeifle knew as well as anyone how to convert thirst into journalism.

One of Pfeifle's most valuable connections was a young attorney named Sidney Siben, whose office in Bay Shore was near *Newsday*. Early in his career, Siben learned that being friendly with *Newsday* meant that his name would appear in the paper, which meant that clients would appear at his door. Siben had first encountered *Newsday* when he was representing a builder who was putting up homes for veterans. "He built roads with holes in them; they had no sewers, and a lot of veterans made complaints to *Newsday*," Siben said. "One day, we had a big rain and there were some puddles, pretty deep, in front of the houses, behind the houses, on the streets. In order to make it interesting, I think it was Alan Hathway who concocted the idea to rent a rowboat." The next day, a big photo of that rowboat, outside the homes built by Siben's client, appeared in *Newsday*, along with what Siben called "the most vitriolic, vicious story." So Siben prepared to sue *Newsday*. Before long, he found himself undergoing the ordeal of lunch with Hathway. "He gave me about five martinis," Siben said. "I can only take two. He had about seven." Siben proposed to Hathway that *Newsday* make amends for the story and the imaginative photo by offering his client free advertising, but Hathway had to check that with Alicia. "She said absolutely not," Siben said. But *Newsday* did give the builder publicity. "He advertised in *Newsday* after that," Siben said, "and they gave him good coverage and good positions in the paper."

In another Siben-*Newsday* confrontation, a returned veteran had too much to drink and stumbled into the wrong house in a row of identical tract homes and fell asleep next to a teenaged girl. When she awoke, she pressed charges against him. The *Newsday* story triggered an avalanche of angry letters to the girl, criticizing her for charging a veteran with a crime. "The girl almost had a nervous breakdown," Siben said. So he called Hathway and they agreed that *Newsday* would pay her medical bills and Siben wouldn't sue. As a result, Hathway said to him, " 'Sidney, I owe you,' " and Siben and *Newsday* continued to build a symbiotic relationship. "Anytime I won a case, big headlines," Siben said. "When I'd lose a case, *Newsday* never even reported it. I can honestly say that my success is partially, if not mostly, due not only to my ability, but to *Newsday*'s help." In return, Siben gave *Newsday* a flow of story tips, access to his clients, and other services — a case of whiskey to the *Newsday* office at Christmas, free legal representation for *Newsday* reporters, the use of his cabin cruiser. Pfeifle, covering county courts in Riverhead, was another beneficiary of Siben's largesse. "He told me, 'Anytime you want to have a drink, stop in the Court Restaurant and charge it to me,' " Pfeifle said.

Pfeifle was by no means the only roguish character that Hausrath inherited. As soon as he arrived in Suffolk, Hausrath noticed that one of his other reporters, Kirk Price, was friendly with Hathway and Jack Altshul. "Right away, I could see that Kirk was Sammy Glick," Hausrath said. "I had the feeling that Kirk Price was too palsy-walsy with too many politicians. I got the feeling eventually that Hathway liked it that way, because it kept me off balance." Hausrath suspected that Price was just waiting in the bushes for a chance to take over.

Though Alicia had a greater affinity for Nassau County than for Suffolk, she visited with Hausrath regularly, sought his views and read the Suffolk edition carefully. She also took concrete steps to make the Suffolk paper grow. Initially, it covered only the populous South Shore towns of Babylon and Islip, stopping short of the huge Town of Brookhaven, which was bigger in area than all of Nassau County. On April 5, 1948, less than four years after the Suffolk paper opened, she expanded it into Patchogue, the prime shopping village in Brookhaven. To help cover the Town of Brookhaven, they hired Frank Mooney, who had already done part-time work for *Newsday*. Mooney sent his copy from Patchogue to the office in Bay Shore on a bus, which stopped outside the office door. This was not big-city journalism, but it was temporarily necessary, if *Newsday* was to keep growing.

A few months later, Alicia ordered another expansion, to the growing North Shore towns of Huntington and Smithtown. The North Suffolk edition of *Newsday* started on October 14, 1948, in Huntington, an increasingly busy shopping village. Kirk Price, beginning his rise, ran the three-room office on Green Street. "He was as autonomous as he could get away with," Hausrath said. The North Suffolk paper ran into the same problem as the South Suffolk paper had confronted — a strong tradition of weeklies. In this case, the opposition was the *Long Islander*, a venerable paper established 110 years earlier by an ambitious teenaged poet named Walt Whitman. So *Newsday* had image problems immediately. "It was not popular in Huntington; it was looked down upon," said Inez Heine, a society reporter for the new paper. "I think *Newsday* was considered yellow journalism." Advertisers were as reluctant as readers. "They wouldn't even talk to me, some of these people," said Elizabeth Casey, then the only woman doing outside ad sales for *Newsday*. "I think they thought our paper was too Democratic, and there were an awful lot of Republicans there. They said, 'We don't need a tabloid.' " But her persistence began to pay off: A year later, advertisers started calling her.

The Suffolk paper began to wear away the resistance gradually, for a number of reasons. It was a daily, which made it more responsive to what readers needed. The early coverage of local high school sports was one thing that a daily could do better than the weeklies. "It was a big factor in the gains in Suffolk circulation," said Lou DeFichy, who left a competitive weekly and became the Suffolk paper's sports editor. Another factor was the proven *Newsday* technique of using the appeal of the carrier boys to make up for the shortcomings of the newspaper. "We had a big banner saying, 'Busy Boys Are Better Boys,' " said John Brignoli, a circulation supervisor in Suffolk. "The boys did a lot to overcome resistance."

Even as the Suffolk paper was gaining acceptance, it was exacerbating a long-term *Newsday* problem. Call it The Oz Factor. From the beginning, young reporters would arrive at *Newsday*, toil in the suburbs for a while and begin looking longingly to the west, where the City of New York gave off an alluring glow on the horizon, like the one that drew Dorothy and her friends toward the Emerald City of Oz. The establishment of the Suffolk paper created a new westward gravitational pull for Suffolk reporters, toward the main office in Nassau, while *Newsday* was striving to grow eastward.

V

AT THE SAME time that *Newsday* was developing the Suffolk paper, the growth of the staff in Nassau kept squeezing more and more people into the tiny showroom in Hempstead.

To cope with the crowding, Alicia had to rely on makeshift arrangements.

Toward the end of the war, for example, they built a balcony in the forward part of the showroom. At various times, it housed the city desk, the sports department, the library and the financial staff. Before the war ended, the advertising department moved out of the showroom entirely and occupied a two-story white house on Main Street, freeing room in the main plant for other uses. Space was not the only problem: Despite everyone's best efforts to insulate the skylight over the composing room, the rain, snow and wind forced their way in. During the winter, some of the printers wore woolen caps at work. In the summer, they tried everything to cool the composing room down, including sprinklers on the roof and large exhaust fans. But the heat was still so bad, John MacCary remembered, that the heavy carts that carried around type would sink into the floor. In the editorial offices, the heat forced Ruth Herrera, a photo retoucher, to sit at her place with her feet in a pot of cold water. Ultimately, putting out a newspaper in an automobile showroom became intolerable. Harry and Alicia had to find a way out. Just as they had recruited editorial writers among their Falaise houseguests, they stumbled upon a solution to their building problems on the estate's tennis court. His name was Albert Wood, Henry Ford's architect.

Wood was born in Manhattan and raised in Boston, and eventually gravitated to Alaska for the great gold rush. Later, he moved to Seattle and learned architecture as an apprentice draftsman. Before World War I, a depression brought construction to a halt in that whole region. So Wood moved to Detroit and ended up on the payroll of the Ford Motor Company. He designed Ford's powerhouse at Highland Park, Michigan, along with plants in this country and abroad, in Ireland and England. He also designed standardized houses for Ford workers at Dearborn, worked on the Henry Ford mansion, Fair Lane, and created the huge Henry Ford Hospital, built almost on the Ford assembly-line principal. Every room was virtually identical to every other room, and there were no large wards, where poorer patients would be lost in anonymity. When the Great Depression hit in 1929, architecture was one of the first casualties. Wood sold his home in Grosse Pointe and moved east in 1930. Looking for a place to live, he settled on Long Island, rented a house in Port Washington and commuted into Manhattan, where he got a job managing the Paramount Building. In 1932, the family launched its own business in Port Washington, Albert Wood and Five Sons, which specialized in designing, building and refinishing furniture. "His idea of starting this firm was a way of combating the Depression," said his daughter, Margaret. "He didn't want his children to be dependent on a job."

Working together turned the Woods inward and made them an unusually close family. So it was natural that when they glided into the orbit of the Guggenheims, that relationship involved the entire family. The Woods came in contact with the Guggenheims through Warren William, a B-movie actor who was friendly with Harry and Alicia and had a relative in Port Washington who knew Albert Wood's son, Francis. One day when the Guggenheims were looking for a fourth for tennis at Falaise, Francis Wood drew the assignment. From that moment on, the Woods were regular tennis partners at Falaise. Alicia became interested in the whole family. She sent wedding presents, then silver cups when the children started coming along. After the marriage of another of Wood's sons, Gardner, the Guggenheims allowed him and his wife to stay at the gatehouse at Falaise until they arranged housing.

Though the relationship between the Woods and the Guggenheims was more than just a tennis friendship, the weekend tennis games at Falaise were a central element of it. Regularly, George Abbott, the theatrical director, would arrive with a group of show girls, whose role was to look on, beautifully, while he played. Harry's friend, Bernard Baruch, would also come by to watch. After tennis, they'd sip drinks and the Woods would pick as many Falaise peaches as they could carry on their racquets. The only jarring note in this pleasant tableau was the occasional tennis argument between Harry and Alicia, whether they were playing on the same team or as opponents. Harry had played tennis at Cambridge, and he considered himself a far better player than Alicia. He was right. "Alicia's really quite poor at sports, but, as with everything she does, she makes up for it with a furious intensity," said Abbott, who suggested that she take lessons from Sam Shore, a local tennis pro. "She wasn't natural, but she came along adequately well," Shore said. "She had a very good idea of how the game should be played, especially in doubles. . . . She had a very good forehand and a conservative backhand." To avoid fighting, they devised a separate-but-equal tennis regimen in which the Wood family was the constant. "Instead of all of us playing together, we'd give Harry his tennis and then we'd stick around and give Alicia hers," Paul Wood said. "He preferred that three of us went out and played with him. . . . We'd go out with George and her and have more of a social game. He'd shower and count his money."

It was at one of these tennis sessions, in 1946, that Albert Wood mentioned that he and Paul had started building an office for the family firm, on Pleasant Avenue in Port Washington. "Alicia said, 'I'd like to see it,'" Paul Wood remembered. "So after the tennis, we drove over here. She looked at it, just half-built, cinder block, the simplest kind of building, and she said, 'That's what I want for *Newsday*.' She didn't want anything fancy." Not long afterward, Albert Wood had lunch with Alicia and the general manager, Henry Page. She told Wood that Harry liked his inexpensive construction. Then she tapped him on the shoulder with a soup spoon and told him that Harry had decided that he should be the architect and start immediately on a site search. Page had in mind a more traditional high-rise newspaper building, with the presses in a semi-basement and offices in the floors above. He wanted to locate this substantial, impressive structure in downtown Hempstead Village, or right in the middle of the Garden City shopping and office district. "My idea of a factory on the outskirts of Garden City had no appeal for him," Wood wrote.

Wood and his wife, Louise, started driving around, looking for the appropriate place. What they came up with was a 10-acre site, zoned for residences, in a sparsely developed area on the eastern of fringes of Garden City. The land was almost 700 feet deep, with 330 feet of frontage on Stewart Avenue, named for the founder of Garden City, Alexander Tunney Stewart, a Scottish immigrant whose dry-goods establishment at Broadway and Chambers Street in Manhattan was considered the first department store in the world. The site had everything *Newsday* needed, including a railroad siding, which made the delivery of newsprint easier. So Alicia sent Harry a note, outlining Wood's plans. "The next morning she phoned me her husband's reply," Wood wrote. " 'Buy the property contingent upon Albert having property rezoned. One or two acres should meet our needs. Arrange to sell balance.' "

Since *Newsday* still was not very profitable, Harry had no desire to spend large amounts of money on a grandiose building and a lot of land. "He always insisted we build no further than three years ahead," said George Schwartzkopf, who had been Harry's aide in the Navy and now was one of his top assistants on the business side of *Newsday*. "His philosophy was to do what we had to do now. . . . We'll take care of the future when it gets here." Wood argued that the plan for the administration building should include provisions for a second floor someday, and Harry wondered why on earth they would ever need a second floor. Ultimately, Wood won the argument and included footings for a second floor.

Wood did not entirely give up on expansion. Without showing it to Harry, he put together a model of a "maximum" *Newsday* plant of the future. "My theory was that growth was inevitable or we face decay," Wood wrote. The immediate plan was to build the plant in several stages — separate buildings joined together as construction progressed. The pressroom would be first, followed by the composing room and finally the administration building. The legal approvals were complicated because the site was within the boundaries of the Village of Garden City, which had a tight building code. "A few feet east would be easier," Schwartzkopf said. "I think they wanted a Garden City address." But finally, they opened the first building, the pressroom, in April, 1947. "That was something of a disaster as far as Harry Guggenheim was concerned," Schwartzkopf said, "because he was led to believe it would be more economical than it was." Nonetheless, it got the pressroom operations out of a converted auto service area and into a real pressroom. It also started what became known as the pony express era of *Newsday* history.

Though the presses were in Garden City, the editorial staff and the composing room were still in Hempstead. So the staff in Hempstead would write and edit the copy, set it in type, and make a cardboard mat, which would later be used in the pressroom to make the cylindrical metal plate that would go on the press itself. In Hempstead, the staff would roll up the mat, place it in a special container to maintain its humidity, and put it in a beat-up old Crosley, and later a Jeep. One of three men — John Hartmann, Bud Ward or Richard Beecher — would drive it through residential streets to the pressroom in Garden City. "Sometimes we were speeding," Hartmann said, and the neighbors called to complain. When the composing room in Garden City was completed in early 1948, the pony express carried edited copy to Garden City, instead of mats. Not all of the mats or the copy always showed up. "This interim period was pure Mad Hatter," Alicia said. "Many were lost en route and the confusion was staggering."

The pony express era ended in April, 1949, when the non-mechanical departments moved into the new administration building, which was at the front of the property, screening the pressroom, paper storage and composing rooms behind it. In the years ahead, the paper's growth would demand addition after addition to this basic plant. But at least *Newsday* was finally in its own building, selling more than 100,000 papers a day, and its infancy was over.

CHAPTER TEN

Levittown

I

THE MASSIVE SHIFT from city to suburbs after World War II was the product of historical trends that had nothing to do with Alicia Patterson or her newspaper. But the potent force of Patterson-Guggenheim luck put *Newsday* in the right place at the right time to profit from the culmination of those trends.

As the postwar tide of development brought hundreds of thousands of new residents to Long Island, the aggressiveness of *Newsday*, plus the nearsightedness of its competitors, turned many of these new Long Islanders into *Newsday* readers. By the time the New York City papers realized what was happening, it was too late. The circulation growth that should have gone to more established, more professional newspapers had gone instead to Alicia's toy. At the start, Harry and Alicia had not understood the paper's growth potential either. Before *Newsday* opened, they had gone to Virginia to tour the *Winchester Star* with Harry F. Byrd Jr., the son of Harry's friend, the governor and United States senator, and they had expressed modest goals. "I remember them saying that they hoped that their paper would be able to hit 25,000," Byrd said. But before they knew what happened, the forces of suburban growth had carried *Newsday* along. "We just got on the escalator," Harry said, "and it started up."

The flight from the city to the suburbs, which provided that dizzying ride upward for *Newsday*, was a total reversal of the original urban order. In the classic European city, almost everyone lived within a mile of the workplace. The city walls protected the inhabitants from invaders and provided a sense of security. The center of the city was the place where the wealthy and powerful wanted to be, and the area beyond belonged to outcasts. But the growth of the cities brought more people, more noise, more dirt, more epidemics. The city came to be seen not as a safe refuge, but as a source of danger. In the earliest European cities, the middle classes and lower classes lived in close proximity, separated only by a rigid caste system. Later, the middle classes began to desire more physical distance from the lower classes. In addition, the nuclear family grew more important, culminating in an Anglican Evangelical movement that made family closeness a religious imperative, to protect women and children from the moral contamination of the city. As a result, the merchant middle class of London began in the eighteenth century to develop the suburb. The first step was the weekend villa, where the family could escape from the city together once a week. Later, the merchants made these villas their primary residences and commuted daily into the city. That idea eventually took full root in nineteenth-century America, where inexpensive land and unprecedented per-capita wealth made possible the profusion of the ideal suburban living unit: a detached home outside the city, surrounded by a yard.

The first true commuter suburb, Kenneth T. Jackson argued in *Crabgrass Frontier*, his comprehensive history of the suburbs, was Brooklyn Heights — across the East River from Manhattan's flourishing downtown. It was the establishment of Robert Fulton's steam ferry service between Manhattan and Brooklyn Heights in 1814 that made possible the development of Brooklyn as a suburban haven for the middle class. In the decades that followed, the development of the electric streetcar, commuter railroads and the automobile eventually brought suburban growth to areas further from the central city. Besides the transportation revolution, another technological innovation was crucial to the growth of the suburbs: the development of the balloon-frame construction method in nineteenth-century Chicago. Using this method, two workers could put up a house more quickly than 20 builders using the heavy timber structure of traditional frame houses.

All of these factors added up to a dizzying rush of suburban growth after World War I. In the first decade when the automobile began to have a serious impact, the 1920s, the suburbs of the 96 largest cities grew twice as fast as the cities themselves. Nassau County nearly tripled in population, from 126,000 to more than 303,000. But the Great Depression brought suburban development to a halt and triggered the creation of two New Deal programs that would profoundly affect the future of the American suburbs. The first was the Home Owners Loan Corporation, created in 1933 to prevent further foreclosures on private homes. The HOLC made the long-term mortgage, with equal payments over the life of the loan, a permanent fixture in American life. In the process, it also codified racial prejudice. In an attempt to standardize appraisals across the country, to make accurate predictions about the future of the housing that it was being asked to finance, the agency developed "Residential Security Maps" that contained four categories of urban neighborhoods — First, Second, Third and Fourth, also described by the letters A, B, C and D or the colors green, blue, yellow and red. Neighborhoods that were African-American — even predominantly white neighborhoods with a handful of black residents — almost always ended up in the D, "red" category. The HOLC actually seems to have extended most of its help to homeowners in the C and D neighborhoods. But its appraisal system helped private lending institutions to make discriminatory lending decisions, which kept mortgages out of the "red" neighborhoods, leading to the term "redlining."

Far more significant than the Home Owners Loan Corporation was the creation of the Federal Housing Administration in 1934. The idea of the FHA was to relieve unemployment in the home construction industry, without a major increase in government spending. The agency did not lend money to homeowners, but encouraged private lending institutions to lend it, by insuring the institution against loss on the loans. Before the FHA, a buyer had to be able to make a down payment of at least 30 percent of the total cost of a house. Once the FHA came along and took the risk out of lending, the buyer could put down less than 10 percent of the purchase price. This fundamental change opened up home ownership to thousands of Americans who could not have afforded it earlier. Besides making houses more affordable, the FHA also made them more livable, by establishing construction standards that governed the whole housing industry. Builders began to construct all of their homes to FHA standards, whether the FHA ultimately insured the mortgages or not, because buyers demanded compliance with those standards. But at the same time, the FHA hastened the decay of the cities. "In practice, FHA insurance went to new residential developments on the edges of metropolitan areas, to the neglect of core cities," Jackson wrote. "Reflecting the racist tradition of the United States, the Federal Housing Administration was extraordinarily concerned with 'inharmonious racial or nationality groups.' " The agency's clear preference was the single-family home in the exclusively white suburb, and that policy had a profound effect in shaping postwar development. Nassau County is a prime example. In the FHA's first quarter-century, from 1934 until 1960, it insured 87,183 mortgages in Nassau County, for a total of $781,378,559 — or $601 per resident. In the same period, the FHA's activity in the inner city was minuscule. In Brooklyn, for example, it insured 15,438 mortgages for a total of $140,330,137, or $53 per capita. As blacks migrated from the South to the cities of the North, whites fled to the suburbs, with the help of the government.

On top of all these factors, Congress enacted in 1944 the Servicemen's Readjustment Act, known as the G.I. Bill, which created the Veterans Administration mortgage program. By the end of World War II, the suburban ideal was firmly rooted in the American psyche and the government was putting its considerable weight into the task of suburb-building. For 16 years, the Depression and the war had stifled the home-construction industry, as the number of marriages and births was soaring. At war's end, millions of servicemen returned home and found that there was no place to live. They had to move in with their parents or live in makeshift housing, such as quonset huts, trolley cars and surplus grain bins. The result of this surging demand, Jackson wrote, was that "the great American land rush after 1945 was one of the largest mass movements in our history." And when the postwar migration from the City of New

York toward Long Island began in earnest, *Newsday* was sitting there in the heart of Nassau County, waiting for it.

II

WELL BEFORE THE end of the war, Alicia had begun to focus on the need for housing. At least part of her education on that issue came from Albert Wood, her Port Washington neighbor, tennis friend and later her architect.

Wood had learned all about cheap housing by serving as the construction engineer for Dearborn Construction Company, the Ford subsidiary that built homes for Ford workers at Dearborn, Michigan. On that project, the key to delivering affordable homes was standardized construction. The process of building the house followed the spirit of the automobile assembly line that Ford pioneered. Instead of the product moving along the line, construction crews moved from house to house, performing the same function. In late 1943, Wood wrote Alicia a letter on housing and sent her a newspaper article about the homes that he had built in Dearborn. A few months later, Alicia ran an editorial that showed she understood what was coming. "During the postwar period we will doubtless see a big increase in our population," the editorial said. "Men coming home from the wars to young wives and new babies will want to settle down in the country so that their children may play on the grass instead of on the pavements of New York City."

Wood wrote Alicia again in September, 1944. "I think it would be conservative to say that ninety percent of all the single homes built in the United States in the decade following this war will have to be priced under five thousand dollars," Wood wrote. This letter obviously impressed Alicia. Starting a week later, *Newsday* carried a five-part series by Madeline Ryttenberg about postwar housing, based almost entirely on an interview with Albert Wood. A month after the *Newsday* series, the *Saturday Evening Post* carried an article, "They'll Build Neighborhoods, Not Houses," detailing the postwar construction plans of a home builder named William J. Levitt. *Newsday* had a good sense of what was ahead, but so did others. It was in the air.

Once the war ended and the veterans arrived home, they began doing some of their own advocacy. A group called the American Veterans Committee was a significant force in the push for housing for veterans. The AVC had two highly visible proponents on Long Island. One was Franklin Delano Roosevelt Jr., the son of the late President. The other was Michael Whitney Straight, a wealthy young man whose parents had founded the liberal magazine *The New Republic*. Straight studied at the London School of Economics and later at Trinity College, Cambridge. There, he joined a Communist Party cell and drifted into the orbit of Anthony Blunt, a Soviet agent in Britain who recruited Straight to spy for Russia. Back in the United States, Straight volunteered for service in the

State Department, where he indulged in a dilettante espionage that never amounted to much more than leaking copies of his own memos. In 1941, he left the government and became the Washington correspondent of *The New Republic*. In 1942, he broke contact with his Soviet courier, keeping silence about his espionage for more than two decades before he told what he knew about Blunt. Following the war, Straight became the publisher of *The New Republic* and began to be active in the American Veterans Committee's push for housing. (The AVC itself, Straight remembered, was a target of Communist Party infiltration at the time, but more in New York City, Chicago and Los Angeles than on Long Island.) Straight lent his name and his Old Westbury estate, Applegreen, to the cause, for a huge housing rally in June, 1946. Since he was running *The New Republic* and commuting back and forth to Manhattan, he left the day-to-day details to a young veteran named Paul Townsend.

Quickly, Straight and Townsend realized that Nassau County Executive J. Russel Sprague was not inclined to treat the housing problems of veterans seriously. "Sprague was sitting on top of the status quo," Straight said. "Why should he be for anything? He didn't have to reach out to the voters." In fact, Sprague was worried about new voters pouring in from the City of New York, who were not likely to be Republicans. "The influx of this new class of people caused a great deal of concern to the leadership in the Republican Party, who were oriented to an extremely conservative, ingrown type of existence," said Joseph Carlino, then a young Long Beach Republican, who later rose to county Republican chairman and Speaker of the Assembly. Long Island was so conservative, in fact, that in the 1920s, it had been a Ku Klux Klan stronghold. "When I first got into politics, some of the older members of the Republican Party were known to have been active Klansmen," said Carlino, who actually saw hooded Klansmen out in the open in Nassau when he was a boy. After the war, the Republican Party developed a welcome-wagon approach to wooing the new residents moving out from the city, but Sprague was still fearful of the influx. "He tried to slow it down," Carlino said. "He wasn't very successful. But the disposition was not to open the floodgates."

So, in early 1946, Townsend looked elsewhere for support. He settled on Alan Hathway, who was more than willing to help, because it gave *Newsday* a chance to nip at the heels of Russ Sprague and his friend at the *Review-Star*, Jim Stiles, just as *Newsday* had done over the issue of legal ads. "He wasn't just an editor," Townsend said. "He was an entrepreneur-opportunist-organizer. This was his first big organizing on Long Island, and he used me — in a nice way. He used me and I was using him." In this symbiotic relationship, the AVC got publicity and Hathway got a sexy, circulation-building issue. "What gave us a base was precisely *Newsday*," Straight said. "He delivered. That gave us leverage, which gave us political power far in excess of our right to it."

Hathway's zeal for the veterans' cause almost cost him his job. In 1946, the Nassau Independent Voters Association, an offshoot of the AVC, was pushing for the construction of 500 garden apartments on a county golf course. The Republican administration argued that no county had the legal authority to build such housing. "Russ Sprague was going to issue an announcement that was going to devastate us," Townsend said. "Late in the afternoon, it was brought around to Alan. Alan called me. He says, 'If you would get over here, give us an answer, I will print your answer at the same time. . . .' Well, I brought Straight over and Alan put us into Alicia's private office, and on Alicia's own typewriter, he helped us write the answer, which he then published the next day in sort of a side-by-side, giving us each equal space." Word of this exercise reached Forrest Corson, Sprague's public relations man, who told his boss. "Russ Sprague called up Harry Guggenheim and said, 'Do you realize what this managing editor of yours has just done?' " Townsend said. "Harry must have told Alicia and said 'Fire that bastard' or something to that effect. Alicia wouldn't fire him, but said to Alan something strong, like, 'Don't you ever do anything like that in my office again. . . .' There were many times that he almost lost his job. He was always going a little far, but Alicia always protected him against Harry."

III

THE YEAR AFTER Alan Hathway began salivating over the juicy housing issue that the American Veterans Committee had presented him, his golden opportunity arrived.

On May 7, 1947, the headline on top of page one was "2,000 $60 Rentals/ Due in L.I. Project." The story, about a huge housing development in the community of Island Trees, gave thousands of veterans reason to hope. "Rental housing — a lot of it — is coming to Long Island," the story began. "Workers will break ground here within two weeks on a sixteen million dollar, 2,000 home project — termed by its builder the largest development of its kind in the nation. When completed, the new homes will rent at $60 per month." The builder was the firm of Levitt & Sons, who had already made themselves into builders to be reckoned with on Long Island. The founder, Abraham Levitt, was a lawyer who had foreclosed on some mortgages, taken possession of the land and decided to build houses on it. From his small start in Rockville Centre, Levitt grew into a builder of substance in the 1930s, turning out homes for $12,000 to $20,000. His partners in the firm were his two sons, Alfred, a soft-spoken designer without formal architectural training, and William, the hard-driving, brash businessman who was the primary spokesman and operator.

During the war, the Levitts gained their first experience in building low-cost housing: 2,350 rental units for the Navy at Norfolk, Virginia. The year before the war ended, the Levitts were already taking the first steps toward realizing their plans for large-scale postwar construction on Long Island: buying land and starting to amass the huge inventory of building materials that would make large-scale construction possible, using the same kind of assembly-line techniques that Albert Wood had used in producing homes for Ford workers in Dearborn. Right after the war, in 1946, the Levitts had built large, expensive houses — five and a half rooms, cellar and garage for $9,990 — but they found that people wanted a smaller house at a smaller price. So they prepared to provide houses for $6,990, available for $60 a month in rent, with a purchase option. In order to produce that inexpensive housing, the Levitts developed a smoothly efficient system: They controlled the price of lumber by shipping it all, precut, from the Levitt mill in California to the Levitt yard in Roslyn. They kept down the cost of other building materials by buying from North Shore Supply Company, a Levitt-owned dealer. To save on the cost of the concrete, they acquired their own fleet of cement mixers. Each day, trucks bearing the precut lumber and other materials rolled out of the Roslyn yard and dropped the materials off at the building site, where swarms of workers moved from house to house, each crew performing its own specialized function over and over again. For all these steps, the Levitts employed subcontractors who worked only for the Levitts and no one else — their fees established by negotiation rather than by bidding.

Almost at the same moment as *Newsday* carried the story of the Levitt plan, the Levitts encountered a major obstacle: They planned to build the homes without basements, on concrete slabs that contained pipes to provide radiant heating. But the building code of the Town of Hempstead required new homes to have cellars. Before the Levitts could proceed, the town would have to change its ordinance. From the first day that it became clear that the cellar issue was the stumbling block, *Newsday* held nothing back. Reporting the problem on May 8, *Newsday* dredged up Alicia's favorite housing expert, Albert Wood, who pronounced cellarless homes the wave of the future. "I do not believe there is a modern architect of top rank from Frank Lloyd Wright, up or down, who recommends cellar construction today," Wood said. The *Newsday* editorial that day, "Construction and Obstruction," made it clear that a minor technical detail should not stand in the way. "We don't want any nonsense to hold up the Island Trees housing project," the editorial said. "The project is a honey. . . . Maybe it was good enough for Grandpappy to live in a baroque chateau propped up over a hole in the ground, but it is not good enough for us. . . . The Island Trees project is big, practical, and ideal enough to make national news. If it were prevented by the code it would make Long Island a national laughing stock."

Despite this ringing editorial endorsement, the reporter who covered many of the Island Trees stories was skeptical. "I was on the side of the nonbelievers," said Bernadette (Berni) Fisher, who later married the *Newsday* reporter George Wheeler, but continued using her maiden name as a byline — at Alicia's insistence. "I said, 'It's cracker-box town,' and I was having this big argument with Hathway: 'This guy isn't the white-haired savior of the veteran. He's just out to make a buck, like anybody else.' " But Hathway's belief in the growth potential of Long Island was intense, and his involvement in the Levitt crusade was total. "He had the plans for the houses in the office," Fisher said, "and Levitt was in the office on occasion."

The Republican leadership in the county was not nearly as enthusiastic as Hathway. "The villages were scared to death with the change of the building codes," Forrest Corson said. "We had never had any experience with radiant heating. . . . Sprague was between Scylla and Charybdis on the goddamn thing." If the opposition of village officials was the rock, *Newsday* was the hard place. "*Newsday* really went to town on that," Corson said. "They never gave us credit for trying to protect the interests of the people." At one point, the editorial writer Stan Peckham was invited to join Sprague, Representative Leonard Hall and Governor Thomas Dewey on a tour through Nassau County that was apparently designed to go through Island Trees. "As we came back," Peckham remembered, "they said, 'Ho, ho, ho, here's Island Trees. This is where that asshole Bill Levitt wants to build these cheap little houses with no cellars. And he wants to change the name of Island Trees. Well, if he does, he should call it Radiant Heat, because it will never work and they will all freeze to death.'"

Naturally, if Sprague had doubts, so did his ally, James Stiles at the *Review-Star*. His paper reported on May 14 that the town board was likely to change the code, but it indulged in none of the *Newsday* hoopla and drum-beating for Levitt. In an editorial on May 22, the *Review-Star* expressed "misgivings" about the code change. "If a revolutionary change in home construction is in process we will have to recognize it and reconcile ourselves to it," the *Review-Star* said. "But we should be extremely cautious not to permit the existing shortage of houses to stampede us into junking all the precautions that have been adopted to protect individual purchasers and the standard of entire communities." By contrast, a *Newsday* editorial that same day made an emphatic plea for a large turnout at the town hearing on the proposed ordinance change. "That means not only people who hope to live at Island Trees, but everyone who seeks Long Island living quarters, and everyone who has the best interests of all our people at heart," the editorial said. "The outcome of this hearing is that important."

In the three weeks between the Levitt announcement and the town hearing, Hathway kept pounding away, with editorials, stories on the number of applications that had flooded into Levitt's offices, reminders of the hearing and quotes from architects who thought cellarless houses were a tremendous idea. With *Newsday* and veterans' groups beating the drum, hundreds of people showed up at Hempstead's town hall on May 27 for the hearing, jamming the second-floor meeting room and overflowing into the hall and down the stairs into the street.

The young veterans and women with babies were orderly, but they made their point. "Cellar or no cellar doesn't mean anything to me or anyone else here," Staff Sergeant Stanley Cokosky called out from the middle of the room. "We want the houses!" Fisher, who had been so skeptical about Hathway's campaign, remembered: "I was almost stunned at the response of this, because

I was young; I was single. What the hell did I know about being without a home and living with your in-laws? I guess I just couldn't believe that people were that desperate for housing. . . . Actually, I found it very moving." The hearing took only 20 minutes. Councilman Ernest Steinbrenner made the motion to repeal the section of the code requiring cellars, and the board unanimously approved. "There was a lot of applause — just an outburst," Fisher said. "I guess they didn't realize that it had all been settled beforehand. There was no way the board was going to come out and have a split vote on anything like this."

Clearly, *Newsday*'s constant pounding helped to create a turnout for the hearing and an atmosphere in which it would have been painful for town officials to reject the code change. But it is less certain how much credit *Newsday* could legitimately claim for the ultimate outcome. There were other potent forces at play that could have brought about the change, even if *Newsday* had been less energetic on the issue. For one thing, the Levitts knew how to grease a political machine. "William Levitt was no slouch either, when it came to political perception," Joseph Carlino said. "He went to Sprague and some of these other guys and said, 'Well, we're going to have an awful lot of insurance here. Can you recommend a broker?' " If there is one skill that the Republican Party of Nassau County had elevated to an art form, it was the recommendation of insurance brokers: always loyal party workers or public officials. In this case, the Republicans recommended Norman Penny, a former member of Assembly who had acquired a place in the Republican pantheon by sponsoring the legislation that allowed on-track pari-mutuel betting, clearing the way for night harness racing at Roosevelt Raceway, which became a rich source of patronage. "He got all the insurance in Levittown," Carlino said. "Not only on insurance but other things, Levitt was very helpful."

There is also reason to believe that the establishment's opposition to the change was not as strong as it may have appeared. In a 1988 doctoral dissertation, Barbara Kelly, the director of the Long Island Studies Institute at Hofstra University, pointed out that the man who sold Levitt much of the land for the original Island Trees project, George Hubbell, was a well-connected figure in Nassau County who could have used his influence to oppose the development. "I see no signs that he opposed it," Kelly said. Hubbell's Merillon Corporation was one of two holding companies created by the heirs to the wife of Alexander T. Stewart, who had bought nearly 9,000 acres of publicly owned land in 1869 to build his model community at Garden City. The community failed initially, because people weren't interested in renting the houses that Stewart's organization built. But the eastern portion of Stewart's land remained intact, out of the hands of spot developers, until the Levitts bought it. "Of the 1,259 acres on which Levitt would build in 1947, Merillon owned 775 acres (61.5%) in 1942," Kelly wrote.

The ownership of so much of the Island Trees land by a holding company also casts some doubt on the validity of an enduring Levittown myth: that Levitt was able to buy so much potato farm acreage because a crop-destroying bug called the golden nematode had drastically curtailed the agricultural value of potato fields. It is true that Nassau County farmers fought bitterly in the summer of 1947 against the state Department of Agriculture, which imposed a quarantine on 4,700 of the 11,000 acres of potatoes in the county. The quarantine prevented farmers from planting on the affected acreage. But Kelly argued that the nematode was a non-issue. "In any given opportunity, residents will drive out agriculture," she said. "You don't need a golden nematode." Besides, more than 60 percent of the original 1947 Levitt land had been owned by Merillon, not by individual farmers. A column in a Roslyn weekly in December, 1947, said: "The fact is the entire tract upon which the present dwellings are rising has not been worked as farmland for many, many years. In recent years it has just been idle grass land." That, of course, does not mean that the nematode infestation had no effect on the price of other land that the Levitts bought. But it seems sensible at least to scrutinize the nematode myth carefully. "I can't buy the idea that the bug came along, the farmers left and therefore the vacant land became houses," Kelly said.

A far more important element in the equation than the golden nematode was the position of organized labor. Levitt had decided to bypass the unions, hire his workers as subcontractors and pay them by the number of units they produced, not by the hour. As a result, the building trades unions picketed Levitt sites in 1945 and 1946. When Levitt moved to get the building code changed to allow cellarless homes, Hathway heard rumors that the most powerful labor leader on Long Island, William C. DeKoning Sr., was trying to pressure the town board to reject the code change. DeKoning ran Local 138, International Union of Operating Engineers, and he had founded the umbrella organization for the construction unions, the Building and Construction Trades Council of Nassau and Suffolk Counties. At the start of the Island Trees project, the council picketed the site. But a few days later, members of Local 138 crossed the picket line, breaking the strike — a step that later caused the council to eject Local 138. "It was the most drastic blow that he could deal to labor," said DeKoning's nephew, John DeKoning, a reformer in Local 138. "We could have broken Levitt." Though union labor paved the roads at Island Trees, Bill DeKoning allowed non-union workers to build the houses, using machines that union workers would normally run. "He was letting the contractor use them without engineers and having people go there and collect from the contractor," said William Wilkens, another Local 138 reformer. "Members were denied those jobs."

Through all of this, *Newsday* continued to be Levitt's staunch ally, except during a series of angry protests by homeowners in 1948. Levitt's first misstep was the grandly immodest decision to rename Island Trees and call his development Levittown. Many of the residents thoroughly disliked that idea, and *Newsday* joined them. " 'Island Trees' is a nice, euphonious name, and already famous," the editorial said. "Why change it any more than the name of Arkansas?" *Newsday* continued to refer to it as Island Trees, then adopted the clumsy dateline "Levittown, Island Trees." A more serious struggle broke out when Levitt announced he planned to raise the rents from $60 to $65 a month. Levitt told the residents of the first 1,882 homes that they had two options: They could continue to rent their homes, for a maximum of one more year, at $65, instead of $60. Or they could purchase their homes for $7,990, without a down payment, by meeting monthly carrying charges of $57.50. In an open letter on the editorial page, *Newsday* argued that Levitt was putting his tenants on the spot. "You are not giving them enough time to decide, Mr. Levitt," the editorial said. "Why not work out a fair compromise with your veteran-tenants there in Levittown, and restore the peace of mind those people deserve?" Levitt's response was a promise that tenants could continue to rent their homes from Levitt indefinitely, but the rents would be adjusted every year to keep up with inflation. The tenants could buy their houses at any time, but the $7,990 price would expire on September 1, 1948.

The firm control that the Levitts exercised over purely economic issues also extended to social matters, such as restrictions on wash lines and fences. On the question of race, the control was absolute. The original Island Trees homes came with "Caucasians only" restrictive covenants. The Levitts argued that white people preferred to live with other whites, and the builders were simply complying with those wishes. It was a firm, unbending rule, even after the Supreme Court of the United States declared restrictive covenants non-binding. When the Committee to End Discrimination in Levittown tried to fight Levitt on the racial issue, he fought back by refusing them permission to use his community meeting hall. And when two families allowed black children to play in their yards, Levitt brought eviction proceedings against them. Behind this opposition, the Levitts hinted, there were sinister forces. *Newsday*, which had been willing enough to criticize Levitt on the name-change issue and the rent increases, swallowed his racial policies whole. "Organizations which appear to be either Communist-dominated or Communist-inspired have been attempting to raise a racial issue at Levittown," a 1949 editorial said. "The issue did not exist until it was fostered by people not immediately affected by it. Their only real motive seems to be to set race against race, and, if possible, to bog down the Levitt building program, which means homes for thousands of people. . . . In this country it is the individual's prerogative, not the state's, to decide where he will live. America will eventually beat bigotry with evolution. But we will never do it with revolution."

In the years following the establishment of Levittown, *Newsday* campaigned hard on the side of growth. If builders such as Levitt were going to create homes for thousands of new residents, that influx of population would create a greater demand for services. So *Newsday* helped, for example, to publicize a campaign to raise funds for the construction of hospitals — in cooperation with the radio personality Tex McCrary, the publicist Paul Townsend and the island's largest private employer, Grumman Aircraft Engineering. Hathway also pushed for the creation of new schools, such as a proposed Nassau campus of Long Island University, on the site of a former estate. When the wealthy landowners in the area opposed it, Hathway jumped in with gusto. One day, the reporter Sheldon Binn was writing a news story on the latest development in the controversy — a public hearing on a zoning amendment. Hathway saw Binn's story, didn't think that it sufficiently conveyed *Newsday*'s support for the college, and, with Binn watching, sat down and wrote this lead: "The North Shore's landed aristocracy got up before noon yesterday in a well-heeled attempt to keep a university out of their millionaire's bailiwick." The story also made sure to mention their "parade of sleek cars with liveried chauffeurs." This was not exactly unbiased journalism, but Hathway saw it as necessary in the crusade for a growing Long Island — in the same spirit as the Levittown campaign.

Added together, *Newsday*'s coverage of Levittown was energetic, thorough, constant. It was on the right side of an important issue: affordable housing. This editorial stand, however, was not exactly a profile in courage. The whole campaign helped *Newsday* at least as much as it helped the veterans. And on the hard issue of race, *Newsday* took the easy position, going along with the majority sentiment and failing to exercise leadership. "In the climate of 1947 in the United States," Barbara Kelly said, "you didn't have to be much of a hero to stand up for housing."

IV

THE ARRIVAL OF Levittown created limitless opportunities for *Newsday* to seize control of its market and turn the corner toward long-term financial success.

On the crudest level, Levittown presented an excellent chance for employees to find a place to live. Right after the Hempstead public hearing, a Newspaper Guild newsletter waggishly predicted: "Bet Levitt will have to name one of the streets Hathway's Lane for all the gang that's going to end up there." From the beginning, William Levitt was more than receptive to *Newsday* employees. Stan Peckham, who wrote the editorials, said that Levitt liked them so much that he told Peckham, " 'You got the first house we complete.' " Since Peckham disliked the suburbs intensely, he didn't take Levitt up on his offer, but Levitt still welcomed others from *Newsday*. "He called Hathway and told him, 'If any of your employees want a place, send them over,' " said Ike Eichorn, the photographer who had covered the May 27 hearing. Eichorn ended up with house number 70.

The *Newsday* employees who got into Levitt houses were veterans, as Levitt required of all his initial tenants. But so were thousands of others whose names were on the list. Being *Newsday* employees seemed to give them an edge. As for Hathway himself, his own dealings with a Levitt house were a source of trouble, because he was not a veteran. His friend, Dick Greenamyer, the owner of a pub in Hempstead, was living in a rented house in Levittown but planning to buy a more spacious, upscale Levitt home in Roslyn Heights. He had already begun the process of getting a Veterans Administration mortgage when marital problems cropped up and he decided not to go ahead. "I think I mentioned it to Alan," Greenamyer remembered, "and he said, 'Why don't you sell me the house?' or 'Let me take over the contract.' I don't remember exactly how it happened." At the time, Hathway was living in downtown Hempstead, in a leaky village-owned house that was just about to be torn down. Greenamyer's house looked attractive, but Hathway's non-veteran status was an obstacle. So the two men went to see William Levitt. "I sat in Levitt's office and we discussed this," Greenamyer said. "Would it be all right for me to turn my commitment over to Alan so that he could take the house instead of me? And it absolutely was perfectly all right with Levitt. He said, absolutely, legally and otherwise it was all right." Levitt said he did not remember any such meeting.

Eventually, Hathway moved into the ranch-style house on Dogleg Lane. Later, Greenamyer, already a World War II veteran, went off to the Korean War. After two years on a destroyer, he returned home. Soon after that, a government attorney came to quiz him about the house. "I guess I was charged with fraud," Greenamyer said. "I was the one who took out the veteran's loan, and they thought that he paid me or something to give him the house, which was ridiculous." So Greenamyer had to go to Washington for a Veterans Administration proceeding. Hathway, who had gotten him into the mess in the first place, was his advisor. "He got me the lawyer; he stood by me through the whole thing," Greenamyer said. In this case, loyalty wasn't enough. Hathway was his usual bullish self in the hearing, which didn't help Greenamyer at all. "He alienated everybody there," Greenamyer said. As a result, Greenamyer lost his veteran's benefits. But luckily for him, he had earned a whole new set of veteran's rights in Korea, which he pointed out in a letter. "So they turned around and they gave it back to me," he said. "They rescinded the entire thing."

The real significance of Levittown to *Newsday* went far beyond the housing needs of its employees. To begin with, it was a marvelous opportunity to build circulation. The *Newsday* circulation department simply followed the parade of moving trucks to the doors of the new homes and found new subscribers. Buddy Chernow, one of the most street-wise of all the *Newsday* circulation supervisors, made it a practice to show arriving homeowners where their electrical fuses were, and at the same time, sell them on *Newsday*. Signing up subscribers was easy, but getting the papers delivered was more difficult. All the families were young, and almost all the children were too small to recruit as carriers. So they used adults. "We had ten of them until we started to import carriers from neighboring territories," said Vinnie Bordash, then third-in-command in the circulation department. "As the years went by, the problem resolved itself." In that effort to exploit the growth of Levittown, one of the paper's major assets, as always, was the competitive enthusiasm of the circulation department — unlike the less energized *Review-Star*, where fear of *Newsday* was not much of a motivation. "The word for *Newsday*'s circulation department was 'gung-ho,' " said Alfred Gilkes, who left the *Review-Star* for *Newsday*. "You did a lot of crazy things, and nobody stopped you. If there was a contest, we went out and we stretched banners across railroad bridges, which was against the law. . . . We dressed in costumes and stood out on the damn street corners. . . . We'd get to these breakfasts, and we'd have a pep man there. His name was George Britting. He was an old-time vaudeville man. He'd get up and he'd start us in, and we had this song we'd sing, 'Cheer, cheer, for all *Newsday* boys.' "

In Levittown, as in other communities that developed later, the circulation department sold the papers and Alan Hathway made sure there was enough coverage of the new community to make the paper attractive. "We get 'em on local coverage, then sell 'em on an overall newspaper," Hathway said. "That's the system, and it works." In addition to all his other traits, good and bad, Hathway was a bit of a huckster. Once, he managed to have copies of the paper on sale at a courthouse within five minutes after the acquittal of a police inspector on bribery charges. "We ran off about 200 copies of the paper with a story on acquittal and 200 with a story on guilty and had them at a distribution depot around the corner from the courthouse," Hathway explained. At the cost of a little wasted newsprint, Hathway had made *Newsday* seem prophetic and at the same time sold a few more newspapers.

Even with the combined skills of Hathway and the circulation department, *Newsday* should logically have been at a competitive disadvantage against the *Long Island Press* in the effort to develop readers in Levittown. "The *Press* had a Sunday product, which we did not," Bordash said. "It was a good selling point for the *Press* in those days, since a lot of people did come from Queens and preferred the *Press*." But neither the *Press* nor anyone else put together the adult carrier network that *Newsday* did. "The *Press* waited too long," Bordash said, "and as a result they blew their chances in Levittown."

The *Press* covered seriously only the part of Nassau nearest to the New York City border. "In those first 10 years, while *Newsday* was fighting the *Review-Star*, the *Long Island Press* didn't have any interest in Nassau," said David Starr, who became the editor of the *Press*. But the *Press* was not alone in this inability to perceive the opportunity that Nassau and Suffolk counties presented. Somehow, all the New York City papers failed to understand that large numbers of their readers were moving to the suburbs. That is one of the enduring mysteries about *Newsday*: Why would sophisticated papers such as the *New York Times* and the *Daily News*, along with second-tier papers with closer ties to Long Island, such as the *Press* and the *Brooklyn Eagle*, fail to capitalize on the explosive postwar population growth of Long Island?

There is no single answer, but there are a number of partial explanations. One problem was the erroneous impression that readers would continue buying the city papers even after the move from Brooklyn or Queens to Long Island. They would simply buy the paper in the city during the day and bring it home on the train. This did not, of course, take into account the readers' desire to read news of their new communities, instead of news of New York City. It also assumed continued commuting into the city. But as Long Island began developing industry, the percentage of Long Islanders commuting into New York declined. Another attitude that clouded the eastward vision of the New York dailies was their day-to-day concentration on serving their own circulation area and advertisers. "Getting additional circulation in an area which is not served by your advertisers is a very expensive proposition," Starr said, "because the advertiser doesn't want to pay for it." In addition, the city papers were coping with expansion in the city itself. "The same thing was going on in their own backyard," Bordash said. "There was growth to be had in the city."

Of all the New York papers that failed to take advantage of the growth of Long Island, the one that was best prepared and most disposed to profit from that growth was the *Brooklyn Eagle*, which had a vision of Long Island as Brooklyn's golden future. "Long Island was the land of promise, the promise of a greater Brooklyn," wrote Raymond Schroth, a Jesuit historian, in his book, *The Eagle and Brooklyn*. "Just as the original city of Brooklyn had grown by annexing its neighbors, they expected that the borough of Brooklyn would continue its own imperialism until it overshadowed its old enemy the isle of Manhattan in population, wealth and power." Even the *Eagle*'s support for the construction of the Brooklyn Bridge was related to its vision for Long Island. "*Eagle* editors who owned Long Island real estate wanted to pull population out there," Schroth said. As a result of this vision, the *Eagle* built up a distribution network on Long Island and published a section of Long Island news. "In its heyday," said Les Hanscom, a former *Eagle* reporter who later came to *Newsday*, "it had had bureaus in every town on Long Island." As a result, the *Eagle* was well positioned to be *the* Long Island paper. "It should have been the *Brooklyn Eagle* that came out here," said Dan Lionel, a former *Eagle* advertising executive. "They had everything going for them."

But well before the postwar growth, the *Eagle* had gone into a period of retrenchment. M. Preston Goodfellow, who became publisher in 1932, effected a series of economies, precipitating a disastrous 1937 strike. "In 1937, against the protests of some of his staff, Colonel Preston Goodfellow pulled the *Eagle* back from Long Island by eliminating the Island News section of the paper," Schroth wrote. "Said Goodfellow, 'There is no future for the *Eagle* on Long Island.'" The last publisher of the *Eagle*, Frank D. Schroth, the uncle of Raymond, also believed that the future of the *Eagle* lay in Brooklyn, not Long Island. "He felt a community of three million was big enough," said his son, Frank D. Schroth Jr. By the time the postwar boom arrived, the *Eagle* was too weak to exploit it. "Alicia Patterson had tremendous resources, which the *Eagle* never had," said Thomas Schroth, the brother of Frank Jr. "Sure, the *Eagle* could have been *Newsday*, with a lot of things changed: a couple of million bucks and a new name. We were in no position to make that kind of a commitment."

The other paper with a logical claim on the Long Island market was the *Daily News*, which did enjoy some circulation growth in the suburbs, but didn't make nearly as strong a push onto Long Island as it could have. "It is true that for many years, this effort was not taken as seriously as it might be by a lot of the people who could have made a difference," said W. H. "Tex" James, who started at the *News* in 1940 and rose to publisher in 1973. "The ability of the big-city newspaper to do it with reasonable cost was blocked to some extent by the onerous labor agreements that had been arrived at over the years." In addition, the *News* may have suffered from an unwillingness to tread on the toes of Alicia, the daughter of the late boss. In fact, Ivan Annenberg, the son of Joe Patterson's close friend Max, had fallen into disfavor at the *Daily News* partly because he had been "holding the *News* back from some parts of Long Island," James Patterson said. In that struggle, Patterson said, Alicia had spoken out on the *News* board in defense of Annenberg.

A later editor of the *News*, Michael O'Neill, insisted that the *News* had not really held back on Long Island out of deference to Alicia. "Jack Flynn, who was the longtime publisher of the *News* following Patterson, did a lot to help Alicia and advise her," O'Neill said. "Flynn was fully recovered from that attitude by the time *Newsday* began to be a significant factor out on the island. . . . There was a sharp competitive attitude toward *Newsday*." But in the 1940s and 1950s, before O'Neill became a power at the *News*, during the crucial time when suburban growth was boosting *Newsday*, others detected a lack of aggressiveness by the *News* on Long Island. "When *Newsday* really began to take off, they didn't do anything about it," said Hal Burton, who moved from the *News* to *Newsday* in that period. "None of them knew quite how to handle this situation. They just sort of didn't do anything out there."

V

THE SAME SURGING postwar population that brought *Newsday* more readers also provided new customers for Long Island retailers, who needed a reliable way to sell them grass seed, lawn mowers and shrubs.

Traditionally, merchants had depended on weekly newspapers in their own villages to attract customers from the immediate area. Then *Newsday* started making the pitch that retailers should think bigger, aiming their advertising to people in other parts of Long Island as well. Once readers had prepared for shopping by searching through the ads in *Newsday*, the advertising department argued, there was nothing to prevent them from getting in the car and driving 15 or 20 miles to the store, since they knew in advance that when they got there, they'd find the right lawn mower at the right price. In meeting its selfish economic need to persuade advertisers that Long Island was one market, *Newsday* became a unifying institution for a huge population area that had no single governmental or social structure tying together its profusion of towns and villages. The driving force behind this process of inventing Long Island was a short, relentlessly optimistic, hard-driving man named Ernest Levy, who had taken over as advertising director after Charles Nicholson left.

Born in Nottingham, England, Levy was about 15 when his father, a tailor and dry cleaner, brought him to Canada. At 17, even before he was legally of age to sign contracts, Levy was selling insurance in Vancouver, British Columbia. Then he drifted into the newspaper circulation business, first in the State of Washington, then in Alaska, as an agent of the *Vancouver Sun*. In 1927, the publisher of the *Sun* sent Levy to Los Angeles, where he started to sell a syndicated health column from coast to coast. Anxious to move east, Levy hooked up with a paper in Paterson, New Jersey, that foundered during the Great Depression, and then he went to work at the *Flushing Daily Journal* as circulation director. From there, he moved to the company that had sold prizes to the *Journal* for distribution to its carriers. Broadening his ambitions beyond working for somebody else's paper, Levy scraped together the financing to become owner and publisher of his own paper in northern Queens, the *Bayside Times*. "He made a living," said his wife, Doris Levy. "It was nothing great." The problem was that he didn't adjust his thinking to the smaller scale. "His big mistake was he ran a little weekly the way he was used to a large daily running," said his daughter, Shirley Young. Levy overextended himself, through such practices as buying equipment instead of renting it, and he soon had to get out of the weekly newspaper business. While he waited for his chance to get back into newspapering, Levy sold Borden's ice cream to retailers. At the start of World War II, he began putting together groups of merchants to buy war bond advertising in newspapers. It was through this enterprise that he came in contact with Charles Nicholson, who offered him a job selling advertising for *Newsday* in 1943. The paper's youth and growth potential appealed to Levy, and his natural skills as a salesman delighted Nicholson so much that he soon sent Levy out to boost the advertising sales of the new Suffolk edition. With Nicholson's departure in 1946, Levy took control of the advertising department.

Soon after Levy took over, he began to implement the strategy of selling Long Island to retailers as a single market. One of his primary disciples in this crusade was David Targe, an outrageously hungry and aggressive salesman. Targe grew up in Hempstead, went into the Merchant Marine, briefly sold encyclopedias, ran his own juice-vending business, then joined *Newsday* as a salesman in 1948, in the middle of the Levittown explosion. Targe was not a pin-striped, polished salesman, but he was ready to do whatever was necessary to win the loyalty of an advertiser. One of those advertisers was a young man with a healthy libido but no discreet place to spend time with his women friends. So Targe regularly turned over his apartment to the advertiser for trysts and stood outside, checking his watch and shivering. In turn, the advertiser gave Targe wide discretion in deciding how many pages of ads the advertiser should run in *Newsday*. With that kind of aggressiveness from Targe and his other salesmen, Levy swiftly changed the mindset of advertisers and helped shape the way Long Islanders saw themselves. "Pre-war, it was a pretty much local-town situation on the island," said John Alogna Sr., an advertising agency executive who first came out to Long Island in 1951 and dealt with *Newsday* for decades. "Getting a so-called regional newspaper pulled Long Island together. It became a place."

There were two other critical elements of Levy's operating philosophy. One could best be described as creative greed. Levy was always suspicious that somewhere there might be an advertising dollar that was going to some other medium, and he hated that thought. "He instilled in many of us who were students of his the philosophy that I'm convinced is what made *Newsday* what it is today, and that was that you take all the money that's there; don't leave any money around," said another early Levy disciple, Michael Forgione. "Anytime we saw someone spending money in something other than *Newsday*, we would talk to those people and ask them why." Levy's covetousness for *Newsday* was so contagious that Targe later took offense when he found an ad on a matchbook cover that he thought should have been in *Newsday*. "We didn't want to share it with anybody," said one of Levy's salesmen, Eugene Higgins.

The corollary of this Levy principle was an aggressive rate-increase policy, founded on advertiser fear. "A retailer, especially a small one, flies by the seat of his pants," said Michael Greene, the proprietor of Wayside Bedding, a furniture store in Hempstead, who advertised with *Newsday* from the beginning. "If it works a little, you're scared to get out." If advertisers feel they must be in *Newsday* to avoid lost business, the only money that they can spend on advertising in another medium is money that is left over after they pay the *Newsday* advertising bill. By raising rates with regularity and daring, *Newsday* aimed to make sure that there was no advertising money left over after the *Newsday* bill was paid. "If you don't leave any money around for your competition," Targe said, "they're not going to be around long."

A second essential element of the Levy method was diversification. "The philosophy was to have as many accounts as possible," Higgins said. "The emphasis was on weekly accounts and away from depending on any big major account. . . . He didn't want all his eggs in one basket." As a result, *Newsday* developed a broad base of smaller merchants, which gave the paper precious independence from the influence of any one advertiser. Some of those little advertisers ended up becoming large chains, such as Pergament, which rose from a paint store to a large chain of home supplies stores, and appliance stores such as P.C. Richard and Newmark & Lewis. One of the merchants who used *Newsday* extensively in the postwar years was Attilio Mancusi, who started out with one store, Tyson Radio, and had 18 by the time he was 21 years old. His primary product was television, which was just becoming popular in the Levittown era. Mancusi had televisions to sell, and he had generous allocations of "co-op money," which manufacturers made available to retailers to encourage them to advertise the manufacturers' products. With the help of the co-op money, he paid very little for his advertising. Add together an advertiser with someone else's money to spend, a product that everyone wants, and an aggressive advertising salesman, such as Targe, and the result was a large amount of advertising in *Newsday*.

In the late 1940s, before *Newsday* developed an art department, the ad salesman had to sell the space, come up with ideas for the ad and lay out the ad himself. Looking for a gimmick for Mancusi, Targe settled on a drawing of a bulldog that he found in a book of stock illustrations, ran it at the top of the ad and announced "Tyson Is Mad." The idea was that he was mad at his competitors, who were angry because he was discounting his prices. That ad quickly hung the nickname "Mad Dog Tyson" on Mancusi's stores. Beyond that, Targe cooked up a series of promotions to bring people into the stores. One was an offer of a $50 discount on air conditioners to anyone who brought in a jar of hot air. "People would actually come into the store with jars and say, 'Can you really get a $50 discount if I give you this jar?' " Targe said. Another promotion was an outrageous piece of huckstering for televisions. "It said, 'See TV in color,' " Targe remembered. "And people came in and all the salesmen gave the people sunglasses. They had the sunglasses on and they saw TV in color." As a result of Targe's imagination and the demands of the market, Mancusi ran as many as 15 pages of ads in one day in *Newsday*. "This was the new, young, vibrant society — people with needs," Higgins said. As those people with needs kept moving to Long Island, *Newsday* kept selling newspapers to the homeowners and ads to the merchants. "What you did was ride wave after wave," Targe said.

That move-and-buy cycle was wonderful for *Newsday*, but those were not always pleasant times for advertisers. During the war and for several years afterward, the newsprint shortage had cast advertisers in the role of beggars. They desperately wanted to get into the paper, but *Newsday* didn't have enough newsprint or press capacity to accommodate them all. So Levy regularly had to reject advertising, as much as it pained him. In addition, advertisers griped regularly about their position in the paper. Every advertiser wants to be the first ad in the paper, or at least to appear near some news. Some advertisers like to appear at the top of the outside columns of a right-hand page. Many newspapers take advantage of those strong preferences by guaranteeing their biggest advertisers their best positions, but *Newsday* refused to guarantee position, with one exception: the Arnold Constable department store, which had been pivotally important in the paper's formative years because it was the first major-league department store to advertise in *Newsday*, and *Newsday* always showed its gratitude. For everyone else, the advertising department tried to rotate position, so everyone got a fair share of the good spots. But no other advertiser got a guarantee. This policy contributed to *Newsday*'s reputation as a company that treated all advertisers the same way: badly. "When you don't give a person what they want, they think you're arrogant," Higgins said, "but we were consistently arrogant."

Advertisers grew unhappy, too, as *Newsday* grew prosperous. The more ads *Newsday* stuffed into the paper, the greater the chance that an advertiser would end up in the middle of a run of ads, instead of on a page opposite news or features. That made them wonder how a customer was going to find their ad. The advertising department developed a standard response to this complaint: A newspaper stuffed with ads is like a department store stuffed with merchandise. It creates what Targe liked to call "buying excitement." That blue-smoke-and-mirrors argument only worked because *Newsday* brought so many customers to the doors of its advertisers. "It became a prime shopper," Alogna said. "You ran an ad in *Newsday*, you got action."

One other annoyance for advertisers was the development of a new way of laying out ads and news on the paper's pages — a magazine-style format that did away with the traditional pyramid ad layout. In the familiar format, pages are arranged so that one column has an ad or ads all the way to the top; the column next to it has a smaller stack of ads, with room for a piece of news on top of the stack; the column next to that has still a shorter stack of ads and a larger hole for news. In this pyramid layout, the reader sees advertising and news in the same vertical column. It benefits advertisers because the ad copy is near editorial copy, but it gives the page a cluttered look and creates the need for tiny news stories whose only real value is that they fit into the small spaces among the stacks of ads. Often, newspapers filled those spaces with nothing more than canned pieces of trivial facts that sound like rejects from a "Believe It or Not" column.

At the start, *Newsday* used the pyramid system, but later Alicia and her designer, Fred Hauck, opted for a cleaner appearance. In breaking with newspaper tradition, they were being true to their philosophy. "What it was was, 'We don't care what other people are going to do; if we don't think it's right, we're not going to do it,' " said Robert Hessler, a young artist who had married Ernie Levy's daughter, Gloria, and came to *Newsday* in 1949 when Levy told him that Hauck was looking for someone to start an art department. Hessler became the liaison between *Newsday* and Hauck at a time when the paper moved away from the old pyramid style toward the magazine approach.

Instead of mixing ads and editorial copy in the same vertical column, the new format required every column to contain all ads or all editorial. "The editorial always ran on the inside and the ads on the outside," Hessler said. The purpose of that was to give the news greater impact than it would have if it were split up and placed on the outside edges of each page. The new format also dictated that there could never be fewer than three columns of editorial copy on a two-page spread. In other words, they didn't want to isolate one narrow column of news on the inside of one page, next to one narrow column on the other page. If one page contained only one column of news, Hessler said, the other page had to have at least two adjoining it. The result was a sharper-looking layout, with editorial copy neatly contained in its own rectangular space and advertising confined to its space. "She thought it looked cleaner," said Al Sarmento, who laid out the paper daily. "I liked the idea."

By switching to the magazine-style makeup, Alicia had reversed the order of things. Once news and advertising began appearing in completely separate stacks, it was no longer the editorial department's job to find tiny stories to fill the odd spaces around the ads. The advertising department had to fill its own holes. Ernie Levy abhorred the idea of plugging any of those precious spaces with a house ad, which promoted the newspaper but brought in no revenue. So he ordered advertising salesmen to stay in the office, working the telephones, until they had persuaded advertisers to buy all of those odd-sized holes for the next day's paper. Only then, often late in the afternoon, were they allowed to go out on the street to sell ads for future papers. The salesmen were able to sell these last-minute spots by phone because many advertisers had weekly contracts that required them to run a minimum amount of lines. So the salesmen would persuade them to run an ad in the currently available hole, in order to meet that requirement. Somehow, despite the difficulties of selling by phone, Levy's salesmen made it work. "When I used to go to meetings and tell other newspapers that we'd stay in the office and sell millions and millions of dollars worth of advertising on the phone," Targe said, "they didn't believe it."

That aggressiveness in implementing the magazine format increased *Newsday*'s dominance, fattened the revenues and, in some ways, added to the advertising department's reputation for arrogance. But *Newsday* could get away with arrogance, because advertisers needed its growing circulation to sell their goods and services to Long Island's rapidly increasing population. By early 1949, the circulation had reached the 100,000 mark, and an editorial marking that occasion proclaimed: "Well, we don't intend to be fat-cat. We still have a long way to go."

CHAPTER ELEVEN

The Start of an Affair

I

IN THE FAMILY of Albert Wood, the architect who designed *Newsday*'s Garden City plant and accepted several commissions for work at Harry Guggenheim's estate, there is an amusing tale about the relationship between Harry and Alicia.

One night, well past midnight, Paul Wood said, Alicia called Albert Wood's home and made an odd, urgent request: " 'Albert, I want you to come over here tomorrow and put a partition down the middle of our bedroom.' " Unless Alicia's request had something to do with the doors between the rooms, a partition would seem to have been superfluous, since the Guggenheims had separate bedrooms at Falaise. Whether it is true or apocryphal, this Wood family lore is instructive about the state of the Harry-Alicia relationship after its earliest years: Everybody seems to have a Harry-Alicia fight story. It was not always that way. There was a strong mutual attraction at the start of their relationship. "I think for a while they were crazy about each other," said Alicia's niece, Alice Albright. "He was so romantic about her sometimes."

Despite the fighting, Alicia remained solicitous of Harry's feelings. If anyone made an anti-Semitic remark, for example, she was quick to defend him. "She couldn't stand it at all," said Hal Burton, who spent many hours with them after he came to *Newsday*. "As a matter of fact, she was critical of Harry, because Harry didn't feel he had to get up and leave the room every time it happened." There were times, in fact, when Harry seemed almost anti-Semitic himself. Alicia's secretary, Dorothy Holdsworth, remembered an occasion when Alicia showed him the guest list for a gathering at Falaise: "He said, 'Good God, Alicia, don't you know anybody but Jews?' " He even poked fun at his own Jewishness.

"I'll send you a book called 'Seed Money' to prove that I'm a Jew," Harry once wrote his friend, John Steinbeck, referring to a book that Harry had commissioned about his family. "I often wondered about the light eyes. Maybe in the days before Frigidaires the ice man cometh." Harry was not much of a Zionist either. In 1948, Alicia and Stan Peckham were uncertain what to say on the editorial page about the creation of Israel, and they asked Harry what he thought. "And he said, 'I don't give a damn whether they have it or not,'" Peckham said. Finally, *Newsday* came down on the side of Israel.

No matter how much they disagreed politically or financially, Alicia did find much to admire in Harry. "She respected Harry, obviously," said her friend, Phyllis Cerf. "He really gave in to her, but led her. He was a good father to her." The relationship, in fact, became far more like father-daughter than husband-wife soon after their marriage. "The sex stopped after a year," one of Alicia's confidantes said. One of Alicia's closest friends said Alicia told her that Harry had become impotent. Others doubted that account, but there seems little doubt from those who knew Alicia best that the relationship stopped being physical very early. "It was totally sterile after the first few years," Burton said. "For some reason, he just simply lost interest in going to bed with her, and she was very hurt by it."

To a large extent, in the 1940s and 1950s it became a stage marriage, in which the primary stage was Harry's mansion on the cliff above Long Island Sound. "She was really just a hostess," Burton said. "She was nice to his friends; he was nice to hers." Even in entertaining at Falaise, they had their differences: After dinner, Harry would take the men downstairs to his trophy room for Cuban cigars, fine brandy and political talk. That left Alicia with the women to carry on their own conversation elsewhere — a segregation that she did not appreciate. The post-dinner routine also included games. In one of them, a guest wore on her back a piece of paper containing the name of a famous person, and she had to ask questions of the other guests until she found out who she was supposed to be. Unenthusiastic about the games, Harry often went to bed early, which is what Alicia's friends wanted. "She had a whole coterie of lady friends who were always grumbling about Harry and encouraging her to grumble about Harry," Burton said. "One or the other woman would say, 'Just wait awhile. Harry gets sleepy about nine o'clock and then we'll have fun.'"

As the frictions grew, Harry and Alicia didn't always hide them well from guests. "Every now and then, when we went down for dinner, they'd have a big fight at the table," said Burton, who lived with his wife in a cottage at Falaise for three years. The Burtons were not the only witnesses to these verbal struggles. "She and I would sit down and have a couple of drinks before she went home," Dorothy Holdsworth said. "Sometimes she'd take me home with her so she wouldn't have to be alone with him. I used to spend many a dinner staring out at the Sound as they gabbed at each other."

They were an odd couple, as they had been from the start. Harry was proper and polite. Alicia was blunt and outspoken. Harry took alcohol in moderation. Alicia liked to drink. Harry liked Lawrence Welk. Alicia liked Cole Porter.

They argued over politics, over tennis, over the two percent that would give her majority control of *Newsday*. She respected Harry's skills and depended on him for financial guidance, but she found herself in a difficult marriage, full of disagreement and confrontation, that gave her little emotional comfort. Just about seven years into this increasingly troubled marriage, Alicia's life intersected again with the life of Adlai Ewing Stevenson.

II

IT HAD BEEN two decades since Alicia Patterson, fresh from her coming-out ball, and Adlai Stevenson, just out of law school, had first become friends.

It isn't certain that Stevenson actually proposed marriage to Alicia in the 1920s, though several of their friends say that may have happened. What is certain is that Stevenson was deeply smitten. "They enjoyed each other's sprightly minds," said Stevenson's sister, Buffie Ives. "She was one of the first girls he was in love with, and she married another man." Of course, Alicia's marriage to James Simpson lasted only a year. Two months after Alicia left Simpson, Stevenson married Alicia's schoolmate, Ellen Borden, in December, 1928. Together, Stevenson and his wife had three sons — Adlai III, Borden and John Fell — and they built a home in Libertyville, near the farm where Alicia had spent much of her childhood.

In the years after his marriage, Stevenson began to move from the practice of law into public policy. His first step was election in 1933 as president of the Chicago Council on Foreign Relations, a force for internationalism in the capital of Midwest isolationism. Not long after his election as president of the council, he left for Washington to work in the New Deal bureaucracy, but he didn't stay long. In the fall of 1934, he returned to Chicago, became involved again in civic affairs and practiced law at the firm of Sidley, McPherson, Austin & Burgess. With the outbreak of war in Europe, Stevenson jumped into the isolationist-interventionist debate. In 1940, as the Nazis blitzed through Europe, the editor of the *Gazette* in Emporia, Kansas, William Allen White, met with others in New York to form the Committee to Defend America by Aiding the Allies. Soon after the committee began, a group of men met in Chicago to put together a local chapter, including Stevenson and Colonel Frank Knox, publisher of the *Chicago Daily News*. The new chapter elected Stevenson as chairman, and he promptly became the target of isolationist attacks from Colonel Robert Rutherford McCormick's *Chicago Tribune*.

Later in the war, Stevenson became less active in the White committee, spent more time on his law practice and began to look around for a suitable government job. One of those he contacted was Frank Knox, by then the Secretary of the Navy, who appointed him his principal attorney. For Knox, Stevenson was a legal jack-of-all-trades, working on the desegregation of the

Navy, writing Knox's speeches, carrying a secret message from Knox to President Roosevelt, and flying with Knox to the South Pacific right after Pearl Harbor. His rise at the Navy Department stalled after Knox died of a heart attack. The new secretary, James Forrestal, was a tough bureaucrat who considered him too fuzzy-headed, which ended Stevenson's Navy career. While he was in Washington, Stevenson contemplated running for the United States Senate from Illinois, then for governor in 1944. After Knox died, he also made a serious but unsuccessful attempt to buy the *Chicago Daily News*. It was during this period that the first major cracks in his marriage to Ellen Borden began to appear — partly because she couldn't stand Washington, partly because she felt overshadowed and deprived of her identity. Later, she told a friend: "I've wanted out of this since 1941 in Washington."

Back in Chicago in early 1945, Stevenson turned down a job offer from Secretary of State Edward Stettinius, because he wanted to be with his family and make a living. Then he reconsidered and became the special assistant to Assistant Secretary of State Archibald MacLeish. In this position, Stevenson travelled to San Francisco in May, 1945, to participate in the conference that drew up the United Nations charter. Following his two months at San Francisco, Stevenson returned briefly to Libertyville, then arranged for himself a seat on the Preparatory Commission in London that was to manage the transition between the signing of the charter and the first meeting of the United Nations. In London, Stevenson became the chief United States spokesman. At the first meeting of the General Assembly, in January, 1946, Stevenson was a senior advisor, rather than a full delegate, but he exerted major influence on the delegation. In the summer, President Truman appointed him an alternate representative to the first General Assembly meeting to be held at the new headquarters of the United Nations, in New York.

On October 16, 1946, Stevenson arrived in New York to begin his work, just as Harry and Alicia were getting ready for their annual post-election day move from Falaise to Manhattan for the winter. No one is certain when Alicia and Stevenson first renewed their friendship, or how it happened. But it would have been difficult for her to avoid him once he came to New York and started moving in the same political and journalistic circles that were open to her. One of Stevenson's own letters to Alicia, dated April 5, 1949, seems to fix the start of their serious relationship at a time 18 months earlier, in the fall of 1947: "If only you were here, you would have all the answers — and besides I'd get to bed earlier," Stevenson wrote. "Do you think you'd love me as much if you saw me more? How could you love a soft, fat, bald old man? I brood too much about the improbability of this mysterious dream that's enveloped me for a year and a half. Are you quite sure you're sane? I'm not at all!" That placed the beginnings of their affair in the fall of 1947. Another woman who was extraordinarily close to Stevenson and met him at about the time he came to the United Nations, Marietta Peabody Tree, said she thought the Alicia-Adlai relationship dated back to the winter of 1946-1947.

The dates, however, are not nearly as important as the central fact: At a time when both Alicia's marriage and Stevenson's marriage were turning sour, they fell into an intense love affair that ripened into a touching, long-distance friendship. For nearly two decades, through Stevenson's campaign for governor in 1948, through his painful divorce in 1949, through his presidential campaigns in 1952 and 1956, into his appointment as ambassador to the United Nations under President John F. Kennedy, they remained loyal, loving friends. Throughout that long friendship, because they could so seldom be with one another, they fell back on letters — hand-written, affectionate, intimate notes, full of teasing, candor and longing. For all his brilliance, Stevenson was a man much given to self-doubt and endless rumination. Should he run for governor? How should he handle the press? How could he maneuver successfully among the political factions in Illinois? Should he run for President? In those moments of reflection, at times when he was weary of the governor's office, or simply because he missed her desperately, Stevenson fell back on his friend Alicia — Elisha, or E Darling, as he affectionately called her. She was his sounding board, his intellectual equal, his lover.

Stevenson was so anxious to share parts of his life with Alicia that he even wanted her to visit him in Libertyville, to meet his wife and his sons. "I want them to grow to love you like their father — well not just like their father," he wrote. "And I want you to know Ellen better. You can probably help me a lot in that direction — not that you're good, but because you are wise; because you are half man and half woman and probably understand both more than anyone else I know." Frequently, Stevenson told Alicia how much he had to learn from her. "Anyway, you must teach me — so many things you know & understand & I don't," he wrote in one letter, discussing her hunting lodge in Georgia. "I can't fish very well, but I can listen, admire and love you."

His letters are full of reliance on Alicia's good sense — mingled in many of his earliest letters with sensual longing. It was a complex love that Stevenson felt for Alicia — an odd combination of buddy-love and puppy-love, admiration for her toughness and desire for her tenderness. He loved her for what he called "her delicious, irreverent voice, her grumpy growls, her realism and loving long loyalty." He loved her for her endurance, referring to her as a "wonderful old war horse." He loved her for what she had done in the newspaper business, in which he'd never been more than a dilettante. "I marvel at you more and more," he wrote in the summer of 1949. "Somehow, never having seen the place and never having let you talk enough, I had not quite realized the enormity of your undertaking and achievement. You've made a great success — in the very field I had once dreamed of working."

At times, it sounded as if he loved her almost androgynously. "The Pantagraph is way off from 1947," he wrote, referring to the financial fortunes of the family newspaper. "But so are they all — except Newsday. What a guy you are." Just as he told Alicia in a letter that she was half man and half woman, he told a *Time* interviewer years later: "I never thought of Alicia as a woman; she always seemed like a man to me." But his letters make it clear he thought of her almost constantly in the traditional romantic way. The letters are filled with the vocabulary of lovers — "my sweet," "darling," hearts drawn at the bottom of pages, constant talk of visions and dreams, long passages of prose straining toward poetry, clumsily searching for new and original ways to say, "I love you." They also contain frequent references to the tension between the demands of his political world and the desire to be with Alicia. "I'd like to throw the whole damn thing out the window and catch a plane to Wyo. and you — dream in the purple twilight; sing in the first mornings," he wrote. "There I go again — off the rails. . . . I must be nuts — or I'm in love like an adolescent."

Like any lover, Stevenson delighted in after-the-fact analysis of their last meeting, wondering how much anyone else was able to guess about what was going on inside their hearts. "I thought I was going to be dreadfully self-conscious & awkward, but I didn't feel that way," he wrote after one meeting. "Did you? Indeed I think we're getting adjusted — if only I didn't want to seize you in a somewhat unconventional way. I hope you appreciated my self-control!" But his self-control seemed to melt whenever mail from Alicia arrived. He'd return to his office in Springfield, find a letter from her on top of the pile, and run off to the men's room to read it in privacy. "Her letters always came to my desk," said his longtime secretary, Carol Evans. "I recognized her handwriting, but I never opened the envelope. I put them on his desk." Once he had them, he hoarded them to read over and over. "These I will keep," he wrote her, "these little scraps of paper scratched with music from a human heart."

But those little scraps of paper from Alicia, the letters that made Stevenson's heart beat faster, have disappeared. If her letters to him were as revealing about *Newsday* as his letters to her were candid about his career and his marriage, they would be the single best source of insight into Alicia's thinking during the time she was running *Newsday*. But they have vanished, leaving behind only Stevenson's letters — a one-sided, incomplete account of their relationship. Stevenson's words give strong clues as to what Alicia was thinking and feeling, but the absence of her letters, along with the absence of almost all her internal *Newsday* correspondence, has muted her voice. One of her few surviving letters, written after she had visited him at Libertyville, was playful and romantic. "I expect I shall never get over wanting to be with you despite your rude remarks about my hands, my tennis, my 'bad' habits," she wrote. "To paraphrase Joseph Medill's immortal remarks

"I do love thee Adalai
Why I do I cannot say
For you do me oft betray
'Tis the woman who doth pay."

Beyond those brief glimpses of her feelings, little remains of what Adlai Stevenson called "your precious letters." Often, Stevenson's letters are preoccupied with his own problems, but it is clear from his written reactions that her letters kept him aware of the major developments at *Newsday*. Just after the paper reached a circulation of 100,000 in 1949, for example, he wrote her a letter of congratulation, in which he appeared both to admire and to fear her toughness. "So you've made it — you indomitable little tiger," he wrote. "I

could bite your ears with savage joy. . . . But why this Napoleonic 'I'll found an empire?' Must Caesar forever gather laurels to be happy? Is this father jealousy-love healthy? I *know* you're a hard little empire-builder — but I *love* a woman — a gentle, wise, compassionate woman — not a mighty, ruthless, determined conqueror. Or do I?" That toughness-gentleness duality constantly intrigued him. "I enjoyed my little walk hand in hand down tobacco road — and I'm still there," he wrote during an airplane flight, after a visit to her hunting lodge. "Indeed I'm afraid I'll still be there for days to come — even after this bird plunges down through the white wool and sets me gently on earth again. I'll see you striding in that solid straight-legged way along the bank and through the pines, all white in sunlight, looking quizzically here and there — half smiling, half panting — but I'll be very circumspect, very casual, very courteous, very banal. I'll resist the awful temptation to sweep you up into a soft white ball, that, magically, unfolds a sharp, savage little tigress."

In contrast, Stevenson often portrayed himself as hopelessly dreamy, goofy and adolescent in his feelings about her. But that didn't prevent him from lecturing her occasionally, like a stern older brother, on her drinking. "I'm wallowing in self pity — as usual, and wondering where you are tonight, what you're doing, how you look, if your [sic] drinking — and I pray you are not — and if you really think of me or just when you write those breathless precious bits." Those admonitions were not confined solely to letters. Sometimes he gave her the same advice when his son Adlai was around. "He'd lecture her about drinking too much, though she never showed any serious signs of excess in my presence," Stevenson said. "She would lecture him — on what, I don't know. I think she volunteered a lot of political advice. She never backed down. That was really one of the endearing qualities. She could be hard and tough and argumentative, but you knew beneath it that she was a softie."

Far more than lectures, though, the letters were filled with the pain of separation. Stevenson was constantly conjuring up ways that he and Alicia could overcome the complex geographical logistics of their lives. Even in the days right after Stevenson was elected governor in 1948, when he had only a short time to put together a government, his letter from Washington was filled with ideas on where they could meet. "I wish I could fly right on to Jax [Jacksonville, near her lodge] & find you waiting with dogs & station wagon and then head for the forest and solitude — and you," he wrote. "Perhaps you should go to the inauguration. Bertie might forgive you." (His letters were full of references to her cousin, Bertie McCormick, who was still Stevenson's resolute political enemy.) Later in the same letter, Stevenson even wrote wistfully about joining Alicia in Europe, where she was covering the Berlin airlift.

Over the years, they met wherever they could find a few minutes together: in Libertyville, in Chicago, at the governor's mansion in Springfield. Constantly, Stevenson wanted to know her plans and how they could intersect with his. And when they couldn't meet, Stevenson insisted that they really were together in spirit — in the cabin of her plane over Berlin or alongside the river that flowed past her hunting lodge. "Good night my love," he wrote in a post-midnight letter from his bedroom. "I *am* with you and you with me."

The letters also display a sense of danger. "Write guarded letters for awhile until I get the secretarial situation down there under control," he wrote just before his inauguration as governor. What did they have to hide? What sort of relationship was it? "I don't think anyone except the two of them can tell you that for sure," said Clayton Fritchey, who later became an aide to Stevenson and eventually a *Newsday* columnist. But their close friends agreed that the relationship had a sexual dimension, at least at the start. "I'm sure it did," said Stevenson's friend, Marietta Tree. "It was quite sexual," said one of Alicia's closest friends. And Dorothy Schiff, who travelled with Alicia to Europe, said they had discussed Adlai. "There was a rumor at that time that Adlai was a homosexual," Schiff said. "His wife had spread the rumor. . . . I asked her [Alicia] and she said that sex was not very urgent with him. I think that she intimated that they had." But the question of whether they did or did not make love is far less important than the undeniable fact that they loved, intensely and for a long time — well after the physical ardor of the relationship had cooled.

Unlike Alicia and Harry, the governor and the publisher shared a basic political world view, although they felt free to argue politics. "Alicia's intellect was equal to his, if not greater," said her friend, Phyllis Cerf. They had sharply different personalities in many ways, but they were both interesting and interested people who knew how to listen. That ability to pay attention to what a person was saying, as if that person were the most important in the world, was a major element of Stevenson's powerful hold on women, and a significant part of Alicia's charm. "She didn't fabricate this interest," said their friend, Jane Warner Dick. "She really was interested. I think that was one thing that probably attracted Adlai to her, because he had that to the Nth degree himself."

It was not a relationship without struggles. In fact, early in 1949, not long after Stevenson's inauguration, Alicia apparently wrote him a letter that asked for a more distant friendship, which wounded him. Uncharacteristically, he began his response with the cool appellation, "My dear 'Friend,' " underlining "friend" three times. The letter, following a visit from Alicia several days earlier, starts out with a description of how he tried to act calmly in front of a secretary when he picked up her letter and read its essential message: " 'Okay, let's be friends. The whole business is Kaput.' " Later, when he was alone, the pain of the letter overtook him. "I've read it all and I'm a little sick," he wrote. Stevenson had to attend a dinner meeting right after he had read the letter, "and I'm talking animatedly and interestedly of their silly problems — and all the time about all I've known of love and genuine interest and personal concern for 10 years is — Kaput!

"Very well, Alicia, I guess I didn't understand. I guess I never will. Maybe we are cut of different cloths as you say. I'm not resentful — I'm deeply grateful for even a few months of what was to be forever. And don't worry about me.

Work has been my refuge for many years — now it will be for many more. I only regret that we couldn't talk. I tried to start that first night here — and again the second but that failed. You *had* drunk too much, altho the hours were precious for talking — wisely, soberly.

"Don't be angry — don't be hurt or prideful. If there's love, there's forgiveness — and I thought there was much, much love . . . but there's only so much time, only so much strength — and now that's run out all over the floor — and I'm a mess and the butler's knocking."

In a few days, he got a letter from her that pulled him out of his funk, and he wrote her: "Darling! — Now I have your letter and I feel very contrite after writing you that long self righteous explosion. I sent it to Newsday. It must have crossed yours and I hope you haven't seen it. When you do please don't read it — just tear it up & lets bury this curious little incident." From his letter, it appears that they fought partly because of Alicia's drinking and partly because of his effort to seem nonchalant about her in the presence of Mark — apparently a reference to the columnist Marquis Childs. "Of course with Mark about I was behaving, play acting, the casual indifference of an old friend, but badly I suspect," he wrote. "I had counted rather on that night — and when you've had too much to drink you are definitely not not [sic] charming! — nor is anyone else. . . . Enough of that — perhaps even at our age the course of true love never runs smoothly. At all events I'm glad you had your little fit of ugly temper, tho I can hardly say I liked it and I think it was the worst 3 days in many years until your sweet letter came. Lets have no more of those — and please spank me roundly if my own petulance gets the best of me."

Somehow, they got past that fight. Somehow, Stevenson got through his painful divorce. Their friendship would survive a sexual cooling-off. It would survive Stevenson's interest in other women. Ultimately, it would set off a chain of events that almost brought Harry and Alicia to divorce. Whatever else happened, the friendship of Alicia Patterson and Adlai Stevenson would continue, just as Stevenson had predicted in one of his letters: "There are years and years and years ahead for us."

CHAPTER TWELVE

The King and the Crash

I

IT WAS THE great misfortune of W. Kingsland Macy that *Newsday* was simultaneously his business competitor and his natural political enemy.

In addition to owning a chain of weekly newspapers in Suffolk County, Macy served as the representative from the huge First Congressional District and as chairman of the county Republican Party. This was a happy combination of circumstances for *Newsday*, which had already perfected in Nassau the technique of stripping legal advertising from James Stiles at the *Review-Star* and at the same time making life uncomfortable for his protector, Nassau County Executive J. Russel Sprague. In Suffolk, *Newsday* didn't bother going after Macy's conduct of his newspapers, although those papers did get significant legal ads from local governments. Provoked partly by Macy's open antipathy to *Newsday* and partly by a naked bloodlust, *Newsday* went directly after Macy's job.

In the 1950 election, *Newsday* threw everything it had against Macy, with little pretense of fairness. Alicia Patterson turned Alan Hathway loose on this crusade, and Hathway did whatever was necessary, almost single-handedly orchestrating the campaign of Macy's little-known Democratic opponent, Ernest Greenwood. "A review of the facts will show that Honest Ernest was merely an incident," Hathway wrote many years later to his colleague and friend, Robert W. Greene. "He happened to be standing there at the time his opponent, W. Kingsland Macy (The Kingfish) . . . had publicly stated that after the then current election, Alicia Patterson and Newsday would be thrown out of Suffolk County.

"She and I consulted and decided that the Kingfish would be thrown out of political power instead. He was. And it was a nitty gritty hassle of which I am still proud. It was not so much to elect Greenwood as to politically murder Macy. Greenwood was a non-entity. When we went into it, I asked the boss, 'Do we do it Chicago style?' She nodded. That meant no holds barred.

"I then said 'Okay, best not ask me any questions.' She didn't and I did a job nobody thought could be done. Politically, we murdered the Kingfish. And that, Pal, is basically how Newsday was able to stay in Suffolk County."

The blueblood victim of this journalistic homicide was the polar opposite of Hathway, his hard-drinking, street-tough tormentor. Macy was a tall, intelligent patrician who continued to wear the trademark high starched collars of the 1920s. He had solid Yankee lineage, coming from an old Massachusetts whaling family and attending Groton and Harvard, where he was a senior editor of the *Harvard Crimson* in 1911. Later, he bought himself a seat on the New York Stock Exchange. Macy was also a senior trustee of the Seamen's Bank for Savings and had served as president of the Union Pacific Tea Company. Long before *Newsday* was even an idea, Macy was a fixture in Suffolk County's upper class. If it had not been for a threat to that class — an effort by Robert Moses to turn their private hunt club into a state park — Macy might have remained content forever to shuttle between the worlds of finance and society, without ever feeling the temptation to move into politics. As a result of his long, unsuccessful battle to thwart the creation of what became Heckscher State Park in the Town of Islip, Macy got into politics and stayed. Quickly, he became chairman of the Suffolk County Republican Party, which he would control for a quarter of a century. Then he wrested the chairmanship of the state party away from the party's Old Guard.

On public policy matters, Macy was an enlightened progressive. It was Macy, for example, who pulled together the Republican votes in the New York State Legislature to establish the Seabury Commission, which investigated municipal corruption in New York City. In contrast to that corruption, Macy enjoyed a reputation for personal integrity. It was not money that motivated him, but political power. In using that power, however, he was every bit as dictatorial and high-handed as Robert Moses. "He was an absolute czar," said Bob Pfeifle, who covered Suffolk County for *Newsday*. "A sparrow couldn't fall and you couldn't have a job without his blessing." Besides controlling patronage through the county chairmanship, Macy wielded power by giving himself elected jobs — first as a state senator and then as a congressman. Wearing a multitude of hats, Macy also served as president of the National Republican Club, a member of the state's Board of Regents, which makes educational policy, and chairman of the Suffolk County Water Authority.

With all his power, Macy was able to treat *Newsday* haughtily when it came along. As a political leader, he dragged his feet about giving *Newsday* results on election nights. As a newspaper publisher, he tried to convince retailers in Suffolk that it would be a mistake to advertise in "that Nassau-minded daily." If *Newsday* established a toehold in Suffolk, he argued, it would help drain customers away from Suffolk and into Nassau. This was a clever argument, but it didn't work. The Macy chain had a certain appeal to smaller advertisers, but *Newsday*'s broader circulation drained larger advertisers away from weeklies in both counties. A perfect example was the *Hempstead Sentinel*, founded in 1858. "When *Newsday* came along, the merchants in Hempstead had to attract people from this bigger area; so they didn't give a hang about advertising in the *Sentinel*," said Kenneth Van de Water Jr., whose family ran the *Sentinel* until competition from *Newsday* forced them to shut it down in 1949, although they continued to do job printing. Similarly, large retailers in Suffolk began to turn away from weeklies as *Newsday* grew. "It was a very tough sell," said Carl Starace, who ran the Macy chain's advertising operations. "In the early '50s, we started to feel it."

For all the economic damage that *Newsday* did to Macy's papers, it is not entirely clear whether that was the motivation for his hostility. "I really don't think so," Starace said. "I think Macy looked on *Newsday* as a political, not at all as a business enemy. Macy certainly didn't in any sense depend on his newspapers. He never made a dime out of the newspapers. He wanted the voice." If Alicia Patterson had wanted to, she could have gone after Macy's voice by attacking his papers on the issue of legal ads, just as she had done to the *Review-Star*. Instead, the club that *Newsday* picked up and started swinging at Macy's head was the issue of illegal gambling in the county.

The gambling revelations began with a tip to Jack Altshul, who was writing his "Heads and Tales" column in addition to serving as city editor. Late in 1949, Altshul was eating in a restaurant when someone told him that a gambling room located behind Frank Friede's Riverside Inn in Smithtown had reopened. Altshul checked the tip and found that it was true. Hathway told Altshul to put an item on the gambling in his column. The tiny item appeared at the top of Altshul's column on a Thursday morning: "Suffolk's most famous gambling den is open again. 'Chicago system' of betting is being used in the horse room." At the same time, Hathway began planning to follow it up by sending a pair of photographers to the horse room: Edna Murray and Dick Morseman, the photo editor. The involvement of Altshul and Morseman in this enterprise was ironic. Altshul was a compulsive gambler. Not long after this story, he married Edna Murray, and gambling remained a source of friction throughout their marriage. Morseman, already on his way to becoming a liquid legend even among the prodigious drinkers at *Newsday*, also enjoyed an occasional wager. He had, in fact, patronized the horse room behind Friede's.

As the bettors went about their business, Murray began surreptitiously taking photographs, using a tiny Contax camera hidden in her purse. "To me, the little click sounded like the atom bomb going off," she said. "I was a little apprehensive then, to put it mildly." Back at the office in Garden City, Murray waited nervously while her negatives were developed, then rushed into the city room with an 11 by 14 photo, still wet, showing the betting charts and a man posting racing information. Hathway, of course, was delighted.

The next day, October 20, 1949, the lead headline was "BIG BET

DEN/BARED ON L.I." Underneath was a huge photo of the betting charts. Inside were stories and more photos, including an aerial shot of the restaurant and the gambling house. The stories hinted broadly that the horse room enjoyed political protection. "In its 20 year history the place has played host to congressmen, judges, high ranking police officials and powerful clergymen," one story said. The same day, *Newsday* carried a small story about an attempted bribe, but it did not identify the briber. "Last Sunday night a public official of Suffolk County approached a reporter for this newspaper offering 'financial arrangements' to the reporter and to executives of Newsday if 'contact' could be made to avoid publicity," the story said. "The reporter promptly refused."

The gambling expose was a perfect story for *Newsday*. Not only did it provide a handy issue to use against Macy, but it buttressed the paper's frequently repeated editorial position in favor of legalizing off-track betting. As delicious as the story was at the start, the Republicans made it even more irresistible by adding the element of persecution. The day after the first *Newsday* story appeared, District Attorney Lindsay Henry, a Republican, announced an investigation. He said that he had been ready to raid the horse room at the first opportunity, but the *Newsday* story had made that impossible. So he subpoenaed a series of *Newsday* employees, including Alicia, Hathway, Morseman and Murray. When the grand jury began hearing testimony, the tone of the questions made it clear that Henry was as interested in proving *Newsday*'s partisanship as he was in ferreting out crime. Called back for a second round of testimony, Hathway read a statement of protest, complaining about the tone of the questions from Assistant District Attorney Harry Brenner. On the same day that it carried Hathway's protest, *Newsday* reported that the grand jury investigation had ended without any indictments, but *Newsday* had found another horse room, this one only 400 yards from Brenner's offices in Huntington.

The day after reporting the grand jury's failure, the paper ran a story, "Lie to Bet Jurors Bared," revealing the identity of the public official who tried to bribe a *Newsday* reporter. Bob Pfeifle had told the grand jury that Smithtown Police Chief Cyril J. Donnelly offered him $100 a month to overlook gambling in Friede's. Donnelly had told the grand jury it wasn't true. Pfeifle's accusation festered for years at *Newsday*, where the police chief had many friends, including Jack Altshul and Pfeifle. "Pfeifle was Cy Donnelly's best friend," said Robert W. Greene, who later came to work at *Newsday*, moved to Smithtown and became close to Donnelly himself. At the time, Greene said, Hathway had been dissatisfied with Pfeifle's work. "Hathway finally said to Bobby, 'You haven't turned in anything in a month; you're fired,'" Greene said. "At which point, Bobby said, 'The reason I haven't is I've been working on something undercover.' And he gave him his best friend. They were best friends. You don't bribe your best friend."

Around Smithtown, Donnelly was known for collecting donated materials and labor for construction projects at local churches and at St. Anthony's High School, a Catholic school that developed an excellent football team and became a popular charity with Irish public officials and newspaper men, including

Donnelly and Greene. "Cy was just a lovable slob," said Tom Renner, who later covered Smithtown. "To my knowledge, Cy never pocketed a nickel." But Hathway continued to nurse a grudge against Donnelly over the bribe allegation. Two years later, in November, 1951, someone murdered a 12-year-old girl named Lyde Kitchner in Smithtown. The following March, Smithtown police and state troopers arrested Harold Lorentson, 13. It didn't take long for Hathway to decide that, if Donnelly's department was making the accusation, Lorentson must be innocent. "He was out to embarrass the police department and the troopers," said Jim O'Neill, who had just joined the *Newsday* staff and was covering Smithtown. *Newsday* began running stories that supported Lorentson, but when O'Neill talked to witnesses who were supposed to testify in the boy's defense, they gave him information that was more damaging to Lorentson than helpful. That enraged Hathway, who fired O'Neill. When O'Neill told Donnelly that Hathway had fired him, Donnelly called the other police agencies in Suffolk and told them not to give any news to *Newsday* until O'Neill was back on the payroll. A few days later, Hathway hired O'Neill back, with a bonus and a raise. But *Newsday* continued to support Lorentson, even to the extent of buying him a horse to replace one that had died. Hathway himself made the presentation. Lorentson won an acquittal, but in 1964, while operating a well-drilling machine, Lorentson hit a high-voltage line and was electrocuted. "I think it was poetic justice," O'Neill said.

II

KING MACY HAD more to worry about in the 1949 election than the *Newsday* crusade against gambling. In his own town, Islip, his candidates for town office faced a challenge by a new coalition of reformers, the Independent Efficiency Party.

The most important town official was Supervisor Charles Duryea, a Macy Republican. Duryea also served as the chairman of the county Board of Supervisors, the legislative body made up of the supervisors of the 10 towns. His opponent was Ernest Greenwood, a Republican running as an independent. Greenwood was a cultured, well-mannered immigrant from England with a wavy mane of silver hair and a British accent, who had taught school in Islip and then had become the headmaster of the Dwight School for Boys in Manhattan. During the campaign, Greenwood focused his attacks on the Macy machine, using the gambling revelations as ammunition. He fell 2,000 votes short of defeating Duryea, but that performance impressed Ralph Hausrath, the *Newsday* Suffolk editor. "I sent a memo to Hathway and said, 'Hey, I think that next year, this Macy outfit could be knocked off,' " Hausrath said. "We got tons of letters in opposition to Macy. I saw that it was a good circulation-builder."

In 1950, when Macy prepared to run for his third term in Congress,

Newsday was more than ready to take him on. The chosen vehicle was Greenwood — a desperate long shot. "He was a pleasant, soft-spoken guy who certainly didn't belong in the same ring with Macy," said Jack O'Grady, who covered Greenwood on and off during the 1950 campaign. "No one gave him a chance." But Greenwood had one powerful asset: Alan Hathway. "I think he *was* the campaign," said Jack Rettaliata, a friend of Hathway and a public relations official at Grumman Aircraft Engineering Corporation, Long Island's major aviation manufacturer. Greenwood needed help in a variety of ways. "He was articulate, but in a Shakespearean way," O'Grady said. "I mean his language was far above the crowd of clam diggers he was talking to, and someone had to pull out those little slogans and teach him how to read it." Occasionally, that someone turned out to be Hathway himself. "Alan had to severely edit his talks," Rettaliata said. "He'd take them away from him and blue-pencil the damn things and give them back, and say: 'Don't say any more than that.' "

Hathway also helped by paying close attention to the way *Newsday* displayed campaign stories. "The copy would come in from Suffolk on Greenwood," said Wes Sheffield, an editor on the night desk at the time. "Alan would hang around and see that it was properly slotted the way he wanted." As a result, campaign accusations against Macy would run upfront, while stories favorable to Macy got less prominent display. "We were giving Ernie Greenwood the best kind of publicity," Sheffield said. "He was given good position and favorably reported." On October 24, for example, the top of page three is the first of a two-part series on Macy's voting record in Congress, under the headline, "Macy One of Congress' Best Loafers." Throughout the campaign, *Newsday* harped on this theme in editorials, columns and news stories. "While other legislators are putting in a five-day week weighing and voting on vital national issues," the story said, "the featherbedding representative from Suffolk and a big chunk of Nassau County, is loafing 75 per cent of the time." Along with that heavily editorialized story, *Newsday* ran a small, unflattering photo of Macy, in which the pattern of light and shadow on his face made him look like a character from a monster movie. Just below the Macy story was a Greenwood photo, four times as large, showing Greenwood with his right hand raised in exhortation. "Greenwood to Wage Street-Corner Fight," the headline on the story said.

The imbalance became so pronounced that Alicia felt compelled to step in. "Miss Patterson called up and said we have to have . . . something about Macy," said the reporter Sheldon Binn. "Bea Jones, who was then on rewrite, was told to go do a story about Macy so we would have equal coverage." That is not to say that Alicia wasn't in favor of murdering Macy. In fact, her rooting interest was well known even as far away as Illinois. "I hope you can get Macy; he's the kind of character that louses up this political business and freezes the bright young hopefuls out," Adlai Stevenson wrote to her.

In addition to *Newsday*'s help, Greenwood got one major lucky break: a complex story that came to be known as "the Hanley letter." It began in the spring of 1950, when the incumbent Republican governor, Thomas Dewey, announced that he was not running for reelection. Lieutenant Governor Joe Hanley became the prime candidate to succeed Dewey, and Macy, a bitter opponent of Dewey, contributed substantially to Hanley's campaign. Then Dewey changed his mind and decided to run. Publicly, Hanley said that he had chosen freely to step aside as a gubernatorial candidate in favor of Dewey. But in a "Dear King" letter to Macy, Hanley told another story: Dewey had persuaded him to accept the nomination for United States Senate and promised him a state job if he lost the Senate race. That was too tempting for Hanley to refuse, since he was heavily in debt. So Hanley stepped aside and ran for Senate. In his letter to Macy, Hanley explained Dewey's offer, acknowledged his indebtedness to Macy and another contributor, the media titan Frank Gannett, and apologized abjectly for backing out.

Somehow, Democrats got hold of Hanley's letter, and accusations started to fly: that Dewey had bought off Hanley, that Macy had leaked the letter himself, to let the world know about Dewey's actions, that Macy's contributions to Hanley represented an effort to control the state, as he controlled Suffolk. The *New York Times* got the story before *Newsday* did, but *Newsday* jumped in enthusiastically, with a huge page-one headline, "HANLEY BARES/DEWEY JOB DEAL," and a theory that Macy had leaked the letter because he wanted the Senate nomination for himself. The whole affair ended badly for Hanley, who got the Senate nomination and lost to Herbert Lehman, and badly for Macy, whose congressional campaign suffered a serious setback. If Macy did leak the letter to help himself, it didn't work. "He destroyed Hanley," said Joseph Carlino, the Long Beach Republican leader, "but he also destroyed himself."

The Hanley letter had given Hathway and Greenwood potent ammunition, but Hathway did not rely on news alone. Taking no chances, he went out into the streets to help Greenwood more directly. To provide Greenwood a campaign song, for example, Hathway went to his friend Ross MacLean, who operated an inn at Roosevelt Field. MacLean was the co-author of a 1947 song called "Too Fat Polka (She's Too Fat for Me)," which Arthur Godfrey had made into a best-selling record. "We got them to agree to let us use it, and we wrote a parody," said Bob Pfeifle, who also covered the campaign for *Newsday*. There was a natural audience for polka music among the large Polish population in Riverhead, in the heart of Macy's district. To make sure that they heard it, Pfeifle took a Polish-language version of the theme song, climbed in a Piper Cub and personally piloted the tape to a radio station in New Haven whose signal covered the East End. Hathway also arranged for a flat-bed truck, Pfeifle said, and he and Hathway helped to hoist a piano onto the truck, so they could use the music to help gather audiences for Greenwood's speeches. "If you had three people show up," Pfeifle said, "then it's a speech and then you can give a fair report of the speech, right? It's a political gathering." In addition, the campaign used sound trucks blaring out Greenwood's message. "One of the things I organized was the sound trucks," Rettaliata said. "They just ran over Long Island day in and day out." Hathway provided tapes of Greenwood's speeches to be played over the loudspeakers and actually went out on the truck himself, Rettaliata said.

Using his own newspapers, Macy attacked *Newsday* for its unfairness. In one editorial, the *Bay Shore Sentinel* described the *Newsday* formula for covering Republicans: " 'Tear into them, boys; knock 'em down and don't stick to fact too closely. Mix it with sex and sensationalism, chuck in a cocktail from the nearest bar, a few lewd pictures, and play up that human failing — gambling, so that we'll be able to have a legalized bookie nearby.' " In cartoons in *Newsday*, Macy appeared with a "Dear King" crown on his head. In Macy's papers, Alicia later appeared as a black-robed witch named Malicia, holding by the neck a dead duck labelled Nassau and a still-squawking duck named Suffolk, poised perilously over a bubbling cauldron labelled "Newsday Circulation."

Besides his battle with *Newsday*, Macy had a long-standing disagreement with J. Russel Sprague, the Nassau Republican leader. That was a real problem, since Macy's district included a significant chunk of Nassau. So Macy went into election day carrying two huge burdens. That night, the final result remained uncertain, and it became clear that the Macy-Greenwood election was one of the closest congressional races in decades, despite Macy's advantages of party enrollment and incumbency. *Newsday*'s campaign had obviously hurt Macy. Two days after the election, Macy's *Bay Shore Sentinel* lashed out at *Newsday* as a "sneering, snarling sheet that deals in dirt, filth and slime; caters to the lowest instincts of humanity and represents the dregs of the newspaper profession." Hathway sent a copy of the editorial to Alicia, along with a note that said: "From one of your dregs."

Almost two weeks after election day, the Suffolk County Board of Elections completed the official canvass and found that Greenwood had beaten Macy by 138 votes. On the same day as the vote count ended, Macy announced that he was resigning as county Republican leader. Under a headline, "Exit the King," a *Newsday* editorial gloated. "The Kingfish has ruled with an unbending hand of iron and regularly stayed away from a Congress he was paid to attend," the editorial said. "This newspaper campaigned for Mr. Greenwood and we believe he will make a good, hard-working representative." Over the next few months, the question of just how hard *Newsday* actually campaigned for Greenwood remained in the headlines. Despite his narrow defeat at the polls and his resignation as chairman, Macy did not fade quietly from the scene. Within days after the final count, Macy began a legal battle to reverse the election on the grounds of voting fraud and irregularities. Macy lost that case all the way up to the Court of Appeals, the state's highest court. The House Campaign Committee also rejected Macy's complaints right after the election. But Macy pursued his appeal in Congress, including accusations about *Newsday*.

Macy's allegations set off a series of loosely structured evidence-gathering hearings in Nassau County, to provide testimony for Congress. At those hearings, Hathway admitted that he had told Greenwood's campaign manager that a sound truck would be a wonderful idea, but *Newsday* didn't pay for it. Democratic party officials testified that they paid for all sound trucks, radio time and recordings. But Ralph Hausrath said years later that *Newsday* played a central role. "*Newsday* had undoubtedly hired the sound truck," Hausrath remembered. "I really didn't see anything wrong. If Hathway seemed to think this was okay, I thought it was okay."

On the question of the leaflets, Greenwood produced his own check to prove that he, not *Newsday*, had paid for the printing. But one of the printers acknowledged that Bob Pfeifle, who was covering the campaign, had placed the order for the leaflets, on an errand from Greenwood. When Alicia testified, she said that the leaflets were intended to boost circulation in Levittown. "The election was a hot issue," she testified, "and we wanted to show the people of that area that we are a virile, vigorous newspaper and not afraid to take a stand on an issue." Apparently, some brochures connected with the Macy campaign came from the job printing shop in Hempstead that had published the *Hempstead Sentinel* before *Newsday* killed the *Sentinel*. "We printed something in connection with that Greenwood thing," said Kenneth Van de Water Jr. of Sentinel Printing. "Alan called me and he said there was something brewing and we could possibly be called to say that *Newsday* had ordered this piece of printing." He wasn't called to testify.

In early 1952, at the end of the hearing process, a House subcommittee rejected Macy's charges and approved a resolution confirming that Greenwood was entitled to the seat in which he had been sitting for a year. Macy fought on and haunted the halls of Congress, cajoling, buttonholing, arguing, even weeping. But the full House of Representatives also accepted Greenwood's election, and Macy lost the fight for his seat — 16 months after he had lost the election.

III

As a CONGRESSMAN, Ernest Greenwood was open, accessible and helpful to his constituents. But in 1952, when he ran for reelection, Greenwood had to overcome the Dwight Eisenhower landslide and an attractive young opponent. This time, Alan Hathway wasn't out in the streets campaigning for him.

Greenwood's opponent in 1952 was Stuyvesant Wainwright, a rich lawyer who had served in the Office of Strategic Services during World War II, then got into politics when W. Kingsland Macy needed someone to do fund-raising. "He was a playboy, more or less, and he wanted something to do," said George Lechtrecker, a Democrat who worked in Greenwood's 1950 and 1952 races. Lechtrecker did some research on Wainwright's background and passed along to *Newsday* the fruits of his work. "They printed it," he said, "but they didn't have the same passion." *Newsday* praised Greenwood's performance and endorsed him for reelection, but there was no all-out campaign for him. In 1950, the goal had been to dethrone a dictator and fundamentally alter the balance of power. Now, *Newsday* was supporting an incumbent Democratic congressman in a

Republican district, in a Republican year. And the incumbent wasn't even someone that Alicia enjoyed. "Greenwood was very straitlaced and very schoolmasterish and I guess Alicia didn't like him too well," Ralph Hausrath said. By contrast, she got along well with Wainwright, who was young, attractive and monied, as she was. Wainwright remembered meeting Alicia at her office, where she pulled out a bottle of whiskey and talked with him, over drinks. "After she chats with me for about 10 minutes," Wainwright said, "she says, 'Now, I want to introduce you to my boss.' And in comes old fat Hathway." The three of them discussed issues and parted on friendly terms, even though *Newsday* was endorsing Greenwood that year.

The endorsement alone was not enough to overcome the Eisenhower landslide, and Wainwright defeated Greenwood. In later elections, Alicia regularly supported Wainwright. "I think Hathway grudgingly accepted me because Alicia said, 'This is our guy,' " Wainwright said. Eventually, *Newsday* became critical of Wainwright as well, and he lost to a Democrat from Riverhead named Otis Pike, one of those who felt *Newsday* had shown a defective sense of loyalty to Greenwood in 1952. "When Stuy Wainwright came along, they kind of hung Ernest Greenwood out to dry," Pike said. "I think they were a little cruel in abandoning him."

That was the nature of the beast that was *Newsday*: A politician could ride the tiger's back for years, but then the tiger might stop suddenly, turn around and eat him. Nonetheless, it was a heady experience to ride the tiger, as Greenwood did, and as a politician named R. Ford Hughes did. Hughes was a tall, roughhewn Texan who had come during World War I to Camp Upton, an Army installation in the woods of Suffolk County, and later opened an insurance and real estate business, entered politics and risen to Suffolk County clerk. When Macy announced his plans to resign as party chairman, Hughes became the heir apparent. But Macy changed his mind about giving up his political power and dug in his heels for a long fight. *Newsday* covered the struggle for the Republican leadership intensely, and strongly supported Hughes. Finally, Hughes won the leadership from Macy in September, 1951.

It quickly became clear that Hathway supported Hughes as heartily as he had opposed Macy. "R. Ford Hughes was someone that Alan could deal with," said Jack O'Grady, who had covered the campaign. "Macy wasn't." Soon, Hathway started to complain about the coverage that Hughes was getting from Frank Mooney, a *Newsday* stringer. Ralph Hausrath defended Mooney, but Hathway angrily ordered Hausrath to tell Mooney his stories were not acceptable. "Mooney got up on his high horse and said, 'Okay, I resign,' " Hausrath said. The next victim was Arthur Bergmann, who started as a reporter at *Newsday* in 1951 and quickly got himself in trouble with Hathway over his coverage of Hughes. Bergmann wrote a story about a speech by Hughes, and when the reaction to the speech turned out to be unfavorable, Hughes squawked that Bergmann had misquoted him. So Hathway called Hausrath to tell him that Bergmann was fired. But Bergmann avoided the axe by getting signed statements from witnesses at the meeting, testifying that Hughes had said exactly what Bergmann had attributed to him. "I went through the whole humiliating thing of getting people to say, yes, that story is correct, and brought it back, and then Hathway called me directly," Bergmann said. "He said, 'I understand that story was correct.' I said, 'Right.' He said, 'Well, don't tell anybody anything about it. But you're not fired. . . . I'm giving you a $10 a week raise.' "

Despite his protectiveness of Hughes, Hathway had warned him from the beginning that Hughes and *Newsday* might someday be opponents. Robert Hughes, the son of R. Ford Hughes, remembered his father's account of what Hathway told him: "Alan had said to dad at the time they were going after Macy and after dad became the leader, he said, 'Listen, you're the fair-haired boy,' but he said, 'you know, the nature of our business is such that one day we'll probably be coming after you.' " Just as Hathway predicted, *Newsday* backed away from Hughes when the Republican Party in Suffolk became enmeshed in a series of scandals that attracted the interest of the State Commission of Investigation and brought about the appointment of a special prosecutor. Hughes was not indicted, and the State Commission of Investigation cleared him of any wrongdoing. But the scandals so badly damaged the party's image that the Democrats took control of the county Board of Supervisors in the 1959 elections. "The voters of Suffolk County threw out the Republicans yesterday," the editorial said. "The machine of boss R. Ford Hughes, weighed down by scandal, was repudiated." The party later rebounded from the 1950s scandals, only to be weakened by a new set of scandals in the late 1960s. In a sense, by dethroning King Macy, *Newsday* had altered county politics irrevocably: Instead of a tightly knit party under a single, powerful party leader who ruled autocratically but was essentially honest, the Suffolk Republican Party became a fragile coalition of 10 warring town leaders.

The defeat of Macy, the first major public official brought down by *Newsday*, was a vivid example of personal, partisan, no-holds-barred journalism. "I don't think they'd do it today," said James Melton, who worked for Greenwood's election and then served as a hearing officer at the hearings that probed *Newsday*'s conduct. "I don't think they would come close to doing anything like that today." Once he was out of power, Macy continued to work on his newspapers, but *Newsday*'s campaign had deprived him of politics. "It was awfully hard on pop," said his son, William K. Macy Jr. In 1961, a decade after *Newsday*'s crusade cost him his seat in Congress and his control of the Republican Party, W. Kingsland Macy died.

IV

THE CRUSADE AGAINST W. Kingsland Macy was manufactured news — invented, shaped and perfected by Alan Hathway. Just three weeks after that election, a far bloodier and more random story came roaring unexpectedly down on *Newsday*, testing its ability to respond to breaking news.

The story came at a moment when *Newsday* was most vulnerable: on the eve of Thanksgiving. Since there was no Thursday paper, everyone had left the office when it all began, a few miles from the *Newsday* plant, in the Richmond Hill section of Queens, a half-mile west of the Long Island Rail Road's Jamaica station. Just before it reached the station, the 6:09 p.m. train from Manhattan to Hempstead had slowed at the approach to a signal, then stopped, with its brakes unaccountably locked. Moments later, a second train, which had left Pennsylvania Station for Babylon only four minutes after the first, bore down on the stalled train in the night and plowed into its rear, shearing it down the middle and leaving a mass of twisted steel, dead bodies and moaning passengers. It was the second major crash on the LIRR in 1950. The first, on February 17, had taken 32 lives in Rockville Centre. That crash had provoked loud demands for the creation of a public authority to take over the LIRR and put an end to its long and spotty history as a privately operated railroad, which had culminated in bankruptcy and receivership.

On the evening of the Richmond Hill crash, Harry and Alicia were at Harry's plantation in South Carolina for Thanksgiving. Alan Hathway wasn't at the plant either. The man who finally found him and told him about the train wreck was Bob Hollingsworth, a reporter and rewrite man. Not many hours before the crash, Hathway had fired Hollingsworth in a dispute over the long hours that Hathway had been working him. On Wednesday night, after leaving *Newsday* for what he thought was the last time, Hollingsworth stopped off for a few drinks at a favorite *Newsday* hangout, the Franklin Arms. Over the noise, he heard a vague bulletin on the radio, about a wreck on the LIRR. "Without thinking about the fact that I had really departed from the newspaper, the first instinct was to find Hathway, because I knew that nobody else was working," he said. Finally, he reached him at the Chungking Royal, the Chinese restaurant owned by Hathway's friend, Arthur Lem. A few minutes later, Hathway appeared in person at the bar and ordered Hollingsworth to get to the crash scene. For the moment, at least, Hathway had put the firing out of his mind.

The city editor, Jack Altshul, had been at home, getting ready to go to a restaurant, when he heard the early radio reports of the crash. "Because it didn't seem too serious, I left for the restaurant," Altshul told Stanley Asimov, a student at the Columbia University Graduate School of Journalism, who wrote a 45-page report on *Newsday*'s coverage of the crash — a report that turned out to be his application for a job at *Newsday*. "Then while I was eating, someone came over to me and said it looked bad. When I tried to check the seriousness of the wreck, the telephone lines were swamped." Eventually, Altshul tracked down Dave Rosenbluth, a reporter who had covered the February crash, and sent him to the scene. "Then I cut my dinner short because it seemed to be building up," Altshul said, "and I came to the office."

By 9:15 that night, enough *Newsday* managers had gathered in the Garden City office to hold a strategy meeting. Only 15 minutes later, they had decided that, even though there was no paper scheduled for the next day, they would put out an extra, with no advertising, devoted entirely to stories and photos of the crash. The decision was unanimous and easy, but actually putting out the paper, with the staff scattered to the winds for the holiday, could have been difficult. As it turned out, it wasn't. Even before the 9:15 meeting, reporters had started calling in, volunteering to come to work and leaving phone numbers where they could be reached. "The remarkable thing on that coverage is that we were all off that night, and they didn't really have to call anybody; we all came in," said Beryl Howell, a reporter, who learned of the crash as she was starting to drive home to Long Island after visiting a relative in Brooklyn. "It was a terrible tragedy, but as far as a newspaper person's feeling of camaraderie, of working together on something, it was great."

Reporters and photographers were scattered all over Long Island when they heard about the crash. Berni Fisher learned about it from a cab driver after she left a movie. Ike Eichorn was on assignment in Glen Cove when he first heard, then went on to take some photographs at a high school basketball game, where a motorcycle cop found him in the locker room and told him his photo editor was looking for him. Dick Morseman, the photo editor, had been at home in Brooklyn, where he promised to spend Thanksgiving eve with his family. Phil Sanborne was emerging from a movie at nearly midnight when he heard about the wreck on his car radio and drove to the office. Bea Jones, a night rewrite woman, was fixing a turkey. When they came in, Hathway and Altshul gave each one specific assignments, to avoid duplication. Keeping track of those assignments on a clipboard, they instructed those who were working outside the office to call in every half hour.

The two photographers at the crash, Ike Eichorn and Harvey Weber, divided up the work between them. At one point, while Eichorn took shots at a different location, Weber was working with a photographer from the *Daily News*. Weber spotted a telephone pole that seemed like a good location to get an overall shot. The *News* photographer helped him to climb the pole and in return, Weber agreed to take a photo for him — a common practice at the time. So the *News* photographer threw a holder of film up to Weber, who slid it into his Speed Graphic camera and took the same shot that he had taken for himself. "Well, when they see two or three flashes going off from the same place," Weber remembered, "the next thing, I got a line down there, about eight guys, all wanting the same thing, which I have to do, in all fairness to everybody."

Perhaps the most haunting image to come from the crash was the sight of a man's face, framed in the window of one car, like a grimly realistic painting. The rubble inside the wrecked car completely surrounded him, leaving only the face visible. His eyes were closed and blood dripped from his mouth and nose. No one was sure whether he was dead or alive. "I personally thought he was dead, but other guys had said they saw his eyes moving," Rosenbluth said. "You really couldn't say." A stunning photograph of the man in the window, taken by a free-lance photographer named A. W. Rossetto, appeared on page one of the *Newsday* extra. Since no one knew whether the man had lived or died, the line above the caption read, noncommittally, "ON HIS WAY HOME."

Organizing his story in his head on the way back from Richmond Hill to Garden City, Hollingsworth reached the office at about 4:15 on Thanksgiving morning, but he held off writing the main story until about five o'clock, to make sure he had the latest available information. Then he sat down and pounded it out in about 45 minutes. A few minutes after Hollingsworth finished writing, the presses started rolling, turning out the first of 150,000 copies of the 16-page extra. The huge front-page headline was "78 DIE IN/LI WRECK," and underneath it was the dramatic close-up photograph of the trapped passenger. Hollingsworth stood in the pressroom as Hathway, who had fired him hours earlier, picked up one of the first copies off the press. "This was the first extra that he had ever put out," Hollingsworth said. "His whole heart and soul were in this thing. . . . He wiped one arm across the paper, like that. Then he opened it up to page three and he looked at it. Tears were streaming down his cheeks. And he wiped his arm across page three again. He turned to me with these tears coming down and he said, 'You son of a bitch.' And I looked at him and I said, 'You son of a bitch.' He smiled, stuck out his hand, and he said, 'Do you want to stay?' And I said, 'Yes.' He said, 'Okay.' And we shook hands. So I didn't leave. It was a memorable moment. It still gets me a little bit when I think about it. It changed my whole life, I think."

The spotlight that night fell on the hard-bitten managing editor and the young reporter who came through on a tough story only hours after being fired. But more than just reporters, editors and photographers were needed to put out an extra. The emergency brought out volunteers from all areas of the paper, such as Elizabeth Casey, the first woman to become an outside advertising salesperson at *Newsday*, who shed her sales role and volunteered to come in and do whatever was needed. Someone told her to bring in whiskey for the editorial staff, and she bought five bottles. When she arrived at the plant, she spent hours on the switchboard, trying to locate circulation district managers, who were spread all over. The managers in turn had to line up the carriers.

All of this, of course, was an expensive proposition. It said something about *Newsday* that its top managers could confidently decide to incur all the costs of putting out an extra, with no advertising revenue, while the majority owner and the editor-publisher were in another state. It said something entirely different about the *Long Island Press*, whose office was within walking distance of the crash, that the *Press* decided not to do anything special about the story. One *Press* reporter, George Wheeler, who later came to work for *Newsday*, had just come in from his police beat and arrived at the *Press* building in Jamaica on Wednesday evening, as the switchboard operator was answering calls about the wreck. So Wheeler quickly telephoned his boss, who was at home. "I said, 'Do you want me to go up there and see what I can do about it?' " Wheeler said. The boss answered: " 'Ah, no, kid. Don't bother. We're not publishing anyway. We'll pick it up by wire.' " Another *Press* reporter, Arthur Perfall, who had covered the earlier Rockville Centre accident, also volunteered and got a nonchalant response. Though *Newsday* readers that Thanksgiving got a 16-page extra, filled with photos, lists of the dead and injured, and staff-written stories, *Press* readers got nothing until the next day.

It was a glorious moment in *Newsday* history, and two days later, the paper took note of it with a chest-thumping story about how the extra came to be. But in the extra itself, *Newsday* was anything but self-congratulatory. Rather, the editorial blamed *Newsday*, among others, for failing to do enough after the Rockville Centre crash to avert the tragedy in Richmond Hill. "We have known for years that the LIRR was in deplorable condition," the editorial said. "The wreck at Rockville Centre tipped us off to fierce dangers to human life that lurk in the LIRR's ill health. Yet we did too little. Now, as far as the new dead and maimed are concerned, it is too late. . . . All we can do is cop a plea, guiltily. The job of alarm we have done has only been fair."

V

IF THE PAPER gave inadequate warning of the tragedy waiting to happen on the Long Island Rail Road, it gave no warning at all about a decision that would shape the lives of readers for decades to come: the construction of the Long Island Expressway.

In the early 1950s, as Robert Moses pushed for construction of this limited-access road linking New York City with eastern Long Island, *Newsday* was something less than a vigilant guardian at the gate. Moses shaped the expressway to his own automobile-dominated vision of society, without seriously considering a proposal for construction of a mass-transit line down the center of the road, and his plan was perfectly acceptable to *Newsday*. Editorially, Alicia had sometimes expressed bland, almost apologetic opposition to a Moses proposal, but she met with him regularly and supported most of his ideas. From the moment when *Newsday* first broke the story of his plans for the expressway on September 1, 1953, the paper swallowed the concept whole, because the road would help Long Island grow. "Master Planner Robert Moses has come up with one of the more masterful of his plans for Long Island highways," the September 2 editorial began. "This is the first concrete action taken by a governmental agency to recognize that Long Island is more than New York's playland. . . . It will open Suffolk County for industry, and will relieve the growing pressure on other east-west routes." With *Newsday*'s full support, Moses developed the expressway just as he had planned, creating a hopelessly overloaded road that quickly became the most visible sign of Long Island's congested highway system.

On more immediate, simple and sensational issues than the future of Long Island, *Newsday* was capable of sounding a deafening alarm. Loud and clear, the paper warned on its front page on January 23, 1951: "Newsday Proves: REDS

CAN LAND/A-BOMB ON LI." To show how vulnerable Long Island was, after the government had closed down Coast Guard stations on the Atlantic Ocean beaches in eastern Suffolk County, a team of *Newsday* reporters had landed a mock atomic bomb on the beach and smuggled it to Times Square. This was alerting the public, Hathway-style, and this stunt story seized national attention at a time when fear of communism was on the rise.

Some critics considered the whole bomb story far-fetched and silly, but a stunt or a crusade did not always have to make sense or cling too close to reality before *Newsday* was willing to try it. All that was really necessary was that Alicia or Hathway get excited about something. One example was a 1952 series by a young reporter named Don Kellermann, who volunteered to commit a burglary and spent seven weeks behind bars, so that he could write about prison conditions from the inside. The series was a dangerous brand of journalism that broke the law and in the long run didn't prove very much, but Hathway could get away with it, because Alicia loved a good stunt story or public service campaign at least as much as Hathway did.

A typically frivolous Alicia story from this era was the one involving Christine Jorgensen, a former soldier who went through a sex-change operation to become a woman. The procedure later became commonplace, but in the early 1950s, it caused a sensation. In December, 1952, Ben White, the former *Newsday* reporter who went to the *Daily News* after World War II, scooped the world on the story of the operation. *Newsday* quickly and gleefully jumped in, carrying wire-service reports with titillating headlines such as: "Texan Dated, Kissed Christine: What a Body!" The following Easter, *Newsday* got a piece of the story for itself after the photographer Jim Nightingale learned in a barroom conversation that Jorgensen was staying with her brother in Nassau County. When Nightingale asked Alicia if she would be interested in a photo of Jorgensen in an Easter bonnet, Alicia was skeptical that he could get it, but she encouraged him to try. So Nightingale went to the house, showed Jorgensen a collection of past Easter bonnet photos, often featuring Alicia's society friends, and persuaded Jorgensen to allow him to photograph her, surrounded by lilies provided by *Newsday*. Then he rushed back to the office and developed the negatives. When Alicia found out that he had the photos, she ran into the darkroom, in a fever of excitement. "Honest to God, she was actually running and she skidded and she came to a sliding halt right up to the hypo tray," Nightingale said. "We held up the negatives in front of that viewing lamp, and she said, 'Goddamn it. I never thought you'd do it.' " The caption treated Jorgensen as if she were any other society lady, mentioning nothing about the sex change operation, and the photo took up the entire page one, with a headline in an Old English-style typeface: "Her First Easter Bonnet."

Not every story that caught Alicia's interest was frivolous. In 1951, for example, she became excited about a crusade to save the birthplace of Long Island's most famous poet, Walt Whitman. She assigned her friend Virginia Pasley, who had just come to work at *Newsday*, to write about the efforts of the Walt Whitman Birthplace Association to purchase the house and keep developers from bulldozing it. The association had raised money for two years, but they had come up with only half of the needed $20,000, and their option to buy the house was about to expire. For weeks, *Newsday* plugged the campaign with stories, editorials and lists of contributors. Finally, *Newsday*'s campaign succeeded where the association had failed. On the day of the deadline, the amount that *Newsday* had collected went past the $11,000 mark. The next day, *Newsday* ran a photograph of a high school girl presenting a check to the elderly owners of the Whitman home, to bind the sale contract.

Another typical Alicia campaign at the start of the 1950s was a series of stories by Bob Hollingsworth, exposing the deadly policies of a dog warden in the Town of Hempstead, complete with an editorial that called the dog pound "Dogdom's Dachau." It was a can't-lose story, because Alicia loved dogs. As if there were any doubt, she once expressed her philosophy forcefully to Dick Morseman, the photo editor, during a discussion of the double truck, or centerfold collection of photographs. "She was very, very unhappy about that day's double truck, whatever it was," said the reporter Helen Dudar. "She apparently went on at some length about this, and finally, in exasperation, he said, 'But Miss Patterson, what *do* you want?' And she went like this, 'Dogs! And cats! And murders!'" Everyone knew that she was an animal lover. At her hunting lodge, for example, she refused to use electric collars, which trained dogs by giving them a small shock, until she had experienced the shock herself. At *Newsday*, when the maintenance man Bud Ward discovered a robin's nest on the outside of her office air conditioner one spring, she told Ward not to turn the air conditioner on until the robin's eggs had hatched. And when one of her dogs, Sunbeam, died on the airplane flight south to her lodge, she was devastated. So Alicia was always receptive to dog stories, such as the saga of Butch, which had filled the pages of *Newsday* a few months before the "Dogdom's Dachau" crusade.

Butch was a homeless Saint Bernard who had made dozens of friends in the City of Glen Cove — mooching food from merchants, riding trains, following children to school and letting them climb on his back like a horse. *Newsday* had celebrated this lovable bum in endless feature stories, and when Butch died, *Newsday* built up his son, Teddy, as his successor. But Teddy had a less lovable set of habits, such as devouring sheep on a North Shore estate. Eventually, Alicia decided to buy a new Butch for the people of Glen Cove, and her staff set out to make a surprise delivery of Butch II. But the priest who had owned the sheep-eating Teddy wanted no part of a replacement. "The voice that came through the window said something about, 'Get the hell out of here,'" the photographer Harvey Weber said. This caused great consternation at *Newsday*, until someone persuaded Mayor Luke Mercadante to accept the dog. As it turned out, despite all the hype, Butch II was no less antisocial than Teddy had been. In time, his physical condition deteriorated, and Butch II began munching on children. So Alicia arranged quietly to send him to her sister's ranch in Wyoming. His behavior there was still bad, but at least he was no longer an embarrassment to *Newsday*.

Beyond her love of animals, Alicia's enthusiasms were eclectic. She devoted hundreds of inches of copy during the 1950s to a campaign to keep the federal government from cutting the budget of the Merchant Marine Academy at Kings Point, for example, and she continued to push for legalized off-track betting, to take away gambling from the racketeers. But if a racketeer was interesting enough, she didn't hesitate to give him space in *Newsday*. In early 1950, at the Waldorf-Astoria, Alicia was having lunch with some friends when Frank Costello, one of the leading gambling racketeers in America, came over and introduced himself. He told her that he was her neighbor in Sands Point, and she and her husband ought to stop by for cocktails sometime. Alicia passed the invitation on to Jack Altshul and asked him to write a story and assign his wife, the former *Newsday* photographer Edna Murray, to take the photos.

As Altshul and Murray sat on the terrace of Costello's home in Sands Point, Costello had a radio tuned to the Yankees game, and the Yankees were losing. Inside, a television carried the Giants game, and they were losing too. Costello was betting on both. "Read the papers and they'll tell you I fix the games," Costello said in his raspy voice. "Maybe that's why I bet the Yankees and Giants today and they're both losin'." Then, as Altshul and his obviously pregnant wife were leaving, Costello asked her whether she wanted a boy or a girl. She wanted a girl. "You got it," Costello said. "Costello can rig anything." The story of the interview took up all of page five, plus a centerfold spread of photos inside. And Edna Murray gave birth to a baby girl, Sara, just as Costello predicted. About a year and a half after their meeting with Costello, Altshul sent Helen Dudar to cover Costello's trial for contempt of Congress, and he asked her to tell Costello that Edna was pregnant again. This time they wanted a boy, and Costello assured them that they'd get one. They named the baby Jake.

CHAPTER THIRTEEN

Alicia, Adlai and Ike

I

DURING THE SAME years when Alicia was falling romantically in love with Adlai Stevenson, she was falling politically in like with Ike, which eventually created a cruel dilemma for her.

Alicia's views of the presidency had first caused her difficulty in 1940, when she backed Franklin Roosevelt, while Harry campaigned for Wendell Willkie. Then she had angered her father by continuing to support Roosevelt during the war. But in 1944, she had joined the *Daily News* and others in detesting the idea of a fourth term. "If Roosevelt is re-elected we will be well on the way to a totalitarian form of government," a *Newsday* editorial predicted. Right after World War II, as she developed an intense dislike for President Harry S Truman, Alicia began to argue in *Newsday* that General of the Army Dwight Eisenhower should be in the White House. In 1948, Eisenhower declined to run for the presidency, and the Republicans chose Governor Thomas E. Dewey of New York to run against Truman. Alicia wasn't enthusiastic about Dewey, but she had no respect for Truman. So she endorsed Dewey, which put her on the same side of the issue as Harry. She even wrote the endorsement herself, when the editorial writer Stan Peckham refused. On election night, Dewey carried Nassau and Suffolk counties easily, but that was one of the few pieces of good news that he got. On the same night, Adlai Stevenson won election as governor of Illinois.

At the end of 1949, Alicia dispatched Peckham to Washington to meet with Stevenson, who was speaking at a dinner honoring Herbert Hoover. "Alicia sent me down there to talk to him about what we could do to revitalize the

Republican Party, which was a curious assignment, he being a Democrat," Peckham said. "As I left, I said, 'Well, governor, the most embarrassing thing that could happen to *Newsday* would be if you and General Eisenhower ran against each other for President.' And he laughed merrily and said, 'Don't worry. That will never happen.' " In fact, there was little reason at that time to believe that Stevenson would ever be running against Eisenhower, then the president of Columbia University. If Eisenhower consented to run in 1952, it seemed likely that Harry and Alicia would agree on a candidate, as they had in 1948. "Alicia was always so gung-ho about Eisenhower," Peckham said.

Even if they agreed temporarily on the question of presidential politics, Harry and Alicia were still feuding over other issues — primarily Alicia's continued request that Harry sell her the extra two percent of stock that she needed to acquire a majority ownership of *Newsday*. Following one of her fights with Harry about the two percent, Alicia complained to Peckham about Harry's intransigence. Alicia said she didn't know what to do, but Peckham dreamed up a devious way for her to strike back. He knew that Alicia's sister, Josephine, was on her way out to her ranch in Dubois, Wyoming, and that Alicia planned to join her there later for her regular summer visit. He also knew that Harry had planned a big party for friends the following evening at Falaise. So Peckham suggested that Alicia head for Wyoming immediately and leave Harry without a hostess for his party. "She thought that was a brilliant idea," Peckham said. "I thought so too. I was Machiavellian." With his wife en route west, Harry had to get through the party as best he could, making lame excuses for her absence. "It was several days, I guess, before it dawned on him that that was where she was," Peckham said. "Then he got in a plane and flew out to bring her back."

In the summer of 1951, the bickering became so severe that Alicia thought seriously of divorcing Harry. In a letter from her sister's ranch, she told Stevenson about it. The woman who had occupied so much of his thoughts was telling him that she was ready to divorce her husband. Far from jumping at the chance, Stevenson sounded almost unnerved by the possibility that Alicia might suggest marriage to him. For all his success in attracting women, Stevenson was not ready to marry again. "I think he was deeply hurt in his first marriage," said his sister, Buffie Ives. "I don't think he could face it." So, when Alicia mentioned a divorce from Harry, Stevenson answered her with almost comical caution.

"I was under the impression somehow that things were going better with you & Harry," Stevenson wrote. "The Sat Eve Post blow up sounded like a not too abnormal fit of jealousy behind some ever sensitive ideas of dignity." A few months earlier, the *Saturday Evening Post* had carried a piece about *Newsday* called "The Case of the Hot-Tempered Publisher." Though the article mentioned Harry, it was overwhelmingly about Alicia, and Harry resented any story that slighted his role. "I wish I knew what to suggest, and about all I *can* suggest is *deliberation*," Stevenson wrote. "Certainly to seek a divorce impetuously would be, I should think, a great mistake. Indeed, I should think it would be your last recourse. Three is quite a lot — even for a brave free spirit! Or a 'tough character,' or all the other epithets you used to hurl at yourself. And then there's your child to think about — Newsday! But if it is no longer tolerable, no matter what the price, I suppose you should do it. . . . And then of course you have *him* to consider, whether you want to or not."

Seeking further advice, Stevenson showed or described Alicia's letter to their friend Jane Warner Dick, who wrote him back: "The more I think about that letter from A the more I think you'll have to be very wary and *much* firmer and more forthright than is your natural wont. . . . I like her as a friend, I like her loyalty — (to everyone but her husband — meeow!). I admire her incisive mind and her point of view about many things; but to say that she is temperamentally unstable, self-centered and demanding puts it very mildly. Qualities that may be interesting, amusing, even appealing in a friend are often not those that work out very satisfactorily in a more intimate sort of relationship. . . . Anyway, just remember — BEWARE AND BE FIRM."

Within a few weeks after Stevenson's letter, Harry and Alicia had reached a truce. "Glad to hear that your home life is more tranquil," Stevenson wrote in September. "Harry's quick conversion speaks well for your diplomacy & tact or is there some other explanation. Maybe he was secretly proud of the Sat Eve Post piece after all. Don't get restless about Newsday. It will never be fat cat or smug with you around — at least until you age a lot more my dear." Though Alicia had decided not to divorce Harry, she continued to be frustrated whenever they fought, because their styles of argument were so different. "He'd always win because she never kept her cool," said Alicia's friend, Virginia Pasley. In the early 1950s, after the introduction of the tranquilizer, Miltown, Alicia used the new drug as a way of equalizing the emotional temperatures in their arguments. Pasley remembered: "She took to taking one a half an hour before she was going to take up something with Harry that she knew was going to be a fight, to keep her calm."

II

WITH THE MAJORITY owner and the editor-publisher in accord on the candidacy of Dwight Eisenhower in 1952, *Newsday* worked hard to get Eisenhower the nomination.

It was not until early 1952 that Eisenhower confirmed that he would leave his position as the commander of all allied forces in Europe to accept a Republican nomination for the presidency, and *Newsday* played a role in that process: Alan Hathway helped to organize an Eisenhower rally at the Garden City Hotel, as a preliminary to a larger rally at Madison Square Garden. "Alan and I staged this rally to organize Long Island's delegation informally," said Paul Townsend, the publicist who had worked with Hathway on the postwar campaign for veterans' housing. The morning after the Garden City rally, the headline on page one of *Newsday* was: "LI CHEERS SPEED/IKE BANDWAGON."

During the week that followed, *Newsday* ran a promotional story about the Madison Square Garden rally, under the headline: "All Roads Lead to NYC for 'I Like Ike' Rally." At the end of the story, *Newsday* ran a list of the names and phone numbers of the rally organizers. On the morning of the rally, *Newsday* ran an advance story on page three. "No paper did more to fill Madison Square Garden than *Newsday*," said John Reagan "Tex" McCrary, the radio personality who was leading the rally, along with Jacqueline Cochran, whose wartime band of women pilots had been so attractive to Alicia. "They publicized the hell out of it for me." The morning after the Manhattan event, *Newsday* led the paper with a huge headline, "33,000 YELL FOR/IKE AT NY RALLY," reporting that there were 15,000 people inside Madison Square Garden, plus another 18,000 outside.

To make sure that Eisenhower understood the support expressed at the rally, McCrary took a canny step. "We did a three-hour kinescope of that whole rally, and Jackie flew it to Ike in Paris the next morning," McCrary said. The general and the pilot watched it together, and when it was over, Eisenhower poured drinks. Cochran raised a toast, "To the President!" she told Stephen Ambrose, an Eisenhower biographer. "I was the first person to ever say this to him and he burst into tears." The rally and the kinescope played a role in Eisenhower's resolve to run for the presidency. Two decades later, Mamie Eisenhower, his widow, wrote to McCrary: "When Jackie Cochran flew over with the film of the 'amateur' rally that you started in Madison Square Garden I admit that it was the first time Ike and myself realized how interested you all were in his coming home to run for the Presidency."

Over the next few months, as Eisenhower's backers maneuvered in the presidential primaries and at the nominating convention, *Newsday* covered the race extensively, prodding the Eisenhower camp and criticizing the more conservative forces of Senator Robert A. Taft of Ohio. Beyond the editorial page, the paper gave clear signals of its sympathies in a variety of ways.

On March 19, *Newsday* reported Eisenhower's huge write-in vote in Minnesota, the home of perennial presidential hopeful Harold Stassen. Eisenhower got more than 108,000 write-in votes, compared to 129,000 for Stassen, whose name *was* on the ballot. On the front page, *Newsday* ran a huge photograph of a grinning Eisenhower, covering the entire page. Further underlining the importance of the event, *Newsday* printed the page in blue ink, a breakthrough that required all-night improvisation. Late the previous night, the production superintendent Allan Woods had called Harvey Broad in the pressroom and asked him to figure out a way to print color. "We had never even thought of running any kind of color," Broad said. "The press was not equipped to run color of any kind." *Newsday* didn't even have colored ink, which forced Broad to concoct a brew of his own, from kerosene and a blue liquid used in the machine shop for marking pieces of metal to be cut. Then Broad sat on the floor, squirting the homemade ink into the press with an oil can. Somehow, this jury-rigged system worked and produced a blue front page. "Miss Patterson came in and she was so happy when she saw that," Broad said. Eventually, he ran out of the makeshift ink. By then, an ink salesman had come around with factory-produced ink, which produced a deeper blue than Broad's homemade concoction had provided. "She saw a copy of it," Broad remembered, "and she said, 'Stop the presses. I don't want that color. It looks like the *Journal-American*.' " For the rest of the press run, the front page went out in black and white, but the brief burst of blue had been *Newsday*'s first color front page — an innovation that flowed entirely from Alicia's enthusiasm for Eisenhower.

Only two months later, Alicia toured Europe and met with Eisenhower himself. The result was an editorial and Alicia's glowing full-page report on Eisenhower. "One quality struck me strongly about Eisenhower," Alicia wrote. "Here was an honest man; here was a man incapable of double dealing. . . . I have talked to many politicians in my life. It was a blessed relief at long last to talk to a man who appears to be above the slime of our present day politics. . . . I am more convinced than ever that I LIKE IKE." *Newsday* liked Eisenhower so much, in fact, that the circulation department made available to the readers a campaign-style button that featured a photograph of the general and a *Newsday* logo. In a familiar *Newsday* typeface, the button proclaimed the paper's position: "WE LIKE IKE."

Given that enthusiasm for Eisenhower, the 1952 campaign would have presented little difficulty for Alicia, if the Democratic Party's needs had not overwhelmed Adlai Stevenson's reluctance. As late as the closing months of 1951, just before the rallies at the Garden City Hotel and Madison Square Garden, Stevenson gave Alicia every reason to believe that he would not become a presidential candidate. "Ike would, of course, be a very strong candidate," Stevenson wrote her on October 16, 1951. "As for me, I don't want any national business." In fact, he didn't even want to run for reelection as governor of Illinois unless the Democratic machine in Chicago was willing to put up a quality candidate for state's attorney in corruption-ridden Cook County, and meet a number of other conditions. A month later, he wrote Alicia again, still indecisive about the Illinois race. The letter started with concern about her health. "And what is this about a threatened collapse!" he wrote. "I want *more* and *exact* and *honest* details and at once!!! What have you been doing — working too hard — why? — Worrying? — about what? Why? Dieting? Why? Drinking? In short, what the hell, and why not act your age?" As to the political situation, Stevenson said: "I literally don't know whether I could physically survive another campaign and 4 more years. . . . Moreover if Ike runs and it turns into a landslide as well it might I'm not sure I could win against the deluge."

But by the end of January, 1952, things had changed for Stevenson. President Harry Truman had decided not to run for reelection, and he had approached Chief Justice of the United States Fred Vinson as his successor. When Vinson declined, Truman had turned to Stevenson. The governor tried to be secretive about his White House appointment during the week of January 20, but the story leaked. Marquis Childs, who had become friendly with Alicia during the war and became a regular *Newsday* Washington columnist, revealed in his column on January 18 that Truman had decided not to run and that he favored Stevenson as the candidate. During the week of Stevenson's meeting with Truman, Stevenson's face appeared on the cover of *Time* magazine and *The Atlantic*. But when Stevenson and Truman met, Stevenson expressed a strong reluctance to run for the presidency.

Right after the Stevenson-Truman meeting, and just a week before the Eisenhower rally at the Garden City Hotel, in which *Newsday* played such a large role, Alicia showed that she had not forgotten her friend. She devoted an entire column on the editorial page to a discussion of the Stevenson furor, including photographs of the *Time* and *Atlantic* covers. In a stroke of Solomonic wisdom dictated by Alicia's growing dilemma, the editorial laid the groundwork for the position that she maintained throughout the campaign, that Eisenhower and Stevenson were both great men: "If the Republicans nominate Dwight Eisenhower for President, and the Democrats choose Adlai Stevenson, it will be a blessing for the country."

The following week, Stevenson wrote Alicia an anguish-filled letter describing his sudden, frenzied immersion in presidential politics. "Never did disaster befall an innocent bystander quite as abruptly as it did me last week," he wrote, complaining of his "great distress of soul and mind about this sudden clamor about the Presidency — in which, thanks to a loving publisher, even Newsday has joined." All he wanted, he told her, was to be reelected governor. In the same letter, he expressed disappointment that he had been unable to spend time with Alicia at her hunting lodge: "I'd dreamed of it, of escape, of the river, of tennis, of sun, of you, my wee, wicked bird. I must to bed — with a prayer that you can forgive my last minute 'chucking' as the English say — an X, another XX, and thanks for the best editorial I've seen regarding that remarkable, virtuous fraud, the Governor of Illinois — who really does know his own measure and has no illusions."

Soon after the Eisenhower rallies, Alicia demonstrated again that her heart was with Stevenson, even though her editorial page was with Eisenhower. She spoke with Harry's nephew, Roger W. Straus Jr., about the possibility that his publishing firm — then known as Farrar, Straus and Young — could publish a campaign biography of Stevenson. "She called me and said this man was going to be very important," said Straus, who later published a book by a writer named Noel Busch. "It was an enormous seller." The publication of the book was helpful to Stevenson, but the suppression of some unflattering biographical material was even more important. That came about because Straus had become friendly with Stevenson's former wife, Ellen Borden, who wanted Straus to help her arrange for syndication of a series of letters in which she questioned Stevenson's virility and his worth as a husband and father. "I sat on them," Straus said. "And I buried them until it was too late for her to be able to use them. Then I returned them to her."

By playing a role in the publication of the campaign biography, Alicia had done what little she could for Stevenson, but Stevenson didn't do much for himself. While Eisenhower was campaigning, and Stevenson-for-President groups were sprouting in Illinois and elsewhere, Stevenson continued to dodge the candidacy. On March 4, he met secretly with Truman and told him that he had made a commitment to run for reelection as governor and he couldn't back out of it. On March 13, he wrote to Alicia: "I will keep out of this thing and concentrate on *being* and *running* for Gov. unless the Democratic convention should nominate me which would seem very unlikely." That letter was the first hint to anyone that he might accept a draft, Porter McKeever said in his 1989 biography of Stevenson. But on April 16, Stevenson issued a statement declining to become a presidential candidate, because of his commitment to run for governor: "I could not accept the nomination for any other office this summer." The optimists saw the use of "could not," instead of something stronger, as evidence that Stevenson might yet change his mind.

Following his statement, Stevenson went to New York to speak at a Democratic dinner honoring New York Governor W. Averell Harriman, whose own candidacy for President could potentially rescue Stevenson from a draft. But Stevenson's speech at the dinner overshadowed Harriman. On his way back to Illinois, Stevenson wrote Alicia that he had performed "too well for my own peace & security from renewed pressure. . . . Harriman did well I thought, but not well enough for the politicians' taste. I 'sold him' as vigorously as I could — and as a President I really believe he would be the best Democratic possibility, indeed a very good President, but as a candidate I suppose they're right and he would be tough to elect against Taft, let alone Ike."

Despite Stevenson's April 16 statement, the presidential drumbeat continued, and he began to wonder whether he should issue the same kind of definitive rejection that General William Tecumseh Sherman had sent to the Republican convention in 1884: "I will not accept if nominated, and will not serve if elected." In May, he wrote to ask advice from Alicia, who was travelling in Greece and elsewhere in Europe. Completely ruling out a run, he told her, would be "a cocky, contemptuous distasteful thing to do and I hate to earn a place in the history books by saying I *won't* do something honorable that has come to few people. Please advise me promptly — shall I say 'No' again and more sharply and decisively; shall I keep still; shall I indicate privately that I would accept a genuine draft — i.e. not let them down if it comes? Help. Help — my wise little bird — my maid of Athens."

Alicia's answer apparently provided him with some comfort. " 'I take my pen in hand' in a bad mood, but rereading my Birdie's sweet letter makes it all feel better," Stevenson wrote. "You're sweet to me and understanding. I really don't want to do it now any more than I did 4 months ago. But I hate to say some further words that may look or sound as tho I deprecate the office or the duty or whatever it is, and, you're right too, that I might well want to try it four years hence." Alicia had also expressed a concern about whether it was safe to continue writing letters, and he reassured her: "There is no reason whatever to discontinue the blue letters; they are never opened at the Mansion — unless of course it makes you feel uncomfortable," Stevenson wrote. "Goodbye my bird — I need you and direct, penetrating logic. So please don't stop the blue envelopes, at least yet."

Up until the end of June, just before the Republican and Democratic nominating conventions in July, Stevenson remained torn. In a June 27 letter, he told Alicia: "I want so much to stay here and do this job . . . but at the same time if the country really needs me, if theres [sic] a touch of destiny about the draft business, then I don't want to thwart it and make a tragic mistake. . . . Any suggestions from the wisest little bird I know would be gratefully rec'd."

III

WHILE STEVENSON WRESTLED inconclusively with himself, Alicia continued to support Eisenhower and to cope with her own problems.

One of the complications was a falling out with Stan Peckham, largely because he felt she was asking him to assume broader responsibilities in her absence than his actual authority equipped him to handle. "She'd come back and ask, 'What in the hell did you let Hathway do that for?' " Peckham said. "Well, hell, Alan wouldn't listen to me. Neither would the advertising manager or anyone else." When Alicia returned from Europe in 1952, they had another fight over that issue, and Peckham decided to take a vacation at his mountain cabin, to cool off emotionally. While he was in Colorado, he got a job offer from the *Denver Post* — a bit of an irony, since that was the paper that Alicia had long ago described to him as the one that she wanted *Newsday* to emulate. When he returned to New York, she summoned him to a meeting at her Manhattan townhouse and gave him a list of orders. "I sat there and said, 'I'm not going to do any of those things,' " Peckham said. "She blew up and said, 'Now Stan, I don't want you to give me any more trouble.' She practically broke into tears. I said, 'I'm not going to give you any more trouble. I am going to work for the *Denver Post*. . . .' Then they had a big party out at Falaise for me. I got a beautiful send-off. From then on, Alicia and I were much better friends then we had ever been when I was working for her." Even if his departure helped their friendship, it also deprived her of a trusted editorial writer in the middle of convention season.

At the Republican convention in early July, *Newsday* consistently supported Eisenhower against Senator Robert A. Taft and his allies. Alicia considered the Taft wing to be the party's Old Guard, and she felt that the Chicago convention was critically important in the struggle between the Old Guard and the more moderate elements in the party. "Here indeed we stand at Armageddon," she wrote, in an analysis piece. "Here will be decided, in my opinion, the final fate of the GOP. . . . It is a struggle to the death between the future and the past." On the same page, Alan Hathway himself wrote the day's lead story — about the Michigan and Pennsylvania delegations moving toward Eisenhower. Besides Alicia and Hathway, the staff at the Republican convention included two veteran reporters whose assignments Alicia controlled personally: Virginia

Pasley and Hal Burton. (*Newsday* even made its convention staff look larger by putting a Chicago dateline on a story written on Long Island by Bob Hollingsworth.) For a suburban newspaper that had only recently become profitable, that was an expensive allocation of staff. But the strength of that commitment enabled *Newsday* to flex its young muscles in national politics, offering advice freely to the most powerful men in America. Alicia even went so far as to suggest to Eisenhower, in another analysis piece, that he should appoint Governor Thomas Dewey attorney general after the election.

A little more than a week after the Republican convention ended, Alicia opened the *Newsday* coverage of the Democratic convention — also in Chicago — with an analysis piece about her friend. "Adlai: The man who doesn't want to run," she began. "The strangest phenomenon of this strange convention is Adlai Ewing Stevenson, the Governor of Illinois, the man who doesn't want to be President.

"Although the Governor has been telling the same story to reporters, to politicians, to friends over a period of months no one has believed him. How is it possible that he could refuse the highest office in the land? Men have lied, men have cheated, men have sold their birthright to become the President of the United States. Stevenson had only to nod his head and he could have been the unanimous choice of the Democratic Party. But the nod has not been forthcoming. Why?

"I have talked to the Governor several times over the past weeks and he is a human in sore distress. He does not want the nomination, neither does he want to serve notice that if drafted he would refuse to run. 'How can I do that,' he asked me, 'when young men are dying in Korea?' "

Then Alicia reviewed Stevenson's record in Illinois and offered her insight into the reasons for his success. "His vote-getting genius is hard to explain," she wrote. "He follows none of the accepted shibboleths of the politician. He abhors histrionics or purple passages or exaggerated gestures. He hasn't the silver tongue of William Jennings Bryan or the physical force of Theodore Roosevelt. But the people love him. Perhaps the answer lies in a curious combination of great wit, great humbleness and great courage. He is the most modest man I have ever met. He never quite believes that this role belongs to him. And yet when the chips are down over some issue he believes to be right, he fights with the ferocity of ten tigers. He doesn't care what politician is hurt in the process or what it will do to the machine." This argument for Stevenson ran on page three, with the news stories, but it reached a rhetorical conclusion more suited to the editorial page. "The only man in Chicago qualified for the job is the man who prayerfully hopes he won't get it," Alicia wrote. "For the sake of this country, it is to be hoped that, in the last extremity the convention will nominate him. Then there will be two good men to choose between. It will be a dark hour for Stevenson but he has the necessary courage to rise above his own desires. And above all he is a patriot."

At the end of that turbulent week's events — a stop-Stevenson drive by Senator Estes Kefauver of Tennessee, struggles between the northern and southern wings of the party, and finally Stevenson's third-ballot victory — the governor of Illinois came before the convention to accept the nomination. Alicia had called him a patriot, but to Burton, who was present for the acceptance speech, Stevenson appeared like a reluctant one. To Burton's horror, Stevenson compared his situation to Christ's agony in the garden, the night before the crucifixion. "I have asked the merciful Father of us all to let this cup pass from me," Stevenson said, paraphrasing Christ's prayer in the garden. "But from such dread responsibility one does not shrink in fear, in self-interest, or in false humility. So, 'If this cup may not pass away from me, except I drink it, Thy will be done.'" Burton was appalled. "I turned to Alicia and I said, 'That kid ain't gonna make it.' She said, 'Shut up!'" His skepticism about Stevenson infuriated her. "I remember Alicia wouldn't speak to me for about a week," Burton said.

Still, for all her pride in her friend, Alicia could not legitimately back down in her support of Eisenhower. "This newspaper, the first in the United States to favor the Presidency of Dwight Eisenhower, does not retreat from that stand, and will use whatever influence is at our command to insure his election this November," the editorial said. "We feel that the country needs a change of administration, needs a Republican President — in short, needs Eisenhower. Nevertheless, an honest appraisal of Adlai E. Stevenson makes clear that if the nation prefers another Democrat, Stevenson will make a magnificent President." Despite *Newsday*'s struggles with the monolithic Republican Party in Nassau and Suffolk, she felt that 20 years of Democrats in the White House was enough. But she was clearly on the horns of a nasty dilemma. "However it comes out," the editorial concluded, "and we hope it comes out with Eisenhower as President, the United States is luckier than it has been in many a year."

The paper's position was so schizophrenic that Jimmy Jenkins, an editor who had the power to reshape the paper in the morning as the presses began to roll, took it into his own hands to keep Stevenson stories out of *Newsday* — even though Stevenson was Alicia's close friend. "He just wouldn't let him in the goddamn paper," said Don Kellermann, who worked with Jenkins. "Stevenson would make a speech and you would never know that there was a campaign. . . . He said, 'Miss Patterson doesn't want him in the paper.' I said, 'What do you mean?' He said, 'We're for Eisenhower. This is a Republican paper.'"

During the campaign, *Newsday* editorials tiptoed down the middle between Eisenhower and Stevenson, criticizing each occasionally. For example, consistent with its stand in 1947, when the paper took advantage of the Taft-Hartley Act to kick out the Newspaper Guild, *Newsday* criticized Stevenson for advocating repeal of Taft-Hartley. But the editorials spoke glowingly about his intelligence and skill as a speaker, and poked fun at Eisenhower's tangled rhetoric. On a far more serious matter, *Newsday* went after Eisenhower's running mate, Senator Richard M. Nixon of California, over an $18,000 personal expense fund that wealthy businessmen had provided for him. After Nixon's televised "Checkers" speech, explaining the fund and defending it, *Newsday* ran an editorial urging him to withdraw from the race. The same editorial found no wrongdoing in Stevenson's own "fund" controversy: an effort to use leftover campaign money to augment the salaries of state officials, after legislators had refused to vote them a raise. "Stevenson was careless or naive in not making a greater effort to tell the people of Illinois about the fund," the editorial said, "but he is not guilty of concealing it." *Newsday* did continue to cover the Stevenson fund story, but it faded away without real damage to his campaign. As to Nixon, when Eisenhower kept him on the ticket, *Newsday* was unhappy. "We do not agree with the public decision," the editorial said, "but in weighing the advantages of Eisenhower against the disadvantages of Nixon, we believe that Ike is worth the cost." On balance, given Alicia's personal attachment to Stevenson, the editorial page did a reasonably even-handed job of commenting on the campaign. And when she chose to run in *Newsday* an excerpt from the Noel Busch campaign biography of Stevenson that she had helped to launch, she ran a similarly large excerpt from an Eisenhower biography the next day.

Outside the pages of the paper, Alicia tried to help Adlai by hosting a September 21 dinner at the River Club, a prestigious Manhattan restaurant, for a group of newspaper publishers, who almost unanimously supported Eisenhower. To give Stevenson an opportunity to spend some time with all the guests, Alicia arranged to leave one chair empty at every table. "Adlai had one course at each table, and that was Alicia's idea, which I think has been copied ever since," said Roger Straus, who was at the dinner. Among the guests were Clare Boothe Luce, the wife of Henry R. Luce, co-founder of *Time* magazine, and Dorothy Schiff, the publisher of the *New York Post*, which was one of the few major papers supporting Stevenson. Mischievously, Alicia left an empty seat between the two high-powered women, which allowed them to skirmish for Stevenson's attention. "Well, it was very funny," said Virginia Pasley, who was covering the campaign for *Newsday*. "I was sitting at another table, but I was close enough to see. Dolly got him first. She wouldn't let him go. So Clare never had a word in edgewise." Despite Luce's breeding, Pasley later overheard her spewing out a stream of four-letter words. "So if Alicia wanted to start a little trouble, she sure did it."

During the evening, Alicia provided another note of mischief by reading aloud a telegram from Harry. The text was gracious, but it contained a sly dig at Alicia's friend: "Tell Adlai how sorry I am not to be able to dine with him. I would like to dine with him anywhere — even in the White House — if we are both guests of Ike." This reading provided a chuckle for the dinner guests, but not for Stevenson's young aide, William McCormick Blair Jr. "I thought it was unnecessary to have read that," Blair said. "I remember I wasn't very amused. I don't think it bothered him, at least that I recall. He was so very fond of Alicia. She meant it in a nice way." The dinner, of course, did nothing to help Adlai Stevenson with the newspapers, which overwhelmingly supported Eisenhower.

At the dinner, Pasley said, Alicia had been suffering from a high fever. Soon afterward, she checked into Doctors Hospital, complaining of the fever and abdominal pains. This was not her first health problem, by any means. She had already had surgery for ulcers and for gynecological disorders. This time, she had a crushing combination of ailments that brought her very low, physically and emotionally. On September 27, doctors performed an exploratory diagnostic curettage, removing tissue that seemed to show that she had uterine cancer. A week later, on October 3, while Adlai Stevenson was setting out on a campaign trip through Ohio, Iowa and Minnesota, a team of surgeons opened up Alicia. They discovered that the cancer was not in her uterus but in her sigmoid colon. They removed that large malignant tumor and found, fortunately, that the cancer had not spread to her lymph glands. They removed her left ovary and took out her uterus, because its lining had atrophied as a result of radium treatments several years earlier, for excessive menstrual bleeding. In addition, they performed a colostomy, creating a temporary artificial anus.

All of this was terribly painful and depressing for Alicia. "She nearly bought it that time," her sister Josephine said. "I went there and stayed with her all the time. She said, 'It's too much pain. I want to die.' She used to say, 'Happiness is surcease from pain.' " Later, Alicia acknowledged how desperate she had been during this period. "I completely lost the will to live," Alicia said. "It was Josephine who restored it to me. She sat by my bedside for hours at a time and cussed me out as a yellowbelly until I got so mad I decided to 'show her.' "

Convinced that she was going to die, Alicia wrote a touching letter to Stevenson. "When you read this I will be residing in spirit by the banks of the black river," she wrote, referring to the St. Mary's River, which flowed past her hunting lodge. She and Stevenson often called it the black river, because the native vegetation discolored the water. "One day perhaps you will pass the St. Mary's & I will turn into a breeze to kiss your nose.

"I am enclosing the letters you wrote me. I think they are beautiful letters and I hope you will not destroy them. Perhaps you would consider turning them over to the Illinois Historical Society to be opened a hundred years hence when all your family will have died.

"How wonderful it would have been if Lincoln had written Ann Rutledge and those letters had been preserved. With your sense of history please think it over.

"I love you so much."

At the height of Stevenson's presidential campaign, instead of being at her desk at *Newsday*, Alicia had to spend more than a month in the hospital, from September 22 to October 25. A month later, she returned to the hospital again, from November 29 to December 14, to have the colostomy closed. Stevenson and Alicia did not correspond frequently during this period, but a few days after her operations, he learned about her condition and wrote her from the state capitol in Springfield. "A letter from Josephine brings me the shocking news about your operations, that you can't talk by phone etc.," Stevenson wrote. "I get to N.Y. toward the end of the ordeal and hope I can catch a glimpse of the convalescent — and also hear about her operations! My prayers are with you — and I can use any you have to spare — not just for victory but for survival."

By the time the campaign neared its conclusion, Alicia was out of the hospital and back at work, supervising the editorial page. The final editorial of the campaign, like those that came before it, was a delicate balancing exercise that reflected her unique dilemma. "Both Gen. Eisenhower and Gov. Stevenson have turned out to be good, hard-working campaigners," the editorial said. "The major issues are still the need for a change, Democratic corruption, tolerance of communism, Far Eastern foreign policy, and labor legislation. . . . Because of these issues, and not because one man is more able than the other, we give our continued backing to Eisenhower. In reaffirming this position, we also reaffirm our high opinion of Stevenson. . . . Because Stevenson is a Democrat, the corruption of the Truman Administration, the waste, bungling and expediency, the toleration of communism would be infinitely harder for him to destroy than for Eisenhower, despite Stevenson's honest devotion to the task. Under Stevenson, there could not be the widespread change from top to bottom that this nation needs." No matter which man won, the editorial concluded, he should make a place for the loser in his administration. "If Stevenson wins, he might do well to appoint Ike Secretary of Defense. If Eisenhower wins, Stevenson would be a good man to head up our United Nations delegation."

When Stevenson lost, Alicia sent him a telegram of consolation, and he answered back two days after the election. "Thanks for your wonderful wire and the letter," he wrote. "I'm glad, so glad, you're mending rapidly. I've no regrets; did the best I could, didn't trim, equivocate or clasp dirty hands." Stevenson ended on an oddly cool, almost distancing note: "Sometime we will talk again — maybe by the black river." But the campaign didn't cause any real rift between them. "Don't worry about *Newsday*," he wrote her the following March, from Palm Springs, California. "I had hoped, of course, but I also understand your situation vis a vis Harry — and also your journey thru the valley of the shadow." Then Stevenson set out on a post-election tour of the world, leaving behind the election and Alicia Patterson.

IV

FOR ALL OF *Newsday*'s talk in the closing editorial of the 1952 campaign about the dangers of "toleration of communism," Alicia was remarkably intolerant of America's most outspoken opponent of communism, Senator Joseph McCarthy of Wisconsin.

"Alicia, in the very beginning, was very anti-Communist," said Forrest Corson, a zealous Communist-hunter who did public relations work for the Nassau County Republican Party and published a "pink sheet," warning of the spread of communism. Over time, he said, *Newsday* editorials took on a different tone. "I perceived them as very viciously anti-anti-Communist." At times in its own history, *Newsday* had been willing to use the threat of communism for its own selfish purposes, such as its crusade to oust the Newspaper Guild in 1947 and its support of the Levitt family's exclusion of non-whites from Levittown. But Alicia could not stomach McCarthy. "She thought he was a punk," Hal Burton said. "She went after McCarthy and never made any bones about that." During the maneuvering before the Republican convention in 1952, for example, *Newsday* linked McCarthy and Eisenhower's opponent as two of a kind. "Taft and McCarthy have lined the same nest for the past two years," one editorial said. "McCarthy is a vulturous type bird who likes to leave the bones of assassinated characters strewn behind. Taft prods him on." The editorial cartoon showed a pair of vultures, labelled Taft and McCarthy, slobbering over a pile of bones labelled "innocent reputations."

Alicia's distaste for McCarthy's techniques propelled her into a 1952 struggle against McCarthyite censorship. She had been appearing on a weekly television show called *Starring the Editors,* along with James Wechsler, the editor of the *New York Post.* At the end of July, Wechsler testified in a libel suit that he had joined the Young Communist League at Columbia University in 1934, when he was 18 years old, and had left the league in 1937. That part of Wechsler's past had been a matter of public record for 18 years, and as an adult, he had spoken out against communism. But the sudden publicity flowing from his testimony in the libel trial alarmed the sponsor of *Starring the Editors,* the Grand Union supermarket chain. Grand Union summarily ordered Wechsler removed from the show because he had become controversial.

Angered by this profile in corporate cowardice, Alicia spoke out forcefully during the August 6 program, along with the other editors on the panel. "I feel strongly that it was a terrible mistake to drop Wechsler from this program," Alicia said. "As editor of the *New York Post,* he has been forthright in his stand against communism. Although I rarely agree with the opinions of the *Post,* it is shameful to have banned him because he joined a Young Communist League at the age of 18 — a fact which he freely admitted many months ago." Alicia condemned the country's drift toward witch-hunting and added: "If we follow that road, we will lose the freedom we first fought to win in 1776." Not content with that brief statement, she also wrote an essay on the Wechsler affair that appeared on the front page of the Bulletin of the American Society of Newspaper Editors in September. "Newspapers cannot be content merely to criticize and condemn these crimes against the public interest," she wrote. "They must fight the witch-hunters with all the weapons and all the vigor at their command. We must fight them for our own sakes, but, more deeply, for the weal of the nation."

Both Wechsler and his boss, Dorothy Schiff, were touched by Alicia's spunky defense of the embattled *Post* editor. "I have just seen the bulletin of the A.S.N.E. and I am even more deeply indebted to you than before," Wechsler wrote her. Schiff liked Alicia's essay so much that she reprinted it in the *Post* and described Alicia in the publisher's column as "a very gallant girl." Schiff pointed out that Alicia's father had once been a Socialist. "In his day this was tantamount to a young man being a Communist in the 1930s," Schiff wrote. "I think her understanding of her father may be a reason why she has shown so much interest and sympathy in the case of James Wechsler." In addition, Adlai Stevenson wrote to congratulate her: "Bravo! Your statement in the Bullètin on the Wechsler case was superb, courageous and wholly right. Thank God you stood up to that one." The following year, when McCarthy summoned Wechsler for a "star chamber" investigation of communism in the 1930s, Alicia again galloped to Wechsler's defense with an editorial and a Cliff Rogerson cartoon showing McCarthy as a hissing snake in the grass, sneaking up on a humanoid rolled-up newspaper, representing The Free Press.

Alicia's stand against McCarthy and witch-hunting didn't entirely stamp out red-baiting attitudes at *Newsday*. Following the execution of Julius and Ethel Rosenberg for espionage on June 19, 1953, for example, Jack Mann wrote a long, carefully observed story about their burial on Long Island. The next morning, he was shocked to see that someone on the desk had edited into his story a gratuitous reference to the Rosenbergs as "the traitors," and had altered his reporting in other ways as well. "I busted my ass covering that story," Mann remembered. "I went to the funeral director. I went to the rabbi. . . . I really did a good job of reporting. For example, I said they were buried in a burnished open casket with the Star of David burned three eighths of an inch deep on the lid. It came out clean pine boxes." Someone on the desk had assumed that, because the Rosenbergs were Jewish and because Orthodox Jews used pine boxes for burials, the Rosenbergs were buried in pine boxes — even though the reporter on the scene had observed otherwise. Further down in the story, Mann had referred to plans to build some sort of religious monument over the grave, and someone on the desk added "even though the Rosenbergs had denied their religion when they became Communists." That infuriated Mann. "I didn't know if they renounced their religion," Mann said. "I didn't know that they became Communist. I didn't know any of those things. And all of this appeared under the byline of Jack Mann. I didn't feel like going to work the day after that. I was so ashamed of it. That was haphazard, half-assed, amateurish work."

The supporters of McCarthy, however, would hardly have noticed an editing injustice done to the Rosenbergs in the name of anti-communism, compared to the constant drumbeat of *Newsday* criticism of the senator from Wisconsin. That consistent McCarthy-bashing was apparently one reason for the frictions between *Newsday* and the Roman Catholic Diocese of Brooklyn, which then covered all of Long Island. The diocesan newspaper, *The Tablet*, was strongly pro-McCarthy, and its managing editor, a fiery conservative named Patrick Scanlan, defended McCarthy against any attack. When McCarthy won a Republican primary in Wisconsin in 1952, for example, Scanlan predicted what his victory would mean. "The party-liners, the 'liberals,' the State Department, the Leftist press whose national anti-McCarthy campaign was the most vicious ever directed against a State candidate for public office, and the entire pro-Communist movement suffered a tremendous setback," Scanlan wrote in his weekly column. At the same time, a *Newsday* editorial deplored McCarthy's victory. "McCarthy is a demagogue, a loudmouth, a character assassin, and a generally reprehensible character — perhaps the nearest kin to Hitler that this democratic country ever saw," the editorial said.

Scanlan didn't point specifically at *Newsday* for its participation in the anti-McCarthy drive, but at about the same time, *The Tablet* excoriated Alicia's paper for what it saw as a nasty anti-Catholic editorial. That controversy arose over the Roberto Rossellini film, *The Miracle*, which many Catholics considered sacrilegious. When a theater in Long Beach exhibited the film, a coalition of Catholic groups threatened a boycott of the theater, and it withdrew the film. *Newsday* responded with an editorial called "Economic Censorship," written by Mark F. Ethridge Jr., whose father was one of the most distinguished journalists in America, and a good friend of Harry and Alicia. "This is just as much censorship as was Hitler's burning of the books," the editorial said. "If the Catholic groups, including the Catholic War Veterans, the Holy Name Society and the Knights of Columbus, believe in law by democratic process rather than by their own dictates, they will make a public apology to the theater and to the public for their conduct."

This prompted a quick, angry response from *The Tablet*. " 'Newsday,' in an unrestrained and vicious outburst of antipathy to the Catholic protest, likened the action to 'Hitler's burning of books' — a grotesque comparison which could only come from a mind either completely stupid or hateful, or stupidly hateful," the *Tablet* editorial said. "Now, if one — either an individual or an organization — has to protest and apologize for loyalty to his religion, and for exercising a constitutional right of protest, it is a sad day for America. But we doubt if such an apology is really wanted. What was desired and utilized was an opportunity to exercise anti-Catholic War Veterans, anti-Holy Name Society, anti-Knights of Columbus and general anti-Catholic feeling. This may be looked upon as a good policy by 'Newsday' but it is repugnant to Americans who oppose religious bigotry and resent it."

At the time of the controversy, Alicia was at her hunting lodge. "I took a look at this, and I said, 'Oh, for God's sake, this isn't going to do,' " Hal Burton said. "I had Alicia's phone number, so I got hold of her in Kingsland, Georgia, and read it to her, and I said, 'Listen, the shit's really going to hit the fan on this one. The church is mad at you anyway.' There had been numerous sermons against *Newsday* in prior times for various things that it said. But, I said, 'This time they've got a genuine case against you. This is insane.' And she said, 'Well, what do you want to do?' And I said, 'I'll write a new editorial and I'll simply apologize.' " The apology ran on September 2, at the top of the editorial column, along with a reprint of an earlier, more temperate editorial about *The Miracle*. "Humans, being mortal, make mistakes and so do newspapers," said the editorial, which carried Alicia's name at the bottom. "The wording of the editorial was unfortunate. We had no intention of offending the members of the Catholic Church and we apologize most sincerely."

Immediately after *Newsday* apologized for the Ethridge editorial, the paper ran a story by Jack O'Grady about a meeting of 350 Catholics who had gathered to protest the editorial, but were calmed by Alicia's apology. The story included a photograph of O'Grady shaking hands with a smiling priest. In *The Tablet*, Patrick Scanlan took note of the apology in his column, but he was not entirely mollified: " 'Newsday' needs constant supervision from its readers and the general public for it is frequently offensive to decent people." The *Newsday-Tablet* skirmishes continued to flare up periodically. "On and off over the years, we publicly criticized *Newsday*," said Don Zirkel, a later *Tablet* editor.

Newsday opposition to McCarthy was part of the problem, and Alicia's uneasy feelings about Catholics may also have contributed. She thought of herself as Irish and liked to sing Irish songs, such as "The Wearing of the Green," but she had grown up Protestant, and she didn't really understand Catholics at all. "Alicia used to refer to the Catholics as the Macks," Burton said. That was a shorthand reference to the slang description of Catholics as "mackerel-snappers," because they ate fish on Fridays. "She said, 'What do you think the Macks will think of this one?' " From the beginning, Alicia was sensitive to potential problems with Catholics. Stan Peckham remembered writing a series about a local health center that gave advice on birth control. The series was already set in type, and was scheduled to run for several days. "Alicia started worrying about it," Peckham said. So she called Richard Clarke, the managing editor of the *Daily News*. "He said, 'Don't run it. You'll wreck the paper.' I think he was a Catholic himself. . . . He said the Catholic Church would ostracize us, and she got scared and wouldn't run it." Her concern was not just imaginary. *Newsday* angered Catholics enough to affect the paper's circulation. "It wasn't unusual to be denounced from the pulpit," said Vinnie Bordash, who had to cope with those circulation crises. "Even the parochial school children were told not to take *Newsday* routes."

Newsday tried a variety of remedies for its friction with Catholics. Hathway and Alicia used Irish intermediaries such as the reporter Jim O'Neill and the photographer Bill Sullivan to soothe the bruised feelings of the Catholic clergy. Another *Newsday* emissary who helped to heal rifts with the church was Ed Igoe, a circulation supervisor who was friendly with church officials because he routinely volunteered his services as a photographer for church events. Hathway himself tried to contribute to the peacemaking effort in typical Hathway style. Dressed in a tuxedo, he attended an event at which Francis Cardinal Spellman made an appearance. Hathway shook the cardinal's hand, made sure that a *Newsday* photographer recorded this friendly exchange, then published the photograph in *Newsday*. It didn't seem to matter to Hathway that Spellman ran the Archdiocese of New York, and most of *Newsday*'s disagreements were with the Diocese of Brooklyn.

Alicia's problems with the Catholic Church continued even after the growth of Long Island caused the creation of a new diocese covering Nassau and Suffolk: the Diocese of Rockville Centre. The bishop was Walter

P. Kellenberg, who was known for his skill at raising money and building new churches, but not for his warmth. Some of his priests gave him a nickname based on his episcopal role and his tough personality: "The German Shepherd." It couldn't hurt *Newsday*, Burton decided, if Alicia paid a visit to Kellenberg and tried to establish a cordial relationship. "She went over and she came back, and I said, 'Well, how was it?' " Burton remembered. "She said, 'You son of a bitch! Don't give me any more advice like that.' I said, 'Why not?' She said, 'I went over there and, in the first place, he kept me standing for 10 minutes. I said that I wanted to see if we couldn't be on better terms. He said, "I could never be on better terms with a newspaper that prints trash like Doris Fleeson and Marquis Childs and Hal Burton." ' That was that."

CHAPTER FOURTEEN

Dethroning DeKoning

I

KNOWING THAT THE press always gets the last word, intelligent public figures have learned to regulate their dealings with newspapers by this sensible axiom: Never pick on someone who buys ink by the barrel. It was partly his failure to follow that principle that brought William C. DeKoning Sr. into conflict with Alan Hathway and *Newsday* — a conflict that resulted in *Newsday*'s first Pulitzer Prize.

For two decades before *Newsday* decided to use large amounts of its ink against him, DeKoning had enjoyed a spectacular rise to power. By 1950, he was clearly the most feared labor leader on Long Island. At a time when the construction of homes and offices was just beginning to explode, he had almost totalitarian control over the industry. His power flowed from his position at the head of Local 138, International Union of Operating Engineers, and his leadership roles in two influential Long Island union councils. Beyond his rule over the construction industry, DeKoning also held a tight grip on the increasingly profitable night harness racing track, Roosevelt Raceway, where he controlled the union representing pari-mutuel clerks. In both of his spheres of influence, DeKoning enjoyed the blessing of powerful Republicans.

The first member of DeKoning's family to achieve prominence in the Operating Engineers was his uncle, a steam mechanic named Bill Callahan, who migrated to America in the 1880s and became a power in the New York City local. But the person who exerted the strongest influence on DeKoning was Joe Fay, the most powerful official in the Operating Engineers. "He was Mister Big," said DeKoning's nephew, John DeKoning, who later became a reformer in the union. "My uncle was his protege. They were very intimate and close. Bill imitated Joe Fay right down to the way he tied his shoes. They were cut from the same cloth, and they were tough, tough guys." It was Fay who chose to send Bill DeKoning in 1930 to Nassau County, where he went to work persuading builders to sign contracts with the union. Soon, DeKoning won a charter for Local 138 of the Operating Engineers, followed quickly by charters for Local 138A and 138B. Later, he put together the Building and Construction Trades Council, an umbrella organization for Long Island's construction unions. He also became president of the Central Trades and Labor Council, which gave him the power to set up picket lines around almost any business on Long Island. DeKoning also derived significant clout from his role as the chief organizer for the AFL on Long Island, which enabled him to unionize any business that seemed suitable.

Branching out beyond the construction trades, DeKoning organized the pari-mutuel clerks at Roosevelt Raceway. Toward the end of World War II, he threatened to scuttle the whole racing season unless the pari-mutuel clerks got the same pay scale that clerks at thoroughbred tracks in New York City received. George Morton Levy, the lawyer who pioneered night harness racing on Long Island, averted that threat by giving DeKoning the power to hire and fire everyone who wasn't a supervisor at the track. That gave DeKoning control of the pari-mutuel clerks, ushers, and even the track's police force. His power at the track reinforced his hold on Local 138: Engineers loyal to DeKoning got undemanding "push-button" construction jobs during the day, such as supervising the operation of a generator that needed virtually no supervision. Well rested from their daytime jobs, DeKoning's loyalists also worked at Roosevelt Raceway in the evenings as pari-mutuel agents. In contrast, those engineers who spoke up against DeKoning got no work at all, or jobs that lasted only a few days. "He controlled everybody's body, mind and soul," John DeKoning said, "because the job is the most important thing that everybody has to have."

This sort of despotic power was enough to make DeKoning a natural target for a young, iconoclastic newspaper such as *Newsday*. Much of the paper's coverage of DeKoning in the 1940s, however, focused on his ostensibly charitable activities. In 1947, for example, *Newsday* reported matter-of-factly the opening of DeKoning's Labor Lyceum — a long, rectangular building in Uniondale, with a huge bar, a restaurant, and a marble bust of Samuel Gompers, founder of the AFL, guarding the front entrance. During DeKoning's lifetime, the story said, unions that belonged to the Central Trades and Labor Council would use the building for meetings and offices. Upon his death, *Newsday* said, the property would become an old-age home for union members. *Newsday* also reported on other DeKoning charities, such as the Nassau-Suffolk Youth Foundation. Cleverly, DeKoning even tried to pull Alan Hathway into the board of directors of the youth foundation in 1949. Hathway wisely ducked, but not until after *Newsday* itself had already mentioned him as a director.

Despite DeKoning's cleverness at public relations, *Newsday* had begun keeping files on him before the end of the 1940s. Publicly, he had brought himself to the paper's attention by threatening the harness racing season at Roosevelt Raceway and by standing briefly in the way of Levittown. *Newsday* also began to get tips from union members who had irritated DeKoning and paid for it by losing their jobs or their self-respect. Privately, DeKoning clashed in menacing little ways with *Newsday* employees. One of those incidents happened when the *Newsday* photographer Ike Eichorn arrived a few minutes late to take a photo of DeKoning handing out Christmas baskets at the Labor Lyceum. "I said, 'Geez, can we set something up?' " Eichorn remembered. "He said, 'I don't give a fuck about you. I don't give a fuck about *Newsday*.' " Eichorn reported that event to Harold Ferguson, the business manager, who passed the word along to Hathway. During the construction of the new plant in Garden City, DeKoning had also fired a warning shot across *Newsday*'s bow, in a conversation with Harvey Broad, who had worked as a pari-mutuel clerk in DeKoning's union before coming to *Newsday*. "He says, 'I'm going to tell you right now, that new plant will never be built,' " Broad remembered. "We wouldn't kick in like everybody." That didn't stop the construction, but Broad informed Hathway about the threat. In that same period, Hathway had a clash of his own with DeKoning over a private business deal: Hathway's part ownership of an arena.

Even before World War II ended, *Newsday* editorials had pointed out the need for a large indoor arena in Nassau County. In early 1944, *Newsday* mentioned it in two separate editorials, lamenting that Nassau County's largest gymnasium could seat only 2,000 people. It is not clear who wrote the editorials, but both of them ran within weeks after Hathway became managing editor. In 1947, *Newsday* ran two more editorials within a month, again complaining about the lack of a decent arena. The reason for both 1947 editorials was that *Newsday*, the local sponsor of the Golden Gloves boxing tournament originated by the *Daily News*, had to turn away 1,000 boxing fans because the gym at Hofstra University was too small.

A year later, in the summer of 1948, the Town of Hempstead granted an application by a group called the Mill Road Garden Corporation for permission to remodel an existing building that had been used for indoor tennis, amateur boxing and horse riding. The group proposed to convert it into an indoor arena seating 3,500 people and name it Hempstead Garden. One of the most prominent members of the corporation was George Morton Levy, the lawyer-turned-racing-impresario. The sports expertise was to come from Anthony "Peanuts" Barbetta, a former boxer who was running sports teams for Grumman, and from Lou Figari, a huge, 350-pound promoter of basketball and auto racing. Among the other members of the corporation were Alan Hathway and Jack Altshul. This was a strange arrangement, to say the least. But apparently Hathway's public-spirited desire to make a larger arena available for Long Island, combined with his private ambition to make some money, overruled journalistic common sense. Obviously, Alicia viewed this venture with some healthy skepticism. A few pages away from the story on the town's approval of the application, *Newsday* ran an editorial that sounded like a warning memo to Hathway and

Altshul. "One thing we wish to make plain is that, while Alan Hathway and Jack Altshul are managing and city editor respectively of Newsday, there is no connection whatever between the newspaper and the arena," the editorial said. "Publicity will be accorded on its news value and in no greater amount than would be given if total strangers owned Hempstead Garden. And that, Alan and Jack, is an order."

Compounding the dubious ethics of owning a share of this arena that his newspaper would be covering, Hathway made *Newsday* one of his customers, using his arena for the Golden Gloves promotions. "Actually, I think he got involved in that *because* of Golden Gloves," said Bob Zellner, then *Newsday*'s sports editor. It was not Hathway himself who made the business arrangements for *Newsday*'s use of the arena, Zellner said, but Jack Mullen, the circulation director. "It was never officially brought up that Hathway was involved in the operation or the ownership, and it was a site that was available and presented as such," Zellner said. "Mullen handled the financial details." Some of Mullen's employees, including Vinnie Bordash, helped to sell Golden Gloves tickets. "This place was packed," Bordash said. "We sold them standing room only for a buck a head. God, my pockets were loaded with bucks."

Whether Hathway directly influenced *Newsday* to use his arena for Golden Gloves or not, he did aggressively pursue another customer: the Republican Party, which *Newsday* regularly bludgeoned in its news columns and editorials. During the 1948 election campaign, when *Newsday* was supporting Governor Thomas E. Dewey for President, and the Republicans were expecting Dewey to win, Hathway called the party public relations man Forrest Corson with a proposition: " 'Forrest, it would be a wonderful thing for *Newsday*, it'd be a wonderful thing for the Republican Party . . . if you could make the Hempstead arena your election-night headquarters.' " Knowing well the value of being on good terms with *Newsday*, Corson went along. "My only consideration was to propitiate Alan," Corson said. The gathering came off as scheduled, at Hempstead Garden. The Dewey victory did not.

Inevitably, given its size and moneymaking potential, the arena became a target for DeKoning. The primary witness to this clash was William F. Mills Jr., who was working part time at *Newsday*, putting out a promotional publication for carriers called *The Go-Getter News*. "Alan or Jack Altshul said to go over and see Lou Figari, that he was looking for somebody like me that knew the island," said Mills, who had come to know Hempstead businessmen while he was in college, selling ads for the *Hofstra Chronicle*. Figari hired him to help promote Hempstead Garden, and in that job, Mills witnessed DeKoning's attempt to muscle the arena. It began when an advance man for a touring ice show came to the arena and began arranging for the installation of additional electric lines and pipes that would provide the ice surface. DeKoning had control over the union workers who would install the equipment. "He threw all sorts of roadblocks," Mills said. "He wanted under-the-table money." Finally, they got the ice apparatus set up, but DeKoning had made it unpleasant for the advance man. "He said that was a terrible experience," Mills remembered.

Ultimately, Hempstead Garden failed, because the crowds were too small for most events. "People just didn't come," said Patricia Barlow, Hathway's daughter. It isn't clear whether the disappointing attendance alone forced Hathway out of the arena business, or whether Alicia finally told him flatly to drop it. But Alicia did not like his involvement. His friend, Paul Townsend, remembered that it was a source of conflict. "Typical Alan," Townsend said. "It almost cost him his job."

DeKoning's clash with the owners of the arena would certainly not be enough, all by itself, to send Hathway running after the powerful labor leader with all guns blazing. But the arena incident illustrates the kind of arrogance that made DeKoning so inviting a target, and Hathway had good reason to know about that abuse of power firsthand. "Alan would never admit defeat, but what I got from him is that he had really been screwed royally," said Robert W. Greene, the young investigator who first came in contact with *Newsday* during the DeKoning investigation and later became Hathway's chosen reporter and close friend. Getting back at DeKoning wasn't just personal, though. It suited *Newsday*'s needs. "The only way *Newsday* was going to be able to make it was to kick a lot of kneecaps," Greene said. "So, DeKoning cost him money, yes. . . . Perhaps that helped to focus his attention on DeKoning, but that was convergent with his basic philosophy that this is what you had to do, and DeKoning was an integral part of that structure, of that kneecap that had to be kicked. So you could add a personal animosity to a philosophical conviction."

II

THE TRIGGERING EVENT that finally pushed Hathway over the edge, prompting him to convert his files on DeKoning into an aggressive series of stories, was not an attack on *Newsday* or a new indignity heaped on union members. It was DeKoning's decision in 1950 to oppose a *Newsday* favorite, Representative Leonard Hall, for reelection to Congress.

Actually, DeKoning announced simultaneously that his political organization, Labor's League for Political Education, would attempt to defeat both incumbent Republican congressmen from Long Island, Hall in Nassau and W. Kingsland Macy in Suffolk. Though he described both congressmen as his targets, DeKoning clearly reserved most of his anger for Hall, an Oyster Bay Republican, purportedly because Hall had supported the passage of the Taft-Hartley Act. At the exact moment that DeKoning announced his "Beat Hall in the Fall" campaign, the congressman was working on *Newsday*'s side in its crusade to save the Merchant Marine Academy at Kings Point from being gutted by budget-cutters. Later in the campaign, an editorial listed some of the reasons why *Newsday* admired him. "He has managed the difficult trick of being at once a good, loyal Republican and an independent one," the editorial said.

"He is no stooge waiting for some Big Boy to tell him what to do." Unlike other Republicans, Hall had *not* forged an alliance with DeKoning and profited from the patronage at Roosevelt Raceway. In addition, Hall feuded periodically with Russ Sprague, the county leader. While Sprague was leaking stories to Jim Stiles at the *Review-Star*, Hall was talking to *Newsday*. "Alan had a pipeline right into Len Hall," Forrest Corson said.

Hall's ties to *Newsday* went even higher than Hathway. After the inauguration of Dwight Eisenhower, Hall became chairman of the Republican National Committee and grew increasingly close to Harry Guggenheim. Within months after Eisenhower took office, Hall was using his influence to arrange meetings between Harry and senior administration officials, including Secretary of State John Foster Dulles, so that Harry could present his views on Latin America. In August, 1953, Harry met with Eisenhower, who offered him a job: assistant secretary of state for Latin America. (Harry declined, arguing that he didn't have enough international prestige.) These meetings were just one example of the warm, cooperative relationship that grew up between Harry and Hall in the years that followed.

Once DeKoning went after Hall, Hathway immediately set in motion a quick, hard-hitting series. The reporter he chose, Helen Dudar, had started out at *Newsday* writing an advice column called "Let Prof. Do-It," while she continued her education at Columbia University every evening. Soon, she began covering the county seat in Mineola, and then moved on to rewrite, where she established a reputation as a skillful, smooth writer. Coming into the assignment, Dudar had a distant memory of DeKoning, who had been a customer in her father's stationery store in the South Shore community of Island Park. "We knew there was something sort of odd and a little shady about him," she said, "but we didn't know what it was." Now, Hathway wanted her to make sense of all the DeKoning allegations that had been floating around and to let *Newsday*'s readers know exactly what was odd and shady about DeKoning.

Dudar brought to the assignment an ability to craft a readable series, with a certain grace and continuity, but she didn't consider herself an investigative reporter. She did know how to take direction, however, and Hathway himself provided one important piece of guidance: a simple suggestion that she check land records for the ownership of DeKoning's Labor Lyceum. "It was a wonderful idea," said Dudar, who discovered that the Lyceum belonged to DeKoning's wife, Rose Mary DeKoning, not to Local 138. That finding appeared at the top of the first piece in the series, which ran on May 11, 1950, the day after the Building and Construction Trades Council of Nassau and Suffolk had expelled DeKoning's engineers because they had crossed picket lines during the construction of Levittown.

"From the lavish Uniondale estate he publicly dedicated to labor and privately deeded to his wife, chunky, pugnacious Bill DeKoning rules a kingdom rich in the unnatural resources of the strong arm and the double-barrelled threat," Dudar wrote in the opening story. Like the rest of the series, this piece carried no byline, because Hathway feared that DeKoning might try to exact vengeance against the writer. The story painted in broad strokes some of the central elements of DeKoning's empire: his domination of employment at the racetrack, in which jobs went primarily to Republican committeemen; his "close friendship with some of the county's most active contractors who have never had to chalk up a single day lost due to picketing" at their construction sites; his heavy-handed insistence that union members at the track patronize the bar at the Labor Lyceum and sell tickets for his frequent social affairs.

The second piece in the five-part series traced DeKoning's background, the structure of his labor empire, his relationship with Joe Fay, and the DeKoning-George Morton Levy connection at Roosevelt Raceway. The next day, *Newsday* offered the first-person story of a member of DeKoning's pari-mutuel union. "Bill's a great one for social affairs," the unnamed insider said. "He keeps saying, 'We want bruddahood and friendship. We should all get togedda.'" Those get-togethers included the "Mule Club," a weekly dinner at the Lyceum that DeKoning forced members to attend regularly. "The fee is $6 a night for all you can drink and eat," the insider said. "Most of the guys I know put in an appearance, register as having attended, and go home after an hour or two." DeKoning's members also had to pay for and attend such events as the spring ball and the summer picnics on the grounds of the Lyceum. Every year, before the start of the racing season, the union members had to appear before the "adjustment committee," which would decide whether they had attended all the appropriate social functions. If a member hadn't sold his dance tickets, for example, DeKoning's men would tell him: "Go square yourself," which meant coming up with the price of the unsold tickets.

Expanding on DeKoning's intimidation techniques, the final piece of the series painted a picture of the fear that DeKoning inspired. "His enemies have learned that it is hard and hazardous to buck Brother Bill, uncomfortable but safer to forget," the story said. "He is a hated man, but the hatred simmers in dark and silent corners." In less than a week, this "preliminary series" had drawn an effective, impressionistic portrait of DeKoning's style and his abuses of power. But it had barely "scratched the surface of his corroding influence on Long Island," the closing editorial admitted, predicting that there was more to come. "Newsday intends to fortify the Long Island labor movement with all the information we can collect on DeKoning and to print it for public judgment," the editorial said. "An informed public will supply the encouragement needed to rid Long Island of a public nuisance."

At the end of Dudar's series, someone who called himself simply "A Good Union Man Incognito" typed a one-page letter to Alicia Patterson. "It is a known fact, that William DeKoning is a past master in the extortion game," the anonymous unionist wrote. "Every county contract that has been awarded, he gets on demand a 2 per cent cut on the amount bid to do the work, on the threat of labor trouble if the contractor doesn't come across. The small home builders, in many cases, pay DeKoning a flat price of $15 for every cellar excavated, although he hasn't an engineer on the job. If they use a small concrete mixer, they must pay to DeKoning's welfare fund $10 each week the mixer is on the job. . . . If the District Attorney will impound the books of the contractors and trace the 2 per cent kickback, a good job can be done on DeKoning." A flood of such tips prompted *Newsday* to announce confidently in early June: "Further chapters in the public and private life of Long Island's labor czar are in preparation and will appear in early issues of this newspaper." But no major new series followed. Of course, *Newsday* continued to monitor the unsuccessful effort to unseat Hall, and it covered occasional flareups, such as DeKoning's reputed role in a violent demonstration by union carpenters against Latvian "displaced persons" who were working at a non-union construction site. Given the loud fanfare accompanying the 1950 series, however, the tone of *Newsday*'s effort on the DeKoning story in the next two years was surprisingly muted.

It was not until 1953 that the tide finally turned against DeKoning. During that eventful year, in addition to the work of its own staff, *Newsday* relied on the efforts of a young investigator for a group called the New York City Anti-Crime Committee. His name was Robert W. Greene.

III

GROWING UP IN a lace-curtain Irish family in Queens, Bob Greene enjoyed an inside view of three professions: the law, politics and medicine.

His father, Francis McLaughlin Greene, was a Manhattan lawyer and a power in Queens politics. His mother, Mary Virginia (Molly) Greene, was the daughter of a physician, William Clancy. During the school year, Frank Greene exposed his son to the ways of the law, taking him to the office, to the courtroom, and to the Bridge Cafe in Manhattan, where the boy sipped ginger ale, munched pretzels and listened to the talk of law and politics. During the summers, Bob Greene visited his grandfather in Massachusetts, went out with him on house calls and read his medical books. Eventually, the pull of the stethoscope overcame the lure of the law, and the boy decided to become a doctor.

Greene's higher education began at Xavier High School in Manhattan, a unique blend of the rigorous Jesuit intellectual discipline and the close-order drill of the Army. But when his father began to drink heavily, causing a precipitous decline in the family's finances, Greene's prospects for finishing Xavier grew dimmer. With contributions from his grandmother and others in his family, he was able to graduate, but along the way, he had to help support himself with a series of jobs. The first was in Ohrbach's department store, where he worked as a "sniffer" in the returns department. His responsibility was to make sure that women did not buy a fancy dress on Friday night, wear it to a party over the weekend, then try to return it on Monday for a full refund. His investigative method was to examine the underarms of the returned dresses for body odors.

Following his graduation from Xavier in 1947, he entered Fordham University's education school, planning to become a teacher and use that salary to save for medical school. While he attended Fordham in lower Manhattan at night, he ate cheese-and-cracker meals at a bar on Broadway, collected small fees from the NAACP for his first professional writing, a pair of black-white morality plays, lived in an apartment in Jersey City and worked at a variety of jobs. One of them, selling sterling silverware to young brides-to-be, required some investigative skill: By reading newspaper announcements about engagement parties and offering free salt and pepper shakers to the women who hosted the parties, in exchange for introductions to the brides, Greene came up with a list of sales prospects. Through all this, his long-term plan was still to become a doctor. But all of his plans changed one day, totally by accident.

At the time, he was dating a Jersey City woman named Kathy Liquari, who later became his wife. One day in 1948, Greene was at her house when a friend of her father's, a Democratic committeeman named Frank Romanelli, showed up and started boasting that he would be attending a rally for President Harry S Truman at a local high school, where only committeemen could get in. That exclusivity irked Greene, who bet Romanelli two cartons of Pall Malls that he would find a way to get into the rally. Equipped only with bravado, a trench coat and a draft card that might look like press credentials if it were flashed quickly enough, Greene got to the school early, bluffed his way in, walked up to a Democratic press aide and announced: "Sir, I'm here covering this for the *Fordham University Curved Horn.*" This display of audacity amused the press aide. So he pulled up a chair and installed it right below the speaker's lectern, in a spot cut out of the stage for a prompter — the closest seat in the whole auditorium to where Truman would be standing. When the rally ended, someone who had noticed Greene's exalted position came up behind him, tapped him on the shoulder and asked him what newspaper he represented. Greene admitted that he was really there only on a bet — a bit of nerve that apparently impressed this gentleman, too. "He said, 'Did you ever think about the newspaper business?' " Greene said. "So I said, 'No.' " Right there, he offered Greene a summer job working on the *Jersey Journal* as a reporter. This benefactor turned out to be Fred Gainesway, the managing editor.

The following June, Greene showed up at the paper and Gainesway put him on the payroll at $23.50 a week, on a trial basis. Gainesway liked his work and offered to keep him on, at $23.50 a week. "If I wanted the job permanently, I'd have to give up school," Greene said. "But all of a sudden, something had occurred to me: I liked this. This was really interesting stuff." Greene explained that he'd like to take the job, but he couldn't end his education for a mere $23.50 a week. "He says, 'I can work that out for you.' " Gainesway's solution was to send Greene to 921 Bergen Avenue, the offices of Frank Hague, the Democratic boss. Hague was to pay Greene an additional $60 a week as a public relations man. Gainesway also sent him to the local YMCA, which would pay Greene an extra $20 a week for public relations work. Later, his fiancee, Kathy Liquari, went to work for Frank Eggers, Hague's nephew, who had been mayor of Jersey City after Hague left office, had lost to John V. Kenny, and was helping to run Hague's organization.

As a result of Greene's unusual arrangements, he would earn roughly 80 percent of his salary from public relations jobs and 20 percent from the newspaper that would be a natural target of those public relations efforts. "I'm not out of any journalism school; I'm not out of any ethics," Greene said. "I'm a man who had just come from selling sterling silver to brides and sniffing armpits." Still, this seemed like an odd way to do business. He asked Gainesway about it, and Gainesway assured him that it was normal: Some reporters were supplementing their salaries by doing public relations work for Mayor Kenny, Hague's enemy, and others were working for Republicans. So Greene took the job. "At that time, I thought it was a perfectly appropriate thing," he said. "I would kill somebody if we were doing it on our paper today."

While he learned to be a reporter on the rough-and-tumble Jersey City waterfront, Greene did well at public relations. "You only really worked during elections," Greene said. "The rest of the time, you didn't do much." His pay from Hague rose to $300 a week, while he was still getting $56 a week from the newspaper — all with the knowledge of Gainesway, whose goal was to help a promising reporter to survive despite the below-subsistence wages that the paper paid him. That was true throughout the newspaper industry at the time, and reporters at many papers — including *Newsday* — were permitted to make additional money in ways that no editor would permit in the 1990s. Greene regularly witnessed one of Hague's aides handing out envelopes of cash to reporters for other papers. During that same era, the Nassau Republican Party gave money to reporters at *Newsday* and other papers — at both election time and Christmas. "I discussed it with Alan Hathway," Forrest Corson remembered, "and he said, 'So long as everybody gets it, including the photographers, I have no objection.' " In all that time, Corson said, only one person at *Newsday* turned the money down. "Stan Asimov refused it," Corson said. "He said, 'Forrest, I don't like to hurt your feelings. I know you don't mean anything by it. I know everybody takes it. But my conscience won't permit me to take it. I hope you understand.' "

Though he was on Hague's payroll, Greene managed to write at least one story that could not have pleased the boss. One night, he was walking down the street in the rain and overheard a loudspeaker inside a building where someone was giving a speech. So he walked in, sat down and listened as some county employees griped about having to kick back part of their pay to the Democratic Party. The speaker was exhorting them to comply, for their own good and the party's. That seemed like a good story to Greene, even though his boss, Frank Hague, controlled the county, and his other employer, the *Journal*, was a pro-Hague paper. Greene's editors were hesitant to run the story without affidavits from the aggrieved employees. So Greene got the affidavits and wrote the story, which the *Journal* displayed prominently. "Gainesway was very unhappy that they played the story on the front page," Greene said. But Hague expressed no anger. "He didn't say a word."

Besides learning about politics firsthand from the Hague machine and getting paid for it, Greene derived another benefit from his Hague connection. It gave him entree to the Irish mob that had controlled the Jersey City docks but was now losing its dominance to the rising Italian mob. "Because the Irish felt that I was on Hague's payroll and so forth, I could be trusted," Greene said. "They're telling me things that you should not tell a reporter — not knowing that in my own head, I am even more reporter than I am Hague." This gave Greene an insight into the way organized crime works and helped give birth to his lifelong fascination with the mob.

Early in his career in Jersey City, Greene began to deal with the mob in dangerously imprudent ways. "I was young and stupid," Greene said. On his rounds, for example, he learned that one of the dock bosses who was aligned with the new Italian mob had threatened to murder Greene if he showed up on the docks. So Greene took steps: First, he acquired a pistol, without a permit. Then, armed illegally, he showed up at a cafeteria on the docks and sat near a group of men loyal to the dock boss who had threatened him. "I pulled out the gun, slammed it on the table and said, in a loud voice, 'Where's the son of a bitch who says he's going to kill me?' " Greene remembered, acknowledging that this was an outrageously dumb thing to do. "Believe it or not, though, it was effective. Everybody then decided I was crazy, and you didn't want to go near anybody who's that crazy."

As Greene's mob expertise grew, his horizons expanded. In 1951, he took a brief leave of absence from the paper to serve as an advisor to Senator Estes Kefauver of Tennessee, whose Senate committee was investigating organized crime. When the hearings came around, Greene had a natural advantage in covering them, since he had worked with the Kefauver committee in developing the evidence. "I knew what they were going to say ahead of time," Greene said. So he was able to stay well ahead of the competing papers. The experience of working with an investigations committee paid off quickly. When S. I. Newhouse bought the *Journal* and the new editor took some steps that made the job less palatable to Greene, his investigative background presented him with a new opportunity. The Kefauver hearings had focused so much attention on organized crime that local anti-crime committees began to spring up all across the country, to gather information on the mob and alert the press. One of them was the New York City Anti-Crime Committee, a successor to the committee that Harry Guggenheim had once served as chairman.

The staff counsel to the committee was a former Manhattan assistant district attorney, William Keating, who had become famous by successfully prosecuting the murderers of a waterfront hiring boss. Now that he was on the anti-crime committee, he continued to focus on the waterfront and became friendly with two Jesuit priests at the Xavier Labor School in Manhattan, the Reverend Philip Carey and the Reverend John Corridan, the inspiration for the waterfront priest in the Budd Schulberg film, *On the Waterfront*. When Keating needed an investigator, Corridan knew a young man who had graduated from Xavier High School, in the same building as the labor school, and had come in contact with Corridan while writing stories on the New Jersey waterfront: Bob Greene.

At the crime committee, Greene began to augment his street skills by learning how to organize large amounts of information. His tutor was the chief investigator, a former FBI agent named John O'Mara, who had developed for the committee a filing system similar to the one at the FBI — carefully cross-filed memos to summarize interviews, with proper names typed in all uppercase letters. "Most of the important things I ever learned, other than self-learned, I learned from John," Greene said. Since Keating was specializing in the waterfront, Greene concentrated on other areas, such as organized crime domination of the garment district. But he still was drawn to Jersey City and the waterfront, which caused him significant grief.

The New York State Crime Commission, an official government agency with actual subpoena powers, wanted to investigate the nexus of the waterfront mob and Jersey City politicians, including Mayor Kenny. Knowing about Greene's waterfront expertise, the commission borrowed his services from the New York City Anti-Crime Committee. During this work, Greene found out from the Hague organization that he might be able to get information from Frank (Biffo) DeLorenzo, who had been Kenny's main operative on the waterfront. DeLorenzo wanted payment for his information, and Greene reported that idea to his two agencies, which decided not to pay DeLorenzo. But Hague's group agreed to put up money to help DeLorenzo to flee when the investigation was over. Greene reported that proposal back to the two agencies, and neither one objected. So he met with DeLorenzo to discuss the payment, and DeLorenzo secretly recorded the conversation. Not long after that, a grand jury in Hudson County indicted Greene and two Hague loyalists, accusing them of offering DeLorenzo $1,100 to lie about Kenny's connections with a dead waterfront mobster, in an effort to defame Kenny.

The apparent goal of the indictment was to help Kenny escape the commission's scrutiny, which became obvious when Kenny announced that he would not appear before the commission, because its own investigator had been indicted. The only two witnesses were Biffo DeLorenzo, who was already under a perjury indictment by the same grand jury, and a detective assigned to Kenny's protective unit. A month after the indictment, DeLorenzo checked into a hospital and died of a heart attack at age 39. Then a new district attorney in Hudson County, a Republican, decided there was never a case to begin with. In September, 1953, a judge in Jersey City dismissed the indictment.

At about the same time that he was struggling with the Jersey City mob and the politicians, Greene became interested in another labor racketeer. Greene's secretary at the crime committee lived on Long Island, and she began bringing him stories from her local newspaper, *Newsday*, about Bill DeKoning. "There was a strong indication that there was more there," Greene said, "but they didn't have it."

IV

ON THE SURFACE, Bill DeKoning did not seem like an appropriate target for the New York City Anti-Crime Committee. "DeKoning, first of all, was not organized crime," Greene said. "Second of all, he was outside of New York City."

But the committee was interested in DeKoning's mentor, Joe Fay, who had been imprisoned for labor extortion. As he learned more, Greene began to feed information to *Newsday*, including a valuable fact that came from Fay's parole records: DeKoning and his son were both regular visitors to Fay in prison — a revelation that tied them even more tightly to the convicted racketeer. On May 13, 1953, *Newsday* reported these visits to Fay. In the same story, it reported that DeKoning had resigned his affiliation with Local 138, accepted the title of president emeritus, and moved to Florida, leaving control of the union to his son.

The tip on Fay's visitors was not Greene's only contribution. As time went on, he talked frequently with Hathway and his reporters. At one point, he began having lunches with Hathway on Long Island and reading to him from his files, while Alicia's secretary, Dorothy Holdsworth, took stenographic notes. "I sat there and just disgorged," Greene said. In this process, Hathway piqued Greene's curiosity about the ownership of the DeKoning-dominated Roosevelt Raceway, and Greene began to investigate. "He understood that DeKoning had some piece of the track, but had no proof of it," Greene said. "He also heard that Russel Sprague had a piece of the track but had no proof of it. They'd all denied it to him. I got the stockholders list for the track."

A full three years earlier, *Newsday* had outlined in broad strokes DeKoning's total control over hiring at Roosevelt Raceway. But it took the bloody execution of a powerful labor figure from another racetrack to set off the chain of events that finally brought DeKoning down. On August 28, 1953, a hood named Snakes Ryan shot down the young labor leader Thomas Lewis, and few minutes later, Ryan died in a gun battle with a cop. The murder of Lewis ignited intense press speculation. The next day, *Newsday* led the paper with an Associated Press story about the murder, under the headline: "LINK RACE UNION/FEUD TO KILLING." The story explained that police were looking for a former employee at Yonkers Raceway who had lost his job on the orders of Lewis, who controlled all hiring at Yonkers, just as DeKoning controlled jobs at Roosevelt.

On September 1, three days after the original story, *Newsday* carried an analysis piece linking Yonkers and Roosevelt, complete with photographs of DeKoning and Lewis. "The Yonkers Raceway, whose employees were ruled by a labor czar slain in ambush last Friday, is some 40 miles away from the Roosevelt Raceway," the story began. "But only inches separate the two titans of the harness racing industry in operating procedure." The author of the story was Stan Brooks, with strong guidance from Hathway. "He would give you the raw material and bombastically shout out, 'That son of a bitch is the same as this son of a bitch,' " Brooks remembered. "He was the one who really came up with the ideas." DeKoning and his wife, the story pointed out, owned 350 shares of Yonkers stock, plus 5,000 shares of stock in the Old Country Trotting Association, which operated Roosevelt. The story also described how the Old Country Trotting Association had used its clout in the Legislature to block the owners of the Yonkers property from acquiring a racing license. That maneuver enabled the OCTA to buy a controlling interest in the Algam Corporation, which operated Yonkers.

The architect of this harness racing empire was the attorney George Morton Levy. He first became involved with racing by representing the operator of a dog-racing track in Mineola, the Nassau County seat. That case gave him a baptism in the arcane law of gambling, but dogs were not Levy's passion. His dream was the establishment of a track for harness racing — a down-home, working-class sport that had traditionally been confined to small county fairs. The first major step toward his goal was a voter referendum in 1939 on a constitutional amendment to authorize pari-mutuel betting, which was designed to allow the state, rather than the bookies, to profit from the human urge to gamble. Once the voters approved the constitutional amendment, Levy helped to shape the enabling legislation that set up the regulation of pari-mutuel betting. A state commission authorized seven trotting associations and gave one of the licenses to Levy's group, the Old Country Trotting Association. Then Levy took over an auto racing track at Roosevelt Field and turned it into Roosevelt Raceway in 1940.

In the years that followed, Levy achieved notoriety by appearing as the first witness before the Kefauver committee's hearings in Manhattan in 1951 and acknowledging that he had paid the racketeer Frank Costello $60,000 to keep bookies away from his track, in order to convince a state racing official that the track was clean. The Costello-Levy connection was a front-page story in *Newsday*, but the furor over the racetrack had long since died down by the time Snakes Ryan murdered Tommy Lewis in the summer of 1953. Coming at the end of the summer, when news is traditionally slow, the Lewis story was red meat for the press. Day after day, the story developed a momentum of its own, growing from the death of one union leader into a broad, spreading syndrome called "the trotting scandal."

One of the first major breaks in this scandal was a revelation about J. Russel Sprague, who had left the office of county executive in 1952 but remained chairman of the Nassau County Republican Party and a member of the Republican National Committee. Sprague, it turned out, was the owner of 4,000 shares of stock in the Yonkers Trotting Association, worth $500,000. But Sprague was a prudent man, and his shares in Yonkers remained in the name of his colleague, Assemblyman Norman Penny, the sponsor of the pari-mutuel betting amendment, who owned 1,000 shares in his own name. Between them, the two men owned a fifth of all the stock in Yonkers.

The Sprague story apparently flowed from several sources: Bob Greene had passed to Hathway information about racetrack stockholders. "I just gave him the names," Greene said. "They unmasked who the names were." Forrest Corson said that it was Sprague's adversary, Leonard Hall, who explained to Hathway that most of the stock listed in Penny's name really belonged to Sprague. In early 1954, a state commission took testimony from Levy, revealing that Sprague's daughter had owned stock and sold it off right after the trotting scandal broke in 1953. Sprague himself told the commission about his fat profits on racing stocks. All these complex transactions showed clearly that Nassau County Republicans, who had played a leading role in the creation of the harness racing industry, had also made sure that they got a healthy cut of the profits.

During the early stages of this process, before all the details had come to light, Sprague had met with Alicia Patterson for lunch. Somehow, he evaded telling her the whole truth about his interests. Corson asked him what he had told Alicia, and Corson knew immediately that his boss had withheld part of the truth. Sprague insisted that he hadn't really lied. "He said to me, 'I told her all that she should know,' " Corson said. That wasn't going to be good enough, Corson felt certain. "I said to him, 'Russ, hell hath no fury like a woman lied to, and Alicia Patterson is going to be furious.' " Soon after, Corson said, Hathway told him: "From now on, kid, we're going after you."

The stain of the trotting scandal quickly spread over Bill DeKoning as well. Less than a week after the story of Sprague's holdings in the Yonkers track broke, the *World-Telegram & Sun* led the paper with a huge two-line banner headline, "$345,000 TRACK EXTORTION/MULCTS ROOSEVELT WORKERS," over a story by Walter MacDonald and Fred Cook. The extortion, of course, was the elaborate kickback setup erected over the years by DeKoning. The *World-Telegram* story carried much the same information that the *Newsday* series had revealed three years earlier, plus one item that *Newsday* had not included: "clambakes" every other Sunday night for track workers, at $16 for two tickets. It was this item that the *World-Telegram* reporters built into a $345,000 kickback, with some quick multiplication based on the 18-week racing season and 1,200 workers. Suddenly, *Newsday* found itself in serious competition with the New York City papers over a story that had begun in Hathway's files not long after World War II and for a long time had been of interest to no one but *Newsday*. Now, the big-league papers were after it, too.

The day after the *World-Telegram* story, *Newsday* published a Hathway interview with Levy, detailing the legal maneuvering behind the establishment of Yonkers Raceway. The same paper carried the big news: Nassau County District Attorney Frank Gulotta announced that he would personally conduct a grand jury investigation of Roosevelt Raceway. Beyond reporting the news, the entire package of stories that day had one overriding purpose: to remind the world that it was *Newsday*, not the *World-Telegram*, that had first broken the DeKoning story. The package included, for example, a summary of what was known about DeKoning, surrounded by a generous collage of past *Newsday* headlines, with labels prominently showing the dates. In the editor's note, *Newsday* minced no words: "Yesterday the New York World-Telegram and Sun published a small part of the story — a story that had been disclosed fully in NEWSDAY long ago."

Only three days after *Newsday* ran this huge package to pooh-pooh the *World-Telegram* story, it faced another embarrassment: a blockbuster story in the *Journal-American* by Guy Richards and Marvin Sleeper, saying that Senate Majority Leader Arthur Wicks, who had been sworn in only the day before as lieutenant governor, had also visited Joe Fay at Sing Sing Prison. On the day that Richards broke the story, there was no Wicks story in *Newsday*, even though *Newsday* had revealed the DeKoning visits to Fay almost five months earlier. Hathway called Bob Greene to ask why he hadn't told him about Wicks. Greene responded by telling Hathway to read the visiting list that Greene had given him. Hathway read it and found the name of Wicks right there. Hathway had been too concerned with DeKoning to bother with anyone else. "They were so totally parochial," Greene said. After *Newsday* had failed to act on Greene's original Wicks information, the committee's counsel had suggested to Greene that they pass it to the *Journal-American*, and *Newsday* ended up eating their dust on the story.

Once the Tommy Lewis murder had aroused the interest of the city papers and they had run a pair of stories that *Newsday* found annoying, *Newsday* became a roaring tiger again on the issue. With the smell of blood in the air, Hathway stayed on top of the story relentlessly. Finally, on October 7, six weeks after the death of Lewis, the Nassau grand jury indicted DeKoning and nine of his aides for extortion, conspiracy and coercion, in connection with his kickback schemes at Roosevelt Raceway. In this moment of triumph, to remind the world that *Newsday* had first broken the DeKoning story, *Newsday* revived a quote from DeKoning's attorney on the question of how the New York papers had learned of it: "They must have read it in Newsday. You've been printing these things for years."

The next day, Governor Dewey announced that he would appoint a special commission to investigate the trotting scandal. This was what *Newsday* had been waiting for — a full investigation into its allegations about DeKoning. And Hathway did his best to make sure that the world thought of this as *Newsday*'s story. On October 9, two days after the indictment, Hathway wrote a letter to Richard Clurman, who was covering the media for *Time* magazine, and outlined *Newsday*'s stories on DeKoning in detail. The resulting article in *Time* was everything that *Newsday* could possibly have wanted. "*Newsday* knew what it was talking about," *Time* said. "Unheeded by other papers or by state officials, *Newsday* had been loudly hammering away for more than three years at corruption at the Long Island track in Nassau County. Last week *Newsday*'s three-year-long campaign finally paid off with a blaze of Page One stories in the Manhattan dailies on one of the biggest state scandals in years."

The next few months were dizzying. *Life* magazine carried a large story on the scandals, mentioning *Newsday*'s role prominently. The state commission began its hearings, providing frequent new insights into the complex scandal. In the November election, the Republican pluralities slipped noticeably. Right after the election, the grand jury hit DeKoning, his son and five of DeKoning's aides with indictments for extortion, coercion and conspiracy — this time in connection with DeKoning's shakedowns of contractors. A third, less significant indictment came a month later. Once this imposing series of accusations materialized over the head of DeKoning and his empire, *Newsday* looked at its work since 1950 and decided it was worthy of a Pulitzer Prize. On January 20, Alicia signed a letter to the dean of the Graduate School of Journalism at Columbia University and sent along *Newsday*'s fat Pulitzer submission. The Pulitzer was to be awarded in the spring of 1954 for work that appeared in 1953, and the *Newsday* submission contained an impressive selection of clips from 1953. But it also contained the entire series written by Helen Dudar in 1950 — buttressing *Newsday*'s claim to have been the first newspaper to jump on DeKoning. Those original stories, the submission argued, contained all the essential elements that appeared more than three years later in the indictments. As a reference, Hathway included Greene's name.

While the Pulitzer process was grinding to its conclusion, DeKoning suddenly cut the legal proceedings short. On April 1, 1954, he agreed to plead guilty to two felony counts of extortion and one of grand larceny, in full satisfaction of 116 counts. His son pleaded guilty to one misdemeanor count of coercion. A week later, Judge Cyril Brown sentenced DeKoning to a year to 18 months in state prison and gave his son a one-year suspended sentence. The next day, the elder DeKoning entered Sing Sing Prison to start serving his sentence.

The sentence was far lighter than what DeKoning could have gotten if he had been convicted at trial, and the columnist Westbrook Pegler later criticized Alicia for tolerating the plea bargain. The prosecutors, seeking to avoid negative editorial comment later, had virtually asked *Newsday*'s blessing on the deal. "Before the plea was accepted, there was a conference with *Newsday*, probably more or less with Hathway," said William Cahn, then a young assistant district attorney who had rounded up DeKoning's records and developed the case. "There was definitely an okay to take the plea. . . . The right thing to do was to take the plea, but to do the right thing and get clobbered for it would be shameful." In an editorial, *Newsday* explained that the light sentence was appropriate, because it saved the taxpayers money. "Whether the sentence was short or long, DeKoning's invincibility is broken," the editorial said. "Long Island working men can breathe free again."

On May 3, Columbia University announced that the Pulitzer Prize for meritorious public service had gone to *Newsday*. Some people at the *World-Telegram* were not only unimpressed, but annoyed. Even though the *World-Telegram* had not submitted its own scandals coverage for the prize, the city editor, Bert McDonald, was angry that the Pulitzer had gone to *Newsday* instead of the *World-Telegram*. "So he insisted we had to write sort of a shameful story . . . sort of belittling *Newsday* and saying that the Pulitzer Prize committee was crazy for not giving it to the *Telegram*," said Fred Cook, who had written about the scandals for the *World-Telegram*. "I had to do it. I sure did hate it. It was buried in the paper somewhere. It was a disgusting performance." This story did not survive in the *World-Telegram* microfilm, but another odd footnote remains in the yellowing pages of the *World-Telegram*'s annual almanac: The 1955 edition contains a list of the 1954 Pulitzer winners, but *Newsday* is not on it. There was also one other omission, unrelated to *Newsday*. In the 1956 almanac, both of the 1955 omissions were rectified. The original omission might have been just a typographical error, but some at *Newsday* suspected that the *World-Telegram* did it on purpose.

"They just hated the idea of this upstart newspaper winning a Pulitzer Prize," said Richard Aurelio, a native of Rhode Island who had worked in public relations at the Mitchel Field air base before joining *Newsday* as a reporter and playing a large role in the *Newsday* coverage of DeKoning. "Anybody who looked at the total record would have to say that *Newsday* contributed more to exposing it than anybody." Greene reached the same conclusion. "The *World-Telegram* was about three days behind *Newsday* in almost anything that they did," Greene said. "I know that they were behind, because they were getting their information from me too." Greene was taking care of *Newsday* first, for several reasons. "*Newsday* had really done all of the work on DeKoning, and nobody else had done any of it," Greene said. "I also lived on Long Island. I was starting to develop a sort of a loyalty to the island." Only a year after *Newsday* won the Pulitzer, Greene came to work at *Newsday*.

The hefty Pulitzer Prize submission contained a long list of bylines — Aurelio, Bernie Bookbinder, Stan Brooks, Arnold Brophy, Val Duncan, Berni Fisher and her husband, George Wheeler, Jack O'Grady, Virginia Sheward, and even one column by Marquis Childs, the Washington columnist. There were other reporters who worked on the story, although their bylines didn't appear in the submission. The primary one was Dudar, whose unbylined 1950 series was so crucial in winning the Pulitzer. But when it was all added together, Hathway was the moving force. He was the father figure whose approval was so important that Aurelio climbed through an open window into the Labor Lyceum to cover a meeting surreptitiously. He was the tough field general who could see clearly what the next move had to be. He was the Front Page-era newsman who focused only on the need to conquer the bad guys, and didn't scruple about the methods. His motives for attacking DeKoning may have been partly personal, due to their clash over Hathway's arena or some obscure business dispute. But once he decided to go after DeKoning, it was Hathway's tenaciousness that carried his small staff through. "No one person at *Newsday* can be cited for the prize," the *Newsday* editorial said. "But if anyone can be singled out above the others, it is Managing Editor Alan Hathway. . . . Hathway spent more hours, more effort, more energy on the story than any other Newsday member."

The Pulitzer was only the start of the campaign to clean up Local 138. The largest part of *Newsday*'s struggle against DeKoning was still ahead. Soon after the Pulitzer, a *Newsday* editorial recognized that reality, outlining a series of further steps that were necessary. "Newsday is proud of having been awarded the Pulitzer Prize for its expose of DeKoning's empire," the editorial said, "but we do not intend to rest on our clippings."

CHAPTER FIFTEEN

No Fat Cats Allowed

I

SEIZING HER NEWSPAPER'S greatest moment of glory, Alicia Patterson decided to use the Pulitzer Prize not as a crown of laurel, but as a whip.

Winning the prize was wonderful, but Alicia was determined to make sure that it didn't give *Newsday* what she called a "fat cat" attitude. It would have been easy for the *Newsday* staff in 1954 to fall into an era of smugness. In addition to winning the Pulitzer, *Newsday* had killed off its first real competitor, the *Nassau Daily Review-Star*. James Stiles had sold control of his strike-weakened paper in 1949 to S. I. Newhouse, who had decided to use it as his foothold on Long Island. Though Stiles continued to serve as publisher, Newhouse sent David Starr out from the *Long Island Press* to be the editor, and the two papers worked out a cooperative arrangement, sharing some stories. That continued until June, 1953, when Newhouse closed the *Review-Star* and moved its staff to the *Press*. "By the time three years were over," Starr said, "it was clear that the *Review-Star* was not a proper vehicle to compete with *Newsday*." A few weeks later, in a speech, Alicia put the demise of the *Review-Star* in context. "We became the only Long Island daily published outside of New York City," she said. "And a New York City paper, with its interests mainly in the five boroughs, cannot hope to properly serve the citizens of a community like Long Island." That left it up to *Newsday* to serve those needs, but it wasn't really ready. Though Alicia's paper had won a major-league journalism award, it was still a minor-league newspaper.

So, in the immediate aftermath of the Pulitzer, Alicia called a staff meeting at the Garden City offices, to discuss what aspects of the paper needed improvement. One of the major criticisms came from Richard Aurelio, a cerebral and impressive young man who had risen from reporter to news editor. "Aurelio pipes up and says, 'Well, I think that what's wrong with the paper is that it's not professional; it's still amateurish,' " Ralph Hausrath said. "So the idea was that what we should get was a copy desk. We didn't have any copy desk." One reason for that was simply that the managing editor didn't care about that kind of detailed editing. "He was more interested in the lead than he was in anything else; he didn't care what was in the second or third paragraphs," Aurelio said. "There was nobody around that really cared about that." As a result, copy editing was comically haphazard. "There was a wire basket in the middle, and there was just a whole bunch of stories piled in there," Aurelio said. "The copy editors would pick anything at random. If they picked something that they didn't like, they'd throw it back and pick another one up. . . . There was nothing consistent about the style. Every editor did his own thing. . . . It was just very sloppy and very unprofessional."

When the time came to do something about this lack of professionalism, Alicia had already established a new pipeline for talent. In the paper's early years, *Newsday*'s slipshod hiring system had relied mostly on the *Daily News*, Hofstra University and other local sources of talent. But in the early 1950s, Alicia had turned south, to the *Winston-Salem Journal* in North Carolina, and hired Mark Foster Ethridge Jr. When Mark Junior came to *Newsday* as an editorial writer, he developed a rocky relationship with the boss. "He and Alicia Patterson fought a lot," said his son, Mark III. Nonetheless, she liked his talent and she still regarded Winston-Salem as a promising place to recruit good young journalists.

In early 1953, when Alicia decided to add a weekly review of the news, she turned again to Winston-Salem. The man she hired, Hal Levy, had grown up in journalism, learning the ways of the city room in Trenton, New Jersey, where his father was the managing editor of the *Star-Gazette*. Arriving at the *Winston-Salem Journal* after World War II, Levy worked on the copy desk, rose quickly to telegraph editor, and eventually became Sunday editor. At the *Journal*, Levy had become friendly with Mark Junior, who recommended him to Alicia. She offered Levy the weekly review job, and he decided to leave Winston-Salem for Long Island. His wife, Bonnie Angelo, who had worked as women's editor at the *Journal* and at the *Richmond Times-Dispatch*, left her job and hoped to find something in New York. On a Saturday in May, 1953, as they drove north for Long Island, they heard an omen on the radio: A horse named Dark Star won the Kentucky Derby. His owner was Harry Guggenheim.

The second weekend they were on Long Island, Levy and Angelo went to lunch with Alicia at Falaise. As they parked in the courtyard, they met Harry, who was on his way out to watch Dark Star race again. Inside, the guests included Marquis Childs, the columnist, and Lester Markel, the Sunday editor of the *New York Times*, a confidant of Alicia. They ate lunch on the glassed-in porch overlooking Long Island Sound, watched sailboats gliding by, and listened to the stories. The next morning, Alicia telephoned Angelo at home.

"She said, 'I want you to work for me,' " Angelo said. The job that they settled on, similar to what Angelo had been doing in the South, involved writing a fashion page and a home furnishings page, and editing a food page. Alicia wanted Angelo, a lively writer, to infuse some new life into the women's pages. "She felt that the women's section was dull," Angelo said. "She felt that it had no style, that it had no sparkle. I don't think she felt the people there could make the break."

At the same time, Hal Levy set about designing the new Weekly Report, which made its debut on Saturday, June 13, 1953. "The first page was whatever happened to be the story of the week," Levy said. "Pages two and three, which were printed as a centerfold, contained six or seven pieces drawn from the week's news. We reprinted cartoons. The fourth page, the back page, was a feature — usually tied to the news. . . . I wrote the whole section and laid it out." In addition, he sometimes filled in as an editorial writer in the absence of Ethridge, and at Alicia's request, he often marked up the paper, writing notes of praise or criticism in red grease pencil.

Given her satisfaction with Levy and Angelo, it was natural enough that Alicia would use the Winston-Salem connection again when she went looking for someone to mold the disorganized copy desk into a force for greater profes-sionalism. The man they recommended had only a few weeks of editing exper-ience, but they had known him in Winston-Salem as a talented writer, with a typically southern linguistic grace. His name was William McIlwain, and he was only 28 years old. McIlwain was a thorough southerner — born in Jones Cross-roads, a rural area outside Lancaster, in northern South Carolina. His father was a farmer who later went to work for the federal Customs Bureau, chasing rum-runners and transferring frequently from place to place in Florida and Alabama and finally settling down long enough for his son to attend school in Wilming-ton, North Carolina, from the sixth grade through high school. While he was still a senior in high school, McIlwain landed a job as the sports editor of the *Wilmington Star*. Right after his graduation in 1944, McIlwain joined the Ma-rines, but he was discharged in the spring of 1945 because of a football injury. Immediately, he took a reporting job in Florida, covering cops for the *Jackson-ville Journal*, and a few months later he moved back to North Carolina, to cover sports at the *Charlotte Observer*. McIlwain was not terribly anxious to go to college, but he won a football scholarship to Wake Forest and decided to go, largely to please his parents. While he was there, he worked summers at the *Winston-Salem Journal*, and once he graduated, McIlwain went to work at the *Journal* full time — covering everything from moonshine to stock car races. Two years later, when he couldn't find a job in New York, McIlwain moved to the *Richmond Times-Dispatch* as a general-assignment reporter. At Winston-Salem, McIlwain had worked for a few weeks on the desk. In Richmond, someone became ill and McIlwain found himself filling in on the city desk. That was where he was working when Alicia summoned him.

Moving into a job for which he felt unprepared was a familiar situation for McIlwain, whose talent and charm had often moved him ahead faster than his experience warranted. "I was, you could say, over my head," McIlwain said. "I was learning them as I was doing them." Now he was moving to a new area, to work at a newspaper that looked like nothing he had ever seen before, at a job that he had never really done. And when he arrived, Alicia was off on one of her European trips. So McIlwain had to settle for a meeting with Hathway, who had only a vague idea of what Alicia wanted McIlwain to do. "I didn't understand anything Hathway was talking about," McIlwain said. "I don't think Alan really understood the job."

So, at age 28, Bill McIlwain came nervously to *Newsday* and began the process of converting a flabby, haphazard copy desk into an all-powerful machine that would rewrite everyone's copy ruthlessly and make generations of reporters grind their teeth in frustration and rage.

II

FOR THE AVERAGE reporter, the definition of a copy desk is this: A group of men and women who toil in richly deserved anonymity, inflicting unnecessary, malicious, unspeakable indignities on perfectly serviceable prose — while the defenseless reporter, after fending off a post-midnight attack of irrelevant questions, sleeps fitfully.

Most reporters sincerely believe that if copy editors could write, they would be reporters. Since they could never construct an acceptable English sentence on their own, these faceless gnomes have to settle for removing all humor, rhythm and grace from someone else's copy and inserting in their place a stultifying mixture of rigid hyper-grammatical structures, awkward transitions and factual errors. The next morning, the reporter opens the newspaper, reads the embarrassing story under her byline, suppresses powerful homicidal urges, and begins a round of humiliating telephone calls to apologize to her offended sources. Meanwhile, the guilty copy editor sleeps peacefully and anonymously.

For the typical copy editor, the definition of a copy desk is more like this: a heroic band of well-educated but under-appreciated scholars, torn away from their families to work cruel night hours, so that they can rescue a herd of illiterate reporters from run-on sentences, split infinitives, misplaced commas and libel. They are the last line of defense before stories are actually set in type and appear in the newspaper. If they do not catch the errors and fill the informational holes by asking insightful questions, the readers get a sloppy, incomplete newspaper. Isolated from much of humanity by the oddness of their working hours and the adversarial nature of their jobs, they develop a fierce tribal loyalty to one another. Ungrateful reporters, whose professional lives they routinely save, may consider them anonymous, but copy editors know that they are bravely brilliant.

At *Newsday*, this eternal struggle took on some distinctive coloration from the unique environment. One significant difference from other papers was *Newsday*'s long production cycle. Reporters turned most of their stories in by early evening, and the presses didn't start until breakfast time the next morning. Another difference was the distribution pattern. Unlike a traditional afternoon newspaper, *Newsday* did not sell large numbers of papers from newsstands to commuters. The goal was to serve the home-delivery readers, and newsstands were secondary. Since *Newsday* relied almost exclusively on school-age carriers, most of the papers did not reach the home until late afternoon, after the carriers returned home from school. Those logistical realities had some profound effects on the way reporters and editors operated.

Since the reader would not be reading the paper until late afternoon or early evening, *Newsday* could not be content with the usual morning-newspaper story that simply told what happened yesterday, which was already old news. So *Newsday* grew into the habit of making the story more complete than a morning-newspaper story, by giving the reader more reaction to the breaking news and telling more about where the story might go next. "A story for this paper has to be angled sharply," Alan Hathway once told an interviewer. "The morning papers have had a shot at it, television has had a shot at it. We have to assume one of two things: no one has seen the story or read anything; or they have both seen and read about it. Either way we have an extra job to do, and that is depth. In effect, we combine the first- and second-day story." That combination, of course, required reporters to pull together more information. If they failed to do that, it was the copy desk's job to make sure the questions got answered and the holes got filled. The long production cycle gave the copy desk all night to do that. "We went to press at 7:30 in the morning," said Stan Asimov, who had come to work at *Newsday* as a reporter in 1952 and moved to the copy desk at about the time of McIlwain's arrival. "You had an awful lot of time to mess around with it. You could always do more with it and do better with it." Once Alicia brought in McIlwain and other strong editors and they began to take advantage of those long hours to improve the paper, what happened in the mid-1950s was nothing less than a total culture change at *Newsday*.

The guiding force in this culture change was McIlwain, whose style was entirely the opposite of Hathway's. Hathway was bluster and bombast and noise. He wasn't much on detail, but when the night's news excited him, he would be all over the newsroom, often drunk, barking out orders. The trick was to figure out which of his orders he would remember in the cold, sober light of morning, and which could safely be ignored. "On big, big stories, God, he just loved it," Aurelio said. "You could see he was frothing at the mouth." Watching Hathway in one of his manic moods was something no one ever forgot. One night, he became enraged because the staff had failed to get comment from a public official on a story that was important to *Newsday*. "We had been trying him all night and his wife said that he wasn't home," McIlwain said. "Alan said, 'Give me the phone.' He got on there and apparently the woman said again he wasn't home. Alan said, 'Madam, if you value your husband's career, you will go out into the night and search for him.' Pretty soon the man was on the phone."

Sometimes, his storms of energy produced inspired results. Late one night in 1952, for example, *Newsday* learned that Russ Sprague and his wife, on their way to San Francisco for a Republican meeting, were among more than 200 passengers stuck in a mountain pass in a blizzard. Quickly, Hathway called the San Francisco airport and left a message for Art Hug, a *Newsday* reporter who was en route there. When Hug called the office, Hathway ordered him to be ready to buy a pair of skis and head for the snowbound train. Fortunately for Hug, Hathway came up with another plan. At one o'clock in the morning, he got on the phone to Nyack Lodge, about five and a half miles from the train, which was stuck in the Donner Pass, northwest of Lake Tahoe. Somehow, Hathway persuaded the proprietor to hire two local men to ski out to the train with a list of *Newsday* questions. At 9:30 in the morning, the proprietor reported that the skiers hadn't returned, but he had found a man who had just come back from a mercy mission to the train. At one typewriter, the reporter Jack Self took notes from the rescue worker, and later from the two hired skiers. At an adjoining typewriter, the rewrite man Charles Gruenberg crafted the story from Self's notes. The resulting coverage that day struck the self-congratulatory tone that pervaded the whole week's coverage, including a huge headline on page one: "NEWSDAY'S/SKIERS TALK/TO SPRAGUE." Those who saw the story unfold in the newsroom remember vividly Hathway's generalship and the simple joy that getting the story brought everyone there.

In contrast to Hathway's hyperkinetic style, McIlwain was slower, softer, more conciliatory, more concerned with the quality of the writing. "The guy had a very good grasp of grammar, of parts of speech; he knew it all," said Stan Green, who as a young copy editor watched this McIlwain transition and in later years replaced him as copy chief. McIlwain's disarming country-boy manner made it relatively painless for reporters and editors to accept his suggestions. "He was a tactician and a diplomat," Green said. "He might say, 'Like I mean now, I see, you know, I see you wrote this here, now, this here word that says that he "affected." Now, that's a good word. But did he really affect the outcome, or do you think that he in some way, you know, I mean, like, do you think we could say. . . .' It was this big ball of words, like a Steinberg drawing in the air." Gently, McIlwain got what he wanted, and the editor or reporter didn't feel violated. McIlwain also added a more cerebral dimension to the desk. "It was different working for Hathway," said Stan Brooks, who worked directly under McIlwain. "You wanted to be tough and show you weren't afraid. Working for McIlwain you wanted to produce literate, stylistic writing, and be real creative, which changed the paper at that point."

The biggest change was that the copy desk became a place where the brightest young journalists at *Newsday* wanted to work, because the new *Newsday* copy desk did far more than add paragraph marks and commas. It offered editors an opportunity to rewrite the most exciting stories of the day. So it was no coincidence that some of the editors who later exerted the greatest influence over *Newsday*'s development began working on the nightside in one capacity or another in the years right after McIlwain's arrival. Several of them came originally from the same tiny source, a mom-and-pop news service in Manhattan called the Park Row News Service, which provided small stories to out-of-town papers that couldn't afford and didn't want their own full-time New York City bureau — including *Newsday*. The first of its graduates to migrate to *Newsday* was a reporter named Al Marlens, followed later by James Hadjin, Richard Estrin and Anthony Insolia. Of that group, Marlens, Estrin and Insolia all became part of the central core that was to govern *Newsday* over its second 15 years, in the era of "the world's strongest desk."

In that period, reporters knew that bad things were going to happen the moment they handed in their copy. "They'd start rewriting it while you were standing there," said the reporter John Cummings. Those who worked on the copy desk were not confined to rewriting small stories that a reporter had fouled up. The desk did rewrites for a variety of reasons: to make stories more intelligible, to give them a broader scope, to impart a lighter touch. "What happened was someone like myself, who was interested in doing as much writing as possible, would work pretty hard at the copy to try and get it out early, so I could play around at one or two o'clock in the morning when it was going to come time to write a story," said Lou Schwartz, one of the editors who would regularly take a story that a reporter had left, add some wire service reports and a phone call or two, and put together a total rewrite. "Then you would get a byline story and it was terrific."

Another reason for rewriting was the growing effort to regionalize stories. *Newsday* and Long Island were both getting too big for *Newsday* to carry a profusion of totally local stories that affected only one small community. So the desk began looking for ways to broaden every story. "The basic thinking was that you could have a newspaper that would say this is a story about Levittown that would interest people in Levittown, or you could write a story about book-burning in Levittown that would interest everybody on Long Island, because it's about book-burning," Stan Asimov said. "If you could find the topic or the story that transcended the geographical limitations of the community in which it was being reported, you would have a story that would appeal to many, many people. . . . This was a major conceptual breakthrough." It was the editors at night — McIlwain, Aurelio and later Marlens — who pushed this notion. If the day editors had not prodded their reporters to make the phone calls necessary to broaden a story out, the night staff took over the job when they came in. That required a round of late phone calls, to reporters and to news sources, which made *Newsday* an infamous disturber of the peace for decades.

The copy desk also expended considerable effort in rewriting stories to make them funny. Often, this meant shameless rewrites of juicy divorce or other gossip stories that had appeared in one of the New York City tabloids. The *Newsday* desk would simply take a story that had been written well in the first place and write it differently, with more humor. "The *News* and *Mirror* would come in at about 11:30 or 12:00 at night and there would be a story about Marilyn Monroe, or Arthur Godfrey, or somebody, written by the best two tabloid rewrite men on the face of the earth," said Jack Mann, one of the brightest of the rewrite lights on the desk of that era. "All I had to do was find the third angle and do it better." The object of the exercise was to come up with readable, funny stories. So, in the late 1950s, the copy desk became known as "The Funny Machine."

One of the primary practitioners of the Funny Machine was Harvey Aronson, who came to *Newsday* in a typical Hathway way. As a reward for his service to the Republican Party, Aronson's father, Izzy Aronson, had acquired a job as a state boxing inspector and had met Hathway during a boxing program at Hathway's arena in Hempstead. Later, Izzy arranged a meeting between Hathway and his son, whose limited writing experience included boxing and humor columns for the *Daily Orange* at Syracuse University and a brief stint at a Jewish paper in Syracuse. At *Newsday*, Aronson quickly developed the art of making serious stories funny and, occasionally, driving reporters crazy. "Very often, the activist desk would get us into terrible hot water with people that they were never going to meet," said Sam Markowitz, one Funny Machine victim. His most painful memory was a story about the suspension of a town police sergeant for stealing buns from outside bakeries at night. Markowitz didn't tap the humorous potential of this story well enough to suit the desk, which decided to take action. "Then Harvey Aronson was given the story, which ran with a cartoon of a big fat cop sitting on the curb, with his cheeks stuffed full of buns," Markowitz said. "It got jazzed up. It was full of puns. There were insinuations." The next day, while Markowitz was engaged in a screaming match with the town police chief over the story and the cartoon, Aronson, the perpetrator, was at home, resting up for the next funny story.

Besides rewriting stories, the desk gave them life in other ways. Newspapers were in the habit in those days of giving criminals nicknames, to make the copy livelier. In 1957, confronted with a series of stories about a slippery robber who had been responsible for a small crime wave, the desk held a contest to come up with a nickname. The winner was Marty Buskin, who decided that "The Eel" was the perfect title for the robber, George Larned. But the *Long Island Press* chose a different nickname, "Mad Dog." Eventually, when Larned was captured, paralyzed for life by a policeman's bullet, *Newsday* mythology holds that he admitted to police, "I'm The Eel." In the *Press*, the headline was " 'MAD DOG' LARNED CAUGHT."

The talented writers on the desk were useful for more than just funny stories. Estrin, for example, became known as someone who could take a complicated science story, or a piece about municipal corruption, and turn it instantly into clear prose. His speed was legendary. "He could write as fast as he could type," said Hadjin, his old colleague at the Park Row News Service. Perhaps Estrin's most famous rewrite job involved the confession of a murderer named Francis Henry Bloeth, who had killed three people in three different Suffolk towns. Taking notes from Tom Renner, Don Drake and Jack Ehrlich, he crafted the 1,200-word main story in 30 to 40 minutes. "You do that in a state of trance," Estrin said.

Beyond the excitement of breaking stories and the fun of the Funny

Machine, the desk also did plenty of donkey work, such as complying with an Alicia directive: Every story that appeared on page one of the *New York Times* had to appear somewhere in *Newsday*. Much of the tedious work of "matching" those stories fell to the copy desk. So every night, *Newsday* slavishly waited for the *Times* to appear, and Aurelio closely checked its page one against *Newsday*'s stories. In the process, Aurelio became an expert on what the *Times* would do. Once, the editor Si Radiloff challenged him to lay out the entire *Times* front page, in advance. "He made up on a copy paper sheet exactly what later turned out to be the front page of that day's *New York Times*," Radiloff said. "There is a feat which I will never forget."

That level of skill was abundant at night at *Newsday*, but not by day. "The nightside were the newer people," Asimov said. "Dayside were the longer-term people. There was much more talent on the nightside than on the dayside." That disparity showed up in the copy that the dayside produced. "The stuff was bad," McIlwain said. As the gap between the day staff and the night staff grew wider, Hathway remained aligned with the older editors, such as Bob Hollingsworth and Jack Altshul. The night kingdom was in the hands of younger, more sophisticated editors, such as McIlwain, Aurelio and Marlens. Eventually, McIlwain said, the nightside began figuring out little ways to circumvent Hathway's lapses in judgment. It wasn't exactly a revolution, but it was at least the start of a substantive challenge to Hathway's authority.

III

MORE THAN MERELY improving the quality of the writing in *Newsday*, Alicia wanted to make the paper more sophisticated, open it up to the world.

In pursuit of that aim, she took a step that drove a wedge between herself and Alan Hathway and created a major new source of friction in her relationship with her husband: She brought in an outsider to help *Newsday* widen its horizons. It wasn't the concept of this broadening that annoyed Harry and Hathway, but the identity and the personality of the man she chose — Richard Clurman, the media writer for *Time* magazine.

Soon after *Newsday* had won the Pulitzer, Clurman had written a *Time* cover story, describing the rise of what he called "the fastest-growing and the most profitable big daily paper started in the U.S. in the last 20 years." The story spoke in glowing terms of Alicia, and her face dominated the cover. In contrast, Harry appeared in the story in a distinctly secondary role, and on the cover, he was nowhere to be seen. "What this did was to put Harry in the position of being a Hollywood husband," Hal Burton said. "He was married to a star." So, when Clurman attended a dinner party with the Guggenheims, Harry was not in a celebratory mood. "Harry was absolutely grim and as near purple as I've ever seen anybody," Burton said. "He departed the party very early indeed and went to bed."

Nonetheless, when Alicia looked around for someone with *savoir-faire*, Clurman was the man she picked. "She wanted an infusion of some outside national journalism," Clurman said. "She said, 'I have the instinct and you have the mind. We can do a lot of things here.'" Actually, Clurman was far from a seasoned national journalist. He had grown up on Long Island, in Rockville Centre, and gone off to the University of Chicago. In 1943, the draft plucked him out of college, and he worked on newspapers in the Army. After his discharge, he went back to the University of Chicago, where he published a highbrow magazine that led him to a minor job at *Commentary* magazine in 1946. With only his three years at *Commentary* and his self-assured manner to recommend him, Clurman landed a job at *Time* in 1949, writing about the press — at the age of 25. When he arrived at *Newsday* in 1955, he was only 31.

Quickly, Clurman's youth and boundless self-confidence annoyed the staff and gave him an image of arrogance and hauteur. "I remember the first day I was there, walking up to the then assistant city editor," Clurman said. "I sat down across the rim and said, 'Tell me what you do.'" Later, he understood how threatening that question could be, coming from a 31-year-old man with all the power of Alicia behind him. But at the time, his purpose was simply to begin to know people. "It seemed to me a legitimate question," Clurman said. "I had never worked on a newspaper. I had no desire to come on as a wimp. I went there with a design. The design was not to run Alan or anyone else out of town, but to add a dimension to the paper." Alicia installed him in an office near hers and made him the editorial director, a new title that made him responsible for the editorial pages, the new Washington bureau, the entertainment pages and the weekly review of news. In this job, he reported only to Alicia — not to Hathway. "It was a very odd construct," Clurman said. "I behaved as if I could dip into any part of the paper. . . . I wasn't very timid about walking into the city room, or calling up at night and saying I didn't think this was right or that was right. If Alan was there I'd talk to him about it. If he wasn't there, I'd do it quite directly, which was very innocent on my part." The problem was more than a question of chain of command. It was the clash of Clurman's worldly style with the unsophisticated tone of *Newsday*. "Clurman came out of a society mix," said Frank S. Johnson Jr., one of the young reporters who arrived at about the same time as Clurman. "You had the impression he thought he was better than everybody else and more sophisticated than everybody else."

If Clurman's confidence and brashness annoyed the young reporters, it had to be even more irritating to Hathway. Alicia didn't specifically tell Clurman to struggle with Hathway and reduce his power, but Clurman's mere presence had that effect. "Clearly, without ever articulating it, she had me there as a counter-weight to Alan's old-style newspapering, and she didn't expect us to love each other," Clurman said. "I think Alan really hated me. Although he never said so to me, I'm sure he did — with reason." The appointment of Clurman signaled clearly that Alicia did not feel Hathway was the right man to lead the paper to new levels of sophistication. "I think she recognized that the paper had passed him by," Dick Aurelio said. "The growth here was incredible, and it was clearly going to be a newspaper that was going to be one of the big newspapers of the future. Hathway was clearly out of step with it. He was from another era." Nonetheless, Alicia respected what Hathway had done for the paper, despite his excesses. "I've always felt that Alan was the one who put the real balls in this newspaper," Bill McIlwain said. "It couldn't have happened if she didn't want it that way."

Alicia had allowed Hathway to roar uncontrolled through the streets of Long Island, but now that *Newsday* was establishing a Washington bureau and attempting to create a national image, she did not want Hathway's blunt, bullish style to be the face that *Newsday* turned toward the world. So she put the bureau under Clurman's control. And she chose two of her newest stars, Hal Levy and Bonnie Angelo, to run it. Until 1955, *Newsday*'s only representation in Washington had been occasional stories from a stringer, Steve Feeley, who covered the Long Island congressional delegation. "This was a period when I think she was really turning that newspaper into a major newspaper, a period during which it became not the second newspaper for so many Long Island people, but the first newspaper," Levy said. "I'm sure she saw the Washington operation as being part of that." Levy and Angelo spent the first few weeks arranging a two-room office for themselves in the National Press Building and getting acquainted with the town. In the process, they encountered the usual obstacles that plagued *Newsday* reporters once they stepped beyond the confines of Long Island: lack of name recognition and clout. Even once they understood what *Newsday* was, few useful sources hurried to return *Newsday* phone calls. Only the Long Island delegation had anything to gain by talking to *Newsday*, but even dealing with them wasn't easy. "All the time we were down there, most of the local delegation hated us," Angelo said, "because most of them were opposed by *Newsday*, and they were hacks anyway."

Beyond the difficulty of establishing themselves in a town that barely recognized their existence, Levy and Angelo also faced the identity question that would plague the Washington bureau for decades: What kind of stories should the tiny bureau cover? "Initially, the emphasis was, don't duplicate the wires," Levy said. If the *Newsday* bureau could not produce a story significantly better than wire-service reports, Levy and Angelo were to "leave it to the wires." Theoretically, that meant that they should focus on in-depth stories or on Long Island-related pieces that the wires were unlikely to provide. But when breaking news happens, editors react to that, and theory goes out the window. So the bureau often had to drop what it was doing and chase the big story. They also grew accustomed to panicked late-night calls from Garden City, in reaction to stories in the early edition of the *New York Times*, which had a far larger Washington bureau than *Newsday* had. "Alicia really never could understand, I think, why *Newsday* couldn't match the *New York Times*," Angelo said. "You cannot match the New York *Times* in a bureau of three people, one of whom had to be doing the local stuff from the Hill."

Eventually, they got help from the home office — a young reporter named Dick Zander, who replaced Feeley. Both of Zander's parents were newspaper people. His father, Harry Zander, had known Hathway in Chicago. His mother, Ruth Reynolds, wrote for many years a series of true-crime stories for the *New York Daily News* called "Justice Triumphs." Despite his connections and his brief experience as a *Daily News* copy boy before he went into the Marine Corps, Zander initially had no luck in persuading Hathway to hire him at *Newsday*. So he went off to Connecticut and worked at the *Bridgeport Herald*. Hathway hired him in 1956 and assigned him to a beat in Nassau County, where Zander began demonstrating his aptitude for politics. It was only about a year later that Hathway asked him to go to Washington. Zander covered the Long Island delegation and other breaking stories, including the Senate rackets committee hearings on Operating Engineers Local 138, which flowed from *Newsday*'s continuing crusade. He stayed in Washington for only 14 months before returning to Long Island politics, but his brief tour was a significant precedent: He was the first of a long line of *Newsday* reporters assigned to cover the Long Island delegation as a full-time responsibility.

As time went on, Levy and Angelo worked out an arrangement that suited their talents. Hal was a solid reporter, well suited to covering the breaking news stories, and Bonnie was a livelier writer who developed her own distinctive magazine-like style and later became *Newsday*'s first space reporter. As they developed a sense of what stories to cover, Levy and Angelo had to navigate through the zany management structure that Alicia had created. "Each day started with a call to Clurman," Levy remembered. "Then I would talk with Clurman again late in the day, before we had filed. Then after we filed, I would be talking with people in the city room. . . . We kind of went through dealing with three shifts, which sometimes made it hard." For the most part, Hathway did not interfere, but several years after the bureau had started, he did assert his power subtly. "There was one time when Hathway I guess decided I should come back and get back in touch with the world, and I came back and spent two or three nights in the city room, editing copy and writing heads and whatnot," Levy said. "That was sort of Alan's demonstration that he still ran the place."

IV

SENDING HAL LEVY to Washington left Alicia without someone to run the weekly news review section that he had started for her. So she dipped once again into the well of talent in Winston-Salem.

This time, Alicia brought north Bill Woestendiek, a close friend of Levy and Angelo. Woestendiek grew up on a farm in upstate New York, near the arts community of Woodstock, but from the time he was in high school, he knew he wanted to be a reporter. Once he had finished his service with the Army Air

Corps in North Africa during World War II, Woestendiek completed his education, majoring in journalism at the University of North Carolina. From there, he
went on to the Graduate School of Journalism at Columbia University, graduating in 1948, and on to Winston-Salem to start his career. At Winston-Salem, he
had risen from reporter to city editor and Sunday editor and won a Nieman
Fellowship. He was happy working in North Carolina, but Levy and Angelo
were persuasive. "They were just so gung-ho and so high on Alicia Patterson and
Newsday," Woestendiek said. "They were selling Alicia Patterson first and
Newsday second."

At *Newsday*, Woestendiek quickly became a member of Alicia's inner
circle. "I was accused of being Alicia's current young man," he said. It is true
that Alicia was a feminist before the word became popular, and she pushed for
the interests of women. "The best thing that ever happened to me professionally was working for Alicia Patterson, a woman who believed that a woman
reporter could do anything," Bonnie Angelo said. But one of the paper's earliest
women reporters, Berni Fisher, noticed a pattern: "Women were hired, and
they were okay, but nobody ever got above a certain level." In other words,
Alicia gave the most senior jobs at the paper to men, like Woestendiek, who
became one of her staunchest loyalists. "I loved her," he said. "I don't mean
romantically. I mean as a person."

In the evolving corporate structure at *Newsday*, there were two distinct
camps. One was the day-to-day staff of editors and reporters who reported the
breaking news and put the paper out every afternoon. The other was the small,
intensely loyal coterie of Alicia's closest associates, the "palace guard." She
controlled their assignments and their work, and they answered primarily to
her. "That paper was very divided," said Bill McIlwain, who managed to keep a
foot in both camps. "Alan tolerated them but didn't like them." Her inner
circle, which had begun at the start of *Newsday* with Stan Peckham and had
expanded to her secretary, Dot Holdsworth, now included Clurman, Woestendiek and Levy and Angelo in the Washington bureau. It also included two
reporters who had come to Alicia through their connections with the *Daily
News*, Virginia Pasley and Hal Burton.

Pasley's husband, Fred, had been a a star reporter at the *Daily News* for
Joseph Medill Patterson. Following her husband's death, Pasley tried to land a
job in the television industry, but Alicia hired her instead in 1951. Her first
major assignment was the campaign to rescue the poet Walt Whitman's birthplace. When Alicia decided to start a program for needy families at Christmas,
called Adopt-A-Family, she chose Pasley to run it. And in late 1954, Alicia gave
Pasley several months to write a long series on the background of 21 American
prisoners of war who had refused to be repatriated after the Korean War and
chose to stay in China. The story took Pasley on a 15,000-mile journey through
America and resulted in a 15-part series, "Escape into Hell," followed by a book
called *21 Stayed*.

Like Pasley, Burton had something beyond his considerable talent to
recommend him as a member of Alicia's inner circle: He was a living link to her

father, as a former outdoor editor and editorial writer for Patterson at the *Daily News*. Burton was born in Little Falls, Minnesota, the hometown of Charles Lindbergh. He got his start in journalism at the *Bismarck Tribune*. Later, after working at the *Detroit Times*, he first got a job at the *New York Daily News* in 1931. But he didn't like New York, and he soon returned to Detroit and became enmeshed in the Newspaper Guild, rising to the position of national vice president. That made him an undesirable in the anti-union Hearst organization. So Burton returned to the *News* in 1933, as a general assignment reporter and rewrite man.

Burton's close relationship with Patterson began to develop one day when Patterson stopped by his desk and asked him about a story that he was writing. Besides his normal rewrite work, on stories such as the fiery crash of the German dirigible *Hindenburg* in 1937, Burton began working directly with Patterson, travelling with the publisher on hunting and fishing trips and writing about them. Then Burton tried out for and won the opportunity to fill in as a vacation editorial writer for Reuben Maury, who had become legendary for his ability to translate Patterson's views into clear, bluntly cogent editorials. Burton's phenomenal writing speed fit neatly with Patterson's standing order that editorials had to be written within 90 minutes after the editorial conference was over. But Patterson's direct relationship with Burton annoyed the managing editor, Richard Clarke, and when Patterson died, Burton knew his own star would decline. So he went off and joined a friend of his in revamping the *New York Daily Mirror* magazine. Soon, he gravitated back to the *News*, working as a substitute rewrite man. Fred Pasley saw Burton in these reduced circumstances and recommended that Alicia hire him. Burton was to work half of the time for Alicia and half of the time doing free-lance magazine writing, primarily for the *Saturday Evening Post*. That lasted until 1952, when it became clear to Burton that the *Post* was headed for the graveyard. So he signed on full time with *Newsday*, which delighted Alicia. "She said, 'You're mine, all mine, dear,' " he said.

Despite his closeness to Alicia, Burton had some rough moments in his early years at *Newsday*. At the *Daily News*, Burton and Hathway had clashed over Newspaper Guild politics. At *Newsday*, Hathway became convinced that Burton was a threat. "He thought I was out to get his job," Burton said. "The last thing I wanted to do was to be a managing editor." His only ambition was to be a writer, not to be part of Alicia's inner circle. Nonetheless, he became one of her closest confidants — taking on assignments at her request, churning out editorials, writing a column called "Change of Pace," and frequently serving as Alicia's lunch partner. For three years, he and his wife even lived in an apartment at Falaise. "Hal Burton, I think, was probably closer to her than anyone," said Francis Wood, another member of Alicia's group. "Hal was really, I would say, the most important pro on the staff."

Wood himself was a prime example of how Alicia's clique worked. The family of Albert Wood had played tennis with Alicia and Harry for years, and as a result, Francis Wood liked to say, he came to *Newsday* on a tennis scholarship. Once he became interested in journalism and decided to leave the family firm in Port Washington, Alicia gave him a summer internship. During the day, he worked as a reporter, and late in the afternoon, he left to play tennis with Alicia. Then she gave him a permanent job in 1956 as a general assignment reporter and allowed him the time to write long reports on issues ranging from the sand mining industry in Port Washington to Long Island's water supply. She also sent him off on a famous *Newsday* stunt story, partly to tweak Harry and his artist friends: Wood pretended to be an artist and infiltrated an exclusive Hamptons club. In addition, Alicia employed Wood's wife, Jean, as a children's book editor. But somehow, Wood's placid personality, combined with *Newsday*'s circumstances, blunted any resentment of his arrangement with Alicia. "The paper was growing so fast," Wood said. "There was plenty for everybody to do."

V

THE DEVELOPMENT OF a real copy desk, the start of a weekly news review and the establishment of a Washington bureau were just a few of *Newsday*'s many needs in the years that followed the first Pulitzer.

Just as the paper had gone for 15 years without a real presence in Washington, for example, it had also been forced to rely almost entirely on wire-service and stringer reports from the state capitol in Albany. That started to change not long after the Washington bureau opened. The first *Newsday* reporter to explore Albany in depth was Stan Hinden, who came to the paper in 1952 and started covering a beat along the South Shore of Nassau County. In 1955, Berni Fisher, who had been covering politics for Hathway, became pregnant and left the paper, and Hinden took her place, developing sources around Long Island and writing a political column. The natural extension of local political coverage is the state Legislature, and Hinden began going up to the capitol to look around. "The first year I was there about half the time," Hinden said. "The second year I went more. By the end of the second year I was there almost full time. I spent nine years in Albany, eventually built up a bureau of three people for the sessions." Over the years, *Newsday* developed a solid reputation for its Albany coverage. In the state capitol, unlike Washington, there was not a huge size disparity between the *New York Times* and the *Newsday* bureaus. So *Newsday* competed equally, scoring its share of victories under Hinden, then Dick Zander and later Albany bureau chiefs.

In the same period, the Suffolk operation changed drastically. For a variety of reasons, Hathway and the others had soured on the longtime Suffolk editor, Ralph Hausrath, a proud, rigid man who had brought a semblance of order to the chaotic Suffolk office after the war. Hausrath had alienated his staff with his authoritarian manner, and he annoyed his editors with his resistance to change. One example of Hausrath's inflexibility was his opposition to the opening of a new Suffolk office in Ronkonkoma, not far from a Long Island Rail Road station, in a section of the county that was still mostly trees. Eventually, the Long Island Expressway would pass within a few hundred feet of the proposed new office. But at the time, Hausrath felt it was foolish to move into the woods and leave behind the rented office in Bay Shore, one of the busiest downtowns in Suffolk. Hausrath lost that battle. In 1956, *Newsday* opened the new office, with the same cinder-block construction that Albert Wood had used in Garden City.

Eventually, Alan Hathway moved Hausrath from Suffolk to Garden City, to run the night Suffolk operation, and he turned the Suffolk reporting staff over to his own protege, Kirk Price. In the Garden City office, Hausrath found himself outvoted by two strong editors who ran the overall night operation: Dick Aurelio and Al Marlens, who had once worked for Hausrath as a reporter. "It was always two to one," Hausrath said. "I was always the one." Locked in a jurisdictional dispute with Aurelio one night, Hausrath made the mistake of appealing to the managing editor. "Hathway said something like, "He's in charge. You understand that? Do you understand that? You're not!' " said Harvey Aronson, who worked under Hausrath briefly, before he left to join the main copy desk. "I feel that Alan broke him. Hathway broke a lot of people." It was a painful confrontation between the old, understaffed, slapdash *Newsday*, and the new, more professional paper that placed a premium on polishing copy to a fine shine. "Ralph didn't really have any skills for that kind of thing," Bill McIlwain said. Finally, in 1957, Hausrath decided to leave *Newsday* and get into teaching, at less than half the pay he'd been getting at *Newsday*.

The departure of Hausrath left the paper with a new Suffolk editor, Kirk Price, but *not* with a more professional operation in the quickly growing county. Price had his strengths, primarily as a reporter, but he had glaring weaknesses as well. He spent much of his energy hanging around with news sources and wielding his power as a journalistic kingmaker, Hathway style. So he had difficulty dealing constructively with his reporters and setting up a workable system for assigning, developing and editing stories. On those occasions when he was sober, Price could be charming and gracious. But like his hero, Hathway, Price was often drunk — especially in the evening. His habit was to supervise the office sloppily by day, then head out for a series of bars. Once Price had gotten a tip in one of these watering holes, he'd telephone the office and order his staff to convert the tip into a story. Often, these leads were fragmentary and nonsensical, filtered through an alcohol haze. "Kirk was a wonderful, wonderful reporter," said Tom Morris, a careful, meticulous professional who became the night editor in Suffolk at about the same time that Price became the Suffolk editor. "He was tenacious and hard-edged when he had to be. My feeling is he never should have been an editor."

For years, Morris had been able to observe closely how Hausrath and Price operated. Morris had first worked for *Newsday* as a messenger in Suffolk in 1945, when he was a student at Babylon High School, and came to the paper full time in 1953. When he became the night Suffolk editor in 1957, Morris tackled the difficult task of bringing to completion the stories that Price had assigned during the day. In the evening, when Morris arrived, Price provided him with a list of developing stories, but the list ranged from informal to nonexistent. "It almost never had any news on it," Morris said. "Maybe some days there would be six stories that he had working. Other days, there'd be one or two. He'd have a yellow sheet with one or two lines — key words on there. He'd say, 'Kind of light today. Kind of light. Nothing much going on. See you later, kid.' He'd take off for the nearest bar. I was in the process of having to go around practically to interview the day people and find out what they were doing." Over time, with the telephoned help of Marlens in Garden City, Morris began to impose a rudimentary structure.

The modernization process was not nearly so bloody and painful in the newspaper's fun-and-games department, sports, as it was in the Suffolk office. In sports, it was simply a question of gently turning the entire concept of coverage upside down. When *Newsday* began, it was obvious that it could not compete with the New York City papers in covering major-league sports. It was, in effect, a supplementary paper. "In those days, the concept was Nassau County," said Bob Zellner, who started working in the sports department before the paper even began publication and became sports editor after World War II. "You were working on the assumption that everyone who took *Newsday* read a New York newspaper." So *Newsday* left serious coverage of the major leagues to the city papers, concentrating instead on covering local high school sports comprehensively. To make readers more aware of its coverage, *Newsday* initiated during the war the annual Thorp Award for the outstanding high school football player in Nassau County. A few years later, when the growth in Suffolk warranted a similar promotion there, *Newsday* established the Hansen Award. These awards, along with the intensity of *Newsday*'s high school coverage, and Zellner's assiduous cultivation of the coaches, helped to make *Newsday* the paper that readers needed if they were to follow local sports.

In the postwar years, Zellner tried to persuade Hathway that some of the annual budget for staff expansion should be used to improve the coverage of professional sports. In this lobbying effort, Zellner got help from Walter O'Malley, the president of the Brooklyn Dodgers. "He used to drop in regularly and visit Alicia, urge her, tell her that it was time we expanded," Zellner said. The first reporter to cover major-league baseball for *Newsday* was Bill Voorhees, who had come to the paper after a tour as the sports editor of the *Herald* in Rutland, Vermont, followed by jobs at the *Nassau Daily Review-Star* and the *Long Island Press*. But the development of full-scale coverage was a slow process. Voorhees didn't go on road trips, because the budget wouldn't allow it, and *Newsday* covered spring training by carrying features written by the Dodger public relations man, instead of sending its own reporter to Florida. By the middle of the 1950s, *Newsday* was still much more heavily oriented toward local sports than toward national sports.

"It was a Long Island group of guys who were afraid of the big city," said Stan Isaacs, a street-wise reporter from Brooklyn who joined the staff in the fall of 1954, after covering major-league sports at the *New York Compass* until it folded in 1952, and then working as a free-lancer writer. "Wherever I had been, you talked sports; you talked about the Giants, the Dodgers. Nobody talked about that. They used to talk about bowling, occasionally about golf. There was no conversation about big-league sports in that department. . . . Voorhees was the only guy who at least had an interest in covering New York sports or expanding."

Outside the sports department, that attitude irked Jack Mann, who was doing rewrites on the copy desk. The incident that made his blood boil involved Satchel Paige, the great pitcher who had toiled in the old Negro leagues for years before baseball's bigotry melted enough to allow him to pitch in the big leagues. That day, Paige won a spectacular extra-inning game, driving in the winning run himself. "One inch, one column inch had been dummied on the sports page for that game," Mann said. "I raised pluperfect hell in the middle of the city room when I saw that. As a matter of fact, I went and got some wire copy out of the sports department, and actually wrote a story myself, and stuck it in the paper. . . . Dick Clurman was around at the time and he heard my noise. He said, 'Could you do it better?' And I said, 'You're goddamn right I could.' "

The beginning of the change was the temporary assignment of Jack Altshul, the city editor, to run the sports department. The next step was the creation of a three-person staff — Mann, Isaacs and Ed Comerford, a sports department veteran — to cover national sports. Zellner remained in charge of local sports coverage, but Mann began to exert more and more influence. Finally, in 1960, Mann became *the* sports editor in title as well as in fact, and Zellner concentrated all his efforts on sports promotions. The process of improving the sports coverage, begun by Zellner, accelerated under Mann. *Newsday* began going on the road with major-league teams and covering spring training. As Alicia loosened the purse strings, Mann started to hire talented young writers. Before Mann took over, the paper had carried Jimmy Cannon's syndicated sports column, but a day later than the *New York Post* ran it. Mann didn't like that arrangement, so he started a new rotation of *Newsday*'s own national columnists: himself, Isaacs and Comerford.

In a short time, the *Newsday* sports department began to forge a small national reputation. The first step was a glorious prank. In 1959, two years after O'Malley had moved the Dodgers to Los Angeles, Mann and Isaacs were covering the first World Series involving the *Los Angeles* Dodgers, and they were outraged to see the 1955 *Brooklyn* Dodgers world championship flag displayed on the wall of a hotel. So they swiped it and brought it back to Brooklyn. Then, in 1961, Mann's distinctive style impressed *Newsweek* enough to make the sports department the subject of a *Newsweek* profile, which reported glowingly on Mann's management techniques and even mentioned his favorite headline. For years, Mann had wanted to write a play-on-words headline that would twist "These are the times that try men's souls" into "These are the souls who time men's tries." Finally, Isaacs suggested a way to get it into the paper: He'd write a story about the fans who came to track meets with stop watches, to time each event and compare those times to the official times. Isaacs wrote the story and

Mann wrote the headline that had been rattling around in his head. Mann even gave himself a byline for the headline. That was an unheard-of piece of egotistical whimsy, but it was part of the reason why the sports department, once so provincial, was beginning to make itself known outside Long Island.

Beyond the improvement in sports, *Newsday* had a long list of needs.

The paper didn't have a real promotion department, for example. So Alicia gave the job to a reporter named John Van Doorn, on the strength of one year's reporting experience and his suggestion for a clever front-page cartoon and headline celebrating the Milwaukee Braves dancing around the casket of the New York Yankees: "The Bier That Made Milwaukee Famous."

The paper didn't have a theater critic, so in 1955 Alicia hired George Oppenheimer, who had written 30 films and originated the long-running *Topper* television series. His presence helped to break down the resistance to *Newsday* among theatrical publicists, who traditionally had taken care of the big New York City papers first.

The paper didn't have a true education editor. It published a school page called Schoolday, written by Gwendolyn Risedorf, who had worked first on the women's pages and then switched to school news. Looking at the school page, Frank S. Johnson Jr., a former Marine Corps combat correspondent who was new to the paper, felt that it was aimed too much at the students, rather than at serious coverage of education. So he talked to Alicia, and she appointed him *Newsday*'s first education editor. Later, he got into a struggle with the city desk about the content of his page and decided to leave *Newsday*. Alicia arranged for him to go to work with Harry at the Guggenheim Museum.

The paper didn't have a good features section, separate from the hard news part of the newspaper. So Alicia established something called the Center Section. The idea was to pull together features that had already been running in the paper and package them in a sensible way that would be more accessible to readers. "That was one of the beginnings of what became a *Newsday* trademark some years later, which was packaging your content," said Art Perfall, who edited the new section. The Center Section was an odd package. In a broadsheet newspaper, it is relatively easy to set up the folding and cutting operation on the press so that the paper consists of two or more separate sections, one behind the other. In the tabloid format, that isn't possible. So the new center section sat inside the rest of the paper upside down, so that readers would be able to find it and pull it out easily. When the new section began, on September 13, 1955, an editorial boasted: "Today NEWSDAY becomes the first tabloid in the U.S. to be printed daily in two complete sections."

Even on the rudimentary level of its physical plant, *Newsday* had endless needs. The plant didn't have air conditioning, for example. When the weather became oppressively hot, the nightside staff would often show up in shorts, to protest the lack of air conditioning. Finally, a petition for air conditioning appeared on the bulletin board. Alicia, who had air conditioning in her own office, signed it, and before long, air conditioning was installed. But that was only one of many changes in the plant. As the paper grew and added employees,

Newsday was forced to add new sections to the building, including a second floor on the administration building. Even with the new second floor, the maintenance staff was forced to shuffle office space. "I took down offices and put them up over the weekend," said Ed Ferguson, one of the maintenance staff. "I never knew when I was going to be told to take down this partition and drag it out another two feet."

So *Newsday* continued to bulge at the seams, adding to its plant, routinely publishing a 144-page paper, reaching the 300,000 circulation mark in 1958, growing fatter financially and physically, always expanding, but somehow avoiding what Alicia feared most: the fat-cat attitude.

CHAPTER SIXTEEN

Patterson v. Guggenheim

I

WHILE ALICIA WAS broadening the paper's horizons after the first Pulitzer, Harry had a full enough agenda of his own, seemingly, to keep him from demanding a bigger share of power at *Newsday*.

Almost a year before the Pulitzer, for example, he had become a member of a special committee of the Jockey Club, the blue-blooded organization of racehorse owners. The committee's purpose was to develop a plan for revitalizing the state's thoroughbred racetracks, to provide stiffer competition to the gleaming new tracks in New Jersey. In 1954, the committee proposed the creation of a not-for-profit corporation, later known as the New York Racing Association, to take over ownership of the Belmont, Aqueduct, Jamaica and Saratoga tracks and pour millions of dollars into modernization. Alicia supported the plan editorially, and later, after the Legislature passed the bill in 1955 and it languished on Governor Averell Harriman's desk, *Newsday* spoke out in favor of the plan again. Harriman finally signed the legislation, and the NYRA eventually closed Jamaica and made major improvements at the other three tracks. In the creation of the NYRA, Harry was not just a name on the letterhead, but a powerful force.

As an owner, Harry had a paradoxical attitude toward racing. "He never liked to be classified as a sportsman, as a breeder and racer of thoroughbred horses," said his private secretary, George Fountaine. "He tried to downplay that, because he apparently had the idea that it was a frivolous pursuit." But Harry was very serious about it. Soon after his horse, Dark Star, had won the Kentucky Derby in 1953, Harry tenaciously pursued the legendary trainer Woody Stephens and finally persuaded Stephens to run his stables. In the years that followed, Stephens accomplished what Harry's other trainers could not: maintaining a long-term relationship with Harry. "I could talk to him, and I am the only one to stay nine years," Stephens remembered. "I could stand up to him pretty well, because I went there not needing the job."

It wasn't easy working for Harry, because he immersed himself in the tiniest details of the operation, down to the pregnancy rate among his mares, and argued with Stephens about the fine points of racing strategy. "He was very opinionated, but fair," Stephens said. Harry didn't want his horses running in mud, for example, and he insisted that a fiery, controversial jockey named Manuel Ycaza was essential to the success of Cain Hoy Stables. So Harry signed an exclusive contract with Ycaza, took care of him financially by providing astute investment advice and helped him to deal with his frequent suspensions for racing violations. Despite the strength of Harry's views, Stephens admired him for his patience with the long-term plan, his understanding of the industry and his willingness to spend whatever was necessary to build a first-class racing stable. In 1959, Cain Hoy became the leading money-winner in the nation, with purses of $742,081. Just as Alicia was not content to relax after the Pulitzer, Harry was not ready to bask in the glow. "The year we led the nation," Stephens remembered, "he said, 'Well, Woody, we've had a great year, but we can't rest on our laurels.' "

That same year, Harry opened the Guggenheim Museum in Manhattan, completing a process that his uncle, Solomon R. Guggenheim, had begun more than five decades earlier. Solomon had started collecting paintings early in the century, primarily works by the old masters. In 1926, he had met the Baroness Hilla Rebay von Ehrenweisen, an Alsatian artist who became his artistic guru, leading him away from the old masters to an appreciation of modern art. In 1939, to make his growing collection available to the public, Solomon set up the Museum of Non-Objective Painting in rented space in Manhattan, and appointed Hilla Rebay the curator and later director. In 1943, Solomon commissioned the architect Frank Lloyd Wright to design a permanent home for the museum. By the end of the following year, the plans were complete, Solomon had bought a site at Fifth Avenue and 89th Street, and the art world expected the museum building to be completed soon. But by the time Solomon died in 1949, his museum was a regular target of art critics, who disliked the way Rebay ran it, and it was still in temporary quarters. The task of turning his uncle's dream into a concrete reality fell to Harry, as chairman of the foundation's board and later as president.

In guiding the museum to completion, Harry needed large stores of patience and diplomatic skill to placate two huge egos: Frank Lloyd Wright and Robert Moses. The architect was so taken with the unique design of his circular concrete tower, for example, that he wanted to call it an "archeseum," but Harry stood fast against that. Wright also feuded with the museum director over the proper way to display paintings on the curved walls of the tower's gravity-defying ramps. Harry resolved these disputes in a series of "Querido Francisco" letters to Wright, who responded with notes to "Lieber Harry the Guggen-heim." More important than his minuet with Wright, Harry faced a struggle with Moses, who controlled construction in the city and detested Wright's design. Though Moses was married to a distant relative of Wright and they exchanged letters addressed to "Cousin Frank" and "Dear Bob the Moses," the process of gaining the necessary approvals from the city was long and tortuous. Somehow, Harry maneuvered past all these obstacles, and Wright's ingenious building at 1071 Fifth Avenue opened to the public on October 21, 1959 — five months after the architect had died. The opening-day crowds included Alicia's tennis partner and designated reporter, Francis Wood, who wrote the *Newsday* account of the event, and Alicia herself, who was a trustee of the museum. In an editorial the next day, she approved strongly of the new museum. "Possibly, this is what the world of painting needs," the editorial said. "Like it or not, the Guggenheim Museum has brought controversy back into a field that seemed doomed to musty decay."

Despite Alicia's support on issues such as the museum and the NYRA legislation, and despite the time that he devoted to those and other interests, Harry began to covet a greater role in decision-making at *Newsday*. As long as it was Alicia's little toy, he seemed relatively content to stay on the fringes, intervening only to save her from fiscal folly. Once *Time* magazine had made *Newsday* famous, however, it took on new importance for him. "His real prob-lem was that he belatedly decided that he was responsible for the paper's success," Richard Clurman said. "None of us paid any attention to Harry's editorial suggestions. That was one of his humiliations. . . . In her mind and in ours, he had no control of the newspaper." Actually, Alicia did allow Harry one indulgence over the years, in deference to his expertise. "Harry was totally influential on the Cuban policy," Hal Burton said. "She gave him that." Beyond that, she kept the editorial pages out of his hands.

In time, Harry's displeasure began to focus as much on Clurman as it did on Alicia. At the start, despite Harry's annoyance over Clurman's piece about Alicia in *Time*, Clurman said that Harry actually seemed pleased that Alicia had hired him. "He was a kind of star-collector," Clurman said, "and I was a sort of little star then." But before too many weeks had passed, Harry summoned Clurman into his presence. "I wandered in in my shirt sleeves and he said, did I consider myself a propagandist for the Democratic Party — not screaming or anything, just quietly," Clurman said. "And I said, 'No, I consider myself a journalist. . . . I'm certainly not a propagandist for the Democratic Party. Why do you ask?' He said, well, he thought that the editorials of the paper were taking that tone. . . . From that moment on, he considered me a dangerous radical, I think."

Then, in 1956, the year after Clurman came to *Newsday*, the Harry-Alicia struggle acquired a new dimension. Adlai Stevenson was thinking about running for the presidency against Dwight Eisenhower again, and this time, Alicia wasn't so sure that she liked Ike nearly as much as she had liked him before Stevenson decided to run in 1952.

II

NOBODY HAD TO drag Adlai Stevenson into the 1956 presidential campaign.

This time, he was not a sitting governor, reluctant to run a race that seemed almost suicidal. As 1956 approached, Stevenson was a self-confident world figure, free of the responsibility of elective office, who had established himself as the Democratic Party's leader, by spending months travelling the country during the 1954 election, retiring his own campaign debt, articulating the party's positions and trying to elect Democrats to the Congress and to the statehouses. In the process, he had set a tone of political discourse that directly foreshadowed John Fitzgerald Kennedy's 1960 campaign against Vice-President Richard Milhous Nixon. Stevenson's rhetoric was an abrupt departure from the Truman-era Democratic slogan, "You never had it so good," which promised rather than exhorted. Instead, his speeches challenged his audiences, calling for fresh ideas and strong national leadership.

Stevenson's campaigning in 1954 was so intense that *Look* magazine published a piece by William Attwood, who had travelled with Stevenson on a world tour after the 1952 election, saying unequivocally that Stevenson had decided to run again for President in 1956. In the final week of the campaign, basking in the attention of an appreciative crowd in Rochester, New York, Stevenson gave a hint that Attwood was right. "I almost wish I were running myself," Stevenson said. Three days later, he spoke at a rally in Great Neck, a wealthy but Democratic community on the North Shore of Nassau County. The crowd of 2,500, which *Newsday* had helped to build, heard Stevenson blast Nixon for conducting a campaign of "smears, slurs, slogans and what-not" and chide Eisenhower for praising Nixon. He spent part of that final campaign weekend visiting Alicia at Falaise. On election day, 1954, the Democrats took control of both houses of Congress and a majority of the statehouses. "There were few if any who left his house in Libertyville Election Night with any doubt that Stevenson would seek, and probably get, the Democratic nomination in 1956," wrote his biographer, John Bartlow Martin. "And many thought he might well win."

The campaign of 1956 began for Stevenson, Martin said, in late November of 1955. In fact, Stevenson began his inaugural four-state political trip by spending several days with Alicia at her hunting lodge, bringing along his aide, W. Willard Wirtz, and Wirtz's wife. A few weeks earlier, Alicia had run on the front page of *Newsday* the results of a poll of Long Island, conducted by Lou Harris of Elmo Roper and Associates. The lead headline on page one was "LI DEMS FOR ADLAI,/ROPER POLL SHOWS." The poll found that local politicians uniformly favored Governor Averell Harriman as the 1956 Democratic candidate, but Democratic and independent voters on Long Island overwhelmingly preferred Stevenson over both Harriman and a more likely candidate, Senator Estes Kefauver. The poll ran one week after President Eisenhower left a Colorado hospital, following his recuperation from a heart attack in September. No one knew whether Eisenhower would decide to run for reelection. So the poll matched Harriman against three potential Republican candidates: Nixon, Senator William Knowland of California and Chief Justice Earl Warren. It showed Harriman losing to all three and Stevenson beating Knowland, losing to Warren and finishing in a dead heat with Nixon. Months later, at the Democratic convention in Chicago, Richard Clurman said, *Newsday* slipped reprints of the poll stories under the doors of delegates.

Before the Roper poll, Stevenson had written to Alicia, complaining that Harriman was "kicking away the first chance in modern times for a major party out of office to agree on its candidate 10 months in advance and concert its effort and resources against the enemy instead of against each other." It is not clear whether it was that letter that prompted her to instruct Clurman to commission the poll, but she definitely asked for it. "It was entirely Alicia's idea," Clurman said. "It seemed too activist for me." Whatever her reasons for doing it, the poll had to be helpful in dampening Harriman's chances of entering the race. If nothing else, it showed that Alicia was willing to help Stevenson any way she could. In 1952, she had found herself boxed into supporting Eisenhower. Now, in the 1956 campaign, she knew going into the year that Stevenson would almost certainly be a candidate, and she no longer had to drag around the weight of several years worth of stories urging Eisenhower to run for the presidency. So she was far more free to advocate Stevenson's candidacy. The Roper poll and an accompanying editorial were a potent start.

Early in 1956, she wrote him a letter filled with campaign gossip and advice. "Whatever happens don't get pushed around by the pols," she wrote. "You can win. 'To your own self be true.' " In another letter, she wrote to tell him about a Democratic dinner at the Sheraton Astor Hotel in New York, where a telegram from Stevenson drew more applause, even though he was campaigning in California, than the speeches of the anti-Stevenson Democrats who were there. "*Well*, boy oh boy what a lot of eggs (not heads) were laid last P.M. at the Astor," she wrote. "If the boys cannot do better than that you have nothing to fear." She also told him that *Newsday* had heard from a senior official of the AFL-CIO that labor would support Stevenson. "Feel mighty encouraged," she wrote. "So must you."

At the end of February, Eisenhower announced that he would run for reelection. The road ahead for Stevenson was clear: a difficult series of primaries against Kefauver, followed, if he won the nomination, by an uphill race against a popular incumbent. The primary season started off disastrously for Stevenson when Kefauver won, uncontested, in New Hampshire on March 13 and then beat Stevenson in Minnesota on March 20. The Minnesota loss was so painful that some of his advisors even discussed whether he should withdraw from the forthcoming California and Florida primaries. Shortly after that stinging loss, Stevenson and his son John Fell showed up at Alicia's hunting lodge in

Georgia, to relax and write a speech that he was to give on April 6 to the Jacksonville Bar Association. Of all the services that she performed for him during the campaign, none could mean more than a few days at her lodge.

For nearly three decades, Kingsland was the place where Alicia went to recharge her spiritual batteries. "She said just a day or two days here and she was a different person," said her caretaker, Walter Merck, who had married Dawn Colson, the daughter of Alicia's original caretaker, Nub Colson. Alicia could be gregarious, but she also had a quieter self that was most comfortable in Kingsland. "She said, 'I don't understand how you lead the life you do, always surrounded by people,' " said her friend, Marietta Tree. "She needed this place where she could go and be by herself for a week at a time."

Alicia and Joe Brooks had bought the 1,800 acres along the St. Mary's River in 1936. Like Alicia, the lodge that they built was unostentatious — a one-story building of weathered clear cypress, with shutters painted a pinkish hue, at Alicia's instruction, to match the color of a fungus on the trees. Those trees were important to her, and once, when she returned to the lodge, she was stunned to find that workers trimming the Spanish moss on a large oak tree had cut it all off. "She loved the Spanish moss," Merck said. "I think that one of the few times I ever saw tears in her eyes was when she saw that oak tree without any moss on it." So they put the moss back.

She loved the river, too. Wearing a broad-brimmed straw hat, she would walk down to the ladder on the river bank and start swimming, even if there were snakes crawling on it. "She'd knock the snakes off the ladder and go right in," said her friend, George Abbott. She'd swim out, keeping her straw hat above water the whole time, and sun herself on a sandbar near a bend in the river. Or she'd climb in a boat with a friend and paddle for hours through remote inlets, exploring and chatting. "We could talk forever," said Abbott, who was occasionally alone with her for a whole week at the lodge. "Harry didn't like that at first. Then he came to the notion that we were really what you call platonic friends."

Alicia used the lodge three or four times a year, between October and April. The times of her visits centered on the quail-hunting season, which ran from November to March. There were other forms of athletics that she had to struggle to master, but shooting quail wasn't one of them. She was as good at it as Harry was, and she was relentless. Even when she broke her leg in a fall, she kept hunting, using a jeep that Harry bought her. "She shot that season with that cast on her ankle, just like always," Merck said. Compared with Alicia's hunting skills, Stevenson's were underdeveloped. Once, Merck said, Stevenson shot at the same bird three times. Stevenson kept missing but the quail kept presenting a target. "He said, 'That was the most obliging bird I ever did see,' " Merck remembered. But that didn't bother Stevenson. "He didn't go to Georgia to hunt," said his son, Adlai. "He went to Georgia to see Alicia." Stevenson was a good tennis player, and Alicia could offer him a competitive game on the court near the lodge, but if he didn't want to be active, he didn't have to be. Merck remembered Stevenson sitting outside the lodge in his shorts, writing his speech, and he remembered Alicia's admonition: " 'I want you to make sure nobody bothers him.' "

Following his brief time in the sun at Kingsland, Stevenson charged back into the campaign, and his fortunes improved. He won the Illinois primary, as he had to, and then he won in Florida and California. Finally, on July 26, Kefauver announced the withdrawal of his candidacy. That still left Harriman's candidacy, but Stevenson beat back that challenge and won the nomination at the Chicago convention on the first ballot. Privately disdaining John Kennedy because he was a Catholic, he threw the vice-presidential nomination open to the delegates, and they chose Kefauver narrowly over Kennedy.

"Once in a long time a man crosses the American horizon who brings to the American people the dream that is America," said the next day's *Newsday* editorial, which followed with an entire column of quotes from Stevenson speeches. Another editorial, after Stevenson's acceptance speech, said: "As the first newspaper in the U.S. to endorse Adlai Stevenson for the Democratic nomination, NEWSDAY is especially pleased that he won it. . . . No one could seriously question that he is far and away the best candidate the Democrats have to offer." Once the Republicans had nominated Eisenhower in San Francisco, *Newsday* echoed its 1952 stance: "Dwight Eisenhower vs. Adlai Stevenson gives the country the best choice we can have." Later, *Newsday* emphasized that it was taking an independent stance in the campaign. "We will make up our mind on the presidential race on the basis of the men, the issues and the campaign," one editorial said.

Just as they had in the 1952 campaign, the editorials bore the outward stamp of objectivity. Reading them without any knowledge of Alicia's personal commitment to Stevenson, the average reader could conclude that *Newsday*'s endorsement decision actually was in doubt. But Long Island Democrats understood the paper's position clearly. "*Newsday* gave us an enormous amount of coverage," said Martin Gross, who worked for Stevenson's candidacy, against the party's leaders. "She went all out — I mean almost a blitz," said John F. English, then a young Democratic lawyer and later the Nassau County Democratic chairman. "It built up a tremendous amount of cadre of Stevenson people out here who became zealots."

At the end of the campaign, Alicia asked Clurman to write two endorsements, one for Stevenson and one for Eisenhower. "I sent her the proofs with a little note on a slip which said, 'Alicia, as I think I've said, I find both these editorials equally persuasive. I'm going to vote for Adlai,' " said Clurman, who had come to know Stevenson through Alicia and had even written a few memos for Stevenson on policy matters, with her blessing. To Clurman, her request for two editorials was not just a charade to convince him that she was impartial. "My analysis of that is that she asked me to do it in good faith," Clurman said. "I think, for her own sense of integrity, she wanted to see the argument."

The result was that Alicia endorsed Stevenson, using an editorial that incorporated much of Clurman's confidential draft. "Our switch to Stevenson is not an easy decision," the editorial said. "In all its history, the U.S. has rarely had two candidates running for the presidency who have had so much to recommend them." While Eisenhower's record was "certainly not bad," the editorial conceded, he had been unsuccessful in lifting the Republican Party to his level; he was saddled with Richard Nixon; relations with Britain and France had seriously deteriorated, and the Republicans had shown no willingness to tackle social issues. "There are a hundred issues and factors that bear on a decision," the editorial concluded. "But on balance we prefer the leadership and promise of Adlai Stevenson's forward-looking 'new America,' to the complacency of Dwight Eisenhower's 'peace, prosperity and progress.' "

This decision for Stevenson came as a nasty shock to Harry. Early in the campaign, at about the time Stevenson was visiting Alicia in Kingsland to write his Jacksonville speech, Harry had sent her a detailed memo, outlining the reasons why an endorsement of Stevenson would be against the paper's best interests. He complained that the coverage wasn't balanced, and she simply answered that she hadn't made up her mind, but the decision would be hers alone. In October, he sent her two more memos, but she didn't reply. Nonetheless, Harry came to the conclusion by the end of the campaign that Alicia was going to endorse the Republican presidential candidate, as *Newsday* had done in 1944, 1948 and 1952. In fact, Clurman said, Harry passed that intelligence along to his friend Leonard Hall, the chairman of the Republican National Committee, just before the final endorsement was to appear. "He told his pal Len Hall that Len had nothing to worry about — his paper was coming out for Eisenhower," Clurman said. Once Harry had made that confident prediction, the Stevenson endorsement became a humiliation that caused an escalation of his marital war with Alicia.

III

THE ESSENTIAL INCOMPATIBILITY that had been there from the start, exacerbated by Harry's refusal to sell Alicia majority ownership during his lifetime, had continued to make the marriage difficult even before the 1956 campaign.

Despite the difficulties, Alicia stayed in the marriage, largely because she knew that divorcing Harry would mean losing her paper. Dot Holdsworth remembered an argument between Harry and Alicia, who were sitting on the couch in the living room of her hunting lodge, when Harry told her bluntly: " 'Well, then, you'll have to leave *Newsday* if you get a divorce.' " Neither Stevenson nor Clurman had caused the long-running conflict. "Adlai Stevenson and I talked her out of divorcing Harry," Clurman said. But Clurman's presence and the endorsement of Stevenson in 1956 triggered the most serious marital crisis of them all, in 1957. It was so knotty, in fact, that Harry and Alicia started communicating with each other through lawyers.

Alicia's attorney was Louis Loeb, a Yale Law School graduate who was a partner in the prestigious firm of Lord, Day & Lord. Loeb served as general counsel to the *New York Times*, and he came to Alicia through the recommendation of her friend Lester Markel, the Sunday editor of the *Times*. Harry's lawyer was Leo Gottlieb, who had been graduated at the top of his class at Harvard Law School in 1920, quickly became a partner in the firm of Root, Clark, Buckner and Ballantine, and in 1946 was one of the founders of a new firm that later came to be known as Cleary, Gottlieb, Steen & Hamilton. He had begun representing Harry in the early 1950s and eventually became one of his closest advisors, on business, on Harry's endless succession of wills and on other personal matters. Harry even showed Gottlieb the drafts of letters that he was writing to Alicia, complaining about operations at *Newsday*.

The role of the lawyers on both sides of the dispute was not to file a suit but to seek some sort of accommodation on the two eternal issues: credit and control. "It all came down to this really: She wanted to have complete, absolute control of the editorial and news departments of the newspaper, and she was perfectly satisfied to have her husband have complete control of the business side," Gottlieb said. But Harry felt that, as the majority owner, his role should be bigger. He also felt that Alicia had a skewed view of the paper's history. "Although she would tell him privately that she recognized fully his great contributions to the success of the enterprise," Gottlieb said, summarizing Harry's view, "she would never say anything when any member of the staff was around which indicated that she recognized these." That was a central element of a memo that Harry and Gottlieb drew up together to give to Alicia. The lack of respect for Harry's contributions went so far, the memo said, that Alicia even caused Harry's name to be removed from the masthead as president. In fact, she had completely dropped the masthead from the editorial page. "APG has done everything possible to create and foster the myth that *Newsday* is solely a Patterson enterprise and not a joint Guggenheim-Patterson enterprise," the memo said. Alicia's lawyers told Gottlieb that the draft memo didn't give Alicia enough credit for what she had done on the editorial side. So Harry wrote out in longhand an addition to the memo, including this sentence: "APG has worked tirelessly and faithfully, has been an inspiration to employees of *Newsday* and has been responsible for knitting together a fighting organization with splendid morale ready to meet any emergencies." Still, his memo argued: "The success of *Newsday* has come about because, in addition to the excellent editorial job which has been done, the newspaper has had the benefit of exceptionally competent business and financial management supplied by HFG. . . . On many occasions APG has made suggestions to better the product of *Newsday* through increased expenditures, but she has never made any suggestions for reducing expenses or increasing income. Indeed, she has opposed most of HFG's programs for reducing expenses or increasing income."

Just a few months earlier, in an incident not mentioned in this memo, Harry had demonstrated his continuing impact on *Newsday*'s financial operations, by helping to increase advertising from an important advertiser. Three major department stores had opened in 1956 on Long Island — Macy's at the new Roosevelt Field shopping mall, Gertz in Hicksville and Gimbels in Valley Stream. Since Gimbels hoped to pull in many of their Long Island customers through ads in the New York City papers, they told Eugene Higgins, the retail advertising supervisor, that they planned to run only 35 pages of ads in *Newsday* in the first few months. Higgins felt that wasn't enough, and Harry agreed. So Harry wrote a polite but tough letter to Bernard Gimbel himself, arguing that there was no substitute for *Newsday* in attracting Long Island customers, and predicting that the small advertising program that Gimbels planned for *Newsday* would be unsatisfactory. "We all feel," Harry concluded, "much as we should like to have Gimbels in, that, until you are ready to use Newsday in a way in which it can be of real value to you, you should postpone coming into the paper." In other words, Harry was telling one of the biggest advertisers in the area that he could just keep his ads. "It was a rather dramatic thing for a growing paper to do," Higgins said. Before long, Gimbels increased its *Newsday* advertising substantially.

Besides emphasizing his contributions to the paper, there was a more practical purpose to Harry's memo to Alicia: increased editorial power, to counterbalance Alicia's control. That shift of power was needed, Harry felt, because Alicia was misusing the paper. "*Newsday*'s objectives require that the personal desires, ambitions and friendships of the editor play no role in the determination of the positions to be taken by the newspaper," the memo argued. "Unfortunately this requirement has not been met by APG in recent years." Obviously, Harry was thinking about the Eisenhower-Stevenson campaign. The editorials during that race, he argued, were often distorted and inaccurate, partly because of the inadequacy of the research. At the end of the nine-page memo, Harry made a plea for a more equal sharing of control, with "full consultation, careful consideration by each of the views of the other, and mutual confidence and respect."

This was not just a squabble over tennis or a disagreement over whether Cain Hoy or Kingsland was the better hunting lodge. This was a deadly serious struggle over the soul of the newspaper. Right in the middle of all this, just a few days after Harry's memo, Alicia and Dot Holdsworth climbed on a plane and headed off for an eight-week tour of Africa that would reunite her with the man whose candidacy had precipitated the struggle: Adlai Stevenson.

In addition to Alicia, Holdsworth and Stevenson, the party on the trip included at various times Stevenson's friend, Marietta Tree; her husband, Ronald, and her daughter, Frances FitzGerald; Adlai Stevenson III and his wife, Nancy, and Stevenson's law partner and political advisor, William McCormick Blair Jr. As she crisscrossed Africa, Alicia took copious notes, for a series that she planned to write. At the same time, she apparently still had the struggle with Harry on her mind. "I remember her talking about her worry that she was going to lose the newspaper," Nancy Stevenson said. During their travels, the two women stayed in the same room one night, and Nancy Stevenson recalled seeing a softer, more vulnerable side of Alicia. "She took down her hair, which she wore sort of tied up in a bun, and it was very long, and she sat brushing it for a long time," she said. "I remember thinking about this as being such a soft and traditionally feminine gesture for someone who played down her feminine qualities, rather than playing them up. We sat and talked like schoolgirls too late in the night that night. It was then that I realized that she was a very warm and vulnerable person. . . . She was quite personal at one point. I grew up in a very openly affectionate family, and I guess I had mentioned that. . . . She told me that she envied me that."

Despite that display of softness, Alicia didn't forget to bring along her toughness and irascibility, and she didn't hesitate to display it. One of those occasions was a visit to Albert Schweitzer's primitive hospital in the jungle. Even though she had been prepared to admire Schweitzer, she reluctantly changed her mind when she saw the unsanitary conditions and observed his refusal to modernize it. It didn't help Alicia's mood, either, that she and FitzGerald had to stay together in a room with no indoor plumbing. "Part of what made her so irritable was that, not only was it what she considered bad medicine, but Schweitzer was imposing himself on her in this way, by insisting that she and all his other guests perform this unnecessary act of self-sacrifice," FitzGerald said. "She'd turn into her hard-bitten journalist self. She could be very tough and very aggressive and very sharp — exceedingly sharp, and very articulate, of course." In her report in *Newsday* on this visit, Alicia wrote: "Like a Prophet from the Old Testament he follows his straightened path, refusing to recognize the changing times. He doesn't want a new world where his Africans, his river, his fatherhood will be challenged."

While Alicia was in Africa, Harry made at least a small effort at conciliation. On their eighteenth wedding anniversary, he sent her a cable: "Did I forget to remember?" And two weeks later: "Please cable me how you are. Love, Harry." In her absence, he continued to exert his influence on overall planning for the paper, but he didn't overstep his bounds. Clurman had offered a plan for improving the paper's business coverage, for example, and Harry had sent him back a memo rejecting Clurman's premise that *Newsday* should make businessmen on Long Island the primary audience. Even though Harry was a businessman himself, he didn't want the paper's business report to aim for a level of sophistication like that of the *Wall Street Journal*. Rather, Harry felt that *Newsday* should speak to the housewife, and a *Journal*-style business section would be "entirely too technical for the housewife." Aside from that kind of guidance, though, Harry refrained from stepping across the line and grabbing control of the editorial pages.

"During her absence I have not overruled the Editorial Director, although I have pointed out what I considered errors of judgment," Harry wrote to Gottlieb. "Since Alicia's return she has made no constructive suggestions to solve our differences. . . ." They couldn't even agree on Harry's desire to commission a Gallup survey of *Newsday* readers, to find out what they liked about the paper and what needed to be changed. In response to the text of a speech by George Gallup, outlining trends in American journalism, Alicia sent Harry a copy of her own speech at Fordham and argued that *Newsday* had already implemented much of what Gallup recommended. "Dr. Gallup has come up with a lot of truisms that have been practiced by good publishers for the past 20 years," Alicia wrote him. "His thinking, it seems to me, is behind the times. A newspaper to be successful must be ahead of the times and I like to think that Newsday has been." She wouldn't object to a survey, she said, but she provided him with her own list of proposed questions. Nonetheless, Harry came away with the impression that she was still resisting. "I think your impression that an appraisal of reader interest will hinder Newsday's progress is wrong," he wrote.

During this continuing duel by memo, Alicia met with Loeb to discuss the controversy, and Harry sat down to draft another statement of the problem, groping for any workable formula. He put together a proposed credo for the paper that he hoped she would find acceptable, and he raised again the need to express his own views on the editorial pages whenever they disagreed. For a brief time, they seemed to be making progress. Alicia accepted Harry's credo for *Newsday* and agreed that, whenever he differed seriously with *Newsday*'s editorial position, she would offer him space opposite the editorial page for a signed statement of his own opinion. She agreed to restore the masthead, with his name. In return, she wanted Harry to promise that his will would give her enough *Newsday* shares to provide her with majority control. But by the end of October, the efforts to resolve their disagreements were looking bleak.

"The difficulties of finding a solution to Newsday's operation are growing in my mind, rather than decreasing," Harry wrote to Gottlieb. To prove his point, Harry attached a copy of the October 29 editorial page, which included a political cartoon by Hugh Haynie, showing a Soviet wizard, carrying a hammer and sickle and sitting on a rocket soaring toward the moon, while a doleful pumpkin with the face of Dwight Eisenhower sat impotently on the ground. "Newsday has been reproducing cartoons by Haynie that are directed to ridiculing, attacking and undermining President Eisenhower," Harry wrote Gottlieb. "I don't know what the objectives are, but the results, if Newsday's editorial page has any influence, would be to undermine the effectiveness of the President."

A little more than a month later, Alicia decided that she had had enough. In the face of Harry's push for control, the thought of continuing to run *Newsday* jointly with him had become even less tolerable than the prospect of leaving. So at the end of 1957, she sat down and wrote two drafts of a statement announcing that she was resigning. "Effective today, I am resigning as editor and publisher of Newsday," one draft began. "It is the most painful announcement I have ever had to make. Newsday — which has been my life's work — has brought me immeasurable gratification and I take pride in what I hope it has accomplished as a newspaper. Rather than let the reasons for my departure 'leak out' and as a result be garbled, I should like to state them unmistakably and as clearly as I am able. . . . Recently, the priority that I have always given journalistic over business considerations, has been challenged. Harry Guggenheim, who put up the original $750,000 to launch Newsday and who retained 51% of the stock while I held a 49% minority interest, has at this late date attempted to exercise more and more control over my editorial management of the paper. Our differences have not been primarily political, although we have had some of those too. . . .

"We have prospered rather than suffered under the theory that journalistic independence and integrity precede balance sheets and business considerations. However in recent months — at the peak of Newsday's success — Harry Guggenheim has increasingly attempted to take control over the journalistic product which he formally can control by virtue of his 51% stock interest.

"My choice was painfully simple. I could stay and preside over the gradual disintegration of those journalistic principles which I believe have made Newsday. I have chosen to resign because I cannot be a part of transforming a living newspaper put out by journalists into a balance sheet controlled by businessmen."

Alicia's rebellion was not simply words on paper. During this long struggle, she also engaged in some overt acts that displayed her anger and frustration. For several weeks, she left Harry and moved in with Bennett and Phyllis Cerf. More important, she hatched a scheme for disposing of her 49 percent of *Newsday* stock in a way that would infuriate Harry. "She said, 'Let's buy the *Daily Mirror*,' which was a dying paper then," Clurman remembered. "She said, 'You be the editor. . . . Let's put the *Daily News* out of business. . . .' She plainly wanted to do that both to stick it to Harry, but also to stick it to her late father and kill the *News*." First, she had to sell her *Newsday* stock to someone, and she settled on S. I. Newhouse, knowing that Harry would be furious. From a hospital room, where he was undergoing treatment for ulcers, Clurman reached Newhouse by phone in Greece. Newhouse was so enthusiastic that he was willing to curtail his trip, but the deal simply didn't work out. "By the time he came back, she decided that she really couldn't do that," Clurman said. "She was very stirred up about doing it, even though she hated Newhouse. . . . I had to tell him that it had gotten so complicated that it didn't seem real anymore."

Early in December, Leo Gottlieb informed Harry that Alicia had decided to resign, effective January 1. But a few days later, while Harry was in South Carolina at his lodge, Alicia called her lawyer, Louis Loeb, and asked him if there was still any chance of working things out. Loeb told her that there might be a chance, especially since Clurman was getting ready to leave *Newsday*. In the first week of the new year, Harry wrote Alicia a memo summarizing those events and outlining once again his proposal for an agreement. This formulation was similar in many ways to earlier versions, but he did concede that "the final decision on editorials will be yours," even though he reserved a right to disagree by writing his own signed editorials. This time, Alicia went along. Though both Gottlieb and Kenneth Ryan, Loeb's partner, said that there was no final written agreement, Alicia and Harry decided to step back from the abyss.

One of the central elements of the solution was the departure of Clurman. Even though Alicia remained friendly with Clurman, she asked him to leave, and she and Harry used his departure as a catharsis. "What became plain was that, in their marital arguments, I was on Alicia's side," Clurman said. "So they would argue about me, rather than arguing about each other. . . . She and I decided that, just or unjust, she had become so paralyzed and I had become so paralyzed in doing what we were doing by this fight that I would get out of it."

Before that paralysis set in, Clurman had exerted a strong influence in shaping *Newsday*'s coverage in a variety of ways. He supervised the start of the Washington bureau; retained a law professor to write analyses of Supreme Court decisions; revised the business coverage, with some advice from his friend Osborn Elliott, then the business editor of *Newsweek*, and published "Hits and Misses," an internal critique of the paper's style, patterned after Theodore Bernstein's "Winners and Sinners" at the *New York Times*. Clurman also had an effect on hiring, such as his effort to replace Cliff Rogerson, the *Newsday* cartoonist. Rogerson was not the kind of artist who conceives of a satirical idea and then draws it, without guidance. "He would offer no substantive views of any kind, and then he would be instructed what to draw," Clurman said. So Clurman reached outside *Newsday* to hire Edmund Duffy, the political cartoonist at the *Saturday Evening Post*, who had won three Pulitzer Prizes at the *Baltimore Sun*. "He was a real cartoonist and didn't take instructions — not that he was impolite about it, but he would just go and do his cartoons," Clurman said. "That was not what Alicia wanted. It was all very genteel, but it just didn't work out."

Perhaps Clurman's most important impact on *Newsday* was his success in getting the paper to think big, even about such mundane matters as the willingness to place transcontinental phone calls. "He was a wonderful influence on that paper," Bill McIlwain said. "He was our first outside big-timer." He had provided the broader vision that Alicia wanted, but he had also exacerbated her explosive relationship with Harry. So he left *Newsday*. The next day, Alicia went to Clurman's Park Avenue apartment for dinner with him and his wife. At one point, she and Clurman went into another room, so they could talk privately. Alicia was on the verge of tears. "We went in the bedroom and she was ranting about Harry and the terrible things he was saying," Clurman remembered. "She said, 'My husband is a crazy psychopath.' "

The resignation of Clurman momentarily eased the tension, but it didn't heal the struggle between Harry and Alicia over the festering issue of credit. One example of this continuing battle was the 1959 piece in the *Saturday Evening Post*, under Alicia's byline, "as told to" Hal Burton. From the outset, Burton was concerned about how Harry would react to it, and he urged Alicia to give Harry some credit in the piece. "She said, 'I hate to give that son of a bitch one dime's worth of credit,' " Burton said. But he finally persuaded her to tell him anything favorable that she could remember. "She said, 'I have to think very hard.' " Burton put together a list of the favorable comments from the piece and sent a copy to Harry, asking him to read and initial it. When the piece appeared in print, Harry called Burton and, in his quiet, toneless voice, suggested that Burton had left out some of the favorable mentions. So Burton sent him a photocopy of the list that Harry had initialed. "About a week later, I got a call: 'Hello, Hal, this is Harry. I guess you're right. Everything's there.' He felt very much neglected. . . . Nobody was paying any attention to him, except, as Alicia said, some little old generals and admirals that he liked to pal around with."

IV

WHILE HE STRUGGLED with Alicia over control of *Newsday*, Harry was also engaged in a long controversy with his daughter over control of her sons. The issue was the future of his fortune and the family reputation.

One of the strongest forces in Harry's life was his conviction that rich families had an obligation to use their money for the progress of the human race. As a result, he had an obsession with making sure that his heir would continue to exercise a prudent stewardship of Guggenheim millions, just as Harry himself would have done it. As 1960 approached, Harry was nearing his 70th birthday and looking for an heir. He had three daughters, but he really didn't believe in women as shapers of the future, even with the example of Alicia — an aggressive, competent, liberated woman — under his own roof.

The closest thing that Harry had to a direct male descendant was his daughter Nancy's first son, Dana Draper. This potential heir had an interesting combination of genes. On his mother's side was the hard-driving Guggenheim strain of business acumen and pursuit of wealth, although Nancy herself exhibited none of these traits. Dana's father, George Tuckerman Draper, was entirely different from the Guggenheims. George Draper's mother, Dorothy Draper, was a renowned decorator who redesigned the interiors of countless hotels and also did some work for Harry at Falaise. His great-grandfather on his father's side was Charles Dana, a legendary managing editor at the *New York Tribune* and later the owner of the *New York Sun*. George Tuckerman Draper himself was a journalist. So Dana inherited from his father at least a small share of the journalism genes.

Early in her life, Nancy Guggenheim had displayed a stout loyalty to her father, choosing to live with him when he divorced her mother, the former Helen Rosenberg. That decision cost Nancy any chance she ever had to develop a relationship with her mother, who expressed no desire to have anything to do with Nancy or her children. Nancy's developing bohemian lifestyle didn't help. She was well outside the Guggenheim mold — a ballet dancer and a freethinker, and her mother didn't approve. "She didn't like her philosophy," said Nancy's older sister, Joan Van de Maele. "She was a little bit too much to the left." Her choice of a husband was also unorthodox for a Guggenheim. Nancy had met George Draper in a public-speaking class at Columbia University in 1934. Later, during the Spanish Civil War, he served as an ambulance driver in the international brigade supporting the Loyalist cause, an enterprise far to the left of Harry's politics. In 1939, Draper married Nancy and they moved west, partly so that he could find newspaper work in San Francisco and partly to escape the Guggenheim influence. There, on June 29, 1940, Nancy gave birth to her first son and named him Dana, an echo of her husband's journalism ancestry. The following year, George Draper was drafted, and the year after that, Nancy gave birth to her second son, George Tuckerman Draper Jr. Soon after he returned from the war, George Draper divorced Nancy. They remarried briefly in 1951, but that didn't last. As a result, Nancy's two sons grew up in San Francisco with no one to look up to as a father figure, except for Harry, who moved into the vacuum and provided a remote, grandfatherly guidance. His advice covered even tiny details, such as their toilet habits. Harry was such a creature of routine that he even made a ritual of defecating as soon as he awoke in the morning, and he urged that practice on his grandsons. "We'd be down at the breakfast table in the morning," George T. Draper Jr. said, "and he would say, 'Boys, have you done your duty today?' "

If Harry had confined his advice to harmless lectures on regular bowel movements, he might not have come into such painful conflict with his daughter. Instead, he badgered her about her choices of schools for the boys, and she fought back. Somehow, she had developed the quaint notion that they were her sons, and she should be the one to decide where they went to school. That ran afoul of Harry's strong feeling that the boys should attend proper, expensive boarding schools. This was no minor matter of preference to Harry. It was an issue of family survival. "These schools are the rich boys' substitute for the school of hard knocks of the poor boy," he explained, urging her to cut the cord tying her to her sons. "If you do not know, please inquire from the medical profession and you will learn that the silver cord is the greatest single developer of homosexuality." Even in the face of this blunt appeal, Nancy was unmoved. "Nancy and I decided to send the boys to public school," George Draper said. "She'd gone to boarding school and hated it, and I'd gone to boarding school for too many years and hated it. We didn't want to subject Dana and George to it."

At his public high school in San Francisco, Dana was anything but a serious scholar. He didn't really know what he wanted to do with his life. He felt no stirring of whatever journalistic blood flowed in his veins. Nor did he feel particularly attracted to follow his grandmother into hotel decorating. Harry provided numerous chances for him to learn about the world: working summers at the Cain Hoy plantation and at one of the family's plants in Chile, where Dana decided he might want to be a surgeon. But Dana didn't deliver good marks. When Dana finished high school in 1958, Harry wrote him a blunt letter of reproval. "I think your lack of real success has been because you have attended an inferior school and because, in addition, you have not applied yourself sufficiently," Harry wrote him. At the time, Dana was planning to enter Menlo College in California as preparation for enrolling in Stanford University, which is the school that Harry wanted for him. To make sure that Dana worked hard, Harry promised to buy him a car if he passed. Manfully, Dana wrote back a "Dear Skipper" letter, defending his high school and taking the blame himself. "I am sorry that you are disappointed in my high school record," Dana wrote. "My trouble has been learning how to study." The problem was that Dana was not nearly as driven as Harry. "I didn't necessarily want to go to Stanford," Dana remembered.

All this warfare over the proper schooling made Nancy's relationship with her father painful and awkward. "Thank you for doing me the kindness of asking me for my views," she wrote him. "If you think back, you have not asked me for my views, you have only told me yours. . . . You want to know what happened to what you refer to as a 'very close and happy relationship' we once had. All I can say to this is that you have repeatedly criticized me severely and unmercifully as to how I have conducted my life and raised my children. This at first hurt me deeply and over the years has caused me to feel antagonism as well as hurt."

Looking back on that time, Dana said that Harry's motives were decent enough. "I think he was trying to be creative and positive," Dana said. "I don't think he was trying to destroy my mother." But the message that came through clearly to Dana as a young man was that his grandfather was powerful and that his mother didn't want that power to overwhelm the Draper family. "I didn't want to basically get into a place where I'm rejecting my mother or rejecting my grandfather," Dana said. "I'm trying to hear him, at the same time I'm hearing her. At the same time, it's real clear I don't know what I want." In the spring of 1959, after an unsuccessful year at Menlo College, Dana decided that, for the time being, his best course of action was to decide nothing, by volunteering for the draft. "The reason I'm entering the service is to get my military obligation out of the way," he wrote Harry. "I will also be able to think about the future."

A few weeks later, Harry and Nancy had an acrimonious disagreement about the schooling of Dana's brother, George. Harry wanted George to attend the exclusive South Kent School, in the Connecticut countryside. Harry and the boy travelled to the school together in Harry's limousine, and while George took the tests, Harry waited. "I felt like it was going to a monastery," George remembered. "I didn't feel comfortable there." But George did well enough on the tests to get into South Kent, and Harry asked him if he wanted to go. "I just felt like I was caught," George said. "I think I might have said yes." But George had second thoughts, and Nancy and her second husband, Thomas Williams, inspected the school and decided that it was not the place for him. Williams remembered vividly Harry's apoplectic reaction when he and Nancy broke the news to him at Falaise. "Brother, it hit the fan," Williams said. "He was screaming at me, threatening me for some reason, threatening Nancy. . . . He is just screaming about disinheritance and, 'You'll get nothing. . . .' He was a dangerous man when aroused."

The thing that aroused Harry most, his relatives and business associates learned, was his feeling that someone he trusted had let him down. In Harry's search for an heir, that would happen more than once, and it would always be painful.

CHAPTER SEVENTEEN

The Reformers

I

IF IT IS proper for a newspaper to rejoice about depriving any man of his liberty, *Newsday* had every right to celebrate its role in the imprisonment of William DeKoning. But the corruption that he had constructed was too powerful to shrivel and die just because he was briefly in prison.

For exposing DeKoning, *Newsday* had won a Pulitzer Prize, but the campaign leading to the Pulitzer had not had a major effect on the day-to-day lives of the union members. "It made a dent, that's all," said William Wilkens, one of the Local 138 members who began to meet secretly and plan ways of reforming the union. Though DeKoning himself was in prison, and his son, William Jr., had to resign his union position as a condition of his suspended sentence, DeKoning cronies still controlled Local 138. But *Newsday*'s Pulitzer had created an atmosphere in which a reform movement could grow and had warned the union's corrupt leaders that they couldn't operate with total freedom. "What it did was it made them more careful," said John DeKoning, the nephew of the imprisoned union leader. "It didn't solve the problem, but it created that big spotlight."

As the reform group grew in strength, its members stayed in close contact with *Newsday*, primarily through the reporter Bernie Bookbinder. On the surface, the thin, soft-spoken Bookbinder seemed an unlikely match for a group of union men who made their living with their muscles. But from the start, he was able to win the confidence of the Local 138 rebels — meeting with them in their homes, interviewing them at their jobs, showing up at crucial moments when the union leadership was trying to crush them. "The guy at *Newsday* I had the most respect for was Bernie Bookbinder," John DeKoning said. "I often was scared for Bernie's life."

In the process of reporting on the reformers, Bookbinder stepped across some journalistic lines. "He wrote our 12-point program," John DeKoning said. "That was the 12 different points we wanted from the union." Once Bookbinder had helped them draft the 12 points — calling for such reforms as annual printed financial statements and secret-ballot elections — he wrote the *Newsday* story, calling it a "revolutionary" program. That kind of participatory journalism would raise eyebrows in the 1990s, but it didn't bother Bookbinder then. "I think we had been so imbued by Hathway — very much to his credit — with the righteousness of what *Newsday* was doing, that it was like covering Nazis," Bookbinder said. "I mean, you abandoned any sense of objectivity." Similarly, Bookbinder was a participant in the process of cleaning up the harness tracks, in the wake of the trotting scandal. The state's Harness Racing Commission began requiring workers at the tracks to have licenses, and Deputy Commissioner Michael Monz interviewed the employees to decide who could work and who could not. Monz, who had become close to Hathway, gave Bookbinder a significant role in the process. "I was permitted to sit in on these interviews, and in fact, was supposed to tip them off if I recognized any guys from the DeKoning ranks who were trying to slip in," Bookbinder said. "I certainly had the power or the authority or whatever it was, unofficially, to prevent people from getting licenses. I felt terrific."

No matter how much help Bookbinder provided, the reform movement would have accomplished nothing without the willingness of the reformers to speak out against DeKoning's abuses. That sense of outrage reached as high in the union's hierarchy as John DeKoning, who had worked closely with his powerful uncle right up until the 1953 indictments. When John DeKoning found that he was among those indicted (his indictment was later dismissed) and sensed that he was to become the "fall guy," he started examining Local 138 more closely. "Then I found out how the union was plundered," DeKoning said. "After many, many, many years of secrecy, it finally came to light and I was completely ashamed that my name was DeKoning." Once he broke with his family and began fighting Bill DeKoning's cronies, *Newsday* made him a hero. With a 1955 story by Bookbinder, the paper ran a photo of John DeKoning on one side and a photo of Marlon Brando on the other, drawing the parallel between DeKoning's break with his family and the rebellion by the character that Brando played in the film *On the Waterfront*.

Another outraged reformer was William Wilkens, who came home from a Nazi prisoner-of-war camp after World War II and went to work almost immediately for the union. His older brother, Lou Wilkens, was the president of the union, until he came into conflict with Bill DeKoning, who could make or break the local's president. Besides observing DeKoning's shabby treatment of his brother, Bill Wilkens learned for himself about DeKoning's gratuitous cruelty. "That particular night, I was so excited, because we had our first child," Wilkens said. "I walked up to DeKoning Sr. and gave him a cigar, saying that I had my first child. And he took a smell of it. He said, 'Oh, El Cheapo,' and threw it on the floor. So that gave me a little initiative to see what could be done."

In the struggle against DeKoning, Wilkens joined forces with a short, fiercely intelligent, tenacious rebel named Peter Batalias, whose name means "warrior." Batalias had first worked in construction when he was still in Newtown High School in Queens, to help support his family. In World War II, he served as a combat engineer and was wounded during the Normandy invasion. Following the war, he formed his own small construction company. Once he started to operate in Nassau County, despite the warnings of friends, and signed a union contract with Local 138, Batalias found out quickly about the power of DeKoning: A Local 138 enforcer demanded that he pay a kickback on his contract with the union, and Batalias refused. A week later, Bill DeKoning showed up at the site in a black Cadillac, with a pair of large associates. "He talked to you like you were dirt," Batalias said. "The windup of it was that I was told I'd have to learn the hard way. Next day, everybody went on a slowdown." On a later job, someone tampered with one of his bulldozers and it blew up. Eventually, Batalias got out of the contracting business and became a heavy equipment operator, which meant that he had to work on a permit from Local 138.

Once Batalias was a part of the union, he learned more about the politics of Local 138. The Connecticut contractor that employed him had beaten out Hendrickson Brothers, which had a monopoly on all major contracts on Long Island. In addition to his executive position in the company, Milton Hendrickson also sat on Local 138's executive board and served as a Republican leader in Valley Stream. Despite the power that this triangular arrangement gave Hendrickson, the Connecticut contractor had somehow gotten a contract, and the Local 138 representatives at the site ordered Batalias and the others to sabotage the contractor's equipment. Unwilling to destroy the machinery, Batalias ran afoul of a former boxer named George Welbourne, also known as George Hayes, one of DeKoning's most fearsome emissaries. "Georgie Hayes stood me up against a wall at Calverton and he started beating my head against the wall," Batalias said. "He was six inches higher than me, and he outweighed me by 100 pounds." Then Local 138 ordered the contractor to pay Batalias what they owed him and let him go. Enraged, Batalias charged into the Labor Lyceum and chased Bill DeKoning Jr. from room to room, in front of a group of politicians. Finally, the younger DeKoning told Batalias he could have his job back. A few months later, Hendrickson Brothers hired him and arranged for him to get a "voting book," which signified full membership in Local 138. Bill DeKoning objected, Batalias said, but Hendrickson had too much clout in the union to be turned aside, and Hendrickson needed his skills.

In time, Batalias and others began writing anonymous letters to *Newsday*, which became part of Hathway's growing files in the period before the Pulitzer Prize, and Batalias began raising questions at meetings. Finally, at a meeting on January 28, 1955, Batalias introduced a motion to liberalize the union's voting procedures. In response, a pack of DeKoning loyalists, including the same George Welbourne who had beaten him years earlier, ejected him. "They hustled me out of one of the side doors and they beat me up in the parking field," said Batalias. Bernie Bookbinder learned of the attack, interviewed Batalias in the hospital and wrote about it for *Newsday*. The paper covered every development in the investigation of the assault, but a judge dismissed charges against Verner Sofield, who ran the union as a surrogate of DeKoning, and a jury acquitted the seven other DeKoning associates accused of the beating.

Physical violence was not the most effective, or even the most frequent, method of enforcing discipline in Local 138. More typically, union leaders dealt with dissidents by making it difficult for them to get work. In addition, the union's leadership staged an elaborate attempt to freeze the reformers out of any role in union meetings. Only two weeks after Bill DeKoning Jr. finished his suspended sentence in May, 1955, and returned to control of the union, Verner Sofield brought charges against Batalias, Wilkens, John DeKoning and others, for bringing the union into disrepute by testifying that Batalias had been beaten. The younger DeKoning suspended both Batalias and Wilkens for five years from union meetings. Eventually, Batalias and Wilkens decided to take their case to the international union's convention in Chicago.

Just before they left New York, Batalias and Wilkens appeared on a radio program with the *New York Daily Mirror* labor columnist Victor Riesel, who had been writing about DeKoning. A few minutes after Batalias and Wilkens left Riesel, someone threw lye in the columnist's face outside a Manhattan restaurant. Though that violence was unrelated to DeKoning, it was still on their minds when they reached Chicago for the convention, where they encountered threats and intimidation and received police protection. In the middle of the night, for example, the phone rang in their hotel room, and a man warned Wilkens: "You had a family when you left home. You better go back." As a result of the threat, Nassau County police put Wilkens' wife and children under 24-hour protection. Throughout the time they spent in Chicago, Bookbinder was with them, filing stories to *Newsday* and serving as an intermediary between the two reformers and the Chicago press. "I was really involved in a very clear, if not conflict of interest, certainly at least a lack of objectivity," Bookbinder said. "I was there sort of as their advance man and PR person."

The trip to Chicago produced nothing for Batalias and Wilkens. So they took an even more drastic series of steps, picketing both DeKoning's Labor Lyceum and the union's international headquarters in Washington. It was not on the picket lines, however, that the reformers finally won their battle. It was in the National Labor Relations Board. In early 1955, Batalias had filed charges with the NLRB, alleging that Hendrickson Brothers and the Nassau-Suffolk Contractors Association dominated Local 138. Since more than 20 percent of the voting members in the union were contractors, the reformers felt that they had to remove the contractors from that position of influence in order to break DeKoning's grip on the union. Throughout the process, Bookbinder covered the NLRB's hearings and wrote long pieces analyzing the cozy relationship between the union and the contractors. In September, 1956, the NLRB examiner found that the abuses were pervasive in Local 138 and ordered the contractors' association to stop doing business with the union. This ruling would have the effect of disbanding the union. "The final end of hoodlum control and DeKoningism on Long Island is now clearly in sight," a *Newsday* editorial proclaimed. It was not, of course, quite that easy. While the examiner's ruling worked its way through the bureaucracy and the courts, the union continued trying to starve Wilkens, Batalias and the other reformers by freezing them out of jobs. So the reformers filed additional NLRB charges, alleging discrimination. It was not until 1969 that the NLRB completed the long, tortuous process of appeals in the Local 138 case. "It took me 15 years to win the final decision, and after the decision was final, it guaranteed seniority, job referrals and everything to union members that were qualified to operate equipment," Batalias said. "Local 138 is still controlled by that decision. That's my claim to glory."

And *Newsday*'s claim to glory was that, at least in the early stages of this decade-long struggle, it provided the Local 138 reformers with the protective shield of public opinion. "We wouldn't be alive, most of us, if it weren't for *Newsday*," John DeKoning said. "*Newsday* took time to help this group. This group of guys changed a lot of things."

II

JUST TWO YEARS after Bob Greene had used his position at the New York City Anti-Crime Committee to help *Newsday* in its pursuit of Bill DeKoning, Greene found himself looking for a new job.

At the committee, Greene had made a major contribution to the literature of organized crime, by alerting the press to a growing form of labor racketeering, the systematic looting of union welfare funds. In his investigation of welfare funds, Greene focused on the International Brotherhood of Teamsters and identified early the rise of an official in the Central States Conference of the Teamsters: James Riddle Hoffa. As Greene amassed information about Hoffa and local mobsters such as John (Johnny Dio) Dioguardi, who was building a kingdom on Long Island, he passed it to journalists, including Murray Kempton, the columnist for the *New York Post*, and A. H. Raskin, who covered labor for the *New York Times*. "Bob was a marvelous source," said Kempton, who got some of his earliest information on Hoffa and Dioguardi from Greene. In providing information to the press, Greene attracted the attention of a subcommittee of the House Government Operations Committee, which was looking into labor racketeering, and the committee asked him to testify.

As he dealt with congressional committees and reporters for the major New York City newspapers, Greene did not forget his friends at *Newsday*. He passed information on Hoffa to Jack Altshul, for example, and Altshul carried a

small but early item in his column, predicting that Hoffa was a good bet to take
over control of the entire Teamsters union from Dave Beck. Greene also told
Altshul about the mob's infiltration of the jukebox industry. In addition,
Greene briefed Bernie Bookbinder on Dioguardi and other mobsters who had
moved to Long Island to live. *Newsday*'s emphasis on the mob persuaded
Nassau County District Attorney Frank Gulotta to set up a rackets bureau in his
office.

Greene's growing closeness with *Newsday* became a precious asset in 1955,
when he resigned from the crime committee after two of his colleagues, William
Keating and John O'Mara, lost their jobs in a complex struggle with Manhattan
District Attorney Frank Hogan. "When O'Mara was let go, I said, 'Screw you,'
and left," Greene said. "I look back at that decision a lot of times and say, at
least once in your life, you stood there and you said, 'Bullshit! This is wrong.' "
Once he started looking for work, Bookbinder suggested that he talk to Hathway, but Greene refused to ask, out of stubborn pride. Bookbinder persisted,
and Greene consented to meet with Hathway and Bookbinder in Mineola.
Hathway hired him at $135 a week, at a time when most of the reporters at
Newsday were making $125.

Greene's first major effort for *Newsday* was a two-part series on the jukebox
rackets. Later in the year, he wrote an ambitious series on mobsters on Long
Island, called "The Mobs Move In," which won a George Polk Memorial Award
from Long Island University. The lead of the first part reminded readers that
William C. DeKoning Sr. would soon be stepping out of the state prison at
Attica, after serving 18 months, and it raised the question of what DeKoning
would be doing next. Naturally enough, Greene drew the assignment of covering DeKoning's release. The way he approached it was typical of the journalistic
melodrama that became his trademark.

At the end of a work day, Greene and the photographer Howie Edwards
climbed into Greene's 1955 Plymouth and started on the eight-hour drive to
Attica. They got to their motel in the middle of the night and arrived outside
the prison at 6 a.m. to wait for DeKoning's release. When DeKoning emerged,
Greene asked for a few comments for *Newsday*. DeKoning responded in two
pungent words, climbed into a car with his wife and a driver and headed off.
Greene and Edwards scrambled into Greene's car and chased DeKoning at high
speeds. Twice during that chase, DeKoning stopped at police stations to report
that a car was following him. Undeterred, Greene kept up his pursuit until he
lost track of DeKoning's car in the Buffalo traffic.

Deducing that DeKoning was going to a hotel and that he'd probably use
an unimaginative alias such as his wife's maiden name, Greene went to the
Hotel Statler to check. He found two suites reserved — one in the name of Mr.
and Mrs. William Matthews, the maiden name of Rose DeKoning, and the other
for Mr. and Mrs. William Callahan, the name of the first of DeKoning's relatives
to rise to prominence in the Operating Engineers. That reservation turned out
to be for DeKoning's son and his wife. Once he knew the DeKonings were
there, all Greene had to do was coax the desk clerk to give him and Edwards an

adjoining room. So Greene pulled out a badge that a grateful law enforcement officer on Long Island had given him. "I lied," he remembered. "I said, 'We're here from the courts. We have been paying very careful attention to this gentleman. He's a terrible felon. . . . We want the room next door to him.'" The hotel had already placed a honeymoon couple in that adjoining room, but Greene asked the staff to make other arrangements. "As Howie and I went up to the room," Greene said, "the honeymoon couple are being led out to an even nicer room."

The next priority was to find out what DeKoning was doing in his suite. "By careful observation, we decide that the medicine cabinet in our room adjoins the bathroom in their room, which has a nice resonance to pick up all the conversations in the adjoining room," Greene said. "So we go in there and we remove the medicine cabinet in our room. Now you can hear perfectly through to the other room." As DeKoning started to make a series of phone calls, Greene listened to DeKoning's end of the conversations through the wall and set up a system for finding out who was at the other end: He arranged for the hotel staff to monitor the calls and send a bellboy up to Greene's room after each one, with information on the number that DeKoning had dialed. On Long Island, Hathway kept one line open to Greene and on another line stayed in touch with a source in the phone company. As soon as Greene found out what number DeKoning was calling, he relayed the number to Hathway, who passed it along to his phone company source, who told Hathway the customer's identity. In this way, Greene found out that DeKoning called Local 138 headquarters to let them know he was back in action, called two of his aides at the union and called the home of Joe Fay, his tutor in the mobsterly arts, who wasn't home. Greene also learned that a powerful local politician, William Mahoney, the former Erie County Democratic leader, had made the room reservations and had met with DeKoning soon after his release.

Unfortunately, this was a Saturday afternoon and *Newsday* still had no Sunday paper to carry the story. So Greene continued his elaborate surveillance routine through Sunday and wrote his story for Monday morning. The page one headline was "DeK FREE, PICKS UP/WHERE HE LEFT OFF," and the story gave the details of DeKoning's phone calls. On Monday morning, as the story was hitting the streets on Long Island, Greene and Edwards were still in bed in Buffalo, recovering from all the drinks that they had consumed in celebration of their coup. "About 8 o'clock in the morning, I hear a phone ringing next door," Greene said. "I get up and I listen." What he heard was enough to convince him that someone on Long Island had read the story and called to tell the DeKonings about it. Greene knew that DeKoning was smart enough to figure out from the story that the reporter who wrote it was living in the adjoining room. So Greene decided that he and Edwards needed to make an immediate exit. As they got on the elevator, DeKoning ran to the door of their room and slammed into it. In later years, Greene talked with the younger DeKoning about what happened once his father had broken into the room they had vacated: "He says, 'He was going to kick the shit out of the two of you. There's nobody there but empty blankets and I'm laughing like hell.'"

III

IT WAS INEVITABLE that Hathway would love a reporter who was willing to chase a labor racketeer at high speeds and eavesdrop for two days from a makeshift listening post.

Greene's flair for crime stories, which had a powerful hold on Hathway's imagination, liberated him from the daily routine of beat reporting and made him into Hathway's hired gun. The managing editor liked organized crime stories so much that he began dragging Greene along to lunch regularly, so that they could converse for hours about the mob, no matter what Greene had been doing for the city desk. "I just became somebody that he liked to talk to at lunch," Greene said. In the course of those long drinking bouts, Hathway often drunkenly fired Greene, only to rehire him as soon as Hathway sobered up. Despite the forced drinking and the periodic firings, Greene thrived on Hathway's presence. "I certainly enjoyed that little leverage of power that came from being with him," Greene said. "He also used me often, if he wanted something done, to organize it, set it up and carry it out. I was always being detached from the desk to carry out these projects."

One of Greene's early assignments from Hathway had a breathtakingly ambitious goal: The complete restructuring of the government of Suffolk County. In 1950, Hathway had single-handedly reshaped the Republican Party in Suffolk by defeating Representative W. Kingsland Macy, the county chairman. Now, Hathway wanted to continue shaping Suffolk's future by giving it a county charter form of government. Greene's role in that crusade was the attempted political murder of Evans Griffing, the supervisor of the tiny Town of Shelter Island, because Griffing stood in the way of the adoption of a charter.

To Hathway, the need for a charter was clear. The form of government in Suffolk County had not changed since colonial times, but the population in the postwar years was exploding — from 77,000 at the beginning of the twentieth century to 475,000 by the middle of the 1950s. Instead of a strong, centralized county government to serve that growing population, Suffolk still divided power equally among its 10 towns. Each town had an elected supervisor, who ran the day-to-day affairs of town government and presided over an elected town board. Each supervisor also sat on a countywide Board of Supervisors that set policy for the county. On that board, every town had one vote, regardless of population. As the county grew in complexity, it became more and more difficult for town supervisors to act as both chief executive in the town governments and legislators in the county government.

Always attuned to issues of Long Island's growth, Hathway felt that only a unified county government could plan rationally for that growth. As a result, he was willing to put the paper's clout behind a charter crusade, and so was Alicia. "You're looking at the princess and the frog when you look at Alan and Alicia," Greene said, "but don't underestimate the rapport that they had." With both Alicia and Hathway behind the charter crusade, *Newsday* went at it wholeheartedly. The earliest efforts included two charter-related series almost back to back in early 1956. The first, written by Arthur Bergmann, tackled the corollary question of the need for a countywide police department to replace the 27 local departments. The basic argument was that the small departments were fine for small crimes, but they couldn't handle homicides. The logo used for the five-part series was blunt and inevitable: "Suffolk's Unsolved Murders: The Case for a County Police Force." Less than two weeks later, *Newsday* started a four-part series by Stan Hinden on the charter itself. This series outlined the county's political history and rolled out *Newsday*'s big gun, Robert Moses, to support a proposed charter that would establish the office of county executive to provide day-to-day administration for the county.

The month after Hinden's series ran, the Board of Supervisors approved a new charter. The state Legislature quickly gave the necessary approval to put the question on the ballot. But Governor Averell Harriman vetoed the bill, apparently because he didn't like the provision for an appointed county executive, rather than an elected one. So the Board of Supervisors appointed a 33-member Suffolk County Charter Commission to draw up a new charter that Harriman would approve. In 1957, the Board of Supervisors and the Legislature passed the needed legislation for another charter, but Harriman again vetoed the bill over the county executive issue. At that point, Hathway decided that *Newsday* was going to have to intervene in a more tangible way.

Hathway began by calling a meeting of community leaders at the Stony Brook Yacht Club, the first step toward the creation of something called the Suffolk Citizens Charter Committee. They chose as the chairman Frank Gulden, the mustard heir — a well-respected, politically neutral businessman. The executive secretary was Hathway's friend, Jack Rettaliata, the Grumman public relations executive. For money, Hathway went directly to Harold Gleason, the vice-president of the Franklin National Bank. "He spoke to me two inches from my face," Gleason said. "I was soaking wet. And he said he wanted to borrow $25,000. I said, 'Okay, you got the loan,' but I booked it as a contribution. How was Hathway or anybody going to repay $25,000?" To raise money, they held a $100-a-plate dinner at a restaurant in Suffolk County, at which *Newsday* bought a table for 10. The dinner raised enough to pay off the loan, and Gleason kept his eye on the money by becoming treasurer of the committee.

Besides creating the committee and arranging the financing, Hathway took one more practical political step. He knew that the East End supervisors were staunchly opposed to the charter, and with good reason: The five tiny East End towns had as much clout on the Board of Supervisors as the more populous five towns to the west. Under a charter form of government, with an elected county executive able to break the traditional 5-5 deadlock between East End and West End on the Board of Supervisors, they'd lose that equality. So Hathway set out to defeat the leader of that anti-charter East End bloc, Ev Griffing.

The campaign began with Greene's courtesy call on the salty, Lincolnesque Griffing. It was a friendly enough evening, as the young Irish reporter and the Yankee Brahmin sipped Scotch and sought some accommodation. "We were really searching around this whole night, to try and find some way in which everything could be satisfied and he would not be politically hurt, in his terms, and also that the East End wouldn't be screwed," Greene said. "But the point is that, no matter how you did it, the East End was going to be screwed. There was no way you could paint it any other way, and we finally both came to this conclusion." That left Hathway with no choice except to run a candidate of his own against Griffing, and it was Greene's job to find one.

"The first thing you do is you look to see if there's a split in the party of the guy that's running," Greene said. "And there was." The anti-Griffing ally that Greene found was Captain Everett Tuthill, the Republican elder statesman, who had served 22 years as Shelter Island supervisor. Tuthill's recommended candidate was Sylvan Pierre Tybaert, a Republican justice of the peace and former chief of police. So Greene approached Lou Price, the town Democratic leader, who agreed that the Democrats would support Tybaert against Griffing. Then he went to Tybaert to float the idea. "I broached it and told him exactly what it was, that if he ran, *Newsday* would back him," Greene said. "I was able to say, 'Here's what we can deliver to you in the package.' " Greene also made it clear that Tybaert would have to pay a price for this package. "I said, 'What is your attitude towards a county charter?' " Greene remembered. "He was honestly for a county charter, which was helpful." Tybaert accepted and ran as an independent candidate, with help from both the Democrats and anti-Griffing Republicans.

Once *Newsday* had a candidate, Greene and another Hathway favorite, Kirk Price, started to work the little island, trying to find soft spots in Griffing's support. For many weeks, Greene operated out of the Ram's Head Inn on Shelter Island, going home only on weekends. Five weeks before the election, Alicia and Hathway sent him down to Miami Beach to cover the Teamsters convention, at which James Hoffa won the union's presidency. In Greene's absence, Kirk Price was to take over the Tybaert campaign. While Greene was gone, Tybaert had a heart attack, but Price remained unwisely optimistic. "When I came back, I said to Alan, 'Do you want me back out there?' " Greene said. "He says, 'No, Kirk says don't worry about it.' " But on election night, the returns showed Griffing beating Tybaert, and Price's optimism turned to nausea. "Price was in the john throwing up all night," Bergmann said.

Though Griffing won, the *Newsday*-backed charter committee continued to put together a proposed charter. This time, they came up with one that called for an elected county executive — largely at Hathway's insistence. But they still had to get the charter approved by the Board of Supervisors, the state Legislature, the governor and the voters. The first break came when East Hampton Supervisor Richard Gilmartin defected from the solid East End opposition bloc, and the Board of Supervisors approved the charter, 6 to 4. Quickly, the Legislature passed a charter bill and Harriman signed it. On November 4, 1958, the voters of Suffolk County overwhelmingly approved the charter, to take effect January 1, 1960.

The day the charter won the approval of voters was not a day of total victory for *Newsday*. In the same election, voters narrowly rejected the paper's candidate for Children's Court judge in Nassau County, Beatrice Burstein. Alicia had supported her Democratic candidacy vigorously, and when the Republican-dominated Nassau Bar Association refused to find Burstein qualified for the job, the October 18 *Newsday* had carried a profusion of Burstein stories. "At least half of that paper was on me," Burstein said. "I absolutely wept when I opened it up." The politically motivated rejection of Burstein annoyed Alicia so much, in fact, that she forced the president of the bar association, James McDonough, to resign as a libel lawyer for *Newsday*. His statement made it sound as if he was jumping of his own will, but it wasn't without a push from Alicia. Despite Alicia's help, Burstein lost the race, but four years later, Governor Nelson Rockefeller appointed her to a District Court judgeship. Burstein never forgot that Alicia came to her aid at a time when women judges were scarce. "Alicia Patterson was really a great feminist," Burstein said. "I'm a judge because she fought for my political life."

Alicia and Hathway had fought hard for Burstein, but they had fought longer and harder for the charter. In the charter crusade, there is little question that the paper went beyond what would be considered acceptable practice under current journalistic ethics. It is also clear that, without Hathway's campaign, the adoption of a county charter would have taken longer. "If there's a void in leadership, then I think it perhaps becomes important for the one who has that view and sees merit to take the bull by the horns, provide the leadership, either directly or bringing people in to get the job done, and I think that he did that," said New York State Supreme Court Justice Arthur Cromarty, who was elected supervisor of the Town of Babylon as a pro-charter candidate in the election of 1957.

Newsday's impact on the shape of Suffolk government did not stop with the adoption of the charter. In the 1959 election, the voters would select the first-ever county executive, who would launch the new charter form of government. In a traditionally Republican county, it would have been reasonable to expect this county executive to be a Republican. But fate and *Newsday* intervened. The first blow to Republican hopes was a state investigation of a series of governmental scandals involving incum-

bent Republicans, which *Newsday* covered relentlessly. The paper also advocated strongly the election of the Democratic candidate, H. Lee Dennison, an
independent-minded engineer who had moved to Long Island from Hornell, a
small city in upstate New York, to work as a highway engineer, first for the state
and then for Suffolk County. In 1951, Dennison issued a scathing report that
criticized the county for lack of planning. With that, Dennison melted into a
career as a private engineering consultant, until he returned in 1959 as the
Democratic candidate for county executive. Impressed by Dennison's emphasis
on planning and his bricks-and-mortar skills, *Newsday* urged voters to elect him,
defeat the Republicans, and hasten the departure of Suffolk Republican Chairman R. Ford Hughes, whom Hathway had supported so strongly when
he replaced Kingsland Macy at the head of the party. At the end of the campaign, Dennison won by a gossamer-thin margin and remained county executive
for 12 years.

On the same day that Dennison took office in 1960, the new county police
department also started operation. *Newsday* had played a major role in its
creation, criticizing the small-town departments in a series of editorials and
biting cartoons. Once the new department was established, *Newsday* played an
important role in the selection of the first commissioner. Hathway bitterly
opposed one potential candidate for the job, and Hughes offered it instead to
Charles R. Thom, the county's chief assistant district attorney. Then Thom had
to meet with Hathway to win his approval. "He wanted to look over the
suspect," said Thom, who met him at a bar and talked with him for hours. "He
wrote a glowing editorial, commenting viciously on what would have happened
if the other guy got it."

Once Thom took office, the paper began to develop an extraordinarily
close relationship with the department through Tom Renner, who had covered
town police for *Newsday* and begun writing extensively about the department
during the months leading up to its formal beginning in 1960. "Tommy knew
more about the routine incidents, arrests and cases than I did," Thom said.
Newsday played a continuing role in shaping the department, pushing Thom to
develop an intelligence unit to combat organized crime. And when Thom left
the job in 1962 to become a judge, Hathway, Greene, Kirk Price and Jim O'Neill
of *Newsday* tried to push Cyril Donnelly, the former Smithtown police chief, as
Thom's successor.

During the 1949 *Newsday* gambling investigation, Hathway had become
convinced that Donnelly offered a bribe to the reporter Bob Pfeifle, but since
then, Hathway and Donnelly had become friendly. In fact, Greene said, he
suspected that Hathway pushed Donnelly for commissioner partly to atone for
the *Newsday* stories about the alleged bribe attempt. They failed in the effort to
get Donnelly appointed commissioner, but they persuaded the new commissioner, John Barry, to make Donnelly chief inspector.

That was the kind of influence that *Newsday* exercised in reshaping Suffolk County — a combination of high energy and questionable journalistic
ethics that had a profound long-term effect on the way the people of the vast

county lived. "*Newsday* changed the face of Suffolk," Renner said. "*Newsday* built the campaign that bridged the change from a rural Long Island to a suburban Long Island."

IV

THE CAMPAIGN FOR the Suffolk County charter was just one item on Greene's agenda in the busy years near the end of the 1950s, when he shuttled back and forth with dazzling dexterity between journalism and government.

In that period, he went to work for Robert F. Kennedy on the Senate rackets committee, came back to *Newsday* in time to work on the charter crusade and cover Jimmy Hoffa's election as Teamster president, returned to the rackets committee, came back again to *Newsday* and played a role in a crucial struggle against labor racketeers, appeared as a witness against those racketeers before the same Senate committee that he had just left, and finally wrote a *Newsday* series on the committee's work.

Greene's expertise on garment industry racketeering had brought him in contact with Kennedy, the counsel to the Senate Permanent Committee on Investigations, which was looking into fraud by garment firms that were selling uniforms to the military. When Kennedy became interested in broader labor racketeering issues, his report on that subject in late 1956 led to the creation of the Senate Select Committee on Improper Activities in the Labor or Management Field, usually called the rackets committee. The chairman was Senator John McClellan of Arkansas. The members included Senator John Fitzgerald Kennedy of Massachusetts and Senator Joseph McCarthy of Wisconsin. As counsel, Robert Kennedy controlled much of the hiring, and one of the first people he chose, early in 1957, was Greene. "I got Hathway to give me a leave of absence, based on the contacts I could bring back to the job," Greene said.

Almost immediately, Greene's presence on the rackets committee stirred up a controversy precipitated by McCarthy. In debate on the Senate floor with Majority Leader Lyndon B. Johnson of Texas, McCarthy asked: "Does the senator know . . . that one of the men whom we had hired as an investigator, and who is now on the payroll, had been indicted for subornation of perjury?" Robert Kennedy knew about the sleazy origins of the Jersey City indictment four years earlier, knew that a judge had dismissed it, and knew that *Newsday* and McCarthy had been at odds. So, shortly after McCarthy raised the issue on the floor, Kennedy spoke to the press in Greene's defense. "I was responsible for hiring Greene, and I would do it again," Kennedy said. "In my opinion, he knows more about labor racketeering in New York than anybody else." Nonetheless, McCarthy was still full of venom toward *Newsday*. During a closed committee caucus, Kennedy later told Greene, McCarthy complained "that he was sick and tired of New York kikes who were writing crucify-Joe-McCarthy editorials in *Newsday*." Greene, an Irishman who had nothing to do with editorials, was so angry that he wanted to punch McCarthy.

The rackets committee referred McCarthy's accusation to a two-person subcommittee, whose members were Senator Karl Mundt, a South Dakota Republican, and Senator Pat McNamara, a Michigan Democrat. A day later, Mundt and McNamara told the committee that they could keep Greene on staff, since the indictment had been "a political frameup — a pure political maneuver to discredit a very able investigator." The committee voted to keep Greene, and afterward, McCarthy approached him to shake hands. "I had one of the great pleasures of my life," Greene said. "I said, 'Go fuck yourself. . . .' I could have done it in a nicer way. I just was so mad." The Greene episode soured the friendship between Robert Kennedy and McCarthy, as the investigative reporter Clark Mollenhoff learned by sitting in Kennedy's office during Kennedy's phone conversation with McCarthy about Greene. "They had considerable conversation, with Bob saying, 'Joe, you're wrong, you're wrong, you're wrong,'" Mollenhoff said. "And then his final thing was, 'Joe McCarthy, you're a shit,' and he slammed the receiver down, and that was the end of their relationship."

Once this crisis was over, Greene continued to work at the committee's offices in Manhattan's Foley Square, concentrating on mob domination of the carting industry and on paper locals — semi-fictional unions that crooked union officials used as weapons to shake down small businesses. In this work, Greene fit well in some ways with Kennedy's sharp-toothed style. "Bob and I were exactly the same type of people," Greene said. But they had disagreements over investigations. Greene and Kennedy differed, for example, on the importance of the hearings about the garbage rackets, because Kennedy had a fixation with Hoffa, and the garbage investigation didn't involve Hoffa. But once the mobster Albert Anastasia was assassinated in a hotel barber chair, Greene convinced Kennedy that the death of Anastasia would enhance public interest in the garbage industry. So they later went ahead with the hearings.

Besides his policy differences with Kennedy, Greene began to have financial problems. The Senate job came with a higher salary than *Newsday* paid him, but Greene often had to pay his own expenses back and forth to Washington, and the Senate took a long time to reimburse him. Then he smashed up his car and asked Kennedy for help in paying the bills, but Kennedy provided none. "I arranged to have Hathway contact Kennedy and end the leave of absence," Greene said. Later, as the committee began to prepare for the garbage hearings, Greene went back to work for them, while *Newsday* subsidized him. Once the hearings ended that fall, Greene stopped working for the committee. But he maintained his ties with Kennedy, and he profited for years from the sources that he had made.

The next time that Greene dealt with the rackets committee, in early 1959, he was testifying as a witness to a bold effort by a labor racketeer to force *Newsday* into a union relationship that it had successfully avoided for two decades.

The major New York City newspapers had direct contractual relationships with the Newspaper and Mail Deliverers Union, an assertive aggregation of truck drivers and other workers that had a chokehold on the flow of newspapers in the city. From the start, *Newsday* had avoided any direct relationship with the NMDU. Instead, an independent distributor, Rockaway News, had delivered *Newsday*. The employees of Rockaway News were NMDU members, but *Newsday* itself did not have to deal with the union, which was exactly what Harry Guggenheim wanted. Harry argued that *Newsday* was not a metropolitan paper, did not have the same access to the city advertising market as the New York papers did, and should not have to live with the same padded work rules. Still, when the NMDU struck the city papers, it usually shut down suburban distributors as well. In those situations, such as a strike against city papers in 1953, *Newsday*'s circulation department delivered the paper by using the cars of circulation employees, who were all non-union.

Toward the end of the 1950s, the fiscal health of Rockaway News became shakier. A new generation of the family that owned the company had come into power, and these two sons did not have as much business acumen as their father did. More important, the company lost its contract for delivery of the *Daily News*, a huge chunk of their business. Inexorably, Rockaway News slid further into financial disarray, falling behind in their payments to the union's pension and welfare fund and encountering increasing friction in their relations with the New York City publishers. To raise additional revenue, the wholesaler increased its rates for delivering the city papers. Finally, the city publishers notified Rockaway News that they were switching immediately to other distributors. The NMDU objected, arguing that they wouldn't work for the new distributors until they could reach an agreement that would protect all the contractual rights that they had with Rockaway. On Thanksgiving Day, the NMDU began refusing to deliver New York City papers on Long Island, and the city publishers promptly sued the union. In rapid succession, the NMDU stopped delivering *Newsday* for Rockaway News, put up pickets around *Newsday*, then struck the New York City dailies. Rockaway News, deprived of all its major customers, filed for bankruptcy and went into receivership.

Starting on December 5, when the NMDU first prevented Rockaway News from delivering *Newsday*, the paper put its own distribution system into effect. They could no longer simply use cars, because the circulation and the size of each paper had grown too much. So they rented trucks and brought in armed guards to ride shotgun and protect *Newsday* circulation employees from NMDU harassment. The union continued to push for a direct contract with *Newsday*, but Harry categorically rejected any direct contract.

The strain of delivering the paper with circulation employees in rented trucks began to wear on *Newsday* as the month went on. So they looked for another solution: forming their own trucking company. In effect, the death of Rockaway News and the accompanying crisis had presented *Newsday* with a golden opportunity. "We were delighted when Rockaway News went out of business, because then we could run our own business and not be subjected to the whims of New York and the membership of the NMDU," said Vinnie Bordash, the top lieutenant to the circulation director, Jack Mullen.

In putting together a trucking company, *Newsday* sought the help of a man named Chester Bornscheuer, whose bus service had delivered *Newsday* during a snowstorm and taken *Newsday* carriers on trips. Bornscheuer, a huge man with the build of a football player, called Charles Lyon, who sold and leased automobiles and heavy equipment. Together, Lyon and Bornscheuer recruited drivers by word of mouth and in truckers' bars. Another source of drivers was Jim O'Neill, the police reporter. "Miss P and Hathway and I met, and she asked me if I could get some people who would drive these trucks without being afraid," O'Neill said. He knew former policemen who could use the work, such as Frank Carey and Frank Graham, and he recruited them. Eventually, these recruitment efforts gathered enough men to start the operation. They named the company Lybco, for Lyon and Bornscheuer, and rented 30 trucks for the first week, not mentioning to the rental agency what they'd be used for.

Lybco started delivering *Newsday* on Monday, December 29, and ran into immediate problems. For one thing, Lybco drivers knew nothing about newspapers, and Buddy Chernow of the circulation department had to train them in handling their routes. The nastier problem was the picketing by the NMDU. In the first week, Lyon said, Lybco lost several of its new drivers, who simply didn't want to keep being threatened. The threats were not directed only at the drivers. The pressmen were also targets. "They threatened all my men," said Harvey Broad, the pressroom supervisor. "They started calling my wife and threatening her. They mentioned where every one of my kids went to school. I had to take my kids out of school." One of the pressmen, John Amrhein, witnessed a group of thugs running another pressroom employee's car off the road, and Amrhein drove back to *Newsday* and told management about it. So *Newsday* decided to house all the pressmen in the Garden City Hotel and shuttle them back and forth to the plant under armed guard.

The central incident of the whole period happened on Lybco's first day, when a group of men slashed the tires of two Lybco trucks at a gas station not far from the *Newsday* plant. On that day, and throughout the struggle with the NMDU, O'Neill and Greene were not just reporters. They were also platoon leaders, enlisting happily in the war against what they considered a thug-ridden union. O'Neill and Tom Renner, the Suffolk police reporter, helped to arrange police protection for the drivers and a police presence outside *Newsday*. And O'Neill, a barrel-chested former football player, served as a bodyguard for the drivers himself. On that first day, O'Neill and Greene heard about the tire slashing. "Jimmy and I race right up there," said Greene, whose photograph appeared in the next day's paper, kneeling next to a truck with a punctured tire. The witnesses gave Greene and O'Neill a description of several men piling out of a car, menacing them with an ice pick and then using it to puncture tires. But the drivers were too frightened to remember more. "We got these guys who can't give a description," Greene said, "but we were playing hardball, and there was one guy who was an ace in the hole, Bill Cahn."

Cahn was a Nassau County assistant district attorney, in charge of the rackets bureau, an office that had come into existence only after Hathway and Greene had advocated it. Greene was an advisor to Cahn, which put him in a perfect position to seek Cahn's help against the NMDU. So Cahn spoke to the witnesses and said it would be a shame if the district attorney's office had to hold them as material witnesses — not a pleasant prospect, with New Year's Eve almost upon them. Suddenly, their memories improved. That led to the identification of four union officials and their indictment a week later. Greene and O'Neill also testified at a court hearing that led to an injunction against the picketing.

On the day that police questioned one of the four NMDU suspects, Greene heard about it and went to the precinct. He brought along with him a visiting friend from the rackets committee — Jerry Adlerman, who later replaced Robert Kennedy as counsel. At the precinct, they encountered William Fello, one of the officers of a distribution firm called Bi-County News, which had built its plant right near *Newsday*'s in Garden City. Fello came up to Greene and admitted that the NMDU officials were friends of his. In fact, Fello suggested, all *Newsday* had to do in order to solve its problems with the NMDU was to hire Bi-County as its distributor. Bi-County would have no trouble with the union, Fello said, and neither would *Newsday*. "Standing next to me is the counsel to the Senate labor rackets committee," Greene said. "Jerry goes back and says, 'Son of a bitch, this is terrific for a hearing.' " As Greene discovered, the driving force at Bi-County was a racketeer named Irving Bitz. His status as a racketeer made him a tempting target for the rackets committee, which began to hold hearings on Bitz and the NMDU. In May, Hathway and Greene both testified about Bitz before the rackets committee. Greene told about his encounter with Fello at the police station. Hathway made it clear that he felt the picketing by the NMDU was part of a scheme to force *Newsday* to use the services of Bi-County News. "We do not think that building their plant a few hundred yards from us was mere coincidence," Hathway testified.

A few weeks after he testified before the rackets committee, Greene appeared before a federal grand jury in New York about Bitz. Once the grand jury had indicted Bitz and 10 others, including six officials of the NMDU, Greene wrote a story about the testimony that he, Hathway and the business manager Harold Ferguson had given. Before 1959 was over, Bitz had pleaded guilty to four charges, including the *Newsday* picketing, and went away to serve a five-year prison term. On the Nassau County charges, the four NMDU members who were accused of slashing the tires on Lybco trucks pleaded guilty to disorderly conduct. Three of the four drew suspended sentences, but Joseph Baer, who had recently been elected president of the union, partly on the strength of the popularity that he gained from his role in the ice-pick incident, went to jail for 10 days. Even when he had served his time, *Newsday* didn't let up. The members of his union had planned a big celebration for the day he got out, but Hathway exerted his influence and made sure that Baer would be released at 2 a.m., when no one would be around to greet him. "He found his way home on public transportation in the middle of the night," said *Newsday*'s attorney, Andrew Hughes.

In the struggle with the NMDU, *Newsday* had not been shy about asking law enforcement officials — the same officials that the paper covered — to help in a struggle that was desperately important for the paper's financial future. "That was our survival," Greene said, "and we do what we had to do to survive, and we did, and no regrets." The ultimate result was that *Newsday* remained free to continue increasing its circulation without constant warfare with the NMDU. "We broke the union's back," Chernow said. "Otherwise, forget it. You wouldn't even have a *Newsday*." From this encounter, Greene developed a long-lasting sense of indebtedness to Cahn, who had helped at the moment of *Newsday*'s great need. "You ask somebody to do something for you," Greene said, "you owe them."

That sense of mutual obligation between *Newsday* and law enforcement authorities was also a major factor in the paper's coverage of a sensational kidnaping in 1956. The story began on July 4, when someone removed baby Peter Weinberger from his carriage on the patio of his home in Westbury and left a ransom note, demanding $2,000 and warning the baby's parents not to notify police. "I hate to do this to you, but I am in great need," the note said. "I am scared stiff. I could ask for more but I am asking only for what I need."

When the kidnaping happened, Jim O'Neill was at his home in Seaford, at a Fourth of July barbecue. He learned about it in a telephone call from a bartender he had befriended in the process of many long nights drinking with cops, to develop them as *Newsday* sources. As soon as he got the tip from the bartender, who had heard one of his customers talking about it, O'Neill made some calls, acquired the address and went to the house. The detective who was running the investigation, Edward Curran, was an admirer of O'Neill, but Curran told him very little. "On a kidnaping, I wouldn't talk to my wife about it," Curran said. "It's just too big." O'Neill learned enough for a good story, but Nassau County police asked him and other papers not to run the story the next day, so that they wouldn't alarm the kidnaper. The kidnaping happened on a Wednesday, and *Newsday* agreed to hold back the story until Friday's paper. But Wednesday evening, when the "bulldog" edition of the Thursday *Daily News* hit the streets, it carried a story on the kidnaping, by Ben White, the former *Newsday* reporter. "I thought we had an assurance that they would not run it," said John McDonald, who did public relations for the police. Somehow, the *News* had run the story anyway. "Ben felt terrible about it," said Sherman Phillips, a police reporter for the *Long Island Press*. "He was with me one night and he started crying about it. It was not his fault."

Once the story appeared in the *News*, the police released all the other papers from their commitments to hold it back, and they went ahead with their stories. *Newsday* led the paper with the headline, "KIDNAP BABY/FROM LI PATIO," and carried a full story by O'Neill and Stan Brooks, along with a sidebar on the neighborhood by David Kahn and Harvey Aronson. That was the start of a long media circus that went on for the next seven weeks, while the Nassau County police and the FBI searched for the kidnaper and the baby. As *Newsday* reporters began to descend on the neighborhood, O'Neill grew progressively more impatient — as he would many times over the years, when *Newsday* routinely covered every big story like an infantry battle, with battalions of reporters. O'Neill was convinced that he knew the cops best, and everyone else was simply getting in the way. "It was my first instance of operation overkill," O'Neill said. "You were stumbling over your own people."

One of those who swarmed to the scene at the start was David Kahn, whose instructions were to lie in some bushes with a view of the Weinberger home and see what happened. When an ice cream truck came by, Kahn momentarily forgot his undercover role and left the bushes to buy some ice cream, attracting the attention of detectives. Right on the spot they questioned him, which assured him a place forever in the lore of *Newsday* overkill. "It was soon discovered that I was a legitimate *Newsday* reporter, and I was let go, and from there, the myth has grown," Kahn said. The swarm also included Greene, who disguised himself as a telephone repairman, along with another reporter, Jim Hadjin, and entered the home of a family that Greene's investigation had turned up as potential suspects. The lead didn't pan out, but Greene was ecstatic about going on a real undercover mission — something different from the kind of document-based investigations that he had been accustomed to doing. "The theory was good; it just didn't work," Greene said. "We all love to play detective."

Weeks later, when O'Neill got a tip that the police were about to arrest a suspect, *Newsday* flooded the streets with reporters and photographers. Their presence prompted the FBI's agent in charge of the investigation to ask Jack Altshul, the city editor, to hold back on printing the story and to pull everyone out of the area, to avoid endangering the baby's life. During these conversations, the agent promised that FBI Director J. Edgar Hoover would issue a statement of praise if *Newsday* complied. Altshul consulted by phone with Alan Hathway, who was at the Republican National Convention in San Francisco, and they decided to hold back the story in the morning. The next day, when the FBI announced the arrest of Angelo John LaMarca, they also released a statement from Hoover: "The cooperation of *Newsday* is another illustration of the splendid assistance the press can render law enforcement. The FBI deeply appreciates the magnificent cooperation it has received from *Newsday*."

As it turned out, all these last-minute negotiations between *Newsday* and the FBI were superfluous. LaMarca, who later died in the electric chair for his crime, had abandoned Peter Weinberger within hours after the kidnaping and the baby had soon died of exposure. But the baby's death didn't alter the reality: *Newsday* had twice agreed to hold back stories, in the spirit of cooperation with law enforcement — a spirit that in later years sometimes became a subject of controversy at *Newsday*.

CHAPTER EIGHTEEN

The Boss Lady

I

THE HELICOPTER STUNT was goofy and impractical, but it was strong evidence of the affection that Alicia Patterson's employees felt for her.

At the end of 1959, when Alicia would normally be attending the zany *Newsday* Christmas party, laughing at the skits that poked fun at her and at Hathway, she was in a Manhattan hospital, recovering from an accident in which she slipped on a rug and broke a bone in her leg. So her staff decided to bring the party to her. They could have done it routinely by driving into Manhattan, but someone decided to rent a helicopter to deliver most of the cast, even though there was no place close to the hospital where it could land. The plan was that the helicopter would buzz Alicia's hospital room, so she could look out and see the sign that was attached to the side of the chopper. "Jack Altshul was telling the guy, 'You have to get right up against the window,' " Harvey Aronson said. "The guy says, 'We'll all die. I can't — the wind currents. I can't get close to the building. . . .' All we did was buzz the hospital and she leans out of the window and waves something red. We went back to LaGuardia and landed. Then we took limousines to the hospital."

The skit that they performed in Alicia's large hospital room was typical of *Newsday* shows: crude dialogue, off-key singing and someone imitating Alicia — in this case, Francis Wood, complete with skirt, cowgirl boots and glasses perched atop a dark wig. At one point in the show, the script called for Mary Pangalos, the tiny reporter who played the hero, to pick up the huge Marty Buskin, dressed as the heroine. Pangalos was small, but her love of horseback riding had given her powerful legs. If anyone ever doubted her stamina, she had proven it earlier in the year, by becoming the first woman to take the strenuous tests given to America's astronauts — an adventure that produced a five-part series in *Newsday*. By comparison to the astronaut tests, picking up Buskin was easy. "After that, this nice, pleasant man came up to me and said, 'How did you do that?' " Pangalos remembered. "And I said, 'Oh, it's easy. You just pick him up using your thighs.' And he said, 'Really?' I said, 'Here, I'll show you.' So I picked him up and walked around with him, and it was Harry Guggenheim."

The underlying reality behind this bizarre excursion was this: Almost universally, the people who worked for Alicia genuinely liked her, respected her skills and felt that, despite her money and breeding, she was one of them — a working journalist. She was often in the city room, talking to reporters and editors, who usually felt comfortable in her presence. "If you had your feet up on the desk, you'd say, 'Hi Miss P, how's it going,' never take your feet down," the photographer Jim Nightingale said. Even the usual horseplay didn't bother her. Early one morning, she strode through the newsroom, into the middle of a sugar-cubes fight. At the moment she arrived, Stan Brooks was crouched in one of the huge wastepaper barrels, seeking shelter from flying sugar. "She looked in and said, 'Good morning, Stan,' and kept going," said John Van Doorn, one of the combatants.

On the question of what had become of her gloves, earrings or purse, or where she had left her glasses (usually on top of her head), Alicia was often forgetful. But she didn't forget her staff. "When I left, I was gone for 15 years," said Jean Cappa Smith, who came to work as a secretary in the circulation department before the first issue of *Newsday*, left in 1948 to raise a family and came back in 1963. "When I returned, she met me in the hall and she recognized me, and she was so nice. She said, 'Oh, are you back with us?' That I couldn't get over, because she had no reason to recognize me." Her familiarity with the staff did not come without effort. Before major *Newsday* events, such as the bowling award dinners or the gatherings for 10-year employees, Alicia would meet with Andrew Miller, *Newsday*'s first personnel specialist, go over the names of those who were to receive awards, and study information about them and their families. "I think most people knew that Alicia didn't know them that intimately," Miller said, "but they appreciated the fact that she went to the trouble to find out."

Another element of her approachable style was her sense of humor, which encouraged people to play practical jokes on her. Once, during a period of friction with the mob, the artist Paul Back bought a large lava rock, attached a threatening note and placed it on the floor of Alicia's office, surrounded by pieces of broken glass, to give the impression that a thug had thrown it through her window. The rock fooled Alicia, and the moment that Back told her it was a joke, she turned the joke on Hathway and anyone else she could find, complaining about lax security in the building. Later that day, she went to lunch at one of her favorite restaurants, and the waiters brought her a platter covered by a big silver dome. Underneath was the lava rock.

She also won the loyalty of her staff by taking the time to praise them and say thank you in large and small ways, ranging from the pot of shamrocks and half day off that she gave Jim O'Neill on St. Patrick's Day, to the $1,000 bonus and extra vacation time that she gave to Harvey Broad after he had worked long hours supervising the installation of a new press. In addition, she remembered the families of her employees, sending gifts for the birth of a baby, for example, or flowers to the ill wife of a photographer. Taken together, her thoughtfulness, accessibility and sense of humor created an environment in which it was possible to disagree with her. She could be tart and short-tempered in an argument, punctuating the discussion with "Fish or cut bait!" or "Shut up and let me think!" But if she got the impression that she had hurt someone's feelings, she would quickly apologize. So her staff felt that it was not fatal to argue with her.

As direct as she could be in outlining her views to a subordinate, she was painfully indirect when it came time to fire or demote someone. "I don't think she had it in her to fire anybody," said her secretary, Dorothy Holdsworth. As a result, when Alicia became disillusioned with someone, she resorted to some odd personnel practices, such as her maneuvers in the women's department. When the women's editor, Nuala Walsh, became pregnant and left the paper, the person in line to succeed her was Lola McManus. But for some reason, Alicia decided to give the job to another woman in the department, Anne Hannan, a close friend of McManus. Instead of giving the title immediately to Hannan, however, Alicia made the change surreptitiously. "Nobody wanted to hurt Lola," Hannan said. "She kept the title and I was supposed to have the responsibility. I was told in secret I could override her anytime. . . . It was an unpleasant way to handle things." When McManus finally left *Newsday*, the other women were angry at Hannan. Similarly, when Alicia grew unhappy with the style of the cartoonist Cliff Rogerson, she found a creative way of easing him out. "She had this grand idea for him that he could work at home and bring the cartoons in," said the artist Paul Back. Rogerson protested that working at home would make it difficult for him to make and receive business calls. So he asked Alicia to arrange for his *Newsday* phone to ring at home. She agreed, despite the protests of her administrative staff. Eventually, they installed the line, Rogerson worked in limbo for several months, and finally left *Newsday*.

If an employee committed a grievous enough offense, Alicia could be tough. A case in point was Ben Kubasik, who was writing movie criticism for the entertainment pages. Occasionally, she would disagree with his reviews, but they got along reasonably well, until their relationship soured over his review of the movie *West Side Story*. Kubasik had loved the stage version, but he hated the film and the immorality that he felt it glorified. The headline was: "West Side Story 'Hate-Filled Failure.' " In the review itself, Kubasik minced no words. "The film's hatred is presented with no redeeming grace," he wrote. "None of this has to do with art, which this reviewer believes is meant to afford hope, to reach out after goodness, to give man an ordered glimpse of the full happiness that somehow always manages to elude his material being." The review in *The New Yorker* was fairly critical, and *Time* magazine echoed Kubasik's views in part. But overwhelmingly, the daily newspaper critics loved the film, and Kubasik sat alone on a slender limb.

Not long after his review appeared, Kubasik heard from Alicia's editorial director. "Bill Woestendiek said, 'She's really unhappy about that review,' " Kubasik said. The breaking point came the following year, 1962, after the film had won ten Oscars, and Alicia asked that Kubasik write an evaluation of that year's Academy Award winners. The way he handled that story only made her angrier. "I wrote that *West Side Story* won all the technical awards, as it should have, because it was exquisite technically, but that the real winner, the one that should have had more notice, even though it won less awards, was *Judgment at Nuremberg*," Kubasik said. The day the piece appeared, Kubasik learned from Robert Rhodes, one of his editors, that they were going to remove him as the film critic — an interesting echo of the way Alicia's father had bounced Paul Gallico as film critic years earlier at the *News*. Through Woestendiek, Alicia offered Kubasik another job: youth editor. "I remember saying to Bill, 'I will be youth editor when she goes back to drawing a comic strip,' " Kubasik said. Deprived of the critic's role, Kubasik decided to leave *Newsday*. His replacement as critic was Mike McGrady, a talented free-lance writer who had arrived just a few months after Kubasik's fateful review. The whole episode appears to have been painful for Alicia, as well as for Kubasik. "I remember running into her one time during this awful period for me," Kubasik said. "I still remember the look on her face — kind of a sadness."

As much as she tried to avoid confrontation, Alicia sometimes caused unhappiness on the staff even when she did nothing. In 1962, for example, she was away from the office, cruising from Athens to Venice on a yacht provided by Agnes Meyer, the widow of Eugene Meyer, owner of the *Washington Post*. The guest list included, among others, Adlai Stevenson and his United Nations aide, Clayton Fritchey, Chief Justice Earl Warren and his wife, the columnist Drew Pearson and his wife, and Bill Attwood of *Look* magazine and his wife. While Alicia was away, her feisty sports editor, Jack Mann, came into conflict with Alan Hathway.

In a short time, Mann had professionalized the sports department in several ways. To begin with, he had started to hire a new generation of writers who later became widely respected columnists at *Newsday* and elsewhere, such as Steve Jacobson and George Vecsey. In addition, acting on a suggestion from the columnist Stan Isaacs, Mann had installed a system that kept reporters from getting stale, by requiring them to rotate rapidly from covering major-league professional sports to local high school sports. For all his success in running the department, however, Mann could be stubborn and high-handed, as he showed in a quarrel with the composing room. The printers were unhappy about the introduction of new equipment designed to automate part of the typesetting process, and they were not being as careful about proofreading copy as they had been. Mann understood their grievance, but he couldn't accept what the protest was doing to sports copy, and he kept complaining to Hathway. "He didn't do anything about it, so finally I did," Mann said. He wrote a crisp memo to the production manager, Allan Woods, with copies to Alicia and Hathway.

"That was on the 19th of July, 1962," said Mann, who remembers the date with precision because it was the day he lost what he considered one of the best newspaper jobs in America. "At 6:11 p.m., my wife was asking me if I was going to be home for dinner, and the phone rang. When I got off the phone I said, 'Well, I'll be home for dinner,' which was very strange to her. Then she said, 'Why?' And I said, 'Because I don't have any place to go. Hathway fired me. Just like that.'" The two people who might have calmed the situation were not available. Alicia was on the cruise with Stevenson, and Woestendiek was in Russia with a group of journalists. "I would have fought Hathway bitterly about firing him if I had been there," Woestendiek said. Hathway gave Mann his severance pay, but Mann refused to accept it from anyone except Alicia, and he returned the money. Later, when she came back from Europe, she sent him his check, with a note: "We owe you at least this much." And the two of them had one final lunch together.

II

IN ALICIA'S LONG line of oblique methods for moving out people who had lost her confidence, the replacement of Jack Altshul as city editor may have been the most unusual.

By the beginning of 1960, the year that *Newsday* turned 20 years old, Altshul had been the city editor, Hathway's second-in-command, for more than 15 years. Almost everyone loved Altshul, but it was becoming obvious that he was ineffective as city editor. The problem was that he had two other big demands on his time: his "Heads and Tales" column and his gambling.

Altshul was a terrible gambler, as his performance during the 1953 Kentucky Derby demonstrated. There are several versions of how Altshul incurred a crushing debt as a result of that race, but perhaps the most reliable comes from the reporter Jack O'Grady, who was with Altshul that day: Out of loyalty to his boss, Hathway decided that he should bet on Harry Guggenheim's horse, Dark Star, even though Native Dancer was heavily favored. So Hathway telephoned Altshul at home and asked him to get a bookie to take the bet. "I hear Jack say, 'Yeah, okay, Alan, don't worry. I'll get it down. Right, Alan,'" O'Grady said. "Then he hangs up and he says, 'Alan wants to bet $50 on Dark Star. Is he crazy? I'm going to book that one.'" Altshul acted as his own bookie, assuming the risks himself. A few minutes later, to Altshul's horror, Dark Star came in first, which meant that Altshul would have to pay off the bet — at odds of 25-1. "He practically convulsed in the chair," O'Grady said.

Altshul would gamble, with equal ineptitude, on almost anything. This was a constant source of friction in his marriage and a major cause of a year-long separation from his wife. His betting also caused him problems at work, where he would often disappear from the office in the early evenings, to place his wagers at the nearby Roosevelt Raceway. At that time of night, while Altshul was at the races, Hathway would frequently call the office to find out what was happening with the paper. "He'd always leave word around, 'If Alan calls, tell him I'm in the can,' " Bob Greene said. "So the famous line was 'Jack's in the can.' " Frequently, Altshul would return from the track just in time to answer Hathway's questions. "Altshul was supposed to have been seeing to everything," said Bill McIlwain, the copy chief. "In truth, he'd get back and say, 'Give me a quick rundown before Alan calls.' I think Alan had become increasingly aware of that."

The column was Altshul's other time-consuming burden. In the restaurants that he frequented, soaking up free meals, Altshul met hundreds of people. He knew everyone and everyone knew him, which enabled him to put together a newsy collection of short items separated by dots and filled with the names of restaurants. The problem was that, although Altshul was an excellent storyteller, he didn't pay close attention to detail. "I gave him a few items, and when I'd give him an item, I'd try to write it in his style, so that he could just pick it up and run it, because I knew anytime I'd give it to him and he rewrote it, he would make an error," Jim Hadjin said. Sometimes the result was litigation. "I had a couple of libel suits with Jack," said Andrew Hughes, *Newsday*'s primary libel lawyer for many years. "Most of his material came from what others gave to him. He was not an investigative reporter. So occasionally things came out wrong." In one case, he used incorrectly some information from Greene and Tom Renner and wrote an item about Suffolk County District Attorney John P. Cohalan Jr. that was libelous. *Newsday* settled the lawsuit for $4,000. Accurate or inaccurate, however, the column conveyed Altshul's warm personality, and it always had high readership. "His columns were very homey — often about his friends, about his family," Hadjin said. "People were very interested in his family, because they'd gotten to know the family, having read his stuff."

Largely because the column and gambling were more important to him than ambition, Altshul became less and less of a force. "Altshul did not take a very active role in the news operation," said Tony Insolia, who had begun to work on the desk at the same time that Altshul was waning. For years, Altshul had toiled as Hathway's loyal lieutenant, absorbing Hathway's verbal abuse and only occasionally fighting back. Over time, however, even Hathway came to understand that loyalty wasn't enough, and that Altshul was not the kind of leader who could replace him when the time came. Alicia came to share this view, with help from the younger editors, who told her about Altshul's shortcomings. "She would agree," Bill Woestendiek said, "but again, she was very reluctant to do anything."

Eventually, Alicia and Hathway adopted a strategy for choosing a new city editor — an odd ploy that became known as "musical chairs." It began with a long memo from Hathway at the start of 1960, announcing that *Newsday* would be completing its second decade later in the year and that it was time for a "reevaluation." So he outlined a plan to shift reporters and editors around to different jobs, to keep them from getting stale. "I have known (and know) too many good reporters who don't have any idea of what happens to their copy after it leaves the typewriter," Hathway wrote. "There are desk men who have been too long from the street digging for a story. . . . We are going to place people in jobs they have never held. We are going to place people in jobs they may have held elsewhere. . . . It is our hope that in the long run, we will all be more vital and aware. And a better paper."

In another memo that same day, Hathway announced: "Jack Altshul is being detached from his regular duties for the period of reevaluation. Jack has had more intimate working association with all sections of the editorial department than any other person here, including myself. Jack will sit in as advisor and director of several departments and will analyse, report and recommend any procedures he deems advisable." In other words, for the duration of the big shuffle, Altshul was no longer the city editor. It isn't clear whether the idea was originally Alicia's or Hathway's, but Woestendiek said: "That was her doing. She kind of operated that way." In effect, this episode of "musical chairs" provided a vehicle for choosing between the two prime contenders to succeed Altshul as city editor: Dick Aurelio, the news editor, and Bill McIlwain, the copy chief. "Dick and I both knew that," McIlwain said.

As the "musical chairs" process unfolded, Altshul apparently had a sense that something was happening to him. In early May, Altshul and Paul Back went on a business trip together to Arizona, to look for candidates to be the *Newsday* promotion manager. "At that time, he told me that that's what was going on," Back said. "He felt that they were sending him to Rome to cover the Olympics and they were going to keep him out of the office as much as they could, because they didn't want him to follow in Alan's footsteps, as he had been promised that he would. He told me flatly that he had been promised by Alan that when Alan left, he would become the managing editor. . . . I think he was greatly disappointed."

Disappointment was a familiar emotion for Altshul. Looking toward the twentieth anniversary of *Newsday*, Alicia had assigned him to research and write a book on *Newsday*'s history. "Altshul wanted to do it," McIlwain said. "I remember Hathway was saying, 'Don't go near it.' " Despite his inexperience at writing any long work of nonfiction, and despite the obvious pitfalls, Altshul had decided to do the book. At the end of this months-long project, Alicia wrote him an encouraging note on the galley proofs: "A fine job, particularly in light of all the difficulties involved." But Alicia told Hal Burton that she didn't think the manuscript had captured the real *Newsday*. Nonetheless, Altshul had the impression that it was Harry who disapproved. "Altshul told me Alicia cried when she told him she couldn't print his book," Burton said.

On top of that painful letdown, Altshul had to live with the disruption of the "musical chairs" period. But he was not the only person who suffered dislocation. Some editors, such as Lou Schwartz, found themselves working as reporters, and some reporters switched beats. Bill Van Haintze, the police reporter, for example, switched with Marty Buskin, who had been working on rewrite. For some, the switch involved the same kind of work, but in a new location — the Suffolk office. The squat white cinder-block building in the woods of Ronkonkoma was a significant change from the atmosphere of the Garden City office for those who made the switch, including Phil Sanborne, Robert Caro and Jane Gerard. "I got the notice that I was sent to Ronkonkoma for two months," Gerard remembered. "I said, 'I don't believe it.'"

Gerard had long since proven herself by writing the kind of story that Alicia would remember fondly from her days on *Liberty* magazine, when she had worked in a variety of occupations and reported on them. Gerard did a series of those participatory stories, tackling such occupations as international airline stewardess. She had all the qualifications to make people interested in her adventures: a splendid writing touch, a playful personality, beauty and endless South Carolina charm. "She was the flashiest feature writer," Sanborne said. Now, Gerard was stuck in Ronkonkoma, living in a boarding house and riding her bicycle around the county. Caro, a promising reporter who had come on the staff only a few months earlier, was stunned. "I started to cry," Caro said. "Jane and I were really sad. We felt we had done something wrong." A few months after her Ronkonkoma tour, Gerard produced the story that left her biggest mark on *Newsday*, a 106-mile walk from Garden City to Montauk Point, the easternmost tip of Long Island. The idea came from McIlwain, who had heard about a female doctor who was walking across America, on a subsistence diet. The *Newsday* twist was that Gerard was to adopt the opposite of a Spartan regimen: She would walk, but she would also sip champagne and eat fattening food. "Every day as I walked, I had to dream up the next day's story," Gerard said. One of the gimmicks she chose was to show up in short shorts, in violation of a local dress code. By the time she arrived in Montauk on the weekend of July 4, 1960, she had built intense reader interest in her walk. "It was hilarious," Sanborne said. "It could have been terribly corny. But it wasn't. It was self-deprecatory, in the sense that she made fun of the whole subject."

Unlike Gerard, some of those who shuffled to new jobs during this period found themselves required to develop an entirely new set of skills. A prime example was Greene, whose closeness to Hathway did not exempt him from the switch. Suddenly, the best investigative reporter on the paper found himself working nights in the composing room as a makeup editor, replacing Howard Halpern, who became a rewrite man. Even though he had never been an editor before, Greene adapted well. "He did it superbly," said Si Radiloff, who supervised him. The only problem with his new job was that Greene, accustomed to working in the streets and collecting expense money, was suddenly toiling inside, where expenses were unnecessary. "So every morning," Halpern said, "after the paper would close, he would come into the newsroom and sit down at a typewriter, and he would spend a good two hours on overtime doing a report, doing a log on what had transpired during the night when closing the paper:

where editors blew it, where printers blew it, where this could have been done better." It was not a device strictly designed to earn him overtime, Greene said, but rather, a report that had to be done, which somehow grew long. As time went on, Greene realized that this report could reflect on the performance of McIlwain and Aurelio, the two contestants for city editor.

It was a gentlemanly competition, in which both McIlwain and Aurelio had different strengths. "Aurelio was the strongest individual — a bit Machiavellian," Greene said. "He was really lining up political support. I mean, he was out campaigning with staff, to line up staff behind him." Of the two men, Aurelio had the most rounded experience. "I thought he was a wonderful newspaperman," McIlwain said. "I thought at that point he was better qualified than I was to get that job." In addition, Aurelio enjoyed the strong support of Hathway, who didn't think McIlwain was tough enough. On the other side, McIlwain had some significant advantages going for him: Alicia and Woestendiek. "Hathway was telling her 'Aurelio' in one ear, and I was saying 'McIlwain' in her other ear," Woestendiek said. It was clear that Alicia leaned toward McIlwain. She liked his smooth southern style, and there was something about Aurelio that she distrusted. "She thought he did not ask the right questions, do the right things," Woestendiek said.

In any situation in which Alicia wanted one thing and Hathway wanted another, the result was inevitable. "All of a sudden, it became quite obvious in my conversations with Hathway that Miss Patterson was going to make the choice," Greene said. "He didn't feel good about that. He always felt that one should be his. He didn't bitch about it." Finally, Alicia made her decision. At the end of October, 1960, right in the middle of an Altshul series about the Guantanamo naval base in Cuba, McIlwain became the city editor. Hathway made the announcement, McIlwain remembered, in a meandering, oblique memo, possibly to soften the blow to Altshul's pride. Not long after McIlwain got the job, Aurelio left *Newsday* and went to work on the staff of Senator Jacob Javits of New York — the start of a political career that later led to his appointment as first deputy to New York City Mayor John V. Lindsay. In fact, it was Aurelio's frustrated desire to cover politics that had first made him think about leaving, even before he lost the job to McIlwain.

"I was essentially a political animal," said Aurelio, who had been interested in an assignment to the Washington bureau. Hathway had supported him, but he also had to get past Alicia's scrutiny, during a lunch at Nino's Restaurant in Westbury. During that lunch, Aurelio became concerned when she started asking him detailed questions about his working-class Italian family in Rhode Island. "I just had the feeling that she thought I just came from too humble or too undistinguished a background," Aurelio said. Whatever Alicia's reasoning, Aurelio did not get the Washington job. Hathway tried to ease the disappointment by giving him a big raise, but the decision made Aurelio start thinking about working elsewhere. Later, the loss of the contest for city editor exacerbated that unhappiness. He had already been talking to Javits, and once Alicia decided to promote McIlwain, those talks accelerated and Aurelio left *Newsday* almost immediately. That quick exit seemed to please his mentor, Hathway. "It was sort of like it was a victory for him," Aurelio said, "almost as if he had said, 'Boy, if you do this, you'll lose Dick Aurelio.' "

So the decision to make McIlwain city editor cost *Newsday* a significant talent, but it also turned day-to-day control of the paper over to a smooth, professional journalist who was far more polished than Altshul. That shift converted Altshul into a full-time columnist and removed him from the center of power. First, he operated out of a rented office across the street from the *Newsday* plant, sharing space with Bob Zellner, the former sports editor, who was working on sports promotions. Later, he moved back to the plant, but in an upstairs office, away from the city room. Through his column, he continued to be a presence, but not a force. "People used to always ask me, because they thought that I would know," said Shirley Graham, who later served as Altshul's secretary, " 'What in the hell really happened with Jack?' "

III

RIGHT AFTER SHE had installed McIlwain as the potential successor to Hathway, Alicia took action to make sure that there would be Patterson blood at the helm of *Newsday* well into the future.

In her 1959 article with Hal Burton in the *Saturday Evening Post*, Alicia expressed her hope clearly. "When the time comes for me to retire as publisher, a good long time from now, the sixth generation of my family may be ready to step in — my nephew, Joseph Medill Patterson Albright and his sister Alice," Alicia said. "I hope both of them have the spark, but it will take hard work on their part to prove it to me." At the moment that the piece appeared, Joe Albright had graduated from Williams College and taken a reporting job at the *Chicago Sun-Times*. His sister, three and a half years younger, was a freshman at Radcliffe College. As they stood on the threshhold of adulthood in 1959, Alicia still hadn't decided between them.

The older of the two potential heirs had started out life in 1937 as Joseph Medill Patterson Reeve. His father was Jay Fred Reeve, a respected partner in a powerhouse Chicago law firm that represented Joe Albright's grandfather, Joseph Medill Patterson, and the *New York Daily News*. At the time Alicia's younger sister Josephine met and married Reeve, she was working as a reporter at the *Chicago Daily News*, a job that her father had helped to arrange. She became a street reporter in the wide-open, mob-dominated Chicago of the early 1930s, covering everything from gangsters to suicidal stockbrokers suffering from Great Depression. "I loved it," Josephine said. "I never had a better time in my life." Along the way, she covered a trial in which one of the attorneys was Reeve. The pin-striped lawyer divorced his first wife and married the rich young reporter in 1936. Joe came along in 1937 and Alice arrived in 1940, two months after the birth of *Newsday*.

The primary influence in Joe Albright's childhood was his mother — not his father. "He was not around much during my life," Joe said. Along the way, Reeve had suffered a painful change of fortunes. He had been such a successful lawyer that he virtually fell apart when he lost an important case. "He'd win 36 cases in a row or something like that," Josephine said. "It was very hard on him. He couldn't believe he lost it." In 1944, the year when Joe turned seven, his mother and father were divorced, and Reeve remarried his first wife. The father figure that Joe grew up with was Ivan Le Lorraine Albright, a short, lively, cheerful artist who became famous for minutely detailed paintings about death, decay and moral rot. Perhaps his most famous work was the series of portraits that he and his twin brother, Malvin, painted for *The Picture of Dorian Gray*, the film version of the Oscar Wilde novel about a handsome London aristocrat who descends into dissolution but retains his good looks, while his portrait gradually becomes hideous. At a party in Chicago, the bachelor artist met Josephine, who was 16 years younger. "It was no romance for a long time; it was just purely friends," Josephine said. "He taught me a great deal about art." The friendship became romance and they were married in 1946. Soon after the marriage, Ivan Albright adopted Joe and Alice and developed a relationship with them that Joe called "ideal." Later, Ivan and Josephine together had two more children, Adam and Blandina.

Even as a young boy, Joe Albright had contacts with *Newsday*, appearing as a regular character in the column that his mother wrote for Alicia in *Newsday*. That notoriety annoyed Joe, who was as cautious and reserved as his sister Alice was outgoing and adventurous. In that way, at least, Alice's personality was like Alicia's. "They both had redhead temperaments, if there is such a thing," said Alice's friend, Frances FitzGerald. "Alice is not at all like Alicia in many ways, but they're both very much out there. Joey is not — much more reserved." Despite those differences, Joe and Alice shared a psychic remnant of their grandfather: a self-consciousness about owning and controlling things that they didn't earn or deserve. "We're both guilt-ridden human beings," Alice said.

As Joe and Alice grew up, Alicia was a powerful presence in their lives. "To some extent, she regarded my sister Alice and me as surrogate children," Joe said. Alicia hovered over them, goading them to do better in school and gradually revealing that there was a place for them, if they could handle it, at *Newsday*. But it was never clear which of them was more likely to assume the throne. "I think that she liked to foster competition among people to bring out excellence," Joe said. "I think she was doing the same thing with us." As her niece and nephew developed, Alicia's views on them changed periodically. "My real sense of it was that she went back and forth, back and forth, back and forth," Alice said. "One would be the favorite, then the other."

Knowing what she had in mind for their futures, Alicia felt free to give child-rearing advice that obviously flowed directly from the way her father had raised her. "She was always after my mother," Alice said, "that my mother was being too soft on us: 'What are you trying to do, make a sissy out of him?' " Actually, growing up in the summers at his mother's ranch in Wyoming, Joe was exposed at an early age to the toughening influence of the west. "He was sent off to work when he was 13, 14," Alice remembered. "He worked on the Indian mission, poor guy, haying for the priest. And it was a tough, tough job. . . . He was so game. He'd get taken along to rodeos, and I can remember him trying to rope, and he did very well, and they'd say, 'little cowboy from Chicago.' It was not too easy. There were some very tough guys out there. They used to beat the shit out of him, too. . . . I remember he had a black eye at the table in the morning, and he was just like it didn't happen, and Aunt Alicia was kidding him a lot about it."

Exposure to a toughening environment was also part of Alice's training. Early in the elementary school years, she briefly attended a school in the Georgia woods, near Alicia's hunting lodge. "Kingsland was scary," Alice said. "They didn't have Yankees going to school there. . . . Aunt Alicia and mother thought it would be a broadening experience." Later, at Chicago Latin School, Alice began to act a little too wild for Alicia's tastes, running her own little newspaper and enjoying boys too much. So Alicia and Josephine shipped her off to the proper Ethel Walker School in Connecticut, where the headmistress made it clear that the girls would grow up and marry corporate vice presidents. "They put me in this school for geishas," Alice said. "They were not being groomed to run newspapers."

The Ethel Walker doctrine on the role of women was just one element in the stream of advice that came to Alice on that subject. Alicia made it clear to her that any woman had to pay a price for operating in a man's world. "I think she was saying to me all the time, 'You're going to have to make some tough choices. To make it as a woman, and to really make it, you have to go after it,' " Alice said. But Alicia gave her another rule that seemed to say exactly the opposite: " 'Never beat a man at tennis, never let a man know you're smart. You catch more flies with honey. Make them think it's their idea.' She also was devastating with men. I think she thought that was her best talent."

Throughout Alice's childhood, Alicia kept providing guidance, incentives and kicks in the pants. When Alice heard a racist epithet and repeated it, without knowing its meaning, Alicia slapped her. When Alice was old enough, Alicia provided her with a summer job at *Newsday*. When Alice thought about going to college at Wellesley, where she could have a good time, Alicia insisted that she go to Radcliffe. When Alicia travelled to Russia with Adlai Stevenson in 1958 after Alice's high school graduation, she took Alice along as bearer, photographer and all-purpose travel aide. At the end of the Russian trip, Alice visited with Alicia at Falaise and had a conversation about her future, in the same bedroom where Alicia used to eat breakfast in bed and allow Alice and the other visiting children to come in for an audience. "It was so seductive to be brought in," Alice said. "I remember after we came back from Russia, my vividest memory was in that bedroom, lying on that bed and saying, 'Oh, I want to be like you. I want to be like you.' And she said, 'Well, it's going to be a lot of work.' "

The role model that Alicia kept holding out to Alice was Frances FitzGerald, who became Alice's roommate at Radcliffe. Alicia called her friend Marietta Tree "Golden Girl" because of her intelligence, beauty and perfect breeding, and she regarded Marietta's daughter Frances as something close to perfect, too. (FitzGerald later proved Alicia a good judge of talent, by winning the Pulitzer Prize for her book on Vietnam, *Fire in the Lake*.) "Alicia was being very hard on Alice, I remember," FitzGerald said. "She wanted Alice to compete. In general, I think she saw Alice as being her successor." At Radcliffe, Alice was far from an underachiever. She was the first woman elected to the editorial board of the *Harvard Crimson*, and in 1959, a small piece in *Time* magazine called her the "Princess of the Crimson."

Before Alice finished college, she had begun drifting in the direction of marriage and away from Alicia's control. First, she dated a British student at Harvard Business School, whom Alicia disliked intensely. Then, working on a summer internship at the *Chicago Sun-Times*, she met a young, blond, talented and immensely self-assured reporter named Jim Hoge, who had started at the paper at the same time as her brother Joe. She spent her last year at Radcliffe shuttling back and forth between Chicago and Cambridge, dating Hoge. And when she graduated from Radcliffe, she married him. That did not please her Aunt Alicia. "I don't think she wanted me to get married," Alice said. "I think she wanted me to have a career." Perhaps as much because she didn't want Alice to marry as because of Hoge's personality, Alicia disliked him and referred to him among her friends as Hog. "We would play croquet and she would always pick on him," said Alicia's friend, George Abbott. "I thought it was kind of rude." By comparison, Joe Albright was providing fewer reasons for Alicia to be displeased. "Alice had rebelled at this point," FitzGerald said. "For Alice to succeed in her eyes, she would have had to stay single. She would have had to really be serious about the newspaper business, and she would have had to stay around Alicia more. So, while Alice was being flaky in her eyes at this point, by going off with these men, Joey was being good, dedicated, loyal, going into journalism."

Like his grandfather, Joe Albright prepared for college at Groton. Then he went on to Williams College in the hills of Berkshire County, in western Massachusetts. There, he applied himself diligently to his studies, earned a Phi Beta Kappa key, and in 1958 submitted a long, detailed history thesis on Joseph Medill Patterson's life that remained, three decades later, the most scholarly, analytical work ever written about his grandfather. On the copy that he gave to Alicia, he wrote in his inscription: "This man is a part of both of us." Between his sophomore and his junior years at Williams, Albright landed a summer job covering cops at the *Denver Post*, with a boost from Alicia's friend, Stan Peckham. "It was something I was doing myself," Albright said. "The family didn't have anything to do with it."

As he got further into journalism, Albright came to feel that both his mother and his sister were better writers than he was, but once he got his degree from Williams in 1958 and went to work at the *Sun-Times*, he began to prove that he was a good reporter. He worked on general assignment, covered courts during the Chicago police scandal and did a six-month tour in the Army at the end of 1959. In 1960, he was part of a *Sun-Times* team covering the Republican National Convention. During the selection of a vice-presidential candidate, Albright came up with a front-page story about a private meeting in a hotel room, at which Richard Nixon told Republican leaders why Henry Cabot Lodge should be the vice-presidential candidate. The word quickly spread around town that Albright had gotten the story by hiding out in a bathroom in the suite, which enhanced his reputation as an aggressive reporter.

Not long after that coup, Alicia began pushing him to come to *Newsday*. Even though Josephine agreed with Alicia's ultimate goal, she felt that her son wasn't ready yet, at age 23. "I thought he needed a little more experience," Josephine said. "I just thought it was asking a lot of a kid that age to suddenly get moved." It is difficult to know why Alicia was in such a rush, but Josephine developed a theory. "I always thought maybe she thought she wasn't going to live that long," Josephine said. "She always said she'd never live to be 60." Whatever her reasons, Alicia thought her nephew was ready, and he wasn't about to disagree. "I was brash enough to think that I was well enough seasoned," he said. "In retrospect, I think my mother was right."

So, in 1961, Albright came to *Newsday* and began making the rounds of all the departments at the paper, obviously in training for a bright future. At one point, he sat in with the management negotiating group during a meeting with Local 915 of the International Typographical Union, which represented the printers. One of the printers wrote a note and passed it along to the others, asking, "Who's he?" A veteran proofreader took the note and scribbled the answer: "The heir apparent."

Universally, the people he worked with found Albright dedicated, hardworking, decent and quietly likable, despite his wealth and his future prospects. But there were some jobs in the business areas that did not fit his skills. Selling advertising was one. "They put me on the Hempstead accounts," Albright said. "I was not nearly mentally tough enough." One example of that was his shyness about collecting money during one sales call. "He came back with the ad, but not the check," said Dave Targe, who supervised him during this advertising tour. "I said, 'You'd better go out and get the check.' This is seven or eight o'clock at night. And Joe said, 'Well, I'm supposed to meet my aunt to have dinner.' And I said, 'Get the check first, then meet your aunt later.' I got a call from Alicia the following week, saying, 'I'm so happy you did that to Joe.' " In circulation, Albright worked out of a district office on Nassau County's North Shore, learning the paper's distribution system. "Everybody who's working had station wagons or something like that, but Joey pulls up in a Mercedes Benz," said Al Gilkes, the canny circulation supervisor who became his mentor. Despite Albright's wealth, he won respect. "He was a worker," Gilkes said. "He was naive as hell, because he came from a wealthy family, and he wasn't used to a lot of the ways of the world. But he got sharped up real quick."

Eventually, Albright showed up in the city room and drew an assignment as a rewrite man. "I didn't really do very well, because I'd never done rewrite," he remembered. "Anyway, it was a shock. People were generally sort of nice, but I suddenly realized that, hey, I had some problems. I hadn't been writing. I thought, 'Here was the big guy coming in from Chicago.' I was going to show these people. It was not that way." Following a brief stay on the copy desk, Albright rotated to his first long-term assignment at *Newsday*, the Washington bureau, where he began to cover the State Department, settle into the routine and feel more comfortable. Albright was a better reporter than he was a writer, and in Washington, he began to come up with good stories. He had acquired an education in the business end of the paper, and now he was back doing what he did best, at the start of what seemed likely to be a number of years of further preparation before he would move up to be publisher.

IV

ONE OF THE most crucial roles of a newspaper's editor is the establishment of an atmosphere of independence, in which reporters can write and editors edit, without worrying about interference by a powerful advertiser or politician.

As to the advertisers, Alicia was an unqualified success. In the earliest days of the paper, she had a relationship with the senior management at Arnold Constable, the first major department store to advertise heavily in *Newsday*. But as the years went on, thanks to a combination of Alicia's attitude and Ernie Levy's strategy of developing large numbers of advertisers instead of relying on a few large accounts, *Newsday* developed the ability to thumb its nose at any advertiser who tried to influence news coverage. If advertisers wanted to reach Long Island customers, they had no choice but to appear in *Newsday*, and if something that *Newsday* wrote made them unhappy, they could withdraw their advertising and *Newsday* would quickly replace them with someone else. So Alicia told Hal Burton that her philosophy was this: " 'If the paper's any good, they're going to have to advertise in it. If it isn't any good, there's no point going out and pandering to them because they won't stay anyway.' " So she avoided entanglements with advertisers as much as possible, and sometimes used a little humor to remind Ernie Levy in the advertising department of that independence. On one occasion, Bill Woestendiek remembered, Levy was planning a special section on sailboats, designed to attract marine advertising, and Alicia got a gleam in her eye and said: "I think I'll call Ernie and tell him we're going to start a big campaign against reckless sailing on the Sound."

As to independence from the influence of her friends and powerful public figures, Alicia's record was more mixed. Her most frequent lapses came in the area of favoring her pals. From the beginning, Alicia's friends participated in writing parts of the paper, and she often dispatched her reporters to do features about the activities of those friends. Many of them, such as George Abbott, were in the entertainment industry, which made them legitimate subjects for stories even if they were the editor's pals. Usually, her transgressions were small and harmless, such as the one involving the engagement of her niece, Alice, to marry Jim Hoge. "When the engagement was announced, it broke a precedent in Paging Women," said Aurelie Dwyer Stack, who worked on the section at that time. "We used to have one-paragraph engagement announcements. . . . You got two paragraphs if you'd gone to college. Alicia's niece's engagement went on for several paragraphs. It was the only one in my memory that went more than two paragraphs."

On the question of columnists, while it is true that Alicia had pushed out Ben Kubasik as the film critic over his review of *West Side Story*, she did give columnists room to disagree. One example was Jo Coppola, the paper's first television critic. She had started at *Newsday* doing the "Let Prof. Do-It" advice column, then had persuaded Alicia and Hathway that the paper should be covering television. In 1948, Alicia had asked her to establish an employee publication, which became known as *Slug*, and when it satirized Alicia and the paper's management, Alicia told her: "You were too kind to me." So Alicia had set a precedent of tolerance, and Coppola called upon it when *Newsday* ran a 1954 editorial that defended the television show, *Strike It Rich*, against the criticism that it degraded the needy people who appeared on it. Coppola thought the show was little more than "public begging," and she wrote Alicia a note asking if she could use her television column to disagree with the editorial. Alicia wrote her back, simply: "O.K. Say that this is your opinion and not that of Newsday — give us hell."

On the more important question of protecting reporters and stories from outsiders, she could be as tough and unyielding as an angry mother bear. But at times it appeared to the staff that she used her power to protect sacred cows, such as Robert Moses, the master builder. Jack O'Grady remembered writing a column that sharply criticized a Moses proposal and giving it to his editor, Ralph Hausrath, for editing. "He read it and he liked it and he said, 'We can't do this. Alicia won't approve of this,' " O'Grady said. "Not that Alicia would have seen it if he had let it go. But Alicia was very fond of Robert Moses." Another Moses story that didn't get into the paper involved a visit that he made to Jones Beach. As Bob Greene heard the story, Moses had draped his towel over a lifeguard stand, and when a lifeguard ordered him to remove it, Moses fired the lifeguard. "We call and we confirm the story with two or three other lifeguards who were there," Greene said. "All of them swore they knew what Moses looked like. We're calling to get comment from Moses, and we're not getting any comment from Moses. The next thing I hear was just we're not going to use the story." Greene had no specific knowledge that Alicia killed the Moses story. It could have been, as in O'Grady's case, the act of a lower-level editor who assumed that Alicia wouldn't like it. In either case, it was clear that she had an inclination to treat Moses gently.

On another occasion, Greene witnessed the killing of a story far more important than the firing of a lifeguard. In 1957, *Life* magazine ran an investigative piece about Jesus Maria de Galindez, a Basque who fled from Franco Spain to the Dominican Republic, became disenchanted with the Dominican dictator Rafael Leonidas Trujillo, left for New York, wrote a doctoral thesis on the corruption of Trujillo and ultimately disappeared. Then an American pilot named Gerald Lester Murphy also disappeared. The *Life* story revealed that agents of Trujillo's government had kidnaped Galindez from a New York City subway, drugged him and taken him by ambulance to Zahn's Airport in Suffolk County, where Murphy was waiting with a plane to ferry him to the Dominican Republic. Murphy was apparently operating under the impression that Galindez was simply a wealthy invalid, not a political prisoner.

At *Newsday*, Jack Ehrlich got some tips about the story from Suffolk police and began working on it. Hathway suggested that Greene should join him. Together, they developed a significant amount of information, including a Greene interview with the editor of a Spanish-language daily newspaper in New York City, who admitted that he couldn't afford to publish anti-Trujillo stories, since Trujillo and other Latin American dictators were major advertisers. They also interviewed Morris Ernst, a well-known liberal lawyer who had been hired by Trujillo to investigate the disappearance. "Morris Ernst was a neighbor of Alicia Patterson," Ehrlich said. "She thought he was the greatest thing since jelly beans. He was a fighter of lost causes. He represented all the poor and downtrodden, and all of a sudden he ended up representing Trujillo. We made him look very, very bad in the series." What the series showed was that Ernst's 95-page report was little more than a whitewash of the Trujillo government.

"The series was written, it was in, it was being advertised," said Ehrlich. In fact, *Newsday* had prepared posters, to be put up on railroad stations, promoting the stories. "Miss Patterson read it and killed it, cold." Ehrlich concluded that Alicia had killed it because it came down so hard on Morris Ernst. Greene heard a different version from Hathway. "Hathway was very hot on it," Greene said. "Alicia read it, and on first glance, she was very much for it. Then she called Alan and me in, and she said, 'Harry doesn't want to run it.' She laid it off on Harry. Alan said that Harry's mining interests had substantial interests in the Dominican Republic."

Whether it was Harry or Alicia who ordered the series killed, it was dead. "We spent one hell of a lot of time," Ehrlich said. "I ultimately became so disgusted with *Newsday* I quit. . . . Bob was more of a professional than I. His attitude was: 'We ate well, we drank well, we travelled first class. So who gives a shit?' I did." Greene was astounded that someone had killed the story. "I always heard there were never any kills on *Newsday*," said Greene. He understood Ehrlich's disillusionment, but he didn't see the need to resign unless he had detected a pattern of kills. There was no consistent pattern to be found. In fact, Alicia's record of making sure that stories got into the paper without interference was better than the performance of many publishers. But it fell well short of perfect.

CHAPTER NINETEEN

APG and JFK

I

THE IDEA OF Adlai Stevenson in the Oval Office still appealed to Alicia in 1960, despite his two losses to Dwight Eisenhower and her painful struggle with Harry after the 1956 campaign.

In that 1956 race, Stevenson had defined the Democrats as a new generation of leaders who could get America moving again after the slothful Eisenhower years. But when 1960 came around and the constitution barred Eisenhower from running again, that new leadership seemed likely to come from John Fitzgerald Kennedy — not from Stevenson. Early in the year, *Newsday* covered primary contests between Kennedy and Senator Hubert Humphrey of Minnesota, and argued editorially that Kennedy's religion ought not to be an issue, but it also occasionally dropped hints about a Stevenson candidacy. One was a cartoon in April showing Stevenson, in a baseball uniform with a bat on his shoulder, waiting to pinch-hit for Kennedy or Humphrey. A little more than a week later, while the American Society of Newspaper Editors was meeting in Washington, Alicia asked Hal Levy and Bonnie Angelo in the Washington bureau to invite some newspaper people over to their home, to meet Adlai. She clearly hadn't given up.

Alicia was not alone in her loyalty to Stevenson. Early in the campaign, it had become obvious to John F. English, the chairman of the Democratic Party in Nassau County, that there was significant support for Stevenson locally. "There's only one person who can do something about that, and that's Alicia Patterson," English told Kennedy. The Kennedy family already had an ally at *Newsday*: Bob Greene, who had worked closely with Robert Kennedy on the

Senate rackets committee. "At Bob's request, I made a pitch for a Kennedy endorsement to both Alicia and to Hathway," Greene said. "I was told that Alicia was committed to Adlai if he ran. I reported this back to Bob. He said that he was aware of the problem. He asked if I could get Alicia to have lunch with Jack." Alicia agreed to meet with Kennedy, and on a cool day in the spring, he arrived, unaccompanied, at the *Newsday* plant and walked into her office. A few minutes later, she took him to a private room at Nino's Restaurant — along with a small group of her staff, including Greene, Alan Hathway, Bill Woestendiek, Jack Altshul, Hal Burton and Stan Hinden. The lunch went smoothly. Even Hathway behaved well, stayed sober and asked intelligent questions. Kennedy answered wittily and worked his Irish charm on Alicia. "She was fluttering,"' Greene said. Before it ended, they had an understanding. "She said, 'If anything ever happens, you're my second choice,' " Greene remembered.

In May, Kennedy scored a smashing victory over Humphrey in West Virginia, a heavily Protestant state, forcing Humphrey out of the race. But Kennedy was worried that Stevenson, who still refused to endorse him publicly, might yet become an active candidate. "He wanted to remain available in case of a draft; he agonized over it a lot," said Bill Attwood, who had taken a leave of absence from *Look* and signed on with Stevenson as a speechwriter. While Stevenson's supporters kept urging him to let them push for a draft and a Stevenson-Kennedy ticket, Stevenson kept asking himself whether he could beat Vice-President Richard Nixon, the likely Republican nominee. "To be beaten by Eisenhower was bad enough," Attwood said.

By the end of May, Kennedy had amassed nearly half of the delegates he would need to win the nomination at the Democratic convention in July. Nonetheless, Alicia carried a signed editorial on May 31, endorsing Stevenson for the presidency. "He is qualified for many reasons but the one overriding reason is that he would be able to deal with the totalitarian powers," Alicia wrote. In a small editorial below, she endorsed Kennedy for vice-president. "Next to Stevenson, Senator John Kennedy is the ablest Democratic candidate," she said. "He has shown a remarkable vote-getting ability in the primaries; his energy and forthrightness have won the hearts of many Americans. But his youth and relative inexperience in dealing with world leaders could be a handicap."

A week later, at the top of the editorial page, Alicia ran a signed editor's note. "On the opposite page, Harry Guggenheim, the president and co-owner of Newsday, states his views on the coming election," she wrote. "He will continue to express his views as the campaign progresses. They will not always agree with those of this editorial column." In 1956, Alicia had stunned Harry by endorsing Stevenson, but he had not written a rebuttal. In this campaign, he had no intention of remaining silent. On the opposite page, his support of Nixon was clear: "We need his leadership for the preservation and extension of the values, spiritual and material, so necessary for the Free World today." Later, *Time* magazine asked Harry about the divergent views. "I don't call it a quarrel," he said. "I'm expressing my own private political view. Of course it can't in any way be separated from my presidency of *Newsday*." The *Time* article concluded wryly: "In short, any time *Newsday* Co-Owner (49%) Alicia Patterson tries to tell Co-Owner (51%) Harry Guggenheim how to vote, Husband Harry can be counted on to put in his extra two per cent's worth."

By the time of the convention in Los Angeles, it seemed clear that Kennedy had the votes to win the nomination on the first ballot. So Alicia adopted a new tactic: On the eve of the balloting, she ran an editorial urging that Kennedy designate Stevenson as his choice for secretary of state. But the editorial was not her only weapon in that campaign. Through Greene, who was in Los Angeles to cover the convention, she actually tried to cut a deal with the Kennedys. "I'd gotten a fairly fast idea that Jack was very close to it on the first ballot, and I'd reported that back down to Alicia Patterson," Greene said. "Then she tried to get hold of Adlai, because Eleanor Roosevelt and Herbert Lehman were there and they had convinced Adlai that he would be able to do well." With his loyalists urging him to seek the nomination, Stevenson did speak to some delegations, but he didn't put on a concerted effort to snatch victory from Kennedy. Still, the Kennedys were worried that Stevenson would raid the Illinois delegation and try to pry loose their votes. Instead, they wanted him to withdraw and place Kennedy's name in nomination.

"Miss Patterson then asked me if I would go back up and see Bobby and find out, if Adlai would drop out and would nominate Jack, would it be possible that he'd be secretary of state," Greene said. He went to see Robert Kennedy, who gave no guarantee, but promised to give Stevenson serious consideration. Greene brought that message back to Alicia. What followed was a frantic tableau in which Alicia tried to close the deal and Stevenson asked for more time to talk with his supporters and decide. "Now she sends me with a letter over to his suite," said Greene, who couldn't meet with Stevenson himself but left the letter with his aides, giving them permission to read it. Then he returned to Alicia and told her. "She says, 'Oh, Lord. I wish you hadn't let them read the letter.' " Finally, the deal fell through. "She says, 'You can tell Mr. Kennedy thank you very much, but he says he just cannot disappoint Eleanor and Herbert, who insist that he has a chance, even though he knows that he doesn't,' " Greene remembered. "She says, 'I'm sure Bob will understand.' So I went up and talked to Bob. He says, 'He still can't make up his rabbit-ass mind.' " Greene's role as an emissary put him in an excellent position to write about the maneuvering over the nominating speech, but none of it brought Stevenson the prize that Alicia wanted for him.

The demise of Stevenson's slim chance to become the nominee did not end the political differences between Harry and Alicia. On October 25, the editorial page began with a note over Alicia's signature: "The opinions of this newspaper are expressed in the editorial column. Today we endorse John F. Kennedy for President of the United States. The reasons for our choice are set forth below. In a column on the opposite page my husband, Harry F. Guggenheim, president of Newsday, states his personal endorsement of Vice President Richard M. Nixon for President." This display of duality did not end with that

one day of conflicting endorsements. Over the next two weeks, Harry took
several more opportunities to express his dissenting views in signed columns
across from the editorial page. It fell to Woestendiek to make sure that Harry
didn't get cheated out of his share of words. In the end, Harry actually got more
space than Alicia in this spousal balancing act. "It was wild," Woestendiek said.
"That was a period during which she was probably the most vehement about
Harry that I remember."

II

IF HARRY DERIVED from the 1960 campaign the satisfaction of standing up to
Alicia and expressing his dissent, Alicia won a much more substantial prize: the
new President's gratitude.

The first evidence of that gratitude appeared a few months after the
inauguration, after Woestendiek wrote Kennedy an open letter that appeared in
Newsday over Alicia's name. Referring to Kennedy's inaugural address, in which
he challenged Americans to ask what they could do for their country, the letter
said: "But still we do not know what it is that must be done, and how you as our
elected leader want us to do it. . . . We want to know so that we can let our
readers know." Just 10 days later, *Newsday* used a full page to carry Kennedy's
answering letter to Alicia. The following day, the *New York Times* ran the text of
Kennedy's letter, across four columns, along with a photograph of Alicia. *Time*
magazine carried a story about the exchange, with a photo of Alicia and the
headline: "Alicia's Pen Pal."

Less than a year later, Kennedy helped Alicia in a far more palpable
way, intervening directly in a long-running controversy that had immense
significance for the growth of Long Island: the future of the Air Force
base at Mitchel Field. This base had opened during World War I, when
Nassau County was still rural. Following World War II, suburban development had surrounded it with an increasingly congested area that included
private homes, stores and *Newsday*'s new plant. Alicia felt that Mitchel
Field was no longer safe or necessary. Beginning in 1955, she had campaigned vigorously for the Air Force to move the facility to another site
that would not endanger the community. That October, she ran a two-part
series by Arnold Brophy, "Is Mitchel Field Necessary?" Soon after the series, as if on cue, a B-26 bomber crashed in East Meadow — near the
home of a *Newsday* compositor, Paul Koroluck — and two crewmen died.
It was the third crash of a plane based at Mitchel Field in two months.
Right after the crash, a *Newsday* reporter had called the base and asked
for details, and the facility's spokesman had blurted out: "There's a plane
down in East Meadow. It's not serious." Next to its editorial, *Newsday*
carried a photo of the crash scene, with a three-word caption: "It's Not

Serious." Just two months later, the paper ran a special supplement, outlining the history of crashes, potential sites farther east, in Suffolk County, and the dwindling justification for the base.

When the Air Force announced in late 1960 that it would close the 1,168-acre facility in June, 1961, the headline on one of the *Newsday* sidebars asked prophetically: "What's Ahead for Mitchel? It's Not Clear." It was clear, however, that the closing was just the start of a complex federal bureaucratic process to determine whether any federal agencies wanted the land and whether the Federal Aviation Administration felt that the field should become a civilian airport. Just before the base was to close, Nassau County Executive A. Holly Patterson appointed an 11-person committee, including Robert Moses, to develop a coordinated plan for the huge piece of land, taking into account the competing demands for use of the property. Both Hofstra, a private institution, and Nassau Community College, a public one, wanted space. But a coalition of businessmen argued that the future economic health of the county depended on the development of a general aviation airport there.

The community college had just opened in 1959, and it was still operating in temporary quarters at the court complex in Mineola. "There was no public higher education in Long Island at the time we came to set up the community college in '59," said Marvin Rapp, who had helped the State University of New York to open community colleges elsewhere and became vice-president of Nassau Community College in 1961. "Not only were you talking about getting Mitchel Field and getting a campus, you were talking about giving an inspiration to public higher education." The community college had a powerful ally, David Starr, the editor of the *Long Island Press*, who was also the secretary to the college's board of trustees. "He helped me, I would suspect, almost more than anybody else," Rapp said. At the same time, Alicia was a trustee at Hofstra. "*Newsday* and the *Press* both campaigned like mad," Starr said.

On the other side, an ad hoc business group called Long Island Planners for Mitchel sprang up, to push for a general aviation airport. Its chairman was Elston Swanson, a scientist-engineer who ran his own electronics firm and was an officer of the Long Island Association, the major business lobbying group on Long Island. "We never thought of it as a jetport or an air carrier type operation," Swanson said, "but merely as a means of getting corporate executives in and out of the area." As long as they got part of the land for an airport, the business group had no objection if some of it went to education. In fact, they argued that the county could acquire the land for free from the federal government if any municipality agreed to run even part of it as an airport, but if the county rejected the airport, it would have to pay for the land. "They just seemed to take an all-or-nothing approach to the thing," Swanson said. "They just did not want an airport there, period."

That attitude was precisely the way Alicia felt. Alan Hathway agreed entirely, even though two of his friends supported the airport idea. One was Jack Rettaliata of Grumman, the largest employer on Long Island. The other was Paul Townsend, the publisher of the *Long Island Commercial Review*, a weekly that

Townsend converted temporarily into a daily, to strengthen his position against *Newsday* and the *Press* on the airport issue. Townsend and Hathway had fought on the same side at other times, including the battle to build housing for veterans after World War II, but on this issue, they were opponents, and Townsend didn't like Hathway's tactics. "*Newsday* was doing terrible things," Townsend said. Many of the crashes that *Newsday* listed in support of its case, Townsend argued, didn't even happen at Mitchel Field. And he felt that *Newsday* was unfair in depicting the businessmen who wanted an airport as selfish fat cats. To Hathway, though, it was the white hats against the black hats, and he reacted angrily to Townsend's alliance with the black hats. " 'Paul, I'm gonna drive you off the island, goddamn it,' " Townsend remembered Hathway saying, after a few drinks at a Christmas party. To show that he was serious, Hathway sent Bob Greene to warn Townsend to back down. "I was delivering Alan's ultimatum to Paul," Greene said. "The point was, 'Why earn yourself all of this problem?' It wasn't in a nasty, threatening way."

There were only two ways that the airport supporters could get what they wanted. Either Nassau County would agree to operate the airport, which it refused to do, or the FAA would have to operate the airport itself. The issue came to a head in January, 1962, when the FAA held two days of hearings in a theater at Mitchel Field. At the start of the hearings, a major witness took center stage: Lieutenant General Elwood R. (Pete) Quesada, the former FAA administrator. As Quesada arrived, Hathway confidently whispered to Townsend: "Wait till you hear this." A few minutes later, Townsend understood why Hathway had been so gleeful: Quesada's testimony supported *Newsday*'s position entirely.

In his testimony, Quesada strongly opposed the idea of the FAA running an airport at Mitchel Field. He emphasized that Senator Kenneth Keating of New York had asked him to appear, but Townsend suspected *Newsday* was really behind it. "Keating may have invited him," Townsend said, "but I'm sure it was cooked up with Alan and Harry." Certainly, Hathway was happy with Quesada's testimony, and Quesada did have a long-time relationship with Harry Guggenheim. Almost a quarter of a century earlier, Quesada had worked with Jimmy Doolittle on the Guggenheim-sponsored experiments in instrumented flight at Mitchel Field. Later, when Harry was ambassador to Cuba, Quesada was his air attache, piloting him on trips around the island. And in 1961, Quesada became the chairman of the Cornell-Guggenheim Aviation Safety Center. Quesada was also part of the coterie of military men who annually visited Harry's Cain Hoy plantation to shoot turkeys by day and the bull by night. "Oh, did we enjoy it," Quesada remembered. "We would sit there night after night, rewriting history." So Townsend had good reason to believe that Quesada was a friend of Harry's. What is not clear is the position that Harry, the aviation patron, took on the airport issue. Quesada did not recall exactly how Harry felt about the airport, but Bill Woestendiek said: "My sense was that he opposed Alicia on it. My feeling from her was that this was kind of another victory for her."

Despite Quesada's testimony, there was still a good chance after the hearings that the FAA would step in and run the airport. Both Oscar Bakke, the FAA regional administrator, and Najeeb Halaby, the administrator of the entire FAA, favored it. "Bakke sort of was on the barricades about it, because he couldn't permit another airport to be lost to the airway system without a struggle," Halaby remembered. "I supported him, but I never went up and was willing to throw myself into the fire about it. . . . It was touch and go, but we thought it could be saved." That was when Alicia got some help from the President.

In late February, a few weeks after the FAA hearings, Alicia told Woestendiek that it would be nice if they could meet Kennedy alone in the White House and chat. Woestendiek knew Kennedy's press secretary, Pierre Salinger, and called him, explaining Alicia's request. "I got that call and I thought, 'Well, I'll tell it to the President, but it's not something that's going to happen in the next couple of months,' " Salinger said. "He got all of a sudden quite eager, and he said, 'Let's do it right away.' " The result was a big surprise to Woestendiek. "Pierre called me back, like two days later, and said, 'The President would like Miss Patterson and you to be his guests for lunch tomorrow in the White House,' " said Woestendiek, who immediately told Alicia. "She just screamed and said, 'Ooh, how did you do that?' " Alicia was so excited that she didn't even want to travel to Washington by plane, for fear that a flight cancellation might make them miss the lunch. So her chauffeur, Noel Dean, drove her and Woestendiek down before dawn the next morning.

When they met Kennedy, Alicia thanked him effusively for the invitation. "He said, 'Well, you were a gracious hostess when I was on Long Island at Nino's that day, and I want to repay the favor,' " Woestendiek remembered. Kennedy offered them Bloody Marys, and the three of them sat down in the family dining room to a lunch of clear soup, veal, beans, salad, rose wine and ice cream cake. As Alicia referred occasionally to her list of questions, they talked about presidential press conferences, the labor problems of the steel industry, nuclear testing in the atmosphere, Ted Kennedy's plans to run for the Senate and Jackie Kennedy's forthcoming trip to India. They also discussed Mitchel Field and the economic disaster that was facing Republic Aviation Corporation, a major Long Island employer. Earlier in the month, *Newsday* had published a special supplement about an Air Force decision to phase out the F-105D fighter-bombers that Republic manufactured. That phaseout, *Newsday* argued, would force the firm to lay off 13,000 of its 15,500 workers and would also shrink employment at other companies.

A few minutes into the discussion of Long Island's problems, Kennedy took immediate action on one of them. "He was sitting in a chair, and he rolled back and picked up the phone and said, 'Get me Jeeb Halaby,' " Woestendiek remembered. "He said, 'Jeeb, we don't need Mitchel Field, do we? Let's shut the damn thing.' Then he turned around, put the phone down. He said, 'It's closed. . . .' That was very impressive." The whole conversation, Halaby remembered, took about three minutes. In answer to Kennedy's question, Halaby conceded that there were problems with an airport at Mitchel Field, but he told

Kennedy why it was needed. By the time they finished, Kennedy had made it clear that he agreed with Alicia. "She persuaded him," Halaby said. "I don't think there was any, 'If you kill the civil airport at Mitchel Field, I'll get you Nassau County,' or something like that. . . . It was just that she was a very persuasive and powerful woman."

After lunch and a brief tour, they thanked Kennedy and left, with his permission to publish a story saying that there would be no airport. "Unfortunately," Alicia wrote in her memo summarizing the lunch, "there was a leak in Halaby's office and all papers carried it the following day." The Mitchel Field development led the paper in *Newsday*: "MITCHEL RULING:/NO AIRPORT." The story, making no mention of Alicia's visit to the President, attributed the announcement to Nassau County Executive Eugene Nickerson, a patrician Democrat who had just been elected in the overwhelmingly Republican county — with a significant boost from *Newsday*. Nickerson said he had gotten the word of the airport decision from Oscar Bakke. "Nickerson also revealed that he had been aware of this development for some time," the story said. "He said that he and Rep. Otis G. Pike (D-Riverhead) were assured last week at a White House meeting that there would be no airport." But two days before Nickerson's announcement, the story reported, Keating had released a letter from Halaby, still supporting the airport. There were other forces pushing Kennedy to close the airport, including the *Long Island Press*, Nickerson and Jack English, the Nassau County Democratic chairman. But it was Alicia Patterson who was sitting at lunch with Kennedy in the White House when he gave the word to Halaby. It is possible, perhaps even likely, that Kennedy had already made his decision and had invited Alicia to lunch primarily so he could make the grand gesture of granting her wish on the spot. It is also possible, as Halaby recalled, that Alicia's arguments at lunch persuaded him. In either case, the President of the United States showed by his actions that he felt he owed a favor to Alicia, who had endorsed him in one of America's most Republican counties, despite her own husband's opposition.

Later, Kennedy also helped with the other problem that they discussed at lunch, Republic Aviation. The *Newsday* supplement had suggested that Kennedy direct other contracts to Republic if the Air Force phased out the F-105D, and the government did exactly that. "We didn't get the airplane," Greene said, "but they did agree to phase it out slower and throw subcontractor work in that kept the thing going for a while."

III

IT WAS JUST as well that Alicia got what she needed from John Kennedy in early 1962, because by the end of the year, *Newsday* had found two ways of alienating the Kennedy family.

The breach began when *Newsday* decided in the spring to cover Edward Moore Kennedy's campaign for the seat in the United States Senate that his brother had held until his election to the presidency. When John Kennedy had vacated the seat, his former college roommate, Benjamin Smith, had moved in. But everyone knew that was only temporary, until the time was ripe for Ted Kennedy to run. The time arrived in 1962, and Bob Greene was the logical choice to cover the race. Besides knowing the Kennedys through his work on the Senate rackets committee, Greene also knew, through his grandparents, the family of Kennedy's opponent at the state Democratic convention, Massachusetts Attorney General Edward J. McCormack Jr., the nephew of John McCormack, the Speaker of the House of Representatives. So Greene went to cover the primary, even though it was unusual in 1962 for a *Newsday* reporter to cover an out-of-state senatorial campaign.

At the convention in Springfield in early June, Greene talked to delegates who planned to vote reluctantly for Kennedy. "They felt that Eddie deserved it, but they were going to vote for Ted," Greene said. "The reason they were going to vote for Ted is because there had not been a postmaster appointed since Jack was elected, had not been a federal judge appointed since Jack was elected, and the whole point was that they weren't going to be, and if you want these in your districts, you've got to vote for Teddy." On the morning after Kennedy won the nomination on the convention floor, Greene wrote the main story and a sidebar that explained this patronage starvation program. Among others, Greene quoted Francis Roche, the Democratic chairman of Cambridge, the home of Greene's grandparents. "We were kept on the waiting list until Ted was old enough to run," Roche told Greene. "Then we were made to understand that if we went along with Ted, we'd get the jobs." The delegates liked McCormack, who had risen through the ranks. He had the support of the party's liberal wing, organized labor and, of course, his powerful uncle. But Ted Kennedy had the White House on his side, plus a compelling argument: He could do more for Massachusetts. So McCormack faced a difficult race in the primary.

As McCormack prepared for his first debate with Kennedy, Greene sat in on the strategy sessions of the McCormack camp. At one meeting, he remembered someone proposing the answer to the ticklish question of how to handle Ted Kennedy. "The whole point is that you've got to show that this is the runt of the litter," Greene said. "Ed McCormack was a brilliant guy and a hell of a good debater. The point was to get him into debates and destroy him in the debates." At the same time, Greene finally got to interview Ted Kennedy. "He says, 'I really don't want to answer any questions unless I have them in writing.'" But Greene did ask him one question, based on a tip that Kennedy had gotten another student to take an exam for him at Harvard. "He says, 'Absolutely not true. Nothing like that ever happened,'" Greene said. "Four days later, in the *Boston Globe*, appears a story." In that story, Kennedy admitted that he had run into a difficult foreign language course in his freshman year and had arranged for another freshman to take a test for him. When the school learned of this, a dean asked Kennedy and his friend to withdraw temporarily. They both later returned to Harvard, and Kennedy was graduated in 1956. This admission, after the denial to Greene, shaped Greene's view of Kennedy forever. "He lied to me, totally lied," Greene said. "At that moment, I think I had the measure of Ted Kennedy." Then Kennedy met McCormack in debate. Kennedy tried to talk about national and international issues, but McCormack moved the focus away from subjects that Kennedy was prepared to discuss, and hammered on Kennedy's inexperience. "If your name were only Edward Moore," McCormack said, "your candidacy — with your qualifications — would be a joke in this state." McCormack won a convincing victory in the debate, but it produced a sympathy reaction that actually helped Kennedy. "Women sat there and said, 'That poor boy,' " Greene remembered.

Newsday covered all this extensively, and Greene's stories caused enough of a stir to be cited on the television program *Meet the Press*. That national attention helped the paper, but it did nothing for Greene's relationship with Robert Kennedy. "Bobby says to me on the phone, 'Look, the kid is just a kid. He doesn't know any better. He'll learn. . . . You're supposed to be a friend of ours,' " Greene remembered. "I said, 'Bob, I'm covering the story.' He says, 'Look, either you're a friend of ours or you're shit.' I said, 'Hey, Bob, I gotta write what I see.' He says, 'Okay,' and he hangs up. That was it." Ted Kennedy went on to beat McCormack in the primary, but Robert Kennedy dropped Greene from his Christmas card list and no longer acknowledged Greene's existence. "Everything stopped," Greene said. "I kept sending Christmas cards, because even though he was mad at me, I wasn't mad at him."

Greene also played a role in another episode that infuriated the White House: a story written for *Newsday* by Alice-Leone Moats, a pal of Alicia's. "Moatsie," as her friends usually called her, was living in Rome, doing free-lance articles for magazines and newspapers, and she occasionally wrote pieces for Alicia. Most of them were inoffensive enough, such as a piece about the Rome wedding of Harry's jockey, Manuel Ycaza, to Miss Universe 1960, Linda Bement. But one of her stories, an account of Jacqueline Kennedy's trip to Rome with her daughter, Caroline, caused a furor. At first, Moats wrote an innocent, shallow little piece about Caroline. Then, she came up with a far more controversial story, the real reason for Jackie's trip. The first lady's once-divorced sister, the former Caroline Lee Bouvier, had married the twice-divorced Prince Stanislas Radziwill. They were both Catholic, but the church declined to recognize their marriage, which embarrassed the Kennedy family. So Jackie was trying to persuade the church to grant annulments of the previous marriages. In this effort, she used an emissary, who met with her on a yacht owned by a prominent Italian industrialist. Moats found out about the story when she spoke to sailors on the yacht.

The job of dealing with this delicate story, which had enormous potential to embarrass the White House, fell to Alan Hathway and to Greene, who worked with the raw quotes and other information that Moats had provided from Italy and made additional calls to fill in the holes. At the end of the process, Greene called Salinger at the White House. "Pierre said, 'I won't honor that question with a reply,' " Greene remembered. He also tried unsuccessfully to get comment from Robert Kennedy. At one point, the President himself requested that *Newsday* not publish the story, but the White House did not deny it was true.

When the time came to run the story, Alicia was in Colorado, just after she had sailed from Greece to Italy on Agnes Meyer's yacht with Adlai Stevenson and others, then had flown to Spain with him. So Hathway sent Alicia a "Dear Boss" telegram in Colorado, with the full text. "Plan this to go tomorrow with adequate biog and pix of Moats," Hathway said. "Have no qualms about this treatment." Alicia had no qualms either, and the story ran on page three, under the headline, "Bare Real Reason for Jackie Trip." This appeared only a week before Greene's coverage of Ed McCormack pounding on Ted Kennedy in their first debate. Together, these stories clearly eroded the good will that Alicia had built up with the Kennedy family.

Trying to placate the President, Alicia sent him a telegram of semi-apology. "Newsday relayed Pierre Salinger's message that you wished me to retract the Radziwill article of August twenty second," she said. "Unfortunately this was impossible as I had authorized its publication after five days of trying to reach someone in authority including the Attorney General and the Press Secretary. It is not Newsday's policy to broadcast gossip but our source was of unimpeachable reputation and lacking denial we felt we must go ahead. I am deeply sorry if the story has caused you inconvenience. As you must know Newsday and I are among your admirers."

The day that the story about Princess Lee Radziwill appeared, Moats remembered, Salinger started calling *Newsday* to complain bitterly, but Alicia stood by her. "She wrote to me and said, 'I'll never be invited to the White House again, but it's worth it,' " Moats remembered. "She stuck with me and she never was invited to the White House again."

CHAPTER TWENTY

The Fire Island Connection

I

ODDLY, ALTHOUGH ALAN Hathway spent his whole adult life in journalism, his closest friend was not a reporter or an editor, but a shrewd restaurateur who came to America illegally, spoke English with a thick accent, and tried to camouflage his business acumen by calling himself a "dumb Chinaman."

The two men spent many hours together at Arthur Lem's restaurant, the Chungking Royal, where Hathway drank an ocean of alcohol over the years. They played an interminable series of bizarre, almost cruel practical jokes on one another. They invested jointly in property on Fire Island, a financial interest that shaped *Newsday*'s coverage of the fashionable barrier beach. And together, they fought against an investigation that turned Lem from a model citizen into a federal prisoner.

Like many Chinese who were frustrated by the harsh, unjust exclusionary laws that America aimed at them, Lem came to this country cleverly, but without regard for the immigration quotas. He was born Chin Doong Art in 1914 in Kwangtung Province. His father had come to America to work on the construction of the transcontinental railroad, saving his earnings to support his family in China. Those earnings were not enough, and the family decided that Chin Doong Art would have to join his father in America, get a job and supplement the family income. Since his father was not a citizen, Chin Doong Art would never be able to get in legally. So his father paid $1,400 to a co-worker named Lem Tong Wing, who had citizenship papers. Lem provided a document attesting that he had a son in China named Lem Bow Quoon. Armed with that document, Chin Doong Art simply had to convince immigration inspectors that he really was Lem Bow Quoon. So, during his four-week ocean voyage from Hong Kong to Seattle, the newly minted Lem memorized a briefing book that contained all the details of his make-believe family. In Seattle, immigration authorities grilled him for three days, and he persuaded them that he was Lem Bow Quoon. Then he joined his father on the East Coast.

Working at a laundry in the Nassau County community of Floral Park, Lem met a Jewish boy named Arthur Levine and adopted his first name. The young Arthur Lem went to school by day and worked in the laundry at nights, until economic necessity forced him to drop out after the seventh grade and work full time. In the depths of the Great Depression, even the laundry business went bad. Lem went back briefly to China, then returned to America, working in laundry and restaurant jobs in New Jersey, and ended up in Hempstead, living over a Chinese restaurant called the Fulton Ideal and washing dishes for $5 a month. As he worked, Lem learned the rudiments of the business from the owner, who became restless and decided to move on, turning over the struggling restaurant to Lem. He renamed it Arthur's and spent most of the rest of the 1930s honing his skills as a restaurateur. Eventually, he acquired another trade, acting as an interpreter for government agencies, such as the Nassau County police, the Immigration and Naturalization Service and the Federal Bureau of Investigation. One of the services that he performed, during the mass roundup of Japanese Americans after Pearl Harbor, was to help government agents to distinguish between the Japanese and the Chinese. During the war, Lem and his wife, Rose, developed a new restaurant on Main Street in Hempstead and named it the Chungking Royal, after the city in China and a successful Brooklyn restaurant, the Fulton Royal. It was at the Chungking that Lem became friendly with Hathway.

The first crucial event in that friendship occurred in late 1945. During a *Newsday* crusade against police protection of gambling, Hathway was anxious to find and interview a recently retired Nassau County police captain who was friendly with Lem. When Hathway came to the Chungking and asked pointed questions, Lem excused himself to get a shoeshine, and instead telephoned the cop, who spent the next few weeks undercover at a farm provided by Lem. This irked Hathway. "He thought I was a bad guy at the beginning," Lem remembered. But Lem's loyalty to his friend impressed Hathway, who prized loyalty highly. "He said, 'You are a very faithful man, Lem.' "

Over the years that followed, Hathway and Lem grew closer and closer. Many days, Hathway would come to work at *Newsday* at ten in the morning, work until noon, adjourn to the Chungking Royal, or "the Chinaman's," as he called it, eat and drink his lunch at the large oval bar, return to the office at about two o'clock in the afternoon, stay there until a little after five o'clock, drop in at the Chungking for supper, then pop back to *Newsday* late in the evening. Besides spending thousands of hours together, Lem and Hathway did each other little favors. For example, as the president of the Upper Main Street Delegation, a merchants' group, Lem exhorted his colleagues to join in a *Newsday* promotion, Hempstead Sales Days, to generate extra pages of ads.

Lem became so identified with *Newsday* that, when Hathway went to the Republican National Convention in 1952 and 1956, Lem tagged along and Hathway listed him as part of the *Newsday* contingent.

It was a friendship of many layers and dimensions, full of ritual. Every Chinese New Year, most of the *Newsday* staff would show up for a sumptuous feast at the Chungking, and Hathway, dressed in formal Chinese garb, recited the ritual in Chinese, which touched Lem deeply. An equally important part of the friendship was the chain of painfully nasty practical jokes that they played on each other. In one prank, for example, Lem planted a pair of women's panties in Hathway's car. That was bound to annoy Hathway's wife, Evelyn, despite her reputation for saintly tolerance of his wildness. In retaliation, Hathway and some other friends acquired dozens of sets of keys, attached phony tags with the Chungking Royal's address and an offer of a reward to the finder, then scattered them all over. Soon, a parade of helpful citizens came to Lem with keys that he didn't even recognize, all expecting a reward. On another occasion, Lem had his employees fill up Hathway's car with garbage. When Lem tried to hurry Hathway into driving home, Hathway coolly bluffed him, saying that he hadn't brought his car that night. Lem quickly sent his employees out to clean the car, thinking it must be someone else's, and Hathway left and drove away in it. The parade of tricks was endless: a potato stuffed in Hathway's muffler, phony photographs of Lem in compromising positions with naked women, even a dead snake rigged by the photographer Cliff De Bear (egged on by Hathway) to jump out of Lem's car when he opened the door. For all the tricks, however, the two men were clearly devoted to one another. "Hathway and Arthur had the most close friendship of any two men I've ever seen," said the photographer Jim Nightingale. It may have been that friendship, Lem came to believe, that led him into the arms of the law.

By the end of the 1950s, Lem had a sterling public image. *Newsday*, which referred to him as perhaps the best known Chinese American on Long Island, had helped to create that image by running Lem's name and photograph frequently, in connection with his community activities. Outside Long Island, through his continuing work as an interpreter, Lem had cultivated an impressive array of relationships with government officials, all the way up to the FBI. Then, at the height of his influence, Lem and his wife suddenly found themselves under investigation for smuggling Chinese into the country illegally. At this moment of need, Hathway stood loyally with his friend. In fact, Hathway became almost frantic with anguish over Lem's plight. One of his first steps was to assign two of his most trusted reporters, Bob Greene and Jim O'Neill, to poke around and see what they could find out about the charges. "It was obviously to help Arthur," Greene said. "Arthur was our friend. If Hathway hadn't said go do it, we would have done it on our own time." So Greene and O'Neill went off to talk to people that Lem had identified as potential witnesses, to learn whether government investigators had offered them deals, threatened them or tried to shake them down. Eventually, Greene and O'Neill testified before the same federal grand jury that was investigating Lem, and a federal prosecutor threatened to indict Greene for obstructing justice. He came back and reported this to Hathway. "Alan said, 'Ah, he wouldn't dare. Keep going,' " Greene remembered.

One of the things that Greene learned was that Hathway and his friend, Leonard W. Hall, the chairman of the Republican National Committee, had helped Lem to get his mother into America as a refugee from China. The help was legal, but Greene felt some prosecutors might want to take advantage of it. "In effect," Greene said, "if you could nail Arthur Lem, you might be embarrassing the hell out of a lot of other people." At various times, Lem and his supporters also suggested that vendettas by the Communist Chinese or by enemies of Hathway had brought about the investigation. Whatever the reason for the government's initial interest, the grand jury indicted Lem and his wife, Rose, in 1959. The government argued that Lem brought Chinese into the country illegally for profit and used their cheap labor in his restaurant. Lem took the position that he was only doing what thousands of Chinese immigrants before him had done: helping others to evade the restrictive immigration laws. "You couldn't get in under the quota," Rose Lem said. "So everybody came as somebody's son."

Following the indictment, Hathway rushed to Lem's defense, even to the extent of recruiting lawyers. "He wanted Arthur out of this mess in the worst way," said Sidney Siben, one of the lawyers that Hathway consulted. "Alan went everywhere. I think it hurt Arthur. Alan went to too many people." One of Hathway's friends, the attorney Emil Cianciulli, who later represented Lem, said that Hathway's loyalty to his friend conflicted with the principles of his craft. "He strained the bounds of his journalistic integrity," Cianciulli said. "He personally injected himself into Arthur's case."

Hathway also hovered over the *Newsday* coverage of the case. At the beginning, when Jim Hadjin covered the trial, Hathway looked at his copy every night. "I anticipated that Alan would want this story written in a certain way, but he didn't," Hadjin said. "He didn't change the story at all." Then Francis Wood began covering the trial — a bit of an odd choice, since the soft-spoken Wood was accustomed to writing feature stories, rather than covering a high-profile trial. Hathway did not bring pressure on Wood to slant the story, but he did insist on seeing it every night. "He wanted to be the first to know what was going to be in the paper the next day," Wood said. Though Hathway did not slant the individual stories, his interest in the case did have an effect. "I think probably Hathway's influence on that trial was that we covered it more than we would have covered a trial had he not known Arthur Lem," said Tony Insolia, then at the start of his editing career. "It was over-coverage rather than steered coverage."

Throughout the trial, *Newsday* helped Lem in little ways. At one point, for example, *Newsday* photographers went to a cemetery to photograph the tombstone of one of Lem's relatives, to help prove a legal point. "We were willing," said Harvey Weber, the photo editor. "We all liked Arthur very much. I'm not even sure it was on company time." Hathway also helped to persuade govern-

ment officials to testify for Lem, and produced a group of *Newsday* employees
for moral support. "Alan had us all come down to his trial so, when the character
witnesses went on, there would be some people in the audience rooting for
Lem," Lou Schwartz said. "Arthur Lem had a lot of friends at *Newsday*."

The trial ended in a hung jury in June, 1960. Between that time and the
scheduled date of the second trial, Lem and Hathway looked at the legal costs
of the first trial and the expected costs of the second. "Alan and I decided, let's
make a deal," Lem said. That deal ended up as a plea of guilty to one count of
conspiracy, and Lem drew a sentence of 18 months. One of his regular visitors
while he was in federal prison was Hathway, his loyal friend.

II

DESPITE THE STRENGTH of their friendship, Hathway and Lem were polar oppo-
sites in many ways, including their approach to money. Hathway could no more
control his finances than he could regulate his temper, but Lem knew how to
make a dollar sing, dance and multiply.

Hathway didn't even *look* prosperous. His clothing was utilitarian at best,
and he wore one ratty brown jacket for years. His automobiles were usually
banged-up used cars, both because he lacked the resources to buy shiny new
ones and because he had trouble steering accurately under the influence. "I
make a small fortune and I don't have anything," he complained to one of his
secretaries, Carmen Hines. But he did have his friendship with Lem, who
rescued Hathway financially, long before Hathway helped Lem with his legal
problems. It was Lem who provided the business acumen and the investment
capital that enabled Hathway to become a real estate operator on Fire Island,
the fragile strip of barrier beach that protects the South Shore of Long Island
from the battering of the Atlantic Ocean. With Lem's help, Hathway acquired a
significant chunk of property there in 1955, before the public's interest in Fire
Island as a summer retreat had yet exploded.

Hathway first introduced Lem to the charms of Fire Island in the 1940s.
Over the years, as Hathway acquired a home on the ocean at Kismet, the island
assumed the same role in Hathway's life as Alicia's hunting lodge played in hers.
"It was dad's way of getting away," said his daughter, Patricia Barlow. "We're all
ocean people. We don't do well away from the sea." In the summer, Hathway
would go out to the island every weekend — sitting on the porch, wearing crazy
hats, swimming, hanging out, drinking. Every year, he'd invite the *Newsday* staff
over for a barbecue at his home. And in the winter, Hathway and a small group
of loyalists, including Lem and Jack Altshul, among others, would head for his
home on the nearly deserted island to perform the annual rituals of the Kismet
Beach Hunt Club. The alleged purpose for the gathering was to hunt ducks, but
the real agenda was nonstop drinking and night-long games of poker. "The only

thing that didn't go on was sleep," said Jack Rettaliata, one of Hathway's regulars.

Eventually, more than 15 years after Hathway first started going regularly to Fire Island, he took the long step from vacationer to entrepreneur — along with Lem and others. That transformation originated with his friend Dick Greenamyer, who had learned to love Fire Island through his friendship with Hathway and had bought a bar there called the Kismet Inn. Hathway helped to launch Greenamyer's new venture by producing a boatload of *Newsday* people to patronize the grand opening. At the request of Hathway, Lem used his contacts in the state government to expedite Greenamyer's liquor license, just in time for the invasion of the thirsty *Newsday* hordes. And Lem taught Greenamyer's wife, Ruth, how to cook. Later, it was Greenamyer who found out that Lillian Cragen, the widow of a New York City judge, had a 17-acre piece of property for sale in Kismet. It was a long, narrow, rectangular piece of land, a little more than 400 feet wide, that ran from the Atlantic Ocean on the south to the Great South Bay on the north. The property lay just east of the Fire Island lighthouse and just west of Kismet Park, a development where Hathway had earlier bought land for his home near the ocean. Greenamyer thought the property was interesting, but he didn't have enough money to take advantage of it. So he told Hathway about the land, and Hathway went to Lem. "He says, 'There's a parcel of land for sale,' " Lem remembered. " 'Can you put up $25,000?' So, with my signature, I got $25,000."

They incorporated themselves as Lighthouse Shores, which at the start included Hathway, Lem and a builder named George Helm, and they bought the land for about $25,000. They had two basic plans for it: small building lots for summer cottages and a boatel on the Great South Bay. In April, 1955, their attorney stood up at a hearing by the Islip Town Board and explained their rezoning application. Most of the land that they were buying was already zoned for summer cottages, but they wanted changes of zoning on two pieces of the property, near the Great South Bay. On one parcel, they wanted the town to adopt a less restrictive residential zoning, so that they could build ten units of "beach apartments," the boatel. On the other, they wanted the residential zoning changed to business, for a use to be determined later. At the hearing, the town clerk counted twelve residents in favor of the plan and nine opposed.

Those who thought it was a terrific idea included Dick Greenamyer, who was not part of the Lighthouse Shores corporation but had become an officer in Lighthouse Boatels, the company that they created to run the boatel. Greenamyer's Kismet Inn was just east of the area of the planned boatel, and he obviously had a chance to derive some additional business from the influx of guests at the boatel. (To Greenamyer's dismay, the Lighthouse Shores partners decided years later to use part of their land to build a restaurant-bar that became a direct competitor of the Kismet Inn.) Those who spoke out against the rezoning included G. Frank Dougherty, the counsel to Robert Moses at the Long Island State Park Commission. State-owned parkland lay just west of the property, and Dougherty didn't want the park surrounded by unsightly commercial buildings. The opponents also included several prestigious residents of the area, such as Thomas F. Murphy, a federal judge, and Max E. Greenberg, a wealthy lawyer.

Despite the opposition, the town granted the rezoning only a week later. Did Hathway use his *Newsday* clout to get the rezoning over the objection of his neighbors? "I don't think so, except that he knew all the members of the town board," said John P. Cohalan Jr., who was the town attorney at the time. "But the boatel was something he was entitled to, I think. I think it was in the proper zone, and after all, you do need accommodations over on the island. . . . It was kosher. It was legal." A week after the rezoning, the purchase from Mrs. Cragen became final.

But the opposition to the project didn't end with the rezoning. Judge Murphy, Greenberg and others filed a lawsuit against the town. Whether or not Hathway used the power of the newspaper in the struggle for the rezoning, he clearly used the same kind of swashbuckling, questionable tactics for his own profit that he had brought to bear on a variety of *Newsday* campaigns. He even used racial politics, bragging about this technique to his friend, Paul Townsend. "He put an ad in a Harlem newspaper, and some black people came over to look at the property," Townsend said. "Can you imagine the son of a bitch stooping to that? But he did. If he didn't get the boatel, they were going to sell it to Harlem residents, to blacks. . . . I guess he was trying to set up the dreadful alternative." In the same spirit, Hathway sought the help of Bob Greene, who was then in his last few months on the staff of the New York City Anti-Crime Committee. "He tried to get me to write a letter to Tom Murphy, the federal judge, from the crime committee, saying that we might be coming out there to investigate race discrimination in Kismet," Greene remembered. "He said, 'You gotta do this, you gotta do this.' " Greene dodged Hathway's request.

Just as he saw nothing wrong in using racial fears to help beat back opponents of his investment, Hathway did not acknowledge any conflict between his financial interest in the development of Fire Island and *Newsday*'s interest in covering that subject objectively. *Newsday* reporters and editors came to understand that, where Fire Island was concerned, Hathway's appetite for stories was bottomless. "Anytime Fire Island came up, Hathway leaped into the picture," said Stan Green, who became the paper's copy chief after Bill McIlwain became city editor in 1960. "He was always asking for the story that you shouldn't write about Fire Island," said Mel Opotowsky, an editor who had to deal with Hathway's Fire Island requests later in the 1960s. "That made me feel a little uneasy."

Sometimes, Hathway's compulsion to cover Fire Island resulted in nothing more than a harmless story. One day in 1954 at the Chungking Royal, for example, Hathway was sitting at lunch, worrying about what Hurricane Edna was going to do to his house in Kismet. As Hathway talked, Dick Aurelio, then still a reporter, made a tactical error. "I just happened to say that, gee, the place to watch this hurricane would be at the lighthouse in Fire Island," Aurelio remembered. "He said, 'That's a good idea.' " Before Aurelio could catch his breath, Hathway had commissioned a boat to take Aurelio to Fire Island, while everyone else was heading the other way, evacuating. Aurelio's orders were to watch the storm from the lighthouse and keep an eye on Hathway's home, a few hundred feet away. Even though the hurricane fizzled, Aurelio played out his role as a combination reporter and security guard: "I had to give him these hourly reports on the hurricane and what was happening on Fire Island, and particularly what was happening to his house."

There were also, of course, legitimate and important stories to be done about the fragile barrier beach. Through the mid-1950s, the biggest continuing story was the controversy over how best to stabilize Fire Island Inlet — the narrow opening at the western tip of Fire Island that allowed boats to travel between the ocean and the bay. The problem was that the natural drift of sand kept making the tip of Fire Island crawl farther west, threatening to close the inlet. The controversy was essentially between Robert Moses, who proposed to use the Army Corps of Engineers to dredge out and stabilize the existing inlet, and Representative Stuyvesant Wainwright, who raised the possibility of creating a new inlet. At one point, *Newsday* offered Wainwright and Moses each a full page to express his views. Wainwright submitted his, but Moses replied imperiously: "I have heard of no controversy. . . ." So *Newsday* ran Wainwright's views on one page and on the opposite page ran only a small photo of Moses, with his one-sentence dismissal. The rest of the page was blank. Another significant Fire Island story in the 1950s was Wainwright's proposal that the federal government buy a large chunk of eastern Fire Island and turn it into a national seashore. Moses opposed this idea, and before Wainwright could get his plan moving, he lost the 1960 election to Otis Pike.

Those were legitimate enough stories, and *Newsday* covered them appropriately. But in 1962 an act of God, followed by an act of Moses, created a situation in which *Newsday* ended up on the wrong side of an issue of great significance to Fire Island's future, raising major questions about whether Hathway's business interest had overshadowed his ethics.

III

IN THE FIRST week of March, 1962, a winter storm slammed into the South Shore of Long Island, chewing up the dunes on the barrier beach, gouging out new inlets between the ocean and the bay, and sweeping dozens of houses into the Atlantic, including Hathway's home at Kismet.

This was a real emergency that any newspaper would have grabbed lustily, and *Newsday* was no exception. In the days after the storm, the coverage included all the expected elements — estimates of the total damage ($10 million), urgent appeals by Governor Nelson Rockefeller for federal anti-erosion funds, disaster declarations by Rockefeller and President Kennedy, and plans to provide flood insurance for the future. Beyond simply outlining the federal aid that storm victims could get, *Newsday* even went so far as to set up a meeting in Bay Shore at which government officials were to explain how homeowners could cope with their storm losses. Any public-spirited newspaper might have done the same thing, but few managing editors would have thrown themselves into it with Hathway's enthusiasm.

"He was just brazen in the way he manipulated things for the benefit of Fire Islanders," said Tom Morris, who had written extensively about the inlet controversy when he was still a reporter. By the time of the 1962 storm, Morris was an editor, but that didn't stop Hathway from drafting him as a reporter, to cover such events as a Hathway-arranged VIP trip to Fire Island, for public officials to assess the damage. Later, Morris also covered the meeting in Bay Shore that Hathway had set up. "He was absolutely drunk as a skunk on the stage," Morris said. "He was grunting and making strange noises. He made introductory remarks, and he had people there from the insurance industry, the Army Corps of Engineers, the Coast Guard. One of the things foremost on his mind was how they could expedite insurance payoffs for people who had lost their property, which was himself. . . . As an editor, it would have been understandable that he would have wanted that kind of a meeting covered, under any circumstances. But he set the meeting up, he made telephone calls, he gave directions as to what was to be done. In other words, he was acting in his own self-interest."

But Hathway's advocacy for disaster relief was only a minor conflict of interest, compared to the way he influenced the paper's position on the most far-reaching proposal for dealing with future erosion — a plan advanced by Robert Moses. The grand dream of the master planner was an oceanfront road all the way from Staten Island, the southernmost point in New York City, to Montauk Point, the eastern tip of Long Island. The Great Depression, the hurricane of 1938 and World War II had effectively killed any chance for building the portion of the road that would have run the length of Fire Island. But by 1962, Moses had already built the Ocean Parkway, running along the dunes from Jones Beach to Captree State Park, on the long section of barrier beach that lay west of Fire Island. He had also completed the causeway leading from Long Island itself down to Captree, and he had proposed the construction of a bridge from Captree across Fire Island Inlet to Fire Island. When Moses first proposed the inlet bridge in 1956, Wainwright and other opponents had seen the bridge as a sure sign that the next step would be a road on Fire Island. The idea that he was pushing a road was "utter nonsense," Moses responded.

Less than six years later, when the storm hit Fire Island, Moses quickly took advantage of the disaster to announce the perfect way to control erosion in the future: an eighteen-foot man-made sand dune that would run the length of the island, with a highway on top. Moses made his announcement in an op-ed piece in the *Long Island Press*, but that didn't stop *Newsday* from falling in line immediately. On the same day that *Newsday* ran the story of the plan, an editorial called "Saving Fire Island" made it clear that *Newsday* loved this "new, progressive proposal that deserves to be accepted enthusiastically and carried out as rapidly as possible."

Not surprisingly, some people with homes on Fire Island expressed alarm over the prospect of a major highway right down the middle of an isolated, environmentally fragile community that had always depended entirely on ferries for its connection to the outside world. One group that jumped into the issue immediately was the Fire Island Voters Association, which had come together in the mid-1950s to fight an earlier, less ambitious proposal by a local group for a road on Fire Island. The association, which soon changed its name to the Fire Island Association, to broaden its appeal beyond voters on the island, had some high-powered members, including the CBS commentator Charles Collingwood, the journalist-historian Theodore White and George Biderman, who had his own public relations firm in Manhattan. Despite the clout of the association's membership, Biderman soon learned that it wasn't going to be easy to combat Moses, *Newsday* and the *Press*.

One of the first skirmishes centered on a fact-finding trip to Fire Island by Interior Secretary Stewart Udall. "Moses heard that I was making the trip," Udall remembered. "He, in effect, offered that he would host and he would show me. I was a little naive and I didn't realize that I was walking into the trap of this incredibly resourceful, powerful figure." When Biderman learned that Moses was going to be leading Udall around by helicopter, he wanted to make sure that the conservationist viewpoint was represented as well. "Collingwood and White and I and a couple of other people were going to meet him and counter Moses on the spot," Biderman said. He tried to reach Udall, but he had already left Washington. An aide to Udall told Biderman to try Jack English, the Nassau County Democratic leader, who had strong influence in the White House. Biderman just missed English, too. "His wife said he'd just left to pick up Alan Hathway," Biderman said. So Biderman and his allies didn't get to fly in the chopper with Udall, but Hathway apparently was able to put in his views.

During their conversations, Moses pointedly reminded Udall that Wainwright had opposed Moses by proposing a national seashore, and he was no longer in Congress. "He sort of shocked me by taking credit for defeating Wainwright," said Udall, who had been friendly with Wainwright in Congress. "What he was trying to do with me was to paint a picture and to say, 'Look, you're a nice young man and you mean well, but this is my bailiwick, and I've been working here for thirty or forty years. . . .' I was, in effect, butting into his program that had been underway for a long time, and why didn't I just be a nice young man and go on back to Washington." At the joint press conference afterward, Udall acknowledged that Moses did not think Fire Island was the place for a national seashore. "I just left it this way: I said, 'Well, if that's what the people up here believe and what they want is Mr. Moses' plan, why of course, we have other things to do.' " Privately, Udall had concluded otherwise. "I left with the feeling that his freeway down Fire Island would be a disastrous mistake and that it should be a national seashore."

Despite Udall's feelings, Moses appeared well on his way to getting the road. The job of analyzing Fire Island's needs had gone to a new Temporary State Commission on Protection and Preservation of the Atlantic Shorefront. The chairman was Assembly Speaker Joseph Carlino, a Long Beach Republican, but the real power was Moses himself. "I was very close to Bob Moses and he dreamed up this commission," Carlino said. "He said, 'I'd like you to be the chair.' " The Fire Island Voters Association tried to discredit Carlino by alleging that he owned property on the island. Carlino showed that he had already sold the property, below market value, to avoid any conflict. Shortly after that minor controversy, the commission held a hearing before about 1,000 people at Jones Beach.

The morning of the hearing, *Newsday* published a four-page supplement, detailing its reasons for supporting the road. At the hearing, Collingwood made some news for the opponents by quoting from a statement made almost a quarter of a century earlier, when Moses was first pushing the road, that "he would save Fire Island the way Hitler is saving the Sudetenland." The next day, *Newsday* leapt to the defense of Moses, calling Collingwood's statement a "vicious smear on Robert Moses, one of our greatest public servants." Before long, the commission members — including the county executives of both Nassau and Suffolk — recommended that Moses get his road. "They all thought it was the right thing to do," Carlino said. "In retrospect, I think it was a mistake. . . . I was reared and guided by Moses, who was the expert on all that stuff."

It was on the day of the commission's hearing that Hathway's business interests became part of the controversy. The *Newsday* supplement included an extraordinary story under the headline, "Managing Editor's Fire Isle Position." It was an excerpt from a story that the *New York Herald Tribune* had carried the day before, outlining the whole issue and repeating allegations by the road's opponents that Hathway could make a lot of money if the road went through. "For example, they charge, Alan Hathway, managing editor of *Newsday* and a leading road advocate, stands to make a killing on his land at the west end of the island," the *Tribune* story said, and then it gave Hathway a chance to respond: "Any suggestion that I'll reap huge profits is ridiculous." For the *Newsday* story, Hathway added: "My interest in Fire Island is, and always has been, as an individual. In no way whatsoever has it ever had any connection with my duties as managing editor of Newsday."

Hathway may have had a partially public-spirited motivation for his position: allowing greater public access to the barrier beach. But the road would also have helped his Lighthouse Shores enterprise, where building lots had not sold well. "Nobody would buy those lots in those days, because you couldn't get there," Rose Lem said. "The ferry wouldn't even go there. If you wanted to go to Kismet, you had to go to Saltaire and then walk over." Similarly, they weren't making much money on the boatel units. "The motel business was lousy," Rose Lem said. "For $800 a season we couldn't rent it." So the Moses proposal could have been beneficial. "The road would help a lot," Arthur Lem said.

From the start, the road's opponents saw Hathway as an enemy. "Our assumption of Hathway's influence was based really on day-to-day coverage, more than editorials," Biderman said. The editorials supported the road, but that could have been because *Newsday* routinely sided with Moses, rather than because Hathway influenced the editorials. "I heard him expound on his reasons for it," said Bill Woestendiek, who ran the editorial page. "He never directly influenced the editorial product at all, unless he did it through Alicia." Whatever Hathway's effect on the actual coverage was, his conflict of interest was a problem. "As I remember," Woestendiek said, "several of us were embarrassed because Hathway's role in the whole thing was not objective." By then, Alicia and Woestendiek had already disagreed more than once over Hathway's behavior in a variety of areas. "I argued that with her constantly," Woestendiek said. "I said, 'You know, you asked me to take this job to improve the image, and you let this guy keep destroying the image,' or words to that effect."

In the case of the Moses road, *Newsday* fell short of the skeptical, question-authority attitude that Hathway himself had done so much to build. While Hathway's paper swallowed the Moses plan whole, a small weekly, the *Babylon Town Leader*, sniped at the proposal from the start and in 1963 began to do the kind of investigative reporting that had made *Newsday* famous. As far back as the 1930s, Judge James Cooper, the *Leader*'s publisher, had clashed with Moses, who had a home in Babylon. Now that Moses had revived his plan for a road on Fire Island, the *Leader* began to examine the merits of a key argument by the road's supporters: Moses had already built the Ocean Parkway between Jones Beach and Captree State Park, and it had worked. "The same type of construction, applied to 17 miles of Jones Beach, has saved it from all but the most minor damage over the past 34 years," said the initial *Newsday* editorial on the road, the day after Moses proposed it. While *Newsday* unquestioningly accepted that argument, the *Leader* began to ask questions.

"We knew that the existing road leading to Jones Beach from Captree was in constant danger of being washed out, so that rather than the road anchoring the beach, they were constantly shoring up the beach to protect the road," said John Maher, who was the managing editor of the *Leader* at the time, and later worked for the *Long Island Press* and *Newsday*. "To establish that, we took Moses to court." The *Leader*, the *Suffolk County News* in Sayville and the *Long Island Commercial Review*, run by Hathway's friend Paul Townsend, joined in the lawsuit, seeking to pry loose the records of maintenance on the Ocean Parkway. In addition, Maher and Karl Grossman, who came to the *Leader* just after the road proposal and covered the controversy for Maher, did some *Newsday*-style snooping. "We were told by an informant in the park commission, John Maher and I, that a lot of this work was done at night, so people wouldn't know it was happening," Grossman said. "And John and I went out with flashlights one night on that Jones Beach stretch, looking for the bulldozers to work. We never found that." Ultimately, the Long Island State Park Commission surrendered the records, and the three small papers ran the story. "It showed that over the past several years, they had been doing an immense amount of expensive dredging to shore up the beach, with the intent to save the road," said Maher, whose story said that the cost had exceeded $4 million over five years. "So it seemed to us a fairly conclusive argument against the proposed road being necessary to save the beach." As the *Leader* went after the story tenaciously, *Newsday* reported the lawsuit briefly, but still supported the road. "In the face of what was a real, true conservationist effort, there was *Newsday* parroting the arguments of Moses," Grossman said. "I don't think it was venal here. I think all it was, was that *Newsday* succumbed — the top editors — to being manipulated by Moses."

Beyond its normal journalistic role, the *Leader* supported the establishment of the second major citizens group aimed at fighting the road, the Citizens Committee for a Fire Island National Seashore, which listed John Maher among its founders. The others who joined in the discussions leading to the establishment of the group included Murray Barbash, a builder who had first become interested in Fire Island when he financed a small development in Fair Harbor called Dunewood, his brother-in-law, an attorney named Irving Like, and Like's law partner, Bernard J. Reilly. Early in its existence, the group made two strategic decisions: First, they couldn't fight something with nothing. If they were to beat back the road plan, they had to have an alternative, and the one that made the most sense was the creation of a national seashore. Second, the opposition to the road would not be successful as long as people perceived it as nothing more than a coterie of rich Fire Islanders trying to protect their homes. The Fire Island Association — with Biderman, Collingwood and Teddy White — had an image as a group of summer residents whose livelihood and primary interests were in New York City. The new committee sought members who were prominent Long Islanders, with an interest in the issue but without obvious ties to Fire Island.

Even though the citizens committee and the Fire Island Association had different approaches to opposing the road, the association did allow the committee to use the services of Paul Townsend, the publicist they had hired to provide them with Long Island expertise. One of Townsend's publicity devices was to line up a DC-3 aircraft to fly members of the citizens committee to Washington to meet with federal officials about a national seashore, then fly over Cape Hatteras National Seashore. But they didn't get much encouragement from Representative Otis Pike, who met with them and explained that the land available at Fire Island was too small for a national seashore. The headline on the story was "Backers of Fire Island Park/Get Little Comfort from U.S." So the trip was a bust. "It was going to be a pro-national seashore story," Townsend said. "It came out in *Newsday* an absolute negative."

Soon it became obvious to the anti-road forces that something had to be done about muzzling Hathway and turning *Newsday* around. The strategy, Biderman said, came from Townsend. "He said, 'I'm sure Alicia doesn't know what's going on, and if she did, she would be deeply offended. So somebody ought to let her know,' " Biderman remembered. Subsequently, Barbash met with Alicia in early 1963, when prospects for the Moses road were beginning to dim: First, at the end of 1962, Governor Rockefeller had clashed with Moses and maneuvered him into resigning as chairman of the state Council of Parks, in favor of his brother, Laurance Rockefeller. In anger, Moses had also resigned as chairman of the Long Island State Parks Commission and the state Power Authority. (Alicia called Rockefeller to intervene for Moses, Hal Burton said, but Rockefeller told her it was too late.) Then, in early 1963, the governor put the project on hold because of a lack of state funds. "If the Ocean Parkway is merely delayed and not abandoned, we of Long Island can accept his action without demur," a *Newsday* editorial said.

It was in that atmosphere that Barbash met with Alicia, in the presence of Hathway. "My recollection is that Alan was tremendously hostile," Barbash said. "If looks could have killed, he would have killed me on the spot." But Barbash got along well with Alicia and sensed that he was making progress. "I liked her very much, because she was a very outspoken lady," Barbash said. "She came right to the point — no wasted time, no pleasantries." Once he had presented his arguments for a national seashore, Alicia asked him a practical question: If she were to support the seashore, how could she be sure that the Department of Interior favored the idea? So Barbash hurdled the bureaucratic barriers and brokered a meeting in Washington between Alicia and Udall.

In the dining room of the Department of Interior, Alicia had lunch with Udall and one of his top aides, Walter Pozen, an ally of the national seashore forces. Pozen, then a young lawyer of 29, was convinced that the Moses road was a dreadful idea. "It was absolutely absurd," Pozen said. So he had taken an advocacy role within the department for the seashore, and when Alicia showed up in Washington, Pozen made a case to her for the national seashore. "She said, 'You know, young man, I think you convinced me,' " Pozen remembered. "I found her to be charming, direct and a very good listener." The meeting with Udall apparently reassured Alicia. Gradually, *Newsday* more and more actively embraced the idea of a national seashore and recognized that the road was dead. The seeds of this change of heart had been there from the start. In an editorial a month after Moses proposed the road, *Newsday* had argued that a national seashore on the eastern end of Fire Island could coexist with a Moses road. "We welcome a National Seashore," the editorial said. "We also know that nothing can interfere with the ocean parkway if Fire Island is not eventually to be washed to sea." Once the road proposal had begun to lose momentum and the seashore proponents had made their case to Alicia, the paper belatedly came around to full support of the seashore — even criticizing Pike in an editorial for not taking a position of leadership on the seashore issue. It was *Newsday*'s final decision to support the idea, Barbash suspected, that led to Pike's introduction of the bill. "*Newsday*, sensing that we were at a stalemate here and nothing was going to get done, took the best doable option, and when it did, boom, that was the end of the whole thing," Barbash said. "We got it. So *Newsday* was incredibly important in that respect. I'm sorry it took so long."

Later, after the Fire Island National Seashore had finally become law in September, 1964, Barbash wrote a letter to the editor, describing Alicia's role. "Her decision that the Seashore was in the best interests of Long Island and

Newsday's strong backing of the proposal were crucial factors in its success," Barbash wrote. This defeat irked Moses for years. When Robert Caro interviewed him at his house on Oak Beach, Moses would grab Caro forcefully by the arm, point across the water to Fire Island and insist: " 'You can see, there should have been a road there.' "

So, in the long run, *Newsday* ended up on the winning side in the creation of a new national seashore, and its reputation did not suffer from the position it had taken initially, in favor of a road that horrified environmentalists. "For some reason," Hal Burton said, "we escaped scot-free." Hathway, of course, was not pleased that Barbash and his allies, including Paul Townsend, had helped turn Alicia around. "And he never forgave me," Townsend said. But there was an ironic footnote to Hathway's unsuccessful efforts in behalf of the Moses road and his opposition to the creation of a national seashore. "His property doubled in value," Townsend said. "Right in front of him, the national seashore bought up that private property between him and the lighthouse, which meant that he sat out there . . . looking out over this beautiful virgin territory that no one could build on."

CHAPTER TWENTY-ONE

Alicia's Choice

I

NEARLY A QUARTER of a century after Harry and Alicia had founded the paper, *Newsday* had grown impressively. But one thing had not changed at all: Harry and Alicia still disagreed sharply on external and internal politics.

Even in the routine transaction of reviewing a new promotional film in 1961, Harry found reason to be unhappy. In a letter to David George, the promotion manager, he complained that the script for the film didn't accurately portray *Newsday*'s business operations. The same day, Harry sent Alicia a testy memo, complaining about the film, about her unenthusiastic handling of a column that he had written about Cuba, about a "mess" in the composing room that he had been forced to straighten out, and about "the never-ending compulsion that you seem to have of distorting, or hiding from the public, my relations and contributions to Newsday." Alicia's response was no warmer than his complaint. "Let me suggest that as President of Newsday you take over my part in the production," she wrote. "I really don't want to be in it anyhow. I do feel, however, that since this is a movie to be shown to school children and community groups the business side of the paper should not be overstressed. The mechanical, editorial and circulation departments have more glamor for the average viewer."

It was the editorial side of the newspaper that had always been the subject of complimentary stories in magazines. It was the paper's content, and not any business decision of Harry's, that caused Alicia's friend Carl Sandburg to write to her in 1961: "I have too long put off sending you a message about Newsday. As a newspaper, it is beautifully affirmative about life. It is sweet, keen, strong and quiveringly alive. It is in terrific contrast to the Los Angeles Times." What was left to Harry was the thankless job of planning *Newsday*'s future as a business. In 1961, for example, he entertained the possibility of buying a Long Island radio station, and in 1963, he considered acquiring timberlands, to reduce newsprint costs. Many of these financial issues were not important to Alicia, but when she did venture into Harry's area, suggesting that *Newsday* get into the syndication business, Harry rejected her.

"Alicia had the idea that she would like to have a news service, a syndicate," said the book publisher Roger Straus, Harry's nephew, who was also friendly with Alicia. At the time, Straus had connections with the family of William Maxwell Aitken, Lord Beaverbrook, the British newspaper proprietor, whose news service was for sale. The North American Newspaper Alliance, a domestic syndicate, was also available. "The idea was to pull them both together," Straus said. "She was going to buy the Beaverbrook thing, buy North American Newspaper Alliance and have a truly international newspaper syndication." Once he and Alicia had discussed the deal, Straus put together a dinner in a private dining room at the exclusive French restaurant, Lutece, where Alicia met with one of Beaverbrook's sons. Harry was not present. The dinner went well, but afterward, Alicia found out that it had all been for nothing. "The point was that this was all set, and then at the eleventh hour, Harry said, 'You can't do it,' " Straus said. "She was very upset, very annoyed."

Despite their disagreements over finances and the editorial page, Harry had at least decided that he would leave to Alicia in his will the two percent of *Newsday* stock that she needed in order to exercise majority control of the paper. His only condition was that they adopt a "cumulative voting" arrangement on the board of directors. Without that, the majority on the board would be able to elect *all* the directors, completely excluding the minority. If Harry was to bequeath majority control to Alicia and make his own heirs minority owners, he wanted to make sure that they would at least sit on the *Newsday* board. With cumulative voting, they would be guaranteed to have representation, and Alicia did not object. For years, Alicia had tried to persuade Harry to sell her the two percent. He had not been willing to do it in his lifetime, and his refusal had caused constant friction between them, but his will now provided that she would get the total control after his death, if Harry died before she did. And that event, Harry told Alicia in a letter outlining cumulative voting, "seems entirely likely."

II

Desperately anxious to please her father by proving that she could be as tough as a boy, and driven by a fiercely competitive spirit, Alicia somehow managed to wring an active, athletic life from a body that frequently betrayed her.

Throughout her adulthood, she had to contend with health problems that ranged from annoying to alarming, including an abscess on her ovaries, menstrual dysfunction that her doctors treated by inserting radium into her body, surgery for an ulcer, and colon cancer, which required a complete hysterectomy and the use of a colostomy. Beyond the damage caused by these acute illnesses, Alicia's body suffered from the chronic effects of her lifestyle. She did not have a severe drinking problem, as her father had, but she did drink too much. And she smoked incessantly. "She was a sick woman in some respects, and she didn't take good care of herself," said her friend, George Abbott. "She was reckless."

In the late spring and the early summer of 1963, her life was going along as it always had, but those who were close to her had begun to notice small signs that she wasn't feeling well. Walter Merck, the caretaker at her hunting lodge in Georgia, remembered that she suffered a brief dizzy spell when she was with him that year. Alicia spent about ten days at the lodge in May, which was unusual for her, since the Georgia weather can be brutally hot and muggy in May. During that stay, her secretary, Dot Holdsworth, noticed that Alicia was much less active than she customarily was. In the spring, Alicia also travelled west — to serve as the godmother for John Fell Stevenson Jr., Adlai's grandson, and to collect an honorary doctorate at Lake Forest College. When Alicia returned to Long Island from her travels, she still wasn't feeling quite right. "She wasn't in the office very much from then on," Holdsworth said. "She would call and say that she didn't feel well."

At about this time, Hal Burton had lunch with Alicia at Nino's, one of her favorite haunts. "Ordinarily, it was a lot of fun to go to lunch with her," Burton said. "This time, I did my best to make her laugh. She was very, very serious indeed." She did continue to make plans — includi   scheduled trip to Italy with her old friend Stan Peckham, where they would stay at a villa that John Cranford Adams, the president of Hofstra University, had rented. But before she could go on the trip, her health got in the way. "I kept beating on her to have the doctor come in," Holdsworth said. Finally, Alicia began feeling dizzy, faint and nauseous. She saw signs of blood in her stool and then vomited blood. So she called a doctor. "He came in, and she went into the bathroom," Holdsworth said. "He followed her into the bathroom, and he saw the blood, and he said, 'You've got to get to the hospital.'"

That same afternoon, June 20, Holdsworth and Alicia got into her car and Noel Dean, her chauffeur, drove them to Doctors Hospital in Manhattan. On the way in, Alicia draped herself weakly across the back seat, but she did manage to carry on a conversation. She even thought to remind Holdsworth to get a copy of a book on the Irish famine that she had promised to Dean. By the time she got to the hospital, she was in shock from the loss of blood. "She was really bled down almost a third," said Dr. Jere W. Lord Jr., the surgeon who attended her. They gave her three units of blood, which brought her blood pressure and pulse back to normal. "She responded to conservative therapy and stopped bleeding," Lord said. Then they administered the standard continuing treatment for ulcers — feeding her intravenously, with no food by mouth.

Once the transfusions and the intravenous feeding had stabilized Alicia's condition, she had a regular stream of visitors. Holdsworth stayed with Alicia in her tenth-floor room all day, reading mystery novels to her and keeping her company. "She loved to be read to," Holdsworth said. Her other *Newsday* visitors included Alan Hathway, who found that Alicia still had her sense of humor, despite the constant flow of blood transfusions. As she improved, the doctors allowed her to sip some sherry, and she even began to think about sports. Just after a series of transfusions, she wrote an optimistic note to her neighbor, tennis partner and architect, Albert Wood, who had sent her some pink carnations. "Two weeks from now I should be just as good as ever — even good enough to take you on at tennis, Albert," she wrote. She wasn't always that optimistic. "She must have been hurting a lot, because she was really on edge," said her niece, Alice Albright Hoge, who visited her several times and played cards. But on the whole, Alicia acted as if she felt that she was going to recover.

As the doctors explained it to her, Alicia had two choices: She could alter her way of life or she could have surgery. "I did not exactly advise changing her lifestyle, but observing a diet, getting more rest and so forth," said Dr. William B. Rawls, her family physician, who had been away at a medical convention when Alicia became ill, but returned quickly to New York. "She did not want to do that, but she wanted to have the operation, so that she could get back to a normal life." One of her staff, John Van Doorn, remembered that Alicia explained her choice colorfully: " 'Darling, they told me it's either this operation or mashed potatoes and skim milk for the rest of my life.' " Her choice of the operation, over the less dangerous alternative of changing her diet, was typical of Alicia. "She was the sort of person who didn't care much about risks," said her nephew, Joe Albright. "She took this gamble. At the time, I don't think any of the executives, and certainly not I, were conscious of it as being a huge gamble." Once she had decided on surgery, she seemed comfortable with it. "She wasn't at all apprehensive about it," said her sister, Josephine. "I didn't try to stop it. I felt the doctors knew what they were doing."

There was no reason why Alicia should doubt the competence of her doctors. Rawls had been treating Harry and Alicia for years, and Rawls felt that Lord, the surgeon, had an excellent reputation. Lord also had a high profile. In 1958, as chief of cardiovascular surgery at New York University Bellevue Medical Center and president of the New York Heart Association, Lord had performed a heart operation on live local television, to educate the general public about heart surgery — one of the first such televised operations in the nation. Lord was the perfect doctor for television — tall, handsome, self-assured, with the long, thin fingers of a surgeon or a pianist. More to the point, he was thoroughly familiar with the operation that he was about to perform on Alicia, a gastric resection — the removal of sixty to seventy percent of the stomach, to treat ulcers. "I did about fifty gastric resections as a resident and helped on about one hundred and fifty, from intern up," Lord said. Later, he went into practice with Dr. J. William Hinton, who became chairman of the deparment of surgery at New York University Postgraduate Medical School. "I assisted him for two years, while I was beginning my own private practice. He had a huge gastrointestinal surgical clientele. I probably helped him on two hundred cases over the two-year period." The operation was a serious one, but it was seldom fatal. "If a person asked me whether, 'Can you die, doctor,' you'd say yes, but two or three percent was a mortality figure on elective operations at that time," Lord said. And a successful resection usually left patients with normal lives. "Most people end up eating three squares a day."

Early in the morning of July 1, Lord made an incision in Alicia's abdomen and began to operate. He found, as her medical history had suggested, that another surgeon many years earlier had treated Alicia's duodenal ulcer by performing a posterior gastroenterostomy. That earlier operation had created a new connection between the stomach and the small intestine, bypassing the ulcerated portion of the duodenum, which is the section of small intestine closest to the stomach. The surgeon had relocated the jejunum, a lower section of small intestine, created a new opening in that, and connected it to the stomach. What Lord found was an ulcer in the jejunum, near the point where it had been joined to the stomach in the first ulcer operation. So he dismantled that earlier connection, removed more than half of Alicia's stomach, connected the remnant of the stomach to the jejunum and closed up the incision. "It all went smooth," Lord said.

Once the operation was over, they inserted a tube through Alicia's nose into her abdomen, to drain any excess secretions. Later in the day, when Lord saw Alicia again, he found reason to be concerned. "The Levin tube was draining fresh bloody fluid, which is extraordinarily unusual," Lord said. "In the two hundred gastric resections that I did, plus or minus, this was the only one that ever did it." In an effort to stop the bleeding without having to perform further surgery, they irrigated her stomach with a cold saline solution. But it didn't work, and Alicia kept leaking blood through the tube. "So we decided the thing to do was to take her back to the operating room and suture the bleeding point," Lord said.

At about 10:30 that night, less than twelve hours after the first operation ended, Lord opened Alicia up again and made an incision in the wall of what was left of her stomach, to search for the cause of the bleeding. He found no bleeding from the place where he had joined the stomach to the jejunum, but he did find something else inside the stomach that he couldn't understand. "The whole entire stomach was blushed red," Lord said. The stomach lining would normally be a pale, yellowish white. "You'd sponge it and then blood would just well up again — not like a spurter, but just like a sponge, when you squeeze a sponge." He also found from 1000 to 1500 cubic centimeters of blood in her abdominal cavity, which mystified him. Lord closed the small hole that he had just made in the stomach and prepared to try something else.

Since the stomach was the source of the bleeding and Lord didn't know what was causing it or how to stop it, one option was to remove the stomach entirely — a total gastrectomy. Even under the best of circumstances, that would have been a poor choice, since total gastrectomies usually left patients severely impaired and unable to lead normal lives. This wasn't the best of circumstances. Alicia had just been through a serious operation, and she was in far less than rosy condition. Lord decided that she couldn't survive such radical surgery. "For me to have performed a total gastrectomy would have been probably signing her death warrant," Lord said. Finally, he decided to do a vagotomy, a procedure that he had rejected as an alternative to the original gastric resection, because vagotomies often left patients with unpleasant post-operative side effects. The goal of the operation was to interrupt surgically some of the impulses carried by the vagus nerve, to reduce the secretion of acid in the stomach. With no real alternative, Lord went ahead with the vagotomy — a tricky operation, since the vagus nerve has multiple fibers that aren't always easy to locate. Lord decided to operate below the diaphragm, in the abdomen, where he already had an incision. That was a more conservative procedure than making a new incision above the diaphragm. "The only thing about a subdia-phragmatic vagotomy is that you can't be absolutely sure it is as complete as the one above the diaphragm," Lord said. "My note shows I got one vagus nerve, but I was not able to identify the other. . . . The vagotomy, even done perfect-ly at the second operation, would not have stopped the bleeding."

Once again, they closed Alicia up and hoped for the best. But by seven o'clock on the morning of July 2, almost twenty-four hours after the first operation, Alicia was not doing well. She was still bleeding, pale and clammy. She was conscious and alert, but she was restless, anxious to get out of the recovery room. Lord discussed the case with Rawls, with a blood specialist and with his own surgical mentor, Hinton, who made an entry on her chart, confi-dently predicting that they could stop the bleeding if they did further work on the vagus nerve. "I didn't want to see surgery the second and third time," Rawls said, "but nothing else was working." So at noon they wheeled Alicia back to the operating room and opened her up again — the third serious surgery in a little more than twenty-four hours.

This time, Hinton performed the surgery, with Lord assisting. They oper-ated on the vagus nerve above the diaphragm, took another look at the stomach and saw the same blushing and oozing. In addition, they decided to remove her spleen — partly because they thought it might be interfering with the coagula-tion of her blood, and partly because the spleen had been torn, probably during this final procedure, Lord said. "Now, it could have been sutured and left in place, but most people at that time thought it best to take a spleen out if there was any injury at all," Lord said. So they took it out and closed Alicia up for the third time.

It was in the recovery room, in the hours after this third operation, that Alicia's sister Josephine saw her for the first time since they had wheeled her away the previous day for her first operation. "She said, 'Tell me true, am I going to die?' " Josephine remembered. Despite Alicia's dreadful appearance, Josephine told her that she wasn't going to die. Later that evening, Josephine left the hospital and went to the Manhattan apartment of Alicia's close friend, Dody Michelson, where she was staying. Not long after, at 11:25 on the night of July 2, roughly thirty-six hours after the end of the first operation, Alicia Patterson Guggenheim died, at the age of fifty-six.

"The thing that led to her death was the bleeding within the remnant, the one third of the stomach or forty percent that remained behind," Lord said. An autopsy showed that the mucous lining of her stomach had essentially disappeared. "So all these little capillaries, blood vessels were just exposed," Lord said. "That's why it just kept blushing and bleeding." The autopsy showed that Alicia had escaped her father's fate: She had a perfectly normal liver. But it gave no clue as to what happened to the lining of her stomach. A quarter of a century later, sitting in his lawyer's office in the *Daily News* building, Lord still had no clue. "The only thing I've learned from this is that if you face that again, you would go ahead and do a total gastrectomy, in spite of making her future life gastrointestinally either miserable or certainly not a very happy one," Lord said. "I'm still disturbed. It took a long time to get over it emotionally."

III

IN THE HOURS after Alicia's death, her family, friends and employees began to cope with a reality that they simply had not expected.

"It never occurred to us she'd die, for God's sake," said Alice Albright Hoge, her niece. When the hospital called to notify Josephine Albright that her sister had died, Josephine was sleeping. Only a few hours earlier, she had assured Alicia that she was going to recover, and Josephine had fully believed that was true. "I always felt terrible about it," Josephine said. "It turned out to be a lie." As soon as she got the word, Josephine rounded up Alice for a trip to Chicago. "We took a plane immediately, thinking we could break the news to my mother," Josephine said. "She greeted us at the door at about seven o'clock in the morning. We said, 'We've got some terrible news,' and she said, 'I know.'"

Despite all the disagreements over the years, Alicia's death hit Harry hard. He had been available to the doctors whenever they needed to consult with him — his usual decisive, controlled self. But when he called Dot Holdsworth to tell her that Alicia had died, he was "shattered," she said. Holdsworth called Bill Woestendiek at his home, and he drove her into Manhattan, where they visited Harry. "He was sitting up in bed," Woestendiek remembered. "He was obviously distressed, looked very pale." Harry reached out for comfort wherever he could find it that night, including his grandson, Dana Draper, who came to the townhouse and spent several hours with him. "He said, 'That wasn't supposed to happen. I was supposed to die first,'" Draper remembered. In his bewilderment, Harry summoned Joe Albright from Washington to help plan the funeral.

"He kind of fell apart a little bit," Josephine said. "He just dumped the whole funeral arrangements in poor Joe's lap."

At the same time that the family was beginning to deal with the reality of her death, the news was spreading to her larger *Newsday* family. A large crowd of reporters and editors, primarily from the Suffolk office, learned about it at a bachelor party for Tom Morris. "The phone rings, Kirk Price answers the phone, and I can see that he was stunned like a statue," Morris said. "It completely changed the tenor of the party. They drifted away very quickly after that." The news even devastated a former employee, Jack Mann, who had left *Newsday* a year earlier. On the afternoon of the day that Alicia died, Mann had gone to the hospital and written a note of encouragement to Alicia. "It said, 'As you once said to me, you're a tough little son of a bitch,' " Mann said. He gave the note to Holdsworth and left. Later, he went to a Yankee game and ended up at Toots Shor's, the popular Manhattan night spot. From a phone booth there, he called the hospital to check on her condition, and someone announced that Mrs. Guggenheim had died. "I got terribly angry and I said, 'Goddamn it! She's not Mrs. Guggenheim. She's Miss Patterson.' Then I went in the other room, and put my head on a table, and cried like a baby."

The Wednesday paper, the morning after Alicia's death, carried a news story on page three, a black-bordered space in the editorial column and a two-page "Informal Appraisal" by Hal Burton. *Newsday* didn't publish on Thursday, July 4, but in the paper on Friday, the day of the funeral, *Newsday* carried a long list of tributes, leading with one from President Kennedy.

The funeral, at the impressive Episcopal Cathedral of the Incarnation in Garden City, was as crowded and colorful as Alicia wanted. Years earlier, during a visit to her hunting lodge, Alicia and Holdsworth had discussed funeral arrangements, and Alicia made it clear she wanted plenty of flowers. Holdsworth made sure that her wish was honored. Flowers were not allowed in the church itself, but they spilled in colorful profusion on the lawn outside the cathedral, and a blanket of orange-tinged roses, a favorite of Alicia's, covered the coffin. The organ belted out a selection of Protestant hymns, plus the music of Bach, Handel and Mendelssohn, closing with "The Battle Hymn of the Republic" as the coffin was carried out. "It was very moving, I thought," said Alicia's longtime friend, Jane Warner Dick. "And it was very much like Alicia. The day, in the first place, was very brisk and buoyant. They had flags all the way up the path to the chapel. There was a wind blowing, and they were all whipping in a very upbeat way."

Nearly a thousand people came to the cathedral, including dozens of political figures and representatives of other newspapers, along with grieving *Newsday* employees. "There were many people at *Newsday* weeping," Albright said. "It was like their whole lives had been ruined." But some *Newsday* employees stayed away, because they had to work. Right after the ceremony, Stan Peckham, who had flown in from Denver to attend, paid a brief visit to the *Newsday* plant. It reminded him of something that Alicia had told him years earlier, when they attended the funeral for Frank Atwood, the crusty old editor who had terrified and charmed the first generations of *Newsday* reporters. "She said, 'Well, when I die, I want my funeral in the cathedral in Garden City, and anyone from *Newsday* who doesn't come is automatically fired,'" Peckham remembered. "I had never seen *Newsday* since they had built on a second story. So someone drove me over there to see it, and I went in. I was amazed to see a staff still working on a paper, and I said, 'You're fired, you're fired, you're fired and you're fired.'"

Once the funeral was over, Harry did the best he could to cope with the little details of grief. He hired Bob Wiemer, a young *Newsday* reporter who occasionally filled in as an editorial writer, to compose dozens of responses to letters of condolence, at one dollar each. He informed his attorney, Leo Gottlieb, that he had no intention to exercise his right as Alicia's husband to override her will and take a significant chunk of her estate. He made the necessary changes in the latest version of his will, which he had completed just before Alicia's death. And he prepared for a ceremonial burial of her ashes at her hunting lodge in Kingsland.

"My original thought that the ceremony on the river should be now, I believe, is wrong," Harry wrote to Alicia's friends. "My idea was to carry out the wish at once, because of Alicia's impatience to be down by her beloved river. I think we are too emotional now and I agree with your idea that the ceremony should be at a time when we can be gay." In the same letter, Harry proposed the language of the plaque that would cover the spot where her ashes would be buried: "A beautiful and spirited lady lived on this land until she died on July 2, 1963. Under this oak tree she watched the river that she loved. She dreamed and thought: 'If there be a paradise on the face of this earth, it is this! It is this! It is this!' A wish has been fulfilled that her ashes mingle here with the earth. Her name was Alicia Patterson Guggenheim. She was born October 15, 1906." When the time came, the family gathered on the lawn sloping down from the lodge to the St. Mary's River, under the tall oak tree draped with Spanish moss. Josephine recited the Lord's Prayer and the Twenty-third Psalm, and they buried her ashes beneath the tree and threw the urn into the river.

Along that river, Alicia had spent many hours with Adlai Stevenson, but he was not there when her family buried the ashes. Nor was he present at the funeral. When Alicia died, Stevenson was in Europe on United Nations business. "Josephine called me up in the middle of the night and told me that Alicia had died, and she said, 'I've been trying to get Adlai on the telephone and I can't get him,'" said Jane Dick, who finally reached Stevenson herself. "He was very broken up, but he pulled himself together." Immediately, Stevenson sent Harry a telegram of condolence: "She was my oldest dearest friend. Returning if possible. Deepest sympathy. Adlai."

There is some question as to how Harry reacted to sharing his grief with Stevenson. "The Captain had him barred from coming to see Alicia when she was in the hospital, just a few days before she died," Woestendiek remembered. "I remember visiting her in the hospital and she said that Adlai had come out to see her and that the Captain had been there and wouldn't let him in." Holdsworth said that Harry had told her that he turned Stevenson away from the funeral. "He called Harry when he got the news and asked Harry if he thought he should come back and Harry said no, he would prefer that he didn't," Holdsworth said. "He was very jealous of Adlai." Alicia's niece, Alice Albright Hoge, actually overheard a conversation between Harry and Stevenson. She had walked from the main house at Falaise to Mille Fleurs, the house that Harry's mother had occupied before her death. As Alice Hoge walked into Mille Fleurs, which hadn't been occupied for many years, she was startled to hear the phone ringing. She picked it up and quickly realized that it was just an extension to the phone in Falaise itself. The conversation she overheard was Harry and Stevenson discussing whether Stevenson would return for the funeral. It may be that Harry told him not to come, she said, but what she remembered clearly was the tone of the conversation. "Harry was very affectionate," she said. "It was like they were both so stunned that she'd died."

Whether Harry specifically disinvited him or not, Stevenson did not come back for the funeral. But Jane Dick wrote him a detailed letter about it, and he wrote her back: "I have read and re-read your letter about the funeral. Somehow, in a few words, you have brought the whole thing to life. It sounds like a suitable *conclusion*, but *why* was a conclusion necessary? It seems unthinkable that she is gone and I, for one, will have a hard time reconciling myself to life without the comforting assurance that she would always be there when needed. I hope when I get back we can talk about her and what she meant to us all — gaily!"

Immediately after Alicia died, Dot Holdsworth made preparations to carry out another of her wishes: that Stevenson's letters to Alicia be returned to him. "After she died, I raced over to the office and opened the safe and got them out and gave them to Bill Woestendiek and told him to put them in his file, because I knew that the Captain would be into that safe," Holdsworth said. Sometime later, Harry called her into the office and asked her to clean out the desk that had been Alicia's. She had already cleaned it, but one of the Stevenson letters, which Alicia had probably hidden in a pile of copy paper, had turned up in the drawer. "He was very cross about it," she said. "I think he read it." Eventually, Holdsworth made an appointment with Stevenson in New York. When she handed him the letters that he had written Alicia, he wept. Stevenson was similarly moved when Woestendiek visited him in his official residence at the Waldorf, and they shared eggs Benedict and reminisced about Alicia. "He started to cry," Woestendiek said, "wheeled his chair around and he said, 'Oh, when I think of how different things might have been.' "

That, of course, was precisely the question: How different could things have been? There is little question of the level of devotion between Alicia and Stevenson. "I think she was probably the one woman he cared for the most," said Stevenson's sister, Buffie Ives. But there is considerable question as to whether they were sufficiently compatible to be married. They enjoyed each other's company immensely, but they were both powerful, strong-willed personalities who knew exactly what they wanted. "He wanted everything one hundred percent his way, and she wanted everything one hundred percent her way," Marietta Tree said. Another woman who was friendly with both Alicia and Stevenson, Ruth Field, said to Stevenson's biographer, John Bartlow Martin: "She told me one time, 'We'd have torn each other apart.' "

But the real problem wasn't so much putting two strong personalities in harness as it was pulling together two disparate worlds. "In many ways, the personalities — the interest in politics, the interest in adventure and travel, learning about the world, and journalism — were very compatible, but the lives were separate," said Adlai E. Stevenson III. "She had her career, her newspaper and her own agenda, and he had his. How you merge those separate lives, I don't know." It seems unlikely that Alicia could have traded in her position of power at *Newsday* to become the wife of a politician, subservient to his needs. If she had asked Harry for a divorce, she would certainly have had to leave *Newsday*, and that was a future that she couldn't face. "She would have had to choose between Adlai and the paper," Marietta Tree said. "I remember her saying, 'I can't leave my baby.' "

IV

IN BUYING A newspaper for Alicia, Harry's modest goal had been simply to keep his playgirl bride usefully busy. No matter what else anyone said about Alicia in the years that followed, she convinced the world that she was not just an idle rich woman, but a serious, working journalist.

Despite her origins, she was never as flamboyant as her aunt, Cissy Patterson, who stirred up Washington society, inspired three full-scale biographies and left behind a newspaper that was swallowed by the *Washington Post* within a few years after her death. Alicia inspired no biographies, but she created a financially and journalistically successful newspaper that was just short of the 400,000 circulation mark when she died. "You've got to give Alicia the credit," said David Starr, the editor of the competing *Long Island Press*. "It was her spirit and her judgment that made *Newsday* into the product that it was. She changed American journalism, in that she created a serious tabloid."

Her tabloid *was* serious, as tabloids go, but Alicia did love tabloid stories, and her prescription for the paper's tone was simple: dogs, cats and murders. Her reporting career was brief, but she had good news instincts. She knew the right questions to ask, she knew a good story, and she knew, as her father knew, how to publish a newspaper that appealed to the masses. "Her idea was very simple: to entertain, to startle, to interest her readers, and through these techniques to inform them as well," Hal Burton said. "She believed that newspapers could be both lively and conscientious but should never be boring. . . . As she said to me, 'I want people to pick up *Newsday* saying to themselves, I wonder what that damn paper is saying today.' " In addition, she never wanted her paper to be complacent. "We want to grow bigger, but far more we want to grow better and wiser and stronger," she wrote on *Newsday's* twentieth birthday. "We want to slay the evil dragons and rescue ladies in distress. We want to keep our ideals always shined up and our courage high. And we want to remember that even the best mousetrap can be improved."

Beyond the newspaper's prosperity, she concerned herself with the future of Long Island, helping to shape a loose collection of small towns and villages into something like a cohesive community, by making *Newsday* its unifying institution. "She really did represent Long Island," said her friend, Phyllis Cerf. "She felt so fiercely about it, as if she'd grown up there. . . . It was her child, as the newspaper was her child."

As successful as her newspaper was, her marriage was not. "She was very happy about *Newsday* and was very proud of it," Dot Holdsworth said. "But as far as her personal life is concerned, she was not happy at all." Her conflicts with Harry were real, continuing and painful. She put up with them because she didn't choose to leave *Newsday*. But for all that sadness, it would be a mistake to think of her simply as a victim. "There was this popular notion around that her life was just one unmitigated tragedy, that she married Harry and that didn't work out, and that Harry was mean to her, and here was this crushed woman," Hal Burton said. "Believe me, she wasn't crushed at all. She crushed him as much as he crushed her." Alicia acknowledged as much in an interview that she gave to J. M. Flagler, who wrote a two-part profile of her for *The New Yorker* that never appeared in print, because of her death. The publication of a profile in *The New Yorker*, an honor accorded to her father twenty-five years earlier, would probably have annoyed Harry. Perhaps sensing that, she tried to give him some of the credit that he always craved. "Not many husbands would have given somebody with so little ability a chance like this," she told Flagler. "Besides, he's showed great forbearance. You know, I'm not such an easy person to get along with."

She wasn't always easy to get along with as a boss, either. She did have a temper, and she had some odd ways of constructing chains of command. She gave Alan Hathway too much freedom and didn't hold his excesses in check as well as she should have. But she was visible. Her employees could talk to her, and she knew their names. Almost universally, they loved her, and beyond that, they respected her skills as a journalist. "She was the greatest newspaperman I've ever known," Jack Mann said. "I don't know if she could dictate a lead on a fire, or write a 5/42 italic headline, but in spirit, she was the best newspaperman I've ever known."

The Newsday Photo Gallery

A few of the more frilly moments of Alicia Patterson's early life: Top right, dressed in finery appropriate for one of Chicago's controlling families. *(de Vos Studio)* Above, at her 1927 wedding to James Simpson Jr. She called the marriage a "self-canceling contest of wills," and it ended in divorce in 1930. *(The Drake Studios)* At right, after her 1931 marriage to Joseph W. Brooks, a sportsman and pilot who was friendly with her father, Joseph Medill Patterson. *(UPI/Bettmann Newsphotos)*

Alicia the fearless sportswoman: as a skillful fisher, right, a pilot who set women's speed records, below, and, in the center of the bottom photo, sharing a rare moment of calm at Roosevelt Field in 1932, with her father and her sister, Josephine. *(Daily News)*

Harry Guggenheim makes the cover of *Time*, below, after his Senate confirmation as American ambassador to Cuba. *(Copyright 1929, Time Inc.)* Right, Harry with his proteges, Robert Goddard, center, and Charles Lindbergh, right. *(Esther Goddard and NASA)* Above, an aerial view of Harry's mansion, Falaise. *(Newsday)*

The new editor-publisher at the controls of the ancient press, above, on *Newsday*'s first day of publication, September 3, 1940. *(Newsday)*

Below, a view of the exterior of the original *Newsday* plant, a converted automobile dealership at 283 Main Street, Hempstead. *(Newsday)*

At top left, Harry plays host to Charles Nicholson, left, the first head of the advertising department, and Harold Davis, right, the first managing editor. *(Newsday)* At left, Harry aboard the carrier *Nehenta Bay*, from which he participated in the strafing of a Japanese-held island in the Pacific in 1945. *(Harry F. Guggenheim Foundation)* Below, Joseph Medill Patterson, right, and his wife, Mary King Patterson, in hat, visit Harry and Alicia at the Hempstead plant. *(Newsday)*

Above, Stanton Peckham, Alicia's editorial writer and confidant. *(Newsday)* At left, Alicia and her friend, the artist Neysa McMein, at work on their short-lived comic strip, "Deathless Deer." *(Newsday)* At top, part of the newsroom, with the city editor, Jack Altshul, writing at right, and one of his key editors, Frank Atwood, in vest. *(Newsday)*

At top left, Alicia and her managing editor, Alan Hathway, after *Newsday* won its first Pulitzer Prize, in 1954, for exposing the corrupt union leader William DeKoning Sr. The Pulitzer Prize put Alicia's face on the cover of *Time* magazine. *(Cover and photo, copyright 1954, Time Inc.)* At left, Hal Burton, who worked at the *News* for Alicia's father and became a confidant of Alicia at *Newsday*. *(Newsday)* Below, Harry in the winner's circle after his horse, Dark Star, won the 1953 Kentucky Derby. *(Associated Press)*

At top, Alicia and Adlai Stevenson, along with his aide, William McCormick Blair Jr., at a Manhattan dinner that she arranged for Stevenson during the 1952 campaign. Bottom left, Harry and Alicia as she leaves for a 1957 African trip with Stevenson. Above, Alicia, foreground, with the Stevenson party in Nigeria. Standing: Blair, Marietta Tree. Sitting: Nancy Stevenson, wife of Adlai E. Stevenson III; former Governor Stevenson; Frances FitzGerald, Adlai E. Stevenson III.

Above, Bob Greene, left, and Alan Hathway testify in 1959 before the Senate, on union intimidation of the paper. *(United Press International)* At left, Jane Gerard during her famous stunt story, a walk to Montauk. *(Newsday)* Below, Bill McIlwain in 1960, when he became city editor. *(Newsday)*

Above, Harry with his biggest big-name writer, John Steinbeck, and his wife, Elaine. *(Newsday)* At left, Harry with Alicia's nephew, Joseph Albright, after Harry named him assistant to the publisher in July, 1963, following Alicia's death. *(Newsday)* Below, Mark Foster Ethridge Sr., Harry's choice to serve as an interim editor of *Newsday* after Alicia died. *(Newsday)*

At top, Harry and Bill D. Moyers meet with *Newsday* employees as Moyers takes over as publisher in 1967, after leaving his position as White House press secretary. Within three years, their sharp political differences turned Harry against Moyers. *(Newsday)*

Above left, Harry and one of the columnists he signed up for *Newsday*, Robert Moses. *(Newsday)* Above right, Harry at the swimming pool at Falaise with his longtime aviation friends, James Doolittle, left, and Charles Lindbergh. *(Newsday)*

Above left, Al Marlens, the intense, immensely talented, intimidating journalist who became managing editor of *Newsday* at the same time that Harry persuaded Alan Hathway to retire and named Bill McIlwain the editor and Bill Moyers the publisher. As Harry grew ill, he became convinced that Marlens was a dangerous leftist, and he asked Moyers to fire him. Moyers refused, even though Marlens distrusted Moyers. Above right, David Laventhol, whom Moyers recruited from the *Washington Post*, to develop the daily newsmagazine style that Moyers wanted. Marlens later clashed with Laventhol and left *Newsday*. At left, William Attwood, Otis Chandler's choice to become publisher after Harry sold *Newsday* to the Times Mirror Company in 1970 and accepted the resignation of Moyers. *(Newsday)*

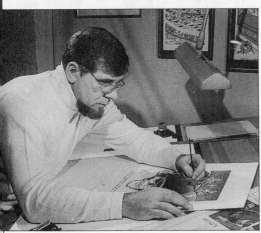

At top, Bob Greene, right, stands in the poppy fields of Turkey with his original heroin trail team: Les Payne, left, and Knut Royce, center. This was the start of a project that won *Newsday* a Pulitzer Prize in 1974. *(Newsday)* Above left, Tom Darcy, who won a Pulitzer in 1970 for his editorial cartoons, at the same time that the Greene Team won for its reporting on land scandals in Suffolk County. *(Newsday)* Above right, Emily Genauer, who won a Pulitzer in 1974 for art commentary. *(Newsday)*

At top, Bob Greene and Karen Hasby on the set of *Inside Newsday,* the short-lived cable television news program produced by *Newsday* in 1983 and 1984. *(Newsday)* Above left, Vincent Bordash, who came to the circulation department before *Newsday* even published its first issue, and later presided over the paper's phenomenal circulation growth. *(Newsday)* Above center, David Targe, who started as an advertising salesman and rose to the top marketing position at *Newsday.* Targe's fierce competitive drive was a major factor in *Newsday*'s sharply rising profits in the 1970s and early 1980s. *(Newsday)* Above right, Anthony Insolia, the editor of *Newsday* from 1978 to 1987, during the difficult early years of the New York edition. *(Bill Senft)*

Above, the rejoicing after *Newsday* won a Pulitzer Prize in 1984, for its coverage of the Baby Jane Doe controversy. *(Newsday)* Below, the 1985 Pulitzer winners at Columbia University. From left: Ozier Muhammad, Murray Kempton, Dennis Bell, Josh Friedman. Kempton won for commentary and the others for covering famine in Africa. *(Newsday)*

Above left, Robert M. Johnson, who became the sixth publisher of *Newsday* in 1986, succeeding David Laventhol. Johnson, a lawyer, is the first non-journalist since Harry Guggenheim to become publisher. *(Newsday)* Above right, Anthony Marro, who became editor of *Newsday* in 1987, succeeding Anthony Insolia. Marro worked on investigations that won the Pulitzer Prize in 1970 and 1974, left *Newsday* and later returned as Washington bureau chief. *(Newsday)* At left, Donald Forst, who became the editor of *New York Newsday* in late 1985. David Laventhol originally brought Forst to *Newsday* in 1971. He left at the end of 1977 to run papers in Los Angeles and later Boston, but Laventhol brought him back to give direction to the growing New York paper. *(Bill Senft)*

BOOK III

The Captain
At the Helm

CHAPTER TWENTY-TWO

The Captain Takes Command

I

JUST A FEW weeks before his seventy-third birthday, at a time when most men are well into retirement, Harry Frank Guggenheim found himself embarking on a new career.

For almost twenty-three years, Alicia Patterson had fought to keep Harry isolated in the business operations of *Newsday* and away from control of the news and editorial pages. Similarly, he had tried to keep her from seeing even the routine profit and loss statements. Now that she was gone, now that he had rejected offers from S. I. Newhouse and John Hay Whitney to buy *Newsday* from him, Harry set about the task of running the whole paper. As he had done with every other endeavor in his life, he attacked the job with vigor. But hard work could not substitute for knowledge of how journalism worked.

To begin with, the rhythms and traditions of editing a newspaper were foreign — even frightening — to him. "Being of German-Swiss descent, he had that old *alles im ordnung* idea, 'everything in order,' " Hal Burton said. "When he got out to *Newsday*, everything was confusion, because that's the way a newspaper is run." In trying to impose Guggenheim order on Pattersonian chaos, Harry was at a serious disadvantage. He had all the fiscal and analytical skills of a successful businessman, but none of the talents of a journalist. "He wrote like a German Swiss, which is what his grandfather was: very, very weighty, as if he had wooden shoes on — clunk, clunk, clunk," Burton said.

Harry's shortcomings as a writer were not crucial, since he didn't do much of it. But his deep-seated fear and distrust of journalists was a crippling disability. Unlike Alicia, who had grown up in an environment where writing about others was the family business, Harry came from a family that was constantly being written about — and not always approvingly. When he was ambassador to Cuba, for example, Harry endured sharp press criticism of his performance. Later, he watched as the press circled hungrily around his friend Charles Lindbergh when a kidnaper took Lindbergh's son. At one of his earliest meetings with the senior staff at *Newsday*, Harry made clear his disdain for journalists. "He said that he didn't trust newspapermen," Burton said, "that they were inaccurate and they frequently lied."

This distrust was not the only gulf between Harry and his employees. Another barrier was the stark contrast between his personal style and that of his staff. He was an Old World gentleman with impeccable manners and perfect tailoring, and he suddenly found himself surrounded by a sloppy, rumpled, profane staff. They were accustomed to a publisher who allowed them to argue back, rather than a boss who liked his employees to call him "Captain," in deference to his Navy career, and obey instantly. It was no small obstacle, either, that Harry was hard of hearing. Most voices, magnified by his hearing aid, sounded like nothing more intelligible than a roaring train. So Harry could barely hear the words, let alone figure out what journalism was all about.

Early in his time as editor and publisher, Harry did take some steps that created good will, such as giving everyone a bonus in memory of Alicia. No matter what he did, however, he could not feel comfortable running the paper. "*Newsday* to him was like a bomb that might go off any minute," Burton said. "All these little details that had to be taken care of in the newspaper, and he never could find anybody that he trusted."

Actually, Harry did have two executives that he trusted implicitly: Ernie Levy, the advertising director, and Harold Ferguson, the business manager. But they controlled the business side of the paper, not the editorial side, where Harry knew he needed help. The first step that he took to get that help was to appoint Alicia's nephew, Joseph Medill Patterson Albright, as assistant to the publisher. At the time he came north from the Washington bureau to supervise the arrangements for his aunt's funeral and then take over a job that he thought would lead to the publisher's seat, Albright was only twenty-six years old. He had shown in Washington that he was an excellent reporter and a workmanlike writer, but he had not yet demonstrated real leadership potential in his two years at the paper. Nonetheless, Harry did need help, and he wanted to honor a request that Alicia had made in a note that she left behind: "You have done so many good things for me; you have been wonderful in giving me a chance in the newspaper. I want Joey now to have that same chance."

The chance that Harry gave him was a job that carried a broad variety of responsibilities, ranging from union negotiations to attendance at the daily editorial conferences with Harry and Burton. This took him away from reporting, but Albright didn't mind, because he had a sense of mission. "Everyone thought the paper *was* Aunt Alicia," Albright said. "People were really bending every sinew to try and keep the magic going. Who knows, in retrospect, what the magic was, or why the formula worked? But at the time, right after her death, we thought that she was such a vital ingredient that we had to really, really stay together and work hard." But Albright was too young and inexperienced to be the editor of *Newsday*. For that job, Harry turned quickly to someone older, wiser and more accomplished: his friend from Kentucky, Mark Foster Ethridge Sr.

Ethridge was a son of the Deep South, born in Meridian, Mississippi, in 1896. In high school, he covered sports for the *Meridian Dispatch*. After only a year at the University of Mississippi, he ran out of money and decided to take full-time newspaper jobs in Georgia, first with the *Columbus Enquirer-Sun*, then with the progressive *Macon Telegraph*. Following service in the Navy in World War I, he returned to the *Telegraph* as city editor. He worked briefly as a writer for the Consolidated Press and the *New York Sun*, but came back to the *Macon Telegraph* as managing editor. In 1933, he went abroad on a fellowship to study postwar Europe, and when he came back, he left the *Telegraph* and took a job with the Associated Press. Fascinated with the *Washington Post*, he signed on there as associate editor and rose to assistant general manager. The following year, Ethridge returned to the South as general manager and publisher of the *Richmond Times-Dispatch*. It was there that he met Barry Bingham, the son of Robert Worth Bingham, who owned the *Louisville Courier-Journal* and *Times*. The younger Bingham persuaded him to leave Richmond, and in 1936, Ethridge became vice-president and general manager of the two papers, the start of twenty-seven years in Louisville, where he rose to publisher and chairman of the board.

At Louisville, well before most southern journalists would have dared to challenge the cruel white supremacist system, Ethridge denounced the poll tax and the white-only primary. His position on social issues fit so well with the Roosevelt and Truman ideology that both presidents called on him for brief tours of public service. When Roosevelt created a committee on fair employment practice in the Office of Production Management in 1941, he named Ethridge its chairman. In 1945, Truman made Ethridge a special representative to Bulgaria and Romania. Ethridge also served on a United States commission investigating guerrilla warfare on the frontiers of Greece and worked as Truman's envoy in the Middle East.

By the time of Alicia's death, Ethridge and his wife, the author Willie Snow, were about to retire — with some bitterness toward the Binghams because the family had failed to give Ethridge the *Courier-Journal* stock that he had expected. "They kind of resigned themselves to the idea of retirement, and it seemed best, but I think the people who knew them knew they might not be entirely happy," said his grandson, Mark Foster Ethridge III. So when his old friend Harry called, it wasn't a painful decision at all for Ethridge to postpone retirement temporarily. Ethridge would live in Garden City, but he would also maintain a home in Chapel Hill, where he would commute on Sunday nights to teach a journalism class on Mondays at the University of North Carolina.

Everyone understood it was not to be a long-term assignment. "The idea, I think, was to stabilize it, run it, figure out what needed to be done and hire a replacement, then go on to retirement," Mark III said. One of his roles may well have been to evaluate Joe Albright and guide him toward the future, as he had done for Barry Bingham's sons. In fact, when Ethridge got the job, *Time* magazine predicted that he would, in effect, be giving Albright a one-man seminar on how to be the editor, and Albright's accession to power at *Newsday* was "only a matter of time."

Given Ethridge's loyalty to the New Deal, he was an interesting choice for Harry, who had opposed Roosevelt in all four presidential elections. But Harry needed him to "help settle some of his internal problems, and also to signalize the fact that the newspaper would continue to be independent and progressive," Ethridge wrote. Besides, whatever their political differences, Harry had known Ethridge for years, through their get-togethers at meetings of the American Newspaper Publishers Association and Harry's visits to Ethridge's home at Kentucky Derby time. Ethridge was also a man of great stature, a confidant of presidents — precisely Harry's kind of man.

"His experience and his accomplishments equip him to carry on the best traditions of Newsday as expressed in its credo, which he enthusiastically supports," Harry said in announcing the appointment on August 12. The "credo" was an editorial that Harry wrote a month after Alicia's death, outlining his views of how the newspaper should conduct itself. The editorial, "This Is Newsday," became his mantra and his calling card. Its description of the way a publisher should operate was a pedestrian, uninspiring effort, but it was harmless. So Ethridge accepted it, and Harry hired Mark Senior, as they all called him, to distinguish him from his son, an editorial writer at *Newsday* a decade earlier.

The morning after Harry announced Ethridge's appointment, their mutual friend, John Steinbeck, read about it at his home on eastern Long Island, at Sag Harbor. "What a brilliant choice," Steinbeck wrote Harry. "He is one of the best men living. Moreover, I think that Alicia would be very pleased for Mark has not only her courage and independence but also her humor." Steinbeck's letter delighted Harry. "When I lost Alicia and the editor of Newsday too," Harry wrote back, "I knew immediately that there was only one man and that was Mark."

II

HARRY GUGGENHEIM HAD little knowledge of the technical details of putting out a daily newspaper, but he did have an abundance of opinions.

The world view that Harry brought to the daily editorial conferences was obviously more conservative than Alicia's. So he wanted to know early whether Hal Burton could be loyal to his opinions after years of fealty to Alicia's. "He said to me, 'Are you sure that you can follow my policies?' "

Burton said. "I said, 'Well, Harry, as far as I've seen them, they are not violently reactionary. They're conservative, but a lot of them are quite moderate. Yes, I can.' "

The real problem with the editorial page in Harry's eyes was not Burton's loyalty to Alicia. The problem was Burton's speedy research style — not at all in keeping with the deliberate approach to opinion-making that Harry had described in "This Is Newsday," outlining the publisher's role. In Harry's view, Burton was churning out editorials too fast and too carelessly. But Burton had always written editorials quickly, at the *Daily News* and at *Newsday*. Alicia's acceptance of Burton's work ethic was one of her few major fights with Burton's boss, Bill Woestendiek, and a few months after Harry took over, Woestendiek continued his criticisms in a memo to Harry and Ethridge. "The foundation of a newspaper is its editorial page and ours is not good enough," Woestendiek wrote.

To improve the editorial page, Harry installed a more systematic approach: The staff would not write editorials on complex subjects unless the editorial writers or the young researchers first generated long, thesis-like reports. "Harry was running it like a ship," said Bob Wiemer, who compiled a report on NATO soon after becoming an editorial writer. "He had staff officers, and I was one of his staff officers. The report would give him the background on an issue, and he'd make up his mind what he wanted to say about it."

That heavy emphasis on research wasn't the only change in the editorial process. The morning meetings also took on a different tone. Harry was clearly in charge, and no one felt nearly as comfortable arguing with him as they did with Alicia. "Mark Senior would argue and could argue with Harry because they were the same age, but it was nothing comparable to the gung-ho and free-wheeling meetings we had with Alicia Patterson," Woestendiek said. At the sessions with Alicia, there were always elements of color — from the presence of her golden retriever, Sunbeam, to her sudden order, after a discussion of fitness, that her editors drop and do pushups. Alicia, of course, joined them and did a few strenuous exercises herself. Under Harry, there was a tight agenda, but there were no dogs, no calisthenics, and little debate. "It didn't pay to argue with him," Burton said, "because he just got stony-faced."

As Harry shaped the editorial page, he moved toward codifying his views into a written canon, just as Alicia would *not* have done. That began only three weeks after her death, when Harry met with his editors and responded to their questions about his opinions. Based on that session, Woestendiek wrote a two-page memo summarizing Harry's views on issues, which were essentially conservative. The memo captured, for example, Harry's reverence for the presidency: "The President and his advisors are in the best position to know our defense needs (regardless of which party) and we must accept their estimates rather than listen to a lot of sour grapes from embittered ex-generals and admirals."

This process of recording for all time the opinions of the publisher did not reach its peak until some time later, after Woestendiek had left *Newsday* and Harry had brought in someone new to run the editorial page in the spring of

1965. Ethridge recommended Stan Hinden, the veteran political reporter who had been running *Newsday*'s Albany bureau. Harry explained the job to Hinden during a lunch at Falaise, Hinden accepted, and Dick Zander replaced him the following year as Albany bureau chief. One of the first projects that Harry assigned to Hinden was to review all the editorials that had appeared in *Newsday* since Alicia's death, analyze them and put together a comprehensive manual of Harry's views — a job that took him weeks. The result was an impressive blue binder, with gold lettering on the cover announcing the title, "Policy Papers," and Harry's signature. "The Captain thought it was very important, because he felt that once he distributed this to everybody on the paper, they would then believe in his ideas and adhere to his ideas and follow his ideas," Hinden said. "Needless to say, he didn't reckon with the kind of skepticism of most people in the news business. I personally delivered it to all the top editors. . . . I remember handing a copy to Al Marlens, who took it, looked at it, and tossed it on a pile of junk that he had in the back of his desk." In addition to compiling the policy papers, Hinden continued and refined the system of long research reports. He also developed an elaborate process for interviewing and making written assessments of political candidates who sought *Newsday*'s endorsement.

It was inevitable that Hinden's adherence to Harry's desire for an orderly process would clash with Burton's far less structured style. Burton grew restless and went in to Harry to complain about Hinden, but Harry stood his ground. "He said, 'I can arrange for your retirement, with extreme generosity,' " Burton said. "Like a goddamn fool, out of pride I didn't take it at that time. I probably could have gotten $25,000, $30,000 a year."

So Burton stayed on, unhappily. One source of his disenchantment was the stream of editorials that he had to write in support of the American presence in Vietnam, because Harry supported the war unwaveringly. "He said, 'If the President of the United States says we're going to win, we're going to win,' " Burton said. "This was his whole approach to the thing." In contrast, Hinden accepted Harry's policy. Joe Albright also brought to the editorial meetings opinions that were "fairly hawkish from time to time, but not hawkish enough for him," Albright remembered. Not even Ethridge shook Harry's views. "Mark, I would judge, just gave up on trying to change him on the subject of the war," Burton said. "It was hopeless."

III

EVEN THOUGH MARK Ethridge brought to *Newsday* a dazzling resume and the admiration of the publisher, nobody really expected him, at age sixty-seven, to alter the paper drastically. But his presence did calm the staff and convince them that the paper was still in safe hands and not lurching abruptly rightward.

"You could have imagined all kinds of bad things happening," Joe Albright said. "We were lucky at *Newsday* to have Harry know somebody who was such a rock in the field of American journalism."

Ethridge's ability to soothe, reassure and stabilize flowed from his towering reputation for journalistic integrity, on issues ranging from his stands on racial justice to his behavior after he had a minor auto accident in Louisville. The police and the other driver were willing to forget about it, but Ethridge wanted to be arrested for drunk driving. The police obliged, and when they allowed Ethridge to make phone calls, he called his newspaper, dictated the story of his arrest and ordered his staff to display it prominently. If the Louisville papers could run a big story about the arrest of Ethridge, he reasoned, nobody had better call and ask him to kill a drunk driving story. With instincts like that, Ethridge didn't have to be afraid of Harry.

If Harry was moving toward taking an embarrassing editorial position, it was Ethridge who had to dissuade him. If Harry developed a powerful but irrational desire to fire someone, Ethridge had to figure out a way to divert him. "He was very good at inventing ways to put off decisions, to humor Guggenheim and to hope that things will go away, and they often did," Albright said.

A typical example of Ethridge's diplomacy involved Harry's clash with John Cummings, a tough, tenacious reporter who developed insubordination into an art form but was so talented that he became one of a small group of reporters who regularly covered national stories. The immediate reason for his painful encounter with Harry was a civil rights story. But the underlying problem was the interest that Cummings had shown, starting before Alicia's death, in one of Harry's areas of expertise: Cuba. First, through his relationship with a Cuban diplomat, Cummings got permission to visit Cuba in the summer of 1962, three months before the missile crisis that brought the world to the brink of nuclear war. "I got out, I came back to Miami, called Hathway and I said, 'The Russians are reinforcing this place. There are things that unquestionably are missiles that are coming in here,' " Cummings said. But editors were skeptical about anything coming out of Cuba in those days, and Cummings felt that *Newsday* softened unnecessarily the missile information in his stories. Hal Hendrix of the *Miami News*, however, managed to get into his paper strong stories about the buildup of Russian fighter planes, which won Hendrix a Pulitzer Prize. Then, in the summer of 1963, just after Harry had taken over for Alicia, Cummings wrote a background piece about the tenth anniversary of the attack on the Moncada Barracks in Santiago de Cuba, led by Fidel Castro. Harry saw it in advance and disliked it. "He went bananas," Albright said. "And he wanted, as I recall, to fire Cummings over having written it." Albright and Ethridge intervened, running a harmless profile of Henry Ford instead of the Cuba piece, and Cummings didn't lose his job.

In the fall of 1963, Cummings began covering the United Nations for *Newsday*, but he found himself bounced from that job after only a few months. Almost as a consolation prize, he ended up travelling through the South in 1964, writing a series about cities that had experienced major integration fights. In

Birmingham, Alabama, he interviewed a devoutly segregationist society matron who ran a local civic group. "I asked her if her committee was integrated," Cummings said. Her answer was: "Well, we've got Jews on it. We're integrated that way." A complaint about the quote annoyed Harry, and he summoned Cummings. During the long conversation, it became clear that the Birmingham story might not have angered Harry so much if it had not been for the earlier Cuba story. The bizarre conversation and the earlier threat of firing shook Cummings and embittered him. "I should have left *Newsday* at that point," Cummings said. "I took it very badly, emotionally." But Ethridge called Cummings in and reassured him, and Cummings stayed.

The palliative function that he served in the Cummings episode and on other occasions was crucial, but Ethridge also made some far more concrete contributions to the shape of the paper. Probably the most visible was the creation of a Saturday magazine, to beef up the scrawny Saturday paper. The magazine, "Weekend with Newsday," started in 1964, with Albright as the editor. It provided an instant outlet for the paper's hot young writers, such as Mike McGrady, Harvey Aronson and Robert Mayer. As Ethridge looked around the paper, he also saw another glaring need. It wasn't obvious to the public, but it was perfectly plain to the reporters: *Newsday*, like most papers, had a woefully inadequate library. Almost twenty-five years of newspaper stories were stuffed into a long row of cabinets that were so full that the drawers were hopelessly clogged. Ethridge and Bill McIlwain asked the news editor, Stan Asimov, to examine the state of the library, and they sought advice from Chester Lewis, the chief librarian at the *New York Times*, who had been a consultant to Alicia. Eventually, they hired a professional librarian, Andrew Ippolito, who started expanding the available space by buying rotary files called Lektrievers. When the machines arrived, Ippolito attached nameplates to two of them, dubbing them "The Captain" and "Mark."

It would have been pleasant if Ethridge could have spent all his time bringing his experience to bear on useful projects such as the Saturday magazine and the library, working his way quietly toward his retirement. But he had to spend far too much energy on the less rewarding task of keeping the peace. One source of conflict was the relationship between Harry and Bill Woestendiek. Alicia was dead, but her shadow still seemed to be grappling with him for control, and the most loyal acolyte of Alicia's ghost seemed to be Woestendiek.

It wasn't that Harry was cold or unfeeling about her death. In fact, he wrote to Alicia's niece, Alice Albright Hoge, a few months after the funeral: "That I should have survived Alicia is a fate that I shall never quite understand." In many ways, he showed genuine concern about her memory. For nearly two years, until the construction of a new wing made changes necessary, he kept Alicia's office basically as it had been at her death — even retaining her family photographs on the walls. He played a strong role in helping her family to get the Alicia Patterson Foundation started. And he commissioned the artist Joan Miro to paint a huge mural with Alicia's name in it, to be displayed at the Guggenheim.

Along with his grief, though, Harry had room in his heart for jealousy. Soon after Alicia's death, for example, Harry asked Woestendiek to arrange a lunch with President Kennedy for him, as he had done for Alicia. Of course, Alicia had endorsed Kennedy in 1960 and Harry had endorsed Richard Nixon. So Woestendiek knew it would be difficult to coax an invitation out of Kennedy's press secretary, Pierre Salinger, but he tried. "Salinger said, 'What the hell has he done for us?' " Woestendiek said. Eventually, Salinger offered an invitation for Harry to a Rose Garden reception. "I told the Captain," Woestendiek said. "He said, 'That's not good enough.' " (Later that year, on September 5, 1963, Harry did get his audience with Kennedy, and presented the same views on Latin America that he had already outlined to Dwight Eisenhower and would later explain to Lyndon Johnson.)

Inevitably, Woestendiek's loyalty to Alicia, combined with his native stubbornness, brought him into conflict with Harry. "He had always been told by Miss Patterson that he would become probably the editor, and that Joe Albright would become the publisher, or some version of that," Bill McIlwain said. Now, Harry was running things — not always to Woestendiek's liking. In fact, at the editorial meetings in the mornings, Woestendiek was often "petulant as hell" with Harry, McIlwain said. More than that, Woestendiek constantly reminded Harry that Alicia operated differently. Tom Dorsey, who came to *Newsday* in 1964 to start the paper's syndicate, remembered one such occasion — a meeting with Harry, Ethridge, Albright and Woestendiek. "Woestendiek walked out in a huff, and as he went out the door, he said, 'Alicia wouldn't want it this way,' " Dorsey remembered. "Harry said to Mark and I, 'Do you think somebody could tell him that Alicia isn't here anymore?' " Ethridge called Woestendiek a "stubborn Dutch bastard" and did what he could to warn him, but Woestendiek persisted.

"I was being honest, and, to me, they were being more pragmatic," Woestendiek said. "They were talking about Harry behind his back, and I was talking to his face." Since Woestendiek didn't back down, Harry eventually decided to take action. Over a pleasant lunch, Harry quietly broke the news to Woestendiek that he wasn't the kind of person that Harry wanted to run the newspaper. "He said, 'I like you. You're a bright young man, but you're too young, too liberal, and you're responsible for all of Alicia's bad thinking,' " Woestendiek said. "I said, 'I'll accept the too young and the too liberal, but nobody told *her* what to think.' " Harry didn't want Woestendiek in charge, but he was willing to give him a lesser job and keep him on the payroll. Woestendiek declined and left without rancor. "He was as much of a gentleman as anybody I've ever worked for — more, in most cases," Woestendiek said.

Woestendiek resigned as editorial director, effective May 1, 1964, and Harry abolished the position. At the same time, he did away with Albright's job as assistant to the publisher and appointed him the editor of the new Saturday magazine. In the same announcement, Harry made two other significant changes: He made McIlwain managing editor and elevated Hathway to the newly created job of executive editor, giving him the functions that had belonged to Woestendiek, but leaving him under the wing of Ethridge, whose arrival had annoyed Hathway immensely. At an election-night party in Harry's office, Hathway vented his anger at Ethridge, poking fun at his diplomatic missions to the Balkan nations two decades earlier. "Hathway had gotten real drunk, and I think really resented Mark, but had never shown it before — at least not very much," McIlwain remembered. "He said, 'What's all this Balkan shit, you phony bastard?' " Finally, Hathway went home, leaving McIlwain and Ethridge, the two southerners, who got along well. With Hathway gone, the outraged Ethridge decided to take action. "He said to me, 'I want you to get him back in here. I'm an old knife fighter, and I'm calling him out,' " McIlwain said. Hathway came back, all shaved, showered and penitent, guided by his keen survival instincts, and apologized.

Hathway didn't have to stifle his resentment of Ethridge for long. In May, 1965, Harry announced that Ethridge would be leaving as editor of *Newsday* and returning to North Carolina to teach journalism. A few months earlier, Harry had discussed with his lawyer, Leo Gottlieb, the names of possible editors of *Newsday*, if anything happened to Ethridge: Harry's nephew, Roger W. Straus Jr., and Lawrence E. Spivak, the host of the television program *Meet the Press*. But when Ethridge actually left, Harry made a different choice: Retaining his titles as president and publisher, Harry assumed the additional title of editor. This provided the *Newsday* staff with some laughs. Everyone knew Harry had brought in Ethridge to train a new editor, and they all expected it to be Albright. But it turned out that Ethridge was really training Harry.

"I think Ethridge's role in keeping *Newsday* on a good path is probably underestimated," Albright said, "because people tend to remember that he drank and that he wasn't perhaps as sharp on copy as the people who were in their thirties, but he made an incredible difference in being able to keep Guggenheim from doing dumb things. For a few years, he was absolutely critical."

IV

ONCE ETHRIDGE HAD left, the staff at *Newsday* had to learn to live with Harry Guggenheim as editor and publisher into the indefinite future. No one knew how long that would last.

In some ways, it was easy enough for his employees to figure out the basic direction of his leadership. They had seen him as publisher for two years and they had a grasp of his central beliefs and his style. But knowing in advance how Harry would act wasn't always so easy, because Harry was a complex man. "I could figure Alicia out in five minutes," Hal Burton said. "I couldn't figure him out in five years."

The passage of time since Alicia's death had done little to make it easier for Harry to withstand the inevitable comparison. Unlike Alicia, Harry often seemed uncomfortable, not quite knowing what to say. "The poor fellow, he wanted to be friends, and he didn't know how to do it," Burton said. "He said to me once, 'The thing people don't realize about me is that I am really terribly shy.'" His basic instincts were to be gentlemanly, if he knew an employee's name and had something to say. But Harry wasn't always good with names. He was constantly mixing up Vinnie Bordash and Buddy Chernow, two of the mainstays of the circulation department, for example, or garbling Stan Hinden's name and referring to him as Stinden. If he saw an employee in the hall and didn't recognize her or didn't want to talk, Harry would simply pass by, saying only "Howdy doooo." His ability to chitchat lightly with journalists was limited. Sometimes, as he did on a limousine ride to Falaise with Tom Collins when Collins became Washington bureau chief, Harry would fill the painful conversational silences by whistling tunelessly to himself.

In his relationships with the staff, Harry was operating with an attitudinal handicap. The same wealth that had given him the capacity for acts of breathtaking generosity had also weighed him down with gnawing suspicion. "Harry was a very lonely man," said Milton Lomask, the author of *Seed Money*, the book that Harry had commissioned to explain the Guggenheims to the world. "I remember his saying, 'To be rich is not to be loved.'" At the same time, he did have some feelings for his personal employees. In fact, one of Harry's warmest relationships in the world was with an employee, his butler, Walter Moulton. Beyond providing simple loyalty and service, Moulton seemed genuinely to like Harry and was able to make him laugh as almost no one else could. Harry paid Moulton a generous salary and provided him with advice on stocks, allowing Moulton to retire in excellent financial condition. On occasion, he carried over to *Newsday* the same benevolent attitude that he showed his servants. One night, for example, Harry and the columnist Mike McGrady were being inducted into the journalism fraternity, Sigma Delta Chi, at a ceremony in Manhattan, and they talked for a few minutes. McGrady mentioned that his grandfather had worked in a Guggenheim copper mine for fifty years and still earned only $1.25 a day at the end. "His eyes filled with tears, and he was really very emotionally moved by this," McGrady said. "The next morning, McIlwain called me in. He says, 'I don't know what you got on the old man, McGrady, but you got a $25-a-week raise.' He was a much more interesting character than people knew."

Despite his limited success in growing close to his employees, Harry displayed sound judgment on the broad business issues — expanding the plant, acquiring new presses, establishing a thirty-five-hour week for everyone on the paper in 1966, once he had agreed to those hours for the printers. He was careful with a dollar, but he didn't hesitate to spend it if he was convinced that it was the right thing to do. On the day of John Kennedy's assassination, for example, most of the regular Friday papers had already rolled off the presses by the time the assassination bulletin moved on the wires. So Buddy Chernow of the circulation department suggested that *Newsday* put out an extra that evening, with no advertising. That was an expensive proposition, but Harry didn't hesitate. Harry also acted without regard to cost when he reacted to Kennedy's death by establishing a policy against accepting gun advertisements. Eventually, the policy lapsed, as the assassination faded into the past and weapons advertisers kept laying money at *Newsday*'s feet.

Since he first took editorial control of the paper, Harry had also been doing the right thing politically. He had always been a staunch Republican, frequently making contributions to candidates and to the party itself. But once Alicia died and his role changed, he adopted a new attitude. Just two months after her death, he wrote a letter to Thruston Morton, who was soliciting funds for the state Republican Party, and made it clear that he could no longer contribute. Even Hathway, who wasn't terribly fond of Harry, singled this attitude out for praise in a 1965 speech. "This does not mean that Harry Guggenheim is no longer a Republican," Hathway said. "It means that he has put his paper above politics."

In the same speech, Hathway said that Harry had a genuine "struggle within himself as to the right thing to do" in the 1964 presidential election. Despite his routine support for Republican presidential candidates in the past, Harry was concerned about Barry Goldwater in 1964. At the Republican convention in San Francisco, Harry told Harvey Aronson why he planned to support Lyndon Johnson over Goldwater: "Barry was right," Aronson said. "Barry had all the right ideas. But Johnson was a son of a bitch. You need a son of a bitch for President." That fall, Harry endorsed Johnson. He also endorsed another Democrat, Nassau County Executive Eugene Nickerson, for reelection. Nickerson was the first Democrat ever elected county executive in Nassau, and even though he had defeated Harry's Republican friends, Nickerson's patrician bearing and his image of honesty and effectiveness appealed to Harry.

As an editor, Harry did not hesitate to suggest stories. "He was always trying to get me to the track: 'You're writing a very good column, Mike, but I notice you never do anything on the sport of kings,' " McGrady remembered. Nor was he shy about ordering stories killed. Once, for example, McGrady wrote a satirical column about the Catholic Church's long-overdue decision to step back from centuries of blaming Jews for the crucifixion of Christ. Harry cancelled it. Similarly, he killed a piece that Aronson had written for the Saturday magazine about life among the homosexuals on Fire Island, before most papers were dealing with that subject. "McIlwain told me it was good; Ethridge told me it was good," Aronson said. "Then they tell me they're not going to run it, because Captain Guggenheim was shocked to learn that this existed and does not believe that a story like this should run in a family newspaper." In contrast, Alicia had done just the opposite. In early 1949, the paper carried several stories about a high school teacher who lost her job because she had tried to break up an affair between two girls in her school, and Alicia assigned Jo Coppola to write a series on homosexuality. "The piece was different than the kind of pieces you would get today, which are pro-homosexuality," Coppola said. Even the headlines, such as "Firm Home

Ties Urged to Cure/Evil of Warped, Abnormal Lives," were so judgmental that they would fill the streets with demonstrators if they appeared in 1990. Unlike Harry, though, Alicia at least faced the issue.

On subjects that he felt he knew, such as Cuba and racing, Harry could be arbitrary and protective. Once, he suggested that the Saturday magazine do a story on fouls by jockeys. The files turned up an old photo of a notorious rough rider, Manuel Ycaza, in the act of fouling another jockey. At the time of the photo, Ycaza had been riding for someone else, but by the time Harry suggested the piece on fouls, Ycaza was Harry's own contract jockey. "All I remember is the Captain walking through the newsroom, standing over my back to look at the proofs," said Lou Schwartz, who was editing the magazine. "He sort of looked at the story and he nodded, but I could see him really getting angry, his face turning almost as blue as his hair. . . . He said, 'But that won't do. That won't do.' And he pointed to the picture of Manny. He said, 'That poor man has suffered enough. I don't want that in this newspaper. . . .' You wouldn't believe how quickly I got another picture in that spot."

V

ASIDE FROM THE structural and ideological changes that he made in the editorial pages, Harry's major journalistic impact was his effort to attract big-name writers to *Newsday*.

Alicia had always liked having big names in *Newsday*, too. A typical example was her idea to record for history a dialogue between two great minds, the architect Frank Lloyd Wright and Alicia's dear friend Carl Sandburg, who knew her father from Chicago newspapers and became a beloved second father figure to her. Alicia sat Wright and Sandburg down in a suite at the Plaza Hotel and recorded their conversation (complete with the sounds of the St. Patrick's Day parade from Fifth Avenue below) while Harvey Weber took photographs. She ran a partial transcript of the conversation under the headline "Meeting of the Titans." When she became concerned about the dangers of subliminal advertising, Alicia and her staff persuaded the novelist Aldous Huxley to write about it for *Newsday*. The result was a twenty-four-page, advertising-free supplement in 1958, called "Tyranny Over the Mind." In effect, it was a nonfiction, book-length sequel to Huxley's novel, *Brave New World*. *Time* magazine called the paper "Brave New Newsday" for publishing it.

Once Harry took over, he set out eagerly to lure big-name writers of his own to *Newsday*. In October, for example, only a few months after Alicia's death, he ran an eight-page piece by the novelist Erskine Caldwell, called "U.S.A. Today," an account of his findings on a cross-country tour. Harry also took another step that later enabled him to offer those big names a broader audience than *Newsday* alone could provide: He started his own syndicate.

While Alicia was alive, he had turned down her proposal to establish a *Newsday* syndicate by purchasing existing properties. But soon after she died, Harry had told Woestendiek that they needed to find someone who knew how to run a syndicate. The name that he turned up was Tom Dorsey, who had learned the business at the *Herald Tribune*'s syndicate and then moved into public relations. So Woestendiek asked him to come in for a meeting with Harry. The meeting at *Newsday* took place in the fall of 1963, at almost the same time that Harry was making two big-name announcements: He was hiring Ruby Hart Phillips, formerly of the *New York Times*, as Latin American correspondent, and signing up the Pulitzer Prize-winning foreign correspondent Marguerite Higgins, to write three columns a week. (Two years after Harry hired Higgins, she contracted a parasitic disease on assignment for *Newsday* in Southeast Asia. While she was ill, two important journalists who were her friends, Peter Lisagor and Michael O'Neill, wrote several columns under her byline, reflecting her views. She died in early 1966.) At his meeting with Harry, the boundlessly self-confident Dorsey laid out his conditions for coming to *Newsday*. Initially, Harry balked at the $25,000 salary that Dorsey asked, but a few weeks later, Harry decided to hire him.

The *Newsday* Specials syndicate began small, with Dorsey and Robert Gillespie, his former colleague at the *Herald Tribune* syndicate, plus an old *Trib* mailing list. Despite those humble beginnings, Dorsey always thought big, never hesitating to spend money in search of sales. Rather than do it by phone, he'd make sure that he flew in to see editors. Dorsey's father had died young, and he was convinced that the same thing would happen to him. So he lived at a fast pace, a man of grand gestures and big entrances. But he knew how to sell syndicated features to editors — not by showing up with visually impressive flip charts, but simply by knowing what the editor's newspaper needed. "I think he was a hell of a judge of features," Gillespie said, "and because of that, he was a damn good salesman."

No salesman can succeed for long with inferior wares, and Dorsey enjoyed some significant success at bringing good writers to *Newsday*. One of his earliest ideas was to sign the novelist John O'Hara to write a regular column. O'Hara's price was high: He would not even roll a piece of paper into a typewriter, he told Dorsey, for less than $1,000. But Harry liked the marquee value of O'Hara's name well enough to pay what he asked. When Harry announced the column, "My Turn," in 1964, *Time* magazine commented: "O'Hara is the captain's most significant catch." Despite the high expectations, many at *Newsday* felt, as Bill McIlwain did, that the column was a waste — typical of the half-hearted efforts that big-name writers turn out for newspapers. The O'Hara column lasted only a year.

Together, Harry and Dorsey also looked for political writers. One of the earliest efforts was a search for a liberal columnist. Harry started out by asking Adlai Stevenson in 1965 to write a weekly column. "You tempt me sorely!" Stevenson wrote. "But it is obvious that I can't even consider this as long as I am in government and I sometimes wonder if I'll even be alive when I'm out of it."

In fact, only four months after he turned down Harry's offer, Stevenson collapsed and died while walking on a London street, with Marietta Tree at his side. The death of Stevenson focused Harry's attention immediately on Clayton Fritchey, his aide at the United Nations. Over lunch at Falaise, Harry and Dorsey discussed with him the potential for a column. Fritchey was a veteran journalist who had also worked in the Truman White House, advised Stevenson during the 1952 and 1956 campaigns and edited the *Democratic Digest*, the magazine of Democratic orthodoxy. But precisely because he was a liberal, Fritchey thought Harry would have a difficult time selling the column to other papers. "He broke in and he said, 'Now, look, Clayton. You may know more about newspapers than I do, but I think I know publishers. The way I intend to present you I feel confident. . . .' He was going to present me, as he would have presented Stevenson, as not a knee-jerk liberal, but as a classical literate, intellectual type of British liberal." Harry was right. The column sold well and lasted for twenty years.

At the other end of the political spectrum, Dorsey reached out to a far more conservative writer: James Kilpatrick, then the editor of the *Richmond News Leader*. Before he became editor, Kilpatrick had been the paper's chief editorial writer, and his conservative views were widely known. Other syndicates had talked to him generally about a contract, but it was Dorsey who flew down to visit him and talk specifics. Dorsey proposed a guarantee of $5,000 for one year, followed by a discussion of future years if the column caught on. They also discussed his views. Kilpatrick had written a book outlining southern beliefs on school segregation, but Dorsey didn't want him writing columns advocating segregation. "I was perfectly aware that I had the reputation in some quarters as an old fire-eating segregationist, one of the fathers of interposition and massive resistance and so on, " Kilpatrick said. "I didn't have any idea of writing columns that would embarrass *Newsday* as being the rabid outpourings of a southern segregationist." So Kilpatrick agreed to write the column. It caught on during the first year, appearing in well over the fifty papers that they had set as a target. But when the time came for *Newsday* to talk about a further contract, the *Washington Star*'s syndicate offered Kilpatrick a succession of five-year contracts and a desk at the *Washington Star*. Harry had made it clear that *Newsday* Specials was not to sign a contract of more than one year with anyone. As a result, Dorsey could not match the *Star*'s offer, and Kilpatrick got away.

Dorsey's greatest success was not in lining up serious columns, but in bringing to the country's attention an obscure housewife from the suburbs of Dayton, Ohio, named Erma Bombeck. She had started in journalism at fifteen as a copy girl at the *Dayton Journal Herald*. When she graduated from the University of Dayton in 1949, she had gone to work in the paper's women's department. She left journalism when her first child, Betsy, was born in 1953. When her youngest child, Matt, went off to school and she found that she had the house clean by 9:30 every morning, Bombeck decided to try writing a column, just to relieve the boredom. So she walked into the *Kettering-Oakwood Times*, a suburban weekly, and volunteered to write. "I did interviews with local people; like Phil Donahue lived across the street," she said. Occasionally, she'd write a column of domestic humor, aimed at universal suburban situations, such as car pools. Her long-term goal was to get the column into one of the daily papers in Dayton, and Glenn Thompson, the editor of the *Journal Herald*, eventually called her and asked if she'd like to write her column for his op-ed page. She started it in early 1965. Soon after Bombeck started writing for him, Thompson had written a letter and sent copies of her columns to Dorsey, arguing that she deserved more readers than he could provide in Dayton. Dorsey and Gillespie quickly signed her up to write for *Newsday* Specials.

The first year of Bombeck's column was difficult. "I knew it was going to be a very tough sell," Dorsey said. "Humor is something editors don't have a lot of appreciation for." One of those editors was Hathway. Even though *Newsday* Specials provided useful exposure for *Newsday* writers by syndicating columns and other features, the editors at *Newsday* considered Dorsey a pushy interloper who enjoyed throwing around the weight that his close association with Harry gave him. "Anything that I suggested or that the syndicate originated they didn't want," Dorsey said. "It was only when Erma Bombeck became a Harry 'must' that it got in *Newsday*." But once that initial year was over, her column started winning friends all across the country. Eventually, the income from Bombeck's column became a major source of the syndicate's profitability for years. Similarly, even though Harry wasn't anxious for Dorsey to sign Jeane Dixon to do a column of predictions, she turned out to be a big money-maker for the syndicate. "It put *Newsday* in the black two years before we were supposed to get there," Dorsey said.

Not every big name that Harry hired was a smashing success. One writer who fell short was Robert Moses, the master builder, who wrote a weekly column, "From the Bridge," for *Newsday*'s Saturday magazine and for the syndicate. Moses had lost much of his power in a confrontation with Governor Nelson Rockefeller, but Harry thought that Moses would have something valuable to say. Even with his power reduced, Moses was imperious. He dictated his columns to his secretary at the Triborough Bridge and Tunnel Authority, and *Newsday* editors almost never got to speak with the great man himself. "If there was a question, we would talk to her," said Stan Green, who edited some of the columns. In fact, Moses complained at one point that *Newsday* was not using the headlines that he had suggested for the columns. So Harry asked Stan Hinden to show Moses how to write headlines that fit properly. "After that, Moses wrote a headline that fit perfectly every time, and we always used his headlines," Hinden said. The columns themselves were less than perfect. "None of the outrageous Moses came across," Dorsey said. "I said, 'This stuff is terrible. You're not getting angry at anybody. You're not getting anybody angry at you.'"

If Moses was disappointing as a columnist, at least his fall into subpar writing did not come from the lofty eminence of a Nobel Prize for literature. That was the fate of the biggest of all Harry's big-name writers, John Steinbeck.

VI

NOT CONTENT TO describe the world only as novelists do, through fictional characters, John Steinbeck also felt the urge to observe it and write about it as reporters do, factually.

"He loved to think of himself as a journalist, and of course he wasn't," said his widow, Elaine. "He was a novelist. He'd hate it for me to say this, but I never really thought he was a very good journalist, because his best pieces were when he could use his fictional talent." Even when he was doing the research for *The Grapes of Wrath*, a searing portrayal of farm workers in the Great Depression, Steinbeck had written nonfiction pieces that flowed from his research.

During the 1950s, Mark Ethridge persuaded him to write some pieces for the *Louisville Courier-Journal* and an ad hoc syndicate about the Eisenhower-Stevenson presidential race. Steinbeck, a profoundly political man, was a staunch supporter of Stevenson, and had provided him with advice and written a foreword in 1952 to a hasty paperback collection of Stevenson's campaign speeches. So, when Alicia and Harry met the Steinbecks at the Ethridge home outside Louisville on one of their Kentucky Derby visits, it was inevitable that Alicia would become friendly with a great writer who shared her admiration of Stevenson, and that she would follow the example of Ethridge and press Steinbeck into service as a reporter.

At the 1956 derby, Alicia persuaded Steinbeck to write a piece for *Newsday* about the experience, his first visit to Churchill Downs. The following year, Steinbeck wrote a piece for the paper's center section about his visit to Rome. On that same European trip, Steinbeck wrote another center section piece on archaeological excavations under St. Peter's basilica and one on the birthday celebrations for the Queen of England. In 1959, Steinbeck made a long visit to England to do research for a book on the legends of King Arthur, and while he was there, Stevenson visited him. When he returned to America at the end of the year, Steinbeck wrote a letter to Stevenson describing his impressions of his own country after his time abroad. It was powerfully pessimistic — full of references such as "a creeping, all pervading, nerve-gas of immorality which starts in the nursery and does not stop before it reaches the highest offices both corporate and governmental." Alicia ran the letter, together with an introduction by Stevenson, across two full pages in the middle of *Newsday*. It prompted a panel discussion in *The New Republic*, which included the historian Arthur M. Schlesinger Jr. and the theologian Reinhold Niebuhr. *Newsday* ran excerpts of that discussion, along with Steinbeck's response.

"Once Alicia and John became friends, there was never any pressure of any kind, nor was there any particular direct action on the part of *Newsday*," Elaine Steinbeck said. "I think that anything John wanted to get off his chest, he knew he had an outlet for." So, by the time of Alicia's death, Steinbeck had established a tradition of writing for *Newsday*. As soon as Harry had designated

Ethridge as the editor, Ethridge had suggested to Harry that they try to persuade Steinbeck to write some pieces for *Newsday* on his planned trip to Russia. "I do hope you will be able to," Harry had written to Steinbeck. "It would be a great kickoff for our battered Newsday team." That request didn't bear fruit immediately, but Harry was a persistent man. In 1965, after Ethridge had left *Newsday*, Harry tried again. This time, he could offer Steinbeck wider distribution, because *Newsday* now had its own syndicate. "Would you be willing to write a column once a week, on anything that comes into your mind, for Newsday and national syndication?" Harry wrote. "Of course you would have complete editorial freedom."

Steinbeck wrote back from Sag Harbor two days later. First, he asked Harry how much the syndication would pay. "I do not write solely for money but a suggestion of it makes good reading," Steinbeck said. Then he enumerated the reasons why it wouldn't be a good idea, mostly because writing pieces on deadline might force him to be dull or to work when he preferred not to work. But he acknowledged that he planned a trip to Ireland and possibly a later one to Vietnam anyway, and writing a column would provide a travel deduction. This letter left the door open for further discussion, and Harry wrote back the next day, offering him a more generous financial arrangement than most syndicated writers got. "Frankly a profit from John Steinbeck's writings is of very secondary consideration to me," Harry wrote. The important point was the prestige that the column would bring to *Newsday* and the euphoria it would bring to Harry.

Finally, Steinbeck wrote back and declined, primarily because he feared the column form. Toward the end of his letter, Steinbeck reached Harry's emotions by bringing up the subject of Alicia. "I loved Alicia very deeply, but I found her guilty of sharp business practices," Steinbeck wrote. "Once she bought a piece from me at a verbally agreed price of one red rose a year in perpetuity. And do you know, after the second year, she defaulted. . . . The memory of princesses is short." With an instinct for the grand gesture, Harry bought and sent to Steinbeck a large rose pin, with a gold stem, jade leaves and coral petals. The card that accompanied it said: "A rose in perpetuity for John the Story-teller from the Princess Alicia."

In addition to the rose, Harry sent a suggestion: Rather than write a regular column, Steinbeck should write irregularly, whenever the mood came upon him. That proposal seemed to turn the tide. Steinbeck wrote back and explained all the reasons why his literary agents were against the idea of his writing for *Newsday*, but this time, the door was clearly open. A week later, Steinbeck proposed that they adopt a loose, non-contract agreement. "I cannot guarantee you copy because I don't know what I will see nor whether I will feel like writing," Steinbeck wrote. "If copy were forthcoming it would probably take the form of letters which allow a variety of fields and subjects to be touched on in a single communication with no sense of outrage to the unity principle." Specifically, Steinbeck proposed a "Letters to Alicia" format — similar to the letters to his wife that had become his book, *Travels with Charley*.

"It is not mawkish nor sentimental," Steinbeck wrote. "The letters would not be to someone who is dead but rather to a living mind and a huge curiosity. That is why she was such a great newspaper woman. She wanted to know — everything. . . . If I write these letters intending to amuse, inform and illuminate (Plato?) Alicia they will do the same to great numbers of people." Harry was so elated that he gave Steinbeck a virtual blank check on expenses. "Live it up or down as it suits your moods and convenience," Harry wrote. "Newsday will pick up the tab."

Once the "Dear Alicia" letters started coming in, the editors at *Newsday* complained that it was odd to be running a series of letters to a dead woman, complete with present-tense references to Alicia's knowledge of Steinbeck's itinerary. "As far as I am concerned this is nonsense," Harry wrote. But Steinbeck acknowledged the problem and suggested that any editor in the syndicate who wanted to drop the "Letters to Alicia" superscription could do that. One of the *Newsday* editors who had strong doubts about the idea was Al Marlens, who also criticized the writing. "I fear that, even as you and I, a writer as good as Steinbeck needs an editor," Marlens wrote.

The first letter to Alicia appeared on November 20, 1965, taking up a full page in the Saturday magazine. At the top of the page was a representation of a postage stamp. The drawing inside it was an artist's palette and a writer's quill pen, because the piece was about government and the arts. In later pieces, the drawing inside the postage stamp changed to reflect the subject of the letter. The mock postmark on each piece contained the name of the location where Steinbeck was writing. The headline, "Letters to Alicia," was in large typewriter-style typeface, and so was the "Yours, John Steinbeck" at the bottom.

At the start of his European tour, Steinbeck was deeply concerned about events on another continent: the war in Vietnam. His son John, whose nickname was Catbird, had just entered the Army and immediately written to his father, asking him to use his influence so that Catbird could get to Vietnam. Catbird also suggested that he write his father a series of letters from the war, potentially for publication. Steinbeck asked Harry about the possibility that *Newsday* could publish such a father-son exchange. "I felt some emotion to know that such a spirit still lives among the young in America," Harry wrote back, receptive to the idea. "With enough of it we can never lose."

Steinbeck's concern with the war showed up vividly in his first published letter from England, about the Viet Cong releasing two American prisoners of war, who questioned the American role. He expressed sympathy for the prisoners themselves, but railed against what he called the Americong, the dupes of the Viet Cong. "These newly come harbingers of peace say we don't belong in Vietnam and we can't win," Steinbeck wrote. "Well, we do belong there and we never wanted to win. But I believe we intend to make sure that Peking doesn't win, either. That's why we belong there."

His next published letter contained another diatribe, this time against draft-card burners. But his enthusiasm for the legends of King Arthur quickly overwhelmed his hawkish views on the war. The following week, his letter was a charming tale of his visit to Alnwick Castle in Scotland, where he found what he at first believed to be a rare and precious manuscript of Sir Thomas Malory's *Morte d'Arthur*, the wellspring of the Arthurian legends that had fascinated Steinbeck since childhood. The manuscript later turned out to be far less significant than Steinbeck had first thought, but that did nothing to spoil his story of finding it, which was filled with excitement and a sense of scholarly adventure, recounted with all of Steinbeck's storytelling skills.

From Scotland, they visited the film director John Huston in Ireland. "He was getting tired," Elaine Steinbeck said. "He said, 'Phone Harry and tell him we're coming home.' " During the phone call, Harry told her that he had hoped Steinbeck would go to Israel. Steinbeck said he was too tired to continue the trip, and she passed that along to Harry and hung up. "I turned to John, and I said, 'After seeing the brain-drain in Ireland and meeting with people who were so backward — all the young, interesting and educated people have left that dead and dying country — there's nothing I would like to do more than see a whole bunch of smart Jews.' Well, John started to laugh, and he said, 'That's a wonderful angle, Elaine.' " So they decided to go to Israel after all. They invited Harry to join them, but he said he wouldn't be much help to them, since he and his family had never been Zionists. Before leaving London, Steinbeck wrote a tragicomic "Letter to Alicia" about his great-grandfather, who had decided in the nineteenth century to go to the Holy Land and convert the Jews to Christianity. When a wandering band of Bedouins ransacked his farm and murdered his brother, Steinbeck's great-grandfather decided to leave the country with his wife and three daughters. As the ship neared Boston, a gang of sailors grabbed the youngest daughter and mauled her so savagely that she died. Steinbeck ended the letter with his favorite understatement, an entry from his grandmother's diary of that voyage: "The crew was over friendly."

In Israel, Steinbeck encountered a hilarious waiter who kept calling him Steinberg, offered an alternate ending for *Of Mice and Men* and asked him how much money he got for the Nobel Prize. Harry printed both the *Jerusalem Post* story about the waiter and Steinbeck's letter to the *Post* editor. Steinbeck also gathered material for "Letters to Alicia" that covered such diverse subjects as the search for his great-uncle's grave, a comparison between the brave Israelis and the war protesters in America, the struggle to bring irrigation to the desert and a visit to the mountain where Jesus uttered the Beatitudes.

Before he returned home, Steinbeck wrote to Harry that the "Letters to Alicia" had turned out not to be a burden after all. "In writing them she came very much alive to me so that it was actually like talking to her," Steinbeck said. Back in New York, the Steinbecks had supper with Harry, who gave them a gift photograph of Alicia. Harry tried to persuade Steinbeck to continue writing letters for publication regularly, but Steinbeck turned him down. "No man has really very much to say," Steinbeck wrote, "but he can easily be convinced that he has more than he has." As it turned out, Steinbeck did have something else that he wanted to write about: the war in Vietnam.

Just as Harry had nudged Steinbeck to write for *Newsday* from Europe, he began cajoling him to do the same from Vietnam, even though *Newsday* had already sent a reporter to the war. In the fall of 1965, McIlwain had sent John Van Doorn, then the night city editor, to the war zone. The sudden assignment to Vietnam was the start of almost four years of foreign travel for Van Doorn, which made him *Newsday*'s first real foreign correspondent. But Van Doorn almost changed his mind about going, after a meeting with Harry. "His last words to me were, 'You know, war is a fine adventure for a young man. You're going to have a wonderful time,'" Van Doorn said. "I almost gagged." Once Van Doorn had been in Vietnam for almost three months, Harry wrote him a letter and said that he had done "an unsurpassable job." A few months later, in 1966, Van Doorn won the Ernie Pyle Award, for his work in Vietnam at the end of 1965. "I know my military friends were quite happy with his objective reporting," Harry wrote Steinbeck. Yet Van Doorn became convinced that Harry's private views were different. "I had turned out to be not what Harry wanted, which he made very clear to a number of people," Van Doorn said. "He wanted me to go over and support the war." What Harry needed was someone who saw the war his way: John Steinbeck.

"Before it is too late someone must tell more about this war than the sensational superficialities that the wires send us throughout the day," Harry wrote Steinbeck. That summer, Steinbeck showed his feelings again when the Russian poet Yevgeny Yevtushenko wrote an open letter in the Moscow literary publication, *Literaturnaya Gazeta*, urging Steinbeck to protest the bombing of North Vietnam. Steinbeck chose to respond in an open letter in *Newsday*. Harry made the Steinbeck letter available to other newspapers, including the *New York Times*, which ran it on page one. The Steinbeck letter caught the attention of Jack Valenti, a top aide to President Lyndon Johnson, and Valenti called Steinbeck to tell him that the letter had inspired the President to rewrite his latest speech on the war. Taking advantage of the opportunity, Steinbeck mailed the President his own proposal for peace negotiations.

The Steinbeck-Johnson relationship had its original roots in Texas, where Elaine Steinbeck had gone to school with Lady Bird Johnson. Once Johnson became President, he began reaching out for the great writer. "He decidedly wanted support in the intellectual community — all the more so after he was roundly denounced by Robert Lowell and the other poets and the other writers of the time," said Johnson's press secretary, Bill Moyers. Given that desire, Johnson was more than receptive to a proposal from Valenti: "I suggested we ought to try to get Steinbeck to try to do some writing for the President." In the summer of 1964, for example, Steinbeck wrote an essay about the President that the Johnson forces distributed at the Democratic convention. Once Johnson had defeated Goldwater, the President asked Valenti to meet with Steinbeck to get ideas for the inaugural address. Valenti took an Army helicopter to Sag Harbor and met with Steinbeck in the little gazebo where Steinbeck did his writing. As the time for the 1965 inaugural address approached, Steinbeck sent Valenti some proposed language, including two paragraphs that the President loved. The final speech contained these words from Steinbeck:

"I do not believe that the Great Society is the ordered, changeless, and sterile battalion of the ants.

"It is the excitement of becoming — always becoming, trying, probing, falling, resting and trying again — but always trying and always gaining."

Given this close relationship and Steinbeck's support of the war, Johnson was as anxious to see Steinbeck go to Vietnam as Harry was. "We both went to Washington, and he went alone to see the President, and he came back to the hotel and said, 'Well, it's settled,' " Elaine Steinbeck said. "I said, 'Oh, good. How?' And he said, 'Well, I said I'd go if I could take Elaine.' " So both Steinbeck and his wife went, with the blessing of Harry Guggenheim and the President of the United States, and Steinbeck did not disappoint either of his patrons. The handwritten "Letters to Alicia" that flowed back to *Newsday* contained some of Steinbeck's eye for detail and storytelling skill, but they were primarily shrill and hawkish.

"They say there's no fool like an old fool, but when I see some of the long-haired young protesting against a life they have yet to live, I don't think we aged have a monopoly on folly," Steinbeck wrote in the first letter of the Vietnam series. "Anyway, Alicia, I'll let you know what I find." The dominant theme of his reports was disgust for those who opposed the war at home, combined with hero worship and awe for the American soldiers. "Can you understand the quick glow of pride one feels in just belonging to the same species as these men?" Steinbeck wrote. "I suppose it is the opposite of the shiver of shame I sometimes feel at home when I see the Vietniks, dirty clothes, dirty minds, sour-smelling wastelings and their ill-favored and barren pad mates. Their shuffling, drag-ass protests that they are conscience-bound not to kill people are a little silly. They're not in danger of that. Hell, they couldn't hit anybody." Not content merely to travel with the American troops, Steinbeck learned how to use weapons. "I don't want to be a dead weight," he wrote in one published letter. "I want to be a guilty bystander, if necessary."

At one point, Steinbeck wrote privately to Harry, complaining about the difficulty of interrogating the Viet Cong, and asking for Harry's help. "Did you ever see scopalomine used, Harry?" Steinbeck wrote. "It doesn't make a man or woman tell the truth, but it makes him a compulsive talker." Such an injection could cut the unit's casualties by at least fifty percent, its commander had told Steinbeck. "I am going to do my best to get some here by any means, if it exists here," Steinbeck wrote. "But somehow I have my doubts. . . . I know your influence with the air force. Would they smuggle some in to me? . . . I wish also for you to ask someone who knows, whether LSD would have any value as an information gatherer. . . . I have no compunction about using any method whatever to that end." Harry's return telegram was cautious. "Am investigating subject your very private letter." A few days later, acting for Harry, Martin Schram of the *Newsday* Washington bureau answered Steinbeck with a cryptic cable: "Expert advice states no medicine able to effect cure. Now working on highly complex measures that could not be administered simply."

In his private correspondence with Harry, Steinbeck also praised General

William Westmoreland, the American commander in Vietnam: "This is a man to watch, Harry. He is not making any mistakes." But in the same letter he criticized Johnson bitterly for his 1967 State of the Union speech, which Steinbeck considered too "wishy-washy" on the war. Harry's response was sympathetic to Johnson. "He is caught between the hawks and the doves and obviously doesn't dare to go too far in either of their directions," Harry wrote. At the same time, Harry repeated his extravagant praise for Steinbeck's reports. "I don't know anyone who is telling the real story but John Steinbeck," Harry wrote. "In single handed combat you're slaying all the doves, peaceniks, beatniks, communists and draft dodgers." In that spirit, Harry recommended Steinbeck for a Pulitzer Prize.

Not everyone at home was as enthusiastic. It was clear to many of the staff at *Newsday* that this was not the same Steinbeck who had championed the downtrodden in *The Grapes of Wrath*. In fact, one of the most famous pieces of *Newsday* bulletin-board writing was a parody by a young editor named Jack Schwartz. His spoof combined the hawkish tone of Steinbeck's Vietnam pieces with an imaginary Steinbeck visit to the fields that had spawned his great novel. "He is offended by these awful-looking grape pickers and strikers and troublemakers and anarchists and radicals and folks like that, who he figures must be put up by outside agitators, like this Tom Joad," Schwartz remembered. "He proceeded to do this column, saying that he has spent a lot of time with real California people, like the owners, and they have told him through their PR guys exactly what's going on."

A more scholarly analyst, Tetsumaro Hayashi, the president of the International John Steinbeck Society, conceded that, although some of the pieces from Europe and the Middle East were entertaining, the Vietnam pieces were not up to Steinbeck's standard. "Very candidly, of course, his quality of writing had declined, because he was not feeling very well to begin with, and he had to write this in a very uncomfortable environment," Hayashi said. Nonetheless, Hayashi tried to persuade Elaine Steinbeck to allow the "Letters to Alicia" to be published as a book. She declined. "I think she wants to avoid publishing anything to do with Vietnam-related writings."

Sadly, Steinbeck's health deteriorated rapidly after he returned from Vietnam, and he died at the end of 1968. "John changed his mind totally about Vietnam while there, and he came home to write it and spent all the rest of the time dying," Elaine Steinbeck said. "That's not just an apology for John. That is true." So the last face that John Steinbeck presented to the world, after a lifetime of identification with the causes of the downtrodden, was the face of a shrill hawk — in the pages of *Newsday*.

CHAPTER TWENTY-THREE

Guggenheim Journalism

I

DESPITE HARRY GUGGENHEIM'S lack of journalistic experience and his emphasis on big-name outsiders, his newspaper made a lasting impact on the community during his years at the helm.

One of his major contributions was to force the officials of Long Island's two suburban counties to start planning seriously for the growth that the paper had promoted from the start. The inexorable demographic forces behind the suburban dream, with *Newsday* cheering all the way, had brought about a stunning population boom. In 1940, the year of *Newsday*'s birth, the United States census reported a combined population of 604,103 in Nassau and Suffolk counties. By 1960, the population of the two counties had more than tripled, to 1,966,955. As the population soared, of course, the circulation of *Newsday* had grown with it. On its first day, *Newsday* sold 16,000 to 17,000 papers. By late 1964, the circulation had reached 400,000.

Profiting so heavily from Long Island's population explosion, however, had not entirely blinded *Newsday* to the consequences. For years, the paper's editorials had been warning government and industry that no one was properly planning for all this growth. Alicia Patterson had understood the dangers. In 1954, for example, as Nassau's population neared 1,000,000, Alicia had run a strong editorial raising the issue. "Nassau has already lost many of its best chances for a planned county, and Suffolk is on the verge of following," the editorial said. "We want a growing population on Long Island. We want new industries, new highways, and new stores. But we do not want to be strangled through our own stupidity, the way New York City has been strangled."

The central problem was that neither county had an effective planning agency. Less than three months after Harry took over as publisher, however, *Newsday* ran a series of stories that finally prodded the two counties into taking the first step toward regional planning for the future.

It began in the second half of 1963 with an assignment from Alan Hathway to one of the few Ivy League-educated journalists that he ever trusted, Robert A. Caro. The Caro-Hathway relationship had started off inauspiciously when Bill McIlwain announced that he had just hired a Princeton graduate. Caro looked the part: earnest and controlled, wearing a proper jacket, tie and often a vest. Hathway preferred street-wise reporters to eager college boys, and he responded to the hiring of Caro with a grumble. At Princeton, Caro had been the managing editor of the *Daily Princetonian*, and after graduation he had gone to work for a small paper in New Jersey, the *New Brunswick Home News*. When he came to *Newsday*, Caro was still unformed.

During Caro's first few days at *Newsday*, someone assigned him to go to a Long Island Rail Road crossing, just east of the office, to get the details on a near-accident. He was so raw that he drove to the west instead, and didn't realize it until he reached Queens. When he finally got to the scene, he found a deaf man with a troubled marriage who had tried to kill himself by parking his pickup truck on the LIRR tracks. "I remember I felt like crying," Caro said. "I mean, this was the first time I had ever been at a human tragedy. I came back and I wrote this story, and I didn't know how to write." Once Caro had written it, Dick Aurelio, the news editor, walked over to him. "He said something like, 'This is a terrific piece of writing, but you don't have a lead on it,' " Caro said. "I, of course, knew in theory what a lead was, but I didn't really know. He said that in the lead you do so-and-so. I did the lead and I brought it up to him and he said, 'Now you need a second paragraph.' He took me through this article. . . . When he finished that, I really understood more about how to write newspaper articles."

In addition to teaching him basic techniques, the *Newsday* environment also began to give Caro something even more important: self-confidence and an understanding of his own skills. Despite his considerable untutored talent, Caro felt so insecure during his probation period that he and his wife, Ina, continued living in New Jersey. One weekend, however, a story came his way that finally made him feel he belonged. The paper had gotten a tip that important documents were available about Mitchel Field, one of Alicia's top priority stories, and Caro went to the Federal Aviation Administration offices at Idlewild (later John F. Kennedy International) Airport and examined the documents. "I always had a great gift for going through files, but I didn't know it," Caro said. He came back to the office and left a detailed memo for Hathway. On Monday, one of Hathway's secretaries, June Blom, called Caro, who was off that day, and told him to come to Hathway's office. "I was sure it was to fire me," Caro said. As he fearfully approached Hathway's desk, Hathway held up his hand, motioning Caro to sit down, and continued reading a document that Caro realized was his memo. "I've won various awards," Caro said, "but I think my most gratifying moment in journalism was when he looked up at me and he said, 'I didn't know someone from Princeton could do digging like this. From now on, you do investigative work.' " Once he attained that status, Caro was not always a popular figure in the newsroom. Some considered him a prima donna who seemed to prefer dealing with no editor below the level of Hathway and Al Marlens, the city editor. But no one could deny that he brought to his work a high level of talent and a searing intensity. For Caro, journalism was a mission, an outlet for his sense of outrage at the world's injustices.

His first major effort was an investigation of the fraudulent sale of vacant land in the Arizona desert. The four-part "Misery Acres" series began on January 7, 1963, including a large photograph of Caro sitting alone in the barren desert, sipping Chianti at a folding table. The project caught Alicia's interest in the last months of her life. "She said, 'You go to Albany and get a law passed,' " Caro remembered. Caro spent weeks in Albany, working for legislation to tighten the loopholes in the law. With the help of Assembly Speaker Joseph Carlino, the *Newsday* campaign succeeded in producing a bill, and Caro posed with Governor Nelson Rockefeller when he signed it into law.

That summer, Hathway asked Caro to take on another project, a look at the economic malaise of Suffolk County. Instead of a quick-hitting story, Caro found a complex reality: No one was really planning for Long Island as a region, even though there was still time to save Suffolk from the haphazard development that had devoured Nassau. "There only seemed to be one guy out in Suffolk who was thinking about this — Lee Koppelman," Caro said. Koppelman was the planning director for Suffolk County, working for H. Lee Dennison, the Democrat who had been elected as Suffolk's first county executive. At lunch with Koppelman at a German restaurant in Smithtown, Caro started by smiling pleasantly and asking Koppelman a series of soft questions. "And I'm waxing poetic about how this new administration is going to guide the future," Koppelman said. "I'm into it for about a half hour, and finally Caro cuts in and . . . reels off a bunch of statistics: Southold was a disaster area. The population was aging. The young people couldn't stay there. The unemployment rate was going up. . . . And he caught me up short."

The result of Caro's reporting was a six-part series called "Suffolk: The Sick Giant," which contained the beginnings of a pitch for regional planning. "I wanted *Newsday* to really campaign to set up a regional planning board and try to put Lee in, because he was the most visionary guy, but to give him real powers," Caro said. "I persuaded Alan of this at great length, and Alan went in and talked to the Captain about it." The series ran from September 30 to October 5, 1963. In January, 1964, Caro followed with another series, "Suffolk: The Still Sick Giant." Then Harry began pushing public officials to set up the regional planning agency. Both county executives — Dennison in Suffolk and Eugene Nickerson in Nassau — favored the idea, but the Republican-controlled Board of Supervisors in each county was far less enthusiastic. One of the strongest opponents in Suffolk was Shelter Island Supervisor Evans K. Griffing, who had also opposed *Newsday* on the county charter issue in the late 1950s. To overcome that obstacle, Nickerson proposed that Harry call Griffing and other elected officials in for a meeting, to explain *Newsday*'s position. Before leaving for the meeting, Griffing made it clear to Koppelman that he opposed the idea, but at the meeting, Harry was persuasive. "It was explained to him," Nickerson said, "and he left the meeting being for it." At the start of 1965, the supervisors of both counties voted to create the Nassau-Suffolk Regional Planning Board. Griffing voted in favor.

Compromising on the makeup of the board, the counties cut a deal: A Nassau politician, Leonard Hall, the former chairman of the Republican National Committee, would be the chairman. The executive director, Lee Koppelman, would come from Suffolk. But before the appointment took effect, Harry summoned Koppelman for an audience in Garden City. "He wanted my concurrence that what we really needed to develop was this grand blueprint," Koppelman said. To underline his point, Harry told a story about inviting the architect Frank Lloyd Wright to Long Island, picking him up in his limousine at the airport and driving past a high-rise apartment complex in Queens. As they drove, Harry told Koppelman, Wright waved his hand at the apartments and said: " 'I give you the slums of tomorrow.' It made a big impression on him, and the Captain says to me, 'We don't want the slums of tomorrow in Nassau and Suffolk.' " The ultimate result of Harry's desire for a "blueprint" was the completion of the bicounty master plan five years later, in 1970. Tom Morris, the veteran reporter and editor, became the paper's full-time planning and transportation specialist, covering the implementation of the plan. "When I look at *Newsday*," Koppelman said, "I look at it as the single most important positive force for the proper development of Long Island."

The planning stories had a lasting effect not only on the growth of Long Island, but on Caro's life. In doing the reporting, Caro discovered how little he knew about planning. So he applied for and won a Nieman Fellowship at Harvard University, where he studied urban and regional planning in 1965 and 1966. While he was there, Caro realized that the best way to explain to the world the way in which politicians use their power to shape the construction of highways, parks and other public works was to write a biography of Robert Moses. His decision to leave the paper, after *Newsday* had supplemented the stipend that he received from the Nieman program, nearly ended that supplement for future Nieman fellows from *Newsday*. But Caro was too committed to the Moses project to stay at *Newsday*, even though it had been the training ground where he had acquired much of his now-legendary persistence and attention to detail. "Everything I learned in that series carried over into my books," Caro said. "Most of what I learned, two people taught me: Alan Hathway and Al Marlens. They're the same techniques I use today."

When he left, Caro expected to return in a year. Instead, he spent seven years on the Moses book, *The Power Broker*, which is now required reading in classrooms across the country. More than a quarter of a century after the *Newsday* series that led to his career as a historian, Caro retained a pride in the establishment of the regional planning board, the creation of the master plan and the preservation of parkland in Suffolk County. "It's so much better than it would otherwise have been, because of Lee Koppelman, because of the bi-county planning commission, and therefore because of *Newsday*," Caro said. But Caro could not have accomplished what he did if Harry had been short-sighted or timid about using the newspaper's power in that campaign. "For all his conservatism," Nickerson said, "he was really interested in good government."

II

ON THE DAY that Alicia Patterson entered the hospital for the last time, the lead editorial in *Newsday* spoke up strongly in favor of John F. Kennedy's proposed civil rights act, because America could "no longer afford the dubious luxury of second-class citizenship." On that same day, the total number of black report-ers employed at her newspaper was zero.

That paradoxical situation neatly sums up *Newsday*'s mixed record on racial issues at the start of the massive civil rights ferment that bubbled up across America in the mid-1960s. Alicia had disapproved of racist language, but she was also capable of a less-than-commendable caution on racial issues. One example was her reaction to the effort of a Nassau County women's group to involve black women. As a feminist, Alicia had cooperated with Elizabeth Bass Golding, the president of the Nassau County Women's Bar Association, in establishing a Women's Forum in 1944, and in the years that followed, Alicia met regularly with Golding and offered advice. "I never had a program that I didn't review with Alicia," Golding said. For the fourth annual forum in 1947, Golding invited a light-skinned black woman, a lawyer from Philadelphia, and suggested that Alicia run a photo of the woman in *Newsday*. "Alicia said, 'That might be very damaging to the paper, because I don't know of any newspaper that has had a picture of a black in it,' " Golding remembered. "I said, 'Then *Newsday*'s going to be the first.' " Alicia ran the photograph. On another occa-sion, Golding told Alicia that the members of the Women's Forum favored making a black woman president. "She said, 'Betty, I don't think you ought to do it,' " Golding said. Despite Alicia's advice, the group later elected a black woman as president. "She felt strongly on social justice, except for the blacks," Hal Burton said.

The paper's editorials themselves made an inconsistent record. In 1943, *Newsday* reacted strongly to a racist editorial in the *Nassau Daily Review-Star* that had recommended locking up "some zoot-suited offenders in Hempstead" and had hinted that hanging might not be a bad idea either. Following the war, one editorial expressed outrage when hotels in New York City refused to accommodate black boxers on the Long Island Golden Gloves team. That editorial ran only a few weeks before Jack Roosevelt Robinson broke baseball's color line by playing for the Brooklyn Dodgers, but strangely, Alicia did not comment editorially on Robinson's debut. Perhaps *Newsday*'s greatest postwar failure on the racial justice issue was its criticism of those who spoke out against the whites-only policy of the Levittown development.

During the 1950s, *Newsday* unambiguously approved of the 1954 decision by the Supreme Court of the United States in *Brown* v. *Board of Education*, banning school segregation; criticized Governor Orval Faubus of Arkansas for resisting integration in the Little Rock schools; repeatedly urged President Eisenhower to speak out publicly during the Little Rock crisis and praised him when he did; decried the election of the racist Henrik Verwoerd as prime minister of South Africa, and counseled local officials to plan for an influx of blacks and Hispanics, to avoid consigning them to slum housing. In general, the paper's position on civil rights was staunchly pro-integration, but against demonstrations, such as the Alabama "Freedom Riders" in 1961.

For the most part, *Newsday* had covered the southern integration battles in the 1950s with wire-service reports. Alicia did send Bill Woestendiek in 1956 to observe the effort of a young black woman named Autherine Lucy to enter the University of Alabama, and Woestendiek wrote a five-part series on the civil rights struggle in the South. Later, Hal Levy and Bonnie Angelo of the Washington bureau wrote about integration in Virginia, and Michael Dorman went to Montgomery, Alabama, to cover the "Freedom Riders" in 1961. Focusing closer to home, in the spring of 1962 Alicia ran a four-part series by Harvey Aronson on housing discrimination on Long Island.

Not until late 1962 did *Newsday* start using its own staff extensively to cover the integration story in the South. First, Bonnie Angelo went to Oxford, Mississippi, to report on Governor Ross Barnett's efforts to keep James Meredith from enrolling in the University of Mississippi. Her replacement, Michael Dorman, covered one integration flashpoint or another through the rest of 1962 and into the summer of 1963. He was there, for example, for the campus riots when Meredith finally enrolled in Ole Miss with the help of federal troops. Dorman also covered riots in Birmingham, Alabama, the violence in Jackson, Mississippi, and the tense standoff in Tuscaloosa between the federal government and Alabama Governor George Wallace. While he was there, Dorman got a tip from a source in the Justice Department that Wallace had developed psychological problems while he was in the Army and was still receiving disability checks. Dorman finally got the story, but *Newsday* declined to run it. (Later in the year, Senator Wayne Morse of Oregon released the same information on the Senate floor.) Dorman's travels in the South that summer ended in the small, tense city of Danville, Virginia, where he met with Dr. Martin Luther King Jr. By late 1963, the year of Alicia's death, *Newsday* as an institution was firmly committed to coverage of the quickly unfolding story. That commitment, along with the paper's coverage of the Kennedy assassination, had thrown *Newsday* reporters together on a regular basis with national reporters from other papers and raised *Newsday*'s profile. "I felt there was an appreciation that *Newsday* wasn't a small-town newspaper anymore," Dorman said.

It is possible that, left to his own devices, Harry might have weighed the value of staff reports from the South and decided that *Newsday* could spend its money more wisely in other ways. In fact, on at least one occasion, Harry had displayed something short of humane sensitivity to the plight of the few black residents of Port Washington, not far from Falaise. Many of the local black residents worked as servants in Sands Point estates and lived in a tiny ghetto along Harbor Road. In the late 1940s, when the Town of North Hempstead's housing authority was looking for a site for a sixty-six-unit garden apartment complex, it focused on property diagonally across from Falaise. Harry disliked that idea. "As an inducement to the authority, Guggenheim proposed that he donate the cost of the purchase of an alternative site for the project," wrote Samuel Kaplan in *The Dream Deferred: People, Politics and Planning in Suburbia.* "The project was eventually approved without much rancor, and built and occupied in 1951 without incident. . . ."

But if Harry wasn't inclined by nature to be a crusader for racial justice, Mark Ethridge was. In addition, the newsroom was filled with editors, such as McIlwain and Marlens, who saw the value of the civil rights struggle as a story, quite apart from the merits of the issue itself. On top of that, by the time Harry had settled into his chair, *Newsday* had actually hired its first-ever black reporter, followed a few weeks later by its second.

On overwhelmingly white Long Island, Hathway had been dubious about the value of black reporters. "He felt that there were many stories that blacks would not be able to cover, because of the prejudice of others," Bernie Bookbinder said. "He said, 'Can you imagine if a black had to cover a Garden City village board meeting?' " Beyond Hathway's doubts, another factor that made the newsroom less than hospitable was the racist judgment — prevalent at newspapers all over the country — that black murder victims were worth less space in the paper than white victims. *Newsday*'s most notable adherent of this view had been Jimmy Jenkins, who was the last editor to touch the paper every morning. "He considered any black murders to be insignificant," Dick Aurelio said. "He was racist, no question about it." In the 1960s, as *Newsday* began covering racial issues regularly, other editors noticed that Jenkins became more racially neutral in his news judgments.

Given those attitudes, plus the failure of the entire newspaper industry to hire black reporters, it took *Newsday* almost a quarter of a century to take its first step. The pioneer was Thomas A. Johnson, who had grown up in New York City, served in the Army, and studied journalism at the Brooklyn campus of Long Island University, graduating in 1954, as one of only two black men in his journalism class. His advisor was supposed to help Johnson find a job, but he would flee whenever Johnson approached, because there simply were no jobs for black journalists, except at black newspapers such as the *Amsterdam News* in Manhattan. Johnson became a free-lance New York correspondent for the *Pittsburgh Courier*, a black newspaper that had seventeen regional editions. He also started a news service that provided stories to black publications. To supplement his income, he wrote liner notes for phonograph records. "I was a hustler, a literary hustler," Johnson said.

Before Johnson approached *Newsday*, he had written to the *Long Island Press* about a job, and an editor telephoned him in response. "He hemmed and hawed and said, 'Are you colored?'" Johnson remembered. He told the editor that he was black, and that ended Johnson's chances. "He said, 'Well, I'm very sorry, and I apologize profusely, but we simply can't hire you, because if we did hire you, it would mean that we could only assign you to cover black people, and that would be discrimination in reverse.'" Then Johnson learned that *Newsday* was looking for a black journalist. So he telephoned McIlwain, who talked to Johnson in his syrupy southern accent and agreed to have Johnson come in and take a writing test.

"I walked in there and there was a Confederate flag on the wall, and an American flag," Johnson said. But McIlwain quickly made it clear that Johnson was welcome. His basic point, as Johnson remembered, was this: "'We're doing a whole lot of writing here about integration, and I look around here, Tom, and I don't see a single Negro on the staff.'" McIlwain offered him a salary that was about $100 a week more than Johnson was making. So he accepted, starting at *Newsday* on July 8, 1963 — less than a week after Alicia's death. "I think they had agreed before I walked in there that, if they found one who could read and write and wouldn't call them too many nasty names, they would hire him," Johnson said. "That was in my favor." And despite his nervous start with McIlwain, Johnson grew to respect him. "I guess it might have been easy to just write him off because of the accent, the flags and all that," Johnson said. "But I found him a good human being."

A month later, acting on a recommendation from Johnson, McIlwain hired another black reporter, Lawrence "Pat" Patterson, an acquaintance of Johnson's from the *Courier*. Patterson had grown up in Queens, a few miles west of *Newsday*, served in the Merchant Marine and in an all-black Army quartermaster unit in the Korean War, had studied economics and journalism at New York University and graduated in 1957. Like Johnson, he found McIlwain's Confederate flag unnerving, but he also became an admirer. With the exception of a few isolated moments, he felt comfortable at the paper. "I do give *Newsday* an awful lot of credit," Patterson said. "Their antennae were out, and I think they were sensitive to a changing climate. In my working professional experience, I've had none better."

During the same summer when Johnson and Patterson arrived at *Newsday*, major civil rights stories were breaking all over the nation, such as the march on Washington, culminating in Martin Luther King's "I have a dream" speech. But that summer, and through the turbulent events of the next several years, *Newsday* did not regularly send Johnson or Patterson to cover these stories in the South. The reporters who covered most of the major civil rights events of that decade were white: primarily John Cummings, Michael Dorman and Bob Greene, and sometimes Harvey Aronson. But neither Johnson nor Patterson complained. "There is a pecking order no matter where you go, and we were not close to the top of the pecking order, having just arrived," Johnson said. Patterson said the situation was awkward, because he didn't want to be pegged as someone who only covered civil rights, but he also wanted to cover the story. "We were pioneers," he said. "You didn't want to rock the boat." Tony Insolia, who became the news director at about the time that Johnson and Patterson arrived, said that it made sense to send other reporters who were more experienced than Johnson and Patterson. "The fact that they were black did not qualify them at that point in their careers to go cover a national civil rights story," Insolia said.

Shortly after he arrived, Johnson did go to the march on Washington as a participant and later, at the request of his editors at *Newsday*, wrote a first-person piece about it. In 1964, after the signing of the civil rights bill, banning racial discrimination in public accommodations, Johnson made news by attempting to register in the old Garden City Hotel, which turned him away, claiming the hotel was filled. But two white *Newsday* reporters telephoned the hotel and were told they could have rooms. (The hotel later claimed that Johnson had asked for a weekend room, and there were none available for the weekend.) He also toured Mississippi with a group from the NAACP and wrote about it for *Newsday*, and he took time off from *Newsday* to join the marchers in Alabama from Selma to Montgomery. Eventually, Johnson's editors let him carve out a local civil rights beat. His reporting brought him into regular contact with the fiery black leader, Malcolm X, and positioned him as well as any reporter in New York to cover Malcolm's assassination in 1965. In addition, he teamed with Aronson to write a long piece for the Saturday magazine in 1966 called "The Negro on Long Island," *Newsday*'s first ambitious look at the way black people lived in the suburbs. Patterson did not cover civil rights as heavily as Johnson did, although he did do occasional local stories about racial issues, such as a five-part series about life in the predominantly black North Amityville neighborhood. And *Newsday* sent him to Memphis to cover the aftermath of Martin Luther King's assassination.

The reporters that the editors did send to the South were tough, talented and experienced, and they represented the paper well. For Greene, it was a unique opportunity. The story required undercover reporting, one of Greene's instinctive skills. But it also required sensitive writing, which did not come naturally to him. "I remember when Greene came there and couldn't write his name," said John Van Doorn, who edited some of his early copy. "He would come up and ask editors, 'Now, who do you really think is a good writer around here?' You would tell him, and you'd find him later, hours after he was supposed to be off duty, back in the library with their clips out." Greene would read the writing of Dick Estrin, Harvey Aronson, Helen Dudar, Virginia Pasley, and others whose work he admired. At night, he'd meet editors in a bar and ask for critiques of his writing. He even honed his skills by producing a poem, "Song to a River," on deadline, as a last-minute replacement for a center section page that had fallen through. "That guy got to the point where he could really turn a phrase," Van Doorn said.

On the civil rights beat, one of Greene's first major assignments started with a phone call from Marlens on a Sunday morning, just after a bombing in Birmingham had killed four little black girls on September 15, 1963. Greene rushed down there in time to file a story about an angry meeting of black leaders, including Martin Luther King. By Tuesday, Greene had come up with a significant story, starting with information from a woman who worked as a waitress and switchboard operator at his hotel. The woman told Greene that she had overheard a phone conversation in which someone (Burke Marshall, the assistant United States attorney general for civil rights) discussed a plan for King to visit the White House. Since the Kennedy administration was still keeping King at arm's length at the time, Greene knew that this was an important development. Greene called Pierre Salinger at the White House, and Salinger denied it. Then he called King in Atlanta, and King confirmed it. Greene wrote a story for the Wednesday paper, saying that King and other black leaders would meet with the President on Thursday. At two o'clock in the morning, Stan Asimov called Greene from the desk in Garden City. "He says, 'Bob, we called Salinger and Salinger says kill the story. It isn't true.' I said, 'Stan, I think it is true. . . .' He says, 'I'm going to go with you, but I'm telling you, I'm taking a hell of a risk doing this.' I said, 'Let's take the risk.' " The paper led with the story of King's planned visit. The *New York Times* didn't carry the story until the Thursday paper. Kennedy met with the black leaders, as Greene had revealed, and called on Alabamans to exercise "restraint and responsibility." For years afterward, Greene told young reporters: "Don't ignore, when you're doing a story, the clerks and all these people. That's where you get some of your biggest stories."

The following year, Marlens and Joe Albright asked Greene to explore reports of the Ku Klux Klan's renewed activity. This gave Greene a chance to work undercover, as a wealthy oil man. To provide confirmation of his identity to anyone who called, Greene set up a system of phony references. One was a friend at a Wall Street brokerage firm. Another was a special phone near Hathway's desk in Garden City. To outfit himself suitably for his role, Greene spared no expense. "I charged *Newsday* for a $350 suit, which at that time was one hell of an expensive suit, and beautiful boots," Greene said. He flew to Jacksonville, Florida, rented a Lincoln Continental, and started driving north, wearing his suit and his oilman's broad-brimmed hat. His first appointment was with Robert Shelton, the Imperial Wizard of the Klan, in Tuscaloosa. At supper with Shelton and his wife, Greene said that he wanted to spend some of his oil wealth on a publication that would tell the world about the noble side of the Klan. Without even checking Greene's phone references, Shelton gave him an official letter, asking local Klan officials to cooperate, plus a list of the key Klan leaders in several states. "He wasn't too bright," Greene said, "but I wasn't too bad an actor, either."

From Tuscaloosa, Greene drove toward Liberty, Mississippi, for a meeting with the head of the Klan in that state. The first night out of Tuscaloosa, he stopped at Meridian for the evening. Taking off his oilman attire and dressing in more casual clothes, he visited the headquarters of the Congress of Racial Equality (CORE) and learned that they had just sent three civil rights workers to investigate reports that whites had burned a black church to the ground. The three men were supposed to have returned ninety minutes earlier, and their friends at CORE were beginning to worry. Greene came back to the CORE office later that night, and the workers still had not returned. "I am the first person, by pure accident, to be there and to know that these guys have not shown up," Greene said. He called *Newsday* and told Marlens, who instructed him to go to the area and bang on every door immediately, in search of the workers. "I said, 'Al, there's nothing to be accomplished there tonight, except maybe getting me killed.' " The next morning, Greene drove to the scene of the burned-down church, interviewed the black people who lived nearby and confirmed that the three civil rights workers had been there the day before, asking about the church fire. Greene filed a story for the next day's paper, the first account in *Newsday* of the disappearance of James Cheney, Andrew Goodman and Michael Schwerner. He stayed in Neshoba County during the early part of the search for the workers, then continued on his Klan odyssey, which provided him with material for a four-part series, "The Klan Rides Again," and for a piece with Tom Johnson on the "Voices of Mississippi." John Cummings replaced him in Philadelphia and covered the rest of the search, until the bodies were found, and the start of the murder investigation.

For the rest of 1964 and much of 1965 and 1966, Cummings and Greene formed a tag-team reporting combination. Cummings covered the Alabama voter registration drive, including the murder of a civil rights worker from Detroit, Viola Liuzzo, and Greene covered the trial of the men accused of killing her. Then Greene covered James Meredith's 1966 march through Mississippi. Greene moved ahead of the march and wrote stories about the mood of towns that lay ahead of the marchers. For that assignment, he wore a big straw hat, dark pants, a tan military shirt, a wide belt and prematurely gray hair in a crewcut. The people he met along the way mistook him for a sheriff, which made it easier to get information. "My personal feelings were enormously pro-civil rights," said Greene, but he disapproved of other reporters who let those sympathies show. "You're not going to get the story, because you're being too partisan." But looking like a sheriff had its drawbacks: The townspeople may have felt more comfortable with him, but the marchers were nervous. "The leaders of that march had to tell the folks who were doing the marching that this guy is okay," Greene said.

Along the route, perhaps the most moving story that Greene wrote was about an old black man, Armisted Phipps, who marched a short distance because he felt he should be part of it all, then collapsed and died — with less than two dollars in his pocket, plus a receipt showing he had paid his poll tax.

"They clustered under the feeble shade of a giant oak tree, ankle high in the lush green grass of a Mississippi meadow, and sang a last farewell to Armisted Phipps yesterday," Greene wrote.

"For just a few moments, the voices of more than 500 freedom marchers drowned out the incessant buzz of the FBI helicopter lazily circling overhead and the raucous taunts of white teenagers gathered just across the narrow, concrete strip of U.S. Highway 51.

"And as they sang the ageless spiritual of the Negro South, four black men tenderly lifted the body of Armisted Phipps from the roadside dust and placed it in an ambulance for the beginning of the final trip to his tiny, weatherbeaten home, 20 miles away. . . . Doctors blamed his death on the fatal combination of a scorching sun and an infirm heart. The Rev. Martin Luther King accused the malnutrition that is often the lot of the Mississippi sharecropper. But Phipps' neighbors diagnosed his fatal disease as an excessive love of freedom."

A few days later, Frank Lynn relieved Greene and covered the rest of the march. Greene returned to Garden City and wrote a six-part series called "Dixie's New Negro," an optimistic assessment of what he had seen on his travels through the Deep South.

Those were exhilarating times for Greene. When he wasn't hopping on a plane to cover civil rights stories, he was back on Long Island, investigating the mob, gambling and the influx of drugs in the high schools. Just as he had dressed as an oil baron or a pseudo-sheriff in the South, Greene pursued those local stories in disguise. Like a large boy, Greene never tired of courting danger — often foolishly — by pretending to be someone he was not.

During a five-week investigation of illegal gambling on Long Island in 1964, for example, Greene and Tom Renner went to a health club that was owned by a mob boss. Hoping to flush the mobster out, Greene didn't give the clerk at the health club his real name or Renner's. Instead, he gave the name of a widely feared mob killer. "The guy's hands were shaking as he wrote the names," Renner said. This was in the middle of a bloody mob war, and the mobster that they were trying to flush out was fearful that someone was going to kill him. So the arrival of a hitman in his health club was likely to make the boss react, and Greene and Renner had convinced themselves that the boss or his underlings might show up at the health club. Just to be safe, Renner ran back outside to the car and brought his pistol into the building. Then he joined Greene in the sauna. "All I kept saying to Greene is, 'They're going to lock that goddamn door, and we're going to be like a lobster,'" Renner said. They survived the sauna, but when they got in their car to drive away in a heavy fog, two cars followed them at high speed and finally caught up. When they saw the press license plates on the car, the mobsters turned away. It was foolish and unproductive, but Greene couldn't resist trying it. "There are times when you have to do things just because they're there," Greene said. "That's what adds all the excitement to life."

The role of a hoodlum suited Greene so well that he tried again in 1966, working with a new reporter named Martin Schram on a series about drugs in the high schools. Some officials were saying that drugs were becoming a major problem, but many parents and even some *Newsday* editors were skeptical: Drugs in schools? Come on! The original assignment went to Schram. He had just come to *Newsday* in 1965, and he quickly found himself swept up in the coverage of the New York City blackout and working on the drug series. Since he was still young looking and had moved north from Miami, Schram posed as a University of Florida dropout and started working on a group of teenagers at a shopping center in Nassau County, asking them for drugs. The leader of the group and two others slammed Schram against a wall and demanded to know who he really was. He produced his Florida driver's license and realized, to his horror, that it listed his occupation as "reporter." Quickly, he grabbed the license back, put his thumb over the "reporter" and angrily waved it at them. A few minutes later, he used a cigarette to alter his occupation on the license to "porter." Once he got past that initial scare, Schram won their trust. But he needed help in dealing with the police, and Greene provided that experience. "Tony Insolia called me and said: 'Would you do me a favor? The kid's got something. Can you come in and help him out?'" Greene remembered.

Toward the end of the project, in addition to providing a liaison with the police, Greene decided to pretend that he was a mob contact for Schram, to see if he could speed up a drug deal. So he met with the leader of the young drug dealers at a bar and put on a boastful hoodlum routine. "We come from heavier people than you people," Greene told him. But the drug dealer was unimpressed. Several cars full of his friends arrived at about that moment, and a few minutes later, they were beating Greene enthusiastically. "Greene looked awful," Schram said. "He was treated and released at the hospital, but he was really bruised and bloodied. His face looked a mess."

Even though Greene's fascination with the mob thrust him into almost comical situations, his coverage of civil rights in the mid-1960s established him as a versatile reporter with the stature to cover national stories. His reporting from the South — along with the work done by Cummings, Dorman, Aronson and others — was a major step in the development of *Newsday*, from a provincial paper to a more sophisticated one that felt increasingly at home operating in the broader arena of twentieth century America.

CHAPTER TWENTY-FOUR

Falls from Grace

I

FOR TWO DECADES, Alan Hathway had often strained Alicia's patience and occasionally embarrassed her. But he had been stoutly loyal, and she had always protected him from the consequences of his follies.

Once Harry took over, Hathway found himself on a far more slippery slope. Harry was hardly in a position to move him out quickly, but it was inevitable that the two men would come into conflict. In fact, they had clashed long before Alicia's death. Supposedly, Harry promised some of his executives cash bonuses, then decided to give them *Newsday* stock instead, and Hathway confronted Harry about it. "Alan said, 'I backed that old son of a bitch up against the wall and told him we wanted $100, and we got it,' " Bill McIlwain remembered. "Of course, he would have been a rich man if he had taken the stock."

Once Harry became publisher, the friction continued. At a Falaise dinner party for Mark Ethridge at the start of his time at *Newsday*, for example, Hathway's behavior annoyed Harry immensely. Hathway was angry that Ethridge was going to be the editor, Hal Burton remembered, and he took his anger out at various points in the evening on Burton and Bill Woestendiek. That broke up the party. The next day, Burton went into Harry's office and Harry wasn't there. While he waited, Burton used the old newspaperman's skill of upside-down reading to peruse a letter on Harry's desk. "This was a letter to Alan, saying, 'No gentleman ever behaved in my house as you have behaved.' " Even when Hathway tried to be careful, he ran afoul of Harry. When a *Time* reporter interviewed Hathway and McIlwain about *Newsday*, they were careful to say favorable things about the boss. But Tom Dorsey, who ran *Newsday*'s syndicate for Harry, said that he acquired a copy of the reporter's raw file, through his contacts at *Time*, and passed it along to Harry. Something in it enraged Harry. "That was when he said, 'Goddamn you, Alan,' " McIlwain remembered. "And that was the only time I ever heard him use profanity."

On a more substantive matter, Harry disagreed with Hathway over his interests in Puerto Rico. In 1956, Hathway had begun travelling there and had formed a friendship with Luis Ferre, a wealthy industrialist and the leader of the island's Statehood Party. Hathway saw him frequently in Puerto Rico, and Ferre came to Long Island, visiting Hathway's home and staying on one occasion at Falaise. Before long, the two men became business partners. "We saw this beautiful property at the beach and we wanted to buy it," Ferre said. "We just had sort of an investment for the future." Ferre and Hathway, plus several of Hathway's Long Island friends — Arthur Lem, Paul Townsend, and George Helm — bought a little more than a hundred acres, with a half mile of beachfront, ten miles from Dorado Beach. The long-term plan for the property, called Mar Chiquita, was to develop a hotel on a rocky promontory overlooking the beach, plus a cottage colony. While they sought the right buyers, Hathway often vacationed at Mar Chiquita. He came to love Puerto Rico so much that be began writing pieces about the island and about other parts of Latin America. To handle his correspondence in Spanish, he hired a Spanish-speaking secretary — Carmen Hines, a Puerto Rican woman whom he recruited at a bar. "He says to me, 'Carmen, I want to live and I want to die in Puerto Rico,' " Hines remembered. In fact, he almost did die in a horseback accident there.

Hathway's *Newsday* reports on Puerto Rico were, naturally enough, "unabashedly sales pieces," said Art Perfall, one of the editors who worked for him. The title of Hathway's five-part series in 1957 sounded like hard-hitting journalism: "Puerto Rico: Our 'Hot Potato!' " But the lead on the first story let the reader know Hathway's perspective immediately: "Ever been to Puerto Rico? No? You haven't lived." Other Hathway stories on Puerto Rico over the years carried such boosterish headlines as "Puerto Rico: An Island Racing into Tomorrow" and "Puerto Rico — Showcase for Latin America." Hathway did deal seriously with important issues, such as the drive for Puerto Rican statehood, but one of his most frequent sources on that subject, was Ferre, his partner. "He felt that was the thing to do, that Puerto Rico had to become a state of the union," Ferre said. "He was a very firm believer in Puerto Rico's future."

Eventually, Harry raised a question about the propriety of Hathway's position. The occasion was a column by Marguerite Higgins, pointing out the danger of Communist gains in Puerto Rico. Harry asked whether Hathway should write a piece in response, and Hathway told him that he should. But Harry had second thoughts, and he told Hathway in a memo: "You want to come to the rescue of the vested interests there. . . . You are one of the vested interests in Puerto Rico." So Hathway didn't write the article. Ultimately, Hathway and his American partners sold their interests to Ferre, who had by then been elected governor of Puerto Rico. The plans for Mar Chiquita still hadn't materialized after more than two decades.

By the time of his disagreement with Harry over Puerto Rico, Hathway was already in decline as the dominant force at the paper. Once McIlwain had become managing editor in 1964 and Hathway had moved up to executive editor, more and more of the daily decisions fell to McIlwain. Hathway could still terrorize employees, but he no longer had the power to deliver — for himself or for his friends, such as William Cahn, the district attorney of Nassau County.

Well before he became district attorney, when he was still a young assistant to District Attorney Frank Gulotta in the early 1950s, Cahn had first earned *Newsday*'s admiration by investigating Bill DeKoning. Gulotta had decided to raid DeKoning's headquarters and confiscate his records, but when Gulotta asked one of his senior assistants to go after the records, the prosecutor refused. So Cahn volunteered nervously for the job, charging into the Labor Lyceum with a group of detectives and gathering the records, then playing a major role in the successful DeKoning prosecution. Later, when Bob Greene came to *Newsday*, Cahn also developed a close relationship with him. Together, they convinced Nassau County Republican Chairman J. Russel Sprague of the need for a rackets bureau in the district attorney's office, and Cahn later became the head of it. In several of his earliest major investigations — of the milk, carting and jukebox industries — Cahn worked closely with Greene. In return for lending Cahn his expertise on organized crime, Greene got back something he wanted: the prosecution of mobsters. "Bill Cahn did something the other DAs didn't do," said Tom Renner, *Newsday*'s organized crime specialist. "He put them in jail for thirty days on contempt, or what-have-you."

For years, Greene had struggled with the mob, but without subpoena power. His ability to influence Cahn, however, gave him the next best thing to a real subpoena. In addition, Greene had a pipeline of information that gave him a distinct competitive advantage. "Cahn was making sure that we had the inside track on everything that he did," Greene said. "That made great stories, and we were stomping on the *Long Island Press* and the *Daily News* — stomping."

By 1962, when District Attorney Manuel Levine resigned to accept a judgeship and Cahn was appointed to succeed him, the Cahn-*Newsday* friendship was a powerful force. That fall, Cahn ran his first race for election to a full term, against a formidably named Democrat, Emile Zola Berman. Even if Cahn had not been a friend of *Newsday*, the paper needed no more reason for endorsing him than the one it gave on the editorial page: Cahn was experienced, and Berman, although brilliant and charismatic, had never been a prosecutor. If the endorsement was defensible, however, some on the *Newsday* staff thought it was far less justifiable for Hathway to allow Greene to write any news stories about the campaign, given his strong commitment to Cahn.

"I felt, and I think other people in the newsroom felt at that time, the assignment of Bob Greene to Cahn's campaign, and the pro-Cahn coverage of that campaign, was really a thank-you for Cahn's efforts on behalf of *Newsday*'s interests," said Stan Asimov, who was then night city editor. Actually, Greene did not write much about the campaign. In September, when Nelson Rockefeller appointed Cahn to replace Levine, Greene wrote the appointment story, referring to his valued source as "Long Island's top racket-buster" in the lead. But *Newsday* didn't begin covering the race until nearly the middle of October, and Greene himself didn't start writing about it regularly until the end of the month. At that point, he wrote stories on Cahn's charges against Berman, while George Wheeler, Michael Dorman and Harvey Aronson wrote about Berman's charges against Cahn. Greene did contribute one major story that could be considered strongly pro-Cahn: a front-page piece about Cahn rounding up welfare cheats — precisely the kind of publicity that his campaign needed.

Even though Greene's total output of copy on the Cahn-Berman campaign was small, both Aronson and Dorman were still wary of his involvement. As the campaign drew to a close, they feared that, if Cahn debated Berman, Greene would slant the story in Cahn's favor. "When I covered Berman, I told Berman, 'Never have a debate with him,' " Aronson said. The two candidates did debate, however, and Dorman and Greene both attended. "It was my impression that Berman cut Cahn to ribbons," Dorman said. But Greene wrote the story, and someone showed it to Dorman. "I didn't think it was an honest story," said Dorman, who wrote an insert to help balance it, and ended up sharing a byline — to his distress. The campaign also left a sour taste in the mouth of Asimov, who remembered getting instructions from either Hathway or Jack Altshul to play Cahn's replies higher than Berman's charges. "I thought that was a total distortion and an indication of very slanted coverage," Asimov said.

To Greene, the coverage of Cahn's race in 1962 was in the tradition of *Newsday*'s previous campaigns for candidates. "Alan certainly didn't say, 'go soft,' or anything else," Greene said. "Nobody would have to tell me that if this guy is your best source and you're getting great stories like this, that if you're going to be covering this, it's going to be very hard not to be writing favorable stories about that person. That doesn't mean that you write derogatory stories about the other person." On election day, Cahn beat Berman easily, and Cahn continued to be a friend of *Newsday*.

If Greene and Hathway admired Cahn's work, however, there were many detractors. "If you analyze any of the *Newsday*-Cahn investigations, they are big, big blurbs in the beginning, tremendous PR, tremendous press, heinous accusations, and they all end up in zilch," said John J. Sutter, a well-known defense attorney. "Cahn couldn't convict Jack the Ripper of double-parking if he had a videotape." A typical case was a long investigation of a group of housewife-prostitutes operating out of bars near *Newsday*. Cahn wiretapped phones in all the bars and recorded the voices of an impressive list of customers — including one hapless *Newsday* employee. When Cahn rounded up the prostitutes, *Newsday* played the story like the end of the world, but the woman identified as the ringleader got off with a suspended sentence. "*Newsday* would never publish with equal space, or position in the paper, acquittals, no-jail sentences," Sutter said. "While there was a pretense of factually reporting investigations, they necessarily were anti-defendant. Trying to get a jury was virtually impossible. That's why I waived a jury in so many cases." Others loathed the insensitivity of

Cahn's roundups of welfare cheats, many of them mothers with small children. "I was appalled," said Judge Beatrice Burstein, who witnessed one of the well-publicized roundups and its effect on the children.

One of Cahn's most vehement critics was Nassau County Democratic Leader John F. English, who had the overall responsibility for the campaigns of Cahn's Democratic opponents. "He felt that Cahn was a very dangerous man," said English's law partner, Emil V. Cianciulli. "He exhausted many nights in barrooms, trying to convince Alan that Cahn was not worthy of the support he was getting, and they never agreed about that." Despite that, English and Hathway, neighbors on Fire Island, remained drinking buddies. English was also friendly with Greene, despite Greene's closeness to Cahn. "The relationship between Greene and Cahn was venal and corrupt," English said. "He'd be in the DA's office and know when they were going to raid someplace and where they they were going to put the wiretaps on. . . . Cahn was a wholly owned subsidiary of Greene."

By the time Cahn ran for reelection in 1965 against former District Court Judge David Gibbons, the *Newsday* equation had changed fundamentally. Hathway was still there, but Alicia was not. In the 1965 campaign, Greene had nothing to do with the coverage, because he was in the South, covering civil rights. Bill McIlwain, who had strong feelings about the impropriety of the Cahn-Hathway relationship, assigned the story to a reporter who shared those feelings, Bernie Bookbinder. It was a nasty campaign, in which Gibbons said it was wrong for Cahn to have a friendly relationship with a jukebox distributor named Irving Holzman, who had a felony conviction in 1943, and Cahn argued that Holzman had reformed and helped him to lock up jukebox racketeers. In covering the campaign, Bookbinder had standing orders from Hathway that he had to call Hathway's apartment every night and read the story to him, before it went to the desk. "I learned quickly to write my leads so that they were Hathway-proof," Bookbinder said. "I devised them in such a way that they couldn't be faulted, but yet were clearly reflecting Cahn's bumbling." Hathway didn't tamper with the stories, but he did accuse Bookbinder of slanting them against Cahn. "It got to the point where he said, 'You're no fucking good. You're a lousy reporter,' " Bookbinder remembered. "It was very painful to me, because he had been kind of a folk hero of mine."

In the end, it was not Bookbinder who turned *Newsday* against Cahn, but Cahn's own temper. "His face would get very red and his jugular veins would stand out," McIlwain said. At some point in the campaign, he met with Harry at the museum and discussed an accusation that Cahn had tapped the phones of County Executive Eugene Nickerson. "He was snotty as hell," Cahn said. "I says, 'Who the hell do you think you are, God?' " This did not make a good impression on Harry. Late in the campaign, Bookbinder attended the editorial board meeting at which they discussed the endorsement and gave his summary of the campaign. Hathway argued for Cahn. The deciding vote, of course, was Harry's. "Guggenheim said that he had seen this man and he was astonished by his behavior; he was no gentleman," Bookbinder said. "And he had no difficulty in believing the things that I had described." So *Newsday* endorsed Gibbons. In 1962, Cahn had won by almost 90,000 votes. This time, he defeated Gibbons by only 10,000 votes. The final estrangement between *Newsday* and Cahn did not happen for another decade, but Cahn's brush with Harry was the beginning of the end.

II

As Hathway's control of the paper was declining, the prospects of Joe Albright, the bearer of Alicia Patterson's hopes, were also slipping.

"At first, I thought things were going well on track for me to become the publisher," Albright said. "Guggenheim and Ethridge were giving me all sorts of encouragement to believe that that's the way that things were going." At the end of 1963, Albright wrote a grateful letter to Harry. "This is a good time to take stock of some of the open-hearted things you have done for my family and me," Albright wrote. "As I look back over this year, the one thing that stands out, besides Aunt Alicia's tragic death, is the way you have brought me into the inner workings of the paper."

Generally, Alicia's family was on good terms with Harry, at least on the surface, in the first two or three years after her death. "We were hoping all would be well," said Albright's mother, Josephine. "I was hoping that Joe would inherit. I was trying to be pleasant." For his part, Harry was thoughtful and generous to the family, sending them gifts, letting them in on his private correspondence with John Steinbeck about Alicia, and offering them encouragement about Albright's progress. "Joe has taken on his new job with enthusiasm and as always is working intelligently, diligently and successfully," Harry wrote Josephine, after Albright had become the editor of the new Saturday magazine.

Below the surface, however, there were storm warnings for Albright. One was Albright's successful effort to prevent Harry from firing John Cummings in 1963, over a piece that he had written about Cuba. "This somehow helped to plant with Guggenheim the notion that I was somehow disloyal, or maybe I was a Commie symp myself," Albright said. "Maybe he also realized, rightly, that I was pretty damn young to be the publisher of *Newsday* at the age of 27 or 28." The encouragement that Harry and Mark Ethridge had offered him began to come less frequently, but Albright didn't pick up that signal immediately.

As assistant to the publisher, Albright attended the daily editorial meetings, and to McIlwain's eyes, he seemed out of his depth. "It was certainly a hard stage for a young man to be appearing on," McIlwain said. In his next job, as the first editor of the Saturday magazine, starting in 1964, he had no major problems. But after that, he became the night city editor in Garden City and a day editor in the Suffolk office, and he had significant difficulties in both jobs.

The news editor had the last word on what went into the paper, but the night city editor ran the reporters, decided what was covered and made sure the copy came in on time. Albright worked hard and stayed all night, but his inexperience made it impossible for him to move quickly enough. "Joey Albright was incapable of making a decision at deadline," said Tony Insolia, who was running the day desk when Albright took over at night, then followed Albright as night city editor. "You've got to juggle ten balls and keep them going, and keep production going, and keep your reporters going and take your telephone calls. It's a very, very stressful job." Insolia was a seasoned journalist by the time he took the job, and his brusque, no-nonsense nature was ideally suited for it, but Albright should not have even tried. "Joe is one of the nicest, most decent, honest people I've ever dealt with," said Cummings. "He should never have been an editor. . . . He'd see all the trees, but he couldn't see the forest. He's a perfectionist in a way. I mean, one time he wanted me to go measure the height of the wall around the governor's mansion in Albany, because somebody had said it was four feet." Over the years, Albright came to recognize as much himself. "I didn't do well in that job," he said. "I kept being late going into the composing room. It was a case where my cockiness, I guess, led me to jump into a job which I hadn't been sufficiently prepared for. . . . I also made the mistake of telling Guggenheim what a big job that they had given me, because I thought this would impress him and please him. The idea that I was deciding what was going to be on page one, he really didn't like."

The next step was a job as a morning editor in Suffolk. It wasn't as stressful, but it also wasn't nearly as important. "I had one reporter," Albright said. "It was really a made-up job." In that job, as in the others, Albright was friendly and well liked, even if his wealthy world was alien to everyone else. "He was the nicest kid," said Ernie Volkman, then a reporter in Suffolk. "You can't take a kid like that, suddenly throw him in with street guys, and not have it show. . . . He lacked all instincts, because he had nothing to give him the instincts." His boss, the Suffolk editor Art Perfall, remembered coming in one day and finding that Albright had badly underestimated the importance of a school fire, and Perfall had to scramble to send more reporters to cover it. "Local coverage really wasn't his thing," Perfall said. "He really didn't think this was very big stuff, which was not the message that I was trying to get across to the staff." Despite Albright's intelligence and talent, he simply was not ready to handle the daily editing jobs that came his way. "They overmatched him, and then they demoted him," his mother said. "It was all very sad."

At the same time that Harry was turning sour on Albright, he was also losing patience with his grandson, Dana Draper, the likeliest heir to Harry's empire. In his long search for an appropriate heir, Harry had occasionally flirted with others, such as his nephew, Oscar Straus II. In the late 1950s, Harry had sought to revive the family's mining operations, and he had entrusted Straus with that task. But the era of Guggenheim dominance had passed. With a small exploration budget, Straus had little chance of competing with larger firms and finding another rich strike, such as the one at Chuquicamata that Harry had run for the family, decades earlier. Harry and Straus quarrelled, and Harry refused even to let Straus use the Guggenheim name on his venture. But Straus was only a brief dalliance. Harry's long-term project was his grandson.

Dana Draper had not attended the right kind of private school, and he had done poorly at Menlo College, instead of going to Stanford and excelling, as Harry wanted. Then he had gone off to the Army in 1959, to gain more time to think about what his future should be. While Draper was at Fort Bragg, North Carolina, he started taking some college courses and expressed a desire to attend Pembroke College, Cambridge, Harry's alma mater. That delighted Harry, who loved Pembroke fiercely, but it didn't work out. Ultimately, Draper decided to enter an American college. Just as he had toyed earlier with the idea of becoming a doctor, Draper started thinking about going into the education field. "My mind is forever changing," Draper wrote Harry. "I just see so many things that I want to learn about." Draper was discharged from the Army in June, 1961, to attend summer school at Columbia University. But before he could start classes in the fall semester, the Army called him back to active duty for a year. He wrote a long letter of protest to his senator, and Alicia ran it across two pages in the center of *Newsday*, and carried an editorial on it — without identifying Draper as Harry's grandson.

Finally, Draper entered Columbia in the fall of 1962, and got better grades than he ever had. A few months after Draper's first-semester grades came in, Harry put him on the board of the Daniel and Florence Guggenheim Foundation, where he was the youngest member ever elected. In addition, Harry rewarded Draper by buying him a Porsche. Harry was so pleased with Draper's progress that he wrote in a memorandum to the trustees of his will later that year: "I have little doubt that in time Dana Draper will qualify as President and Joseph Patterson Albright as Publisher or Editor of Newsday."

But before the end of 1964, Draper had begun to disappoint Harry, by announcing that he planned to marry a Columbia student named Marilyn Kirshner. In a meeting with Leo Gottlieb, his attorney, Harry made it clear that he was beginning to doubt whether Draper wanted to undertake the family responsibilities that Harry had in mind for him. He told Gottlieb that his nephew, Roger W. Straus Jr., "might be a solution for him" as a beneficiary and as editor of *Newsday*. And he complained about Kirshner's influence on Draper. It was not her working-class background that bothered Harry, but her ideas. "Mr. Guggenheim was somewhat disturbed to find views somewhat similar to his daughter Nancy's views about the higher utility of things other than money-making," Gottlieb wrote, in a memo after a meeting with Harry. "I don't think I ever used the word 'money' in our conversations," Kirshner explained later, "but I certainly talked to him about other things that were going on in the world, like Vietnam."

Once Draper had married Kirshner, Harry's fierce determination to mold his grandson into his heir seemed to overwhelm his concerns about Draper's wife. Draper spent some time at Harry's plantation in the spring of 1965 and made a two-and-a-half-page report on its operations that seemed to give Harry disproportionate pleasure. Only two months after Draper's report, Harry outlined the provisions of his will and explained that it would be necessary for Draper to spend a large portion of his time at *Newsday*, to prepare himself to become the paper's president. By early 1966, in an effusive letter to Draper, Harry was full of confidence for the future. "I have had one great hope that the good Lord has granted me," Harry wrote. "I wanted to see you prepared by education and talents so that you could continue to build on the works that generations before you have made for the progress of mankind if you had the ambition and desire to do so." They agreed that, in the fall, Draper would come to work at *Newsday*. Draper was still uncertain about what he wanted to do with his life, but the romance of his own father's newspaper career appealed to him, and he saw the *Newsday* experience as a way to find out what he was really meant to be. When he returned from a vacation in Europe, Draper moved into Falaise and started work at *Newsday* on October 3.

For training and evaluation, Harry turned Draper over to McIlwain. The experiment started on an inauspicious note, when Draper misspelled the name of Columbia University, his alma mater, on his application. Then Draper took the test for incoming reporters. When it was over, McIlwain gently explained his findings. "He said basically, 'You're a Guggenheim, so you're in,' " Draper remembered. "But he said, 'Otherwise, you don't have the journalistic skills of the caliber that *Newsday* has.' " McIlwain told him that the test results showed that Draper might make a good minister. Nonetheless, Draper liked McIlwain and McIlwain liked him. "The thing I remember about Dana was his eyes," McIlwain said. "He had these fawn-like, doe-like — just the kindest, gentlest, least-combative eyes you ever saw." McIlwain passed this gentle man along to Insolia, one of the toughest editors at *Newsday*. "I followed a reporter around — different reporters," Draper said. "I would write up some copy and they would write up some copy. Then I'd hand my stuff in to one of the editors, and they'd ink it up real good. . . . It was a lot of stress. Everybody's looking at the stuff and I'm not feeling at all confident about my communications skills anyway." It quickly became apparent to Draper and to Insolia that he had no future in the newspaper business, and Insolia briefed him candidly on his strengths and weaknesses. "He thanked me very much," Insolia said. "He was a very nice, gentle kid who just didn't have it." After only seven weeks, the experiment ended.

Ultimately, Draper had to break the news to Harry. "I said basically I didn't want to work at *Newsday*," Draper said. "He didn't say anything." But the news was a great disappointment to Harry, who had convinced himself that his grandson could be something for which he had no real aptitude. As always, Harry didn't listen well enough or understand what people really were. Instead, he projected onto them his own high expectations. "So much of it had to do with his fantasies," Draper said. When people failed to live up to those fantasies, Harry's anger was monumental. In the months that followed, as Draper found a job as a social worker, Harry made his displeasure clear. In one letter, he informed Draper coolly that he would not sponsor him again for membership on the boards of two family foundations, and he went on to outline his grievances:

"I have ever tried to convince you — but I am afraid I failed — that all the preparation I had attempted to give you was not in my interest but yours, so that you would lead a full, fruitful and dedicated life to your fellow man in our family tradition.

"This tradition must and will be carried on by those who consider it a privilege and a rare opportunity, and not merely an obligation or for one's special benefit. I hope with greater maturity you will come to that conclusion, and try to find some way to retrieve the opportunity you have discarded, and serve."

Years later, when Draper found something that truly engaged and interested him — an arts project called Sculpture in the Environment — he wrote an enthusiastic note to Harry and said he'd like to talk to Harry about what he was doing. "I got no answer," Draper said. "I didn't push real hard."

Dana Draper had lost his chance to be the heir. Joe Albright had somehow disappointed Harry and lost any opportunity to take over *Newsday*. But Harry desperately needed someone to take control of his empire and to run the newspaper that he himself understood so poorly. In the closing months of 1966, as Draper's big chance came and went, Harry turned for an answer to the one human institution that he revered above all others: the White House.

CHAPTER TWENTY-FIVE

The Captain and the Minister

I

IT WAS ONLY a page and a half long, but at the time, it was the most important piece of writing that Bill Moyers had ever done.

At the age of nineteen, Moyers already felt an attraction to public affairs, and he had an instinctive grasp of how to operate politically. So, when he sat down to compose a letter to Senator Lyndon Baines Johnson, volunteering to work in Johnson's 1954 reelection campaign, Moyers made all the right points. At the time, Moyers lived at North Texas State College in Denton, a short drive northwest of Dallas, but he wrote the letter on the stationery of the *Marshall News Messenger*, where he had worked as a reporter, starting during his high school days, and where he still worked during summers and vacations. The first two words in the letter were the name of his mentor, Millard Cope, the publisher of the *News Messenger*. Cope completely supported Moyers in this effort to attract Johnson's attention, which became the turning point in his young life.

Billy Don Moyers was born in 1934, the second son of John Henry and Ruby Johnson Moyers. When he was still an infant, the family moved from Hugo, Oklahoma, to Marshall, Texas, a small railroad town on Route 80, east of Dallas and just west of Shreveport, Louisiana. It was a typical southern town, with a legacy of slave holding and racial segregation. Demographically, Marshall was solidly working class. Henry Moyers made his living at a variety of jobs, from picking cotton to driving a truck, and never earned more than $325 a month. So his sons helped the family financially by holding part-time jobs.

While he was in high school, Moyers worked at a supermarket, bagging groceries. His older brother, James, had gone to work as a reporter for the *News Messenger* and become its city editor. One day, James passed him on the street outside the supermarket. "I had my arms full of packages, carrying them out to the car for a lady, and my brother said something to the effect of, 'You know, there's a better way to make a living,'" Moyers remembered. That suggestion made sense to Moyers, who had already become a prodigious reader and had developed an interest in journalism. So, when the publisher himself came by and invited him to work at the *News Messenger*, Moyers agreed. From that moment, Millard Cope began to exert as pervasive an influence on Bill Moyers as he did on Marshall. "I used to watch him walk down South Marshall Street and stop at every store and greet by their first name every shopkeeper," Moyers said. "He was just in the sinew, the warp and woof of the life of that town."

The first assignment for Moyers was to write about Marshall boys who were entering the armed forces during the Korean War. "That led to features, not only about them, but about other things, and I developed into a fairly productive young reporter," Moyers said. Cope encouraged him to go beyond that, to cover the school board and later the courts and elections. Extending his influence into the rest of Moyers' life, Cope helped him to get a Rotary Club fellowship to North Texas State College. Before the end of his sophomore year there, Moyers had served as the president of his freshman and sophomore classes, joined the Young Democrats Club, run the college radio station, and made some plans for his future. "I had decided I wanted to be a political journalist," Moyers said. "So I decided I needed political experience." After discussing it with Cope, he sat down to write the letter to Johnson.

"This, we both want you to understand, is not a request for a political favor; it is a request for an opportunity to work and learn, which I believe a job with you would offer," Moyers wrote to Johnson. "Mr. Cope tells me that it probably would be a 20-hour-a-day job; that is fine with me. I think I understand just what such a job would require: typing, mimeographing, building platforms, driving and perhaps some writing. Whatever needs to be done, I would try to do. What I definitely would like to do is to help you reach the thousands of 'young voters' — those people on the college campus who so often are neglected in a campaign race."

At Johnson's office, his top aide, Walter Jenkins, plucked the letter from the pile when he saw that Moyers had worked for the *News Messenger*, and he put it on Johnson's desk. Johnson called Cope, who gave Moyers a ringing endorsement. Then Johnson wrote Moyers a brief note. "I am impressed by your letter," Johnson wrote. "You appear to be the kind of ambitious, energetic young fellow whom I like to have associated with me."

That summer, Moyers worked in Johnson's Washington office, rising quickly from addressing envelopes to a far more responsible position. Johnson took an interest in his future, persuading him to transfer to the University of Texas at Austin and to support himself by working at a radio and television station that the Johnson family owned. While he studied journalism in college, Moyers put it in practice in the station's newsroom. He earned his journalism degree in 1956 and won an award for compiling the highest four-year scholastic record of any senior journalism student. He also won a Rotary fellowship that allowed him to study religious history for a year at the University of Edinburgh, Scotland. From there, he wrote a column for the *News Messenger* about British criticism of America's failings on racial equality. A few virulent racists back home in Marshall wanted the Rotary Club to withdraw the fellowship, but Cope deftly smothered the "recall" effort. In that episode and in many other ways, the publisher was so important to his life that Moyers named his first son William Cope Moyers.

Following his year abroad, Moyers enrolled in a Baptist seminary, worked full time as its director of information while he was a full-time student, served as a rural pastor on weekends and earned a bachelor of divinity degree. Rather than go into preaching, he planned to lecture on Christian ethics, but he began having second thoughts about whether that was the proper stage for his gifts. Then Lyndon Johnson brought his influence to bear and persuaded Moyers to join his staff in late 1959 and help him run for President of the United States. Throughout Johnson's campaign for the presidency and the vice-presidency in 1960, Moyers lived in the finished basement of Johnson's Washington home, while Judith Moyers and their children remained in Texas. During those intense months, the young preacher became indispensable to Johnson, forging a relationship with him that was closer than that of a father and a son. In ways that older men could not, Moyers was able to organize and channel Johnson's feral force. Moyers also provided something that other "Johnson men" could not give him: a liaison to the Kennedy campaign. Many of John Kennedy's closest advisors disliked Johnson, but they saw in Moyers an intellectual equal, worthy of their trust.

Once the campaign ended and Johnson became vice-president, Moyers decided that there were more exciting places in the new administration than in the office of the vice-president. During the campaign, the idea for a Peace Corps, enunciated by Senator Hubert Humphrey and others, had caught on with Kennedy and Johnson, and Moyers had written a version of it into one Johnson speech. Now that the idea was about to become a reality, Moyers wanted to be a part of it. Johnson was reluctant to let him go, but Moyers finally persuaded him. Along with Sargent Shriver, the director of the new agency, Moyers played a pivotal role in drafting the enabling legislation, in lobbying Congress to enact it and in recruiting volunteers. Within two years, he had risen to deputy director.

In the fall of 1963, Kennedy's aide, Kenneth O'Donnell, asked Moyers to tackle a quick assignment outside his Peace Corps duties: mending some political fences in Texas and coordinating arrangements for a dinner for the President in Austin. Moyers balked, fearing that such an overtly political chore would hurt the Peace Corps. But when President Kennedy himself called and asked him to go, Moyers agreed. The afternoon of the dinner, Moyers was at lunch in Austin when he learned about the assassination of Kennedy. As soon as he had confirmed the news, Moyers acted. "I suppose I was presumptuous, but

I didn't mean to be," he said later in a magazine interview. "All I could think was that Johnson was President now and that he might need help. I knew there would be unfamiliar people all around him. I thought it would help him just to have somebody there he knew and understood, and who knew him. So I went out and chartered a plane and went to Dallas."

When he arrived at the Dallas airport, he commandeered a state police car and ordered the trooper to drive him to the hospital, where he assumed he would find Johnson. On the way, they learned on the radio that Johnson was already aboard Air Force One at the airport that they had just left. So they turned around and sped back there. A Secret Service agent prevented Moyers from getting into Johnson's stateroom, but Moyers did persuade him to pass a brief note to Johnson: "I'm here if you need me." Just as Moyers had thought, the shaken Johnson was anxious for the help of someone who had served him before. Moyers witnessed Johnson's swearing-in, served as his liaison to the Kennedy staff on the flight back to Washington and helped draft the statement that Johnson made when he stepped off the plane that night.

From that moment of tragedy, Moyers glided smoothly into a position of crucial importance at the White House. First, when Johnson expressed a wish for a broad domestic program that would put his stamp on the presidency in 1964, it was Moyers who set up and guided the task forces that produced a sweeping list of domestic initiatives, which became the basis for Johnson's Great Society program. In the 1964 presidential campaign, when Johnson set out to crush Barry Goldwater, to remove him not only as a presidential opponent but as a roadblock to the enactment of Johnson's social agenda, he turned to Moyers to help him carry out that strategy. In the process, Moyers demonstrated that behind his baby face and gentle voice, there was a core of political toughness.

"We had gotten very concerned at the Republican convention in '64, when it appeared that Goldwater, having achieved the nomination, was going to make a headlong dash for respectability, putting behind him all of his damn-fool remarks about nuclear weapons," Moyers said. So Johnson instructed Moyers to make sure that the voters didn't forget everything that Goldwater had said before the convention, and Moyers brought that directive to the campaign's advertising staff. The most famous result of his request was a devastating commercial showing a young girl counting daisy petals, followed by a nuclear explosion. "Without even mentioning Goldwater's name, it kind of buried him," said Sid Myers, an art director at the advertising agency of Doyle, Dane, Bernbach, who worked on it. Moyers, of course, gave his approval for the ad. It only ran once, raising howls of protest from the Republicans, but it hung a nuclear albatross around Goldwater's neck. "It could be, certainly, the most effective commercial that was ever produced for anything," said Maxwell Dane, the founder of the agency.

The following year, 1965, Johnson asked Moyers to take on another difficult assignment: to improve the President's deteriorating relationship with the press, by serving as his press secretary. Moyers already enjoyed a reputation with the press as Johnson's "good angel." So Johnson decided his best tactic was to make Moyers his primary spokesman to the world. In that job, Moyers gained even further visibility. His name and face became familiar to millions of Americans, including Harry Guggenheim.

Despite his busy schedule, Moyers had found time in early 1965 to send Harry a brief note after Harry met with Johnson to outline his views on Latin America. "And thanks for those continuing fine editorials," Moyers said in a handwritten postscript. In July, when Moyers became press secretary, Harry sent him a congratulatory note, then a letter the following week, asking Moyers to be helpful to Tom Collins, the senior reporter in the *Newsday* Washington bureau. At the end of that letter, Harry wrote: "Sometime I would like to talk to you about information of a more confidential kind." A year after that note, Harry and Moyers met for lunch at the Metropolitan Club in Washington, and Harry asked Moyers to come to Long Island and run *Newsday* for him. "I was flabbergasted," Moyers said.

By that time, after a year in the press office, Moyers had already begun to think about leaving the White House and going back to Texas. His relationship with Johnson, so close for so long, had begun to develop strains. The war in Vietnam was part of it. At first, he had worked primarily on Johnson's domestic program and had not focused on the war. But when he became press secretary, Vietnam became a central element of his work. "One of my first jobs was to announce the buildup of troops in July of 1965," Moyers said. He started out believing the arguments of Johnson and his national security advisors, but he began to have doubts. "To me, the essence of democracy is the relationship of means to ends," Moyers said. "What we had to gain in Vietnam didn't seem to me to be squared with the means we were using."

Moyers converted those doubts into serious policy advice when Johnson asked him to provide a second channel for information and opinions on the war. In developing Johnson's domestic program, Moyers had skillfully cultivated members of Washington's permanent government. Now, he used that network-building skill to get from moderate bureaucrats the kind of factual information that would serve as a counterweight to the hawkish views that constantly flowed to Johnson. In his role as a source of moderate advice, Moyers helped to persuade Johnson to stop the bombing of North Vietnam at Christmas, 1965. But the bombing halt did not bring about the movement toward peace that its advocates had hoped for, and Johnson felt that those who advised him to stop the bombing had served him badly. "I would go to meetings and he would say, 'Here comes Stop-the-Bomb Bill,' " Moyers said. "He said it as if it were a jest, but it was really a mocking comment. . . . He was so desperate for sympathy and understanding that anybody who raised a question about the relationship of means to ends became anathema to him."

The war was not the only reason — perhaps not even the most important one — for the growing estrangement between Moyers and his patron. One point of friction, for example, was his advice on the economy. "I had lobbied inside for a tax increase," Moyers said. "I didn't think that we could pay for the

Great Society and the war in Vietnam with deficits." In late 1965, he went to see Defense Secretary Robert McNamara and urged him to support a tax increase. "That got back to the President," Moyers said, "and he just reamed me out." A more long-lasting and nettlesome source of conflict was the dizzying balancing act that the press secretary had to perform. "Trying to be the press' reporter to the White House and his interpreter to the press caught me in a crossfire that just steadily reduced my effectiveness with both," Moyers said. "The more I would try to help the press, the more he thought I was on the side of the press. The more I tried to explain him to the press, the more the press disbelieved me." Nonetheless, most reporters genuinely liked and admired Moyers. The more they wrote positive stories about him, in contrast to their criticism of Johnson, the more Johnson came to distrust Moyers.

In addition to feeling sandwiched between Johnson and the press, Moyers disliked the administrative detail of the press office and wanted a more substantive job, involving foreign policy. When McGeorge Bundy stepped aside as Johnson's national security advisor, Moyers was interested in succeeding him, but that job went to Walt Whitman Rostow. Then George Ball resigned as undersecretary of state, and newspapers carried speculative stories saying that the job should go to Moyers. Even though Moyers did not encourage those stories, Johnson thought that Moyers was campaigning for the job. Instead, Johnson gave the job to Nicholas Katzenbach and told Moyers he wanted him to stay right where he was.

All of these strains, real and imagined, led Johnson to begin treating Moyers much more coolly than he had at the height of their relationship. Despite that internal change, the world beyond the White House still admired Moyers immensely. In fact, the same high-profile national image that annoyed Johnson was a major reason why Harry saw Moyers as the perfect man to run *Newsday* and elevate it instantly to a more visible plane. For all his wealth and power, Harry was oddly prone to hero worship. Beyond that, Harry saw in Moyers the same qualities that had attracted Johnson: luminous intelligence, integrity, smooth southern charm — everything that a man could want in a son or an heir. But Harry seems not to have understood the estrangement between Johnson and Moyers, or the role that the war in Vietnam played in it. "He once told me that his whole perception of me had been formed from watching me on television," Moyers said. Just as he had misperceived his grandson Dana Draper, he appears from the very start to have seen in Moyers only what he wanted to see: a brilliant and famous man who worked for the only Democratic President that Harry had ever really supported. What he could not or would not see, even though Moyers made no effort to hide it, was that Moyers was a liberal Democrat, by anyone's definition.

"I remember when he said, 'I'd like you to come down and help me run the paper,' I laughed," Moyers said. "It was surprised laughter. It wasn't the laughter of ridicule. I said, 'Captain, I know about your editorial policies, and I'm on the other side of the fence philosophically.' " But Harry insisted that there was no reason to fear a conflict. They didn't even talk very much about the war in Vietnam. "He said, 'But you have supported the President on the war.' I said, 'Yes. I have some doubts, though.' He said, 'We all have doubts about it.' Of course, I didn't realize at the time his doubts were that we should have been in there all the way." In any case, Harry explained, he would take care of the editorial policy and Moyers would guide the paper's growth, make certain that it had a first-rate news operation and fend off the challenge from a new daily paper that was about to start publication in Suffolk County.

At that initial lunch, the issue seemed academic, since Moyers didn't think he was interested. "Somewhere in late August, I told him no," Moyers said. "I did so reluctantly, because the chance to come to a newspaper that was taking off was rare in our society." Just about two weeks later, an unexpected tragedy jolted Moyers and began to alter his thinking. His older brother, James, who had joined the White House staff a year earlier, at about the same time that doctors found that he had cancer, killed himself with an overdose of prescription medicine. Moyers wanted to help his brother's family financially, but he was also worried about his own family, since he had no real savings. In that light, he began to think more seriously about Harry's offer, which would mean a significant increase in pay. Soon after his brother's funeral, Moyers left for Asia to prepare the way for a presidential trip, then returned to Washington and went on the trip with Johnson. On his travels, Moyers had dinner one night in Bangkok with the *Time* magazine correspondent Hugh Sidey and Bonnie Angelo, the former Washington correspondent for *Newsday*, who by then had gone to *Time*. "Bill kept pumping me about *Newsday*: 'Tell me about *Newsday*. Tell me about Harry Guggenheim,' " Angelo said. In Seoul, South Korea, Moyers ran across the *Newsday* columnist, Marquis Childs, and also asked him questions about *Newsday*.

"After my brother died," Moyers said, "in genuine remorse and reflection on 'Okay, what now,' in the realization I had about paid the price that one could pay for public life, and wanting to get out of the spotlight and wanting to concentrate on my family after four uproarious years, I called him back and I said, 'Captain, I think I'm changing my mind.' " So Harry came down to Washington and they met again at the Metropolitan Club in November.

"We had not talked money or title, although he had been talking about my succeeding him as publisher," Moyers said. "I said, 'All right, let's do it.' He said, 'You're going to make a good associate publisher.' And I said, 'Wait a minute. We haven't talked about titles, but you talked about my succeeding you, and being associate publisher is not the way to do it. . . . I'll be half a man in that role. If you want me to come, I've got to come as publisher.' " Harry thought about it for a couple of days, then called Moyers back and told him he would be the publisher and Harry would be the president and editor-in-chief. "He did not intend to give up that editorial page," Moyers said. "To be very frank, and it was probably a mistake on my part, I thought that his keeping control of editorial policy would actually be to my benefit. I didn't want to come out of the White House and appear to turn on Johnson immediately. . . . Even though he and I were at odds, I didn't want to be an agent of further misery for him. I thought, 'That is really the way to do it. Harry Guggenheim writes the editorials.' "

II

ONCE HARRY AND Moyers had agreed that Moyers would become the publisher of *Newsday*, both men had some loose ends to tidy up. Moyers had to deal with President Johnson's reaction and Harry had to prepare the *Newsday* staff for the new publisher's arrival.

The day after Thanksgiving, Moyers and the President spent hours riding around Johnson's Texas ranch in a jeep, as Johnson tried to persuade Moyers not to leave the White House. Then, once he understood that Moyers would not stay in Washington in any event, Johnson urged him to return to Texas and get into politics. "I told him I didn't want to go into politics," Moyers said. "I told him I wanted to get into the newspaper business."

Moyers also wanted to inform Senator Robert Kennedy of his decision — not just because Kennedy was a senator from New York, but because they had become friends. Johnson knew of their relationship, of course. Kennedy and Moyers had even made the same proposal on the war. "We both had offered to go to Vietnam as ambassadors," Moyers said. So Kennedy and Moyers had lunch together at the Sans Souci restaurant, near the White House. Once Moyers announced his resignation, the Washington gossip mill added that announcement to the San Souci lunch and deduced that Kennedy had gotten Moyers the job at *Newsday*. That was absurd on the face of it, since Harry would hardly make a hiring decision on the basis of a recommendation from Kennedy, whom he despised. But Johnson's fear of the Kennedys, plus his resentment of the connections that Moyers had with them, made it easy for him to believe that Kennedy was behind it all. "I have a letter from Drew Pearson, saying that he was in the President's bedroom the night that I announced my resignation, and that Johnson had wept in lament and bellowed in anger, Pearson said, and used all kinds of foul language about Bobby Kennedy stealing my affections and all of this," Moyers said. The Kennedy conspiracy was myth, but Johnson's pain over the loss of his surrogate son was real. "I know he felt deep down that he would never be able to replace Bill," said George Christian, who succeeded Moyers as press secretary. "Of all the people on the White House staff, Moyers was the only one who touched every facet of what Lyndon Johnson was about."

The appointment of Moyers also brought significant pain to the *Newsday* plant. The biggest casualty was Hathway. In Harry's view, Hathway was totally unsuitable as the highest-ranking editor under Moyers. So Harry called in Bill McIlwain, who had been making most of the day-to-day decisions, and secretly told him that he planned to remove Hathway before Moyers arrived in Garden City and make McIlwain editor and Al Marlens managing editor. Once he had broken the news to McIlwain, Harry sent him down to Washington to meet Moyers. "The thing I felt at the time, and I'm sure that outsiders must have felt too, is that given the difference of these two men, how do they think that they will get along with each other?" McIlwain said. "Yet they both just seemed that they thought it would work just fine."

The news began to spread at *Newsday* one day when someone telephoned June Blom, Hathway's secretary, and asked her if there was any truth to the rumor that Moyers was coming to *Newsday*. When Hathway returned from lunch, she told him about it. Hathway went to speak with Harry and later returned disconsolately to his own office. "I remember he took a handkerchief out," Blom said. "I waited a few minutes and went in. Then he told me. So then we both took out handkerchiefs. He said, 'I'm going to be retiring.' "

The only thing left for Hathway was to seek a financial settlement. "Alan said, 'I'm going to see what kind of alimony that old son of a bitch will give me,' " McIlwain remembered. Hathway reported to his friend Arthur Lem that Harry was willing to give him $16,000 a year. Lem went in to plead Hathway's case with Ernie Levy, the advertising director, who had Harry's confidence. The final agreement was that Hathway would retire on January 31, 1967 — before Moyers arrived — and he would get $26,000 a year, plus a $6,000 annual consultant fee. But the money was not enough to heal the hurt that he felt. "He was devastated," said his daughter, Patricia Barlow. "His job was his life." Harry made the departure of Hathway and the appointment of Moyers official in an announcement on December 14, 1966 — his grandson Dana Draper's last official day at *Newsday*.

The Moyers appointment was also frustrating for Joe Albright. "Naturally, I was disappointed that Joe seems to find himself off the ladder," Josephine Albright wrote Harry. "However, the choice of Moyers seems to me to be brilliant and will add much luster to the paper. Some day I would like to talk to you about your ideas on Joe's future." Prompted by the Moyers announcement and his own growing uncertainty about his worth to the paper, Albright himself had a long talk with Harry and expressed his concerns. He asked Harry whether he should leave *Newsday* for the *Daily News* or for a Nieman Fellowship. "You have temporarily been delayed in your rise on the editorial staff because you did not succeed in getting the best results when in charge of fairly large numbers of personnel," Harry wrote after their talk. "I have opened every door to you at Newsday. It would be unfair to Newsday and its stockholders, and to you in the long run, if I attempted to do more than this for you."

If the arrival of Moyers meant pain for Hathway and doubt for Albright, it was a source of almost childish joy for Harry. Nothing was too good for Moyers. In the five-year contract that he gave Moyers, Harry agreed to pay him $75,000 a year, more than twice his White House salary, bought him a comfortable home in Garden City, where Moyers was to live rent-free, and provided him with a company car. Then Harry arranged a huge welcoming lunch at the Garden City Hotel for February 17, 1967, two days after Moyers took over. Almost nine hundred people came to the lunch, including Nelson Rockefeller, both of New

York's senators, Kennedy and Jacob Javits, and the most powerful people in the worlds of business and government on Long Island.

At the lunch, Moyers made a graceful, thoughtful speech, filled with his concept of what a newspaper must be about. "I have always shared W. H. Auden's conviction that true democracy begins with free discussion of our sins," Moyers said. "A newspaper ought to provoke it. . . . Like a public servant, a newspaper ought to give, by precept and by example, the clearest vision of what a community can achieve and contribute."

The new publisher's eloquence made him the star of the afternoon, but the occasion really belonged to Harry. In a long life of accomplishment, few moments had brought him greater pleasure than this one: He had coaxed an immensely talented young man to leave the President of the United States and take over *Newsday*. Harry was convinced that he had assured the newspaper's future. To his friend Leonard Hall, the former chairman of the Republican National Committee, he boasted: "Len, I've got a star." A few weeks after Moyers took over, in letters to Steinbeck, Harry still bubbled with joy and relief. "Bill Moyers at long last is on the job," Harry wrote, "and is already everything that I had anticipated."

III

SUDDENLY PARACHUTED INTO a strange land and surrounded by tough newspaper professionals, Bill Moyers was in one sense a vulnerable outsider.

But his sophistication in the ways of the world more than made up for any deficiency in technical knowledge. He had helped Lyndon Johnson win reelection, had shared in the creation of the Peace Corps, had grappled at the highest levels of government with the pain of the war in Vietnam. He was a smooth practitioner of global politics, a polished veteran of the world beyond Long Island — a world that almost no one at *Newsday* had really mastered.

"Interestingly, I hadn't been at a newspaper in a long time, but I wasn't intimidated by coming here, nor a stranger to the newspaper business, because I thought of newspapers more sociologically than editorially," Moyers said. "I saw the country sociologically and anthropologically, and I saw the role of a newspaper in it. . . . My job was to think about the paper institutionally and not editorially when I first came here, to think about *Newsday*'s role on this island in the next twenty-five years."

Moyers had known Long Island from the outside. To study it from the inside, even before he actually took the job, Moyers came to Long Island and listened to its voices. "I read the local weeklies," Moyers said. "I stopped and talked to people. I talked to politicians. What I realized was this was a community of people more concerned about the nation than they were about their own neighborhoods, and that the genius of *Newsday* would be to be both the best local paper it could, but also treat its readers as national citizens, which they were. So my argument to Harry was we've got to spend more money to cover Long Island, even as we embrace a larger beat." Harry listened, trusting Moyers to lead *Newsday* into the future, no matter what the cost. "Harry cared about profits, but never exclusively," Moyers said. "I said to him, 'We're going to have to spend a million dollars over the next three years to improve the editorial product, to hire people.' He said: 'That's all right. Go right ahead. . . .' To his credit, he agreed to do that before I presented him with a detailed blueprint of where I would spend it." Moyers told Harry only in general terms that he wanted to hire new writers, increase salaries, add more columns, bolster the Albany and Washington bureaus and send more reporters to Vietnam.

In the same way that he studied Long Island, Moyers trained his eye on the operations of the paper itself, drawing knowledge from an odd assortment of people. At the start, he established a bond with Jack Mullen, the skinny, hard-drinking circulation director, who sent Moyers out on *Newsday*'s delivery trucks, to meet customers and circulation employees. He became friendly with Hal Burton, who could tell him about the paper's past. "If I had been able to spend a week with Hal Burton before I took the job," Moyers said, "I probably wouldn't have come." And he began to learn the mysteries of *Newsday*'s night kingdom from Dick Estrin, who had ridden his reputation as a brilliant, light-ning-fast rewrite man into the powerful position of news editor. "I'd go down at midnight and stay till three, and sit there and watch him, talk to him," Moyers said. "I learned more from Dick Estrin about the newspaper business than from almost any other teacher."

As he talked to the staff and the readers, Moyers began to draw some conclusions about the newspaper and about the community — a diffuse suburb that was so different from the tiny, cohesive town of Marshall, Texas. In spite of that dissimilarity, Moyers recognized a parallel between *Newsday* and the small Texas newspapers of his youth. "It was a frontier newspaper," Moyers said. "When I got here, *Newsday* was like a rodeo at which it was the cowboys who were wild. What I found was a marvelous and charming menagerie of idiosyn-cratic journalists having a wonderful time publishing a newspaper that was feisty, irreverent and fun, while not recognizing that they had a lot more potential than they could see, because they were having such a good time."

As the outsider, looking at the paper afresh, Moyers felt he could see horizons that the staff could not. "My sense of things was that *Newsday* had a pronounced sense of its place on Long Island, but that the people of *Newsday* had a limited sense of Long Island's place in the world," Moyers said. "There was a sense both on Long Island, and at *Newsday*, of an inferiority complex, that we were parochial, that we were in the shadows of New York." But he looked at Long Island and saw a cosmopolitan community that needed a newspaper to match. "Much of what was really fine about *Newsday* was none of my responsi-bility," Moyers said. "I hadn't started it, and I didn't commission all of that terrific reporting that they did. My job was to refine it into a more sophisticated publication, as the island became more sophisticated — more metropolitan is the term we kept using. . . . This is a local newspaper with a metropolitan constituency, I kept saying, because the people on Long Island were coming from everywhere." The paper that was serving that readership was lively and aggressive, but it had rough edges. "It had a kind of adolescent exuberance about it that kept it from being dull, but the definition of news was rather orthodox."

As Moyers refined his vision of where the paper should go, he ran into the limitations of the staff that had to get it there, such as the drinking. Unlike many Baptists, Moyers enjoyed an occasional drink and smoked skinny cigars, but he hadn't expected the boozy atmosphere that he found at *Newsday*. One editor drank so much at a party at Moyers' home in Garden City that he passed out three times. At the next party, two others passed out in the backyard. "I was astonished, because neither in the seminary, the White House or the Peace Corps did people drink very much," Moyers said. "It wasn't only the playfulness that I began to realize was an excessive barrier to the professionalism. It was the personal self-destruction that was going on." One of the hardest drinkers was the man who would have to work most closely with him: Bill McIlwain, the newly named editor. The first time that Moyers went to lunch with McIlwain at the Sulky, McIlwain drank four martinis. At a later lunch, he had seven, Moyers said. "I was appalled, not only at what it meant to the paper, but what it meant to him."

Despite McIlwain's growing alcohol problem, he and Moyers respected each other's skills. "Bill didn't have much newspaper experience," McIlwain said. "But then you would suspect, and it turned out to be true, that any man that smart would probably be able to do most anything that he set out to do." Everywhere he went in his early weeks, Moyers impressed the staff by displaying in abundance all the best of the traditional political skills — the ability to make people feel important by knowing who they were, by listening and absorbing what they told him. Like Alicia, Moyers didn't know everyone's name immediately, but like Alicia, he took the trouble to find out a person's name before meeting him, and that person came away with the feeling that Moyers did know him.

At the start, Moyers needed all those political skills. "I understood before I got here that my biggest problem would be acceptability by the working journalists," he said. "If I had been there, and Harry Guggenheim had hired Richard Nixon's press secretary to come and be publisher of this paper, I would have said, 'What's going on here?' " So he worked hard at meeting people and acclimating himself to the paper. As he began to fit himself into the stream of *Newsday* history, he would sometimes ask Dot Holdsworth, who had been Alicia Patterson's secretary for 15 years, what Alicia would have done in a given situation. "He was a great admirer of hers," Holdsworth said. "We talked a lot about Alicia."

The exposure to the new publisher during his learning process convinced many on the staff that Moyers was everything they could have asked for in a publisher. Nonetheless, some senior editors were still suspicious. To Harry,

Moyers was a towering figure who would make *Newsday* a nationally important voice, but to these editors, he was a potentially partisan outsider who might want to lay unholy hands on the *Newsday* tradition. "I look back at it and I just realize how unreal it was and just how totally we rebuffed Bill from having anything to do with the newspaper," McIlwain said. "It was like it was our paper. We shut Bill off from it." McIlwain was part of that attitude, but the editor who viewed Moyers most suspiciously was the man who had taken Alan Hathway's position as the most feared editor at the newspaper: the new managing editor, Al Marlens.

IV

IMMEDIATELY AFTER HIS graduation from the City College of New York in 1949, Al Marlens had started in journalism as a reporter, first at the tiny Park Row News Service in Manhattan and then in the Suffolk office of *Newsday*. But he figured out quickly that his natural habitat was not the streets, but the desk.

"Al did not like to knock on doors after accidents and that kind of thing," said his wife, Hanna. "He was really very interested in how stories were played, in layout and what went where." So, after a brief tour in the Army during the Korean War, Marlens came back to *Newsday* and became the assistant to Ralph Hausrath, the Suffolk editor — a move that created the first major struggle between Marlens and another editor. "They had judgment conflicts down the line," Tom Morris said. Later, Marlens moved into the Garden City office, where he rose from night city editor to news editor to city editor, displaying along the way the skills and the compulsions that made him a dominating force at *Newsday* throughout the 1960s. "Marlens was the most extraordinary person I've bumped into in my entire life," said Bob Wiemer, who worked under Marlens as a reporter and as an assistant news editor. "He really burned with a hard flame, a very intense person, and absolutely cared about the job."

To begin with, Marlens knew a story when he saw one, even when others didn't see its full potential. "He had this sense of where the bodies were buried and what questions to ask that would get you a much better story than you thought you had," said Robert Mayer, who worked on rewrite under Marlens. Unlike many editors, Marlens didn't simply react to the news. He thought ahead to where the story was going, and demanded that his reporters do the same. "If you hadn't included that in the story, or if you didn't know what was going to happen next," Wiemer said, "he would call you a damn fool."

Unlike Hathway, who excelled at inspiring reporters to chase down stories but paid little attention to the finer details, Marlens was a maniacal perfectionist. "He was, I guess, the most obsessed editor I've ever seen," McIlwain said. Marlens detested sloppiness by reporters who had not asked enough questions to fill all the holes in a story. "I was day editor for a while and I tried to think of every question," Stan Brooks said. "Al would come in and he'd look over the copy and say, 'Okay, what about this and what about that?' "

His intense scrutiny didn't end when the story left the desk and found its way into print. "Every day when you would come in, there would be a copy of the paper and just about every story in the paper would have comments scrawled in red grease pencil," said Art Perfall. "Marlens decided he wanted us each, every night, to do a full memo answering all of these questions. . . . We tried it for about two or three days, and then we left him a note saying he had a choice: Did he want us to write a memo about yesterday's newspaper, or to put out today's?" This onslaught of grease pencil didn't do much for morale. "I remember going up to him one time finally after many months of this," Tony Insolia said. "I said, 'I come to work every day full of enthusiasm and the first thing I see when I come in is the paper you've got marked up on how we failed yesterday. It cuts your enthusiasm.' "

Nonetheless, his relentlessness rubbed off on others and set a tone. It taught young reporters such as Robert Caro how to be persistent and to ask the right questions, and it helped to make the editing process at *Newsday* as rigorous as any in America. Those editing skills earned him a nearly mythic reputation. "He's one of the greatest editors I have ever worked for," said Frank Lynn, who covered politics at the *World-Telegram*, at *Newsday* and later at the *New York Times*. If his skills inspired awe, his hard-edged management style created fear. "He was very abusive," Wiemer said. "In fact, I used to chant to myself, when I was first working under him, 'I'm not going to quit tonight.' " Marlens was such a perfectionist that he thought nothing of embarrassing publicly anyone who fell short of that perfection. One of the most frequent targets of that cruelty was Stan Asimov, who worked loyally under Marlens for a decade.

Like Marlens, Asimov had decided early in his career that he preferred the anonymous satisfactions of editing to the gritty glory of reporting. He had been involved with newspapers since his childhood, when he sold them at one of the candy stores that his parents operated in Brooklyn. He had earned a master's degree in journalism from Columbia and joined *Newsday* directly from there in 1952. Originally, he planned to spend two years at the little suburban paper, then move on to the big-time, at a paper such as the *Providence Journal*. But once he became an editor, Asimov blended smoothly into the *Newsday* way, establishing a reputation as a professional and reliable journalist and rising to the difficult position of night city editor. Along the way, he had developed a nearly mystical faith in *Newsday* and shelved any thoughts of moving to another paper. In the newsroom, there were occasional unkind cracks about the relative brilliance of Stan Asimov and his older and more famous brother, the prolific writer Isaac Asimov. "I've never had difficulty about it, and I think it's because I have a sense of my own worth," Stan Asimov said. "I can appreciate my brother and being in my brother's shadow without being blacked out." In a sense, living in the shadow of his brother prepared Asimov well for important jobs at *Newsday*, working in the shadow of editors with higher profiles and larger egos. But nothing prepared him for the abuse that Marlens heaped on him.

Asimov was a true believer in Marlens. "I have always admired him as being one of the best newspapermen I've ever met," Asimov said. But Marlens constantly found fault with Asimov. "He would just completely demoralize him, chew him out in front of the entire staff, talk down to him," Perfall said. "It was absolutely cruel." John Van Doorn, who considered Asimov an excellent editor, also watched it every night. "I loved Al Marlens in almost every way," Van Doorn said, "but that's one thing I could never forgive him."

In addition to criticizing Asimov in front of others, Marlens regularly deprived him of the chance to do more layout, for which Asimov was amply qualified. "The one thing that he didn't do very well was that he didn't delegate very well," Asimov said. "He didn't give you too much of an opportunity to spread your wings." Oddly, despite his cruelty in the office, Marlens could be charming to Asimov outside. "You could be having dinner with him, socializing with him, and he was the warmest, friendliest kind of person, very thoughtful, and you'd get along very well," Asimov said. "You'd walk into the office and it was almost as if a different person had arrived." That aloofness in the office was a conscious strategy. "Al prided himself on sort of not winning brownie points with the troops," Hanna Marlens said. He had no tolerance for editors who worried about whether the staff liked them. "I don't come to work to be loved," he told people. "I get all my loving at home."

As a result, few at *Newsday* loved Marlens. He won few hearts, but he did change lives. "Probably because of Al — and maybe this is a mark of deficiency on my part — I sort of gave up the battle and became more of Bill McIlwain's assistant than Al Marlens' assistant," Asimov said. That led Asimov more and more away from handling copy and into the administration of the newsroom, which shaped the rest of his career. The same was true of McIlwain. He came to *Newsday* in the first place because he was a strong writer, but the more Marlens took command of words on paper, the more McIlwain was reduced to administration. "In my heart of hearts," Asimov said, "I do believe that McIlwain was affected by Al as much as I was affected by Al." As McIlwain slipped further and further into alcoholism, more and more of his power fell to Marlens. "McIlwain at that point was abdicating very much his responsibility," Insolia said. "Al became the controlling editor of the paper."

In some ways, McIlwain remembered, Marlens offered him support, such as recommending that he see the same psychiatrist who had been treating Marlens. But McIlwain still resented the constant need to protect Marlens from being fired — by Alicia Patterson, by Alan Hathway, by Harry Guggenheim — while Marlens was free to play the role of journalistic knight. "It was kind of like he could wear the white hat," McIlwain said. "And that always, the more I reflected on it, pissed me off."

Unlike Hathway, Marlens had an almost puritanical vision of journalistic integrity. His view of society was essentially liberal, but he wanted nothing to do with either the Democrats or the Republicans. He took his children to antiwar protests during non-working hours, but he wrote a stern memo telling the staff not to wear antiwar buttons while on assignment, and he warned Frank Lynn not to identify with the civil rights groups that he was covering. Hathway, for all his excesses, had given *Newsday* its courage and vigor. Marlens brought to the paper its sense of journalistic standards.

"For a long time, he gave the place a conscience," Bob Wiemer said. But it was a fierce, unyielding conscience. "He was overly principled," Hanna Marlens said. As a boy, he had stood on the street corners in Brooklyn and argued politics and public policy heatedly. "We were all like that," said Elton Rayack, his childhood friend. "Everybody took a strong stand on the issues." As an adult, Marlens had little room in his conscience for nuance. "He had a sense of right and wrong," Asimov said. "I can identify wrong pretty well, but I think there are many rights. But not to Al. He could see something, and he knew what was right, and by God, if you had another opinion, you weren't right. You were wrong."

And Moyers, as far as Marlens was concerned, was wrong. "He really hated Bill Moyers," Asimov said. "He thought that Bill Moyers was coming in to further his political ambitions, that he was using the paper for political purposes, and this was totally contrary to Al's sense of right and wrong." To Marlens, the logic was simple: Moyers was a politician. Therefore, he must be planning to use *Newsday* as a mouthpiece to help him gain whatever political goal he had in mind. Though Moyers had rejected Lyndon Johnson's advice that he get into politics in Texas, he could never free himself of the suspicions that he had a political agenda. At the very start, Ted Lewis, the Washington bureau chief of the *Daily News*, wrote a column saying that Moyers was establishing a base and he should think about running for the United States Senate from New York. That fueled the speculation. "Harry later told me that a number of his Republican friends clipped that column and sent it to him," Moyers said.

If the rumors about his plans were imaginative, the external pressure on Moyers to get into politics was real enough. Former New York Governor Averell Harriman invited Moyers and his wife to his home in Sands Point, for example, and suggested that Moyers try the Senate. Similarly, Nassau County Executive Eugene Nickerson occasionally urged him to run. "People were always bringing it up," Moyers said. "I don't remember ever bringing it up with anyone. . . . I had no interest in running for office in New York." Nonetheless, his obvious talents made him desirable as a candidate. "He was the only man I ever worked with and knew well that might someday be president, and would be a good president," McIlwain said.

Elective office wasn't the only political lure that someone dangled in front of Moyers. In 1968, Secretary of Health, Education and Welfare John Gardner, who had earlier worked under Moyers on one of the task forces that led to the Great Society, called and asked him to take a leave of absence from *Newsday* and serve as executive director of the Urban Coalition. Moyers asked Harry to write Gardner a letter turning him down, and Harry did. That same year, Senator Eugene McCarthy of Minnesota and Senator Robert Kennedy of New

York both sought his help for a presidential race. "Bobby Kennedy asked me to run his campaign for president, not because he thought I was a great strategist but because it would have been a wonderful story that he had Lyndon Johnson's former fair-haired boy," Moyers said. He turned Kennedy down out of loyalty to Johnson and to Harry, but Moyers couldn't win: Harry was annoyed that Kennedy visited Moyers in the hospital in Mineola and that Moyers flew with Kennedy to the funeral of Martin Luther King. Moyers told Harry, with a smile: "If you can shoot quail at Cain Hoy with all these right-wingers, I surely can take one trip with Bobby Kennedy to a funeral."

None of the political overtures to Moyers succeeded. "I had made a decision to join this side of the crowd," Moyers said. "While these things came up, I resisted them all without any temptation. I knew that I couldn't carve out this new life and play around politically." But Marlens never really believed that, and he made it clear in a variety of small ways that he didn't trust Moyers. "We used to have what they called verb headlines, where the headline led with a verb and no subject," said Allan Wallach, who was then editing the entertainment pages, before a long career as the drama critic at *Newsday*. "Moyers ruled that out, because he felt they were confusing. Marlens put out a memo that we were no longer to use them, in a way that indicated just contempt for the whole change."

The resistance to Moyers was sometimes subtle, sometimes overt, but it was always there. Myron Waldman remembered an incident that happened after McIlwain sent him to cover Senator Hubert Humphrey during the 1968 presidential campaign. Moyers liked his work so much that he called Waldman and invited him to fly up from Washington for a party at his home. At the party, Moyers praised Waldman's reporting on the campaign. "Moyers says, 'When are you going out again, Mike?' " Waldman remembered. "And I said, 'Gee, I don't know. They haven't told me.' " The moment Moyers walked away, Waldman found out. "An editor who was with the old guard immediately came up to me and said, 'I have news for you: You're never going out again.' "

Even though the major editors in the newsroom did their best to dilute his impact on the news pages, Moyers was simply too potent a force. For a man who had shown the ability to penetrate the federal bureaucracy in service to President Johnson, the *Newsday* hierarchy was a far less formidable puzzle. Inevitably, as the months rolled on, the paper began to reflect his presence.

V

WITHOUT HAVING TO take a single substantive step, beyond moving to Long Island and allowing his name to appear on *Newsday*'s masthead, Moyers had an immediate effect on the newspaper's image.

For all of Hathway's fiery crusading, for all of McIlwain's gifts of language and soft southern charm, for all of Marlens' rigid ethics, *Newsday* was still very much a local paper when Moyers arrived — unknown by most of the world outside of Long Island. But the presence of Moyers changed that almost overnight.

Before 1967, *Newsday* advertising salesmen would show up at agencies in Manhattan, announce that they were from "*Newsmmm*," and often the receptionist would think they meant *Newsweek* and allow them into the inner sanctum. Once Moyers arrived, executives in advertising agencies *knew* what *Newsday* was. "We started to get identity in the national business when Bill Moyers came aboard," said Michael Forgione, then the national advertising manager. Similarly, in telephoning people outside the immediate area, reporters could simply mention the name of Moyers, instead of giving the usual explanation of what *Newsday* was. Moyers also used his contacts to help reporters in the Washington bureau get important interviews with government sources. So his mere presence had created an incipient national image for the paper. All Moyers had to do was to fill in the outlines of that image, to shape *Newsday* into something more sophisticated.

At the start, Moyers reached out to people he knew and arranged for them to write for *Newsday* — an echo of Harry's emphasis on big names. At the outbreak of war in the Middle East, for example, he signed up the novelist Saul Bellow to cover it. "I wanted to cover the war for a daily newspaper and I remembered I knew Moyers," Bellow said in a magazine interview. Moyers also got Daniel Patrick Moynihan, a friend of his, to write an analysis of urban unrest, "How Liberals Failed the Negro." The Moyers touch showed, as well, in the publication of a thoughtful series of essays called "The Condition of the American Spirit," in the Saturday magazine, with contributions from a broad spectrum of public figures, such as Bellow, Marya Mannes, Billy Graham, J. Edgar Hoover, Bayard Rustin, Arthur M. Schlesinger Jr. and Erich Fromm. Moyers also tried to persuade John Steinbeck, the biggest of Harry's big names, to keep writing for *Newsday*. He didn't like Steinbeck's "Letters to Alicia" from Vietnam, but he admired Steinbeck's earlier work. "I had been greatly influenced by Steinbeck's *Travels with Charley*," Moyers said. "I had hoped to get him to retrace the path he took every ten years in *Travels with Charley* for *Newsday* and syndication. . . . I wanted to try to encourage him to be a journalist-anthropologist, and I said, '*Newsday* will pay for you going and doing a profile of each state.' " But Steinbeck's health was already in precipitous decline, as Moyers saw when Steinbeck visited his home in Garden City. "He was so depressed," Moyers said. "He couldn't fight this depression, and he never was productive after that."

The Steinbeck overture didn't work out, but even Moyers' more successful efforts to get occasional pieces from well-known writers could not by themselves permanently change the tone of the paper. He needed an infusion of writers and columnists, and he found them both inside the paper and outside. One of his early steps was to hire Pete Hamill, a pugnacious street columnist who had made a name for himself at the *New York Post* and had met Moyers during the presidential trip to Southeast Asia in 1966. Moyers offered him more money and a chance to write a column from Washington. Hamill had started out writing a New York column, but he went to Vietnam for the *Post*, and his column had begun to criticize the war and Johnson. That was the columnist that Moyers hired. "It wasn't like they were getting a mystery writer or anything," Hamill said. "They knew who I was and what I did."

At the same time that he hired Hamill for Washington, Moyers had found a new chief for that bureau — someone of his own choosing to replace Tom Collins. "I didn't get the sense that Moyers had a tremendous amount of confidence in me," Collins said. "I sent word to McIlwain: Hey, get me out of here, in so many words, before I'm pushed out and he brings his own man in." The man that Moyers chose was Nick Thimmesch, then a New York correspondent for *Time*, who had experience covering national issues. "He had a style of writing that was analytic," Moyers said. "I felt that he saw Washington of a piece, and that he would be able, with a small staff, to give us a reflection on the news that would compensate for our inadequate coverage of the news. We could never have a large enough bureau at that time, with our resources, to cover Washington originally, except on certain stories. We had to be creative in how we covered that city." So Thimmesch took over the bureau and promptly ran into Hamill, whose liberal views clashed with his conservatism. "Pete had an office in one corner and Thimmesch had an office in the other, and they would be at each other's throats," Myron Waldman said. "I thought they were going to kill each other."

Predictably, Hamill's full-page columns had a strong, assertive point of view, ranging from criticism of Johnson on his conduct of the war to a wistful elegy at the death of Che Guevara, the Cuban revolutionary. Hamill made it clear to Thimmesch that he would write what he chose, but he wasn't always successful in explaining that to Marlens. He wrote a column, for example, about the disintegration of the Johnson administration, and Marlens refused to put it in the paper. "So I said, 'What the hell am I going to write about now? I've got two hours before I have to put a column in,'" Hamill said. "He got really pissed off and said, 'Write about the snow. I don't care.'" So Hamill turned out an improvised column that started with a snowstorm in Washington. A few weeks later, miffed by the killing of that column and unhappy in Washington, Hamill decided to leave, after only four months with *Newsday*. "To blame Al Marlens for it is silly," Hamill said. "I've got to blame myself for being a hothead." But he did understand why Marlens resisted him. "It was imposed on the editors almost immediately after Moyers took charge," Hamill said, "so there might have been some real resentment there."

A few months after the Hamill experiment failed, Moyers and his editors also had to take corrective measures with the other combatant in the Hamill-Thimmesch wars. The new bureau chief was not very smooth in his dealings with his two reporters, Waldman and Martin Schram, who both enjoyed solid reputations among the editors. At one point, Thimmesch threatened to send Waldman back to Long Island. On another occasion, Insolia left a message for

Schram to call him in Garden City, which prompted Thimmesch to wonder anxiously why Insolia was calling Schram and to threaten Schram with firing if he returned Insolia's call. It turned out that Insolia simply wanted to congratulate Schram on a story. "Nick was in many ways a very nice guy and fun to be around," Schram said, "but he was prone to moments like that." In addition, Thimmesch was not ideally suited, after so many years as a magazine writer, to the rhythms of daily journalism. So *Newsday* sent Joe Albright down to Washington to work with him.

As a reporter in Washington in the early 1960s, Albright had done well. Now Moyers was sending him down to shore up Thimmesch and show how good he could be, but the Thimmesch-Albright relationship was rocky. Thimmesch admired Albright's hard work and reporting skills, but he was less than politic with Albright. "One day I forgot myself," Thimmesch said. "Joe had irritated me in a small way and I said, 'Joe, you act like you own this place.' " (Albright and his sisters and brother, of course, together owned almost half of the place.) Before long, McIlwain adopted a more drastic solution to the bureau's problems, making Albright the bureau chief and allowing Thimmesch to remain in the bureau as a columnist. "I think, frankly, that McIlwain and Marlens wanted someone who was more aggressive as bureau chief," Thimmesch said. Albright was far better as a reporter and bureau chief than he had been as an editor, and he worked smoothly in harness with Waldman and Schram.

A few weeks after he had first hired Thimmesch and Hamill from outside, Moyers also played a role in signing up Emily Genauer, the former art critic of the *New York Herald Tribune*. Harry knew her through his art museum, and he called her as soon as the *Tribune*'s successor paper, the *World Journal Tribune*, folded. "He and Bill Moyers drove up to this house one morning, and they sold me this paper," she said. "And they told me what their plans for it were."

In addition to hiring outsiders such as Thimmesch, Hamill and Genauer, Moyers made columnists out of two writers who had good reputations at *Newsday* as facile rewrite artists on the "Funny Machine." The Harvey Aronson column, announced in June, was based on Long Island. The Robert Mayer column, which began in September, was a bolder step: Mayer was to work in and write about New York City, which *Newsday* had almost ignored until the late '50s and early '60s. In the summer of 1967, just before becoming a columnist, Mayer had covered the urban riots in Detroit and distinguished himself with a touching portrait of a bright young black man caught up, Job-like, in the pain of the ghetto. As he began the new column, he decided that his mandate was to keep Long Islanders informed of New York City's pains and problems, on the theory that they would soon be Long Island's problems. His first columns covered a strike by school teachers in the city, including one in which he revisited his old school in the Bronx. The next day, Mayer came into the office and found a copy of the column, with a note across it from Moyers: "Beautiful."

Harry, however, didn't always consider Mayer's column beautiful. Like Hamill, Mayer had strong views on the war in Vietnam, and he found ways of expressing them, even though the column was supposed to be about New York City. The Mayer column alternated on the first page of the paper's center section with Hamill's, just a flip of the wrist away from Harry's editorial page. The Hamill column disappeared after four months, but Mayer continued writing and occasionally raised storms of protest. Despite any negative reactions from Harry or from the readers, the Mayer column had to be considered a success. He wrote it for four years, and twice he won the Meyer Berger award, named for the late Pulitzer Prize-winning *New York Times* writer and given annually to the reporter who does the best writing about the City of New York. So the choice of Mayer gave the paper an almost immediate impact in the city. Another Moyers initiative, a major improvement of the paper's anemic business coverage, brought about a further foothold for *Newsday* in the big city.

During the last years of Alicia's life, Richard Clurman had pushed for an expanded business report, but in 1967 it was still little more than small stories on Long Island firms, written by Frank Wood, one of Alicia's old palace guard. The business report contained no regular stock tables, puny coverage of Wall Street and little attention to national business trends. Harry sought the advice of Harold Gleason, the vice-president of Franklin National Bank, and suggested that Gleason come to *Newsday* in some capacity to oversee the business section, but nothing came of that. So when Moyers arrived, business coverage was still a major deficiency, and he directed his editors to look for ways to make it better. McIlwain recommended that they hire Warren Berry, a former financial editor at the *Herald Tribune*, who responded to McIlwain's inquiry with a proposal for an expanded business staff, operating out of New York City. Ultimately, *Newsday* decided to do just that, hiring Berry and renting a small suite of offices in the old *Herald Tribune* building in Manhattan — *Newsday*'s first permanent office in the city.

Once he was on the staff, Berry hired Dennis Duggan from the *New York Daily News* and Clarence Newman from the *Wall Street Journal*, recruited George Wheeler from *Newsday*'s Garden City office to cover the stock market, and brought in as the staff's junior member Prudence Brown, a former secretary at the *Tribune* who had written free-lance pieces. Berry was unable to persuade the editors to run daily stock tables, but he and his staff did begin to emulate the *Journal* in another way, by writing full-page features every day that were similar in tone to the page one "leader" pieces that ran in the *Journal*. In time, *Newsday* increased the visibility of its expanded business section by moving the lead business page to the back page of the paper. The impetus for this expansion of business coverage had come directly from the publisher. "Bill Moyers wanted to go first cabin in everything he did," Berry said. "It was Moyers behind it."

Beyond journalistic issues such as the columnists and the business report, Moyers also had to wrestle with finances. Even though that was not his area of greatest strength, he invested much of his time in it. In one business matter, Moyers used his journalistic skills of observation to make a shrewd decision. He looked at the eight-page section of mediocre comic strips distributed with the

Saturday paper and wondered whether he could drop it and spend the money better on Washington and Albany coverage. "One of the first things I knew about newspapers was watching my own children," said Moyers, who had noticed that when television cartoons on Saturday became popular, his children stopped reading Saturday comic strips. Jack Mullen, the circulation director, argued that discontinuing the section would hurt circulation, but Moyers was confident from his own experience that Mullen was wrong. So he killed the separate color comics section, leaving intact the black-and-white comics that ran in the paper itself. "We were paying over $2,000 a week buying those colored comics," said Vinnie Bordash, Mullen's lieutenant. "We cut them out and there were only three calls from Levittown. . . . So Moyers really paid his salary by eliminating the comics."

Grappling with union issues wasn't nearly as simple. "I didn't like, and had no special talent for, labor negotiations," Moyers said. But only a few months after he arrived, Moyers had to cope with a nasty dispute between the production department and Local 406, the pressmen's union. The contract called for the union and *Newsday* to go through "reopener" negotiations on wages, and the union wanted those scheduled talks to include the issue of how many pressmen would work on each press. As the paper added presses, Local 406 wanted a higher level of staffing than *Newsday* did.

Coming on top of earlier disputes about working conditions, this issue energized the younger, more activist officers of the union. "We had a terrible relationship with *Newsday*," said George Tedeschi, then a Local 406 vice-president. Tedeschi precipitated direct action, by arranging for several journeymen printers from outside the company to report for work in the pressroom, so that the union would have enough men to handle the extra positions. But when the men showed up, the company directed uniformed guards to usher them out of the building, then told the remaining pressmen to go ahead with the press run, shorthanded. "I, with a small group of close friends, proceeded to slow down the pressroom," Tedeschi said. "The company reacted like we were doing something, but they couldn't prove it. We made sure that when company officials were around, we worked like hell."

Beyond slowing down, the union didn't sanction any sabotage, Tedeschi said. But the production manager, Floyd Main, sent Harry a memo listing evidence of sabotage. A week later, on the recommendation of Moyers, Harry stood up in the pressroom and spoke to the pressmen. In his brief speech, Harry listed the acts of sabotage and asked for calm. The pressmen had decided in advance not to applaud, but to listen and quietly file out at the end. "It was pathetic," said Harvey Broad, who ran the pressroom. "Here's a millionaire getting up on a box, pleading with the boys to be good."

Ultimately, it was Moyers who began to bring peace to the situation, calling in Tedeschi and another union leader, Len Mayer. His willingness to meet with them was an important first step. "Here's the press secretary of the President of the United States, and here I am in my early twenties, sitting down with this guy in his office," Tedeschi said. Moyers won them over by listening to their complaints and agreeing that they were correct about the working conditions in the pressroom. "It was not that everything changed overnight," Tedeschi said. "We still had wars sporadically." But Moyers elevated the level of the discourse and lowered the level of combat, which was what Harry wanted. "Harry cared more for peace than he did for money," Moyers said.

To help Moyers handle such day-to-day details, Harry gradually decided that the new publisher needed help. "Though he never told me particularly what he intended, Guggenheim was making it clear that he wanted me to do more for him than *Newsday*," Moyers said. "He was talking about the museum. . . . He was asking me to meetings of his foundation. He was gradually introducing me to his business affairs. And he said, 'As I needed somebody, you're going to need somebody.' " One somebody that Harry considered was Jim Hoge, a rising young editor who was married to Alicia's niece, Alice. Hoge had impressive academic credentials — Exeter and Yale — and he had become the managing editor of the *Chicago Sun-Times*. The principal custodians of Alicia's memory, Dot Holdsworth and Josephine Albright, heard that Harry was considering Hoge and complained, arguing that Alicia had disliked him. Hoge came to New York and discussed with Harry and Moyers the proposed job: Hoge would be the general manager, running the whole business operation. But he liked his new job in Chicago, and he politely turned them down.

The understudy that they did snare came to them as a result of a typical *New York Times* power minuet. He was Sydney Gruson, who had covered Europe for the *Times* for two decades, served as foreign editor, then returned to Europe to reverse the losses of the *Times* international edition. Gruson recommended and helped to bring about a merger with the Paris edition of the *Herald Tribune*. As he understood it, he was to become the publisher of the merged paper, but that agreement vanished, and Gruson ended up back in New York. Turner Catledge, the executive editor, told him to hang around there for a few months, to see what developed. "When Catledge said this to me, I think I got as angry as I can," Gruson said. "I just picked up a phone and called Harry Guggenheim, whom I'd known socially."

Gruson went to Harry's townhouse for dinner. "I said, 'I'm going to leave the *Times*. Is there anything at *Newsday*?' He said, 'There just might be.' " Soon after that, he visited with Moyers in Garden City and agreed on a job a week later. From Paris, he mailed Moyers an acceptance letter and sent a series of notes to the demigods at the *Times*. "It's a good paper and I think I can make it considerably better," Gruson wrote to James "Scotty" Reston. To Lester Markel, the Sunday editor, who had been Alicia's friend, Gruson wrote: "It will not be the New York Times, but then what is?"

Laboring under that *Times*ian blend of hauteur and condescension, plus the Anglophile manner that his years in London had bred in him, Gruson did not make fast friends among the senior editors at *Newsday*. "He looked upon *Newsday* as a bit like the hicks who were going to be civilized by his involvement," Asimov said. "He was resented by people in editorial." In one conversation with Marlens, Moyers asked just what it was about him that Marlens didn't

like, and Marlens mentioned the mere presence of Gruson as a major annoyance. The nickname that Marlens applied to Gruson, Tony Insolia remembered, was "The Dilettante." Bill McIlwain had a different designation. "I
called him The Gunfighter," McIlwain said, "because he's a real quick and a
sharp little guy."

Gruson was decidedly not in the classic *Newsday* mold, but he did know
something about newspapering. Moyers entrusted him with much of the daily
operation of the paper and asked him to supervise the first redesign of *Newsday*'s appearance. The time had come, both Harry and Moyers felt, for *Newsday*
to look less like the *Daily News*. When Moyers asked Gruson and the editorial
art director Paul Back to create that new look, he drew on the ideas that had
flowed from an earlier effort to produce a national edition of *Newsday*.

"Harry had a deep and pronounced ambition to make *Newsday* a national
force," Moyers said. "That was his idea, to do a national edition. It was my job
to try to give flesh to it." What Harry wanted was an edition of *Newsday* that had
no local news and emphasized national stories. It would do, in effect, what
Gannett did years later with *USA Today*. Moyers tried to convince Harry that
Newsday had only to improve the quality and breadth of its reporting to take
advantage of the national audience that already existed in Manhattan, the
media center of the world. Dressed casually in a short-sleeved shirt, Moyers
rode the New York City subways, watched carefully what went on at the
newsstands at 72nd Street and Broadway, and did research on the role of those
newsstands in the city's intellectual life. "I wrote him a note about the major
subways, the major newsstands, and I said, 'If you printed another 30,000 copies
and we could get them to these newsstands every day, you could have the
impact in Manhattan that you want,' " Moyers said. But Harry was not convinced. " 'I think we need a separate identity,' he said. 'I don't think people will
read a local newspaper for national impact.' "

Settling down to Harry's idea of exploring a national edition, Moyers
turned to John Denson, the editor who had once been so influential in shaping
the *New York Herald Tribune*'s modern look. "We brought in Denson for one
version of it, and paid him to draw up a mock edition," Moyers said. "Harry
didn't like that, and then we assigned our own people to do it." He sent Paul
Back, Al Marlens and Dick Estrin to a third-floor office for months and asked
them to come up with something. It was a difficult task, because *Newsday*
simply didn't carry enough national material at the time. "The whole idea was
flawed," Estrin said. But they plugged away at it, while Vinnie Bordash and
Buddy Chernow from circulation struggled with the problem of distribution,
exploring knotty questions such as the feasibility of flying the paper to airports
by helicopter. Bordash decided that the cost would be prohibitive, which
turned out to be the factor that killed the idea, in early 1968. "I finally had a
version I could take back to Harry," Moyers said, "and he changed his mind." At
the end of the process, Moyers made a counter-proposal. "I said, 'Don't start a
paper. Buy a paper.' " So he met with Dorothy Schiff, the publisher of the *New
York Post*, to discuss whether *Newsday* could buy the *Post*. But Harry and Schiff

disliked each other too much. "I could never get them together," Moyers said. "It wasn't a good idea anyway."

The national edition had failed to fly, but the project helped Moyers to visualize more clearly what he wanted the paper to look like. "I liked Denson's mockup," Moyers said. "It was a newsmagazine mockup — not as small as a newsmagazine, and therefore, tolerating more white space. It had a clean and inviting look to it." Moyers was convinced that the more analytical approach of the newsmagazines was exactly what *Newsday* needed. "One of the things I learned about people out here when I spent the week wandering around is how much a part of their information flow television had become, diminishing the time they had for all the reading material," Moyers said. "The most compact way of helping one understand the news was to read the news weeklies. And how do you do that on a daily basis? How do you expand the scope of your coverage and organize it so that it is available for people on a daily basis in a helpful way, with succinct depth?" The work that Denson and the *Newsday* staff had done on the prototype for the national edition showed the way. "I said to myself, 'Why can't we make the daily newspaper look like they are proposing the national *Newsday*?' "

Gruson supervised and provided some broad ideas for the redesign project, but Back did the actual design. Back had joined *Newsday* in 1952, when all of the paper's artists worked for the advertising department, because Alicia Patterson wanted Ernie Levy controlling them, rather than Alan Hathway. Later, he worked briefly as an editorial cartoonist and lobbied for the creation of an art department that served only the paper's editorial needs, separate from advertising. Just before Moyers asked him to redesign the paper, Back had created a promotion campaign: "Who says a tabloid has to be sensational?" The whole point of the redesign was to make the paper look less sensational. So Back set about attacking those elements of the paper's appearance that made it too loud: the lack of white space and the square, heavy sans serif typeface on the front page.

"Sans serif typeface has inherent power, boldness — screaming, if you will," Back said. "You can't scream in Century. Century is not a typeface that screams, no matter if you make it eight feet high." So he replaced the sans serif faces with the Century family of typefaces. The serifs at the top and bottom of the letters helped them to blend gently together, giving the page more grace, elegance and calm. Beyond the change in typeface, the other key element of the redesign was a radical realignment of the front page. Unlike a broadsheet, a tabloid front page almost always holds only one major story, with a huge headline above and some large photo below. That structure often inflates the importance of a story on a slow news day, when no story really *needs* a huge headline, but the format demands that the front page have a huge headline anyway. Back's solution was to use small boxes on the bottom of the page, in which editors could put headlines for other stories in addition to the primary one. "Essentially, what you're doing is putting five headlines on a front page," Back said. For a broadsheet, that was nothing new. For a tabloid, it was a major innovation.

Back's redesign quickly won the approval of Gruson, Moyers and Harry, and it showed up in the paper for the first time on July 8, 1968. A few years later, Harold Evans, the editor of *The Sunday Times* of London, wrote a book about newspaper design and called *Newsday* "an advanced example of what a serious tabloid might be." In his handwritten inscription, Evans referred to Back as "designer of the world's best tabloid."

In addition to his small role in the redesign, Gruson was a minor actor that year in a couple of other moments of history and near-history.

When Tom Dorsey saw a chance to sign up the Pulitzer Prize-winning cartoonist Pat Oliphant to work for *Newsday* and its syndicate, Dorsey flew to Denver to meet with him. Oliphant was interested. Then Gruson arranged for a meeting at the Denver airport between Dorsey and Moyers, who was flying through Denver, and Moyers gave his enthusiastic approval. A few days later, at a Falaise dinner, Gruson explained the Oliphant deal to Harry. Then Gruson conveyed the bad news to Dorsey: " 'Harry says the guy can't draw.' " So the paper lost its chance to hire one of the best cartoonists in America.

Gruson also supervised the hiring of a small group of talented young black men for a summer's training as journalists. "In Washington, it was very obvious to me that the civil rights movement was being covered primarily by white males," Moyers said. "Every newspaper was delinquent." So he asked Gruson to see what *Newsday* could do to correct that. "Gruson, who was a very good delegator and not a very good doer, delegated it," Asimov said. "The problem came in that minorities who were interested in journalism did not exist at the time." So Asimov decided to look for talented non-journalists and inspire them to be interested in newspapers. When Asimov found them, Gruson turned them over to McIlwain for training. "Everybody agreed at the end of the summer that this was a mistake," Asimov said. "Maybe we were good newspaper people, but we were not very good teachers." That same year, Asimov did hire two black men who *were* journalists, worked briefly at *Newsday* as reporters, then went on to success elsewhere — Bob DeLeon as managing editor of *Jet* magazine and Ron Smothers as a reporter for the *New York Times*. And Moyers continued to push in 1969 for greater efforts at minority hiring, creating a special fund in addition to the regular budget to hire six permanent minority employees — a project McIlwain and Marlens asked Tony Insolia to supervise.

The delegation of the minority hiring project to Insolia was an example of the way his supervisors in the newsroom relied on him to get things done. McIlwain and Marlens considered him trustworthy, competent and steady. Still, the Moyers years were the most difficult time for Insolia since he had first arrived at *Newsday*. Insolia had grown up in Tuckahoe and Mount Vernon, in Westchester County, north of New York City. His father was an Italian immigrant from a small town in Sicily, and his mother had been born in America, of Italian parents. While he was still in high school, Insolia developed journalism fever, largely through watching movies about reporters. He delivered the *Mount*

Vernon Daily Argus, worked as a kitchen helper, and paid his way through college by working in a Gristede's supermarket. Insolia started at Columbia University, stumbled academically, and got drafted into the Army, just in time to serve with the occupation troops in Germany. When he returned from Europe, he went back to work at Gristede's and studied journalism at the New York University campus in nearby White Plains. Following graduation in 1949, Insolia took a job in the circulation department of the *Daily Argus*, then moved to the *Yonkers Times* as a reporter. Simultaneously, he also held jobs at Gristede's and as a maitre d'. When the *Times* management fired a friend of his, Insolia and several others walked off the job, and he ended up at Park Row News Service with Marlens. Then he moved to a reporting job in Stamford, Connecticut. On his second try, he arrived at *Newsday* in the fall of 1955. Four years later, he followed the example of Marlens and became an editor.

In the Moyers years, Insolia's title was news director — a unique appellation that *Newsday* had concocted because they couldn't really have a city editor, since the circulation area was a suburb. Regardless of the title, he was really the city editor, working under Marlens and exercising increasing influence. But he began to wonder why Marlens and McIlwain kept making a point of telling Gruson and Moyers to watch how good his work was. "I came to find out later this was in response to criticism of me from them," Insolia said. He suspected that it was Gruson who had convinced Moyers that he did not have the right stuff to rise any higher, but Gruson said: "Bill was totally unimpressed with Tony. He had reached that conclusion before I got there." The real whispering against Insolia came from Dorsey. "Dorsey tried to poison me about everybody," Moyers said. "Dorsey was just one of those office schemers."

Insolia's image problem arose because his strengths — impeccable news judgment and dogged attention to detail — were not obvious to someone who didn't see him work every day. But his weakness — a relentless honesty that often crossed the line into bluntness and earned him the nickname of "Tony Insult" — was easy to detect. In his own mind, he traced his bluntness to his days as a soldier in postwar Europe, where he fell in love with a young German woman. When he returned to America, he had been too vague about his intentions, and he ended up hurting her feelings, breaking off the relationship by mail. From that time forward, Insolia had always said exactly what he thought.

A typical example of Insolia's style involved the reporter Robert Ellis Smith, who took a leave of absence to be a consultant to the Kerner Commission, which studied the causes of the urban riots of 1967. When he returned to *Newsday*, he expressed distress that Insolia had assigned other reporters to revisit the riot cities. Insolia sent him a brusque memo, explaining that Smith had yet to prove himself. "I have matured since then and have learned it's not necessary to crush somebody in saying no to them," Insolia said. Smith passed the note along to Moyers, who did not remember the note or the incident. "I had very little dealings with Tony," Moyers said. "There's no indication that Tony's career was hurt by whatever my impression might have been."

Even if Moyers thought Insolia did not have the potential to be *the* editor of *Newsday*, he did give him more responsibility, but with one catch. In July, 1969, Moyers promoted Insolia from news director to day managing editor and Perfall from Suffolk editor to night managing editor. McIlwain called Insolia, who was on vacation, and told him about the change. "I said, 'It sounds like I'm going up one rung and Perfall is going up two,' " Insolia remembered. "It didn't bother me, but I was now sharing a level of authority with someone who was subordinate to me previously."

It was so painful a period, in fact, that Insolia even explored the idea of becoming managing editor of the *Dayton Daily News* in Ohio. But he decided to stay at *Newsday*. Despite the ups and downs of his career in the Moyers years, Insolia demonstrated that he was able to survive in the Byzantine arena of *Newsday* politics. As it turned out, his polar opposite, Sydney Gruson, did not survive for long.

VI

FOR NEARLY THE first eighteen months that Moyers was publisher, Harry Guggenheim was a constant presence at the paper, clinging steadfastly to his control of the editorial pages and leaving the rest to Moyers. But in the summer of 1968, Harry's deteriorating health forced him to start loosening the reins.

"I am not as alert as I was," he wrote to his daughter Diane in June. "I have a combination of hepatitis and arthritis. . . . I have lost about 18 pounds." At the suggestion of his friend, John Hanes, Harry began wearing a copper bracelet to ease the pain. But before the year was over, Moyers and Harry both knew that his health problems were more serious than a copper bracelet could cure: Harry had cancer of the prostate gland. "He began to absent himself more and more," Moyers said, "although we would talk almost every day."

It was in the context of that altered working arrangement that Moyers and Harry approached the 1968 presidential election. In early October, Moyers wrote Harry a ten-page memorandum on his views of the two candidates, Vice-President Hubert Humphrey and former Vice-President Richard Nixon. Displaying an erudite sense of humor and an accurate perception of the trickiness of the decision, Moyers listed the subject of the memo as "Charybdis and Scylla," a nasty pair of mythological monsters who confronted Odysseus on his voyage through the Strait of Messina.

"*Newsday's* endorsement will be and should be your decision," Moyers wrote. "But if my choice and yours are different, one of us is going to have a forum and the other will not. Because I feel the way I do about public issues and because I believe in speaking out, any difference between us on this question will present me with a dilemma: silence in so important a matter about which I have deep convictions."

Not surprisingly, Moyers chose Humphrey. The first reason was broadly ideological. "Nixon as President would be leading a party whose dominant majority, when the chips are down, is not only resentful of fundamental social changes but philosophically and impulsively reactionary toward the crises we shall inevitably be enduring," Moyers wrote. "This is especially true in regard to minorities. Most of us are not black and we are not poor; it is all the more important that we be governed by men who try to realize what is like to be black and poor. . . ." His second reason was Nixon himself. "Let me be clear in stating my disagreement with those people like Herblock and George Ball who believe Nixon is some kind of amoral, unprincipled, and devious charlatan. He may not be the best man the Republicans could have nominated, but in addition to being intelligent he is well trained for the job, experienced, aware of the difficulties at home and abroad and anxious to try to deal with them. It is not that Nixon is unprincipled but that his principles and mine are so incompatible that for me to support him would be to negate those programs and ideas for which I have worked and in which I have believed." Finally, Moyers argued that Humphrey would be a joyful, grudgeless, compassionate, inspirational leader at a time of painful transition.

It was a reasonable, articulate argument from a man who knew the inner workings of public policy far better than Harry did. But Harry's mind was made up. With the exception of Lyndon Johnson in 1964, he had always supported the Republican nominee. Now Johnson had stepped aside, and it was Humphrey, a classic liberal, against Nixon, a tough, conservative Republican. They had exchanged brief "Dear Dick" and "Dear Harry" letters in the months after Nixon lost to John Kennedy in 1960, and Harry still felt a strong affinity for Nixon. In fact, just before Moyers wrote his memo, Harry had dictated to Hal Burton some notes on why Nixon should be elected.

A week later, on October 16, *Newsday* carried a full-page signed editorial in which Harry endorsed Nixon. On that same day, the page-two news story that announced *Newsday*'s endorsement also carried a statement from Moyers, conceding that the prerogative of endorsements was Harry's, but disagreeing with Harry's choice. "My own position is clear," Moyers said. "Because of his deep and sustained commitment to justice for the poor and the black, because he realizes that ending the war in Vietnam must be the first task of the new President, and because his decent and humane qualities are so clearly recognizable, I intend to vote for Vice President Humphrey."

It wasn't quite the same thing as the opposing editorials that Harry and Alicia had written in the 1960 campaign, but it was close enough. "He never said this, but in Guggenheim's mind that was blatant disobedience and disloyalty," said Stan Hinden, the editorial page editor. If Moyers was disloyal politically, his actions showed that he was still loyal to Harry personally. The day after the endorsement, Moyers consulted by phone with a doctor from the Mayo Clinic about Harry's cancer and put together a memo explaining what the doctor had told him: "If you have to have cancer in your 70s, this is the cancer to have." That provided reason for optimism about Harry's health, but a few weeks later, when Nixon beat Humphrey, Moyers had more reason for pessimism about the future of his complex, delicate relationship with the owner.

On election night, Harry and Moyers entertained several editors in Harry's office. Finally, it became clear that Nixon had won. "Harry said, 'Well, now it's over; he's President of all of us,' " Hal Burton remembered. "A voice in the room said, 'He's not my President.' " Harry's suspicions later turned toward Marlens as the source of the comment, Burton said, but whether Marlens said it or someone else did, the result was clear. "It was a very serious matter," Moyers said. Neither he nor his wife even noticed it when it happened, because the evening had been filled with banter and comments about both candidates, but Judith Moyers did detect Harry's growing sense that he was surrounded by aliens. Early Wednesday morning, Harry picked up a ball-point pen and wrote a complaint to Moyers.

"The reaction of the people in my office last night confirms my worst suspicions," Harry wrote. "They were pathetically praying for the defeat of Richard Nixon and their deep-seated hostility toward him was obvious in their dismay on their faces and in their comments. They will never give him a chance. They are just like Flora Lewis, who told me the other day that she was frightened about the prospects of a Nixon victory. . . . I am sure you will find a way to free Newsday from the clutches of propagandists and polemicists who are so deeply prejudiced that they cannot see what is right for their country."

The next day, Moyers answered. "Frankly, I did not notice the 'hostility' or 'dismay' in the group that watched the returns in your office," Moyers wrote, arguing that the paper had been fair in covering the campaign. "As for the other matters, if Newsday is going to be truly independent, we must be free to criticize as well as praise the new President. If you think that is not the way we should maintain our independence, let's talk; you have the right to obtain a publisher who puts out the kind of paper you want, but if you want a paper that hews to any undeviating line on any President, I shouldn't be running it."

In the weeks following this unsettling exchange of letters, Harry did not act as if he had decided he wanted someone other than Moyers to run the paper. On November 13, Harry's lawyer, Leo Gottlieb, met with John Peeples, the mining associate that Harry had installed as a vice-president at *Newsday*. Peeples told Gottlieb that Harry had informed him that he wanted Moyers, not Peeples, to succeed him as president of *Newsday* — contrary to Harry's previous wishes. On November 25, Harry signed a third codicil to his will of May 8, 1968. The codicil left Harry's mining interests in four equal shares: one to Moyers, one to Peeples, one to Harry's daughter, Joan, and her husband, and one to Peter Lawson-Johnston, Harry's cousin. Before that codicil, Harry had left those interests solely to Lawson-Johnston. Finally, after Harry had entered Doctors Hospital in December, he officially designated Moyers as the vice-president who would take over for Harry if he died or became disabled.

So, while Harry and Moyers had disagreed publicly on politics, Harry showed no sign that he had given up on the relationship. But that election night became a sharp line of demarcation, after which Harry was almost never at *Newsday*. "Something happened to him after the election of '68, and he began to stay away not only because he was ill, but because he was disgusted," Moyers said. "Somehow, he identified what was happening in society as a repudiation of everything he believed about America."

Increasingly, Harry looked at the pages of *Newsday* and saw evidence of dangerous liberal tendencies. He began warning Gruson that the staff was turning leftist, and he followed those warnings one day with a bizarre request: He wanted Gruson to get rid of two liberal columnists — Clayton Fritchey and Flora Lewis. "He said, 'They've become Communists,' " Gruson remembered. "I said, 'Harry, you hired both of them, and I'm not going to fire them. Besides, Flora Lewis is my wife.' "

At the start of Gruson's time at *Newsday*, the publisher of the *Times*, Arthur Ochs Sulzberger, had written a letter to Harry, announcing that Sulzberger would do everything in his power to wrest Gruson back. The whole time he was at *Newsday*, Gruson regularly drove from Garden City to Manhattan to have lunch at the *Times*, and Sulzberger kept wooing him. It wasn't until Harry asked Gruson to fire his own wife that he took the final step. Gruson returned to the *Times* at the end of 1968, after working a bit less than eight months at *Newsday*. "He was here on the way back to the *Times*," Moyers said. "It was a mistake. I liked Sydney personally, but he is not of *Newsday*."

The departure of Gruson and the withdrawal of Harry, at about the same time in late 1968, left Moyers alone at the top of *Newsday*.

CHAPTER TWENTY-SIX

The Suffolk Scandals

I

SPRAWLING SPACIOUSLY INTO the Atlantic Ocean, Suffolk County in the 1960s was still the Wild East, Long Island's last frontier.

The lure was the land — more than 900 square miles, larger than New York City and Nassau County combined. Once the flow of population from New York had gobbled up the easily available real estate in Nassau, it rolled farther east and began to overwhelm Suffolk in the 1950s and 1960s. The new residents had massive needs — for gas stations, supermarkets, appliance stores. To meet those needs, thousands of property owners asked the towns to take land that was zoned for homes and rezone it for the heavier density that stores and other businesses needed.

The accepted goal of zoning is to help governments to plan growth rationally, but it is also an alluring form of economic alchemy: It allows government, in effect, to create wealth. By rezoning a piece of land, politicians can substantially inflate its value, since an acre of stores can bring in far more income than an acre of houses. As rezoning applications flooded into town halls in Suffolk, a few politicians decided to grab some of the wealth that they were creating. Using their power and knowledge, they bought land, ballooned its value through rezoning and reaped profits that might otherwise have gone to less well-connected citizens.

Bad government, of course, is the raw material of good journalism. In this case, the greediness of a few public officials and party leaders provided an irresistible target for *Newsday*. At the end of the 1960s, Bob Greene and a platoon of reporters seized upon the slick zoning practices

of Suffolk politicians and broke new ground in the craft of investigative reporting in order to dig up the story.

A decade before Greene and his team did their own investigating in 1967,
Newsday had already gotten a taste of Suffolk scandals, covering a long, state-
initiated inquiry into corrupt practices by town and county officials. It began in
1955 when two auditors from the state's Department of Audit and Control
walked into the county offices in Riverhead for a routine review of records.
They found evidence that the county treasurer's office had used improper
procedures in selling land that the county had acquired when the owners failed
to pay property taxes. Gradually, they brought in more auditors, and the investigation spread, creating five years of turmoil. In the five years that followed,
State Investigations Commissioner J. Irwin Shapiro joined the investigation;
District Attorney Harry Brenner, a Republican, resigned rather than prosecute
friends; Governor W. Averell Harriman appointed George Percy, a Democrat, as
district attorney; Percy lost the next election; Harriman appointed a special
prosecutor, Edward Rigney, who resigned after Harriman's successor, Nelson
Rockefeller, squeezed his budget, and a second special prosecutor, Edwyn
Silberling, took over.

"This was a perfect situation for the corruption that springs from one-party
power," Silberling said. "What you had were political leaders with unchallenged
power. They were running the government, not the elected officials. . . . And
the political leaders not only were running the government, they were lining
their pockets." Reacting to the scandals, Suffolk voters turned over to the
Democrats control of the county Board of Supervisors and the new county
executive's office. "It was just a marvelous, invigorating change," Silberling
said. "You had a feeling that the politicians no longer felt they had complete
immunity — for a short while."

That momentary caution had dissipated by the time the 1960s rolled
around, and hints of corrupt zoning practices began to surface in the Town of
Islip, on Suffolk's South Shore. Despite the Democratic victories in 1959, Islip
was monolithically Republican. In Islip, as in most of Suffolk's ten towns, the
Republican-dominated town board made the zoning decisions, with little oversight from the feeble Democratic Party. So corruption was almost inevitable.
But it was not until 1967 that a tangled combination of events finally brought
about a full-scale *Newsday* investigation.

One of the earliest events leading to the *Newsday* investigation was a 1964
announcement by Islip Supervisor Thomas Harwood: The town planned to pay
$90,000 for a small parcel of land just east of the town hall parking lot and use it
to build additional town office space. Manny Topol, who had just arrived at
Newsday as a reporter from the *Long Island Press*, later asked the town attorney,
Walter Conlon, who owned the property. "He says, 'Oh, I'm not sure. I'll have
to look it up,' " Topol remembered. Topol mentioned that to another reporter,
Alan Eysen, who came to *Newsday* in 1961 from the *Middletown Record* in
upstate New York. Eysen checked and found out that the corporation that
owned the land was located at the same address as Conlon's law firm, and

the president of the corporation was the brother of Conlon's law partner.

Eysen also got some information on zoning in an interview with a widely feared carpenters' union enforcer named Julius Klein Jr., who complained that Islip politicians had treated him badly when he sought some rezonings for his own construction firm. The information from Klein, added to what he had heard elsewhere, led Eysen to continue digging into the records. The pattern he found was this: Ordinary citizens would apply for a rezoning and the town board would vote them down. Disgusted, the owners would sell the land, and the town board would later grant the new owners a rezoning. Those new owners often turned out to be well-connected politicians and their friends, hiding their interest in the land behind a dummy corporation. Once he wrote what he knew about this, Eysen took his findings to the district attorney's office in 1965, presenting them to James M. Catterson Jr., the chief of the rackets bureau.

One of Catterson's key witnesses was Klein, who testified that he had made payoffs to Islip officials for rezonings. The grand jury heard about fifty witnesses, including all of the top officials of Islip, but the investigation produced only one victim: Eugene Verratti, a member of the town planning board, refused to sign a waiver of immunity, and Supervisor George Raven fired him. In January, 1966, the grand jury completed its work, and a new district attorney, a Babylon Republican named George Aspland, took office. The grand jury returned no indictments and made no report. "I knew it was there someplace, but I couldn't put it together," Catterson said. "I wanted to come out with a report, Aspland didn't want to, and that's how it died."

Despite the failure of the grand jury to indict anyone, Eysen and others were still interested in the story. But the Suffolk editor, Kirk Price, was not. Price did have a high level of interest in another Islip story — the growth of MacArthur Airport, a town-owned facility that had the potential to become something much more than a small suburban airport. While Price was running the Suffolk office, he and his reporters wrote a stream of stories about the future of the airport. "I did one story on MacArthur Airport, and he got so excited," Topol remembered. What Topol did not know was something that Price had once told Ralph Hausrath, his predecessor as Suffolk editor. "He said, 'I'm buying some tax land up around MacArthur Airport,' " Hausrath said. As Eysen continued reporting during 1965 and 1966, Democrats told him that Price was involved in land deals with the Republicans. Eysen asked Price about that as they drove into Garden City for a meeting to discuss Eysen's proposal for a broader investigation. "Kirk said, 'Well, I'm glad you raised that question with me,' " Eysen said. "He said, 'I want you to know that not only have my land dealings been approved of by Alan Hathway, but by Alicia Patterson." So there was no conflict, Price insisted. At the meeting with Hathway, nothing decisive happened, and the investigation stagnated.

Information about Price's land deals also came to Tom Renner, who was covering Suffolk police. "I apparently dug a little bit too deep and the word got back to him, and he came down on me and went to Alan to have me fired," Renner said. "Bob Greene somehow found out and talked to me about it."

Greene and Renner were good friends, and Greene had worked closely with Eysen in 1963, investigating the Suffolk County Water Authority. If anyone could help clear the way for the two reporters to investigate further, it was Greene, who was friendly with Price and close to Hathway. In fact, they were so close that Hathway had told him about his own business dealings. "I loved Alan Hathway," Greene said. "At the same time, Alan was doing things that right now I'd probably send him to jail for." The modern journalistic code of ethics didn't exist then, Greene said, and Hathway saw nothing wrong with dabbling in business. "He was generally in there fighting for the good," Greene said. "He was going to help himself a little bit while he fought." All along, Price knew what Hathway was doing. "I generally think that Kirk's feeling was, 'Hey, if there was nothing wrong for Alan, why is there something wrong for me?' " Greene said. Price had told Greene, without detail, that he was buying land. In addition, Greene knew Price's second wife, Margo, a brassy, ambitious real estate operator. "Margo was obsessed with making money," Greene said. So, when he heard about the problems that Renner and Eysen were having, the possibility that Price might be involved in shady land deals seemed real enough.

His first step was to talk with Price. "Kirk maintained to me there was nothing going on wrong down there," Greene said. Then, rather than go to Hathway, Greene approached Al Marlens, the prickly conscience of *Newsday*. Soon after that, Hathway summoned Greene to a meeting, which Marlens didn't even attend. (Greene asked the normally forceful Marlens afterward why he hadn't attended the meeting and hadn't been more helpful. "You never heard anybody more subdued," Greene said.) At the meeting, Hathway demanded to know who was saying these terrible things about Price, and Price kept insisting that nothing was wrong. Despite Hathway's declining power and despite their friendship, Greene had failed to move him toward a wider investigation.

For the rest of 1966, the Islip story languished. Then, in early 1967, a fortuitous combination of events took it off the back burner. First, Harry Guggenheim hired Bill Moyers and forced Hathway into retirement. Then, only a month later, as Price was on his way to a meeting of the county Board of Supervisors in Riverhead, he collapsed. Price died the next morning of a cerebral hemorrhage. Art Perfall, who was with him at the time, became the Suffolk editor. The twin obstacles to the story were gone. "Everybody got very brave," Greene said.

Perfall had been interested in the story all along, working under Price, as Suffolk news editor. "The stench was there," Perfall said. "But I could never get any movement from Kirk. That was not unusual, because the traditional thing was, 'Hey, we don't have the manpower to spare.' " Now Price was gone. At the same time, events outside the office continued to raise suspicions. Since June, 1965, when Islip Supervisor Thomas Harwood had resigned, a number of other important Republican politicians in the town had either quit or been fired. In June, 1967, the political reporter in Suffolk, Arthur Bergmann, wrote a story about the departures, then followed with a column on the same subject, under the headline: "11 Overboard: a Coincidence?" Soon after Price's death, Perfall ordered some preliminary reporting on the situation in Islip, but it turned up nothing concrete. It was at about that time that Perfall, along with Al Marlens and Tony Insola, decided that there was only one person who should lead a full-scale investigation of Islip: Robert W. Greene.

II

IN HIS FIRST decade at *Newsday*, Greene had been Hathway's hit man.

Unlike other reporters, Greene had no geographic beat. When he was not on assignment from Hathway, Greene worked on whatever interested him, usually on organized crime. He also travelled out of town on major stories. Before the Islip story, in fact, Greene had established a reputation as a master of the expense account. On a three-week assignment in New Orleans in early 1967, for example, Greene covered District Attorney Jim Garrison's bizarre investigation of the assassination of President Kennedy and indulged in a spiraling expense war with a reporter for the *Daily News*. When he returned to Garden City, he wrote an account of this expensive struggle in *Slug*, the internal publication. Even the frugal Harry Guggenheim laughed. On this *Newsday*-subsidized diet, Greene had grown to huge proportions — a startlingly round figure beneath a full head of prematurely gray hair. By the time Hathway left, Greene's talent and his larger-than-life style had made him a dominant presence. But he was primarily a lone operator. Now, at a point when a less canny reporter might have lost influence because his patron had been forced out, Greene actually increased his clout — by becoming the leader of a team.

The first member of the team was Eysen, who had already done a significant amount of reporting. Eysen didn't mind working with Greene, but one aspect of that collaboration irked him. "It was Greene's salesmanship, more than the material that I found, that ultimately sold this as a project," Eysen said. "Greene gave me lessons in how to write memos to editors, how to conduct a session with an editor. I don't know whether he's the world's greatest investigative reporter, but he's certainly one of the greatest salesmen of investigative stories."

One of the most important selling points is the establishment of a minimum and maximum expectation for the investigation. In this case, the minimum was a story about a *Newsday* editor engaged in questionable real estate practices. The maximum was a scandal that would engulf the whole government of Islip. To get that broader story, *Newsday* would have to assign to the project a significant part of the Suffolk staff. That was not going to be easy, because the paper was in the early stages of competing with a new daily newspaper, the *Suffolk Sun*. But McIlwain, Marlens and Insola quickly gave Perfall approval to do whatever was necessary to get the story. At the same time,

Harry Guggenheim had authorized an increase in the size of the Suffolk staff, to combat the *Sun*. The result was the largest commitment of time and staff to a single project that *Newsday* had ever made — its first extended piece of gang journalism. The rest of the staff, including a prodigiously productive pair of rewrite men, Maurice Swift and Jim Scovel, would just have to work long hours to turn out the daily stories while the Greene Team pursued its mission.

The team started small, with Greene, Eysen and Ray Larsen. They had some early help from John Cummings, but Cummings quickly found out that working under Greene wasn't easy. Before the project began, Cummings had made plans to go on vacation with his family. So he left. Greene, who had become accustomed to working endless hours, did not understand. When Cummings returned, his place on the team was gone. "I was universally a son of a bitch," Greene said. "I would never let Cummings back in it. Without question, I feel that I was wrong. At that point, I just felt any guy who would walk away from a story like this doesn't deserve to come back. . . . His values were probably better values than my values."

When Greene decided to replace Cummings, Perfall called on Ken Crowe, who had joined *Newsday* in 1963 from the *Syracuse Herald-Journal*. Perfall called him at home, where he was on vacation, and asked him to come to the office. As soon as Perfall told him about the story, Crowe knew he had a problem: While covering courts, he had become very friendly with Frank Conlon, an assistant district attorney, whose son was Walter Conlon, the former Islip town attorney and one of the central figures in the story. "Frank Conlon adored his son," Crowe said. "I didn't want to be part of hurting him." Then he met with Greene, who explained that each reporter on the project would have a target, and Crowe's target would be Walter Conlon. "I said, 'Well, I'm not going to do it,' " Crowe said. "Greene is a master salesman. He said, 'If you could prove Walter Conlon is innocent, then he'll be off the hook.' I said, 'Okay.' "

Walter Conlon was a perfect target: an increasingly high-profile public official. He had started to rise politically during Governor Nelson Rockefeller's reelection campaign in 1966, when Conlon had helped put together a Long Island rally and served as a keynote speaker. A month after Rockefeller won, he appointed Conlon to the State Tax Commission, in which Conlon supervised development of the state's lottery. The governor had noticed Conlon because Suffolk delivered a huge plurality for him and because Conlon had political talent: intelligence and powerful Irish warmth. "Walter Conlon is one of the most charming people you'll ever meet," Greene said. Once Rockefeller appointed him to the tax commission, Conlon found himself involved in some of the discussions about a Rockefeller presidential candidacy. He also heard rumors that Rockefeller's counsel might be moving on and Conlon might replace him. "It was heady stuff," Conlon said.

As Conlon daydreamed about his future, Crowe began digging into his past. In Syracuse, Crowe had learned how to work with documents: deeds, mortgages, contracts — the building blocks of modern investigations. In fact, when the Islip investigation started, Crowe had more experience with real estate records than Greene did. As the investigation went on, Crowe demonstrated impressive talent for finding real estate documents, analyzing them and figuring out how hundreds of "deals" had worked. But documents alone would not get the job done, since the politicians who had made money from rezoning had hidden their identities in dummy corporations. It was Greene who found a way around that veil. "In about two weeks, I developed *the* source, the dream type of source that a reporter asks for all his life and never gets," Greene said. The source, code-named "Zip," had known Greene for years. Just before Greene agreed to take on the Islip story, the source had worked on a federal investigation of Islip, and he had access to detailed information on the dummy corporations and the names of the politicians who had formed them. In effect, Zip had given Greene a road map through the deeds and mortgages. But Greene's team still had to spend countless hours digging out the right documents to use with that road map. Once they did, Greene now knew, he would have far more than the small story on Kirk Price that he had set out as his minimum.

In going through those steps, the Greene Team encountered obstacles, including Islip Town Clerk Fred Pfifferling, who had custody of town records. "He affected a friendly manner when the process started, but by the end of it was pretty openly hostile," said Brian Donovan, who had come to *Newsday* from the *Rochester Democrat and Chronicle*. "To be fair to him, we did put a heavy burden on them, in wanting to see just about every scrap of paper in the whole town hall." As they got further into the search for records, they needed more help. First, Rosemary Skapley, an editorial assistant in Garden City, checked records. Then she became pregnant and recommended another editorial assistant, Geraldine Shanahan, as her replacement. Shanahan had left a job selling ice cream a year earlier, to work in the *Newsday* library. Later, she had moved to the city desk, where she answered phones, sharpened pencils and got lunch for reporters. Greene and Perfall plucked her out of that position and made her an investigative clerk. She had no experience with documents or reporting of any kind, but Crowe trained her. Quickly, she became a critical member of the team — one of the squirrels who went out foraging for acorns to lay at the feet of the big squirrel, Greene.

"It was a tremendous education to work for Greene," Donovan said. "We would all be out in the field all day, gathering documents, talking to people. We'd come back into the office in the early evening. Greene would be sitting there, having spent much of his day on the phone, and we would each report what we had collected. Greene had an incredible ability to see connections that the rest of us hadn't seen. . . . He had a near-genius mind for assimilating this material and for not just seeing broad patterns, but remembering very tiny details." If working for Greene was often enlightening, it was not always easy. "I think it frustrated Bob that he couldn't do all of this legwork himself, because he always worried that the reporters were only bringing him back eighty-five or ninety percent of what was in the file, or of what could have been gleaned in the interview," Donovan said. "And he pushed you to go from eighty-five to ninety percent to the ninety-five to one hundred percent level."

At the same time that Greene was managing the team, Perfall was running the rest of the office, leaving Greene on a long leash. "You don't control Greene," Perfall said. "You cajole him." In the evenings, after Greene had read the day's material, he and Perfall would meet at a restaurant to discuss the day's findings. They would also meet periodically with the editors from Garden City, usually at someone's home. "What we did was take a recitation from Greene on all the things we had and what he thought the story lines were," said Insolia, who later did the line-by-line editing of the stories. "We'd take notes and we would come to a consensus."

As the summer went on, working out of its own little space in the back of the Ronkonkoma office and writing nothing for the daily paper, the team grew increasingly isolated from the rest of the staff. "You couldn't tell anybody what you did that day, because it didn't make any sense," Shanahan said. "So we just told each other." Not even Knut Royce, who came to the paper during the investigation and covered the town that the team was investigating, was privy to their work. "They had this tremendous aura of secrecy, and they wouldn't share diddly," Royce said. But the mere knowledge that the team was digging into Islip, Royce felt, scared sources into talking to him.

Gradually, the team acquired more and more documents, analyzed them, interviewed the minor characters and prepared for the showdown interviews with the targets themselves. "The person answers your questions at the end because you have so much knowledge, they think you know everything," Crowe said. In the case of Walter Conlon, the grand interview came at a long lunch with Greene and Crowe. At the time, Conlon saw no reason not to show up, but he did not expect the list of detailed questions that he would face. "I guess if I were ever going to do it again," Conlon said, "I would have my own preparation of material." In the memories of Greene and Crowe, the alcohol they drank at that lunch played a central role. "What he doesn't realize is that I'm going into the men's room every once in a while and shoving my hands down my throat and throwing up," Greene said. "So I'm staying reasonably sober." Eventually, Greene said, Conlon began making admissions about some of the deals that they had investigated. "He got caught because he thought he could outdrink us that afternoon," Greene said. "He couldn't." Conlon didn't remember getting very drunk, and he saw the whole lunch as less significant than Greene did. "Those articles were going to be written anyway," he said.

Another of their major targets, former Islip Republican Leader Edward McGowan, was not as cooperative. Only four years earlier, in his role as a member of the Suffolk County Water Authority, McGowan had come across as a decent public servant, offering to help make records available to *Newsday*. By 1967, he was a more powerful figure — the chairman of Rockefeller's Long Island-New England Bridge Study Commission — but he was less outgoing. "He wasn't dumb enough to be cooperative," Crowe said. McGowan said that he did agree to an interview with Greene alone, but when Greene showed up with Donovan, McGowan asked for an interview with just Greene. So the two reporters left.

The McGowan investigation was also more complicated because buying and selling real estate was not just a sideline for him, but his livelihood. So he was involved in thousands of transactions. As the reporting went on, Greene asked Marlens for more reporters, and the team expanded to include the newly hired reporters Jim Toedtman, Carole Ashkinaze and Gurney Williams, plus additional help from others. "There was so much property," Greene said. "I can remember at times in the city room we would have deeds laid out from one end of the city room to the other."

The suspense finally ended for Islip politicians on September 28, 1967, when the first stories appeared. The lead story on the first day showed that Conlon, while he was town attorney, had secretly been involved in a real estate deal with Julius Klein, the union enforcer. Even two decades later, Conlon thought it was a frivolous story, since it was already public knowledge that he had represented Klein in the past. Conlon's prosecutors agreed that the Klein-Conlon deal was not significant in the case against Conlon. "He became prominent in his own way," Conlon said. "I became prominent in my own way. And so, 'Let's put the two together.'"

In the next day's paper, *Newsday* began prodding public officials to react to the revelations. Crowe and Donovan managed to get quotes from a Rockefeller aide in New York, and from the governor himself. The story said only that Rockefeller's counsel would look into the allegations, but that was good enough for the headline: "Probe of Conlon/Ordered by Gov." The same day's paper carried the details of Conlon's hidden interest in the property next to town hall. As town attorney, the story said, Conlon "negotiated" unsuccessfully with the owners (who included himself), before the town decided to acquire the land by condemnation (a procedure that provided tax benefits to Conlon's partners). Conlon eventually asked the town board to assign another attorney to the case, but by then, the condemnation had been set in motion. In addition, the stories described an earlier deal, before Conlon became town attorney but while he was a special assistant town attorney, in which Conlon and his partners paid a $9,000 "finder's fee" to Councilman Donald Kuss for official actions that enabled them to make a $64,000 profit. The stories also outlined how Conlon had profited from his interests in land near MacArthur Airport, at the same time that he was advising the town on airport expansion.

The airport was the focus of the third-day stories, which showed how Kuss supervised airport development for the town and also acquired an undisclosed interest in prime land at the airport entrance, without paying any cash. On the same page, a two-column headline announced the results of the Kirk Price investigation: "Editor Tied to Kuss Deal." The story said that Price and his wife, Margo, had invested only a $50 binder in a choice piece of airport property and later made a profit of $33,000 when they and their partners sold the land to a syndicate that included Kuss. All the other owners had invested $10,000, but

Price's wife got credit for $7,500 in brokerage and finder's fees, and Sidney Siben, the Bay Shore attorney who provided tips and other help to generations of *Newsday* reporters, lent the Prices $2,500 and recovered that loan later out of the profits. "Kirk brought the deal to me," Siben remembered. "I liked the deal, but they didn't have any money."

Pushing the Islip story one step further, Greene decided to force District Attorney George Aspland to investigate Kuss and Conlon. Like many other investigative reporters, he was not content to let the story rest on its own merits. He wanted indictments. So Greene looked through the state penal code and found an obscure section that he thought applied. Then he called his former *Newsday* colleague Jack Ehrlich, a prosecutor in Aspland's office. If Aspland declined to prosecute, Greene warned Ehrlich, *Newsday* would print a box in the paper containing the appropriate section of the law and let the readers decide whether Aspland was acting properly. As Greene arrived at Aspland's office, Aspland had just finished telling the *Long Island Press* reporter Karl Grossman that he would let the voters pass judgment, rather than launch an investigation. A few minutes later, Greene had persuaded Aspland to investigate. "George was not an experienced prosecutor when he got in," said his assistant, Catterson. "You never announce an investigation and you never start a grand jury investigation unless you have one or two felonies in your pocket to begin with. . . . When a newspaper is on your case and you don't resist it, then you fall prey to 'Gee whiz, I'd better come up with something. Maybe we'd better indict somebody.' "

A few weeks later, less than a week before the local election day, *Newsday* dropped the other shoe: the McGowan phase of the series. The stories said that McGowan, as town Republican leader, had sat in executive sessions of the town board as the "sixth man" and used his inside knowledge to help his own real estate deals. In response, McGowan held a press conference, but he refused to talk about anything except allegations that he had used blockbusting techniques and "exploited racial prejudice" to help build his empire. "Being called a blockbuster seemed to get to him in a way that just being called corrupt didn't," Donovan said.

Not surprisingly, the drumbeat of scandal stories had a profound effect at the polls. Democrats swept into control in three towns: Islip, Babylon and Huntington. One of the casualties was Islip Town Clerk Fred Pfifferling, who had stalled *Newsday* in its search for records. *Newsday* was directly responsible for all the upheaval. "Most politicians think, "What the hell, I can take a one-day shot,' " said Edwin M. Schwenk, who became the county Republican leader in the aftermath of the 1960s scandals. "But man, when they work you over for a week or ten days like they did, that had its effect."

In early December, the grand jury indicted Conlon and Kuss under the section of the penal law prohibiting the acceptance of unlawful fees, in connection with the $9,000 finder's fee mentioned in the series. The same day, Conlon resigned as a member of the State Tax Commission. At the end of that week, McGowan resigned as a member of the Suffolk County Water Authority. "Water

Authority meetings became a circus," McGowan remembered, "attended by *Newsday* photographers who followed me around the clock."

Right after the indictment, Aspland announced that he had hired an outsider, Maurice Nadjari, an experienced prosecutor from the Manhattan district attorney's office, to prosecute the case and serve as his chief assistant. Using the *Newsday* series as his prosecution outline, Nadjari soon decided it wasn't going to be a difficult case. Until the Greene Team developed techniques for unearthing real estate deals, no one on Long Island had ever before looked over the shoulder of the politicians, and they hadn't been as careful as they should have been in their land deals. "They left trails as wide as a four-lane highway," Nadjari said.

On October 22, 1968, a little more than a year after the Islip series ran, a jury in Westchester County convicted Conlon and Kuss and the judge later sentenced both to a year in jail. Even after he went through the stigma of imprisonment, however, Conlon retained his ability to charm. As a prosecutor, Catterson had investigated Conlon, but later, as a counsel to Assembly Republicans, he pushed through a bill that allowed Conlon to apply to the courts for reinstatement as a lawyer. As a reporter, Greene helped put Conlon in jail. As a person, Greene liked him: "I could see a lot of other people who, in my own preference, I would rather see go away than Walter."

The consequences were not as drastic for McGowan. "We never made a case against him," Nadjari said. "We just couldn't get the evidence." No one accused him of a crime, and no one moved to revoke his real estate license. "I did not use political influence or inside knowledge," McGowan said. "Any transactions I had were done in the normal course of business in the same manner I conducted myself prior to my role in politics." In the end, McGowan continued to deal in real estate and to prosper. "All these charges have gone down the tubes," McGowan said. "I didn't do anything wrong. They wasted their time. It was just plain nastiness."

III

IT TOOK NO special brilliance for the Greene Team to realize that the techniques that they had developed in Islip would work in other towns. "You can do this anywhere," Geraldine Shanahan said. "The corruption was just there."

The next logical focus was east of Islip, in the huge Town of Brookhaven, the most significant focus of suburban growth in the metropolitan area. By early 1968, when they started working on Brookhaven, the team had lost one of its original members. Alan Eysen had decided to leave Greene and return to the daily staff. "I found him too overwhelming an individual to deal with," Eysen said. "I really did not care to be in his shadow." Ken Crowe wasn't always comfortable with Greene, either. "He once said openly he considered me the team's accountant," Crowe said. "I resented being called an accountant, because I felt I was a full-fledged reporter." But the potential of the story outweighed his annoyance. "I knew that we would win a Pulitzer Prize sooner or later," Crowe said, "and I wanted to win a Pulitzer Prize."

During the four-month Brookhaven project, the Greene Team didn't have the same kind of inside information as Greene had developed on Islip from his federal source, "Zip." So they started almost from scratch. "We would put a zoning map on the wall and draw a circle around every gas station, garden apartment and major shopping center rezoning and just backtrack it," Crowe said. "We did it on our own, and we did it successfully." The result of their work was a series of stories that started on May 1, 1968. The primary targets were Brookhaven Republican Leader Richard D. Zeidler and Councilmen George Fuchs and Clarence Hough. The most colorful was Zeidler, an automobile dealer who ate well, smoked big cigars, drove large cars and carried himself like a big-city political boss. Typically, Zeidler reacted to the series with bravado. "I will buy a piece of land with anybody if they put their money up and it's a good investment," he said. Nonetheless, before the first week was over, he suspended himself without pay from his position as chairman of the Suffolk County Water Authority.

One of the most interesting deals involved the construction of a regional shopping center, Smith Haven Mall. Both Fuchs and Hough voted for the rezoning, and afterward, private firms in which they were involved got $700,000 worth of business in the mall's construction. The major store at the mall was to be Macy's, and the headline was: "Macy's Good for Returns." During the reporting, Brian Donovan had worried that someone would frown on the use of a prime *Newsday* advertiser's name in a scandals story. But this story demonstrated that, in the *Newsday* environment, editors did not question stories that might annoy advertisers. "No one ever pulled the plug," Donovan said. "No one ever slowed us down."

A little more than three weeks after the series began, the scandals grand jury returned its first indictments in Brookhaven, against Fuchs, Hough, and three others. But the pursuit of Fuchs and Hough turned out to be more difficult than the case against Conlon and Kuss. The first case to come to trial involved Fuchs and his son. The attorney for Fuchs, John J. Sutter, outsmarted Chief Assistant District Attorney Maurice Nadjari by waiving a jury, which deprived Nadjari of his strength: convincing juries. The trial ended in an acquittal. When the courts had disposed of all his other charges, either through acquittal or dismissal, Fuchs pleaded guilty to a misdemeanor charge of income-tax evasion and drew a $2,500 fine. Before Hough could come to trial, he died of injuries from an automobile accident.

The stories about Zeidler produced no indictments, and County Republican Chairman Edwin Schwenk failed in his effort to oust Zeidler as town Republican leader. But at the end of 1968, the Greene Team produced another story that did hurt him. It showed how Zeidler had used his knowledge as chairman of the Suffolk County Water Authority to become a partner in a land deal, knowing that the authority planned to sink a well nearby, which would increase the value of his land. Nadjari found no criminal violations by Zeidler, but Zeidler did lose permanently his job as authority chairman. The series also produced a significant legislative change: In 1968 and 1969, the New York State Legislature adopted laws requiring zoning applications to disclose the names of the principals.

The next town that the Greene Team took on was Babylon, at the southwest corner of Suffolk County. The initial break came involuntarily from Babylon Republican Leader Fred Fellman. With his squat body, his crew cut and his nickname, "Duke," Fellman looked and sounded like a club fighter. As a young man, he had worked in construction. Later, he helped his brother Raymond, an architect, to build Frontier City, an amusement park in North Amityville, and he operated an Italian-ice concession there. Then he became a Babylon Republican committeeman and a member of the Zoning Board of Appeals. In 1966, he rose to town leader. In that job, Fellman showed a gift for turning public policy into private gain. "The only way you raise funds is illegally," Fellman explained. "You raise funds from people who expect tremendously big favors back." His facility with funds, legal and illegal, made him popular. "He was not a greedy crook," said his former wife, Lillian. "He shared the wealth with the people around him." With his honest admission of his dishonesty, Fellman amused Greene, even though Greene knew from Fellman's own mouth that he was a crook. "We all knew, but we hadn't been particularly working on Freddie," Greene said. Then, in 1969, a story about Fellman fell into Greene's lap.

The story had begun when Fellman's marriage started to crumble. That long process culminated on national television at the 1968 Republican convention, when a network camera focused on the New York delegation and came to rest briefly on Fellman, in close company with a woman. His wife didn't see the broadcast, but she found out about it months later. After an angry fight, Fellman moved out of their bedroom, but he continued living in the house. During this period, she came upon some of the financial records of the trailer park in which he was a partner with a prominent attorney named Eugene Blumberg. She told her husband that she had the records and suggested that she might call Blumberg and tell him. "He was like a lunatic," she remembered. Fellman had good reason to be upset: He was taking a $300 kickback from the manufacturer on each trailer sold, without the knowledge of Blumberg or Arthur Cromarty, the other partner in the business.

Fellman's wife mentioned the confrontation over the records to a Babylon Republican named Edward "Skippy" Waldman, who was living with her sister. Waldman had started out life honorably, working as a *Newsday* master carrier and earning perfect attendance pins in church. As an adult, he fell into the rough-and-tumble garbage business and learned to cope with shotgun blasts and other forms of violence. In one business dispute, he lost the use of his wrists when his rivals placed them in the trunk of a car and sat on the trunk lid. Later, he got into politics, as a Republican zone leader, town sanitation commissioner and deputy highway commissioner. Waldman met Fellman when Fellman was putting together the amusement park, and they were friendly for years. By the time Fellman and his wife were heading toward a divorce, however, Waldman and Fellman were feuding. After Lillian Fellman had spoken with Waldman about her husband's papers, Waldman suggested a course of action, and she went along. "Freddie's attache case was in the trunk of his car, and I just turned all the lights out in the driveway and opened the trunk of his car," she said. "Somebody came along and picked up the attache case, and that was it." In the trunk were Fellman's business records, including the trailer park documents. Lillian Fellman's motivations were simple: "Just to screw him," she said. "I didn't want to hurt anybody. I just wanted Freddie to get the business." As for Waldman's motives, she wasn't sure. "For his own reasons, he wanted those papers," she said. "I had no idea and didn't care."

Once Waldman had the papers, he went to town and county officials and told them about the documents. He insisted that he simply wanted the officials to force Fellman to provide suitably for his wife. But Greene's sources told him that Waldman was actually looking for political jobs for himself and for Lillian Fellman, plus the removal of Fred Fellman as town leader. Whatever his motives, none of the officials offered Waldman any help. So he talked to Greene. At the time, Greene was involved in another investigation, and he was uncertain of Waldman's reliability as a source. Waldman interpreted that as Greene's reluctance to tackle a Fellman story. "His question: Why do I want to hurt Freddie?" Waldman remembered. Waldman also talked to Karl Grossman at the *Long Island Press*, who decided not to write a story, but to tell the prosecutors. "I just felt it was bigger than me to deal with," Grossman said. "It was a criminal thing." Finally, Greene called Waldman and arranged for Ken Crowe to pick up the papers. "When we opened the suitcase, I remember telling the other team members that Freddie was so likable it was almost a shame he was going into the soup, particularly inasmuch as I was trying to build him into a source," Greene said. "But there was never a question about what I would do or how fast. I immediately put the other investigation on hold."

The documents came to Greene at the end of a frenetic few months, in which he had been balancing the Suffolk scandals with his own coverage of breaking news. At the beginning of 1969, he had covered the California trial of Sirhan Bishara Sirhan, the murderer of Robert F. Kennedy. And during the summer, Marlens sent him to cover the aftermath of Senator Edward Kennedy's auto accident on Chappaquiddick Island, which killed Mary Jo Kopechne. Greene flew to Massachusetts and joined Jon Margolis, the Albany bureau chief, then asked the office to send up Tony Marro, who had joined *Newsday* in 1968, directly from the journalism school at Columbia University. Greene and Marro separated themselves from the herd and made their contribution with basic reporting. They decided, for example, to jump into the water at the scene, except that Marro ended up diving in alone, minus Greene — an exercise that proved nothing. The more meaningful story came from a walk along the route that Kennedy had taken the night of the accident, without stopping to call for help. At each house, Greene asked who was home that night, how late people stayed up, and how many lights were on. Greene also told the photographer Ken Spencer to shoot photos of the darkened houses with lights on. The photographs came out only as points of light, but the story came out strong: a step-by-step retracing of Kennedy's path, showing that there were six houses where he could have stopped for help, and that four of them had had lights on.

At the same time, the Greene Team was working on an investigation of State Senator Edward Speno of Nassau County, based on information they had gathered in Brookhaven. But when the Fellman papers came in, Greene and Crowe turned their attention to making sense of them, breaking them down into a series of deals. "On a lot of these, unless you put in one hell of a lot of work, you're going to have to have some admissions," Greene said. That was what he wanted from Fellman. So Greene called Fellman and arranged for a meeting at the Sayonara Motel, not far from Fellman's home. At the motel, Greene spread out six folders of Fellman's papers on one bed and six on the other, then made his proposal. "I said, 'You probably have very bad tax consequences on some of these. Others you don't. You give me admissions and tell me how you did it and I'll let you choose three from Column A and three from Column B, so you can leave out the ones that are your six biggest tax problems,' " Greene remembered. Fellman made as good a joke as he could. "I said: 'Bob, can I have it all?' " Greene, of course, declined. What Greene wanted was admissions about Fellman's partner in the trailer park, Cromarty, the former supervisor of Babylon and former Republican county chairman, who was by then a sitting Supreme Court judge. In 1957, when he was first elected supervisor, Cromarty had supported the idea of a county charter, which made him a *Newsday* favorite. Now he was a target, and Fellman agreed to help Greene in the hunt.

The source of Fellman's papers, Waldman, was angry that Greene did not deal more harshly with Fellman, and he argued that Greene treated Fellman leniently because they were friendly. Several years later, a *Newsday* story led to the indictment of Waldman and another public official for perjury and criminal contempt, during an investigation of their business dealings with Joseph Petrizzo, a garbage carter suspected of having ties to organized crime. Waldman pleaded guilty to attempted second-degree contempt and drew a sentence of probation. *Newsday*'s role in this process made Waldman suspect that Greene was persecuting him because of Waldman's antipathy to Fellman. But Greene saw Waldman as just another errant public figure to be investigated and nailed. It is true that Greene was not overjoyed about having to shoot Fellman out of the water, but he did pull the trigger. "He didn't shy away from going where the story was headed," Marro said.

Using the Fellman papers that Waldman had provided, plus additional reporting, the Greene Team — Crowe, Geraldine Shanahan, Marro and another recent arrival named Jim Klurfeld — finished its reporting at the end of September. The chief target, Cromarty, sat for an interview with Greene and came away thinking he had answered all the questions. "I thought I would have gotten a fair shake, having taken that opportunity to explain," Cromarty said.

The story that came out pounded heavily on Cromarty. Fellman was in the stories, but the headlines were all Cromarty. Over a span of seven years, one story said — as supervisor, county leader and then judge — Cromarty had held a secret interest in the trailer park and profited from a series of town rezonings and other actions. That and other stories triggered an inquiry by the Appellate Division of the New York State Supreme Court, which found that Cromarty had done nothing wrong. The district attorney's office saw no reason to prosecute Cromarty, Greene's real target, but it did go after Fellman. "I think Greene might have preferred it the other way around, but the evidence just wasn't there," Nadjari said. "The evidence pointed to Freddie and not to Cromarty."

The scandals grand jury indicted Fellman, along with his brother Raymond and three others. A judge dismissed the charges against Raymond Fellman. Two of the other three men indicted were acquitted. The third was convicted of stealing $700 in Republican Party funds, but an appeals court later reduced his ninety-day jail sentence to an unconditional discharge. Fred Fellman himself ended up pleading guilty to one felony count of grand larceny, for stealing $4,074 from one of the trailer firms, and the judge sentenced him to three years in prison, of which he served sixteen months.

Of the five men indicted by the scandals grand jury in the aftermath of the *Newsday* story, Fellman was the only one who went to prison. As badly as the deal at the Sayonara Motel worked out for him, however, it turned out gloriously for Greene. *Newsday* had won no Pulitzer Prize for the 1967 Islip revelations or for the 1968 Brookhaven stories. But in 1970, only a few months after the 1969 Fellman-Cromarty story broke, *Newsday* won a Pulitzer Prize for public service. The medal referred to the three-year effort, but it was ironic that *Newsday* finally won the prize only after the Babylon stories, which dropped into Greene's lap and produced few long-term results, except for the prison sentence for Fellman, whom Greene liked. Typically, Fellman showed up at the Pulitzer celebration, months before his own sentencing, and reminded the *Newsday* staff that the paper owed its Pulitzer to him. Fellman, of course, owed his later imprisonment to *Newsday*. "I did it, so I can't blame *Newsday*," Fellman said. "If it weren't for Bob Greene and his investigative team, ninety percent of this stuff in Suffolk County would be going on undetected."

Despite the scandals stories, Republicans remained dominant and Suffolk didn't develop into more of a two-party county until later in the 1970s, after the Watergate scandal. If the Greene Team did not leave a lasting imprint on the local government, however, it did advance the craft of investigative journalism. The traditional newspaper investigation had usually involved the leak of a report from a prosecutor or other government agency. But Greene had shown that reporters could go directly to the documents and do the basic work themselves. That success helped to popularize the notion of permanent investigative teams.

The *Newsday* experience had a particularly strong impact on the *Boston Globe*. On a year's sabbatical, Tim Leland of the *Globe* spent time in London, studying the "Insight Team" of *The Sunday Times*. But the concept was almost unknown in this country. The only two that Leland knew about were at the *Washington Post* and at *Newsday*. The *Post* experiment had ended, Leland said, and Benjamin Bradlee, the *Post* managing editor, advised him not to start a team, because it would create morale problems in the newsroom and take too long to accomplish too little. "So then I went up to *Newsday* and fell into the wonderful embrace of Bob Greene and had a completely different story from him," Leland said. As a result of Leland's recommendation, the *Globe* established its Spotlight Team in 1970 and won a Pulitzer in 1972.

At the same time, Greene's strategy after the scandals stories, pushing a prosecutor into indictments of dubious value, raises a serious question: Should newspapers urge prosecution or simply expose corrupt practices in print and let the law take its course? Since prosecutors are elected officials, political factors enter into indictments often enough, without additional pressure from newspapers. In fact, the scandal series demonstrated that a paper doesn't have to send people to prison in order to perform a public service: figuring out the inner workings of a corruption that the average citizen sensed, but could never decipher on his own. "He told people how they did it," Marro said. "That's what Greene was good at."

CHAPTER TWENTY-SEVEN

The Setting of the *Sun*

I

JUST AS SUFFOLK County was ripe for political corruption in the 1960s, it also showed signs of being ready for journalistic competition.

Newsday had started its Suffolk edition in 1944, but two decades later, the Suffolk paper was not yet the real *Newsday*. Internally, many reporters and editors looked at Suffolk as a temporary exile on their way back to Garden City. Externally, there was not enough competition to sharpen *Newsday*'s performance. The New York City dailies were not a major factor in Suffolk, and the primary local competitor, the *Long Island Press*, concentrated on Queens and didn't establish a full-time Suffolk operation until the late 1960s. Those factors had produced a Suffolk *Newsday* that wasn't in fighting trim. That was especially true in the East End, where the tiny year-round population had no loyalty to *Newsday*.

The signals of weakness had reached Gardner "Mike" Cowles, the communications mogul who had been the publisher of the *Des Moines Register*, the founder of *Look* magazine and the owner of a string of dailies. Cowles had become fascinated with *Newsday* more than a quarter of a century earlier, when Alicia Patterson told him of her plans to start a new newspaper in an automobile dealership. "Mike said, 'That's the craziest thing I ever heard of in my life. Don't do that. You'll lose your shirt,' " said John R. Harrison, Cowles' former son-in-law, who was a Cowles executive and later a vice-president of the *New York Times*. Alicia proved Cowles wrong, of course. "He thought it was one of the great success stories he had ever seen," Harrison said.

In the years after his inaccurate prediction to Alicia, Cowles had expanded his newspaper holdings. In the early 1960s, for example, he had studied the growth of Florida and decided to acquire the *Gainesville Sun* and the *Lakeland Ledger*. Cowles installed Harrison as publisher in Gainesville and his son, Gardner (Pat) Cowles III, as publisher in Lakeland. Just as Cowles had predicted, the two papers profited mightily. "That's what convinced Mike Cowles," Harrison said. "He kept saying, 'I want another drink of this.'" So Cowles turned to Suffolk, counting on the rapid population growth and *Newsday*'s relative weakness there.

Before going ahead, Cowles asked his son and son-in-law to study Suffolk. Advertisers grumbled about *Newsday*, but Harrison saw clearly that a new paper couldn't give them the same clout that *Newsday* did. "The cost per thousand of *Newsday* was so terribly attractive," he said. "The report said under no conditions should he start the newspaper called the *Suffolk Sun*. There was absolutely no way on God's green earth that the paper could ever make it." The Gannett chain had reached a similar conclusion. After buying a group of papers north of New York, in Westchester County, Gannett had looked at Suffolk and other markets, including Cocoa, Florida. Gannett, too, saw that *Newsday* was weaker in Suffolk than in Nassau. "That doesn't mean that we felt that they would necessarily stay weaker if a competitor came in," said Al Neuharth, the former Gannett chairman. "That was a major reason why we did not go in there, because we thought *Newsday* would react aggressively." Since they expected a weaker reaction in Florida, Gannett decided to start a paper in Cocoa called *Today*.

Despite the negative report and the bad omens, the temptation of Suffolk was too great for Cowles. He commissioned a Lou Harris survey, which left the question of advertising largely untouched and focused on potential readership. "The people in Suffolk County are ready for a paper of their own," the study said. "The goal of 50,000 households in the first six months should be within easy reach for the right product."

As the publisher of the new paper, Mike Cowles chose his son, who was not as pessimistic as Harrison. "I was twenty-nine and had had relatively good success in Lakeland," Pat Cowles said. "At that age, you feel you can conquer the world pretty much." That choice spawned a joke at *Look*: that the paper should have been named the *Suffolk Son*. But Harrison rejected the idea that Cowles started the paper for his son. "Mike Cowles never started anything in his entire life for anybody other than Mike," he said. "Mike was a brilliant, wonderful, dear, loving man, but he was a man with an ego that had to be fed. This was a way to do that."

Once Cowles had decided to go ahead, he paid an hour-long visit to Harry Guggenheim at *Newsday*. He had known Harry and Alicia for many years, and Harry's daughter, Joan Van de Maele, had served as the godmother for Cowles' daughter, Virginia. So it was awkward for Cowles to tell Harry that they would now be competitors. Harry insisted that his competitor in Suffolk might as well be Cowles, since they knew and admired each other. But he did issue a gently ominous warning. "A battle of this kind sometimes gets very bloody and we both may well be spattered," Harry told him. When Cowles said that they wouldn't really be competing, since the *Sun* would be a morning paper, Harry answered firmly: "I don't want to go into the morning field, but if we find that you are succeeding, that a morning paper can be successful here, why then we will go into the morning field and compete with you." The message beneath the polite tones was clear: *Newsday* would fight to make the *Suffolk Sun* bleed from a thousand tiny holes. "It was a knot in his stomach," Bill Moyers said. "It was a matter of ego to him that he not lose the terrain that Alicia had claimed. . . . He wanted to fight 'em. He didn't want to buy them out. He didn't want to woo them, merge with them. He wanted to fight 'em."

II

THE FIGHT BEGAN even before the *Sun* published its first issue.

Through his sources in the industry, Vinnie Bordash of the circulation department had learned that the *Sun* planned to emulate the early success of *Today* in Florida. So Bordash made an appointment with Al Neuharth, for himself and for Ernie Levy and Dave Targe of the advertising department. In their meeting with Neuharth, they grilled him on what *Today* had done right. Then they flew to Florida and met with the general manager of the *Orlando Sentinel*, to find out what the *Sentinel* had done wrong in allowing *Today* to move into the market. They used this knowledge to improve their incentives for carriers and district managers. They also split up existing routes, to make more *Newsday* routes available and lure away the best carriers who might otherwise go to the *Sun*. "We'd leave them the trash," Bordash said.

In addition, Bordash went a step further, ordering one of his salesmen to call up 300 potential *Sun* customers, pretend to be working for the *Sun* and find out how many sales he could get. At the end of each call, the salesman would falsely tell the customer that the *Sun* would start on Monday, and that the customer should think about discontinuing *Newsday*. "Now what does that do to the person on the other end?" Bordash said. "They think, 'That son of a bitch. That *Suffolk Sun* is very unethical.' In the meantime, the paper never came." Beyond sowing ill will for the *Sun*, this ploy showed Bordash that the *Sun* had the potential to sell 70,000 to 100,000 papers. To combat that, *Newsday* increased its telephone sales and other campaigns. Whatever money they needed in these efforts, Harry gave them. He had told Cowles that *Newsday* had a $5 million "war chest," plus his own fortune, to fight competition, and he spent it willingly. In early 1967, for example, *Newsday* adopted a $550,669 list of budget revisions to fight the *Sun*, ranging from new reporters and editors for Suffolk to a service that provided stock information to readers by phone.

When the first issue of the *Sun* rolled off the presses at its new plant in

Deer Park on November 21, 1966, a small group of *Newsday* circulation supervisors followed the *Sun* trucks, to see where their routes were. "They thought we were some goons, and there was some wild driving going on," said John Brignoli, the *Newsday* supervisor in charge of the spy mission. That convinced *Sun* employees that *Newsday* would actively sabotage the new paper. "Did we follow their trucks? Sure we did," Bordash said. "Did we scare the hell out of the truck drivers at three in the morning? Sure we did." But, he insisted, they committed no sabotage.

The advertising department was as fierce as circulation was. "They were the soul of *Newsday* as a business operation," Moyers said. "God, they were feisty! I really enjoyed them." The advertising salesmen fought hard against the *Sun* because they remembered how the *Nassau Daily Review-Star* had failed to crush *Newsday* and paid for that mistake with its life. "It served as a lesson to us," said Michael Forgione, one of the key advertising supervisors. "If we did it to someone else, they could do it to us." If they needed any further motivation, Ernie Levy provided it. One *Newsday* salesman, Len Partiss, remembered how Levy ridiculed the uniform that *Sun* ad salesmen wore, green blazers with yellow sunbursts. Levy used the jackets as a battle cry: " 'Does that sell advertising? Go out and kick their ass.' "

The strategy that Targe used in obeying Levy's command had two elements. One was based on the mistake that the *Orlando Sentinel* had made in fighting *Today*: They cut advertising rates to attract advertisers. Those rate cuts left advertisers with more money to buy ads, but the advertisers invested it in the new paper, *Today*, instead of keeping it in the *Sentinel*. So Targe wanted to make it difficult for an advertiser to afford ads in both *Newsday* and the *Sun*. "We raised our rates and we kept raising them for the years that they were here," Targe said. "There just wasn't any money left over. We virtually sponged out their advertising." For those advertisers who dared to take advantage of the *Sun*'s lower rates and ran ads in the new paper, *Newsday* worked hard to convince them that ads in the *Sun* were not helping them to sell goods. If an ad appeared in the *Sun*, someone from *Newsday* had to be at the door of that advertiser the same day and persuade her not to use the *Sun*. In addition to the efforts of the salesmen in their territories, Targe set up a "killer" team, whose members had *no* other job except to visit *Sun* advertisers and kill *Sun* ads. The team included career salesmen such as Bob Hirsch and John Tewksbury, plus Don Trimboli, a gentle and imposingly tall man who was studying to become an Episcopalian priest the whole time he worked as a *Sun*-slayer.

If mere argument failed to shake an advertiser loose from the *Sun*, Targe used rougher methods. Since the volume of ads and the lack of space often made it difficult for advertisers to get into *Newsday* anyway, it was easy to keep out of the paper entirely anyone who advertised in the *Sun*. If the advertiser complained, Targe had a logical argument. "If you as an advertiser were using the other paper, well, you were in the market," Targe said. "So you didn't need us. And the people who were just using *Newsday* counted on us." If *Sun* advertisers griped that *Newsday* was burying their ads in the back of the paper,

Targe had a fanciful explanation. He just told them that the man in charge of making up the paper every day, Al Sarmento, hated the *Sun*. That, of course, was untrue. Sarmento was a sweet, reasonable man. So Targe removed the phone from Sarmento's desk, to prevent advertisers from calling him. "He was our mystery man," Targe said.

One vivid example of this squeeze was the case of Flower Time, a gardening outlet with a new store in Huntington. Robert Ench, the canny businessman who created Flower Time, knew that he had to have *Newsday* ads to launch the store. So he bought a two-page ad for a Friday. But the day before his ad was to run in *Newsday*, he ran one in the *Sun*. That day, Ench got a call from someone in the *Newsday* advertising department, who told him he was wasting money in the *Sun* and also mentioned that there was a sudden change in the Friday paper. " 'Gee, we don't have room for your two pages of ads. Which page do you want? The right or the left? The GRAND or the OPENING?' Then they said, 'Well, what we can do is shrink down both ads and combine them for you into the one page.' " Ench protested immediately to Gene Higgins, the retail ad manager. "I had to call him and tell him that this was against the law," Ench said. "I played on his honesty and his integrity. Of course, I got my two pages. . . . That was my first introduction to hardball at *Newsday*."

At the same time that *Newsday* was using tactics that bordered on restraint of trade, the mere presence of the *Sun* also forced *Newsday* to tone down its monopoly attitude, which agencies and advertisers had always considered arrogant. "It made us sharper," Higgins said. "We got better. Our relationship with agencies also improved tremendously."

III

As MUCH AS the *Newsday* advertising and circulation departments loved to tell war stories about *Sun*-bashing, the new paper's death was much more a suicide than a murder.

One of its costliest mistakes was the size of its circulation. At the start, they discussed putting out a modest paper of 25,000 circulation, but that wasn't enough. "Macy's, A & S, Sears, Martin's, all said they'd come in, but only if we had 100,000 circulation," Pat Cowles said. So the *Sun* guaranteed the 100,000 — an almost impossible promise to keep. "You just don't turn on the faucet and come up with 100,000 net paid, especially when you're up against quality papers," said Bruce Rubino, who became the *Sun* circulation director in 1969. "It sometimes takes generations of intensive work before a newspaper is totally accepted," said Lou Fabian, a *Sun* home delivery supervisor.

The difficulty of reaching 100,000 paid readers forced the paper to fib. "The circulation department was issuing a lot of gains and so forth that were not necessarily all accurate," said Henry Downs, who became the paper's production manager in 1968. "We all got a little gold key chain thing when they hit 80,000. . . . I was only printing 67,000 each night at the time." The pressure for 100,000 also forced them to give away free samples and to start circulating in Nassau, which diluted the *Sun*'s strength and inflated the huge cost of delivering the paper. "It was just eating us up alive," Pat Cowles said. "It took an enormous amount of money to feed this animal."

The *Sun* also miscalculated in its choice of staff. "I hired some for advertising from Florida, and the advertising business is a lot different in Florida," Cowles said. They didn't understand the competitive New York market, and they didn't know how to work with large department stores. Eventually, S. O. Shapiro, the circulation director at Cowles Communications, urged Pat Cowles to replace his friend, Bob Powell, the advertising director. Shapiro did the replacing for him, and in Powell's place, they hired a veteran advertising man named Daniel Lionel, who had worked at the *Brooklyn Eagle*, the *New York Herald Tribune* and the *New York Post*. "Lionel could relate to the market much better," said Chuck Milas, one of his salesmen. "He was the best thing that the *Suffolk Sun* ever did." Despite *Newsday*'s advantages, Lionel's professionalism steadily improved the *Sun*'s advertising performance, but it was not enough to offset the heavy burden of the paper's costs.

On top of its advertising and circulation problems, the *Sun* also had labor and production difficulties. At the start, Cowles reached a contract with the printers that allowed them to represent all the crafts at the paper — an arrangement that might have been acceptable in Florida, but not in New York. The pressmen objected, and pickets surrounded the building. "I felt that it was a mistake right off the bat," said Juergen Jaenicke, one of the printers at the *Sun*, who later came to work at *Newsday*. "It was totally against traditions." The plant itself had neatly color-coded furniture and gleaming equipment, but it was an old-fashioned letterpress operation, when many papers were converting to offset printing. "We built a state-of-the-art dinosaur," said Robert Williams, the *Sun*'s assistant managing editor. To run the plant, Cowles had a parade of production managers, starting with a friend of his father, who set it up and served three tours as production manager, plus four other men — a total of seven regimes. "When I came in the door," Henry Downs said, "I was known as Henry the Eighth." Together, the production problems, the circulation costs and the initial inadequacy of the advertising staff added up to a severe handicap. "It was mostly on the business side," Moyers said, "because they didn't put out a bad editorial product."

The *Sun* was a six-day morning broadsheet that emulated the small papers in Florida by running daily color photographs. "The color was always a problem," said Harry Beery, a former rewrite man and editor at the *Herald Tribune* who was a copy editor and day news editor at the *Sun*. "They could never get it in register." *Newsday* didn't have that problem. "I didn't think we needed to go to color," Moyers said. "But I did take some steps. I wanted Suffolk beefed up. I wanted to pay more attention to Suffolk politics." In addition, bowing to the importance of symbols, the paper had also quietly added a new line at the top of page one, three months before the *Sun*'s first issue: "Published for Long Island by Long Islanders." The obvious purpose was to point out that the *Sun*'s staff was full of outsiders. There was certainly some truth to that. Early in his time at the *Sun*, for example, Beery had to change a headline that referred to Democrats from "Demos," the Florida usage, to "Dems," the style on Long Island.

The Florida flavor in the newsroom was understandable enough: Pat Cowles had worked and made contacts there. His admiration for the *St. Petersburg Times* led him to its managing editor, Cortland Anderson, a hard-drinking, sometimes profane editor with a booming voice. Cowles made Anderson the *Sun*'s editor, and Anderson recruited a managing editor from Florida: Rick Tuttle, a quiet, docile man who had risen to night city editor at the *Miami Herald*. Once Tuttle came north, he persuaded Bob Williams to leave the *Herald* and join the *Sun* as news editor. The Florida connection also produced two reporters who became standouts at *Newsday* after their *Sun* days: Fred Bruning and Jon Margolis.

The staff that the *Sun* gathered was, in many ways, like the early *Newsday* staff — a mixture of raw, inexperienced reporters and cynical veterans. "Surprisingly, the *Sun* had a lot of talent there," said one of the editors, Bill Soriano. "It was almost like a revolutionary army of sorts. We got people from all over the place." The staff ranged from an intern named Fred Tuccillo, who had worked with Soriano on a weekly paper in Smithtown and started at the *Sun* as a high school senior, to more hardened reporters such as Bob Dolan, who came to the *Sun* from the papers in Binghamton, New York. As different as they were, they shared a sense of challenge. "The spirit of the thing was: 'Well, there's *Newsday* out there, and *Newsday* covers the earth, and we're just little people trying to get this niche here,' " said Michael Schefer, a reporter and editor at the *Sun*. " 'Maybe we'll do it and maybe we won't, but we're going to have a good time trying.' "

In some ways, working at the *Sun* was fun, especially for those who got to cover stories that they couldn't possibly cover on a more mature paper. Tuccillo started out taking scores of high school games, but he soon found found himself, while still in college, covering the Mets, the Yankees and major news stories, such as crashes on the Long Island Rail Road. "Frankly, even I wouldn't have trusted me," Tuccillo said. "In retrospect, it was kind of crazy." Similarly, Chris Weber, who had never covered courts before, found himself writing about the trial of Conlon and Kuss, the targets of *Newsday*'s Islip scandals stories. And Ed Hershey, whose journalism experience included only work as a high school sports stringer for the *New York Post* and the *Journal-American* and a brief tour at the *World-Telegram*, got to cover the championship year of the Jets. He couldn't get to the Super Bowl, because the *Sun* couldn't afford it, but he did get to cover the AFL championship.

The fun at the *Sun*, however, was mixed with real problems. Inside the plant, the staff faced a lack of guidance from the senior editors. Frequently, Cowles, Anderson, Tuttle and others would adjourn for long lunches at the Sky Lounge, a bar at a small airport near the plant. "It was very disheartening for a young staff to see all the bosses go out several days a week for long periods of time in the heart of the day," Bruning said. More important, those long lunches didn't produce a unified vision of what the *Sun* should be. "It was conceived of by half the people who had a say in it as a metropolitan paper, covering national and international news," Williams said. "It was conceived of by the other half as a suburban paper. . . . We never were able to tap into the psyche of our market."

Outside the plant, the reporters faced *Newsday*. No matter how much enthusiasm they brought to bear, mere energy was not enough to beat *Newsday*. "We outnumbered them," said Jim Toedtman, one of the reporters hired to fight the *Sun*. "Both the numbers and the time gave us a huge advantage editorially." As a morning paper, the *Sun* had earlier deadlines, which allowed *Newsday* reporters to stay at meetings later and get the full story, while *Sun* reporters had to rush back and write. In the morning, if the *Sun* had a good story, *Newsday* could read it and put a version of it in that day's paper. "*Newsday* went into a semi-paranoid posture about this newspaper," said John V. N. Klein, then the chairman of the county Board of Supervisors. "I was starting to get telephone calls from *Newsday* reporters at 8:30 in the morning. What they were trying to do was make last-minute revisions in their stories, to be competitive with the *Suffolk Sun*." So the struggle was painful for the *Sun* staff. "There were good, healthy competitive feelings about *Newsday*, along with sort of despairing feelings about how hopeless it was, how much they had and how arrogant they were," said Rebecca Klock, a young reporter and editor who later came to *Newsday*. "They were very intimidating." *Newsday* made matters worse by breaking story after story in the Suffolk scandals investigation, which the *Sun* couldn't match. "We were just eating *Newsday*'s dust on the story," said Bob Dolan, who had the melancholy duty of covering Islip during the scandals. "We'd have to attribute it to *Newsday*. We couldn't really ignore it."

At the same time, the costs of the *Sun* were getting the attention of Cowles Communications, which was having troubles of its own with *Look*. Television, the rise of specialty magazines and a business recession had begun to cut advertising revenue, while the soaring circulation raised the magazine's costs. "The circulation became an albatross," said Jack Squire, the *Look* promotion manager whose slogan, "LOOK IS BIGGER THAN LIFE," helped to develop that circulation. In that environment, the *Sun*'s losses began to hurt the whole corporation's credit standing. William Attwood, then the editor-in-chief at Cowles Commununciations, recalled the losses at $16 million. Pat Cowles said they were $8 million or $9 million. In either case, they hurt.

That reality subjected Pat Cowles to a series of unpleasant meetings at the corporate headquarters and visits by corporate advisors. Cowles was a quiet man with simple tastes, who enjoyed putting on jeans and tinkering with his car, but never liked the Manhattan meetings. Many at the *Sun* saw him as a pleasant but weak leader, but John Harrison attributed many of his problems to corporate meddling. "If they had let Pat Cowles do it, the *Suffolk Sun* may have made it," Harrison said. "Pat Cowles is good. He's a plugger."

In the closing months, as rumors of the paper's demise increased, the turnover grew and they had to find staff where they could. Ed Lowe, for example, was teaching English, after previous rejections by *Newsday* and the *Sun*, but when he approached Anderson for a job in 1969, he got it. That summer, they also hired Jim Bernstein, who had just graduated from Long Island University and worked briefly for a paper in New Jersey. No one bothered to tell him he was climbing on a sinking ship. So he moved from New Jersey to Long Island, hopeful for the future. Not long after Bernstein arrived, Pat Cowles went to one last meeting in Manhattan in the late summer of 1969. He argued that the *Sun* was about to make a profit, but that didn't work. Cowles Communications decided right then to close the *Sun* and instructed Pat Cowles not to pass the word at the paper yet.

Finally, on Friday, October 17, 1969, Mike Cowles announced in Manhattan that Saturday's *Sun* would be the last. At the office in Deer Park, Tuttle stood on a desk and told the staff. Most of them melted away immediately. So Ed Lowe, who had been hired only a few months before, ended up writing three front-page stories, without bylines, for the last issue. The closing was especially difficult for Weber and his wife, Mary Anne, who also worked at the *Sun*. She had just brought their new son, Douglas, home from the hospital, and they were sipping champagne when they learned that the *Sun* was setting. Sudden unemployment for both of them was terrifying. But Chris Weber and Lowe, like others at the *Sun*, ended up working at *Newsday*, and Tuttle helped others find jobs elsewhere.

At the end, Pat Cowles tried to sell the *Sun* to *Newsday*, but Harry was uninterested. Cowles ended up selling the *Sun*'s circulation lists to the *Daily News* and its equipment wherever he could. Less than two years after the *Sun* closed, Mike Cowles announced the end of *Look* magazine. "The *Suffolk Sun*, I think, was responsible for the early demise of the whole organization," Attwood said.

Years later, some of those who worked for the *Sun* still felt that there really had been a market for a second paper in Suffolk, but the *Sun* simply failed to take advantage of it. "It was a sad paper and did not deserve to continue," Bruning said. But it was a blessing for *Newsday*: After long neglect by the Garden City office, the Suffolk paper had grown sharper, more competitive and better staffed. "In the overall scheme of things," Bob Williams said, "the *Suffolk Sun* was probably the best thing that ever happened to *Newsday*."

CHAPTER TWENTY-EIGHT

The Man in the Gravy-Stained Tie

I

As BILL MOYERS reached his second anniversary at *Newsday* in early 1969, he found himself coping with a sick and unhappy owner, an alcoholic editor, a rebellious managing editor, and his own difficult, unfinished agenda for change.

For two years, he had been trying to shape *Newsday*, always conscious of Lyndon Johnson's advice: The best fertilizer for a ranch is the footprint of the boss. Attempting to leave those footprints and define his vision, he sat down and wrote a nineteen-page memo to Bill McIlwain and Al Marlens. It conceded that *Newsday* was a fine paper, but focused primarily on weaknesses: an absence of imagination and consistency.

"There are days when we read like the AP report," Moyers wrote. "There are exceptions — we can be brilliant in handling news explosions like LBJ's withdrawal and RFK's assassination. And we are good with our series. But in handling the daily flow of news we are erratic. We are also often boring." *Newsday* concentrated too much on traditional breaking news and failed to provide an interesting blend of lifestyle pieces. "Not all news is a happening," Moyers wrote. "Ideas are news." The paper was also boring because of the writing. "It is consistent only in blandness," he wrote. "We have a reputation as a paper that cannot keep good young creative people because we ask them to write their stories not so much with their own intelligence or as they saw it but as some formula requires. . . . It's not a question of competence. If anything, Newsday is staggeringly competent, the most adequate newspaper in the neighborhood. But that's not enough. Something is missing. I think it is personality."

In addition to these broad criticisms, the memo was full of specific recommendations on makeup and features. It also focused on "the split personality" of *Newsday*. "Reporters have constantly told me of their frustration at being handed an assignment by one editor, turning his copy in to another editor who accepts it, and having still a third editor change it himself or call the reporter to change it for reasons that have to do mostly with the fact that a new party can always see another way of doing something," Moyers wrote. "Some of this has to be, I know, but I also know that the night-and-day division of our labors is too great for us to achieve the kind of harmony and consistency I want." Far from harmony, *Newsday* had created a "harsh and impersonal process" that ground down reporters. "One of your veterans told me last week: 'This is not a happy place to work right now,'" Moyers wrote. "That must change."

If Moyers could have interviewed every reporter, he would have learned that "not a happy place" was a vast understatement. "I hated it," said Tony Marro, one of the best of the new reporters to arrive at the paper under Moyers. "I think there were people who were calculatedly abusive." Marro had jumped joyfully into the newspaper business as a high school student in Rutland, Vermont, because he knew of no more exciting place than the city room of the *Rutland Herald*. But arriving at *Newsday* in 1968, he found nothing like that charm. "I thought newsrooms were wonderful, fun places to be," Marro said. "This place was nasty."

The chief source of pain was the continued dominance of the night desk, under the news editor, Dick Estrin. "He wasn't a very pleasant person to work with," Tony Insolia said. "He was like a bully, always challenging. When he got away with it, I think he exulted in winning those kinds of battles." More than his personality, it was his microscopic scrutiny of stories that drove reporters and editors mad. He would sit at his desk, his head shaking nervously from side to side and his pencil flying over a piece of copy, and then pass it on to the copy chief to get the holes in the story filled. Then a copy editor would have to grill the reporter or the assigning editor. "He'd have thirty-five questions on every story," said Richard Sandler, who watched Estrin first as a copy editor, then as a night editor in Suffolk. When a copy editor relayed Estrin's questions, Sandler would make it clear how ridiculous he considered them. One of those editors was David Hamilton, who repeatedly had to ask questions raised by Estrin. The one that he remembered most vividly involved a story by Bob Wyrick, about scientists discovering that the universe was twice as big as they had thought. Estrin asked: "What does this mean to LI?" Hamilton had no choice but to gulp hard and call Wyrick at home. That nightly process took its toll even on the street-wise Wyrick, who had been through the toughening experience of a prison term for robbery before he came to *Newsday*. "It was a man-killer," Wyrick said. "I was tough and it damned near killed me."

The persistent pressure changed the way editors edited and reporters reported. "You found yourself asking every question conceivable, not for the story, but for the editors," Ken Crowe said. The desk was so dominant that it became known as far away as the state capital. "In Albany, it was a sort of joke that late at night, in the reporters-legislators bars and restaurants, if the phone would ring, they'd go, 'Oh, it's the *Newsday* desk,' " said Jerry Edgerton, who joined *Newsday* in 1966 from the Associated Press. "I feel like it made me a better reporter, but I think the same values could have been inculcated with a considerably lower level of fear, loathing and abuse."

The editing structure was so daunting that it helped to drive away a reporter who won one Pulitzer Prize before coming to *Newsday* and a second after he left. Gene Goltz arrived in 1966, after winning the Pulitzer for a series of pieces about municipal corruption in the blue-collar suburbs of Houston. One of his problems at *Newsday* was that Goltz had developed his own rhythm in Houston, and the *Newsday* desk wanted results in what he considered an unreasonable rush. Tony Insolia sent him to Long Beach on an investigation and promised him as much time as he needed, for example, but another editor reversed that decision and ordered Goltz back to the office before he could finish the project. In addition, Goltz said, new shifts of editors constantly countermanded what the previous shift had ordered him to do. "There was absolutely total war between the dayside and the nightside," he said. "My God, that's excruciating." Finally, after a year, Goltz left for the *Detroit Free Press*, where he promptly won a Pulitzer for covering the urban riots. In both Houston and Detroit, his colleagues regarded him highly, but editors at *Newsday* saw him as a good gatherer of facts who could not organize his information in the *Newsday* way. When word of Goltz's Detroit Pulitzer came in, a new reporter named Bradford O'Hearn remembered standing at the wire machine as Insolia read the story and commented: " 'I still say he's no goddamn good.' "

Against that formidable editing machine, which still did not trust his motives, Moyers had no real allies, except for two bright young men who joined the paper soon after Moyers arrived. To the veterans at *Newsday*, these new employees seemed to fit neatly in the tradition of Alicia Patterson's old palace guard system. One was Robert Ellis Smith, a Harvard graduate, who had worked at the *Trenton Times* and the *Detroit Free Press* before a mutual friend recommended him to Moyers. Smith worked as a reporter, then transferred to *Newsday*'s syndicate. Another was Ralph Keyes, who had graduated from Antioch College and studied at the London School of Economics. Even though his journalistic experience included only a few free-lance pieces and a short tour as a copy boy at the *Toledo Blade*, Keyes sat down one day and wrote a cheeky letter to Moyers, suggesting that *Newsday* wasn't covering the student revolt very well. To his astonishment, Moyers offered him a job. What Keyes did not know was that Moyers had started his career the same way, with his letter to Lyndon Johnson. "I pay attention to letters," Moyers said, "because letters changed my life."

When Keyes came in, with shoulder-length hair and a bushy beard, he started as a special assistant to Moyers — doing research for speeches, drafting letters and performing other chores. He also reinforced the publisher's own views about the need to cover emerging social trends. "It was a very, very effervescent time," Keyes said, "but you wouldn't have known that, for the most part, from reading *Newsday*." It was inevitable that newsroom veterans would be wary when Keyes took reporters out to lunch and talked with them, apparently to learn the concerns of the staff. "He was a spy," said Dick Zander, the crusty political reporter. Keyes struck Bob Greene the same way. "Moyers didn't help by bringing in kids with beards and jeans to sit in the back of the city room and suddenly do report cards," Greene said. But Greene and others missed the point: Moyers was providing an opportunity for the young, as Johnson and Millard Cope had done for him. "That had nothing to do with any sense of palace guard," Moyers said. "I benefitted greatly from being older men's protege, and I've always tried to return the favor."

Neither Smith nor Keyes had a major impact on the newspaper, but in his work at *Newsday*'s syndicate, Smith did help create the first syndicated comic strip drawn by a black man about issues of race. Reading the civil rights magazine *Freedomways*, Smith admired the work of an artist named Brumsic Brandon Jr., who lived on Long Island. So he called Brandon and suggested that the time was right for a black comic strip. Since Brandon had already submitted ideas for black comic strips to others, without luck, Smith's suggestion delighted him. The head of *Newsday* Specials, Tom Dorsey, and his assistant, Bob Gillespie, discussed it with him and suggested a black version of *Skippy*, a strip that featured young children exploring philosophical issues. So Brandon started sketching a group of black children and named the strip *Luther*, after Dr. Martin Luther King. *Newsday* Specials couldn't sell *Luther*, but Brandon did find a home for him. Smith had sent copies of the strip to *The Manhattan Tribune*, an experimental weekly. Its managing editor was Pat Patterson, who had been the second black reporter hired by *Newsday*. Patterson liked *Luther* and started running it. A few months later, Smith said, Marlens wrote a memo to Moyers, suggesting that *Newsday* pick up *Luther*. So *Newsday* became the first daily newspaper to carry the strip, which the *Los Angeles Times* Syndicate later distributed for fifteen years. And the whole idea had started with Smith. "I have always considered him to be *Luther*'s godfather," Brandon said.

Bright but inexperienced young men such as Smith and Keyes could bring new voices to *Newsday*, but they were not enough to reshape the paper the way Moyers wanted. He needed someone with real newspaper experience who shared his views. "I knew the strengths of Marlens and Insolia and all of those people," Moyers said, "but I didn't think their strengths added up to the capacity to adapt to where I wanted to take the paper." He also knew that McIlwain, whose drinking was getting worse, could not help him move the paper toward the daily newsmagazine approach that he wanted. "I saw Bill teetering," Moyers said. "I knew that Bill was heading for a problem, and I had to build around that."

For a time, Moyers talked with Edwin Diamond, who was editing the back-of-the-book sections of *Newsweek*, and asked him to come to *Newsday*. Diamond felt that his future was in newsmagazines, and he declined. It was just as well, because anyone from a newsmagazine would have faced fierce resistance from *Newsday*'s daily journalists. "If I could find someone from the newspaper business whose credentials were unquestionable," Moyers said, "then he would at least not have that barrier."

In 1969, Moyers found what he wanted, in Washington. "The Style section of the *Washington Post* was evolving in the very direction that lay at the heart of both my feelings about a daily newspaper's becoming more like a newsmagazine on a daily basis and John Denson's and Al Marlens' own work on what a new look to *Newsday* might be if it became *Newsday National,*" said Moyers. So he wondered: "Who is this guy who is doing this at the *Washington Post?*" His name was David Laventhol.

II

FOR STUDENT JOURNALISTS at Yale in the 1950s, it was easy to become so focused on the *Yale Daily News* that all else seemed secondary.

"It was considered very, very uncool to be seen to be a serious student in those years," said Larry Bensky, a Yale friend of Laventhol. "He majored in the *Yale Daily News,* with a minor in drinking." When they were not at the offices of the *News,* they would adjourn to a bar that they called The Dimey, in a disreputable quarter of New Haven, where a thirsty student could drink beer for a dime a glass. But for Laventhol, The Dimey was just a pastime. The *Yale Daily News* was a passion. Newspapering was in his genes.

Both of Laventhol's parents were born to families recently arrived in America from the Ukraine, near Kiev. His father, Jesse, worked for several newspapers in Philadelphia, covering politics and government. In 1936, when David Laventhol was three years old, his father became the state bureau chief and moved the family to the capital, Harrisburg. Later, he went from journalism into government, editing a publication called *Pennsylvania Highways.* In 1940, they moved back to Philadelphia, and Jesse Laventhol did public relations for the Anti-Defamation League. His job with the league took the family in 1944 to Washington, where he later worked in Harry Truman's 1948 campaign. Following the election, he took a job in the new Office of the Coordinator of Information in the House of Representatives and worked there until he retired.

Plunging into his father's craft, David Laventhol edited the school paper at Woodrow Wilson High School in Washington, worked as a copy boy at the *Washington Star* and produced high school sports pages for the *Washington Daily News,* then in 1951 started at the *Yale Daily News.* "No one ever worked harder," said Mike McGrady, then a *Yale Daily News* sports columnist. But Laventhol didn't work as hard on his studies. "After my second year at Yale, they recommended that I go in the Army," Laventhol said. "I was a bad boy." So he spent two years in the Army, repairing radios, then returned to Yale. This time, he trimmed back slightly on his hours at the newspaper, but he still worked at it hard enough to be elected managing editor.

Around the campus, Laventhol developed a reputation for being quiet and unprepossessing. "He was widely admired for his lack of ambition," said one of his Yale acquaintances, the columnist Calvin Trillin. But beneath the unimpressive facade, Bensky saw real talent. "The man is ferociously intelligent," Bensky said. Even in college, Laventhol turned that intelligence toward editing, rather than reporting. "It was kind of *declasse* even to think about being a reporter at Yale," Trillin said. "He wanted to be a desk man." That held true when he was graduated from Yale in 1957 and went to work at the *St. Petersburg Times*. He started out as a reporter, but only three months later, he switched to the desk. Taking a brief detour after two years of editing at St. Petersburg, he went off to earn a master's degree in English at the University of Minnesota, where he took a creative writing course with the poet and critic Allen Tate and learned that creative writing wasn't his strength. His first step back to journalism was a tryout for a copy editing job at the *New York Times*, where an editor told him: " 'Well, Mr. Laventhol, let's not be Pollyannish about it. Your editing is erratic.' " So he returned to St. Petersburg in the summer of 1960 and became the editor of the national news section.

Controlling a whole section of his own, Laventhol had the opportunity to do everything: pick the wires to use, rewrite them, lay out the pages, write headlines, crop pictures. "It was a terrific job, and in some respects it was probably the best job I ever had," Laventhol said. "I had a lot of freedom to experiment with a lot of different things." Given that latitude, he began to act on his intuitive sense of the need to package news differently, to fit the needs and tastes of readers who were getting more and more of their news from television. "The whole process by which people receive information was becoming different, but newspapers woke up to that very slowly," Laventhol said. At St. Petersburg, he developed an activist style of editing: grinding up wire service copy and dressing it up with imaginative graphics that made the news more easily digestible — much like a newsmagazine. Once Laventhol had finally decided to leave Florida, he applied to both the *Washington Post* and the *New York Herald Tribune*. The *Tribune* was in the middle of the disastrous New York newspaper strike of 1962-1963. So Laventhol signed on at the *Post* in March, 1963, as night world editor. He had barely settled into his routine there when the New York strike ended and the *Tribune* offered him a job as assistant foreign editor. When Laventhol arrived in the spring of 1963, the *Tribune* was perhaps the most exciting place in all of American journalism: a great newspaper with a rich history, struggling to survive.

Searching for a way to reverse the loss of millions of dollars a year, Walter N. Thayer, the *Tribune*'s president, had reached into *Newsweek* and hired away an authentic genius, John Denson, as his editor. Since Denson had made his reputation at *Newsweek* as a master of graphics, and since the *Tribune*'s losses didn't allow it to spend much money on hiring more staff, his mission was to increase the paper's appeal by altering its appearance. Denson's manic energy and flair for exciting layout brought quick circulation gains, but his compulsive tinkering with the front page disrupted the whole production process. Finally, Thayer forced Denson out and replaced him with one of his four executive editors, James Bellows, whose job was to retain the liveliness introduced by Denson but reduce the chaos.

Arriving in the *Tribune*'s grimy city room, Laventhol quickly grasped what the paper was trying to do. "I don't think they ever said, 'Hey, we're in the television age; we've got to put out a different kind of newspaper,' " he said. "But they had things like a news summary on page one. They had a tremendous amount of compression of the news to organize it more cleanly for people, a tremendous amount of rewriting — a lot more like a magazine in many ways than a newspaper." So Laventhol sat at the *Tribune* foreign desk and rewrote wires and staff reports to make them intelligible and lively. "When he came, it was like fresh battalions had been thrown into the trenches," said his boss, Harry Rosenfeld. "Not only did he bring his newspaper skills, of which he had ample amount, he brought a scope of interest in the world and in national affairs."

On the foreign desk and later on the news desk, Laventhol learned firsthand that Bellows insisted, as Denson had, that the paper look exactly right every night. "On the front page at that time, Bellows wrote all the headlines himself," Laventhol said. "I think I wrote sixty-five headlines before one was ever accepted." At first, Bellows found Laventhol externally unimpressive. "I remember so well the pencil, the way he'd write," Bellows said. "I'd say, 'Can this guy really do things, and is he competent?' " It didn't take long, though, for Bellows to see beneath that exterior to his skills. When the city editor, Dick Schaap, asked to be relieved of that job and to return to writing, Bellows chose Laventhol to replace him. "He was cool, easy, comfortable, and he had great common sense," Bellows said. "He got along with people."

When Laventhol took the job, he had only been at the paper for a year and a half, and he was just thirty-one years old. So his appointment prompted some complaining. And he was easy to mock. It was painful for him to carry on small talk with strangers, for example, and nearly impossible for him to eat a meal without leaving coffee or gravy all over his tie. "David Laventhol had a running nose for the first three years I knew him," said Richard Wald, who became managing editor under Bellows. These traits made Laventhol a perfect target for other editors. One of his tormentors was Don Forst, a clever little man with a choirboy face and a mongoose manner, who worked as an editor on the city desk, as national editor and as executive news editor. Another was Danny Blum, the bald, cigar-smoking day city editor, who had been crippled by polio a decade earlier and ran the desk from a wheelchair. Despite the mockery, Laventhol soon showed that he was competent and that he knew how to translate Bellows, who communicated his wishes with mumbles and imprecise gestures. "Jim probably partly wanted me in there because I would do what he wanted me to," Laventhol said. "Jim was very difficult to understand. . . . I thought I understood what Jim was doing, and I agreed with him."

In the end, Bellows and Laventhol could not rescue the *Tribune* from its financial wounds. The management attempted to put together a new entity, along with the struggling *Journal-American* and *World-Telegram & Sun*. But the unions objected strenuously to that merger and the Newspaper Guild struck. Idled by the union dispute, Laventhol ended his *Tribune* career running elevators in the old building in downtown Manhattan that had belonged to the *World-Telegram*. Then he looked for work. His former *Trib* boss, Rosenfeld, had already gone to the *Washington Post* and strongly recommended Laventhol to the new *Post* managing editor, Benjamin Bradlee.

Laventhol started at the *Post* in the fall of 1966, and soon became night managing editor, running the news desk. Unlike *Newsday* or other editor-dominated papers, the *Post* news desk laid out the paper but did not control the actual content. Bradlee wanted that changed. "It was a passive desk," Bradlee said. "We encouraged David to take the authority himself." Impressed by Laventhol's work with hard news, Bradlee turned to him in 1968 for a completely different job: the development of a new section, to be called Style. The old women's section, "For and About Women," was a traditional blend of reports on embassy parties and formal teas, plus advice on such subjects as etiquette. Bradlee wanted to "treat women like people" and organize the paper better, to pull everything that involved the reader's leisure time into one section.

The creation of Style wasn't a universally loved idea. "The business side of the *Post* really didn't want to do it, and didn't like changing, and Katharine Graham was lukewarm," Laventhol said. "So we said we'd do it without additional staff." As a result, Laventhol and his colleagues put in extraordinary hours. In that creation process, Laventhol showed a strong sense of what the section should become. "He was clearly the visionary," said David Lawrence Jr., who worked with him on the project and later became the publisher of the *Detroit Free Press*. "In terms of pure smarts about newspapering, I don't know anybody smarter."

The Style section began boldly in early 1969. "What we didn't do was we didn't change gradually," Bradlee said. "We did it POW!" Some people groused about the reduced coverage of society parties and other revisions, but the section began to take hold. "Very quickly, it became a huge hit with readers, and very quickly after that, a huge hit with advertisers," Bradlee said. "It really was by far the most widely copied thing that this paper's ever done." One of its big admirers was Bill Moyers.

In the spring of 1969, Laventhol was a tired man, after months of putting out the new section with a minuscule staff. He enjoyed his work at the *Post*, but the *Dayton Daily News* was wooing him to come to Dayton as managing editor (just as they courted three *Newsday* editors, Tony Insolia, Art Perfall and Stan Asimov). Laventhol enjoyed the thought of running his own paper, but at the same time, another suggestion came in. Laventhol was in New York for a wedding and ran into McGrady, his old colleague from the *Yale Daily News*. "At Mike's urging, I went to see Bill," Laventhol said. Moyers dangled a bigger salary and the title of associate editor in front of Laventhol and persuaded him to come to *Newsday*. "We offered David some stock and tried like hell to keep him," Bradlee said. "He was really the first guy that we lost that we cared like hell about. . . . He played a big role in the rebirth of this paper."

III

ALMOST FROM THE moment David Laventhol walked in the door at *Newsday*, he could sense the hostility.

As associate editor, he was responsible for the special sections, such as the Saturday magazine, for developing the paper's coverage of "non-happening" lifestyle news, and for putting together a staff of reporters to cover those trends. At the same time, Moyers gave Laventhol an assistant, Lou Schwartz, who had been the editor of the magazine. The announcement said nothing about Laventhol supplanting McIlwain or Marlens. "I didn't think that far ahead, in the sense of personnel," Moyers said. But the editors sensed that Laventhol wasn't going to remain a mere associate editor for long, and with a few exceptions — Schwartz, McIlwain and Asimov — they gave him a frosty reception.

"I was not in a friendly camp," Laventhol said. "I didn't think that people were real happy to see me." Just as editors at the *Tribune* had identified him as a creature of Bellows, those at *Newsday* who distrusted Moyers viewed Laventhol as his man. And he was. "I felt that Bill was grappling with the kinds of issues that I had been grappling with as an editor and that newspapers in general needed to deal with," he said. Laventhol's goal had always been to edit a paper to suit the needs of the reader, but the philosophy he found at *Newsday* was: " 'We put out the best possible newspaper. We put it out for us.' " Laventhol was impressed by the competence of the editors, but he disagreed, as Moyers did, with excessive focus on breaking news. "*Newsday* did very well in the watchdog role, in reporting on the functions and follies of government, in investigative reporting," he said. "We also put out a very orthodox newspaper for the times." So he began doing what he could, with his limited authority, to move the paper away from that orthodoxy, toward covering social and cultural news in the way that he had pioneered at the *Post*.

Laventhol came to *Newsday* in September, 1969, and on the first day of October, he gave Moyers and the others a four-page memo outlining his plans. "This is a proposal for a daily Newsday section about people, the way they live, and the kind of world they live in," Laventhol said. "The new section will replace the present family and entertainment sections. . . . Emphasis will be on people rather than events, and on articles that define community and society rather than on day-by-day reports of occurrences within community and society."

Turning his broad concepts into improved coverage of society was not painless. The coverage of television was an early example. "I knew from Washington that television had become the new campfire," Moyers said. "It now substituted for the weather as the bond that people had with each other, even when they were strangers. . . . So that one of the first things I did was to say, I want two more pages for television, and I want some new writing about television." Moyers had become interested in a free-lance writer, Marvin Kitman, who was covering television for a small journal called The *New Leader*. "What I was doing there was evolving this different way of writing about television, which is not just to review the programs, but to review the setting of the programs and question basic premises of television," Kitman said. So Laventhol and Schwartz met Kitman for lunch and offered him the job and a steady salary. He eagerly accepted. Then Laventhol told Barbara Delatiner, who had been the television critic for thirteen years and had won several awards. He offered her a different job, but she decided to leave. "It was rather hurtful to the ego," she said. "Obviously, they wanted a change, and I was not doing the job they wanted." Moyers made the formal announcement on December 1.

Moving out Delatiner was just one source of friction. Laventhol also had problems convincing other editors that *Newsday* needed specialists in some of the subject areas that the new section would cover. One example was Ken Briggs, an ordained minister who came to *Newsday* to cover religion. "I would have wanted a newspaperman who would have just gone out and learned religion," said Mel Opotowsky, one of the editors who questioned the need for specialists. "I think he turned out to be right on that." In addition to Briggs, Laventhol hired new reporters such as Kevin Lahart to cover behavior and Harry Pearson to cover the environment, and gave other specialist jobs to reporters who were already on staff, such as David Zinman, who covered science and medicine. Laventhol also appointed an editor, Jack Schwartz, just to supervise the specialists.

In addition to the corps of specialists, the new section used the skills of a splendid generalist, a painfully shy but elegant writer named Leslie Hanscom. Growing up in Maine, Hanscom came to New York in 1949, right out of Yale, and went to work for the *Brooklyn Eagle* as a copy boy and later a reporter. When the *Eagle* folded in 1955, Hanscom worked at the *World-Telegram & Sun* as a reporter-rewrite man, reviewed books at the *World-Telegram* and at *Newsweek*, worked as an editor at the *Saturday Evening Post*, joined the Peace Corps, writing reports on Peace Corps programs, and eventually signed on at the *Philadelphia Inquirer*. In 1969, suffering from job turbulence at the *Inquirer* and marital problems at home, he came to *Newsday* as a suitable place to hide out. At the start, he even used a fictitious byline. Then, as Laventhol prepared to start the new style section, to be called Part II, they found a more public way to use Hanscom's talents — a feature called Long Island Diary.

One important audience for the column was *Newsday*'s young reporters, Moyers said to Hanscom. "He told me that one of the things that he wanted this diary to do was to show that you could cover the suburbs with a big-city reporter's kind of imagination," Hanscom said, "to demonstrate to the younger reporters that the suburbs were not as boring as they thought." So they gave him two weeks to roam Long Island and soak up its rhythms, to begin noticing things about the day-to-day lives of Long Islanders that would provide the raw material for his column. When Part II began on February 9, 1970, Long Island Diary was the first feature the reader came to, on page two of the new section. Later, Laventhol moved it to the front of the paper, where it remained a fixture.

While Laventhol and Lou Schwartz were working to put Part II together, Laventhol's status changed abruptly. The reason was McIlwain's drinking. "McIlwain was one of those gifted drunks who continued to radiate charisma and was capable even of good decisions about people," Moyers said. "It took me a while to realize that we were suffering." As McIlwain drank more and more, Moyers had warned him, but he ignored the warnings. "I felt Bill would have to accept my drinking and my brilliance; I had helped make *Newsday* one of the finest newspapers in the world and I had done it while drinking," McIlwain wrote in his book, *A Farewell to Alcohol*. "I believe now — but didn't then — that I was becoming paralyzed in my job, a drunk figurehead who no longer was making great contributions to my newspaper." By 1969, McIlwain was keeping a half-gallon of vodka at home, a half-gallon in his office and a half-gallon in the car, washing it down with lemon-lime soda. "He was becoming the object of concern, if not rebuke, among the younger people," Moyers said. "He thought he was handling it, but there were too many signs. People didn't understand why this was being tolerated." The last straw for Moyers was election night, 1969. "He was standing in the middle of the newsroom with a martini in his hands," Moyers said. Drinking in the newsroom, especially on the copy desk at the end of the work week, had been a *Newsday* tradition. But this time it was too much for Moyers.

Soon after that night, Moyers and McIlwain had lunch with James Ralph Scales, the president of Wake Forest University, McIlwain's alma mater. Afterward, Scales called McIlwain and offered him a job as a writer in residence. McIlwain told Scales that he couldn't possibly leave his *Newsday* job, but Scales urged him to talk with Moyers. To McIlwain's surprise, Moyers thought it was a wonderful idea. McIlwain didn't know until later that Moyers had arranged the whole thing. "I took the initiative and called James Ralph," said Moyers, who told Scales: " 'If you will give him a position of esteem, I will make the salary and pay the cost of rehabilitation.' " A key element of the deal was that McIlwain had to agree to enter an alcoholism program. It was the ultimate white-collar firing. "Bill was real, real sweet to me," McIlwain said.

Moyers told the staff in December that McIlwain was leaving for a one-year leave of absence in February, 1970, and Laventhol was filling the new position of executive editor immediately, to start an orderly transition. (McIlwain did not return in a year. From Wake Forest, he went into an alcoholism center, then on to an editing job in Toronto, with a strong recommendation from Moyers, followed by a series of other editing jobs.) Suddenly, David Laventhol, snubbed and roundly distrusted by *Newsday* editors when he arrived in September, was their boss.

A few days after the announcement, at the end of 1969, Moyers gave Laventhol a memo outlining basic principles that he wanted the new executive editor to follow in running the paper. "Our first obligation is to help the people who read Newsday to know everything that is worth knowing about Long Island," Moyers wrote. He also exhorted Laventhol to make the paper more readable, more newsy, less boring. "You once told me that you wanted a chance to shape a news department according to your philosophy and leadership," Moyers wrote. "You now have that chance."

That philosophy showed up by the end of the month, in the last issue of *Newsday* in the 1960s. The front page was classic Laventhol: not a standard news headline, but a magazine-style cover, with a photograph of the earth taken from moon orbit, a headline that said simply, "Into the '70s," two brief quotes on the bottom, and acres of white space. That kind of conceptual cover became a familiar *Newsday* technique under Laventhol, but some of his more traditional editors resisted those revisions, just as some editors had done at the *Tribune* and the *Post*. "Somehow," Laventhol said, "I always seem to get into these newspapers in the middle of this period of change."

CHAPTER TWENTY-NINE

Guggenheim v. Moyers

I

BY THE TIME Bill Moyers had found the editor for *Newsday*'s future, his own deteriorating relationship with Harry Guggenheim was threatening to make Moyers a part of *Newsday*'s past.

From the start, Moyers had reminded Harry that they had sharply different political ideas, and Harry had insisted that they could work together anyway. A series of events, however, had overwhelmed that fragile agreement. Perhaps the earliest of those events occurred in the spring of 1967, when Mike McGrady sat down and wrote a memo to Harry and Moyers. In reaction to John Steinbeck's hawkish "Letters to Alicia" from Vietnam, which McGrady intensely disliked, he made a bold suggestion: *Newsday* should send McGrady to cover the war and write a series called a "A Dove in Vietnam." Moyers liked the idea. "I carried it to Guggenheim and persuaded him to do it," Moyers said. So McGrady went to Vietnam and wrote pieces that exposed the war's folly and aroused Harry's anger. "He never forgave me for it," Moyers said. In time, *Newsday*'s criticism of the war, and of President Richard Nixon's policies, became the central theme of the Moyers-Guggenheim struggle.

At first, for almost two years, Moyers kept a low profile on national and international issues, but not on local concerns. "I knew that if the domestic programs for which I had been partly responsible in the White House were to work, they had to come out the other end of the conduit, at the local level, and be effective," he said. "My views were fairly formed on domestic policy. It was international affairs — to which I had come, at Johnson's request, late — about which I still did not have formed opinions." By contrast, Harry's opinions —

especially on the war — were not only formed but frozen. "Some of our longest discussions were on Vietnam," Moyers said. "He was a committed hawk, and even though he finally admitted that the war was wrong, both morally and as an exercise of American power, he defended it as a place to test weapons. That would bring a grimace to the face."

Despite their clash on Vietnam, Moyers admired Harry in many ways. "I mean, there was a decent man in there, trying to overcome the limitations that had been imposed by his political circle of friends and a protected environment, in which great wealth often traps some people," Moyers said. "His intuitions I found all admirable. It was his opinions that were not, and his information that was often flawed." On the war, for example, Harry argued that the solution to the impasse was continued bombing of North Vietnam, but Moyers offered factual insights that he had gained in the White House, showing that the bombing was ineffective. "He brought that kind of judgment that nobody in an editorial board normally has," said Phil Sanborne, who attended the editorial meetings as a substitute editorial writer. "He brought inside information." That insider knowledge impressed Harry, but facts didn't alter Harry's position: If the President thought the bombing was working, then the bombing was working. The paper's adherence to that view began changing in early 1969. First, Harry started staying away from the paper almost entirely after the 1968 election. Then Nixon became President. Harry's absence gave Moyers more latitude on Vietnam, and Nixon's presence allowed Moyers to form those views without appearing disloyal to an administration that he had served. He owed that loyalty to Johnson, but not to Nixon.

Even before Nixon's inauguration, Moyers hired a chief editorial writer with a distinctive voice, who would later become a factor in his estrangement from Harry. The writer was Patrick J. Owens, a temperamental, hard-drinking, immensely gifted native of Montana. Owens had written editorials at both the *Arkansas Gazette* and the *Pine Bluff Commercial*, then had become the primary labor reporter for the *Detroit Free Press*. There, he worked with Robert Ellis Smith, who later became a Moyers protege at *Newsday*. Toward the end of 1968, Smith had arranged a contact between Moyers and Owens. Moyers decided that Owens had the qualities that he wanted and hired him to become chief editorial writer, starting in January, 1969.

Before he even began work at *Newsday*, Owens read the paper's editorials. "They were strangely pro-Nixon, among other things," Owens said. They also lacked a consistent voice. "One day they'd say one thing and the next day they'd say another thing." Quickly, Owens identified Stan Hinden, Harry's handpicked editor of the editorial pages, as the agent of the pro-Nixon bias. "I essentially was Guggenheim's man there," Hinden said. "That was my job, to help reflect his views." When Owens wrote Vietnam editorials, Hinden edited them heavily and made them more pro-war and pro-Nixon. "He would take my copy and he would change it to suit himself or Captain Guggenheim," Owens said. "Then he would have it retyped. So Moyers never saw my copy. . . . Eventually, I complained to Moyers, but that took a long time, because I'm an enlisted man at heart."

In the early months of 1969, *Newsday*'s editorials on Nixon were more than willing to give him a chance to move toward peace. The comment on his inaugural address, for example, was upbeat and friendly. "The new President's speech was remarkable for its reach beyond partisanship and Republican dogma," the editorial said. "The stress was on peace and accommodation with other nations, not on armaments and the rigid defense of assumed American prerogatives. . . . The inaugural established that Nixon has his priorities in order, with peace abroad and unity at home leading his agenda." At the start of March, however, *Newsday* began to prod Nixon gently. "We need a policy now to end the fighting," an editorial said. "One year ago, campaigning for the presidency, Richard Nixon said he had just such a plan. He refused to discuss it on the grounds that he did not wish to inject Vietnam into domestic politics. Nixon has been President for six weeks now, and the country anxiously is awaiting his plan. . . . Act fast, Mr. President, before more young men go senselessly to their deaths." Moyers followed that admonition with two days of full-page editorials that examined the options and recommended several, including a withdrawal of 50,000 to 100,000 American troops.

Through the spring and summer, the editorial page presented a balanced view of Nixon, commenting evenhandedly on his first hundred days, praising him for a "candid and canny" speech on Vietnam, for example, but taking him to task for his attack on critics of American military policy. The editorial on his withdrawal of the first American troops was typical of this balanced approach. "President Nixon's decision to withdraw 25,000 troops from Vietnam is no giant step forward," the editorial said, "but perhaps a man dragging the country out of a bog into which he did not lead it can be allowed to begin with a small and cautious step." It was not long after that editorial that Moyers took a bolder step of his own — moving Hinden out as editor of the editorial pages.

"He was a sweet man who was nonetheless not his own man," Moyers said. "I liked Stan personally, but I didn't think his mind was fetching enough to produce an editorial page for a metropolitan newspaper." That contrasted with his perception of David Gelman, his own choice for the job, who had worked with Moyers in the Peace Corps. "Gelman was a facile mind that had looked at the world whole and had worked with me," Moyers said. Gelman's background had been in journalism, but in 1962 he joined the Peace Corps, evaluating its programs in a variety of countries, then rising to director of the special projects division. When Gelman left the Peace Corps in 1966, he worked for *Newsweek* for two years, then in a private firm that ran training programs for the hardcore poor. In early June, 1969, Moyers invited Gelman and his wife to a combination thirty-fifth birthday party for Moyers and Peace Corps reunion at the Moyers home in Garden City, and Moyers hinted at the job offer. Later, they had lunch at Harry's townhouse in Manhattan. It went smoothly enough, and Gelman got the job.

The firing of Hinden was not nearly as smooth. Hinden had admired

Moyers as a talented writer and had often encouraged Moyers to write the editorials himself, but once Moyers decided to make a change, that admiration turned to disillusionment. "He charmed everybody out of their shoes, and later out of their jobs," Hinden said. "What I resented about it was that he gave me the bad news by leaving a letter in my typewriter." They discussed the question of what Hinden would do next, and decided finally that he would work in the Washington bureau. "I went to see Guggenheim at Falaise, before I went to Washington, to say goodbye," Hinden said. "He asked me the question, 'What is it that Moyers is trying to do?' He was very distressed about Moyers."

II

THE SUMMER OF 1969 was a time of both anguish and triumph for Harry.

The triumph came from the success of the American space program, which Harry had helped to nurture, by financing the work of Robert Goddard. The federal government had formally acknowledged its debt to Goddard and the Guggenheims in 1960, making a $1 million payment to settle a copyright infringement claim brought by Goddard's widow and by the Daniel and Florence Guggenheim Foundation, which owned the rights to his patents. So when Neil Armstrong walked on the moon, Harry's employees gave him a mat of the *Newsday* front page, inscribed: "To Captain Guggenheim, who has made many dreams come true." Only a week after the moon walk, Moyers made the official announcement that Gelman was becoming editor of the editorial pages — a clear signal that Moyers was putting his own stamp on the paper. Soon after that, Harry had another rude shock: a piece of soft-core pornography that worsened his relationship with Moyers.

The pornography episode had begun three years earlier, in June, 1966, with a small group of *Newsday* reporters sharing drinks and lamenting the state of American literature. In that group, John Cummings and Harvey Aronson were writing novels, and McGrady was still recovering from an interview with the novelist Harold Robbins and wondering how such unliterary writers as Robbins and Jacqueline Susann churn out best-sellers time after time. The answer, of course, was sex. It was then that McGrady suggested it: Why couldn't a group of reporters and editors from *Newsday* turn out a novel — a chapter each, as steamy and poorly written as possible — and watch it climb the best-seller charts? That same June night in 1966 — months before Bill Moyers came to *Newsday* — McGrady sat down to write a memo outlining his plan. "As one of *Newsday*'s truly outstanding literary talents, you are hereby officially invited to become the coauthor of a best-selling novel," he began. "The entire best-seller will be written in a single week — between Monday, June 20, and Monday, June 27." Then he described its guiding principle: "There will be an unremitting emphasis on sex. Also, true excellence in writing will be quickly blue-penciled into oblivion."

The central characters were to be William and Gillian Blake, the stars of *The Billy and Gilly Show*, a morning radio program that celebrated the joys of middle-class marriage. In contrast to the wholesome broadcast image, Gillian was to be wildly promiscuous off the air. "Gillian, as the book opens, learns that William has been conducting an affair with one of their production assistants, Esther," McGrady wrote. "She is unfaithful at first to even the score. She is unfaithful for a while because she enjoys it. She is unfaithful, finally, because she makes it a goal to destroy the seemingly happy marriages that surround her." The plot was thin, but good enough to attract a wide variety of volunteer coauthors.

One of the most famous scenes in the book came from Cummings, a foul-mouthed former high school football player who grew up near Pittsburgh and later joined the Marine Corps. His chapter was about Ernie Miklos, a foul-mouthed former high school football player who grew up near Pittsburgh and later joined the Marine Corps. In the scene, Gillian Blake uses an ice cube to bring her liaison with Miklos to a memorable end. It was no great accomplishment to coax a chapter out of Cummings, who was born to write that scene. But McGrady's idea proved so irresistible that he even got a chapter from Stan Green, one of the most literal and cautious editors at *Newsday*. McGrady also acquired contributions from, among others, Martin Buskin, the widely respected education editor, Tony Insolia, the news director, and Bob Greene, whose fixation on organized crime moved him to write about a mobster who pays for his few minutes with Gillian by losing his life in a mob assassination. The highest-ranking of the *Newsday* coauthors was Bill McIlwain, the editor. McIlwain's chapter focused on a crippled, 104-year-old advertising tycoon called The Baron. The real-life inspiration for The Baron, everyone understood, was Harry.

Sharing the editing duties, McGrady and Aronson trimmed ruthlessly, combining some chapters and killing others entirely. During the editing process, Moyers arrived at *Newsday*. Since the editor of *Newsday* had contributed, McGrady and Aronson tried to get a chapter from the new publisher. They gave a copy of the manuscript to Moyers, who returned it later to Aronson, expressing his distaste silently.

Even without a chapter from Moyers, the book had more than enough coauthors. But there would be only one byline: Penelope Ashe. First, the authors made up the name. Then they searched for a real-life woman to play the role in radio and television promotional appearances. They settled on McGrady's sister-in-law, Billie Young, an unpublished novelist with a strong resemblance to Jacqueline Susann. The title they picked was *Naked Came the Stranger*. The publisher was Lyle Stuart, who had handled a variety of sex books and was well known in the industry as a boat-rocker. They signed a contract and began making plans to market it in the summer of 1969.

Perhaps the most crucial element in that marketing was the design of the book's jacket. The one that they chose left little to the imagination: a rear-view photo of a strikingly proportioned naked woman. As soon as Lyle Stuart unveiled the jacket at the annual booksellers' convention, some buyers objected, but Stuart persuaded many of them to order copies anyway. Before the advertisements, before the reviews, even before the July publication date, the book began to sell. "They get stopped by the jacket," one sales clerk told Stuart. "The damnedest thing. I mean it's just a nude."

Building on the initial momentum, Stuart spent unusual amounts of money on advertising. The most effective ads, which appeared in the *New York Times*, sprang from the brain of one of the coauthors, Bernie Bookbinder. The ads used individual photos of the authors, representing the characters they had created. In one of them, featuring McIlwain in sunglasses and a Panama hat, the copy read: "Meet the Baron. Tired Old Tycoon. . . . Hardhearted invalid. . . . He found a new use for his wheelchair when . . . Naked Came the Stranger."

By the end of the first week in August, 20,000 people had bought the book — not knowing that it was a hoax. But reporters in Detroit became suspicious when they recognized the face of their colleague, Gene Goltz, the former *Newsday* reporter, in one of the ads. Soon, *Newsweek* and the *Los Angeles Times* were chasing the story too. Then McGrady gave an interview to Marlene Cimons, a former *Newsday* reporter who had just moved to the Washington bureau of the *Los Angeles Times*, and he asked her to hold it awhile. Within a few days, the *Wall Street Journal* and the *New York Times* were also sniffing around. Finally, the Associated Press carried the story, letting loose a flood of other stories all over the country. The *Times* story, on page 28, carried photos of McIlwain, Aronson and Jack Schwartz from the advertising campaign, identifying them in the captions. On Long Island, the *Newsday* version was buried on page 48A, deep in the paper's entertainment section. But the *Suffolk Sun* splashed the story across the top of page one. "The *Suffolk Sun* played it very big, and that bothered Bill and it bothered the Captain," McGrady said.

· At the time, McGrady and his coauthors didn't understand how much the book annoyed Harry. They were enjoying the laughs too much. "The rest of the world considered it a hilarious joke," McGrady said. Whatever else it did, the book certainly spread *Newsday*'s fame. "It was just one of the most incredible put-ons on the literary taste of America," Greene said. It also became a small windfall for the authors. Greene, for example, earned about $10,000 for less than four hours of work, which paid for a large portion of his son's college tuition.

The mastermind of this lucrative hoax was not aiming to sabotage Bill Moyers. As a movie critic and as a columnist, McGrady had been one of the paper's best writers, and he knew that Moyers wanted *Newsday* to become more of a writer's paper — just as McGrady did. So McGrady felt comfortable offering his ideas on the paper's future in a pair of long memos, which included a proposal for the expanded use of magazine-style cover stories on the front page, even before Laventhol arrived and began moving *Newsday* in that direction. "He not only encouraged that kind of thing, but he took it and ran with it," said McGrady. "I consider him the most remarkable person I ever worked for." So, the last thing McGrady wanted was to drive still another wedge between Harry and Moyers, but his columns from Vietnam, followed by *Naked Came the Stranger*, had done exactly that.

At first, Moyers himself didn't grasp the extent of the damage, but it began to become clear when he arrived at Falaise for lunch not long after the story broke. Harry was sitting there, with a copy of the book and some of the reviews, and he was weeping. " 'They would never have done this to Alicia,' he said," Moyers remembered. " 'Why do they do it to their own paper? Why do they do it?' " Moyers thought the book was a silly and unprofessional thing to do, but he didn't think it would really hurt *Newsday*, and he tried to move Harry toward that view. "I wound up in a series of meetings defending their right to do this, and therefore, becoming more in Harry's mind on the other side," Moyers said. "Harry Guggenheim believed that I should have prevented that, that I could have prevented that. . . . He never forgave me for them."

III

As SUMMER SLID into autumn, *Newsday*'s editorials reflected the nation's growing skepticism about the slow unfolding of President Nixon's plan for ending the war.

Nixon's announcement of the withdrawal of 35,000 more troops provoked a verdict of "welcome, but less than comforting" in an editorial, accompanied by a Tom Darcy cartoon showing a huge Nixon face trapped behind the White House columns, as if in a jail cell, with the caption: "Prisoner of War." At the start of October, another editorial proclaimed: "Americans are profoundly weary of this war, and we do not undermine our President or do him any disservice by reminding him, while he counsels with his generals and his political strategists, that there are other voices which must also be heard."

Those voices reached a crescendo on Vietnam Moratorium Day, a nationwide demonstration against the war on October 15. In New York City, one of the major events was a daylong service at Trinity Church in Wall Street. One of the speakers was Moyers, who delivered a thoughtful, balanced speech. "Because of my own experience I have too much sympathy for the new President to demand more from him than his duty to his office will permit," Moyers said. But a few paragraphs later, he gently chided Nixon for his refusal to be moved by the dissent: "At the same time I would urge the President to remember Winston Churchill's definition of democracy as 'the occasional necessity of deferring to the opinions of other people.' " It was certainly possible to question whether a newspaper publisher ought to be speaking at all at the service, but the tone of his speech was conciliatory. "This is both a sad and remarkable day in American history — sad because it is necessary; remarkable, perhaps, because it is possible," Moyers said, both in the speech and, with minor revisions, in the lead of the October 15 editorial.

If Harry reacted to the speech, Moyers didn't remember it, but *Newsday*'s coverage of the moratorium did prompt Harry to write a bitter memo to Moyers. "Newsday was sucked into the deception perpetrated by the organizers of the Moratorium to the effect that overwhelming numbers of people supported their efforts," Harry wrote. "Our left-wing city room accepted the propaganda without question. . . . We were also wrong in stating that the moratorium was organized by the young people. They were merely dupes for known organizers, all of them not very young, who are trying to destroy our way of life on directions from outsiders."

No matter how much Moyers argued that *Newsday* was being evenhanded, no matter how true it was that the editorials criticized Nixon politely and praised him when praise was possible, Harry was convinced that *Newsday* was out to get the President. To David Gelman and Patrick Owens, who were writing the editorials, Moyers mentioned Harry's unhappiness only briefly. "He had to pass it on, almost apologetically," Gelman said. "He continued to be very protective of us. He was as honorable about this as we could have asked. He was loyal. We never personally got in a jam over this. He took the heat, and we knew he was taking the heat, from the Captain." Moyers may have been a bit more cautious than Gelman and Owens, but they agreed on the basic policy. "We didn't take him anywhere he didn't want to go," Owens said.

The publisher's willingness to run blunt editorials may have earned him Harry's enmity, but it won him the loyalty of his staff. Even when an editorial or a viewpoints piece offended Long Island's defense industry, Moyers routinely allowed it to appear and then absorbed personally whatever external heat it generated. For example, one controversial viewpoints piece by Ernie Volkman sharply criticized the F-14 fighter, the primary product of the Grumman Corporation, the Island's largest employer. "I showed him the piece," Volkman said. "He said, 'Terrific. Print it.' Never hesitated a second, never blinked. I developed, along with everybody else, a great respect for Moyers."

Right after the tiff between Moyers and Harry about the moratorium, another source of conflict popped up. During the investigation of the Suffolk land scandals, Greene's researcher, Geraldine Shanahan, had come across a document that was bound to be embarrassing to State Senator Edward Speno, a powerful Nassau County Republican. The document showed that Speno owned a piece of land in Suffolk with a notorious gambler named Harry Soccorso and others. At the time she found it, the Greene Team was still working on the Suffolk land scandals, but Greene was looking for future stories that would keep his team intact. So he filed the information on Speno away. In 1969, Greene went after Speno with a team of Shanahan, Tony Marro, Ken Crowe and Jim Klurfeld. They produced a five-day series that began on October 27, just before the local election. It also hit at an inopportune time for Speno, who was planning a 1970 run for United States Senate. The first day's stories told of his deal with the gambler and outlined how he had received more than $1,000,000 in unsecured loans from the Franklin National Bank at a time when he was a member of the Senate Banks Committee and the Republican leader of Nassau County and Hempstead Town, which put him in a position to help banks. At an angry press conference the afternoon of the first stories, Speno attacked Moyers personally as a "partisan political activist," adding: "I call on Harry Guggenheim today to remove Bill Moyers as publisher of Newsday."

The day after that challenge appeared in *Newsday*, Harry wrote Moyers: "Leonard Hall told me at dinner that his friends think Newsday is becoming a Democratic newspaper. He has no brief for Speno but he believes the timing of the series is designed to help the Democrats in next week's elections." Moyers minced no words in his reply. "Leonard Hall is wrong," he wrote. "Of course, his friends in the Republican Party do not want their friends exposed for corruption. But that does not mean that Newsday is becoming a Democratic newspaper." As for the timing, Moyers explained, *Newsday* had to run the stories before the election because the *Daily News* was preparing to run a less ambitious version of its own. In contradicting Hall, Moyers was going up against a powerful Republican who had always been close to Harry and was at the time representing him in his efforts to leave Falaise to Nassau County in his will. "I'm convinced that Len Hall went to him and inflamed Harry's already paranoid partisanship," Moyers said.

The struggle with Harry became more intense at the end of 1969. "People like Flora Lewis, Clayton Fritchey, Robert Mayer and all the other left-wingers have only one motive: to destroy Richard Nixon and turn America over to their own kind," Harry wrote. "I trust the President far more than I trust the punks who write for newspapers." Increasingly, Harry focused his attacks on one man: Al Marlens. That left Moyers in the ironic and difficult position of worsening his relationship with Harry by defending an editor who had suspected and resisted Moyers from the start. In his personal politics, it is true, Marlens was far from conservative. "I would classify him as left-liberal, certainly sympathetic to somebody like Norman Thomas," said his childhood friend, Elton Rayack. But on the corner in Brooklyn where they all argued politics, Rayack said, Marlens was also "passionately anti-Communist," a strong advocate of free speech. When Harry looked at Marlens, however, he saw no such distinctions. "All liberals today are left-wingers," Harry wrote Moyers. "Al Marlens is one of them. . . . McIlwain was not the one to move out. Marlens is." Even though Harry asked Moyers three times to fire Marlens, Moyers stood his ground. "I simply cannot dismiss a man when the charges against him are unfounded and false," Moyers wrote. "I had to move Bill McIlwain out because he is an alcoholic, but my differences with Marlens are not sufficient for me to remove him as managing editor. . . . I urge you to trust my judgment on this."

Harry declined to accept that plea, Moyers felt, in large part because Harry's own judgment was so impaired by ill health. Moyers had tried to help Harry cope with that declining health. He had arranged for Harry to be seen at the Mayo Clinic, for example, and he had rushed to Falaise in the middle of the night, in response to a frantic phone call from one of Harry's attendants, to get

Harry to a hospital. "If we hadn't got him there in time," Moyers said, "he would have been gone." Despite that help, Leo Gottlieb, Harry's attorney, said that one reason for the estrangement was that Harry felt Moyers had moved in too fast to assume more power during one of Harry's illnesses. Harry said something similar when Hal Burton asked him later what Moyers had done wrong. "He said, 'Well, he tried to get my job,'" Burton remembered. That struck Moyers as an odd accusation. "He brought me here to take his job," Moyers said, "and then resented me for trying to fulfill his expectations."

Whether or not Gottlieb was correct about Harry's resentment of Moyers moving in too fast during Harry's illness, failing health was definitely a factor in the deterioration of the relationship. On top of his continuing struggle with cancer, Harry had begun to experience strokes. His daughter, Joan Van de Maele, was with him in Saratoga when he had a major one at the time of his eightieth birthday in August, 1970, and his attorneys knew of another one about eight months earlier. In addition, Harry had what looked to Moyers like a mild stroke in the fall of 1969. "That was the dividing line," Moyers said. "I've read a lot about strokes. . . . They make you a different person in the same body. And that's what happened to Harry Guggenheim." Whatever the exact timing of the strokes, it seems clear that Harry became a more difficult person as his health declined. Even Gottlieb, who had worked amicably with Harry for fifteen years, found it much harder to deal with him in that period. "He was crotchety, he was unreasonable, he was suspicious," Gottlieb said. "He was suspicious of everybody."

Once Moyers could no longer sit face-to-face with Harry, at the office or at Falaise, the battle was lost. "The man that I used to be able, with humor and argument and civility, to keep true to himself, became impossible to connect with," Moyers said. "That communication just stopped, and it was all in notes, where you had not the impetus of the voice or the fluency of the language or the gesture or the personal chemistry that bonds you to a colleague. . . . I'm convinced that much of what happened would never have happened if he hadn't had the stroke. Everything was manageable up until the stroke, everything — and after that, totally unmanageable."

CHAPTER THIRTY

Harry and Norman and Otis

I

ALL OF HARRY Guggenheim's anger at Bill Moyers would have accomplished nothing if Harry did not have an alternative. But he had two successors in mind — one to inherit the Guggenheim empire, and the other to take over *Newsday*.

Following his long, unsuccessful search for a suitable son, Harry found the right man practically under his nose. He was a true Guggenheim, the grandson of Harry's uncle, Solomon R. Guggenheim. His name was Peter O. Lawson-Johnston. Uncle Sol's daughter, Barbara, had married John Robert Lawson-Johnston, whose family had established Bovril, the British beef soup concentrate firm. Since his mother and father were divorced not long after he was born, young Peter's male role model was his grandfather, Solomon. They spent endless hours together, at Solomon's plantation in South Carolina and at his Sands Point home, Trillora Court. Harry's estate was close by, but when he was growing up, Lawson-Johnston barely knew his much older cousin.

When he was ready for a career — after service in the Army in Italy at the end of World War II and graduation from the University of Virginia in 1951 — Lawson-Johnston did not choose the Guggenheim mining enterprises. Instead, he tried the *Baltimore Sun* — first as a reporter, then as yachting editor — but he and his wife decided that $35 a week was not enough. "Then I had a couple of public relations jobs, which paid a lot, but which were dead-end," he said. "So when I was about thirty, I started all over again and went into the family business."

Initially, Harry offered Lawson-Johnston a job in the nitrate fields in Chile, but his wife's family didn't want her living in the Chilean desert. So Lawson-

Johnston chose wife over career and declined, which made a poor first impression on Harry. But another Guggenheim partner, Albert Thiele, who had been Solomon Guggenheim's closest aide, gave Lawson-Johnston a job with a subsidiary of one of the family corporations. In a short time, he had handled positions in North Carolina, New York and Malaysia and established himself as an effective member of the family business. Then, despite his less-than-successful relationship with Harry a few years earlier, he made contact again.

"People knowing of my heritage would ask me questions about the Guggenheim Museum, and I had nothing to do with it," Lawson-Johnston said. "So I got an appointment with him, and the purpose of my visit was to ask him whether I could be put on the mailing list, so that when people asked me questions, I wouldn't be a complete idiot." Lawson-Johnston had no desire to be on the board of the museum named for his grandfather, but Harry looked into what he had done since their earlier contact, liked what he saw, installed him on the museum board in 1964 and made him vice-president for business administration. "He also made me a partner of the firm at the same time," Lawson-Johnston said. In 1969, Harry promoted him to president of the museum, vaulting him over Thiele. Harry also started involving him in some of his other ventures, such as his Cain Hoy plantation.

Clearly, Lawson-Johnston was the perfect heir for Harry: well-educated, well-groomed, a dependable married man with a family. As early as 1965, when Harry was still hoping that his grandson, Dana Draper, would be his heir and president of *Newsday*, he began including Lawson-Johnston in his often-changed wills, making provision for him to inherit ten percent of Harry's mining interests. In early 1967, soon after Draper's brief trial at *Newsday*, Harry told Leo Gottlieb that he was seriously considering substituting Lawson-Johnston for Draper as his primary heir. During 1967 and 1968, Harry codified that intention in his wills, and then revealed to Lawson-Johnston that he was to be the chosen heir, in a memorable encounter in Harry's hospital room at Memorial Sloan-Kettering in Manhattan.

As they met, Lawson-Johnston held a manila envelope that he had received from George Fountaine, Harry's personal secretary. "He said, 'Now, open up the envelope. I want you to read it,' " Lawson-Johnston said. "It was his will. I was pretty stunned." While Lawson-Johnston tried to digest the news that the mantle of millions was to fall on his shoulders, Harry explained why. "He said, 'You've got a wonderful family, you've got common sense, you've got good judgment and you're a gentleman,' " Lawson-Johnston said. In a memo to his executors, Harry said in formal language what he felt in his heart: that the Guggenheim legacy was only safe if he focused his wealth on one man, rather than spreading it around ineffectually. Somehow, in the speechlessness of that moment, Lawson-Johnston did not meet Harry's need for gratitude. "I just said, 'Harry, I'm overwhelmed,' " he remembered. "A day or two later, Bill Moyers called me up very confidentially and he said, 'Peter, I think you should know that the Captain thinks that you were a little ungrateful. . . .' That was an awfully nice thing for Bill to do." That thoughtful warning gave Lawson-

Johnston a chance to tell Harry again how much he appreciated his generosity.

The pivotal meeting in the hospital seems to have taken place in the first week of August, 1969, at about the time that the world found out that *Naked Came the Stranger* was a hoax and the Moyers-Guggenheim relationship began a precipitous decline. Nonetheless, at the time when Lawson-Johnston discovered that he was to be the heir, and for months after that, Harry still planned a significant role for Moyers. "I want Mr. Moyers, as President of Newsday, to be in full charge of the operations of the newspaper," Harry wrote, "but I would want him to seek the advice and approval of the Trustees of my Newsday stock before undertaking any major new commitment for Newsday." The trustees of the Newsday stock were to be Moyers, Lawson-Johnston and Harry's mining colleague, John Peeples. But by early 1970, Harry's feelings about Moyers had hardened. It was only then, in an unexpected phone call to his home, that Lawson-Johnston found out how fundamentally the relationship had changed. "I was lying in bed in Princeton, and the phone rang, and Harry was in Florida," Lawson-Johnston remembered. "He said, 'Peter, I'm going to sell my newspaper. I'd like your help.' "

Lawson-Johnston quickly flew to Florida and went to Harry's oceanfront suite at the Golden Strand Hotel in Miami Beach. The other party to their meetings was John Wesley Hanes, one of Harry's most trusted friends. Harry and Hanes knew each other primarily as horsemen, serving together on the Jockey Club committee whose report led to the creation of the New York Racing Association and to the modernization of the state's thoroughbred tracks. Beyond his knowledge of racing, Hanes also moved with impressive skill in the worlds of business and finance. Born to North Carolina tobacco wealth, he started out in business selling cigarettes, built his own rubber company, then moved to New York and became a senior partner in one of the largest brokerage houses on Wall Street, Charles D. Barney & Co. In 1938, he left Wall Street for a position on the Securities and Exchange Commission and later became an undersecretary in the Treasury Department. Following his return to private business in 1940, Hanes worked for William Randolph Hearst in a total restructuring of the Hearst newspaper empire and served as a consultant to John Olin Industries, guiding Olin through a huge merger with Mathieson Chemical. With that high-powered background, Hanes would find the sale of a newspaper a yawningly uncomplicated transaction.

As Harry asked Hanes and Lawson-Johnston to help him make the deal, they saw that he needed no help at all in deciding who the new owner should be. Three decades after starting it as a small country newspaper in a converted automobile dealership, Harry was determined to sell *Newsday* to the Times Mirror Company, the owner of his friend Norman Chandler's *Los Angeles Times*. Realizing that Harry's suspicion of Moyers was the central reason for the sale, Lawson-Johnston suggested that Harry move Moyers out by giving him a generous financial settlement, instead of selling. But Harry was adamant. "Harry had already decided that he wanted to sell it to Times Mirror," Lawson-Johnston said. "He never questioned about who he was going to sell it to."

II

THE IMAGE OF the *Los Angeles Times* that glowed reassuringly in Harry's mind in 1970 was that of the stolid, conservative newspaper that Norman Chandler had published in the 1940s and 1950s.

For decades, the *Times* had been a journalistic joke — a pseudo-newspaper whose obvious purpose was to build Los Angeles and serve the interests of the Chandler family, with little pretense of serious journalism. But it was Harry's kind of paper: antagonistic to unions and friendly to Republicans. It had essentially invented the city of Los Angeles, even more actively than *Newsday* had invented Long Island. And it had created Richard Nixon, Harry's hero. Most important of all, Harry just *knew* that Norman Chandler would run *Newsday* in the proud conservative tradition of the *Los Angeles Times*.

The rise of Norman Chandler's family began when young Harry Chandler left New Hampshire for the west, in 1883. As a freshman at Dartmouth, he had caught pneumonia during a frigid swimming prank, and he hoped that the California climate would cure him. Selling grapefruits in the San Fernando Valley, he amassed a $3,000 bankroll and invested it in *Los Angeles Times* circulation routes. As he rose to a circulation clerk at the *Times*, he continued acquiring routes — not only of his own paper but of its competitors. That control enabled him to squeeze the competing *Tribune* until it folded and to buy its production equipment, which helped the *Times* meet its own expansion needs. That coup impressed the owner of the *Times*, a tall, tough, opinionated, Civil War veteran from Ohio named Harrison Gray Otis. It started Chandler on his rise at the *Times*, to circulation manager and then business manager. Cementing his relationship to Otis, Chandler married his daughter, Marian.

Over the next half century, using the *Times* as the instrument of his commercial pursuits, Chandler built Los Angeles and profited mightily, buying desert land cheap and using political skill to turn it into lucrative subdivisions. Besides buying and selling land, he created the climate for growth. When it became obvious, for example, that the city could not keep growing without a plentiful outside supply of water, a syndicate that included Otis and Chandler grabbed up the rights to the water of the Owens Valley, more than 200 miles northeast. Then the *Times* pushed for the construction of a giant aqueduct to bring the water south, completing what became known as the rape of the Owens Valley. To provide an economic base for the city, Chandler played a major role in attracting both the movie industry and the aircraft industry to Los Angeles.

As much as the *Times* worshiped industry, it despised labor. Otis was himself a former union printer, but when the printers struck in 1890, he fought back bitterly and brought in nonunion workers. As the keystone of an anti-union coalition called the Merchants and Manufacturers Association, the *Times* became the target of labor's wrath. On October 1, 1910, a series of explosions shook the *Times* building and started a huge fire, killing twenty employees.

Despite the services of Clarence Darrow as their attorney, two young unionists, J. B. McNamara and his brother, J. J. McNamara, pleaded guilty and went to prison for the bombing.

Not even the paper's battles with the unions interfered with Chandler's drive to build the city and his own profits. In the years after Otis died in 1917, Chandler was a leader in building the California Institute of Technology, the Hollywood Bowl and the Los Angeles Coliseum. As he was promoting Los Angeles, however, he neglected the finances of the *Times*. That job fell increasingly to his son Norman, who was neither a fiery ideologue like Harrison Gray Otis nor a real estate baron like Harry Chandler. Norman became assistant general manager in 1934 and began tightening up the paper's sloppy business practices.

Following Harry Chandler's death in 1944, the *Times* remained devoutly Republican under Norman. But Norman was not built for political brawling. He left that job to Kyle Palmer, the powerful *Times* political editor, whose word built careers and destroyed them. It was Palmer, for example, who discovered a young lawyer named Richard Nixon, brought him under the wing of the Chandlers, guided him through the start of his congressional career, nudged him to run for the Senate, cushioned him against the effects of the slush fund scandal that almost cost him his place as Dwight Eisenhower's running mate, and helped him in the maneuvering that led to his presidential nomination in 1960. But that same year, the *Times* made a major shift in its executive suite that would eventually alter its attitude toward Nixon: Norman Chandler stepped back from direct control of the *Times* to concentrate on the business of the parent Times Mirror Company, and his son Otis succeeded him as publisher.

Otis Chandler came to the job equipped with more than simply his wonderfully dynastic name. To begin with, he was tough. That toughening process began early. In the space of about two years in his boyhood, he had survived first a kidnap attempt and then a nearly fatal fall from a horse. Despite that accident, Chandler discovered early that he had abundant athletic skills, and he pushed himself — at summer camp, at Phillips Academy in Andover, Massachusetts, and later at Stanford University — to excel. When he left Andover, he was tall and lanky, but he willed himself to grow, plunging into weight-lifting and shot-putting and bulking up from 155 pounds to an all-muscle 190 by the time he entered Stanford. He joined the varsity track team in his freshman year and became a record-breaking shot-putter. Later, he barely missed a spot on the 1952 Olympic team. Throughout his education, his goal was to stand out as a man of excellence — on his own, without help from his name.

Beyond his toughness and fierce competitive spirit, Otis Chandler brought to the publisher's office a record of thorough preparation. When he got out of the Air Force in 1953, his father immersed him in a seven-year training program that would teach him the inner workings of every part of the *Times*. Norman Chandler insisted that his son learn even the dullest, least rewarding jobs on the paper — starting in each new department at the lowest salary paid in that department. Only when he got to be a reporter did the paper really seize his interest and hold it. But no matter what part of the *Times* he worked in, he plugged away, recording in notebooks his suggestions for change. As a result, by 1960 he was more than ready to be publisher.

The problem for Otis Chandler — and therefore, for his mother — was that his father's family didn't want him in the job. Dorothy Buffum Chandler — everyone called her Buff — came from a substantial California family of her own. Her father, Charles, had been mayor of Long Beach, and the Buffums operated a successful department store chain. As Norman Chandler's wife, she had become a formidable fund raiser in such causes as the construction of the music center that became the Dorothy Chandler Pavilion. She exerted powerful influence on her cautious husband, pushing him constantly to change the *Times* and keep it abreast of the new California. She was a strong, forceful, intelligent woman, but she was not a Chandler. The Chandler family — particularly Norman's oldest sister, Ruth — didn't trust her. By extension, they didn't trust her son either. As a result, if Norman Chandler listened to his wife's advice and decided to step aside as publisher, the family wanted the job to go to his brother, Philip, the paper's general manager. But Otis Chandler was better prepared to be publisher than anyone else was, and he had the force of his mother's iron will on his side. So he won.

Under Otis Chandler, the *Times* did not immediately stray from tradition. In the 1960 presidential election, the paper enthusiastically supported Nixon, but the Chandlers were stunned and angry when he lost a race that they thought he should have won. A few months later, Nixon ate dinner with Norman and Dorothy Chandler to discuss a campaign for governor in 1962. Despite their past support, they showed no inclination to help Nixon against the popular Democratic incumbent, Pat Brown. Instead, the *Times* expressed skepticism about Nixon's candidacy and covered his campaign hard and straight. When he lost and issued his famous "You won't have Nixon to kick around anymore" declaration, Nixon was clearly directing his anger at the *Times*. In 1964, the *Times* endorsed the liberal New York Governor Nelson Rockefeller over Barry Goldwater in the Republican primary. In the general election, despite his own conviction that Goldwater should not be President, Otis Chandler bowed to his father's wishes and allowed the *Times* to endorse Goldwater.

At the same time that the paper was showing signs of changing its political attitudes, Chandler moved far more quickly to erase its image as a joke and move it toward excellence. The Chandler family was often distressed with the changes, but no one could deny that the paper was becoming more profitable or that he was showing signs of sharp business instincts. Within six years after Otis Chandler became publisher, his father had seen enough of his business skills to start pushing him to become chairman of the parent company, allowing Norman Chandler to move upstairs as chairman of the executive committee. Otis Chandler declined, preferring to stay with the *Times* for a few more years. Instead, Franklin Murphy, the chancellor of UCLA, became Times Mirror chairman. But the signs were clear: Norman Chandler was approaching seventy and gradually

distancing himself from day-to-day operations, and his son was gradually increasing power.

Sitting in Florida, dying of prostate cancer and consumed with the fear that
Newsday was lurching leftward under Bill Moyers, Harry Guggenheim seemed
to understand none of this. He didn't correctly perceive the power shift from
Norman Chandler to Otis Chandler. Nor did he seem to understand that the
Times was no longer quite as conservative as it had been during the years when
its reputation was so bad that it prompted S. J. Perelman's often-repeated joke
about a stop in Albuquerque on a cross-country train trip: "I asked the porter to
get me a newspaper and unfortunately the poor man, hard of hearing, brought
me the *Los Angeles Times*." Nor did he seem to know that Otis Chandler was a
good friend of one of the men Harry despised the most, Robert Kennedy. Just as
he had with Dana Draper and Bill Moyers, Harry saw only what he wanted to
see. He was dying, and he wanted his paper safe in the hands of Norman
Chandler. Peter Lawson-Johnston and John Hanes had a better grasp of the
changing reality in Los Angeles, and they mentioned it to Harry, but it didn't
alter his thinking. All he kept talking about was Norman Chandler.

It was not that Harry didn't know Norman's son. Otis Chandler and his
wife, Missy, had often attended publishers' meetings with Harry and Alicia and
had been guests at the small dinners at their townhouse in Manhattan. In many
ways, even though Harry didn't seem to grasp their political differences, Otis
Chandler was precisely Harry's type of man, just as Lawson-Johnston was: well-
educated, self-assured, carefully trained, impeccably groomed, sharp in his
business judgments. But Otis Chandler had developed a closer kinship with
Alicia Patterson than with Harry. "If I had someone in the country that I really
looked up to, from the standpoint of being a good reporter — not an owner, but
a news person, a professional — it was Alicia," Chandler said. "She cared
passionately about *Newsday*, and she was so proud of it."

When he became publisher, he regularly read *Newsday*. "I liked the
tabloid format," he said. "I thought it read well." More than that, he
liked the paper's profitability. This was not simply idle, long-distance admiration. Chandler wanted a paper in the New York market for Times
Mirror. "I was working the street," he said, "and I became convinced that
that was a tremendous property." So, when Mark Ethridge took over as
editor after Alicia's death, Chandler asked him if there was any chance
that Harry might ever sell *Newsday*. "He kept saying, 'Well, I don't think
so. I don't know, but I'll keep you informed and I'll talk to Harry,' "
Chandler said. He also courted Dorothy Schiff, the publisher of the *New
York Post*. "When Dolly said yes, I said, 'Well, let me think about it,' " he
said. The New York City unions and the competitive environment in New
York worried him, and he had second thoughts. It was at about that time
that Harry made his decision. "So it was wonderful timing when we got
the call," Chandler said. The call, as he remembered, came from Harry to
his father, who called him in to listen to the conversation. Harry told
them: " 'I've decided that I want to sell the paper, and I want to sell it

to you and Otis, and I don't want an option, and I don't want to get into outside third-party forces. I don't want brokers. I want to make a clean and simple sale.' "

III

THE NEGOTIATIONS BETWEEN Harry's emissaries and Times Mirror management would be, as Harry wished, clean and simple. But Harry himself introduced an element of complexity: From the beginning, Harry had made it clear to Hanes and Lawson-Johnston that he didn't want Moyers to know anything about it.

"He knew that when Bill got wind of that, that Bill would try to see that the paper got into the hands of people closer to his ideological view," Lawson-Johnston said. It was Lawson-Johnston's job to gather the necessary financial information from people at *Newsday*, in order to establish a proper price, *without* letting Moyers know. Ernie Levy was his contact, and Levy's secretary, Martha Fox, remembered gathering the numbers at Levy's request. Later, Hanes flew out to California to meet with some of the top Times Mirror executives, including Robert Erburu, then a senior vice-president, Albert V. Casey, a member of the board of directors, and Otis Chandler himself.

"My question to Hanes was, 'Well, now, when are we going to announce it? How's it going to be announced? I assume that Harry's talked to Bill,' " Chandler said. But Hanes insisted that no one must tell Moyers anything. "I kept arguing — well, suggesting — to this nice man that this is not particularly a very good way to do it, and that I didn't understand it, and I thought Bill would be really upset," Chandler said. "My hands were tied. My father's hands were tied. And after all, it wouldn't be up to us to call the publisher of a paper we were buying and say, 'By the way, the owner's selling the paper.' "

It was also not Chandler's role to remind Harry who was now in charge at Times Mirror. "He did not know my editorial policy, which I had put in since 1960, and how different it was from what he perceived the *Times* policy to be," Chandler said. "All Harry had to do was send for some clips from the *Los Angeles Times* on various key issues, and he would have known that the *Times* was a far different paper than he had earlier thought it was when my father was publisher. . . . But for some reason, he did not pursue the subject of who was in charge of the editorial policy of the *Times*, or he just assumed that I was in my father's mold." Whatever Harry's reasons, neither the secrecy nor his fixation on Norman Chandler really mattered to Times Mirror. "If you're offered an opportunity to buy *Newsday*," Erburu said, "you don't say: 'Do you know what you're doing?' We were thrilled."

Since both sides were so anxious to make the deal, hard bargaining was unnecessary. During the visit that Hanes paid to Los Angeles and a later trip that Erburu and Casey made to see Harry in Miami Beach, they all worked pleasantly together. "Al would say, 'Whatever you want, Harry,' " Lawson-Johnston remembered. "There was never any haggling over price, never one minute of haggling over price." Once they had come up with the basic outlines of a deal, Harry instructed Leo Gottlieb not to do anything to negotiate the price upward. It was such a good deal, in fact, that for years afterward, other publishers asked Chandler: "How did you pull that one off, Otis?" Eventually, the purchase of Harry's fifty-one percent of *Newsday* cost the Times Mirror Company $31.6 million.

The only real problems arose when Moyers and the rest of the world learned of the proposed sale. Moyers was vacationing with his family in the Caribbean in February, when Harry called and asked him to come and see him in Florida. "That's when he told me he was going to sell the paper; he'd already negotiated the sale," Moyers said. "Death was on his face — melancholy more than death. He was the most melancholy man I've seen." To save Harry the necessity of taking the drastic step of selling the paper, Moyers offered to resign. "But he was adamant and irrational about it," Moyers said. "There were moments when he would become angry, but you couldn't tell what he was angry at — at life, I think."

Since his offer to resign had failed to dissuade Harry from selling, Moyers tried to put together enough money to buy the paper himself. The financiers that he contacted, at Chase Manhattan Bank and elsewhere, assured him that the money was available. "What I said to him was, 'Whatever they've offered you, we'll give you $10 million more,' " Moyers said. "He kept saying, 'I want to sell it to Norman Chandler.' " Months earlier, another potential buyer had visited Moyers at his Garden City home and expressed an interest: William Casey, the law partner of Harry's powerful friend, Leonard Hall. "He came over here and said to me, 'You know, I can put together a group to buy this, if you can persuade Harry to do it,' " Moyers said. "And I said, 'I don't want to persuade Harry to do it. . . . The paper's in good hands.' " Once the Times Mirror deal became public, Casey visited Moyers again and told him: " 'We can offer Guggenheim $20 million or $30 million more.' " As one of the original investors and a director of the media conglomerate Capital Cities Communications, Casey had access to the money. Besides, he and Hall were solid, Guggenheim-style Republicans. Hall had been the party's national chairman, and Casey had worked in every Republican presidential campaign since 1948 and later ran the Securities and Exchange Commission under Nixon and the Central Intelligence Agency under Ronald Reagan. But nothing came of his offer.

Besides trying to buy the paper from Harry, Moyers attempted to show him that he was wrong about the politics of the *Los Angeles Times*, by asking Stan Asimov to put together a systematic comparison of *Newsday* and *Times* editorials. "It showed that the *Los Angeles Times* had taken the exact same positions that *Newsday* had taken," Asimov said. "Only we had taken it more articulately and in a better journalistic way." No argument worked, however, and Harry pressed forward. On March 12, the day after Moyers posted a notice to the staff that Harry was talking with Times Mirror, the story of the proposed deal appeared on page one of the *New York Times*, and the shock and uncertainty began to spread, inside *Newsday* and out.

In Manhattan, a former United Press International reporter and editor named Bill Sexton was on a city bus, on his way to work, when he read the story. At the time, Sexton was working at Publishers Hall Syndicate, and Moyers had already made him an offer to run *Newsday*'s syndicate. Its former director, Tom Dorsey, had resigned in a conflict over his use of expenses and his handling of the payments that he owed *Newsday* reporters for stories that he had syndicated. Sexton had agreed to come to *Newsday* and clean up *Newsday* Specials, but he had not yet given notice at Publishers Hall, when the *Times* story broke the news. "I called up Asimov, and I said, 'Do I still have a job?' " Sexton said. "And he replied, to the effect, 'Do *I* still have a a job? None of us know.' "

That same day, Moyers wrote a "My dear Captain" letter to Harry, describing his own hurt feelings and the reaction at *Newsday*. "The news broke here like a bomb shell, and people like Marty Buskin, for one, were weeping in the city room," Moyers wrote. "These people love Newsday. They have enormous respect for you. And you know how I feel. I have been honest in saying that I do not want to see Newsday's independence turned over to anyone else. The independence of Newsday has given it a character and soul unique in American journalism. And so I repeat: In the interest of the people who work here, and in the interest of Newsday's independence, I would think it best if I stepped aside, and left quietly, so that you would not feel compelled to carry through with this proposal."

The employees themselves took several steps. For one thing, they signed a petition asking the minority owners, Joe Albright and his family, to preserve the paper's independence. The Albrights sent a telegram back to the staff and hired an attorney. The staff also set a mass meeting for the Garden City Hotel, to decide what to do. Those who attended voted to form a *Newsday* Editorial Caucus, elected Martin Buskin chairman and instructed him to write to Harry, seeking more details. When the meeting was over, some of the staff stayed behind and talked with a representative of the Newspaper Guild. Moyers reported to Harry on the meeting: "One reporter later told an editor: 'If you had taken a vote last week for the Guild, there wouldn't have been one vote for it. Today there wouldn't be one vote against it.' " Moyers asked Harry to offer the staff some word of reassurance, but Harry was not in a reassuring mood. The other party to the deal, Otis Chandler, had left for a tiger-hunting safari at the same time that the story broke. So, in the absence of a calming message from anyone, the staff was skittish and worried about a loss of independence.

The only hope for that independence, as many employees saw it, was Joe Albright's family. "Pray for Joe," one note on the bulletin board said. When the story broke, Albright's mother, Josephine, returned from Italy and started telephoning Harry, but his response was chilly. "I said, 'Give us a break here. Alicia would have wanted it,' " she remembered. "He said, 'Your children are all New Left, and I don't approve of that. . . .' I said, 'Can you just hold off a little bit and give us a chance to get some money together and buy this thing?' He said, 'No, I've made up my mind.' "

Harry wanted the Albrights to sell their stock at the same time as he sold his, because that would soften the tax consequences of the sale for him. Instead, their attorney, David Washburn, proposed a restructuring of *Newsday* stock that would give Harry tax benefits, plus editorial control during his lifetime, but would eventually allow the Albrights to run the paper. "He didn't want to listen to any alternative except their selling at the same time that he did," Gottlieb said. Washburn had made his reorganization proposal in a letter on April 13, but by that time, it was really too late. Otis Chandler had returned from his safari a week earlier, and the negotiations had gone smoothly. The day after Washburn's letter, Hanes, Lawson-Johnston, Gottlieb and his partner, Thomas Hagoort, met with Albert Casey and Robert Erburu at LaGuardia Airport and reached agreement on the acquisition of Harry's fifty-one percent. The next day, April 15, Gottlieb wrote a letter to Washburn rejecting the Albright proposal, and late that afternoon, at *Newsday*, David Laventhol tacked on the bulletin board an announcement that Harry and Times Mirror had reached agreement. At the time, Moyers was in Switzerland for an international conference that had been scheduled months earlier. A few on the staff were miffed that Moyers was not around when the agreement was announced, but there was nothing that he could have done to stop the sale. Times Mirror signed the agreement on April 30 and Harry signed on May 1.

Toward the end of April, with the deal now in place, *Time* magazine quoted Joe Albright on Times Mirror: "I'll be very interested to find out what they mean by independence." On April 29, he met with Otis Chandler in Los Angeles to find out Chandler's plans. "I sort of maybe naively thought that by making a good impression on him, he would somehow realize that it was in his interest to let me run the paper," Albright said. But it wasn't a terribly equal meeting, between the young Washington bureau chief and the tall, powerfully built new owner, surrounded in his home by the heads of wild animals that he had hunted down. "He was not one of my favorite people," Chandler said. "He was not of my style." Chandler was considerably more impressed when he met with Laventhol at the Waldorf in Manhattan. Chandler, the perfectly muscled and tanned California WASP, took one look at the frumpy Laventhol and realized that their personal styles were starkly different. But as they talked, Chandler warmed to him. Laventhol had other options — including a standing offer to return to the *Washington Post* — but it didn't take long for Chandler to decide that Laventhol would be acceptable to him as the editor of *Newsday*.

In early May, Chandler made his first appearance at *Newsday*, where he could read the staff's hostility right on the bulletin boards. "I didn't feel, though, that it was a personal hostility toward me as an individual or the *Los Angeles Times* or Times Mirror," Chandler said. "It was simply, 'Goddamn it, we've been independent all our lives, we built this great paper and then without any warning we get sold to this thing in the West.' " As Chandler stood in the Ronkonkoma office, making a polite little speech, the phone rang and Bob Greene answered it. "It sounded like he was talking to a beat reporter: 'Yes.

Thank you. Good. Fine,' " Chandler said. But when Greene hung up, Chandler found out what the call was all about: *Newsday* had won a Pulitzer. A few minutes later, a second phone call announced another Pulitzer. The Greene Team had won for its investigation of the Suffolk scandals, and Tom Darcy had won for his cartoons — mostly focused on the war in Vietnam. "That was a wonderful omen for me, because I think it broke the ice a little bit, gave me a chance to talk a little bit more about editorial quality and our number one interest in maintaining it," Chandler said. "I'll never forget that day, as long as I live."

The Pulitzers had arrived just in time for the new owner, but *Newsday* had earned them under Bill Moyers as publisher. In the next morning's paper, Moyers issued a graceful statement that used in the first sentence the word that everyone was thinking, "independence." The statement was among his last acts at *Newsday*, because Harry Guggenheim had made it abundantly clear that he wanted Moyers out as publisher before Times Mirror took over. That was a Guggenheim decision, not a Times Mirror one. In fact, Chandler would have entertained the idea of hiring Moyers in some other capacity. "To this day, I regret that circumstances prevented us sitting down and getting together to talk about Bill Moyers," Chandler said. "He would not have been my choice for publisher, but he might have been my choice for editor, if he'd given me a chance to evaluate it." Moyers knew he might well have been better as an editor than as a publisher, but he wasn't interested. "If Chandler had come and said, 'Would you be editor,' I would have said no," Moyers said, "not because I had been publisher, but because I really don't believe you can do that with owner-ship 3,000 miles away." Instead, Moyers prepared to leave the paper, and the gears of Harry's legal machine ground efficiently to accomplish that departure.

"He wanted to be generous with him in the severance, but he didn't want him to have anything to do with *Newsday*," Gottlieb said. Moyers had told Gottlieb that he would leave it to Harry to determine how generous he wanted to be, but Moyers reminded him that he had turned down two job offers in the past six months that would have paid more than *Newsday* did. Moyers had a little less than two years remaining on his five-year contract, and Gottlieb proposed that they give Moyers a $100,000 settlement. "I thought that was generous, and I put it up to Harry, and he said he wanted to do better than that," Gottlieb said. The final settlement gave Moyers $300,000 in severance pay and deferred compensation and allowed him to remain temporarily in the home that *Newsday* had provided for him in Garden City.

At the same time as they worked on the settlement, Harry was preparing to cut Moyers out of his will. Oddly, despite Harry's burning distrust of Moyers, he had provided generously for Moyers in the most recent will, signed in Miami on March 12, a few hours after the story of the sale broke. It gave Moyers $100,000 in cash, plus twenty percent of Harry's mining interests. But within a few weeks after he had signed the will, Harry and his lawyers started working toward a codicil that would eliminate the bequests to Moyers. On May 8, four days after *Newsday* had won the two Pulitzers, Harry signed the codicil, removing the

$100,000 cash bequest and leaving all his mining interests to Lawson-Johnston. The old idea of a committee, with Lawson-Johnston and Moyers cooperating to run Harry's empire, was dead. Moyers was not the only one slighted. The will entirely omitted Harry's grandson, Dana Draper, and made limited bequests to his granddaughter, Diane Carol Langstaff, and his three daughters, in comparison with what he gave Lawson-Johnston. Harry had anticipated that the will might cause some grousing, but he felt that he had already taken care of his daughters amply in other ways. "If I were to provide for all of my family equally," he wrote in the will, "none of them, in my opinion, would be in a position to carry on the family tradition effectively."

With the question of the financial settlement and the will resolved, the divorce between Harry Guggenheim and Bill Moyers — and between Harry and *Newsday* — was almost complete. All that remained was Moyers' resignation, announced on May 12, and the formal closing of the Times Mirror purchase of Harry's fifty-one percent, which took place in Los Angeles on May 19. The resignation statement was brief, but it underlined what Moyers had argued all along with Harry: the paper's evenhandedness. "To have published a newspaper beholden to no party, ideology or interest group is a rare and rewarding experience, and I will not soon forget either the experience or the people who have contributed so much to the joy of it," Moyers said. "There are too few newspapers deeply committed to fearless inquiry, and I have been fortunate to work for one that has maintained such a commitment for 30 years."

If his resignation statement was filled with a sense of accomplishment, his leave-taking from Harry was an exercise in melancholy. "The last thing he said to me when I shook hands with him before leaving — he had a tear in his eye, and he said: 'I deeply admire the way you and Judith are trying to bring up your children,' " Moyers remembered. "That, to me, was not a personal compliment, because we were flawed parents, like everyone else. It was a comment on his own family life, which was ruptured by discord and an absence of intimacy. He was a sad, sad man."

IV

SUDDENLY, ONLY EIGHT months after walking into a newsroom where he was surrounded by hostility, David Laventhol was running the paper by himself, without a publisher.

In the few months since Laventhol had become executive editor, he had enjoyed the benefit and the burden of close supervision from Moyers, who had sent Laventhol a stream of daily memos that critiqued the paper sharply. Now, Moyers was gone and Laventhol's only boss was 3,000 miles away. The problem that Laventhol faced was not a sudden, wrenching change of philosophy. In fact, Otis Chandler agreed with the basic Moyers-Laventhol vision of the paper.

His mission, in fact, was simply to maintain order and put out a paper every day, until Chandler could find a publisher.

With no publisher available to mediate disputes between Laventhol and Ernie Levy, who was running the business side of the paper, Laventhol had to rely on weekly notes between himself and Chandler, plus visits from Richard Robinson, a Times Mirror official designated as Chandler's surrogate. It didn't take long for Laventhol to see how tricky this interim period would be. The first jolt, on the morning after Moyers announced his resignation, came from Jim Bellows, Laventhol's former boss at the *New York Herald Tribune*. At the time, Bellows was an associate editor at the *Los Angeles Times*, dispatched to *Newsday* to report back on the paper's condition. On that first post-Moyers morning, something that Bellows had said at a *Newsday* gathering came out in the *New York Times* like this: "A Los Angeles Times official, James Bellows, told staffers on his first visit to Newsday recently that the Los Angeles organization wanted a Republican for the post and planned to make changes in Newsday's editorial policy, particularly as it touched on Vietnam and the Nixon Administration." Since the staff knew that Bellows had clout in Los Angeles, this report unnerved them. Quickly, Laventhol issued a calming statement: "Jim says he didn't say that and wouldn't say that." Soon after that, the *Los Angeles Times* itself provided strong evidence that Times Mirror would not reverse *Newsday*'s posture on the war. "The time has come for the United States to leave Vietnam, to leave it swiftly, wholly and without equivocation," a *Times* editorial said on June 7, less than a month after Harry Guggenheim had sold *Newsday* because he didn't like what its editorial pages were saying about the war and Nixon.

Even if Bellows did not say to the staff that Times Mirror would seek a Republican publisher, that is what he recommended privately to Chandler. In his twelve-page report, Bellows said: "The type of man I believe you want — i.e., a high-integrity, important, intellectual, Eastern Republican — is in very short supply." Among the names he suggested were Henry Kissinger, Nixon's national security advisor, Yale President Kingman Brewster and the CBS correspondent Walter Cronkite. In addition, the report was full of insights into the strengths of *Newsday*, the problems facing Laventhol and the need for Times Mirror to bring stability to the situation. "Alicia Patterson started Newsday and maintained it with tremendous in-plant editorial room power and fierce editorial room independence from the pressure of other departments in the newspaper," Bellows wrote. "What I'm trying to emphasize at length here is that these features of the Newsday operation are treasured there, and it will be important for TM to value them just as highly. Otherwise, I fear we'll be gutting the spirit that has helped that paper grow to the great stature it has today. And it is very important to TM to find a publisher who has equal respect for Newsday's great integrity." In the meantime, Bellows said, *Newsday* would be in safe hands with Laventhol. "He is a creative future-thinker and a very competent technician," Bellows wrote. "He is a proven leader in getting things done, but he is not the dynamic sort."

The difficulties that Laventhol faced, Bellows wrote, included living

with a 1970 editorial budget drawn up the previous summer by Moyers, McIlwain and Marlens, "all of whom are gone or will be gone by the end of this
month." Moyers was resigning, McIlwain was struggling against his alcoholism
at Wake Forest, and Marlens had seen the future of *Newsday* and realized that it
belonged to Laventhol, not to him. There was never a chance that Marlens
could work peacefully with Laventhol. "He wasn't a sharer," Laventhol said.
"My desire to draw on the strengths that he had and, at the same time, to bring
in the kind of things I would like to see done just didn't work with him. . . . He
sent me an angry note, essentially: 'The paper is yours, all yours. Do whatever
you want with it.'"

So Marlens left, working briefly and unhappily at *Time*, then moving to the
New York Times, where he rose to editor of the News of the Week in Review.
For all his brilliance and his journalistic integrity, he had simply been unable to
work with Laventhol or Moyers. "The irony of it all is that I think that,
intellectually, Moyers and Marlens were the two strongest people in *Newsday*'s
history, and probably would have made a magnificent team, could they ever
have gotten together," said John Van Doorn, who worked with Marlens at both
Newsday and the *Times*. "To his dying day, Marlens thought that Moyers was a
terrible person." But Marlens did not know how Moyers had prevented Harry
from firing him. Years later, Van Doorn and Moyers discussed Marlens over
lunch. "He said, 'I saved him, and he hated me,'" Van Doorn remembered. In
1977, Marlens died playing tennis and was buried in his tennis clothes. But the
standards that he established continued to exert an almost mystical influence
on generations of *Newsday* editors.

Laventhol's struggles with Marlens ended quickly, but he still had a dance
card full of nervous minuets with others. One of them was Pat Owens, the chief
editorial writer. David Gelman had moved from editor of the editorial pages to
the newsroom, to run the national desk. That left Owens doing the same work
that Gelman had done, but he still had the title of chief editorial writer, *not*
editor of the editorial pages, which annoyed him. He also was in a sour mood
about the 1970 Pulitzers. *Newsday* had won two, but Owens felt that his 1969
editorials — primarily on the war in Vietnam — should have won the third. In
fact, the Pulitzer jury had chosen his work, but the Pulitzer board reversed that
decision and gave the prize to the *Washington Post*. "According to Pat Owens,
the world is pecking away at his soul moment by moment," Bellows wrote.
"And he suffers! God, how he enjoys suffering." As a result, those were difficult
times for both Owens and Laventhol. Owens didn't like it, for example, when
Laventhol killed one of his editorials. He also thought Laventhol accepted the
Times Mirror takeover too meekly, and he kept telling Laventhol to change the
masthead and make him editor of the editorial pages. Laventhol kept declining.
One night, Owens finally decided to take matters into his own hands and
altered the paper's masthead to include his own name in large type. Laventhol
found out about it in time to keep the new masthead from appearing in the
paper, then called Owens at home. "He said, 'Send me my severance pay in a
cab,'" Laventhol remembered, growling in imitation of Owens. "I said, 'That

was really not a good idea to do that, Pat, and let's not do that anymore.' A couple of months later, I made him a columnist."

Another problem that Bellows pinpointed for Chandler was the question of pay. Since *Newsday* did not have a systematized salary structure like the one in Los Angeles, the result was widespread inequity. "Newsday had been flown — very well, too — for a long time by the seat of Alicia's matriarchal pants," Bellows wrote. "She fawned on the editorial people as her gifted but deprived children, and it worked beautifully — as long as it was a small, tidy operation. But it's too big now. . . . Some of the best people have been given adequate (maybe more than adequate) raises regularly. Others have been slighted; they have not even received annual token raises." Not even Brad O'Hearn, one of the most active in the drive to unionize *Newsday*, saw malevolence behind the inequity. "I would think it was simply inattention," O'Hearn said. "I just don't think that they realized that they had allowed these disparities to creep in. . . . They paid attention to the squeaky wheels." The pay inequity, combined with dissatisfaction over health and retirement benefits, added up to a fertile environment for a union drive.

Whatever the underlying grievances, it was the presence of Times Mirror itself that had made employees start thinking about unions. That was obvious from a clever piece of bulletin-board satire about Times Mirror's historical antipathy toward unions, created by one of *Newsday*'s most inventive writers, Lewis Grossberger. On top of that, many on the staff were angry that Moyers had been booted out — even though Harry, not Times Mirror, had done it. "He was so widely respected, and thought of as one of us, in a way that publishers nowadays aren't," said Fred Bruning, who had come to *Newsday* from the *Suffolk Sun* a few months earlier. Despite the fears and angers, any union would have a difficult time organizing *Newsday*. "There was a lot of resistance and an astonishing amount of ignorance about unionism," Bruning said. "There was a kind of a comfort zone that *Newsday* had created for enormous numbers of people, and I think there were lots of folks who felt, why ruin a good thing?" That made the organizing task difficult for those, like Bruning, who saw a union as necessary.

The first question was: Which union? The traditional choice for reporters was the Newspaper Guild, which had already had its day at *Newsday* in the 1940s, but had had no luck since then. As recently as 1967, they had tried an organizing drive. O'Hearn had been president of the Guild in Allentown, Pennsylvania, and he agreed to help, but that earlier drive had gotten nowhere. "There was a good deal of distrust of the Guild," O'Hearn said. "The thing that came up all the time was the sweetheart contract that the Guild had with the *Long Island Press*, because we had a lot of people who had come over from the *Press.*" So they tried other unions. "The committee wrote and contacted every possible union," said Maureen O'Neill, who became chairwoman of the organizing committee at one of the first meetings. "We had different people do reports on each of the unions." The union that caught on was the United Auto Workers — a powerful union with an admirable social record under Walter Reuther.

One of the key supporters of the UAW was Greene, who had soured on the Guild during his time at the *Jersey Journal*. Since he had lived across the street from the UAW regional director, Charles Kerrigan, Greene called him and asked him if the UAW would be interested. "He went to Walter, and Walter was delighted," Greene said. But there were strong voices of dissent. "That was a silly idea," said Owens, who knew the UAW from his days as a labor reporter in Detroit. "Reuther certainly never considered it." But the UAW's strength and liberal image made it appealing. "People were also caught up in the first syndrome," O'Hearn said. "We would be the first journalistic union to become part of the UAW. . . . That was a lot of the sex appeal of the UAW, I think."

To settle the issue, the caucus held a straw vote in the *Newsday* parking lot, after the company refused to allow the vote in the building. The UAW beat the Guild, eighty-seven votes to fifty-two, and started an organizing drive that made waves and generated publicity. "We really had the newspaper industry scared shitless," Greene said. "UAW could really bother them." Laventhol did what he could to blunt the union drive, conducting a review of the salary structure and issuing a three-page memo that made a telling point: "I do argue that you should give the new ownership and the newsroom management a reasonable chance to make their own record."

As it turned out, *Newsday* didn't have to do much to overcome the UAW. Walter Reuther died in an airplane crash at almost the same time as the straw vote, and in the aftermath of his death, the Guild flexed its muscle. In a ten-minute meeting in a VIP lounge at Washington's National Airport, the president of the Guild, Charles Perlik, made his plea to the new UAW leader, Leonard Woodcock. "I told him that we weren't organizing automobile plants, and I'd appreciate it if he didn't organize newspaper plants," Perlik said. "He was in complete agreement right off the bat. . . . I think Reuther would have done exactly the same thing." On August 11, *Newsday* announced to the staff that the UAW had withdrawn its representation petition. The UAW defection angered Maureen O'Neill, who had worked so hard on the drive, and infuriated Greene, who had brought the UAW's Charles Kerrigan to *Newsday* and thrown his weight behind the UAW. When the drive died, others began to suspect Greene's motives. "Everybody always felt that somehow or other, I had something to do with that thing going out," Greene said. "Charlie died about a year later, and I was still so mad I didn't go to the wake." But the UAW's withdrawal worked out perfectly for Laventhol. It bought him time to deal with other problems, while the Guild was heating up its own organizing drive.

In some ways, the union drive was not as nettlesome for Laventhol as the resistance that he encountered from some of the paper's senior editors — including Mel Opotowsky, the Suffolk editor, whose opposition prompted Laventhol to refer to him as "my hair shirt," and Art Perfall, the night managing editor.

Perfall had had no contact with Laventhol until Laventhol suddenly vaulted over Marlens to become executive editor. " 'Who is this guy and why the hell isn't Marlens being named?' " Perfall remembered wondering. "So then I met him, and as they like to say in the corporate suites, it was a matter of chemistry." Not only did Perfall dislike Laventhol because he was not Marlens, but because his style was not Perfall's. In editing investigative stories, for example, Laventhol brought too much of a magazine perspective to suit Perfall, who was more attuned to a straight, hard-news approach. Nor did Perfall like it when Laventhol sometimes played columnists in the front of the paper, or when he increased the paper's coverage of New York City. Another source of friction between Laventhol and Perfall was Laventhol's inability to get Dick Estrin, the news editor, to do things his way. "He kept seeing things in the paper that bothered him that Estrin was doing," Tony Insolia remembered. "Perfall was very ineffective in controlling those things." Later, Laventhol handled that by switching Insolia to nights and Perfall to days. In addition, Laventhol began to curb the copy desk's historic function of heavily rewriting stories and he ordered the desk to consult with reporters before making major changes.

As much as Perfall rocked the boat, Insolia went along with the program. Whatever his lack of polish may have done to stall his career under Moyers, Insolia's essential competence, plus his willingness to work with Laventhol, raised his stock quickly. "I think that Tony had more wisdom and flexibility in his own way than Al Marlens did," Laventhol said. For the time being, while he was trying to maintain the status quo, Laventhol had to derive what comfort he could from those who were willing to work with him, such as Insolia and Lou Schwartz, and deal as best he could with Perfall.

V

WHILE THE PRIMARY mission for David Laventhol during the spring and summer of 1970 was to run a smooth ship, he and Times Mirror did take some initiatives that moved the paper forward.

The first was an effort to deal with the concerns of the tiny contingent of black reporters. *Newsday* had not hired its first black reporters until Tom Johnson and Pat Patterson in 1963, and the numbers had remained minuscule. In 1969, Moyers had made a push to hire six minority reporters outside the normal budget, but the people that *Newsday* hired eventually looked at this minority recruitment effort and found it flawed. "What was immediately clear to us is that we were not being treated the way other reporters were being treated," said Les Payne, one of the original six. "This program of setting aside six slots kind of became an informal training program." That left them considerably short of equality. "I think some of our white colleagues — not all of them — sort of looked at us as if the only reason they hired us was for image," said Michael Alexander, who came to *Newsday* with a journalism degree from Ohio State.

So the black reporters began meeting as a caucus and discussing their concerns. One of their earliest joint efforts was a short note to the editors in 1970, protesting the overuse of the term "black militant." Then they sought permission to attend a convention of black journalists in Missouri. "We talked to Insolia and Asimov and could get no satisfaction," said Payne, who had already begun making a reputation by covering the Black Panthers with Patrick Owens. "You have to deal with the top person." So they set up a meeting with Laventhol. The caucus had no formal leader, but the role fell to Payne, because he was the most experienced in the group — not in journalism but in life. Payne had grown up in the intensely segregated atmosphere of Tuscaloosa, Alabama, and later felt the more subtle racism of Hartford, Connecticut. He had gone from the University of Connecticut into the Army and had stayed in almost six years, rising to the rank of captain and serving a tour in Vietnam, where his duties in the public information office included writing speeches for General William Westmoreland. In 1969, he had come to *Newsday*, with a recommendation from Bill Nack, who had worked with him in Saigon and then started at *Newsday*. "He just was a lot more worldly than the rest of us," Alexander said. So Payne carried the debate with Laventhol.

"The whole idea we argued to Laventhol was that we found ourselves in a hostile situation," Payne said, "that we were all rookie reporters, for the most part, that we were not treated fairly and we could not relate to the experience of white younger reporters at the paper." The Missouri conference was important, they argued, because senior black journalists would be there, and they could share information on how to deal with their common problems. Laventhol's fallback position, Payne said, was that he would permit three of the group to go. "I said, 'You can't do that; we can't accept that, Dave,' " Payne said. The central quality of the conference, Payne insisted, would not be the specifics of what was said, but the interaction among black journalists. "I used a metaphor from physics," Payne said. "I said that a meeting is like a colloidal suspension: You have these charged particles bouncing around. . . . Almost immediately after that, he said, 'Okay, you all can go.' " So nine black reporters and photographers from *Newsday* became the largest single group at the conference, which played a major role in the development of the National Association of Black Journalists. Laventhol's decision didn't please some of the white staff members, who put a note on the bulletin board. "It said that there was going to be an Italian-American meeting somewhere, and they wanted to send all the Italian reporters," Payne said. "There was resentment." But Laventhol emerged from this awakening of the black caucus with a decent working relationship with them. In his first turbulent months, that was enough.

Another *Newsday* innovation in the summer of 1970 was a strange piece of journalism called *The Summer Journal of Morton Pennypacker*. It sprang from the brain of Jim Klurfeld, who had just shared in the Pulitzer as a member of the Greene Team, and his friend, Howard Schneider. At Syracuse University, they had both edited an underground paper, and they later set one up on Cape Cod and called it *Poor Howard's Wednesday Afternoon Post*. When they had trouble selling ads for *Poor Howard's*, they had written to Moyers and asked if he'd be interested in running an underground newspaper at *Newsday*. Moyers had expressed interest in the idea. Then Klurfeld joined *Newsday* and Schneider followed him there in the summer of 1969. When he first met Moyers, Schneider renewed the idea of an experimental supplement that would take the youngest journalists at *Newsday*, give them complete freedom, and allow them to publish things that no traditional newspaper would touch. Although Moyers liked the concept, the more traditional journalists, such as Insolia and Opotowsky, didn't. "I just didn't grow up on a newspaper that took its most inexperienced people and gave them their head," Insolia said. "To me, it was college journalism."

Moyers resigned before he had a chance to implement the idea, but Laventhol decided to go ahead with it. "This was a time of great social change," Laventhol said. "It seemed like an innovative kind of approach. . . . I doubt that we'd do it now." To publish *Pennypacker*, named for a Long Island historian, they picked a rotation of ten reporters, who would work for two weeks each on stories that interested them, and they augmented the staff with high school and college students. They decided to publish it five times that summer — every other Saturday. They gave it a distinctive look by turning loose the art director, an eccentric genius named Gary Viskupic. In addition to his bold conceptual illustrations, he came up with a bottom-of-the-page design that knit the stories together with a running strip that contained quotes and small photos and illustrations. The editors did odd things such as sending high school students to do reporting on racial unrest, asking them to write memos, then publishing the memos. They sent Ed Hershey out to write a piece about being a cop and Victoria Mares, a member of the black caucus, to write a piece about being a house cleaner in a white, middle-class home.

Not every story in *Pennypacker* was whimsical. Perhaps their most impressive effort was a serious, powerful piece about migrants, by Payne, which appeared in the first issue of *Pennypacker*. To find out about conditions in the migrant camps on the East End, Payne went undercover, calling himself "Bubba," and living with the migrants. His story, "Waiting for the Eagle to Fly," captured brilliantly the rhythms of their speech and the shape of their lives. When the story appeared, both Insolia and Opotowsky jumped on Schneider for allowing Payne to go off on such a risky assignment without backup. But *Pennypacker*'s spirit of daring in 1970 and 1971 helped *Newsday* to begin reinventing itself as a daily magazine. "I think it speeded up some of the innovation at *Newsday*," Schneider said.

A funky experiment such as *Pennypacker* did not bother Times Mirror, which was more concerned with another innovation: increasing the profits. At the same time that *Newsday* was unveiling *Pennypacker* in the summer of 1970, Times Mirror was preparing to scrap a long-standing policy of Harry Guggenheim: his refusal to increase the price. The paper had cost five cents since 1950. Often in the 1960s, the circulation department had told Harry that he could increase the price to seven or eight cents without losing circulation permanently. He refused. To him, it was more important to get *Newsday* into every household than to make a few more dollars of profit. Partly as a result of that strategy, *Newsday* had become so dominant in its area that it was essential for advertisers. On the other hand, *Newsday*'s after-tax profits in 1969 had only been about $2.4 million — nothing to be ashamed of, but not nearly what the paper could make if it had a Sunday paper and a higher price. Starting a Sunday paper was a complicated process that would take many months, but Times Mirror could increase the price easily and quickly. So they did. On September 21, 1970, they doubled the price of *Newsday* from a nickel to a dime. As it turned out, the increase was not painless. At the time, the circulation was hovering around 450,000, and the price increase caused an almost immediate loss of about ten percent of that. It took *Newsday* until 1976 to overcome that loss and reach a higher annual average circulation, but ultimately, the price increase did improve profits.

Somehow, newspapers often follow a price increase with a big story or a design change — something dazzling to help make up to the reader for the additional cost. A week after the price doubled, *Newsday* carried the start of the latest Greene Team effort — the result of a nine-month investigation of the Nassau County Democratic Party and the administration of County Executive Eugene Nickerson. This was not the first time that *Newsday* had nipped at the heels of a politician that it had supported, but it was easily the biggest bomb that they had ever dropped on the Democrats. Most of *Newsday*'s investigative reporting over the years had been directed at the Republicans, simply because the Republicans were almost always in control. But Eugene Nickerson had overcome that monolith in 1961 to become Nassau County's first Democratic county executive.

In 1961, County Executive A. Holly Patterson had thrown the Republicans into turmoil by stepping down as party chairman and deciding not to run for re-election. For a variety of reasons, the logical candidates to succeed him couldn't run. So the former county chairman, J. Russel Sprague, found a total unknown, Robert Dill, collector of customs for the Port of New York, to make the race. Dill had such a shaky grasp of the issues that the Republicans tried to keep him under wraps, and *Newsday* chided him for not agreeing to a debate. At one point during the campaign, Dill met with Alicia Patterson to discuss that and other matters. "He said, 'Now, Mrs. Patterson,' " Hal Burton remembered. "She said, 'Miss Patterson!' He said, 'Well, Mrs. Patterson, I think you and I ought to get a room and go in it together and lock the door and have this out man to woman.' She said, 'Mr. Dill, that sounds deliciously sexual.' " For Dill, that was one of the few amusing moments of a campaign that got more difficult as it went on.

Toward the end of the campaign, one of Nickerson's aides, Mitch Lipson, discovered that Dill's brokerage firm owned shares in companies that did business with the port while he was collector, and the Democrats accused him of conflict of interest. Enraged, Dill lost control during an appearance before a women's group in Levittown. "He got up and he really got carried away," said Dick Zander, who covered the event for *Newsday*. "All of a sudden you hear this stuff coming out of his mouth." Among other things, Dill called the Democrats "greasy, slimy pigs." Zander wrote the story, and the Democrats jumped on it, dressing in pig suits to ridicule Dill. Throughout the campaign, *Newsday* treated the race as a serious one, which was all Nickerson needed. "I wouldn't have won without *Newsday*," Nickerson said. "That's clear."

The election of Nickerson brought to Nassau, momentarily, the two-party system that *Newsday* had always wanted. But that didn't deter Greene when he learned that the Democrats were using their power to perpetuate themselves, just as the Republicans had. "If you wanted to get some kind of viability for this team," Greene said, "it had better work Democrats." So the team — Greene, Crowe, Shanahan, Marro, Bob Wyrick, Michael Unger, Sidney Schaer and Carole Ashkinaze — spent months running down information that the Democrats were granting non-bid personal service contracts to architects and others, then milking them for campaign contributions. The resulting series showed that the county had let $36 million in personal service contracts of more than $10,000 each and reaped $800,000 in contributions to the Democratic Party.

The series on the Nassau Democrats was not the only excellent journalism that *Newsday* accomplished during the difficult months of 1970. One example was a major series by Tom Morris on the adoption of the new bicounty master plan — the fruit of *Newsday*'s long campaign for better planning. Another was the coverage by Ed Hershey, Drew Fetherston and Pete Bowles of a bus crash in Pennsylvania that killed seven children from a Hebrew school in Lawrence, followed by the discovery that the bus driver had a horrendous driving record. While the staff worked on those stories and others, and while Laventhol struggled to keep the paper running smoothly, everyone waited anxiously to see who the new publisher would be.

At the start of his search, Otis Chandler had offered the job to Richard Wald, the former managing editor of the *Herald Tribune*, who was then executive vice-president of NBC News. "I thoroughly loved the idea," Wald said. "But I had given my word to NBC that I would stay there. That was a very delicate period at NBC." Nonetheless, Chandler talked at length with Wald about who might make a good publisher. "Otis' interest was that the person who take this job be someone who did not have a personal political ambition," Wald said. "He didn't care what the person's politics were."

In Nassau County, a group of influential Republicans cared very much about the new publisher's political orientation. They wanted him to be someone favorably disposed toward the Republican Party. They wanted it so much, in fact, that they set in motion a bizarre plan to name a publisher of their own choosing. The central actors in this coup were William Casey, the mumbling power broker who had tried unsuccessfully to buy the paper from Harry, and Tex McCrary, the radio personality who had played such a major role, with *Newsday*'s help, in launching the candidacy of Dwight Eisenhower. The man they chose as their candidate was Frank Sorg, a Port Washington resident with only the most tenuous connections to publishing: As a student, he had worked on the presidential poll that appeared in the first issue of *Newsday*, and as an adult, he had run a printing company that turned out financial documents. He was also active in a variety of community affairs on Long Island, including the presidency of North Shore University Hospital. "It was my idea," McCrary said. "He was Mister Long Island." That was his entire resume for the job — except that he was a registered Republican who was on friendly terms with Nixon and with his friends, Bebe Rebozo and Robert Abplanalp.

One morning that summer, Casey invited Sorg to his home for breakfast. When Sorg arrived, he found McCrary, Casey and two high-powered lawyers: Casey's partner, Len Hall, and Ben Frank, who had run Casey's unsuccessful race for Congress, worked in Nelson Rockefeller's 1966 campaign and later became a deputy commissioner in the state's Office of General Services, where he worked to build Rockefeller's futuristic government mall in Albany. This gathering of movers and shakers told Sorg that he could become the next publisher of *Newsday* and provide Nixon with a friendly newspaper. "I'm saying to them, 'You guys are nuts,' " Sorg remembered. But they convinced him that Nixon could nudge the process along. "I decided, yeah, okay, I'll do it."

To make sure that Nixon approved, Sorg asked Abplanalp to discuss the plan with the President himself. "The report came back: Fine, beautiful, wonderful," Sorg said. The next step was for Nixon's longtime friend, Robert Finch, to make contact with Otis Chandler. "I thought I was going to be the new publisher," Sorg said. "I got to the point where I was actually thinking of what I was going to say to the employees the first day." There was just one major flaw in the putsch. "We contacted everybody but the guy that can make the decision," Sorg said. "Everybody was contacted but Otis Chandler." Finally, in the middle of the night, McCrary called Sorg and said that he had just found out that Otis Chandler had named a new publisher of *Newsday*. It wasn't Frank Sorg. It wasn't even a Republican. It was an Adlai Stevenson-John Kennedy Democrat named William Attwood.

BOOK IV

The Golden West
And the Big Apple

CHAPTER THIRTY-ONE

Enter the Ambassador

I

ONCE RICHARD WALD had told Otis Chandler that he felt obligated to stay at NBC, rather than become the publisher of *Newsday*, Wald shifted into the role of an informal advisor.

In their conversation, Wald listened as Chandler described his vision of *Newsday*. "He didn't have the words for it, but what he wanted was a daily magazine," Wald said. So Wald thought immediately of someone who had magazine experience and would soon be looking for a job — the editor-in-chief at Cowles Communications, Bill Attwood. Wald knew that the look of death was on the face of *Look*, and running that magazine was eighty percent of Attwood's job at Cowles. The first step was a lunch at the Century Club in Manhattan, with Wald, Attwood and a mutual friend, the columnist Art Buchwald. "I mentioned that I thought the day of the general magazine was passing, and I was interested in looking around and doing something else, maybe in television," Attwood said. "They said nothing about anything — nothing at all. Then I got a call out of the blue from Otis Chandler."

The meeting between Attwood and Chandler in Los Angeles was brief. "I'd just broken my shoulder, and I was in terrible pain," Chandler said. "It's a wonder we got along." Attwood candidly discussed his strengths (editing and motivating a staff) and his weaknesses (corporate finance), and Chandler found him acceptable. "When it was over, he said, 'Okay, let's go up and tell my father,' " Attwood said. "He didn't say, '*ask* my father.' He said, 'tell my father.' " So they went to see Norman Chandler. Despite Harry's expectations about the elder Chandler's political orthodoxy, it didn't seem to bother Norman

Chandler that Attwood was not a Republican. "He said, 'What are your politics?' " Attwood said. "I said I was a registered Democrat. And he said, 'Okay, welcome aboard.' " So much for the rumor that Times Mirror would pick a Republican publisher. "Otis understood the importance of continuity on Long Island, and that, even though the Republican establishment didn't like it particularly, to change the personality of a paper is always bad," Attwood said. "So he was looking for somebody who was more or less in the Moyers mold."

Like Bill Moyers, Attwood was a liberal Democrat whose career was an amalgam of government service and journalism. But the two men had starkly different backgrounds. Moyers came from a poor family in Texas, but Attwood was born in Paris and educated at Choate and Princeton. Following his World War II Army service, Attwood signed on to work as a copy editor on the cable desk of the *New York Herald Tribune*. Quickly, he decided he'd rather be writing stories in Europe than editing them in New York. There was an opening in the *Tribune* Paris bureau, and Attwood did speak French, but the foreign editor suggested that Attwood first accept an assignment to Washington, where he could demonstrate his competence. The postwar ferment of Washington provided him the chance to cover such stories as the dawn of the atomic age and the creation of the Central Intelligence Agency. Then, a few weeks later, he was in Paris. During the next fifteen years, Attwood covered the development of the cold war in Europe and at the United Nations, and he travelled extensively — first for the *Herald Tribune*, then briefly for *Collier's* and over the course of a full decade for *Look*. It was his work for *Look* that first brought Attwood in contact with Adlai Stevenson, which led to a second career, in government.

In the aftermath of his crushing defeat by Dwight Eisenhower, Stevenson set out in 1953 on a world tour, agreeing with Gardner Cowles to provide a series of articles for *Look* about his travels. To make sure that Stevenson met his deadlines and turned out 3,000 readable words every two weeks, Cowles sent along Attwood, then *Look*'s European editor, as a literary valet. Attwood did research, arranged for photos and made sure the copy was filed on time. Stevenson did much of the actual reporting, with help from other members of the party and a diary that Attwood kept. On that trip, the politician and the writer developed a rapport, and in 1956, Attwood contributed to Stevenson's speeches during his second presidential campaign. In late 1959, Stevenson asked Attwood to take a leave of absence and assemble speech material for the 1960 campaign, in case Stevenson decided to run again. Attwood agreed, and one of Stevenson's friends, Agnes Meyer, the widow of the *Washington Post* owner Eugene Meyer, paid Attwood the equivalent of his *Look* salary during the campaign. Once John Kennedy was nominated, Attwood joined Kennedy's speechwriting staff, and the Kennedys detached him to help Stevenson mobilize the liberals for Kennedy.

Once the 1960 campaign was over, Attwood returned to *Look*, declining Stevenson's offer to serve as his public affairs officer at the United States mission to the United Nations. But when Chester Bowles, the new undersecretary of state, asked Attwood for the names of potential appointees, Attwood casually mentioned that he himself would like to be ambassador to Guinea. To Attwood's surprise, President Kennedy appointed him. It was during his two-year tour in Guinea that Attwood contracted polio, which left him with a permanent limp. When Attwood came back to America in 1963, Kennedy sent him to work with Stevenson at the United Nations, as an advisor on African affairs. Following Kennedy's assassination, President Lyndon Johnson made Attwood his ambassador to newly independent Kenya. (Later, in his book, *The Reds and the Blacks*, Attwood wrote about the corruption that he saw in Kenya, and the government there banned both the book and the author.)

By the spring of 1966, Attwood was ready again for a change. When his former boss, Gardner Cowles, visited him in Kenya and asked him to return to New York as editor-in-chief of Cowles Communications, Attwood accepted. Over the four years that followed, Attwood suffered a heart attack, followed by an episode of clinical depression and a second heart attack. In the midst of that physical pain, he was surrounded by the inexorable decline of *Look*. So, when Otis Chandler offered him the *Newsday* job, he was more than ready for a change. Chandler announced the appointment on September 1, effective at the start of November.

"He said that there were certain things he wanted me to look into on a priority basis," Attwood said. "One was the Sunday paper. He couldn't understand how they did without a Sunday paper." Attwood was to increase profits and clear away "dead wood" on the staff, and Chandler was to give him autonomy. "I expected general instructions, but nothing too specific. It would be a bunch of easterners running an eastern newspaper. We would play down the whole Times Mirror connection as much as possible," Attwood said. "He agreed with that."

While Attwood was winding down his affairs at Cowles Communications and preparing for his arrival at *Newsday*, Times Mirror was concluding its negotiations with Alicia Patterson's heirs for the purchase of their forty-nine percent interest. It had not taken long for Joe Albright and his family to realize that ownership of forty-nine percent of the stock gave them no clout on the board of directors. The relationship with the Times Mirror directors was cordial enough, but one meeting of the board gave the minority owners a vivid reminder that Times Mirror was in charge.

"It was a fairly dramatic meeting," said David Washburn, the attorney for the Albrights. One item on the agenda was a routine approval for Times Mirror to take *Newsday*'s revenue and invest it, paying *Newsday* back at the prime rate — just as they did for other subsidiaries. The Albrights voted against it. With one of the Times Mirror directors absent that day, the vote ended up in a tie, and the proposal didn't carry. Chandler and Times Mirror were miffed. "We believe that was a motivating factor for the offer that came fairly shortly after the board meeting to buy out the Albright interests," Washburn said. In fact, Times Mirror offered them more for their forty-nine percent than it had paid Harry Guggenheim for his fifty-one percent. Besides, the Albrights saw no evidence that the new owner was an evil empire. "You sort of envisioned a chain as being like Newhouse, that the worst would come about, that they'd do these horrible things," Joe Albright said. "That didn't happen." So they reached an agreement to sell their interest in *Newsday*.

Harry had sold his fifty-one percent for 500,000 shares of Times Mirror common stock, plus $10,000,000 in notes and an additional 100,000 shares of common stock, contingent on *Newsday*'s 1971 profits. That part of the deal turned out to be worth $31.6 million, as Times Mirror computed it. For the forty-nine percent owned by the Albrights, Times Mirror offered 1,042,500 shares of common stock, plus 2,610 shares of convertible preferred stock — a total of $37.5 million. In all, said Phillip Williams, then the Times Mirror vice-president for finance, the company paid $69.1 million for *Newsday*. Many in the industry considered it a steal. Despite *Newsday*'s long-term profit potential, however, Chandler argued: "That was a very full price. *Newsday* was only making a couple of million bucks after taxes."

Times Mirror announced the agreement with the Albrights on October 27, 1970, clearing up the last substantial obstacle to full Times Mirror control of the paper, just before the arrival of Attwood as publisher at the start of November.

II

TO THE TASK of shaping *Newsday* in the Times Mirror image, Bill Attwood brought a quarter of a century in journalism and government, but only a limited knowledge of the newspaper. What he knew about *Newsday* he had gleaned from reading the paper, from John Flagler's unpublished manuscript about Alicia Patterson for *The New Yorker*, and from a ten-page memo provided by Stan Asimov.

Under Moyers, Asimov had risen to the position of assistant to the publisher, but the departure of Moyers had left Asimov in limbo. Asimov and Moyers remained in contact by mail while Moyers crossed the country to gather material for his book, *Listening to America*, and Asimov remembered receiving an envelope from Moyers addressed to "the assistant to an empty chair." When Asimov first met the new publisher, Attwood didn't do much to reassure him. "He sat down next to my desk," Asimov said, "and his first words were, 'I've never worked with an assistant before, but we'll give it three months and try it out.' Well, that was sort of a shock." But Attwood did ask Moyers about Asimov. "He said, 'Don't lose him,' " Attwood remembered. "Moyers said he was indispensable. As it turned out, he was."

About two weeks before Attwood actually started, Asimov sent him a memo outlining the issues that faced him, such as the Sunday paper, the slow progress in introducing modern technology and the problem of dealing intelligently with the aspirations of the paper's black reporters. Asimov also suggested several initiatives. He urged Attwood, for example, to study the feasibility of expanding *Newsday* westward into New York City's easternmost county, Queens. "There are as many people living in Queens as in all of Nassau and Suffolk," Asimov wrote. "They regard themselves as suburbanites and would be a natural area for expansion."

The Asimov memo contained no details of the paper's Byzantine office politics, but Attwood began to learn about those in another communication: a complaint about a plan by Laventhol to replace the departed managing editor, Marlens. Instead of naming a single managing editor, Laventhol wanted to create a system of three managing editors: Insolia, Perfall and Lou Schwartz, the assistant managing editor who had worked with him on the soft-news side of the paper. "He didn't probably know who he really wanted to do the job," Insolia said. "I would imagine he really didn't want to create somebody with too much authority, since his was not firm yet." Insolia didn't think it was a good idea, but he agreed to go along. Perfall's reaction was more extreme.

"When it came now to a vacant managing editor's spot, I felt I had a right to it, rather than sharing it with him and Lou Schwartz," said Perfall, whose candidacy had the support of important figures such as Greene and Opotowsky. In addition to his distaste for this specific idea, Perfall was not terribly impressed with Laventhol. "Art always used to say, "God, I hate that man. He's so stupid,' " said Pat Byrne, then Perfall's secretary and later his wife and his ex-wife. So Perfall decided to contact Attwood before he arrived at *Newsday* and seek his help in derailing Laventhol's plan. "I wrote Attwood a letter, saying that I thought this was a mistake and it was unfair," Perfall said. "I felt it wasn't good for the paper and I felt that I could do a better job."

Perfall sent a copy of the letter to Laventhol, but that didn't soften the effect of his action. "It was really not very smart of Perfall," Insolia said. "From Laventhol's point of view, here he's got a renegade going to Attwood and telling him this is a stupid thing, and you've got Insolia, who's saying, 'I don't think it's a very good system, but if this is the way, we'll make it work. . . .' Dave has always trusted me from that point on." Neither Laventhol nor Attwood responded to the letter. Instead, one of Attwood's first acts as publisher was to announce that he was promoting Laventhol from executive editor to editor and naming three managing editors beneath him: Insolia to run the paper at night, Perfall to direct news coverage and Schwartz to run Part II and special supplements. Perfall had lost the battle, and his final slide had begun.

The question of the three managing editors was just one of several personnel matters on Attwood's agenda. One was the need to start knitting together the paper's departments, which had become accustomed to operating like independent fiefdoms. "That's when we instituted the staff meetings, where everybody talked about their own problems and shared them," Attwood said. "I was just amazed at these first staff meetings. I almost felt that I had to introduce these people to each other." Shortly after his arrival, Attwood also filled a vacancy that had caused problems for Laventhol during the no-publisher months, by appointing Bernie Bookbinder, the veteran reporter and rewrite man, to be editor of the editorial pages. Of all his immediate personnel problems, however, the one with the most potential to alter the way *Newsday* operated was the Guild organizing drive.

Once the United Auto Workers drive had died during the summer, the Guild had rushed in to fill the void, and a representation election was set for January 14, 1971. Attwood and Chandler saw it as an early test for Times Mirror. "He just said: 'I leave it to you, but this is one we want to win,' " Attwood said. Even before he arrived, Attwood had announced a general salary increase, based on an analysis of the existing salaries. The union organizers used the raises as an argument *for* a union. "If the mere threat of a Newsday Guild can move management in this manner," the organizing committee said in one December bulletin, "it seems reasonable to believe that the actuality of a Guild at Newsday will gain us our share of the prosperity and security which we have helped bring to Newsday."

Both sides issued the predictable memos, explanations, charges and countercharges, but the battle was not terribly bitter. For one thing, a nasty campaign would have weakened the company's case, which was based on trust. "The company came on with a very effective argument," said Brad O'Hearn, one of the key organizers. " 'Give us a chance. We're new. We mean well. We realize there have been things that went on in the past that shouldn't have. But this is a new corporation now. . . .' For the people who were on the fence and who were wavering, this was a powerful argument." The company also relied heavily on the same lingering doubts about the Guild that had created a movement toward the UAW. In the end, the Guild lost convincingly, 167 to 90 — almost exactly the result that Asimov had predicted. "The Guild defeated itself," John Cummings said. Nonetheless, Times Mirror gave Attwood credit for the win. "We are all delighted," wrote Richard Robinson, the vice-president who supervised Attwood. "It's a great way to launch your career as a new publisher."

On the January night when the votes were counted, Attwood invited some of the union representatives into his office for drinks. In the morning, recovering from the all-night party, Attwood decided that as long as he felt so rotten, he might as well tackle an unpleasant chore: notifying the circulation manager, Jack Mullen, that he had to retire. There was a certain irony in Attwood's taking action while suffering a hangover, since the major issue with Mullen was a severe drinking problem, which Attwood had discovered when he first visited Mullen's office. "I got up there around two o'clock, and he was still out to lunch," Attwood said. "I went back up at 2:30, and he was drunk — quite drunk. . . . It turns out he was never really sober after twelve." Once Attwood discovered that Harry Guggenheim had left Mullen with a separation agreement that would take care of him amply, Attwood decided there was no reason not to make him retire. So he ordered his staff to write a press release, announcing the retirement of Mullen and the appointment of Vinnie Bordash to replace him. Then he asked Mullen to read it and check it for accuracy. Mullen started to read it over, not understanding its meaning at first, then suddenly stopped. "He said, 'Hey, wait a minute. It says something here about my resigning,' "

Attwood remembered. "I said, 'That's right, and we're accepting it.' "

At the same time that Attwood was removing this mainstay of the Guggen-heim-Patterson *Newsday*, the surviving founder was nearing death. The pre-vious June, just after Harry had sold his stock to Times Mirror, the report on his health was mixed. His prostate cancer was quiescent, but he was experiencing a growing weakness in his legs, and one of his doctors suggested that the cause might be cancer-related pressure on his spinal cord. A little more than two months later, his health declined drastically during his annual visit to Saratoga for the racing season. On August 23, his eightieth birthday, he suffered another stroke. His daughter, Joan Van de Maele, was with him. Together with Harry's secretary, George Fountaine, she arranged for a private ambulance to take him down to Memorial Sloan-Kettering Cancer Center in Manhattan. He stayed there for a little more than three weeks and returned to Falaise. That is where he spent the last months of his life, primarily in a hospital bed that his staff had installed in Alicia's former book room, on the first floor.

As Harry lay in the book room, attended by private nurses twenty-four hours a day, he had very few visitors. Not even Fountaine, who had worked closely with him for fifteen years, was among them. His most constant compan-ion was his daughter. His sister, Gladys Straus, also visited him. The two men who had helped him sell *Newsday* to Times Mirror, Peter Lawson-Johnston and John Hanes, came regularly. So did Charles Lindbergh. "He didn't make much effort to see people who were ill, but he did make an effort to see Harry," Anne Morrow Lindbergh said. "He felt very drawn to Harry."

During those final months, Harry was unable to speak. "Since he couldn't talk, there was tremendous pressure to carry the conversation," Lawson-John-ston said. "I remember one time in particular, I had just come back from South Carolina, and I was just trying to think of everything I could think of about Cain Hoy. He took it all in, and at the very end, he said, 'Good report.' That's the only thing he ever said that I ever understood." Van de Maele felt that he could understand what his visitors were saying, but she didn't know whether he understood what was happening at *Newsday*. Just a week after Harry's stroke, for example, Times Mirror announced the appointment of the liberal Attwood to succeed Moyers. "He would have had a fit," Van de Maele said. In a later letter to Chandler, Lawson-Johnston said: "As you know, Harry was disappoint-ed that Newsday's anti-administration editorials persisted after the sale." But in the last months of his life, as lawyers for Times Mirror and the Albrights made the acquisition final, *Newsday* was no longer Harry's primary concern. To the extent that he was able to focus on anything, Harry worried about his plantation and his home.

Harry was tremendously proud of Falaise and its role in history — so proud that he had installed a plaque in his own living room to commemorate the 1929 discussion there with Lindbergh that had led to their long association with Robert Goddard. In his last years, Harry had gone to great trouble to make sure that Nassau County would preserve the estate exactly as it had been during his lifetime. His instructions covered the smallest details, including the way his military uniforms were to be displayed in his bedroom closet. He displayed that concern right to the end. "Our last talks related to Falaise, its grounds and their condition," Lindbergh wrote in a 1973 reminiscence. "I had walked over the grounds so I could keep him accurately informed." Then Lindbergh left on an overseas trip, and soon after that, in the early morning hours of January 22, 1971, Harry Frank Guggenheim died.

For those who worked at *Newsday* in the years right after Alicia's death, his indelible image is that of a very old, very conservative man, suffering from deteriorating health, which made him suspicious and paranoid, convinced that there were leftists behind every typewriter. Despite that, Harry was a man of unassailable ideals. He believed firmly that his family should use its immense wealth for the progress of humanity, and he could be stunningly generous with it. At the end, he used much of it to establish a foundation with the high-minded but vague goal of finding peace by studying and eradicating the human urges to dominance and aggression.

Harry tried hard to maintain a loving relationship with his family, but true intimacy was difficult for him, and he was neither warm nor very happy. Despite his emotional shortcomings, however, Harry was a man of great accomplishment. He knew how to get things done, in the diverse fields of business, art, science, horse racing, and even — despite his total lack of technical journalistic skills — in the world of newspapering. Harry did underestimate the paper's growth and kept such a tight hold on its finances that he infuriated Alicia, but his prudence finally made the paper financially successful. Harry did act irrationally in pushing Moyers out the door, but he was also canny enough to hire Moyers in the first place, which brought *Newsday* immediate respectability in the world outside its own region. Harry did sell the paper out of ignorance of what Times Mirror had become, but even that worked out well. "I realized he had done the right thing for the wrong reasons in choosing Times Mirror," Moyers said, "because I thought they would protect it as a good newspaper." Even though Harry died at the start of the Times Mirror era, his decision to hire Moyers continued to shape the course of *Newsday*, because Moyers hired Laventhol, who had a larger impact on the paper than anyone else in the first fifteen years of Times Mirror ownership.

With Harry's death, *Newsday* had only one remaining dynastic connection to the Guggenheim and Patterson families: Joe Albright, the Washington bureau chief. It was obvious to Albright and to everyone else that there was no place in the upper levels of *Newsday* for him. The reorganization of *Newsday* as a Times Mirror subsidiary became final on February 11, 1971, and the axe fell on Albright less than a month later. In the years that followed, without the benefit of being Alicia Patterson's nephew, Albright established himself as a first-rate foreign correspondent with Cox Newspapers. But in 1971, neither Albright nor the performance of the Washington bureau impressed Attwood very much. So he worked out an arrangement that would allow Albright to announce his resignation in March, effective April 15 — a decade after he first came to *Newsday*. To replace him as bureau chief, Attwood and Laventhol chose Russell

Sackett, who had run the *Life* Magazine investigative team for three years.

A few days after Albright's resignation, Attwood announced still more changes. Ernie Levy was retiring after twenty-eight years at *Newsday*, and Attwood was appointing four vice-presidents — David Laventhol to run the editorial department, David Targe to pull together all of the paper's marketing functions and oversee both circulation and advertising, Frank Farrell to run the finances, and an outsider, a Times Mirror veteran named James Grider, to serve as general manager. All these changes marked a clear end to the Harry Guggenheim-Alicia Patterson era at *Newsday*, as Attwood acknowledged when he first discussed the Albright move with Laventhol. "He said, 'But he's related to Guggenheim,'" Attwood remembered. "I said, 'That's all over now. *We're* not related to Guggenheim.'"

III

THE ODD TROIKA of managing editors that David Laventhol had created, with the blessing of Bill Attwood, continued to have one major flaw: Art Perfall.

"It wasn't going to work with Perfall," Laventhol said. "Eventually, I thought, 'I've got to have my own person here.'" The person that he chose was his old *Herald Tribune* colleague, Don Forst. Following the death of the *Trib*, Forst had worked briefly and unhappily at the *New York Times*, supervising daily coverage of New York City's cultural life. Leaving the *Times* after three years, Forst had joined another *Tribune* alumnus, Dick Schaap, editing sports books. When Laventhol brought him to *Newsday* in early 1971, Forst ran the national desk. But Perfall took one look at the canny, intensely ambitious Forst and knew: "This was going to be my replacement."

Just about six months after Forst arrived, Laventhol decided to move Perfall out as managing editor and move Forst in. Perfall was to lose his office in the newsroom and move to an office upstairs, near the cafeteria. At the time of this management-by-furniture decision, Perfall was on vacation. That timing angered Perfall's secretary, Pat Byrne, but her protests were in vain. So she moved Perfall's possessions to the new office while he was still on vacation and decorated it for him. For several months, they worked together in the second-floor office, Byrne as his secretary and Perfall as an associate editor, supervising investigations and special reporting projects. "It was obviously a non-job," Perfall said. "I started looking around." In early 1972, he left *Newsday* for a public relations job with a bank.

In the early months of his tenure, Attwood did some imaginative ousting of his own. It didn't take him long, for example, to see that one of Harry Guggenheim's legacies, the column by Robert Moses, was unacceptable. So he met with Moses, using diplomacy rather than a frontal assault. "I said, 'You know, I've been reading your column now that I'm at *Newsday*, and I have the feeling that you're constrained. . . . You've got a lot to say, but you can't say it in a 700-word format,' " Attwood remembered. "I said, 'Why don't you write a longer column on a different frequency — once every month. That way, you can really let yourself go. . . .' It worked. Of course, what happened was he'd forget to turn it in, forget to do it." Moses soon dropped out of the paper entirely — remaining on good terms with Attwood.

As Attwood was beginning to make changes in the paper, Times Mirror gave him a relatively free hand. "The interference, such as it was, was innocent and not deliberate," Attwood said. "It did not have to do with the content or the quality or with the newspaper. It had to do with accounting matters and financial matters." Some of those matters were extraordinarily tiny, such as the repeated suggestion that *Newsday* use the Times Mirror logo on its letterhead, which Attwood ignored. Some were more weighty, such as the requirements for financial reporting and budget planning, which occupied important *Newsday* executives for many more hours than they had ever spent during the Guggenheim-Patterson years. But primarily, the emphasis was on the bottom line.

"Times Mirror paid a very high multiple for the Albright family's minority interest in Newsday and we therefore have to show considerable earnings growth over the next several years if we hope to add several cents a share to the consolidated earnings of Times Mirror," Otis Chandler wrote Attwood. "And this, obviously, is the point of the Newsday purchase: to increase Times Mirror earnings." Attwood's own incentive payments depended on how much he increased after-tax profits, which were only $2.5 million in 1970. "The best way to increase profitability is to improve the editorial product," Chandler wrote. "But one has to proceed very cautiously with improving the editorial product, particularly if it involves a substantial increase in costs." So Chandler urged Attwood both to push the paper's marketing and install tight expense controls.

In the newsroom and on the editorial pages, the primary worry was not profits. "One of the big fears was that Times Mirror would attempt to dictate *Newsday*'s editorial or news policies," Bernie Bookbinder said. Though Attwood felt that "editorial autonomy was one hundred percent," Chandler didn't hesitate to comment on the tone of the paper's editorials. Attwood actually prompted one Chandler comment by telling him about columns on successive days by Patrick Owens and Robert Mayer, both advocating the impeachment of President Nixon. Attwood and Laventhol planned to meet with them and ask them to write that kind of column "more carefully and with less emotion, if indeed it has to be written," Attwood said. Commenting on the Mayer column, Chandler called it "quite hysterical and not deserving of the quality of Newsday," and went on to ruminate about a *Newsday* editorial on the war in Vietnam. "You obviously feel very deeply about the moral aspect of the Indochina war," Chandler wrote. "I agree, but this is not the most important aspect of the problem to me. Our major concern should be one of self-interest, or what is best for the United States. I agree we have to get out and I think Nixon is getting us out. . . . I do not dismiss the moral argument; but I think that all wars are immoral and I do not see why this country for the first time should suddenly become so righteous and moral about what we are doing in Indochina." A few sentences further down, as if to reassure Attwood, Chandler added: "In any case, I think it is well and good that Newsday and The Times do not see eye to eye."

Internally, Attwood did not always see eye to eye with his editorial board. For one thing, the new publisher annoyed his underlings with his obsessive focus on writing style. "I fussed much too much at first," Attwood said. "I found myself rewriting them. That's the last thing a publisher should do." Attwood also admonished his editorial writers constantly to pay close attention to a small book of wisdom, *The Elements of Style*, by William Strunk Jr. and E. B. White. The staff believed in Strunk-White, but they didn't want to be badgered about it. So Bob Wiemer brought in a purple altar cloth and votive candles and propped up *The Elements of Style* on it, like a prayer book. Then they turned out the lights and chanted: "Omit needless words." Attwood walked in on this bizarre scene, took it in silently and left.

More important than the question of style, Attwood struggled with his editorial writers on the matter of tone. The publisher and the writers were in substantial agreement on the issues themselves. Attwood intensely disliked Nixon, for example, and he opposed the war in Vietnam. But he wanted the emotional temperature of the editorials far cooler than the writers did. "He constantly depassionized the editorials, on the grounds that we were seeking to espouse a liberal position in an essentially conservative area, and if we were to have any success, it would be through subtlety," Bookbinder said. "We felt that, if you have a podium, stand up there and say it." One influence on Bookbinder's view was a congratulatory letter from Moyers when Bookbinder took over the editorial pages. "I pray for your righteous indignation," Moyers wrote, "that it know no quarter." Rather than indignation, Attwood sought calm and reason. "I didn't see that we stood to gain by being strident," Attwood said. "In the back of our minds, we had to think of Los Angeles, too. . . . They had a great feeling that we should be a respectable tabloid."

As a result of that Times Mirror desire for respectability, Chandler strongly criticized one 1971 Bookbinder editorial, supporting a bill to create a congressional inquiry into American war crimes in Vietnam. Chandler prefaced his comments by reaffirming *Newsday*'s independence. "I will never ask you to parrot us or pattern Newsday after the Los Angeles Times or, indeed, any other newspaper," he wrote. But Chandler could not hold back his intense dislike for the editorial. "I frankly thought it was an emotional, hysterical and immature position to take and not worthy of Newsday. . . . Some of my senior editors saw this editorial come in over the UPI wire and were amused by its obvious immaturity and emotionality. I think they were also saddened and a little embarrassed to be associated with such an outstanding newspaper on the East Coast that would take such a sophomoric position."

Attwood, who had edited and approved the editorial, shrugged Chandler's criticism off. "I welcomed your comments on Bernie's War Crimes editorial," Attwood wrote. "Not because I agreed with them but because I like guys who don't mince words." Attwood was less tolerant, however, of Fred Bruning, who wrote many of the Vietnam editorials — with enthusiasm. "I would go to work in the morning, I would bash Richard Nixon for seven or eight hours a day and they paid me for it," Bruning said. But Attwood kept resisting Bruning's editorials and taming them down. "He did not want what he called any ad hominem attacks on anybody, including Richard Nixon, which immediately made the fun go away for me," Bruning said. To resolve their differences, Attwood decided to make Bruning go away (to a job on Part II, as it turned out), and he delegated that unpleasant task to Bookbinder. "It was my worst experience at *Newsday*," Bookbinder said.

Bookbinder himself also became a target of Chandler, as Laventhol reported to Attwood in an early 1972 memo, describing a telephone conversation with Chandler. "He was 'extremely unhappy' about the editorial page," Laventhol wrote. "He said that the rest of the Newsday editorial product just kept getting better and better all the time, so why couldn't we do something 'about the Bookbinder problem.' " In a handwritten note a few weeks later, Chandler told Attwood that the editorial page was "still the weakest part of Newsday." At about that time, Laventhol sent out a memo suggesting an in-depth look at suburban life, and Bookbinder responded with a memo proposing a "sociological Greene team." Laventhol liked the idea and asked Bookbinder to run the team as a senior editor for projects. "I remember him saying, 'I'm going to make you a senior editor to protect you,' " Bookbinder said. "I was very aware that this was a move to get me out of there. I was not unhappy to be leaving, because I had felt pressure and dissatisfaction from Attwood." So, only a month after Chandler's critical note to Attwood about the weakness of the editorial page, Laventhol announced the appointment of Bookbinder as a senior editor and Bill Sexton, Laventhol's assistant, as the new editorial page editor.

Given all the energy Attwood spent on preserving a reasonable tone in his editorials, it is ironic that it was not an editorial that brought Attwood and Times Mirror into painful controversy with the Nixon White House, but a carefully worded series of investigative reports a few months later by the Greene Team.

CHAPTER THIRTY-TWO

Stalking Nixon

I

OVER LUNCH ONE day in early 1971, three men sat down and decided to turn the talents of the Greene Team away from local scandals and focus them on the President of the United States.

In 1970, the team had won a Pulitzer Prize for investigating corruption in Suffolk County. Then it had taken aim at a county government, reporting on the fund-raising practices of the Democratic administration in Nassau County. Now Bob Greene wanted to take the next logical step. "I felt that we had sharpened our teeth on these little things," Greene said. "Why not go for the highest? Why not go for the biggest?"

At the lunch in the John Peel Room, a traditional *Newsday* dining spot, Greene discussed possible investigative targets with Laventhol and Art Perfall, who was nearing the end of his career at *Newsday*. The most interesting Nixon cronies that Greene mentioned were Charles G. (Bebe) Rebozo, a millionaire who was Nixon's closest personal friend, and former Senator George Smathers, a Florida Democrat, who in 1951 had introduced Nixon to the Key Biscayne area and to Rebozo. By the time the lunch was over, Laventhol had agreed to let Greene do some preliminary reporting, called a "smell" or a "sniff," to find out whether a full-scale investigation was justified.

The team that started in early January included Greene, Ken Crowe, Bob Wyrick, Geraldine Shanahan and Tony Marro — with some help from Martin Schram of the Washington bureau, who knew the Miami area well, but was too wary of working in Greene's shadow to become a full-time member of the team. One of the primary elements of the sniff was an exhaustive chronology of

Rebozo and his business deals that Crowe put together from clips, a few interviews and long hours in government offices in Miami. Even for someone as skillful as Crowe, it was difficult to operate in a strange environment. "We ran into a state where we didn't get cooperation," Crowe said. "We worked the clerks in that Dade County courthouse like crazy, and they started feeding us stuff. I went out to so many lunches in Cuban restaurants with clerks."

During the sniff, the team also ran into personnel turbulence. Bob Wyrick, legendary for his toughness, had a fight with Greene because Wyrick was in a bar with a source and was late in contacting Greene. So Wyrick left the team. "I didn't need anybody to kick me in the ribs to get more work out of me, when I was already working my guts out," Wyrick said. His replacement was John Hildebrand, a journalism school graduate who had only joined *Newsday* a few months earlier, after three years in the foreign service.

At the end of the sniff, in March, Laventhol passed Greene's findings to the Washington bureau chief, Russ Sackett, who agreed that the project was worthwhile, but warned Laventhol: "It seems to me what we'll wind up saying is that Smathers is a first-class crook, that Rebozo is sort of a third-class corner-cutter and implying that Nixon, by extenuation, is something of a crook himself. I'd be happier, for lack of really hard stuff on Nixon, if we simply concentrated on Rebozo-Smathers." That was exactly how the story evolved.

From April through June, the team camped in the Royal Biscayne Hotel, not far from the presidential compound, and went at it. Typically, Greene drove his reporters constantly, forcing them to live, work and eat together — until they began to yearn for the company of almost anyone else. One night, Marro remembered, Greene became "absolutely furious," when Schram wanted to go out someplace different to eat and listen to some jazz. "It was like being in a velvet prison," said Crowe, who broke free long enough to take a canoe trip that he had promised his children. "Greene made sure that there was always enough to do over the weekend," said Marro, who had been pulled away from a tour in the Albany bureau to join the team. "He made clear he didn't want us leaving." Just before Memorial Day, Marro's wife complained to Laventhol. "It is now over five weeks since I have seen my husband," Jackie Marro wrote. "What kind of company sends an employee away from his family for such a long period of time and then tells him that if he wants to go home for a holiday weekend he must pay for the trip out of his own salary?"

Compounding the pains of their journalistic incarceration, they also suffered from the frustration of knowing that the story was falling short of expectations. "It was set up like a typical Greene investigation, and yet, unlike the stuff that was done in Nassau County, the bad stuff of the Nixon administration was in private records rather than public records," Marro said. What they did find was interesting, but they didn't find anything truly damaging to Nixon. "It was a failed investigation," Shanahan said. "Everybody knew it. The dogs in the street knew it."

The assignment was particularly difficult for Hildebrand, who hadn't been with them on previous stories and developed bonds with the others. To Crowe and Shanahan, he remained the outsider. "They were being increasingly rough on Hildebrand," Greene said. Finally, at a dinner on Long Island celebrating the end of the project, their frustrations bubbled to the surface. The powerfully built Crowe and the much smaller Hildebrand exchanged insults and almost traded punches. "That night, at that affair, I said: 'I think it's probably about time we break up the Yankees,' " Greene remembered. "That was the end of that team. . . . It shouldn't have happened."

II

FOLLOWING A RIGOROUS editing process, during which David Laventhol placed more emphasis on magazine-style writing than the team had ever experienced, the six-part Rebozo series began on October 6, 1971.

The first day's package was the story of how Rebozo became a millionaire. The series ended a week later with a story headlined "The Florida of Richard Nixon," which described the President's Florida lifestyle, his friends and his investments. *Newsday* devoted acres of space to the series every day, including a full page in front, summarizing the story inside. On the surface, it was an impressive debut for the Greene Team in the national arena, but many of its readers — from the publisher of *Newsday* to members of the team itself — felt that the series had not accomplished its mission.

For a series that had aimed at the President of the United States, the obvious question was: How much had it damaged Richard Nixon? When the series hit the streets, Marro later found out, a group of reporters and editors at the *New York Times* bought copies and started reading hurriedly for the Nixon material. "All of the heads came up, one after another," Marro said, "and they said, 'They ain't got him.' " The same assessment came from Laventhol and Attwood. "I yield to no man in my feelings about Richard Nixon," Attwood said. "On the other hand, in retrospect, I wish we'd cut the thing short. We promised a lot and didn't deliver. . . . Nixon himself was not guilty of anything except going fishing with a friend who, it appeared, was in with the Florida big-money wheelers and dealers." That was part of the reason why Laventhol pushed for softer leads, rather than the hard-news leads that might have made it easier for wire services to carry parts of the series, but might also have given the impression that it revealed more than it really did. "We couldn't make the final connections," Laventhol said. "At the same time, we very clearly had the flavor of Richard Nixon in a way that was ahead of its time."

Despite the failure to nail Nixon, the series did produce some excellent journalism. "The individual stories would hold up anywhere," Marro said. "What they didn't do was make a compelling portrait, I don't think, of a malfeasance by any administration." *Time* magazine's report on what it called "an encyclopedic — indeed, numbing — 70,000-word" series called *Newsday* a leader in the growth of investigative reporting across the country. The series also got the attention of a Times Mirror-owned publishing house that wanted to run it as a book, tentatively entitled *The Florida of Richard Nixon*. "Peter Ritner, editor-in-chief of World Publishing Company, now has possession of the series," Laventhol wrote in a memo a few days after it ended. "He is so enthusiastic that he is moving the book into production in advance of sending us a contract to sign." That enthusiasm quickly vanished, however. Not long after Laventhol's memo, he called Greene and told him that they were both wanted in Attwood's office. "We were standing there and he said, 'Now, what do you intend to do next?' " Greene remembered. "I said, 'We've got four more aspects of Nixon to do, and each one of them is better than the next one.' And he said, 'Well, I don't think we want to do any more Nixon. Out on the coast, they feel that it's an election year coming up, and we don't want to look like we're out to get him.' You could feel in your gut that this was not Attwood talking." Attwood also told Greene that World wouldn't be publishing the book, either.

At the time, Attwood told David Wise, the author of a book called *The Politics of Lying*, that killing the book was his own idea. "It would have looked like a campaign hatchet job," Attwood said. "We explained this to Los Angeles because World books was a subsidiary. It was just the wrong year." But in an undated, handwritten comment on someone else's memo about the book, Attwood told Laventhol: "Robinson called. Shaw has informed Rittner [sic], as of this a.m., that it is not being published." Robinson was Richard Robinson, the Times Mirror vice-president who was Attwood's direct supervisor. Robinson said he did not recall the memo. Shaw was Christopher Shaw, the president of World Publishing, who also had no recollection of the transaction. When he was shown the 1971 memo, Attwood confirmed that he had written the line about Robinson, and he remembered more clearly that Times Mirror had wanted the book stopped. "It would look as though we were being more partisan than they wanted to be," Attwood said. "That's the way they felt."

Whether the decision to back off Nixon was made in Los Angeles or in Garden City, the Watergate investigation later made clear just how closely the White House was watching *Newsday* — before, during and after the series. "I know that the FBI agent in charge of the Nassau office called John Cummings and then also called Tommy Renner, in an attempt to learn when we were going to be out," Greene said. That interest is also apparent in a memo written almost a month before the series appeared, and later revealed after Watergate. In the memo, a White House investigator, Jack Caulfield, told Nixon's counsel, John Dean, that "a discreet look at the newspaper's publication calendar has been accomplished," and the series would not run in September. "A trusted member of the newspaper's staff has stated that outside pressure is being exerted to uncover the details of the story before publication. This pressure is *independent* of the efforts being programmed from my office." In later memos, Caulfield and another White House aide, David Wilson, discussed possible antitrust action against the *Los Angeles Times*, but rejected it. The men around Nixon were persistent, however, and they quickly came up with other methods for showing their displeasure.

Right after the series, Nixon's press secretary, Ron Ziegler, became pointedly unavailable to Schram, the *Newsday* White House correspondent. And when the bureau chief, Sackett, asked for accreditation for two new Washington reporters, Warren Berry and Tony Marro, the White House still hadn't responded three months later. The silence was trivial, however, compared to what the White House did to Schram in early 1972. At that time, every major newspaper was jockeying for one of the limited press seats for Nixon's historic trip to China. Finally, Ziegler called Schram in for a meeting at the White House. "I said as soon as I sat down, 'Well, Ron, am I going to China?' " Schram wrote in a memo that day. "Ziegler replied: 'Well, Marty, the reason I called you in here was because I wanted to tell you personally that Newsday is not on the China list and that it doesn't have anything to do with the Bebe Rebozo series. . . .' " Then Ziegler ticked off the criteria for the trip: Any newspaper on the list had to have sent reporters on Nixon's foreign and domestic trips and regularly covered the White House. Schram argued that *Newsday* met them all. "Ziegler could not cite any specific criteria," Schram wrote, "but he said: 'We just had to make some decisions. . . . We had a space problem.' " Schram did not go on the trip. A month later, Ziegler admitted to Sackett and Schram that all the petty snubs were a result of the Rebozo series. " 'I didn't think the series represented good journalism,' " Ziegler told them. But he still insisted that the series had nothing to do with the China decision.

The White House response did not stop there. Greene and Laventhol found themselves stuck with tax audits. Both Dean and Caulfield later admitted during their Watergate testimony that they had sought to instigate a tax audit of Greene by New York State tax authorities. "The first time I was ever introduced to John Dean," Marro remembered, "he said: 'Did we pull your taxes?' " As it happens, Marro said that after the series the government did audit a tax return on which he had claimed few deductions. Otis Chandler also felt that the White House was responsible for a messy scandal that blew up in his face. A close Stanford friend of his, Jack Burke, had founded GeoTek, an oil-drilling firm. Chandler had helped him to find investors, and in return, Burke had given him stock and finder's fees. When the company went broke, Nixon's Securities and Exchange Commission investigated. The government accused Chandler and others of making false statements about their investments, and he spent $1 million in legal fees to fight the charges, which were later dropped. The whole affair was an acute embarrassment to Chandler in 1972 and 1973, at the same time that his reporters were digging in the Watergate scandal.

Despite White House anger at *Newsday*, Nixon did give Attwood, a few weeks before the 1972 election, something that he wanted very much. Since 1968, *Newsday* had campaigned in its news columns and on its editorial pages for the designation of Nassau and Suffolk counties as a Standard Metropolitan Statistical Area, separate from New York City. This was hardly the kind of cause to make ordinary Americans march in the streets, but it was vital to *Newsday*.

The reasons that most often appeared in the paper were that the creation of a new SMSA would stimulate job growth, make it easier for local governments to apply for federal aid, and provide a new sense of Long Island identity. The more selfish reason was that it would help *Newsday* sell ads. Finally, Nixon announced the Long Island SMSA during a campaign visit to Long Island. Those new statistics on Long Island as a separate entity, the advertising department gleefully predicted, would help them show advertisers how rich a market Long Island was. In fact, on the day that Nixon announced the SMSA, Attwood issued a boosterish press release. "For years, we have been advising national advertisers to recognize Nassau/Suffolk for what it truly is — a leading market in its own right, independent of the New York metro market," Attwood said in the press release. *Newsday* almost immediately followed up with a promotional campaign based on the SMSA designation.

During the same campaign season, *Newsday* had already given Nixon a present: It declined to endorse anyone for President of the United States, which withheld an important source of comfort from Nixon's opponent, George McGovern. In every race since 1940, *Newsday* had taken some position on the presidency, even if they were occasionally schizophrenic. In 1972, the new owners didn't expect *Newsday* to endorse Nixon, as the *Los Angeles Times* was doing. But Otis Chandler did discuss the endorsement question with Attwood. "He said, 'I know you would never endorse Nixon, knowing how you feel. But, gosh, I hope you don't endorse McGovern,' " Attwood said. "He didn't say, 'Don't do it.' He just said, 'I hope you don't.' I immediately said, 'We're not. We're not going to endorse either of them.' " Bernie Bookbinder, who by then had left as editorial page editor, wrote a memo arguing against the policy. *Editor & Publisher* also criticized it in an editorial. But Attwood stuck with it and insisted, without convincing many, that it was a policy that had worked well for him at *Look*, and it had nothing to do with Times Mirror or with his unwillingness to choose between Nixon and McGovern. Even without an endorsement, however, *Newsday* didn't let Nixon completely off the hook. Most of its presidential issues editorials supported McGovern's views. "Otis later said: 'Geez, you guys are pretty clever. You didn't endorse McGovern, but you agreed with all his positions on the issues,' " Attwood remembered. "And I said, 'Well, yeah, his positions happen to coincide with a lot of things we think.' We never did say, vote for McGovern."

Throughout that campaign and beyond, *Newsday*'s Washington bureau was scrambling to catch up with the *Washington Post* on the Watergate scandal. "You went in there every day behind the curve," said Marro, who had started covering the story right after the burglary, when Schram sent a policeman to the tiny, telephoneless schoolhouse that Marro owned in Vermont, and asked Marro to call his office. Marro immediately got on the trail of Bernard Barker, one of the burglars, in Miami. "You were always being called to account for hurrying up and getting *Newsday* into the game," Marro said. "I got worn down by it. Marty thrived on it." Schram, in fact, broke an early story about the payment of hush money to the burglars. At the end of 1972, Schram became bureau chief, replacing Sackett — one of the first Attwood-Laventhol appointees. They had plucked Sackett from the world of magazine journalism, on the theory that his investigative experience at *Life* would allow *Newsday* to make an impact with thoughtful investigative pieces. But Sackett was more of a writer than an investigator, and his writing rhythm was not suitable for daily stories. When they decided that Sackett wasn't working out, Sackett recommended Schram as his successor, and Tony Insolia pushed for the appointment of the rising young star who had waited for the bureau chief job through the tenure of Nick Thimmesch, Joe Albright and Sackett.

Schram's hush-money story was not the only significant one that *Newsday* broke during Watergate. Another came from Judith Bender, who had joined the paper in 1969 from the *Knickerbocker News* in Albany. Anxious to do some national reporting, she had simply taken her vacation, showed up at the Democratic National Convention in Miami, and offered her services to the editors. One night, having a late supper at a coffee shop, she ran into one of her Albany sources, who had a relative working at the Committee for the Re-election of the President (CREEP). The conversation turned to Watergate and to something that Bender's source had heard about an employee of CREEP named G. Gordon Liddy, whose name had not yet surfaced. "What hadn't come out yet was that Liddy had been fired the previous Saturday, for failing to cooperate with the FBI," Bender said. Bender passed the information along to Don Forst, the managing editor. When nothing appeared in the paper over the next day or two, she called Marro, who got the rest of the story. Bender and Marro shared a byline on the story, which appeared a month after the break-in. "That was the first time anyone had heard of Liddy, who became a critical figure," Bender said. In their book, *All the President's Men*, Carl Bernstein and Bob Woodward of the *Washington Post* acknowledged *Newsday*'s role in the Liddy story. But most of the time, *Newsday* was trying to catch up to them.

The Watergate story in 1972 gave a new life to the 1971 Bebe Rebozo series, which could help reporters at other papers understand some of Nixon's connections. Suddenly, the copies of the series that Marro had saved became very popular. "Inside of two weeks after Watergate, they were all gone," Marro said. The Nixon-Rebozo investigation might have turned out to be even more helpful, Greene is convinced, if *Newsday* had chosen at the end of 1971 to pursue it further. One of his proposals was to subject Nixon's California investments and friendships to the same scrutiny that they had brought to bear on Florida. "I think if we had been able to complete this whole thing," Greene said, "we could have certainly had one hell of a good shot at the President of the United States."

CHAPTER THIRTY-THREE

The Heroin Trail

I

ON THE HEELS of the decision not to pursue Nixon further, Attwood soothed Greene's disappointment by making a proposal that caught his imagination: a chance for the Greene Team to go international.

"Laventhol and Greene and I were sitting in the Westbury Manor having dinner one night," Attwood said. "After a couple of drinks, we were saying, 'What is the investigative team going to do next?' I had read in the paper that morning there had been fifty-three heroin overdose deaths on Long Island, and I said, 'Well, how about drugs?' Somebody else said, 'All drugs?' I said, 'No, let's think of heroin. That's where the overdoses came from.' "

Since reporting on drugs on an international scale would entail chasing the mob, Greene couldn't resist. Since Greene had never been to Europe, he also complied happily with Attwood's suggestion that he fly to Paris and discuss a joint project on drugs with two key journalists at the newspaper *France Soir*: the chief foreign correspondent, Michel Gordey, and the managing editor, Robert Villers. His weekend visit to France did not produce a concrete agreement for a *Newsday-France Soir* project, but Greene did get the names of some experienced French reporters who were prepared to help.

Following his Paris trip, Greene began to feel that the project had to cover a broader sweep than just the United States and France. "That missed the other leg," Greene said. "Where was this stuff coming from originally, and how come it was being allowed to come?" That question brought Turkey into the equation. For many years, Turkish farmers tilling poppy fields in the hills of Anatolia had been a major source of the heroin flowing through France to the

United States. But in 1971, the Turkish government had declared a ban on the growing of opium poppies, effective after the harvest of the 1971-1972 crop. To encourage this ban, the United States offered $35 million in aid. But Greene doubted that any ban could shut down an industry so important to the economy of Turkey. To learn more about that industry before any final decisions were made on what he called Project Snowflake, Greene flew to Miami and interviewed a police official who had befriended him during the Rebozo investigation: Salvatore Vizzini, the chief of the South Miami Police Department, who had worked for two decades for the federal Bureau of Narcotics and Dangerous Drugs in Turkey, France, and Southeast Asia.

The result of the Miami trip was a six-page memorandum to Laventhol and to Don Forst, who would directly supervise the project. The memo described the heroin process at length: from the harvesting of the congealed sap of the opium poppy, through the laboratories in France where mob chemists converted the boiled-down sap, called morphine base, into heroin, and finally to the port of Marseilles, where much of it left for the United States. Beyond explaining this system to Greene, Vizzini had also given him the names of contacts who could help him get started in Turkey, plus a short list of top heroin dealers. That was the first step toward Greene's goal of charting the heroin flow, from the poppy fields to the veins of heroin users in America. Then Greene set out to find reporters for this dangerous expedition.

At one point, Greene wanted to take along a police detective, Matt Bonora, but that idea didn't work out. His other choices were more orthodox. One was Knut Royce, who had come to the paper during the Suffolk scandals investigation. Later, Royce had joined Greene in investigating the Metropolitan Transportation Authority's operation of Republic Airport on Long Island. Besides sharp reporting skills, Royce had a suitably international background: He was born in Marseilles and grew up speaking French, Portuguese and British-accented English. He didn't move to the United States until he was nearly eleven years old, in 1951. When he was graduated from Dickinson College in Pennsylvania, Royce joined the Peace Corps, served in Ethiopia and decided that he wanted to become a foreign correspondent. Instead of covering Africa, once he had earned a master's degree in journalism from the University of Iowa, Royce soon found himself working in the Town of Islip for *Newsday*. When the heroin project came along, his Marseilles origins, his fluency in French and his reporting skills made him a natural for the story.

For different reasons, Greene decided that Les Payne was also a perfect choice. In a little more than two years since he had completed his Army service and come to *Newsday*, Payne had already established himself as an aggressive and fearless journalist and as a leader among the black reporters. Greene had not experienced his skills directly, but he had noticed that the tall and physically imposing Payne did not flinch from danger. The story that impressed Greene most was Payne's 1970 piece from a migrant camp, which showed exactly the traits that Greene wanted: a willingness to work undercover and to put his life at risk. In his analysis of Payne, Greene saw no negatives: "professional military experience as an officer; can handle himself physically; very good reporter when motivated; can take orders; has very strong motivation in sense of doing something for his people." Until drug abuse spread to the white suburbs and attracted Nixon's attention, its victims were not young people in the countries where the drugs originated, but inner-city American blacks. "That kind of pattern struck me all the way through this thing," Payne said. "It was also one of the motivations for me, in addition to the obvious one as a reporter." At the time when Greene sat next to Payne at a crowded *Newsday* party in early April, 1972, and asked him to join the heroin project, Payne had been thinking about leaving *Newsday* to work for *Ebony* magazine. But Project Snowflake quickly changed his mind.

One of the team's first steps was Greene's request for equipment, including guns. Vizzini, who was thoroughly familiar with Turkey, had recommended strongly that the team should be armed. "Particularly in the interior of Turkey there is danger from an assortment of bandits, nationalist-extremists, smugglers and wolves," Greene wrote. "It is best to always have some weapons." Attwood took one look at the proposed spending — including the guns, a house and servants in Istanbul and a four-wheel-drive Land Rover — and told Laventhol: "Much of the expenses appear to be quixotic and counter-productive. Bob Greene's servants bidding him a tearful farewell as he departs his Istanbul villa with his arsenal of weapons en route to a rendezvous by Land Rover with imaginary wolves strikes me as rather too conspicuous a way to conduct this investigation." Attwood refused the Land Rover, but he later allowed the weapons. So Greene sent Payne out to buy a shotgun and rifles, and the three team members took shooting lessons. Going a step further, Greene decided to bring along a length of piano wire. In the mob world, piano wire is a quiet, efficient weapon, but Greene wasn't planning to strangle anyone. The idea was to use it as a trip-wire, to warn them of invaders, if they had to sleep outdoors. "We never took lessons on the piano wire," Royce said.

Besides the weaponry and three weeks of Turkish language lessons, Greene focused heavily on codes, secrecy and cover stories — some of his favorite parts of journalism. Rather than carry along files that could fall into the wrong hands, for example, they wrote a long list of sources, informants and drug dealers on one page of rice paper for each team member. They were to hide it in a corner of their wallets and, in an emergency, swallow it. Greene also concocted code names for each of them: Big Daddy for Greene's girth, The Bear for Royce's grizzly gait and The Moor for Payne's dark skin. They also invented a cover story, to fool the Turkish government: The team would be touring the continent for a series of stories about modern Europe. "Bob Greene, Les Payne and Knut Royce are going overseas to do some special reports on Europe in the '70s," David Laventhol wrote, in the middle of a routine memo to the staff. "They will be filing political, economic, social and travel pieces."

The concern for security extended all the way up to the publisher, who asked the Central Intelligence Agency to keep an eye on the team. As an ambassador, Attwood had dealt regularly with CIA station chiefs in Guinea and

Kenya, and he found the agency neither mysterious nor sinister. In fact, he had once written a magazine piece, "A Few Kind Words for the CIA," for *Look*. With that background, he didn't hesitate to ask for help from the agency's director, Richard Helms. "I saw him and said, 'They're going to be dealing in a story that's going to be pretty dangerous in Turkey, France and other places. It would be nice if you could alert your station chiefs to what they're doing, and if they're in trouble, have a phone number they can call,' " Attwood said. The CIA was to perform a variety of services for the team. "If we needed some information checked, they would try to check it for us," Greene said. "If we were really being shot, they would try to move a helicopter in or something else to move our asses out of there."

So, comforted by the blessing of the publisher, the presence of their arsenal and the watchful eyes of the CIA, the team set out for Europe in the first week of June, 1972. But before they got to Turkey, Greene took one more precaution, lighting three votive candles in Rome to invoke divine protection for their journey. "It made me feel better."

II

FOLLOWING MONTHS OF planning and meticulous preparation, the *Newsday* invasion of Europe began like the opening scenes of *The Marx Brothers Stalk the Poppy*.

The first hurdle was the difficulty of getting their weapons overseas. Reacting with extreme caution after a bloody terrorist attack on an airport in Tel Aviv, an airline official in New York ordered their weapons removed from the plane. The team got the weapons back on the plane, but the problems continued when they arrived in Rome and a group of colorfully uniformed Italian policemen escorted Les Payne and the weapons to an overnight customs storage area. That night, at an expensive hotel, they found a refrigerator full of champagne, and the worldly-wise Royce assured Greene that it was all free. Like the winning team in the World Series, they not only drank it, but sprayed it and washed Royce's socks in it. The following morning, the hotel presented them with a $169 bill for the bubbly. The follies continued in their first few hours in Turkey, when a businessman who was friendly with Sal Vizzini, Greene's source, met them at the airport and escorted them to their rented house in the suburbs of Istanbul. When he saw their armaments, he was shocked, because Turkey was under martial law. "You can be shot on sight for those," he told them. Later, they stored with police the rifle that was most likely to cause them trouble, and they retrieved it when they left the country.

The headquarters that they had rented through Vizzini's businessman friend was a pleasant two-story house with a garden full of fruit trees, plus the services of a cook-housekeeper named Martha and a driver-guide named Genghis. The house was comfortable, and Turkey was in many ways a pleasant place to be — especially for Payne, because Turks considered blacks to be good-luck charms and treated them well. But the domestic arrangements couldn't compensate for the galling lack of success in their first few weeks. Vizzini could deliver them a house and servants and put them in touch with a potentially helpful informant, but he couldn't make the man talk.

The contact was Galip Labernas, a former Turkish police narcotics official. Right after they arrived, Greene contacted Labernas, who promised to help them, but seemed to trust only Vizzini. Greene wrote to Vizzini to get him to prod Labernas by mail, but Labernas continued to stall. While they negotiated with Labernas, they began filing their cover stories and did some reporting in the village of Degirmendere, not far from Afyon, the principal city of the province of Afyon — both named for the province's chief product, the opium poppy. Payne also began making contacts among black-market operators in the American military, who could provide a secure mail drop through the Army post office system and might later lead him to information on drugs. Despite those signs of progress, they felt that they were moving very slowly. "We drank an awful lot of tea, just meeting with people — newspaper people, government people, police people," Payne said. That intricate process of getting sources to talk was also depressing Greene. "At times," Greene wrote to Forst, "we feel as if we are bogged down in a football field filled with Jell-O."

Just three days later, their luck changed. Labernas delivered to their villa a person he identified as Ali Adnan Ozpetek, who had once been involved in the heroin trade. Ozpetek agreed to study their list of questions and come back again. That same afternoon, Labernas brought in two Syrian brothers who were engaged in smuggling morphine base into Bulgaria. The brothers gave them the names of a few top smugglers and a briefing on the drug trade, then returned two days later and agreed to help the team get the story of the Bulgarian connection. The big break came almost a week after their first meeting with Ozpetek, when he returned to their villa and supplied them with a list of more than fifty names — the biggest drug dealers in Turkey.

The interview with Ozpetek was a major step toward one of Greene's primary goals: naming in *Newsday* the names of Turkey's key heroin traffickers. As the team developed its list of names from Ozpetek and other sources, they confirmed the names with Labernas, with the CIA and with Orhan Erbug, the director general of the Turkish National Police. For his help, Ozpetek got about $5,000 — despite the long-standing newspaper reluctance to pay for information. "I made the decision we do it," Greene said. "I don't regret it." Forst agreed. "I don't know if I would call it checkbook journalism," Forst said. "The conclusion was that it was appropriate." It was also expensive. In mid-July, Greene asked Forst to have Laventhol bring over an additional $10,000 in cash when he visited. Laventhol's stop in Turkey, during a longer trip through Europe, was a source of concern for the team, which was sensitive about its slow start. "We thought they were going to kill the project," Payne said. But the worrying turned out to be unnecessary. "We sort of went over what they had and discussed it," Laventhol said. "They were very much on course."

From the time they got the names from Ozpetek, the team's momentum began to build. In visiting Cyprus, Payne got an important interview with its president, Archbishop Makarios, which was far above the quality of the other cover stories. A few days later, Greene and Royce drove to Sofia, Bulgaria, and met with the two smuggling brothers. At an outdoor cafe outside the hotel, Royce took several photos, with Greene in the foreground and the smugglers in the background, at a table with a man that they later identified as a major smuggler of morphine base. Once Greene left, Royce stayed behind and photographed the brothers standing outside a building that another source had identified as the new headquarters of Kintex, the Bulgarian agency reported to be involved in the heroin trade.

Early in August, two months after arriving in Turkey, Greene and Payne enjoyed a brief reunion with their wives, who went to Europe at *Newsday*'s expense. Then the two wives stayed on in Turkey while the team completed its interviews, revisited Afyon and photographed properties owned by the major Turkish drug dealers. The team came away from Turkey with a detailed knowledge of how the opium traffic worked and a firm conviction that the poppy ban was unlikely to succeed. At the end of August, as they prepared to start the French phase of the investigation, Greene couldn't resist another touch of melodrama. The germ of the idea had come to him in July, as he and his driver returned from Bulgaria to Turkey, and he noticed that the border guards were nonchalant in inspecting his car. Now, to demonstrate how lax the border security was, he took two clear one-kilo packages of white confectionery sugar and packed them conspicuously in their luggage. First, they flew from Istanbul to Vienna, then drove in a rented car through crossings on the borders of Austria, Yugoslavia, Germany, France, Switzerland and Italy — with Greene and his wife in front and Royce in back, with a camera. As the trip went on, they put the mock heroin in more and more obvious places, finally displaying it on the dashboard. But no one searched them. When the series ran, the story of this odyssey took up a full page, and a map and photos filled the opposite page, under a two-page headline: "When You Crisscross Europe With Two Bags of 'Heroin.' " In the Garden City office, the sugar caper inspired a bulletin-board cartoon depicting one border guard saying to another: "Here comes the fat guy with a bag of sugar again."

III

As SOON AS the team arrived in France, Don Forst asked them to sit down in their villa on the Riviera at Le Lavandou, take their notes from Turkey and turn them into stories.

To guide them through the writing, Forst spent two weeks with them, sitting on the terrace overlooking the Mediterranean and editing. "I've got to admit, it wasn't the toughest duty in the world," Forst said. "The toughest part of that was not having the pages blow off." Once Forst returned to the states, they resumed their reporting. In Turkey, they had concentrated on the government's ban on poppy farming and on the widespread corruption that made heroin traffic possible. In France, they hoped to show how the government had developed a close relationship with the mobsters who moved the heroin. The roots of that relationship went back to 1961, when European extremists in Algeria formed the *Organisation Armee Secrete* (OAS) to thwart the effort by President Charles de Gaulle to reach a conclusion to the Muslim rebellion against French colonial rule there. In the struggle against the OAS, de Gaulle accepted the help of mobsters, who worked in counter-terrorist brigades organized by the French counterpart to the CIA, the *Service de Documentation Exterieure et du Contre-Espionage*, (abbreviated SDECE and pronounced *steck*). This arrangement included one of the team's prime targets, a heroin dealer named Marcel Paul Francisci, who not only supplied men to fight the OAS, but also campaigned for the Gaullists on his native island of Corsica.

In reporting on these government-mob connections, the team stirred the curiosity of both sides. "We were safer in France, because we were followed by the underworld and the French government, whereas in Turkey it was usually just the underworld," Payne said. The French government suspected that the team represented an American government agency. "The French just could not accept the fact that a newspaper from Long Island would be mounting such an extensive operation in their country," Greene said. One transaction that stirred the government's curiosity was a phone call between Payne in Le Lavandou and Greene in Paris. The two men discussed Payne's arrangements to fly home, where his wife, Violet, was giving birth to a son, Jamal. Later, Greene learned from the CIA that the French had intercepted this conversation and decided that Payne was really flying to New York because the team had made a major discovery. "The French were convinced that 'baby' was a code word and demanded that the CIA explain the code to them," Greene said.

Never reluctant to play cloak-and-dagger, Greene took to this kind of intrigue with enthusiasm. If he talked to *Newsday* by phone, he resorted to codes that he would make up and explain as he went along — a long-distance game of charades. Once, he tried to tell Tony Marro, who was running the American end of the investigation, about a heroin smuggler named Andre LaBay. To get Marro to guess what he meant, Greene kept naming American bays: " 'Big Peconic, Little Peconic, Chesapeake. What do they have in common?' " In the same spirit, Greene went to great trouble to elude anyone who wanted to follow him. When he travelled from Le Lavandou to Paris, for example, Greene used evasive procedures that added a half hour or more to his trip. "It might have been dumb," Greene said, "but it made me feel better." Even his Paris headquarters had a cloak-and-dagger background: It had once been Madame Claude's, a high-class brothel frequented by government ministers with a taste for women and whips. In 1972, it was known as a place where lovers could meet for careful trysts. Since French police discreetly ignored it, Greene could meet with sources freely there.

The man who set Greene up at this location was Jean-Pax Mefret, who came to the team's attention through a high-ranking former French intelligence official. Mefret had been a colonist in Algeria, and he knew many Algerian settlers working in French government agencies. Several days a week, Greene would go to Paris and meet with sources steered to him by Mefret. At the same time, Greene said, Payne ran into such virulent racism in southern France that it became difficult for Payne to operate effectively. So they decided, since Payne spoke German but not French, that he would spend time in Munich, a major transshipment point for morphine base. When he wasn't in Munich, Payne was with Knut Royce. On those occasions, they would awaken in Le Lavandou early in the morning, drive two hours to Marseilles, work all day, drive back to Le Lavandou, type out their memos to Greene and get to bed at one o'clock in the morning. Toward the end of their period in France, the long hours took a toll on Royce, who had a heart attack. While Royce was still in a French hospital, Greene arranged for a replacement — Chris Cook, a young reporter in the Suffolk office who spoke fluent French because he had grown up in England and France, where his father was a foreign correspondent.

On Cook's first day in the villa, he got a taste of Greene's love for intrigue: Greene tried to explain their arrangement with the CIA to him, without saying the agency's name out loud, in case the house was bugged. " 'If everything comes right down to it, Chrissy, and we need some help, we're going to be bailed out,' " Cook said, mimicking Greene's rumbling, gravelly voice. "And then he says, 'We'll get some help from . . .' and he goes C-I-A with his fingers." Cook had no idea what Greene was doing, until the third repetition of the finger signals. Then Cook blurted out, loud enough for any listening device to pick up, "Oh, CIA!"

For the remainder of the project, Cook spent his time providing French translation for Payne. At the same time, Greene travelled with another rein-forcement, Pucci Meyer, a young woman who had worked as a home editor on the new Sunday magazine, then as a Part II feature writer. Meyer, who also spoke fluent French, helped Greene in a bizarre scheme to get information about Michael Victor Mertz, a captain in the French secret service who had also been a major heroin smuggler. Mertz was ostensibly in prison, but Greene was certain that his imprisonment was just a charade to satisfy American drug enforcement officials. To get further information on Mertz and his connections with SDECE, Greene decided to pass himself off to Mertz's wife as a lawyer and tell her that someone had left money to Mertz, who could not collect it unless he was a French citizen in good standing. Greene typed out an actual seven-page will, and Meyer arranged for an impressive set of calling cards and stationery for the fictional California law firm of Laventhol, Forst and Greene. Armed with this phony documentation, he met with Madame Mertz. She told them that her husband was expected to get out of jail in February, 1973. That would mean, the team figured out, that Mertz was serving only eight months of a five-year sentence — if indeed he actually served any time at all, which they doubted. During this meeting, Greene persuaded her that, since her husband was in jail, they would need the names of people who would confirm that Mertz was a good citizen. At a later meeting, she provided Greene with several names, including that of a retired former supervisor of Mertz at SDECE, which confirmed for the team that he had worked for SDECE and provided an indication that SDECE would still not disown him, despite his heroin dealings. Mertz became a key figure in the team's story about French secret service agents who had been part of the heroin trade. It was important information, even though Greene's impersonation of a lawyer was unorthodox. "I figured that was what reporters did to get stories," Meyer said. "I didn't know."

Greene's impersonation on the Mertz story was bold, but not nearly as dangerous as the mission that he chose for Cook and Payne: a visit to Corsica, the island south of France that was the home of many major heroin traffickers — including Marcel Francisci. Everyone warned the team to stay away, including the head of the Bureau of Narcotics and Dangerous Drugs in Europe, Payne and Cook said. The trip would be particularly difficult for Payne, who would be the only black man on the island. But Greene insisted that his sources told him the visit would not be dangerous. Besides, he said, Cook and Payne volunteered, although neither of them remembered being anxious to go.

In Corsica's typically Mediterranean capital city, Ajaccio, Cook and Payne went to take a photograph of a cafe that had once been the scene of a mob shootout. Sitting on a park bench, they were preparing to take photos with a miniature camera, when Payne noticed someone pointing a movie camera at them from the cafe. "That's when I said, 'Holy shit. We're going to be on the seven o'clock mob news,'" Payne said. "There's no question that we were scared shitless." Reaching their hotel just ahead of a group of men who were chasing them, they got into the tiny elevator, which groaned as it rose slowly to their floor, while their hearts pounded. "We decided we're getting the hell out of this," Cook said. "We're not going to get ourselves chopped up because of Bob Greene."

As they packed hurriedly, they looked out in the street and noticed the hotel desk clerk talking with the men who had just followed them. Cook and Payne went down to the lobby and told the clerk to call a cab. She moved as if to come out from behind the desk, and Payne blocked her, so she couldn't get to the street and report to the men who had followed them. A few moments later, the cab came, Payne retrieved from beneath the pillows of a sofa some files that he had hidden there, and they jumped into the cab. Suspecting that the driver wasn't really taking them to the airport, Cook loosened his belt for use as a weapon. But the driver got them to the airport a few steps ahead of the posse, and just barely in time for the plane. "I have never, ever, ever seen a coastline look as great as the French coastline did when we were getting out of this place," Payne said. Back at Le Lavandou that night, despite all the griping that they had done about Greene's arsenal, both of them slept with a rifle.

Not long after they returned from Corsica, the French phase was over, and

Greene ordered Payne and Cook to pack up and prepare the weapons to clear customs. Finally, the whole team ate a farewell dinner at an exquisite Paris restaurant, inviting Cook's mother to join them. At the end of the meal, Cook's mother drove them toward their hotel. Just before they reached the hotel, Greene asked her to stop the car, and he supplied a grandly gallant explanation. "He says, 'My dear lady, your son and I must take our leave of you here. We have some more business to conduct,' " Cook remembered. Reluctantly, Cook and Payne piled out of the car and stood with Greene across the street from Fouquet's, a restaurant partly owned by Marcel Francisci. Despite all their efforts, they had not been able to interview Francisci, and Greene had been wanting to make one last attempt, in Fouquet's. So he chose this moment. " 'Whatever it takes, we're going to find Marcel Francisci,' " he told them, and they lurched across the Champs Elysees and into Fouquet's. Elegantly removing his shabby raincoat from his shoulders and swirling it like a velvet cape, Greene presented it to the host and asked for seats at the bar.

"Off to the right of us, sitting in a booth, is a man who looks remarkably like Marcel Francisci," Cook said. Greene looked at the man and turned to Cook. "He says to me, 'Chrissy, I want you to take a note in French.' " Cook grabbed a scrap of paper, an airline ticket envelope, and took dictation: " 'Dear Mr. Francisci: Since we have not had the opportunity to meet upon the field of challenge, may I extend my invitation to you to discuss your business dealings? Sincerely, Robert W. Greene.' " The restaurant staff insisted that Francisci wasn't there, but Greene gave the bartender the note anyway, along with one hundred francs, asking him to get it to Francisci. They didn't find Francisci, but they did get out of France in one piece, relieved to be heading home after six months of cloak-and-dagger work on the heroin trail.

IV

THE STORY THAT excited Tony Marro in 1972 had nothing to do with heroin. It was about a bungled burglary: The Watergate scandal was unfolding, and he very much wanted to stay with it.

Late in August, he got a telephone call from Laventhol, summoning him to Garden City, to discuss his role in the heroin project, as the head of the United States team. That was a major responsibility for someone who had been with the paper only four years. But in that short time, Marro had impressed the editors with his reporting skill and his capacity for hard work.

Growing up in a blue-collar neighborhood in the marble and railroad town of Rutland, Vermont, Marro had been working hard since childhood. His father's family came to America from a town near Naples at the end of the nineteenth century. His mother, born a short distance from Rutland, sprang from a working-class Yankee family. Frankie Marro met Esther Butterfield one day when he was out on his route, selling beer, and they were married just before he went into the service in 1941. Anthony Marro, their first child, was born in 1942. After the war, they settled down to raise their family in a wood frame house at 264 West Street, a few feet away from the grocery store operated by Frankie's brother at the corner of West and Meadow, in the part of town that was variously known as Nebraska or The Gut. In time, Frankie developed serious drinking problems, which threw much of the burden of supporting the family on the shoulders of Esther. So, from elementary school on, Tony Marro worked in a variety of jobs — as a caddy, as a pinboy at the bowling alley, and as a carrier for the *Rutland Herald*. While he was still in high school at Mount Saint Joseph's Academy, his uncle helped him to get a job with the *Herald*, covering sports and other high school events.

More than simply working for the *Herald* as a schoolboy stringer, Marro almost lived there. In school, Marro was the object of teasing because of his stuttering, but at the *Herald*, even though he was far younger than the reporters, he was an accepted, well-respected fixture. "They indulged me," he said. "They used to treat me like a grownup." After hours, he would spend his leisure time with the reporters Kendall Wild and Tom Fagan. During the day, he would perform small chores, such as helping reporters who were working on stories about Sunday shopping laws, by going to stores and reporting what he had been able to buy. "He sort of seemed to pick it up on his own," Fagan said. "This kid could do anything." So, in the summer of 1963, a few months after Wild had become managing editor, he hired Marro as a full-time reporter. Marro took a semester off from the University of Vermont, where he also held down three jobs, and concentrated on the *Herald*. He returned to college in January of 1964, but came back to the *Herald* in the summer of 1964, covered the Goldwater-Johnson campaign for them that fall in Burlington, covered the legislature during a break from school and arrived at the paper permanently after his graduation in 1965. That same year, his mother started a long career at the *Herald*, as a receptionist and confidante to the young staff.

As a full-time reporter, Marro immersed himself in the *Herald* around the clock. He got to cover a broad variety of stories, from the arrest of a Rutland minister by segregationists in a small North Carolina town to a Sunday evening car crash on Route 7 that killed five. Before long, Wild became confident enough in his work to assign him permanently to the state government in Montpelier. In the tiny world of the press room under the dome of the capitol, the person who taught Marro the most was Vic Maerki, the *Burlington Free Press* correspondent, who was older and more cynical. "I held the legislature in obvious, open contempt," Maerki said. One day, in fact, something that a senator said during debate struck Maerki and Marro as so ridiculous that they both broke out laughing, and a few minutes later the Senate voted formally to censure them. Marro knew how to laugh, but Maerki remembered him most for his doggedness. "Tony was always serious about his work," Maerki said. "He understood that hard work was really important. Although he had strong views on things, he went where the story took him."

Marro was not particularly anxious to leave Vermont, but a combination of factors in 1967 drew him away, including active duty in the reserves, the chance to get a master's degree in journalism from Columbia and the desire of his wife, Jackie, to work in the fashion industry in New York. So, when he finished Columbia in 1968, he went directly to *Newsday*, with the help of Stan Asimov, who taught at Columbia and took another teacher's recommendation about Marro. He had a shaky start, when his editors discovered that he was not suited to general-assignment reporting and needed a regular beat to flourish. But it soon became obvious that he was a strong reporter — first in Nassau County, then in Albany and Washington. Bill Moyers took note of those skills and sent him a handwritten letter to dissuade him from leaving to work in the Senate campaign of Philip Hoff, the Kennedyesque Democratic governor of Vermont who had occasionally had drinks with Marro at a bar in Montpelier. Bob Greene saw his talent and kept requesting him for assignments. Marro had already won one Pulitzer with Greene, in 1970, and now Greene wanted him on the heroin trail team, which might well win another.

Even though Marro acknowledged that Greene, along with Wild and Maerki, taught him to be a reporter, he was not anxious to work on another Greene project. So, as he rode north on the Metroliner for his meeting with Laventhol, Marro wrote on a yellow pad all the reasons why he should not be pulled away from Watergate. But when he got to Laventhol's office and saw a huge photo of Greene, Royce and Payne in the fields of Turkey, his heart sank. "I realized it was too late to get out of this one," Marro said. He made his case, but he lost. Laventhol assigned him to create a team that would trace the flow of heroin within the United States.

The team that Marro recruited included Joe Demma, who had started at *Newsday* as a clerk and made himself into a tough, street-smart reporter in Suffolk; Jim Sullivan, a hard-drinking rewrite man who had worked at the *New York Herald Tribune* before *Newsday*, and David Behrens, who wrote about youth issues for Part II and had just done an 8,000-word piece about the death of a heroin addict. Behrens was to track down addicts and ex-addicts; Demma was to work with police agencies on LI; Sullivan was to concentrate on New York City, and Marro was to work on federal agencies. The goal was to follow a shipment from Turkey all the way into the arm of an addict, but it quickly became obvious to Marro that they wouldn't be able to trace any shipment that completely. They decided instead to begin with a few high-visibility heroin cases in the United States and trace them toward Europe. "I got a chain of heroin that went back to Marseilles," Marro said.

To provide more detail on the dealers, Greene asked Tom Renner to infiltrate a drug ring. "I said it was an insane idea," Renner said, "because reporters don't infiltrate drug rings in this country and not get hurt." But the domestic team did have its share of scary moments, such as Demma's wild ride through the Bronx with a former Suffolk County heroin dealer. On the ride, he announced that he had a pistol, and kept asking Demma: " 'Does Greene know where you are?' " Before the informant would show him the drug location that he had promised, he directed Demma to a bombed-out apartment house and demanded that Demma go in with him. Demma refused. Then the informant demanded that Demma pay him the money that *Newsday* had promised him for acting as a tour guide. To buttress his argument, he pulled out his pistol. "I started to pass out," Demma said. Finally, the informant's teenaged stepson, who had come along for the ride, persuaded him to calm down. They found the drug site and headed back to Long Island.

In his search for addicts, Behrens also got himself into a troublesome situation. A Nassau County addict told Behrens his story and agreed to meet Behrens at a motel, so that the *Newsday* photographer Mitch Turner could photograph him shooting up. Behrens persuaded him that they needed to take a bag of his heroin back to *Newsday* for chemical analysis, so they could be sure that it was really heroin that he had used in the photographs. With the bag in his hand, Behrens was both elated and wary. "I drove as slowly as I could back to the office," he said. "The last thing I wanted in the world was to be stopped for anything and then to explain, how did I get this heroin." When he got to the office, he told Laventhol about the heroin and left the bag behind for safekeeping. The following morning, he found out that Laventhol had become jittery about possessing a bag of heroin and flushed it down a toilet. "We were furious," Behrens said. Marro wasn't always happy with Laventhol during the project either. "At one point," Marro said, "I got in a big argument with Laventhol and told him he had no business running a major American newspaper."

Behrens encountered a different kind of frustration in his interviews with drug counselors. "They were actually somewhat upset about our preoccupation with heroin, because they felt that we had missed the boat," Behrens said. The problem on Long Island, they said, was not so much heroin addiction as the abuse of multiple drugs, such as amphetamines and barbiturates. The series did take account of that phenomenon in passing, but *Newsday* remained convinced that heroin, with all the crime and misery that it generated, was the sexy part of the drug story. Similarly, Behrens came upon another troublesome fact that didn't fit *Newsday*'s needs. Laventhol had decided to run a small profile of one heroin overdose victim each day. Since the series ended up running for thirty-two days, that was a tall order. The list that Behrens developed from the medical examiner's files included about fifty overdose deaths in the previous year, but only about half of them were from heroin. Luckily for *Newsday*, the medical examiner listed methadone deaths in a "heroine-related" category, which enabled the paper to use them. Together with the reporter Tony Schaeffer, Behrens wrote the daily profiles of heroin victims, which became a source of pain and embarrassment to the survivors.

At the end of trail, *Newsday* named American names, including Ralph Eboli, the brother of a deceased organized crime leader. During a conversation with Demma, complaining that he should not have been on the list of dealers, Eboli blurted out that he had accepted $5,000 from a federal narcotics agent to buy drugs, then took a vacation in Puerto Rico instead of delivering the goods. Demma wrote about that admission, and a few days later, Eboli found himself under indictment, on the strength of Demma's story about his Puerto Rico vacation. That made Eboli perhaps the only person indicted in the aftermath of the series. (Eboli later paid a $1,000 fine, which left him $4,000 ahead.)

Just as naming names of dealers in the domestic part of the series caused repercussions, some on the team felt that it was inappropriate to name the foreign dealers without giving them a full chance to respond. "We didn't confront these people," Marro said. "It's a basic philosophical issue." Another issue was the confidentiality of sources. Royce had dealt closely with the two Syrian smugglers, and he was outraged when *Newsday* used their real first names and ran their photos with only a strip of black obscuring parts of their faces. Royce said that he argued with Greene and Forst, but he lost. Given issues such as those, plus the complexity of the reporting, it was inevitable that the final writing and editing would be difficult.

First, they had to decide on a writing style. "It was really a book," Laventhol said. "It had to be written like a book." So, while the team was still in France, Laventhol told them that they should write it in the style of the novelist John Dos Passos. "I said, 'Fine. All right, we'll think about that,' " Greene said. "I put down the phone and I turned around to Les and said, 'Who the fuck is John Dos Passos?' " In Paris, they found the *U.S.A.* trilogy and examined the imaginative narrative devices that Dos Passos had developed. "It's a mixture of a report of what you found, and then interpolating into it your own personal action, like putting the reporters into the story," Greene said. Back in America, the team warmed to the Dos Passos style. "Don loved it; Dave thought it was great," Greene said. "It went to Attwood, and from what I understand, Attwood says, 'What's this Dos Passos crap? I want a report.' " Still, the final version did contain touches of what happened to the reporters, such as a low-key account of the chase in Corsica and a full rendering of Greene's disguise as a lawyer.

Once the writing was finished, the editors struggled to trim the series. Still, the final version ran to thirty-two parts. "If you can't tell any story in less than ten installments," Attwood said, "you're just overwriting." The verdict of *Newsweek* was similar: "The series can be faulted only for being perhaps *too* responsible; it is weighty, unsensational and so thorough that it can be heavy reading in spots." The series was so long, in fact, that it later had to be edited *down* to fit into a book. It was the book, not the series itself, that led to a libel lawsuit by one of the men named as a Turkish heroin dealer. At the end of a difficult trial, a jury brought back a verdict that exonerated *Newsday*.

V

JUST AS ED Hershey was getting into the rhythm of his new assignment, covering New York City for *Newsday*'s suburban audience, Forst called and asked him to put the new job aside and seek governmental reaction to the heroin series.

Early in this process, Hershey sat down in his hotel room in Washington one night and read a book called *The Politics of Heroin in Southeast Asia*, by a Yale graduate student, Alfred McCoy. The book was about the heroin trade in the golden triangle, the mountainous region where the borders of Thailand, Burma and Laos met, but it had a section about the Turkey-Marseilles connection. To Hershey's surprise, not only did the book contain information about Marcel Francisci, SDECE and other important elements of the *Newsday* series, but it called the Turkey connection obsolescent. "During the 1960s local arrests, internal warfare, and international law enforcement activity progressively weakened the Turkey-Italy-Marseilles narcotics axis," the book said. Hershey saw that the book had been published in 1972, before the series ran. "I'm reading this thing, and I'm going to pieces," he said. "Greene and Royce and Payne had just spent all this time and money . . . and this guy McCoy is telling you how now it's *passe*."

In this agitated state, Hershey called Marro, who had given him the McCoy book, and told him what he had just read. Marro told Hershey that he had known about the problem all along. Immediately after Laventhol asked him to work on the project, Marro had shown his awareness of the shift from Turkey to Southeast Asia — in a memo to Sackett, then in his last months as Washington bureau chief. "If he can't prove that the illegal flow will continue," Marro wrote, "whatever series Newsday runs will be dated and someone will begin asking why Greene went to Turkey instead of to Asia." One answer is that reporters go to their strengths, and Greene's strength was organized crime, which dominated heroin traffic in Turkey, but not in Asia. Greene's own answer is that Turkey was where the heroin was originating. "Every major authority we had in the United States government — and the United Nations and everybody else — was telling us that the major route was Turkey out," Greene said. The comparative importance of the heroin trade from the two areas was certainly a public issue, however, before and during Greene's time in Europe.

All summer long, starting a few weeks after Greene arrived in Turkey, the newspapers and television had focused on a debate about the Southeast Asia drug trade. The cause of the debate was McCoy's assertion that the CIA was guilty of complicity in the heroin traffic in Southeast Asia. McCoy had begun looking into Asian heroin traffic during a break from his doctoral studies on Southeast Asian history at Yale, when he visited Paris and talked to political exiles from Vietnam and Laos and to French officials who had served in that region. What he learned in Paris was enough to persuade Harper & Row to finance a trip to Southeast Asia. In all, he conducted more than 250 interviews, surviving a barrage of mortar and automatic rifle fire along the way. The result of his reporting was the book that Harper & Row planned to publish in August, 1972. An excerpt from the book appeared in *Harper's* in July. But even before that, McCoy made headlines with his testimony about the heroin trade before congressional committees.

On June 2, just before Greene left for Turkey, McCoy appeared before a Senate subcommittee, accused the CIA of complicity in the heroin dealings of

American allies in the region, and gave them his assessment of the heroin flow — starkly different from Greene's view: "Southeast Asia is fast becoming the major supplier of illicit narcotics for America's growing population of heroin addicts," he testified. "The drugs now flowing from Southeast Asia in effect make all the funds and effort expended reducing Turkey's opium production totally irrelevant as a final solution to our problem." A week later, McCoy told another congressional committee: "Even at its peak in 1967-1968 Turkey produced an estimated 100 tons of illicit opium, equivalent to only 5% to 7% of the world's total illicit supply." By contrast, McCoy said, the golden triangle produced 1,000 tons of raw opium a year. "This is equal to more than 70% of the world's illicit opium supply."

Soon afterward, the CIA asked Harper & Row for a chance to review McCoy's manuscript before publication — a struggle that appeared on the front page of the *New York Times* and in television interviews. Over McCoy's objections, the publisher let the CIA see the manuscript and submit a critique, but then Harper & Row went ahead with publication. When the book appeared, the *Times* reviewed it twice, once on a weekday and once on the cover of its Sunday book review section. Despite the high visibility of this controversy, no one from Greene's team called McCoy. "I never got a whisper from them," he said.

Greene's team did no reporting on accusations about CIA complicity in the Asian drug trade, but it went to great lengths to show that the French equivalent of the CIA had dirty hands in the European traffic. "In Europe, the CIA was in no way connected with the drug dealers," Bill Attwood said. "So they wished us Godspeed." Not only did they wish *Newsday* luck and provide advice in Europe, but at the end of the series, the CIA asked a favor in return. Bronson Tweedy, a CIA official who knew Attwood from Princeton, came in and asked him to delay publication so that the series would not affect the forthcoming French elections. Attwood refused to delay the series, and it began on February 1, 1973.

The payoff at the end of the long, expensive trail was the 1974 Pulitzer Prize for meritorious public service — one of two Pulitzers that *Newsday* won that year. The second went to Emily Genauer for her art criticism. There were some at *Newsday*, however, including the national editor, Ernie Volkman, who felt that the focus of the series was skewed. "It was off the point, off the mark," Volkman said. "But it had the desired effect. It won the new *Newsday* a Pulitzer Prize." McCoy himself felt that the team could have done a better job by reporting on the growing importance of the Southeast Asia routes and the CIA's role, but he also found that the reporting that the team did under difficult circumstances was excellent in many ways. "I admired the quality of the Newsday reporting about the Turkey-Marseilles connection and feel that their Pulitzer Prize was richly deserved," McCoy said. "If I were being brutally honest, I would be forced to admit that I was a bit jealous about the Pulitzer award going to Newsday for its reporting. I took far greater risks, reported a more difficult story and came up with extremely controversial findings that stood the test of very close scrutiny. . . . By reporting the Turkey-Marseilles route, Newsday picked a more conventional drug story and avoided taking on any of the volatile political issues that I faced in my work."

Just a month after the Pulitzer, one of the key members of the team jolted *Newsday* by deciding to leave the paper. In Marro's work in the Washington bureau, he found the bureau chief, Martin Schram, too stifling. "He wanted everybody to think like him, to report like him, to write like him," Marro said. "Without meaning to, he'd beat you into the ground. . . . Some of it, too, was having stayed too long at the fair. It was time to move on." So Marro left to cover Watergate for *Newsweek* — a powerful dose of bad news for *Newsday*, on the heels of the Pulitzer euphoria. "I thought at the time that the loss of Tony Marro was on the scale of the loss of Al Marlens," Tony Insolia said. "His growth potential was immense."

Despite the departure of Marro, and despite any criticism of the series, 1974 was a benchmark year for *Newsday*. The Pulitzer greatly enhanced *Newsday*'s reputation as a newspaper that was willing to spend unlimited resources on important projects — a level of resources that even the *New York Times* and the *Los Angeles Times* did not regularly commit to a story. The series was far from perfect, but it did help to show that the Times Mirror version of *Newsday*, in addition to generating increasing profits, could also produce high-profile journalism.

CHAPTER THIRTY-FOUR

The Seventh Day

I

IT TOOK ONLY two years for *Newsday* to expand from five days of publication to six. Then, for almost three decades, Harry Guggenheim resisted the next step.

"A Sunday edition would be very costly and probably would not successfully compete with the New York Sunday newspapers, and so could be a disaster," Harry wrote Alicia in 1956. Besides, Ernie Levy warned Harry that a Sunday paper would drain advertising away from the daily paper. In contrast, Otis Chandler knew that *Newsday* would be far more profitable if it had a Sunday edition. The country itself was changing in ways that made a Sunday paper more essential, such as the gradual erosion of the "blue laws," which had strictly limited Sunday sales. That erosion led to the rise of Sunday shopping and a greater demand for Sunday advertising. There were also changes in reading habits. "Younger people were not buying papers seven days a week, and lower-income group people weren't," Bill Attwood said. "So you had a growing group of Sunday-only readers."

As a result, Attwood made Sunday a top priority, appointing a committee headed by Stan Asimov to study such questions as how much circulation a Sunday edition could expect. Times Mirror, which was anxious to launch the seventh day and reap the profits, predicted rosily that the Sunday paper would start out with the same circulation as the daily, about 450,000. But the circulation department said that it would sell about 225,000 copies initially. The advertising department was also pessimistic. "Dave Targe came up with a linage projection," Attwood said. "When we cranked it into the equation, the paper wouldn't be profitable for two years. So I said, 'We want to start this paper, Dave. See if you can restudy those figures.' So he came up with a whole new set of figures, which turned out to be very accurate.' "

Another important issue was how to sell it to readers. One approach was a "forced buy," which meant that all subscribers would have to accept the Sunday paper. "In California, the style was forced," said Vinnie Bordash, the circulation director. In the more competitive Long Island market, he felt that such an ultimatum was dangerous. Over the years, *Newsday* had angered large groups of readers with one story or another, and Bordash knew that a take-us-or-leave-us attitude would prompt many of them to stop subscribing. Targe agreed with him, and Chandler understood. So they decided to make the new Sunday paper optional.

A few months after Attwood arrived, on May 26, 1971, Chandler gave him a final go-ahead to launch the Sunday paper. Two weeks later, Laventhol produced a detailed plan for it, predicting an increased cost of $955,000 in the editorial department in 1972, to hire forty-six new employees, and proposing some interesting concepts, such as a broadsheet section that would contain sports, a money section and classified advertising, all wrapped within the tabloid main section. It also provided for a freestanding TV listings book, half the size of a tabloid page, and a full-color rotogravure magazine. To develop the prototypes for the Sunday paper, he appointed Lou Schwartz as his primary agent, with the artist Paul Back as the designer.

With the creation of a rotogravure magazine, the first casualty of the Sunday paper would be the black-and-white Saturday magazine section. Since the new magazine would have a much longer lead time between the conception of an idea and its appearance in print, it was essential to get it started early. So Attwood chose the editor quickly: Clive Irving, a successful British magazine editor recommended by Harold Evans of *The Sunday Times* of London. Stan Green, who had run the copy desk and later worked on the Saturday magazine, became the new magazine's managing editor. The first crucial choice they made was to limit it to Long Island subjects. So Schwartz proposed that they name it *LI*. They also decided early to make the comic section a broadsheet rather than a tabloid, so it could serve as a wrapper for the rest of the paper. But choosing the shape of the section was far easier than getting the comics, because other papers had the best comics locked up. So they came up with the idea of running a page of more easily available older comics and selling it to readers as nostalgia. In addition to the old cartoons, the Sunday edition of *Newsday* would help to break some new ground in the New York metropolitan area by offering an emerging cartoon called *Doonesbury*, which had already started in the daily paper in 1971.

No matter what the new paper looked like, it would not succeed unless they could sell the *idea* of a Sunday paper. "We'd spent thirty years teaching Long Islanders they didn't need a Sunday newspaper," said Bill Sexton, who helped Laventhol to shepherd the Sunday project. "So we sat down and we did an analysis of what there was in *Newsday* which was a part of people's daily life — even if they couldn't stand the editorial page or the news stories — and did a series of eight or ten ads, each of which focused on one thing that *Newsday* does for people." This "Newsday at Your Service" campaign evolved into "Newsday at Your Service Every Day" and a promotion mantra: The Seventh Day of *Newsday.*

The decision to include a separate TV book turned out to be a significant part of the Sunday paper's appeal. "I think if the *News* put out a TV book, they would have somewhat slowed down our growth," Targe said. As the startup date approached, the *News* did hire a new editor for its magazine, upgrade some features and add some other staff. But one *News* editor said bravely: "We have had a Long Island edition for 25 years, and we don't believe the loyalty will change." Besides, the *News* could not afford to do much to meet the *Newsday* threat. "It is true that *Newsday* did a lot of things when they went Sunday, which perhaps the *News* should have sought to match or better," said W. H. "Tex" James, who became the publisher of the *News* a few months after the *Newsday* Sunday paper began. "The newspapers in New York had made such onerous deals with unions over the years that our costs for doing anything were considerably more costly than those for *Newsday* or the *Newark Star-Ledger* or the Westchester-Rockland papers, for example." The *Times* reacted to the forthcoming Sunday *Newsday* by inaugurating a new freestanding Brooklyn, Queens, Long Island (BQLI) section on Sunday, September 12, 1971.

Besides provoking reaction outside *Newsday*, the Sunday paper ignited labor friction inside, with Local 406, International Printing Pressmen and Assistants Union, which had represented the pressmen for years and had recently organized the drivers. The dispute focused on whether the union members should be paid double time for working on the Sunday paper or get straight time, plus a five-dollar bonus, as newer sections of the contracts provided. At the end of March, the president of Local 406, George Tedeschi, notified management that his men would not work on Saturday night, April 8, to print the Sunday paper. Just in case it became necessary, Targe asked a group of advertising salesmen to volunteer to learn how to run the presses, and they went to Pennsylvania for training. "We were laughing about it," said Al Gaeta, one volunteer. "We said, 'My God, we have no aptitude.' " They didn't need any. *Newsday*'s lawyer, Andrew Hughes, and its labor negotiator, Dan Mannix, got a court injunction and served it on Tedeschi at his home. The union complied and later lost the pay issue at arbitration.

The initial press run was nearly 483,000 copies. The newsstand price was twenty-five cents, but for the first three weeks, they gave the Sunday paper away free to to all home delivery customers. The fourth week, they delivered the paper and sent the carriers to collect the money. "Now it was up to them to say, 'I never ordered the paper,' " Targe said. "And a lot of people did. For the next few weeks, each week we used to meet here on Saturday night at twelve o'clock when the figures came in. Each week, those figures went down. They kept falling week after week, until it stabilized." By the end of May, the slide had stopped and circulation leveled off at 340,000.

It took five years for the Sunday circulation to pass the daily and reach

500,000 — an event that provided the excuse for a massive party at the huge
Colonie Hill catering hall. Selling the Sunday paper to major advertisers took
even longer, because they were satisfied with their existing ads in the Sunday
News, *Times* and *Long Island Press*. "We didn't really have a successful product
until the 1978 city newspaper strike," said Carey Gates, one of the paper's
salesmen during the Sunday paper's first few years. During the strike, major
advertisers *did* need *Newsday*. When the strike ended, the paper retained much
of the additional linage that it had gained.

The launch of Sunday *Newsday* brought a number of personnel shifts, such
as the departure of the magazine editor, Clive Irving, right after the first issue.
"What was wrong with the magazine under Clive was that it was a little too
British, a little too sophisticated," Schwartz said. Perhaps the most significant
change was the movement of Dick Estrin, the brilliant and widely feared ruler
of *Newsday* by night, from the news desk to the Sunday paper. The new paper
had also created an opening for a Sunday books editor, and Laventhol gave that
job to Leslie Hanscom, whose graceful writing had started the Long Island
Diary feature so successfully two years earlier. To replace him, Laventhol hired
John Pascal, formerly of the *Herald Tribune* and the *New York Times* and more
recently a coauthor of the musical, "George M." The Sunday paper also brought
in dozens of other reporters and editors who played an important part in
Newsday's success in the '70s and '80s.

Beyond personnel changes, the Sunday paper provided an immediate increase in the "news hole," which meant room for more stories. It also stimulated technological innovation. On the presses, Pete Falagario, who had helped to
perfect the device that enabled *Newsday* to put thumbholes in the daily paper
to separate its sections, developed a "skip-slitter" cutting arrangement that
allowed the tabloid presses to turn out a broadsheet sports section. In the
collating area, Walter Enderley devised a makeshift system to put a dab of glue
on the TV book and prevent it from falling out of the color package.

The most important effect of the seventh day, of course, was its impact on
profits and on the competition. The *Daily News* suffered significantly. Its
average net paid Sunday circulation in Nassau and Suffolk for 1972 was 367,642.
At the start of the new decade in 1980, that average was down to 226,781. The
Sunday *Times* did not suffer nearly as much on Long Island, declining from
155,004 in 1972 to 141,396 in 1980.

Not content with the growth that the Sunday paper brought, Attwood and
Times Mirror looked for other ways to increase both circulation and advertising.
One immediate change was the acceptance of preprinted advertising brochures
that *Newsday* would deliver to readers with the newspaper. Just as Ernie Levy
had opposed a Sunday paper because it might drain ads from the other six days,
he detested preprints because he feared that advertisers would use those and
cut back on ads in the newspaper itself. In the years before the Sunday paper
started, as the use of preprints by advertisers was soaring everywhere, Levy held
fast. But Times Mirror changed that policy, realizing that advertisers loved
preprints. The brochures, often printed on high-quality glossy paper, offered

more flexibility than the newspaper did, and they had a longer shelf life. "It gives that advertiser the feeling of its own mini-newspaper," said Tom Taylor, who took over the new preprint section in 1973. Initially, *Newsday* could only deliver preprints to its entire readership. Later, the paper developed the capacity to deliver to Nassau only or Suffolk only, and eventually, to deliver to smaller and smaller zones. In time, as Levy had predicted, the revenue from preprints grew at the expense of advertising in the paper itself. "He was right," Targe said. "There has been a tremendous shift."

Accepting preprints was not Times Mirror's only reversal of longtime *Newsday* policy. At about the same time, *Newsday* also started trying to sell more papers at newsstands. For three decades, *Newsday* had believed that the best way to sell newspapers was through home delivery. Home delivery subscribers have to go to some trouble to cancel the paper, but those who get their paper at a newsstand can cancel it for that day simply by not stopping to buy it. Bordash hated the idea of making it that easy. Besides, advertisers considered home delivery a more reliable way of spreading their message. As a result, eighty-five percent or more of each day's paper went to home delivery. *Newsday* didn't even deliver to newsstands until after lunchtime, which guaranteed poor street sales, and there wasn't even a pretense of trying to curry favor with newsstands. Richard Czark, who became the assistant single-copy manager early in the '70s, remembered asking Bordash for money to buy *Newsday* aprons for street vendors, and Bordash told him to get the old ones washed instead.

The resistance to single-copy sales finally fell because Attwood wanted more profits and because readers wanted their papers earlier. More and more women were going to work, which meant that in many cases, no one was at home to receive the paper late in the afternoon. So, in January, 1972, *Newsday* made the press start two hours earlier, which made it possible to produce an early edition of the paper to reach commuters going to work. In addition, Bordash appointed a home delivery supervisor, Chic Lawrence, to run an expanded single-copy sales effort, with Czark as his assistant. It wasn't an easy job. "We had a terrible reputation with newsstands," Czark said. "You had to go out and apologize." Besides, there was still skepticism inside *Newsday*. "You felt sometimes with the single-copy department against home delivery like there was a battle going on," Lawrence said. But in 1972 and 1973, *Newsday* at least began making a real commitment to selling more papers in the morning at newsstands.

Besides growing by taking advantage of new time periods, *Newsday* also began to examine growth through expansion into new territories. One early study looked at the possibility of a Queens paper, but Attwood rejected it. Attwood also explored the feasibility of starting a new edition of the paper in Fairfield County, Connecticut, a suburban county north of New York City. But in 1977, Times Mirror bought the existing dailies in Stamford and Greenwich, which ended *Newsday*'s flirtation with the area. Even without geographical expansion, however, the period after the start of the Sunday paper was a time of energy, growth and maturing. In 1974, *Time* magazine confirmed that coming of age, including *Newsday* on its list of America's ten best newspapers. "Times Mirror came along at just the right time in *Newsday*'s development," Laventhol said, "because it was time to grow up." But with the growth came a time of pain and confrontation.

II

TWO YEARS AFTER they had soundly rejected the Newspaper Guild in a representation election, *Newsday* editorial employees began to look around for another union.

The Guild had lost because most of the staff distrusted it, and because Attwood and Laventhol had cleverly argued that the new owners should have time to prove themselves. "We gave them a chance," said Brad O'Hearn, one of the prime organizers. "There was a growing consensus that the company had not kept its promises." Besides the discontent among long-term employees, there was a whole new core of staff who came in with the Sunday paper. "Now we had a large number of people who did not have a *Newsday* heritage," Asimov said. "A short-term person says, 'What have I got to lose?' "

One overriding concern was the salary inequity that still existed, because *Newsday* had had no formal salary structure for years. By 1973, the company had at least started to develop a system of pay ranges, but employees didn't know about it. "The problem was, we were very secretive," said Ken Brief, who became Laventhol's assistant in 1972 and represented him on union matters. "You couldn't tell people, 'Yes, we have these pay ranges, and here's what they are. . . .' There was a general reluctance on the part of management here to share with employees the intricacies and inner workings of salaries."

Another major factor was distrust of Times Mirror. Some felt, for example, that the new, more profit-oriented *Newsday* was becoming too concerned about the feelings of advertisers. One incident involved pressure on Jerry Morgan, who had started writing a real estate column the day before the Sunday paper began. "My opinion of a column was facts with some comment on them," Morgan said. His approach was to examine accepted real estate practices critically, such as the one percent fee that lawyers got at closings. But Laventhol and Attwood thought there was too much comment in the columns. "Opinion on the real estate business wasn't really what we were looking for," said Laventhol, who let the column go for a time and liked it less and less. Late in 1972, Morgan went to lunch with Laventhol, Lou Schwartz, and his editor, Roy Hanson. "Laventhol said, 'The column we wanted you to write was who's opening what developments,' " Morgan said. "I said, 'That's what advertising pages are for.' " After the lunch, Morgan no longer wrote a pure column, but a news analysis — without heavy doses of his opinions. A second incident that added to the mood of distrust was a large photo spread in the news pages about the opening of a

Bloomingdale's store on Long Island. The editors argued that the opening of such a major store was a legitimate news story, but the play of the story was a source of concern. "Most people thought it was extremely bush," Morgan said. "There was a feeling of creeping commercialism." Finally, Laventhol met with the staff to hear these concerns. In the middle of this, some participants remembered, Laventhol moved out from behind his desk and sat among the reporters, a small symbolic act that helped ease the tension. "The man is a genius politically," Morgan said. "We had a hearing. We had a very long, unprecedented hearing." That soothed feelings, but suspicion of Times Mirror continued.

All the suspicion and unrest became action when the reporter Ed Hershey returned from his temporary assignment writing follow-up stories after the heroin trail series. During that period, one of his editors had forced him to write a lead that focused on a minor element of the story. That, along with other issues, put Hershey in a sour mood. So he began asking people about potential unions and placed a call to George Tedeschi at Local 406, who had dinner with him at a steak house. "I told him I was willing to talk to other people in the editorial unit," Tedeschi said. "I told him I wanted this done on a secretive basis." But Hershey destroyed the secrecy by putting a note on the bulletin board, announcing a meeting at a public library. That infuriated Tedeschi, who grabbed him, pushed him up against a wall, and demanded: "What the hell are you doing?"

Despite that confrontation, the union drive got off to a relatively smooth start. The meeting at the Plainview library drew about sixty people, and soon after that, Local 406 developed a sufficient show of interest to support a petition to the National Labor Relations Board for a representation election. "First of all, this was not the Guild," said Bruce Lambert, who had been a Guild president in Rochester before coming to *Newsday*. "It was a local union, already at *Newsday*. So it wasn't New York City. It was a union that had never had a strike, that had a low dues schedule." Though Local 406 had never struck *Newsday*, the editorial workers knew that a union that represented reporters, pressmen and truck drivers *could* close the paper down, if necessary. The question was whether blue-collar workers would stand solidly behind white-collar members. "That was certainly one of management's arguments: 'What do you have in common with them? You're better than that,' " O'Hearn said.

The stakes were high for *Newsday* management. No one had to remind them that beating back the union would make them look good in Los Angeles. Beyond that, some editors took the union drive almost as a personal affront, wondering why employees didn't trust them. That was true of Tony Insolia, although he had started out his career with an act of insurrection against management, resigning from the *Yonkers Times* in protest over the firing of a colleague. "I worked for places that a labor union would have helped us, but they were always so small that the Guild would never get involved," Insolia said. "Since they were never willing to be there when I needed them in the places I worked, when I came to *Newsday*, I always felt that at this newspaper, you don't need a union."

Once the campaign began, the company went at it with enthusiasm, but not always with skill. "We did some things that were wrong, in that we relied on the judgment of a couple of managers who were out of touch with their departments," Asimov said. "The company's perception was very, very far off." On the night of the vote, September 7, 1973, the managers gathered for the counting of the ballots, and a photograph clearly showed the intensity in their faces. The tally was 149 votes for Local 406, 138 against. Another fourteen employees cast ballots, but the union asked the NLRB to review them, on the grounds that they were supervisors or had access to confidential correspondence on labor policy. If all fourteen turned out to be votes against the union, it could lose the election. Nearly six months later, after the union had dropped its challenge to six of the ballots, the NLRB counted them, and all six went against the union, leaving Local 406 with a slim 149 to 144 lead. The NLRB held a series of hearings on the remaining eight challenged ballots and upheld the union's position on seven of the eight. Finally, on January 29, 1975, more than sixteen months after the vote, *Newsday* notified the NLRB that it would not challenge the hearing examiner's findings. Two days later, the NLRB certified Local 406 as the bargaining agent for editorial employees.

Often, after a long lag between the representation election and certification, unions lose momentum. In this case, despite the loss of dozens of employees through normal attrition, Local 406 signed up a significant number of members. For one thing, the company froze salaries, until negotiations could take place. "That was a big strategic error, because it seemed punitive," Lambert said. "What I said to people was, 'The only way you're going to get a raise is through the union.' " The list of salaries, which showed the discrepancies, also helped. When Lambert showed it to the artist Gary Viskupic, for example, he decided on the spot to join the union.

The contract talks began in May and dragged on for months, while Local 406 was busy trying to organize the circulation department. "It would not have been advantageous for us to come up with a settlement in negotiation with the editorial department that would have enhanced the union's position in trying to organize," said Dan Mannix, the labor relations expert who came to *Newsday* in 1971 and ran the negotiations for the company, along with Insolia, Ken Brief and Sylvan Fox, the Nassau editor. Another problem was the company's demand that the union give up the unlimited sick pay that editorial workers had enjoyed and accept the kind of limits that existed for others at the paper. "For the most part, it was good-natured," Lambert said. "But there were times when Tony, in particular, would get outraged." At those times, Mannix would act as a calming force, just as Tedeschi had to calm Hershey or other union negotiators. "Mannix was a true professional," Tedeschi said. Finally, on September 28, 1975, the union took a vote and agreed to support a strike if necessary. "The strike vote was a standard, to-be-expected ploy," Insolia said. "The union clearly had no stomach for striking." Insolia insisted that the vote had no real effect on management's position, but within days after the vote, the two sides agreed on a thirty-month contract, which the union ratified on October 5. It raised salaries and codified the existing practice, but it restricted sick leave for new employees. "That was the price of the contract," Lambert said.

Some members were dissatisfied, but they ratified the contract by a large margin. The union had won what it wanted: a first contract, something to build on. The company had won a victory on sick pay and held the cost of the contract below budget. Attwood and Laventhol had lost the battle to keep the union out, but they didn't lose their jobs. "The most amazing thing is that Times Mirror didn't hold it against anybody," Brief said. "If it was a Gannett company, you would have seen the publisher and editor change instantly."

III

AT THE SAME time that *Newsday* managers had to accept a union in the newsroom, they had to swallow another painful reality: Inspired by the rising tide of feminism in America, women at *Newsday* were accusing the all-male management of discrimination.

Ironically, it was an enlightened 1971 *Newsday* editorial, calling on the federal government to hire more women, that prompted one of the first overt acts. The editorial caught the eye of Annabelle Kerins, a reporter in the Suffolk office. "I wrote a note to Dave Laventhol, saying: 'Dear Mr. Laventhol, I am confused. I read the editorial: Government should hire women. Then I read the masthead. Why is it the only woman on the masthead has been dead a good number of years?' " Kerins said. "I got a photocopy of it back with a note that said, 'You're absolutely right.' " The only woman on the masthead was Alicia Patterson. In fact, in the post-Alicia era, even the position of editor of the women's pages had gone to men, Lou Schwartz and Stu Troup.

A few months after her memo to Laventhol, Kerins began reaching out to other women. They met at the Manhattan apartment of an attorney named Harriet Rabb, an expert on employment discrimination, and in July, 1972, they met with the management, including Attwood, Laventhol, Insolia, and the attorney Andrew Hughes. In advance, the women decided that they would remain silent and let Rabb speak for them. "They couldn't get over the fact that we weren't talking to them," Kerins said. "I would write down what they said, and Laventhol would lean over my shoulder and go, 'She's writing down what I said! She's writing down what I said! She's writing down what I said!' He went crazy. All of them did. Insolia said: 'You, Annabelle, tell me one instance of discrimination. You, Marilyn, I defy you to tell me one instance of discrimination. . . .' We left saying we would develop information for them."

The job of gathering evidence fell to Kerins, who spent weekends and vacation days in the library, looking for patterns of discrimination in the assignment of women reporters. "She was a real terrier about finding things out," said Rebecca Klock, one of the leaders of the movement. The resulting report argued that stories written by men appeared in the paper more prominently than those written by women, and men drew travel assignments more often. Kerins showed it to her boss, Mel Opotowsky. "He looked at the byline statistics and he looked at me and said, 'Where's their production?' " Kerins said. "I said, 'Oh, my God.' " She had left out a key variable: the number of stories the men had *produced*, compared to the women. So she had to spend additional time digging for that information in the daily news budgets. In the end, she produced a 117-page report called "A Brief in Support of 14 Points."

Beyond assignment statistics, the women also needed to know the salaries of men. "We simply asked each and every man we could, and almost without exception, they gave us what their salary history was," Kerins said. Once Kerins had transferred to the copy desk, she and Geraldine Shanahan used the early morning hours to find information another way, by looking through open files, as they had seen men doing. "One night we came in and the file was locked, so I looked in the file next to it, and lo and behold, there were all the keys to everything," Kerins said. "I decided we really needed a key in case they locked this file." So she borrowed a duplicate key and had copies made. Eventually, management discovered and stopped these raids, but by then, Kerins and Shanahan had photocopied dozens of memos about salaries.

In the summer of 1973, Rabb dropped out of the case and the women retained an all-female law firm, Bellamy Blank Goodman Kelly Ross & Stanley. Attwood tried to deal with the demands of the women through the newly established affirmative action committee, but that effort failed. Finally, in December, 1973, the women filed a formal complaint with the federal Equal Employment Opportunity Commission, the first step on the way to a federal lawsuit. On January 13, 1975, the women filed a class-action lawsuit that became known as *Carter* v. *Newsday*. The four named plaintiffs were the reporters Sylvia Carter and Marilyn Goldstein, the telephone operator Jane McNamara and Marian Leifsen, a journalist for a New York City weekly, who had applied to *Newsday*, but had not been hired.

The complaint was filled with dry statistics, but it also contained a small, peripheral allegation that the women knew would catch the attention of the media. In a six-month evaluation of Kerins at the end of 1970, her supervisor, Richard Sandler, had written: "Annabelle Kerins is an A all around. Works hard, understands what she is doing, has a nice writing touch and nice legs." (In the same memo, Sandler said of a male reporter: "I don't know about his legs.") Opotowsky recommended to Laventhol that she be kept on staff and he also mentioned her legs. The women read Laventhol's scrawled comment on the memo and decided that he had said: "Let's look." The company insisted that Laventhol said: "Let's talk." The legs memo was hardly a central issue, but it did provide a colorful anecdote to humanize the story.

From the start, there was no chance that the suit would end quickly, because the managers believed that they had done nothing wrong. "God, that annoyed me," Attwood said. "Women were simply not discriminated against at *Newsday*. They just absolutely were not." So both sides settled in for a long struggle. After almost two years, U.S. District Court Judge John R. Bartels decided that the case could proceed as a class action, which forced *Newsday* to react to broad allegations, instead of focusing on individual cases. "The instant he decided it was a class action, we were dead," Asimov said. "This meant we were in for the long haul." The suit was terribly expensive for both sides. Asimov had to spend large amounts of his time gathering statistics. David Hamilton, who became an assistant to Laventhol in 1975, had to put together point-by-point rebuttals. And the legal fees soared. But *Newsday* and Times Mirror had far more resources than the women did. So the women dreamed up a variety of fund-raising schemes. One of them involved cooking for the Local 406 Christmas party, but some felt that this simply reinforced a stereotype of women as cooks. "It did seem to be a bitter irony," Sylvia Carter said. "But at that point we desperately needed $2,000."

As the decade went on, *Newsday* hired more women and gave them more prestigious jobs, but that didn't always create good will. The company reached into the 1974-1975 Nieman Fellowship class at Harvard, for example, and gave good jobs to three women from outside *Newsday*: Dee Wedemeyer, Elaine Shannon and Sheryl Barnett. "We knew exactly why we'd been hired," Barnett said. "And quite rightly, the women who were there felt that we were taking things that they had earned." Nonetheless, the suit did open doors. "I think the women's suit had a lot to do with the fact that I was given opportunities," said Susan Page, who finished at the top of her journalism class at Columbia, came to Newsday in 1974, and went to the Washington bureau a little more than four years later. "I feel to this day that the women who filed the suit paid a price from which I benefitted. I absolutely feel I owe a debt to those women." Similarly, Phyllis Singer attributed the growth of her career as an editor to the suit. "I think they pushed me along extremely rapidly," Singer said. "I think it speeded up the process for all of us."

Eventually, after the two sides had assembled a massive pretrial record, *Newsday* made a motion for partial summary judgment, asking Bartels to decide whether the paper had discriminated in its hiring practices. Bartels ruled in late 1981 that *Newsday*'s hiring had not discriminated against women in the editorial department and dismissed the complaint of one plaintiff, Leifsen. That ruling significantly narrowed the scope of the suit. "The fact that we prevailed in that summary judgment was ultimately pivotal in persuading the plaintiffs, now it's time to get down and work out a reasonable arrangement here," said Mark Jacoby, the attorney who represented *Newsday* in the late stages of the suit. Another incentive to settle was a concern about how well the elderly Judge Bartels could perform in a long trial. And *Newsday* had spent $1 million on the case and didn't want to spend a similar amount on a two- or three-month trial. Finally, in early 1982, *Newsday* and the women agreed to an out-of-court settlement. The company agreed to pay a total of $130,300 to as many as 740 current and former women employees and to follow specified affirmative action goals. Not every woman approved of the terms. "I don't think it was as good a settlement as we provided them the basis for," Kerins said. But the women at least came out of their long, difficult legal struggle with a tangible result.

In the end, the suit took much longer than either side really wanted. "It was a ten-year sore on *Newsday* for no good journalistic purpose," said Amanda Harris, who became active in the women's suit as soon as she came to the paper in 1974. "Nobody wanted blood. Nobody wanted *Newsday* to pay through the nose. All anybody wanted was for women journalists to be treated just like men journalists."

IV

IN THE MIDDLE of all this turbulence, *Newsday* found time to act as the midwife at the birth of a new level of technological sophistication that set a standard for the rest of the industry.

For a long time, the paper had been computer-illiterate. "*Newsday* got its first business computer in 1968," said Dennis O'Leary, who supervised that acquisition. "We were roughly eight years behind the times." But by the early 1970s, it was clear to the editors that the future of journalism lay in computers.

Inevitably, computers would take work away from printers. They had already gone through the introduction of typesetters that generated a punched paper tape, which fed through a device on the Linotype and turned out metal type. The company had retrained the printers to use the standard typewriter keyboard of the new typesetters, and the union had survived that change. But the next step was more threatening: Instead of a printer entering a story into type on a Linotype, reporters would enter stories directly into a computer. The advent of offset printing at *Newsday* would also render the hot-type process obsolete, which would further erode jobs. Unlike New York City locals, which had contractual bars against the use of new technology without the union's permission, Local 915 had no such protection. "We had the freedom to do what we wanted contractually," said Andrew Hughes, *Newsday*'s labor lawyer. "That doesn't mean that you have the freedom to do it practically. . . . You still had to deal with your people and you had to have the people content."

So *Newsday* and the union took a pioneering step in 1974: *Newsday* guaranteed for life the jobs of the printers then working in the composing room — excluding some apprentices and substitutes — and in return got a guarantee of a peaceful introduction of new technology. That would allow *Newsday* to reduce the size of the composing room, as the printers on the guaranteed list retired. "We were the first in the industry to negotiate job security," said Joseph Gagnon, then the chairman of the negotiating committee for Local 915, International Typographical Union. To help the union sell this to their members, the company gave each one a certificate explaining the guarantee and listing by name the printers whose jobs were protected. Still, some printers were concerned that they would end up in non-skilled jobs. But *Newsday*'s growth over the years following the contract provided plenty of demand for printers, and none of them ended up behind a broom, despite the new technology.

The year before the new contract with the printers, *Newsday* had begun exploring that technology. Attwood didn't understand it himself, but he appointed a new technology committee, headed by Jim Grider, the general manager, with the help of Asimov. The editorial department appointees on the committee were Insolia and Ken Brief, the assistant to Laventhol. In the summer of 1973, Brief wrote a detailed, twelve-page memo on "New Technology and the Newsroom," laying out the alternatives. One was a system in which reporters typed stories on electric typewriters, and a device called an Optical Character Reader scanned the stories and converted them to computer impulses. From that point on, editors handled the copy on video display terminals (VDTs). The second would allow reporters to write their stories directly onto VDTs. *Newsday* flirted with the first process, then chose the second.

Examining the alternatives, Brief and Insolia travelled the country, looking at existing computer systems. Perhaps the most advanced was the Hendrix system at the *Detroit News*, but it had its limits. The system allowed editors to edit on computers, but it did not give the newsroom full control over the actual production of type. But *Newsday* had few options, because the big manufacturers, such as Hendrix and Harris, would only sell the off-the-shelf system that they sold to everyone, without modifications. Then a tiny company installed a computer system for a Times Mirror subsidiary, the legal publishing firm of Matthew Bender, and a computer expert at Times Mirror mentioned the company to *Newsday*. The company's name was Atex.

The founding father of Atex was Doug Drane, an engineer who also had developed marketing skills at the Harvard Business School. His first jobs were with the defense contractor, Raytheon, and with a small company called Computech, which developed a pioneering "intelligent terminal" but didn't make any money. He left Computech in 1972 and two months later incorporated Atex. His partners were two brothers, Charles and Richard Ying, computer geniuses born in China. Charles Ying had worked at Hendrix, where he designed the hardware for the *Detroit News* system, and had worked with Drane at Computech. Richard Ying, whose specialty was programming, had worked as a consultant to Hendrix. Together, they wanted to perfect a system for processing newspaper and magazine copy. "We had these ideas about how to make writing easier," Richard Ying said. "To us, it was pretty obvious." Like *Newsday*, Atex started out in a makeshift plant, a $100-a-month room on the second floor of an old country store in East Lexington, Massachusetts. Its first significant contract was a system at *U.S. News & World Report*. Then it installed a small system at the *Beverly Times* in Massachusetts. But it was still an infant company when its top executives came to meet with Asimov, Brief and a technology subcommittee.

"We said, 'We'd like to work with you. We'd like to deliver you an eight-terminal system,' " said Drane, who impressed them with his willingness to invent a system right at Garden City to do what *Newsday* wanted. Asimov asked

Drane if Atex could produce a 240-terminal system. "My mouth dropped," Drane said. "And Charlie launches right into it: 'Sure, and here's the way we'd construct it.' " By the time Atex began working with *Newsday*, they had moved to bigger quarters, a storefront of 2,000 square feet in Burlington, Massachusetts. But it was still tiny. "They gave us a $2 million contract when we were eight people in a storefront," Drane said. "That was pretty courageous."

Together, *Newsday* and Atex set out to allow the ultimate users, editors and reporters, to design the system. Atex worked closely with Insolia, Asimov, Brief and the editors Harry Beery and Howard Halpern. In addition, the editors even brought in a reporter with no technical skill, Sidney Schaer, to look at the system and give advice. These consultations covered the tiniest issues, such as the shape of the keyboard. "The original Atex terminal looked like a Linotype keyboard," Asimov remembered. "We said no." Instead, they pushed for a keyboard just like an IBM typewriter. They didn't want reporters and editors to fumble with a series of commands to execute one function. So the system allowed anyone to accomplish the most important functions by hitting one clearly labelled key. Instead of using computer language to label keys, they used newspaper terms, such as "next story" and "previous story." The result was a system that was better suited to newspaper production than any that had come before. "All these things were invented there," Drane said. "They had not existed before."

The terminals started arriving in the newsroom in early 1975. Reporters and editors were skeptical, but fear quickly turned to acceptance. Artie Schmidt, who arrived at *Newsday* as an employee when Atex was installing the system, remembered one reporter's reaction when Schmidt installed his VDT. The reporter hugged his typewriter protectively and said: "You're not taking my baby." A few weeks later, Schmidt returned to adjust the same reporter's VDT, and the reporter hugged the VDT tightly, as if Schmidt were threatening to take it away.

As part of the original contract proposal, *Newsday* had asked Atex to design a system for processing classified ad orders and billing advertisers. That was a bumpy ride, because Atex wanted to put the new system on line before *Newsday* thought it was ready. "There were lots of fights, lots of screaming," said Fran Curran, the advertising department's representative in the development of the system. "It was a two-way street, because they were learning. They really ended up with an excellent classified system, which they sold to a lot of newspapers."

Newsday, in effect, became a showroom for Atex, which paid *Newsday* a royalty for helping to develop the system. "It was the proving ground for a lot of things, both on the editorial side and the classified ad side," said Jonathan Seybold, whose *Seybold Report* is the bible for users of newspaper computer systems. "It drew everything together and set the standards that everybody followed, from that point on. The *Newsday* installation was seminal."

CHAPTER THIRTY-FIVE

Big Daddy, King of Suffolk

I

AT THE END of the heroin trail, Bob Greene was weary and burned out.

For six years, he and his team had conducted investigations of national and international scope, leading *Newsday* to new levels of prestige. Along the way, he had often alienated his colleagues by demanding of them a commitment of time that left little room for family, but he had made the same demands of himself. Typically, during the heroin trail, he had stayed in France rather than return home for the wedding of his wife's younger sister, who had grown up with them as almost a second daughter. Beyond that, he felt the pressure of having to replicate his past success. "I was stressed to the teeth," Greene said.

At that point, *Newsday* politics provided an alternative that would keep him closer to home: the job of Suffolk editor, which had belonged to four men in six years. When Kirk Price died in 1967, just before the Greene Team proved that he had been a partner in a shady real estate deal with an Islip politician, Art Perfall had succeeded him and guided the staff through the Suffolk scandals stories. Then Moyers made Perfall night managing editor in 1969 and gave the Suffolk job to Tom Collins, the former Washington bureau chief. That was a short-lived and unhappy arrangement. So Laventhol moved Collins out and made him the media writer. "Tom was not a good manager," Moyers said. "Tom is, I think, the best media writer today on a newspaper." Laventhol replaced Collins with Mel Opotowsky, a fine editor with one flaw: He didn't see eye to eye with Laventhol. In late 1972, Opotowsky decided to take a management job at the *Riverside Press-Enterprise* in California. That left a vacancy.

To Greene, the job was attractive because it was obvious that Suffolk

County was *Newsday*'s future. Running the Suffolk office would give him broad autonomy, since the editors in Garden City seldom trekked to Ronkonkoma. He could continue playing reporter, and he would have good sources, since he had done so much investigation in Suffolk. The job would also make him a powerful figure on Long Island. "I've always had an Irish emotional feeling about Long Island," Greene said. So he took the job, starting in March, 1973, just after the heroin series ended.

By the time Greene arrived, the *Suffolk Sun* had died. The only daily competition was the *Long Island Press*, which Greene weakened by hiring away a productive reporter, Mitchell Freedman. "The only other place you could compete against was Nassau," Greene said. Many of his staff, feeling that Suffolk was just a farm team, had already asked for transfers to the main office in Garden City. So Greene tried to fight that second-best attitude by driving the staff into a frenzy of productivity, to make sure that Suffolk stories pushed Nassau stories out of the Suffolk edition.

In that competition with Nassau, Greene was a fierce turf warrior. Outraged to find the bylines of Nassau reporters on Suffolk stories, for example, he staged a retaliatory strike by sending the rookie reporter A. J. Carter to pretend to cover the Nassau County Board of Supervisors, even though Nassau reporters were there — a tactic that annoyed other editors, but vividly made Greene's point. To help give his staff a sense of identity, he persuaded Laventhol to change page one of the Suffolk paper so that it was clearly a separate edition, instead of forcing readers to decipher a cryptic symbol on the inside pages to figure that out. He also went to great lengths to make sure that his reporters won at least as many monthly prizes as the Nassau staff did.

The result of this competition was an outrageous appetite for stories, which made the Suffolk reporters consider their assigning editors a pack of wild dogs with an endless craving for red meat. The pressure was just as great on the editors. "I probably aged ten years in the five years I worked for him," said Bob Samsot, one of Greene's key assigning editors. If the tidal wave of stories made reporters in Suffolk nervous, it made editors in Nassau furious. "The man could make no distinction between quantity and quality," said Tom Stites, who had worked with Greene in Suffolk, then moved to the news desk in Garden City. "He and I went at it hammer and tong, night in and night out, because he wanted all of his stories on page one and in the front of the paper, and he didn't give a shit about anybody else's stories."

To create this flow of copy, Greene relied primarily on stimulating his reporters to dig more stories out of their beats. "I was going to try to experiment in giving reporters far more input into what was happening, what was going to be covered," Greene said. "Obviously, this always requires a returning commitment on the part of reporters." The instrument that Greene chose to develop that commitment was a weekly memo called a "beat note," a list of story ideas and coming events on each beat, prepared by the reporters, for the guidance of the assigning editors. On a big-city newspaper, the rapid-fire explosion of daily events keeps reporters so busy that there is little need to plan stories. But in the slower universe of suburban towns, it is essential to plan coverage in advance, to predict where news might break out — at a town board meeting where a controversial rezoning was on the agenda, for example.

Ideally, the beat note would keep a reporter so busy executing her own suggestions that she would escape the story ideas of editors. Almost as if to show how painful life could be when reporters didn't provide their own story ideas, Greene came up with inspirations of his own that could be humiliating. At Halloween, for example, he sent Carter into the streets in a devil costume, complete with red tights. On another occasion, Greene decided to prove that the laws of New York required banks to cash checks written on any sort of surface. So he sent reporters to cash checks written on objects ranging from a T-shirt to a chimpanzee's paw. In addition to dreaming up ideas himself, Greene got many of them from Fred Fellman, the former Babylon Republican leader. Whenever Fellman visited the office, a memo from Greene to the staff was sure to follow, with political tips from an unnamed source. His meetings with sources such as Fellman allowed Greene to play reporter, to pass tips on to his staff, and to see if they were as knowledgeable about what was happening as he was. It was unsettling for reporters, however, to know that their boss was talking to some of the same sources that they were using.

Despite this profusion of his own ideas, Greene really was serious about giving reporters more power to set the agenda for themselves. He underlined that commitment by developing a group of beat leaders, the lead reporters on each town beat and on the county government beat. When management was slow to give merit raises to beat leaders to compensate them for the added responsibility of compiling the beat note, Greene invented his own form of merit raise: paying beat leaders guaranteed overtime every week. At the same time as he was acting to empower reporters, however, Greene was finding ways to annoy them, bringing to his new job the same demanding style that had caused friction when he ran the investigative team.

"He came out with a paternalistic, patronizing and often militaristic attitude," said the reporter Ed Lowe. One early example of that paternalism was "Big Daddy's Bible," a three-page memo from Greene that codified office policy. His predecessor, Opotowsky, had put out an annual policy memo, but Greene did it with a bit too much zeal. One verse from the bible that particularly rankled reporters was this: "Given the standard daily work load it is almost impossible to adequately develop sources in your area. Therefore it is strongly suggested that you use some of your own time to develop sources. . . . Of course this is entirely voluntary on your part. But this is what measures the difference between a reporter and a recording clerk." His theme was correct: Good reporters do not work banker's hours. But something about the tone of the messenger made the message unpalatable.

Besides using the written word, Greene also taught his methods through the large gesture. One of the most memorable was his response when the rewrite man Jim Bernstein confused two Long Island hamlets in the lead of a story, writing Farmingville instead of Farmingdale. "He called me in and he said, 'I am going to teach you the difference between Farmingdale and Farm-ingville in a way that you will never forget,' " Bernstein said. Greene instructed him to drive from one to the other and measure the exact mileage. The high-strung Bernstein wouldn't even think of trying to evade compliance. So he went out on a cold, rainy night and spent two hours in traffic, following Greene's directions to the letter, measuring thirty-three miles between the two areas, and putting a total of about sixty miles on his car. Greene was right: Bernstein never forgot that night. Nor did anyone who heard about it.

Like his impact on reporters, Greene's enthusiasm for stories was larger than life. A fabled example was the 1974 kidnaping of an eight-year-old boy, John Calzadilla. Almost two decades earlier, Greene had jumped excitedly into the search for the kidnaper of Peter Weinberger, and he saw no reason to treat the Calzadilla case more lightly. So he deployed platoons of reporters in the neighborhood, complete with all the paramilitary touches that he loved, from walkie-talkies and binoculars to code names. Reporters worked around the clock on stakeout, and Greene sat at the desk, barking orders like a general and keeping long hours that everyone else had to match. "Those were some of the worst days of my life here," said Bernstein, who assembled the stories on rewrite. "I got heart palpitations." The sense of urgency didn't even decrease when the kidnapers let the boy loose after about thirty hours, and his family prepared to bring him home. "We'd gotten word they were going to sneak the kid into the house some way, probably wrapped in a blanket," A. J. Carter said. "I had instructions, when a car pulled up, to run up to any blanket and ask it, 'Hello, Johnny, how are you?' " And when *Newsday* learned where the boy had been held in New Jersey, Greene's reporters went there, to search the garbage outside. "We were fairly sure we had the right trash," said Larry Eichel, a Harvard graduate reduced by the story to garbage duty. The saturation coverage began to seem even more excessive later, when it turned out that the leading kidnapers were not unknown desperadoes, but the former brothers-in-law of the boy's father. "When it was all over," said Gail Meadows, one of the assigning editors, "it turned out to be a joke."

The effect of Greene's demanding, production-oriented management style was a pervasive tension. Like a large, playful puppy with no sense of how much damage he is doing to the furniture, Greene irked reporters more than he realized or intended. In that and many other ways, he resembled Alan Hathway, his role model. Like Hathway, Greene was an editor who continued to be a reporter. Like Hathway, he felt an editor should be engaged with the communi-ty, not neutral and above it. "There are a lot of Alan things that rub off," Greene said. "He was a live human being who had dimensions to him and went out there and did things."

By the time Greene became Suffolk editor, Hathway had been gone from *Newsday* six years, living in Puerto Rico and in Florida, out of sight and out of power. "Here's this guy who's used to being a lion," Greene said, "and nothing happens when he roars." So, whenever Hathway was on Long Island, Greene tried to pull him back into *Newsday*. Finally, he persuaded Hathway to visit the

Suffolk office, to make him feel part of things, and to let the young reporters see him. "He came in that one day, and he stayed a little while and looked like it was just too painful," Greene said. "It really ripped you if you knew him."

About a year later, Hathway died of cancer. He had told his great friend, Arthur Lem, that he wanted to die on Lem's birthday. True to his word, Hathway died early on the morning of Lem's birthday, April 15, 1977. At the grave, Lem tossed a dime in, to allow Hathway's spirit to buy a drink on the other side. Greene's mentor was gone, but he never stopped patterning himself after Hathway: "I loved the son of a bitch."

II

FOR ALL THE tension that his style of leadership generated, Greene was an excellent teacher of reporting techniques.

"I learned how to be an investigative reporter from Greene, and in many ways, I learned to be a reporter from Greene," said Stuart Diamond, who came to *Newsday* from the *New Brunswick Home News* in New Jersey a few months after Greene took over. "There were a lot of people at *Newsday* who didn't like Bob Greene, because he had a gruff manner sometimes, because he was demanding. Those are the reporters who lost out, because Bob Greene is a phenomenal journalist, certainly one of the very best I've ever known. . . . I didn't care how he delivered whatever criticism he was going to deliver to me. I just wanted to sit at his feet and learn what he had to say." Greene assigned Diamond to cover the Town of Brookhaven, and Diamond turned up a series of tough stories about the patronage and campaign financing practices of the town Republican leader, Richard Zeidler.

Diamond's stories on Zeidler led one Republican to tell John Cummings that *Newsday* was not without corruption itself. That tip led to a painful story by Cummings and Drew Fetherston about Arthur Bergmann, the former *Newsday* political reporter who had left the paper in 1971 to become chief deputy to County Executive John V. N. Klein. While he was still covering politics for *Newsday*, they reported, Bergmann had regularly ghostwritten a weekly newspaper column for the Republican supervisor of Brookhaven and had done a small piece of writing for Zeidler himself, accepting a total of $18,000 to $20,000 in Republican Party funds over three years. Even though Greene had witnessed the less-than-delicate ethics of the Hathway era, Bergmann's admission shocked him. "There was an incredible sense of betrayal," Greene said. "Back in those days in Suffolk, lots of people were taking jobs. . . . If that had been out in the open, I don't think anybody would have complained."

Oddly, Bergmann's role had not come to light in 1972, when Bob Wyrick wrote an investigative piece for *Newsday* about reporters on political payrolls. Wyrick was a dogged and skillful reporter who earlier in 1972 had written a major, high-impact story about Nassau County Republicans coercing town and county employees to kick back one percent of their pay to the party. But Wyrick hadn't found out about Bergmann's job. While Greene was in Europe working on the heroin trail, however, Wyrick had heard rumors that Greene had worked on the campaign payroll of his ally, Nassau District Attorney William Cahn, and Laventhol had called Greene in France to ask about it. "I said, 'Absolutely not,' " Greene said. "I've never taken a nickel from anybody."

Greene continued to feel that *Newsday* owed some loyalty to Cahn as an excellent source, but the paper no longer showed Cahn any deference. In 1971, for example, David Zinman had found Cahn's official car speeding wildly, had followed him and recorded his speed several times, and then had written a piece for the Saturday magazine called "Investigation of a Public Citizen Above Suspicion." That was just a petty annoyance, though, compared to stories that *Newsday* ran in 1974, during Cahn's campaign against Denis Dillon. A well-known gadfly named Dr. Ralph Sorley had said for months that Cahn was travelling excessively in his role as president of the National District Attorneys Association and billing the county for expenses that the association also paid. But *Newsday* didn't pay attention initially. During the campaign, Dillon also began to focus attention on Cahn's out-of-town trips, and Bruce Lambert wrote about the issue in *Newsday*. After Dillon had defeated Cahn, a federal grand jury indicted the former district attorney in 1975, and he was later convicted and sent to prison. During those hard times, there was no way Greene could help his old friend. "Cahn was coming to me, coming to me," Greene said. "I said, 'Bill, there's nothing I can do.' "

Though Greene couldn't help Cahn, some reporters were concerned that Greene's closeness to important Suffolk politicians might prompt him to help them. At least once a year, Greene went fishing with the three men who controlled the Suffolk Republican Party: County Chairman Edwin (Buzz) Schwenk, Assemblyman Perry B. Duryea Jr. of Montauk, who served as speaker of the Assembly and later minority leader, and Smithtown Republican Leader Nicholas Barbato. He also met regularly with Barbato at Smithtown restaurants. Not content to hear about the power brokers from others, Greene wanted to see for himself. "I find it fascinating to get in close with them, to talk with them, get a sense of who they are, how they think, how they move," Greene said. "In any conversation, even if a person doesn't want to tell you things, he's telling you things. He's telling you things by the things he suddenly stops talking about."

So Greene would listen to the politicians, hoping to pick up information, and the politicians would listen to him, hoping to learn what he knew. That sort of jousting happened often with Barbato. Greene had visited Barbato's farm stand in Smithtown for years and enjoyed his company, but once Greene became Suffolk editor, they had a tacit agreement that the friendship would not interfere with the adversarial relationship of journalist and politician. "It's always been sort of understood: foxes and hounds," Greene said. Often, after an unfavorable story, Barbato would walk into the *Newsday* office and ostentatiously give Greene a plant or some vegetables from his farm. "Bob would say, 'You're hurting me with my reporters. They think we're friends,' " Barbato said. Similarly, Barbato's colleagues in the party often asked him whether he was giving Greene information. But they kept meeting. "We became a challenge to each other," Barbato said. "I might have helped him, but he certainly helped me to be sharp, too."

In the case of Duryea, Greene proved early that he would not shy away from a solid story. Cummings and Fetherston had found out that the county legislature had enhanced the profitability of a twenty-two-acre parcel of land that Duryea owned, by removing it from a list of sites that the county planned to acquire, through condemnation proceedings, for parkland. By that time, Duryea was already hypersensitive about *Newsday*. A year earlier, Alan Eysen had written about a state investigation of a phony election committee that Assembly Republicans had set up to siphon votes away from Democrats and give them to Liberals in close races. Duryea was indicted, but the charges were dismissed in 1974. A few weeks after the dismissal, Cummings and Fetherston were after him about the parkland story, and Duryea was livid. He squawked to one of his Hamptons constituents, Juan Trippe, the founder of Pan Am, where Otis Chandler served on the board, and Trippe mentioned it to Chandler. "I frankly never paid any attention to it at all," Chandler said. "I didn't interfere." But Duryea did get a meeting with Greene, who listened to him for four hours. "What he laid out proved that what they were saying was exactly right," Greene said. With Greene's approval, *Newsday* ran the story, but Duryea didn't stop fighting it. He wrote a letter to Chandler, starting off with Trippe's name, and asking Chandler for a meeting. Chandler asked Attwood about it, accepted his assurances that the story was accurate, and wrote to Duryea: "I would point out to you that Newsday, like all Times Mirror newspapers, has complete editorial autonomy. . . . I do not presume to tell the editors of Newsday how to cover Long Island."

Despite Greene's steadfastness on the Duryea story, some on the staff still considered him capable of bending a story. Perhaps the most troublesome accusation of unbalanced coverage flowed from a wild and woolly piece of Suffolk County politics. In the Watergate year of 1974, a Democrat named Henry O'Brien won the office of district attorney in Suffolk County — the first time that anyone could remember a Democrat in that job. Only seven months after taking office, O'Brien got into a nasty struggle with Police Commissioner Eugene Kelley, a Republican. First, Kelley attacked O'Brien for failing to protect police informants. Then O'Brien announced that he was investigating Kelley for "misconduct in office." A few weeks later, Kelley accused O'Brien of sexual abuse of a twenty-one-year-old male client. Even for Suffolk, where politics was a Wild West shootout, that was a startling story.

To Greene, neither Kelley nor O'Brien was a classic good guy. Kelley liked to ride around in a leather jacket on police motorcycles, which seemed overly ostentatious. "Everybody regarded Gene Kelley, including myself, as sort of a jerk," Greene said. As for O'Brien, even though he had set up an office to investigate political corruption, Greene was unimpressed. "They were running around there accomplishing nothing," Greene said. At *Newsday*, the reporters liked O'Brien, who was friendly, down-to-earth and, they felt, a straight arrow. Greene's view, tinted by his conversations with his sources among the police, was harsher: "He was a bad district attorney." Nonetheless, Greene said, he set out to provide a balanced investigation.

To O'Brien, however, and to some of Greene's reporters, the *Newsday* investigation looked one-sided, aimed primarily at O'Brien. "They went out to try to find out what Harry's lifestyle was and whether or not he was a homosexual," said Paul Gianelli, who became O'Brien's chief assistant during the controversy. Knut Royce, who had worked with Greene on the heroin trail and later left *Newsday* to work for O'Brien, had the same perception. "The scrutiny was all on Harry," Royce said.

For days and days, *Newsday* reporters searched for information about O'Brien and his sexuality, primarily in bars in Deer Park, where O'Brien often drank. The investigative hypothesis was that O'Brien was using poor judgment in hanging out at the bars, which could have compromised him somehow. Once O'Brien understood that emphasis, he stopped talking to *Newsday*. Kelley chose another tactic. "Kelley was trying to get the upper hand by professing openness and talking to reporters on a regular basis," said Bob Samsot, who put together the team of reporters for Greene. As the investigation unfolded, Samsot grew angry over what he thought was its skewed focus. "I went in and told him, 'This is a crock of shit. I don't want to have anything more to do with it,' " said Samsot, whose protest set off a heated, desk-pounding argument with Greene.

The story that flowed from this investigation found no evidence of wrongdoing by either Kelley or O'Brien — the same conclusion that the special prosecutor and the grand jury later reached. "I have no apologies for the way it came out," Greene said. "The sum impression of that story was that both of these people had incredibly bad judgment." But the story didn't *look* balanced. It devoted a full page to the allegations against O'Brien and less than half of that to Kelley. "The story might have been a different story, had Harry O'Brien cooperated," said A. J. Carter, who regularly covered O'Brien and worked on the project. "But I think that by then there was a perception in his mind that *Newsday* was so anti-him and pro-Kelley that it was useless." The whole experience left O'Brien bitter. "It was such an enormous amount of coverage against me," O'Brien said. "There was no investigation of the possibility of fake charges being made against me. . . . Why didn't they talk about that possibility, of people trying to get me to stop my investigations?" When O'Brien lost the next election, he made his unhappiness clear: "I lost the election by one vote, the vote of Robert William Greene."

CHAPTER THIRTY-SIX

The Arizona Project

I

FOR MORE THAN a quarter of a century, like Captain Ahab in search of the white whale, Bob Greene had chased organized crime relentlessly.

Repeatedly, starting in the mid-1950s, Greene found strong evidence of mob influence: in the juke box industry, in garbage carting, in gambling. That obsession with the mob spawned a thousand stories, but perhaps the most frequently told of all revolves around a 1976 incident at a Smithtown restaurant owned by Peter Raneri, a friend of Greene.

In the weeks before the incident, Suffolk police had been investigating a series of threats against Raneri and passing information to Greene's protege, Joe Demma. The detectives told Demma that they thought the mob was unhappy with Raneri for hiring the developer Ronald Parr to build a new restaurant for him. The mob was angry because Parr had thwarted their attempt to infiltrate a quarter-horse racetrack that he owned. Demma had been an eyewitness to that scheme, after he left *Newsday* in 1973 to do public relations for Parr's track. Once Demma and Parr detected the mob's intentions, Parr ordered Demma to leak documents to Greene — without the knowledge of Demma's boss at the track, the former *Newsday* office boy Nick Grande. The secrecy was necessary because they suspected that Grande was helping the mob. The result of Demma's information and the *Newsday* investigation was a 1974 series by Greene, Tom Renner, John McDonald and Carole Agus. Among other things, the series said that Grande had regularly recommended that Parr hire contractors who turned out to have mob connections. It also showed that Grande had met frequently with Andimo Pappadio, identified by police as the boss of a mob family, and with John Del Mastro, a businessman who associated with mob figures and had become a favorite target of Greene. "That was, to my mind, the single best investigation we ever did at *Newsday*," Greene said. "It was picture perfect. We uncovered organized crime there to the teeth." A few months after the series, Demma returned to *Newsday* and started reporting on the threats against Raneri — threats serious enough to prompt the police to provide protection for Raneri and Parr and to set up a telephone monitoring system at the restaurant. Before Demma could break the story, someone attacked Raneri's, where Greene was sitting at the bar, with his wife, Kathy.

The night of the attack, Greene telephoned Demma at home and ordered him to get to Raneri's quickly. At the scene, Demma found some of the detectives who had been investigating the threats. They told him that they had examined the hole in the window and the hole in the back wall and decided from the trajectory that someone had fired a .22-caliber weapon. They theorized that the shots were connected to the threats. So Demma wrote a story about the incident, using it as a news peg on which to hang the broader story of Parr, Raneri and the mob. His story quoted Greene on what it felt like during the attack. "It must have passed an inch in front of my nose," Greene told him. "You can feel that pressure of the bullet go by." The headline on page three said: "Mob Link to Shots in Smithtown."

As the police investigated further, they failed to find a bullet in the wall. Then a woman who had been standing across the street from the restaurant called police and gave them the license plate number of a car that she had seen stopped in front of Raneri's. When police traced the license plate, the rest of the mystery unraveled. The attackers were not part of the mob. They were three teenagers, including two former employees of Raneri. The weapon was not a gun, either. It was a slingshot and rocks. The detectives broke the news to Demma at home, and Demma gulped hard and explained it all to Greene. The next day, *Newsday* had to carry a second story — not by Demma — with a headline that retracted the first one: "No Mob Link to Restaurant Incident."

In the guffaws that followed, no one stopped to remember that the police had had substantial reason to think the mob was involved. In fact, when Raneri eventually moved to his new location, organized crime figures continued to pressure him. "The mob bled the restaurant to death," Greene said. At the time of the incident, however, the only thing that anyone talked about was Greene's melodramatic quote. "I certainly was the butt of a lot of jokes, most of them from inside *Newsday*," Greene said. "But I didn't feel embarrassed. The cops said it was a bullet, as Joe can attest. The rest was fact." Despite the momentary laughter, his reputation as an organized crime fighter was so strong that, within weeks after the Raneri's incident, he found himself playing a central role in a mob story that brought about a precedent-setting investigation.

The story began a few minutes after 11:30 on the morning of June 2, 1976, when a bomb exploded in a white Datsun in the parking lot of the Clarendon House hotel in Phoenix, Arizona. Within hours, reporters all across the country learned that the bomb had mortally wounded Don Bolles, an investigative reporter for the *Arizona Republic*. Until that explosion, the spring of 1976 had been a heady time for investigative reporters. The film *All the President's Men* was holding out to a whole generation of young people the image of journalism as a glamorous profession that would allow them to bring down even the President of the United States. At the same time, a new group, Investigative Reporters and Editors, was preparing for its first convention — the start of a mechanism that would help investigative reporters to share techniques and information, as they had already been doing informally. Bolles had been an important member of that informal network and had occasionally traded information with Greene. Both men had joined the IRE within a short time after it came to life in 1975.

By the time the IRE convention opened in Indianapolis, Bolles had died. Much of the hallway conversation focused on what the IRE could do in response to the murder, which had shattered the basic assumption that no one would dare kill a reporter. Those discussions produced a proposal to put together a team of reporters from all over the country and send them to Arizona to turn the state upside down. Inevitably, they turned to Greene, one of the best known investigative reporters in the country, and asked him to examine the feasibility of such a project. The idea appealed to Greene, even though he had rejected a suggestion from Attwood and Laventhol that he put together a *Newsday* investigation. A *Newsday*-only team, he feared, would subject the paper to accusations of showboating, but a cooperative effort was acceptable. So he agreed to take a look at the idea.

Greene began with a visit to Phoenix and conversations with the city editor of the *Arizona Republic*, Robert Early, who pledged his help. Returning to Long Island, Greene wrote a memo to Laventhol, proposing that he be allowed to lead the IRE project. "It would be a concerted statement by the press of America and working newspaper people that the assassination of one of our own results in more problems than it is worth," Greene wrote. The object of the exercise, he emphasized, would *not* be to solve the murder. In fact, soon after the bombing, police had settled on a minor hoodlum named John Harvey Adamson as the man who had lured Bolles to the Clarendon House by promising him information about Arizona land frauds. The Arizona papers would continue to cover the investigation of Adamson and his coconspirators. The IRE team would work on everything else in Arizona: land fraud, growing mob influence and the complicity of the power structure in that corruption — exactly the kinds of stories that Bolles had done.

The *Newsday* contribution to this project would be to allow Greene and Tom Renner to work on it for about six months. Renner had become a full-time mob specialist a decade earlier, after a presidential commission recommended that every newspaper appoint one. He had been ill and wasn't ready for a long project, but Greene persuaded him. *Newsday* would also provide the services of Tony Insolia, who had long experience in editing investigative stories. The paper's libel lawyer, Andrew Hughes, would give legal advice.

To gather his team, Greene began calling dozens of reporters and asking them to seek permission from their own papers to spend time on the project. Some editors were generous, such as Bill Woestendiek, the executive editor of the *Arizona Star* in Tucson. Woestendiek, the former editorial director for Alicia Patterson, had started making calls to *Newsday* and other papers after the bombing, encouraging them to send reporters to Arizona. So he contributed Alex Drehsler and John Rawlinson, who stayed on the project from beginning to end. Bob Early at the *Arizona Republic* gave Greene the services of John Winters for the duration. Greene also got contributions from other Arizona sources, including professors and journalism students from both Arizona State University and the University of Arizona. "Whatever we did was never going to have any effect in Arizona unless the people there were aware that this wasn't some outsiders coming in to trash you, that this was your own people too — your own university system, your own newspapers," Greene said. Beyond Arizona, Greene got reporters from all over the country. Many would be able to spend just a couple of weeks on the project. Some were able to give long stretches of time, such as Myrta Pulliam and Richard Cady of the *Indianapolis Star*, another property of the Pulliam family, which owned the *Arizona Republic*.

The recruiting effort succeeded in producing a solid reporting team, but Greene had less success in selling the idea to the elite of journalism. The most caustic reaction came from Ben Bradlee at the *Washington Post*, who felt that investigative reporters had such large egos that they couldn't work well on a joint project. At the *New York Times*, A. M. Rosenthal argued that a joint project would damage the diversity of the press. To Greene, the putdown by Rosenthal was simply normal *Times* elitism. "I didn't feel that Abe was out to destroy the project," Greene said. "I felt much differently about Bradlee." Like a canny football coach, he used Bradlee to inspire his team, displaying in the office a copy of Bradlee's quotes and a photograph suitable for darts.

While Greene was still assembling the team and gathering funding, he sent Renner out in late summer as an advance scout. For more than two weeks, Renner travelled through Ohio, Michigan, California, New Mexico, Texas and Arizona. At the end of his trip, Renner wrote a long report to Greene that became the cornerstone of the team's work. Then Greene packed up and headed for Phoenix to set up the project's offices in the fall of 1976.

II

THE HEADQUARTERS OF the Arizona Project in Phoenix reflected Greene's preoccupation with keeping his reporters safe and keeping them together in a velvet prison.

Greene had arranged for a series of rooms on the top floor of the Adams Hotel in downtown Phoenix, including a large suite that served as the city room, plus other rooms where the reporters slept. He had insisted on an office that didn't face nearby buildings, from which someone could observe or even shoot at them. "There was no line of sight to that room all the way to the south mountains," Greene said. Further, to prevent anyone from planting a bomb in one of their rented cars to kill a specific member of the staff, Greene rented five identical cars and threw the keys in a drawer, so that different people would use them every day. He also warned the reporters to avoid any situations that could compromise them, such as dalliances with strange women. "My biggest worry was people trying to set us up," Greene said. "If they got one person set up, they could blow the whole project."

It was in this office-dormitory complex that Greene spent most of his time, sitting at the desk, deploying his reporters, reading their daily memos, deciding what leads they should pursue, and marking the memos up so that the clerks could cross-index them in a file that grew to 40,000 index cards. "I remember walking into a smoke-filled room, a lot of women filing stuff, and in the dark back corner, this smoky corner, is this massive silver-haired man," said Steve Wick, who had been working on land fraud stories for the *Colorado Springs Sun* when he got an invitation to join the team. "In front of this man are piles of memos from reporters, intelligence documents, land records, deeds — every conceivable thing." The only opening in the paper pile was a space for an ashtray. "The ashtray is overflowing with cigarettes," Wick said. "They are falling into his lap and through his legs, if that's possible, and onto the rug under his chair, which was simply burned to the concrete floor. He looked to me like a mob figure."

Every morning, Greene would roll out of bed in a room adjoining the office and hold a meeting with the staff, to brief them on the contents of the memos. From the shards of information that the reporters had brought in, Greene built in his mind a cohesive mosaic and gave them a sense of where the story was going and where they should focus their work that day. At the end of the day, they would gather for a typical Greene meal, then return to the office, where they would go to their rooms and retire for the night, while Greene stayed up most of the night reading their memos.

Besides the memos from the staff at the hotel, Greene got regular reports from Renner. To assure his law enforcement sources that their cooperation with him wouldn't backfire, Renner stayed undercover, living at the home of an agent. His only contact with the project was through meetings with Greene, which they arranged by phone, using the standard confusing Greene telephone codes. "The team never actually saw me until the last month," Renner said. "I was just someone nobody ever knew." But they did see his memos. "They were filled with details that I, as a new reporter, never thought that any reporter could get," Wick said.

In the reporting, the team began to focus on three men who dominated Arizona: Senator Barry Goldwater, his brother Robert, and Harry Rosenzweig, the former Republican state chairman. The team's scrutiny of the senator's brother covered a variety of issues, including his partnership with an associate of the mob underboss Peter Licavoli Sr. in a restaurant chain, and his partial ownership of Arrowhead Ranches, a Phoenix citrus farm. To examine the substandard working conditions of the illegal aliens who worked at Arrowhead, Greene's team staged a full-fledged raid, complete with walkie-talkies and military-style evasion tactics.

The team also looked closely at a Phoenix liquor millionaire named Kemper Marley Sr. Though they were not trying to solve the Bolles murder, they did pursue suspicions by editors at the *Arizona Republic* and others that Marley may have ordered the killing. Those suspicions were rooted in a controversy that swirled around Marley just before the murder of Bolles. In early 1976, Governor Raul Castro had appointed Marley to the Arizona Racing Commission, and Bolles had written a story that rehashed criticism of Marley's performance in a previous appointive job, on the State Fair Commission. At about the time when the Bolles story appeared, Castro asked Marley to resign from the racing commission. Within months after Marley's forced resignation, John Harvey Adamson lured Bolles to the hotel parking lot and placed a bomb in his car. Later, investigators identified a Phoenix contractor named Max Dunlap, who had business dealings with Marley, as the person who hired Adamson to kill Bolles. After striking a plea bargain with prosecutors, Adamson told police in an affidavit that Dunlap had said that Marley wanted Bolles dead because Bolles had given Marley "a bad time" over the racing appointment. But Greene's team found out that Castro's change of heart about Marley had nothing to do with the Bolles story.

Early in Renner's reporting, he discovered an FBI report in which an informant said that Marley had been involved with a mob racing wire service in the 1940s. The Arizona Department of Public Safety also had that information, but Castro told Greene's team that he had not learned about it until *after* he had nominated Marley. "The Department of Public Safety had that in its own memorandum, and when Castro had asked for a background check on Marley, Castro said they were late in getting it in," Greene said. "We felt that Kemper Marley was convinced that Bolles would get that memo. Bolles never knew about that." As a result, even though it became clear to Greene's team that the Bolles story had not really caused Marley's ouster, some of those involved in the case developed a "rangeland justice" theory: that Marley wanted Bolles dead for reasons of revenge and self-protection. But no one ever formally charged Marley in connection with the murder. In 1977, a jury convicted Dunlap of murder, for hiring Adamson. The same jury also convicted a plumber named James Robison, who was accused of actually setting off the remote-controlled bomb. But an appeals court later overturned both convictions. So, more than fourteen years after the murder, the origins of the alleged conspiracy remain murky.

Another major target was Ned Warren Sr., a real estate operator who developed land fraud in the Arizona desert into an art form. Together, Greene and Drehsler held a long interview with Warren in his plush circular home overlooking Phoenix, then continued the interview at a nearby restaurant. Strangely, although prosecutors were circling hungrily around his empire, Warren agreed to talk openly, with one condition: "He says, 'Anything I say, unless we agree that it's not on the record, will be on the record. But you can't take any notes,' " Greene remembered. So, for the next seven hours, while Warren spewed out a stream of colorful quotes, the two reporters concentrated hard on every word. Then they rushed back to the office and sat down at separate typewriters to type out what they remembered, including Warren's candid acknowledgment of his roguishness: "I was a thief. And I was a good thief." For hours, the two men typed, without speaking to each other, for fear that they might contaminate each other's memory. Then Greene merged the two versions, which matched almost exactly in many areas, into one memo. A few days later, Warren visited the team's office and Greene showed him the memo. "He read the memorandum and he made two little corrections," Greene said. "Then he says, 'How did you do it?' "

At the start of 1977, Insolia flew out to Phoenix and burrowed down among the piles of memos, to get a sense of what the team had found. A few weeks later, once the team started to turn the memos into stories, Insolia came back and edited them. Then Hughes read the huge series for libel, along with two other lawyers. Toward the end, Jack Driscoll, the assistant executive editor of the *Boston Globe*, came out to do rewriting and editing. The Associated Press also sent a rewrite person, to start boiling down the stories. Then Greene dispatched the final report to participating papers, giving them time to edit it and ask questions. The stories would start running on March 13, 1977, nine months after Bolles died.

Though *Newsday* and a few other papers decided to run the series in its entirety, the newspaper that had employed Bolles, the *Arizona Republic*, declined to run it at all. Instead, it ran a brief box, explaining that it didn't want to run a story whose accuracy it couldn't verify itself. Following all the cooperation that Early at the *Republic* had given, that decision stunned Greene. "Early wasn't told about this," Greene said. "I believe Early one hundred percent, and I still believe him to this day. . . . The editorial board down there made their decision." The *Republic*'s blackout prompted other papers in Arizona and the *Denver Post* to print extra copies and sell them in Phoenix. But in some of the largest cities in America, such as Los Angeles, San Francisco and Chicago, major newspapers chose not to run the series at all. One newspaper executive who didn't like the idea was Otis Chandler, who expressed reservations and followed up with a personal letter to Greene. "I think your work on the Phoenix project was professionally superb," Chandler wrote. "I happen to have a personal disagreement as to the concept of the IRE and, specifically, I do not like the Phoenix project. I wish we had not participated in it." Even Attwood expressed doubts years later. "In the end, I think a newspaper should do these things on its own and not get mixed up as a posse," Attwood said. "We looked like we were trying to smear Goldwater."

The project produced some unpleasant side effects, such as a draining lawsuit by Marley, who denied all of the allegations in the series. The lawsuit kept Greene in the witness chair day after day after day, but Marley's effort to hold the team legally liable ultimately failed. The stories also earned the enmity of Joseph Bonanno, the mob leader who had moved to Arizona and had become an important target of the series, which Bonanno later criticized in his autobiography. Soon after the series ran, federal agents combing routinely through Bonanno's garbage found a piece of paper with a cryptic, possibly threatening reference to Greene. So they informed Suffolk police, who assigned Greene a bodyguard for weeks.

The series also ignited an internal squabble between Greene and one of his reporters, Mike Wendland of the *Detroit News*, who wrote a book about the project, infuriating Greene. "We had an absolute pact that nobody would make a single nickel on this," said Greene, who had tried to get the media writer Ben Bagdikian to produce a book, to generate revenue for the IRE. "That's really what made me say, 'If he's going to do it, I'm going to do it,' " Wendland said. More than a decade later, the mere mention of Wendland's name caused Greene to bristle. For his part, Wendland acknowledged how much he had learned from Greene about reporting, but he said that he had come to doubt some of the team's findings. "We bought the line of the Kemper Marley 'rangeland justice' theory," Wendland said. "There are few people, if anybody, who would say that Kemper Marley had anything to do with this now."

Despite the turmoil surrounding the series, it did create a stir in Arizona for a time. Bruce Babbitt, who was the state's attorney general during the project and later became governor, summarized that effect at a 1982 gathering of journalists on the fifth anniversary of the series. "Arizona did wake up," Babbitt said. "The citizens of this state were aroused to a level of indignation that was truly awesome. . . . The legislature acted. They picked up an agenda that law enforcement had had in front of them for a long, long time." In addition, Renner said, he later learned of a Chicago mobster who warned an associate not to harm an employee of the *Chicago Tribune*, because he didn't want an Arizona-style invasion of journalists. "It did a tremendous amount in terms of protecting reporters," Renner said.

As long as reporters talk about investigations, the Arizona Project is likely to continue to be a subject of controversy. But one thing seems absolutely incontrovertible: Greene was probably the only journalist in America who could have pulled together such an unprecedented effort, which required of its leader a unique combination of investigative skills, larger-than-life energy and insatiable zeal for hunting the mob. Whatever anyone else thought of the project, Greene saw it as a triumph: "That is without question the proudest accomplishment of my life."

CHAPTER THIRTY-SEVEN

Long Island Moves West

I

DEFYING THE EVIDENCE of the senses, *Newsday*'s definition of the Real Long Island had always excluded Brooklyn and Queens, the two boroughs of New York City at the western end of the island. Only the suburban counties of Nassau and Suffolk really counted.

That feat of geographical nearsightedness intrigued a group of reporters in the Suffolk office who were concocting an imaginary *Newsday* history movie in the early 1970s. So they decided to allude to it in the film. "The opening scene was going to be a huge fish, with a voice-over that said, 'The Deity's Long Island is shaped like a fish,' " said Ed Lowe, one of the make-believe movie's creators. "Then a cleaver would come down behind the gills and wipe away the head, and the voice-over would say, '*Newsday*'s Long Island . . .' "

The paper had ignored the two populous counties, to begin with, because *Newsday* had to convince advertisers that there was a huge gulf between the city and Nassau-Suffolk, in order to sell them on the idea of Long Island as a separate market. "Newsday's circulation exceeds that of all other newspapers on the Real Long Island," said a 1950 house ad. "New York City slop-over circulation can't do the job."

Newsday also avoided the city because Harry Guggenheim feared the huge costs of New York City union work rules, such as the "bogus" clause. That practice started after advertising agencies began to supply newspapers with completed mats for local ads, ready to be made into plates for the press. Fearing that this would cost them jobs, printers insisted on a new work rule: When one of these mats came into the composing room, printers had to set a bogus version of the same ad by hand, then throw it away. Harry refused to accept this wasteful rule. The International Typographical Union was unhappy, but its Local 915 went along with Harry, largely because many of its members had moved to Long Island, and they were anxious to work at *Newsday*, to avoid commuting to Manhattan. So, at the same time that bogus and other costly work rules were draining the city papers, *Newsday* was growing economically robust.

More than just shunning the city, *Newsday* developed a scornful attitude about it. Alicia Patterson herself referred to the city as "a dying community," and later told the journalism educator John Hohenberg: " 'I don't have to go into New York. New York will come out to me.' " So she resisted suggestions that the paper expand into New York — or elsewhere. "She said this was a Long Island newspaper, and we're not going to go venturing into other areas that we don't know anything about," said Bill Woestendiek. That anti-city view sometimes found its way into the paper, as it did shortly before Alicia's death, when *Newsday* called the communities in Queens "way stations on the road to Hell-in-Manhattan."

Despite *Newsday*'s negative attitude toward New York City, its reporters felt drawn to Manhattan papers. "Everybody wanted to put on a trench coat and cover New York City and City Hall, which was more glamorous than covering a Nassau County planning board — or perceived as being more glamorous," Don Forst said. "I think that's one of the things that in the past has hurt *Newsday* and possibly always will."

As for coverage of city news, *Newsday* did little of that. "In the '40s, Newsday was provincial to the point of being hicky," the former sports columnist and editor Ed Comerford wrote. "If it didn't happen in Nassau or Suffolk, we didn't cover it, as though the Great Wall of China had been rebuilt on the Queens border." In the early 1950s, if *Newsday* wanted city stories, it would usually acquire them from the tiny Park Row News Service. Later, in the early 1960s, *Newsday* began assigning its own reporters to cover city news. The first one permanently based in the city was Maureen O'Neill. She had started out commuting — covering trials and hearings in New York, driving to Garden City to write, then returning to her home in the Bronx. Not long after Alicia's death, the editors decided that O'Neill should have an office in the city. Through Alan Hathway's connections, she got a desk in the United Press International newsroom in the *Daily News* building, and worked full time on city stories.

About a year after O'Neill left the city job and became an assigning editor in Garden City, the new emphasis by Moyers on business coverage led in 1967 to the establishment of *Newsday*'s first Manhattan bureau, in the *Herald Tribune* building. That same year, Moyers had assigned Robert Mayer to write a regular column from New York. Later, after Mayer had left *Newsday*, Laventhol assigned Ed Hershey to cover New York. David Gelman, the former editorial page editor and national editor, became a national correspondent and also wrote pieces from New York. Always, *Newsday* covered the city selectively, writing about major events and giving readers a sense of the city's life. "In our absolutely correct drive to be a paper that met the needs of the people of Long Island, we almost covered New York as if it were Chicago or Los Angeles," Laventhol said. "I'm not sure we ever got it exactly right."

For the few *Newsday* reporters who covered the city in the late 1960s and early 1970s, the job was glamorous, but they had little impact. "The one frustration that we always had in those days was that the work was not seen in New York City," Mayer said. "It didn't get the feedback that you would for a New York paper." *Newsday* did sell papers in New York, but only on the eastern fringes of Queens. The purpose was to fend off any effort by the *Daily News* or the *Long Island Press* to expand their circulation on Long Island. But *Newsday* made no effort to put more city news into the papers sold in Queens. Those readers got the same edition of *Newsday* that went to Nassau County.

The sale to Times Mirror seemed unlikely, at first, to change that timid approach to New York. When *Time* magazine asked Otis Chandler whether he would expand *Newsday* into the city, he gasped: "Good Lord, no! Why in heaven's name would you want to involve it in city problems?" In *New York* magazine, the headline on an article by the media writer Edwin Diamond asked: "Will Big Otis Try to Cross the East River?" Diamond hinted that a New York edition of *Newsday* would allow Chandler to strike back at the *New York Times* for invading his turf in 1962 with a short-lived West Coast edition. But Chandler denied any such plans. "We have all but ruled out coming into the New York City field with *Newsday*," Chandler said.

A year later, however, the decline of the Queens-based *Long Island Press* prompted *Newsday*'s long-range planning committee to begin studying the idea of a Queens edition. Within a month, *Newsday* had assembled a contingency plan for a Queens newspaper. In the planning process, they began to realize how shaky the *Press* was. It had reached an all-time circulation high of 444,500 by the end of 1969, a year and a half after absorbing another Newhouse paper, the *Long Island Star-Journal*. But in 1970, the *Press* had doubled its price in Queens to a dime and suffered a sharp circulation loss, just as *Newsday* did the same year. By the end of 1971, *Press* circulation had slipped to 391,000 in Nassau, Suffolk and Queens. At the same time, advertising linage had fallen off severely. In 1969, the *Press* had reached an all-time high of 25,429,623 lines, but in 1971, it ran only 20,600,000 lines.

The root problem was that the *Press* had failed for three decades to expand forcefully into Nassau-Suffolk. "They didn't think the influx of population would be so great so fast; they figured, hell, Queens is the place," said the Long Island advertising agency executive John Alogna Sr. "Then, when the *Press* realized they had some real tough competition in contemplating moving east, it was too late."

Meanwhile, *Newsday* had been building a large, diverse group of advertisers, to avoid relying on a few dominant ones. By focusing on Queens, the *Press* had been unable to achieve the same diversity. "There weren't as many thriving small businesses in Queens as there were in Nassau-Suffolk," said David Starr, the editor of the *Press*. "We had Jamaica, and we had Flushing, and that was it." Those shopping areas began to decline at the same time that *Newsday* was beginning to prosper in Nassau-Suffolk. As the minority population in Queens grew, the force of racist fear prompted middle-class whites to flee to Long Island, leaving behind minorities that had lower purchasing power. That white flight simultaneously sapped the vitality of the prime advertisers of the *Press* in Queens and helped strengthen the Nassau-Suffolk market. "The stores in Queens began closing, one after another," Starr said. "It was brutal."

One vivid symptom of the shift to the suburbs had been a decision in the 1950s by Gertz, the Jamaica department store that was the largest *Press* advertiser, to open a store in Hicksville. At that point, Gertz started advertising heavily in *Newsday*, although it continued using the *Press*. "We had to be in the *Press*, because *Newsday* wasn't in Queens," said Roger Cruz, then the Gertz advertising director. But Gertz did hurt the *Press* when the store's new president, Paul Dowd, decided to move much of its advertising to the *New York Times*. Cruz and his predecessor, Harold Merahn, argued that *Times* readers weren't Gertz customers, but Dowd insisted on the shift. That weakened the *Press*, but Gertz alone did not send it spiraling toward oblivion. "The *Press'* downfall was their lack of aggressiveness in Nassau County," Cruz said. "It had nothing to do with one store or two stores supporting it."

By the beginning of the 1970s, those trends had weakened the *Press* so much that its vulnerability forced *Newsday* to think seriously about doing something in response. Laventhol argued for action in 1973, when labor contracts at the New York papers were scheduled to expire. "Based on previous discussions, the editorial department is planning to budget for a pilot Queens staff in January, 1973," Laventhol wrote Attwood in the summer of 1972. "My proposal is that we start a limited Queens edition on March 1." Just a week later, Chandler made his views clear to Attwood. "I am not enthusiastic, as you can tell, about expansion into Queens," Chandler wrote, "but I am willing to listen and be convinced." Two months after that, in a talk at the Overseas Press Club, Attwood said: "The city's advertising revenues flow into the three big dailies, and it would not be economically feasible for Newsday to insinuate itself into that market."

So the Queens idea remained dormant for a time, but it didn't die. In early 1973, Attwood told Richard Robinson at Times Mirror: "We are now considering adding Queens news and features only to the Sunday paper, stressing street sales and holding home delivery to the areas we are already serving." Even if the additional Queens sales didn't bring in much new advertising, Attwood said, they would at least help boost Sunday circulation closer to the level of daily circulation. All the planning and discussion produced no real movement into Queens in 1973 — or 1974, 1975, or 1976. But the lack of action didn't change the reality: *Newsday* had to find new ways to grow. "As we look ahead to the 1980s, we see that the growth that has symbolized Long Island has begun to slow down," Stan Asimov wrote to Attwood in 1974. "Therefore, it is necessary for us to determine whether we can better secure our economic base on Long Island by expanding outside of Long Island."

Times Mirror wanted growth, too, but the corporation took a while to decide how to do it. Before Times Mirror bought *Newsday*, Chandler had thought about buying the *New York Post*, and in the mid-1970s, Chandler had asked Attwood to study ways of making the *Post* work as a Times Mirror property. *Newsday* did the study, but nothing came of it. Eventually, the growth imperative began to make the idea of expanding *Newsday* into Queens more acceptable to Times Mirror. "There is a principle in the human condition: You either go backward or forward," said Phillip Williams, who succeeded Richard Robinson as Attwood's immediate superior at Times Mirror. "You had Dave Targe and a lot of other very gifted newspaper executives who said, 'Well, now, we don't want to sit on our hands or our laurels. Maybe what we ought to do is take a very measured, carefully planned foray into Queens.' "

All along, Laventhol kept nudging the idea forward. "Here you had *Newsday*, an enormously successful newspaper, and a wonderful newspaper journalistically, and somehow, all that good stuff ought to be spread on a broader canvas," Laventhol said. Some *Newsday* veterans were not as enthusiastic as Laventhol. Tony Insolia, for example, worried that a Queens paper might bleed resources from Mother *Newsday* on Long Island. But if the organization's decision was to go ahead, Insolia was ready. "I grew up with Long Island *Newsday*," he said. "It was one innovation after another. I didn't grow up with a fat, lazy operation. I was used to change."

Finally, *Newsday* and Times Mirror agreed to take the first step: a Queens newspaper that would appear on Sunday only, starting on January 9, 1977. It was a delicate toe in the water, and Attwood was careful to keep expectations low when he announced it: "I want to emphasize that Newsday has no intention of 'invading' New York City and that this is simply a limited effort to satisfy those of our readers who live in Queens and those of our advertisers who want to reach them."

The layout of the new Queens Sunday paper gave it basically the same appearance as the Nassau-Suffolk version, but the first day's paper did have a healthy share of Queens news, including a lead story about a mysterious fire at a restaurant frequented by Queens politicians, a profile of Queens District Attorney John Santucci, a Queens Diary column by Ken Gross and coverage of Queens politics by the veteran political writer Dick Zander. This Queens-oriented paper boosted the existing circulation, but only by about 3,500 copies. As unimposing as the Queens Sunday paper was, however, it did seize the attention of the management at the *Press*. "You got the sense that they were running scared," said Peter Gianotti, a *Press* reporter who suddenly had to scurry to match *Newsday*'s community profiles.

In early 1977, as *Newsday* was learning how to put out a Sunday paper for Queens, declining advertising revenue forced the *Press* to cut costs wherever it could. "Everybody was doing three jobs," said John Maher, who was running the editorial page, handling letters to the editor and working Saturdays on the city desk. "When somebody left for another job, the feeling in management wasn't, 'How are we going to replace this valuable person,' but, 'Isn't it great that there's one less paycheck?' " Circulation had also continued to plummet. So the managing editor, Sam Ruinsky, knew it was only a matter of time before the *Press* folded. A few weeks after *Newsday* started its Sunday Queens paper, Ruinsky ran into Attwood at a public event, and Attwood asked him how he would feel about coming to *Newsday*. Ruinsky was interested, but he told Laventhol that he didn't want to leave while the *Press* was still alive. Someone had seen Ruinsky and Laventhol at lunch, though, and the word got back to the *Press* that Ruinsky was on his way to *Newsday*, which stirred resentment toward him at the *Press*.

At about the same time, two months into the Sunday experiment, *Newsday* shifted strategy. When Attwood announced the Sunday Queens paper, he had told the staff: "No daily Queens edition is contemplated." But in late February, Laventhol wrote a memo proposing a daily Queens paper. Finally, on March 18, Laventhol announced the decision to the staff: "A daily Queens edition of Newsday will start on Monday, March 28." A week after that memo, David Starr walked into the city room of the *Long Island Press* at five o'clock on the morning of March 25 and asked the staff to replace a page-one feature with a story announcing that the *Press* was printing its last edition that day, the eighty-third edition of its 157th year.

On Monday, March 28, just seventy-two hours after the demise of the *Press* and almost six years after *Newsday* had first begun seriously studying the idea of moving substantially into Queens, the presses in Garden City started turning out the first daily edition of *Newsday* edited specifically for Queens readers. "People were just dumbfounded how we could have moved so fast into the vacuum," Attwood said. "It was pure coincidence. . . . It really was *Newsday* luck, because we expected to be competing with them, and the competition vanished."

II

NO ONE AT *Newsday* or at Times Mirror approached the Queens venture as a snarling, bloodletting brawl with the New York City dailies. It was, from the start, an exercise in gradualism.

"It was done with the idea of having what I call a golden bridge of retreat," said Phillip Williams, who supervised the excursion for Times Mirror. If it looked as if the experiment were failing, they had the option to cut their losses. "This was not going to be a major new newspaper," said Howard Schneider, the assigning editor who ran the small band of Queens reporters. "What we did was very tentative and not very ambitious, when we could have really jumped in in a big way." If it had bought from the defunct *Press* its Queens subscriber lists, for example, *Newsday* might have built the edition's circulation quickly. But *Newsday* didn't, the *New York Post* did, and the *Post* reaped the benefit.

One of the major reasons why *Newsday* was uninterested in the *Press* list was that most of its circulation had been outside the sector of Queens that *Newsday* had chosen as its turf. In planning the edition, *Newsday* had decided to focus on the part of Queens that most resembled Nassau and Suffolk. This northeast quadrant — whimsically dubbed The Tenderloin — included communities such as Little Neck and Douglaston, full of single-family homes and well-tended lawns, like the suburban landscape that had become so familiar to *Newsday*.

As they developed the edition, the top management at *Newsday* had to resolve an argument that had been going on since the first Queens studies in the early 1970s. "The linchpin of the debate was: What is a Queens person? Is he or she a New Yorker or is he or she a Long Islander?" said Ken Brief, who helped with those early studies. "Some of us felt strongly they were New Yorkers, but we were in the minority." The key decision-makers looked at the semi-suburban lifestyle of the homeowners in The Tenderloin, realized that many of them shopped at malls or went to movies in western Nassau County, and came to what they considered the inevitable conclusion. "Queens was Long Island," Attwood said. "Basically, they think of themselves as Long Islanders, not as urbanites." That dictated the coverage: Besides providing the same report that *Newsday* gave Long Island readers on the world, the nation and the state, the Queens paper would offer local stories focused narrowly on Queens. It would not cover Manhattan issues heavily, although that was the seat of city government. In *Newsday*'s view, Queens readers didn't care about Manhattan.

"It was an unusual way to cover any kind of municipality," said Gianotti, who signed on with *Newsday* within hours after the *Press* folded. "There were selected communities where presumably the circulation drive would be taking place, and they would be covered to death." This approach made no sense to Dennis Duggan, a veteran of the *Herald Tribune*, the *Times* and the *News*, who had come to *Newsday* in 1967 to work on the upgraded business pages and became the paper's New York City bureau chief in 1971. "It was a strange vehicle," he said. "It in a sense meant you were covering one fifth of the city. It was sometimes rather embarrassing. . . . I remember vividly there was a story about a track meet and somebody from Queens finished fifth, and that was the lead." That small-town approach irked the reporters. "There was an enormous sense of frustration," Gianotti said, "in that they were trying so much to create this niche in Queens, to create this identity in Queens, that the most minor item was magnified." If there were truly major city stories, the staff covered them, but Queens news was the priority. "I was forever looking for stories that were connected to northeastern Queens," said Joe Treen, who worked out of city hall in Manhattan, but constantly had to leave city hall behind, to chase stories more closely related to The Tenderloin. "Going down to city hall meant touching base, saying hello and then going out and covering another story." At the same time that *Newsday* was placing all this emphasis on small-town coverage of Queens, Gianotti felt that the *Post* and the *News* were also working hard to stay on top of neighborhood stories. "I think it was in response to what was seen as an opportunity, with the *Press* folding," Gianotti said. "There'd be hostage situations that today wouldn't warrant sending a reporter, and you'd have these three musketeers from the different papers out there, acting as if it was the Lindbergh kidnaping."

In that period, the reporters realized what the management didn't. "The lowliest intern on the streets of Astoria for five minutes concluded that obviously, the people in New York have a slightly different sensibility," said Kate McCormick, who came to *Newsday* in 1977 and moved to the Queens edition as a copy editor at the start of 1978, when a separate Queens copy desk came into existence. "New Yorkers wanted a whole different pace to the way they got the news — a much faster pace, shorter stories, more action on the page. You couldn't help but understand it. Unfortunately, I think management was slow to respond to that." These differing perceptions caused frequent clashes between Treen and Howard Schneider, who controlled his assignments. "Anything that was west of the East River wasn't Queens, and therefore, he didn't care about it," Treen said. "We had lots of trouble over that."

Besides making coverage of New York City parochial, the Queens-is-Long-Island concept also created other distortions. "Management could see no problem at all in our having to pick up huge stories about corporal punishment in the Commack schools and the future of MacArthur Airport and whither Riverhead planning," McCormick said. The Queens paper also had to swallow decisions of the Long Island news desk about the front page. "Very often, we would have a better New York story than the national story that was fronting the Long Island *Newsday*," said Dan Lynch, the night Queens editor, "and we had to use the Long Island *Newsday* front." As a result, observant readers quickly figured out that they were not getting a genuine city newspaper. "Somebody wrote to us saying that they had complained to the Better Business Bureau or the consumer affairs bureau in the city that this was consumer fraud," Schneider said. "We were all embarrassed by that letter, because we knew it was true. That led Tony Insolia to propose the next phase, which was that Queens would have a separate copy desk, and we would make over as much of the paper as we could. . . . That was the beginning of thoughts that we had to do more."

At the same time that readers griped about Long Island stories in the Queens paper, the staff grumbled about their inability to get good New York City stories into the Long Island paper. "Curiously, if we said we had this great story in the city, and would they want to carry it in the Long Island paper, it was the most threatening thing in the world," McCormick said. "They were tremendously resistant in insisting that people on Long Island were not interested in those city things." That fear of allowing too much New York copy into the Long Island paper emanated from the highest levels of *Newsday*. "There was a motto laid down, a kind of dictum laid down by Dave Laventhol, that the tail must not wag the dog," said Sylvan Fox, who supervised the Queens and Nassau editions. "They were always erring on the side of caution, not putting things into regular *Newsday* from the Queens edition, on the theory that, if they did so, it would appear that the tail was wagging the dog." As a result, Fox had an unhappy group of Queens reporters on his hands. "It was a difficult morale problem," Fox said. "At this point, the sense of adventure was being overcome by the feeling that people were writing for a handful of readers, and this was a little depressing. The circulation was infinitesimally small. Here we had this huge circulation on Long Island, and they couldn't get a crack at that." So the reporters often felt that they were dropping their stories into a void. "We were like the Columbia University School of Journalism: We were putting out a mock paper," said Ed Hershey, one of the original Queens reporters. "The overwhelming problem was that, whatever we were doing, we weren't publishing a newspaper."

III

SINCE THE QUEENS edition was an odd construct based on an inaccurate perception of the readers, it seemed fitting that its staff should be a zany blend of talent, inexperience, manic enthusiasm and discontent.

To lead this colorful staff, Laventhol had chosen Sylvan Fox, the Nassau editor, and asked him to keep running Nassau as well — consistent with the effort to keep expectations for the Queens edition modest. Later in the year, Fox became the national editor and took the Queens operation along with him. Since Queens was a secondary concern for Fox, he left the day-to-day assignment of the Queens staff in the hands of Howard Schneider. Together, they were a journalistic odd couple, a veteran and a young editor with sharply different styles and backgrounds.

Fox brought to the job an unusual resume: He was both a Juilliard-trained pianist and a Pulitzer Prize-winning journalist. With a Juilliard education and a master's degree in music history, he thought about teaching music in college, but he was also interested in writing. So he took a job in 1954 as a reporter at the *Little Falls Evening Times* in upstate New York, followed by tours at the *Schenectady Union-Star* and the *Buffalo Evening News*. In the summer of 1959, Fox came to *Newsday* as a reporter-rewrite man. Before long, he fell for the lure of New York and went to work at the *World-Telegram & Sun*, despite Hathway's warning that he was making a big mistake. In 1962, Fox was working rewrite at the *World-Telegram* when a plane crashed at LaGuardia Airport. He spent the whole day writing about it, and that night, he told his wife, Gloria: "If I ever won a Pulitzer Prize, I won it today." In 1963, the Pulitzer Prize for local general reporting went to Fox and two *World-Telegram* reporters who had covered the crash. Not long after the prize, Fox became the city editor of the *World-Telegram*. When it folded in 1966, he took an interim press relations job with the New York City Police Department, then went to the *New York Times* as a rewrite man. After a year's leave of absence, during which he and his wife lived in Jerusalem and Fox worked as a consultant to the Israeli government, he returned to the *Times* and became the Saigon bureau chief in late 1972. By the spring of 1973, Fox had lost forty pounds and any desire to remain at the *Times*. So he ended up back at *Newsday*, despite Hathway's threat fourteen years earlier that he could never return.

By comparison, Schneider was almost a rookie. Following graduation from the journalism school at Columbia, he had taught English for two years in New York City and arrived at *Newsday* in 1969 as a reporter. With the creation of *The Summer Journal of Morton Pennypacker*, the experimental weekly that went to *Newsday* readers with the Saturday magazine, he had established a reputation for energy and creativity. When the Sunday paper started in 1972, he became the Long Island culture writer, followed by brief assignments running the paper's summer East End section, working on the copy desk, covering real estate and supervising projects in the Suffolk office. A few weeks after the Queens daily paper started, Schneider signed on with Fox to run it.

Just about the only thing that the two men had in common was a Brooklyn childhood. "We had a contentious relationship early on," Schneider said. "The famous saying is that I was the son Sylvan wished he never had." For one thing, they approached journalism from totally different perspectives. Fox had been a prodigiously fast rewrite man, feeding off the excitement provided by the breaking news that is the heart of big-city journalism. Schneider had grown up at *Newsday*, where breaking news was more the exception than the rule. This difference became clear to Schneider one day when five or six good breaking stories in the Queens paper made Fox excited and proud. "Suddenly, I for the first time knew what it was to be in a city where the news comes flying at you," Schneider said. "On the other hand, this was not *Newsday*. I didn't feel particularly proud, the way I felt proud when we broke a story in Suffolk or we enterprised a story in Nassau."

More important than their contrasting newspaper experience, Fox and Schneider had completely opposite styles. Fox was cool, laconic, almost sleepy. Schneider was enthusiasm incarnate: spewing out ideas, gesticulating wildly, his entire metabolism vibrating at an outrageously high frequency. "Howard can cram more words into a thirty-second burst than anybody I've ever met in my life," Dan Lynch said. "Sylvan's goal in life was to get through the day with as little bullshit as possible. Howard would come up, waving his arms and saying, 'Okay, Sylvan, we've got to do this, we've got to do that.' Sylvan would go: 'Are you crazy? Are you crazy?' "

Schneider's rapid-fire ideas and enthusiasms also drove the reporters wild, despite his fierce intelligence and basic decency. "There were staff rebellions on a regular basis," Gianotti said. The tiny Queens staff worked egregious amounts of overtime and operated in a fog of fatigue, which left them in no mood to chase after Schneider's sudden inspirations. "He's very creative, very energetic, but he doesn't seem to get great ideas until about five to five in the afternoon," Treen said. "It wasn't the kinds of stories. It was the timing and the pacing that was aggravating." All during that time, Treen kept a diary, filled with references to the struggle with Schneider. "He calls dozens of times a day, hysterical, wanting things, making impossible demands," Treen wrote. "The bottom line on Schneider is that he has everyone running around doing things but there is no story at the end of the day." After almost a year of this, Fox and Schneider had dinner with the staff and discussed the conflicts. "There was a sort of a catharsis," Treen remembered, "and Howard toned down."

If the Fox-Schneider combination was strange, the reporters themselves were also a bizarre ensemble. They called themselves "The Dirty Dozen," a reference to the film about a band of misfit soldiers recruited to carry out a suicidal commando raid against the Nazis. "They apparently used the creation of the Queens edition to bury a lot of people that nobody else wanted to deal with," Lynch said. A prime example was the skillful but fractious veteran reporter John Cummings, who had clashed with his boss, Bob Greene, repeatedly. Finally, Greene took Cummings off investigations and assigned him to the somnolent Town of Smithtown. Greene insisted that he had an investigative agenda for him there, but Cummings saw it as punishment. "He said I wasn't performing the way I should," Cummings said. "I just wouldn't show him homage or put flowers under his statue." So Cummings left the Suffolk office and started commuting into Queens every day to cover courts. In his new assignment, he was still not easy to manage. "Cummings' idea of recreation was to challenge every decision the desk ever made," Lynch said.

Similarly, Ed Lowe fled Greene and ended up in Queens, by a circuitous route. First, he flirted with an offer from the *Daily News*, then accepted a temporary assignment on *Newsday*'s Sunday magazine, followed by a tour on the Nassau desk, where he worked for Fox and had the sense that he was still somehow being punished for revolting against Greene. The desk assigned him to do "view from" pieces on small communities and later to write a column for the Sunday paper — a collection of short anecdotes that showed he had a feel for a column. Finally, Laventhol offered him the chance to write a column for the Queens paper. "I was called in by Laventhol, who introduced the conversation by saying, 'You know I hate columnists,' " Lowe remembered. "I said, 'Well, you know me. I've never had a whole lot of use for editors, either.' " Lowe took the job and went about the business of riding through Queens neighborhoods every day, looking for stories about ordinary people doing ordinary things — like the Long Island Diary column that Leslie Hanscom had pioneered in the Nassau-Suffolk paper.

"I used to drive around that whole area from Bayside down to Queens Village every day," Lowe said. "Now what I have to do is summon up the courage to go up to a total stranger and say, 'Hi. This is going to sound a little weird, but my name is Ed Lowe, and I write a column for *Newsday* about people doing whatever they're doing, and I noticed what you were doing is sweeping out your store, and I thought maybe if we talked for a while, I could write a column about you sweeping out your store.' Now this is Queens. So the first thing out of his mouth — and I'm telling you, fifty times I heard this — was: 'You got ID?' I'd say, 'Yeah, sure,' and I'd show him my ID, and he'd say, 'So, what is this? Does this cost? I mean, what do I have to do to do this? What are

we talking about here?' In other words, what is the scam? I would approach
people sometimes and then say, 'I can't do it,' turn around, get back in the car
and ride around for another hour, because it was so humiliating." But Lowe
stuck with it. After about a year of writing for the small audience in Queens, he
graduated to writing a column for the Long Island paper. It generated torrents
of mail from readers, and it made Lowe's walrus-mustached face one of the
most familiar symbols of *Newsday*.

The reporter that Lowe replaced as the author of Queens Diary was Ken
Gross, a gifted writer who had come to *Newsday* in 1969, at the invitation of Bill
Moyers. "The joke was Queens Diary was really a diary," Gross said. "We were
the only ones who read it. . . . In a way, there was a nice kind of privacy to it."
Even though very few people in the streets were reading it, the editor of
Newsday was. "I did a few and Laventhol hated them," Gross said. That was
when Lowe arrived and brought a completely different style to the column. But
Gross continued to be a mainstay of the Queens paper, writing features and a
wide variety of news stories with a deft and entertaining touch. "I pretty much
called my own agenda," Gross said. "I ran to the sirens." Everyone recognized
his talent and put up with his high-strung personality. "Some people call in
sick," Lynch said. "Gross used to call in depressed." Despite his quirks, Gross
provided the Queens edition with an entertaining, distinctive voice.

Perhaps the strangest reason for an assignment to Queens was Joe Treen's.
By the time the Queens paper began, he had been at *Newsday* almost a decade
and had already been a Nassau beat reporter, served as the first Sunday Nassau
editor, and worked as a general-assignment reporter for the national desk out of
the New York bureau, covering big stories, such as the Middle East and Watergate. Then, in 1976, he hurt his back, and when he returned to work, his editors
wanted him to operate out of the Garden City office on rewrite. But his ailing
back wouldn't allow him to sit still in a car and drive from his apartment in New
York to Long Island. So he preferred riding the subway to work, standing up,
and the advent of the Queens paper gave him that chance.

On the surface, Treen didn't look troublesome. He had a smooth, confident bearing and an authoritative midwestern voice. He was an excellent writer
and a thorough, meticulous reporter. Like Cummings, however, he had his
share of struggles with the desk. "I used to hang up on editors all the time,"
Treen said. "I was a real prima donna." One of those crises came during the
summer of 1977, when police were hunting Son of Sam, the serial killer who was
shooting at couples seated in parked cars. *Newsday* jumped on the case hard,
even to the extent of sending the reporter Leonard Levitt out to sit in a parked
car with an editorial assistant named Carol Gulotta and wait for the killer to
show up. Levitt and Ed Hershey became the paper's Son of Sam experts, and
Treen resented being asked to act as merely a helper for Levitt. One night,
Lynch called him at home and asked him to rush to police headquarters and
cover the arrival of the suspect, because Levitt couldn't get there for a while.
Treen cursed and slammed down the phone. "I probably just got myself fired,"
he wrote in his diary. He survived that outburst and went on to do some

excellent work for the Queens paper, including a tough series of stories about City Councilman Eugene Mastropieri, for wrongdoing that ranged from failing to pay parking tickets to maintaining a financial relationship with a mob figure. But he couldn't shake the prima donna image. "I had a reputation that I had gone overseas, and therefore, I had a really big head," Treen said.

The same kind of post-glory trauma affected Ed Hershey, who had been part of the award-winning *Newsday* coverage in the aftermath of the bloody prison riot at Attica, had nearly won a Pulitzer with Drew Fetherston for their coverage of a 1970 bus crash that killed seven Long Island school children, and had served as a New York correspondent for *Newsday*. When he found himself working for an edition that reached only a handful of readers, he saw a correlation between that and his role in the successful union organizing drive in 1973. "I knew right away that I was being buried," Hershey said. "I was doing these great stories that were printed in 18,000 papers." That drove Hershey to distraction. Two years after the Queens paper started, he left *Newsday* to do public relations for New York City's jail system.

Not everyone looked at the Queens paper as punishment. The staff also included eager young reporters who worked ridiculously long hours and grumbled, but found it a terrific opportunity. "There were so few of us in the beginning and there were so many big stories that you did get your share of stories," said Marianne Arneberg, who had worked at *Newsday* as a Part II intern until Schneider dragooned her for emergency duty on the Queens paper. "It was great for me. I was young. I was working in the big city for a big newspaper." The same was true of Alison Mitchell, a Harvard graduate who had started in journalism as a *Newsday* intern, worked at the *Bergen Record* and came to *Newsday* as a reporter in early 1977. Dressed in jeans and boots, with a head of dark, unruly hair, and full of noisy, manic energy, she reminded everyone of a crazed revolutionary. But beneath her high-volume cackle, there was a natural talent. "We watched her grow up, and she was everybody's little sister," Treen said. "She's first-rate."

Soon after she joined the Queens staff, Mitchell began covering a school integration struggle in the predominantly white Rosedale and primarily black Laurelton sections of Queens, which drew her into an internal *Newsday* controversy. "I discovered in passing that none of the people that lived in Laurelton seemed to be getting the paper," Mitchell remembered. She was not alone in that perception. "We covered Laurelton; we didn't circulate there," said another reporter, Caryn Eve Wiener. "Credibility was hard to come by in minority neighborhoods." In a note to Insolia, Hershey made the same complaint. "The black neighborhoods of St. Albans, Springfield Gardens, Laurelton and Cambria Heights are wealthier than some of the white neighborhoods in Queens where we now deliver," Hershey wrote. "They are contiguous to Nassau County, closer to Newsday than some of the areas now receiving home delivery. And, judging by everything we have heard on the hustings, they are eager to receive the paper." What *Newsday* was doing, the reporters argued, was "redlining" black neighborhoods. "We didn't skip over them, really," David Targe said. "In black areas, because of the demographics, it's very difficult to get carriers to operate. . . . Your circulation was not as good there, in black areas. . . . Over the years, we've been very careful about redlining, very conscious of not skipping any low-income areas." Nonetheless, the reporters and editors who covered those communities continued to see that pattern. "They were only comfortable in what they saw as Long Island-style neighborhoods, which were white," Hershey said.

Besides the assortment of rookies and malcontented veterans on the reporting staff, the crew of castoffs on the Queens paper would not have been complete without Dick Estrin. By then, Laventhol had long since removed him from dominance over the daily newspaper as news editor and shipped him off to other jobs — first to the Sunday paper and later to Part II. But when Laventhol saw the need for a separate Queens desk that would remake the paper every night, he had decided that Estrin was the best person to accomplish that, even though everyone knew how difficult he could be. "All the stories about Estrin turned out to be true — extraordinarily talented, seriously demented, without a doubt the single most confrontational human being I've ever met," Dan Lynch said. "With Estrin, you had to fight. If you didn't, he would whittle your testicles off."

Given the makeup of the staff, talented but undersized and sometimes contentious, and given the flawed strategic concept, the Queens edition was not an easy place to work. But the very idea of starting a new edition in the City of New York, which had been burying newspapers regularly, did provide a certain excitement. And the new paper did have brief moments of glory, such as its coverage of the 1977 New York City blackout, which even put the boss, Sylvan Fox, back in harness as a rewrite man. At a time when the New York City papers were momentarily crippled by the loss of electricity, the fledgling Queens edition of *Newsday* flooded the streets with reporters and provided an outstanding package. "We thought we had a shot at winning a Pulitzer," said Lynch. By putting the usual huge *Newsday* credit box on the package, instead of giving bylines to Fox and a few reporters, Lynch felt, they diluted their chance. "If I had put one or two bylines on it, Sylvan would have won a second Pulitzer." The edition also had moments of humiliation, such as the way the *Times* woke from its slumber and outgunned *Newsday* on the Son of Sam story. "For two days, we beat everybody on Son of Sam," Lynch said. "Then the *Times* got serious, and that was the end of that."

In addition to fighting the New York City competition, the *Newsday* management had to struggle internally to figure out what the Queens paper should be. "They kept changing the focus of what they wanted to do," said Bob Tiernan, who worked under Estrin on the copy desk. In the eyes of some, the Queens paper was too comprehensive and plodding, and not lively enough. "We were more like the *New York Times* than the *Daily News* in terms of coverage," Tiernan said. "There was always a sense on the part of Lynch and Estrin that we needed to be more like the *Daily News*."

Beyond the tactical questions of layout and coverage, the broader issue was still this: How serious should *Newsday* be about competing in New York City? "They wanted to encroach block by block," Ken Gross said. "They thought nobody would notice, and they were right: Nobody noticed." But by the end of the decade, as the edition approached its third anniversary, there were signs that *Newsday* was willing to think more boldly. At the beginning of 1979, for example, Fox and Ken Brief prepared a study of a Manhattan edition of *Newsday*, beyond the Queens paper. Not long after that, Fox and Schneider took the first step toward laying down some roots for the Queens paper, by finding a permanent office in the Rego Park section. That gave *Newsday* an office on Queens Boulevard, one of the primary streets in Queens, in addition to its small midtown bureau at 1500 Broadway, which had replaced the *Tribune* building in the mid-1970s as *Newsday*'s Manhattan enclave.

Before the end of 1979, the founding editors of the new edition had moved to other jobs — Fox to editor of the editorial pages and Schneider to Nassau editor — and effectively ended the first stage of the Queens expansion. As *Newsday* entered 1980, the Queens paper was still an evolving project, but the management had begun to learn some lessons. The most important was that their perception of Queens readers as suburbanites had been off the mark. "It was wrong," Schneider said. "I think the value of that period, although it was a lost opportunity, was that it helped later on, when we established our presence in New York, to know what did work. We couldn't be a Queens paper. We had to be a city paper." Beyond covering the local issues of Queens, *Newsday* had to cover the broader issues and personalities of the city as a whole. "You could see that the level of commitment was going to have to be significantly higher for us to be a success," Schneider said. "You couldn't do this as a halfway measure."

CHAPTER THIRTY-EIGHT

At the Crossroads

I

WHILE THE QUEENS edition was searching for an identity in its early months, the Long Island paper was struggling with a question closer to its suburban heart: How could Long Island, a hopelessly fragmented collection of government units, pull itself together to confront its future intelligently?

For years, *Newsday* had recognized this lack of unified leadership. It was a 1976 editorial, bemoaning that vacuum, that gave birth to an ambitious *Newsday* project designed to address the issue. The editorial described Long Island's problems, complaining: "And in neither the private nor the public sector are leaders coming forth to say, 'Let's get together and solve some of these problems.' " The paper's planning writer, Tom Morris, read the editorial and wrote a memo to Bob Greene, proposing a series on that lack of leadership. "It doesn't seem likely that the regional planning board would get out front on this kind of campaign," Morris wrote. "Would Newsday?" Simultaneously, the real estate writer Jerry Morgan was also examining the issue, from the perspective that a one-year economics fellowship had given him. "We were coming out of the recession much more slowly than anybody else," Morgan remembered. "The rate of growth had slowed. But more, there was this sense that nobody had a handle on it." So he wrote a memo of his own.

At the same time, Attwood kept hearing about the island's economic malaise in his encounters with businessmen, and Greene was meeting regularly with a group of business and government leaders to discuss the economy. The organizer of these meetings was Paul Townsend, the editor of the *Long Island Commercial Review*. "Paul Townsend had written for years about this problem, but nobody was paying much attention to him," said Dan Kahn, who covered Long Island business for *Newsday*. "He was saying we needed some sort of overall plan." All those currents of thought came together near the end of 1977, and *Newsday* decided: If no other institution would take the lead, then *Newsday* would.

To run the team, Laventhol chose Greene, the best big-project leader at *Newsday*. This assignment would be different from Greene's normal crime-and-corruption projects, but it would allow him to act on his beliefs about a newspaper's proper role. "Does a newspaper remain totally away from the things that intimately affect its community, or does it become a community leader, as well as the community's source of information?" Greene said. "Being a community leader, do you literally screw up your ability to objectively inform? That's a tough one." Greene himself had always come down on the side of involvement. When St. Anthony's High School in Smithtown wanted to build its image by starting a football team, for example, he helped establish a gridiron club, chose the team colors, and persuaded even Al Marlens and Tony Insolia, who were both suspicious of engagement with causes, to let their names be used. So he jumped enthusiastically into a project that could help shape the island's future.

"He had a hypothesis, which is fairly normal in a project like this, that Long Island was stalled, that growth had pretty much reached the limit, that what was needed was some dramatic initiatives," said Richard Galant, one of the reporters on the project. Greene had picked up ideas for initiatives in his meetings with businessmen, and he expounded them in long staff meetings, startling the younger reporters with his habit of falling asleep in mid-meeting, then waking abruptly minutes later, without missing anything that anyone had said. "He would lean back and look up at the ceiling, scratching his belly in his characteristic way, and go into a monologue that might go thirty or forty minutes, on what the island could be like," Tom Morris said. Then the reporters had to seek reaction from experts to those ideas, such as the creation of a regional wholesale market on the island and a deepwater port on Long Island Sound, near a proposed Long Island-to-Connecticut bridge.

The bridge to Connecticut was a central element of the series. For years, *Newsday* had argued that a bridge would end the island's geographical isolation and clear the way for growth. "We felt we had to get an East End exit," said Harold Gleason, the influential banker who had served, at *Newsday*'s request, on an earlier bridge-study commission that recommended an Orient Point-to-Rhode Island bridge. "We had to de-island the island." The master builder, Robert Moses, favored a bridge much farther west: from Bayville, in northern Nassau County, to Rye, in Westchester County. In fact, he built an entire road, the Seaford-Oyster Bay Expressway, to carry traffic to the bridge. Starting in the late 1960s, Governor Nelson Rockefeller sided with Moses and regularly vetoed a bill by Assemblyman Joseph Reilly of Glen Cove and Senator Ralph Marino of Muttontown that would have banned the Bayville bridge. Finally, in 1973, Rockefeller dropped his support for the bridge, and the plan died. That left only the Suffolk-to-Connecticut option, and in his meetings with business leaders, Greene had found strong support for it. "It was a given that we would push the bridge," Morris said. "This was not an effort to go out and report everything totally down the middle."

Most Connecticut officials felt that a bridge would only benefit Long Island, but *Newsday* managed to find one voice of support: former State Senator Paul Amenta, who had been the chairman of a special Long Island Sound bridge committee. He supported the idea because he thought it would help the economy of the Naugatuck Valley, but that support was costly: His opponent had used the bridge issue against him in 1970 and won. "I was a hero on Long Island," Amenta said, "but I wasn't running on Long Island." Some of the same antagonism haunted Attwood when he went to Connecticut to testify at a hearing about the bridge. Critics accused him of supporting the bridge so he could commute more easily between *Newsday* and his Connecticut home, even though his route across the Throgs Neck Bridge in Queens was quicker than any Suffolk-Connecticut route would be.

Toward the end of the project, Stuart Diamond wrote a detailed memo about the adverse environmental impact of a bridge, but it had no real effect on the series. Another skeptical memo came from the Albany bureau chief, Joel Kramer, whose only connection to the project was to keep asking New York Governor Hugh Carey about the bridge. "Carey was making fun of us, and I thought he was right," Kramer said. Finally, Kramer wrote a memo to Laventhol, criticizing the handling of the project. "In my entire career at *Newsday*," Kramer said, "it was the only real bad moment I had with my top bosses."

Despite the concerns of the reporters that they were working toward preordained conclusions, the project produced some excellent reporting. Among others on the team, Galant concentrated on quality-of-life issues, Kahn on business, Morgan on housing, Morris on transportation and planning, Diamond on energy and environment, John Hildebrand on education, David Zinman on science and technology, and Susan Page reported on the island's lack of a sense of identity. Michael Alexander gathered a long series of pithy quotes from a cross-section of community leaders, for use throughout the series. The pithiest quote of all came from an interview that Kahn and Galant had with Peter Goldmark Sr., the inventor of the long-playing phonograph record, who had written about the impact of working at home on the future of society. During the interview, Goldmark uttered the quote that later appeared prominently on the first day of the series: "Long Island could be a paradise or Long Island could be hell. And it's all going to be decided in the next twenty-five years."

Somewhere in the middle of that reporting, the central concept switched from an examination of what Long Island would be like in the year 2000 to a study of Long Island at the Crossroads, which became the final title of the series. "In doing the year 2000, we were focusing on what the problems were now, and what would happen if there was nothing done," Kahn said. The switch in emphasis forced them to do what they considered hurried and incomplete reporting on potential solutions. But Greene felt that they had already done some of the reporting on the solutions simply by researching the problems. "It

became apparent that without conclusions, without some kind of recommendations, the whole exercise was sort of a useless thing," Greene said.

When the time came for writing, the reporters got another jolt: The main
story in each subject area was to be 2,500 words long. "They asked me to cover
all of energy in 2,500 words, and I didn't think it was possible," Diamond said.
So Diamond wrote 9,000 words and turned the story in. When he had finished
answering the questions, it was 11,000 words long. "He said, 'Now I've said
everything I want to say about the subject. You trim it,' " said Jean Patman, who
helped to edit the project.

The series began with a twenty-four-page wraparound supplement that ran
in the paper on Sunday, March 19, 1978. That giant package outlined the
problems facing Long Island. Starting the next day, the series displayed the
result of the reporting at the end of the process: a group of stories about
potential solutions. "The indictment of the present system was much, much
better than the solutions," Galant said. On the final day, March 31, the series
offered *Newsday*'s recommendations: "Ten Priority Projects for LI." Some
reporters on the project, along with others on the paper, felt *Newsday* should
have made those recommendations on the editorial page — not on the news
pages.

The first recommendation turned out to be the most journalistically troublesome. *Newsday* concluded that Long Island needed a formal power structure
to make choices for the island's future, as a coalition of community leaders had
done in Kansas City. So Greene pulled together a group that became known as
the Long Island Action Committee. It was Greene who called up Long Island
leaders, Greene who chose the influential Republican, William Casey, as its
initial chairman, Greene who sold Casey to others, and Greene who hovered
over the committee's early meetings. "I have always been far more hands-on
than most newspaper people would be," Greene said. But Laventhol soon
decided that *Newsday* should disassociate itself from the committee, and
Greene pulled back. "I think a lot of these people read *Newsday* walking out as
meaning that no longer would they have the full force of that newspaper behind
them," Greene said.

Whether Greene's continued presence could have averted it or not, the
committee slid gradually into impotence — studying the problems instead of
doing something about them. "We called it the inaction committee," said Kahn,
who wrote regular follow stories after the series, along with Tom Morris and Jim
Scovel. "The action group didn't deliver, and then *Newsday* got stuck looking
like ninnies," said Lee Koppelman, the executive director of the regional
planning board. In retrospect, Laventhol felt that *Newsday* should not have
helped to create the committee and set the agenda. "We were probably getting
into a role that wasn't proper," Laventhol said. "The problem was that nobody
on Long Island really could put the thing together except *Newsday*."

In the end, the series did produce some change — primarily symbolic.
Since Long Island had little sense of identity, *Newsday* urged the use of the
words "Long Island" on regional entities, such as the Long Island Regional

Planning Board instead of the Nassau-Suffolk Regional Planning Board, and Long Island MacArthur Airport instead of Islip MacArthur Airport. The series also won some important recognition, a prestigious award from the Amos Tuck School of Business Administration at Dartmouth. But many at *Newsday* remained disappointed in the results.

"The fact that Long Island had no center, which was why we wrote the series, is eventually what made it sink — the fact that there was nobody there to grab hold of it once we did it," Morgan said. "We were, in effect, writing for the vacuum we were deploring." If there was any chance of solving that problem, Greene argued, *Newsday* destroyed it by disengaging from the action committee. "We had created, essentially, a way out of that vacuum," Greene said. "But then, the minute we created it, without perfecting the machinery of it, we abandoned it."

II

ONE OF THE most critical issues examined by the Crossroads series was the pollution of Long Island's fragile underground water supply, a problem that led to a long-running, Byzantine story of corruption and ineptitude.

Unlike New York City, which draws its drinking water from upstate reservoirs, Long Island gets its supply from subsurface soils. With the postwar growth of housing and industry, a broad range of pollutants seeped into the groundwater, contaminating one well after another, first in Nassau County and then in Suffolk. That pollution forced politicians into a massive public works project, a sewer district for the southwest corner of Suffolk County. Rather than let homes and businesses dump their wastewater directly into the ground through cesspools, the Southwest Sewer District would gather the waste, remove most of the pollutants and dump the treated effluent into the ocean. Beyond its environmental effects, that plan also had a major political impact: By funnelling huge amounts of money to construction contractors through politicians, it almost guaranteed graft.

A month before a 1967 referendum on the district, *Newsday* endorsed the concept, but with reservations. "The sewer system is meritorious, but people have to know what it will cost them," the editorial said. At the same time, Greene and Ray Larsen took a closer look and wrote a four-day series, "Problems in the Pipeline," which began with this assessment: "Suffolk County's program for a critically needed sewer system is steeped in politics and plagued by poor administration and its estimated cost may be far more than taxpayers are being told." Consequently, *Newsday* carried an editorial on the last day of the series, urging voters to reject the district. The voters turned it down overwhelmingly.

Only two years later, *Newsday* decided that the Suffolk Sewer Agency had replaced partisanship and garbled information with professionalism and candor. So an editorial urged voters to approve the district, and they did. But by mid-1976, the district had become mired in controversy. A combination of a statewide fiscal crisis and the district's swollen cost estimates forced the county to pledge countywide sales tax revenue in order to keep the district from sliding into default. During those difficult years, *Newsday* examined the project, seeking evidence that Republicans had taken kickbacks from the contractors, but the story was elusive. "There's no way we can look at the books and records of a sewer district and learn a goddamn thing," Greene said. "You have to have an inside source."

Finally, one day in 1977, a source turned up and met with Fred Tuccillo, the reporter on the Suffolk County beat who regularly covered the district. "It was clear that he knew things," Tuccillo said. "But he seemed to be probing to see what protection and what benefit this could yield to him. There was even talk of payment. That pretty much ended the discussion at that point, because I told him that *Newsday* did not pay for information. So he disappeared, really, for months after that." Eventually, the source came back to Tuccillo and started feeding him information on the inner workings of the county's Department of Environmental Control, which was overseeing the district. The source used the code name Lowell, which was actually the first name of his brother, a television journalist who had given Greene some information for the Arizona Project. His real name, which only became public many months later, was Martin Bergman.

Tuccillo's source was wary of *Newsday*, primarily because the paper had supported the sewer district in 1969. "Largely for that reason, he began talking to me almost immediately about wanting to be put together with the FBI," Tuccillo said. "He would talk to us and give us information, but he also wanted to make sure something real was going to happen." Greene set up a meeting with John Good, the agent in charge of the FBI's Hauppauge office. Though Greene considered Bergman self-serving and unproductive, the source's contact with the FBI gave them information that they found useful later. "He had, from internal gossip in the department, some sense of how tests might be rigged on pipe that was being used in the project," Tuccillo said. At the time, the FBI was not actively investigating the district, and Bergman's information helped get them started. "Over the months that followed," Tuccillo said, "they would become disenchanted with Bergman, not because his information wasn't good, but because he was uncontrollable and indiscreet."

As Tuccillo worked with Bergman and other sources, and the FBI and the county legislature scrutinized the district, the scandal produced one story after another in 1978 and 1979: delays in the opening date, nepotism, the firing of a whistle-blower, the rigged purchase of laboratory equipment, fraudulent stress-testing of pipes, an outfall pipe that floated away in the ocean and the indictment of the firm that supplied the district's concrete pipe. Even blood and sex entered the picture: Within hours after a grand jury had indicted the former commissioner of the Department of Environmental Control, John Flynn, and Flynn had agreed to tell what he knew about the corruption, his lover and former employee, Sue Quinn, stabbed him to death. She later acknowledged that she killed Flynn because he had told her he planned to end their relationship, but the timing of the death looked conspiratorial, which was still another painful twist for Suffolk County Executive John V. N. Klein, who had vowed to push the district through to completion. "I had the feeling that I was the driver of a runaway cement truck," Klein said. "Everything was going wrong. Every day was a new disclosure. Every day was a new disaster. The media in general went into a feeding frenzy." In particular, though, he blamed Tuccillo. So he called Greene and asked for a meeting to air his gripes. Greene listened politely, but that was all he did. "Greene conducted himself admirably," Tuccillo said. "He did not give an inch."

Though Tuccillo's stories caused trouble for Klein, some critics of the district suspected that Greene allowed his friendship for Klein's mentor, Smithown Republican Leader Nicholas Barbato, to soften *Newsday*'s coverage. But the pages of the paper carried ample evidence that Greene did not prevent his reporters from pounding Barbato. In 1977, in fact, it had been Greene himself who forced a judge to unseal court papers that showed how a Smithtown insurance broker, George Tobler, had shared his premiums with Republicans, kept Barbato on his payroll for $200 a week, and allowed Smithtown Republicans to use part of his building, rent free, as a headquarters. For the rest of 1977, 1978 and early 1979, the reporter Carole Agus kept pressing Tobler for more information. Finally, in early 1979, Greene decided to let Agus pursue the story to Tobler's home in Sea Island, Georgia, but he sent Tuccillo along with her.

Staying at condominiums near Tobler's home, Tuccillo and Agus worked at loosening Tobler's tongue, plying him with liquor and questions. Agus played her natural role — nervous, excitable, unpredictable — and Tobler turned for support to Tuccillo, who remained quiet and calm. "He would just come up to the edge of confirming things," Tuccillo said. "He was filibustering us with anecdotes." Finally, they went to his house and he began to show them documents. Agus told him that they could not help him unless he trusted them. "I said, 'I want every piece of paper in your house,'" Agus remembered. "He thought I was a lunatic. . . . Fred said, 'I don't think she's crazy. I think she's right.'" For a long time, they sat silently, waiting for the next step, until Tobler finally decided to let them have the papers.

Wasting no time, Tuccillo put down his notebook and began scooping up Tobler's records and carrying them out to the car. Agus got on the phone and tried to maintain her calm while she told Joe Demma on the Suffolk desk what was going on. Not long after they left Tobler, with a car full of documents, the dimensions of their coup suddenly hit them. "He stopped the car in the middle of the street and we just laughed and laughed and laughed," Agus said. "He said that was the highest high you could get in reporting." When they returned to Long Island, Greene greeted them like conquering heroes. "Something he had chased for years had suddenly fallen in his lap," Tuccillo said. "Greene insisted on taking us out to dinner. I've never seen him so happy about anything."

With help from Drew Fetherston, Agus and Tuccillo sat down and started to figure out Tobler's papers. The biggest story that the documents produced was a link between contractors on the sewer district and Barbato, who had been a major supporter of the project. Fetherston and John Cummings had earlier discovered that Barbato and Perry B. Duryea Jr. were partners in a Bahamian land venture with the contractors Mario Posillico and Carl Lizza when Duryea was the speaker of the Assembly. Tobler's papers suggested what Lizza and Posillico might have gotten out of the deal: A steep increase in the cost of oil-based materials had forced contractors to seek state and local legislation allowing them more money on their contracts. At the same time, Duryea and Barbato were experiencing financial trouble on the Bahama property. Not long after the contract adjustment bill passed, giving Posillico and Lizza an extra $556,000, they invested in the Bahama land. In another story, Barbato admitted that Twin County Transit Mix, a sewer district contractor, had put him on its payroll for $200 a week as a salesman and public relations man.

Besides carrying the stories based on Tobler's papers, *Newsday* made both Tobler and the papers available to the FBI, and Tobler testified before a federal grand jury investigating the sewer district. Soon after that, a county grand jury indicted Barbato for extortion: forcing Tobler to pay him more than $100,000 over nine years, in exchange for the county insurance contract. At about that time, Klein met with Greene, who advised him that he had to ask Barbato to step down as town leader. Barbato did resign, but that didn't help Klein, who lost a Republican primary to Peter Cohalan and soon found himself out of office. A judge acquitted Barbato of the state extortion charge, but in 1981, a federal grand jury indicted Barbato and Bowe Walsh & Associates, the sewer district engineer, for a system of kickbacks that allowed Bowe Walsh to win the contract. Once again, Barbato won acquittal, but his primary codefendant, Charles Walsh, was convicted. Finally, in 1982, Barbato ended the long chain of criminal charges by pleading guilty to two misdemeanor perjury counts, in connection with his testimony before the county grand jury.

Oddly, during the long *Newsday* pursuit that led him into the courts, Barbato developed a strong dislike for Tuccillo, but continued his friendship with Bob Greene. "Our relationship never changed," Barbato said. "He didn't write the story. He had to do what he had to do." Despite the concerns of his staff about his closeness to Barbato, Greene had not flinched. "If Nicky went to jail, I'd feel terrible, because I like him," Greene said. "But that doesn't mean I wouldn't set into motion all the things that would catch him."

III

THE SEWER SCANDAL and the Crossroads series absorbed thousands of reporter-hours in the late 1970s, along with other high-profile local stories, such as the Franklin National Bank's collapse and the lawsuit by the Levittown schools that persuaded a judge to declare the state's school-financing system unconstitutional. But during that period, it was the assignment of a lone reporter to a foreign story that came closest to bringing *Newsday* a Pulitzer Prize.

The reporter was Les Payne, who had already won a share of a Pulitzer for his work on the heroin trail with Bob Greene. The year after the heroin trail, Payne had spent weeks covering the kidnaping of the newspaper heiress Patricia Hearst and trying to understand the radical group that staged it, the Symbionese Liberation Army. At the same time, he started hinting that *Newsday* should send him to South Africa. Then a 1976 rebellion in the black township of Soweto, bloodily suppressed by the government, thrust South Africa into the headlines. "When Soweto broke out," Payne said, "Dave Laventhol said right away I could go."

Black journalists, of course, had a difficult time getting visas for South Africa. So Payne turned for help to Arthur Ashe, the black tennis star, who had visited South Africa. Ashe was friendly with Doug Smith, Payne's college roommate, who had come to *Newsday* as a reporter with Payne's help. In Payne's behalf, Ashe communicated with the minister of sports and information, Piet Koornhof. Even with the help of the minister's name, Payne had to wait four months for a visa. He got to South Africa at the end of September, 1976, escorted by Andrew Hatcher, an American public relations consultant working for the South African government.

"I was doing mealymouthed stories, skills I had picked up on the heroin trail," Payne said. "Then they stopped watching me very carefully." So Payne asked the government to extend his visa from thirty days to three months, and they granted his request. "That's when I dropped out of sight," Payne said. His agenda was to develop as soon possible an in-depth knowledge of what was really happening in the country. "What I was doing was exploring parachute journalism, which *Newsday* pioneered in a way," said Payne, referring to the practice of sending an aggressive reporter into a country long enough to develop a sophisticated understanding of its economy and culture, then pulling him home to write hard-hitting reports, without the constraints that would face a reporter who had to continue living in that country. "After about two months, I really began to understand the country."

The government made black townships such as Soweto off limits to foreign journalists without permission, but Payne ignored that rule and went into Soweto daily. "They thought I was an African returning home after work," Payne said. "There are places in Africa where I would not look like an African. But in South Africa, clearly that's probably where my forebears came from." With this access to the township, Payne began to focus on the death toll from the Soweto uprising. The government was saying that about 200 blacks had died in the Transvaal Province, including Soweto, but the residents were telling Payne that the total was anywhere from 400 to 700. To find out the real figures, Payne interviewed the owners of funeral homes. "The guy would invariably tell me, 'You'll be back in New York and I'll be in prison if I were to tell you how many people I buried that were riot-related,' " Payne said. But in one funeral home, he spoke to a young woman employee instead of the owner, and he made his plea: "The world should know. These are not mosquitoes or cockroaches. These are human beings." She reacted emotionally, because her nephew had died and her husband had been injured. So after closing hours that night, Payne came back and she gave him a list.

On his rounds of funeral homes, Payne learned that the recorder's court in Johannesburg had figures on the deaths. "Somebody told me that the riot-related names in the inquest record had an 'R' by them," Payne said. So he showed up at the courthouse with a black journalist, Enoch Duma, posing as ordinary citizens looking for the name of a relative. A clerk brought out a ledger book and let them look at it. "Boom, we looked and there were the Rs," Payne said. "When she went to lunch, we started writing down names like crazy." By the end of the day, they had 150 names. They came back the next day, this time with a camera. As a result of his counting, Payne wrote two pieces about the death toll in late 1976, including one that showed that the toll in Soweto alone was 332 — at least seventy-five percent higher than the government estimate — and the toll for the whole country was in excess of 435. Then, after he returned to America, Payne wrote an eleven-part series in early 1977.

Soon after the Pulitzer Prize awards in 1978, Tony Insolia called Payne and explained to him that the Pulitzer jury had chosen Payne's South Africa series, but the advisory board had overturned that recommendation and given the prize to Henry Kamm of the *New York Times* for a series about the Southeast Asian refugees. Payne decided not to say anything that might anger the Pulitzer board, because by then, he had been to Rhodesia and written an eight-part series in early 1978 that he considered better than the South Africa series. But others grumbled loudly about the "overturn" phenomenon. An Associated Press story revealed that the board had overturned juries that year in five of eleven categories. So Tom Collins, *Newsday*'s media writer, launched an investigation of the Pulitzer process and wrote a three-part series on the issue.

"That was the first year that the records of the minutes for previous years were open for examination, and *Newsday* was the first to take advantage of it," Collins said. "One of the greatest satisfactions I ever got on this media beat was calling up people around the country to tell them how close they came to a Pulitzer. They were as pleased as if I had just awarded it to them. We were the first ones to ever get that information to the newspaper community." The Collins series, of course, came too late to help Payne, who added a new title to his resume: Pulitzer Prize loser.

CHAPTER THIRTY-NINE

Newsday Moves East

I

FROM THE START, the simple cinder-block plant that Albert Wood designed for *Newsday* had been an awkward compromise between the paper's immense growth potential and Harry Guggenheim's fiscal caution.

But the explosive development of Long Island in the 1950s and 1960s forced Harry to approve one space addition after another, as *Newsday* grew. "It was a rabbit warren," said Michael Youchah, who first saw the plant when he joined Times Mirror in 1974 as director of management services on the East Coast. "There were at least seven different roof levels, and there were many parts of the building that could not be accessed without going outside and coming in another door. So we had these strange little alleys."

The inadequacy of the plant was obvious, but the solution was not. The building codes in Garden City made it impractical to add new space on top, and the land on either side of *Newsday* wasn't available. So, by the time Youchah arrived, *Newsday* had concocted a plan for a makeshift addition of 30,000 square feet on the only land they *could* use: the lawn. "The 30,000 feet out front was never going to solve even yesterday's problems," Youchah said. After significant study, the idea of expanding in Garden City fell apart, and *Newsday* began looking for another site — somewhere to the east, because everyone assumed that the future growth of the paper's readership would be in Suffolk County. The plan was to close both the Ronkonkoma office in central Suffolk County and the Garden City plant in central Nassau County and build a single plant somewhere along the Nassau-Suffolk border. But Bob Greene in the Suffolk office waged a lonely and ultimately unsuccessful campaign against the proposal for selling the Ronkonkoma acreage where he and his reporters worked.

Journalistically, Greene argued, moving into a plant at the Nassau-Suffolk border would put most of the reporters into an office farther away from their beats. Financially, he insisted that it made good sense to keep the Ronkonkoma office site and install presses, because the land was between a Long Island Expressway entrance, which gave trucks quick access to the roads, and a Long Island Rail Road siding, which would speed the delivery of newsprint. But a satellite plant had drawbacks. "You couldn't move copy the way you can today, electronically," said James Fitzgerald, a senior vice-president of *Newsday*, whose headaches included the physical plant. "Either you'd have to have two composing rooms, which is very costly, or try to set copy in Garden City and then race it out to Ronkonkoma." So *Newsday* decided on one central plant.

Finding a site was not easy. To begin with, once a major corporation starts looking for real estate, prices can spiral. So, when Youchah started his search, he used subterfuges to hide his corporate affiliation: He directed mail and phone calls to a company owned by a neighbor of his in Manhattan, and he didn't even tell the broker that he represented *Newsday*. He would meet the brokers at their office, view potential sites, then drive home. "They told me a couple of times they had great temptations on some occasions to trail me home to see where I went, but I used to take different routes every time," Youchah said. "It was cloak and dagger."

In looking for a location for the plant, Youchah and *Newsday* established a corridor: within two miles of the Long Island Expressway, anywhere from just east of the Nassau-Suffolk line to a point about fifteen miles east of that. They also wanted the site to have a rail siding, just as the Garden City plant had. If they had to settle for a plant without rail access, they could only receive newsprint by truck, which could make the paper vulnerable to a truckers' strike. But when Youchah started looking along the Long Island Rail Road tracks, he found nothing suitable. "There was nothing there that would not be a pure heavy-industrial kind of site, and that was not what we were looking for," he said. "We wanted to make a statement. We didn't want to look like another factory."

The absence of sites near rail sidings complicated an already difficult search. "I looked at over 120 sites," Youchah said. One of them was a former drive-in movie right at the intersection of the expressway and Route 110, the main north-south road just east of the Nassau-Suffolk border. "It would have made a major, major statement," Youchah said. But the price was prohibitive and the truck access was complicated. Youchah looked at another site with high visibility, a little farther south on Route 110. Otis Chandler liked it, and *Newsday* went so far as to take an option on it, but its size and shape presented too many problems. Finally, the searchers settled on a location on Pinelawn Road in Lower Melville, just south of the expressway. Ironically, this was one of the first sites that Youchah had seen, but it had fallen into disfavor because it had no rail siding and it sat across the road from a national cemetery. By the time *Newsday* and Times Mirror decided to take the site that they had dubbed "The Boneyard," they were willing to settle for a rail siding three miles away, which they felt would provide a backup in the event of a trucking strike.

The rectangular site was made up of three parcels totaling 32.8 acres. The front half, on Pinelawn Road, belonged to the Rottkamp family, which had been growing vegetables there since 1950 and had recently sold the back half for development. "We were trying to make a living and we couldn't anymore," said Cyril Rottkamp, one of the three brothers who farmed the land. For Youchah, accustomed to dealing with corporate executives and real estate brokers, closing a deal with the Rottkamps was a pleasant dose of reality. They met to discuss price and arrangements in a rough greenhouse — plastic sheeting draped over pipes — where the Rottkamps grew flowers. "Cyril sat in the tractor seat," Youchah said. "The rest of us sat on old wooden kitchen chairs with the backs cut off. So you weren't too comfortable. It was a real down-home kind of a thing. You knew you were dealing with real people. . . . They were just as sweet and as honest as they could be." Youchah shook Cyril Rottkamp's huge hand on the deal, and Rottkamp presented him a purple passion plant for his wife.

Early in 1977, *Newsday* completed the purchase of the Melville site, at a cost of just under $2 million, and on June 2, Attwood turned the ceremonial first shovelful of dirt. In the first six months of 1977, *Newsday* had opened a two-front war, moving its circulation area west into Queens and its headquarters east into Suffolk.

II

RIGHT IN THE midst of building a new plant, *Newsday*'s top management suddenly had to rebuild itself.

At the core of this reshuffling was an ennui that came over Bill Attwood once he had launched the plant project. "I didn't have the zest," Attwood said. "I was no longer making decisions. I was cutting a lot of ribbons and handing out safe-driving awards." Without major new decisions to make, the day-to-day bureaucracy of the corporation simply annoyed him. From Times Mirror's point of view, the company was hardly intrusive. "This is not a heavily bureaucratic company," said Attwood's corporate boss, Phillip Williams. "The sense that we try to convey is one that the publisher of *Newsday* is the chief executive officer in all respects." Still, Attwood thought that Williams wanted too much financial information. "He was correct, but he was a worrywart," Attwood said. "He'd call, usually at 5:30 in the afternoon, and ask me about something in great detail. . . . It was spinning wheels." Attwood was an experienced editor and reporter, and Williams was a cautious businessman who had no newspaper background before coming to Times Mirror in 1969. During one discussion, Attwood remembered, Williams told him: " 'Your problem is that you're a journalist. . . .' He was totally a money man, and the more money we made, the more he used to worry about it."

As the construction of the new building got under way, Attwood also began to think about how much farther he would have to travel every day from Connecticut. "It would have been an impossible commute," he said. "I had some books in me I wanted to write. I wanted to try something I never had, which was teaching journalism." So, about two years before he actually left *Newsday*, he spoke with Otis Chandler about an early retirement. "I said: 'I would hope my successor would be David Laventhol,' " said Attwood, who had already pushed Laventhol to become more involved in the business side of the paper. "He said: 'I share your feelings about Laventhol, because I saw how he held that place together during the summer of 1970.' " So, in 1977 and 1978, Attwood sensed that his days with Times Mirror were winding down. "I think we were bored with each other," Attwood said. "Everything that I'd been sent there to do we'd done — the new plant, the Sunday edition, reorganizing the staff and the executives. . . . And so, our time was up." Chandler had also begun to feel restless about Attwood. "Bill did a good job as publisher and he put together a good team and developed fine esprit de corps and unity," Chandler said. "But I think in time, we felt — Times Mirror felt, I felt personally and Phil Williams felt — we felt that we needed a stronger person there as leader. Bill is a fine person, but he's kind of a mild-mannered, feet-up-on-the-desk type of person. . . . We just felt maybe the time had come. So we talked to Bill about it and he said, 'I've enjoyed my time here. But if you guys want somebody else, I'm not going to stand in your way.' "

The precipitating event was a planned Paris conference of the United Nations Educational, Scientific and Cultural Organization in the fall of 1978. At this conference, UNESCO was expected to adopt a declaration that would allow governments to control the press. A group of American journalists approached Attwood, because of his diplomatic experience and fluency in French, and asked him to attend the conference and try to modify the declaration. "That, of course, took place in October and November, which was during our whole budget cycle," Attwood said. "It made more sense for Laventhol to take over the publishing job then." So, early in September, 1978, the top executives of *Newsday* gathered for a morning meeting in Attwood's office and listened to Chandler tell them that Attwood was leaving immediately as publisher and Laventhol was taking over. Attwood was to stay on as chairman of the board until his retirement in July, 1979. Some *Newsday* executives had understood that Attwood wanted to remain publisher until the company took over the new building. So, when he stepped down months before the completion of construction, they saw his departure as strangely sudden. That perception spawned a flood of rumors, but the truth seems to be simply that Attwood was tired of Times Mirror and Times Mirror was tired of him, and the UNESCO conference made a quick decision necessary. "There was no firing and no resignation," Attwood said. "It was just sort of a mutually agreed-upon parting of the ways."

In eight years as publisher, Attwood had steered the paper through the unsettling aftermath of the Times Mirror purchase and presided over a series of major business decisions, such as the start of the Sunday paper and the Queens edition. Editorially, he had shown his cautious, diplomatic side when he decided that *Newsday* would no longer endorse political candidates. But he had also demonstrated that he was open to new ideas, such as a column by Stan Isaacs on television coverage of sports, and a feature that began in 1978 and achieved instant popularity: *Kidsday*, a section for and about children, written and prepared mostly by the children themselves. In addition, he had some ideas of his own, ranging from the profoundly serious heroin trail project to the light-as-air Sunday section that covered the summer scene in the Hamptons, with Bob Greene cast improbably as the gossip columnist.

On balance, Attwood was a comfortable fit for that period of *Newsday*'s development. Even though he devoted significant attention to the business side of the paper, Attwood remained basically a journalist. He was willing to operate in the new Times Mirror corporate environment, but ready to evade the absentee owner in small ways. He would send to Los Angeles the minutes of his staff meetings, for example, but he wouldn't send them minutes from the meetings of the executive committee, for fear that the committee's brainstorming about the future would alarm the cautious Times Mirror management. In a letter to the heroin trail team after visiting them in France, Attwood expressed that slightly maverick attitude, admitting that he missed being a reporter, but that being publisher gave him some satisfaction: "I can help keep the money men at bay and thus keep Newsday not just a good paper but a rare paper — that is, one which spends money on things it doesn't *have* to spend money on in order to make money." By the time he left, Attwood's style had earned him a measure of affection from the staff, which turned out en masse for a lavish farewell party for him, a few weeks before his tour as chairman of the board expired in 1979.

Attwood's departure thrust David Laventhol suddenly into the role of publisher — not a job that he had expected to have — and Laventhol made Tony Insolia his successor as editor. "I didn't think I would ever be editor of the paper, even when I got to be one of the three managing editors," Insolia said. "I remember telling someone that there was only one way that I would ever become editor of this paper, and that was if the selection was made by Dave Laventhol. . . . I knew that he understood my value to this newspaper and he knew my strengths better than anyone else." Despite those strengths — steadiness, loyalty and day-to-day competence at the complicated craft of putting together a newspaper — his roughhewn personality had convinced many people at *Newsday* that Insolia was too blunt to be *the* editor. "He never bullshitted anybody," said the editor Tom Stites. "I appreciated the fact that if you went to Tony, he'd tell you right in your face, and maybe with hobnailed boots and four-wheel-drive vehicles and everything else, go right up your chest, and tell you what he meant." In later jobs, at the *New York Times* and elsewhere, when a problem of news judgment confronted him, Stites would try to imagine how

Insolia would handle it. "His news judgment is just perfect," Stites said. "Tony has a way of going to the heart of the matter."

Laventhol felt so strongly about Insolia's value that he had acted, months before Attwood stepped down as publisher, to give Insolia primacy: At the end of 1977, he had promoted Insolia to executive editor, dismantled the three-managing-editor system and left Lou Schwartz as the sole managing editor. Before that announcement, the third managing editor, Don Forst, had told Laventhol that he was leaving *Newsday* to try to save the ailing *Los Angeles Herald Examiner*. "I left the paper because David seemed to be set for a good long run as editor," Forst said. "I wanted a challenge."

The final step in the management reshuffling in 1977 and 1978 was Insolia's announcement that he was appointing five assistant managing editors. The most significant of these were Phyllis Singer's appointment to run the feature sections, which gave *Newsday* a woman's name high on the masthead, and Bob Greene's appointment as assistant managing editor for Long Island, which solidified his control over the local news-gathering operation. The Nassau staff, which had laughed from afar at his emphasis on productivity in Suffolk, had started to become nervous a few months earlier, when Greene became Long Island editor and took control of the Nassau staff as well. His appointment to assistant managing editor, plus the impending unification of the two staffs in one building, exacerbated their fears. "They were looking to run places," said Bob Samsot, who had left Suffolk and was an editor in Nassau, "and I was saying: 'Hey, give the guy a chance.' "

One group that seemed especially edgy was the black caucus. Earlier in 1978, a member of the caucus, Sam Washington, had committed suicide. The *Newsday* obituary not only gave the details of his death, but mentioned that he had beaten his wife. The caucus was outraged that Washington's obit contained such details, but that the obits of white *Newsday* employees who had taken their own lives had omitted the painful facts. "This treatment was not surprising, for we know, as Sam reluctantly and quite painfully discovered, that the Suffolk editor particularly treats blacks in a dehumanizing manner," the caucus said in a memo. The memo did not identify its author, but the cadences were unmistakably Les Payne's.

The black caucus was convinced that the villain was Greene. But Cathy Davidson, who wrote the obituary, said that Greene did not shape it. Gail Meadows had assigned the obituary during the day and Joe Demma edited it at night. "We all thought that we did a very sensitive, telling piece," Demma said. A major reason for the use of so much detail on Washington's death was that Davidson and others had felt it was wrong not to have written the truth when their colleague Maurice Swift committed suicide, and that *Newsday* should be honest about the deaths of its own people. So the caucus memo stunned Davidson. "I thought that I was on this great mission of truth-telling," she said. "I still don't think I was racist, but I think I was wrong."

Yet it was Greene who was the primary target of the anger. This was a vivid example of the complex relationship between Greene and Payne. They had worked closely together on the heroin trail, and Greene later was among those who recommended that Payne apply for the job of national editor. In the Sam Washington case, Greene felt he had done everything he could to help Washington, but that didn't deter Payne from calling him a racist. "I feel that Les sometimes, for political purposes, feels he has to do some things," Greene said.

While the staff coped with Greene's ascendancy, and Laventhol and Insolia tried to make their imprint on the paper, the construction of the new plant went forward. That involved a constant push-and-shove between *Newsday* and Times Mirror over costs. Times Mirror didn't want to build more than *Newsday* would need in the near future, but nobody wanted the plant to be too small, either. "We increased the size of the building before we got off the drawing board," said James Fitzgerald. The final size of the building was about 325,000 square feet, roughly double the size of the Garden City plant.

Beyond the basic concerns of size and cost, one of the key issues was the configuration of the presses. Jim Grider, who had come to *Newsday* from Times Mirror in 1971 as general manager, had strongly recommended that *Newsday* abandon letterpress printing and go to the more modern offset process, for two reasons. "The first one was quality," Grider said. "Metropolitan newspaper letterpress quality is pretty damned poor. Secondly, I felt that to stay competitive in the media marketplace, that it would become imperative eventually to go to color." Offset made good sense for smaller newspapers, but Times Mirror was skeptical about using offset at a paper as large as *Newsday*, because offset wastes more newsprint than letterpress does. As for color, Phillip Williams at Times Mirror was hesitant about that, too. "He was saying, 'Well, there is no color in New York,' " said Grider, who argued that the lack of color capacity at other papers was precisely the reason why *Newsday* should have it, to gain a competitive advantage.

The correct number of presses was also a difficult decision. From the start, *Newsday*'s circulation had grown so fast that it strained the capacity of the presses to print enough papers. So the plant had to have sufficient press capacity to keep up with growth, but not so much that the cost of the presses bloated the budget. Youchah argued for six presses, but they ended up leaving space in the pressroom for expansion to six presses but starting off with five eight-unit Goss offset presses. They also compromised on the issue of color, installing a modest capacity for full-color pages. "Had we looked a little farther in the future," Grider said, "we would have added more color capacity." Once the presses were installed, the production staff set up the system that *Newsday* had developed for punching thumbholes in the papers at Garden City, to help readers find different sections. But they had to abandon that when they realized that the finicky system wouldn't work as well on offset as it had on letterpress.

All during this period, while the staff continued to work in the antiquated, crowded Garden City building, the hopeful motto became: "It will all be better in the new building." Finally, the plant opened — over budget and a year behind schedule — in October, 1979. "The original budget was something like $33 million, and we wound up spending closer to $44 million," Fitzgerald said.

"More of our concern than staying on budget was staying on time. . . . When you prolong a building, you're carrying a heavy capital investment that you get no beneficial use out of. . . . That's more expensive than if the damn building goes over a few million dollars, but it's not as readily identifiable."

The building came complete with controversy, including a lawsuit by the subcontractors and a tax abatement that *Newsday* won from the state's Job Incentive Board for building its plant in the Town of Huntington — as if *Newsday* would have moved to Iowa without the incentive. The abatement later became an issue during a struggle in the state Legislature about job incentive programs. Despite the controversy, the delays and the cost, *Newsday* was finally able to leave behind its old, inadequate plant and occupy one that seemed more than ample for the paper's future.

III

AS THE LAST year of the decade began, *Newsday* had a new publisher, a new team of managers and a nearly completed new plant, but it still did not have a single foreign bureau.

Over the years, *Newsday* had covered foreign news primarily through the eyes of the wire services. Alicia Patterson had supplemented the wires by arranging for reports from veteran correspondents who were stationed abroad, writing for a variety of publications, such as Edmund Stevens in Moscow and Alice-Leone Moats in Rome. Alicia had also made regular foreign trips of her own, which produced reports on Russia, the Middle East and Europe. Once Harry Guggenheim took over, he sent John Van Doorn, John Steinbeck and Mike McGrady to Vietnam and assigned Van Doorn permanently to foreign coverage. Van Doorn travelled widely, but his base was Long Island, not a foreign city. Early in the Times Mirror era, a few reporters spent significant time abroad, including Joe Treen in the Middle East, Marilyn Berger at the Paris peace talks and David Gelman in Vietnam. In an echo of Alicia's travels, Laventhol visited China with a group of American editors in 1975, and Bill Attwood, Laventhol and Bill Sexton toured Russia in 1976 and reported on *razryadka,* the easing of tensions. *Newsday* had also spent money freely in developing the kind of "parachute journalism" that Les Payne practiced in covering Africa.

In contrast, the *Los Angeles Times* under Chandler had built up its foreign staff the traditional way, with overseas bureaus. At one point, after *Newsday* had sent someone abroad on a temporary assignment, David Laventhol discussed *Newsday's* occasional-coverage approach with Chandler. "He said, 'That's good, but that isn't really the way to do it. Really, the only way to do it is to have people overseas,' " Laventhol remembered. To do it right, Laventhol told him, *Newsday* would need ten people. "He said, 'Well, of course, it would all have to be within your budget.' I said, 'Actually, if we were going to spend a million dollars a year, I'm not sure I'd spend it on foreign correspondents.' "

At that point, the discussion was theoretical. But at the end of 1978 and in early 1979, *Newsday* faced a practical reality that confronted Laventhol with one of his first major decisions as publisher. On December 15, 1978, President Jimmy Carter announced that the United States would formally recognize the People's Republic of China on January 1, 1979, and would upgrade its mission in Beijing to an embassy on March 1. The opening of China to the west was a story of immense scope, and major news organizations immediately began filing applications with the Chinese for permission to open bureaus in Peking. It was clear that the first wave of papers to open bureaus that spring would be such industry giants as the *New York Times*, the *Washington Post*, the *Los Angeles Times* and the *Wall Street Journal*. But Laventhol decided that *Newsday* had nothing to lose by trying. So, when the *Newsday* reporter Arnold Abrams went to China in March, part of his mission was to sound out the Chinese on *Newsday*'s chances. Abrams went to the spokesman for the foreign ministry, Yao Wei, who had met Abrams in the United States, during a visit by Vice Premier Deng Xiaoping. "I was mandated to ask what the Chinese position would be," Abrams said. "Yao Wei was blunt with me." He made it clear that China wasn't happy about admitting foreign correspondents to the country, but that they were grudgingly going along. Later in the year, Laventhol was at a Long Island dinner with a number of visiting Chinese, and one of them came up to him. "Out of the clear blue sky, he says: 'I understand you have applied for a bureau in China.' I said, 'Yes. How did you know?' And he said, 'Well, call so-and-so at the consulate in Washington and you will have good news about that.' That's how I heard about it. We decided it was such an unusual opportunity that we would take it, even though that was our first foreign bureau. There was tremendous interest in China at the time."

Then the question was, who should get this incredible plum? Though Arnold Abrams spoke Chinese and had worked as a journalist in Asia, no one offered him the job. "I was hurt," Abrams said. "At the very least, I felt I had earned the right to be asked." Tony Insolia had different ideas. "The first person I offered that job to was Bob Greene," Insolia said. "Because of Bob's contribution to this newspaper, he had earned the shot." That was the primary motivation, but the turbulence that surrounded Greene as an editor was a consideration. "There's always a degree of dissatisfaction with Bob as a manager, and there was some here also," Insolia said. But Greene declined. Then Insolia turned to someone who had even worse problems relating to his staff, Bill Sexton, the editor of the editorial pages.

Years before, Mel Opotowsky, who had known Sexton at UPI, had urged Laventhol not to give Sexton a management position. "When it came to running a staff, I felt, he would be a disaster," Opotowsky said. But Sexton had served as Laventhol's assistant and won his admiration in helping to plan the Sunday paper. Right after the Sunday paper started, Laventhol had put him in charge of the editorial pages. By the time the end of 1979 came around, his staff had grown restless under his leadership. "I'm a good detail manager, in that people get their raises, people get thanked if they do a good job," Sexton said. "On the other hand, I'm not a warm and cuddly personality that's a natural manager." Besides his writing skill and intelligence, Sexton did have legitimate credentials as a foreign correspondent. He had worked for seven years in the UPI London bureau, and for *Newsday* he had gone to Russia in 1976, Japan in 1977 and China in 1978 and written extensively about each tour. But the friction between him and his staff was part of the reason why Insolia chose him. "I had faith in Willie's ability to carry through," Insolia said. "It also solved my other problem. . . . He didn't belong in charge of that operation." The day the notice went up announcing Sexton's departure for Asia, his staff exploded in glee. "I heard the cheer," Insolia said. So Sexton went to China and Sylvan Fox took over the editorial pages.

Starting the first *Newsday* foreign bureau was a difficult chore. For a year, Sexton operated out of a small hotel room, with few sources in China and no real foreign desk back in Melville to guide him. "The biggest problem was *Newsday*'s unreadiness to deal with the fact that we were now doing foreign coverage," Sexton said. "There was none of the kind of support that you took for granted." But Sexton did have the help of his wife, Bonnie, who had experience as a *Newsday* researcher, and he had the contributions of an informal pool of reporters from other countries. He also had a natural story: the first glimpse for *Newsday*'s readers of a vast, fascinating country. He worked hard, travelled widely and broke an occasional big story, such as China's abandonment of communes. Even those who had been angriest at him at *Newsday* conceded that he represented the paper well as it marched into the 1980s with its broader, more global vision of how it should serve its growing audience in Nassau, Suffolk and Queens.

CHAPTER FORTY

Crossing the River

I

IT WAS NOT much consolation to the editors of *Newsday* in 1980 that the Queens edition was covering Queens more thoroughly than any other New York newspaper, because the readers didn't seem to notice at all.

Late that summer, *Newsday* assigned Raymond A. Jansen Jr., the classified advertising manager, to scrutinize every aspect of the Queens paper and report back. Though he found that *Newsday* was replating, or making over, twelve pages of its Nassau paper every day to put in Queens news, that coverage had not won *Newsday* much name-recognition — even a short distance west of the Nassau border. "You could literally go a couple of blocks, and it was as if *Newsday* didn't exist," Jansen remembered. And those who did know about *Newsday* did not consider it relevant to Queens. "Certainly our newspaper in its present state has value for the Queens consumer, but the perception that Newsday is a 'Long Island paper' negates that value," Jansen wrote. "There appears to be a genuine feeling of general dislike."

As a result, newsstand sales were "lackluster," and Jansen predicted that by the end of the year, the Queens paper would have only 16,000 home-delivery subscribers. That was a discouraging number, especially since *Newsday* had sold 10,000 papers in Queens in 1972, before it even had a separate Queens edition. Though the increase in circulation was tiny, *Newsday* was spending more money on it than anyone had realized. The editorial staff alone was twenty people in late 1980, but the Queens paper was not generating significant additional advertising revenue to offset those costs. So Jansen conducted a top-to-bottom review of the whole project, asking even the basic question: Should *Newsday* continue the experiment at all? "I would like to think this caused some more serious thinking about really what the mission should be," he said. "What we were doing wasn't going to get too far too fast."

Instead of giving up on the Queens paper, *Newsday* began taking steps in early 1981 to improve it, such as hiring Murray Kempton, one of the most widely respected — and loved — journalists in America. For years, as a columnist at the *New York Post*, Kempton had been a beacon of civilized, literate liberalism. But his newspaper had changed to a shrill, right-wing propaganda sheet under the ownership of Rupert Murdoch. Despite their political differences, Murdoch treated Kempton well, but Kempton began to wonder how much longer Murdoch would keep paying a good salary to a columnist whose voice was so starkly different from the *Post*'s. Gradually, he began to think about leaving the *Post*, and when he did, he thought of *Newsday*. "I went in to see Tony Insolia and I got along with him very, very well," Kempton said, "and he offered me the job."

At the same time that Kempton's column began giving *Newsday* a more cosmopolitan image, the Queens edition launched another initiative in almost exactly the opposite direction: saturation coverage of one Queens neighborhood, Bayside. "It was an attempt to see whether intense coverage of a neighborhood would translate into intense purchase of a newspaper," said Bob Heisler, one of the Queens assigning editors at the time. One of the primary instruments of this push was Caryn Eve Wiener, who had started at *Newsday* as a secretary, moved to writing book reviews, left to work as a reporter in Middletown, New York, and returned to *Newsday* as a Queens reporter at the end of 1979. (In 1990, Wiener changed her name legally to Caryn Eve Murray.) She moved into an apartment in Bayside, and her place of residence became part of a campaign to convince Bayside residents that *Newsday* really cared. They took a photograph of Wiener interviewing Bayside merchants, and they ran a series of ads in *Newsday* itself and in Queens weeklies, proclaiming: "Caryn Wiener doesn't just cover Bayside. She lives it." And they took Bayside very seriously, slugging it out with the weekly newspapers for dominance in coverage of community news. "I can remember people saying to me, 'Hey, today we beat the *Bayside Times*,' " said Wiener, astounded that a daily paper of *Newsday*'s size could get so excited about beating a weekly.

Motivated by this emphasis on Bayside, the Queens edition turned trivial events into stories and legitimate stories into blockbusters. One example was the controversy over Fort Totten, a waterfront military post where the federal government declared some of its land surplus. The community's effort to agree on a use for the land was a real issue, but the Queens edition inflated some of Wiener's stories on it far beyond their worth. "I think it was the first major Bayside story, and it was a joke," she said. "I saw 'Fort Totten Land Deal Challenged' on the front page, the words Fort Totten in forty-eight-point bold type, and I thought, 'This isn't that important. Who cares?' "

The advertising department also put heavy emphasis on Bayside, setting up for the first time a separate sales territory in Queens. "In April of '81, we assigned two salespeople to start working in the Bayside-Little Neck-Douglaston area," said the advertising supervisor Dick Beekman. They began to enjoy some success in selling advertising for the Sunday paper's North Nassau regional section, which went to readers in Queens. In response, the *Daily News* started a weekly northeast Queens section, charging rates fifty percent lower than *Newsday* was asking for regional ads.

Over the next few months of 1981 and through early 1982, the *News* had far bigger worries than competing with *Newsday* in Queens. The first major jolt was the decision in August to fold its year-old *Tonight* edition, an abortive and expensive attempt to sell an upscale version of the *News* in the afternoon. Then the parent Tribune Company took a look at the marginal profits of the *News* in the 1970s, followed by a $12 million loss in 1981, and made a stunning decision: A week before Christmas, 1981, the president of the Tribune Company, Stanton Cook, announced that the company was ready to sell the *News*.

In the torrent of analysis that followed, media writers pointed out that the *News* circulation had remained in the vicinity of 2,000,000 throughout the 1960s and early 1970s, but had dropped by 500,000 since 1976, to 1,500,000. "Perhaps its biggest blind spot concerned the growth of the suburbs," *Newsweek* said. "It had virtually no home-delivery network, which meant that it had no way of following its readers when they moved — as hundreds of thousands did — to suburban New York and New Jersey. Though that should have concerned News executives, it didn't. Nor did the rapid growth of a small Long Island daily tabloid called Newsday."

At the same time that readers were fleeing to the suburbs, advertisers were losing interest in the blue-collar readership of the *News* and trying to reach a more upscale audience. Under a new editor, Michael O'Neill, the *News* began in the second half of the 1970s to clean up and elevate its sex-and-crime image and to provide more solid journalism. In the middle of that improvement, however, another setback hit the *News*: an eighty-eight-day newspaper strike in 1978, which sapped the strength of the *News* more than that of the *Post* or the *Times*. (*Newsday* decided not to sell papers outside its circulation area during the strike, but it did increase its press run and it sold as many as 100,000 more papers a day in Nassau, Suffolk and Queens.)

In the years before the *News* calamity, the parent Tribune Company had been through some bumpy times of its own. The major event was the expiration of the McCormick-Patterson Trust, the legal device set up by Robert Rutherford McCormick and Joseph Medill Patterson to keep tight family control over the company's stock. Once the trust expired in 1975, the Tribune Company's ownership became far more fragmented. Then the company had gone through changes in the executive suite in Chicago, a major capital program, a decline in both advertising revenue and circulation at the start of the 1980s and the purchase of the Chicago Cubs. If the *Daily News* was in trouble, many *News* employees felt, the Tribune Company had to share the blame. "The major cause of all the problems they had was that the Tribune Company was a poor owner and hadn't paid a great deal of attention to the *News* in many years," said Robert Keane, then an assistant managing editor at the *News*. "*Tonight* was the coup de grace."

For years, Michael O'Neill had been convinced that there was a market in New York for a lively afternoon paper that was *not* the *Post*. He had put together a prototype, and the *News* had tried to sell the idea to the parent company. "It went to the Tribune Company board and was rejected," Keane said. Then, in 1979, a top Tribune Company executive, Robert Hunt, came to New York and succeeded W. H. (Tex) James as the publisher of the *News*. It was Hunt who decided to start the *Tonight* edition. To pay for the additional costs of *Tonight* and upgrade the rest of the paper, the Tribune Company invested more than $20 million in 1980.

Quickly, the *News* hired more than one hundred new staff members and steamed ahead excitedly — and sometimes imprudently. Concerned that all the fanfare over *Tonight* would make readers of the morning paper feel short-changed, for example, the executives decided to improve the morning paper as well, by introducing a series of theme sections. The plan was to phase them in gradually, but Hunt soon dropped that approach. "Everything started the same week," Keane said, "and it was just absolute chaos." Similar confusion surrounded the *Tonight* edition itself, despite the high-quality journalism that it often provided. "There was no planning done, in terms of basic things, like what time of day it ought to come out," said Tom Curran, the news editor of *Tonight*. "The first edition came out so late that trucks couldn't get to Wall Street in time." Besides the logistical problems, *Tonight* suffered from a clash between its upscale voice and the blue-collar tone of the morning *News*. "It was an irrevocable crack down the middle," said Dennis Duggan, who had worked at the *News* and covered its travails for *Newsday*. "It was a fight for the soul of the paper, and as a result, it really lost its spirit."

The goal that Hunt had set for the *Tonight* edition was a circulation of 200,000 to 300,000, but the actual figure dropped from a high of about 100,000 to 70,000. "The minute it started, it started to die," said Keane, who drew the sad duty of laying off one hundred employees as soon as the *News* closed the edition down in 1981. After *Tonight*, Hunt proposed a plan to rescue the *News*: He would persuade the unions to accept cuts that would trim the paper's costs, and in return, the Tribune Company would invest $60 million to modernize the paper's Brooklyn printing plant. Instead, the Tribune Company decided to cut its losses and sell the *News*.

Throughout the life of the *Tonight* edition, *Newsday* had monitored its progress, but that had not prepared *Newsday* for the Tribune Company's decision to offer the *News* for sale. "That was like a wet fish in the face to us," David Laventhol said. "What it said is that the *Daily News* is on much shakier ground than we had ever thought and you could get to the day when the *Daily News* wouldn't be there anymore." *Newsday* had made plans for the demise of the

Post, including a 1978 prototype *New York Newsday*, aimed at commuters in Manhattan, that would contain some features from a defunct *Post*. But they had not anticipated the death of the *News*. So, at the beginning of 1982, *Newsday* flew into a frenzy of planning.

A few days after the Tribune Company announcement, the key managers at *Newsday* organized a *Daily News* committee and a smaller subcommittee, to study several options for the heartland of the *News*, Brooklyn and Queens, where several major *Newsday* advertisers had stores. The least ambitious plan was simply to broaden *Newsday*'s distribution in Queens. They also considered a plan to sell *Newsday* in both Queens and Brooklyn, plus an option to move into Manhattan as well. On the possibility that *Newsday* might expand into Brooklyn, they commissioned a report on that borough from Sam Ruinsky, the former *Long Island Press* managing editor who had joined *Newsday* in 1977, and paid for a reader survey by Social Data Analysts, which did frequent polling for *Newsday*. The survey found that the residents of Brooklyn knew very little about *Newsday*, but they thought that it resembled the *News*. That finding lent weight to one plan for the post-*News* era: buying the name *Daily News* from the Tribune Company and selling a *Daily News* edition of *Newsday* in the city. So, when the managing editor Lou Schwartz and the staff developed a prototype for a separate version of *Newsday* for New York, it looked much like the *News*. It had the sans serif *News*-style headline typeface, which *Newsday* had abandoned in 1968, and a *News*-style centerfold, another feature that *Newsday* had dropped. It also made provisions for *Daily News* writers such as Jimmy Breslin to appear in *Newsday*.

Not everyone at *Newsday* liked the rushed atmosphere surrounding the prototype. "I was really appalled at that," said Gary Hoenig, who had come to the paper from the *Washington Star* in 1981 and developed a reputation for his knowledge of graphics. "They were doing unbelievable things — designing logos that looked like the *Daily News* logos, things that so indicated a lack of confidence in *Newsday* as an institution and that so crudely imitated the superficial qualities of what in my view had been a failing newspaper for twenty years."

As the planning continued, Laventhol concluded in one draft memo that the *News* was "almost certainly about to close." That belief ignited a sense of urgency that went beyond the mere writing of "Plan A" and "Plan X" and began affecting the operation of *Newsday* itself in small ways. The managers feared, for example, that they would be in an awkward position if the *News* died and *Newsday* had to invade Manhattan with papers that included a Sunday magazine named *LI*. So, at the start of 1982, they quickly changed it to *The Newsday Magazine*, without any real effort to come up with a more imaginative title. The belief in the imminent demise of the *News* was so strong that *Newsday* looked into acquiring rental furniture and computer terminals for a possible larger New York office. This sense of imminence even filtered down to the reporters. "We were on call," Wiener said. "If the *Daily News* went under, we just had to show up on a moment's notice."

While *Newsday* prepared for the death of the *News*, the efforts of the Tribune Company to sell the paper ran into obstacles. The biggest roadblock was the need to reach agreements with the paper's unions on steps designed to cut costs. That proved too big a hurdle for the most serious suitor, Joe Allbritton of Allbritton Communications, who dropped out of the bidding in late April, 1982, after his representatives failed to persuade the unions to agree to $70 million worth of cost savings. Actually, court papers later showed, the Tribune Company offered to *give* Allbritton $100 million to take the *News*, and made the same offer to the developer Donald Trump. But Trump, Allbritton and the Tribune Company all had the same fear: the costs of closing the paper down, including the drain of lifetime job guarantees to hundreds of employees. Those costs, estimated at somewhere between $200 million and $400 million, were a major reason why the Tribune Company decided not to close the *News* after all. "We're Here to Stay," the *News* headline crowed. Finally, before 1982 was over, the *News* and its unions agreed that the Tribune Company would invest in a modernization program and the unions would consent to the elimination of more than 1,300 out of the paper's 5,000 full-time jobs. For the time being, at least, the *News* was alive.

Until the *Daily News* scare of 1981-1982, *Newsday* had concentrated its planning for New York City on the limited goal of expanding its coverage of Queens, fighting a small border skirmish with the metropolitan papers. But the long agony of the *News* had changed the entire equation. "What it says is that there could be an opportunity for *Newsday* to be a full New York paper, because if the *Daily News* isn't there, what's going to happen to all the people in New York who don't want to read the *Times*?" Laventhol said. "Even though they came back, we said that clearly the idea of the *Daily News* not being around there anymore is now a potential reality in the future, and let's regroup, let's reassess, let's figure out what we're going to do with them *in* business."

II

AT A TIME when it was starting to move more boldly into its New York City future, *Newsday* decided to find leadership for this venture by reaching into its Long Island past.

More than a decade earlier, Bill McIlwain had left *Newsday* because Bill Moyers feared for the paper's future under an alcoholic editor. Since then, McIlwain had gone through an alcohol rehabilitation program in North Carolina, had begun recovering and had worked at five newspapers: the *Toronto Star*, the *Bergen Record* in New Jersey, the *Boston Herald American*, the *Washington Star* and the *Arkansas Gazette*. In Arkansas, McIlwain and his publisher were knocking heads on a variety of issues, and McIlwain was ready to leave. Simultaneously, after the Tribune Company decided not to sell the *News* and *Newsday* started looking around for someone to give direction to a more ambitious Queens paper, McIlwain's name popped into Tony Insolia's head. "I needed somebody very strongly people-oriented," Insolia said. "Otherwise, we were going to have a morale fiasco."

One of the reasons for the morale problem was the lack of unanimity at *Newsday* about the Queens paper. The architect of the whole enterprise, Laventhol, faced discontent from two directions. On one side, the Queens staff was frustrated by the gradual approach. "I left *Newsday* in 1981 because we weren't serious about what we were doing," Bob Heisler said. On the other side, many in the Melville office were worried that the New York effort would hurt the Long Island paper. One of those doubters was Insolia, who liked to remind others of the priorities by saying: "Mother *Newsday* lives in Melville." Into that schizophrenic setting, Insolia added McIlwain.

With his soft stream of vague southern phrases, McIlwain had always had a facility for soothing anger and bringing a measure of calm to a situation. Despite his drinking and his distaste for confrontation, which had made him less than an ideal ally in an office political struggle, the staff had liked him during his first tour at *Newsday*. "McIlwain was just totally charming," said the rewrite man Lewis Grossberger. "He'd always make you feel like a million bucks, although you had no idea what the hell he was talking about. . . . You had to love McIlwain." So, when he returned to the paper in September, 1982, McIlwain felt wanted. "It was like being awash in a sea of love," he said.

McIlwain began by sitting at a temporary work space in a corner of the Melville newsroom, envisioning what the new, more New York-oriented Queens edition would be like and what audience it would serve. "It always seemed to me like there was a middle ground in there, that maybe years ago the *Herald Tribune* served, that wasn't like the *News* or the *Post*, and yet wasn't like the *Times*," McIlwain said. "And the *Times* didn't cover New York worth a damn, anyhow." To give life to that broad notion, McIlwain needed a strong news desk to make the thousands of nightly decisions that would complete the paper's image. So he acted in the true *Newsday* spirit, focusing initially on the structure of the editing staff.

In its earliest days, Dick Estrin had run the Queens news desk, but he had lost a series of battles to give the edition more of a city look. "I was trying to do a lot, and they were coming down on me," Estrin said. "Every other day, they wanted something different. They could never get a consistent policy." Estrin had been so persistent in his attempts to remake the paper, stretching the capacity of the composing room and the patience of his bosses, that they moved him off the news desk and put him in charge of the edition's daytime operation. That left decisions about the Queens paper more directly under the control of the Long Island news desk. Confronted with that weakened news desk, McIlwain had to decide whether to put it in the hands of Estrin, who had been a nemesis to him during his earlier tour at *Newsday*. In his book about his alcoholism, McIlwain had mentioned his inability to confront an unnamed news editor and tell him: "Don't sit here like a damn kid resisting everything in sight." The unnamed editor was Estrin. At the start of his second tour at *Newsday*, some editors warned McIlwain: "Estrin will ruin it." But McIlwain opted to accept Estrin's personality, in order to take advantage of his genius for making up a newspaper. This time, McIlwain did not shrink from confronting Estrin when it was necessary, and it worked. "I'd changed an awful lot," McIlwain said, "and he and I really built up a lot of respect for each other."

In the new operation, McIlwain made Estrin executive news editor, moved the news desk to a different part of the newsroom, off on its own, and created an atmosphere that allowed the Queens paper to become more distinct. "Virtually from the start, he wanted a paper that would have a more New York flavor, and he made it clear from the beginning that he wanted one with as little Long Island in it as possible," said Kate McCormick, who worked on that desk. "He won for us for the first time the right to refuse certain pieces that were written for the Long Island paper." So the Queens news desk began to flex its muscles more often, to give the edition a distinctive look. "We started doing what we should have been doing," Estrin said. "All of a sudden, we were doing it right."

Besides giving Estrin control at night, McIlwain decided that he wanted a real metropolitan editor in Queens, working face-to-face with the reporters, instead of dealing with them by phone from Melville. His choice was Charlotte Hall, who had worked with him at the *Bergen Record*, in Boston and in Washington, and had come to *Newsday* in 1981, running the copy desk. McIlwain gave her control over the small reporting staff, which he started to build. "We began to try to cover a little bit more citywide things, although with twelve reporters, it's pretty hard," Hall said. "We did have people in Manhattan, but our coverage was still geared more towards the Borough of Queens."

McIlwain's effort to remove unnecessary Long Island stories from the Queens edition also extended to the feature section. He didn't have enough staff to produce a completely separate Part II, but he and Insolia did appoint a Queens Part II editor: Stuart Troup, a *Newsday* veteran, who had left in the summer of 1980 to join the *Daily News* when it opened its *Tonight* edition. He quit the troubled *News* at the start of 1982 to return to *Newsday* and helped Lou Schwartz develop the prototype of the New York paper that *Newsday* would publish if the *News* died. Now Troup's job was to tailor Part II to the needs of city readers, within the limits of the staff. Not long after McIlwain and Troup began working together, Troup got a phone call from another refugee from the *Tonight* edition of the *Daily News*, Tom Curran. Once *Tonight* folded, Curran had spent two unhappy years as editor of the *Trenton Times* in New Jersey, and then called Troup at *Newsday*, who told him: " 'They're going to start to take New York seriously.' " Soon after Curran arrived at *Newsday* at the start of 1983 to work on the desk with Estrin and later as a deputy to Hall, Curran remembered, McIlwain gathered the staff in a conference room and gave them a pep talk: "He said, 'You are going to be doing the most exciting newspapering in America.' " That kind of rhetoric, plus McIlwain's concrete steps to improve the edition, gave his staff new hope.

A few months after McIlwain's arrival, *Newsday* took the next big step: On

January 18, 1983, *Newsday* stopped calling its city paper "Queens Edition" and dubbed it "City Edition," signifying the effort to spread the paper's horizons beyond Queens. Soon after that, *Newsday* made another noticeable change. Using some of the color capacity of the new presses, it began to print the *Newsday* flag, at the top of both page one and the last page, in blue ink. This splash of color prompted irreverent newsroom comments that the paper had become "*Bluesday*," but it also served an important purpose: calling more attention to the city edition on newsstands.

Another highly visible form of recognition that *Newsday* acquired at the same time was a pair of signs at Shea Stadium. For the 1983 season, the Mets had one spot available on the main scoreboard. James Nagourney, the Mets vice-president who handled advertising, had offered it to Sam Ruinsky, who was running the community affairs operation at *Newsday*, and to Yashica, the camera manufacturer. Yashica came up with the $70,000 before the ponderous *Newsday* bureaucracy could stir itself, and *Newsday* lost that spot. As a former Nassau County official, Nagourney had a strong aversion to annoying *Newsday*, and he went home looking glum. When his young daughter, Adrienne, asked what was wrong, he explained his dilemma, and she came up with a solution: " 'Why don't you put up another sign?' " So the Mets developed a new location, near the auxiliary scoreboards at each foul line — an even better spot than the main scoreboard. "Every time a home run was hit to right or left field, the *Newsday* sign was on," Nagourney said. For the first year, *Newsday* got this prime location for $35,000 in cash and $15,000 worth of ads in the sports section. The *Newsday* signs angered *Daily News* executives, who later got a sign for the *News*, but in a less desirable spot in the ball park. The signs also irked another group. "The beat reporters covering the Mets for *Newsday* were very unhappy about it," Nagourney said, "because they thought that it in some way compromised their integrity."

The *News* lost the struggle over the signs in 1983, but it won a skirmish later in the year, by pushing *Newsday* into a silly panic. *Newsday* knew that the *News* planned to start carrying *Parade*, the nationally circulated Sunday supplement. At various stages before and after *Parade* began appearing in the *News*, one of its top executives offered *Parade* to *Newsday*, but *Newsday* and *Parade* could not reach agreement on terms. So it became clear that the *News* would pick up *Parade*. To counteract that step, *Newsday* decided to rush into a drastic change: Instead of printing one version of *The Newsday Magazine*, which went to readers in New York and Long Island, management decided to produce two separate magazines. Scrambling to create a New York magazine quickly, Lou Schwartz flew into a burst of layouts, plans and personnel changes, transferring the copy editor Patricia Fisher from Part II to the magazine and persuading Caryn Wiener to work for the magazine as a writer. Wiener feverishly gathered gossip items for a magazine column and quickly gave the column to Schwartz. A few hours later, he called her into his office and stunned her with the news that *Newsday* had dropped its plans for a New York magazine. Someone had finally studied the figures and decided that the costs would be enormous. So Fisher and Wiener both returned to their old jobs, only days after their goodbye parties, and someone tacked up a photo of Fisher in the magazine's office, with the caption: "Never mind!"

Despite all *Newsday*'s efforts to give its city edition a distinct image, thousands of New Yorkers said in 1983 readership surveys that they still viewed *Newsday* as a Long Island paper. Then *Newsday* took the next step, renaming the city paper again. On September 11, 1983, the "City Edition" of *Newsday* became *New York Newsday*, a clear symbol that *Newsday* had decided it had the resources and the will to march ahead boldly in New York. "I always said, 'We've got to hold the name *New York Newsday* until we're really ready,' " Laventhol said. At about the same time as the name change, *Newsday* was making plans to move its Manhattan office from the small, overcrowded New York bureau on Broadway, which was no longer adequate to the paper's needs, to a new skyscraper on Third Avenue.

All these administrative steps would have meant nothing, however, if Laventhol and Insolia had not given McIlwain total freedom to create a New York identity for his edition and to control the hiring. McIlwain was the first editor of the city paper who had the freedom to choose his own staff, rather than settling for those who were unhappy or unwanted on the Long Island paper. In running that staff, as Insolia had expected, McIlwain's warm, fuzzy style worked. "When he came to us and spoke to us, he was a presence," Wiener said. "That was the golden age for many, many people." But at the end of 1983, the golden age started to crumble.

The initial crack in the facade was Charlotte Hall's decision to leave as metropolitan editor of the city paper to work on the Long Island desk, because she knew that the new office in Manhattan would be opening, and she didn't want to commute every day from Huntington. Her replacement as metropolitan editor was Bob Sales, who had covered sports and worked on the night city desk at *Newsday* and later served as managing editor of the *Boston Herald American* and executive editor of the *Toledo Blade*. Only a month after the appointment of Sales, Insolia made an announcement that stunned the whole city staff: Bill McIlwain was leaving to become the editor of the *Sarasota Herald-Tribune*, one of the regional papers owned by the *New York Times*.

"People were shocked, because nobody foresaw it," Tom Curran said. Actually, McIlwain hadn't foreseen it either. He had started out by telling a *Times* executive that the perfect choice for Sarasota would be Robert Brandt, a former colleague of his at the *Washington Star* who had come to *Newsday* in 1981 to run the news desk. But the executive, John Harrison, found McIlwain an even more attractive prospect. McIlwain was happy at *Newsday* and certain that he was building a solid foundation for the New York paper. "Maybe that's the cleanest piece of work that I've ever done, the one I'm the proudest of," he said. But he also wanted someday to move back to a warm climate, and the Sarasota paper was a chance to be *the* editor of a newspaper. So he took the job.

In only a year and a half back at *Newsday*, McIlwain had taken the first critical steps toward making the city edition a serious newspaper. "It was a real establishment of significant independence for the edition," Kate McCormick said. Now that McIlwain was on his way out the door, however, his staff's optimism quickly changed to discouragement. For the next eighteen months, *New York Newsday* lurched uncertainly along, trying one combination of editors after another, in an effort to regain the momentum that McIlwain had generated. It wasn't easy.

III

THE DEPARTURE OF McIlwain left Insolia with both a headache and an opportunity. He had to find someone who could run *New York Newsday* during the search for a new editor, and he had to find a way to get Lou Schwartz out of Melville.

Insolia and Schwartz had worked together well for years, but a chain of events that began at the end of 1978 had created a quiet but growing friction between them. It started when Martin Schram, the gifted Washington bureau chief, decided to leave *Newsday*, which was a real setback. "Schram did a great job in making *Newsday* a presence in Washington," said Jim Klurfeld, who worked with him in the bureau for two years. Schram had strong newspaper instincts and had developed to an art form the *Newsday* "ticktock" story, a detailed chronological treatment of a major event, such as the one that he and Klurfeld wrote together on the Camp David peace accords in 1978. But Schram wanted to write for a newspaper that had real clout in the capital, which *Newsday* did not. "It's the frustration that every out-of-town paper has here, with the exception of the *New York Times* and the *Wall Street Journal*," Schram said. Once Schram quit, Insolia wasted no time in telephoning Tony Marro, who had left *Newsday* partly because he had felt stifled working under Schram. But Marro was happy at the *New York Times*, and he felt no urge to become a manager. "I said, 'I don't want that job, Tony,' " Marro remembered. "He said: 'Don't be an asshole. Stop and think about it.' " Then Marro flew to New York and met with Insolia at a hotel near LaGuardia Airport. Ultimately, Marro decided that the ability to set his own reporting agenda as bureau chief outweighed the disadvantages of being a manager. So, at the start of 1979, he accepted the job.

Once Marro had been in Washington a while, Insolia began to think about a broader role for him. Just two years after he became bureau chief, Marro took a step up: In early 1981, Insolia announced that Phyllis Singer, the assistant managing editor who ran Part II and other features, was taking a maternity leave starting in April. He replaced her temporarily with David Hamilton, the assistant managing editor for national, foreign and city news, and he brought Marro up from Washington to replace Hamilton, leaving Jim Klurfeld running the Washington bureau. Marro figured that he would only be in Melville briefly, but in middle of 1981, only two months after Singer's leave began, Insolia made Marro the managing editor of *Newsday*.

The difficulty in the Marro appointment was that Insolia already had a managing editor: Schwartz, whose easygoing manner and goofy sense of humor had earned him the office nickname of "Chuckles." Despite his lighthearted approach, Schwartz had built a reputation as a strong "packager," especially in the area of features. But in the time since Insolia had made him managing editor and his responsibilities had grown to include hard news as well, Insolia had been disappointed. "I needed him to take over more and more of the operation, as I became more and more involved with a lot of the planning and the business side of the editorial department," Insolia said. "As he took over more of the operation and became responsible for more, those were not his strengths. His strengths are not juggling ten balls. He seemed to have a low attention span. Assistant managing editors complained that he wouldn't give them an answer."

So Insolia made Schwartz executive editor at the same time that he made Marro managing editor, moving Marro ahead of such *Newsday* veterans as Bob Greene, the assistant managing editor for Long Island. Soon after the appointment, Marro said, the reporter Ken Crowe came up to him and said: " 'Just think, ten years ago, you used to work for Bob Greene, and now he works for you. Isn't America great?' " Greene respected Marro, and he wasn't sure that he wanted to be managing editor himself, because he didn't like the administrative details that came with the job, but he was angry that Insolia did not discuss it with him before giving the job to Marro. Once the appointment took effect, however, Greene was polite and correct to Marro. That left Marro with the more difficult problem of developing a working relationship with Schwartz.

"Everything had to be a two-step process," Marro said. "You had to do it in a way that didn't look like you were undercutting." At the same time, Schwartz needed to carve out a role for himself. "The one place where I could continue to be most helpful, where I had strengths which he didn't have, was in news editing and display," Schwartz said. Despite that division of labor, there were clashes, including one battle over a series by Bob Wyrick and Patrick Owens about the Reagan administration's effort to throw people off the disability rolls. Once it ran, the series had a major impact on public policy, but during the editing, Schwartz questioned its value. Marro exploded, slamming an office door so hard that he knocked pictures off the wall. "There were shards of glass all over the place," Marro said. In time, Insolia concluded that the Schwartz-Marro tandem wasn't working. "Lou was in the way too often," Insolia said. "He prevented Tony from being as effective in some areas as he could." So, when McIlwain left, Insolia sent Schwartz to Manhattan to oversee *New York Newsday*. "I felt great about it, because there was a situation where I did have clearcut things to do," Schwartz said. "It was clear that Marro would keep his hands off that."

One of the earliest major landmarks of Schwartz's tenure was the move to the new Manhattan office, at 780 Third Avenue, in the summer of 1984. In keeping with its history of misperceptions and shaky decisions in the first seven years of running a city edition, *Newsday* unaccountably decided, soon after the Manhattan office opened, to close down the editorial offices in Rego Park. "Basically, they abandoned Queens coverage for all intents and purposes," said Al Cohen, one of the Queens editors. That left only Caryn Wiener and Kristen Kelch in Queens, operating from desks in *Newsday*'s advertising office there, while the bulk of the city edition staff worked in the spacious, air-conditioned new Manhattan office. A few months later, *Newsday* realized that Queens was still the heart of its strength in the city, even if the flashy new office was in Manhattan. So reporters and editors began moving back to Rego Park. Then Bob Sales and Tom Curran came up with an idea to prove to Queens readers that *Newsday* still cared: assigning Kelch and Wiener to produce daily "neighborhood pages," which offered listings, feature stories and news briefs, focused tightly on Queens neighborhoods.

At the start, producing the neighborhoods pages with only two reporters was a grind. Even after the Rego Park staff grew, the neighborhoods pages caused morale problems. If a reporter wrote a piece for the front of the paper and the editors held it for lack of space, they would often shuffle it to the neighborhoods page, where production bottlenecks prevented it from running for another day or two. Further, the reporters saw the Rego Park office as something like a place of exile, where women and minorities stayed for a long time, while white males moved rapidly on to the Manhattan office — much like the practice at other New York newspapers. "We nicknamed it Soweto Park," Wiener said.

Besides the morale problems in the Rego Park office, Schwartz had to deal with a more painful conflict: a feud between the metropolitan editor, Bob Sales, and the executive news editor, Dick Estrin. "I was sort of in the middle," Schwartz said, "and neither one of them had much good feeling for me." Estrin and his boss, David Hamilton, felt that Sales had erratic news judgment. But the New York reporters, who genuinely liked Sales, disagreed. In 1983, the reporters Leonard Levitt and Gerald McKelvey had given the New York paper high visibility by finding an internal police department report that cleared Police Commissioner-designate Benjamin Ward of suspicion that he had given an order in 1972 that led to the release of twelve suspects in the fatal shooting of a police officer at a Black Muslim mosque. But a year later, Levitt ran into a wall of frustration when he tried to get Hamilton and Schwartz to run an embarrassing story about the inability of police officials to find Ward for three days after a bloody mass murder on Palm Sunday. After a week of delays, Levitt said, it was Sales who finally overcame objections by Schwartz and Hamilton and got the story into the paper.

Schwartz did what he could to calm the Sales-Estrin feud, but he also caused some disputes of his own, by making last-minute suggestions for changes in the New York paper, either in visits to the Melville newsroom on the way from the *New York Newsday* office in Manhattan to his home on Long Island, or in telephone conversations with Hamilton. The ideas themselves were often good, but Schwartz's last-minute timing was frequently disruptive. "I told him if he thought that was the way he wanted to do that job, he should find a new dog," Hamilton said. "Lou never understood why I was so angry."

While Schwartz was grappling with these personnel problems, *Newsday*'s key managers took two days away from their normal work in the fall of 1984 to discuss the New York paper, in a management retreat at Great Gorge, New Jersey. A young Harvard MBA named Julie Raynor, Laventhol's assistant, put together a long case study of *New York Newsday*, to serve as raw material for the small-group discussions. Those groups produced some serious recommendations on strategy, such as the question of how to promote the New York paper.

"I always felt *Newsday* would never make it big in New York unless it did big-time marketing," said the promotion director, Jack Squire, who persuaded his discussion group that *New York Newsday* had to use television advertising to make itself felt in the market. *Newsday* had always relied on barter with New York radio stations, exchanging advertising space in the paper for commercial time on the stations, but had steered away from paying cash for television time. That was in keeping with the advertising department's long-held belief that advertising Long Island products on New York television was a waste, because the signal reached too many people who lived outside Long Island. Now, Squire argued, *Newsday* could no longer afford to avoid it. He was the only one making that argument, and the other managers laughed when he proposed it. But the following year, *New York Newsday* began running television commercials, with the actor Telly Savalas and the new New York Mets catcher Gary Carter. Like the Shea Stadium signs in 1983, the Carter commercials annoyed the *Newsday* sports reporters, who did not want to be in the position of covering a player who was also a spokesman for the paper. "I felt that was inappropriate," said Richard Sandler, the sports editor. "But I wasn't going to throw myself under that train. There was no way I could stop it." Over the next five years, television advertising became a central element of the *New York Newsday* promotion program.

Beyond giving managers a chance to make specific plans for New York, Laventhol felt, the retreat had helped many of them to shed some of their skepticism about the New York edition, simply by talking seriously about it. That was the perfect time for an increase of managerial energy, because a few months after the retreat, Laventhol and Times Mirror made an even greater investment in New York. "I had the confidence that *Newsday* could do this," Laventhol said. "I mean, this is one of the most difficult things that any newspaper has ever done. But nonetheless, I thought *Newsday* was ready."

In the space of a few weeks in the early spring of 1985, the paper hired thirty new people for the editorial staff, expanded its distribution area in Queens, increased its newsstand sales in Manhattan and Brooklyn, began the major television campaign with Carter and Savalas, cut the newsstand price temporarily from thirty cents to twenty cents on April 15 and introduced a new gossip column, "Inside New York." The creation of the gossip column was in itself a statement that *Newsday* was getting more serious about New York, but its structure showed a strong trace of continuing caution. The column had one reporter who spent full time in New York: Ben Kubasik, who had left *Newsday* a quarter of a century earlier in a dispute with Alicia Patterson about his movie reviews, had worked as a publicist for years and finally approached Insolia with a proposal for a column at exactly the moment that Insolia was trying to start a gossip column. But the primary writer, the *Newsday* veteran Warren Berry, retained his job as the editor of special sections and remained on Long Island. A couple of nights a week, he got into the city for events, but he did most of his reporting by phone and wrote the column in Melville. To the world outside *Newsday*, however, that little note of caution was minor. What everyone saw was the new sense of resolve about the New York paper.

The name *New York Newsday* had come into existence in September, 1983, but until the spring of 1985, *Newsday* had simply not promoted it aggressively. As a result, the concerted promotion campaign that began in the spring of 1985 became the watershed in the young paper's history. That push came at the same time as rumors that the owner of the *New York Post*, Rupert Murdoch, would have to sell the *Post* to comply with Federal Communications Commission regulations, because he had bought six Metromedia television stations. It seemed possible that Murdoch might not find a buyer and might fold the *Post* instead — a scenario that increased media interest in *Newsday*'s new effort in New York. A headline in *New York* magazine referred to it as "*Newsday*'s Big Move," and *Business Week* proclaimed: "*Newsday* Knocks Harder/On New York City's Door." The spotlight was clearly on *New York Newsday*, more intensely than ever before.

IV

FACED WITH THE corporate decision to increase the size of the New York staff rapidly, Tony Insolia was still not satisfied with the management structure of *New York Newsday*.

The sudden growth of the New York staff caused him to question the adequacy of editors who had once seemed acceptable, when they ran a smaller staff. "They started being judged much more harshly, because the stakes were up," Insolia said. As a result, he kept adding editors, both on the assigning desk in New York and on the New York news desk in Melville, looking for the right blend of talent.

Even before the big push in 1985, Insolia had reached out to the *Daily News* to hire Robert Keane, an executive with strong experience as a news editor, to strengthen the news desk. At the time, Keane had been in the administrative field for years at the *News*, but he had grown tired of having to fire people, and he was ready to return to a newsroom. He started in the fall of 1984, working under Estrin on the news desk and running the Sunday New York paper. Keane had no promises from Insolia for the future, but everyone knew that a former assistant managing editor at the *News* was not going to remain in a second-level job forever. "Clearly, he knew something about editing a tabloid newspaper for the streets of New York that none of us did," David Hamilton said. "He's a terrific news editor." The obvious person for Keane to replace was Estrin, whose stubborn independence was still annoying Insolia. As Insolia pushed Hamilton to bring Estrin under control, Hamilton kept urging Estrin to give more responsibility to Keane. "If I would say to Dick, 'Why don't you let Keane do that,' he would say, 'Well, are you sure he's ready for it? I'd rather do that myself,'" Hamilton remembered. Then, within a few weeks in the early spring of 1985, at the same time as the big promotion push, the whole fragile editing structure flew apart.

First, Schwartz decided that he had gone as far as he could go at *Newsday*. The next editor of the paper, it was clear, was not going to be Schwartz, but Tony Marro. But no one came to him, Schwartz said, to tell him that formally, or to ask him to help prepare Marro for it. "I always look at it as a succession problem that was not handled gracefully," Schwartz said. "Had it been handled gracefully, I might not ever have left." Instead, Schwartz decided to pull up stakes and accept a job as the president of the *Los Angeles Times* Syndicate. "That's the way the ball bounces in upper management," Schwartz said. "It shouldn't be taken as a point of great shame."

A little more than a month after that announcement, the hammer fell on Estrin: Insolia made Keane the executive news editor and Estrin the Sunday editor. "I felt I was being mistreated," Estrin said. "The man who was being brought in as my assistant was suddenly going to be my superior." Again, Estrin's prickly personality had triumphed over his immense talent. "I have never learned, I guess, to say nothing when I think I ought to say something," Estrin said. A week after Insolia announced this change, he told the staff that Estrin was resigning after thirty years at *Newsday*, to work for McIlwain in Sarasota.

The Schwartz solution had lasted only a year, and now Insolia was faced with yet another nagging problem: Bob Sales was the top assigning editor at *New York Newsday*, and Insolia no longer trusted him to run the growing operation. Insolia had not hired Sales to run the paper alone, but to be a number-two man to McIlwain. "I still think that would have been a fine job for him," said Jim Toedtman, the former *Newsday* editor who had worked with Sales in Boston and recommended him to Insolia. "Bob was in an impossible situation. He had not been in New York for twenty years. He had no knowledge of *Newsday*." Those were serious handicaps for a man whose job was to understand the city and to maneuver in the schizophrenic *Newsday* corporate culture. To Insolia, it seemed that *Newsday* had just solved the rivalry between the Nassau and Suffolk staffs, by moving them all into the same building, and now a new rivalry was growing, between the New York staff and the Long Island paper. To Sales, that rivalry was a motivational tool. "Melville" became a battle cry that he could use to forge unity on his own staff.

Though Insolia and Marro were growing more nervous about allowing Sales to shape the young New York staff, the reporters themselves were fiercely loyal to him. "Sales was a very fine person, a very fine newsman, who was just a babe in an internal political snakepit," said Jim Dwyer, one of the young reporters who began to flourish under him. On the surface, Sales seemed to be trying out for a role in the classic newspaper play, *The Front Page*. He sounded like an old-time newspaperman, with his gravelly, big-city voice, and he tried to look old-fashioned as well, wearing a bowler hat and buying the same antique-style telephones that reporters used in 1920s films. Below that eccentric exterior, however, his staff detected a warm heart. They considered him a reporter's editor and an ally against what they saw as the hopelessly suburban attitudes of the management in Melville.

If Sales lived up to the journalistic stereotype in the heads of his staff, he did not fit at all the traditional *Newsday* image of an editor: a careful maker of lists and schedules, planning prudently ahead. "He was a hang-loose type person," said Al Cohen, one of the editors who worked for him and liked him. "Sometimes details slipped through the cracks. . . . He kept a lot of things in his back pocket, and that didn't work well when we got to be more than a half-dozen people." Besides, his knowledge of the city seemed dated. "He always seemed much more at home talking sports than talking New York City," said Neill Rosenfeld, one of his reporters.

Early in 1985, a few weeks before Schwartz accepted the Los Angeles job, Insolia tried another tack, propping Sales up with a strong deputy. His choice for the job was an ironic one: John Van Doorn, who had left *Newsday* in 1970 and returned in late 1984 as an editor on the national desk. Just before returning to *Newsday*, he had been the executive editor at the *Toledo Blade*. His predecessor there had been Bob Sales, who lasted only about a month before his conflicts with the eccentric publisher prompted him to leave town. Van Doorn had lasted there about a year and then had come back home to *Newsday*, as so many others had. "There are only a handful of places to go, and the *Newsday* of our memory was the best newspaper property in the world to work for," he said. "It was naive and sort of innocent of everybody, in a way, to believe that you could somehow go back and get that." The *Newsday* that Van Doorn found was no longer the hellacious paper that he remembered. Standing in the newsroom in Melville one day, surrounded by the insurance-office decor and the surprising quiet, Van Doorn fell into a conversation with Insolia and Marro, who asked him how the new *Newsday* was different from the old. His reaction was a comment on the paper's caution, which was so different from the hip-shooting style of the Alan Hathway era: "A hunch would die in this room right now."

When Van Doorn came back to *Newsday* and worked on the national desk, there were no promises about his future, but he was interested in becoming *the* editor of the New York paper, and he convinced himself that he had a chance. "I heard what I wanted," he said. "I misread the whole thing, from start to finish." In early 1985, Insolia sent him into Manhattan as deputy metropolitan editor, to shore Sales up and bolster him. "I kept saying to Tony Insolia, 'You can't bolster from below, my friend,' " Van Doorn remembered. If Insolia was dissatisfied with Sales, Van Doorn argued, there was another alternative: " 'Make me the editor. It really won't work from below. You're asking me to undermine the guy.' " From the moment that Van Doorn arrived in Manhattan, no one had much doubt about what was happening. So Sales was understandably sensitive about the presence of Van Doorn, who had briefly been his boss at *Newsday* many years earlier. At one of their first meetings, Sales made his point bluntly. " 'Don't forget who the fuck is in charge here,' " Van Doorn remembered Sales saying. "I went back and told Insolia, 'It's not going to work. This guy is pissed off, and I don't blame him.' So Insolia got furious and climbed all over Sales, or had somebody climb all over Sales."

As Van Doorn began working with Sales, he could see immediately why the reporters liked him. "He's avuncular," Van Doorn said. "He listens to their problems. He's got a quirky, amusing mind, and they would listen to him." He could also see why the editors in Melville had decided that the organization was now simply too big for Sales to manage. "There was no organization of any kind. I'm not terribly organized, but I felt like a CPA coming in there after Sales." At the same time, Van Doorn discovered that he himself had been too long away from the day-to-day grind of a newsroom to work directly with reporters. "I was no longer really a city editor type," Van Doorn said. "I hadn't really the temperament or patience to run reporters and do it right. . . . I think we all made an error in putting me in there."

Only two months after Van Doorn showed up in Manhattan, Insolia tried one more plan to bring order to the New York paper. On the suggestion of Tony Marro, Insolia announced that the Long Island editor, Howard Schneider, would temporarily start commuting to Manhattan regularly to "oversee" the news-gathering operation in the city. This assignment was something of a homecoming for Schneider, who had worked on the Queens paper in its earliest days, before returning to the Long Island desk as a manager. On Long Island, he had demonstrated a mastery of the *Newsday* style of editing, which required a complex structure of future files, beat notes from the reporters and careful planning of the daily report. That was the *Newsday* system that Insolia expected Schneider to create in New York. "The push is on; the people are in place," Insolia wrote in a memo to Schneider and Sales, the day he announced the Schneider appointment. "The shakedown period must be short. I expect to see improvements and progress in days and weeks, not months."

Almost as if the announcement of the Schneider solution were not enough to jolt Sales, *Newsday* followed that a few days later with another change. "On the morning he woke up from having malignant polyps removed from his throat," Jim Dwyer said, "he picked up *Newsday* and found that his name had been removed from the masthead." A tiny box on page two of the New York paper had shown four names: Schwartz as executive editor, Estrin as executive news editor, Sales as metropolitan editor and Stuart Troup as Part II editor. But the departure of both Schwartz and Estrin from *Newsday*, plus the transfer of Troup to a new job as a jazz writer, rendered that masthead obsolete by the end of April. So, even though Sales was still metropolitan editor, *Newsday* simply eliminated all four names from page two. "It wasn't intended as a slap," Insolia said. But in combination with his illness, his battle with Van Doorn and the arrival of Schneider, that sudden anonymity stung Sales.

The new arrangement was wrenching for Schneider, too. "This was a difficult position for me," Schneider said, "and I was encountering hostility and aggravation, more than the usual." One source of that hostility was Van Doorn. "I resisted every inch of the way," Van Doorn said. "I was not pleasant with Howie Schneider. I said awful things to him." Not long after that, Van Doorn became the New York editor of Part II and briefly the editor of all of Part II. But neither of those jobs worked out for him or for *Newsday*, and he soon left the paper, for the second time.

Beyond the hostility, Schneider also had to cope with a style of journalism that was alien to him. On Long Island, editors and reporters would sit down in advance of a major event, such as the release of a county budget, and plot it out, like the invasion of Normandy. In New York, Schneider found a nonchalant, let's-just-go-and-see-what-happens approach. "I remember vividly the city budget coming out," Schneider said. "I think it was a day or two before, and somebody said, 'Well, tomorrow we've got the city budget.' I said, 'We've got the city budget? What are we doing? What's the plan? How many slugs? What does it say in advance? What do we know? What are we doing graphically? Who's doing the analysis?' Everybody looked at me."

If the New York paper was a revelation for Schneider, his frenetic enthusiasm, already legendary on Long Island, was astonishing to the New York reporters. "Howard came in and seemed to want to energize the place," Dwyer said. "I think it's very appropriate if you're covering a place that does not have twenty-five bona fide candidates for page one a day, like New York does. It's appropriate to get people out and racing like crazy. . . . But in New York, you walk across the block and you can find a story." Just as the staff had to adjust to Schneider's energy level, he had to adjust to that New York pace. So did the lieutenant that he pulled in from the Long Island office to help him: James "Hap" Hairston, a large, unkempt editor who had built a reputation on the Nassau desk for brilliance in assigning and editing stories and occasional deviousness in dealing with reporters. "One of the things that took all of us a while to understand is that Long Island is not big-time newspaper business," Hairston said. "When I was the Nassau editor, if you got murdered on Wednesday, I didn't have to put it in the paper on Thursday. I could choose to make it a takeout and put it in the paper Sunday."

As Schneider and Hairston learned to cope with the competitive New York environment, they gradually imposed a *Newsday*-style discipline on the process of assigning stories and making up the daily budget. But the New York paper still had its setbacks in the middle of 1985. One of them came from the hiring of Don Singleton, a veteran general-assignment reporter and rewrite man who had worked at the *Daily News* for two dec-

ades. Singleton was not a household name in New York, an automatic circulation-builder, but he was the first significant reporter that *New York Newsday*
hired away from its prime competitor, the *News*. So his new bosses treated him
royally, giving him choice assignments, such as a three-day stay at the Plaza
Hotel to cover a strike by hotel employees. But as the weeks went on, he began
to miss his friends at the *News* and miss the impact that its huge circulation had
given him. "I don't think I got a single letter for anything I ever wrote for
Newsday," Singleton said. Its minuscule circulation made *New York Newsday*
seem like a toy, by comparison to the *News*. "There was a certain atmosphere
reminiscent of a college newspaper," Singleton said. "They were doing something parallel to putting out a newspaper at *Newsday*, but it wasn't *it*." Besides,
despite the new emphasis on *New York Newsday*, it still didn't feel like a real
New York City paper to him. "They were definitely on a leash from Long
Island. Howie Schneider was like the voice of reality." What would happen,
Singleton wondered, if *Newsday* pulled back its horns in New York? Would he
have to move to the Long Island paper? So he decided to return to the *News*,
only a few weeks after he had left. His brief sojourn at *Newsday* got Singleton a
better deal at the *News*, but his departure stunned *Newsday*.

The Singleton fiasco was a fitting punctuation mark for the whole period
from the departure of McIlwain in early 1984 to the Schneider regency in 1985.
It was a time of tremendous dislocation and uncertainty, mixed with growth and
optimism. The way the reporters saw it, the constant flux was not the fault of
any of the editors in New York. "I think the senior management of the paper is
to blame for not establishing a clear figure of authority," Jim Dwyer said. And
Laventhol, the most senior manager of them all, acknowledged that the constantly shifting plan for New York had made things difficult for the staff.
"Change is likely to be more effectively executed if it's very clear what it is that
you're going to do," Laventhol said. "I think in the early years in New York, it
wasn't perhaps as clear the direction that we really wanted to take as maybe it
should have been."

Once Schneider began to conform the New York paper to *Newsday* tradition, however, both Insolia and Marro were satisfied that they were finally
moving in the right direction. But Schneider could not continue running both
the New York paper and the Long Island paper indefinitely. They needed a full-
time, long-term editor for New York. One possibility was to give the job to
Schneider himself, and Insolia and Marro both felt comfortable with that idea.
But at the start of the summer of 1985, Laventhol went in another direction
entirely. In keeping with the seemingly endless parade of former employees
who had returned to *Newsday* and worked on the New York paper, Laventhol
decided to entrust the future of *New York Newsday* to another figure from
Newsday's past: the same former colleague from the *Herald Tribune* that he had
lured to *Newsday* for the first time in 1971, his old friend Don Forst.

CHAPTER FORTY-ONE

Newsday and the Nuke

I

THE WIRE-SERVICE story was short and perfunctory, just a few paragraphs of purple ink on yellow paper. But the moment Stuart Diamond saw it, he knew that this was a shattering event.

It was 9:30 on the morning of March 28, 1979, just after Diamond had arrived for work in the Ronkonkoma office of *Newsday*. The story in front of him described an accident at the newly opened Three Mile Island nuclear plant, located on an island in the Susquehanna River, south of Harrisburg, Pennsylvania. It gave few details, but it did report that the accident had occurred at about four o'clock in the morning, and a state of general emergency still existed at 7:30. That was enough for Diamond. "Nuclear accidents are over immediately, or they're never over," Diamond said. "I knew that an accident that began at four, that wasn't over at 7:30, was the big one."

The average reporter would not have been so familiar with the doomsday details of nuclear accidents, but Diamond had been gaining expertise in the subject since a few months after his arrival at *Newsday*. His boss, Bob Greene, had started that process in 1974 by encouraging him to learn everything that he could about nuclear power. That was part of Greene's solution to a perennial *Newsday* problem: keeping young reporters content to cover suburban towns. By assigning additional fields of specialization, beyond the town and county beats, Greene was attempting to give his reporters more variety in their work and to improve morale. In Diamond's case, the subject of nuclear power was an obvious one. His beat, the huge Town of Brookhaven, contained a major nuclear research facility, Brookhaven National Laboratory. Later, at the start of 1977,

Diamond had dropped the town beat and become the paper's full-time energy and environment specialist. "So, for five years, I was getting ready to cover that accident," Diamond said. As a result, when the Three Mile Island accident happened, Diamond was ready.

As soon as he read the wire story, Diamond drove home, loaded his car with files, his list of phone numbers, and a two-week supply of clothing, and headed for Three Mile Island. The news editor in the Washington bureau, Jim Toedtman, had prepared to leave for Pennsylvania too, and he made arrangements for Diamond to work from a desk at the *Harrisburg Patriot-News*. Soon after Diamond got there, he placed a call to an official of a Pennsylvania state agency that was monitoring the accident. "He gave me, for two and a half hours or so on the phone, the complete chronology of the accident and the fact that it was caused principally by human error — a chronology that was almost perfect in its detail, which stood up months later," Diamond said. "I had great stories that day. I had great stories the next day. I thought, 'Man, I'm really something.' " But a few months later, Diamond found out that his success was not entirely a result of his own expertise. One of his sources at Brookhaven National Laboratory told him that scientists at the lab had guessed that Diamond would be going to the scene. So they telephoned the Pennsylvania official, told him that Diamond would be calling, and asked him to tell Diamond everything he knew. "Those people were wonderful to me," Diamond said.

In the days that followed, the editors of *Newsday* put together saturation coverage of the worst nuclear accident in American history, sending the reporter Susan Page and the photographer Audrey Tiernan to join Diamond at Three Mile Island, and dispatching platoons of additional reporters to produce sidebars from Washington, Pennsylvania and Long Island. The paper's interest in the story was intense, because Long Island had a significant stake in the question of nuclear safety: At the moment of the accident, the Long Island Lighting Company was building its own nuclear power station on the North Shore of Suffolk County, at Shoreham. LILCO was also preparing for the resumption of state hearings on the utility's plans to build two more nuclear plants farther east, in Jamesport.

Only three days after the accident, the story had its first major impact on Long Island: Governor Hugh Carey repeated his opposition to the Jamesport plants and vowed to prevent their construction. The following week, *Newsday* carried a typically comprehensive Part II package on "Choices: The Future of Energy on Long Island." Later in April, Diamond wrote a series on "The Lessons of Three Mile Island," which included a prophetic headline: "After 25 Years of Promises/A Public Debate Begins."

Well before Three Mile Island focused the attention of the average citizen on the debate, *Newsday* had evolved an editorial position favoring nuclear power. That process began in 1965, when LILCO first disclosed plans for a nuclear plant. In 1966, *Newsday* reported that LILCO had decided to buy land for the plant in Shoreham. A few weeks later, in its first editorial comment on the plans, *Newsday* was vague and noncommittal. Then, as the Atomic Energy

Commission began its long hearings in 1970 on a construction permit for the Shoreham plant, *Newsday* editorials sounded repeated notes of caution, urging the AEC to consider safety and environmental questions. But just before the AEC's decision to grant the permit, *Newsday* made up its mind, concluding that "a safe, strictly regulated and scrupulously operated nuclear plant at Shoreham is preferable to the prospect of oil wells off our beaches."

For the rest of the 1970s, *Newsday* remained a supporter. The editorials still urged caution, but they gradually made it clear that *Newsday* wanted nuclear power because there was no other way to sustain Long Island's growth. In 1977, for example, *Newsday* pounced on Suffolk County Executive John V. N. Klein when he opposed the Jamesport plant because no one had proven the future need for its power. "Alas, he may be right," the editorial said. "But given the present flabby state of the local economy, Klein's first duty should be to promote orderly growth. And few resources will be more vital to that growth than readily available, competitively priced electricity."

By 1979, *Newsday* had developed a reputation as a good friend of LILCO. Privately, Bill Attwood regularly ate meals at the Westbury Manor during the 1970s with the chairman of LILCO, John J. Tuohy. "LILCO and *Newsday* were the two things that really held Long Island together," Attwood said. "All we were doing was having a sociable time. He was good company." When Attwood's son, Peter, was graduated from college and started to look for work in the computer field, Tuohy arranged an interview for him, and LILCO hired him. Later, when *Newsday* moved to Melville, LILCO bought the old *Newsday* Garden City plant, for future expansion of a substation. Publicly, the editorials kept up a steady drumbeat of support for the nuclear plant. "It was apparent to me from the beginning, when I got involved in advocacy in the '70s, that LILCO and *Newsday* went together," said Richard Kessel, whose opposition to LILCO was the start of a long career as a consumer activist.

At the time, *Newsday* was not the only newspaper that supported nuclear power. "Before Three Mile Island, people believed the nuclear industry, including LILCO," Diamond said. "Until a couple of years after the oil embargo, LILCO was a very well regarded utility with reasonable rates." But Three Mile Island was a jolt that forced *Newsday* to look more seriously at nuclear energy on Long Island. So the editorial page began a reassessment, bringing in nuclear power experts from across the country for briefing sessions. At the end of this process, *Newsday* carried a series of editorials, written by Elisabet Van Nostrand, who had come to *Newsday* in 1975 from the *Vancouver Columbian* in Washington, where she wrote editorials against a plan for five new nuclear plants. At *Newsday*, she had argued strenuously on the editorial board against LILCO's plans for more plants at Jamesport. In the post-Three Mile Island reassessment, her view prevailed, and the editorials came out against the construction of Jamesport, largely because the increase in demand for electricity had flattened. By contrast, however, the editorials decided, "despite all the shortcomings, continuing work on Shoreham still appears to be the best way to meet Long Island's short-term energy needs."

At the same time that the editorial page was reaffirming its support for Shoreham, David Laventhol decided it was time for *Newsday* to do serious reporting on the problems that had pushed the scheduled completion date of the plant back from 1973 to late 1980 and had swelled the projected cost. When LILCO announced the purchase of the land for the Shoreham plant in 1966, the estimate for the cost of the plant was $65 million to $75 million. By 1969, it had grown to $261 million. At the time of Three Mile Island, it stood at somewhere between $1.2 billion and $1.3 billion. Something was wrong, and *Newsday* didn't know what it was. So Greene assigned Diamond to find out.

II

EVEN BEFORE THE Shoreham project, Stuart Diamond had established himself as a demon reporter, an obsessive gatherer of information who drove editors insane by plowing ahead with his reporting long after they felt he had done more than enough.

Right after Three Mile Island, for example, Diamond had to leave behind the LILCO story temporarily to join Bob Wyrick and Brian Donovan in an investigation of the national gasoline shortage. Their reporting showed that the Carter administration and the oil companies had taken actions that helped to cause, worsen and prolong the crisis. But getting Diamond to wind up his reporting was not easy. "When it came time to write, somebody'd have to lock him up in a house to write the stuff," Wyrick said. Once the oil series was done, except for occasional interruptions in late 1979 to do follow-up stories on Three Mile Island, Diamond focused his omnivorous appetite for information exclusively on the pursuit of the Shoreham story. "I knew I had to learn that plant bolt by bolt, rivet by rivet, pipe by pipe, system by system," Diamond said.

The first thing he did was to go to the public document room at the library in Shoreham and spend weeks and weeks reading the paperwork on the plant. "I began to establish what became a 500,000-page filing system," Diamond said. "One of the things that I did toward the end is I read the 20,000-page licensing hearing for Shoreham from 1970 to 1973. I indexed every paragraph for subject. I compared every promise that LILCO and the contractors made to what transpired, and I found that they had overpromised, made mistakes." Besides reading all the documents of the Atomic Energy Commission and its successor, the Nuclear Regulatory Commission, Diamond went to Albany and read every document that LILCO had filed with the state's Public Service Commission since 1965. "They had told the NRC one thing and told the PSC another thing about the price of that plant," Diamond said. "That was one of the first things I found."

Beyond the reading, Diamond began to do extensive interviewing. Some names he got from Kessel, the anti-LILCO gadfly. Others he knew from his previous work on energy issues. Still others were unhappy union workers who were disgusted over what was happening at the construction site. In all, he interviewed more than 700 people, including some who feared that talking to him meant endangering their lives, but met with him secretly and felt compelled to tell what they knew. "I'd see people in strange diners at one o'clock in the morning," Diamond said. "It was just like in the movies. These people gave me internal documents that were just devastating."

At first, with Three Mile Island fresh in his mind, Diamond focused on trying to find out whether the plant was safe. But Greene argued with Diamond that the safety issue was going to be inconclusive. "People will argue safety back and forth forever," Greene said. Instead, Greene urged him to focus on the spiraling costs of Shoreham, which were destroying any hope of producing reasonably priced electricity. "This is a compelling argument against this thing being completed," Greene said. Some critics of *Newsday*'s pro-Shoreham editorial stand hinted that *Newsday* imposed on Diamond a strategy of ignoring safety issues and focusing on less volatile economic issues. "Absolutely not," Diamond said. "I couldn't find anything which indicated to me this reactor was particularly unsafe." But the opponents of the plant continued to be suspicious of *Newsday*. In late 1980, an article in the magazine *Media People* articulated some of those suspicions.

The author of the *Media People* article was Ernie Volkman, the former *Newsday* national editor. Volkman was a talented editor who developed a disdain for the *Newsday* hierarchy that he made no effort to conceal. He had disagreed with them on a variety of issues, and they had come to resent what Tony Insolia considered his arrogance and lack of loyalty toward his bosses. Eventually, they had moved him out as national editor and made him a national correspondent. Finally, when Volkman and John Cummings wrote an investigative piece for *Penthouse* in 1977, Insolia formally reprimanded Volkman, claiming that Volkman had not received *Newsday*'s permission to write the piece. Volkman took severance pay and left the paper, rather than accept another reassignment.

While he was still national editor, Volkman had concluded that *Newsday* editors had become touchy and overly sensitive on LILCO stories. In early 1973, Volkman had come across an investigative piece by the reporter Ken Crowe, who had done some revealing work on the interlocking directorates that tied LILCO closely to major banks. Crowe had also discovered strong financial links between LILCO and Stone & Webster, the engineering firm that had won the Shoreham contract, despite lower estimates by other firms. Once he had written the story, Crowe remembered, it disappeared for months. "The difficulty apparently was subject matter," Volkman said. "They didn't want to run it." So Volkman waited for a moment when the senior editors were occupied with a training program and quietly persuaded someone in the Money section of the paper to run it. The memory of the Crowe episode was fresh in Volkman's mind when he wrote the *Media People* piece, in which he concluded: "Put bluntly, many of its readers no longer trust the paper's coverage of the issue. . . ." One of his points was that a former *Long Island Press* reporter, Karl Grossman, had broken a story about inadequacies at the Shoreham plant, based on documents that someone had thrown into a garbage dump, and *Newsday* had done little with the story. But *Newsday* had seen the same documents and rejected them as worthless, and by the time the article appeared in *Media People*, Diamond had read many more documents himself. By then, in late 1980, Diamond was confronting LILCO with his preliminary findings.

On September 8, several weeks before the *Media People* article, Diamond had written a nine-page memo to Ira Freilicher, the LILCO vice-president for public affairs, detailing all the questions that Diamond proposed to ask LILCO about the plant. "There was a real debate within LILCO as to whether we should cooperate," Freilicher said. By then, Freilicher had already complained to Greene about the barrage of small news stories about Shoreham's problems, and he got the impression from Greene that Diamond's series was an attempt to step back and take a broader look at the whole project. In that context, LILCO decided to go along. So Diamond began interviewing LILCO executives, and when he asked questions that went outside the area of competence of individual officials, LILCO began setting up groups of executives to meet with him. "I interviewed essentially the entire board of LILCO, all the inside directors of the company, around a big conference table, my brain against theirs," Diamond said. "I measured my reporting against those statements." The question, of course, was whether LILCO had made a mistake in agreeing to talk so extensively with Diamond. "I probably would not have given *Newsday* the kind of access that they had," said Michael Patterson, a former *Daily News* reporter and former press secretary to Governor Hugh Carey, who took over LILCO's press operation several months after the mass interview. "They totally opened the door."

The interview with LILCO's executives was not the conclusion of the process. In fact, it was just about the halfway point. For the next year, Diamond continued his reporting, like a runaway train. Greene and the editors below him, Joe Demma and Howard Schneider, tried repeatedly to make Diamond cut off his reporting. "Stuart would keep saying, 'I have to get more. I have to get more,' " Greene remembered. "I was going over there with the scissors, threatening to cut his telephone wire in front of everybody in the office." But Diamond knew that he had an immensely important story, and he was driven to get all of it. "If you want a case study on what went wrong with the nuclear age, this was the plant," Diamond said. "Wild horses weren't going to stop me from doing this story."

It wasn't enough, for example, to sense that LILCO's management wasn't equal to the task. Diamond wanted to determine which engineering schools had produced LILCO executives and which schools had produced the executives of utilities that had built nuclear plants properly. It wasn't enough to show that the plant was too expensive. Diamond felt the need to spend three months examining LILCO's estimates of the future need for power. All that work ended up trimmed to a small sidebar, but it proved that LILCO had made bad estimates. Even Diamond's chronology of Shoreham was endless — twenty-four single-spaced pages, starting with the invention of the light bulb. This open-ended orgy of reporting could have been shortened, some editors later felt, if someone had worked one-on-one with Diamond all along. Diamond wasn't so sure. "This series required one person, me, to be an expert and an authority," Diamond said. "It took me two years to become an expert."

Finally, Greene ordered Diamond to produce at least a first draft, and in late 1981, Diamond sat down at his computer and churned out thousands of words. Greene read it and produced a list of questions, and Schneider decided to assign the whole project to one editor, Fred Tuccillo. As the lead reporter on the investigation of the Southwest Sewer District at the end of the 1970s, Tuccillo had solid experience with complex projects. By late 1981, Tuccillo had been an editor on the Long Island desk for two years. Dissatisfied with his progress there, he was thinking about becoming a reporter again or leaving *Newsday*. "I figured this was an opportunity to prove myself," Tuccillo said, although others consid-ered editing the huge project a dubious honor. "The consensus was that I had been thrown an anchor and had agreed to catch it."

At the start, Tuccillo took home the first draft and sat down with it. "The more I read, the sicker I got," Tuccillo said. "The problem was it was just completely disorganized. It had no focus at all." The reporting, of course, was impressive, but Tuccillo had to do something with the structure. "I began to take what he wrote apart, literally, and put it back together in a different set of stories," Tuccillo said. "What he would then have to do is not simply rewrite but do some re-reporting, and also go back to his notebook on some of this." This process might have angered Diamond, except that it was better than Schneider's original proposal: that Tuccillo rewrite the series. Tuccillo preferred to have Diamond do the rewriting himself, with Tuccillo's guidance. That was fine with Diamond, because he would have the byline all to himself, and he had a reputation as a fierce defender of the sanctity of his own byline.

Over a period of about three months, Tuccillo fed Diamond the revamped stories one at a time, along with questions and comments that led to more reporting. "Stuart worked six, seven days a week on this stuff," Tuccillo said. "Mostly out of exhaustion, I think, he began to get more ornery." At one point, Diamond wrote a memo to Tuccillo, Schneider and Greene, protesting: "Your deadlines are inhuman, unrealistic, and enforced under the threat of turning over this series to rewrite." One of the biggest fights was over the lead of the opening story. Tuccillo and the other editors felt it was too wordy, but Diamond thought it was so all-inclusive and prophetic that its absence killed his chance to win a Pulitzer Prize. By the time it was all over, Diamond was so angry that he picked up a typewriter as if to throw it at Tuccillo, before common sense prevailed and he backed down.

Finally, the seven-part series began on November 15, 1981, with a front-page headline that read "SHOREHAM: What Went Wrong." The three-para-graph copy block that went with it summarized the project's problems in a few devastating words:

"It was to be in operation by 1973. It still isn't.

"It was to cost $65 million. The current estimate is $2.49 billion.

"It was to provide quick relief for LILCO customers. It won't."

On page five, Diamond began a three-page *summary* of the whole series with these two paragraphs:

"The Shoreham Nuclear Power Station has become the nation's most expensive atomic power plant.

"It is a living catalog of all the ills that have beset the nuclear industry since the days when the atom was viewed as the ultimate answer to America's energy needs."

The summary gave a quick overview of those ills: the unproductive union work force, poor management, inconsistent scrutiny by federal regulators, the utility's heavy borrowing to pay the soaring costs, the declining need for Shoreham's power, and on and on. Inside the paper, in addition to the three-page summary, the first day's report took up six pages of *Newsday*. On the morning the story appeared, Patterson called his LILCO colleague Freilicher at home. "I remember saying to him, 'I think it's going to win a Pulitzer Prize,'" Patterson said. "He said, 'Do you see any inaccuracies?' I said: 'A couple, but I think you could get them on the back of a matchbook.' He concurred." Accurate or not, the series floored Freilicher. Even before it ran, he had realized that it wasn't going to be what he had thought. "We were very, very shocked when the focus of the story shifted from the overall project, an objective look at its pluses and minuses, to 'What Went Wrong,'" Freilicher said. "If the subject matter of the story is what went wrong, you can't win. . . . What they did was they telescoped fifteen years of mistakes, without looking at any of the successes, and without looking at all of the obstacles that had been overcome." The president of LILCO, Wilfred Uhl, had the same view, but Patterson, with a journalist's perspective and an Irish wit, asked him: "What would you call it, 'Shoreham: What Went Right?'"

Whatever the reactions within LILCO, there was no doubt about the impact of the series. At the time it began running, LILCO had just reached a tentative agreement with Suffolk County officials that would have answered the county's concerns about the plant and avoided any litigation. "After the *Newsday* series, it collapsed," Patterson said. "Everybody backed off. It was a radically changed atmosphere. The forces in the county who were always there, who wanted to go in another direction, had the political leverage at that point to do it." Suddenly, attacking LILCO became politically desirable, because the series had damaged the Shoreham project so badly in the eyes of the public — for the wrong reasons. "Nobody read it," Freilicher said. "It was too long for anybody to read. So the public believed that it was a story that said Shoreham was unsafe."

Even anti-Shoreham activists such as Kessel and Irving Like, who had felt that *Newsday* had been too friendly with LILCO editorially, acknowledged the effect of the series. For one thing, Diamond identified so much waste that the state's Public Service Commission later conducted a long "imprudency" pro-

ceeding, to determine how much of the plant's final costs were due to imprudent management and could not be charged to the ratepayers. "There's no
question that Stu's articles contributed to the eventual successful outcome of
those hearings," Kessel said. "A lot of the imprudency was cited in Stuart
Diamond's series, years before that decision came out."

Despite Diamond's series, the paper continued to carry editorials advocating that Shoreham be opened, even after Governor Mario Cuomo began to
argue that the plant should be closed because there was no safe way to evacuate
Long Island in the event of an accident. Throughout most of the 1980s,
Newsday continued to display a sharp dichotomy between support for the plant
on the editorial pages and news stories that reported its continuing woes. To
Freilicher, at least, it was clear that the net result was "dreadfully negative,"
because the news stories hurt much worse than the editorials helped. "Clearly,
the paper was editorially supportive," Freilicher said. "It was our belief that
that view was certainly not shared over on the news side of *Newsday*, and that
the news side went out of its way terribly to counteract the editorials. Our
feeling then was that *Newsday*, with this so-called schizophrenia, was salving
their conscience for doing a perpetual hatchet job in the news pages on the
plant by writing the nice editorials. They could always turn around and say,
'What are you talking about? We're in favor of it. We love it. . . .' Nobody reads
editorials. They read headlines."

But the opponents of Shoreham *did* read the editorials, and the paper's
pro-Shoreham editorial policy made many of them skeptical of *Newsday*'s ability
to cover the story objectively. "The uninformed person was constantly accusing
us of being in LILCO's corner," said Richard Galant, the editor who ran
Newsday's LILCO coverage for most of the 1980s. One of those critics was the
free-lance reporter Karl Grossman. "I think there's been a substantial breakdown of *Newsday*'s normally highly aggressive investigative reporting when it
came to Shoreham and LILCO," said Grossman, who expanded on that theme
in his 1986 book, *Power Crazy*. But the developer Maurice Barbash, one of the
most outspoken of the anti-Shoreham leaders, said: "By and large, *Newsday* has
allowed its reporters free rein to report the story as they see it."

Throughout the 1980s, LILCO writhed in agony, moving closer to a
decision to scrap the Shoreham plant — a decision in which *Newsday* would
ultimately play a pivotal role. Along the way to that previously unthinkable
course of action, Diamond's series — arguably the best sustained reporting ever
done by a single reporter on one project at *Newsday* — had been the first step.
"It destroyed the project," Freilicher said. "It was the single greatest cause of
Shoreham's demise."

CHAPTER FORTY-TWO

Bad Times for Big Daddy

I

SURROUNDED BY THE technology of the electronic age, some planners in the newspaper industry have developed a nightmare vision of the future: that cable television will destroy reading skills, gobble up newspaper advertising, and shrink circulation to the edge of extinction.

In that nightmare, viewers push a few buttons in their living room, commanding the television to deliver only the advertisements or news stories that interest them, and they stop reading newspapers, which deliver a wide variety of stories and ads that don't interest them. That nagging possibility prompted newspaper publishers in the late 1970s and early 1980s to examine the potential of getting into the cable television business themselves, in self-defense. In *Newsday*'s market, there was already a group of cable companies, and the list of subscribers was rising. As a result, a young analyst in the management services department, Julie Raynor, began studying electronic information delivery in 1980.

One of the cable operations that Raynor visited was the Gateway system in California, owned by *Newsday*'s parent company, Times Mirror. At the time, Gateway was one of the country's two interactive cable systems, which allowed subscribers to control the flow of text information through the screen. "That was the long-term objective," Raynor said. In time, *Newsday* settled for a less ambitious intermediate step: a non-interactive "videotex" system. It would provide cable viewers with classified ads, news briefs and other information, but the text would appear on a fixed schedule, beyond the viewer's control. To make the proposed cable system more attractive, *Newsday* decided to break up the long stretches of videotex with a few hours of taped programming, including an hour-long local news show in the evening. That decision created a need for someone at *Newsday* to serve as the anchor for the news show. Just as they had appointed Bill Sexton in late 1979 to run the China bureau, and simultaneously eased the tension that he had been causing as a manager, they decided to use the TV job as a way of removing Greene from control of the Long Island staff.

At the time, Greene had recently added new luster to his larger-than-life image, by playing a pivotal role in *Newsday*'s coverage of an FBI sting operation that became known as ABSCAM. During the investigation, an impressive list of powerful people — lawyers, state and city officials, seven congressmen and one United States Senator, Harrison Williams of New Jersey — showed a willingness to use their offices to help a phony Arab sheik, in exchange for wads of his money. More than three months before the FBI was ready to make arrests, Greene had learned of the sting. He later passed his information along to Tony Marro in the Washington bureau, who completed the reporting and wrote a thorough account that appeared when the FBI swooped down on the suspects in early 1980. "The most detailed early reports were in Long Island's *Newsday* and the New York *Times*," *Time* magazine said. Later, Greene wrote a book on the case, *The Sting Man*, about a central figure in ABSCAM, a Long Island-based con man named Mel Weinberg. The whole episode reinforced Greene's reputation as a reporter and added to his marquee value. But reporting wasn't his real job. *Newsday* was paying him to be an assistant managing editor. By early 1983, other editors — including Marro, who had become Greene's boss — were unhappy with the way he was managing.

In the decade since he had become an editor, Greene had developed a tightly controlled system that revolved entirely around "Big Daddy," as he called himself. From the start, his stated goal had been to empower reporters by making them more responsible for generating their own stories, but his system for reaching that goal had become comically rigid and bureaucratic. Reporters would write weekly memos outlining coming events and potential stories on their geographic beats, and Greene would read these beat notes and mark each story idea with a symbol that was supposed to tell the reporter what Greene thought of it. But the system of symbols got so complicated that Greene had to explain it in a memo. In time, his emphasis on the beat notes seemed almost to overshadow the stories themselves. "With a few exceptions, the beat notes stink," Greene and Howard Schneider said in one 1981 memo. "Newsday must have strong beat notes. Without them, we cannot serve our readers."

Even Greene's considerable skill as a teacher of reporting methods seemed to fall victim to excessive structure. During a series of seminars on "sourcing," for example, he issued a detailed memo with common-sense recommendations on developing sources. Many of his ideas were time-tested and unassailable, but some reporters laughed at seeing them in print at all, and some grew angry over such items as his recommendation that reporters make loans to sources "at your own risk." Oddly, despite his emphasis on the importance of developing sources on the town beats, Greene and his sub-editors sometimes shuffled reporters en masse from beat to beat, disrupting source development. In perhaps the clumsiest such shuffle, they moved one reporter, Amanda Harris, from the Suffolk County beat to the Hempstead Town beat — a move that she and her colleagues considered a demotion, even though Greene argued it was not — and replaced her temporarily with her husband, Drew Fetherston. Greene also disrupted the sourcing process, many reporters felt, by continuing to play reporter himself. He usually passed along to reporters any tips he got, but he never seemed to understand that reporters often resent hearing information after another journalist has it, especially their own boss.

More than his handling of reporters, however, it was Greene's dominance over his editors that worried Insolia and Marro. Big Tony and Little Tony, as they became known, were concerned that Greene was keeping his editors on too tight a leash, requiring them to check in with him on all but the most routine matters. "He allows reporters to grow into aces, but he doesn't allow subordinate editors to grow," Insolia said. "We had a very bright young guy like Howie, and we felt sooner or later we had to find out how far he could go." The other concerns included Greene's failure to develop more minority reporters and editors, and his grudging acceptance of Marro's efforts to improve communication among editors. By the end of 1982, a year after Marro had become managing editor, both Tonys had become convinced that they had to move Greene out of control of the Long Island staff. It was at exactly the same time that the cable project came along.

At the time, one of Greene's extra duties involved serving as a host of a radio talk show that featured *Newsday* reporters discussing their stories. He enjoyed that, and he liked his occasional television appearances. But when Laventhol began asking Greene to do the cable show, Greene balked. "I said, essentially, this looks to me like just a way of trying to move me out of here," Greene said. "So I said to Dave, no, and I said to Tony, no. . . . Then Tony Insolia calls me in and says, 'You have to go there.' " Insolia explained that Greene was "too strong" and was not letting the editors under him grow. Greene protested that he was already allowing Schneider ample room to show his skills. "I was letting Howie virtually run the whole thing, with just that idea, of developing Howie," Greene remembered. But Insolia still kept pressing him to take the television job. Greene said no again, asking Insolia to find him a job at another Times Mirror paper. Then Greene and his wife decided they didn't want to leave Long Island. "So, finally, I went back to Tony and I said, 'All right, I'll do it,' " Greene said. "So I went and did it — not because I wanted to."

In late 1982, Insolia issued a memo announcing Greene's role in the cable project, "in addition to his other responsibilities." The memo said that Schneider would take over the daily job of running the Long Island staff, but he would "continue to report" to Greene. But everyone, including Greene, knew that he couldn't do both jobs at once, and whenever his role in the cable project ended, he wouldn't be running the Long Island operation again.

II

FROM THE BEGINNING, *Newsday* approached the cable project as a cautious venture into unfamiliar territory, holding down the costs and minimizing the risks.

"Part of our overall objective was to be conservative financially," said Julie Raynor, who became the manager of the cable channel. "We were always working carefully within a budget." With that approach, *Newsday* and Times Mirror saw no reason not to give it a try. If they had to, they could always pull the plug, just as they had done several years earlier on another *Newsday* innovation that didn't work out: an effort to publish regional telephone books.

In the telephone book project, the competition was a company called Yellow Book, which published regional phone books in the New York area. *Newsday* decided that it could publish better directories, with community information sections and fold-out maps. "We were cocky," said Dick Beekman, the *Newsday* advertising supervisor who ran the project. "We couldn't fail." But selling small ads in telephone books, usually to service companies such as cesspool cleaners or exterminators, was more difficult and less profitable than selling large ads in the newspaper to major retailers. "We had thousands of advertisers, but the average sale was a $200 sale," Beekman said. They also didn't count on the aggressive reaction of Yellow Book. "They improved the book one hundred percent," Beekman said. With a better grasp on the advertisers and an improved product, Yellow Book beat back *Newsday*. The project, launched in late 1976, folded in late 1978. David Targe was convinced that *Newsday* could eventually have made a profit, if Times Mirror had been more patient. Beekman was more blunt: "This was a major failure, this project."

Despite that painful financial flop, *Newsday* decided less than five years later to get into another business that it didn't know, and to leave the project in the hands of an executive who had just arrived at the paper: Robert M. Johnson, the new president. His predecessor, Donald Wright, had come to *Newsday* from the *Minneapolis Star* in 1977 as general manager and became president a year later. It was Wright who launched Raynor's study of the cable industry, but at the start of 1982, Wright left *Newsday* to become president of the *Los Angeles Times*, creating the vacancy that Johnson later filled. Like Wright, who was a mechanical engineer and business administrator, Johnson was not a journalist. He had a management and marketing degree from Louisiana State University and a law degree from the University of Michigan Law School. Even though his father had been a union member and Johnson had grown up in a blue-collar environment, he went directly from law school to work in the Washington office of a Chicago firm that represented management in labor negotiations: Seyfarth, Shaw, Fairweather and Geraldson. After representing newspaper executives for a while, Johnson became one himself. He was serving as vice-president and general manager of the *Columbus Dispatch*, in Ohio, when an executive recruiting firm brought him to the attention of Laventhol.

On the surface, Laventhol and Johnson were strikingly different. In contrast to the perennially shy and rumpled Laventhol, Johnson was trim and impeccably dressed, with a neat mustache and every hair on his head obediently in place. Like many others before and after him, Johnson at first found Laventhol unimpressive. Later, he began to change his mind, after a long lunch with Laventhol in San Francisco, during a publishers' convention. "I came away from that session with the sense that here was a man who really had a vision," Johnson said. Then Laventhol gave Johnson a helicopter tour of Long Island, which persuaded Johnson's wife that she might like Long Island after all. Johnson accepted the job.

When Bob Johnson came to *Newsday* in the summer of 1982, Stan Asimov had already done much of the preparation for the cable project, including negotiations with the largest cable company on Long Island, Cablevision. In October, Laventhol signed a complex agreement with Cablevision, under which Cablevision would provide *Newsday* with studio facilities and access to a channel, and *Newsday* would provide Cablevision with programming and advertising space. It was Johnson's job to oversee the *Newsday* channel, and with his experience on the telecommunications committee of the American Newspaper Publishers Association, Johnson looked at the project and saw no reason to be fearful. "It just seemed to everybody to be a low-risk kind of venture to undertake," Johnson said. "We knew eventually somebody was going to do it, and we said, 'Why not us?'"

At the same time, the attitude of the anchor man, Bob Greene, could fairly be described as "Why me?" Despite his reluctance, Greene went about the job with his customary energy. First, he read voraciously about television and began writing a series of memos to Johnson and Asimov, filled with ideas. Then, with the *Newsday* television book editor Tony Gentile, Greene spent a day watching Dan Rather and his staff put together the CBS evening news. Later, he visited public television's MacNeil/Lehrer news program. Those experiences left him worried. Rather's staff was huge, but he was only on the air for a few minutes out of each broadcast, because CBS correspondents were on camera the rest of the time. By contrast, Greene would have a tiny staff, and he would be on the air for almost the entire one-hour show. So he fought to shorten the news show from an hour to a half-hour, but he lost that crucial battle and set out to prepare for a full-hour news show.

Early in the preparations, *Newsday* had some good luck: Channel 21, the local public broadcasting station, had dealt with a budget squeeze by scrapping its nightly Long Island news show. That left a vacuum for *Newsday* to fill on the air, and it provided the first television professional for the new *Newsday* channel. Bob Civiello, who had started at Channel 21 as a nightly news producer and risen to a top administrative position, had a sense that public television was coming into hard times, and he wanted to try cable. So he joined *Newsday* in February, 1983. Right away, Civiello saw what Greene was beginning to realize: The plan for the show was not going to work. "It was a talking-head show," Civiello said. "What it was, basically, was a bunch of *Newsday* reporters sitting around for an hour, talking about what was new." Civiello argued that they had to broaden the concept by providing camera crews to tape footage of breaking news. Sending out camera crews was going to cost money, for salaries, cameras and other equipment, but Johnson gradually won permission from Times Mirror to make that investment. In addition to changing the show's shape, Civiello also helped by recruiting Karen Hasby, who had worked at Channel 21 as a reporter, an anchor and a news director. Her arrival, as a reporter and Greene's coanchor, gave the new operation a professional on-camera performer. To round out the reporting staff, Greene reached into the newsroom and recruited Rex Smith, a good reporter who also had television-style good looks and a resonant voice.

Beyond changing the format to include taped reports, *Newsday* made another critical decision about the news program: Instead of broadcasting from Cablevision's studios, as they had planned, they opted to build the set for the news show right in the *Newsday* newsroom. That plan eliminated the complicated logistics of ferrying *Newsday* reporters back and forth between the newsroom and the studio several miles away, and it allowed the reporters to stay in the newsroom, where they would be less nervous. More important, the newsroom setting would provide the viewer with a sense of being inside *Newsday*. In fact, they named the news show *Inside Newsday*. "I liked the concept of the newsroom," Hasby said, "because the thing the show had going for it was its affiliation with *Newsday*."

As a result of the decision to do the show from *Newsday*, which had no direct video connection to the cable facilities, the news show would have to be taped, rather than live. If *Newsday* had invested in expensive microwave transmission equipment to beam the signals from its plant in Melville, the show could have been live. But *Newsday* and Times Mirror thought that was too big an investment. The solution was to tape the show and rush the tape to Cablevision and the two other cable companies that planned to carry it — a solution that later led to major problems.

Finally, after months of planning and dry runs, the *Newsday* channel went on the air on May 1, 1983. Each day's programming consisted of twenty hours of text on screen and four hours of taped shows, including the one-hour news show. In every hour of text, there were thirty minutes of classified ads and thirty minutes of information: news briefs, movie and restaurant reviews, local events, health tips and other items. As a result of the topflight graphics equipment that *Newsday* bought, the videotex was perhaps the most impressive-looking aspect of the channel. But in time, it became clear to everyone, including Bob Tiernan, the young editor who ran the videotex operation, that viewers just weren't interested in text on a television screen. "It's not something you sit down to watch like a program," Tiernan said. As it turned out, people preferred to get their information in a more traditional way. "The browsing function of newspapers is irreplaceable," Raynor said. "I think that is one of the great lessons to be learned."

The taped programming included local special events, such as the *Newsday*-sponsored Long Island marathon or the finals of a local spelling bee, and several regularly scheduled shows, featuring *Newsday* employees. One was *The*

Newsday Magazine, an interview show that Rex Smith called "the most boring half-hour on television." Once, he remembered, he interviewed the reporter Kimberly Greer for fifteen minutes about lawn furniture. Another regular show featured *Newsday* critics chatting with Laventhol's assistant, Steven Isenberg, until Times Mirror made Isenberg publisher of its papers in Stamford and Greenwich, Connecticut, and the assistant managing editor David Hamilton took his place. The channel also carried a Wall Street show with Warren Berry and Alan Wax and a regular half-hour series of one-on-one interviews with local newsmakers.

It wasn't the videotex or the other programs, however, that attracted attention and caused strains within *Newsday*. It was the news show, which had to struggle every day with enormous problems of production and distribution.

The primary production problem was the shortage of full-time camera crews, which kept Greene from building up a backlog of tape to use on slow days. "I started every morning with nothing," Greene said. "We had nothing in the can." So they had to fill an entire one-hour news show every day with that day's taping, despite the lack of camera crews to do it. To supplement the full-time crews, Greene hired free-lance cameramen on a regular basis, including Bob Wolf, who made his living as a plumber. Sometimes, *Newsday* would call Wolf to come in for a story, and his beeper would go off while he was fixing someone's sink. Wolf, like the other cameramen, often ended up doing bizarre stories on slow days, simply because there was nothing else. On one such day, Greene decided to run a story about the cauliflower crop in the rural East End, spoke to a farmer by phone and told him what to talk about, then sent a free-lance cameraman out to tape the farmer, without a reporter. On another tight day, Johnson asked Greene to send a camera crew to an awards ceremony for *Newsday*, when Greene had other plans for the crew. Greene reluctantly complied, and that night he included in the show six minutes of boring tape about the awards program, to make the point that the president of the newspaper should not meddle in news decisions. "He was a stand-up, straightforward person on that," Greene said. "He never interfered again." But the staff shortage continued, forcing everyone to work exhaustingly long hours. "We were holding this together with our pride, literally," Greene said. "The stress level was just incredible."

The show also caused stress in the newsroom, where the lights and the noise broke the concentration of reporters and editors, right in the middle of trying to put out a paper. "You can't produce a TV show while you're trying to run a newsroom on deadline," said Carl Pisano, then an editor on the national desk, who had worked in television before, but still resented the commotion. Some editors began registering their protest by wearing old-fashioned green eyeshades, and in some cases, jungle-style helmets. The newsroom was not always the easiest environment for a television program, either, with its constant noise, Chinese food deliveries and other distractions. "It had a certain charm to it," Tiernan said. "You'd have people walking across the camera eating french fries or bopping people in the head with paper wads."

One of the most noticeable visual problems was Greene himself, because the camera seemed to magnify his huge size, in contrast to Karen Hasby. "We used to call it 'The Beauty and the Beast Show,'" Bob Wolf said. Greene did what he could to improve his appearance — buying new suits and investing in contact lenses, so he wouldn't have to wear glasses to see the TelePrompTers. (He never had to wear the lenses, because *Newsday* did not invest in the TelePrompTers.) But Greene had never been a television anchor, and it showed. "It was sad to see this man, who had distinguished himself as much as anyone in the nation as an investigative reporter, in effect reduced to this role of TV bimbo," Rex Smith said. Nonetheless, Hasby saw real potential in him. "Given the right amount of time and training and tools, he could have cut it," said Hasby, who said she learned more about reporting from Greene than she had ever learned from anyone else. "He could have been a great character. People love those sort of personality quirks."

A far more important problem than Greene was the difficulty of getting the show aired on time. Often, they finished taping it less than an hour before air time, then sent messengers to Cablevision and the two other systems that were carrying the news show. "It was a terrible system," Hasby said. "Sometimes the messengers would have a flat tire, or it would snow, or they would get lost, or they didn't realize they had a deadline and would stop for a cup of coffee." If the tape got to one of the two secondary cable systems late, they would simply substitute other programs. Even if the tapes got there on time, they were still tapes, rather than a live show, with all its immediacy. "It just cried out to be done live and then satellited out to the cable stations," Hasby said.

The decision not to buy microwave equipment not only deprived the viewers of live news, but helped keep down the size of the audience. *Newsday* had hoped to set up a connection with all the local cable companies, in addition to Cablevision, but could not do it without the microwave equipment. As a result of that and other factors, the audience was small, which began to erode the advertising support. "Advertiser after advertiser tried promoting special merchandise to test it, and it did not pull," said Targe, who thought the programming was far too amateurish to compete with the nearby New York City stations. "It was homey, but it was not what people are used to seeing in this market." The result was not good for *Newsday*'s powerful image. "They looked totally stupid," said John Alogna Sr., an advertising agency executive who had dealt with *Newsday* for years. "Here they were, real pros in a print medium, and they tried to transplant this great expertise into a sight-and-sound medium. It was an embarrassing bust. I was ashamed of *Newsday*."

To correct the deficiencies, *Newsday* called in Don Kellermann, a Times Mirror executive who had worked at *Newsday* and later in television, and asked him to examine the operation. Kellermann brought about a few cosmetic changes and efficiencies, but he knew that the project needed much more. "The conclusion of his group, which I concurred in, was that we would have to spend $5 million to $10 million a year to do this in the way it should be done," Laventhol said. *Newsday* tried to solve the problem by negotiating with

Cablevision for a joint venture, but the talks fell apart when Cablevision asked for editorial control and *Newsday* refused. The failure of those negotiations framed the issue in stark terms: Did *Newsday* want to spend the money on its own? "Ultimately, it got down to the question of, do we put the resources here, or do we put the resources against our expansion in New York?" Johnson said. Since the long-term profit potential of the New York paper seemed far greater than that of the cable operation, the choice was clear. In April, 1984, just short of a year after the channel opened, *Newsday* closed down the news show and the other taped programs, although it continued the less expensive videotex service for an additional two years.

At the end of 1986, Cablevision started its own twenty-four-hour news channel, News 12 Long Island, committing to it the kind of money that *Newsday* had declined to invest — a 1987 budget, for example, of nearly $7 million. The artistic success of News 12 showed what *Newsday* could have accomplished. "I believe we made a dramatic mistake not putting more resources behind it," Johnson said. "I believe we could have done even better than News 12." But the continuing lack of profitability of News 12 sent another message. "My ego on the one hand says we could have done it; we could have made it work," Johnson said. "On the other hand, it would not have been a moneymaking venture." Still, Johnson insisted that *Newsday* had done the right thing in trying the cable project, and might eventually have a second chance: "I think it's going to come around again."

Following the cable experience, Greene did come around again — not to the power he had enjoyed as an editor, but to his original strength, running the investigative team. His title remained assistant managing editor, but his role shrank from directing the whole Long Island staff to supervising a handful of reporters in a small office, remote from the daily action of the newsroom. Greene looked at the assignment as an internal exile, but even in exile he could not shed the habit of long hours and hard work, and he soon threw himself back into his accustomed pursuit of the mob. By his own admission, Greene had not been "a great manager," but he felt he had no apologies to make for his time as one of the paper's most powerful editors. "If I make a mistake, it's probably in bigger letters than other people might," Greene said, insisting that they were not mistakes of malice. "I never did anything in terms of intentionally hurting any human being."

CHAPTER FORTY-THREE

Baby Jane and the Famine

I

ON A SLOW day in the criminal courts, when there are no juicy trials, no developments in major investigations, no unusually nasty criminals appearing for arraignment, the reporter who covers courts has to use her wits.

That was the challenge facing Kathleen Kerr one afternoon in the fall of 1983 as she prowled the hallways of the H. Lee Dennison Building in Hauppauge, which housed many of Suffolk County's criminal courtrooms. "I was basically just sort of scouting around for a story, pestering people," said Kerr, who had joined *Newsday* in 1979 from the *Hudson Dispatch* and had started to cover the Suffolk district attorney's office and the courts earlier in 1983. As she went from lawyer to lawyer, searching for a story, an attorney named Charles Hickmann offered her one. "He said, 'We have an Infant Doe case. I know you probably don't know what that is. I'll explain it to you,' " Kerr remembered.

Actually, Kerr knew exactly what Hickmann was talking about: the controversy over the care of severely handicapped infants. The issue had most recently come to the public's attention in 1982, as the result of a struggle over a child born in an Indiana hospital with Down's syndrome and a deformed esophagus. The parents asked the hospital to withhold feedings and refused permission for surgery to repair the esophagus. When the hospital asked a local judge to order the operation, the judge refused. A higher state court upheld that ruling, and the baby died before the case could reach the Supreme Court of the United States. In response to pressure from right-to-life groups, the Reagan administration ordered federally funded hospitals to post signs warning that doctors who withheld treatment from the handicapped would be violating the law — a policy that became known as the "Baby Doe Rule." Later, a federal judge struck it down. "For some reason," Kerr said, "I was really, really interested in that case."

Standing in the hallway, Hickmann began explaining to Kerr the details of a local case. It involved a baby girl who had been born less than a week earlier with a combination of deformities, including an opening in the spine, called spina bifida, an abnormally small head, water on the brain and a variety of neurological defects. The parents had refused to permit surgery, and an attorney named A. Lawrence Washburn Jr. had heard about the case from local right-to-life activists and intervened. Hickmann knew about the case because he was active in right-to-life issues himself and had worked with Washburn on other cases. Over the weekend, two days before Hickmann met with Kerr, Washburn had persuaded Supreme Court Justice Frank DeLuca to order a hearing on the case for that week. The same day that DeLuca acted, a Saturday, Washburn remembered calling *Newsday* about the story. On Monday, Washburn called again and spoke briefly with the Suffolk editor, Richard Galant, who looked around the newsroom for a reporter. "I was the closest to his view," said Joe Calderone, who had come to *Newsday* two and a half months earlier, from the *Philadelphia Daily News*. Calderone took the information from Washburn and shared a byline with Kerr on the first story about the case, which ran the next morning, at the bottom of page four. "It was our story alone that first day," Galant said. But the story revealed that the hearing would take place the next morning, which guaranteed that other newspapers would begin to cover it.

Following the long hearing before Judge Melvyn Tanenbaum, Kerr continued to cover the case through Tanenbaum's decision to order the surgery, the reversal of that decision by the Appellate Division of the State Supreme Court, and an appeal of that ruling by the baby's court-appointed guardian. The week after the initial hearing, Kerr wrote a large Part II piece about the case, with a sidebar about a similar case by the health and science writer, B. D. Colen. Then Kerr covered the argument before the state Court of Appeals in Albany, which later upheld the right of the parents to refuse permission for surgery. That story contained hints, however, that the case wasn't over. An official of the federal Department of Health and Human Services, which had tried unsuccessfully to get the child's medical records from the hospital, said the department was studying the ruling to decide what to do next. The government decided quickly: The Justice Department filed a lawsuit to obtain Baby Jane Doe's medical records from the University Hospital at the State University at Stony Brook, to determine if the hospital had violated her rights.

As the federal lawsuit began to elevate Baby Jane Doe from a good local issue to a terrific national story, Kerr arranged two important interviews: one with Surgeon General C. Everett Koop, about the government's decision to sue the hospital, and one with the still-anonymous parents, Dan A. and Linda A., at the home of their attorney, Paul Gianelli. In the first few weeks, Kerr's editors did not think the story was important enough to cut her loose from her normal responsibilities. "They said, 'Kathy, go back to the courthouse. This story will take its course. It's a big deal, but not that big a deal,' " she remembered. So, every morning, Kerr would go to the courts and check on other stories, then make calls on the Baby Jane Doe case. Eventually, the editors detached her from the court beat and assigned her full time to Baby Jane Doe. Then, one piece of information suddenly seized the attention of her editors and made the story even hotter: On a Sunday television program, Koop said that the government had already asked for records in forty-eight similar cases. The next day, the government released a list of those cases. "Then we realized that we could really take a look at this as a national story," Galant said. "Everybody on the Long Island desk felt that this was something really worth pursuing."

The obvious way to pursue the story was to gather the details of the other cases and produce a package of stories for the following Sunday. The traditional *Newsday* method for developing such an ambitious package on such short notice was to throw a lot of people at it. "Kathy may have felt during this period that somehow things were passing her by," said Howard Schneider, the Long Island editor. "The reality was: This no longer was a one-person story." In fact, Kerr was a reporter who guarded her own stories fiercely, and she did feel left out. "I didn't get an assignment," she said. "I was asked to give people that were on the team sources and information. That was my assignment. That was the extent of anything that I did."

Despite Kerr's hurt feelings, the assignment of a big team of reporters made sense, since the story had spread nationwide. Schneider and Galant sent three reporters out to interview families: Geraldine Baum to Florida, Joye Brown to Chicago and Irene Virag to Colorado. On Long Island, another group of reporters stayed behind and pursued different aspects of the story: Michael Alexander, Joe Calderone, Michael D'Antonio, Robert Fresco and Steve Wick. A key member of the team was Colen, who had come into the project with an expertise in issues involving the care of children born at risk, since he had written a book on the subject. At the start, Colen hadn't been able to devote much time to the project, because he had a contract for a quick book on Acquired Immune Deficiency Syndrome. In 1982, two years after arriving at *Newsday* from the *Washington Post*, Colen had written a four-part series on AIDS — one of the earliest major projects on this subject. Once the book publisher had backed away from the AIDS book, Colen gave more time to working with Kerr on Baby Jane Doe.

To tie all the reporting together, the editors assigned Adrian Peracchio, who had come to *Newsday* in 1978 from the *Boston Herald American*. In five years, he had demonstrated a sharp analytical mind, a grasp of modern issues and a smooth writing touch, which made him perfect for complex projects. Using his own reporting on the ethical and political aspects of the case and notes from the other reporters, Peracchio crafted the main story for Sunday. At the end, he ended up working well past midnight on Thursday and Friday nights. "Everyone was incredibly energized by this story," Peracchio said. "It was not an artificial story. It was real and it was happening and it was happening all over the place." The result of this project, which began in the chaos of

Tuesday, election day, was a six-page report that Sunday, November 13. The editors gave bylines to Peracchio, Brown, Virag, Colen and D'Antonio, and put the rest of the names, including Kerr's, in a credit box. "It was sort of a miracle that it could be done under these kinds of circumstances," Galant said. "It was really a triumph of team journalism."

Once the crash project was over, Kerr and Colen were the primary reporters on the case. "We were talking about it almost every day," Kerr said. "He'd come in one day and say, 'Oh, they should let the baby die,' and I would say, 'No, they should let the baby live.' Then I'd go home and think about it, and we'd come in the next morning and have coffee, and he'd say, 'I was thinking about it. You're right.' I was saying, 'No, I was thinking about it. You're right.' That was helpful, because it showed both of us that the questions were really very difficult questions." Eventually, the parents resolved their own difficult question by consenting to surgery, and the baby went home to begin her life — a life made difficult by her handicaps, but not as difficult as her parents had feared.

In early 1984, *Newsday* submitted its coverage of the story for a Pulitzer Prize, and Kerr and Colen went to work on a series on medical ethics called "Hard Choices." Just as that series was starting to run, *Newsday* learned that it had won a Pulitzer for its coverage of Baby Jane Joe. But that joyous news came mingled with some pain. To begin with, two other *Newsday* writers had just missed winning Pulitzers. Morris Thompson had gotten himself to Grenada within hours after the American invasion, and he was among the finalists for the foreign reporting prize. Dan Cryer, the book critic, came even closer: In the jury for the criticism category, Cryer had emerged as the first choice, but the Pulitzer board chose Paul Goldberger, the architecture critic of the *New York Times*. Unfortunately, word had already leaked to Cryer that the jury had recommended him. When the board chose Goldberger, Tony Marro had to inform Cryer that he had not won after all. "It was one of the worst moments of my life," Cryer remembered. "It just hurt so bad. I went home and cried."

The other painful piece of business that day was the question of whose photographs would appear in *Newsday* the next day as sharers in the glory. Kerr and Colen disagreed strongly with the decision of the editors to forward no specific names to Columbia University as major participants, a decision that meant that the records of the prize would always reflect *Newsday* as the winner, rather than individual reporters. "How many times does this happen in a lifetime of journalism," Colen said, "and our names are not at Columbia." As to the question of credit, Kerr and Colen felt that it should not go beyond themselves and Peracchio. But Insolia and Marro decided otherwise: They would run photographs of Kerr and Colen on page three, underneath the headline about the prize. On page twenty-two, there were fourteen more photographs. Two of those were the near-winners, Cryer and Thompson. The rest were reporters and editors on the Baby Jane Doe story, including Schneider, Galant, all the reporters who had worked on the Sunday project and Dennis Hevesi, who had written several early stories on rewrite, including Kerr's interview with the parents.

Despite the haggling over credit, it was a high moment for *Newsday*, and a front-page photograph showed Kerr and others deliriously happy. Though Kerr had heard about the prize in advance and called the child's parents to prepare them for some unseemly post-Pulitzer merriment, some of the staff felt embarrassed over the contrast between the anguish of the family and the giddy joy of the photograph. The happiness was hard to contain, however, and the Pulitzer was sweet, because it wasn't the result of an airplane crash or a tornado, the kinds of disasters that often produce Pulitzers, but the product of routine local coverage — broadened to a national issue by a team project that became a key element in the Pulitzer submission. "The nice thing about the prize was that we didn't set out to win a prize," Galant said. "We just did what we tried to do all the time."

II

FOR MOST OF the people of Long Island, one of the richest suburbs in America, the grinding poverty of the Third World seems distant and unreal.

But in the early 1980s, as *Newsday* grew more interested in covering the world, the paper began looking more seriously at Third World issues. The first step was the assignment of Bob Wyrick to an investigation of American firms exporting hazardous products to developing nations. One of the roots of the project was a controversy over Tris, a flame-retarding substance that manufacturers used in children's pajamas, to comply with federal regulations that required sleepwear to be fire-resistant. When Tris turned out to be carcinogenic, the government banned the domestic sale of Tris-treated clothing, which left manufacturers holding a huge inventory of useless pajamas. So they sold them overseas. Marro was aware of this issue, because his wife, Jackie, had taught at the University of Maryland, which did research on the flammability of clothing. "It was that issue that first got Tony Marro's interest," Wyrick said. The result, after a year of reporting, was a powerful nine-part series in late 1981, "Hazards for Export," showing how American companies victimized consumers, endangered workers and polluted the environment overseas — often selling goods or using practices that were prohibited in America.

That same year, *Newsday* began exploring the issue of global hunger in depth — a decision that eventually produced some searing journalism and a Pulitzer Prize, but not without badly bruising some egos. The initial project was a look at the entire problem, starting in late 1981. One of the first concrete proposals on the hunger issue had come a year earlier from the reporter Dennis Hevesi. Hevesi had left *Newsday* at the end of 1978 to study hunger for a year, with support from a private, not-for-profit foundation. When he returned, as a part-time copy editor, he gave Tony Insolia a ten-page proposal for a series on solutions to the hunger problem. That helped to get *Newsday* thinking about hunger, but Insolia and others felt that Hevesi was too much of an advocate, which would make it difficult for him to cover dispassionately the hunger agencies. So the project went to Drew Fetherston and Adrian Peracchio, who decided to write an occasional series of moderately sized pieces, instead of the traditional *Newsday* blockbuster series of 50,000 words in one week, which intimidates readers. Rather than just describe the scope of the problem graphically, they examined the causes and scrutinized the governmental and private agencies that were fighting hunger. The series won them a prize donated by the singer Kenny Rogers through the United Nations: a large cash award, plus individual statuettes of a silver spoon on a globe.

Two years later, *Newsday* took the next logical step, a closeup examination of hunger in a crisis situation: the drought in sub-Saharan Africa. Before that decision in 1984, the only reporter who had spent significant time in the area for *Newsday* was Les Payne. But in 1980, Payne had become a weekly columnist and then the paper's national editor, which gave him less time to travel in Africa — although he did get there in 1982, in connection with the hunger series. At first, Payne supervised both the domestic and the foreign report as national editor. Then, in 1983, Insolia created a separate foreign desk and appointed Jean Patman, who had been the executive news editor, as the first foreign editor. In the first half of the 1980s, the creation of a separate foreign desk — and the addition of bureaus in London, Mexico City and Cairo to the original *Newsday* bureau in Asia — was a significant element of David Laventhol's long-term strategy of making *Newsday* a complete paper, so that readers wouldn't have to depend on any other newspaper. Anxious to build the paper's foreign report through major reporting projects, Patman decided in conversations with Payne that the sub-Saharan drought was a natural. "There had been a couple of small *Washington Post* pieces that said, here's the scope of it, but nobody had gone on the ground to take a look at what was happening," Patman said. So, on one of her long-term planning memos, she proposed a drought project. "Laventhol apparently read all these memos," Patman said. "He's the one who said, 'Let's go do that.'"

In late summer of 1984, Patman began to pick the staff for the project. Though Payne no longer had responsibility for foreign coverage, she relied heavily on his advice. They were both looking for people who could function in the Third World, but Payne was also looking for something else: the proper racial makeup. "I think the key to reporting is access," Payne said. "My experience in Africa had been that blacks have greater access. . . . A lot of what has passed as journalism and reporting out of that continent, by an overwhelmingly white foreign correspondents' corps, has not been quite the truth." On the principle of blacks covering Africa, Patman didn't disagree, but the reporter she chose to head the team was Josh Friedman, a white man. Friedman had already had significant experience in Third World countries, first in the Peace Corps and later as a reporter. He had come to *Newsday* two years earlier from the *Philadelphia Inquirer*, where he had been part of the team that won a 1980 Pulitzer Prize for its coverage of the Three Mile Island nuclear accident. At *Newsday*, Friedman had already broken new ground in the investigation of municipal corruption in Nassau County, travelled to Cuba after the invasion of Grenada, and covered the explosive situation in Beirut. "He just delivered," Patman said. "So I thought, 'He's a natural.' " Payne used the same term to describe the other reporter on the team, Dennis Bell, who came to the project with a fascinating background.

Bell grew up in Michigan, attended the University of Michigan for a year, joined the Army, and came to Long Island in 1971. At night, he worked at Hofstra University, sweeping classrooms. By day, because he was an employee, he attended class for free. But he had to interrupt his education and move back to Michigan, to help run his father's small grocery store. Then Bell moved back to Long Island and eventually took a job at *Newsday* as a porter, sweeping floors in the pressroom. A few months later, he became a proof boy in the composing room. When *Newsday* switched to offset printing and cold type, the opportunities in the composing room narrowed. Besides, Bell was ready for something else. "I decided that I was sick of this working just with my hands," Bell said. So he took a substantial pay cut and got a job as a clerk in the newsroom, then moved up to the sports department to handle box scores and other sports agate. Soon, Bell began to tire of the drudgery and to despair of getting a job that would make use of his intelligence. "Part of the job was to get editors and reporters coffee," Bell said. "I said, 'I'm twenty-nine years old, going to work to get some white folks coffee.' " The next day, his wife, Norma, brought home from *Newsday* a brochure about a summer training program for minority journalists. Bell applied and spent eleven weeks in Berkeley learning how to be a journalist. The problem was to arrange a job for himself at *Newsday* once the program ended. In that, Payne was his ally. "Les was working behind the scenes, trying to get *Newsday* to take me back," Bell said. Finally, *Newsday* did hire Bell as a reporter, assigning him to a beat in Nassau County. Later, he transferred to a court beat, where he began covering the controversy over the victims of Agent Orange contamination in Vietnam. In less than a decade, Bell had gone from porter to reporter at *Newsday*. Now, Payne thought he was ready for the Africa project, and Patman concurred.

The third member of the team was the photographer Ozier Muhammad, who had already been to Africa twice, and whose family had significantly influenced the lives of African Americans: His grandfather, Elijah Muhammad, had been the leader of the Nation of Islam, usually known as the Black Muslims. Ozier Muhammad had come to *Newsday* in 1980, with eight years of experience at *Ebony* magazine and the *Charlotte Observer*, and he had quickly established himself as a gifted, sensitive photographer. He also had a gentle disposition that enabled him to get along with anyone. That turned out to be an essential quality on this project, because Bell and Friedman had trouble working peacefully with each other.

"They were at loggerheads a bit before the project began," Muhammad said. "The issue was, I guess, ego. I think that both of them felt that they should be in charge." But Patman had chosen Friedman, because of his foreign experience. "I thought she had good reason to make him the team leader,"

Muhammad said. In the weeks-long period of preparation before they left for Africa — reporting on the general situation, contacting embassies, applying for visas and making logistical arrangements — the conflict between Bell and Friedman affected Muhammad. "Josh would want to go in one direction with the timetable — what country to start with and where to go to next — and Dennis had another idea that was contrary to that," Muhammad said. "In a way, it sort of had me spinning around."

When they finally left for Africa in mid-October, all the preparation began to pay off. Not quite two weeks after they had arrived and started reporting in Mali, Niger and Ivory Coast, Friedman learned that their long-awaited visas for Ethiopia had finally come through. At the same time, Patman was in New Jersey, at the *Newsday* management retreat in Great Gorge, when she saw on the late news a wrenching free-lance film of the relief camps in Ethiopia, jammed with victims of the famine. "That was the first real look inside Ethiopia," she said. A few minutes later, she found Tony Marro at the retreat and they decided to change the schedule and get the team to Ethiopia immediately. They had intended to have the team make the full tour of Africa and return to America to write, but the film clip suddenly made Ethiopia a major breaking story. *Newsday*'s long preparations, which had been an office joke, had now put the team in position to be the first American journalists to get into Ethiopia and report on the famine. "I picked up the phone and told Josh, 'We're going in,'" Patman said. The advance work made it possible for them not only to get into Ethiopia, but to travel freely, while other American journalists were still trying to wade through the bureaucracy. "The guy I had spoken to on the phone is waiting for us; the world is our oyster," Friedman said. "We were the only reporters, for at least a couple of weeks, who were able to go anywhere."

While Bell remained in the capital, Addis Ababa, covering the relief efforts, Friedman and Muhammad went out to the refugee camps, where they had to struggle to control their emotions, because they could do nothing to help the dying people in front of them, beyond telling their story to the world. "On many occasions, we were mistaken for doctors," Muhammad said. "They beseeched us to help them." At one camp, he remembered coming upon a distraught man, worried about his desperately ill wife. "The man was saying to us, through an interpreter, 'Please help me. My wife is dying,'" Muhammad said. "That took a lot out of me, and I couldn't quite function the rest of the day after that." To honor the dignity of the starving, they adopted a code of procedure. "I refused to photograph people dying in front of me," Muhammad said. "Folks who I thought were not going to make it, I respected their situation."

The tour of the camps turned up such vivid material that Patman offered a large package of stories and photographs for the Sunday paper of November 4 — the first on-the-scene report by an American newspaper about the Ethiopian famine. Not long before that Sunday, Muhammad had attended a routine weigh-in at the Korem relief camp and captured the most stunning photograph of the entire trip: a painfully emaciated child, with enormously sad eyes, sitting in a sling, being weighed. When Muhammad's film reached *Newsday* at about three in the morning, it was immediately apparent to Patman that the shot of the child was *the* photograph. It appeared on page one, the impact enhanced by acres of white space surrounding it, under the headline: "Ethiopia: A Nation Dying." Inside, there were additional striking photographs, plus Friedman's searing account of the camps and Bell's story about the failure of the relief effort.

It was during those weeks that Bell and Friedman had what Bell called "a screaming match" in the Addis Ababa Hilton, over the coverage of the story. "Josh did all the wandering around in Ethiopia," Bell said. "I didn't particularly care to be relegated to Addis, and Josh didn't particularly like the focus of some of my stories, or the way I went at it." Soon after Bell and Friedman had their screaming match, Patman called Bell. "She said, 'You do what Josh says or you come home,' " Bell remembered. He was becoming increasingly depressed with the way the story was going, and he began to consider going home. That was when he spoke to Payne, who was not his editor, but his advisor.

Though Payne had risen to a high position in management, most black reporters and editors still admired him and trusted his judgment. Some, however, grumbled that *Newsday* was using Payne's success as evidence that black people at the paper were making progress, and Payne was cashing in on that, without corresponding gains for the others. "There came a time when the other reporters, I found, were referring to me as 'Supernigger,' behind my back, of course," Payne said. Nonetheless, most black journalists on the staff felt that Payne was the most talented and forceful in the group and was providing better leadership than anyone else could have. "Could you see Dave Laventhol and Tony Marro taking *me* seriously when I come in there — Miss Temper Tantrum?" said Sheryl Barnett. "What would I be able to negotiate with these guys? What was Betti Logan going to negotiate, or Mike Alexander, or Scott Minerbrook, or Charles Moses? If we didn't have Les, we'd be in deep shit. Three quarters of the people in the newsroom are afraid of him."

Given all that, it was not surprising that Bell consulted Payne on whether he should quit the project and return to Long Island. "Les convinced me to stay, to do what was necessary to get the job done and contribute my voice to this package," Bell remembered. "He said: 'This is the way it is: If there's going to be a voice of truth, it's going to be you. So stay.' " Payne was actually sending Bell a dual message — Bell's value to the project and the need for blacks to cover Africa. "My idea at that point was to cross the Rubicon with black reporters and journalism," Payne said. "It was a specific point to him, but really, my larger point was to say that, hey, Africa is important, and I think that the degree to which Americans understand it at the next level is going to be the degree to which black reporters get in there."

It was a tricky situation: Payne talked with Bell but not with Friedman, the team leader, and Friedman began to feel that, under Payne's influence, Bell was not sharing information freely with the team. So, in his telephone conversations with Patman, Friedman criticized Bell's work. "Josh was terrific in a situation as a reporter, but as a team leader, he wasn't that great, because he'd complain about Dennis doing this and Dennis doing that," Patman said. "It's really hard, this many miles away, to figure out what's his ego and what's the truth." When Friedman became ill after their time in Ethiopia and had to spend about ten days in a Nairobi hospital, even that became a source of friction. Patman told Bell and Muhammad to throttle back somewhat on the reporting and get some needed rest until Friedman recovered, and Bell felt insulted that the work couldn't continue at the same pace without Friedman. Payne agreed that cutting back on the reporting was "silly." During this whole difficult time, the voice of reason was Muhammad, whose placid personality and sure sense of himself provided a buffer between the bruised egos of Friedman and Bell.

Despite the frictions and the internal politics, the team accomplished its mission. The thorough preparations had given them an enormous lead over all other American papers on the breaking story in Ethiopia, and they added reports on the situation in Kenya, Zimbabwe and the nations of West Africa. As a result, they produced a comprehensive package of stories about the entire region. That thoroughness, along with the impact of the breaking story, helped *Newsday* to win the Pulitzer Prize in 1985 for international reporting. The assignment and its aftermath left scars on the relationship between Payne and Friedman, but in the spring of 1985, the Pulitzer Prize overshadowed all that.

In winning the big prize in 1985, right after the 1984 prize for Baby Jane Doe, *Newsday* had won Pulitzers in consecutive years for the first time in its history. It was also the paper's first Pulitzer in the foreign reporting category. Besides the prize for the famine stories, the paper's staff won a second Pulitzer that carried absolutely no history of conflict or dissension, because the winner was Murray Kempton, a great favorite among his colleagues at *Newsday* and elsewhere in journalism. Kempton won for his work at *Newsday* in 1984, but there was a general feeling that he should have won years earlier, at the *New York Post* or the *World-Telegram & Sun*. The reason that he had finally won, Kempton felt, was probably that *Newsday* was more "respectable" than the *Post* and promoted his work more heavily. With typical self-deprecation, Kempton cited one other factor: "I think it was my age." Whatever had brought the Pulitzer to Kempton, he knew that the next day, he'd still have to be "out in the streets looking for something to write about." In the same spirit, one day after accepting the applause of his colleagues, Dennis Bell was back at work in the Nassau County courts. That day, Bell forever endeared himself to working reporters at *Newsday*, by gracefully shifting from the glory of covering global famine to the chore of writing about a dog brought into court by its owner to establish that the dog was safe and gentle.

On the same day that *Newsday* won the two Pulitzers, another prestigious prize went to Jeff Sommer, the Asia bureau chief. Sommer, who spoke fluent Mandarin Chinese, had replaced Bill Sexton in Asia at the end of 1982. In 1984, he had covered several major stories in India: the chemical plant disaster in Bhopal, the assassination of Indira Gandhi and violence among the Sikhs. The combination of those stories won him an Overseas Press Club award. Together, the two prizes for foreign coverage demonstrated that *Newsday* had grown beyond a merely local paper and was capable of solid reporting in the international arena. The global papers, such as the *New York Times* and the *Washington Post*, continued to beat *Newsday* regularly on the broad scope of their foreign coverage, but *Newsday* was beginning to show that it could compete with anyone on individual foreign stories. On the day that the story of *Newsday*'s Pulitzers appeared, for example, Myron Waldman continued his dogged, agenda-setting reporting on President Ronald Reagan's plans to visit a German cemetery in Bitburg, which contained the bodies of Nazi SS officers. And earlier in the decade, the London bureau chief Patrick Sloyan had turned in a legendary job of responding to a breaking foreign story, arriving in Cairo after the 1981 assassination of Anwar Sadat and quickly producing a surpassingly well-crafted main story under the pressure of the bloody moment.

The 1984 and 1985 Pulitzers, based on excellence in local and foreign reporting, helped to give *Newsday* an identity as a tabloid to be taken seriously. But that boost to the paper's self-image did not solve the lingering problem that was absorbing much of *Newsday*'s energy and concentration in 1985: how to bring consistent leadership to the turbulent New York City edition of the paper and give *New York Newsday* a vital, separate identity all its own.

CHAPTER FORTY-FOUR

Tab Wars

I

COMPARED WITH THE emotional strain of running moribund newspapers in two different cities, returning to *Newsday* to shape the future of a young and vigorous new paper was a pleasant prospect for Don Forst, despite the complex management structure that came with it.

When he left *Newsday* in 1977, Forst had accepted an offer from his former boss at the *New York Herald Tribune*, James Bellows. By then, Bellows had left jobs at the *Los Angeles Times* and the *Washington Star* and had become the editor of Hearst's *Los Angeles Herald Examiner*. Hearst had foolishly conceded to the *Times* a monopoly in the mornings, in exchange for a *Her-Ex* monopoly in the afternoon. As the demand for afternoon papers shrank everywhere, the *Times* flourished and the *Her-Ex* withered. Despite that, Bellows thought Forst could help him revive the paper. Intrigued by the idea of challenging the stuffy *Times*, Forst accepted the job of executive editor in early 1978.

Immediately, Forst tried to infuse some life into the pages by hiring eager young reporters who would accept low pay in exchange for a job in the big city. One of the first was Denis Hamill, the brother of the *New York Post* columnist Pete Hamill. In 1977, working for the *Village Voice*, Denis Hamill had won the Meyer Berger Award, given to the reporter who best captures the rhythms of New York in his work. By the time Forst reached Los Angeles, Hamill was writing a column for *New York* magazine. Forst called him and offered him a chance to write a column like Jimmy Breslin's New York column. Quickly, Hamill attracted attention, because he was the only columnist in Los Angeles who gave the reader a feel for the streets and dared to criticize Hollywood icons.

"I really scoured the streets, which hadn't been done before," Hamill said. Another typical recruit was Scot Paltrow, a young reporter in Memphis who wrote Forst a note reminding him that Paltrow had been a *Newsday* intern. "He picked up the phone and offered me $175 a week and the city lights," Paltrow said, "and I took it." While he was hiring young, inexpensive reporters, Forst was also firing older employees. "Within a year, I was the most senior person on the staff," Paltrow said. "You'd come back from lunch every day, and somebody else would have been laid off."

Aggressive hiring and firing shaped the staff in Forst's image, and his manic capacity for hard work energized them and nurtured a crusading spirit. More than that, he brought to the job his ability to focus on the story that everyone in town will be talking about, and to present it in an attention-grabbing way. A typical example was the "Hippo Watch" that he ran on the front page after a hippopotamus named Bubbles escaped from a wild animal park. Reacting emotionally to this daily update on the attempt to rescue Bubbles, readers paid close attention to the *Her-Ex* while it was going on. Similarly, when a young boy developed cancer, Forst mounted a campaign to call attention to his plight, referring to him in the headlines as "Tumor Boy." That headline raised a storm of outrage about Forst's taste, and later, he admitted that it was "dreadful, insensitive, awful, unthinking, ugly, terrible." (Earlier, at *Newsday*, Forst had evoked protests with his headline, "They Can Pull the Plug," describing a court decision that allowed doctors to disconnect the coma victim Karen Ann Quinlan from a respirator. "I don't think that was a bad headline," Forst said. "I think that absolutely encapsulated and said what the court said, in street language, and I think headlines should be in street language, within certain bounds.")

In a short time, Forst found ways to motivate the young staff and improve the editorial quality of the *Her-Ex*. With increasing frequency, the *Her-Ex* actually beat the wealthy *Times* on local stories. But at the end of fourteen months, Forst had a chance to become *the* editor of a paper, and he took it, leaving Los Angeles to take control of the *Boston Herald American*, another troubled Hearst newspaper fighting for its survival against a smugly dominant competitor, the *Boston Globe*.

Like the *Her-Ex*, the *Herald American* had steadily been losing circulation, from a high of 525,000 in 1972 to 264,000 when Forst arrived. Besides the dominance of the *Globe*, the problem was that the *Herald* was an amalgam of two starkly different papers: Hearst's *Record American*, a working-class tabloid, and the patrician *Herald Traveler*. Hearst combined the two staffs, who didn't get along, to produce the broadsheet *Herald American* — a combination that simply didn't work. Before Forst arrived, Bill McIlwain had been the editor and had tried to persuade Hearst to convert the paper into a tabloid, to set it apart from the stuffy *Globe*. Hearst refused. Later, worn down by the demands that he save money by cutting features, McIlwain had left for the *Washington Star*. When Forst arrived in 1979, the *Herald* was still a broadsheet, still losing ground to the *Globe*.

In Boston, Forst applied the same basic formula that he had used in Los

Angeles, starting with long hours. "He was an absolute workaholic," said Charlie O'Brien, the city editor. That intensity quickly rattled some of his staff. At one early meeting, Forst noticed one editor's absence and asked O'Brien where he was. "I said, 'He called in sick today,' " O'Brien remembered. "Don sort of smiles with that little smile that he has, and he says: 'He saw the fin in the water, I guess.' It was absolutely true: He had scared the hell out of this guy. I don't think he ever came back. He's a tough, tough guy to work for."

As he had in Los Angeles, Forst began cleaning house and firing people. One of the victims was Murry Frymer, the editor of the Sunday magazine, who had worked with Forst at *Newsday* and hadn't enjoyed it. By the end of Forst's first week in Boston, he and Frymer clashed after a magazine story needed last-minute changes. Working past midnight, Frymer ran into Forst and told him that he was about to take the revised story to the airport and send it by air freight to the printer in Kentucky. Instead, Forst ordered him to fly down to Kentucky *with* it. "I made the ridiculous mistake of saying something like, 'no,' " Frymer said. Then he had second thoughts, deciding to find out whether he could arrange a passenger flight that would get him to Louisville as quickly as the freight plane would get the story there. He couldn't. So he sent the story by freight after all, and he went home. The next morning, Forst asked why he wasn't in Louisville. Frymer explained, but Forst rejected the explanation. "He fired me right on the spot," Frymer said. At the time, Frymer had a new house, a large mortgage, three small children and no other income. Once his two weeks of severance pay ran out, he collected unemployment for months, until he found a job — in California. "It was a very rough time for me," Frymer said. He was not the only victim. As circulation kept shrinking at the end of 1979, Forst got orders to cut twenty-six people from the staff. By the twenty-third person, Forst said in a magazine interview, he cried. But he didn't always display such tenderness. "I think there's a sadistic streak there," Frymer said.

As much as Forst's toughness scared some of the people on his staff, he saved his real hostility for the *Boston Globe* and its editor, Thomas Winship. "He called once, I think, and he very graciously said, 'Dave Laventhol says you're a hell of a nice guy. I'd like to meet you and get together,' " Forst remembered. "And I said, 'Tom, I never want to meet you. I just want to poison your well and slaughter your sheep, pillage your villages, sack your house and rape your women. I want to have nothing to do with you, because I have to wake up in the morning wanting to kill you. . . .' In my particular, peculiar makeup, I needed to have that burn every morning when I got up."

The primary weapon in Forst's war with Winship was the front page — the same brand of cheeky, irreverent front page that he had done in Los Angeles. When Carl Yastrzemski collected career base hit number 3,000, for example, Forst ran the word "hit" 3,000 times on the front page. "He's a very original thinker," said Betsy Buffington Bates, who worked with Forst at the *Herald*. "He thinks visually, which is not true of a lot of newspapermen." Behind his great strength, devising an eye-catching page one, there were weaknesses: He did not focus well on long, explanatory stories. He did not deal effectively with administrative detail. And he flew off too easily into excess. So, to provide a check on his excesses, Forst appointed an executive editor: Jim Toedtman, a serious, cautious journalist who had worked with him at *Newsday*. Forst also hired Bob Sales, another former *Newsday* employee, to work under Toedtman. The familiar faces around Forst also included Denis Hamill, who wrote the same kind of street column in Boston as he had in Los Angeles. Like Hamill, the rest of Forst's staff vividly conveyed to the reader a sense of the city, which made the *Herald* more competitive with the *Globe* than it should have been. "The *Globe* is so fat and lazy that they didn't even make any attempt to cover local news," said Penny Raynor, then a *Herald* copy editor. "So we could get some good stories on them."

In time, the paper's progress persuaded Hearst to make an investment in the future by turning it into a tabloid, as Forst had urged. "We put together a design that, of course, looked tremendously like *Newsday*," Toedtman said. "The readers voted, and they liked it. The advertisers voted, and they didn't like it." So the paper continued to die, and the staff grimly compared their situation to the hopeless French battle against the Vietnamese at Dien Bien Phu. "This was the original death barge in American journalism," Toedtman said. "We were losing anywhere from $12 million to $20 million a year, and it just seemed to be unstoppable. There was nothing that we could do."

Finally, Forst made a desperate attempt to save the paper from closing, by trying to convince the Australian publishing lord, Rupert Murdoch, that buying the *Herald American* from Hearst would be a good investment. Murdoch did decide to buy the paper and make it over in his image, but he also decided that he wanted someone other than Forst to run it. So Murdoch moved Forst out as editor and made him associate publisher — a job that wasted his considerable talents on trivial tasks. Murdoch did offer him other jobs, including managing editor at the *New York Post*. But early in 1983, Forst resigned from the *Herald*. "He did everything humanly possible to try to keep that paper going, and it worked," Bates said. As he left, the staff gave him a gold medallion with the inscription: "To Don Forst. Thanks for the best years of our lives."

For part of 1983, the Hearst organization employed Forst as a consultant and tried to persuade him to return to Los Angeles. But Forst was wary of the continuing problems there, and his new wife, Starr Ockenga, didn't want to go to California. Later in the year, the publisher of *Boston Magazine*, which had carried a long article on Forst's days at the *Herald*, offered to make him the magazine's editor. In that job, Forst learned about magazine graphics and magazine writing, but he also discovered that the pace was far too slow. In 1984, a few months after he joined the magazine, he got another newspaper offer: James Hoge, the new publisher of the *New York Daily News*, asked Forst to be his editor. Forst turned him down. Then his old friend David Laventhol, who had brought him to *Newsday* fourteen years earlier, asked him to return, as the editor of *New York Newsday*.

Laventhol and Forst had sharply dissimilar personalities and management styles, but they shared a genius for packaging daily newspapers. So Laventhol felt Forst was the perfect person to carry out his vision for *New York Newsday*. "I felt that he knew and understood *Newsday*, knew and understood New York, knew and understood competitive journalism, knew and understood tabloid journalism," Laventhol said. "So I called him and asked if he would be interested." Forst vacillated: "Did I want to come back to New York? Did I want to leave a cushy job in Boston? Did I want to accept the restrictions that came with the job? Did I want to participate in a strange mechanism?" In that mechanism, Forst would be the New York editor, but he would report to the overall managing editor, Tony Marro, who seemed certain to become *the* editor of *Newsday* when Tony Insolia retired.

At one point, Marro said, Forst turned Laventhol down, and they began to think seriously of giving the job permanently to the temporary overseer, Howard Schneider. But Laventhol kept pursuing Forst. Eventually, Forst met with Marro and Insolia in a hotel near LaGuardia Airport, and they explained to him exactly how it would work. In addition to the requirement that he report to Marro, Insolia gave him one more caveat: "We're going to do it within the bounds of *Newsday* journalism." Finally, Forst decided that *New York Newsday* was going to fly, and he wanted to be part of it: "I had confidence that, with my talents, the money Times Mirror was willing to put up against it, the marketplace, the marketing strategy, the smart people, that it could be done, with a lot of hard work."

II

THE ANNOUNCEMENT OF Forst's appointment as the editor of *New York Newsday* created a conflicting set of emotions on the staff, ranging from euphoria to fear.

For the metropolitan editor, Bob Sales, it was good news. Insolia had lost faith in his ability to run the growing staff, and Sales had endured the imposition of John Van Doorn and later Howard Schneider as temporary solutions. But Sales had worked closely with Forst in Boston and looked forward to his arrival. At the same time, some of the *Newsday* women were so concerned about Forst that one of them taped to a mirror in the ladies' room a copy of a critical article from the *Boston Phoenix*, with the ominous headline, "Forst Upon Us." The story began by raising questions about Forst's treatment of women: "What would you say about a newspaper executive who enjoyed calling women on his paper's staff and asking them embarrassing sexual questions?" The next paragraph tried to strike a balance: "And would you say the same thing if you were informed that he is *also* described as a sweet and sensitive man whose closest friends are women?"

Some women at *Newsday* had worked with Forst during his first tour, and it was not the sweet side that they had seen. They had heard him regularly use short, vulgar, offensive synonyms for the word "woman." They knew that he had asked women personal questions about their sexual preferences and had described his own fantasies in graphic detail. None of those women felt that Forst was actually soliciting sex from them, but his comments left them at a loss for a response. That was a central element of Forst's style: saying breathtakingly outrageous things to throw people off balance. One example came from Penelope McMullan, who worked at *Newsday* as a reporter during Forst's earlier tour. McMullan was getting ready to take a job at the *Daily News* and telephoned Forst to tell him about it. At the time, he was at a management retreat with a group of other editors. "In his true prick way, he says, 'I know why you're calling. You're going to the *Daily News,*' " said McMullan, who later changed her name to McMillan at the *News*. She asked him how he knew the reason for her call, and he said: " 'I know everything.' " She was proud of her work at *Newsday* and happy about her move to the *News*, but in their phone conversation, Forst belittled her new job and didn't say anything kind or gracious about her performance at *Newsday*. So, in the emotion of the moment, McMullan's voice cracked as she talked to him. Not long after they had finished talking, he called back and said: " 'Guess what I've got?' " He played back a tape recording of their conversation, and she soon learned that he had also played the tape for the amusement of the editors at the management retreat. That set off waves of outrage in the newsroom. Later, Forst regretted it. "It was her effort to do something that was very serious and important to her," he said, "and it was just stupidly sloughed off by me."

The women also remembered an incident during the women's suit in the 1970s. One complaint had been the absence of women reporters in the Washington bureau, and the editors responded by sending a reporter named Lynn Rosellini to Washington. That choice was bound to annoy the women, since they knew that Forst had once had a romantic relationship with Rosellini. At the time, Rosellini was young and untried, but immensely talented. The women all liked and admired her, but when her appointment to Washington was announced, some of the women said, they suspected that Forst was using her assignment partly to thumb his nose at their demands. "That wasn't my intent — absolutely not," Forst said. "If they read it that way, they read it that way." Whatever his intentions, the object of the women's suspicion was Forst, not Rosellini, who went on to do a prize-winning job in Washington. Through it all, Rosellini still considered Forst her friend. She had heard accounts of his hostility to women, but those stories seemed out of keeping with the man that she knew. "What I never understood was how he could be so 'vicious' toward women and yet turn around and in a personal, one-on-one relationship, be so tender and loving and considerate," Rosellini said. "This was a guy who was capable of real love, real, real caring and real softness. That's the side I saw of him and, frankly, that's the side I've always seen of him. To this day, I hear these horror stories, and I think, 'Who is this man?' It's almost like the Dr. Jekyll and Mr. Hyde thing. This is not a man I know. It's weird."

Though Forst had caused women discomfort with his graphically sexual remarks, they did not see him as holding women back professionally. So he was not a target in the women's suit. Nonetheless, in 1985, the women were worried about his return. The other cause of concern was the fear in the Melville newsroom that Forst would turn *New York Newsday* into a lurid clone of the *New York Post*. At one early meeting in Melville, editors and reporters from the national and foreign desks questioned him sharply about his plans, and Forst calmly described to them the emotional tone that he hoped to set: If the *Times* was quiet at zero and the *News* was noisy at ten, Forst wanted to make *New York Newsday* a six.

Whether the women or the staff in Melville trusted Forst or not, *New York Newsday* needed *someone* to bring order out of the chaos that the departure of McIlwain had created. With the heavy promotion of the New York paper that had begun in the spring of 1985, it was more visible than ever, but without a real leader, it was going nowhere. "From the time McIlwain left until the time Forst came, there was nobody clearly in charge of the paper who was committed to New York City," the editor Tom Curran said. "None of them had the vision and the feel for what a paper in New York City needed to be."

On Forst's first day in New York, even Laventhol made a little joke about Forst's reputation, asking two members of the staff in a hallway: " 'Is Don behaving himself?' " In the months that followed, many of those who had worked with Forst at *Newsday* in the 1970s detected a softening of his hard edges, a "new Don." They attributed that to the benign influence of his second wife, Starr Ockenga, an intelligent, well-bred New Englander, the daughter of a Congregational minister. But at the start, Forst showed that he was still ready to display his legendary toughness. In a meeting with Van Doorn, who was at the end of his troubled tenure as deputy to Sales, Forst began softly. He knew that Van Doorn was disappointed not to be *the* editor in New York, but he assured Van Doorn that they could work together. Then, Van Doorn remembered, Forst said: " 'Or, if you want a shit fight, you've got it.' " Still, Forst impressed him. "I had a certain admiration for the way he conducted himself, coming in and editing a paper in which he's sort of the editor, but not really the editor," Van Doorn said. "While he carried himself as a bantam rooster and a tough guy, he nonetheless made intelligent decisions."

Some of Forst's earliest decisions concerned layout. During his years in Boston, he had watched *Newsday* from afar and had seen it become "stolid, predictable, and conservative." Taking over in New York, he was able to impose his more freewheeling style quickly by controlling the front page and working with the news editor, Bob Keane, who had just taken over from Dick Estrin a few months earlier. "Even when Dick left and I moved in and started doing it, we didn't really have the free hand to change the paper around, to make it look dramatically different, until Don arrived," Keane said. "Tony Insolia and the folks who were running *Newsday* understood it had to be a little bit different, but didn't think the differences necessarily should be radical." With Forst's encouragement, Keane installed a busier, more Forstian layout: shorter stories and more items on each page, to make the paper look more exciting and fast-paced, in order to make it fit more comfortably in the New York market.

Besides altering the layout, Forst began changing the tone of some of the paper's features, such as the "Inside New York" gossip column that Warren Berry had been writing from Long Island, with help from Ben Kubasik. Despite Berry's writing talent, many editors were uncomfortable with a New York gossip column written from Long Island. Only two months after Forst arrived, Berry returned full time to editing the paper's special sections, and Forst hired a magazine writer, Anthony Scaduto, to work with Kubasik. That put the entire staff of the column in Manhattan, under Forst's eye. A few weeks later, he hired Susan Mulcahy away from the *New York Post* to work with Scaduto and Kubasik. In one move, the hiring of Mulcahy strengthened *Newsday*'s gossip column and jolted the *Post*, where she had been running Page Six, the widely read gossip section.

At the same time that he was hiring Mulcahy away from the *Post*, Forst recruited another of its most promising young writers, Mike McAlary, who had worked for Forst in Boston. In the next few weeks, Forst also hired Richard Esposito from the *Post*, Anthony DeStefano from the *Wall Street Journal*, and Maurice Carroll, a veteran rewrite man at the *New York Times* who had worked with Forst at the *Herald Tribune*. DeStefano and Esposito became important parts of the paper's coverage of criminal justice, and Carroll was a facile writer with valuable experience covering New York City politics. Of all the people that Forst hired in those first few months, however, McAlary would eventually make the most noise at *Newsday*.

McAlary grew up in Brooklyn and New Hampshire, covered sports for papers in New Hampshire, and landed a job on the sports pages of the *Boston Herald American* soon after his graduation from Syracuse University in 1979. He stayed at Boston for a year, signed on with the *New York Daily News* in 1980 and got laid off the following year, in the bloodletting that followed the closing of the *Tonight* edition. After a brief tour in Rochester, McAlary landed a job in late 1982 with the *Post*, where he covered the Yankees and the Mets. But for McAlary, sports was simply a means to an end. "Always, my idea was to wind up a columnist, a cityside columnist," McAlary said. "I had conversations with Forst about that, back when I first got out of college." McAlary wanted the same kind of high-profile column that Jimmy Breslin was writing at the *Daily News*, and he consciously set out to train himself for it. "Sports was a place where I believe you're free to write, develop a style," McAlary said. By the time Forst arrived in New York, McAlary was ready to make the jump from sports to the city desk. So he called Forst and began the discussions that led to his hiring.

For McAlary, working for *New York Newsday* made perfect sense, because Forst not only could give him a column someday, but could teach him how to write it. "I think he knows the most about editing a column of anybody around," McAlary said. "He understands what a story is. He understands how to tell a story. He understands how to take a small piece of something and make it representative of the bigger story. . . . He understands tempo and orchestration." But before McAlary could even think about a column, he had to learn how to work in the streets, instead of the stadiums. "I never wrote a news story before January of 1986," McAlary said. He started in the Queens office, covering cops and prowling the streets. One of his first stories was a summary of every murder in Queens for a month, which gave him a good start toward a strong relationship with the police. A few months later, that network of sources would bring him the story of his life.

While McAlary learned about news, in hopes of writing a column someday, the New York paper had no shortage of columnists. Murray Kempton, who had just won a Pulitzer, was the lead columnist. Dennis Duggan, who had been working for *Newsday* in Manhattan since 1967, had written a column for the New York paper since 1982. Ken Gross had briefly written a Queens Diary column when the edition first started in 1977, returned to writing features, then became a columnist again in 1980. But Forst's arrival began to change the alignment of columnists.

Soon after Forst took over, he arranged for his protege, Denis Hamill, to come to *Newsday* as a columnist. At about that time, Forst asked Gross to take on some temporary assignments. One proposal, Gross remembered, was a column that would focus entirely on the subways. Gross declined, convinced that Forst was planning to take away his general column. "That was always his paranoia, but that wasn't true," Forst said. Still, Gross felt threatened. "There was never any doubt, by anybody who was privy to it, that I was in Hamill's way," Gross said. During that period, as Gross was growing unhappy at *Newsday* for a variety of reasons unrelated to Forst, he got a lucrative offer from *People* magazine. In early 1986, roughly six months after Forst arrived at *New York Newsday*, Gross left the paper and took the job at *People*. "When he came in, he said, 'In six months, you won't be writing a column,' " Gross remembered. "As history shows, he was right."

The hiring of Hamill raised questions on the staff, partly because of his closeness to Forst and partly for more substantive reasons. "There was a lot of resentment when he brought in Hamill: yet another male, yet another Irishman," said Neill Rosenfeld, then an education reporter. "Why in New York City didn't we have a columnist of color? Why didn't we have a woman?" Hamill, of course, was none of those things. He was a hard-drinking denizen of the streets, who wrote tough, unyielding prose, sprinkled with tales of his own encounters with flashing knives in bucket-of-blood bars. But he sensed quickly that *Newsday* was entirely unlike the desperado papers where he had worked with Forst before, in Los Angeles and Boston. "It's like the *New York Times* without a fold," Hamill said. And right from the start, Forst made clear how Hamill was to work. "He read me the rules," Hamill said. "He wanted me to do down-and-dirty, but it had to be within certain guidelines — no more red meat to the carnivores."

Despite Forst's guidelines, Hamill still wrote blunt descriptions that outraged people. In one column, for example, he wrote about a convention of the American Bar Association: "I used to think it was a stereotype to say most lawyers are bald, but God Almighty, there were so many Chrome Domes

yesterday that you could have set up business to sell symbols to hock shops."
Reading that column on a subway train, the *Newsday* reporter Richard Sandomir, who had already lost much of his hair, became enraged, went back to the
newsroom and spent the rest of the day writing a parody of Hamill's style, which
became an underground classic at *Newsday*. "I wanted to catch the gratuitous
descriptions," Sandomir said. "I wanted to get the pseudo-tough-guy, I've-
been-everywhere-and-been-protected-by-Don-Forst-everywhere."

While Forst worked closely with Hamill, editing his column personally for
the first few months, Forst also continued to push for a subway column. Forst
liked to tell people that he stole the idea from a mass-transit column called
"The Phantom Rider" at the *Philadelphia Daily News*, whose former editor, F.
Gilman Spencer, had come to New York to edit the *New York Daily News*.
Though it wasn't Forst's own concept, it made sense to him. "On the island,
there are a couple of common denominators," Forst said. "One is *Newsday* and
one is the car. The common experience in New York City, it seems to me — *the*
most prevailing common experience — is the subway." Looking for someone to
create a subway column, Forst talked to Dennis Duggan about it. Duggan
perceived it as a step down from his general column, and he didn't relish
spending most of his working day in the filthy, crime-ridden subways. So he
stalled, but he eventually went along, with assurances that it was just a three-
month assignment. "Forst's instructions were: 'I don't want to see you in the
office,'" Duggan said. "I felt in a sense like I had to take off the ermine robes
and dress like a Welsh miner." Not surprisingly, Duggan found it difficult to
create a new kind of feature, limited to the subways, and generate enough ideas
to keep it going. "Red Smith used to say: 'God will provide,'" Duggan said.
"You have to think that way. Sometimes it was a little dicey."

III

As FORST WAS beginning to shape the staff, fine-tune the layout and impose his
own standards on the paper, a major news story broke, severely testing *New
York Newsday*'s ability to compete with the established dailies.

It began in the early morning hours of January 10, 1986. At about one
o'clock in the morning, on the Grand Central Parkway near Shea Stadium in
Queens, police spotted someone driving erratically and stopped him. The
driver was one of the city's most powerful politicians: Donald Manes, the
borough president of Queens and the Democratic leader of Queens County.
When the police found him, Manes was dazed and bleeding from a gash on his
wrist. A few days later, Manes told investigators that two unknown men hiding
in the back seat of his car had abducted him, forced him to drive around
Queens, and attacked him.

While police were starting to sort out the details of the Manes story and search for the attackers, another story broke: Federal authorities arrested a Manes associate, Geoffrey Lindenauer, the deputy director of the city's Parking Violations Bureau, and accused him of extorting $5,000 from the head of a firm that had won a city contract to collect delinquent parking fines. As the scandal in the Parking Violations Bureau continued to spread, with the ouster of its director, detectives announced that they couldn't substantiate the story that Manes had told them, and they believed he had tried to commit suicide. Finally, on January 21, Manes read a brief statement to reporters in his hospital room, acknowledging the truth. "The wounds I received that night were self-inflicted," Manes said. "There were no assailants and no one but me is to blame."

Within forty-eight hours after Manes had revealed his suicide attempt, the *Daily News* hit the streets with a story by Jimmy Breslin that went a long way toward explaining why Manes was so despondent — a story that made a few people at *New York Newsday* feel a despondence of their own. "Michael Dowd, a Queens Blvd. attorney, last night told the United States attorney's office in Manhattan that Donald Manes, the Queens borough president, extorted money from him for a period of 18 months," Breslin wrote. "This revelation causes the city's Parking Violations Bureau scandal to detonate." Dowd was a criminal lawyer who practiced his trade near the Queens County courts in Kew Gardens, which had been Breslin's turf for years. One of Dowd's side businesses was a collection agency. In order to get contracts from the Parking Violations Bureau to collect money from delinquent violators of the parking laws, Dowd told Breslin, he had to pay bribes. Manes himself had instructed Dowd to pay Lindenauer, and Dowd had paid $36,000 before he finally refused to pay any more. Once Dowd had told Breslin this story, Breslin had persuaded him to tell federal prosecutors, and then Breslin had broken the story in the *Daily News*. The day that Breslin's story appeared, federal officials said that Manes was a target of their investigation, and Mayor Edward Koch said that Manes should consider resigning.

Breslin's front-page story was a devastating embarrassment for *New York Newsday*, because Queens was still the center of its universe. If *New York Newsday* was going to beat the other city papers on any story, it *had* to be on a mushrooming scandal based in Queens. But Breslin had just beaten *Newsday* with a shattering scoop. Later in 1986, Breslin won a Pulitzer, largely on the strength of his columns about another Queens scandal: police brutality. Based on his performance in the Manes story, Breslin predicted that he'd win a Pulitzer in 1987, too. "Who could you give it to next year and not give it to me?" Breslin asked. (Breslin's prediction turned out to be more confident than accurate. He didn't win a Pulitzer in 1987.)

The story came as a particularly nasty shock to Jim Dwyer, a young reporter who had been working on scandal stories for *New York Newsday* in Queens. Dwyer was a native of New York, a former editor of the *Fordham Ram* and a graduate of the journalism school at Columbia. He had come to *Newsday* in 1984 after working at a series of papers in New Jersey. Before the Breslin story broke, Dwyer had become familiar enough with the scene around the court-house to identify Dowd as a potentially good source. "I tried everything to get in to see him, and there was a young lawyer in his office who kept dealing with me all day and putting me off," Dwyer said. "The young lawyer finally said to me, 'Listen, he doesn't know anything about it. I don't know enough about it, but I can tell you, he was not involved in the payoffs.' So the next morning, at a quarter to seven, Tom Curran telephones my house and starts reading me the front-page column by Jimmy Breslin about Michael Dowd having gone to the U.S. attorney's office. I was almost vomiting. . . . We got beat on the biggest story going, and I got beat. I was terribly upset about it, and Forst came in and said, 'Don't worry, we'll get back.' We put a few on the scoreboard then." Soon after Breslin's scoop, a source phoned Dwyer, apparently feeling compassion for him in his moment of defeat, and offered a tip: Richard Rubin, a counsel to Assembly Speaker Stanley Fink and the executive secretary of the Queens Democratic organization, had placed one of his private legal secretaries on the Assembly payroll, but she did no real work for the Assembly. Dwyer wrote the story and a federal grand jury later indicted Rubin, who was convicted and sentenced to three years in prison. "My consolation prize was Richard Rubin," Dwyer said.

If the Breslin story was a stomach punch for Dwyer, it carried a certain ironic pain for Forst as well. With encouragement from Forst, his old colleague from the *Herald Tribune*, Breslin had written a column for the *Newsday* view-points pages in 1972, before *Newsday* had a real city presence. The column was only temporary, and the suburban pages of *Newsday* were simply not the right place for his distinctly urban voice. Nonetheless, Breslin and Forst remained close over the years, and Breslin felt that Forst really understood the art of writing a column. When Forst was in Boston and Breslin was at the *Daily News*, Breslin learned that the *News* had offered Forst the editor's job and Forst had turned them down. Breslin was outraged. "He called me in Boston and said, 'Drop dead; I never want to talk to you,' and he hung up," Forst said. "The day I started here, he called me and said, 'What's doing?' And from the first day I started here, I thought if we could, we ought to get him." Instead, Breslin remained at the *News* and blew *Newsday* out of the water with the Dowd story.

The sudden explosion of a big-league scandal story, right at the start of his watch, was a difficult development for Forst. "I said, 'Holy shit! What do I do?' " Forst remembered. To begin with, he invested considerable time and staff in it. "I put Tommy Curran in charge," he said. "We put together a task force that met every morning and figured out how to take the story forward." It was a slippery story for Curran, Bob Sales and the staff to follow, but it was an opportunity for some reporters in the Queens bureau to get to Manhattan. "Basically, people rode Manes into New York," the reporter Ellis Henican said. "That's what I did." Along the way, each day brought jarring new develop-ments, such as the second suicide attempt by Donald Manes. This time, he succeeded, piercing his heart with a kitchen knife, but his death did nothing to halt the spread of the story. So the staff of *New York Newsday* had to keep struggling through it. It was painful when they fell behind the other papers, but the story was also fun. "It was thrilling," Curran said. "It was serious, competitive newspapering."

On balance, despite the pain of the Breslin scoop and other losses along the way, the city scandals turned out to be a strengthening experience. "In my mind, I know when we came of age in New York, and that was on the Donald Manes story," Forst said. "It was like being a Division III school and discovering somebody has scheduled you to play Notre Dame. Sometimes we got run over, but we kicked some field goals, we scored a few touchdowns, but most of all, we weren't run off the field."

IV

WHILE IT WAS struggling with the scandals story in 1986, *New York Newsday* made progress in other areas. Perhaps the most visible coup was the hiring of a columnist who had already won a Pulitzer at another New York newspaper: Sydney Schanberg.

In 1976, Schanberg had won the Pulitzer for his coverage of the bloodbath in Cambodia for the *New York Times*. His account of those days became the basis for the movie, *The Killing Fields*. Later, he became the metropolitan editor of the *Times*, but in 1980, he asked to be relieved of the job, because he disagreed with the way his bosses were forcing him and his staff to cover the city — without enough sensitivity to minority groups. His next assignment was to write a column about New York City affairs. Aggressively scrutinizing life in New York, he inevitably irked some of the powerful real estate and other interests in the city. Eventually, the column began to displease his bosses, especially the executive editor, A. M. Rosenthal. Finally, just before leaving on vacation in the summer of 1985, Schanberg wrote a column criticizing the press for concentrating on fluff and failing to cover serious issues, such as the Westway highway project, which the *Times* supported editorially. While he was on vacation in upstate New York, he got a call from Sydney Gruson, the deputy to the publisher, Arthur Ochs Sulzberger. "I said, 'What's it about?' " Schanberg remembered. "He said, 'Well, there's some unhappiness here with the column you wrote.' "

When Schanberg returned from vacation on a Monday, he started to write a column for the next day, but Gruson interrupted him with a phone call and asked Schanberg to come to his office. Gruson told him that Sulzberger had not been happy with the column for some time, and the paper was going to discontinue it, after a run of four years. The *Times* told the world about this on Tuesday with a two-paragraph announcement. The next day, the "Inside New York" column in *New York Newsday* commented tartly: "The *Times* has asked Pulitzer Prize-winner Schanberg to stay on in another position. What would that be? Kneeling?" Actually, the *Times* asked Schanberg to be a roving correspondent for the Sunday magazine, but he rejected that and other proposals. "What I wanted to do is what I had been doing," Schanberg said.

In early 1986, Schanberg left the *Times*, which prompted people at *Newsday* to realize that a Schanberg metropolitan column would be a major boost for the New York paper. Laventhol, who had known Schanberg since Laventhol's days at the *Herald Tribune*, talked with Schanberg himself. They quickly and amicably reached agreement. In coming to *New York Newsday*, Schanberg would be writing for a paper with much less clout than the *Times*, but that didn't bother him. "By nature, I identify with an underdog," Schanberg said. "I mean, I wouldn't call *Newsday* an underdog, but *Newsday* in New York I would call an underdog — the new guy on the block, having to break into somebody else's territory. . . . So I thought: 'What a great chance to make a contribution to this new thing and maybe have some role in affecting its shape.' " Besides writing the column, Schanberg was to be an associate editor, which didn't entail regular administrative duties, but did give him a chance to participate in discussions and meetings in the newsroom. In the process, he found that *New York Newsday*, whatever its faults, was paying serious attention to the city, unlike the *Times*. "On balance, since I've been here," Schanberg said, "*New York Newsday* has covered the city better than any other paper."

At about the time that Laventhol was closing the deal with Schanberg, Forst was completing the top management of *New York Newsday*. Just as he had done in Boston, Forst brought in Jim Toedtman to handle administrative details and to protect Forst from his own excesses. When Forst called him in late 1985, Toedtman was the editor of another declining newspaper, the *Baltimore News-American*, which had once had a strong blue-collar readership, but had lost circulation as Baltimore became more of a white-collar city. Toedtman stayed in Baltimore for several more months and came to *New York Newsday* in March, 1986. With Toedtman's arrival, Forst had in place the same group of top managers that he had assembled in Boston: himself as editor, Toedtman as managing editor, and Bob Sales as metropolitan editor. Almost as soon as Toedtman arrived, however, Sales decided to return to Boston as the executive sports editor of the *Herald*. That decision had nothing to do with Toedtman. Rather, it was the product of the bitterness that Sales felt toward the powers on Long Island, who had made clear that their confidence in him had evaporated, even though Forst felt that Sales had been an excellent teacher for the young reporters and had recruited some of the paper's top talent. "Bob went away because he hated *Newsday*," Forst said. "He felt he got fucked before I got here, by Insolia."

Once Sales was gone, Forst had to find another metropolitan editor. Forst would continue to shape page one and bring a more New York perspective to the columns and features. Toedtman would administer. Hap Hairston, who had come to New York during the post-McIlwain turmoil and had developed into a solid New York assigning editor, would work directly with the reporters. But Forst needed someone above Hairston and below Toedtman, someone who could look beyond the day's news and figure out where stories were going next. To fill the role, Forst chose John Cotter, a journalist with an unusually varied background.

Cotter was the oldest of nine children of a pediatrician in the mining town of Pittston, Pennsylvania. After a thoroughly Jesuit education, at Scranton Prep and Scranton University, and a brief tour in the Coast Guard Reserve, Cotter landed his first job in journalism, at the *Harrisburg Patriot-News*. From there, he hooked up with the Associated Press, working as a reporter in the Pittsburgh bureau and later the Philadelphia bureau, then moved to a supervisory job on the AP general desk in New York. Before long, the AP made him enterprise editor. As his job became more and more administrative, Cotter decided to get back into reporting, as a free-lance reporter on the national desk of the *New York Daily News*. During that time, he attracted some attention by writing a long series about the followers of the Korean cult leader, Sun Myung Moon. Then the managing editor of the *New York Post*, Craig Ammerman, asked Cotter to run its coverage of Pope John Paul II's visit to New York in 1979. That led to a more permanent role at the *Post*, as an associate editor and later as a day city editor. Growing weary of the Murdoch-era *Post*, he went to work at a weekly supermarket magazine, *Woman's World*. The pay and the perks were good, but Cotter soon succumbed to the lure of daily journalism again, signing on as a Reuter correspondent. Following a variety of assignments, from domestic politics to revolution in Haiti, Cotter was only a few months away from going to South Africa as the chief Reuter correspondent there when he got a call from Don Forst.

At first, Cotter didn't think much would come of it, but two things helped to change his mind. One was a set of harsh restrictions that the South African government imposed on the press, which made his new assignment less palatable. The other was Forst himself. "Forst is a great salesman," Cotter said. "He needed somebody that had done the city and could bounce with these guys and could walk right into a competitive situation and kick ass. . . . You can't walk away from something like that." Then Cotter met with Laventhol, who asked him for his impressions of *New York Newsday*. "It was real flat," Cotter said. "The reporting was excellent, but it wasn't as sharply angled as it should have been. . . . But the potential was obviously there."

Quickly, Cotter evolved what he called a "fuck-you" relationship with Forst: They could call each other names, yet spend hours together every day. "I'd go in there early, because if you work for Forst, you're in early," Cotter said. "Some mornings, Forst would call me at home at 6:30." For the rest of the day, Cotter would spend much of his time with Forst, thinking through potential stories for page one, or gliding through the newsroom and talking with reporters. "That's my style," he said. "I hate meetings." His style also included a motto: The best plan is no plan. None of that, of course, was in keeping with the heavily structured *Newsday* way.

There was no way of quantifying what Cotter did, but many of his young reporters developed an appreciation for it. "John's way of working was basically to nudge the paper, to go to people in his kind of laid-back way, sort of lean on the desk and say, 'What you got?' " Ellis Henican said. "He might say: 'What about this angle or what about that angle,' or 'Did you push it to the next step? We could get ahead of it like this.' It was totally unstructured. But in the end, I think, you had a situation where a whole lot of stories every day, particularly the main stories of the day, which is what he focused his attention on, were thought out and were sort of pushed, particularly in a competitive sense." Together, Cotter and Toedtman were Forst's closest advisors — Toedtman as the voice of caution and moderation, Cotter as the advocate of daring. "In the constellation of people he deals with at *Newsday*, basically everybody is telling Don no: 'You can't do that. That's too flashy. That's too cheap. That's too expensive. That's not the way we do it. That's not *Newsday*,' " Henican said. "Cotter was the one who was saying, 'Oh, of course you can do it. Do it twice.' "

On top of this unique mix of managers running the editorial staff, *Newsday* added yet another element to the odd structure of the New York paper: an associate publisher who was to work in New York as a surrogate for the publisher of *Newsday* itself. The new associate publisher was Steven Isenberg, a tall, bearishly friendly, bountifully garrulous man whose education and odd career path had amassed for him a bottomless vault of conversational currency that he handed out to everyone he met.

From the public schools of Los Angeles, Isenberg had done his undergraduate studies at the University of California at Berkeley. After toiling as a manuscript reader at McGraw-Hill in New York, he acquired a literature degree from Oxford and thought about working for a doctorate. Then he executed a sharp change in course, entering Lyndon Johnson's Great Society bureaucracy as an employee of Upward Bound. One of his colleagues in that program had contacts in the administration of New York City Mayor John V. Lindsay, and Isenberg moved to New York as an analyst in Lindsay's budget office. Later, Isenberg campaigned for Robert Kennedy in California in 1968 and stood about one hundred feet away when Sirhan Bishara Sirhan assassinated Kennedy. Over the next several years, Isenberg completed an education at Yale Law School while continuing to work for Lindsay — in the budget office, in the 1969 mayoral campaign, as a mayoral assistant overseeing the volatile Department of Sanitation, as chief of staff, and as a state coordinator in Lindsay's 1972 presidential campaign. Soon after he left city hall in 1974, he settled down to the practice of law, as a litigator for Breed, Abbott and Morgan. It was there that an executive recruiter found him and passed his name to Laventhol.

Even though Isenberg had no newspaper experience, Laventhol liked his intelligence and scope, and he hired him in 1982 as an assistant to the publisher. "He said, 'I'm going to give you the office next to mine, and we're going to teach you the business, and we'll see where it goes from there,' " Isenberg remembered. Only fifteen months later, Isenberg became the publisher of the Times Mirror papers in Stamford and Greenwich, Connecticut. Then, early in 1986, the events leading up to his return to *Newsday* began. Laventhol had been devoting more and more time to his other job, as a Times Mirror vice-president in charge of its eastern newspapers. Eventually, Laventhol had to lighten his responsibilities at *Newsday* to concentrate on the broader corporate agenda. So he glided out of the publisher's seat at *Newsday* and became its chairman, elevating Bob Johnson from president to publisher at the start of 1986. Laventhol had persuaded Johnson to come to *Newsday* in the first place, and now he was making him the sixth publisher in *Newsday* history, just at the moment when the New York paper was beginning to take off.

A few months later, Laventhol took the next step in his ascent of the corporate ladder, when Times Mirror announced that he would become the corporation's president on January 1, 1987. It was a stunning breakthrough for Laventhol, an easterner from a Ukrainian Jewish family, to reach the presidency of Times Mirror, a heavily WASP enterprise, traditionally dominated by golden westerners. In fact, given Laventhol's unprepossessing style, his Yale classmate, the columnist Calvin Trillin, had said that if he wrote a biography of Laventhol, he would call it *Unlikely Mogul*. When Trillin learned of Laventhol's promotion, his reaction was: "There must be some mistake."

Soon after the announcement of Laventhol's ascent to the presidency of Times Mirror, he and Johnson brought Isenberg back from Stamford to act as the publisher of *New York Newsday*. Isenberg would have a certain level of autonomy, but he would take his orders from Johnson, just as Forst reported to Marro, who moved up from managing editor of *Newsday* in late 1986 to executive editor — obviously in preparation for the day when Insolia would retire as *the* editor and Marro would take his place. To any business school class, this flow chart would seem hopelessly convoluted. "We do have a complex governance here," Isenberg said. "But you know something? We manage it."

V

IN THE BYZANTINE relationship between the New York paper and Mother *Newsday* in Melville, there was general agreement on the strategy for dealing with the enemy outside the walls — primarily the *Daily News* — but there was also inevitable friction between Forst and editors on Long Island.

The strategy against the *News* was simple: take away their readers and erode their advertising in Queens and Brooklyn. As Johnson and Isenberg saw it, even though the *News* had significant circulation in the suburbs around New York City, advertisers still had to buy space in the strong suburban papers, including *Newsday* on Long Island. "So what's the *Daily News'* claim to fame in New York City?" Isenberg said. "Well, take out Manhattan, because the *Times* and the *Post* would give you those. Now you're really talking about the Bronx, Brooklyn and Queens. If this other huge paper comes in and takes Queens, and takes a big bite out of Brooklyn, the *Daily News* is no longer the umbrella buy here." In other words, once *Newsday* developed a strong enough presence in

Brooklyn and Queens, advertisers would be able to cover Brooklyn, Queens and the lucrative Long Island market with *Newsday* alone, which would weaken the appeal of the *Daily News*.

Just before Isenberg's arrival in New York, *Newsday* had taken a major step toward perfecting this strategy: "unbundling" the newspaper, or separating the advertising in New York more distinctly from the advertising on Long Island. From the time that *Newsday* had started its Queens edition, advertisers who bought space in the Long Island paper had been getting the extra circulation in Queens without an extra charge. The circulation was so small that for years *Newsday* could not risk "unbundling" the paper and asking advertisers to pay more for Queens. "If we started charging too early, nobody would pay for it," said John Tewksbury, who took over advertising for the New York paper and studied the issue extensively. As a result, even though the editorial content of *New York Newsday* was growing more distinct from that of the Long Island paper, the advertising in the two editions still looked much too similar. But the New York circulation moved past 60,000 in the middle of 1985, and in the spring of 1986, it hit 100,000. So, in early 1986, *Newsday* decided to make the necessary changes in the production process to unbundle the paper.

"We went around and told advertisers, 'By the way, we're giving you 60,000 circulation, at no charge at all,' " David Targe said. Actually, they had really been paying more for the Queens circulation all along, because Targe had been raising the paper's overall advertising rates twice a year as the growth of the New York paper swelled *Newsday*'s total circulation. "But we went out and built up the idea in their mind, 'You've been getting this for nothing.' At the next rate increase, we then said, 'As we told you, we can't continue to give you this for nothing. We're going to have to charge you something for it — not a hell of a lot of money. We're going to charge you a hundred dollars a page. . . .' Now, the hundred dollars was a hundred dollars on top of what the hell they were paying, so now they're paying twice for it. . . . What the hell do they know?" When Targe went to Los Angeles and explained this to the conservative officials of Times Mirror, they were amazed. "You'd have twenty guys shaking their heads," Targe remembered, "saying, 'How the hell do you sleep nights?' "

With the unbundling, the larger advertisers, such as Macy's, simply paid the extra charge for the New York circulation. In the years that followed, the added cost for that circulation kept escalating, so that an advertiser such as Macy's ended up paying almost $500,000 a year for it. The smaller advertisers, who didn't need that circulation anyway, dropped out of the New York paper. This winnowing process began to make the New York paper smaller than the Long Island paper. That diminished the revenue growth, but the reduced bulk of the paper also helped to cut down slightly on the costs of distribution.

In order to make the New York paper more attractive to both readers and advertisers at the time that they unbundled the paper, *Newsday* had already gone to considerable time and expense to enhance one of its biggest competitive advantages: the ability to run full-color photographs on the front page and full-color advertising inside. In late 1984, looking for ways to expand that color capacity and plan the growth of the pressroom to keep pace with the New York circulation, Johnson had recruited a well-trained printing professional, James Norris, from the *Detroit News*. Norris learned that when the paper moved to Melville in 1979, its five Goss presses had the capacity to print color, but not much. "They could not run process color without giving up page capacity," Norris said. "The color decks were located in the wrong position to run color on page one." In the early 1980s, *Newsday* did occasionally gear up to run full-color photographs on page one, but only for special events, such as the inauguration of Ronald Reagan or the arrival of Sandra Day O'Connor as the first woman on the Supreme Court. But by the time Norris arrived at the start of 1985, even though *Newsday* had expanded to six Goss presses, the circulation growth was already straining their ability to turn out enough papers, and they still didn't have enough color capacity. So Norris had to find a way of meeting both needs. The answer came from an aggressively innovative Japanese company called TKS, which found a way to "straddle" additional color units over the six existing presses, to add color capacity. TKS got that done in time to provide extra color for the unbundling in early 1986.

The regular use of color on page one was an important factor in helping *New York Newsday* to gain ground on its black-and-white competitors. "It was an easy way to distinguish a newspaper in a market with very fixed reading habits," said Gary Hoenig, who supervised the paper's graphics during the expansion of the color capacity. "In many markets, color is just something one paper does and then the other one has to do. In this particular market, it gave us a real marketing advantage." In time, *Newsday*'s possession of this marketing advantage forced even the good gray *New York Times* to make plans for adding color capacity. And within *Newsday* itself, the regular use of front-page color created a whole new genre of conversation at meetings of editors: Should the headline on a story about football, for example, be pink? For anyone familiar with Alan Hathway's loathing for meetings, it is amusing to imagine his reaction to two journalists discussing the merits of puce over beige.

At the same time *Newsday* was adding regular color, Forst was fighting a series of internal battles with editors in Melville over his desire to give the paper more of a New York feel. One of those struggles centered on Part II, the paper's daily magazine. Over the years, Part II had won several awards, but Forst found it too slow-paced for the city audience. It usually began with a small news feature on page three and a two-page news feature on pages four and five, with the entertainment stories farther back. Forst wanted a livelier pace and more emphasis on entertainment. As he pushed for a glitzier Part II, he inevitably clashed with Phyllis Singer, the assistant managing editor in charge. "Don was frustrated by not being able to control everything — Part II, the national desk, everything," Singer said. "He always worked in settings where it was him and three other editors running the whole show, and that's just not the way it is at *Newsday*." At one point, Forst became so enraged during a telephone argument with Singer, over the editing of a story, that he picked up his computer terminal and threw it on the floor.

The pressure from Forst was one of the major factors in a series of changes in both staff and emphasis on Part II. One change was the increased focus on entertainment news. "The entertainment sections of *Newsday* had never been news sections," Singer said. "They had been review and preview sections." In one early attempt to beef up that news coverage, *Newsday* hired the reporter Kevin Goldman from *Variety* to cover the television industry. "I think he really changed the face of television news reporting in New York," Singer said. "I mean, we were beating the *Times* every day." Less than three years later, Goldman justified *Newsday*'s confidence by obtaining a copy of a memo from Bryant Gumbel, the host of the *Today* show, which criticized some of his colleagues. That story led the paper in *New York Newsday* and dominated the news for days.

Other changes were far less popular, such as the reassignment of the Part II editor, Roy Hanson, a soft-spoken, competent editor who had led the section to several of its awards. "Roy was wonderful, and one of the greatest people we'll ever know, but toward the end, things got a little bit gray," Singer said. "There was a certain lack of spark to the section. There was tremendous, tremendous pressure on me to produce a sparkling section." So, early in 1986, Singer arranged for Hanson to move from Part II to a job supervising the science staff on the national desk. "In this whole process of building New York," Singer said, "everybody's feelings have been hurt, at one time or another."

The paper's music and drama critics were among those who felt the pain. "There was a feeling that our critics, while all good, weren't quite as lively as we felt they ought to be," Singer said. One was Allan Wallach, who had been writing theater criticism for *Newsday* for two decades. First, *Newsday* killed Wallach's Sunday column. Then, in late 1986, they announced the hiring of Linda Winer, a critic-at-large for *USA Today*, to write an entertainment column. In 1988, Winer replaced Wallach as *Newsday*'s primary drama critic. Wallach and Winer were able to develop a good relationship, but that didn't erase the hurt that Wallach felt over being pushed aside.

The same kind of thing happened to the music critic, Peter Goodman, when *Newsday* hired Tim Page from the *New York Times*. Page had studied at the Tanglewood Music Festival and at the Mannes College of Music, and later became the classical music coordinator for a small Manhattan paper, the *Soho News*, and hosted his own classical music radio program on WNYC. In time, he became a prodigiously productive free-lance contributor to the *Times*, writing music reviews, obituaries of musicians, and news stories. Tom Wallace, who had been an editor at the *Times* and worked briefly as an entertainment editor at *Newsday*, knew Page and asked him to come to *Newsday* as a music critic. "One of the first things I said when I was asked was, 'How does Peter Goodman feel about this?' " Page remembered. Wallace told him that Goodman was unhappy, but that if Page turned the job down, *Newsday* would still hire someone else. "I respected Peter and I liked his work," Page said. "On the other hand, it was too damn good a deal. Once I was told that somebody was going to get it, why not me? Peter and I went to lunch and we hashed it out almost immediately." Once

Page came to *Newsday*, in the spring of 1987, he treated Goodman considerately, making sure that Goodman got a fair share of the plum assignments. But Page was the chief music critic, and Goodman wasn't. "I like Tim, and I'm glad he's working for *Newsday*," Goodman said. "But I wanted that job, and I felt that I had earned it."

These and other changes stirred resentment among reporters who had worked for Part II all along. "There was a real feeling in Part II when the New York paper started that the opportunity to work in New York was going to be their reward for years of good service," Sheryl Barnett said. "Most of them, including me, were extremely angry when it didn't happen." But the end result was a faster-paced Part II, with entertainment stories toward the front of the section and fewer long news features, usually starting farther back in the section. In New York and on Long Island, Part II does fewer stories that don't relate directly to the circulation area. And when Part II does do non-local stories, the editors in Melville have tried to compensate for the hurt feelings of Long Island-based Part II reporters by giving the vast majority of the travel assignments to them — not to New York reporters.

On balance, despite the internal turbulence, Forst's efforts to improve the paper for New York also provided benefits for Long Island readers. Sports was one major example. "Every time they upped the ante in New York, sports came out with more space, more hires," said Richard Sandler, who had become the sports editor in 1973, before the New York paper, and remained in that job throughout the early years of its growth. In the spring of 1986, for example, at the same time that *Newsday* began running color every day on the front and back pages, Sandler added a "Baseball Special" section to the sports pages — a heavy dose of additional statistics and other coverage — and appointed a full-time baseball editor, Bob Herzog. Its primary purpose was to make the New York paper more competitive, but Long Island baseball fans derived the same benefits. By the end of the 1980s, *Newsday* had such comprehensive coverage of sports in both New York City and Long Island and such a highly regarded staff — including the regular columnists Joe Gergen, Stan Isaacs and Steve Jacobson — that the Associated Press Sports Editors designated *Newsday* as the only paper in the New York area that ranks among the top ten in the nation in all three major categories: daily, Sunday and special sections.

Similarly, the New York paper caused a bountiful flow of money to the business pages, which had been a traditional subject of concern at *Newsday*. In the early 1980s, the business staff had expanded, to meet the needs of the new real estate section on Saturdays and the stand-alone Monday business section that *Newsday* established as part of its development of daily Part III sections on such subjects as fashion, homes, food and science. But the greatest breakthrough came after Forst's arrival. In 1986, the assistant managing editor who supervised both the business pages and the paper's graphics, Gary Hoenig, sat down with his staff and developed a five-year plan for expanding the business staff further. "Two weeks later, Tony Marro comes in to me and says, 'Laventhol's thinking about accelerating hiring in business next year. Give me your wish list,' " Hoenig remembered. "I had a wish list, and I had sixteen jobs on this wish list — sixteen jobs. They gave me every single one of them." Hiring sixteen people at once was difficult, but the existence of the New York paper made it far easier to attract high-quality business reporters than it would have been a few years earlier at *Newsday*.

Besides increasing the business staff to about fifty, *Newsday* took another major step in improving business coverage: the introduction of daily stock tables. *Newsday* had not provided the tables in the past, because most readers got the paper late in the afternoon, more than twenty-four hours after the previous day's stock market closing. But with a newspaper in New York and the expansion of deliveries earlier in the day, stock tables made sense. So *Newsday* began running the tables.

Along the way, Forst bruised more than his share of egos in his first months at *New York Newsday*, but he also had his successes, such as the subway column. Duggan had gotten the column started, but he was happy a few months later when he was able to return to his regular column. In the middle of 1986, the reporter who replaced him was Jim Dwyer. "I thought about it for two seconds and said that sounded pretty good, because I sure wasn't going to get a column any other way," said Dwyer, who thought it was a great beat. "This is sort of the grazing rights to the great public common of New York."

Dwyer's first column was about a group of subway buffs who rented old cars from the Transit Authority and rode around in them all day, making movies of the event. "Forst called me in after I wrote it and he said it was fine, but this isn't about crazy people," Dwyer said. "He wanted to keep me on the path that he envisioned for this thing, which was that it's not a lunatic asylum you're writing about. It's about what normal people experience down there — the lunacy *they* experience." Forst offered further course-corrections, mostly in the direction of reminding Dwyer to keep riding the subways for his stories. Eventually, Dwyer developed a feel for the beat that enabled him to negotiate the dizzying tightrope walk of writing a column. "Now I don't feel like this is an impossible job," Dwyer said in 1988. The column reminded him of his father's town in Ireland, where there was no running water in the houses, but a spring at the bottom of a cliff provided abundant water, if people were willing to carry it in buckets. "I feel the same way about the subways," Dwyer said. "The well is deep. You only have to have the strength to draw from it."

Not long after Dwyer took over the subway column, one of Forst's hand-picked reporters brought *New York Newsday* a sudden flash of visibility, beating the other New York City papers soundly on a major story. It began in late September, with the revelation that Charles J. Hynes, the state's special prosecutor in New York City, was investigating police officers for shaking down narcotics dealers for money and drugs. The first package of stories contained a list of thirteen officers at the 77th Precinct in Brooklyn who had been suspended. Then the police Internal Affairs Division ordered the thirteen officers to surrender for arrest and arraignment on November 6. The evening before that surrender, one of the cops called Mike McAlary, who had been working on the story, and asked to meet with him. That night, McAlary spent four hours with Officer Brian O'Regan at a diner in Rockaway Park, listening to his story. The next morning, O'Regan failed to surrender as scheduled. The following day, *New York Newsday* carried McAlary's story of the interview with O'Regan, with a page-one headline: "Confession of a Scared Cop."

While New Yorkers were reading that story on Friday morning, police were searching for O'Regan. On Friday afternoon, they found him, when the owner of a small motel on Long Island's East End looked into one of her rooms after the occupant had failed to check out. On the bed inside, she saw Brian O'Regan, with one bullet hole in his head. He had killed himself. The next morning, *New York Newsday* carried a first-person account by McAlary of his meeting with O'Regan and the events that followed, starting with a page-one byline — a rarity in *Newsday*. McAlary described how he had begun to fear for O'Regan's life as soon as he heard that O'Regan had failed to surrender. Then, McAlary had called police to tell them about his meeting with O'Regan and to suggest where they might look for him. On the night table in that motel room, McAlary said, there was a copy of *New York Newsday*, with his story about O'Regan's confession to him. "It didn't seem fair," McAlary wrote. "I felt furious and sad, puzzled and sick." Out of that sadness, though, McAlary emerged with a book contract and a glowing reputation as a reporter. And *New York Newsday*, which had looked so impotent a few months earlier on the Manes scandal, suddenly looked as if it could compete with the established papers on a major breaking story.

VI

THE EARLY MONTHS of 1987 were a heady time for *Newsday*.

In 1986, the first full year of Bob Johnson as publisher of *Newsday* and Don Forst as editor of *New York Newsday*, the city paper had passed the 100,000 circulation mark and made significant progress in elevating both its visibility and its performance. Despite the deficit of $10 million to $15 million on the New York paper, the overall profitability of *Newsday* had been strong — more than $90 million before taxes. All that impressed *Adweek* so much that the magazine named Johnson "newspaper executive of the year" and put a smiling photograph of Johnson on the cover of the issue of April 28, 1987. At about the same time, Johnson and *Newsday* were getting ready for a major circulation and editorial push from Queens westward into Brooklyn, another strike at the heartland of the *Daily News*. It was a time of high optimism, when *New York Newsday*'s advertising boasted that it was "on top of the news and ahead of the times."

In the middle of this era of optimism, Johnson was working quietly on a coup that would rock the *Daily News*. For months, both Forst and Laventhol had wanted to lure Jimmy Breslin away from the *News*. In time, as Forst and Breslin talked on the phone, Forst got a sense that Breslin was growing disillusioned with the *News* and was ripe for the right pitch. "I don't think he felt that he had anybody there who he could really relate to as an editor," Johnson said. "They all found him to be a pain in the ass, which he can be." At *Newsday*, of course, Breslin would be working with Forst, who spoke his language and was willing to listen to Breslin's complaints about the way the paper was covering the city. "I really think it's that relationship between Don and Jimmy that's the key to the whole thing," Johnson said. At the *News*, Breslin had a long-term contract, expiring in late 1988, but it didn't have options and other clauses that protected the *News* from Breslin's sudden departure. That gave *Newsday* a chance to pry Breslin away, and Johnson decided to handle the negotiations himself.

"Breslin came in and said, 'I want to be made a millionaire, and I want a whole bunch of shares of stock,' " Johnson remembered. Johnson offered him a long-term deal, with much of the compensation deferred until the end of the contract and beyond. That would provide Breslin something like a pension, in exchange for his agreement not to compete with *Newsday* once the contract expired. Though Breslin's *News* contract would not expire until October 10, 1988, nearly eighteen months after he signed the agreement with *Newsday* on April 29, 1987, Johnson knew that *Newsday* couldn't keep it a secret. So he announced it to the staff on May 4. The hiring of Breslin and the anticipation of his arrival provided a momentary rush of excitement for *New York Newsday*, followed by its highly competitive coverage of a racial incident in the Howard Beach section of Queens in which a black man fell under the wheels of a car while fleeing an angry white mob. But before the year was out, *New York Newsday* went from euphoria to dissension and sorrow, almost overnight.

It began with complaints by women that the newsroom in New York had taken on the air of a men's locker room — too many crude and offensive epithets flung at women, too many sexual jokes and anti-gay putdowns. In the early fall of 1987, three women met at the Lion's Head restaurant in Greenwich Village to discuss the problem: Amanda Harris, the editor of the weekly City Business section, Laura Durkin, an editor on the metropolitan desk, and Marianne Arneberg, a New York reporter. Soon after that, a group of more than twenty women met at Arneberg's Manhattan apartment on a Sunday afternoon. Rita Ciolli, a talented reporter who was also an attorney, briefed them on the background of the women's suit, which had been settled only five years earlier, and they discussed current issues: assignments, promotions and the atmosphere in the New York newsroom.

Not long after that brunch, the metropolitan editor John Cotter had a few drinks one evening with Mike McAlary and Arneberg in a bar downstairs from the *New York Newsday* offices. For several hours, they talked shop, including a discussion of the women's complaints. One of the subjects that raised the temperature of the conversation was money. "People were very upset about the merit raises," Arneberg said. The women felt that men had received higher merit raises than women, and McAlary had received one of the biggest. "Mike thought that this whole thing was a frontal assault on him," Arneberg said. "Cotter was going on about how I am ruining everything that *New York News-day* stands for and that Long Island was going to come in and take over the paper. 'Is that what you want?' " At one point, Arneberg — a tough-as-nails reporter — was in tears.

Finally, the conversation took a fateful turn. "John was going on and on about how he runs the paper," Arneberg said. "I said, 'You don't run this paper. Hap runs this paper.' " In fact, Hap Hairston was the editor who put the budget together every day, and his contribution was certainly more quantifiable than Cotter's unstructured methods. But Cotter couldn't let her comment pass without a response. "I told her a story, and I used the word, 'nigger,' " Cotter said. "It was thirty seconds in a three-hour conversation. It was a funny story, and I would have told it in front of Hap. I didn't think anything of it." The story he said he told was this: Earlier that day, a group of editors in New York — including Cotter, Forst and others — had been talking about a forthcoming meeting, at which the women were to discuss their complaints with Marro. "Hap came in and said, 'I've been warning you guys for a year about this,' " Cotter remembered. "He kept going on, like saying, 'I was innocent. I didn't do anything. I warned you guys.' It was such bullshit." The other editors in the group laughed, because they felt that Hairston was as foulmouthed as any of them. When Hairston left the room, one of the editors uttered a line that Cotter couldn't fully remember, except that it ended in: " 'Then that's one dumb nigger.' But it was not malicious. Was it a bad line? Yeah, looking back." That was not quite how Arneberg remembered it. Cotter simply said the offensive words on his own, she said, without quoting someone else's joke.

The following Tuesday afternoon, Marro came into the New York office and met with the women. This was one of the first tests of Marro's conciliatory skills since he had replaced Insolia as the editor of *Newsday* in June. Rising to editor in 1978 when Laventhol became publisher, Insolia had faced the difficult task of providing the administrative skills to convert Laventhol's vision for *Newsday* into concrete reality. His nearly nine years as editor spanned a complicated era that included three Pulitzer Prizes but presented tricky managerial problems, ranging from running the newsroom during *Newsday*'s failed cable venture to coping with the explosive growth of the New York paper. For most of those years, it was Laventhol who set the agenda and persuaded Times Mirror to authorize the spending, but it was Insolia who executed Laventhol's ideas. That entailed, for example, managing the significant expansion of the paper's foreign and domestic bureaus and creating a separate foreign desk. It also involved trying again and again to put in place the right management structure for the New York paper. Through all that, Insolia's brutal bluntness sometimes bruised those who ran afoul of it, but he still managed to convey an impression of essential fairness and competence to his top subordinates. Once he had chosen Marro as his ultimate successor, Insolia grew so enmeshed in the administrative details and so distant from the journalism that the job lost its attraction for him. Then he found a retirement spot in South Carolina and began gradually ceding control of the paper to Marro and moving toward early retirement. By the time he left, he had brought *Newsday* much closer to becoming the complete newspaper that Laventhol wanted, and he had installed the editors who would run the paper into the 1990s: Marro at the top, with Forst and Toedtman working under him in New York and Howard Schneider and Robert Brandt on Long Island.

Now, as the editor, Marro had the ultimate responsibility for such knotty problems as the women's concerns. At the meeting, he listened to the grievances and gave the women reason to believe that he was taking them seriously. "He was really the voice of reason," Arneberg said. "It was a really positive meeting." Toward the end, Arneberg talked about the need to curb anti-gay jokes and other gutter humor. "I said, 'I'm not going to go in every cubicle, and I'm not going to be part of the language police,'" Cotter said. "I think that pissed Tony off."

In the hours after the meeting, as Marro returned to the Melville office, two black reporters who had heard about Cotter's remark to Arneberg at the bar, Ron Howell and Larry Bivins, went to Cotter's office. "I wanted to make the point that I wanted it to stop," said Howell, who said that Cotter had used the word "nigger" even before the conversation with Arneberg. "He kept saying, 'Let's go in to Don,'" Howell said. "I kept saying, 'I just want to get it off my chest.'" Finally, Cotter went in to Forst and told him about the allegations. "He got Marro and Johnson on a speakerphone," Cotter said. "I sat in my office for, I guess, ninety minutes." During that time, while Forst gathered more information about the incident, Marro and Johnson in Melville considered their options. "If that allegation were to see the light of day and *Newsday* did not do anything, I thought it would be an indefensible position," Johnson said. "I don't think that there were any true racial overtones in what was said. But that's not the kind of thing that I think you can explain to today's world." So that same evening, they accepted Cotter's resignation. "My career was ended," Cotter said. "My career was over — twenty-two years, wiped away, and I knew that instantly."

The resignation of Cotter, fully reported in the city's other papers, caused a profound reaction at *Newsday*. Many of the women were miffed, because it had taken only one racist remark to oust Cotter, and they felt that he had made a long string of insensitive comments about women, without any consequences. In contrast, some reporters who liked and respected Cotter were outraged, directing their anger at Arneberg. More substantively, they were angry at the perceived lack of due process for Cotter, and they saw the whole thing as the powers in the Long Island office somehow striking at Forst and the New York paper through Cotter. For the editors in Melville, Cotter was simply too much of a Murdoch-style tabloid journalist and not enough of a *Newsday* type, his friends felt. "The reality was that there were people gunning for Cotter on Long Island, who didn't like his way of working, didn't like his personal demeanor, didn't like his view of what the paper ought to be, and wanted to get rid of him for a long time," one New York reporter said. *Newsday* continued to keep Cotter on the payroll for a year, but the paper went without a metropolitan editor until the start of 1989, while Forst, Marro and Johnson considered a variety of candidates from outside the paper. Finally, Marro proposed Richard Galant, a veteran editor from the Long Island paper, and Forst eagerly accepted. Soon after that, Cotter signed on as metropolitan editor of the *New York Post*. The scars from Cotter's resignation healed, but for a time, it acted as a wedge between the New York staff and the rest of *Newsday*. One of Cotter's admirers, McAlary, said: "That whole thing killed a year off the paper."

VII

IF NOTHING ELSE, the Cotter incident demonstrated how painful it can be for a newspaper to stand naked in the scrutiny of its competitors in New York's tabloid wars.

In this intense atmosphere, where big stories explode constantly and opposing papers carry slurpy little items of gossip about each other, the internal strains of any newsroom can grow even more vexing. For *New York Newsday*, an evolving paper with a complex relationship between the staff in New York and the main office in Melville, those strains can be immense. A case in point was the story of a black teenager named Tawana Brawley, who disappeared from her upstate home in late 1987 and told police that a group of men had abducted her, raped her, smeared her with feces and scrawled racial slurs on her body. The attackers, she said, included a law enforcement officer. As investigators began to doubt her story, Brawley insisted that it was true, and an ad hoc group of advisors protested that the criminal justice system was failing her.

At *Newsday*, the story ignited a tug-of-war between the editors of *New York Newsday*, which wanted the best possible coverage of the hottest story in town, and the national desk, which was supervising the Brawley coverage from Long Island. One element of that disagreement was the continuing hostility between two black editors, the assistant managing editor Les Payne and the New York assigning editor Hap Hairston. Before the Brawley story broke, Hairston had declined to hire a black reporter, Michael Cottman, for the New York paper, and Payne had objected. "Les Payne calls me up and says, 'You racist dog. You Uncle Tom,'" Hairston remembered. Payne said that others at *Newsday* shared his concerns about Hairston's treatment of black reporters and trainees, and Payne felt that Hairston had not done nearly enough to hire black journalists. "He's been considered an enemy of the best interests of black people at this paper," Payne said. *Newsday* did hire Cottman, to work as a minority affairs specialist in Melville, and when the Brawley story broke, Cottman was one of the reporters that the national desk sent upstate to cover it. Not surprisingly, since Hairston had not hired Cottman, he was critical of Cottman's work and the overall coverage that the national desk provided, under Payne's supervision. "Greater *Newsday* decided not to make it a sensational story, and consequently got their asses kicked," Hairston said. "Brawley was universally embarrassing."

As the story unfolded, *Newsday* sent the veteran investigative reporter Joe Demma to serve as a team leader. The New York paper contributed Elaine Rivera and Rita Giordano, two young reporters who made up for their lack of experience with hard work. "There are a lot of people who feel we didn't do well, like Steve Isenberg and Don Forst," Demma said. "Les Payne and Tony Marro will tell you that, for what we did, we did extremely well. We went out and documented with eyewitnesses what happened. We went out and documented with eyewitnesses what didn't happen. . . . What we did not have was the leaks of interim reports and documents that the *Times* had."

In the end, the disagreement between Payne and Hairston over the story resolved itself ironically: In 1989, Hairston left *Newsday* for the *Daily News* and Payne wrote a front-page *Newsday* story in which Brawley's boyfriend admitted that Brawley had told him she invented the abduction story to prevent her mother's live-in lover from beating her. The headline was: "Tawana Made It Up." Some people in the black community reacted angrily to the story, calling Payne a "traitor" and a "disgrace," though he had established a reputation in his weekly column as an articulate voice against the oppression of African Americans. Eventually, he blunted the criticism, he said, by "pointing out that the old ladies who contributed their rent money to Brawley had a need to know that her story was a bogus."

As *Newsday* was struggling to stay even with the other papers on the Brawley story in early 1988, the tab wars raged on several fronts.

Publicly, a new society column by the *New York Newsday* reporter James Revson fired a withering blast at the queen of society columnists, the *Post*'s Suzy. "I want Suzy's job," Revson began. "It's fun. It's simple. It's such a breeze. She doesn't even have to leave the house." Revson explained that he had read Suzy's column, which contained a list of society figures who had attended the opening of an exhibition at the Metropolitan Museum of Art. Revson had been at the opening, and several of the people that Suzy mentioned hadn't been there. With a little bit of reporting, he found out that she had written the item *before* the party, from a press release, and hadn't attended. Suzy responded with a blast at Revson, calling him a "rat" and a "jerk," among other epithets, and threatening to boycott any party that included Revson on its guest list. This tabloid feud raged for days, on the pages of *Newsweek*, the *Wall Street Journal*, and elsewhere — a meaningless but exhilarating tiff that lifted morale at *New York Newsday*, by showing that it could set the agenda in New York. (Suzy had the last laugh: Only two years after Revson's Suzy-bashing debut, *Newsday* discontinued his column.)

Privately, the war between *Newsday* and the *Post* was even more serious. The real estate developer Peter Kalikow had bought the paper from Murdoch, and promptly asked Forst to be the editor of the *Post*. Forst turned him down, but that didn't end the *Post*'s attempt to raid *Newsday*. The *Post*'s new publisher, Peter Price, knew that the paper needed to improve its woeful image with advertisers. So he telephoned David Targe and asked for recommendations. That soon evolved into an effort to woo Targe away from *Newsday*. Price's call caught Targe at a vulnerable time. After a long period of dominance, he was facing a new set of realities that he found unpleasant. From the moment Laventhol had brought Bob Johnson in as president, Johnson was aware that Targe's revenue-raising success had made him difficult for any publisher to control. "Basically Dave Laventhol had said to me, 'If you can handle this guy, you can handle the operation,' " Johnson said. Laventhol wanted Johnson to be the paper's chief marketing officer and to develop a close relationship with major advertisers, which was bound to bring conflict with Targe.

The initial skirmishes between Targe and Johnson escalated after Johnson succeeded Laventhol as publisher in 1986. For one thing, Johnson disliked Targe's twice-a-year rate increases. Even more than the actual cost of the increases, advertisers hated the uncertainty they created, which disrupted their ability to plan budgets. Johnson also was anxious to shore up advertising linage in the newspaper itself, which had been slipping as advertisers increased their use of preprinted brochures that *Newsday* delivered for them. Targe had helped to create that trend by raising the rates for preprints more slowly than the rates for ads in the newspaper. To reverse the trend, Johnson wanted to offer advertisers incentives for running the same number of pages in the daily paper as they had the year before — either a given percentage discount once the advertiser reached the required number of pages, or additional pages of ads free. Targe considered that plan to be contrary to the *Newsday* tradition, and he hated it.

The final blow for Targe was Johnson's decision to bring in a neighbor and sailing buddy, Douglas Fox, as a vice-president for marketing. Johnson and Fox had become friendly because they were both young men in highly responsible jobs, who moved to Long Island from Ohio at virtually the same time — Johnson to work at *Newsday* and Fox to develop a marketing department at Tambrands, which sold feminine hygiene products. As they sailed together, they discussed business philosophies, and Johnson decided that Fox had views compatible with his. Fox was a successful, intelligent, trained marketing executive — in the modern business-school style. But his only experience with selling newspapers had been as a carrier for a small weekly in Lyndhurst, the Cleveland suburb where he grew up, and filling in occasionally for his brother on a daily newspaper route. His entire career, first with Procter & Gamble, then with Tambrands, had involved the sale of packaged goods. Nonetheless, it was clear to everyone that he would be Targe's replacement.

"At this point, I had every plan to work until sixty-five," Targe said. "I felt that, with a year and a half to go, two years, we should bring somebody in. I was disappointed that I didn't have the opportunity to help select my successor. . . . Doug has his own specific idea of how to do marketing. His philosophy and my philosophy are totally different." Like Johnson, Fox wanted to cooperate with advertisers, not to bully them. "I don't believe that in the long run, having customers hate you and hate your practices is a particularly wise strategy," said Fox, who found a universal hostility toward *Newsday* among the advertisers. "We've been arrogant, we've been condescending and we've jammed the price increases to them at a rate that's multiples of inflation." Given their differing views, the arrival of Fox was not a happy time for Targe. Two months after Fox came to *Newsday*, Targe got his first phone call from Price at the *New York Post*, who had met Targe years earlier. "I liked his style a lot," Price said, "because he was very straightforward, no bullshit, what-you-see-is-what-you-get."

In a series of meetings with Price and Kalikow, Targe kept expressing his hesitance to leave *Newsday*, and they kept increasing the offer: a huge salary and bonuses, plus a company car and an apartment in Manhattan. Some at *Newsday* thought Targe's knowledge of the market would enable him to lure important advertisers to the *Post* immediately. Fox thought that, if Targe left behind the clout of *Newsday* and went to the financially weakened *Post*, advertisers would do nothing to help someone who had bullied them for years. Targe, of course, disagreed: "There wasn't any doubt in my mind I could turn it around." Finally, Laventhol asked Targe to fly to Los Angeles and discuss it with him. "He said, 'We've talked about it, we're very concerned if you leave, and we'd like very much for you to stay,' " Targe remembered. "I said, 'Well, based on that, if you think it would really hurt the company and hurt people, I'll turn down the offer.' And that was it." Following a discussion of consulting services that Targe could perform for Times Mirror after retirement, Targe turned right around and got on a late-afternoon plane for New York. The next day, he wrote a letter to Kalikow, turning down the offer.

Less than a year later, *Newsday* paid for a grandiose retirement party for Targe at a country club, with a sit-down dinner for hundreds of employees, advertisers and guests. There were a series of giant television screens, all showing a comic videotape about Targe's career, called "Targe Mahal." There was Bob Johnson, the buttoned-down publisher, wearing a fireman's helmet and raincoat — an allusion to a fire that had gutted Targe's house. There was an array of gifts. There was a marching band. There was Laventhol, reciting *Newsday*'s revenue growth in the Targe years — from $5 million in 1948 to $400 million in 1987 — and recounting the question an advertiser had asked him about Targe's retirement: " 'You think we'll only get one rate increase a year now?' " The answer was yes: Johnson had cancelled the second rate increase in 1988, despite Targe.

At the end of the evening, as Targe's staff straggled out of the room, there were mixed emotions: relief that this often difficult man was leaving, plus fear of what *Newsday* would do without his fierce competitive fires, at a turbulent period in its history. Targe was the last major link to the infant *Newsday* of the 1940s, the last highly visible remnant of the advertising department that had helped killed off three competing daily newspapers on Long Island and turned *Newsday* into a monopoly. Now, Targe was leaving at just the moment when

Newsday was facing sharp competition in the difficult New York market.

Even though the *Post* had failed to woo Targe away from *Newsday*, the *News* had more luck with Mike McAlary. By the time Johnson announced in the spring of 1987 that Breslin would join *Newsday* in the fall of 1988, McAlary had done so well as a reporter that Forst promised him he'd still be a columnist, even with Breslin on the paper. "He knew he had a column a year up the road," Forst said. But the *Daily News* was dangling in front of McAlary the chance to replace Breslin as the lead columnist. "The more I thought about it," McAlary said, "the more I realized it was a once-in-a-lifetime shot to get that piece of real estate, to be the lead columnist on the *Daily News*." So in April, 1988, before Breslin even joined the staff, McAlary told Forst that he was leaving for the *News*.

A few months after that painful jolt, Forst went through an even greater trauma. At a Brooklyn shopping center, Denis Hamill ran into a man who introduced himself as Frank Genova, a New York City correction officer, and gave Hamill details of life among famous inmates at the city jail on Rikers Island. Forst put the story on page one, with photographs of four inmates and quotes on each, under the headline, "Inside Rikers." When the story appeared, city officials denied that anyone named Frank Genova worked at Rikers, or anywhere else in the city system. *Newsday* had to carry a second story, admitting: "Hamill said he did not check with correction officials to verify the employment of the man." The hoax was a major embarrassment for both Forst and Hamill. "I was devastated," Hamill said. "I felt like I was raped." Despite the embarrassment that the incident caused *Newsday*, Forst stood by Hamill. "He wasn't happy, but he was supportive," Hamill said. "I offered my resignation, but he refused it." Still, Forst was nervous about Hamill's next column, and the metropolitan desk sent the reporter Rita Giordano out to fact-check the column — an unpleasant assignment for Giordano that became even worse when the *Post* found out about it and called her. The headline on the resulting *Post* story was: "Newsday watching problem writer."

The anger at *Newsday* focused as much on Forst for putting the column on page one as it did on Hamill for writing it. "The issue wasn't Frank Genova," one *New York Newsday* reporter said. "That becomes a surrogate for bigger battles. Denis ultimately is supported by those who support Don and despised by those who don't like Don." Right after the hoax, Forst wrote a memo to the staff, discussing the "lesson for all of us to learn." Someone posted it in the office on Long Island, and an angry staffer added a footnote in red pen: "What's this 'us' and 'we' and 'our' shit? *We* didn't screw up!"

The relationship of Forst and Hamill survived the Genova fiasco, but less than two years later, in the spring of 1990, Hamill created further turbulence, this time by engaging in a loud argument with a court officer during the tense trial of two white teenagers from Bensonhurst, who were accused in the racially motivated murder of a black youth named Yusuf Hawkins. In the aftermath of Hamill's confrontation with the court officer, Forst finally lost patience with his protege, took away his column and gave him a less prestigious assignment — all of which the *Daily News* reported in its Apple Sauce gossip column. Rather than accept the new assignment, Hamill finally decided, at the beginning of June, to leave *New York Newsday*.

A few weeks after the Genova incident in 1988, *Newsday* began preparing for the arrival of Breslin, by running a series of teaser ads in the paper. One showed only Breslin's eyes, without mentioning his name, and said: "These are the eyes, sharp and keen, that well remember all they've seen, that now see fit to see New York only in Newsday." Another in the series said: "This is the shadow in New York that's cast by the man who's taking a walk from the Daily News he left behind to write only in Newsday." Later, posters sprang up all over the city, carrying a message that was certain to sting the *Daily News*: "Breslin switched. How about you?"

Only days before Breslin's first *Newsday* column was to appear, McAlary wrote an exclusive front-page column for the *Daily News*, revealing that heavyweight champion Mike Tyson had tried to kill himself by driving his wife's car into a tree. The column seemed like a warning that McAlary wasn't intimidated by the prospect of competing with Breslin. Compounding the pain, the Press Clips column in the *Village Voice* later reviewed Breslin's first column unfavorably and called Breslin a "$400,000 gorilla," a reference to the estimated salary figure most popular at the time. "Unhappily for *Newsday*," the column said, "Breslin's expensively touted debut came hard on the heels of Mike McAlary's Tyson front-pager in the *News*."

Despite that criticism, it didn't take Breslin long to hit his stride. Watching the presidential debate between George Bush and Michael Dukakis, Breslin went right to the heart of the troubled Dukakis candidacy in his column: "The first thing they asked Michael Dukakis last night was how he would feel if somebody raped and murdered his wife. Dukakis said he wouldn't feel a thing. I hope that when the election results come in sometime next month, he also will register no pain." Forst was with Breslin, watching the debate and then watching Breslin write his conclusion: that the rape question was the undoing of Dukakis. "He spotted that in the first thirty seconds of the debate," Forst said. "Nobody woke up to it for four days. He saw it, spotted it, wrote it." A few weeks later, on the twenty-fifth anniversary of the assassination of John F. Kennedy, *Newsday* ran a reprint of the brilliant column that Breslin had written from the hospital in Dallas for the *New York Herald Tribune*. In the front of that day's paper, Breslin's current column ran. Forst looked at the two pieces of work, separated by a quarter of a century, and glowed with pride: "I sat back and I said, 'The son of a bitch hasn't lost a step.' He's still in his prime."

Breslin's work could be wildly uneven. Early in 1989, for example, he predicted flatly and, as it turned out, inaccurately: "Rudolph Giuliani is the next mayor of New York. He will win the election easily." Then, just a week later, he wrote a powerful interview with Willie Horton, a black convict who had been freed on furlough in Massachusetts and went on to commit other crimes, providing George Bush with a club to use on Michael Dukakis. "Although Willie Horton had more to do with George Bush winning the election than anyone,"

Breslin wrote, "he won't be at the inauguration today because of a case of murder." No matter how brilliantly he performed, however, Breslin could not shake McAlary at the *News*, who escalated the tabloid warfare in New York City by scooping *Newsday* on Long Island with a front-page story revealing the key suspect in the murder of Kelly Ann Tinyes, the biggest story on Long Island at that moment.

At *New York Newsday*, the McAlary scoop was a delicious turn of events, because many on the staff still liked McAlary as much as they disliked the Long Island paper that was generating the revenue that paid their salaries. Just as the Long Island staff grumbled about Forst's outrageous front pages, the New York staff griped that they were being stifled by the hopelessly suburban outlook of Mother *Newsday* in Melville. The city paper, they felt, was at least trying to be hip and daring. By contrast, they thought the Long Island paper was dull and stodgy. At a party in late 1988, after the New York paper reached a circulation of 200,000, Bob Johnson indirectly acknowledged that dichotomy when he told the New York staff that someday they'd overcome the "stigma of Long Island" that the competing papers were trying to hang on *Newsday*. That was a perfect illustration of the precarious tightrope act that Johnson faced in running such a schizophrenic operation. On Long Island, he had to placate readers who watched all the television ads for *New York Newsday* and concluded that the paper cared only about the city, and in New York, he had to reassure the staff that suburban concerns wouldn't stifle them.

Despite the vexing problems, by the time of that party in late 1988, the New York edition had grown from a tiny, bogus newspaper published in a remote corner of Queens, to a truly competitive paper, slugging it out with the established dailies. And, for all the controversy around Forst, *New York Newsday*'s most explosive growth had happened during his first two years as its editor. Forst's detractors in Melville wondered whether that growth would have happened in any case, without quite so much turmoil and without so many front pages of questionable taste. Still, the New York paper did achieve growing influence in the city under Forst in those two years and it did establish an identifiable voice for itself. "No matter what anyone says about Forst," said John Van Doorn, who started out as anything but a Forst admirer, "one has to say, but look at the product."

CHAPTER FORTY-FIVE

The New *Newsday*

I

A HALF CENTURY after its birth, *Newsday* is no better at forecasting its own future than it was in the beginning.

When *Newsday* built its Garden City plant at the end of the 1940s, Harry Guggenheim saw no reason even to plan for a second floor. Three decades later, *Newsday* had to build a new plant in Melville, which opened at 325,000 square feet — almost double the size of the Garden City plant. "The new plant is planned to comfortably accommodate production and personnel through the year 2000," one memo predicted. But the millennium came early: It took *Newsday* less than a decade to outgrow the plant.

One of the unexpected developments was a rapid expansion in the number of preprints that *Newsday* distributed, which generated a need for more storage space and more employees. In addition, the increase in morning newsstand sales and the growth of the New York paper created a need for more presses. The plant started with five presses, but by 1990, it had grown to ten. The development of multiple editions — in Brooklyn, Queens and Manhattan, plus regionalized editions on Long Island — also created a need for more truck bays and a better computerized system for directing the right bundles to the right truck. To accommodate those needs, *Newsday* expanded and gobbled up parking space on the south side of the building. The loss of that space and the growth of the staff forced *Newsday* to buy an additional seventeen acres for parking, which they could have bought originally, if they had seen the need when they originally moved. "We were leaving ten acres in Garden City," said James Fitzgerald, the senior vice-president for finance and administration. "We said: 'Thirty acres? My God, that's triple. Shouldn't that be enough?' "

In 1987, before the new plant was even eight years old, the growth of the staff forced *Newsday* to rent space in a nearby office complex and to begin a series of additions to the building. The constant movement of departments and the recurring appearance and disappearance of walls, for so many years a fact of life in Garden City, became the norm in Melville. By the end of the decade, the plant had nearly doubled in size, to about 600,000 square feet, and *Newsday* had bought another building a few hundred feet away, which added almost another 200,000 square feet — and named it for Alicia Patterson. In other words, between the beginning of 1979 and the end of 1989, *Newsday* quadrupled the space that it occupied. During that period, the capital improvements cost nearly $300 million, on top of the plant's original cost of $44 million. By 1993, the investment was expected to reach about $420 million, making *Newsday* a more heavily capitalized company than ever before.

Similarly, Times Mirror and *Newsday* had not foreseen the rapid growth of the staff in New York, which quickly rendered its offices at 780 Third Avenue obsolete. When the first staff moved into the building in 1984, it was unusually spacious, with an array of empty desks on the floor that *Newsday* occupied. Within five years, *Newsday* and Times Mirror occupied a total of six floors in the building, but the space was so inadequate that they had to make plans for a move to a new office on two larger floors at 2 Park Avenue, which eventually took place in March, 1990. If Times Mirror had been willing to sign a lease in 1984 for the amount of space that it occupied by 1989, the owners would have been willing to name the Third Avenue building for Times Mirror or *Newsday*. But no one anticipated that *Newsday*'s need for space would grow so quickly.

Even with the commitment to a long-term presence in the volatile New York City market, the paper's future growth is no easier to predict than it was in 1940. But its present is clear: It is vastly different, not only from the little country paper that Harry envisioned, but also from the paper that he sold to the Times Mirror Company in 1970. The haphazard, informal management style is a thing of the past, along with the hiring of reporters in bars, the boozy parties on the copy desk at the end of the week, the abhorrence of meetings. The new *Newsday* is an archetypically corporate newspaper, where every day is a procession of meetings: meetings on stories, meetings on graphics, meetings on the budget, meetings on prizes, meetings on the food in the cafeteria, meetings on the proper way to handle bylines. It is a newspaper that lives on planning, on memos, on formal evaluations of employees.

That emerging corporate culture starts at the top of the company, with the publisher, Bob Johnson, who began a fundamental redirection of the paper's management style when he first arrived in 1982, as president. Much like Bill Attwood in 1970, Johnson discovered that cooperation among departments was scarce. One of his solutions was a technique used with increasing frequency in other corporations: an employee opinion survey that sought the views of the workers on how the company was operating. "I basically wanted to show every department that they had problems, that nobody was simon-pure," Johnson said. "It gave me an objective data base from which I could begin to make moves, and it was going to be very difficult to argue that I was attacking the wrong issues." The survey showed generally high levels of job satisfaction, but it revealed dissatisfaction with some managers, and in a few cases, it was the final push that led to the removal of those managers. The survey also found that managers hadn't had enough training. So Johnson arranged a series of seminars to teach supervisors how to listen to employees better and lead them more effectively. The survey showed that employees didn't know what their bosses thought of them. So Johnson instituted a formal employee evaluation system.

By the time David Laventhol made him publisher at the start of 1986, Johnson had made a significant imprint on the way *Newsday* operated. As Laventhol prepared to turn over control, however, he felt it necessary to leave Johnson a memo explaining the role of the publisher. It concentrated especially on the newsroom, since Johnson was not a journalist by training. "Journalists are moralists," Laventhol began. "They're primarily in the business to make a better world, to improve society through revelations of its sins and glories. . . . Newsday is something special in this respect: its journalists have been able to flourish in an environment where they are able to 'practice the craft' better than almost anyone, freer of restraints from business, advertising and community pressures than at most newspapers." The memo went on to describe the publisher's role in setting editorial policy and the publisher-editor relationship. "I was infuriated when I first got it," Johnson said. "It's so typically David. He's not going to leave anything to chance. I was incensed, and I got about half through it and I thought it was terrific."

Even though Johnson had no real journalism background, in some ways his approach was easier on the newsroom than the hands-on style of Laventhol. "There were days, when Dave Laventhol was still here, when I'd come in and he was fiddling with the page, moving pictures around and columns around," Johnson said. "That's not my thing. Everybody gravitates to what they like to do and think they do best. I think one of the things that, frankly, I do best is represent *Newsday* to the outside world. There's a great demand for it. . . . I'm more active in the community than David was." In representing *Newsday*, Johnson accepted important roles in community organizations, as chairman of the Long Island Philharmonic and as a director of the Long Island Association (LIA), the primary advocate for Long Island's business community. But his roles in those institutions caused some members of the staff to worry about potential conflicts with his responsibility as publisher.

That broad philosophical question sometimes became a very practical one for Peter Goodman, in his coverage of the Long Island Philharmonic. In late 1987, for example, schedule conflicts made it difficult for him to review the philharmonic one weekend. When a public relations man for the orchestra learned that Goodman planned to ignore both of its concerts, he called Goodman's editor to complain. Then the public relations man called Johnson, who was his own ultimate boss at the orchestra, as well as Goodman's ultimate boss at *Newsday*. In the end, Goodman's editor told him to do the right thing, and he chose not to review the philharmonic. Though he felt that he had clearly displeased Johnson by ignoring the philharmonic, Goodman suffered no practical effects. But Johnson did make his views known. "I think it's ludicrous for this newspaper not to have a reviewer at every concert of the largest cultural institution that's serving Long Island," Johnson said later. The incident led to the hiring of more free-lance reviewers, to make sure that *Newsday* could cover more concerts, but it had no effect on reviews. "In no way at *Newsday* was I ever encouraged to give special favoritism to people," said Tim Page, the chief music critic. "My reviews of the Long Island Philharmonic have been mixed."

On another occasion, Goodman found out that the philharmonic had chosen a woman, Marin Alsop, as its new music director. Goodman called Johnson for his comment as the philharmonic's chairman. Though Johnson had played a role in the selection of Alsop, he was noncommittal. The story ran anyway, breaking the news earlier than the orchestra wanted. Later, at the press conference announcing Alsop's selection, Johnson joked about his schizophrenic response to Goodman's story: As chairman of the orchestra, he had been angry. As publisher of *Newsday*, he had been proud. "I know Peter's a little uncomfortable about it, but I also believe that the publisher of an institution like *Newsday* has to bear his or her share of community leadership responsibilities," Johnson said. "I think in many respects this is one of the least controversial institutions that I could become involved with. I think my involvement with the LIA could potentially be more difficult for some." In fact, it was in Johnson's dual roles as a business leader and publisher that he played a part in the resolution of a far more important issue than the selection of a conductor: the controversy over the Long Island Lighting Company's Shoreham nuclear plant.

From the time of Stuart Diamond's series in 1981, it had become popular for politicians to urge the Nuclear Regulatory Commission not to allow the plant to open. Within weeks after the series, Suffolk County backed away from its agreement to work with LILCO in developing an evacuation plan for the area. In 1983, county legislators concluded that there was no safe way to evacuate, and the newly elected Governor Mario Cuomo said that the state would not override the county. Since state and local governments refused to participate in the evacuation plan, the plant's opponents argued that LILCO should drop its efforts to open Shoreham.

Despite the opposition to the plant, *Newsday* continued to urge editorially that LILCO be allowed to open it. That stand became so unpopular that the editorial writer responsible for the issue, Elisabet Van Nostrand, began to get nasty calls at home. "I mean, people would call up and even tell my kids, 'Do you know that your mother's trying to kill us?'" she said. The favorable editorials did not placate the new LILCO chairman, William Catacosinos, who blasted *Newsday* for letting its reporters cover all the controversy, but they did have some effect. "It may have scared some people into not opposing Shoreham as early as they should have," said Richard Kessel, the longtime LILCO opponent, who became executive director of the state's Consumer Protection Board under Cuomo. "I certainly know of two or three major public officials who didn't want to oppose Shoreham because *Newsday* was in favor of the plant."

The editorials didn't frighten Cuomo, however. Regularly, he met with the *Newsday* editorial board over lunch and argued against the plant. Cuomo sometimes grumbled to others about the board and about Johnson, but *Newsday*'s stand didn't surprise him. "A lot of other responsible newspapers felt exactly the same way," Cuomo said. "I don't believe there was anything but a solid, sincere judgment. They were viewing it from a business point of view — Bob Johnson particularly. . . . He had the businessman's position, which is, 'You need this. There is no alternative to it.' I never believed that."

Eventually, LILCO's prospects grew bleaker and bleaker: Backup diesel generators developed cracks. The state's Public Service Commission ruled that LILCO had mismanaged construction, and the PSC ordered LILCO's stockholders to absorb $1.35 billion of the plant's cost, instead of charging ratepayers. Hurricane Gloria struck Long Island, and LILCO's slow restoration of power further angered its critics. Then, a few weeks after the Chernobyl nuclear disaster in the Soviet Union, the state Legislature created a new agency, the Long Island Power Authority, to study a public takeover of LILCO and the closing of Shoreham. As all this went on, the editorial page editor Sylvan Fox began to adopt a softer position: The plant had to open, *unless* someone could come up with a better alternative. Once Fox retired and the former Washington bureau chief, Jim Klurfeld, took over the editorial pages, that openness to an alternative continued. "I basically felt that the plant was never going to open," Klurfeld said. "I felt that we had become too shrill on the Shoreham issue. . . . My sense was that it was good for Long Island to get beyond the Shoreham issue. Enough was enough, already."

Faced with a possible government takeover, Catacosinos began negotiating with Cuomo's representative, Vincent Tese, for a settlement of the issues. That was when Johnson became involved. "I got a call from Vince Tese," Johnson said. "Vince said to me, 'Bob, we think we've got a settlement worked out.' " Tese asked Johnson to meet with him, Catacosinos and their investment bankers for a briefing. For three hours, Johnson listened as they outlined the deal to shut Shoreham and keep LILCO alive. "They said to me, 'Can you help us get the various political people together to listen to this and see if they'll support it?' " Johnson remembered. "My response was, 'I will be glad to call people that I have been talking to about this and tell them that it appears to me that you have reached a settlement and that I think it would be worth their while to sit down and listen to what you have to say. But I'm not going to do anything further. I'm not going to endorse it. I'm not going to reject it.' "

So Johnson called influential Republican legislators on Long Island to persuade them to let Catacosinos brief them on the settlement. When the story of that briefing appeared in *Newsday*, it included a mention of Johnson's involvement. In the newsroom, his role troubled many on the staff. A few days later, the *Daily News* jumped on the story with a small item in its Apple Sauce gossip column: " 'We all understand the concept of an activist publisher,' a Senate source told our Joel Benenson. 'But this was a little too activist.' " At the time, Cuomo complained to Johnson that the publisher had acted prematurely. But looking back at it, after LILCO had agreed to turn the plant over to the state for decommissioning and the state had promised rate increases, Cuomo said: "He has been very constructive. Whether he should do it as a publisher, that's for you guys."

Johnson's intervention in the Shoreham settlement was unusual, but he has regularly taken a far more intense interest in setting editorial policy than Laventhol did — especially on local issues, where he feels that he has firsthand knowledge. When Tony Marro became the editor of *Newsday*, Marro made it clear that he didn't think the paper's editor should also run the editorial page, as Insolia had under Laventhol. That left the paper's editorial policy in the hands of Johnson and Klurfeld. Immediately, they agreed that they wanted a sharper, more assertive page than the one that Laventhol and Fox had produced. "If the editorial page doesn't state how things ought to be, who's going to do it?" Klurfeld said. In Johnson's view, that change in tone has worked. "I don't think people were reading the page," Johnson said. "I think people are reading the page now."

People were certainly reading when *Newsday* ran a heavily researched series of editorials in 1989, written by Larry Levy, challenging the Long Island power structure to rescue the island's economy, through such steps as consolidating school districts and governmental units, increasing class sizes, and limiting pay increases for public employees. Those editorials prompted angry responses from teachers' unions and other groups, but they demonstrated again that *Newsday* remains one of the few unifying institutions on Long Island, that only *Newsday* exerts a pervasive enough influence to stimulate fundamental change in the island's fragmented governmental system. And Johnson intends to involve himself in that community, even if that worries people in the newsroom. "I think journalists inherently distrust their publisher," Johnson said, "especially if their publisher doesn't have a journalistic background."

II

THOUGH MANY IN the newsroom have raised questions about Johnson's views on the publisher's role, he still enjoys a reputation as a talented businessman. Given the difficult times facing *Newsday* in the early 1990s, he had better be.

At many American corporations, when management decides to take on an initiative as costly and energy-consuming as *New York Newsday*, it avoids tackling other big new ventures at the same time. But *Newsday* is trying to accomplish a whole agenda of radical changes simultaneously. Besides the New York initiative, it is shifting from an afternoon to a morning newspaper and battling against the gains of weekly newspapers on Long Island by developing a series of daily and weekly regional editions. The question is whether it is crazy for *Newsday* to attempt so much at the same time. "It absolutely is," Johnson conceded. "It is scary." Some nights, Johnson said, he sits down and wonders: "Am I really capable of managing this, or is this a big charade?" Nonetheless, in his view, those difficult initiatives also offer a useful ferment that wards off corporate complacency. "I think the level of complexity of this place is really one of the reasons that we're able to attract the talent that we're able to attract," Johnson said. "That's why I think we can manage all of the craziness."

Of all the projects, the conversion to a morning paper is perhaps the most inevitable. "We're the only afternoon paper in the country that is growing," Marro said, "and we're growing in the morning." What Bill Attwood sensed in the early 1970s is still true: More and more, people want the paper in the morning. For years, late afternoon delivery had enabled *Newsday* to provide far more complete stories than those that appeared in the morning papers, but completeness has become less crucial than timeliness. "You had a wonderful, full editorial product, but the fact is that since 1980, Long Island's afternoon home delivery has been shrinking," said Robert Brandt, the managing editor in charge of production at night. "I think that people are telling us something."

The conversion to morning delivery has put immense strains on the production operation. Delivering the paper earlier means printing it earlier, which is especially difficult at *Newsday*. In its first three decades, *Newsday* didn't start running the presses until after breakfast time, which was fine for late afternoon delivery. "We basically had a seven-hour publishing cycle," Johnson said. "We could do more with fewer presses." That ability to get by with less capital equipment was one of the factors that helped make *Newsday* so profitable. But in the 1980s, with the simultaneous growth of the New York City paper and the movement toward morning delivery, *Newsday* had to install more presses. By 1990, the paper had ten presses with ten units each. In addition, the presses had to start earlier and earlier, until they started running at midnight. That means that the pressroom has to turn out from 700,000 to 800,000 papers between midnight and about 4:30 in the morning. In the next few years, that figure is expected to climb to something like one million, which leaves very little margin for error in the production process.

The shift to morning delivery has also drastically changed the circulation system. *Newsday* built its home delivery strength on an army of 10,000 young carriers who would return home from school in the afternoon, pick up their papers and deliver them by about 4:30 in the afternoon. Several factors cut that army to about 5,500 by early 1990. At one time, *Newsday* could urge carriers to greater productivity by offering incentives, such as radios, sports equipment and even bicycles. Now, between the money that their parents give them and what they can earn at fast-food restaurants, carrier-age children have enough money without the hard work of a paper route. "One time, giving the kids a bicycle for fifty orders was a big thing," David Targe said. "Now the kids laugh at you: 'Get off my back, and I'll give *you* a bicycle.' " On top of that, the new emphasis on early-morning delivery makes it even more difficult to attract school-age carriers. As a result, *Newsday* has had to rely more and more on a growing corps of adult carriers, who deliver *Newsday* in the morning, then go on to other jobs in the afternoon.

In order to make the job profitable enough to attract adults, *Newsday* has to assign each adult the same number of papers that four youth carriers used to deliver. The adult is able to deliver that many papers by using an automobile, and by dropping the paper at the end of the driveway, instead of stopping at each house to carry it to the front door, as youth carriers have traditionally done. "It's hard to get an adult who's got 175 to 200 papers to get out of that car," said Harold F. Woldt Jr., the vice-president for circulation. Beyond the problem of the quality of delivery, the increasing use of adult carriers has affected the way that *Newsday* sells subscriptions. Youth carriers have always done their own soliciting for new orders to build up their routes, but adult carriers don't have the time. That has forced *Newsday* to rely more on telephone circulation sales and other methods.

Despite the complexities involved, *Newsday* is firmly committed to the goal of becoming a one hundred percent morning paper. At the same time, Johnson wants to move morning readers away from buying their papers at the newsstands and toward morning home delivery, which is more valuable to advertisers and more stable. By early 1990, the entire *New York Newsday* circulation, both home delivery and newsstand sales, was reaching the reader by seven o'clock in the morning. On Long Island, about twenty percent of the home delivery papers were getting to homes before seven o'clock, and another thirty-three percent by noon. Eventually, *Newsday* wants to make the paper even more attractive to early commuters by getting it into the home before six o'clock. "If you could market that," Woldt said, "nobody could beat you."

The problem is that *Newsday* still lacks the press capacity to shorten the printing cycle further and print papers earlier. And every time *Newsday* adds another 60,000 to 70,000 in circulation, it needs to buy another press, just to stay even. To keep up with circulation increases and complete the movement toward morning circulation, the ten presses that *Newsday* had at the start of 1990 would not be nearly enough. "You're looking at anywhere from fourteen to sixteen presses that you're going to need to do that, if you continue to print collect," said James Norris, the vice-president for operations. "The press runs at 25,000 revolutions per hour. In the collect mode, it produces one paper per revolution. In the straight mode, it produces two papers per revolution. In the collect mode, the capacity is 256 pages. In the straight mode, it's exactly half of that, 128 pages." Since *Newsday* sells enough advertising to run 256 pages regularly, it has been forced to use the slower collect mode of printing, which has held press capacity down. "You can buy more presses and continue to print collect, or you can convert to straight-running presses," Norris said. But squeezing more presses into the Melville plant is impractical, and a satellite plant is too expensive. "To buy and build a four-press satellite plant, you're probably looking at something in the range of $200 million to $250 million, plus all the overhead."

So Norris proposed to increase the output of the presses by converting them to the straight mode, without diminishing their page capacity. The "Norris plan" is to realign the paper's contents so that it can be printed in two separate sections of roughly equal size. One section, containing all of the entertainment and feature material, would roll off the presses starting at about nine o'clock at night and be stored on inserting machinery provided by FERAG, a Swiss manufacturer. While that section is coming off the presses, editing and other production work would continue on the main section of the paper, which would contain breaking news, sports and business. At midnight, the presses would start to produce the main section, and the FERAG equipment would insert the feature section inside it, as the presses roll. The plan is to continue printing *New York Newsday* in the current collect mode, and to use the FERAG insertion equipment to assemble the Nassau and Suffolk editions that go to newsstands. At the start, because of the limited number of FERAG insertion drums that *Newsday* is buying, home delivery papers for Nassau-Suffolk will leave the plant in two pieces and be assembled by the carriers. Even with the initial limited installation of four FERAG systems, however, this arrangement significantly increases the effective press capacity for $35 million — a far smaller investment than the cost of a satellite plant.

There are risks connected with the Norris solution, including the danger of housing so much production capacity under one roof. But Norris predicted: "It's going to work." If it does, *Newsday* can make steady progress toward keeping up with the growth of the New York paper and converting completely to morning delivery by 1993. "We're going to have the capacity to circulate one million a.m. newspapers out of this plant," Johnson said, "zoned daily for eleven different zones — four in Nassau, four in Suffolk and three in the city."

The publication of regional sections is another heavy burden on the production process. But *Newsday* made a firm decision in the second half of the 1980s that the paper had to publish regionals, to combat the weekly newspapers that were wooing smaller advertisers who could not afford and didn't need ads that run throughout Suffolk County or Nassau County. The purpose of the regional sections was to offer advertisers a smaller audience, closer to their place of business, at a lower rate.

Besides the advertising rationale, there was a legitimate editorial argument for the creation of regionals. By adding to its foreign and national staffs, *Newsday* had made itself a more complete newspaper — the long-term goal of David Laventhol. But that increased staffing led to more competition for space in the paper. In the early 1970s, when a reporter went to cover a town board meeting, there was a strong chance that even a routine story from that meeting would run in the front of the paper. By the end of the 1980s, however, a routine town board story was highly unlikely to appear upfront. Further, the space crunch was so tight that the daily list of holdovers — stories that didn't make it into the paper at all — had grown depressingly long. The regionals offered a partial solution.

The first step was a freestanding weekly regional called *In Brookhaven*. Internally, it caused unrest. "The reporters resented working on *In Brookhaven*," said Howard Schneider, who ran the task force that developed the concept. "They felt like suddenly they were working for a second-rate weekly newspaper." Externally, it made a weak impression. "What we learned is that our strength is that we're there every day," Johnson said. "By just being out there one day a week, we really weren't building any kind of true regional following." The next step, in late 1987, was the establishment of daily regional pages. There were four separate regionals five days a week in Suffolk. By running four regional sections in Suffolk, *Newsday* could make extra room in the paper by using the same page four times, with four different sets of stories. Initially, the lack of press capacity prevented *Newsday* from regionalizing the Nassau paper, but in 1988, Nassau regionals began running once a week, on Wednesdays.

Newsday had been thinking about regionalization for years before the daily regionals began, but Johnson finally pulled the trigger only a few months after a significant event: the entry into the Long Island market of a publisher named Ralph Ingersoll II, who had already built a ring of free-distribution papers around St. Louis. In 1987, an Ingersoll-dominated company called Community Newspapers Inc. bought an eighty percent interest in a Long Island chain of free-distribution weeklies called Chanry Communications, run by a former *Newsday* circulation manager, Stan Henry. Soon after that purchase, Chanry boasted that it reached more than 900,000 homes on Long Island, with eventual plans to reach 1.2 million homes. A few months later, at a meeting with *Newsday* managers, Johnson said that *Newsday* had never before faced a chain of weeklies that could offer advertisers something close to one hundred percent saturation in Nassau-Suffolk, as Chanry could. "We believe that basically Ralph Ingersoll believes that *Newsday* is so focused on New York that it is going to forget the homeland," Johnson said, "and he can come in and pick up the scraps." A major goal of *Newsday*'s daily regionals was to block that strategy.

Within two years after the start of the daily regionals, Chanry hit *Newsday* with a one-two punch. First, in early 1989, Chanry hired away a *Newsday* advertising supervisor, Frank Gallagher — one of several to defect. A few weeks later, in April, Henry announced that on May 6 Chanry would merge its *Pennysaver* and *Weekender* newspapers into a regionalized weekly tabloid called *This Week*, which would reach about a million homes with seventy-six editions. In advertisements in trade weeklies, Chanry boasted that *This Week* would offer better penetration of the market and lower advertising rates than *Newsday*. Those claims were little more than "hype and smoke," said Doug Fox, the *Newsday* senior vice-president for marketing. But *Newsday* acted quickly to counteract the threat, by publishing weekly "specials" reaching ten different zones in Nassau and Suffolk. *Newsday* had been planning these for some time, but the advent of *This Week* accelerated their debut. In weeks, the specials began to turn a profit — well ahead of what *Newsday* expected.

If Chanry wanted to battle with *Newsday*, Johnson was in a fighting mood. "*This Week* has declared war on *Newsday*," Johnson told a group of supervisors, soon after the launch of the weekly specials. "They want to take the dollars out of our pockets." One of the major weapons was Chanry's willingness to cut prices. Just the week before Johnson's briefing, *Newsday* had been forced to restructure its contract with a major discount store, to keep it from bolting to *This Week*, and Johnson predicted that *Newsday* would have to do that often. "We may be holding on to the business," Johnson said, "but getting less revenue than we otherwise might."

In addition to addressing the threat of *This Week* and other weeklies, the regionals have caused strains at *Newsday*. One problem is the need to develop a lead story of about 1,200 words each week for each of the ten weekly specials. In the process of regionalizing, *Newsday* hired additional reporters, but Tony Marro and Howard Schneider, the managing editor of the Long Island paper, made a decision not to hire a separate staff to do only the weekly sections, because that would create a two-tier reporting system. As a result, the same reporters who cover breaking stories in the towns also turn out the weekly specials. Schneider argues that each story should find its natural level — in the daily regionals, the specials, or the front of the paper — but the reporters think that the need for copy in the specials sometimes keeps a story out of the main paper. "The specials just act like a vacuum, sucking everything up," one Long Island reporter said. Despite the profitability of the specials and their acceptance by advertisers, reporters feel that readers don't pay attention to them. "I have never gotten a reaction to a special," one reporter said. "It's an advertising vehicle, more than anything else."

The rise of the regionals has created a painful paradox: The salary structure and overall excellence of *Newsday* have generated a flood of job applications from reporters, which enables *Newsday* to reject almost any reporter with fewer than three or four years of experience. But the need to fill the daily and weekly regionals has created a demand for the kind of local stories that most of these new reporters thought they had outgrown before they came to *Newsday*. Further, reporters coming to a newspaper with a total circulation of 700,000 are often shocked by the minuscule size of the audience for the regionals. "I didn't come to *Newsday* to write stories for 40,000 people," one Long Island reporter said. Marro deflects those complaints by telling reporters that, if they cover towns well, there are more appealing jobs at *Newsday* than ever, as feature writers, specialists or correspondents in foreign and domestic bureaus. In fact, the Moscow correspondent, Alison Mitchell, started out covering small neighborhoods in Queens. "I'm not going to apologize for the fact that we're a Long Island newspaper," Marro said. "If they're half the reporters that they think they are, they should know that before they get here."

The reporters also face another problem partly caused by the daily regionals: the backward march of deadlines. When Times Mirror acquired *Newsday* in 1970, *Newsday* reporters could work all night, write a comprehensive story just before dawn and get it into every copy of *Newsday*, while the other papers had to run fragmentary stories in earlier editions. By 1990, the production demands of the New York paper and the regionals had pushed deadlines back so far that reporters often have to turn in stories well before six o'clock in the evening, and sports reporters who used to write one story a night now routinely have to write three versions. The earlier deadlines also mean that *Newsday* can no longer wait for the late-moving stories on the *Los Angeles Times-Washington Post* news service. So, there is a greater burden on the Washington bureau to cover breaking stories, in addition to writing enterprise pieces.

Beyond those practical problems, the regionals pose a philosophical question that goes to the core of *Newsday*'s self-image: How local a newspaper should *Newsday* be? "The endless problem is trying to deal with stories that are of great interest in a community and of no interest anywhere else," Marro said. In the 1950s and 1960s, *Newsday* solved that dilemma by trying to broaden out stories: If something happened in Islip, the editors pushed reporters to find out if the same thing was happening in other towns and write a story that was interesting to people beyond that community. Now, many reporters and editors feel, the daily regionals are going in exactly the opposite direction. "They're Balkanizing it," said Art Perfall, the former managing editor, who pushed for years to broaden stories. "It's crazy. *Newsday* made its reputation on being the only unifying force on Long Island."

Criticism of the regionals has also come from outside. "I get complaints constantly from politicians, from public relations people, who say, 'Now I've got to go out and buy five or six editions of *Newsday*, to make sure I'm staying on top of everything that's going on in Suffolk County,'" Johnson said. "Our solution to that is going to be an on-line data base that they can all tap into, to get all the different regional stories. . . . The other thing we're looking into is a regional faxpaper." The editors also try to handle that problem by the way they juggle stories from one regional edition to another. "We can play these stories big in the local community and small in the other communities," Marro said. "That gives us a chance to do five times as much news."

Whatever the drawbacks, the regionals seem to have had an effect on the competition. Certainly, whether *Newsday* had anything to do with it or not, *This Week* was in shakier condition at the end of 1989 than it was six months earlier, when it began. In early December, Chanry decided to scale back on its plans, switching some of its weeklies back to the old *Pennysaver* designation, with a smaller news content. The decreased emphasis on news allowed Chanry to cut back its editorial staff. At the same time, *This Week* appointed a new publisher, only three weeks after the previous one had taken over. Then, early in 1990, the parent corporation of Chanry, Community Newspapers Inc., along with Ingersoll Newspapers Inc., lost their debt rating from Moody's Investors Service. Soon after that, Community Newspapers offered Chanry for sale. In the spring of 1990, Chanry announced that it was planning to convert its entire chain of papers back to the less ambitious *Pennysaver* format, which allowed Chanry to trim its news staff even further. Then Ralph Ingersoll's problems spread south: Only seven months after Ingersoll launched the tabloid *St. Louis Sun*, its lagging circulation, high costs and lack of advertising forced him to shut it down.

Chanry's troubles were welcome news at *Newsday*. "They're writing it off to the economy, and clearly that has hurt him, just like it's hurt us," Fox said. "But the fact of the matter is that we've just absolutely kicked their butt. . . .

Ads in their publication aren't pulling people into the stores to buy the products. Ours do." To back up that boast, *Newsday* did research to demonstrate that *This Week*'s one hundred percent penetration of the market is illusory. "We had photographs of landfills full of *This Week*s that had never been unbundled," Johnson said. "We never used the photographs, but we did do research for any of our advertisers who were interested in the research." Beyond the delivery problems, Johnson argued, Chanry made other important mistakes: "I think they assumed that *Newsday* did not have the ability to respond quickly, both with the regional program and also, frankly, with a change of attitude towards the advertisers."

In battling Chanry, *Newsday* did try to turn a friendlier face toward the advertisers than it had in the past, before the stiff competition from New York dailies and Long Island weeklies. So Fox pushed his sales staff to emphasize *Newsday*'s willingness to work with advertisers to help their business grow. But advertisers remained skeptical, remembering all the years of aggressive rate increases. If they deserted *This Week* and came rushing back into the arms of *Newsday*, they asked Fox, " 'Will you be abusive in the future?' " Despite *Newsday*'s arguments that *This Week* was not delivering customers to their doors, advertisers clung to it because its rates were cheap, and the competition helped to keep *Newsday*'s rates in line. As a result, *Newsday* was still fighting a difficult battle in early 1990 to wrestle away from *This Week* its most important advertisers: the supermarkets.

Every week, the supermarket chains send out hundreds of thousands of flyers with coupons and sale prices of their food. The presence of those flyers inside the free-distribution weeklies is the major reason why homeowners pick them up off the driveway and take them into the house. In the past, *Newsday* could not compete with the weeklies for these flyers, because supermarkets wanted to be able to change them at the last minute, if a carload of produce came in from California spoiled, for example. The free-distribution papers could accept last-minute changes and still deliver the flyers on Saturday, but *Newsday* had to have the flyers in the plant a week before delivery. "We just didn't have a system that answered their needs," said Carey Gates, who became *Newsday*'s advertising manager in 1989. So the weeklies got the business, and *Newsday* did not.

To fight back, *Newsday* and Times Mirror made a strong investment in equipment. Under the new system, those who do not subscribe to *Newsday* get their food flyers from *Newsday* in the mail on Saturday, wrapped in something called *Newsday Plus*, which contains a few pages of features normally seen in the newspaper itself. *Newsday* subscribers get their supermarket flyers with the Sunday paper. The initial goal was to coax four major supermarket chains to sign up with *Newsday*, but the struggle went slowly, as *Newsday* had a hard time competing with *This Week*'s rates. "If we go in and say three cents apiece," Gates said, "they'll say two cents apiece." At the start of 1990, *Newsday* had one major chain, King Kullen, plus two smaller chains, and was struggling to woo Pathmark and Waldbaum's away from Chanry.

III

THE TUSSLE WITH the weeklies was not the only financial struggle that *Newsday* faced at the start of the 1990s. Following an unprecedentedly long period of expansion, the national economy began to slow down, and the robust, defense-oriented Long Island economy began experiencing post-Cold War contraction.

The boom created by the Ronald Reagan defense buildup began to go bust in 1987, when Fairchild Republic Company lost its major contract and went out of business. At about the same time, the largest employer on Long Island, the Grumman Corporation, began paring its work force. In 1989, Grumman had to fight to persuade Congress to continue production of its primary product, the F-14D fighter. The company won a temporary victory, but Grumman continued cutting employment, and other defense contractors did the same. From early 1987 to mid-1989, 12,000 of the 60,000 defense workers on Long Island lost their jobs. That was a clear warning of hard times ahead, as defense budgets shrink. "I think the cycle for us on Long Island is going to be deeper and longer and more fundamental," Fox said. "It isn't just a dip. We've got to go through a metamorphosis on Long Island, not unlike the Route 128 corridor around Boston. We've got to find our reason for being, beyond the defense industry. If we don't, we're going to have some real problems."

The slide in the economy severely hurt *Newsday*'s advertising linage. The decline in defense jobs, for example, meant a loss of recruitment ads, a major element of classified ad revenues. Another large segment of classified, automotive advertising, slowed as car sales dropped. The other significant category of classified ads, real estate, also declined sharply. In addition, the growth of retail advertising suffered, as consumers spent less, because of defense budget cuts, high taxes and housing costs on Long Island, and the impact of the stock market crash. This sharp downturn cut deeply into profits. In 1986, Johnson's first year as publisher, *Newsday*'s pretax profits were more than $90 million, sources within Times Mirror said. But in 1989, they dipped below $30 million. That is still a tidy profit, far better than the picture at the *Daily News* or the *Post*, but it is a worrisome trend.

Declining revenues have forced *Newsday* to look at the expenditure side of the ledger more closely than ever before. "We've grown so damned fast, and our profitability has been so strong that, frankly, nobody cared," Johnson told about 300 supervisors at a cost-containment breakfast in a country club in the early summer of 1988. Later that year, Johnson made an announcement that demonstrated he was serious about cost containment: *Newsday* was changing the company's health insurance plan to increase employee contributions. Then, at the start of 1990, the paper laid off five employees — the first real layoffs in *Newsday*'s history. At the same time, the paper gave smaller salary increases to managers than in previous years, and made a strong effort, in negotiations with the editorial unit of Local 406, to hold down wage increases for union workers.

This retrenchment would be painful enough for a company whose management is already fully in place and set for the future. But the decline in revenues and the rise of cost containment all came at a time when Johnson was still trying to fulfill one of David Laventhol's mandates: to find, train and develop a new generation of managers for *Newsday* — especially in the two revenue-producing departments, advertising and circulation. As Johnson looked around, he saw no one on the staff that he considered qualified to become president of *Newsday* and relieve Johnson of one of his two hats. That was part of his reason for hiring Doug Fox, as a future president. When Fox arrived, one of his first priorities was to evaluate the advertising managers and determine who should lead the department in the post-Targe era. In the spring of 1989, Fox made his changes in advertising, offering several managers lesser jobs and hiring Lou Gazitano from the *New York Times* to run the department. Most of the managers accepted the changes quietly, but one demoted supervisor, Tom Taylor, made noise. Fox asked him to relinquish control of the preprint department and accept a job as an automotive advertising salesman, but Taylor balked. In a meeting with Fox, Taylor argued his case in vain, then told Fox: "Doug, you know, you're not a very compassionate person." Fox exploded in a torrent of salty language, both men remembered. Taylor insisted that Fox fired him, which Fox denied. Taylor left *Newsday*, enraged by the demotion and Fox's personal style, and after an unsuccessful negotiation over severance pay, he filed an age-discrimination complaint against *Newsday*.

Beyond the advertising department, Fox's hard-driving style and lack of newspaper experience made him an object of suspicion and fear in some parts of the newsroom, where it was widely known that he was Johnson's choice to be president of the company. In 1989, Fox made some people in the editorial department nervous by taking a major role in two journalistic projects, despite the *Newsday* taboo against the commercial side of the paper meddling in editorial matters. The first project was the rescue of *The Newsday Magazine*. The magazine had once offered something that no other part of the paper could: color ads and photographs. As the rest of the paper gained that capacity, the rationale for a magazine with a six-week lead time became weaker, and advertisers found it less attractive. But the high costs continued. Johnson had wanted for years to kill it, and David Laventhol had wanted to distribute *Parade* magazine with the Sunday paper. But Fox and Tony Marro agreed that *Parade* was not up to *Newsday* standards. "Did I infuse myself in that?" Fox said. "You're goddamn right I did, but why not? What was the alternative?" Setting out to find a way to save it from the axe, Fox decided that the magazine needed glossier paper and a better overall appearance. Bernie Bottomley, the director of administrative services, found a printer in Buffalo who could do the magazine on better quality paper and make other improvements, in return for an agreement to cut its size slightly. Fox pushed for that solution and changed the bonus plans of his advertising salesmen to force them to sell space in the magazine more aggressively. Marro accepted Fox's proposal, and they prolonged the life of the magazine.

Similarly, Fox jumped into the middle of efforts to cut the costs of the weekly television guide. In 1987, learning that Cablevision was planning to publish an improved guide, *Newsday* beat them to the punch by creating its own improved television book, with a glossy cover and several pages of glossy stock inside. They expected to lose money on it, but by 1989, the losses had grown too large, and Fox took a lead role in cutting the losses in half. That involved discarding the glossy pages inside and changing the format of the listings, among other things. Some in the newsroom felt Fox had gone too far by involving himself in that kind of design decision. "My life is going to be easier if my product is easier to sell," Fox said. "What's really important, if you're a team player, is that at least you invite and you listen to somebody else's point of view. Does that mean that the commercial side strays a little bit into the journalistic side? Right, it does. Does that mean that they have to accept it, carte blanche? No." Despite the suspicions on the staff, Marro and Fox found ways to work together. "He's new to this business," Marro said. "He's also a smart guy."

The problem for both Fox and Johnson is that, while they are both well-trained, intelligent managers, their rise to power has come at a bad time: They cannot yet cite the company's bottom line to prove that their ideas work, because the bottom line has been sliding steadily. They believe strongly that the old arrogant *Newsday* approach to advertisers only hurt the company in the long run. But that philosophy did produce many years of rising revenues and swelling profits. Johnson and Fox expect their advertiser-friendly approach to lead *Newsday* to even greater profit margins, but it has not yet, largely because of the general downturn in the economy. "Right now, *Newsday* is one of the worst-performing large newspapers in the nation," said one security analyst, Susan Decker, in an interview with the *Newsday* reporter Charles Zehren, who wrote a long piece in late 1989 about *Newsday*'s battle with the weeklies. (Zehren's piece, edited by Marro, amazed people outside *Newsday* with its candor, but it disturbed Johnson. "He thought we were giving major competitors an advantage and a credibility they didn't deserve," Marro said. Johnson let his pique slip out during a speech at a *Newsday* awards dinner, then met later with the business staff to soothe bruised feelings.)

Despite the paper's declining performance, the management at Times Mirror has taken into account similar declines at some of its other papers and has been patient, worrying less about quarterly profits than about the future. "These guys are sharp enough long-term businessmen that they recognize that there are business cycles," Fox said. "I think they really believe, more so than the average businessman, in the long pull."

IV

AT A TIMES Mirror meeting a few months after the start of the 1985 promotional drive for *New York Newsday*, someone questioned the basic assumptions behind the New York paper, and Phillip Williams, one of the most cautious executives in the company, spoke up with finality: "We've already made that decision."

The decision to take on New York came gradually, in fits and starts, but once Times Mirror had finally made it, the commitment was irrevocable. Times Mirror is a company that believes in the need to stand by long-term plans, even in the face of short-term difficulties. Beyond that, it is convinced of the essential soundness of the New York strategy, which Williams called a "creeping acquisition." *New York Newsday* is in the red, anywhere from $10 million to $20 million a year, but Times Mirror has looked at those annual losses as an investment. Eventually, the company believes, *New York Newsday* will be profitable, and Times Mirror will have acquired a newspaper in New York City for much less than the cost of buying a paper outright in many large cities. Before Laventhol became president of Times Mirror, he had to work hard to sell the New York idea, but support for the strategy now pervades the corporation. "I will guarantee you Dave Laventhol could get hit by a truck and it wouldn't miss a beat," Johnson said. "Everybody is on board one hundred percent."

The broad agreement on the strategy, however, is not enough to guarantee the success of the complex relationship between *New York Newsday* and the paper's management in Melville. That requires a tricky day-to-day balancing act between the observance of traditional *Newsday* standards and the New York paper's need to operate autonomously. The central figures in that balancing act have been Forst and Marro. In the Melville newsroom — where Marro is widely respected as a reasonable and honest editor who understands reporters because he was a first-rate one himself — one of the few substantial criticisms of Marro is that he does not do enough to tame Forst. But Marro has consciously held himself back from meddling, to let Forst do what he does best: call attention to the paper. "It took two years before he realized I wasn't going to try to be the New York editor," Marro said.

The two men have sharply contrasting approaches. Marro is a serious journalist whose judgment of a story's value tends to focus on its *importance* compared to other events of the day. Forst looks primarily at a story's conversational value on the streets, even if it isn't important. On one day in early 1990, for example, the main cover story of the Long Island paper was a serious issue: President George Bush's visit to Colombia to attend an anti-drug summit, where his safety was a major concern. But the New York front page focused instead on the juicy details of a multimillion-dollar divorce struggle between the developer Donald Trump and his wife, Ivana. The next day's New York front page went one step further: It was a cartoon about the Trumps by Pulitzer Prize-winning cartoonist Doug Marlette, hired by *Newsday* in 1989. (The *Post* was far more graphic, leading the paper with a huge photo of Trump and a headline quoting Trump's reputed girlfriend: "Best Sex I've Ever Had.") To many at *Newsday*, the Trump front pages appeared frivolous. Forst also drew criticism for a front-page headline on a story about the trial of Imelda Marcos, the widow of Philippines President Ferdinand Marcos. The trial revolved around issues of greed in high places, and one day's front-page headline, describing allegations that Mrs. Marcos used a Philippine bank in New York as her personal piggy bank, said simply: "OINK!" Similarly, after John Fitzgerald Kennedy Jr. failed to pass the New York State bar exam, the *New York Newsday* front page carried a bare-chested photo of Kennedy and the headline: "The Hunk Who Flunked." The rationale behind the lurid emphasis on these stories was simple: These were the stories that everyone in New York was talking about at the time. "There's one thing I think I've learned from Don," Marro said. "To be a useful newspaper, you not only have to tell people how their government works. You have to be able to help them engage in the kind of conversations they have every day."

Despite Marro's understanding of Forst's style, the two men still have disagreements on front pages. No matter how effectively Forst's proposed front page would call attention to *New York Newsday* on the newsstands, Marro sometimes has to decide that it doesn't belong in any paper carrying the name *Newsday*. When Lebanese terrorists hanged an American hostage in 1989, for example, Forst would have liked to use a page-one headline that he had seen in a British newspaper in a different context: "Bastards!" But that was unacceptable to Marro. (Forst called his former *Newsday* colleague John Cotter, the metropolitan editor of the *New York Post*, and offered the headline to him. The *Post* used it.) Despite the occasional disagreements, though, Marro recognizes Forst's value: "Don is very important to this paper."

Similarly, the operation of the *Newsday–New York Newsday* tandem requires a smooth relationship between the editor of the editorial pages on Long Island and the editor of the *New York Newsday* editorial pages, who reports to him. For three years, the New York job belonged to Tom Plate, a former *Newsday* editor who had left in 1972 for *New York* magazine, later worked with Forst in Los Angeles, then moved to *Time* magazine and to *Family Weekly*, before Laventhol brought him back to *Newsday* in 1986. "Dave wanted a nonconventional editorial page," Plate said. "He wanted it to be very New Yorkized. He wanted it to have some flair." At the time, Jim Klurfeld had not yet taken over the editorial pages from Sylvan Fox, and there had been no full-time *New York Newsday* editorial page editor.

The discussions with Laventhol were smooth, but Plate ran into some opposition from Fox, who raised basic questions: " 'How could one paper have two editorial page editors, and also, why couldn't it be done out of Long Island?' " Within a few months, however, Fox and Plate had developed a good relationship, and that continued when Klurfeld took over the pages. "My job was to give New York as much autonomy as possible," Klurfeld said. "They're very local pages. You have to be doing it from a New York perspective. You cannot have someone who's sitting on Long Island directing New York editorial policy." Most of the foreign and national editorials come from the Long Island staff, and the New York paper edits them down to its needs. "We've structured this section to be very New York," Plate said. "We run far fewer national and foreign editorials than does Mother *Newsday*."

By the time Plate left *Newsday* in 1989 to run the editorial pages at the *Los*

Angeles Times, he had shaped the New York pages into a voice to be reckoned with in the city. "The paper has an impact among newsmakers in government really far beyond what 230,000 circulation seemingly would earn you," Steve Isenberg said at the start of 1990. In the 1989 mayoral race, for example, *Newsday* was the only major daily to endorse David Dinkins in the Democratic primary. Reacting to that endorsement, the *Amsterdam News*, perhaps the most widely read paper aimed at New York's black community, said that *New York Newsday* had "reported on the neighborhoods of this city as no other newspaper has ever even tried . . . and with a staff that really reflects the ethnic, racial and religious diversity of a city that they so clearly love." Later in the campaign, *Newsday* was also the paper that broke a series of stories by Joe Calderone of Bob Greene's New York investigative team, raising questions about the propriety of Dinkins' private financial dealings. That became a major campaign issue, but Dinkins survived it and became the first black mayor of New York.

The growth of the paper's clout, however, has not erased the painful reality that the staff faces every day: Even though many magazine articles on the New York newspaper wars credit *New York Newsday* with covering the city better than any other paper, it is still at the bottom of the pecking order. "Nobody returns your calls," one New York reporter said. "Leaks always go to the *Times* night rewrite." Even with the circulation at nearly a quarter of a million, the staff still faces the frustration of writing for a paper that isn't as widely available as the *Times* and the *News*. People still complain to reporters that they don't see the paper, and reporters still have to make photocopies of their stories for sources.

At any newspaper, reporters gripe, and *New York Newsday* provides all the normal reasons for complaint, such as the Brooklyn bureau's illogical location, far in the south of the borough, away from the courts and the politicians. But in addition, the complex New York-Melville relationship provides a separate set of complaints unique to *Newsday*. The *Times*, the *News* and the *Post* all made offers to the subway columnist Jim Dwyer, for example, and *Newsday* increased his salary substantially to keep him. (Later, the paper assigned Dwyer to write a general column and gave the subway column to Ellis Henican.) Other reporters didn't begrudge Dwyer his raise, but the whole episode emphasized the sharp distinction between the New York paper and Mother *Newsday*: Long Island columnists, such as Ed Lowe, Paul Vitello and Marilyn Goldstein, do not have a competitive situation to provide them with salary leverage — even though Lowe is the most well known Long Island writer and Vitello has repeatedly won *Newsday* prizes for his sensitive, carefully crafted work. A few years ago, when Dwyer joined it, the New York edition was still an infant. Now, reporters in New York have access to the glitzy stories that bring book contracts and job offers and force *Newsday* to deal with them through agents. Reporters in Melville, for the most part, do not. As a result, many Long Island reporters both want to work in New York and resent the attention lavished on *New York Newsday*. "We *expect* everybody to hate us on Long Island," one New York reporter said. "They make the money and we spend it. Who wouldn't hate us?"

As a result of all these complexities, the delicate task of regulating the unusual machinery of the new *Newsday* is seldom easy for Marro and Forst, and there are times when it can be excruciatingly painful. In the spring of 1990, for example, they both lived through a hellish week brought on by their highest-priced, most visible columnist, Jimmy Breslin. It began when Breslin wrote a column griping about his wife, Ronnie Eldridge, a newly elected member of the New York City Council. Her offense: paying more attention to her council duties than to her husband the columnist. The same column railed at women officials in general: "I hate official women!" This column did not amuse Ji-Yeon Yuh, a young Korean-American woman working as a reporter in the Queens office of *New York Newsday*. So she sat down at her computer, wrote a brief message of protest to Breslin, accusing him of spewing sexism, and pushed the button that sent the message to Breslin's computer queue.

The day after the column appeared, Breslin read Yuh's message, emerged from his office, fuming, and reacted to her criticism with a thundering series of epithets aimed at both her race and her sex. Yuh was not in the newsroom to hear it, but those who were there said that his choice of words included "bitch," "yellow cur," "slant-eyed" and a brief anatomical word that is particularly offensive to women. Beyond that, Breslin sat down and typed a computer note to Forst, complaining about Yuh's note. "I absolutely will not tolerate being bothered," Breslin wrote. In his anger, Breslin failed to keep this note secure, and angry colleagues quickly spread copies of it across computer screens in New York and Melville.

Almost immediately, another Asian-American reporter, Jessie Mangaliman, wrote a note of protest to Marro, signed by more than forty others. By late that afternoon, Breslin had sent a note of apology to the staff: "I am no good and once again I can prove it. I intended to make noise, not offend nice people. I'm sorry. I said things I shouldn't have said. The racial and sexual insults I spewed are never appropriate. Again, I'm sorry." Forst also sent out a note to the staff: "Jimmy Breslin's remarks in the newsroom this morning were offensive and inexcusable. I told him that immediately. There is no place in this company for racial or sexual insults." The competing tabloids, the *News* and the *Post*, displayed the story prominently the next day.

The controversy didn't end with one apology or one day of stories. The following Monday, May 7, *Newsday* carried Breslin's column, which apologized further, but the paper also contained a story about a coalition of Asian-American groups calling on the paper to fire him. On Tuesday, *Newsday* and the other tabloids reported on demands by state legislators that Marro suspend Breslin. On Tuesday evening, Marro and the other editors met with a group of Asian-American reporters to discuss the issue. At the meeting, Yuh described to Marro a telephone interview that Breslin had done on a radio show earlier in the day, in which he joked about the controversy and said: "All my apologies, however, are carbons." Following the meeting, Marro and the other editors listened to a tape of the radio interview and quickly concluded that Breslin was still insensitive to the furor that he had created. "I said, 'The guy doesn't get it; he just doesn't get it,' " Marro said. So the *Newsday* management decided to suspend Breslin without pay for two weeks.

The next morning, Marro wrote a three-page memo to the staff, summarizing the meeting with the Asian-American reporters, explaining the paper's actions and responding to criticisms that *Newsday* had a double standard: It had accepted John Cotter's resignation in 1987 after he made racial remarks about his deputy, a black man, but Breslin drew only a two-week suspension for making angry racial remarks about an Asian-American woman. The difference, among other things, Marro wrote, was that Breslin's offense was "an outburst by an individual, and was the first of its kind. John Cotter, in contrast, was a part of the senior management of Newsday, responsible for the hiring and assigning and daily oversight of the staff, representative of the whole institution." In the same memo, Marro, who became the target of criticism in the Melville newsroom because he hadn't taken strong disciplinary action before Breslin spoke on the radio, reacted angrily to a note from twenty-four members of the staff in Melville. In addition to deploring Breslin's conduct, that note went on to complain about a variety of transgressions by the New York paper and to urge that "no disciplinary action of any kind should be taken against Yuh." Reporters on the New York paper didn't like the use of the Breslin incident as an excuse for the staff on Long Island to bash *New York Newsday*, and Marro said in his memo that he deeply resented the suggestion that *Newsday* would seek "retribution" against Yuh. The day after Marro's note, the paper carried a large package of Breslin stories, including a statement by his wife and columns by two of the paper's best columnists, Murray Kempton and Robert Reno. Those columns annoyed some on the staff because, even though they deplored Breslin's behavior, they also seemed to defend him.

All this furor, created by a columnist who had prided himself for decades on being the voice of the downtrodden, was terribly painful for a newspaper that had done more than any other major paper in New York to hire Asian-American reporters. It came right in the middle of a period of ethnic conflict throughout the city, including a black boycott of Korean grocers in Brooklyn and the trial of two white teenagers in connection with a racially motivated murder. Breslin's carefully cultivated persona had always included loud, angry, vulgar outbursts, but in the New York City of 1990, where growing ethnic friction made it especially necessary for everyone to be careful of everyone else's feelings, his tirade against Yuh had come at the worst possible time. It did nothing to heal the divisions of the city that Breslin loved or to build unity at the schizophrenic newspaper that provided him with a bountiful livelihood. "It was hurtful and harmful to everybody he worked with in there," Marro said.

At the same time that *Newsday* had to cope with the internal friction created by the Breslin incident, it had to continue navigating through a difficult and unpredictable external competitive environment. The *Daily News* began the year determined to cut costs by seeking sweeping concessions in contract negotiations with its unions. That meant that *Newsday* had to prepare for contingencies ranging from a settlement that would strengthen the *News* for years to come, to a strike that would offer *Newsday* a chance to sell 300,000 more papers in the city. Whatever the fate of the *News*, it is clear that *Newsday* faces for the next several years a continuing struggle. But behind all the background noise of external competition and internal frictions, the basic reality is that *New York Newsday* has survived its most turbulent years. It is gaining circulation. It is adding editorial staff, up to a total of more than 250 by early 1990. It is solving long-standing problems, such as the lack of female and minority columnists, which it has attempted to remedy by developing columnists from within: Sheryl McCarthy, a black woman, and Carole Agus, a white woman. And it is convincing the city's power brokers that it is a serious newspaper. No matter what its problems in the past, it is too far along now to back off. As long as it takes, Times Mirror seems prepared to keep reaching into its deep pockets and battling the competition in New York. "They'd love us to take our foot off the pedal," Steve Isenberg said. "It ain't going to happen."

V

THE FIRST THING she would notice, of course, is the building. By comparison to the auto dealership in Hempstead or the plant in Garden City, it is a huge structure, looming large in a landscape of squat, relentlessly similar office buildings and factories, including one that bears her name.

Inside, she would stand in the giant newsroom, crammed with insurance-office-modern work stations and dozens of blankly staring computer screens. She'd visit the quiet, antiseptic composing room, without a trace of the incessant clanking of Linotypes that once surrounded her in her windowless cubicle in Hempstead. In late afternoon, she'd sit around a conference table in the editorial conference room and listen to the editors discuss the next day's story budget with another group of editors, distant and disembodied, offering their comments on a speakerphone hookup from Manhattan and Queens. In the evening, she'd listen disbelievingly to the near-silence of the great newsroom, as a legion of absurdly young copy editors stare intently into their computer terminals and put the final touches on the day's stories — with none of the liquor-guzzling gusto of the early years. Getting past those first physical impressions, if Alicia Patterson could come back for a visit, it would take a few weeks of reading the paper before she could figure out whether any trace of her influence remained in the new *Newsday*.

The most visible difference is the dominance of graphics. Almost every day, *Newsday* puts out a weekly newsmagazine-style front page, instead of the traditional headline-and-photo format. On days when a traditional news photograph is not the best graphic element for the front page, the paper uses concept photos — such as two Halloween pumpkins, one smiling and one frowning, for a story about a proposed Halloween curfew. If a concept photo won't work,

Newsday can fall back on a front-page illustration from an art department that grew exponentially in the 1980s, as *Newsday* struggled to overcome its grayness and learned to live in color. At the start of the 1980s, *Newsday* could barely put together a simple locator map for the next day's paper. Now, it works every day with computer-age graphics, including such wonders as a system called Scitex, which can edit photographs in such startling ways that it raises ethical questions about how much a newspaper should alter visual reality through the use of electronic wizardry.

Another dominant quality of the current *Newsday* is the frequent assignment of large reporting teams for many months to produce stunningly thorough series that run for page after page, day after day. The *Newsday* of Alicia Patterson's time didn't have enough of a staff to allow the commitment of so many reporters for so long. Today's *Newsday* has an editorial staff of well over 800 people — ten times the size of the paper's total original staff in all departments — and that wealth of journalists makes long projects possible. The stories that these projects produce are so long that they provoke a constant debate among the editors about how much a reader can take. But the assignment of platoons of reporters, plus the emerging use of computers to help those reporters in analyzing the facts, allows *Newsday* to provide thoughtful, nuanced scrutiny of complex problems. In the 1980s, those reports included such difficult subjects as a telephone rate structure that discriminated against Long Island residents, unfair assessment practices throughout Long Island, and a systematic effort by the City of Long Beach to revive the city by driving out its poor.

The project that most vividly exemplified the large-team approach was a 1987 series on the garbage-disposal problems of Long Island and the nation. The idea sprang from the ridiculous odyssey of a barge filled with Long Island garbage, looking for weeks for a place to unload. From that starting point, the reporter Thomas Maier suggested a series on garbage. It began with a staff of two: Maier and the environmental reporter Mark McIntyre. By the time it ended six months later, it involved about twenty-five people, stuck in a small office called "The Garbage Room." The series was ten parts and 55,000 words — a typically encyclopedic *Newsday* length.

In addition to taking on projects that are far longer and more involved than Alicia's paper usually attempted, the new *Newsday* has aimed at some targets that would surprise her, including one of *Newsday*'s great heroes — William Levitt, the builder of Levittown. In a 1986 series, the reporter Kimberly Greer showed how Levitt's empire had crumbled. Similarly, the old *Newsday* did not often question the way prosecutors and police worked. But in late 1986, a small reporting team of Maier and Rex Smith produced a series that showed how police in Suffolk County relied excessively and often improperly on confessions to get convictions. Another target that would surprise Alicia has been Mario Cuomo, one of the most powerful governors in America. As Albany bureau chiefs, Alison Mitchell and later Miriam Pawel set the agenda for other papers by examining fearlessly the governmental performance behind Cuomo's brilliant rhetoric, including Pawel's 1985 series on the governor at midterm and her investigation of the state's borrowing practices under Cuomo — a dauntingly complex project that the original *Newsday* would never have attempted.

There is no doubt that today's *Newsday* produces a more thoroughly researched, endlessly edited brand of journalism than the paper of Alicia's time, or that the paper's journalistic ethics are sharper than they were under Alan Hathway. But to some of those who worked at the *Newsday* of years ago, something important is missing. "It's like looking at this perfect being without a soul," said Bob Greene, the last real remnant of Hathway journalism at *Newsday*. "We don't take up things with heart and gusto. We're so afraid of crusading." Greene has contributed more than any other single reporter to the paper's success. As he approaches retirement, he no longer has the high profile that he enjoyed when he ran the entire Long Island staff. In the final months before his retirement, Greene takes his satisfactions from teaching journalism, from wielding influence in the Investigative Reporters and Editors organization that he helped to launch, and from turning his investigative skills to a promising new field: the City of New York. Looking back on the *Newsday* that Hathway and Alicia hatched, Greene misses its spirit. "It might not have been as straight as it is now, but it sure was a lot of fun," Greene said. "We all got Calvinist someplace along the line."

If *Newsday*'s history can be viewed as a struggle between the crusading, worry-about-ethics-later style of Hathway and the higher journalistic standards of Al Marlens, the Marlens philosophy has clearly won. But if Alicia Patterson could come back and spend a few weeks reading the paper, talking with the editors, and perhaps chatting about old times with Bob Greene, she would learn that an important part of her spirit lives in *Newsday* still. The daughter of Joseph Medill Patterson learned at her father's knee that fear was unacceptable, that winning his approval required her to demonstrate courage — hunting wild animals, breaking speed records in an airplane, and finally, starting a tabloid newspaper against her own father's advice, simply because she knew that it would work. That little tabloid grew up, and it began a long struggle with her father's newspaper, the *News*, for survival in New York City — an arena that has killed so many old newspapers and defeated so many efforts to launch new ones. If she could see that, she would probably decide that *Newsday*, like Alicia Patterson, is not afraid.

Interview List

Bibliography

Source Notes

Acknowledgments

Index

Interviews

THE PROCESS THAT ultimately produced this book began in late 1983, with a series of oral-history interviews conducted by Bernie Bookbinder, then the *Newsday* senior editor for projects. Bookbinder gave the tapes of those interviews to the author, who began interviewing at the end of 1986 and took on the project full time in April, 1987.

In the cases of some women who have changed their names, through marriage or otherwise, this list contains parenthetical notes of other last names by which they have been known.

BERNIE BOOKBINDER INTERVIEWS

Arnold, Marty, May 23, 1985; Aronson, Harvey, March 20, 1984; Asimov, Stanley, December 27, 1983, January 4, 1984, January 6, 1984, January 11, 1984, January 12, 1984, January 17, 1984; Attwood, William, August 21, 1984; Binn, Sheldon, May 20, 1985; Blom, June, April, 6, 1984; Bordash, Vincent, March 8, 1984, March 12, 1984, March 14, 1984, March 21, 1984; Brooks, Stan, May 20, 1985; Burton, Hal, January 25, 1984; Chernow, Buddy, April 3, 1984; Clurman, Richard, February 22, 1984; Corson, Forrest, March 26, 1984; DeFichy, Lou, June 14, 1985; Diamond, Stuart, May 29, 1985; Farrell, Frank, April 1, 1984; Fisk, Alan, May 23, 1985; Fontaine, Andre, July 17, 1985; Forst, Donald, May 28, 1984; Gebhard, Jacqueline Gilbride, February 23, 1984; Golding, Elizabeth Bass, April 5, 1984; Grider, James, September 22, 1984; Gruson, Sydney, May 23, 1985; Halpern, Howard, November 7, 1984, November 19, 1984; Hinden, Stan,

March 1, 1985; Holdsworth, Dorothy, March 31, 1984; Hollingsworth, Bob, July 18, 1984, July 23, 1984, January 22, 1985, January 24, 1985, January 30, 1985, February 1, 1985; Insolia, Anthony, June 11, 1985, June 12, 1985, June 20, 1985, June 26, 1985, July 24, 1985; Jenkins, Evan, May 20, 1985; Kellermann, Don, September 24, 1984; Levy, Hal, May 18, 1984; Lynn, Frank, May 14, 1984; Mann, Jack, May 18, 1984; Margolis, Jon, May 18, 1984; Mayer, Robert, September 14, 1984; McIlwain, William, February 2, 1984, February 8, 1984; Miles, Martha, May 29, 1985; Murray, Edna (Turi), June 24, 1985; O'Grady, Jack, May 17, 1984; O'Neill, Jim, June 13, 1985; Opotowsky, Mel, September 23, 1984; Pasley, Virginia, September 24, 1984; Peckham, Stanton, September 11, 1984, October 2, 1984; Quantrell, Marie (Hanning), March 6, 1984; Schram, Martin, March 2, 1985, March 3, 1985; Schuon, Marshall, May 23, 1985; Schwartz, Jack, May 29, 1985; Schwartz, Lou, May 7, 1984, May 11, 1984, June 18, 1984, June 29, 1984, November 20, 1984; Sheffield, Wes, August 6, 1984; Sheward, Virginia, February 16, 1984; Targe, David, May 21, 1985, May 22, 1985, June 10, 1985, July 1, 1985; Thimmesch, Nick, May 17, 1984; Woestendiek, William, July 18, 1985.

AUTHOR INTERVIEWS

Abbott, George, February 4, 1987; Abramowicz, Frank, March 11, 1988; Abrams, Arnold, December 1, 1989; Adinaro, Ernest, January 12, 1988; Agus, Carole, February 16, 1989; Albright, Alice (Arlen), June 1, l987, October 14, 1988; Albright, Joseph, December 13, 1986, July 8, 1988; Albright, Josephine, March 11, 1987, March 26, 1987, August 1, 1988, April 17, 1989; Albright, Madeleine, October 6, 1987; Alexander, Michael, September 16, 1988; Allard, Dean, October 1, 1987; Alogna, John, Sr., January 29, 1988; Amenta, Paul, October 22, 1988; Amrhein, John W., February 4, 1988; Angelo, Bonnie, March 2, 1988; Annenberg, Ted Max, September 9, 1987; Annenberg, Walter, September 9, 1987; Arneberg, Marianne, November 18, 1988; Aronson, Harvey, January 7, 1988, August 16, 1988, September 20, 1989; Asimov, Stanley, October 27, 1987, August 18, 1988, March 4, 1989; Attwood, William, November 16, 1988, February 9, 1989; Aurelio, Richard, January 9, 1988.

Back, Paul, February 8, 1988; Baker, Seth, October 12, 1987; Barbash, Maurice, March 8, 1988, November 7, 1988; Barbato, Nicholas, October 3, 1989; Barlow, Jerome, November 17, 1987; Barlow, Patricia, November 17, 1987; Barnett, Sheryl, December 21, 1988; Barra, Carl, March 16, 1988; Batalias, Peter, January 25, 1988, April 27, 1988; Bates, Betsy Buffington, December 2, 1988; Beekman, Richard, October 7, 1988; Beery, Harry, May 20, 1988; Behrens, David, October 17, 1989; Beichman, Arnold, August 4, 1988; Bell, Dennis, December 5, 1988; Bellanca, August, May 13, 1987; Bellows, James, April 7, 1988; Bender, Judith, November 30, 1988; Bensky, Larry, June 27, 1988; Bergmann, Arthur, January 15, 1988, February 9, 1988; Bernstein, James, May 18, 1988, September 13, 1988; Berry, Warren, May 3, 1988, January 10, 1990; Bialla, Rowley, December 6, 1988; Biderman, George, January 14, 1988, March 9, 1988, June 23, 1989; Bishop, Kathleen, May 29, 1987; Bitter, John, May 6, 1987; Blair, William McCormick, Jr., May 27, 1987; Blank, Diane, September 25, 1988; Blom, June, November 19, 1987; Bombeck, Erma, May 19, 1988; Bookbinder, Bernie, June 1, 1987, January 19, 1988, August 2, 1988, May 3, 1989; Bordash, Vincent, December 29, 1987, October 5, 1988; Boro, Walter, December 22, 1987; Bradlee, Benjamin, July 13, 1988; Braff, Phyllis, May 15, 1987, May 19, 1987; Brandon, Brumsic, Jr., June 9, 1988, September 11, 1989; Brandt, Robert, February 7, 1990; Brief, Kenneth, October 10, 1989; Brignoli, John, February 19, 1988; Broad, Harvey, October 8, 1987, October 16, 1987, October 10, 1988; Brooks, Arthur, February 16, 1988; Brooks, Stan, May 8, 1989; Brown, Crystal, December 24, 1986; Brown, Louis, November 7, 1988; Brown, Marian (Sprague), April 27, 1988; Bruning, Fred, May 11, 1988, June 20, 1988, August 31, 1988; Burstein, Beatrice, October 15, 1987, February 23, 1988; Burton, Hal, June 29, 1987, February 25, 1988, March 7, 1988, March 28, 1988, February 9, 1989, March 15, 1989, April 11, 1989, April 21, 1989, July 18, 1989; Byrd, Harry F., Jr., May 13, 1987; Byrne, Patricia, June 24, 1988.

Cafiero, Edmond, June 27, 1988; Cahn, William, June 28, 1989; Calderone, Joe, November 29, 1988; Callison, Charles H., March 9, 1988; Carey, Frank, February 9, 1988; Carey, Rev. Philip A., March 11, 1988; Carlino, Joseph, March 31, 1988, March 16, 1989; Carlson, Marie, February 5, 1988; Caro, Robert A., July 21, 1989; Carroll, Maurice, December 15, 1988; Carter, A. J., September 15, 1988, September 30, 1988; Carter, Sylvia, September 6, 1988; Casey, Elizabeth (Sarmento), March 15, 1988; Casselman, William, January 13, 1988; Catterson, James, June 2, 1988; Cerf, Phyllis (Wagner), September 16, 1987; Chandler, Otis, October 29, 1987; Chernow, Buddy, October 1, 1987, April 26, 1988; Chichester, Bill, October 25, 1988; Childs, Marquis, March 8, 1988; Chopin, Josephine, January 5, 1988; Christian, George, October 20, 1988; Cianciulli, Emil V., December 17, 1987; Ciolli, Rita, November 25, 1988; Civiello, Robert, November 7, 1988; Clark, Leroy, June 16, 1987; Clavin, Donald, October 9, 1987; Clurman, Richard, May 28, 1987, February 18, 1988, March 18, 1988, May 16, 1989, June 15, 1989; Cohalan, John P., Jr., February 4, 1988; Cohen, Al, November 28, 1988; Colen, B. D., January 29, 1990; Collins, Thomas, May 2, 1988; Comerford, Ed, October 21, 1987, August 17, 1988; Conlon, Walter, June 2, 1988; Cook, Christopher, September 21, 1988; Cook, Fred J., March 21, 1988; Coppola, Jo, January 14, 1988; Corson, Forrest, October 14, 1987, October 15, 1987, October 21, 1987, February 12, 1988, August 17, 1988, May 3, 1989; Cotter, John, December 21, 1988, May 10, 1990; Cowles, Gardner, III, May 2, 1988, June 9, 1988; Cowles, Jan, June 10, 1988; Cressman, Robert, October 1, 1987; Cromarty, Arthur, February 19, 1988, July 22, 1988; Crowe, Kenneth, May 23, 1988; Cruz, Roger, December 22, 1988; Cryer, Dan, January 22, 1990; Cummings, John, January 30, 1987, September 19, 1988, October 12, 1988, July 12, 1989, July 26, 1989, December 8, 1989; Cuomo, Mario, January 19, 1990; Curley, Joseph, March 23, 1988; Curran,

Edward, February 29, 1988; Curran, Fran, September 20, 1988; Curran, Thomas, December 19, 1988; Czark, Richard, August 30, 1988.

Dane, Maxwell, May 17, 1988; Davidson, Catherine Mary (Kerr), September 19, 1988, September 20, 1988; Dean, John Noel, April 21, 1987; Deas, Monsignor George T., January 26, 1988; De Bear, Cliff, December 23, 1987; DeFichy, Lou, March 22, 1988; de Florez, Suzanne, September 25, 1987; de Koenigswarter, Baroness Nica, September 17, 1987, December 9, 1987; de Koenigswarter, Janka, September 25, 1987; de Koenigswarter, Patrick, September, 25, 1987; DeKoning, John, February 8, 1988, May 25, 1989; Delatiner, Barbara, August 21, 1989; DeMarinis, Janet (Chandler), March 17, 1988; Demma, Joseph, September 22, 1988, November 2, 1989, November 27, 1989; Diamond, Edwin, September 11, 1989; Diamond, Henry, March 9, 1988; Diamond, Stuart, October 21, 1988, December 31, 1988; Dick, Jane Warner, April 9, 1987; Dillon, C. Douglas, June 20, 1989; Dolan, Robert, May 31, 1988; Donovan, Brian, June 28, 1988; Doolittle, James, October 22, 1987; Dorman, Michael, March 23, 1988, July 25, 1989; Dorsey, Thomas D., October 30, 1987, June 20, 1988; Douglas, Jack, January 13, 1988, May 11, 1988; Downie, Leonard, November 29, 1989; Downs, Henry O., May 4, 1988; Drane, Douglas, September 8, 1988; Draper, Dana, October 28, 1987; Draper, George T., Sr., December 9, 1987; Draper, George T., Jr., December 11, 1987, December 14, 1987; Dudar, Helen, December 21, 1987; Duggan, Dennis, December 1, 1988; Dunne, Richard, October 21, 1988; Dwyer, Jim, December 8, 1988.

Eberlein, Roxane, November 2, 1987; Edgerton, Jerry, September 27, 1988; Ehrlich, Jack, June 14, 1988; Eichel, Larry, September 19, 1988; Eichorn, Ike, December 2, 1987; Eisner, Peter, January 12, 1989; Ench, Robert, November 22, 1988; English, John F., October 9, 1987; Erburu, Robert F., October 30, 1987; Estrin, Richard, February 11, 1988, October 12, 1988, December 12, 1989; Ethridge, David, April 18, 1988, July 12, 1989; Ethridge, Mark F., III, April 8, 1988; Ethridge, Margaret, April 18, 1988; Evans, Carol, September 6, 1988; Eysen, Alan, May 24, 1988, September 15, 1988, November 28, 1988.

Fabian, Lou, June 9, 1988; Fagan, Thomas, March 10, 1987; Falagario, Pete, April 1, 1988; Farrell, Frank, October 15, 1987, September 27, 1988; Feinberg, Arthur, July 10, 1987; Fellman, Fred, August 18, 1988; Fellman, Lillian, June 2, 1988; Ferguson, James Edward, September 29, 1987; Ferguson, Ruth, September, 29, 1987; Ferre, Luis, August 16, 1989; Fetherston, Drew, November 10, 1988; First, Wesley, March 22, 1988; Fisher, Bernadette (Wheeler), July 30, 1987, December 22, 1987, October 20, 1988; FitzGerald, Frances, March 21, 1988; Fitzgerald, James, October 28, 1988, January 10, 1990; Fontaine, Andre, October 20, 1987; Foreman, Gene, September 27, 1988; Forgione, Michael, December 21, 1987; Forst, Donald, September 23, 1988, December 9, 1988, November 16, 1989, April 5, 1990; Fountaine, George, May 21, 1987, October 2, 1987; Fox, Douglas, March 2, 1989, February 6, 1990, February 13, 1990; Fox, Martha, January 5, 1988; Fox, Sylvan, April 7, 1988; Frank, Ben, June 18, 1988;

Fresco, Robert, February 3, 1989; Freilicher, Ira, January 15, 1990; Friedman, Josh, January 15, 1990; Fritchey, Clayton, May 27, 1987; Frogge, John, October 20, 1987, October 27, 1987, March 14, 1988, September 12, 1988; Frymer, Murry, January 29, 1990.

Gaeta, Al, September 7, 1988; Gagnon, Joseph, March 17, 1988; Galant, Richard, October 24, 1988, November 8, 1988; Gates, Carey, March 10, 1989; Gatewood, Dallas, October 19, 1988; Gebhard, Jacqueline Gilbride, October 6, 1987, November 5, 1987, March 17, 1988, March 15, 1989; Gelman, David, November 14, 1988; Genauer, Emily, December 30, 1988; Genovese, James, January 28, 1988; Gerard, Jane (Chekenian) November 19, 1987; Gianelli, Paul, September 16, 1988; Gianotti, Peter, October 13, 1988; Gibson, Jack, June 16, 1988; Giddens, Dale, December 3, 1987; Gilkes, Alfred, January, 4, 1988; Gillespie, Robert, May 6, 1988; Giordano, Rita, December 30, 1988; Gleason, Harold, November 11, 1988; Golding, Elizabeth Bass, June 21, 1988; Goldstein, Marilyn, October 5, 1988; Goltz, Gene, June 1, 1988; Goodman, Peter, December 13, 1988; Gordon, Willie, April 27, 1988; Gottlieb, Leo, April 30, 1987, May 21, 1987, June 11, 1987, September 10, 1987, April 19, 1988, September 23, 1988; Graham, Shirley, June 15, 1988; Grause, Edward, March 14, 1988; Green, Stanley, March 30, 1988; Greenamyer, Richard, November 18, 1987; Greenamyer, Ruth Herrera, February 5, 1988; Greene, Mary, January 29, 1988; Greene, Michael, January 26, 1988; Greene, Robert W., January 23, 1988, March 1, 1988, May 18, 1988, June 20, 1988, September 5, 1988, September 17, 1988, October 25, 1988, November 29, 1988, January 14, 1989, April 29, 1989, May 3, 1989, May 13, 1989, September 23, 1989, October 2, 1989, November 25, 1989, December 16, 1989; Greenley, Fred, June 12, 1987, November 3, 1987; Grider, James, December 2, 1989; Gross, Kenneth, October 14, 1988, January 31, 1990; Gross, Martin, February 9, 1987; Grossberger, Lewis, September 29, 1988; Grossman, Karl, March 9, 1988, March 10, 1988, June 6, 1988, October 24, 1988; Grossnick, Roy, October 1, 1987, January 11, 1988; Gruson, Sydney, October 26, 1988.

Hadjin, James, May 18, 1988; Hairston, James, November 14, 1988; Halaby, Najeeb, March 30, 1988; Hall, Charlotte, December 12, 1988; Hallion, Richard, June 15, 1987; Hamill, Denis, February 6, 1990; Hamill, Pete, May 6, 1988; Hamilton, David, September 20, 1988, November 23, 1988; Hanes, Hope, September 18, 1987; Hannan, Anne (Radiloff), November 5, 1987, August 15, 1988; Hanscom, Leslie, June 30, 1988; Harris, Amanda, September 6, 1988; Harris, Wallace, January 18, 1988, March 15, 1988, March 8, 1989; Harrison, John R., June 1, 1988; Hartmann, John, December 30, 1987; Hasby, Karen, December 8, 1988; Hauck, Janet, April 5, 1988, April 17, 1989; Hauck, Jenny (Ward), February 3, 1987; Hausrath, Matte Prince, October 10, 1987; Hausrath, Ralph, October 10, 1987; Hayashi, Tetsumaro, April 6, 1988, July 18, 1989; Heine, Inez, January 27, 1988; Heisler, Robert, December 9, 1988; Henican, Ellis, December 29, 1988; Hershey, Edward, July 27, 1987, January 20, 1988, June 28, 1988; Hessler, Robert, December 28, 1987; Hevesi, Dennis, January 23, 1990; Hickmann, Charles, November 29, 1988; Higgins, Eugene, November 17, 1988; Hildebrand, John, September 8, 1988; Hinden, Stan, July 18, 1988; Hinds, Rita, September 25, 1987; Hines, Carmen, March 4, 1988; Hoenig, Gary, November 17, 1988; Hoge, James, June 30, 1988; Hohenberg, John, June 8, 1988; Holden, Stewart, February 18, 1988; Holdsworth, Dorothy, May 11, 1987, May 26, 1987, November 18, 1987, April 5, 1988; Hollingsworth, Bob, April 13, 1989; Hoover, Julie, June 29, 1988, July 13, 1988; Howell, Beryl, June 30, 1988; Howell, Ron, December 22, 1988; Hoxie, R. Gordon, March 29, 1988; Huesch, Heinz, January 7, 1988; Hug, Arthur, April 18, 1989; Hughes, Andrew, May 21, 1987, September 10, 1987, April 29, 1988; Hughes, Robert L., April 11, 1989.

Iacona, Phil, April 22, 1988; Ibarguen, Alberto, March 24, 1989; Insolia, Anthony, June 4, 1987, October 31, 1988, November 1, 1988, July 26, 1989, January 10, 1990, January 23, 1990; Ippolito, Andrew, July 7, 1989; Isaacs, Stan, May 15, 1989; Isenberg, Steven, December 1, 1988, January 16, 1990; Ives, Elizabeth, March 29, 1988.

Jackson, Kenneth T., April 19, 1989; Jacoby, Mark, November 22, 1988; Jaenicke, Juergen, May 6, 1988; James, W. H., December 22, 1989; Jansen, Raymond A., Jr., January 8, 1988, December 6, 1989; Jinks, Larry, May 10, 1988; Johansson, Paul, December 15, 1987; Johnke, William, April 22, 1987; Johnson, Frank S., Jr., March 14, 1989, May 17, 1989; Johnson, Robert M., June 4, 1987, December 12, 1988, December 27, 1988, January 3, 1990; Johnson, Thomas A., April 19, 1988, July 27, 1989; Jones, C. H. Tunnicliffe, June 18, 1987.

Kahn, Daniel, October 24, 1988; Kahn, David, February 16, 1988; Kappler, Frank, March 21, 1988; Keane, Robert, November 15, 1988, December 8, 1989; Kellermann, Don, October 29, 1987; Kelly, Barbara, March 16, 1989; Kempton, Murray, May 20, 1989; Kerins, Annabelle, September 12, 1988; Kerr, Kathleen, November 25, 1988; Kessel, Richard, November 9, 1988; Keyes, Ralph, June 1, 1988; Kilpatrick, James, May 4, 1988; King, Cynthia, February 3, 1987; Kinsolving, Charles, November 8, 1988; Kirshner, Marilyn (Draper), December 7, 1987; Kitman, Marvin, August 22, 1989; Klappert, Herman, October 26, 1987; Klein, John V. N., June 8, 1988, November 30, 1988; Klinger, Laura, March 2, 1987; Klock, Rebecca, May 5, 1988, September 15, 1988; Klurfeld, James, December 12, 1989; Knoll, Joseph, December 30, 1987; Knott, James, April 15, 1987; Koppelman, Lee, December 18, 1987; Kramer, Joel, September 9, 1988; Kubasik, Ben, June 30, 1988; Kunkel, Albert, October 23, 1987.

La Corte, John, July 7, 1987; Lambert, Bruce, October 10, 1988, October 13, 1988; Laventhol, David, December 22, 1986, December 30, 1986, October 30, 1987, January 18, 1989; Lawrence, David, Jr., June 13, 1988; Lawrence, Francis, August 30, 1988, January 11, 1989; Lawson-Johnston, Peter O., June 12, 1987, October 31, 1988, September 20, 1989; Leahy, John, October 17, 1988; Lechtrecker, George, April 6, 1988; Lefkowitz, Louis, September 20, 1988; Leland, Timothy, May 31, 1988; Lem, Arthur, April 21, 1988, May 19, 1988;

Lem, Rose, June 21, 1989; Levitt, Leonard, December 8, 1988; Levitt, William, December 18, 1987; Levy, Doris, February 12, 1988; Levy, Hal, July 19, 1988; Lewis, Chester, July 11, 1989; Like, Irving, March 9, 1988, November 7, 1988; Lindbergh, Anne Morrow, January 13, 1989; Lionel, Daniel, May 4, 1988; Lipson, Milton, August 2, 1988; Littlejohn, Francis, January 11, 1988; Lobsenz, Norman, November 12, 1987; Lomask, Milton, June 23, 1987; Lord, Jere W., Jr., March 18, 1988, November 9, 1988; Lowe, Ed, May 12, 1988, October 18, 1988; Luchsinger, John, May 9, 1988; Lynch, Daniel, June 3, 1988; Lyon, Charles, February 17, 1988.

MacCary, John W., October 19, 1987; Macy, William K., Jr., May 8, 1989; Maerki, Vic, May 27, 1987; Maher, John, March 9, 1988, June 8, 1988, October 24, 1988; Mancusi, Attilio, February 1, 1988; Mann, Jack, June 24, 1988; Mannix, Dan, November 2, 1988; Mapel, Evelyn, December 4, 1987; Marciante, Bonita, January 8, 1988; Margiotta, Joseph, November 22, 1988; Marino, Ralph, October 20, 1988; Markowitz, Sam, August 31, 1988; Marlens, Hanna, August 16, 1988; Marro, Anthony, February 27, 1987, May 28, 1987, November 25, 1987, May 12, 1988, November 17, 1988, September 5, 1989, January 2, 1990, February 14, 1990, May 11, 1990; Martenhoff, James, November 20, 1987; Maynard, Kathryn, October 8, 1987; McAlary, Mike, December 19, 1988; McAllister, Connie, June 8, 1989, July 18, 1989; McCaffrey, Daniel X., February 19, 1988; McCaffrey, Sandra, February 19, 1988; McCormick, Kate, November 10, 1988, December 12, 1989; McCoy, Alfred, September 2, 1988; McCrary, John Reagan, June 17, 1988; McDonald, John, June 10, 1988; McGowan, Edward, June 8, 1988; McGrady, Michael R., April 28, 1988, September 15, 1989, September 22, 1989; McGuire, James W., Jr., January 11, 1988; McIlwain, William, February 11, 1988, February 23, 1988, July 20, 1988, August 3, 1989, September 18, 1989; McIntyre, Mark, August 29, 1989; McLaughlin, Irene (O'Sullivan), December 30, 1987; McMullan, Penelope (McMillan), September 21, 1988; McNulty, Diane, December 23, 1988; Meadows, Gail, September 12, 1988; Melton, James, April 5, 1988; Merahn, Harold, December 28, 1988; Merck, Dawn, September 1, 1988; Merck, Walter, February 3, 1987, September 1, 1988; Messer, Thomas, April 11, 1988; Meyer, Pucci, September 29, 1988; Michelson, Dorothy (Livingston), December 23, 1986, February 3, 1987; Milas, Charles J., June 10, 1988; Miller, Andrew, April 16, 1987; Mills, William F., Jr., June 16, 1987, December 11, 1987; Mitchell, Alison, December 4, 1988; Moats, Alice-Leone, December 7, 1987; Mobilio, Al, September 28, 1988; Mollenhoff, Clark, March 7, 1988, November 20, 1989; Mollison, Andrew, October 17, 1989; Morgan, Jerry, June 23, 1988, October 19, 1988; Moritsugu, Henry, September 26, 1988; Morris, Tom, April 15, 1988, October 7, 1988; Moyers, Bill D., February 20, 1988, September 24, 1988, August 14, 1989, September 28, 1989; Muhammad, Ozier, December 15, 1988; Murchison, Charles, March 12, 1987; Murray, Edna (Turi), October 7, 1987, February 10, 1989; Murray, Will, October 18, 1988; Myers, Sid, May 17, 1988.

Nadjari, Maurice, June 29, 1988; Nagourney, James, October 17, 1988;

Neuharth, Allen H., July 1, 1988; Nickerson, Eugene, July 21, 1988; Nightingale, Jim, July 31, 1987; Noble, J. Kendrick, Jr., February 13, 1990; Nofziger, Lyn, September 7, 1988; Norris, James, December 6, 1989; Novinski, William, January 14, 1987; Noyes, Florence (Carleton), May 14, 1987.

O'Brien, Charles P., November 11, 1988; O'Brien, Henry F., September 8, 1988, April 17, 1989; O'Grady, Jack, January 15, 1988; O'Hearn, Bradford W., June 17, 1988, September 21, 1988; O'Leary, Dennis, January 15, 1987; Oliphant, Pat, May 11, 1988; O'Neill, Jim, November 18, 1987, February 1, 1988, February 13, 1988, May 9, 1988, June 22, 1988; O'Neill, Maureen, August 19, 1988; O'Neill, Michael, September 6, 1988; Opotowsky, Mel, October 18, 1988; Orshan, Ed, June 16, 1987; O'Sullivan, Frank, December 30, 1987; Owens, Patrick, September 15, 1989; Ozechowski, Joseph, December 12, 1987.

Pacca, Carmine, March 10, 1987; Page, Susan, December 5, 1988; Page, Tim, December 23, 1988; Paltrow, Scot, December 21, 1988; Pangalos, Mary (Manilla), May 9, 1988; Partiss, Leonard F., Sr., December 16, 1987; Patman, Jean, December 16, 1988; Patterson, James, June 22, 1987; Patterson, Lawrence, April 22, 1988, July 26, 1989, September 11, 1989; Patterson, Michael, November 25, 1988; Payne, Les, September 20, 1988, October 20, 1988, December 20, 1988; Peckham, Stanton, July 2, 1987, July 9, 1987, July 16, 1987, October 22, 1987, February 18, 1989, August 24, 1989; Pell, Art, May 7, 1987; Peracchio, Adrian, November 23, 1988; Perfall, Arthur, March 2, 1988, April 13, 1989, October 12, 1989; Perlik, Charles A., Jr., June 28, 1988; Petersdorf, Nicholas W., February 9, 1988; Pfeifle, C. Robert, January 19, 1988, January 21, 1988, April 26, 1988; Phillips, Sherman, February 3, 1988; Pierzgalski, Chet, September 28, 1988; Pike, Otis, March 7, 1988; Pisano, Carl, November 8, 1988; Plate, Thomas, July 19, 1989; Pozen, Walter, March 10, 1988; Price, Peter, December 12, 1988.

Quantrell, Marie (Hanning), December 28, 1987, February 17, 1989; Quesada, Elwood R., March 30, 1988; Quinn, Marie De Carmine, January 6, 1988.

Rabb, Harriet, November 6, 1989; Radiloff, Si, November 5, 1987, August 15, 1988; Rapp, Marvin, March 24, 1988; Raver, Anne, November 9, 1988; Rawls, William B., January 26, 1988, November 29, 1988; Rayack, Elton, September 1, 1988; Rayack, Jean Radlauer, September 1, 1988; Raynor, Julie, January 5, 1989; Raynor, Penny, November 11, 1988; Reilly, Adrianne Baker, April 27, 1987; Reilly, Bernard J., March 9, 1988; Renner, Thomas C., June 21, 1988, October 13, 1988; Reno, Robert, January 31, 1990; Rettaliata, Jack, December 29, 1987, February 9, 1988; Riegel, O. W., June 16, 1987; Risedorf, Gwen, November 17, 1987; Risedorf, Lucy, November 5, 1987, March 27, 1989; Ritter, Bill, January 20, 1989; Robinson, Richard, October 12, 1989; Rodgers, James, April 5, 1988; Rosellini, Lynn, November 21, 1989; Rosen, Murray, April 26, 1988; Rosenbluth, David, March 28, 1988; Rosenfeld, Harry, June 28, 1988; Rosenfeld, Neill, July 19, 1989; Rottkamp, Cyril, December 1, 1989; Rovegno, Jack, June 2, 1987;

Royce, Knut, July 18, 1988; Rubino, Bruce, June 8, 1988; Ruinsky, Sam, October 17, 1988; Ryan, Kenneth, June 16, 1987.

Salinger, Pierre, June 29, 1989; Samsot, Robert, September 12, 1988, October 3, 1988; Sanak, James, December 10, 1987; Sanborne, Philippe, August 17, 1988; Sandler, Richard, November 28, 1988; Sandomir, Richard, January 31, 1990; Sanford, Marian, May 11, 1987; Sarmento, Al, February 12, 1988; Scales, James Ralph, May 17, 1988; Schaer, Sidney C., September 30, 1988; Schaffler, Jeffrey, May 6, 1988; Schanberg, Sydney, December 9, 1988; Schefer, Michael, May 5, 1988; Schiff, Dorothy, March 1, 1988, March 2, 1988; Schindler, William, May 10, 1988; Schmidt, Art, October 25, 1988; Schneider, Georgia, April 27, 1988; Schneider, Howard, October 11, 1988, December 16, 1988; Schram, Martin, October 13, 1989; Schroth, Frank D., Jr., July 20, 1988; Schroth, Raymond, August 15, 1988; Schroth, Thomas, July 20, 1988; Schwarner, Carlton, June 8, 1988; Schwartz, Jack, May 3, 1988; Schwartz, Lou, December 27, 1988; Schwartzkopf, George, April 23, 1987, March 28, 1988; Schwenk, Edwin, May 25, 1988; Scovel, Jim, September 13, 1988; Seaman, Lewis, December 7, 1987, April 26, 1988; Seldes, George, August 31, 1987; Selvin, Barbara, December 29, 1988; Senft, William, May 11, 1988; Sexton, William, December 28, 1988; Seybold, Jonathan W., September 9, 1988; Shanahan, Geraldine, May 26, 1988; Shapiro, S. O., May 17, 1988; Sheward, Virginia, October 16, 1987, October 19, 1987, March 31, 1988; Shipp, Bill, June 1, 1988; Shore, Sam, April 21, 1987; Siben, Sidney, January 7, 1988, April 29, 1988, May 26, 1988; Silberling, Edwyn, June 16, 1988; Singer, Phyllis, November 20, 1989; Singleton, Don, January 10, 1990; Skapley, Rosemary, September 14, 1988; Smith, Bernard C., June 6, 1988; Smith, Don, June 19, 1989; Smith, Jean Cappa, December 14, 1987; Smith, Rex, November 18, 1988, March 29, 1989; Smith, Roane, October 28, 1988; Smith, Robert Ellis, May 27, 1988, September 11, 1989, September 18, 1989; Smothers, Ronald, August 15, 1988; Solow, Seymour, May 5, 1988; Sorg, Frank, June 16, 1988; Soriano, William J., June 9, 1988; Squire, Jack, May 12, 1988, January 9, 1990, January 10, 1990; Stack, Aurelie Dwyer, July 29, 1987; Starace, Carl A., July 13, 1987, October 7, 1987; Starr, David, October 17, 1988; Steinbeck, Elaine, September 16, 1987, February 5, 1988; Stephens, Woody, March 24, 1988; Stevens, Edmund W., September 27, 1988; Stevenson, Adlai E., III, March 5, 1987, April 8, 1987, November 2, 1987; Stevenson, John Fell, May 13, 1987; Stevenson, Nancy, April 8, 1987; Stites, C. Thomas, September 28, 1988; Straight, Michael, January 6, 1988; Straus, Oscar, II, May 20, 1987; Straus, Roger W., Jr., May 20, 1987, June 28, 1989; Strum, Charles, October 10, 1988; Sturcke, Peter A., January 12, 1988; Sutter, John Joseph, June 7, 1989; Swanson, Elston, March 28, 1988.

Targe, David, October 12, 1988, November 21, 1988, January 13, 1989, February 20, 1989; Taylor, Thomas, September 15, 1988, July 26, 1989; Tedeschi, George, January 16, 1987, October 25, 1988; Tewksbury, John, April 13, 1988; Thom, Charles R., July 1, 1988; Tiernan, Robert, October 27, 1988; Tilton, Katherine, July 10, 1987; Toedtman, James, December 15, 1988; Topol,

Manny, March 15, 1988; Townsend, Paul, December 9, 1987, March 11, 1988, March 24, 1988, March 15, 1989, June 21, 1989; Tree, Marietta, April 30, 1987; Treen, Joseph, October 14, 1988; Trillin, Calvin, June 13, 1988; Trimboli, Rev. Donald J., September 2, 1989; Tuccillo, Fred, May 16, 1988, November 15, 1988.

Udall, Stewart, March 7, 1988, March 8, 1988; Ulmer, Ursula, November 15, 1988; Umbria, Claire, January 25, 1988.

Valenti, Jack, April 25, 1988; Van de Maele, Joan, June 11, 1987, July 15, 1987, November 11, 1988; Vanden Heuvel, John, October 13, 1988; Vanderbilt, Alfred G., October 27, 1987; Van de Water, Kenneth, June 16, 1987, October 13, 1987, May 11, 1988; Van Doorn, John, October 2, 1987, July 29, 1989, January 31, 1990; Van Haintze, William, May 16, 1988; Van Nostrand, Elisabet, December 2, 1988; Villa, Jacqueline, October 26, 1987, March 19, 1988; Viskupic, Gary, October 19, 1988; Volkman, Ernest, September 29, 1988, January 12, 1990; Voorhees, William K., February 2, 1988.

Wainwright, Stuyvesant, May 25, 1988; Wald, Richard, June 15, 1988; Waldman, Edward, May 27, 1988; Waldman, Myron, December 5, 1988; Waldrop, Frank C., October 20, 1988; Wall, Adele, May 19, 1987; Wallach, Allan, April 11, 1988; Ward, Bud, December 9, 1987; Washburn, A. Lawrence, Jr., January 22, 1990; Washburn, David, June 24, 1988; Weber, Chris, May 23, 1988; Weber, Harvey, April 15, 1988; Weber, Mary Anne, June 6, 1988; Wechsler, Nancy, January 11, 1988; Wendland, Michael, November 17, 1989; Wheeler, George, April 14, 1988; White, Theresa Kiernan, August 21, 1989; Wick, Steve, October 6, 1988; Wiemer, Robert, September 2, 1988; Wiener, Caryn Eve (Murray), December 6, 1988; Wild, S. Kendall, March 10, 1987; Wilkens, William, January 28, 1988; Williams, Robert, May 24, 1988; Williams, Phillip, October 4, 1989; Williams, Roger, June 11, 1987; Williams, Thomas, January 19, 1988; Woestendiek, William, February 24, 1988, March 25, 1988, April 5, 1988, December 20, 1988, June 15, 1989, June 23, 1989; Woldt, Harold F., Jr., February 12, 1990; Wolf, Bob, November 23, 1988; Wolling, Elaine, May 4, 1988; Wood, Francis, January 19, 1987, March 29, 1988; Wood, Gardner, May 7, 1987; Wood, Jean, January 19, 1987; Wood, Margaret (Shaw), April 11, 1987; Wood, Moyer, May 7, 1987; Wood, Paul, January 14, 1987; Wyckoff, Edith, October 8, 1987; Wyrick, Bob, December 5, 1988.

Ying, Richard, September 23, 1988; Youchah, Michael, October 26, 1988, February 9, 1990; Young, Shirley, February 12, 1988.

Zander, Dick, March 8, 1989; Zellner, Robert, April 28, 1987, January 13, 1988; Zinman, David, October 21, 1988; Zirkel, Don, January 21, 1988.

Bibliography

BOOKS

AMBROSE, STEPHEN E. *Eisenhower: Soldier, General of the Army, President-Elect*. New York: Simon and Schuster, 1985.

ANDERSON, PATRICK. *The Presidents' Men: White House Assistants of Franklin D. Roosevelt, Harry S Truman, Dwight D. Eisenhower, John F. Kennedy and Lyndon B. Johnson*. Garden City: Doubleday, 1968.

ARTHUR, REGINALD WRIGHT. *Contact! Naval Aviators Assigned Numbers 1 to 2000*. Washington: Naval Aviator Register, 1967.

ASHE, PENELOPE. *Naked Came the Stranger*. New York: Lyle Stuart, 1969.

ATTWOOD, WILLIAM. *Making It Through Middle Age: Notes While In Transit*. New York: Atheneum, 1982.

———. *The Twilight Struggle: Tales of the Cold War*. New York: Harper & Row, 1987.

BENJAMINSON, PETER. *Death in the Afternoon: America's Newspaper Giants Struggle for Survival*. Kansas City: Andrews, McMeel & Parker, 1984.

BERGER, MEYER. *The Story of the New York Times, 1851-1951*. New York: Simon and Schuster, 1951.

BERGES, MARSHALL. *The Life and Times of Los Angeles: A Newspaper, a Family and a City*. New York: Atheneum, 1984.

BERNSTEIN, CARL, and BOB WOODWARD. *All the President's Men*. New York: Simon and Schuster, 1974.

BIRMINGHAM, STEPHEN. *Our Crowd*. New York: Harper & Row, 1967.

BISHOP, LOUIS FAUGERES. *The Birth of a Specialty*. New York: Vantage, 1977.

BONANNO, JOSEPH, with SERGIO LALLI. *A Man of Honor: The Autobiography of Joseph Bonanno*. New York: Simon and Schuster, 1983.

BRENNER, MARIE. *House of Dreams: The Bingham Family of Louisville*. New York: Random House, 1988.

BROWN, ALDEN V. *The Tablet: The First Seventy-Five Years*. Brooklyn: The Tablet Publishing Company, 1983.

CARO, ROBERT A. *The Power Broker: Robert Moses and the Fall of New York*. New York: Vintage Books, 1975.

CHAPMAN, JOHN. *Tell It to Sweeney: The Informal History of the New York Daily News*. Westport: Greenwood Press, 1961.

COCHRAN, JACQUELINE, and MARYANN BUCKNUM BRINLEY. *Jackie Cochran: The Autobiography of the Greatest Woman Pilot in Aviation History*. New York: Bantam Books, 1987.

COLE, WAYNE S. *Charles A. Lindbergh and the Battle Against Intervention in World War II*. New York: Harcourt Brace Jovanovich, 1974.

COWLES, GARDNER JR. *Mike Looks Back: The Memoirs of Gardner Cowles, Founder of Look Magazine*. New York: Gardner Cowles, 1985.

DAVIS, JOHN H. *The Guggenheims: An American Epic*. New York: William Morrow, 1978.

DE KOENIGSWARTER, JULES. *Savoir Dire Non*. Paris: de Koenigswarter, 1976.

DICK, JANE WARNER. *Volunteers and the Making of Presidents*. New York: Dodd, Mead, 1980.

DORMAN, MICHAEL. *We Shall Overcome*. New York: Delacorte Press, 1964.

ELLIS, L. NATHAN. *Newsprint: Producers, Publishers, Political Pressures*. New Brunswick: Rutgers University Press, 1960.

ELSON, ROBERT T. *The World of Time Inc.: The Intimate History of a Publishing Enterprise, 1941-1960*. New York: Atheneum, 1973.

EVANS, HAROLD. *Newspaper Design: An Illustrated Guide to Layout*. New York: Holt, Rinehart and Winston, 1973.

FISHMAN, ROBERT. *Bourgeois Utopias: The Rise and Fall of Suburbia*. New York: Basic Books, 1987.

FORD, HENRY, and SAMUEL CROTHER. *My Life and Work*. Garden City: Doubleday, 1922.

FOWLER, GENE. *Timber Line*. New York: Covici Friede, 1933.

GANS, HERBERT J. *The Levittowners: How People Live and Politic in Suburbia*. New York: Pantheon, 1967.

GIES, JOSEPH. *The Colonel of Chicago*. New York: Dutton, 1979.

GILLESPIE, ROBERT B. *The Crossword Mystery*. New York: Raven House, 1982.

GORDON, MAX. *Live at the Village Vanguard*. New York: St. Martin's Press, 1980.

GOTTLIEB, ROBERT, and IRENE WOLT. *Thinking Big*. New York: G.P. Putnam's Sons, 1977.

GREENE, ROBERT W. *The Sting Man*. New York: Dutton, 1981.

GROSSMAN, KARL. *Power Crazy: Is LILCO Turning Shoreham into America's Chernobyl?* New York: Grove, 1986.

GUGGENHEIM, HARRY F. *The Seven Skies*. New York: G.P. Putnam's Sons, 1930.

―――. *The United States and Cuba: A Study of International Relations*. New York: Macmillan, 1934.

GUGGENHEIM MEDAL BOARD OF AWARD. *The Guggenheim Medalists: Architects of the Age of Flight*. New York: The Guggenheim Medal Board of Award, 1964.

HALBERSTAM, DAVID. *The Powers That Be*. New York: Knopf, 1979.

HALLION, RICHARD P. *Legacy of Flight: The Guggenheim Contribution to American Aviation.* Seattle: University of Washington Press, 1977.

HEALY, PAUL F. *Cissy: A Biography of Eleanor M. "Cissy" Patterson.* Garden City: Doubleday, 1966.

HODGES, ARTHUR L. *Long Island's Greatest Newspaper.* Rockville Centre: *Nassau Daily Review,* 1931.

HOGE, ALICE ALBRIGHT. *Cissy Patterson: The Life of Eleanor Medill Patterson, Publisher and Editor of the Washington Times-Herald.* New York: Random House, 1966.

HOSOKAWA, BILL. *Thunder in the Rockies: The Incredible Denver Post.* New York: William Morrow, 1976.

HOYT, EDWIN P., JR. *The Guggenheims and the American Dream.* New York: Funk and Wagnalls, 1967.

JACKSON, KENNETH T. *Crabgrass Frontier: The Suburbanization of the United States.* New York: Oxford University Press, 1985.

JOHNSON, WALTER, and CAROL EVANS, editors. *The Papers of Adlai E. Stevenson,* Volumes 1 to 8. New York: Little, Brown, 1972-1979.

KAPLAN, SAMUEL. *The Dream Deferred: People, Politics and Planning in Suburbia.* New York: Seabury Press, 1976.

KEATING, WILLIAM. *The Man Who Rocked the Boat.* New York: Harper & Brothers, 1956.

KLUGER, RICHARD. *The Paper: The Life and Death of the New York Herald Tribune.* New York: Knopf, 1986.

LAZO, MARIO. *Dagger in the Heart: American Policy Failures in Cuba.* New York: Funk & Wagnalls, 1968.

LEHMAN, MILTON. *This High Man, The Life of Robert H. Goddard.* New York: Farrar, Straus and Company, 1963.

LINDBERGH, ANNE MORROW. *Bring Me a Unicorn.* New York: Harcourt Brace Jovanovich, 1972.

——— . *Hour of Gold, Hour of Lead.* New York: Harcourt Brace Jovanovich, 1973.

——— . *War Within and War Without.* New York: Harcourt Brace Jovanovich, 1980.

LINDBERGH, CHARLES A. *Autobiography of Values.* New York: Harcourt Brace Jovanovich, 1976.

LITTLETON, MARTIN W., and KYLE CRICHTON. *My Partner-in-law: The Life and Times of George Morton Levy.* New York: Farrar, Straus & Cudahy, 1957.

LOMASK, MILTON. *Seed Money.* New York: Farrar, Straus and Company, 1964.

MARTIN, JOHN BARTLOW. *Adlai Stevenson of Illinois.* Garden City: Doubleday, 1976.

——— . *Adlai Stevenson and the World.* Garden City, Doubleday, 1977.

MARTIN, RALPH G. *Cissy: The Extraordinary Life of Eleanor Medill Patterson.* New York: Simon and Schuster, 1979.

McCOY, ALFRED W. *The Politics of Heroin in Southeast Asia.* New York: Harper & Row, 1972.

McGIVENA, LEO E. *The News: The First Fifty Years of New York's Picture Newspaper.* New York: News Syndicate, 1969.

McGRADY, MIKE. *A Dove in Vietnam.* New York: Funk & Wagnalls, 1968.

——— . *Stranger Than Naked or How to Write Dirty Books For Fun and Profit.* New York: Peter H. Wyden, 1970.

McILWAIN, WILLIAM. *A Farewell to Alcohol.* New York: Random House, 1971.

McKEEVER, PORTER. *Adlai Stevenson: His Life and Legacy.* New York: William Morrow, 1989.

MEDVED, MICHAEL. *The Shadow Presidents: The Secret History of the Chief Executives and Their Top Aides.* New York: Times Books, 1979.

MEEKER, RICHARD H. *Newspaperman: S.I. Newhouse and the Business of News.* New York: Ticknor & Fields, 1983.

MITGANG, HERBERT, editor. *The Letters of Carl Sandburg.* New York: Harcourt, Brace & World, 1968.

MOLLENHOFF, CLARK. *Investigative Reporting.* New York: Macmillan, 1981.

MORGAN, GWEN, and ARTHUR VEYSEY. *Poor Little Rich Boy.* Carpentersville, Illinois: Crossroads Communications, 1985.

MOYERS, BILL. *Listening to America: A Traveler Rediscovers His Country.* New York: Harper's Magazine Press, 1971.

O'CONNOR, HARVEY. *The Guggenheims: The Making of An American Dynasty.* New York: Covici Friede, 1937.

PASLEY, VIRGINIA. *21 Stayed.* New York: Farrar, Straus and Cudahy, 1955.

RASCOE, BURTON. *Before I Forget.* New York: The Literary Guild of America, 1937.

ROBERTS, CHALMERS M. *The Washington Post: The First 100 Years.* Boston: Houghton Mifflin, 1977.

ROSS, WALTER S. *The Last Hero: Charles A. Lindbergh.* New York: Harper & Row, 1964.

SALISBURY, HARRISON E. *Without Fear or Favor.* New York: Times Books, 1980.

SANDBURG, CARL. *Abraham Lincoln: The War Years.* New York: Harcourt, Brace & World, 1926.

SCHROTH, RAYMOND A. *The Eagle and Brooklyn: A Community Newspaper, 1841-1955.* Westport: Greenwood Press, 1974.

STEPHENS, WOODY, with JAMES BROUGH. *Guess I'm Lucky.* Garden City: Doubleday, 1985.

TALESE, GAY. *The Kingdom and the Power.* New York: World, 1969.

TEBBEL, JOHN. *The Story of the McCormicks, Medills and Pattersons: An American Dynasty.* Garden City: Doubleday, 1947.

UHLAN, EDWARD. *Dynamo Jim Stiles: Pioneer of Progress.* New York: Exposition Press, 1959.

WALDROP, FRANK C. *McCormick of Chicago.* New York: Prentice-Hall, 1966.

WENDLAND, MICHAEL F. *The Arizona Project.* Kansas City: Sheed Andrews and McMeel, 1977.

WISE, DAVID. *The Politics of Lying.* New York: Random House, 1973.

WOODS, ALLAN. *Modern Newspaper Production.* New York: Harper and Row, 1963.

PERIODICALS

ABRAMS, ARNOLD. "Product of the Times." *The Newsday Magazine*, October 4, 1987, pages 14-37.

ALEXANDER, JACK. "Vox Populi." *The New Yorker*, August 6, 1938, pages 16-21; August 13, pages 19-24; August 20, pages 19-23.

ARCHITECTURAL FORUM STAFF. "A Complete House for $6,990." *Architectural Forum*, May 1947.

ARONSON, HARVEY. "The Captain and the Kid. *New York*, March 30, 1970, 44-47.

BRUNING, FRED. "Goodbye Levittown: 40 Years Later, It's Just Another Suburb." *The Newsday Magazine*, October 4, 1987, pages 8-12.

BUCKLEY, THOMAS. "How the C.I.A. Got Hooked on Heroin." *Penthouse*, June 1973, pages 54-122.

BUSINESS WEEK STAFF. "*Newsday* Knocks Harder on New York City's Door." *Business Week*, May 27, 1985, pages 40-42.

CLURMAN, RICHARD. "Alicia in Wonderland." *Time*, September 13, 1954, pages 52-58.

DIAMOND, EDWIN. "Will Big Otis Try to Cross the East River?" *New York*, August 14, 1970, pages 42-45.

――――. "Queens' Ransom." *New York*, April 1, 1985, pages 16-19.

FORTUNE STAFF. "The Industry Capitalism Forgot." *Fortune*, August 1947, pages 61-170.

HAUSRATH, RALPH. "The Early Days of *Newsday*." *Long Island Forum*, July 1975, pages 128-135; August 1975, pages 148-155; September 1975, pages 170-178.

――――. "The Sea Took Heavy Toll in 1951." *Long Island Forum*, September 1977, pages 172-177.

――――. "'King' Macy's Last Campaign." *Long Island Forum*, April 1978, pages 82-87.

――――. "*Newsday*: The Postwar Years." *Long Island Forum*, January 1979, pages 4-11.

――――. "*Newsday*: The Suffolk Operation." *Long Island Forum*, February 1979, pages 40-46.

――――. "*Newsday*: The Berlin Airlift." *Long Island Forum*, March 1979, pages 64-70.

――――. "The Train Wrecks of 1950." *Long Island Forum*, October 1980, pages 212-218.

――――. "When *Newsday* Came to Suffolk." *Long Island Forum*, April 1987, pages 72-75.

――――. "A Birthday Party at Falaise." *Long Island Forum*, June 1987, pages 120-125.

――――. "Winning a Pulitzer and the Kentucky Derby." *Long Island Forum*, August/September 1987, pages 172-177.

HOLAHAN, DAVID. "Les Payne." *Northeast Magazine*, June 15, 1986, pages 12-19.

HOLLINGSWORTH, KENT. "Patrons of the Turf: John Wesley Hanes." *The Blood-Horse*, December 21, 1963, page 1758.

LARRABEE, ERIC. "The Six Thousand Houses That Levitt Built." *Harper's*, September 1948, pages 79-88.

LIFE STAFF. "Nation's Biggest Housebuilder." *Life*, August 23, 1948, pages 75-78.

――――. "The Story of a Dark International Conspiracy." *Life*, February 25, 1957, pages 24-31.

———. "Costly Whitewash of Black Charges." *Life*, June 9, 1958, pages 105-106.

MITGANG, HERBERT. "Policing America's Writers." *The New Yorker*, October 5, 1987, pages 47-90.

NEWSDAY STAFF. "Silver Anniversary Edition." Special supplement to *Newsday*, September 10, 1965.

———. "40 Years With *Newsday*." Special supplement to *Newsday*, September 9, 1980.

———. "A Decade of Sundays." Special supplement to *Newsday*, April 4, 1982.

O'BRIAN, DAVE. "Forst Upon Us." *The Boston Phoenix*, June 3, 1980, pages 6-18.

O'BRIEN, GREG. "Rupert Buys Hub Rag: Wingo in, Forst Out." *Boston Magazine*, May 1983, pages 113-155.

O'LEARY, NOREEN. "Newspaper Executive of the Year: Newsday's Robert Johnson." *Adweek*, April 28, 1987, pages 3-5.

PATTERSON, ALICIA. "The Case Against Wechsler." *Bulletin of the American Society of Newspaper Editors*, September 1, 1952, pages 1-2.

———, with HAL BURTON. "This Is the Life I Love." *Saturday Evening Post*, September 21, 1959, pages 19-51.

PAYNE, LES. "What Big Brother Put Into My File." *LI Magazine*, September 26, 1976, pages 7-19.

———. "Out of Harm's Way." *The Newsday Magazine*, May 11, 1986, pages 13-33.

RADOLF, ANDREW. "Who will be tabloid king of the city?" *Editor & Publisher*, 2/21/87, pages 12-49.

———. "Long Island battleground." *Editor & Publisher*, July 30, 1988, pages 14-15.

ROBINS, NATALIE. "The Defiling of American Writers." *The Nation*, October 10, 1987, pages 367-372.

ROWAN, ROY. "Secrets of the Tribune Tower." *Fortune*, April 5, 1982, pages 66-74.

SACHAR, EMILY. "Arch Rivals." *NewsInc.*, November/December 1989, pages 16-23.

SELIGSOHN, LEO. "The Power Writer." *The Newsday Magazine*, November 21, 1982, pages 22-46.

SPARKES, BOYDEN. "They'll Build Neighborhoods, Not Houses." *Saturday Evening Post*, October 28, 1944, pages 11-46.

THEOHARIS, ATHAN. "How the F.B.I. Gaybaited Stevenson." *The Nation*, May 7, 1990, pages 617-636.

U.S. NEWS & WORLD REPORT STAFF. "A media baron's suburban strategy." *U.S. News & World Report*, April 24, 1989, pages 49-50.

VOLKMAN, ERNEST. "How They Didn't Bring the News from Shoreham to Long Island." *Media People*, November 1980, pages 69-72.

WELLES, CHRIS. "The Battle for Control of the Daily News." *New York*, March 31, 1975, pages 50-56.

WERTENBAKER, CHARLES. "The Case of the Hot-Tempered Publisher." *Saturday Evening Post*, May 12, 1951, pages 36-118.

WICKER, TOM. "Bill Moyers: Johnson's Good Angel." *Harper's*, October 1965, pages 41-49.

WILKENS, WILLIAM, as told to BERNIE BOOKBINDER. "We're Battling the Mobsters in Our Union." *Coronet*, October 1956, pages 61-66.

UNPUBLISHED MANUSCRIPTS AND SCHOLARLY PAPERS

ALBRIGHT, JOSEPH M. P. "Joseph Medill Patterson: Right or Wrong, American." undergraduate thesis, Williams College, 1958.

ALTSHUL, JACK. Untitled *Newsday* history manuscript, 1960.

ASIMOV, STANLEY. Untitled 1952 manuscript about the 1950 Long Island Rail Road crash in Richmond Hill, Queens.

BRIMMER, DONALD ROSS. "Ambassador Harry Frank Guggenheim in Cuba." Master's thesis, Old Dominion College, 1969.

FLAGLER, JOHN M. Untitled two-part manuscript about Alicia Patterson for *The New Yorker*, 1963.

HAYASHI, TETSUMARO. "John Steinbeck and the Vietnam War (Part I)." Steinbeck Monograph Series, The Steinbeck Research Institute, Ball State University, 1986.

KELLY, BARBARA. "The Politics of House and Home: Implications in the Built Environment of Levittown, LI." Doctoral thesis, State University of New York at Stony Brook, 1988.

LIELL, JOHN THOMAS. "Levittown: A Study in Community Planning and Development." Doctoral thesis, Yale, 1952.

LIVINGSTON, ROBERT TEVIOT. "Economic Survey of Long Island," Columbia University, 1940.

SILVERMAN, ARNOLD R. "Defense and Deconcentration: Defense Industrialization During World War Two and the Development of the Contemporary American Suburb." Suburbia Reexamined Conference, Hofstra University, 1987.

TREEN, JOSEPH. Excerpts of an unpublished diary of his career at *Newsday*.

WAX, ALAN. "Alicia Patterson's Growing Vision: The Growth of America's Largest Suburban Daily Under Its First Editor and Publisher." University of Missouri, 1971.

WOOD, ALBERT. "Suburbia With Love," unpublished manuscript, 1971, with a supplement, "The Newsday Story."

Source Notes

THE PRIMARY SOURCES for this book were the author's nearly 900 interviews with more than 650 people, the *Newsday* reporter Bernie Bookbinder's oral history interviews with 52 people, and a large collection of letters, memoranda and other documents.

The documents include such collections as the papers of Harry F. Guggenheim (referred to in these source notes as HFG papers), at the Library of Congress; the papers of Alicia Patterson (APG papers), gathered at *Newsday* from a variety of sources; the papers of Joseph Medill Patterson (JMP papers), at Donnelley Library, Lake Forest College; the papers of Mark Foster Ethridge Sr. (MFE papers), at the University of North Carolina at Chapel Hill; the papers of Stanley Asimov, donated by Asimov from his files at *Newsday*; the papers of William Attwood, at the State Historical Society of Wisconsin; the papers of Walter Johnson, at the Illinois State University at Normal; the papers of Robert M. Hutchins, at the University of Chicago; the papers of Adlai E. Stevenson, at Princeton University; the papers of Lester Markel and of James Wechsler, at the State Historical Society of Wisconsin; the papers of Gardner Cowles Jr., at Drake University; the papers of Carl Sandburg, at the University of Illinois; the papers of John Steinbeck, at Stanford University; the papers of Frances FitzGerald at the Mugar Library in Cambridge, Massachusetts.

Smaller collections of documents came from Patricia Barlow, who contributed papers of her father, Alan Hathway, from the Reverend Philip Carey, S.J., Stuart Diamond, Leo Gottlieb, Robert W. Greene, Anthony Insolia, Robert Johnson, David Laventhol, Francis Lawrence, Local 406, Graphic Communications International Union, Ed Lowe, Anthony Marro, Tom Morris, Bill D. Moyers (referred to in these notes as BDM papers), Richard Sandler and Fred Tuccillo. Other materials came from the Lyndon Baines Johnson Library in

Austin, Texas; the Dwight David Eisenhower Library in Abilene, Kansas; the John Fitzgerald Kennedy Library in Boston, Massachusetts; the Mundt Foundation at Dakota State College; the Oral History Research Office at Columbia University, and the National Aeronautics and Space Administration. In addition, the author has drawn from a variety of books, periodicals, unpublished manuscripts and scholarly papers, listed in the bibliography.

NOTE:

1) If an entry in these notes is followed only by a date, with no specific indication of source, the entry refers to an issue of *Newsday*.

2) The typographical style for this book follows the recommendations of *Words into Type*, Third Edition, published by Prentice-Hall in 1974.

3) In the chapter text, if a quote comes from a written source, the quote includes the original spelling, punctuation and typefaces of that written source, even if they are inconsistent with the typographical style of the rest of the book. *Words into Type* recommends, for example, that the names of newspapers be italicized, but many of the written sources quoted do not use italics for newspapers.

CHAPTER ONE: The Honeymooners

Page 3: Background on Robert Goddard: Lehman, *This High Man*; Hallion, *Legacy of Flight*; *New York Times*, 7/18/29, 7/21/29, 10/14/29, 12/15/29.

Page 4: "Goddard's faith . . ." *This High Man*, page 211.

Page 4: Wedding ceremony in Jacksonville: Interviews with Dorothy Michelson, John Bitter and Charles Murchison.

Page 5: Discussions with Goddard about cooperative research: *This High Man*, pages 267-269.

Page 5: Max Annenberg telegram: Altshul manuscript, pages 3-4; 20th Anniversary recollections of HFG, in *Newsday* files.

Page 5: Annenberg background: Chapman, *Tell It to Sweeney*; Tebbel, *An American Dynasty*; Morgan and Veysey, *Poor Little Rich Boy*; McGivena, *The News*.

Page 5: "Max's telegram was . . ." 20th Anniversary recollections of HFG.

Page 5: " 'Everybody ought . . .' " Patterson and Burton, *Saturday Evening Post*, 2/21/59, page 21.

Page 6: "On the arrival . . ." 20th Anniversary recollections of HFG.

CHAPTER TWO: Bourbon Joe

I

Pages 7-10: Background of Medill, Patterson and McCormick families: Morgan and Veysey, *Poor Little Rich Boy*; Tebbel, *An American Dynasty*; Chapman, *Tell It to Sweeney*; Hoge, *Cissy Patterson*; Healy, *Cissy*; Martin, *Cissy*; Sandburg, *Abraham Lincoln: The War Years*; *Dictionary of Literary Biography* entries on Joseph Medill, Joseph Medill Patterson, Cissy Patterson and Robert Rutherford McCormick.

Page 10: "My mother hated me . . ." *Poor Little Rich Boy*, page 24.

II

Pages 11-12: JMP at Groton and Yale: The best source is a 1958 history thesis at Williams College, Massachusetts, "Joseph Medill Patterson: Right or Wrong, American," by his grandson, Joseph P. Albright. Another useful source is the three-part 1938 profile of Patterson in *The New*

Yorker, by Jack Alexander.
    Page 12: JMP view of Hearst: Albright manuscript, page 26.
    Page 12: JMP wedding: *Chicago American*, 11/20/02.
    Page 12: JMP election to Illinois Legislature: Tebbel, *An American Dynasty*, page 280; Morgan and Veysey, *Poor Little Rich Boy*, pages 76-77; Albright manuscript, pages 27-30.
    Page 12: "I was through being . . ." Interview in *Cincinnati Enquirer*, 10/23/10, quoted in Albright manuscript, page 52.
    Pages 12-13: JMP as commissioner of public works: *An American Dynasty*, page 280; *Poor Little Rich Boy*, page 84; Albright manuscript, pages 32-34.
    Page 13: "I have hardly read . . ." *An American Dynasty*, page 281.
    Page 13: "My son is of age . . ." *New York Times*, 3/4/06.
    Page 13: "I have an income . . ." *The Independent*, 1906.
    Page 13: "I still maintain . . ." Carl Sandburg to JMP, 9/17/26, in JMP papers.
    Pages 13-14: Cissy's marriage: *Poor Little Rich Boy*; *An American Dynasty*; Hoge, *Cissy Patterson*; Healy, *Cissy*; Martin, *Cissy*; *Dictionary of Literary Biography* entry on Cissy Patterson.
    Page 14: JMP in Wisconsin: Albright manuscript, page 41.

CHAPTER THREE: "Keep Alicia Moving."

I
    Page 15: Door-slamming story: Interviews with Josephine Albright, Janet Hauck, Hal Burton and Jack Mann.
    Page 15: "He had wanted . . ." Patterson and Burton, *Saturday Evening Post*, 2/21/59, page 44.
    Page 15: "When I think . . ." Handwritten, undated recollection of Alicia, in APG papers.
    Page 16: "In fact, she took . . ." *Saturday Evening Post*, 2/21/59, page 44.
    Page 16: "I don't know what . . ." *Saturday Evening Post*, 2/21/59, page 44.
    Pages 16-17: Alicia's ear infection: Cablegrams between James Keeley of the *Chicago Tribune* and his Berlin correspondent, 4/15/12, 4/16/12, 4/17/12, 4/18/12; letter, JMP to Marie Kleiner, 4/16/12, in JMP papers.

II
    Page 17: Debs, Dunne campaigns: Albright manuscript, page 38.
    Pages 17-18: Patterson as a writer: Albright manuscript, pages 41-48; Morgan and Veysey, *Poor Little Rich Boy*, pages 98-100; Alexander, *The New Yorker*, 8/13/38, page 20; Tebbel, *An American Dynasty*, page 286.
    Page 18: James Keeley background: *An American Dynasty*, pages 75-91; *Dictionary of Literary Biography*, Volume 25, pages 144-151.
    Page 18: Medill McCormick at the *Tribune*: *Poor Little Rich Boy*, pages 100-102, 116.
    Page 18: JMP and Robert R. McCormick become officers of Tribune Company: *An American Dynasty*, pages 75-76; *Poor Little Rich Boy*, pages 116-118; Albright manuscript, pages 60-61.
    Page 18: Annenberg methods: Rascoe, *Before I Forget*, pages 269-276.
    Pages 18-19: Division of labor between Patterson and McCormick: *Poor Little Rich Boy*, pages 119-120.
    Page 19: Comic strips: Chapman, *Tell It to Sweeney*, pages 32, 147-160; Hoge, *Cissy Patterson*, 124-127.
    Page 19: Movie listings, rotogravure: Gies, *The Colonel of Chicago*, pages 46-47.
    Page 19: "I never had . . ." Waldrop, *McCormick of Chicago*, page 181.
    Page 19: JMP as a war correspondent in Mexico: Albright manuscript, page 72; *Poor Little Rich Boy*, page 128.
    Page 19: JMP and McCormick on the Mexican border: Albright manuscript, pages 72-75; *Poor Little Rich Boy*, pages 164, 175.
    Page 20: Meeting between JMP and McCormick in France: *Tell It to Sweeney*, pages 13-17; *An American Dynasty*, pages 102-104; *Poor Little Rich Boy*, pages 220-224.
    Page 20: "I said we would . . ." *Tell It to Sweeney*, page 16.
    Page 20: "So far, our printing . . ." Albright manuscript, page 134.
    Page 20: Lack of letters: *Tell It to Sweeney*, page 71.
    Page 20: *News* circulation: McGivena, *The News*, page 51.
    Page 20: Tribune Company keeps publishing the *News*: *Tell It to Sweeney*, page 77.

Page 21: "No more killing, Max. . . ." Albright manuscript, page 105.

III

Page 21: Early nicknames: Interview with Josephine Albright.
Page 21: "Father seemed to get . . ." Flagler manuscript, Part I, pages 14-15.
Page 21: "Black Mane was bigger . . ." Handwritten, undated recollection of Alicia Patterson, in APG papers.
Page 22: "Long after I had grown up . . ." Patterson and Burton, *Saturday Evening Post*, 2/21/59, page 44.
Page 23: "Most likely Elinor . . ." Alicia to JMP, 2/23/21, in JMP papers. NOTE: In the large correspondence between Alicia and her father contained in the JMP papers, most of Alicia's letters are undated. These source notes will only refer specifically to those letters that have dates.
Page 23: "I don't know . . ." JMP to Alicia, 2/25/21.
Page 23: "I am awfully . . ." Alicia to JMP, 2/27/21.
Page 24: "Really you oughtn't . . ." JMP to Alicia, 12/22/20.
Page 24: "Groton was very . . ." JMP to Alicia, 10/8/21.
Page 24: ". . .general obstreperousness . . ." *Saturday Evening Post*, 2/21/59, page 44.
Page 25: "Last Sunday night . . ." Elizabeth Risser to Alice Patterson, 11/9/24, in JMP papers.
Page 25: "I certainly would not . . ." JMP to John Drake, 12/2/24.
Page 25: "What a bad girl . . ." JMP to Elinor, 11/6/24.
Page 25: "Alicia, please try . . ." JMP to Alicia, 11/26/24.
Page 25: "Keep Alicia moving . . ." *Saturday Evening Post*, 2/21/59, page 45.
Page 25: "I got two proposals . . ." Alicia to JMP, 2/18/25.
Page 25: "I am glad at least . . ." JMP to Alicia, 3/6/25.
Page 26: Debutante ball: *Chicago American*, 12/30/25.

IV

Page 26: "Last year . . ." Undated JMP manuscript, in JMP papers.
Page 26: "The thing simply . . ." Undated JMP manuscript.
Page 27: ". . . in the corner clipping . . ." Patterson and Burton, *Saturday Evening Post*, 2/21/59, page 45.
Page 27: "She had actually . . ." Undated JMP manuscript.
Page 27: "Much that I learned . . ." Speech by Alicia at Fordham University, 7/15/53, in APG papers.
Page 27: ". . . whose husband . . ." Fordham speech.
Page 28: "When she told me . . ." Undated JMP manuscript.
Page 28: "Bertie was . . ." Flagler manuscript, Part I, page 20.
Page 28: "Maybe one of . . ." Undated JMP manuscript.

V

Page 28: "Sometimes we talked . . ." Wertenbaker, *Saturday Evening Post*, 5/12/51, page 37.
Page 28: "I was in love . . ." *Saturday Evening Post*, 5/12/51, page 113.
Page 29: "Jim Simpson is coming . . ." JMP to Elinor, 5/5/27.
Page 29: ". . .a place where hurry-up . . ." Associated Press, 8/19/27.
Page 29: "Miss Patterson certainly . . ." Associated Press, 8/19/27.
Page 30: "He knows now . . ." Alicia to JMP, 2/15/28.
Page 31: Payment for fox-hunt story: JMP to Alicia, 3/23/28.
Page 31: ". . .self-canceling contest . . ." Patterson and Burton, *Saturday Evening Post*, 2/21/59, page 45.

VI

Pages 31-32: *Liberty* Magazine pieces: Selling magazine subscriptions, 7/21/28; selling dresses, 11/3/28; flying, 3/20/29, 9/7/29.
Page 31: "My father had . . ." *Liberty*, 9/7/29, page 19.
Page 32: Cleveland to New York flight: *New York Times*, 11/7/30.
Page 32: Sladang hunt: *China Press*, 4/24/31.
Page 32: "It is the most . . ." Associated Press, 4/30/31.
Page 33: "When she first . . ." Wertenbaker, *Saturday Evening Post*, 5/12/51, page 114.
Page 33: "Account inquiries . . ." JMP to Alicia, 10/30/31.

Page 33: "Furious at . . ." Alicia to JMP, 10/30/31.

Page 34: "That is because . . ." JMP to Alicia, 1/6/32.

Page 35: "As the years went . . ." Patterson and Burton, *Saturday Evening Post*, 2/21/59, page 45.

CHAPTER FOUR: Ghetto to Gold Mine

I

Pages 36-37: Guggenheim background: Davis, *The Guggenheims: An American Epic*; Hoyt, *The Guggenheims and the American Dream*; Lomask, *Seed Money*; O'Connor, *The Guggenheims*.

Page 37: "Every wealthy family . . ." *Seed Money*, page 44.

Page 38: Letters between Daniel and Harry: *Seed Money*, pages 55-62.

Page 38: Aviator numbers: Arthur, *Contact! Naval Aviators Assigned Numbers 1 to 2000*, pages 308-309.

Pages 38-39: Disagreement over Chuquicamata: O'Connor, *The Guggenheims*, pages 413-415.

Page 39: Background of Howard Gould estate: Historic Buildings Evaluation, Nassau County Historical Museum.

II

Pages 40-41: Background of Daniel Guggenheim Fund: Hallion, *Legacy of Flight*; Lomask, *Seed Money*; interview with Hallion.

Page 40: "Don't show this . . ." *Legacy of Flight*, page 29.

Page 41: "What's the use . . ." *Legacy of Flight*, page 32.

Page 41: "I remember looking . . ." *Seed Money*, page 92.

Page 41: "I spent about three . . ." Recollections of Harry F. Guggenheim and Falaise, by Charles A. Lindbergh, 4/30/73, in the papers of the Nassau County Museum.

Page 41: "Frankly, I don't . . ." *Seed Money*, page 93.

Page 41: Lindbergh's cross-country tour: *Seed Money*, pages 94-95, *Legacy of Flight*, pages 152, 154-158; Lindbergh, *Autobiography of Values*, page 81.

Page 42: Charles Lindbergh-Anne Morrow flight from Falaise: Lindbergh's recollections of Harry and Falaise, 4/30/73; *Memories of Falaise*, by Anne Morrow Lindbergh, 10/73, in the papers of the Nassau County Museum; Anne Morrow Lindbergh, *Bring Me A Unicorn*, page 183; interview with Anne Morrow Lindbergh.

Page 42: Blind flying experiments: *Legacy of Flight*, pages 114-124; *Seed Money*, pages 97-102; interview with Doolittle.

Pages 42-43: Origins of Guggenheim-Goddard relationship: Lindbergh's recollections of Harry and Falaise, 4/30/73; *Seed Money*, pages 141-145; *Legacy of Flight*, pages 174-176; *Autobiography of Values*, pages 336-343.

Page 43: "May be the answer . . ." *Seed Money*, page 142.

Page 43: "Do you . . ." *Autobiography of Values*, page 343.

III

Pages 43-44: Harry as ambassador: Lomask, *Seed Money*, pages 66 to 71; Hoyt, *The Guggenheims and the American Dream*, pages 302-308; *New York Times*, 9/15/29, 9/17/29, 9/20/29, 9/22/29, 1/11/30, 2/16/30, 5/9/30, 10/4/30, 10/6/30, 4/9/31, 5/15/31, 5/17/31,5/23/31, 8/11/31, 8/15/31, 8/26/31, 7/5/32, 3/28/33, 8/20/33, 10/27/33; *Time*, 10/21/29; Brimmer, "Ambassador Harry Frank Guggenheim in Cuba."

Page 45: ". . .easily fatiguable . . ." Malcolm Goodridge to HFG, 4/4/32, in HFG papers.

Page 45: "You know perfectly . . ." Carol Guggenheim to HFG, 10/18/37, in HFG papers.

Page 45: ". . .departing with . . ." HFG to Carol, 2/3/38.

Page 45: "You know it to be . . ." HFG to Carol, 3/7/38.

Page 45: Citizens Committee on the Control of Crime: *Seed Money*, pages 71-72; *New York Times*, 12/16/39, 5/13/40; interview with Arnold Beichman.

CHAPTER FIVE: Alicia Says Yes

Page 47: "Dear Miss King . . ." JMP to Mary King, 1/29/23, in JMP papers.

Page 47: "Dear Mr. Patterson . . ." Mary King to JMP, 4/4/23.

Page 48: "Make it look . . ." *Tell It to Sweeney*, page 27.

Page 48: Kirkland meeting with Alice Patterson: Kirkland to JMP, 9/14/37.

Pages 48-49: Pre-divorce agreement, 6/16/38, and pre-nuptial agreement, 6/27/38, in the files of the Surrogate Court, County of Westchester.

Page 49: "Alicia is a very fine . . ." Nancy Guggenheim to Diane Guggenheim, 5/25/39, in HFG papers.

Page 49: Press announcement of Harry-Alicia wedding: T. J. Ross to HFG, 6/29/39, in HFG papers.

Page 49: Cissy Patterson's purchase of the *Times* and *Herald*: Hoge, *Cissy Patterson*, pages 162-163; Martin, *Cissy*, page 399.

Page 50: "I doubt whether . . ." HFG to Charles Murchison, 7/10/39, in HFG papers.

Page 50: "I had terrible . . ." Wertenbaker, *Saturday Evening Post*, 5/12/51, page 115.

Page 50: "I wonder if . . ." 20th Anniversary recollections of HFG, in *Newsday* files.

CHAPTER SIX: Mr. Newhouse Regrets

I

Page 54: New plant for *North Shore Daily Journal*: Interviews with Forrest Corson, Paul Johansson and Bill Ritter; *New York Times*, 1/15/33.

Page 54: J. Russel Sprague instructions to James Stiles: Interview with Corson; Uhlan, *Dynamo Jim Stiles*, page 93.

Page 54: Strike against *North Shore Daily Journal*: Interviews with Corson and Johansson; *Editor & Publisher*, 2/6/37, 3/20/37, 4/17/37, 5/1/37, 6/19/37.

Page 54: Newhouse buys *Long Island Star*: *New York Times*, 6/21/38; *Editor & Publisher*, 6/25/38.

Page 54: *North Shore Daily Journal* goes out of business, merges with *Long Island Star*: *New York Times*, 9/10/38.

Page 54: Merger of *Nassau Daily Review* with *Nassau Daily Star*: *Dynamo Jim Stiles*, pages 54, 55, 164.

Page 54: T. Harold Forbes approach to Sprague about buying *Review-Star*: *Dynamo Jim Stiles*, page 92.

Page 55: Demise of the *Nassau Daily Journal*: *New York Times*, 3/2/39, 3/11/39; *Editor & Publisher*, 2/25/39, 3/18/39.

Page 55: Newhouse labor troubles at *Long Island Press* and *Long Island Star*: *New York Times*, 4/6/37, 4/8/37, 4/22/37, 4/25/37, 5/1/37, 5/7/37, 6/26/38, 7/10/38, 7/12/38.

II

Pages 55-56: William Mapel background: Interview with Evelyn Mapel; *Newsday* obituary, 4/1/84; *New York Times* obituary, 4/2/84; *Bronxville Review-Press* obituary, 4/5/84; *University of Missouri Bulletin*, page 102; *Who's Who in America*.

Page 56: Nassau farming: United States Census; Livingston, "Economic Survey of Long Island."

Page 56: Sprague background: 10/29/54, 12/24/56, 4/6/61; obituary, 4/18/69.

Page 57: "By the end . . ." 3/11/49.

Page 57: "When I said . . ." Altshul manuscript, page 8.

Page 58: "I thought . . ." Meeker, *Newspaperman*, page 245.

CHAPTER SEVEN: What's In a Name?

I

Page 59: HFG and Goddard: Lehman, *This High Man*, page 291, 293-295.

Page 59: HFG in Willkie campaign: *New York Herald Tribune*, 8/15/40.

Page 59: ". . .readable, entertaining . . ." Patterson and Burton, *Saturday Evening Post*, 2/21/59, page 51.

Page 60: "I favored a tabloid . . ." Speech, Fordham University, 7/15/53, in APG papers.

Page 60: Nicholson and the advertising department: Altshul manuscript, pages 9, 13.

Page 60: "If you haven't . . ." Altshul manuscript, page 9.

Page 61: Mullen background: Mullen to Jack Altshul, 6/10/59; obituary, 2/21/72.
Page 61: Finletter subscription: *Newsday*, 3/11/49; interview with Stan Peckham.
Page 61: Finletter background: *Encyclopedia Americana*.

II

Page 63: Hiring of Harold Davis: Altshul manuscript, page 9.
Page 63: Davis background: *Newsday* obituary, 1/10/55.

III

Page 66: "A light began . . ." Altshul manuscript, page 12.
Page 66: HFG gift to APG of $4,000 share in *Newsday*: F. A. Collins to William Mapel, 9/25/40, in HFG papers.

IV

Page 67: Grande's trip: Altshul manuscript, page 15.
Page 69: Circulation figures: Altshul manuscript, page 16.
Page 70: ". . .for all the help . . ." HFG and APG to Joseph Medill Patterson, 9/3/40, in APG papers.

CHAPTER EIGHT: Newsday Goes to War

I

Page 71: Building dimensions: Architect's drawings, 4/17/40 and 9/5/44, in *Newsday* files.
Page 72: "The turnover . . ." *Miami Herald*, undated, in APG papers.
Pages 72-73: Letters to the editor: Interviews with Andre Fontaine, Jackie Gebhard; Chapman, *Tell It to Sweeney*, page 71.
Page 73: "I wouldn't give . . ." Patterson and Burton, *Saturday Evening Post*, 2/21/59, page 45.
Page 74: "Let's git going . . ." 11/18/42.
Page 75: "As to your . . ." JMP to APG, 7/26/43, in JMP papers.
Page 75: "I think I am . . ." JMP to APG, 8/9/43.

II

Page 77: Skunk's Misery Road column: 2/5/41.
Page 78: Nursing home series: 2/5/41 to 2/17/41.
Page 78: Nursing home editorial: 2/19/41.
Page 78: Nursing home death: 5/14/42, 5/15/42, 5/18/42, 5/19/42, 7/3/42.

III

Page 79: Hathway background: Interviews with Patricia Barlow, Hal Burton, William Casselman, Jackie Gebhard, Bonita Marciante.
Page 80: "I'm *still* Alan . . ." Interview with Dick Greenamyer.
Page 80: "BABOON TERRORIZES . . ." 6/29/43.
Page 81: Gas-rationing: Altshul manuscript, pages 40-41.

IV

Page 81: Atwood background: Altshul manuscript, pages 36-38.
Page 82: Frances Story background: 20th Anniversary recollections, in *Newsday* files.
Page 84: Altshul background: Altshul columns, 7/13/80, 6/7/81, 3/14/82.
Page 85: Berserk barber and Super Fortress stories: Altshul manuscript, pages 49-50.

V

Page 87: Stiles background: Uhlan, *Dynamo Jim Stiles*, pages 1-17.
Page 87: "*The Nassau Post* will be . . ." Hodges, *Long Island's Greatest Newspaper*, page 35.
Page 87: Stiles weeklies: *Dynamo Jim Stiles*, pages 28-30, 59-60.
Page 87: "He never . . ." *Dynamo Jim Stiles*, pages 84-85.
Page 87: "He was generous . . ." *Dynamo Jim Stiles*, page 96.
Page 88: "Don't spread out . . ." *Dynamo Jim Stiles*, page 93.
Page 88: Republicans help Stiles buy out his competitor: *Dynamo Jim Stiles*, pages 88-90.

Page 88: ". . .got in plenty . . ." *Dynamo Jim Stiles*, page 94.
Page 88: "On the opposite . . ." 1/23/42.
Page 88: Comparative tax lists: 1/27/42.
Page 89: "Loses Home . . ." 1/26/42.
Page 89: "What Is Your . . ." 1/28/42.
Page 89: Editorials on "Courtesy and Cooperation" campaign: 4/7/45, 4/11/45.
Page 89: "With 25 years . . ." 4/7/45.
Page 90: Stiles fund raising: *Dynamo Jim Stiles*, pages 64-65.

VI

Page 91: DiDonato-Kelland debate: 10/4/40.
Pages 91-92: "I can remember . . ." 10/29/40.
Page 92: JMP and FDR during the Depression: Chapman, *Tell It to Sweeney*, pages 186-200; Tebbel, *An American Dynasty*, pages 258-260.
Page 93: "Only --- days . . ." *An American Dynasty*, page 225.
Page 93: ". . .the noblest . . ." Martin, *Cissy*, page 324.
Page 93: "Suppose the . . ." *Tell It to Sweeney*, page 193.
Page 93: "If it averts . . ." *Tell It to Sweeney*, pages 197-198.
Page 93: "He lied . . ." Hoge, *Cissy Patterson*, page 182.
Page 93: ". . .virtual power . . ." Hoge, *Cissy Patterson*, page 183.
Pages 93-94: Lindbergh speech: Ross, *The Last Hero*, pages 289-320; Cole, *Charles A. Lindbergh and the Battle Against Intervention in World War II*, pages 171-185; Lindbergh, Anne Morrow, *War Within and Without*, pages 220-222; interview with Anne Morrow Lindbergh.
Page 94: JMP meets FDR: Memo, Steve Early to General E. M. Watson, 12/10/41, Watson to FDR, 12/10/41, J. Romagna to Watson, 12/10/41, in FDR library; memo, JMP for files, 1/29/42, in JMP papers; Hoge, *Cissy Patterson*, page 185; *Tell It to Sweeney*, pages 181-210.
Page 95: "All I want . . ." Hoge, *Cissy Patterson*, page 185.
Page 95: "Father and I . . ." *Time*, 10/6/41.
Page 95: JMP and Representative Holland: Hoge, *Cissy Patterson*, page 195; *An American Dynasty*, page 165; *Tell It to Sweeney*, page 210.
Page 95: "Joseph Medill Patterson who wrote . . ." 8/5/42.
Page 96: JMP snubs Alicia over Ayer award: Feature story, Wide World, 10/4/42, in APG papers.
Page 96: "I am going . . ." APG to JMP, 8/19/43.
Page 96: *Daily News* helps *Newsday* with newsprint: APG to R. C. Holliss, 4/12/46; R. C. Holliss to JMP, 4/15/46, in JMP papers.
Page 96: Advertising squeeze: Altshul manuscript, page 44.
Page 97: JMP approves sale of press to *Newsday*: R. C. Holliss to JMP, 9/13/44, in JMP papers.
Page 97: HFG meets Stiles: Altshul manuscript, page 30.

VII

Page 98: "I considered joining . . ." Patterson and Burton, *Saturday Evening Post*, 2/21/59, page 50.
Page 98: "I'm going back . . ." *Saturday Evening Post*, 2/21/59, page 50.
Page 98: "What would those . . ." *Miami Herald* clip, undated, in APG papers.
Page 98: "I do not know . . ." Draft of letter, HFG to Thomas Cochran, 7/14/27, in HFG papers.
Page 98: Commendation for strafing Sakashima: Interviews with Dean Allard, Bob Cressman.
Page 99: Background of Jules and Nica de Koenigswarter: Gordon, *Live at the Village Vanguard*, pages 117-122; interviews with Nica, Patrick and Janka de Koenigswarter.
Page 102: "You've raised . . ." Wood manuscript, page 122.
Page 102: Shorts story: 8/14/41.
Page 102: Cancer photos: 5/3/45.

CHAPTER NINE: The End of Infancy

I

Page 103: "Three of the Big Ones . . ." Tebbel, *An American Dynasty*, page 270.
Page 104: "Apology" for O'Donnell column: *Daily News*, 10/13/45.

Page 105: "It is purely . . ." *Current Biography 1942*, page 651.

Page 105: "Let's do . . ." Chapman, *Tell It to Sweeney*, page 43.

Page 105: Transferring Gallico: *Tell It to Sweeney*, pages 43-46.

Page 105: Hatchet in JMP's bathroom: Alexander, *The New Yorker*, 8/6/38, page 20.

Page 105: "It was a wonderful . . ." Patterson and Burton, *Saturday Evening Post*, 2/21/59, pages 19 and 21.

Page 106: McCormick refuses to give APG power: Hoge, *Cissy Patterson*, pages 220-223; Martin, *Cissy*, pages 456-459; Morgan and Veysey, *Poor Little Rich Boy*, page 398.

Page 106: "You have done . . ." Cissy Patterson to APG, 9/10/45, in APG papers.

Pages 106-107: Cissy Patterson's overtures to APG: Hoge, *Cissy Patterson*, pages 223-225; Martin, *Cissy*, page 451; *Poor Little Rich Boy*, page 380; *New York Journal-American*, 6/8/63.

Page 107: Death of Cissy Patterson: Hoge, *Cissy Patterson*, pages 224-237; Martin, *Cissy*, pages 465-476.

II

Pages 107-108: "For some . . ." APG to HFG, 11/4/46, in HFG papers.

Page 108: "As you know . . ." HFG to APG, 11/7/46.

Page 108: "You people . . ." Altshul manuscript, page 52.

Page 108: *Newsday* losses: Montgomery Angell to HFG, 7/29/46.

Page 109: Amberg departure: *Newsday*, 3/17/49.

Page 109: "I couldn't stand . . ." *Time*, 9/13/54.

Page 109: "So in the future . . ." HFG to APG, 5/1/44.

Page 109: "I have decided . . ." HFG to APG, 7/26/44.

Page 110: "Well you certainly . . ." HFG to APG, 11/12/48.

Page 110: "I have read . . ." HFG to APG, 11/22/48.

Page 110: "The natives are half . . ." *Liberty*, 3/29/30.

Page 111: "Even the birds . . ." 12/22/48.

Page 111: "Didya hear . . ." 12/23/48.

Page 111: "Moses, it is now . . ." HFG for files, undated.

III

Page 113: Invitation to unions: Interview with Stan Peckham.

Page 113: Salary dispute with pressmen: 4/16/46.

Page 113: "So we had . . ." Altshul manuscript, pages 53-54.

Page 114: "The philosophy of the Guild . . ." Undated, unsigned *Newsday* memo, in HFG papers.

Page 115: "We do not believe . . ." Richard Amberg to Irving Gilman, 11/1/47, in HFG papers.

Page 115: "The New York Guild . . ." Amberg to staff, 11/3/47.

Page 115: Blue Cross coverage: Amberg to staff, 11/14/47.

Page 115: Vacation policy: Amberg to staff, 11/19/47.

Page 115: Loan fund: Amberg to staff, 11/21/47.

Page 115: Recreation fund: Amberg to staff, 11/24/47.

Page 115: Guild election: *Guild Reporter*, 6/24/49.

Page 116: "On Friday, the ITU . . ." HFG to APG, 11/22/48.

Page 116: "Space Reserved . . ." *Newsday*, 11/19/48.

Page 116: "We are in . . ." HFG to APG, 11/22/48.

Page 116: "Whenever these . . ." HFG to APG, 7/20/61, in *Newsday* files.

Pages 116-117: *Review-Star* dispute with ITU: 10/1/47, 11/11/47.

Page 116: "If Stiles had . . ." Uhlan, *Dynamo Jim Stiles*, page 316.

Page 117: Sale of *Review-Star* to Newhouse: *Dynamo Jim Stiles*, pages 268 and 273; *Newsday*, 1/20/54.

IV

Page 118: Bill Steele background: Altshul manuscript, pages 43-44.

V

Page 122: Albert Wood background: Interviews with Margaret Wood Shaw, Francis Wood, Gardner Wood, Moyer Wood and Paul Wood.

Page 122: Henry Ford Hospital: Ford, *My Life and Work*, page 216.

Page 123: "Alicia's really quite . . ." Flagler manuscript, Part I, page 60.
Page 123: Albert Wood lunch with Alicia: Wood manuscript, pages 115-117.
Page 123: "My idea . . ." Wood manuscript, page 118.
Page 124: "The next morning . . ." Wood manuscript, page 119.
Page 124: "My theory was . . ." Wood manuscript, page 121.
Page 125: "This interim period . . ." Speech, Fordham University, 7/15/53, in APG papers.

CHAPTER TEN: Levittown

I

Page 126: "We just got on . . ." Interview with Hal Burton.
Pages 126-129: Suburban history: The best sources are Kenneth T. Jackson's *Crabgrass Frontier* and Robert Fishman's *Bourgeois Utopias*.
Page 127: Brooklyn Heights: *Crabgrass Frontier*, pages 25-30.
Page 127: Nassau growth: United States Census.
Page 128: "In practice, FHA . . ." *Crabgrass Frontier*, pages 206 and 208.
Page 128: Nassau-Brooklyn comparison: *Crabgrass Frontier*, page 211.
Page 128: ". . .the great American . . ." *Crabgrass Frontier*, page 282.

II

Page 129: Albert Wood and Dearborn Construction: Undated clips in the Wood papers.
Page 129: Albert Wood letter about Dearborn: Mentioned in letter, APG to Albert Wood, 11/8/43, in the Wood papers.
Page 129: "During the postwar . . ." 2/16/44.
Page 129: "I think it . . ." Wood to APG, 9/21/44, in the Wood papers.
Page 129: Ryttenberg housing series: 9/28/44, 9/29/44, 10/2/44-10/4/44.
Page 129: "They'll Build . . ." Sparkes, *Saturday Evening Post*, 10/28/44.
Pages 129-130: Background of Michael Straight: *Current Biography 1944*, pages 653-655; *New York Times*, 12/27/82; Lewis Lapham review of Straight's autobiography, *After Long Silence*, in *New York Times*, 2/20/83; *Newsday*, 2/23/83; interviews with Straight and Paul Townsend.
Page 130: AVC housing rally: Press release, 5/21/46, in the papers of Michael Straight.
Pages 130-131: Opposing viewpoints on garden apartments by Sprague and the AVC: 9/17/46.

III

Pages 131-132: Levitt & Sons background: Sparkes, *Saturday Evening Post*, 10/28/44; *Architectural Forum*, May 1947; *New York Sun*, 6/6/47; *New York Times*, 6/7/47; *Fortune*, August 1947; *Life*, 8/23/48; Larrabee, *Harper's*, September 1948.
Page 133: "Cellar or no cellar . . ." 5/28/47.
Page 134: "Of the 1,259 acres . . ." Kelly, "The Politics of House and Home," page 55.
Page 135: Nematode quarantine: 7/21/47, 7/23/47, 7/25/47, 8/2/47, 8/16/47, 9/3/47.
Page 135: Ejection of Local 138 from Construction Trades Council: 5/11/50.
Page 135: Renaming Island Trees: 1/5/48, 1/9/48, 2/25/48.
Pages 135-136: "Island Trees is a nice . . ." 1/9/48.
Page 136: "You are not giving . . ." 7/20/48.
Page 136: "Organizations which . . ." 3/12/49.
Page 137: "The North Shore's landed . . ." 7/19/50.

IV

Page 137: "Bet Levitt . . ." *Guilday*, 6/11/47, in HFG papers.
Page 139: "We get 'em . . ." Wertenbaker, *Saturday Evening Post*, 5/12/51, page 117.
Page 139: "We ran off . . ." *Editor & Publisher*, 2/9/46.
Page 140: "Long Island was the land . . ." Schroth, *The Eagle and Brooklyn*, pages 116-117.
Page 140: "*Eagle* editors who owned . . ." Interview with Raymond Schroth.
Page 140: "In 1937, against . . ." *The Eagle and Brooklyn*, page 275.

V

Page 146: "Well, we don't intend . . ." 3/11/49.

CHAPTER ELEVEN: The Start of an Affair

I

Page 148: "I'll send you . . ." HFG to John Steinbeck, 5/28/66, in HFG papers.

II

Pages 149-150: Adlai Stevenson background: Two of the best sources are John Bartlow Martin's exhaustive two-volume biography, *Adlai Stevenson of Illinois* and *Adlai Stevenson and the World*, and Porter McKeever's more readable one-volume work, *Adlai Stevenson: His Life and Legacy*.

Page 150: "I've wanted out . . ." *Adlai Stevenson of Illinois*, page 196.

Page 151: "I want them to grow . . ." AES to APG, probably summer, 1949, in the papers of Walter Johnson. NOTE: Excerpts from many of Stevenson's letters to Alicia appear in the biographies by Martin and McKeever, or in the eight-volume collection of Stevenson's papers, edited by Walter Johnson. But none of these works published the letters in their entirety. As a result, the research for this chapter included a check of copies of Stevenson's handwritten letters, in the papers of Walter Johnson, maintained by the Illinois State University at Normal, Illinois. Wherever possible, the exact quotes in this book come directly from copies of those handwritten letters themselves, or from transcripts of those letters done for Johnson. Otherwise, these notes specify the book in which the letter appears. As to dates, both Alicia and Stevenson often wrote undated letters. In some cases, context clues provide approximate times. In others, a postmark on an attached envelope gives an actual date.

Page 151: "Anyway, you must . . ." AES to APG, 7/10/49.

Page 151: ". . .her delicious . . ." AES to Mrs. Daniel Caulkins, 7/13/63, *The Papers of Adlai Stevenson*, Volume 8, page 430.

Page 151: " '. . .wonderful old war horse . . .' " Susie Zurcher, quoted in *Adlai Stevenson of Illinois*, page 385.

Page 151: "I marvel . . ." AES to APG, early September, 1948.

Page 151: "The Pantagraph is . . ." AES to APG, 2/28/49.

Page 151: "I never thought . . ." Stevenson said this in a 1954 interview with a *Time* correspondent, who included it in an internal memorandum that Richard Clurman used in writing a *Time* cover story of 9/13/54. Clurman remembered the quote in an interview with the author.

Page 152: "I'd like to throw . . ." AES to APG, early September, 1948.

Page 152: "I thought I . . ." AES to APG, spring, 1949.

Page 152: "These I will keep . . ." AES to APG, 3/8/49.

Page 152: "I expect I . . ." APG to AES, probably 1952.

Page 152: "So you've made it . . ." AES to APG, 3/8/49.

Page 153: "I enjoyed . . ." AES to APG, probably summer, 1949.

Page 153: "I'm wallowing . . ." AES to APG, 3/8/49.

Page 153: "I wish I could fly . . ." AES to APG, 11/12/48.

Page 154: "Good night, my love . . ." AES to APG, May, 1949.

Page 154: "Write guarded . . ." AES to APG, 1/3/49.

Page 154: AES and sexuality: The FBI Director J. Edgar Hoover received an unsubstantiated report that Stevenson was homosexual, and Hoover kept this raw information in a secret file that he maintained in his office. See Theoharis, *The Nation*, 5/7/90.

Page 154: " 'Okay, let's be . . .' " AES to APG, 2/17/49.

Page 155: "Darling! Now I have . . ." AES to APG, 2/22/49.

Page 155: "There are years . . ." AES to APG, 11/3/48.

CHAPTER TWELVE: The King and the Crash

I

Page 156: "A review of the facts . . ." Hathway to Greene, 11/27/75, in the papers of Patricia Barlow.

Page 157: W. Kingsland Macy background: Altshul manuscript, page 72; Hausrath, *Long Island Forum*, April 1978, page 82; interview with William K. Macy Jr.

Page 157: Macy's struggle with Robert Moses: Caro, *The Power Broker*, pages 154-155, 182, 184-203, 211-217.

Page 157: ". . .that Nassau-minded daily . . ." *Long Island Forum*, April 1978, page 83.
Page 158: Tip to Altshul about gambling: Altshul manuscript, pages 73-74.
Page 158: "Suffolk's most famous . . ." 10/13/49.
Page 159: District attorney's investigation: 10/22/49.
Page 159: Hathway protest to grand jury: 11/30/49.
Page 159: "Lie to Bet Jurors . . ." 12/1/49.
Page 160: Arrest of Harold Lorentson: 3/6/52.
Page 160: Hathway presents horse to Lorentson: 4/9/52.

II

Page 161: "I hope you can get . . ." AES to APG, 11/5/50, in the papers of Walter Johnson.
Page 162: "HANLEY BARES . . ." 10/17/50.
Page 163: "Tear into them . . ." *Bay Shore Sentinel*, 10/26/50.
Page 163: "Malicia" cartoon: *Suffolk Every Week*, 8/7/51.
Page 163: ". . .sneering, snarling . . ." *Bay Shore Sentinel*, 11/9/50.
Page 163: "From one of your dregs . . ." Wertenbaker, *Saturday Evening Post*, 5/12/51, page 36.
Page 163: "Exit the King . . ." 11/21/50.
Page 164: Greenwood produces his own check: 3/10/51.
Page 164: "The election was a hot . . ." 4/20/51.

III

Page 166: "The voters of Suffolk . . ." 11/4/59.

IV

Page 167: "Because it didn't . . ." Asimov manuscript, page 7.
Page 169: "78 DIE . . ." 11/23/50.
Page 170: "We have known . . ." 11/23/50.

V

Page 170: Long Island Expressway: *The Power Broker*, pages 944, 948-949.
Page 171: Kellermann series: 10/20/52 to 10/25/52.
Page 171: "Texan Dated . . ." 12/5/52.
Page 171: "Her First Easter Bonnet . . ." 4/4/53.
Page 172: Culmination of Walt Whitman campaign: 10/16/51.
Page 172: "Dogdom's Dachau . . ." 2/3/50.
Page 172: *Newsday* gives Glen Cove Butch II: 1/28/49, 3/11/49.
Page 173: Costello interview: Altshul manuscript, pages 82-83; interview with Edna Murray; *Newsday*, 6/1/50.

CHAPTER THIRTEEN: Alicia, Adlai and Ike

I

Page 174: "If Roosevelt is re-elected . . ." 11/3/44.
Page 175: "I was under . . ." AES to APG, 7/16/51, in the papers of Walter Johnson.
Page 175: "The Case of the Hot-Tempered Publisher . . ." Wertenbaker, *Saturday Evening Post*, 5/12/51.
Page 176: "The more I think . . ." Martin, *Adlai Stevenson of Illinois*, page 478.
Page 176: "Glad to hear . . ." AES to APG, 9/14/51.

II

Page 176: "LI CHEERS . . ." 2/1/52.
Page 177: "All Roads Lead . . ." 2/5/52.
Page 177: "33,000 YELL . . ." 2/9/52.
Page 177: "To the President . . ." Ambrose, *Eisenhower: Soldier, General of the Army, President-Elect*, page 523.
Page 177: "When Jackie Cochran . . ." Mamie Eisenhower to Tex McCrary, 2/16/72, in the papers of Tex McCrary.
Page 178: "One quality struck me . . ." 5/22/52.

Page 178: "WE LIKE IKE" buttons: 4/2/52.

Page 178: "And what is . . ." AES to APG, late November, 1951.

Pages 178-179: Truman-Stevenson meetings: Martin, *Adlai Stevenson of Illinois*, pages 517-524, 537-538; McKeever, *Adlai Stevenson: His Life and Legacy*, pages 176-181.

Page 179: "If the Republicans . . ." 1/25/52.

Page 179: "Never did disaster . . ." AES to APG, 1/29/52.

Page 180: AES hints he might accept a draft: AES to APG, 3/13/52; *Adlai Stevenson: His Life and Legacy*, page 182.

Page 180: "I could not accept . . ." *Adlai Stevenson of Illinois*, pages 560-562; *Adlai Stevenson: His Life and Legacy*, pages 187-188.

Page 180: ". . .too well for . . ." Letter, AES to APG, 4/19/52.

Page 180: ". . .a cocky, contemptuous . . ." AES to APG, 5/15/52.

Page 180: "I take my pen . . ." AES to APG, 6/11/52.

III

Page 181: "Here indeed we stand . . ." 7/9/52.

Page 182: "Adlai: The man who . . ." 7/21/52.

Page 183: "I have asked . . ." *New York Times*, 7/26/52.

Page 183: "This newspaper, the first . . ." 7/26/52.

Page 183: Criticism of AES on Taft-Hartley Act: 9/3/52.

Page 183: Comments on Eisenhower and AES as speakers: 9/8/52.

Page 184: "Stevenson was careless . . ." 9/24/52.

Page 184: "We do not agree . . ." 9/26/52.

Page 184: Excerpt of Noel Busch campaign biography: 10/13/52.

Page 184: "Tell Adlai . . ." Phyllis Cerf column, 10/2/52.

Page 185: "I completely lost . . ." Patterson and Burton, *Saturday Evening Post*, 2/21/59, page 44.

Page 185: "A letter from . . ." AES to APG, 10/12/52.

Page 186: "Both Gen. Eisenhower . . ." 11/3/52.

Page 186: "Thanks for your . . ." AES to APG, 11/6/52.

Page 186: "Don't worry about . . ." AES to APG, 3/2/53.

IV

Page 187: "Taft and McCarthy have lined . . ." 7/3/52.

Page 187: "I feel strongly . . ." 8/7/52.

Page 187: "Newspapers cannot be content . . ." Patterson, *Bulletin of the American Society of Newspaper Editors*, 9/1/52.

Page 187: "I have just seen . . ." James Wechsler to APG, 9/3/52, in the Wechsler papers.

Page 187: ". . .a very gallant . . ." *New York Post*, 10/5/52.

Page 188: "Bravo! Your statement . . ." AES to APG, 9/14/52.

Page 188: Snake-in-the-grass cartoon: 4/30/53.

Page 188: Jack Mann on the Rosenberg funeral: 6/22/53.

Page 188: "The party-liners . . ." *The Tablet*, 9/13/52.

Page 189: "McCarthy is a demagogue . . ." 9/11/52.

Page 189: "This is just as much . . ." 8/27/52.

Page 189: " 'Newsday,' in an unrestrained . . ." *The Tablet*, 8/30/52.

Pages 189-190: Jack O'Grady story about Catholic protest: 9/4/52.

Page 190: " 'Newsday' needs . . ." *The Tablet*, 9/6/52.

Page 190: Hathway photo with Cardinal Spellman: 4/28/55.

CHAPTER FOURTEEN: Dethroning DeKoning

I

Pages 192-193: William DeKoning background: *Newsday*, 5/11/50 to 5/17/50; interview with John DeKoning.

Page 193: Opening of Labor Lyceum: 4/17/47.

Page 193: Youth foundation: *Newsday*, 6/29/49; William DeKoning to Alan Hathway, 6/20/49; Hathway to DeKoning, 8/22/49, in *Newsday* files.

Page 194: Editorials on the lack of a large arena: 2/4/44, 2/12/44, 1/28/47 and 2/21/47.
Page 195: "One thing we wish . . ." 8/17/48.

II

Page 196: DeKoning announces drive to unseat Hall and Macy: 3/18/50, 4/18/50, 3/19/50.
Page 196: Hall and Merchant Marine Academy: 3/23/50, 3/31/50.
Page 196: "He has managed . . ." 10/11/50.
Page 197: Hall arranges White House meetings for HFG: HFG to Hall, 8/18/53; Hall to HFG, 8/27/53; Hall to HFG, 10/26/53; HFG to Hall, 10/29/53; HFG to Hall, 11/20/53; HFG to Hall, 1/6/54; John Foster Dulles to HFG, 6/15/54, in HFG papers.
Page 197: Eisenhower offer to HFG: HFG to Eisenhower, 1/6/54.
Pages 197-198: Dudar series: 5/11/50, 5/12/50, 5/15/50 to 5/17/50.
Page 198: " . . .scratched the surface . . ." 5/18/50.
Page 198: "It is a known . . ." Anonymous, to APG, 5/19/50, in *Newsday* files.
Page 199: "Further chapters . . ." 6/3/50.

III

Page 203: John Kenny investigation: *New York Times*, 4/19/52, 5/28/52, 6/19/52, 9/5/52; interview with Robert W. Greene.
Page 203: Indictment of RWG: *New York Times*, 12/6/52.
Page 203: Kenny refuses to testify: *New York Times*, 12/12/52.
Page 203: Death of Biffo DeLorenzo: *New York Times*, 1/8/53.
Page 203: Dismissal of indictment: *New York Times*, 9/24/53.

IV

Page 204: Thomas Lewis murder: *Newsday*, 8/29/53; *Life*, 10/16/53.
Page 204: "LINK RACE UNION . . ." 8/29/53.
Page 205: Background of George Morton Levy: Littleton, *My Partner-In-Law*.
Page 205: Pari-mutuel legislation: *New York Times*, 3/3/39, 11/7/39, 11/8/39, 11/9/39.
Page 205: Levy testimony on Costello: *Newsday*, 3/12/51; *My Partner-in-Law*, pages 185-227.
Page 205: Norman Penny holds stocks for Sprague: 9/23/53.
Page 206: Levy, Sprague testimony: 3/4/54, 3/5/54, 3/6/54.
Page 206: "$345,000 TRACK . . ." *World-Telegram*, 9/28/53.
Page 207: Guy Richards-Marvin Sleeper story on Arthur Wicks: *Journal-American*, 10/2/53.
Page 207: Dewey names commission: 10/9/53.
Page 207: Hathway letter to Richard Clurman: Contained in Pulitzer submission, in *Newsday* files.
Page 207: "*Newsday* knew . . ." *Time*, 10/19/53.
Page 207: Decline in Republican pluralities: 11/4/53.
Page 208: Additional DeKoning indictments: 11/6/53, 12/19/53.
Page 208: Pegler column: *Journal-American*, 4/11/54.
Page 208: "Whether the sentence . . ." 4/10/54.
Page 209: "No one person . . ." 5/4/54.
Page 209: "Newsday is proud . . ." 5/14/54.

CHAPTER FIFTEEN: No Fat Cats Allowed

I

Page 210: "We became . . ." Speech at Fordham University, 7/15/53, in APG papers.

II

Page 214: "A story for this . . ." *Time*, 11/4/66.
Page 215: "NEWSDAY'S SKIERS . . ." 1/16/52.
Page 217: "The Eel" arrested: *Newsday*, 7/26/57; *Long Island Press*, 7/26/57.
Page 217: Francis Henry Bloeth confesses: 8/14/59.

III

Page 218: " . . .the fastest . . ." Clurman, *Time*, 9/13/54.

IV

Page 222: "Escape into Hell" series: 9/8/54 to 9/28/54.
Page 224: Francis Wood sand series: 9/17/56 to 9/21/56.
Page 224: Wood water series: 3/5/57 to 3/8/57.
Page 224: Wood artist series: 4/14/61 to 4/17/61.

V

Page 227: *Newsweek* piece on sports department: 3/27/61.
Page 227 : "These are the souls . . ." 1/21/61.
Page 228: "The Bier That Made . . ." 10/11/57.
Page 229: 300,000 circulation: *Newsday*, 10/24/58.

CHAPTER SIXTEEN: Patterson v. Guggenheim

I

Page 230: Jockey Club plan: 9/22/54, 2/23/55.
Page 230: Editorials on Jockey Club plan: 9/22/54, 4/28/55.
Page 230: Harriman signs NYRA bill: 5/2/55.
Pages 230-231: Cain Hoy Stables: Stephens, *Guess I'm Lucky*, pages 79-91; interviews with Stephens, George Fountaine and Leo Gottlieb.
Pages 231-232: Background of the Solomon R. Guggenheim Museum: Lomask, *Seed Money*, pages 164-218.
Page 232: "Possibly, this is . . ." 10/22/59.

II

Pages 233-237: Adlai Stevenson campaigning in 1954 and 1956: Martin, *Adlai Stevenson and the World*, pages 102-148, 242-398; McKeever, *Adlai Stevenson: His Life and Legacy*, pages 311-390.
Page 233: "I almost wish . . ." *Adlai Stevenson and the World*, page 142.
Page 233: "There were few . . ." *Adlai Stevenson and the World*, page 148.
Page 233: Great Neck rally: 10/30/54.
Page 233: "LI DEMS FOR ADLAI . . ." 11/18/55.
Page 234: " . . .kicking away . . ." AES to APG, 10/11/55, in the papers of Walter Johnson.
Page 234: "Whatever happens . . ." APG to AES, early 1956.
Page 234: "*Well*, boy oh boy . . ." APG to AES, early 1956.
Page 236: "Once in a long . . ." 8/17/56.
Page 236: "As the first . . ." 8/18/56.
Page 236: "Dwight Eisenhower vs. Adlai . . ." 8/23/56.
Page 236: "We will make up . . ." 9/17/56.
Page 236: "Our switch to Stevenson . . ." 10/25/56.
Page 237: HFG to APG on the Stevenson campaign: Mentioned in memo by HFG, 5/21/57, in the Gottlieb papers.

III

Page 238: "APG has done . . ." HFG to APG, 5/21/57, in the Gottlieb papers.
Page 239: "We all feel . . ." HFG to Bernard Gimbel, 10/3/56, in the papers of Eugene Higgins.
Page 240: "Like a Prophet . . ." 10/14/57.
Page 240: "Did I . . ." HFG to APG, 7/1/57, in HFG papers.
Page 240: "Please cable . . ." HFG to APG, 7/15/57, in HFG papers.
Page 240: " . . .entirely too technical . . ." HFG to Richard Clurman, 7/1/57, in the Gottlieb papers.
Page 240: "During her absence . . ." HFG to Gottlieb, 9/9/57, in the Gottlieb papers.
Page 241: "Dr. Gallup has come up . . ." APG to HFG, 8/5/57, in the Gottlieb papers.
Page 241: "I think your impression . . ." HFG to APG, 9/5/57, in the Gottlieb papers.
Page 241: APG agrees to HFG's credo for *Newsday*: Louis Loeb to Gottlieb, 10/15/57, in the Gottlieb papers.
Page 241: "The difficulties of finding . . ." HFG to Gottlieb, 10/30/57, in the Gottlieb papers.

Page 241: "Effective today . . ." Draft of resignation statement, December 1957, in APG papers.

Page 242: " . . .the final decision . . ." HFG to APG, 1/5/58, in the Gottlieb papers.

IV

Page 245: "These schools are . . ." HFG to Nancy Draper, 9/9/53, in HFG papers.

Page 245: "I think your lack . . ." HFG to Dana Draper, 6/9/58.

Page 245: "I am sorry . . ." Dana Draper to HFG, 6/13/58.

Page 246: "Thank you for . . ." Nancy Draper to HFG, 2/12/59.

Page 246: "The reason I'm . . ." Dana Draper to HFG, 5/23/59.

CHAPTER SEVENTEEN: The Reformers

I

Page 248: 12-point program: 2/12/55, 2/24/55.

Page 248: John DeKoning and Marlon Brando character: 2/1/55.

Page 250: Beating of Batalias at union meeting: 1/29/55, 2/2/55, 3/1/55, 3/3/55, 3/4/55, 3/5/55.

Page 250: Charges against Batalias and Wilkens: 6/9/55.

Page 250: Attack on Victor Riesel: 4/5/56.

Page 250: Batalias and Wilkens at union convention: *Newsday*, 4/7/56, 4/10/56, 4/11/56, 4/12/56, 4/13/56, 4/14/56; Wilkens and Bookbinder, *Coronet*, October 1956.

Page 250: Reformers picket: 8/10/56, 8/15/56.

Page 250: Complaint to NLRB: 2/19/55, 4/19/56.

Page 251: "The final end . . ." 9/20/56.

II

Page 252: Jukebox series: 6/6/55 to 6/7/55.

Page 252: "The Mobs Move In . . ." 10/6/55.

Page 253: "DeK FREE, PICKS UP . . ." 10/10/55.

III

Page 254: Population figures: United States Census.

Page 255: "Suffolk's Unsolved . . ." 1/30/56 to 2/3/56.

Page 255: Stan Hinden on the charter: 2/14/56 to 2/17/56.

Page 255: Harriman vetoes charter bill: 4/30/57.

Page 257: Voters approve charter: 11/5/58.

Page 257: Bar association president resigns: 11/3/58.

Page 258: Endorsing H. Lee Dennison: 10/30/59, 11/2/59.

Page 258: Election of Dennison: 11/6/59.

IV

Page 259: "I was responsible . . ." 3/5/57.

Page 260: " . . .a political frameup . . ." 3/7/57.

Page 261: 1953 strike: 2/2/53, 2/5/53, 2/7/53, 2/11/53.

Page 261: Rockaway News bankruptcy, dispute with NMDU: 11/28/58, 11/29/58, 12/13/58, 12/17/58, 12/29/58.

Page 262: Photo of Bob Greene with punctured tire: 12/30/58.

Page 263: Indictment of NMDU leaders: 1/7/58.

Page 263: Irving Bitz background: 12/31/58, 5/6/59.

Page 263: "We do not think . . ." 5/6/59.

Page 263: Greene's story on indictment of Bitz: 6/24/59.

Page 263: Bitz guilty plea and sentencing: 8/4/59, 11/17/59.

Page 263: Guilty pleas by NMDU officials: 10/21/59.

Page 264: "I hate to do this . . ." 7/5/56.

Page 264: "KIDNAP BABY . . ." 7/5/56.

Page 265: Request to *Newsday* to withhold story of Angelo LaMarca's arrest: Altshul manuscript, pages 97-98; interview with Jim O'Neill.

Page 265: "The cooperation of . . ." 8/24/56.

CHAPTER EIGHTEEN: The Boss Lady

I

Page 266: Alicia's accident: Thomas Byrd to HFG, 11/28/59; Josephine Albright to HFG, 1/7/60; HFG to Josephine Albright, 1/12/60, in HFG papers; interview with Dr. William Rawls.

Page 267: Series on astronaut tests: 6/22/59 to 6/26/59.

Page 268: "Fish or . . ." Flagler manuscript, Part II, page 31.

Page 268: "The film's hatred . . ." 10/19/61.

Page 269: Other reviews: *The New Yorker*, 10/21/61; *Time*, 10/20/61.

Page 269: Academy Awards for *West Side Story*: 4/10/62.

Page 269: Guests on 1962 yacht trip: Martin, *Adlai Stevenson and the World*, page 713; Attwood, *Making It Through Middle Age*, page 105; interview with Attwood.

II

Page 272: "I have known . . ." Hathway to staff, 1/7/60, in the papers of Michael Dorman.

Page 272: Jane Gerard on stewardesses: 10/7/58 to 10/10/58.

Page 274: Altshul series on Guantanamo: 10/26/60 to 10/28/60.

III

Page 275: "When the time comes . . ." Patterson and Burton, *Saturday Evening Post*, 2/21/59, page 51.

Page 275: Jay Fred Reeve background: *Chicago Tribune* obituary, 7/24/56; *New York Times* obituary, 7/25/56.

Page 276: Ivan Albright background: *Current Biography 1969*, pages 3-6; *Newsweek*, 11/23/64; *Newsday* obituary, 11/20/83.

Page 278: "Princess of the Crimson . . ." *Time*, 2/16/59.

Pages 278-279: Joe Albright background: *Newsday* internal biography, January, 1969; interview with Albright.

Page 279: Albright on 1960 convention: *Chicago Sun-Times*, 7/29/60.

IV

Page 281: Editorial on *Strike It Rich* program: 2/4/54.

Page 281: "O.K. Say . . ." APG to Jo Coppola, undated, in the papers of Jo Coppola.

Page 281: Coppola columns on *Strike It Rich*: 2/5/54, 2/10/54.

Page 282: Articles on Galindez: *Life*, 2/25/57, 6/9/58.

CHAPTER NINETEEN: APG and JFK

I

Page 283: Cartoon of AES: 4/13/60.

Page 284: JFK victory in West Virginia: 5/11/60.

Page 284: "On the opposite page, Harry . . ." 6/8/60.

Page 284: "I don't call it . . ." *Time*, 6/20/60.

Page 285: Endorsing AES for Secretary of State: 7/12/60.

Page 285: AES convention maneuvers: Martin, *Adlai Stevenson and the World*, pages 517-528; McKeever, *Adlai Stevenson: His Life and Legacy*, pages 452-464.

II

Page 286: "But still we . . ." 5/5/61.

Page 286: JFK letter to *Newsday*: 5/15/61; *New York Times*, 5/16/61; *Time*, 5/26/61.

Page 286: "Is Mitchel Field Necessary?" 10/19/55, 10/20/55.

Page 286: B-26 crash: 11/2/55.

Page 287: Special supplement on Mitchel Field: 1/9/56.

Page 287: "What's Ahead for Mitchel . . ." 11/29/60.

Page 287: Appointment of Mitchel Field committee: 4/28/61.

Pages 288-289: FAA hearings: *Newsday*, 1/17/62, 1/18/62; hearing transcript, in the papers of Marvin Rapp.

Pages 289-290: Details of APG lunch with JFK: Memo, APG to files, 2/27/62, in the APG papers; interviews with Bill Woestendiek, Pierre Salinger and Najeeb Halaby.

Page 289: Republic Aviation supplement: 2/8/62.

Page 290: "MITCHEL RULING . . ." 2/28/62.

III

Page 291: "We were kept . . ." 6/9/62.

Pages 291-292: Edward Kennedy at Harvard: *Boston Globe*, 3/30/62.

Page 292: "If your name were . . ." 8/28/62.

Page 292: Manuel Ycaza marriage: 12/14/62, 12/28/62.

Page 293: "Plan this to go . . ." Alan Hathway to APG, 8/21/62, in APG papers.

Page 293: "Bare Real Reason . . ." 8/22/62.

CHAPTER TWENTY: The Fire Island Connection

I

Pages 294-296: Arthur Lem-Alan Hathway relationship: Interviews with Patricia Barlow, Emil Cianciulli, Cliff De Bear, Ike Eichorn, Dick Greenamyer, Ruth Greenamyer, Bob Greene, Arthur Lem, Rose Lem, Jim O'Neill and Jack Rettaliata.

Page 297: Indictment of the Lems: 6/30/59.

Page 298: Lem trial ends in hung jury: 6/6/60.

Page 298: Lem pleads guilty: 5/9/61.

II

Pages 299-300: Fire Island land transactions: Deeds and mortgages in the office of the Suffolk County Clerk, Riverhead.

Pages 299-300: Zoning hearing: Islip Town Board minutes, 4/19/55.

Page 300: Zoning granted: Islip Town Board minutes, 4/26/55.

Pages 300-301: Dick Aurelio's report from the lighthouse: 9/13/54.

Page 301: Fire Island Inlet: 6/25/56.

Page 301: "I have heard of . . ." 6/26/56.

Page 301: Stuyvesant Wainwright proposal for a national seashore: 7/13/56, 7/23/56, 7/24/56.

III

Page 301: Coverage of winter storm: 3/7/62 to 3/10/62.

Page 302: " . . .utter nonsense . . ." 6/27/56.

Page 302: "Saving Fire Island" editorial: 3/26/62.

Page 304: Controversy over Joseph Carlino's Fire Island land: *Newsday, New York Times*, 6/28/62.

Page 304: Special supplement on Fire Island road: 7/10/62.

Page 304: " . . .vicious smear on . . ." 7/11/62.

Page 304: Temporary state commission approves road: 7/28/62.

Page 304: Criticism of Hathway's Fire Island position: *New York Herald Tribune*, 7/9/62.

Page 305: "The same type construction . . ." 3/26/62.

Page 305: Lawsuit by weeklies to get information on Ocean Parkway: *Babylon Town Leader*, 2/7/63; *Newsday* 2/12/63.

Page 306: Cost of maintenance: *Babylon Town Leader*, 3/21/63.

Page 306: "Backers of Fire Island Park . . ." 9/22/62.

Pages 306-307: Rift between Rockefeller and Moses: 12/1/62, 12/3/62; Caro, *The Power Broker*, pages 1074-1080.

Page 307: "If the Ocean Parkway is merely . . ." 2/27/63.

Page 307: "We welcome a National Seashore . . ." 4/23/62.

Page 307: Editorial criticizing Otis Pike: 4/11/63.

Page 307: "Her decision . . ." 9/1/64.

Page 308: "You can see . . ." Interview with Robert Caro.

CHAPTER TWENTY-ONE: Alicia's Choice

I

Page 309: Complaint about promotional film: HFG to David George, 5/19/61, in the Gottlieb papers.

Page 309: " . . .the never-ending . . ." HFG to APG, 5/19/61, in the Gottlieb papers.

Page 309: "Let me suggest . . ." APG to HFG, 5/22/61, in the Gottlieb papers.

Page 309: "I have too long put off . . ." Carl Sandburg to APG, 7/11/61, in the Sandburg papers.

Page 310: Possible purchase of a radio statio and timberlands: Interview with Leo Gottlieb.

Page 310: " . . .seems entirely likely . . ." HFG to APG, 7/21/61, in the Gottlieb papers.

II

Page 312: "Two weeks from now . . ." APG to Albert Wood, 6/28/63, in the Wood papers.

Pages 313-314: Description of operations on APG: Medical records; interviews with Dr. Jere W. Lord Jr. and Dr. William B. Rawls.

III

Page 316: Description of funeral: 7/6/63.

Page 317: HFG decision not to override APG's will: Interview with Leo Gottlieb.

Page 317: "My original thought . . ." HFG to Janet Hauck and others, 7/8/63, in HFG papers.

Page 317: "She was my oldest . . ." Martin, *Adlai Stevenson and the World*, page 765.

Page 318: "I have read and re-read . . ." *Adlai Stevenson and the World*, page 765.

Page 319: "She told me one time . . ." Martin, *Adlai Stevenson of Illinois*, page 386.

IV

Page 320: "We want to grow . . ." 20th Anniversary recollections of APG, in *Newsday* files.

Page 320: "Not many husbands . . ." Flagler manuscript, Part II, page 55.

CHAPTER TWENTY-TWO: The Captain Takes Command

I

Page 339: Profit and loss statements: Interview with James Fitzgerald.

Page 339: Whitney and Newhouse purchase offers: HFG memo to file, 6/28/66, in HFG papers.

Page 340: Criticism of HFG in Cuba: Interview with Hal Burton; *New York Times*, 8/26/31; Brimmer, "Ambassador Harry Frank Guggenheim in Cuba: 1929-1933."

Page 340: Charles Lindbergh and the press: Anne Morrow Lindbergh, *Hour of Gold, Hour of Lead*, pages 271-272; interview with Anne Morrow Lindbergh.

Page 340: HFG's hearing problems: Interviews with Cliff De Bear, Hal Burton, George Fountaine, Virginia Sheward, Joan Van de Maele.

Page 340: Bonus after APG death: Interviews with Hal Burton, Leonard Partiss Sr. and Bill Woestendiek.

Page 340: HFG trusts Levy and Ferguson: Interview with Burton.

Page 340: "You have done . . ." Quoted in letter, 1/11/67, HFG to JPA, in HFG papers.

Page 341: Ethridge background: *Current Biography*, 1946; *Current Biography*, 1949 (Barry Bingham); *The Annual Obituary*, 1981; obituaries, *Newsday* and the *New York Times*, 4/7/81; interviews with Harry F. Byrd Jr., David Ethridge, Margaret Ethridge, Mark F. Ethridge III, Georgia Schneider, William Sexton.

Page 341: Ethridge bitterness at retirement: Brenner, *House of Dreams*, page 282.

Page 341: Commuting to Chapel Hill: Interviews with Georgia Schneider, Mark F. Ethridge III, David Ethridge.

Page 342: " . . .only a matter . . ." *Time*, 8/23/63.

Page 342: " . . .help settle . . ." MFE to William Friday, 8/9/63, in MFE papers.

Page 342: "This Is Newsday." *Newsday*, 8/5/63.

Page 342: Steinbeck on Mark Ethridge: Steinbeck to HFG, 8/13/63; MFE to HFG, 8/16/63; HFG to Steinbeck, 8/22/63, in HFG papers.

II

Page 343: "The foundation of a newspaper . . ." Woestendiek to MFE, HFG and JPA,

11/26/63, in HFG papers.

Page 343: Woestendiek on Harry's views: Woestendiek to HFG, JPA, Hal Burton, 7/26/63, in HFG papers.

Page 344: Stan Hinden appointment to editorial pages: Interviews with Hinden, Burton, Jim Hadjin, Bob Wiemer, Dick Zander.

III

Page 345: Ethridge drunk driving: Interviews with William Sexton and David Ethridge.

Page 345: Cummings series from Cuba: 9/4/62 to 9/8/62.

Page 345: Cummings on the 26th of July: 7/27/63.

Page 346: Birmingham desegregation: 5/13/64.

Page 346: Ethridge and the library: Stan Asimov to Ethridge and McIlwain, 2/18/65, in *Newsday* files; interviews with William Sexton, Andy Ippolito, Chester Lewis.

Page 346: "That I should have survived . . ." HFG to Alice Albright Hoge, 3/5/64, in HFG papers.

Page 346: Keeping APG's office unchanged: HFG to Josephine Albright, 4/14/65, in HFG papers.

Page 346: Miro mural: HFG to Joan Miro, 11/19/65; dedication speech, 5/18/67, in HFG papers; interviews with Thomas Messer, Emily Genauer.

Page 347: HFG meeting with President Kennedy: HFG memo for files; HFG letter to JFK, 9/9/63, in HFG papers.

Page 347: HFG meeting with LBJ on 2/23/65: HFG memo for files, in HFG papers.

Page 347: Woestendiek resignation: *Newsday*, 4/22/64.

Page 348: Ethridge departure: *Newsday*, 5/18/65.

Page 348: Possible replacements for Ethridge: Interview with Gottlieb.

IV

Page 349: Thirty-five-hour work week: Memo, HFG to staff, 5/31/66, in *Newsday* files.

Page 350: Ban on gun ads: Interview with David Targe.

Page 350: "This does not mean . . ." Alan Hathway speech to Copley Newspapers seminar, 5/14/65, in the Hathway papers.

Page 350: Endorsement of Lyndon Johnson: 10/19/64.

Page 350: Endorsement of Eugene Nickerson: 10/20/64.

Pages 350-351: Jo Coppola series on homosexuality: 3/16/49, 3/17/49, 3/18/49, 3/21/49, 3/22/49.

V

Page 351: Carl Sandburg-Frank Lloyd Wright conversation: *Newsday*, 4/20/57; interview with Harvey Weber.

Page 351: Huxley supplement: 5/31/58; letter, Woestendiek to Huxley, 5/23/58, and news release, 7/1/58, in *Newsday* files; interviews with Richard Clurman, John Van Doorn.

Page 351: Erskine Caldwell piece: 10/5/63.

Page 352: Ruby Hart Phillips announcement, 10/24/63.

Page 352: Marguerite Higgins announcement: 10/12/63.

Page 352: Marguerite Higgins death: *Newsday*, 1/4/66; interviews with Michael O'Neill, Thomas Dorsey.

Page 352: O'Hara announcement: *Newsday*, 9/15/64; *Time*, 9/25/64.

Page 352: HFG's request to Stevenson to write a column: HFG to AES, 2/2/65; AES to HFG, 3/3/65, in HFG papers.

Page 353: Stevenson's death: Martin, *Adlai Stevenson and the World*, pages 862-863; McKeever, *Adlai Stevenson: His Life and Legacy*, page 563.

Pages 353-354: Signing Erma Bombeck: Letter, Glenn Thompson to Thomas Dorsey, 1/15/65, in *Newsday* files.

VI

Page 355: Nonfiction based on *The Grapes of Wrath*: Interviews with Tetsumaro Hayashi, Elaine Steinbeck.

Page 355: Steinbeck and Stevenson: Martin, *Adlai Stevenson and the World*, page 512; McKeever, *Adlai Stevenson: His Life and Legacy*, page 210; interviews with Hayashi, Elaine Steinbeck.

Page 355: Early Steinbeck pieces for *Newsday*: Kentucky Derby, 5/7/56; Brooklyn boy in Rome,

5/16/57; St. Peter's, 5/21/57; Queen's birthday, 6/20/57.

Page 355: Steinbeck letter to Adlai Stevenson: 12/22/59; Steinbeck response to critics, 3/1/60.

Page 356: Request to Steinbeck for stories from Russia: MFE to HFG, 8/16/63; HFG to Steinbeck, 8/22/63, in HFG papers.

Pages 356-357: Request to Steinbeck to write a column: HFG to Steinbeck, 8/9/65; Steinbeck to HFG, 8/11/65; HFG to Steinbeck, 8/12/65; Steinbeck to HFG, 8/14/65; undated, Steinbeck to HFG, acknowledging rose; HFG to Steinbeck, 8/17/65; Steinbeck to HFG, 9/7/65; Steinbeck to HFG, 9/9/65; HFG to Steinbeck, 9/15/65; Steinbeck to HFG, 9/20/65; HFG to Steinbeck, 9/23/65.

Page 357: Editors dislike "Letters to Alicia" format: HFG to Steinbeck, 11/10/65; Al Marlens to HFG, 11/12/65; Steinbeck to HFG, 11/17/65.

Page 357: Proposal to publish letters between Steinbeck and his son: Steinbeck to HFG. 12/9/65; HFG to Steinbeck, 12/15/65.

Page 357: "Letter to Alicia" on the Americong: 12/18/65.

Page 357: "Letter to Alicia" on draft-card burning: 12/24/65.

Page 358: "Letter to Alicia" on Alnwick Castle: 12/31/65.

Page 358: Israel trip: Steinbeck to HFG, 1/15/66; HFG to Steinbeck, 1/20/66.

Page 358: "Letter to Alicia" on Steinbeck's great-grandfather in the Holy Land: 2/12/66.

Page 358: Steinberg and the waiter: *Jerusalem Post*, 2/11/66, 2/16/66; *New York Times*, 2/17/66; *Newsday*, 2/28/66.

Page 358: "Letter to Alicia" on brave Israelis: 3/5/66.

Page 358: "Letter to Alicia" on irrigation: 3/12/66.

Page 358: "Letter to Alicia" on the mount of the Beatitudes: 3/19/66.

Page 358: "In writing them she came very much alive . . ." Steinbeck to HFG, 2/19/66.

Page 358: "No man has really . . ." Steinbeck to HFG, 4/4/66.

Page 359: ". . . an unsurpassable . . ." HFG to Van Doorn, 10/28/65.

Page 359: "I know my military . . ." HFG to Steinbeck, 6/7/66.

Page 359: "Before it is . . ." HFG to Steinbeck, 10/10/66.

Page 359: Open letter to Yevgeny Yevtushenko: *Newsday* and *New York Times*, 7/11/66.

Page 359: LBJ rewriting speech: Steinbeck to HFG, 7/14/66.

Pages 359-360: LBJ inaugural speech: *Newsday*, 1/21/65.

Page 360: "They say there's no fool . . ." 12/3/66.

Page 360: "Can you understand . . ." 1/7/67.

Page 360: "I don't want to be . . ." 12/31/66.

Page 360: "Did you ever see . . ." Steinbeck to HFG, 1/4/67.

Page 360: "Am investigating . . ." HFG to Steinbeck, 1/9/67.

Page 360: "Expert advice . . ." HFG to Steinbeck, 1/14/67.

Page 361: "This is a man . . ." Steinbeck to HFG, 1/19/67.

Page 361: "He is caught . . ." HFG to Steinbeck, 1/26/67.

CHAPTER TWENTY-THREE: Guggenheim Journalism

I

Page 362: Population figures: United States Census.

Page 362: 400,000 circulation: 10/2/64.

Page 362: "Nassau has already . . ." 3/23/54.

Page 363: Caro background: Interview with Caro; Seligsohn, *The Newsday Magazine*, 11/21/82; *Current Biography Yearbook*, 1984.

Page 363: Caro story on attempted suicide: 9/19/59.

Page 364: "Misery Acres" series: 1/7/63 to 1/10/63.

Page 364: Photograph of Rockefeller and Caro: 4/27/63.

Page 364: "Suffolk: The Still Sick Giant" series: 1/20/64 to 1/24/64.

Page 365: Creation of regional planning board: 1/12/65.

II

Page 366: Editorial on civil rights act: 6/20/63.

Page 366: Editorial criticizing *Review-Star*: 6/23/43.

Page 366: Editorial against racism in sports: 3/1/47.

Page 367: Editorial against critics of whites-only policy at Levittown: 3/12/49.

Page 367: *Brown* v. *Board of Education* editorial: 5/19/54.
Page 367: Editorials on Orval Faubus: 9/7/57; 9/10/57; 9/16/57; 9/21/57; 9/15/58; 8/14/59.
Page 367: Editorials urging President Eisenhower to speak out: 9/5/57; 9/12/57; 9/17/57; 9/24/57.
Page 367: Editorial on election of Henrik Verwoerd: 9/8/58.
Page 367: Editorials on influx of minorities: 12/1/59; 12/5/59.
Page 367: Editorials on Freedom Riders: 5/23/61; 5/26/61; 5/31/61.
Page 367: Woestendiek series on southern integration: 3/2/56, 3/5/56 to 3/8/56.
Page 367: Aronson series on housing discrimination: 4/30/62 to 5/3/62.
Page 367: Angelo on James Meredith: 9/20/62, 9/21/62, 9/24/62.
Page 368: "As an inducement . . ." Kaplan, *The Dream Deferred*, page 88.
Page 370: Johnson piece on Washington march: 8/29/63.
Page 370: Johnson and the Garden City Hotel: 7/3/64, 7/6/64.
Page 370: Johnson report from Mississippi: 7/9/64.
Page 370: Johnson on Malcolm X assassination: 2/22/65.
Page 370: "The Negro on Long Island . . ." 1/8/66.
Page 370: North Amityville series: 8/15/66 to 8/19/66.
Page 370: Patterson on Martin Luther King assassination: 4/6/68, 4/8/68, 4/9/68.
Page 370: "Song to a River . . ." 8/1/61.
Page 371: Greene story after Birmingham bombing: 9/17/63.
Page 371: Greene story about Martin Luther King and John Kennedy: 9/18/63; *New York Times*, 9/19/63.
Page 371: ". . . restraint and responsibility . . ." 9/20/63.
Page 372: Greene on missing civil rights workers: 6/23/64.
Page 372: "The Klan Rides Again . . ." 6/6/64 to 6/9/64.
Page 372: "Voices of Mississippi . . ." 8/8/64.
Page 372: "They clustered under . . ." 6/10/66.
Page 373: "Dixie's New Negro . . ." 6/25/66 to 7/1/66.
Page 373: Gambling series: 1/13/64 to 1/15/64.
Pages 373-374: Drug series: 1/4/66 to 1/7/66.

CHAPTER TWENTY-FOUR: Falls from Grace

I

Page 376: Five-part series on Puerto Rico: 3/18/57 to 3/22/57.
Page 376: ". . . Island Racing . . ." 3/20/59.
Page 376: "Showcase for Latin America . . ." 3/11/61.
Page 376: Marguerite Higgins column: 3/8/65.
Page 376: "You want to come to the rescue . . ." HFG to Hathway, 3/15/65, in *Newsday* files.
Page 378: "Long Island's top racket-buster . . ." 9/12/62.
Page 378: Welfare cheats story: 10/18/62.
Page 378: Housewife prostitute roundup: 2/4/64.
Page 380: Cahn defeats Gibbons: 11/3/65.

II

Page 380: "This is a good time . . ." JPA to HFG, 12/25/63.
Page 380: HFG generosity to Albrights: HFG to Josephine, passing along Steinbeck correspondence, 11/16/65, in HFG papers.
Page 380: "Joe has taken . . ." HFG to Josephine, 10/22/64.
Page 382: "My mind is forever . . ." Draper to HFG, 2/5/61.
Page 382: Draper discharge: HFG to Draper, 12/6/61; *Newsday*, 12/6/61.
Page 382: Draper enters Columbia: Draper to HFG, 2/18/63.
Page 382: HFG appoints Draper to foundation: HFG to Draper, 5/10/63.
Page 382: HFG buys Draper a Porsche: George Fountaine to North Country Motors, 6/11/63.
Page 382: "I have little doubt . . ." HFG to trustees, 1/64, in the Gottlieb papers.
Page 382: ". . .might be a solution . . ." Memo for file, Gottlieb, 9/15/64, in the Gottlieb papers.
Page 382: "Mr. Guggenheim was somewhat . . ." Memo for file, Gottlieb, 9/15/64, in the

Gottlieb papers.

Page 383: Draper's report on Cain Hoy: Draper to HFG, 6/18/65; HFG to Draper, 6/22/65, in HFG papers.

Page 383: HFG tells Draper he will have to spend time at *Newsday*: HFG to Draper, 9/13/65, in the Gottlieb papers.

Page 383: "I have had one great . . ." HFG to Draper, 1/6/66, in HFG papers.

Page 384: "I have ever . . ." HFG to Draper, 5/2/67, in HFG papers.

CHAPTER TWENTY-FIVE: The Captain and the Minister

I

Pages 385-390: Moyers background: Anderson, *The President's Men*; Medved, *The Shadow Presidents*; *Current Biography*, 1966, 1976; *Contemporary Authors*; interviews with Bill Moyers.

Page 386: "This, we both . . ." BDM to LBJ, 2/7/54, in LBJ library.

Page 386: "I am impressed . . ." LBJ to BDM, 2/12/54, in LBJ library.

Page 387: "I suppose . . ." Wicker, *Harper's*, October 1965, page 44.

Page 389: "And thanks . . ." BDM to HFG, 2/29/65, in HFG papers.

Page 389: Congratulatory note: HFG to BDM, 7/12/65, in HFG papers.

Page 389: "Sometime I would . . ." HFG to BDM, 7/19/65, in HFG papers.

Page 391: Death of James Moyers: *New York Times*, 9/18/66, 9/21/66.

Page 391: BDM conversation with Marquis Childs: Childs to HFG, 12/20/66, in HFG papers.

II

Page 393: Terms of Hathway's departure: Agreement, 1/20/67, in *Newsday* files.

Page 393: "Naturally, I was . . ." Josephine Albright to HFG, 12/67, in HFG papers.

Page 393: "You have temporarily . . ." HFG to JPA, 1/11/67.

Page 393: Terms of employment for BDM: Contract, 2/15/67, in *Newsday* files.

Page 394: "I have always . . ." Speech by Bill Moyers, 2/15/67, in HFG papers.

Page 394: "Len, I've got . . ." Hal Burton notes on an interview with Leonard Hall, 9/17/74.

Page 394: "Bill Moyers at long last . . ." HFG to Steinbeck, 3/6/67, in HFG papers.

III

No source notes in this section.

IV

Page 399: "I don't come to work . . ." Interview with Stan Green.

Page 400: Prohibition against antiwar buttons: Marlens to staff, 11/19/69, in *Newsday* files.

Page 400: Job offer from John Gardner: John Gardner to HFG, 2/24/68; HFG to Gardner, 2/28/68, in HFG papers.

V

Page 402: "I wanted to cover . . ." *Newsweek*, 8/28/67.

Page 402: "How Liberals Failed the Negro . . ." 8/5/67.

Page 403: Hamill column on Che Guevara: 10/12/67.

Page 403: Hamill column on the snowstorm: 12/2/67.

Page 404: Announcement of Aronson column: 6/27/67.

Page 404: Announcement of Mayer and Hamill columns: 9/11/67.

Page 404: Mayer profile of Detroit riot victim: 7/27/67.

Page 404: Mayer columns on teacher strike in New York City: 9/11/67, 9/13/67, 9/27/67.

Page 405: HFG tries to recruit Harold Gleason: Interview with Gleason.

Page 405: Recommendation to hire Warren Berry: Memo, McIlwain to HFG and BDM, 8/18/67, in HFG papers.

Page 406: Background of Local 406 controversy: Memo, HFG to Local 406 members, 9/22/67, in the papers of Local 406; interviews with Harvey Broad, Frank Farrell, Joseph Ozechowski, Bill Schindler, George Tedeschi, John Vanden Heuvel.

Page 406: Order to pressmen to run presses without extra men: John Reynolds, president of Local 406, to Floyd Main, *Newsday* production manager, 9/14/67, in the papers of Local 406; interview with Tedeschi.

Page 406: Listing of sabotage: Memo, Floyd Main to HFG, 11/6/67, in *Newsday* files.
Page 407: Sydney Gruson accepts a job at *Newsday*: Gruson to BDM, 3/6/68, in *Newsday* files.
Page 407: "It's a good . . ." Gruson to James Reston, 3/19/68, in *Newsday* files.
Page 407: "It will not be . . ." Gruson to Lester Markel, 3/21/68, in *Newsday* files.
Page 409: Background of the art department: Interviews with Paul Back, Robert Hessler.
Page 410: " . . .an advanced example . . ." Evans, *Newspaper Design*, page 100.
Page 412: Insolia promotion: 7/28/69.

VI

Page 412: "I am not as alert . . ." HFG to Diane Meek, 6/25/68, in HFG papers.
Page 412: HFG wears copper bracelets: George Fountaine to Walter Moulton, 7/1/68.
Page 412: "Newsday's endorsement will . . ." BDM to HFG, 10/8/68, in HFG papers.
Page 413: Letters between Richard Nixon and HFG: HFG to Nixon, 11/10/60; Nixon to HFG, 12/9/60; HFG to Nixon, 6/23/61; Nixon to HFG, 6/30/61, 9/15/61; HFG to Nixon, 9/27/61.
Page 413: HFG notes on Nixon endorsement: Memo by HFG, apparently to files, 10/7/68, in HFG papers.
Page 413: "If you have to have . . ." BDM to HFG, 10/17/68, in HFG papers.
Page 414: "The reaction of . . ." HFG to BDM, 11/6/68, in BDM papers.
Page 414: "Frankly, I did not . . ." BDM to HFG, 11/7/68, in BDM papers.
Page 414: Peeples conversation with Gottlieb: Memo, Gottlieb, 11/19/68, in the Gottlieb papers; interview with Gottlieb.
Page 414: Description of third codicil: Memo for file, Gottlieb, 12/24/68, in the Gottlieb papers.
Page 414: Designation of BDM to succeed HFG: HFG to secretary of *Newsday*, 12/11/68, in the Gottlieb papers.

CHAPTER TWENTY-SIX: The Suffolk Scandals

I

Page 417: Background of the 1950s Suffolk scandals: 1/20/55, 10/6/55, 10/7/55, 12/12/55, 3/17/56, 6/8/56, 12/8/56, 3/16/59, 12/14/60.
Page 417: Islip purchases parking lot property: 6/25/64.
Page 418: Julius Klein testimony: 10/22/65.
Page 418: Islip fires Eugene Verratti: 10/7/65.
Page 418: Grand jury returns no indictments: 1/29/66.
Page 419: Kirk Price's death: *Newsday*, 3/14/67, 3/17/67; interview with Perfall.
Page 420: "11 Overboard . . ." 6/22/67.

II

Page 420: Greene's expenses on Garrison story: *Slug*, March, April-May, 1967.
Page 421: Appointment of Conlon to tax commission: 12/23/66.
Page 423: McGowan and the Suffolk County Water Authority: 7/13/63.
Page 424: McGowan agrees to meet with Greene alone: Letter, Edward McGowan to author, 8/8/89.
Page 424: "Probe of Conlon . . ." 9/29/67.
Pages 424-425: Stories on Donald Kuss and Kirk Price: 9/30/67.
Page 425: Aspland agrees to investigate: 10/6/67; interviews with Bob Greene, Jack Ehrlich, James Catterson.
Page 425: McGowan press conference: 11/6/67.
Page 425: " . . .exploited racial prejudice . . ." 11/3/67.
Page 425: Democratic victories: 11/8/67.
Page 425: Conlon-Kuss indictment: 12/5/67.
Page 425: McGowan resignation: 12/9/67.
Pages 425-426: "Water Authority meetings . . ." Letter, Edward McGowan to author, 8/8/89.
Page 426: Appointment of Maurice Nadjari: 12/19/67.
Page 426: Kuss-Conlon convictions: 10/23/68.
Page 426: "I did not use . . ." Letter, Edward McGowan to author, 8/8/89.
Page 426: "All these charges . . ." Interview with McGowan.

III

Page 427: "I will buy . . ." 5/2/68.
Page 427: Zeidler suspends himself as chairman of Suffolk County Water Authority: 5/4/68.
Page 427: "Macy's Good for Returns." 5/9/68.
Page 427: Brookhaven indictments: 5/25/68.
Page 427: George Fuchs pleads guilty: 5/11/71.
Page 427: Death of Clarence Hough: 2/14/70.
Pages 427-428: Zeidler uses his knowledge as chairman of the Suffolk County Water Authority: 12/17/68.
Page 428: Legislature tightens zoning laws: 5/24/69.
Page 428: Fred Fellman takes kickbacks on trailers: 7/13/71.
Pages 429-430: Reexamination of Ted Kennedy's walk on Chappaquiddick: 7/25/69.
Page 430: Indictment of Waldman: 7/12/74.
Page 430: Waldman's guilty plea: 2/24/76.
Page 431: Stories on Arthur Cromarty: 10/1/69.
Page 431: Appellate Division finds no wrongdoing by Cromarty: 7/2/70.
Page 431: Indictment of Fred and Raymond Fellman: 2/4/70.
Page 431: Charges against Raymond Fellman dismissed: 11/11/71.
Page 431: Acquittals of two other defendants: 10/13/71, 12/71.
Page 431: Conviction of a third defendant: 7/7/71, 9/9/71, 7/25/73.
Page 431: Fred Fellman pleads guilty: 5/11/71, 7/13/71, 11/13/72.

CHAPTER TWENTY-SEVEN: The Setting of the Sun

I

Pages 433-434: Expansion of Cowles Communications: Cowles, *Mike Looks Back*, pages 208-212.
Page 434: "The people in . . ." *A Study of Suffolk County*, Louis Harris and Associates, July, 1966, in *Newsday* files.
Page 435: "A battle of this kind . . ." Memo, HFG for files, 6/28/66, in the Gottlieb papers.

II

Page 435: Budget revisions for *Suffolk Sun*: Memo, Frank Farrell to HFG and BDM, 3/2/67, in HFG papers.

III

Page 439: "Published for Long Island . . ." 8/23/66.
Page 441: Announcement by Gardner Cowles that the *Sun* was closing: *Suffolk Sun*, 10/18/69.
Page 441: The demise of *Look* magazine: *Newsday*, 9/17/71.

CHAPTER TWENTY-EIGHT: The Man in the Gravy-Stained Tie

I

Page : "There are days . . ." BDM to McIlwain, Marlens, 2/26/69, in *Newsday* files.

II

Pages 447-448: The hiring and firing of John Denson: Kluger, *The Paper*, pages 603-646.
Page 448-449: The death of the *Tribune*: *The Paper*, pages 724-745.
Page 450: Appointment of Laventhol as associate editor: BDM to staff, 7/9/69, in *Newsday* files.

III

Page 450: "This is a proposal . . ." Laventhol to BDM, McIlwain, Marlens and others, 10/1/69, in the Laventhol papers.
Page 451: Appointment of Marvin Kitman: 12/1/69.
Page 452: "I felt Bill . . ." McIlwain, *A Farewell to Alcohol*, pages 14-15.
Page 452: Announcement of McIlwain's departure: BDM to staff, 12/9/69, in *Newsday* files.
Page 453: "Our first obligation . . ." BDM to Laventhol, 12/15/69, in BDM papers.

Page 453: "Into the '70s . . ." 12/31/69.

CHAPTER TWENTY-NINE: Guggenheim v. Moyers

I

Page 454: McGrady memo on Vietnam: 4/26/67, in HFG papers.
Page 456: "The new President's . . ." 1/21/69.
Page 456: "We need a policy . . ." 3/3/69.
Page 456: Series of Vietnam editorials: 3/25/69, 3/26/69.
Page 456: Editorial on Nixon's first 100 days: 4/30/69.
Page 456: " . . .candid and canny" Vietnam speech: 5/15/69.
Page 456: Editorial on critics of military policy: 6/6/69.
Page 456: "President Nixon's decision . . ." 6/10/69.
Page 456: Announcement of Gelman appointment: 7/28/69.

II

Page 457: "As one of *Newsday*'s . . ." McGrady, *Stranger Than Naked*, pages 10-11.
Page 457: "There will be . . ." *Stranger Than Naked*, page 13.
Page 458: "Gillian, as the book . . ." *Stranger Than Naked*, page 17.
Page 458: The *Newsday* contributors to *Naked Came the Stranger*: Barry Abisch, Harvey Aronson, Marilyn Berger, Bernie Bookbinder, Carol Burton, Martin Buskin, Ken Byerly, John Cummings, Val Duncan, Merle Goldberg, Gene Goltz, Stan Green, Bob Greene, Tony Insolia, Stan Isaacs, Mal Karman, Jane Margold, Robert Mayer, Mike McGrady, Bill McIlwain, Jack Schwartz, George Vecsey, Bob Waters, Robert Wiemer.
Page 459: "They get stopped . . ." *Stranger Than Naked*, pages 107-108.
Page 459: "Meet the Baron . . ." *Stranger Than Naked*, page 115.
Page 459: Local stories on *Naked Came the Stranger*: *Suffolk Sun*, *Newsday*, 8/7/69.
Page 459: Cover story suggestion: Mike McGrady to Bill Moyers, 3/28/69, in the Laventhol papers.

III

Page 460: " . . .welcome, but less than . . ." 9/17/69.
Page 460: "Americans are profoundly . . ." 10/1/69.
Page 461: "Newsday was sucked into . . ." HFG to BDM, 10/20/69; BDM to HFG, 10/21/69, in BDM papers.
Page 461: Viewpoints piece on the F-14: 1/7/70.
Page 462: "I call on Harry . . ." 10/28/69.
Page 462: "Leonard Hall told me . . ." HFG to BDM, 10/29/69, in BDM papers.
Page 462: "Leonard Hall is wrong . . ." BDM to HFG, 10/29/69, in BDM papers.
Page 462: Hall representing HFG on gift of Falaise to Nassau County: Hall to HFG, 11/7/68, in HFG papers.
Page 462: "People like Flora Lewis . . ." HFG to BDM, 12/18/69, in BDM papers.
Page 462: "All liberals today . . ." HFG to BDM, 12/27/69, in BDM papers.
Page 462: "I simply cannot . . ." BDM to HFG, 1/1/70, in BDM papers.
Page 463: Stroke in early 1970: Memo for file, John F. Ward, 9/4/70, in the Gottlieb papers.

CHAPTER THIRTY: Harry and Norman and Otis

I

Page 465: 1965 will provisions: Gottlieb to HFG, 6/8/65, in the Gottlieb papers.
Page 465: 1967 will provisions: Memo for file, Gottlieb, 1/6/67, in the Gottlieb papers.
Page 465: HFG memo to executors on Peter Lawson-Johnston: 7/28/69, in the Gottlieb papers.
Page 466: Timing of the meeting in the hospital: Memo for file, Gottlieb, 10/10/69, in the Gottlieb papers.
Page 466: "I want Mr. Moyers . . ." HFG to executors, 7/28/69, in the Gottlieb papers.
Page 466: Hanes background: Hollingsworth, *The Blood-Horse*, 12/21/63, page 1758; *Daily Racing Form*, 4/23/82.

II

Pages 467-470: Chandler family and *Los Angeles Times* background: Berges, *The Life and Times of Los Angeles*; Halberstam, *The Powers That Be*; Gottlieb, Robert, and Wolt, *Thinking Big*.
Page 470: "I asked the porter . . ." *The Powers That Be*, page 101.

III

Page 472: BDM announcement about sale: 3/11/70, in *Newsday* files.
Page 473: "The news . . ." BDM to HFG, 3/12/70, in the Gottlieb papers.
Page 473: Response of the Albright family: Telegram, 3/14/70, in *Newsday* files.
Page 473: "One reporter . . ." BDM to HFG, 3/17/70, in the Gottlieb papers.
Page 473: "Pray for Joe . . ." Aronson, *New York*, 3/30/70, page 45.
Page 474: Restructuring proposal by the Albrights: David Washburn to Gottlieb, 4/13/70; Gottlieb to Washburn, 4/15/70, in the Gottlieb papers.
Page 474: Meeting at LaGuardia: Memo for files, Thomas Hagoort, 4/15/70, in the Gottlieb papers.
Page 474: Times Mirror signs the agreement: Hagoort to Arthur Schmutz, 5/4/70, in the Gottlieb papers.
Page 474: "I'll be very interested . . ." *Time*, 4/27/70.
Page 475: Moyers statement on Pulitzers: 5/5/70.
Page 475: Drafting of codicil: John F. Ward to HFG, 4/8/70, in the Gottlieb papers.
Page 476: "If I were to provide . . ." HFG will, 3/12/70, page 33.
Page 476: "To have published . . ." 5/13/70.

IV

Page 477: "A Los Angeles Times official . . ." *New York Times*, 5/13/70.
Page 477: "Jim says he didn't . . ." Laventhol to staff, 5/13/70, in *Newsday* files.
Page 477: "The type of man . . ." Bellows to Chandler, 5/10/70, in the Laventhol papers.
Page 480: UAW straw vote: *Editor & Publisher*, 5/16/70.
Page 480: "I do argue . . ." Laventhol to staff, 6/15/70, in *Newsday* files.
Page 480: Walter Reuther's death: *New York Times*, 5/10/70.
Page 480: UAW withdraws petition: Frank Farrell to staff, 8/11/70, in *Newsday* files.

V

Pages 481-482: Memo on the term "black militant," 5/12/70, to *Newsday* management, from Robert DeLeon, Robert Imbriano, Angela Dews, Les Payne, Kent D. Smith, Laura Blackwell, Victoria Mares and Michael Alexander, in *Newsday* files.
Page 483: "Waiting for the Eagle to Fly," 7/11/70.
Pages 483-484: Price change: 9/21/70.
Pages 484-485: Dill-Nickerson campaign: *Newsday*, 5/25/61, 6/1/61, 9/15/61, 10/26/61, 10/27/61, 10/28/61; interviews with Forrest Corson, Joseph Carlino, John F. English, Dick Zander, Stan Hinden, Edith Wyckoff, Mitch Lipson, Eugene Nickerson and Hal Burton.
Page 485: Nickerson series: 9/28/70 to 10/5/70.
Page 485: Master plan series: 7/13/70 to 7/18/70.
Page 485: Initial stories on Pennsylvania crash: 7/16/70 to 7/18/70.

CHAPTER THIRTY-ONE: Enter the Ambassador

I

Pages 490-491: Attwood background: Attwood, *Making It Through Middle Age* and *The Twilight Struggle*; interview with Attwood.
Page 492: Agreement between Albrights and Times Mirror: 10/28/70.

II

Page 492: Attwood's knowledge of Flagler manuscript: Attwood to Otis Chandler, 10/14/70, in the Attwood papers.
Pages 492-493: Asimov memo to Attwood on issues at *Newsday*: 10/21/70, in the Asimov papers.
Page 493: Promotion of Laventhol to editor: 11/2/70.

Page 494: Salary increase: Attwood to staff, 10/28/70, in *Newsday* files.

Page 494: "If the mere threat . . ." Newsday-Guild Organizing Committee, 12/10/70, in the papers of Bruce Lambert.

Page 494: "We are all delighted . . ." Robinson to Attwood, 1/15/71, in the Attwood papers.

Page 494: Appointment of Bordash to replace Mullen: 1/19/71.

Page 495: Description of HFG health: Dr. Jerome B. Posner to HFG, 6/3/70, in HFG papers.

Page 495: Return to Falaise from Sloan-Kettering: George Fountaine to Joan Van de Maele, 9/16/70, in HFG papers.

Page 495: "As you know, Harry . . ." Lawson-Johnston to Chandler, 2/8/71, in Attwood papers.

Page 495: Development of plaque for living room at Falaise: Lindbergh to HFG, 6/17/66, in HFG papers.

Pages 495-496: HFG instructions on display of Falaise: Interview with Phyllis Braff.

Pages 496-497: Resignation of Albright and appointment of Sackett: 3/9/71.

Page 497: Ernie Levy retirement: Press release, 3/11/71, in *Newsday* files.

III

Page 498: "Times Mirror paid . . ." Chandler to Attwood, 12/16/70, in the Attwood papers.

Page 498: ". . .more carefully and with less emotion . . ." Attwood to Chandler, 2/5/71, in the Attwood papers.

Page 498: ". . .quite hysterical . . ." Chandler to Attwood, 2/16/71, in the Attwood papers.

Page 499: "I pray for . . ." BDM to Bernie Bookbinder, undated, in the Bookbinder papers.

Page 499: War crimes editorial: 3/22/71.

Page 499: "I will never ask . . ." Chandler to Attwood, 3/26/71, in the Attwood papers.

Page 499: "I welcomed your comments . . ." Attwood to Chandler, 3/30/71, in the Attwood papers.

Page 500: "He was 'extremely . . .'" Laventhol to Attwood, 2/2/72, in the Attwood papers.

Page 500: ". . .still the weakest . . ." Chandler to Attwood, 3/30/72, in the Attwood papers.

Page 500: Appointment of Sexton to replace Bookbinder: Laventhol to staff, 4/28/72.

CHAPTER THIRTY-TWO: Stalking Nixon

I

Page 501: Lunch meeting on Nixon investigation: Greene to Laventhol, 1/11/71, in the Greene papers.

Pages 501-502: Rebozo chronology, Ken Crowe to Greene, 2/25/71, in the Greene papers.

Page 502: "It seems . . ." Sackett to Laventhol, 3/15/71, in the Greene papers.

Page 502: "It is now over . . ." Jackie Marro to Laventhol, 5/26/71, in the Laventhol papers.

II

Page 503: "The Florida of Richard Nixon . . ." 10/13/71.

Page 503: ". . .an encyclopedic . . ." *Time*, 10/25/71.

Page 504: "Peter Ritner, editor-in-chief . . ." Laventhol to Attwood, 10/18/71, in the Greene papers.

Page 504: "It would have looked like . . ." Wise, *The Politics of Lying*, page 224.

Page 504: "Robinson called . . ." Undated memo, in the Greene papers.

Page 504: "A discreet look . . ." Jack Caulfield to John Dean, 9/10/71, in the Marro papers.

Page 504: Antitrust action: John J. Caulfield to John Dean, 11/2/71; David Wilson to John Dean, 12/1/71, in the Marro papers.

Page 505: Accreditation difficulties: Sackett to Gerald Warren, 2/18/72, in the Laventhol papers.

Page 505: "I said as soon as I sat down . . ." Schram for file, 2/7/72, in the Laventhol papers.

Page 505: "I didn't think . . ." Sackett to Laventhol and Volkman, 3/23/72, in the Laventhol papers.

Page 505: Caulfield and Dean on Greene's taxes: 5/28/74.

Page 505: GeoTek: Halberstam, *The Powers That Be*, pages 631-633; Berges, *The Life and Times of Los Angeles*, pages 158-162.

Pages 505-506: Nixon announces Long Island SMSA: 10/24/72.

Page 506: Attwood press release on SMSA: 10/24/72, in the Attwood papers.

Page 506: SMSA promo campaign: Attwood to Robinson, 12/29/72; Robinson to Attwood, 1/12/73; Attwood to Robinson, 1/22/73.

Page 506: Bookbinder on non-endorsement: Bookbinder to Attwood, 9/5/72, in the Bookbinder papers.

Page 506: *Editor & Publisher* on non-endorsement: 9/9/72.

Page 507: G. Gordon Liddy story: 7/22/72.

Page 507: Comment on *Newsday*'s Liddy story: Bernstein and Woodward, *All the President's Men*, page 35.

CHAPTER THIRTY-THREE: The Heroin Trail

I

Page 509: Greene interview with Vizzini: Greene to Laventhol and Forst, 2/28/72, in the Greene papers.

Page 509: " . . .professional military . . ." Greene to Laventhol and Forst, 4/17/72, in the Greene papers.

Page 510: "Particularly in the interior . . ." Greene to Laventhol, 5/8/72, in the Laventhol papers.

Page 510: "Much of the expenses appear. . ." Attwood handwritten comments on memo from Greene to Laventhol, 5/8/72, in the Laventhol papers.

Page 510: Rice-paper lists: Greene to Arthur Klein, undated, in the Greene papers; interview with Les Payne.

II

Page 511: "You can be shot . . ." Greene to Arthur Klein, undated, in Greene papers.

Page 512: "At times . . ." Greene to Forst, 7/4/72, in the Greene papers.

Page 512: Meetings with Ozpetek: Greene to Forst, 7/7/72 and 7/13/72, in the Greene papers.

Page 512: Meetings with Syrian brothers: Greene to Forst, 7/7/72 and 7/9/72, in the Greene papers.

Page 512: Confirmation of names by CIA: Greene to Forst, 8/9/72, in the Greene papers.

Page 512: Confirmation of names by Orhan Erbug: Memo for file, Les Payne, 8/21/72, in the Greene papers.

Page 513: Greene-Royce trip to Bulgaria: Greene to Forst, 7/21/72; memo for file, Knut Royce, undated, in the Greene papers.

Page 513: "When You Crisscross . . ." 2/8/73.

III

Page 514: OAS against de Gaulle: *Newsday*, 2/11/73; *Encyclopedia Americana*.

Page 514: Marcel Francisci and the Gaullists: 2/15/73.

Pages 515-516: Greene impersonation of a lawyer: *Newsday*, 2/13/73; interviews with Greene, Meyer, Cook, Attwood.

Page 516: Chase scene on Corsica: *Newsday*, 2/17/73, interviews with Les Payne and Chris Cook.

IV

Page 520: Story on suspected Long Island dealers: 2/25/73.

Pages 520-521: Ralph Eboli indictment and conviction: 2/27/73, 3/13/73, 8/25/73; interview with Joe Demma.

Page 521: Photographs of Syrian smugglers: 2/6/73.

V

Page 522: "During the 1960s, local arrests . . ." McCoy, *The Politics of Heroin in Southeast Asia*, pages 52 and 57.

Page 522: "If he can't prove . . ." Marro to Sackett, 8/30/72, in the Marro papers.

Page 522: McCoy background: Buckley, *Penthouse*, 6/73; interview with McCoy.

Page 523: "Southeast Asia is fast . . ." Transcript of hearings before Subcommittee of the Committee on Appropriations, 6/2/72, in the McCoy papers.

Page 523: "Even at its peak . . ." Testimony of McCoy, 6/9/72, before the congressional inquiry on international narcotics traffic, in the McCoy papers.

Page 523: Reports of CIA-Harper & Row controversy: *New York Times*, 7/22/72, 7/24/72, 8/9/72; *Newsweek*, 8/21/72; transcript of NBC News program, "Chronolog," 7/28/72; transcript of CBS Morning News with John Hart, 8/8/72.

Page 523: *Times* reviews of McCoy's book: 8/31/72, 9/3/72.

Page 523: "I admired the quality . . ." Letter, Alfred McCoy to author, 9/2/88.

CHAPTER THIRTY-FOUR: The Seventh Day

I

Page 525: "A Sunday edition would . . ." HFG to Alicia, 3/23/56, in the Gottlieb papers.

Page 526: Announcing Chandler's approval of Sunday paper: Attwood to Laventhol and Targe, 5/28/71, in the Attwood papers.

Page 526: Laventhol outline for Sunday: Laventhol to Attwood, 6/10/71, in the Attwood papers; Laventhol to Attwood, 2/26/71, in the Laventhol papers.

Page 527: "We have had a Long Island edition . . ." *Newsweek*, 11/8/71.

Page 527: Notification by pressmen: George Tedeschi to James Genovese, 3/31/72; Genovese to Tedeschi, 4/4/72, in the papers of Local 406.

Page 527: Local 406 loses at arbitration: Tedeschi to members, 12/22/72, in the papers of Local 406.

Page 527: 340,000 circulation: Asimov to Attwood, 6/1/72, in the Attwood papers.

Page 528: *News* and *Times* circulation figures: Audit Bureau of Circulations.

Page 529: Earlier press start: Laventhol to staff, 12/3/71, in *Newsday* files.

Pages 529-530: *Newsday* among 10 best papers: *Time*, 1/21/74.

II

Page 531: Petition to NLRB: Laventhol to staff, 6/1/73, in *Newsday* files.

Page 532: Local 406 election results: Laventhol to staff, 9/10/73, in *Newsday* files.

Page 532: Six challenges won by *Newsday*: Laventhol to staff, 3/6/74, in *Newsday* files.

Page 532: Certification of Local 406: Laventhol to staff, 1/29/75, in *Newsday* files; Certification of Representative form, 1/31/75, in the papers of Local 406.

III

Page 533: Women meet management: Attwood to Robinson, 7/13/72, in the Attwood papers.

Page 534: Lawsuit: Complaint, 1/13/75, in the Asimov papers.

Page 534: "Annabelle Kerins is an A all around . . ." Richard Sandler to Mel Opotowsky, 12/17/70, in the Sandler papers.

Page 535: Ruling on class action: *Media Report to Women*, 12/1/76, page 5.

Page 535: Bartels decision on partial summary judgment: *Newsday*, 10/2/81; *Editor & Publisher*, 10/10/81.

Page 535: $1,000,000 in legal fees: John Wills to Asimov, 10/27/81, in the Asimov papers.

Page 535: Settlement terms: *Newsday*, 2/27/82; consent decree, 2/26/82, in the Asimov papers.

IV

Page 537: "New Technology and the Newsroom . . ." Ken Brief to Laventhol, 7/10/73, in *Newsday* files.

CHAPTER THIRTY-FIVE: Big Daddy, King of Suffolk

I

Page 541: "Given the standard . . ." Greene to staff, 3/19/73, in the Greene papers.

Page 542: Calzadilla kidnaped: 3/7/74.

Page 543: Hathway obituary: 4/16/77.

II

Page 543: Arthur Bergmann story: 1/18/75.

Pages 543-544: Wyrick story about reporters on political payrolls: 10/26/72.

Page 544: Wyrick story about one-percent kickbacks: 4/16/72.

Page 544: "Investigation of a Public Citizen . . ." 5/22/71.

Page 545: Alan Eysen on phony election committee: 6/13/73; indictment, 12/13/73; dismissal of indictment, 1/25/74.

Page 545: Cummings-Fetherston on Duryea's land: 4/14/74.

Page 545: Duryea plea to Chandler: Duryea to Chandler, 5/2/74; Chandler to Attwood, 5/10/74; Attwood to Chandler, 5/13/74; Chandler to Attwood, 5/20/74; Chandler to Duryea, 5/29/74, in the Attwood papers.

Page 545: O'Brien investigation of Kelley: 7/12/75.

Page 545: Kelley accusations against O'Brien: 9/4/75.

CHAPTER THIRTY-SIX: The Arizona Project

I

Pages 547-548: The mob and the track: 12/6/74 to 12/10/74.

Page 548: "It must have passed . . ." 4/7/76.

Page 548: "No Mob Link . . ." 4/11/76.

Page 549: "It would be a concerted . . ." Greene to Laventhol, 7/19/76, in the Greene papers.

II

Pages 551-552: Goldwater, Rosenzweig stories: 3/14/77 to 3/18/77, 3/20/77.

Page 552: Kemper Marley Sr. story: 3/22/77.

Pages 552-553: Ned Warren stories: 5/23/77 to 5/25/77.

Page 553: Arizona series: 3/13/77 to 4/4/77.

Page 553: "I think your work . . ." Chandler to Greene, 4/12/77, in the Attwood papers.

Page 554: Joseph Bonanno criticism: Bonanno and Lalli, *A Man of Honor*, pages 346-348.

Page 554: "Arizona did wake . . ." Speech by Bruce Babbitt, 3/27/82, in the Greene papers.

CHAPTER THIRTY-SEVEN: Long Island Moves West

I

Page 555: "Newsday's circulation . . ." 8/12/50.

Page 556: "a dying community . . ." Patterson and Burton, *Saturday Evening Post*, 2/21/59, page 21.

Page 556: " . . .way stations on the road . . ." Flagler manuscript, Part II, page 23.

Page 556: "In the '40s, Newsday . . ." 3/4/85.

Page 557: "Good Lord, no . . ." *Time*, 4/27/70.

Page 557: "Will Big Otis . . ." Diamond, *New York*, 8/14/70.

Page 557: 1971 decision to study Queens: Asimov to Jim Grider, 10/25/71, in the Asimov papers.

Page 557: Contingency plan: Referred to in memo, Laventhol to Sexton, 11/17/71, in the Asimov papers.

Page 557: *Long Island Press* decline: Grider to Attwood, 6/19/72, in the Asimov papers.

Page 558: "Based on . . ." Laventhol to Attwood, 7/5/72, in the Asimov papers.

Page 558: "I am not enthusiastic . . ." Chandler to Attwood, 7/14/72, in the Attwood papers.

Page 558: "The city's advertising . . ." *Editor & Publisher*, 9/16/72.

Page 558: "We are now . . ." Attwood to Robinson, 2/15/73, in the Attwood papers.

Page 558: "As we look ahead . . ." Asimov to Attwood, 11/25/74, in *Newsday* files.

Page 559: "I want to emphasize . . ." Attwood to staff, 12/20/76, in the Asimov papers.

Page 559: Circulation figures on Queens Sunday paper: Attwood to Chandler, 1/11/77, in the Attwood papers.

Page 560: "No daily Queens . . ." Attwood to staff, 12/20/76, in the Asimov papers.

Page 560: Proposal for daily Queens edition: Laventhol to Asimov, 2/24/77, in the Asimov papers.

II

Page 561: Dennis Duggan appointment as New York bureau chief: Laventhol to staff,

3/15/71, in *Newsday* files.

III

Page 563: Sylvan Fox becomes national editor: Laventhol to staff, 12/14/77, in *Newsday* files.
Page 567: Mastropieri failure to pay tickets: 6/14/78.
Page 567: Mastropieri and mob figure: 12/28/78.
Page 567: "The black neighborhoods . . ." Hershey to Insolia, 3/29/79, in the Asimov papers.
Page 569: Manhattan edition study: Fox and Ken Brief to Asimov, 1/12/79, in the Asimov papers.

CHAPTER THIRTY-EIGHT: At the Crossroads

I

Page 570: "And in neither . . ." 7/25/76.
Page 570: "It doesn't seem . . ." Morris to Greene, 7/27/76, in the Morris papers.
Page 572: Other reporters on Crossroads team: Robert E. Kessler, Jim Scovel, Jane Snider, Susan Soper. Photographer: Dick Kraus.

II

Page 574: "The sewer system is . . ." 1/27/67.
Page 574: "Problems in the Pipeline . . ." 2/21/67 to 2/24/67.
Page 574: Editorial urging rejection: 2/24/67.
Page 575: Editorial urging approval: 10/29/69.
Page 575: Firing of whistle-blower: 4/25/78.
Page 575: Rigged purchase of laboratory equipment: 6/13/78.
Page 575: Fraudulent stress-testing: 6/27/78, 7/13/78.
Page 575: Runaway outfall pipe: 11/29/78.
Page 575: Indictment of pipe supplier: 2/16/79.
Pages 575-576: Murder of John Flynn: 6/16/79.
Page 576: Unsealed court papers: 7/31/77.
Page 577: Bahamas story: 3/20/79.
Page 577: Barbato on Twin County payroll: 3/19/79.
Page 577: Barbato's indictment on state charges: 5/1/79.
Page 577: Barbato's acquittal on state charges: 8/31/79.
Page 577: Barbato's indictment on federal charges: 4/10/81.
Page 577: Barbato's acquittal on federal charges: 10/24/81.
Page 577: Barbato's guilty plea on perjury: 4/28/82.

III

Page 579: Payne on Soweto death toll: 11/22/76, 12/12/76.
Page 579: Payne South Africa series: 1/30/77 to 2/9/77.
Page 579: Payne Rhodesia series: 1/22/78 to 1/29/78.
Page 579: Tom Collins Pulitzer series: 6/4/78 to 6/6/78.

CHAPTER THIRTY-NINE: Newsday Moves East

I

Page 582: Price of land: Interview with James Fitzgerald.
Page 582: Groundbreaking: *Inside Newsday*, 6/15/77.

II

Page 583: Laventhol named Attwood's successor: 9/6/78.
Page 584: "I can help keep . . ." Attwood to Greene, 9/25/72, in the Attwood papers.
Page 585: Departure of Forst, promotion of Insolia: 12/1/77.
Page 585: Appointment of five assistant managing editors: Insolia to staff, 10/19/78, in *Newsday* files.

Page 585: "This treatment was not surprising . . ." Black caucus to Attwood and Laventhol, 5/4/78, in *Newsday* files.

III

Page 587: Series on *"razryadka"* in Russia: 4/19/76 to 4/25/76.

Page 588: Recognition of China: 12/16/78, 1/2/79, 3/2/79.

Page 588: Appointment of Sexton to run editorial pages: Laventhol to staff, 4/28/72, in *Newsday* files.

Page 589: Sexton series on Japan: 5/22/77 to 5/26/77.

Page 589: Sexton series on China: 10/22/87 to 10/27/78.

Page 589: Appointment of Sexton to run China bureau: Insolia to staff, 10/12/79, in *Newsday* files.

CHAPTER FORTY: Crossing the River

I

Page 590: Assignment of Jansen to study Queens: Asimov to Laventhol, 7/8/80, in the Asimov papers.

Page 590: "Certainly our newspaper . . ." Memo, Ray Jansen, 11/80, in the Asimov papers.

Page 592: *Daily News* Queens regional section: Interview with Dick Beekman; memo, 7/2/81, in the Asimov papers.

Page 592: Tribune Company plans to sell *Daily News*: *Newsday*, 12/19/81, 12/20/81; *New York Times*, 12/19/81; *Editor & Publisher*, 12/26/81.

Page 592: "Perhaps its biggest . . ." *Newsweek*, 1/25/82.

Page 592: *Newsday* circulation during strike: Report, 11/78, in the Asimov papers.

Page 592: Tribune Company's travails: Welles, *New York*, 3/31/75; Rowan, *Fortune*, 4/4/82.

Page 593: $20 million investment: *Editor & Publisher*, 12/26/81.

Pages 593-594: Planning for the post-*Post* era: Laventhol to Attwood, 6/20/78; study, "Demise of the New York Post: Circulation Plans and Estimates," 6/28/78, in the Asimov papers.

Page 594: Establishment of *Daily News* committees: Asimov to Laventhol, 12/22/81; Gerald Tryhane to Laventhol, 12/23/81, in the Asimov papers.

Page 594: Initial options: Tryhane to Laventhol, 12/23/81, in the Asimov papers.

Page 594: Reports on Brooklyn: Ruinsky to Laventhol, 1/5/82; Social Data Analysts, 1/82, in the Asimov papers.

Page 594: " . . .almost certainly about to close . . ." Draft memo, Laventhol, 1/3/82, in the Asimov papers.

Page 595: Allbritton drops effort to buy *News*: *Editor & Publisher*, 5/1/82.

Page 595: Tribune Company offer to Donald Trump and Joe Allbritton: 1/18/90.

Page 595: Decision by Tribune Company not to sell the *News*: 5/1/82, 1/18/90.

Page 595: "We're Here to Stay . . ." Quoted in *Wall Street Journal*, 5/5/82.

Page 595: Final *News* agreement with unions: *Newsday*, 10/25/82; *Editor & Publisher*, 11/20/82.

II

Page 596: Announcement of McIlwain as *New York Newsday* editor: Insolia to staff, 8/24/82, in *Newsday* files.

Page 596: "Don't sit here . . ." McIlwain, *A Farewell to Alcohol*, page 14.

Page 597: Departure and return of Stu Troup: Insolia to staff, 7/31/80 and 1/5/82, in *Newsday* files.

Page 598: Start of *Bluesday*: Laventhol to staff, 4/1/83, in *Newsday* files.

Page 598: Plans for separate Sunday magazine: Minutes of executive committee meetings, 7/26/83, 7/17/83, in *Newsday* files.

Page 599: Transfer of Hall: Insolia to staff, 11/15/83, in *Newsday* files.

Page 599: Hiring of Sales: Insolia to staff, 12/14/83, in *Newsday* files.

Page 599: Departure of McIlwain: Insolia to staff, 1/16/84, in *Newsday* files.

III

Page 600: Martin Schram-Jim Klurfeld "ticktock" on Camp David: 9/24/78 to 9/25/78.

Page 600: Appointment of Marro as Washington bureau chief: Insolia to staff, 1/9/79, in *Newsday* files.

Page 600: Temporary transfer of Marro to Long Island: Insolia to staff, 2/3/81, in *Newsday* files.

Page 601: Appointment of Tony Marro as managing editor and Schwartz as executive editor: Insolia to staff, 6/8/81, in *Newsday* files.

Page 601: Bob Wyrick-Patrick Owens series on disability: 3/20/83 to 3/22/83.

Page 602: Benjamin Ward and the mosque: 11/17/83.

Page 602: Benjamin Ward and the massacre: 10/24/84.

Page 604: "*Newsday*'s Big . . ." Diamond, *New York*, 4/1/85.

Page 604: "*Newsday* Knocks . . ." *Business Week*, 5/27/85.

IV

Page 604: Hiring of Keane: Insolia to staff, 8/24/84, in *Newsday* files.

Page 605: Departure of Lou Schwartz for Los Angeles: 3/8/85.

Page 605: Demotion and departure of Dick Estrin: Insolia to staff, 4/16/85 and 4/23/85.

Pages 606-607: Appointment of Van Doorn as deputy metropolitan editor: Insolia to staff, 2/28/85, in *Newsday* files.

Page 607: Appointment of Schneider to "oversee" the New York paper: Insolia to staff, 4/23/85, in *Newsday* files.

Page 607: "The push is on . . ." Insolia to Marro, Schneider, Sales and Hamilton, 4/23/85, in *Newsday* files.

Pages 607-608: New masthead without the name of Sales: 4/30/85.

Page 607: Transfer of Troup to jazz coverage: Insolia to staff, 4/16/85, in *Newsday* files.

Page 608: Van Doorn moved to Part II: Insolia to staff, 9/6/85, in *Newsday* files.

CHAPTER FORTY-ONE: Newsday and the Nuke

I

Page 611: Carey opposes Jamesport plants: 4/1/79.

Page 611: "Choices: The Future of Energy . . ." 4/4/79.

Page 611: "After 25 Years of Promises . . ." 4/24/79.

Page 611: LILCO's plans to buy land at Shoreham: 4/13/66.

Page 611: First editorial comment on Shoreham: 5/7/66.

Page 612: " . . .a safe, strictly regulated . . ." 4/3/73.

Page 612: "Alas, he may be right . . ." 8/4/77.

Page 612: Post-Three Mile Island editorials: 6/24/79 to 6/28/79.

Page 612: " . . .despite all the shortcomings . . ." 6/25/79.

Page 613: Cost estimates: 4/13/66, 4/4/79.

II

Page 613: Oil crisis series: 8/26/79 to 8/30/79.

Page 614: Crowe on LILCO: 3/22/73, 3/24/73.

Page 614: "Put bluntly . . ." Volkman, *Media People*, November 1980, page 72.

Page 616: Chronology of Shoreham: Diamond to Schneider and Tuccillo, 7/7/81, in the Diamond papers.

Page 616: "Your deadlines . . ." Diamond to Tuccillo, Schneider and Greene, 9/28/81, in the Diamond papers.

Page 616: Shoreham series: 11/15/81 to 11/20/81, 11/22/81.

CHAPTER FORTY-TWO: Bad Times for Big Daddy

I

Page 620: Background of ABSCAM: *Newsday*, 2/3/80; *Time*, 2/18/80; Greene, *The Sting Man*.

Page 620: "The most detailed . . ." *Time*, 2/18/80.

Page 620: "With a few exceptions . . ." Greene and Schneider to staff, 9/9/81, in *Newsday* files.

Page 620: " . . .at your own risk . . ." Greene to staff, 3/23/81, in *Newsday* files.

Page 621: " . . .in addition to his other . . ." Insolia to staff, 11/12/82, in *Newsday* files.

II

Page 622: Background of Wright: 8/3/77.

Page 622: Hiring of Johnson: 7/15/82.

Page 623: Arrangement between *Newsday* and Cablevision: Agreement, 10/1/82, in *Newsday* files.

Page 627: Termination of the news show: 4/27/84.

Page 627: News 12 budget: *New York Times*, 1/24/88.

CHAPTER FORTY-THREE: Baby Jane and the Famine

I

Page 629: First story on Baby Jane Doe: 10/18/83.

Page 629: Decision by Tanenbaum: 10/21/83.

Page 629: Reversal by Appellate Division: 10/22/83.

Page 629: Appeal to Court of Appeals: 10/25/83.

Page 629: Part II piece: 10/26/83.

Page 629: Court of Appeals argument: 10/27/83.

Page 629: Court of Appeals decision: 10/29/83.

Page 629: Federal lawsuit: 11/3/83.

Page 629: Interview with Koop: 11/5/83.

Page 629: Interview with parents: 11/4/83.

Page 630: Koop admits intervention in other cases: 11/7/83, 11/8/83.

Page 630: Colen book: *Born at Risk: The Dramatic True Story of the Struggle for Life in an Intensive Care Nursery*. New York: St. Martin's Press, 1981.

Page 630: AIDS series: 9/12/82 to 9/15/82.

Page 631: "Hard Choices" series: 4/15/84 to 4/19/84.

Page 631: Thompson lands on Grenada: 10/28/83.

Page 631: *Newsday* wins the Pulitzer: 4/17/84.

II

Page 632: "Hazards for Export" series: 12/13/81 to 12/18/81, 12/20/81 to 12/23/81.

Pages 632-633: "World Hunger" series: Occasional stories, starting on 10/18/81.

Page 633: Appointment of Payne as a columnist and national editor: Insolia to staff, 3/14/80 and 9/25/80, in *Newsday* files.

Page 633: Creation of separate foreign desk: Insolia to staff, 6/14/83, in *Newsday* files.

Page 633: Appointment of Patman as foreign editor: Insolia to staff, 11/15/83, in *Newsday* files.

Page 633: London, Mexico City and Cairo bureaus: Insolia to staff, 2/3/81, 6/14/83, 7/18/85, in *Newsday* files.

Pages 635-637: African famine stories: 11/4/84, 11/13/84, 12/2/84, 12/9/84, 12/23/84, 12/24/84, 4/21/85.

Page 637: Pulitzer Prizes: 4/25/85.

Page 637: " . . .out in the streets . . ." 4/25/85.

Page 637: Bell's dog story: 4/26/85.

Page 637: Appointment of Sommer as Asia bureau chief: Insolia to staff, 12/16/82, in *Newsday* files.

Page 637: Overseas Press Club award: 4/25/85.

Page 637: Sloyan on the death of Sadat: 10/7/81.

CHAPTER FORTY-FOUR: Tab Wars

I

Page 639: Departure of Forst: 12/1/77.

Page 640: "They Can Pull the Plug . . ." 4/1/76.

Page 640: *Herald American* circulation figures: O'Brien, *Boston Magazine*, May 1983, page 116.

Page 641: Forst cries: O'Brian, *Boston Phoenix*, 6/3/80, page 18.

Page 641: Forst front pages: *Boston Phoenix*, pages 6-7.

Page 642: Forst meets Murdoch: *Boston Magazine*. pages 113-116.

Page 642: "To Don Forst . . ." *Boston Magazine*, page 155.

II

Page 643: Hiring Forst: Insolia to staff, 7/30/85, in *Newsday* files.
Page 643: "What would you . . ." O'Brian, *Boston Phoenix*, 6/3/80, page 6.
Page 646: Hiring Scaduto: Insolia to staff, 11/8/85.
Page 646: Hiring Mulcahy and McAlary: Insolia to staff, 1/6/86.
Page 646: Hiring Esposito and DeStefano: Insolia to staff, 1/30/86.
Page 646: Hiring Carroll: Insolia to staff, 2/10/86.
Page 647: McAlary on murders in Queens: 2/9/86.
Page 647: Start of Duggan column: Insolia to staff, 11/12/82.
Page 647: Start of Gross column: Insolia to staff, 11/20/80.
Page 647: Denis Hamill column: Insolia to staff, 12/2/85.
Page 647: Departure of Gross: Insolia to staff, 3/28/86.
Page 647: "I used to think . . ." 8/13/86.

III

Pages 648-649: Chronology of city scandal: 3/14/86.
Page 649: "The wounds I received . . ." 1/22/86.
Page 649: "Michael Dowd, a Queens . . ." *Daily News*, 1/23/86.
Page 649: "Who could you give it to . . ." *Newsweek*, 5/12/86.
Page 650: Dwyer on Rubin: 2/10/86.
Page 650: Breslin suburban column: 7/28/72.
Page 650: Manes commits suicide: 3/14/86.

IV

Page 651: Schanberg's *Times* column ends: *New York Times*, 8/20/85.
Page 651: "The *Times* has asked . . ." 8/21/85.
Page 652: Announcement of Schanberg column: 3/14/86.
Page 652: *News-American* background: *New York Times*, 5/28/86.
Page 652: Departure of Sales: Insolia to staff, 4/30/86.
Page 653: Hiring Cotter: Forst to staff, 7/15/86.
Pages 654-655: Isenberg as associate publisher: 5/14/86.
Page 655: Laventhol becomes Times Mirror president: 5/1/86.
Page 655: Marro to executive editor: 11/6/86.

V

Page 657: Early uses of full-color on front page: Reagan inauguration, 1/21/81; swearing in Sandra Day O'Connor, 9/26/81.
Page 658: Hiring Goldman: Insolia to staff, 6/16/86.
Page 658: Goldman on Gumbel: 2/28/89.
Page 658: Reassigning Hanson: Insolia to staff, 2/14/86.
Page 658: Hiring Winer: Insolia to staff, 11/14/86.
Page 658: Winer to theater critic: Marro to staff, 2/22/88.
Page 660: Stock tables start in LI paper: 9/15/87.
Page 660: List of suspended police officers: 9/24/86.
Page 661: "Confession of a Scared Cop . . ." 11/7/86.
Page 661: "It didn't seem . . ." 11/8/86.
Page 661: McAlary's book: *Buddy Boys*. New York: G.P Putnam's Sons, 1988.

VI

Page 663: Marro replaces Insolia as editor: 6/9/87.
Page 664: Cotter resigns: Forst to staff, 11/11/87.
Page 665: Cotter becomes the *Post*'s metropolitan editor: *New York Post*, 7/29/89.

VII

Page 666: "Tawana Made It Up . . ." 4/27/89.
Page 666: "I want Suzy's job . . ." 3/24/88.
Page 666: Original Suzy column: *New York Post*, 3/22/88.

Page 666: Suzy response: *New York Post*, 3/30/88.
Page 669: "Inside Rikers . . ." 7/29/88.
Page 669: "Hamill said he did not . . ." 7/30/88.
Page 669: "Newsday watching . . ." *New York Post*, 8/5/88.
Page 669: " . . .lesson for all of us . . ." Forst to staff, 8/3/88.
Page 669: Hamill incident at Bensonhurst trial: *Daily News*, 5/2/90; interviews with Marro, Asimov.
Page 670: Mike McAlary on Mike Tyson: *Daily News*, 9/7/88.
Page 670: "Unhappily for . . ." *Village Voice*, 9/20/88.
Page 670: "The first thing they asked . . ." 10/14/88.
Page 670: "Rudolph Giuliani is . . ." 1/12/89.
Page 670: "Although Willie Horton . . ." 1/20/89.
Page 671: McAlary on Tinyes: *Daily News*, 3/22/89.

CHAPTER FORTY-FIVE: The New Newsday

I

Page 672: "The new plant . . ." Report to staff, 9/7/77.
Page 674: Employee opinion survey results: *Inside Newsday*, January/February, 1984, pages 3-5.
Page 674: "Journalists are moralists . . ." Laventhol to Johnson, 12/18/85, in the Johnson papers.
Pages 675-676: Background of LILCO settlement: 5/15/88, 5/29/88, 6/17/88, 11/20/88, 2/15/89, 3/1/89, 3/2/89, 6/29/89.
Page 676: $1.35 billion imprudency finding: 6/14/85, 6/27/85.
Page 676: Johnson and LILCO: 5/10/88.
Page 676: " 'We all understand . . .' " *Daily News*, 5/20/88.
Page 677: Levy editorial series: 9/25/89 to 10/1/89.

II

Page 681: Announcement of Nassau regionalization: 6/1/88.
Page 681: Background of Chanry Communications: Radolf, *Editor & Publisher*, 7/30/88; Sachar, *NewsInc.*, November/December, 1989; *U.S. News & World Report*, 4/24/89; Zehren, *Newsday*, 10/16/89.
Page 681: " . . .hype and smoke . . ." 4/14/89.
Page 681: Announcement of weekly regional sections: 6/18/89.
Page 683: Chanry cuts back plans for *This Week*: 12/7/89.
Page 683: Loss of bond rating: *Wall Street Journal*, 2/6/90.
Page 683: Chanry for sale: 3/24/90.
Page 683: Complete conversion to *Pennysaver* format: 4/21/90.
Page 683: Death of *St. Louis Sun*: 4/26/90.

III

Page 685: Defense job gains and losses: 6/19/89.

IV

Page 688: Trump and drug summit stories: 2/15/90, 2/16/90.
Page 688: Hiring Marlette: 2/7/89.
Page 688: "Best Sex . . ." *New York Post*, 2/16/90.
Page 689: "OINK!" headline: 4/4/90
Page 689: "The Hunk Who . . ." 5/1/90.
Page 690: " . . .reported on the neighborhoods . . ." *Amsterdam News*, 9/16/89.
Page 691: "I hate official . . ." 5/3/90.
Page 691: "I absolutely . . ." Breslin to Forst, 5/4/90.
Page 691: Mangaliman note to Marro: 5/4/90.
Page 691: "I am no good . . ." Breslin to staff, 5/4/90.
Page 691: "Jimmy Breslin's remarks . . ." Forst to staff, 5/4/90.
Page 691: "All my apologies . . ." 5/9/90.
Page 692: " . . . an outburst by an individual . . ." Marro to staff, 5/9/90.

Page 692: Reno, Kempton columns on Breslin: 5/10/90.

V

Page 693: Pumpkin cover: 10/12/89.
Page 694: Telephone rate series: 2/15/81 to 2/18/81.
Page 694: Assessment series: 5/12/85 to 5/17/85.
Page 694: Long Beach series: 4/19/87 to 4/23/87.
Page 694: Garbage series: 12/13/87 to 12/18/87, 12/20/87 to 12/23/87.
Page 694: William Levitt series: 2/16/86 to 2/18/86.
Page 694: Confession series: 12/7/86 to 12/11/86.
Page 694: Cuomo at midterm: 9/6/85 to 9/8/85.
Page 695: Borrowing under Cuomo: 9/22/86.

Acknowledgments

INCLUDING THOSE WHO generously consented to be interviewed and those who assisted in the development of the manuscript, more than 700 people have had a hand in the creation of this book. I am grateful to all of them, but especially to three people who have done the most to make it possible.

The first is my wife, Judith Ann Dempsey Keeler, who not only handled patiently the dozens of family responsibilities that I left unattended during this project, but also read the entire manuscript, making valuable editing suggestions. Without her loyal help, I could never have written this book.

The second is my researcher, Kathy Geiger, who heroically endured my compulsiveness, performed endless tedious chores, and did a first-class job of finding thousands of pages of documents and turning them into a cohesive, professional filing system.

The third is Stanley Asimov, whose sense of history brought this project into being, and whose optimism, energy, wisdom and journalistic skill have guided me kindly through the valleys. I merely researched and wrote this book. Stan Asimov *willed* it.

I owe a special debt to the publisher of *Newsday*, Robert M. Johnson, and to the editor, Anthony Marro, for showing the integrity and courage to let me write this book with absolutely no interference. My gratitude also goes out to the former editor of *Newsday*, Anthony Insolia, who read the entire manuscript at his home in South Carolina and offered sensible and cogent criticisms during the editing process; to my patient editor at William Morrow, Harvey Ginsberg; to Alan Williams, the editor who first expressed interest in the book at William Morrow; to Martin Levin, who helped me to attract the interest of William Morrow, and to Lori Ames, the experienced promotion expert at Morrow who helped spread the word about the book. I am also grateful for the wise advice and the splendid example of Richard Kluger, the author of what I consider the best newspaper history ever written, *The Paper: The Life and Death of the New York Herald Tribune.*

In the interview list, I have included the names of all those who consented to interviews, and I am grateful to all of them for their candor and their time, whether I quoted them extensively in the chapter text or used very little of their information. But I would especially like to thank Robert W. Greene, who played such a large role in the paper's history and shared more hours with me than anyone else did. He knew from the start that parts of the book might be painful for him, but he still made himself available for interviews whenever I needed him, and he patiently answered what must have seemed like an endless series of computer-messaged questions. Similarly, I would like to mention the generous contributions of the late Dorothy Holdsworth, Alicia Patterson's secretary, who went out of her way to help us acquire Alicia's medical records, and the late Leo Gottlieb, Harry Guggenheim's attorney, who devoted many hours to searching through his records to provide information on Harry and Alicia, with the tireless help of his secretary, Betty Landis.

Those at *Newsday* who helped immensely included, in roughly the chronological order of their contributions, Elaine Goldman and David Hoffman, who made time in the middle of their normal duties in the library to spend many hours digging creatively and persistently for information for this book; Pearl Granat, who somehow found whatever out-of-print books I needed; Lucy West, who made copies of hundreds of pages of *Newsday* from the library files, with assistance from Mildred Smallwood; Mary Ann Skinner and Elizabeth Whisnant, who run the library and made it possible for their staff to help; Bill Senft, who took a series of photographs of current Newsday executives and employees; Dora Potter, who helped with research and dozens of administrative details; JoAnn Volk, who helped with research in Albany; Artie Schmidt, the manager of publishing systems, and Bill Chichester, who set up a process to ensure that the electronic version of the manuscript didn't disappear into the cosmos; William Berry, Frank Lima, Thomas Neri and Howard Rosenthal, who late every night performed the procedures that protected the disc containing the manuscript and my notes; Mike Weippert, the scrupulously careful and reliable technician who patiently produced many thousands of pages of printouts of different versions of the manuscript; Pam Robinson, who provided gentle, skillful and professional copy editing and careful reading of the final proofs; Nancy Richman, who read the entire manuscript and offered astute advice on matters of libel and copyright law; Bill Davis, whose computer genius created the formats that enabled *Newsday*'s tabloid news layout system to generate the type for the book, and who was amazingly patient with me through all my last-minute tinkering with page proofs; Mike Schroeder, who managed the overall production process and arranged for the indexing of the book; Kathy Cashman and William Robert Moyer, who did the bulk of the hands-on technical work of producing the type electronically, with assistance from Rose Chin, Diane Xenakis and Bob Suter; Bob Eisner, who helped immensely in the design of the jacket, and Jack Squire and Bob Delboy, who designed the promotional material that appeared in *Newsday*.

Beyond those who contributed as a part of their jobs at *Newsday*, I benefitted from the generosity of those who helped simply because they are good people, including my friend Ken Spencer, who took the jacket photograph and often encouraged me through the darker days; Monsignor George T. Deas, who taught me the first useful things that I ever learned about writing, three decades ago, and offered wise counsel about knotty questions involved in this book; Karen Ann Roach, who first did research in Albany when she was working there for *Newsday*, and then, after her departure from the *Newsday* staff, faithfully read the manuscript and offered cheerful encouragement; Amanda Harris, one of the most fundamentally sound journalists at *Newsday*, who generously read the entire manuscript and provided excellent, professional advice for trims and changes; Renee Kaplan, who read the whole manuscript, asked intelligent questions, kept me informed about developments at modern-day *Newsday* while I was sequestered in my cubbyhole, and helped during the proofreading process; Pamala Griset, who found time away from work on her own book to read part of my manuscript and make insightful comments; Hal Burton, Dan Cryer, George Juergens, Stan Peckham, Martha Sandlin and Bill Woestendiek, who also were kind enough to read parts of the manuscript, and Alexis Jetter and Miriam Pawel, who gathered groups of young *Newsday* reporters to give me their perspective on the paper.

In addition, Kathy Geiger joins me in expressing gratitude to those who were especially helpful to her during her research: Phyllis Braff, for providing us information about and access to Falaise whenever we needed it; Richard A. Winsche and Gary R. Hammond of the Nassau County Museum, for providing useful advice and easy access to their valuable collection; Garold L. Cole, the history reference librarian at the Milner Library, Illinois State University, for helping us to collect the correspondence of Alicia Patterson and Adlai Stevenson from the papers of Walter Johnson, and Janice L. O'Connell, at the State Historical Society of Wisconsin, and the researcher Fritz Knoebel, for their help in gathering the papers of Bill Attwood.

The jacket of the book contains my name, but all of these generous people helped to put it there.

Index